DATE DUE			

The Long View

The Long View

BASIL WRIGHT

Alfred A. Knopf

New York, 1974

For KASSIM

'Men require of their neighbours something sufficiently akin to be understood, something sufficiently different to provoke attention, and something great enough to command admiration.'

A. N. Whitehead

'Allons! La marche, le fardeau, le désert, l'ennui et la colère. A qui me louer? Quelle bête faut-il adorer? Quel sainte image attaque-t-on? Quels coeurs briserai-je? Quel mensonge dois-je tenir? Dans quel sang marcher?'

Arthur Rimbaud

'All things are beautiful if you have got them in the right order.'

John Grierson

CONTENTS

	Acknowledgments	xi
	Preface	xiii
SIGNPOST—1895:	The Year of the Lumière Brothers	1
CHAPTER 1.	Free for All	4
SIGNPOST—1915:	The Year of 'Birth of a Nation'	23
CHAPTER 2.	Stars and Stripes	28
SIGNPOST—1927:	The Year of 'The Jazz Singer'	66
CHAPTER 3.	All Talking, All Singing, All Dancing	70
SIGNPOST—1939:	The Year of 'Gone With The Wind'	148
CHAPTER 4.	War	153
SIGNPOST—1945:	The Year of 'Rome—Open City'	216
CHAPTER 5.	Neo-realism, Witch Hunts and Wide Screens	220
SIGNPOST—1956:	The Year of 'Pather Panchali'	400
CHAPTER 6.	Iron Curtain and Points East	408
SIGNPOST—1960:	The Year of 'A Bout de Souffle'	476
CHAPTER 7.	New Waves, Angries and Undergrounds	487
SIGNPOST—1970:	The Year of 'Woodstock' and 'Gimme Shelter'	645
CHAPTER 8.	Whatever Next? ·	659
	A Note on Dates	695
	Select Bibliography	697
	Index of Films	follows page 709
	Index of Names	
	General Index	

ACKNOWLEDGMENTS

First and foremost I express my deepest gratitude to my old friend and colleague Michael Ayrton, who not only suggested the idea of this book but also propelled me into the welcoming arms of Tom Rosenthal and thus into a contractual obligation from which not even my natural sloth could rescue me. I am under additional obligation to Michael and his wife Elisabeth for having taken the time and trouble to read the manuscript and make a number of valuable criticisms and suggestions.

I wish also to record my indebtedness to E. H. Gombrich and R. H. Wilenski, whose writings in a parallel albeit higher field served as inspiring models even though I could not hope ever to emulate them. I am especially beholden to the latter, since it was from passages in *Modern French Painters* that I picked up the idea for the Signpost sections which precede each chapter of the book.

I am also particularly grateful to Tom Milne for his patient and perceptive editing; and to John Wolfers for his skilful and sympathetic pilotage throughout the whole enterprise.

Beyond this, my indebtedness is legion, and it is with apologies for what I fear may be many omissions (however unintentional) that I express my thanks to:

The staffs of the British Film Institute's Library, Information and Education departments, of the National Film Archive and of the National Film Theatre; to Fred Zentner of Cinema Bookshop, London, for a constant high-speed supply of books, many of them unobtainable from any other quarter; to Henri Langlois and Mary Meerson of the Cinémathèque Française, not least for allowing me to share with them something of their special affection for the medium; to Herman G. Weinberg for much valuable information and encouragement; to Dilys Powell for her exemplary filmic appreciation and meticulous accuracy which I have benefited from (and often envied) over so many years; to Bramwell Chandler and to his successor as European Representative of the National Film Board of Canada, Wilfred Jobbins; to K. L. Khandpur, Director of the Films Division of the Government of India; to Professor Satish Bahadur of the Film Institute of India; to Ahmad Al Hadary of the Visual Images Technical Centre, Cairo; to Margaret Grierson, Lewis Jacobs, Muir Mathieson and Paul Rotha for much useful information and advice; to Charles and Kitty Cooper and Charles Hedges of Contemporary Films, London; and to Edgar Anstey, Dallas Bower, Kevin Brownlow, Mrs Robert Burns, Denis and Helen Forman, Lewis Gilbert, Richard Hawkins, Peter Hopkinson, Stanley Read, Gaston Roberge, David Robinson, Marie Seton, Alexander Shaw and Colin Young. Finally my thanks to Gavin Shaw for his invaluable help in the indexing of this book.

I also express my gratitude to the Editors of *The Spectator*, *Sight and Sound* and *Film Quarterly* for permission to reprint extracts from some of my writings for those journals.

PREFACE

This is neither a history of the film nor a technical study. It is, rather, the record of a love affair with the film medium which began in 1913 when my grandmother took me to the cinema for the first time. This apocalyptic experience set the course of my life and made it inevitable that I would become a film-maker.

Thus I saw most of the Chaplin shorts as they were released, to say nothing of Fairbanks and Pickford; likewise Griffith (the Gish Sisters took little heed of the warnings I shouted to them from the four-pennies), Stroheim, early Lang, early Hitchcock, early Clair and early Cavalcanti – to say nothing of individual revelations like Pabst's *Secrets of the Soul*, Czinner's *Nju*, Galeen's *Student of Prague* or Robison's *Warning Shadows*. Similarly, I saw such of the early Soviet films as the British Home Secretary would permit, and in due course travelled to Germany to see the rest. Thus, too, I sprang idiotically to the defence of my love when threatened with violation by synchronised sound, until a few films like *Broadway Melody*, *Blackmail*, and *Sous les Toits de Paris* brought me to my senses. Later I was less disturbed by the arrival of the wide screen (indeed I gave *The Robe* a by no means unfavourable review), though I found the brief 3D period a little hard to bear.

But love affairs – true ones at any rate – tend to be stormy, and this may be reflected from time to time in the pages that follow. I can only plead a lover's privilege and hope that, just as in the end the lover, despite angers and despairs, looks only for the best in the object of his affections, so here I may manage to reveal a little of the creative achievements and the extraordinary organic growth of this new art, whose existence still spans less than a century.

This is a time when the nature of the moving picture as we have known it is entering a period of radical change. Hollywood, for so long the centre of the film world, has collapsed. In addition to the vast development of television as a mass medium, we now have the arrival of things like VTR and the cassette, while at the same time the process of film production is becoming simpler, cheaper and easier every day. All this suggests a need to stand back a little and take stock; and this, within the bounds of my own selectivity and prejudice (or, if you prefer, bloodymindedness), I have tried to do.

Here I must enter a caveat or make an apology. Like many people (I suppose) I suffer from certain blind spots in relation to the arts. I have to admit, with shame, that I am incapable of appreciating Wagner, Bruckner, Carlyle, Thackeray, Titian and Gauguin. With equal shame I must now add, in film terms, the names of Ingmar Bergman and Michelangelo Antonioni. Heaven knows I have tried hard enough. At times, as with Wagner and the rest, a faint glimmer of comprehension comes my way – in *Wild Strawberries*, for instance, or *The Red Desert* – but alas!, as I pursue, it fades. In view of this handicap I have thought it best not to waste the reader's time by further parading my incomprehension. If without knowing it I am even now treading the road to Damascus, no one could be better pleased than myself; for I know I am missing a very great deal indeed.

Conversely I have, in a book which makes no pretence of comprehensiveness, made at times noticeably brief references to film-makers whose work I deeply admire. Let me emphasize that in 'taking for granted' much of the output of, say, Buñuel, Delluc, Langdon, Lloyd, Keaton, Kuleshov, Pabst and Renoir, I am paying compliments.

Other gaps and omissions are due to different factors. Such film criticism as I have written has been in my spare time from film-making; so, unlike the real critics, I have not seen all the films all the time. Moreover, absence on location, especially in distant lands, has often cut me off from current releases for long periods of time. During the writing of this book I tried hard to catch up, and have managed to see a considerable number of films which I had missed over the years. Meantime the increasing flood of new films, especially over the past ten years, has made it increasingly difficult to keep up; and to this must be added the fact that the time-lag between delivery of the manuscript and publication means that, with a very few irresistible exceptions, no films released after June 1972 can be included.

The writing of the last chapters was clouded by the death of my very dear friend John Grierson, to whose genius as a producer I owe any small success I may have achieved. I shall always cherish the memory not only of his teaching but also of that warm and loving friendship which was the inner secret of his tremendous personality. It is a source of some comfort to me that in his last illness he had the goodness to read and, in general, approve the first six chapters of this book.

Then, while this book was in the press, came two more sorrows – the untimely deaths of Arthur Elton and Olwen Vaughan, both of them friends of forty years' standing. *The Long View* owes much to Elton's pioneer work in the development of the expositional film no less than to his contribution to scientific cinema which has put the world in his debt.

Of Olwen I have written and spoken elsewhere. Here let me say only that her precious friendship, linked with her love of film and her phenomenally encyclopaedic memory, made the writing of this book a happier and easier task than I had ever dared to hope it would be.

The Long View

SIGNPOST - 1895

THE YEAR OF THE LUMIERE BROTHERS

IN FRANCE

On March 2nd, in Paris, the brothers Louis and Auguste Lumière project a film in private to members of the Society for the Encouragement of Science. On June 10th, 11th and 12th they give private demonstrations of their films to the Photographic Congress at Lyons. On June 15th they present their first complete programme of films at the Revue Générale des Sciences in Paris. And it is in Paris, on December 28th, that the Lumières mount the first public showing, to a paying audience, of their programme. This takes place at the Grand Café, Hotel Scribe, and marks the beginning of cinema as we know it today.

Dreyfus, falsely convicted of treason and publicly degraded, is refused a new trial by President Faure.

Vollard puts on a retrospective of works by Cézanne which is partly a genuine success and partly a *succès de scandale*.

Cézanne, who is 56, completes his painting of the Boy in the Red Waistcoat.

Sarah Bernhardt and Lucien Guitry co-star in Rostand's *La Princesse Lointaine*.

Berthe Morisot dies, also Louis Pasteur.

Manet and Gauguin hold successful exhibitions, and Toulouse Lautrec makes his series of drawings of May Belfort.

Still in their teens, Vlaminck and Picasso are painting vigorously.

André Gide marries his cousin, writes *Paludes*, and visits Florence where he meets D'Annunzio.

Erik Satie composes his *Messe des Pauvres*.

Verdi, in his 80th year, attends a performance of his *Falstaff* at the Opéra Comique.

IN THE UNITED STATES

Thomas Armat successfully fits an intermittent movement to Edison's Kinetoscope, as a result of which he is able to screen clear motion pictures; from this prototype will come Edison's projection machine known as the Vitascope. Woodville Latham demonstrates his Panoptikon to the press in New York; Edison claims that it infringes the patents of his Kinetoscope. Nevertheless the Latham 'film' of a boxing match (running time four minutes) is screened on Broadway.

Gillette invents the safety razor.

Stephen Crane writes *The Red Badge of Courage* which, 56 years later, will be made into a film by John Huston.

President Cleveland, in pursuit of the principles of the Monroe Doctrine, tries to force Britain to submit her dispute with Venezuela to arbitration.

IN BRITAIN

R. W. Paul patents a cinematographic apparatus. He shoots some exterior scenes including *Seascape* (also known as *Rough Seas at Dover*) and the Derby. He also plans with H. G. Wells, in relation to the latter's pioneer work of science fiction *The Time Machine*, a synaesthetic happening which, had the right machinery been available, would have been years ahead of its time.

The Liberals are defeated in the General Election and Lord Salisbury forms a government.

Sir Arthur Pinero writes *The Notorious Mrs Ebbsmith* and Oscar Wilde, after the triumph of *The Importance of Being Earnest*, loses his libel action against Lord Queensberry, is convicted and sent to prison.

T. H. Huxley dies.

Henry Wood inaugurates his Promenade Concerts.

The first Automobile Exhibition is held in London.

Thomas Hardy completes *Jude the Obscure* and Joseph Conrad *Almayer's Folly*.

IN GERMANY

Max Skladanowsky patents his Bioscope and presents a not very successful programme of film at the Wintergarten in Berlin.

Wilhelm Röntgen discovers X-rays.

Richard Strauss completes his tone poem *Till Eulenspiegel*.

The Kiel Canal is opened.

Frank Wedekind writes *Der Erdgeist*, the first of two plays about Lulu which will, in the Twenties, be filmed by G. W. Pabst.

Elsewhere, on the eve of the arrival of the Lumière films, the following events may be noted:

IN RUSSIA

Tolstoy writes *Master and Man* and Tchehov completes *The Seagull*; Petipa and Ivanov create the ballet *Le Lac des Cygnes* to music by Tchaikovsky; and Rachmaninov writes his First Symphony.

IN ITALY

Marconi invents Wireless Telegraphy.

IN POLAND

Henry Sienkiewicz completes his novel *Quo Vadis?*, which will be filmed in Italy in 1912 and 1924, and in the United States in 1951.

IN AUSTRIA

Gustav Mahler embraces Roman Catholicism and composes his Third Symphony; Hugo Wolf completes his opera *Der Corregidor*; the Czech composer Anton Dvorak writes his Cello Concerto; and Sigmund Freud, with his *Studien über Hysterie*, founds Psychoanalysis.

CHAPTER I

1895 - 1915

FREE FOR ALL

The invention of photography not only signalled the decline of realistically representational painting, thus opening the way to Impressionism, Cubism, Dadaism, and suchlike; it also laid the foundations of a new Art – the first new art to be discovered by man since the dawn of civilized existence.

Man's desire to reproduce natural movement, to *make* pictures move, whether in order to propitiate the gods, tyrannize over the superstitious or add a new dimension to ceremonial drama, had up to this point been limited, indeed frustrated by the absence of a continuum. The illusion of movement, based on the long-understood principle of Persistence of Vision, had for years been achieved on the general lines of the animated, or cartoon film of today; but the length of action available was very restricted. The little episodes depicted on the zoetropes, praxinoscopes and thaumatropes were limited to the revolution of a small circular system, and lasted only a few seconds. Moreover they only worked on the peepshow principle, viewable by one person at a time. They were in essence toys; the magic of the images could never provide a communal experience.

For a shared experience, for an audience of spectators there were the alternatives of the shadow plays (especially those of Malaya and Indonesia, known as Wayang Kulit) and, later on in the West, the magic lantern, which was in effect a projector of inanimate pictures and, with the development of photography, a new element in education and information. In its later versions like the film-strip and the epidiascope, it remains much in evidence today. The shadow play, which could very effectively disport itself on a large screen in front of a large audience, had of course the basic defect that it was just as dependent on a crew of human beings as was a travelling theatre; and it was left to Lotte Reiniger in the mid-twenties to transfer this enchanting form of expression to film with *The Adventures of Prince Achmed*.

4

Thus although the principles of animated motion and of public projection had long been known, the problem of bringing the two together still awaited solution, as did that of showing images of real persons in real places and in real actions and relationships.

Photography solved the latter problem (though some of the early pioneers like Julia Margaret Cameron did everything possible to make their studies as *unrealistic* as possible). A means of projecting a long series of photographs in an action sequence, and onto a screen visible to a number of people, was all that was needed for the cinema to be born.

Photography and electricity existed. What was lacking was the right mechanism and the right material to carry the photographs. Thus, as soon as there became available a new material – celluloid – tough enough to stand the strain of intermittent movement in a projection machine and sensitive enough to accept the photographic image, the invention of the cinema was an immediate and foregone conclusion.

That is why the cinema was invented almost simultaneously in a number of different countries, with resultant claims and counter-claims which still reverberate from time to time and are usually based on regrettably chauvinist attitudes. However, the whole subject has been dealt with so exhaustively, particularly by Georges Sadoul and Terry Ramsaye,[1] that it would be superfluous to try to repeat it here. Sadoul's brilliantly compressed summary may suffice:

'In 1879 Muybridge produced the first actuality scenes in which rapid motion was broken down into its component parts. The invention of still photography on gelatine bromide, followed by the creation of "films", made it possible to construct cameras. Marey . . . in October 1888 was very probably the first man to produce really good photographs on film. Then Edison, in 1889, in conjunction with Eastman's factory, made transparent film on celluloid, long, supple and perforated – a standard product which is still in use today. With Dickson as his assistant . . . he put his Kinetoscope on the market in 1894; this apparatus opened a path for the whole world towards the invention of *projected* moving pictures.

'The first person to present a series of prolonged sessions of projected animation pictures was Emile Reynaud in 1892. The first photographed *films* were projected onto the screen – during laboratory experiments – by Le Prince, Friese Greene, Edison and Dickson (all

[1] Georges Sadoul, *L'Invention du Cinéma*, 1832–1897, Editions Denoël, 1946; *Les Pionniers du Cinéma*, 1897–1909, Editions Denoël, 1947.
Terry Ramsaye, *A Million and One Nights*, Simon and Schuster, 1926.

in 1889), Marey and Demeny (1893), etc. These were followed in 1895 by public showings (with admission charges) by Le Roy (February), Latham (April), Armat and Jenkins (September), Skladanowsky (November) and Lumière (December). But the Lumière apparatus, called the *Cinematograph*, was the only one which achieved great success, and in fact started the new industry of the production of moving pictures.'

(*L'Invention du Cinéma*, p. 338)

Despite the number of claimants and the disputes over patents and chronology which ensued in succeeding years, it is historically clear that the Lumière brothers, Louis and Auguste, deserve their recognition. Although later on their vision of the possibilities of the film became blurred, it was at this stage that they clearly realized certain things which completely eluded Edison, who seems to have regarded his own invention, the Kinetoscope, more or less as a toy; a profitable toy. The Kinetoscope was essentially a peepshow. A battery of them in an arcade could bring in a reasonable income (gross receipts from five American cities in 1895, $48,144).[1] But only one person at a time could see the programme whose length, also, was almost as limited as that of the old zoetrope. Edison in fact failed, until it was very nearly too late, to see the real point. But the Lumières did.

To Edison's Kinetoscope they opposed public projection on a large screen. To Edison's electrically-driven system running at 48 pictures per second they opposed a hand-cranked apparatus moving at 16 pictures a second, which provided the cameraman or projectionist with a physically convenient movement of two turns of the handle per second. To Edison's cumbersome apparatus, immobilized in its 'Black Maria' studio, they opposed a comparatively lightweight apparatus which one man could carry around with him. Moreover, they combined projection with photography; their representatives returned not only with box-office receipts but also with new films, shot during their travels, which formed the basis for future programmes. Nor did the Lumières have Edison's compulsive fixation on electricity; they evolved an ether lamp which ensured that they could project films in those many areas to which electric power had not yet come.[2] Finally, and most importantly, they showed *actuality*. It was in its documentary

---

[1] See Appendix to *A Million and One Nights* by Terry Ramsaye.
[2] Sadly enough it was an ether lamp, not the film apparatus itself, which caused the disastrous Charité fire in Paris in 1897 which killed many of the most illustrious aristocracy, and which earned cinema a bad name from which it took a long time to recover.

capacity that the cinema first captured its audiences. They saw themselves, or people like themselves, moving naturally about in settings they could recognize. Workers coming off shift at a factory, a train bringing commuters into a station, baby's breakfast in the garden – these fascinated, these struck home. Edison's vaudeville what-the-butler-saw Kinetoscopes had nothing like the same appeal and, of course, they lacked the all-important *shared enjoyment* of an audience.

At almost the last minute Edison realized his mistake and switched to screen-projection with his Vitascope. Soon after this a savage patents war eliminated the Lumières from the American scene. Nevertheless it was the Lumière projector and the Lumière camera which set the standard for cine-apparatus for years to come; and it was the Lumières' use of actuality for their subject matter which caused the new invention to sweep across the world in an incredibly short space of time.

After the first public showing in December 1895, Lumière films covered all of Europe, including Russia and the Balkans, during the following year, to say nothing of Egypt, India and China. By 1897 they were current in Japan, by this time in competition with Edison's Vitascope, which shows how rapid was the competition as well as the expansion of the new medium.

From this point on there was nothing to hinder the development of this new art form except the stupidity and cupidity of human beings. Some regarded it as a novelty whose interest value would soon fade. Others, perhaps in a confused way, saw it as a potential gold-mine. Others, like doctors Doyen and Comandon, instantly saw its value as an instrument of teaching and for the exchange of scientific knowledge and technique. But at this early stage practically no one saw it for what it really was and is – a new and very powerful sort of magic based, like the real magic of the aborigines, on the inner meaning of the animate and inanimate actuality which surrounds us, and in which we live and move and have our being (or which lives and moves in us). The gradual realization or discovery of this fact through trial and error, despite ignorance and because of instinct, is the significant factor of the first twenty years of the moving picture.

The successful film-makers, surely, have always been those who realize and have access to this deeply rooted, almost ceremonial and magical affinity.

As Claude Lévi-Strauss points out in *The Savage Mind*, 'Art lies halfway between scientific knowledge and magical or mythical thought'. So one of the first people to call on the Lumière brothers after their pioneer public showing in 1895 was a well-known conjurer and illusionist from the Théâtre Robert-Houdin, Georges Méliès.

By a curious paradox Méliès, while of course snatching at the new medium as an almost unbelievable, almost illimitable extension to the craft of the illusionist, somehow stumbled on the idea of reality as well. In addition to his illusion films he also – having no doubt noted the success of the Lumière 'documentaries' – went to tremendous trouble to reconstruct (nowadays one would say fake) contemporary news events, including the Potemkin episode, the Dreyfus Case and the eruption of Mont Pelée. The interesting thing is that in those early days these reconstructions, whose falsity to us is more than obvious, were often accepted by audiences as newsreels.

Today we revere Méliès as the first genius of cinema because he was a fantasist; because he saw the literally fantastic possibilities of the new medium. It is likely, however, that we may not realize what were the real reactions of his contemporary audiences. Of course he did not expect his fantasies to be taken completely seriously; one of his best films is entitled *Voyage à travers l'Impossible*. Yet today, when we sit in the theatre and watch the marvels of *2001—A Space Odyssey*, are we quite sure we know exactly how Méliès' spectators viewed his film?[1] I think it must be true that at that time people participated with a psychological naïveté which we have lost today. And this may bring us back to the Lévi-Strauss attitude.

The magico-mythological element of the motion picture, as opposed to the scientific-technological aspect, involves a double aspect of reality. A film can give an impression of actuality – a reality which we accept as being in line with our daily experience of the world. But a film can also give an impression of super-reality – the reality of one of those dreams whose circumstance we do not accept as part of our daily experience, but whose intensity seems to produce a conviction of reality superior to actuality itself. (Such indeed must, in part, be the experience of the visionary.)

Surely then the reaction of Méliès' audiences to his films, seen in a mytho-magical light, must raise the question of the relationship between films and dreams. No doubt the aspect of this matter which will come quickest to mind is that of wish-fulfilment, an attribute which for many years film-makers were accused of valuing above all else in terms of extracting maximum cash from the film-going public. In other words, they were trying in their films to reflect, indeed to

---

[1] The press pictures of the Soviet moon vehicle published in 1970 gave the impression that it had been personally designed by Méliès.

pretend to satisfy vicariously the unspoken desires, ambitions and daydreams of ordinary folk. Indeed in 1950 an eminent anthropologist published a study of Hollywood as a dream factory;[1] and there is that familiar phrase 'Dreams that Money Can Buy' used, among others, by Hans Richter as the title for his anthology of experimental films.

Early on in his *Psychology of the Unconscious*, Jung puts forward one of what were to be a large number of developing definitions: 'The dream arises from a part of the mind unknown to us, but none the less important, and is concerned with the desires for the approaching day'. This, of course, apart from anything else, implies elements of anxiety and of prayer; and if one could make a film on the same 'wavelength' so as to resolve, or appear to resolve, these desires and prayers, the spectators might well enjoy a vicarious impression of wish-fulfilment not at all unlike that of a genuine dream.

If we move forward with Jung's developing thoughts, we come to his theory of the collective unconscious and of the archetypes – heritages, he claims, shared by the whole of humankind. If, as he suggests, dreams are capable of arousing in individuals 'not only the contents of personal conflicts but also manifestations of the collective unconscious',[2] might not films, if only to a degree, have something of the same ability? If the dream has its own purposiveness unknown to our own consciousness, this may mean that 'one does not dream; one is dreamed. We "undergo" the dream; we are the objects'.[3] Could it not then be said that in certain cases we may voluntarily 'undergo' a dream experience in the course of seeing a certain type of film? Furthermore if, as is possible, our subconscious is in fact dreaming continuously while our conscious only perceives this in a state of sleep, might not the film, again in certain circumstances, tap this continuous 'dream' activity with results almost identical with those of the dream itself?

To quote Jung yet again, the dream 'is a series of images which are apparently contradictory and nonsensical, but arise in reality from psychological material which yields a clear meaning'.[4] Here we have an extremely filmic statement suggesting, for example, the condition of a film before it is edited and, more particularly, Dziga Vertov's theory of the Kino-Eye (Kinoki), in which the primary function of expression passes largely from the film-maker to the camera itself, so that what the

---

[1] *Hollywood, the Dream Factory*, by Hortense Powdermaker, Secker and Warburg, 1951.

[2] Jung, *Psychology of the Unconscious.*

[3] Jung, *Seminar on Children's Dreams*, 1938.

[4] Jung, *Psychology of the Unconscious.*

camera has recorded represents a kind of jigsaw puzzle out of which the film-maker must make for the screen a pattern intelligible to his audience. Suzanne Langer picks up this point when she writes that 'The percipient of a moving picture sees with the camera. . . . The camera is his eye (as the microphone is his ear – and there is no reason why a mind's eye and a mind's ear must always stay together). *He takes the place of the dreamer*, but in a perfectly objectified dream – that is, he is not in the story. The work is the appearance of a dream, a unified, continuously significant apparition.'[1] (We can note here Vertov's mistake in giving the camera *total* priority.)

Earlier in her book Langer discusses the image of time in relation to music, pointing out that music liberates us from ordinary time as we normally know and accept it, and creates its own 'virtual' time, as she calls it. I think that the idea of filmic time has something in common with this. Film involves us in the three linked factors of time, memory, dream. All our big experiences are likely to involve interference with, or distortion of, one or all of these factors; and this is especially true of aesthetic experience. For instance, that impression we sometimes get that we know exactly what is going to happen next is a memory-distortion in which we seem to be trying to make our time-sense work in the opposite direction (unless it is something more than this, as suggested by J. W. Dunne in *An Experiment with Time*).

Simulacra of this can be found in terms of cinema. In my own *Song of Ceylon* certain religious images (of Buddhist provenance) are shown only in brief flashes early in the film, not being explained as themselves but placed in an acceptable context involving the flight of birds at dawn; but their real significance is not known until the last reel. So too in Resnais' *L'Année Dernière à Marienbad*, the flash-forwards of the woman sitting up in her bed are designed to make us participate in the dislocation of time which is part of the man's compulsive and continual approaches to her. We may note too that new cinematic styles, such as the substitution of arbitrary jump-cuts (often within a single set-up) instead of 'normal' film continuity, accentuate the dream-like quality of film by further dislocating temporal and, to a degree, spatial apprehension.

Langer also remarks that 'Drama is "like" action in being causal, creating a total imminent experience, a personal "future" or Destiny. Cinema is "like" dream in the mode of its presentation: it creates a virtual present, an order of direct apparition. That is the mode of

[1] Suzanne K. Langer, *Feeling and Form: A Theory of Art*, Routledge and Kegan Paul, 1953.

dream'. On the other hand Jung eventually came to conceive of the structure of the dream rather along the lines of classical tragedy. On this basis a dream will consist of (a) Time, place and dramatis personae; (b) Exposition (probably of a theme supplied from the unconscious); (c) Peripeteia, in which the plot develops to a crisis – catastrophic or otherwise; and (d) Lysis – the solution, the relaxing of tension, and possibly (in psychoanalytic terms) a meaningful conclusion.

As classical tragedy is a major repository of archetypes, and as, at least until recently, the fiction film has remained, broadly speaking, within the Aristotelian boundaries, this idea suggests a strong affinity between film and dream. I wish Jung had paid more attention to cinema, especially in terms of those filmic illogicalities which are often, as with Resnais, only acceptable in terms of dream (for the apparent logicality of a dream is rejected by the wakened brain), but can, perhaps, be accepted as signals reaching us from inner rather than outer space. It is still a question of wavelength.

Apart from *Hiroshima Mon Amour*, *L'Année Dernière à Marienbad* and *Je t'Aime*, *Je t'Aime*, there are two films, Cocteau's *Orphée* and Chris Marker's *La Jetée*, which particularly involve the spectator in powerful dislocations of the sense of time and space. *Orphée*, partly by reason of the realism and modernity of its settings, tends to evoke the feeling of a waking dream; indeed whenever I see this film I emerge into the street in a condition of doubt about the nature of reality – my own and that of the traffic and people who surround me. Is this perhaps a tapping of that part of our subconscious which, as some suppose, dreams continuously, night and day, sleeping and waking, throughout our lives? As for *La Jetée* – by eschewing all movement *within the frame* (except for one seismic moment) it involves us almost formally in a depth of dream, or in this case nightmare, whose 'reality' we try vainly to reject, not merely because of the fear aroused by the theme but also because the overt attack on our time-sense is almost too much to be endured. To this film, to *Je t'Aime*, *Je t'Aime* which partly derives from it, and to *Hiroshima Mon Amour*, I shall devote a little more space later in this book.[1]

The Orpheus legend is, of course, in Jungian terms, a perfect archetype. It has been the source of inspiration for many artists in many periods, and at this particular time, when civilized man is living among the images of his own death, standing, like the acrophobe, on the edge of the precipice from which he fears to fall and yet almost

[1] See chapter 5. Unfortunately Roeg's *Don't Look Now* appeared too late for discussion and analysis.

certainly will leap, this legend of man's contest with death, the known and unknown quantity, loses nothing of its power.

The whole of Cocteau's film has a dreamlike quality which arises, at least in part, from the realistic element I have already mentioned. Death's bodyguards are motor-cyclists – or should we now say Hell's Angels? The mysterious messages from Hades ('L'oiseau chante avec ses doigts', etc) are received on a car radio. Hades is a blitzed city. And Death itself, beautiful and terrible Death, turns out to be a secret agent, elegant and perhaps royal, who is in the end seen to be subject to the arbitrament of an anonymous tribunal in a dirty cellar – a tribunal acting for . . . well, for whom? To which Cocteau gave his own cryptic answer. The Princess, the agent, 'is Orpheus' own death, a satellite of death itself'.[1] So the film continues in 'that half-light in which enigmas flourish', and when Orpheus tries to follow supposed Death through the mirror in a deserted villa it is no longer 'glassy . . . translucent' like Sabrina's wave; it is adamantine. He swoons, and we see both himself and his reflected self slide to the floor. The reflection is repeated, but this time it turns out to be a puddle, and as he regains consciousness and raises his head, the camera withdraws to reveal that the deserted villa has disappeared and that Orpheus is lying in a drab suburban wasteland. Another image is that of Orpheus' journey into the kingdom of death, through a ruined city in which a chilling wind blows about the hair of the dead but not of the living until, at a certain corner, it becomes universal, and both leader and led are swept by the Plutonic gale along the side of a wall.

Langer quotes R. E. Jones as saying that films 'project pure thought, pure dream, pure inner life'. To this flattering and somewhat over-compendious compliment she adds her opinion that 'the "dreamed reality" on the screen can move forward and backward because it is really an eternal and ubiquitous virtual present. . . . The dream mode is an endless Now'. The subconscious too may be an endless Now – the agent perhaps of the collective unconscious; and it may be that by these paths we can pursue the mystery of film aesthetic.

But at the aesthetic level Professor Gombrich sounds a mild warning. In considering Dali's painting *Apparition of Face and Fruit-dish on a Beach*, with its disturbing visual puns and provocations which flow in and out of shape and focus before our eyes, he describes it as an attempt to 'imitate (the) weird confusion of our dream-life' in which 'some things . . . stand out with unexpected clarity while other shapes remain vague and elusive'. He goes on:

[1] *Cocteau* by Francis Steegmuller, Macmillan, 1970.

'Dali's sea-shell which is also an eye, his fruit bowl which is also a girl's forehead and nose, may send our thoughts back to the first chapter of this book, to the Aztec rain-god Tlaloc, whose features were composed of rattlesnakes.

'And yet – if we really take the trouble of looking up the ancient idol we may receive something of a shock – how great is the difference in spirit for all possible similarity of method! Both images may have emerged from a dream, but Tlaloc, we feel, was the dream of a whole people, the nightmare figure of the dire power that held sway over their fate; Dali's dog and fruit-bowl reflect the elusive dream of a private person to which we hold no key.[1]'

This is a very neat analysis of the difference in communication represented by the Jungian theory (Tlaloc), which must in the final issue be seen to be universal, and the private, the in the original Greek sense 'idiotic' message of Dali which may or may not get through and, if it doesn't, has no more than surface significance, like the wrapping on a box of candy which one cannot or does not want to open. We can continue to bump back towards the asphalt road of hard practicalities by noting the following from Arnold Hauser:

'Film production owes its greatest successes to the realization that the mind of the petty bourgeois is the psychological meeting place of the masses. The psychological category of this human type has, however, a wider range than the sociological category of the actual middle class; it embraces fragments of both the upper and the lower classes, that is to say, the very considerable elements who, where they are not engaged in a direct struggle for their existence, join forces unreservedly with the middle classes, above all in the matter of entertainment.'[2]

If we strip this statement of its doctrinaire jargon and allow also for the fact that it is based on the assumption that Hollywood and the systems it represented were indestructible – which we now know was not the case – it still remains true that even at this low level of appreciation there are psychological considerations in relation to the box-office, if only in its aspect of wish-fulfilment, which have to be borne in mind. And on Dr Hauser's petty bourgeois level, if not somewhat higher, an experiment carried out in 1970 by Dr Christopher Evans of the National Physical Laboratory may be of some interest. Dr Evans was concerned

[1] *The Story of Art* by E. H. Gombrich, Phaidon, 1950.
[2] *The Social History of Art, Part 4*, by Arnold Hauser, Routledge and Kegan Paul, 1951.

in a theory involving comparison between dreaming and computer programme clearance. With the cooperation of the Weekend Supplement of a Sunday paper he submitted a questionnaire which had one simple object – to find out from people what films reminded them of their own personal dreams; it deliberately went no further than that.

Somewhat to Dr Evans' surprise, no less than 30,000 people filled in the questionnaire, and out of their replies over one hundred films emerged. The 'Top Twenty' from these provided some surprises (*The Graduate, Dr Zhivago*) as well as some certainties including *Orphée, The Seventh Seal, Wild Strawberries, L'Année Dernière à Marienbad*, and *2001*. The two latter headed the voting list; *Orphée* came rather low down, but this may well be accounted for by the fact that it has not been in wide circulation in recent years.[1]

In evaluating these results Dr Evans pointed out that below the surface of verbal and aural communication there must be a mass of ineffable material. While we share our external world with each other, we all have our own interior worlds which cannot be shared. Dreams, while on the one hand helping us to process information received during the day, may on the other hand be helping us to map out our inner world.

The information obtained by Dr Evans may indeed help with his computer world. But neither the knowledge of what films most resemble people's dreams nor of what films people dream about most (as in the *Picturegoer* survey used by J. P. Mayer in his *Sociology of the Film*, published in 1946, in which Deanna Durbin, Bette Davis, Gene Kelly,[2] *Gone with the Wind* and *The Song of Bernadette* featured quite markedly) can be as important as the resemblance between experiencing a film and experiencing a dream. That this is only a part of the whole philosophy of aesthetics is obvious, but the newness of the film as an art suggests

---

[1] The full list was: 1 *L'Année Dernière à Marienbad*, 2 *2001*, 3 *Juliet of the Spirits*, 4 *Alice in Wonderland* (the Jonathan Miller TV production), 5 *Wild Strawberries*, 6 *Yellow Submarine*, 7 *8½*, 8 *The Trial*, 9 *Blow-Up*, 10 *Orphée*, 11 *Dr Zhivago*, 12 *Incident at Owl Creek*, 13 *Repulsion*, 14 *Belle de Jour*, 15 *The Seventh Seal*, 16 *A Man and a Woman*, 17 *Barbarella*, 18 *The Graduate*, 19 *Rosemary's Baby*, 20 *Fantasia*, 21 *La Belle et la Bête*.

[2] For example: 'I am 18 years of age, and films mean a great deal to me . . . films have appeared in my dreams sometimes I seem to be a part of them, and sometimes scenes from different films appear for instance I had a dream recently in which I danced with Gene Kelly fantastic, I know, but that was the dream. Scenes from *Rebecca, Dark Victory, Now Voyager* and *Cover Girl* have appeared in my dreams, stars also appear these include Bette Davis, Spencer Tracy, Gene Kelly, Paul Henreid, Stewart Granger and many others. Well I think that is all I can tell you about myself except that I am 5 ft 9½ins tall, have blue eyes, brown hair, weight 10 st 2 lbs.' (Mr X (Scotland).)

a need for someone of the highest calibre to make a deep study along these lines.

Recent research has indicated the probability that people deprived of dreaming may become mentally disturbed or worse. One need not proceed from this to claim that people deprived of moving pictures would show similar symptoms; although in Ray Bradbury's book *Fahrenheit 451* the withdrawal of the perpetual television programme is the severest sanction short of death which the State can impose – and science fiction is constantly being overtaken by reality. But it may well be that there is something in the motion picture which can sometimes help to give a sort of expression to the ineffable within us. We shall have to come back to this later when the possible relationship, in terms of effect, between the modern hallucinogens and the coming development of psychedelic or synaesthetic multi-media production demands consideration.

On the more ordinary level, of course, we might say that in terms of the motion picture the human being is as gullible as they come; and being willingly and delightedly gulled is not quite the same thing as suspension of disbelief. And in those early days the impact of the film may indeed have been much stronger, perhaps sometimes in its feeling of Magic quite traumatically so, than it is today, and so has become extraordinarily closely knit with the simple ideas and simple dreams of ordinary people; and perhaps of extraordinary people too. At any rate Tolstoy, on his 80th birthday in 1908 said of the film, 'this swift change of scene, this blending of emotion and experience – it is much better than the heavy, long-drawn-out kind of writing to which we are accustomed. It is closer to life. In life, too, changes and transitions flash by before our eyes, and emotions of the soul are like a hurricane. The cinema has divined the mystery of motion. And that is greatness.'[1]

Meantime there was Georges Méliès realizing, within his own particular limitation, many of the potentialities of cinema and, from 1896 to 1913, pouring a cascade of pictures into the rapidly growing market. As he himself wrote, 'It is the intelligent use of trickwork which enables us to make visible the supernatural, the imaginary, even the impossible; and to create truly artistic pictures which are a veritable feast for those who can understand how all aspects of Art are synthesized in their creation'[2] – a statement which in some ways foreshadows Eisenstein's remarks during one of his London lectures in 1929, 'The

[1] Quoted in *Kino* by Jay Leyda, Allen and Unwin, 1960.
[2] *Centenary of Georges Méliès*, Cinémathèque Française, 1961, p. 63.

historical moment has come at which we are to find the synthesis of art and science in an entirely new form of picturization'.[1]

Méliès had the *instinct* for cinema – that was the important thing. And the instinct was passed on. In 1910 Dadasaheb Phalke, a forty-year-old Indian from Bombay who had just recovered from an attack of blindness, happened to see a film on the Life of Christ.[2] He was so impressed that he went to see it again, and thereupon decided that, come what may, he would devote the rest of his life to film-making. Phalke was a photographer, a skilled art printer, and like Méliès an expert magician; he was now to become the virtual founder of the Indian Film Industry. By 1911 he had raised enough money to visit England, whence he returned early in 1912 with a movie camera, full laboratory equipment, and enough film stock to keep him going for several months.

Phalke's basic idea was to film the mytho-religious stories of the Hindu gods and goddesses. His first film was *Rajah Harischandra*, a pioneer spectacular lasting some 45 minutes, which opened in Bombay in 1913. It was a smash hit, mainly because it was the first film ever made about India for Indians; Phalke was bringing them their own legends, their own gods, their own magic. The impact was tremendous. 'When Rama appeared on the screen in *Lanka Dahan*, and when in *Krishna Janma* Lord Krishna himself at last appeared, men and women in the audience prostrated themselves before the screen'.[3] Cinemas showing Phalke's films were besieged by crowds day and night. Some cinemas kept open for 18 hours out of 24.

Phalke embarked on a programme of hundreds of films, using trick work and effects on at least as large a scale as Méliès and with similar success. Sections of some of his films, miraculously preserved in view of the effect of heat on nitrate film, are in the hands of the Film Institute of India; their production values are extremely impressive.

So from 1913 onwards a basic pattern was set for Indian film-making; and although later on other styles and subjects were developed, a large volume of contemporary Indian film production follows the magical-mythological vein whose import Phalke, in a more conscious manner than Méliès, so successfully exploited.

Anyone who visits India and experiences the beauty and the horrors of that fascinating, frightening and tantalizing subcontinent, will understand how Phalke's vision brought to millions of ignorant,

[1] *Sergei M. Eisenstein* by Marie Seton, The Bodley Head, 1952.
[2] Probably either Zecca's of 1905 or Jasset's of 1908.
[3] *Indian Film* by Erik Barnouw and S. Krishnaswamy, Columbia University Press, 1963.

poverty-stricken, under-nourished but deeply religious people a regular source of spiritual comfort and experience which must have been literally beyond price. You can, of course, particularly in hindsight, call it exploitation of superstition, if you feel so inclined. You can point out that it involves, or originally involved, large profits on comparatively small outlays. But in the end the Indian example differs little from what happened in America or Europe in terms of the revelation of what this new medium could mean to ordinary people everywhere in the world.

One of the results of the Industrial Revolution was cultural starvation of the masses. As long as life involved the village and the market town, the old traditions of drama and dancing and so on could persist. But the proliferation of factories and the resultant population explosion produced circumstances of deprivation little different from those with which Phalke was later to be concerned under the British Raj. With the expansion of the moving picture the whole situation changed in a few years. Millions who had never had a communal experience beyond a strike or a lockout were suddenly offered, *at a price within their competence*, all the riches and romances of a visual world. The cinema restored to the great mass of humanity the magic and the myths from which it had for so long been cut off.

Thus to the workers in Europe and America, too, the cinema became an all-pervasive cult, or a popular escape-hatch from the misery of working conditions and slum life. It was not only the *Charité* disaster which kept the 'respectable' classes away from the cinemas in the early days; it was also the sense that films were a form of entertainment specially provided for the 'lower classes'.

Yet it was those films which appealed to those same 'lower classes' which won out in the end, and from which basically the real art of the moving picture grew.

Thus it was that the instinct of film-makers like Ferdinand Zecca proved superior to that of Méliès. Zecca, who began as an imitator of Méliès, later went to meet the masses on their own ground. His early successes like *Les Victimes de l'Alcöol* or *L'Histoire d'un Crime* – made around 1902 – could be readily appreciated and understood (from experience) by audiences in fairgrounds and suchlike places which were the main exhibition centres for the early films. As in the case of the early Lumière films, they could identify directly. The swing to pictorial realism or representationalism became stronger and stronger; by 1913 Méliès' market had vanished.

Zecca was in fact influenced by the early work of British pioneers like George Albert Smith, James Williamson and others; and in general it may be said that the early developments of the medium followed the same patterns almost everywhere. Various methods turned out to lead up blind alleys, such as the formalized Films d'Art, in which the particular properties of the motion picture were totally ignored. As late as 1916 the young Abel Gance was being reproved by his producer for shooting close-ups; but the fixed camera position and the stilted exaggeration of the acting of the Film d'Art was bound to ensure its demise, as can be seen by contrasting Sarah Bernhardt's films with the brooding intensity of Eleonora Duse in *Cenere*. The differencehere is simply between incomprehension and comprehension. Bernhardt and her producers had failed to understand the medium; whereas in *Cenere* (her only film) Duse and her director actually anticipated the Neo-Realist style of the late Forties. She had entered into the inner spirit, had realized the magical attraction, of the moving picture.

In the first twenty years of cinema no one country attained predominance; and all countries were involved in similar trials and errors. By the time the errors had been more or less eliminated there survived, by 1915, the melodramas (serial or otherwise), the comedies, the westerns, the travelogues and the super-spectaculars. All of these survived because they partook of the essential nature of cinema. They survived because they had nothing to do with the theatre; which does not mean that they had nothing to do with the drama. They were of course dramatic. They ranged about in street and field, house and palace. They were full of dramatic movement. I remember it. A fire brigade! A car chase! A custard pie in full flight! A train smash! Red Indians on the warpath! These are visual images as vivid today as when I first saw them – to say nothing of more specific images such as the babies being thrown into the white-hot maw of Moloch's belly in *Cabiria*, or the sickening thuds[1] of the pillars falling on to flesh and blood in *The Last Days of Pompeii*.

They really were convincing, those movies. The suspension of disbelief could be absolute. One entered into the action on the screen body and soul. One did not observe the performance; one lived it. One identified – how one identified; with Charlie cocking a snook at society, with the mother expecting her darling son from the wars and receiving him in a coffin draped with the American flag (I can see the change in her expression now as she came out of the front door at the top of a flight of steps), and, of course, with the dream-like, octopus-ridden sea-world of Annette Kellerman (thank you, Herbert Brenon).

[1] The fallacy of the so-called 'silent' film will be dealt with shortly.

If today we are looking at these early films, it is worth remembering that it is as important to adjust our sense of appreciation of them as it is when we read Chaucer's English or cast our eyes on a painting by Uccello. In this way, by an effort, we may get to an approximation of what they meant to the spectator at the time.

The spectator at the time was of course the victim, or at least the guinea-pig (willing, probably) of the emergent tycoon; and patterns were being set from which the film industry would not depart for years to come. The tycoons were born of the sudden realization that an almost unlimited number of copies of a single film could be shown all over the world, at the same time, to countless people. Their story is one of vision, opportunism, sharp dealing, foresight and skullduggery – the story, in a word, of the new god Box-Office.

It is curious that it was the inventors who failed to see the opportunities. The Lumières went so far, and then withdrew, feeling that the novelty value of cinema had been fully exploited; while Edison found himself, in frantic hindsight, trying to protect (patent-wise or otherwise) the invention which he had originally regarded as a passing novelty. In doing this he began an internecine conflict in the United States which led to a westward migration and the establishment of Hollywood.

Basically the actions of Edison and his associates were 'anti-American' in the sense that they were aimed at evading the Sherman Anti-Trust Act of 1890. They thought that they could get away with a swingeing monopoly of production, distribution and exhibition if they based their position solely on the possession of existing patents. This worked well for a while: but soon some of the independents such as Carl Laemmle and William Fox, who had been making all their money in a wild free-for-all market, fought back. They carried the battle into the enemy's camp by going into production themselves and, despite actual violence used as a deliberate policy by the Patent Company, they refused to be intimidated. By 1912, when the Woodrow Wilson administration decided to slap down the Patent Company, the battle was in fact won. Hollywood was to be the centre of American film-making, and, a couple of years later, the names of soon-to-be-famous film companies – Universal, Fox, Paramount – were already established, with others, to be associated with such names as Goldwyn, Mayer, Lasky and Warner, just under the horizon.

So far, however, no country had achieved a world monopoly in terms of film. Although Méliès and Pathé had been members of the Patent Company racket, this was only, from their point of view, one facet of the general export market from France. Basically, in Europe as well as Asia, the cinema world was a world of free trade. Most countries produced films; and most countries exported and imported films. The only exception was that films from oriental countries, largely owing to alleged differences of custom and culture, seldom came westwards. Japan and China, on the contrary, tended to show an increasing demand for American and European film – though it may be noted that when Phalke brought his first three films to London in 1914 they were respectfully received and reviewed; and as early as 1904–1905 the Japanese pioneer Kenichi Kawaura took various indigenous newsreels and travelogues to the United States, not without success.

It is hardly surprising, then, that the development of the film industry in various countries followed more or less the same pattern. After a tentative start came the realization of the almost unlimited financial possibilities. Films became longer, more elaborate, more expensive – and none the less more profitable. Thus the super-film came into fashion: from Britain came Will Barker's epic *Jane Shore* (with torn-up paper running sadly short towards the end of the snowstorm scene) and, importantly, the sensational Kinemacolor film of George V's Durbar in New Delhi; from Italy *Cabiria*, *Quo Vadis?* and others; from France *La Vie de Notre Seigneur Jésus Christ* and Feuillade's *Fantômas*; from India Phalke's mytho-religious dramas; from Russia *The Siege of Sevastopol*; from Japan *The Loyal Forty-Seven Ronin*; from Germany the early versions of *The Golem* and *The Student of Prague*; while, brewing up in the background with *Judith of Bethulia*, D. W. Griffith was preparing to blow everything sky-high with the scope and sweep and novelty of *Birth of a Nation* – a film which was not only to change the whole conception of cinema but would also, as Europe plunged into all-out war, signal the establishment of a world-wide monopoly of the film by the United States.

All this time, as ever in film history, a less spectacular element continued to develop – the academic and the scientific. Doctors, scientists and educationists, who had been, like Doyen and Comandon, among the first to recognize the potential of cinema in their own work, were still pressing on, unpublicized. At the same time there were others who were beginning to theorize and to write about the aesthetics of the new medium. In Hungary, for instance, Cecil Bognár, a Benedictine monk with an interest in philosophy and psychology, was writing on film well before 1915 at a time when Sándor (later Sir Alexander) Korda was directing his first films in Budapest. Cecil Bognár took the attitude that 'the film itself is actually only an instrument, a raw material, like paint or type', and went on to point out that while film may produce art, it may also be a means of scientific communication, of information and even of *perception* – in this anticipating some of the later speculations of Rudolf Arnheim. And it was in 1915 that there appeared the first real book on cinema, Vachel Lindsay's *Art of the Moving Picture*.

But the final arbiter was the audience – the great grey anonymous masses who had taken the cinema to their hearts. Here, for them, were the purchasable dreams, reasonably priced. Here too were warmth, and the privacy of darkness. Here too, soon, would be luxury as well – the Picture Palace, aptly named. At these early stages the arguments and battles – puritanical, political or progressive – over the 'influence' of the film were yet to come, though even in the earliest days the rumblings had begun. Maxim Gorky, for instance, in writing about the first showing of the Cinematograph in Nizhni-Novgorod in 1896:

'Without fear of exaggeration, a wide use can be predicted for this invention, because of its tremendous novelty. But how great are its results, compared with the expenditure of nervous energy that it requires? Is it possible for it to be applied usefully enough to compensate for the nervous strain it produces in the spectator? A yet more important problem is that our nerves are getting weaker and less reliable, we are reacting less to natural sensations of our daily life, and thirst more eagerly for new strong sensations.[1]

'The cinematograph gives you all these – cultivating the nerves on the one hand and dulling them on the other! The thirst for such strange fantastic sensations as it gives will grow ever greater, and we will be increasingly less able and less willing to grasp the everyday impressions of ordinary life.'[2]

Whether or not this can be regarded as an early example of Leninist-Marxist Socialist Realism, Gorky certainly foresaw with some clarity the general direction in which cinema was to develop. But whether, in the event, the cinema industry could be accused of pandering to, or alternatively underestimating the tastes and values of its audiences, the plain fact remained that, by 1915, the movie was a magnet, and a powerful one.

All this took place despite the fact that up to this point, and

[1] This was written after the appalling Khodinka disaster when more than 5,000 people were trampled to death in a panic during the personal appearance of the Tsar. This had been filmed by two Lumière employees, Moisson and Doublier – but their film was confiscated and destroyed.

[2] Quoted in *Kino* by Jay Leyda.

indeed for another ten years after, the film medium was hampered by the lack of synchronous dialogue, and had to rely (outside Japan, where the benshi, or narrator, tyrannized) on the crude explanatory shorthand of the subtitle.

Yet maybe, in these early stages, this very malformation contributed to the cinema's success. It was a medium in which language barriers did not exist; international distribution was simplicity itself, the cost of translating and making titles being minimal. Moreover, the inability to reproduce speech put a premium on miming, and this, at its best, gave us Chaplin, Keaton, Langdon. Indeed, the comics may have survived better than any other films of the period because they formalized their movements almost as strictly as did the great *maîtres de ballet*. These formal movements, satisfying expectations but at the same time pregnant with surprises, are to be observed not only in individual artists but also in groups like the Bathing Beauties and the Keystone Cops. In the dramas of the period, on the other hand, one finds (with exceptions) too many echoes of Vincent Crummles, too much exaggeration of gesture to compensate for being dumb (a word, incidentally, which the Americans equate with 'stupid'). The one exception in melodrama is seen in the action pictures – cops and robbers or redskins and cowboys – where the melodrama is transmuted into an acceptable pattern by the presence of the horses and buffaloes and the majestic and illimitable perspectives of the American West.

The comics, the westerns, and the revolution known as D. W. Griffith; these are the golden legacies of the first twenty years of the moving picture.

SIGNPOST - 1915

THE YEAR OF 'BIRTH OF A NATION'

IN THE UNITED STATES

Theda Bara, the first vamp, scores a tremendous success with *A Fool There Was*, based on the Rudyard Kipling poem *The Vampire* (which in turn had been inspired by a painting by Burne Jones); Douglas Fairbanks makes his debut as a screen actor in *The Lamb* produced, somewhat reluctantly, by D. W. Griffith; Charles Chaplin completes 17 films under his $1250 a week contract with Essanay, including *The Champion*, *Shanghaied*, and *Carmen*. Cecil B. De Mille directs his own production of *Carmen* starring Geraldine Farrar; Mary Pickford is under contract to Adolph Zukor for the unprecedented sum of over $100,000 a year; Herbert Brenon's aquatic films with Annette Kellerman are at the height of their popularity, while serial films, including the first episodes of *The Exploits of Elaine*, with Pearl White, are all the rage. A film version of Brieux's *Damaged Goods* (a drama on the subject of venereal disease) grosses $600,000 against a production cost of $40,000. Carl Laemmle establishes Universal City, a new studio in the San Fernando Valley, California; and the Fox Corporation is founded. The poet Vachel Lindsay writes the first book of real film criticism – *The Art of the Moving Picture*.

The Panama Canal, completed in 1914, is now opened to world shipping.

The *Lusitania* is torpedoed and sunk by a German submarine, with great loss of life.

Camille Saint-Saëns composes *Hail! California!* for the Panama Pacific Exposition and brings the score personally to San Francisco.

Henry Ford develops the first farm tractor.

Harry Leon Wilson publishes *Ruggles of Red Gap* which will be filmed in 1923 with Edward Everett Horton and in 1935 with Charles Laughton.

Edgar Lee Masters brings out his *Spoon River Anthology*.

Anthony Comstock, Secretary of the Society for the Suppression of Vice, dies.

IN FRANCE

Abel Gance directs *La Folie du Docteur Tube*, never shown to the public but a pioneer film in the development of cinema. Henri Krauss directs *Le Chemineau*, and Louis Feuillade, at the height of his powers, makes his serial *Les Vampires*.

Aristide Briand becomes Prime Minister of France.

Henri Gaudier-Brzeska is killed on active service with the French Army; and Georges Braque is wounded.

Modigliani abandons sculpture for painting; Picasso concentrates on Cubism; Renoir paints his *Femme au Corsage Rose*, *La Liseuse Rose* and *Paysage Bleu*; and Marcel Duchamp starts work on *La Mariée Mise à Nu par ses Célibataires, Même*, which will not be completed until 1923.

Rémy de Gourmont dies; and Sarah Bernhardt has her right leg amputated.

Romain Rolland receives the Nobel Prize for Literature.

Debussy composes his *Twelve Etudes for Piano*.

Diaghilev produces *Le Soleil de Minuit* with Massine, to music by Rimsky-Korsakov and decor by Larionov.

IN BRITAIN

Cecil Hepworth directs (among others) *Barnaby Rudge*, with Stewart Rome and Chrissie White; *Sweet Lavender* by Sir Arthur Pinero, with Henry Ainley and Alma Taylor; and *The Man Who Stayed at Home*. Will Barker launches his spectacular historical film *Jane Shore*. George Pearson directs his thriller *Ultus the Man from the Dead*.

Herbert Asquith forms a coalition government.

Hubert Parry sets William Blake's *Jerusalem* to music; and Gustav Holst composes *The Planets*.

Joseph Conrad's *Victory* is published, as is Somerset Maugham's *Of Human Bondage*; D. H. Lawrence's *The Rainbow* is declared obscene, the publishers are fined and all copies of the book destroyed.

Henry James becomes a British citizen and five months later has a stroke.

James Elroy Flecker dies of tuberculosis and Rupert Brooke (while serving in the Royal Navy) of septicaemia.

IN GERMANY

Paul Wegener directs his first version of *The Golem*, playing the title part himself; he will re-make it in 1920.

The Germans use flamethrowers and poison gas for the first time.
Einstein enunciates his Theory of Relativity.
Max Ernst is serving in the German Army.
Richard Strauss completes his Alpine Symphony.

IN ITALY

Eleonora Duse makes her only screen appearance in *Cenere*, a film much ahead of its time and anticipating in some measure the neo-realist films of the late Forties. Pirandello is working on his novel about the film world, to be entitled *Si Gira*.

Italy enters the war on the side of the Allies.
Chirico paints *Jouets de Prince* and *Mélancolie du Départ*; and serves in the Army.
Respighi's *Sinfonia Drammatica* receives its first performance in Rome.

IN RUSSIA

Vsevolod Meyerhold directs a screen version of Wilde's *The Picture of Dorian Gray* in which he also plays the part of Lord Henry Wotton; the part of Dorian is played by a woman, and the decor and lighting make an extraordinary impression. Chaliapin appears as Ivan the Terrible in a film based on Rimsky-Korsakov's opera *Pskovityanka*, directed by A. Ivanov Gai.

German and Austrian armies invade Poland, and the Russian forces retreat from East Prussia and Galicia.
Scriabin dies.
Chagall paints *Le Poète Allongé* and is conscripted into the Russian army.
Rasputin is now the effective ruler of Russia.

IN DENMARK

Asta Nielsen and Valdemar Psilander appear in *The Dark Dream* and Benjamin Christensen directs *Night of Revenge*.

Women in Denmark get the Vote.

IN HUNGARY

Sándor (later Sir Alexander) Korda and Michael Kertesz (later Curtiz) are making their first films.

Italy declares war on Hungary.

IN TURKEY

The shooting of the first Turkish feature film is abandoned because of the war; said to be loosely based on Molière's *Le Mariage Forcé*, this film, entitled *The Wedding of Himmet Aga*, was eventually to be completed in 1918.

Turkish forces are thrown back from the Suez Canal and also defeated at Kut-el-Amara in Mesopotamia.
    Bombardment of the Dardanelles is followed by Allied landings in Gallipoli.

IN INDIA

The mytho-religious films of Dadasaheb Phalke sweep the country; because of his mastery of trick work he is hailed as the Indian Méliès.

Indian troops are largely used by the British in the defeat of the Turks in Mesopotamia.

IN JAPAN

Kiyomatsu Hosoya directs *Katusha,* an adaptation of Tolstoy's *Resurrection,* made in the modern *shingeki* (new theatre) style.

Japan's 'Twenty-one Demands' on China are, due to representations from Europe, only partly met.

Japan undertakes not to make a separate peace with Germany.

CHAPTER 2

1915 - 1927

STARS AND STRIPES

I

Birth of a Nation is neither a pleasant nor, in the ultimate issue, a particularly good film. It is overly melodramatic – even for its time – though this failing, of which he never cured himself, was something that Griffith could on occasion turn into a virtue, as in *Way Down East* and *Isn't Life Wonderful?*. It is, at any rate in its second part, rampantly racist, climaxed by the saintly Ku Klux Klan riding to the rescue (the original title, significantly enough, was *The Clansman*). Historically it is all too over-simplified; and of course we now know that the real film on the Civil War was not to come until 1939 with *Gone With the Wind*.

Nevertheless *Birth of a Nation* was in its own way a revolutionary film, and its timing in the history of the medium was impeccable. Its appearance signalled an era of tremendous expansion in the American film industry, both culturally and financially. This is reflected, I think, in the breathtaking nonchalance with which Griffith forced every director from now on to raise his sights. In this perhaps lay his genius. It was not that he 'invented' close-ups and parallel action specially for this film. He and others had been using these for some time. What he did was to demonstrate how the mobility of the camera and the presti-digitation of the cutting bench could be used to express big ideas through principles of construction which must be just as important to film as those already existing were to drama or the novel.

The reason we can still be excited by *Birth of a Nation* today is that in it, for the first time, and in a way which the makers of the Italian super-films had never understood, we see someone deploying nearly all the possibilities of film to a definite and preconceived purpose. On this basis we can still thrill (ideology apart) to the ride of the Klan, with its parallel action suspense and its brilliantly shot and edited tracking shots (surely the first low-angle tracks ever taken); and to the tremendous sweep from the group of weeping women on the hillside to a vista of a whole army on the march.

This film must have been to Griffith what *Strike* was to Eisenstein. In each case the experience gained, and the expressiveness achieved, laid the foundations for a masterpiece – in one case *The Battleship Potemkin* and in the other *Intolerance*.

Intolerance is still arguably the biggest film ever made; the Babylonian sets are certainly the biggest ever built. Its conception is of course breathtaking, even arrogant, in size, ambition and boldness. By presenting a series of historical episodes plus one (type-cast) modern story, and interweaving these at a steadily increasing tempo; by also imposing a kind of rhythm on the film through the internal structure of the sequences as well as through the repeated Mother symbol, Griffith succeeded in giving a shape to his grandiose conception which otherwise would have fallen into a mass of confused fragments.

How far the cinema-going public of the time appreciated all this is a different question. There was, among other things, its title. As Terry Ramsaye pointed out, 'The conception denoted by the word "Intolerance" is an abstraction of thought. A motion picture which has to be thought about is in the same status as a joke which has to be explained . . . The public never goes anywhere to intellectualize. It went to *Intolerance* in just sufficient numbers to find out that it did not know what it was about . . . To Griffith the scenes of Lillian Gish rocking a cradle did mean "a golden thread" denoting the continuity of the human race and binding his fugue (sic) of period pictures. But to the movie audience a picture of a cradle is a hieroglyph meaning "there is going to be a baby", "there is a baby" or "there was a baby".'[1]

In this sense Ramsaye may be right in calling *Intolerance* a magnificent failure; he may on the other hand have underestimated the power of the contemporary audience. In any case, to people of that period who were willingly learning to appreciate the new medium, this film was a revelation. It was not only the grandiose conception, it was the manner in which Griffith organized and controlled, *in the cutting room*, his cataract of fabulous images. As the tempo increased the multiple climaxes became compressed, jostling and crushing each other, almost overlapping, but yet each separately racing to its own dénouement. It was an intoxication, a new experience. Cinema-going would never be the same again, on the one hand because no one could or would beat Griffith at this particular game, and on the other because

[1] Terry Ramsaye, *A Million and One Nights*, vol. II, pp. 758–9.

he had revealed the almost limitless horizon of cinematic possibilities. From now on the cinéaste could approach each new film with the hope of a new artistic revelation; that he was only too often disappointed (as much as was Terry Ramsaye's public) is another matter.

Sadly enough, and although people did not realize it at the time, *Intolerance* marked the beginning of the end for D. W. Griffith. The huge cost of the production could not be recouped – largely owing to the suspicion and incomprehension of the distributors and exhibitors. In a lordly way he took up the slack himself, thus landing himself with debts from which he never fully freed himself. To begin with he managed to continue to use his own studio and to make independent productions; but gradually the smog of mortgages closed in, and he had to work for others. Despite the box-office success of *Way Down East* and *Orphans of the Storm*, he never really equalled his previous achievements, except perhaps in *Isn't Life Wonderful?* (1924–1925, with Carol Dempster), which he shot on location in Germany amid the misery and starvation of the Inflation period; which he shot with his own money; of which Lillian Gish said 'It was the only picture he made after I left him that I thought worthy of him. Honest, moving, but grim, the film found scant audiences in America. It lost money'; and of which Lotte Eisner has written 'Le grand Griffith, ce génie du cinéma, a su donner une véritable cavalcade du désespoir et de la faim sans jamais tomber dans la facilité sentimentale'.

While Griffith was making *Intolerance* in America, most of the rest of the world was locked in the most terrible war the world had ever known. Before being sucked into it herself the United States had, not unnaturally, cornered the world market in films; and the expansion of Hollywood was explosive.

The gradual realization by the budding tycoons that the ubiquity of cinema could mean an unheard of multiplication of income from each film made led to two main results. Firstly, and logically, an expansion of the means of production and so of production itself. Hollywood grew very fast from 1915 on; and the constantly increasing takings and profits led, through competition, to higher and higher production budgets, for after Griffith nothing could be quite the same again. Secondly, the hitherto exploited screen actors began to realize their real value and took up strong bargaining positions. It is sometimes forgotten that Edison's Patent Company group (which included Biograph and Pathé) resolutely refused to permit any screen credits whatsoever. It was the independents like William Fox and Carl Laemmle who started to use screen credits in order to tempt actors and actresses away from the Patent Co, thus laying up plenty of future trouble for themselves, as Adolph Zukor, in particular, soon found out; as soon as the girl known hitherto to the public as 'Little Mary of Biograph' became identifiable as Mary Pickford, it became clear that 'The World's Sweetheart', backed by her mum, could strike a very hard bargain. In fact the cases of Pickford and of Chaplin give a pretty vivid picture of what the expansion of Hollywood really involved.

In 1909 Mary Pickford received $5 for her appearance in Griffith's *The Lonely Villa*. By 1910 Carl Laemmle was paying her (with what reluctance one can guess) $175 a week. In 1912 Charles Chaplin started his screen career at $150 a week. By 1914 Mary Pickford was 'getting expensive' to the tune of $1,000 a week from Adolph Zukor, while Chaplin was drawing $1,250 a week from Essanay. In 1915 Zukor, realizing that at all costs he must hang on to a good thing, contracted Pickford for $104,000 a year; and in the following year, after a tremendous struggle, he still kept her, but at the cost of a contract guaranteeing $1,040,000 over two years, plus a bonus of $300,000 plus 50% of the profits. In that same year, 1916, Chaplin drew a total of $670,000 from Mutual. Then in 1917 First National – a group representing powerful and wealthy exhibitors – cornered both Chaplin and Pickford, paying each of them $1,075,000 for the year. In 1918 Chaplin built his own studios, and in 1919 he, Pickford, Fairbanks and Griffith formed their own company, United Artists. 'The lunatics' as someone remarked 'have taken over the asylum'. One may note, finally, that in 1924 *The Gold Rush* cost Chaplin about $750,000 to produce. It then took $2,500,000 from the United States market, and about the same amount from the rest of the world. From this film Chaplin personally made $2 million.

Meantime the movie tycoons themselves were not doing too badly. They exploited the market and, wherever possible, each other, with ruthless persistence. They indulged in nepotism on the largest scale. The power wielded by people like Laemmle, Zukor, Lasky and Fox was almost incredible. But somewhere inside themselves there must have been a nagging element of uncertainty. Was this just a mad dream from which they would suddenly awaken? Was Fate even now preparing a Mickey Finn? And, above all, was the Puritan element in America going to attack them on moral grounds? And it was the last-named which caused the first big panic, triggered off, as everyone knows, by the unfortunate and almost certainly innocent Fatty Arbuckle. Seeking to protect their interests, they acquired the po-faced Will Hays to run a voluntary censorship code on their behalf, thus putting a creative strangulation on American film production which was only finally broken in the 1960s.

It is probable that the ten years from 1915 to 1925 were the period of the greatest production freedom in Hollywood. The tycoons had not yet seen exactly how they could control the creative people without whom their films could not be made. Laemmle accepted von Stroheim's early extravagances not only because they paid off in the end but also because, at that stage, he didn't know how to cope with the man. During the same period it was remarked of Griffith that there were times when 'he would rather make pictures than make money'. Such ideas were not likely to appeal to a front-office executive.

With the formation of the big studios with their complex and nepotic organization, and with the introduction of banking investment as opposed to the earlier jollity of living on lucrative picture turnover, the tycoons began to regain their confidence and, indeed, to believe that they knew best about everything. Anyway, they could make or break. The creative artists were brought to heel. Thus the tycoons were at best tyrants, and very few could stand up to them, though Frank Capra's value to Harry ('I don't have ulcers, I give them') Cohn was such that he was given absolute freedom on all his films. (It was Capra who, in 1939, frightened the front-offices by organizing a strike of directors and thus ensured the full recognition of the Director's Guild.)

Soon, too, operators with considerably more sophistication invaded the market. There were A. H. Giannini, who was probably the first financier to realize the potentialities of large-scale investment in the new industry; Howard Hughes – to this day still a man of mystery – whose *Hell's Angels*, shot in 1928 and converted to sound for 1930 release, cost $4 million and still made a profit; and Joseph P. Kennedy (father of John F. Kennedy, Robert and Edward, and Ambassador to the Court of St James in 1940) who bought Film Booking Office of America in 1926, was instrumental in the setting up of, amongst other corporations, RKO, and after less than three years in the industry bowed out with a multi-million fortune, one of his final acts being to persuade Gloria Swanson to sack von Stroheim and cancel her production of *Queen Kelly* – an episode from which neither Swanson nor Stroheim ever fully recovered.

For most of this period the American industry had 80% of the world market. As the US home market consisted of no less than 21,000 theatres (1925), it was extremely difficult to lose money; and from the cinemas of the rest of the world, which numbered around 30,000, the profits were money for jam. (In Great Britain in the mid-Twenties not more than 5 % of the films shown in the theatres were of British origin.) This all added up to the fact that America was in the position to make some 700 feature films a year; and the box-office receipts from these amounted to around $550 million.

Apart from the circumstances of World War I which eased Hollywood into this world monopoly, it is only fair to remark on another factor. The population of the United States was, and is, a conglomeration of people from literally all over the world. This diverse audience prevented any narrow nationalism in the making of films. Producers and directors served up to their home public material which owed much to various European traditions (notably those of Italy, Germany, Scandinavia and Eastern Europe), and this catholic approach made the pictures all the more suitable for the world market – though as time went on a superimposed Americanism moved in; but this did not happen until world audiences had become conditioned and ac-climatized to the whole tradition of the American film.

II

Only in India and Japan at this time did some elements of in-dependence persist; and this was due more to cultural factors than anything else. So in India, though some 80 % of the films released were American, there was also a steady market for the mythological films started by Phalke and continued by directors like Debaki Bose. To these were added the comedies of actor-director Dhiran Ganguly and, importantly, the 'social' films pioneered by Chandulal Shah with *Gun Sundari* (*Why Husbands Go Astray*) featuring the fabulous Gohar, archetypal film-star of India. These 'socials' became as much a part of indigenous cinema as the mythologicals. They were concerned with marital and familial problems, and to some degree with relations between the classes and professions within the essentially bourgeois areas of Indian city life; they were often influenced by the 'flaming youth' formulae of Hollywood, and soon had as by-products a haze of fan-magazines. It is easy to sneer at both styles; but it has to be remembered that, regardless of content or quality, these were true Indian films concerned with things which were totally outside the province of the occupying power, the British Raj, whose only real achievement in the field of cinema was to set up a system of censorship of a stupidity which had to be experienced to be believed.

In Japan, meantime, the cinema became dominated by a figure unique in film history – the benshi, or narrator. Just as in the early days of European cinema, before films became long enough to need subtitles, some form of compère, or even barker, was used, so in Japan, to whose people the West was still mysterious, there was urgent need for someone to explain. To explain, indeed, everything; for, as Donald Richie points out, 'the audience was not sure how the projector worked, and this they had to be told. . . . Furthermore, Japan has a theatrical tradition of treating the necessary mechanics as part of the performance. . . . This interest in the machine . . . was most apparent when one of the early showmen placed his projector at the right side of the stage and the screen at the left. Most of the spectators, if they could see the screen at all, viewed it quite obliquely, but at least they had an excellent view of the projection crew in action.'[1]

The benshi soon became established as an integral part of any film show; in fact a movie was nothing without him. Certain benshis became as famous as, sometimes more famous than, the film-stars themselves. In their explanations they often went far beyond mere description, dramatizing the parts, improvising dialogue and providing sound effects. A vivid description of the benshi *mystique* is provided by Oswald Wynd, a European whose childhood was spent in Japan:

'I can recall all those silent Hollywood epics of the Cecil B. de Mille school made glorious by the wailings and palpitating enthusiasm of the benshi. This gentleman by no means confined himself to merely reproducing dialogue but enlarged his function until he was practically the Japanese version of the cinema organ, holding in reserve a repertoire of noises which would unquestionably have embarrassed a Wurlitzer. . . .

'Although as an occidental I was supposed to prefer the English sub-titles to the Japanese vocalisation, the mere dullness of the printed word had no chance of competing with the dramatic roarings of a silk-robed genius. I listened . . . to the benshi and discussed his respective merits with my friends much in the same way as I might now . . . argue about the acting ability of Sir Cedric Hardwicke.

'A film, I think it was called *The Eleventh Hour*, remains fixed in my mind, not due to its excellence, but simply because on that

---

[1] *The Japanese Film* by Joseph L. Anderson and Donald Richie, Tuttle, 1959. The benshi of course emerged from the various narrative traditions of Kabuki and of the Bunraku puppet shows.

occasion the benshi surpassed himself. There was a shot . . . of a submarine sinking and we were presented with photography of a tin model subsiding slowly to the bottom of a porcelain bath. The benshi, appreciating the weakness of the film . . . treated us to an absolute onslaught of sheer artistry. Each bubble which emerged from the synthetic wreck was accompanied by a most incredible assortment of desperate and horrible gurglings. The tin model sank, and we were harrowed by a symphony of aquatic noises interspersed with fiendish screams which suggested all too realistically the agony of dying men. That miserable fake shot became a stark reality and an obvious fraud was converted, for those of us in that Tokyo cinema, into a drama of vital intensity'.[1]

It was in part because of the dominance of the benshi that the indigenous Japanese film developed rather slowly; and it was not until 1920, when Minoru Murata made *A Woman Standing in the Light*, that a really cinematic film appeared. Then in 1922 the same director made *Souls on the Road*, which in its impact was in a way Japan's *Birth of a Nation*. One of the great attributes of the Japanese film is its unconcern with elaborate plot-structure; the audience is glad to empathize with a series of events arising from a given situation, and they are especially glad if the situation is recognizable from their own experience. On top of this they do not in general make overmuch distinction between the real and the ghostly. These attitudes explain the popularity of *Ugetsu Monogatari* and *Rashomon* on the one hand, and of *The Lower Depths* and, for the modern student generation, Oshima's *Diary of a Shinjuku Thief* on the other. It was Murata's *Souls on the Road* which more or less discovered and set this style. Although it began with the great attraction of the popular stars Haruko Sawamura and Denmai Suzuku, it finally impressed by the conviction of its location shooting and of its characters – two groups of wanderers of different class and background.

It was at this time, too, that Kenji Mizoguchi and Teinosuke Kinugasa appeared on the scene. Kinugasa's film, *A Page of Madness* (also known as *A Page out of Order* and *A Crazy Page*), made in 1927 on a shoestring budget, with the sets decorated with silver paint to mitigate the shortage of lighting, was a great success[2]; and he followed this in 1928 with *Crossroads* (also known as *Shadows of the Yoshiwara*), with which the pre-dialogue cinema of Japan attained maturity. In this

[1] Article in *World Film News*, August 1937.

[2] In 1972 Kinugasa found in his garden shed a perfect print of *A Page of Madness*; released with a music and effects track, it proved to be even more ahead of its time than its reputation had suggested.

extraordinary film the hero, wounded and delirious, has lost all sense of time and, as Donald Richie has pointed out, the director thereupon constructed his film without any chronology. The audience therefore had to find its own sense of time. It also had to identify to a very great degree with the hero's fevered sufferings. 'The pain becomes a visible hallucination when the water he is drinking turns into steam; the most ordinary of objects are transformed – the cat, for example, turns into a great and mythic beast, attracted by the bloom of his open wounds'.[1]

For the rest, Japanese cinema was in competition with a flood of American films, just as was India. The difference between the two countries, in the event, was that the Japanese cinema progressed greatly in quality as the years went by, while the Indian film remained bogged down in mediocrity. The fact that India was occupied by an alien power and that Japan was independent may have something to do with this. The films of both countries were equally ignored by the West.

III

Meantime the American industry was taking its profits from these exotic markets as well as from everywhere else. The position of the British, French, German and Scandinavian film industries in relation to Hollywood was one of subservience – at any rate economically and financially. Even the Soviet Union, which was attempting to build its own monolithic industry without interference from outside, found itself in the mid-Twenties importing American films 'by lack of domestic production and force of demand'.[2] All this, of course, apart from the tremendous creative influence of Griffith's work on the first generation Soviet directors like Kuleshov, Pudovkin and Eisenstein.

But the time at which the European and Russian cinemas were going to have a considerable creative (rather than economic) influence on Hollywood was not far off.

In the meantime the Hollywood film-tsars, as American as chutzpah could be, continued to dominate the world of screen entertainment; and the dreams of millions were American dreams, dreams concocted at the behest of tycoons whose origins, as often as not, were in the slums or ghettos of Central or Eastern Europe, or of Ireland. Hollywood had embarked on 'the mass production of prefabricated

[1] Donald Richie, *The Japanese Movie*, Ward Lock, 1966.
[2] Terry Ramsaye, *A Million and One Nights*, vol. II, p. 826.

daydreams' and was trying, not without success, 'to adapt the American dream, that all men are created equal, to the view that all men's dreams should be made equal'.[1]

This communal dream-world of cinema – built on the magic of visuals and still without the vital element of the human voice – created for itself, with logical inevitability, the Star System. As we have already seen, the cinema appealed particularly to the deprived, the under-nourished and the uneducated. As Phalke had found in India, the answer is Worship and/or Identification; on the one hand the admirable but admittedly unattainable,[2] and on the other the admirable with which self-identification could be, if only in theory, possible.

Vachel Lindsay, whose book *The Art of the Moving Picture*, published as early as 1915, entitles him to be recognized as the first real film critic, had this to say about Mary Pickford:

'Why do people love Mary? Because of a certain aspect of her face in her highest mood. Botticelli painted her portrait many centuries ago when by some necromancy she appeared to him in this phase of herself . . . The people are hungry for this fine and spiritual thing that Botticelli painted in the faces of his muses and heavenly creatures. Because the mob catch the very glimpse of it in Mary's face, they follow her night after night in the films'.

This may be compared with Miss Pickford's own reminiscence of what the public wanted:

'The crowds were even thicker this time. They pressed in very close and Douglas and I were soon aware that a frantic and un-inhibited souvenir hunt was on. When we took inventory later in the day, Douglas had lost all the buttons off his coat and vest, and I had surrendered my handbag, powder case and handkerchief. Even the hairpins in my curls were gone. It was a most flattering thought that here on the Isle of Wight . . . people actually knew and loved us as if they were our neighbours in Beverly Hills . . .

' . . . On all sides the crowds were thick as bushes, waving and shouting wildly. Suddenly a voice called out, "Shake hands with me, Mary!" While my two companions were looking the other way I put out my hand. Immediately I felt it lock in an iron grasp. Then someone else grabbed my other hand, and two or three other people reached for the rest of me (*sic*). I was quietly but surely sliding over the back of the moving car, when Douglas turned his head and

[1] Hortense Powdermaker, *Hollywood the Dream Factory*, Secker and Warburg, 1951.
[2] Unattainability does not preclude imitation: compare Thomas á Kempis.

quickly lunged out for my ankles. The car stopped, and as Douglas held on, a frightened and bewildered (George) Grossmith began gesticulating wildly.

'"I say, please unhand the little lady, won't you", he spluttered, "Can't you see she's in danger of her life?".'[1]

It is said that some primitive tribes desire to eat their gods. At any rate, here was a modicum of attainability.

This passionate mass-love, these amalgamations of a million self-identifications, reached their height in the Twenties, and by glancing through the fan magazines the popularity of the stars, waxing or waning, can be gauged. But the top stars remained fixed – Valentino, Garbo, Pickford, Fairbanks, Mix, Chaplin, Nazimova – fixed until, for a few, came death; or, for the rest, until the public tired or they retired.

The apotheosis of the Idea of the Star came in 1926 with the death of Valentino, which was the occasion for a fantastic surge of mass hysteria. 'The myth of a fatal lover . . . sustained by publicity and many imitators, now rushed back to its original source in his dying body intensified by the very real sense of fatality the event engendered'. Thus Alexander Walker in his book *Stardom*. He completes his comments on Valentino, and indeed on the starry heights, by saying:

'And anyway stardom is not a matter of nomenclature, but of attitude. "Who are you, my lord? I do not know your name," the dancing girl enquires of the sheik she has met in the temple ruins. "I am he who loves you," comes the answer with splendid certainty, "Is not that enough?"
'It was. It is.'

Gods and Goddesses. Heroes and heroines. Gods and Goddesses who, as in Greek mythology, partook of human attributes and came down to earth to meddle in human affairs. The hearth goddess like Pickford and the moon goddess like Garbo. When the stars faded it was because the heroic coinage had become debased. As Penelope Houston pointed out:

'The magnetic personality beaming or glowering his way through a series of highly coloured adventures would do only for an age which strove itself to achieve the grandiose, which possessed an optimism to which the simpler heroic virtues were not alien, and whose mass audiences had never before experienced the opulence and the rather tawdry splendour to which the screen introduced them.

---

[1] Description of a visit to England in 1920, from *Sunshine and Shadow*, Heinemann, 1956.

Since the twenties, the public has demanded a cinema whose relaxations into the older style resemble the attempt of a tired business man to join in the children's games. The hero is no longer dominating and active, but cowed under pressures of his age'.[1]

Thus came Bogart, Cagney, Gabin, James Mason. Only in the world of the Western did the hero remain a Type of virtue – and by now even he has disappeared in the blood and violence of Peckinpah and the rest. James Dean alone – the rebel without a cause – revived in his tragic and violent death a burst of supercharged emotions on the pattern of Valentino's; and even here the angry grief of disappointed and frustrated teenagers was a pale shadow of the universal dolour of 1926.

With the larger-than-life development of the stars came the larger-than-life development of films and their directors. In his own way Griffith was a star; and to a lesser degree the schoolboy megalomania of Cecil B. De Mille put him near the star class, thanks among other things to a superb publicity machine which always made the most of the spectacular vulgarity of his productions.

IV

It is likely, however, that the man who sums up this whole period is the one to whom some inspired publicist attached the slogan 'The Man You Love To Hate'. Beside Erich von Stroheim's works, the whole corpus of De Mille's output from 1914 to 1959 looks somewhat ridiculous.[2] De Mille reduced big ideas to small ones and then inflated them into huge films. Stroheim was not really interested in the size of his films; he was obsessed with the size of his ideas. That is what makes him a great director. *Blind Husbands*, for instance, is not visually a spectacular film except in so far as it is located in the Alps. The spectacle is internal; it is to do with the intensity with which Stroheim (who also plays the principal rôle) projects his extremely simple story. There is one particular sequence, not of any great length, which takes place at a dinner table at a mountain inn. The camera concentrates on a young honeymoon couple from the point of view of the man who intends to

[1] *Sight and Sound*, Oct.-Dec., 1951.
[2] This is not to denigrate De Mille's flair for film-making – for example *The Plainsman* – or the technical virtuosity of his spectaculars which, leaving aside all question of subject matter and treatment, was invariably superb.

seduce the wife; the would-be-seducer is, of course, Stroheim. The couple's innocent sexuality, including certain movements of hands beneath the table cloth, is in some strange way built up to an orgasmic intensity which is not so much in them as in the audience which is being made to identify with Stroheim himself.

Of all the directors who managed, one way or another, to get at loggerheads with the commercial film industry, and especially Hollywood at its most powerful, Stroheim and Orson Welles are probably the most noted. Both were concerned with extremes in subject matter, in ambition, and in the portrayal of monsters. Both needed total control of production if they were fully to express themselves. Behind both of them lies a trail of unfinished or never started projects, most of them of great potentiality.

Welles, of whom more later, managed to stay in the race; but Stroheim's stormy career ended in 1932, when his *Walking Down Broadway* was taken away from him and partly remade by Alfred Werker under the title *Hello, Sister*. From then on he was to be an actor – a very distinguished actor – and a prolific writer of screenplays some of which, rewritten as novels, he published. As actor he played many parts, as witness his magisterial performances in *The Great Gabbo*, *As You Desire Me* (with Garbo), *La Grande Illusion* and *Sunset Boulevard*. Unlike Welles and De Sica in later times, however, he does not seem to have raised sufficient funds from acting to be able to finance – even to the point of first money – any of his proposed productions.

Only two Stroheim films gave unalloyed pleasure to the tycoons – his first, *Blind Husbands* (1918), which delighted Carl Laemmle since it was not over-expensive and made a lot at the box-office, and his second, a lurid offering called *The Devil's Passkey* (1919) which few people seem to have seen and which appears to have vanished.

It was *Foolish Wives* (1921) which revealed the real Stroheim for the first time. In *Blind Husbands* the story and the cast, despite some melodramatics, were acceptably normal; in *Foolish Wives* the story, like most of the characters, was monstrous – Stroheim not least. It was also an extremely ambitious film which he designed to be released in two separate parts as was, later on, *The Wedding March*. A crazy epic of wealth, crime and degeneracy laced with many episodes of social comment,[1] with larger-than-life acting against a background of the luxury hotels and the lush land- and seascapes of the Côte d'Azur, this

---

[1] It seems possible that Vigo, in his first film *A Propos de Nice*, may have been influenced by this element in *Foolish Wives*.

film by the very intensity of its extravagances attained a certain magnificence. One remembers Stroheim, as Karamzin, making his elaborate morning toilet, perfumes and all; his various methods of seduction (not least the boat scene with the American Ambassador's wife); that fabulous dénouement when the false princesses (Maude George and Mae Busch) remove their wigs; and the final disposal of Karamzin via the main drain into the Mediterranean Sea.

Stroheim completed *Foolish Wives* in 18 reels. Universal cut it by two-thirds and put it out as a single feature; after which they re-employed him on *Merry-Go-Round*, from which he was sacked by the new whizz-kid Irving Thalberg. Little of this film, which was completed by Rupert Julian, was representative of Stroheim, though I do remember being very impressed by the atmosphere and movement of the opening fairground scenes which led to the first meeting between the Count and Mitzi (the exquisite Mary Philbin). Incidentally von Sternberg, in his autobiography, has a caustic passage about Thalberg's big purge of MGM which, in addition to Stroheim and Sternberg himself, included Victor Sjöström, Mauritz Stiller, 'Frank Capra who next made *It Happened One Night*. . . . William A. Wellman whose next film was the successful *Wings*, and . . . Frank Borzage who next made the beautiful film *Seventh Heaven*.'[1] Another method of dealing with recalcitrant directors was through censorship, as Stroheim himself described:

> 'In *Foolish Wives* I started a new school in films, the real axis of things, love and sex, which had been overlooked by producers who treated the public as infants. It was new, and shocked meddlers, people who had no sex outlet themselves. Freud has a name for them. *As part of the publicity campaign* (my italics), Universal invited twenty-two censors to come free of charge to Hollywood to view *Foolish Wives*. They came with their scissors. These people, some petty shyster politicians, drunk with their own importance, came, looked – and cut.'[2]

Next came *Greed* which, even in the mutilated form in which it has come down to us, must be recognized as one of the great cinematic masterpieces. So much has been written about it that it seems impertinent to expatiate further. It is necessary however to emphasize once again that some of the criticisms of Stroheim's work in this film are

[1] *Fun in a Chinese Laundry*, Secker and Warburg, 1966.
[2] Interview with Leslie Perkoff, *World Film News*, Sept. 1937. A less emotional and probably more accurate description of this episode is in *Stardom*, by Alexander Walker. (Michael Joseph, 1970.)

based on misconceptions. I am thinking in particular of the frequent
complaint about the unintentional humour of the subtitle in which
Trina is made to say to McTeague 'Let's go over and sit on the sewer'.
The fact is that this and other titles, like the ludicrous 'Such was
McTeague' early in the film, were inserted, in a desperate search for a
new continuity, by one or other of the many butchers who hacked the
film about. These titles were never in Stroheim's script. In any case the
titles are the least indication of the vandalism committed in cutting the
film to ten reels from Stroheim's already shortened version of twenty-
four.[1] It is obvious that the result of all this truncation must have been
that little was left in the film beyond the highlights of each dramatic
episode; it became a film of meaningless climaxes in which the dramatic
build-up and the psychological motivation of the characters had been
left out. Anyone seeing *Greed* for the first time should acquaint themselves first with the shape and content of the film as Stroheim designed
it.[2] It is especially important to realize that two complete sub-plots –
one concerning Maria and Zerkow and the other involving the matter
of McTeague's drink-sodden father – have been removed from the
film altogether. The absence of these makes a nonsense of the changes
in Trina's character during the film, and provides no adequate background to certain aspects of the character of McTeague himself. As
Finler puts it,

'The mutilation of *Greed* is not confined to a reduction in length,
but has resulted in the complete destruction of the original balance
between the realistic and naturalistic, and the weird, bizarre or
subjective elements. . . . *Greed* . . . had originally much more in
common with his other films than is generally realized. All that
remains is the realistic core of a film which was meant to combine
many different elements, the underlying realism being used by
Stroheim to give an added force to the strange and unrealistic
aspects of the story. . . .'[3]

Given this knowledge, it is easier to appreciate some moments in
the film as it stands where this mixture of elements takes place – not
least perhaps in the extraordinary sequence of the wedding breakfast.
Here the realistic lighting and meticulous details of the crowded,

---

[1] Stroheim's *first* version was forty-two reels.

[2] Fortunately this is easy to do by consulting Joel Finler's excellent book *Stroheim*
(Studio Vista, 1967), the same author's complete edition of the script (Lorrimer, 1972),
and Herman G. Weinberg's magnificent pictorial reconstruction from stills, some of them
rare and hitherto unpublished, in *The Complete Greed* (Arno Press, 1972).

[3] op. cit., p. 43.

fussily decorated apartment clash with the strongly over-emphasized activities of the players. Shot on a real San Francisco location, this is nevertheless nothing to do with documentary; it is a hunk of schizophrenia in which the audience must participate in stormy and mysterious emotions undergone by the main characters, and *feel* the bodements of future fate. That is why, at the height of the episode, Stroheim suddenly forces us to look out of the window, over the shoulders of the guests, at a funeral passing in the street outside. This culmination of an already great sequence is for me one of the great thunderclaps in movie history. And in a strange way it reminds me of the 'Rosebud' sequence in *Citizen Kane*, with Toland's ultra-deep-focus set-up stretching our vision from the plotting adults in the foreground to the as yet innocent child far away in the white snowscape outside the window – a hundred worlds away. Here, as in *Greed*, the meaning of the image is multifold, magnified, ineffable.

Like Dickens, Stroheim mingled realism with fantasy and exaggeration; the Zerkow excised from *Greed* is a kind of Quilp. He is wholehearted in his creation of ogres like Karamzin in *Foolish Wives*, Sadoja in *The Merry Widow* or Schani in *The Wedding March*.[1] As for obsession – his films are full of foot fetish. Many of his heroines have leg trouble; in *The Wedding March* not only does Cecelia have a crippled foot but Mitzi hurts her leg right at the start and spends most of the film on crutches. It is indeed by insisting on obsession that Stroheim achieves his greatest effects. Thus his orchard scene with Mitzi, all religious sweetness, sentiment and sunlight, is countered by a contrast which deliberately goes to the furthest opposite extreme – a downpour of rain and an attempted rape in a blood-boltered butcher's shop.

But if the outlines of some of his films – like the synopses of some operas – occasionally seem somewhat comic in cold print, the actual impact from the screen itself remains something quite else. Stroheim has the capacity to make everything he screens seem real. He regarded himself as a realist, and this attitude is supported by the comparatively recent discovery that a great deal of his original material for *Walking Down Broadway* still remains embedded in *Hello, Sister*.

When we trace the Stroheim material in this film, it becomes clear that he was moving into an area of human relationship in which there is a realism of treatment not seen since *Greed*; and a contemporaneity – the scene is New York – which is almost unique in Stroheim's

---

[1] We may note the terrifying mutations of these figures which appeared some 45 years later as Sonny, Brasi and Neri in *The Godfather*.

work.[1] *Walking Down Broadway*, or as much of it as remains, is a
simple story of love, jealousy and misunderstanding. Two girls, new to
the city, meet two boys via their acquaintance with a tough prostitute
with the proverbial heart of gold. The men quarrel over one of the
girls, who soon becomes pregnant; the other girl, through jealousy,
tells the boy that the child will not be his; but at the last moment she
tells him the truth, and during a big blaze at the apartment house all
ends happily as he rescues her from the roof. Not perhaps the most
inspired of stories, and hardly improved by the introduction of a
dipsomaniac (shockingly overacted) whose hobby it is to collect
gelignite;[2] nevertheless there is enough in much of the direction and
in the quality of some of the settings to mark a number of sequences
as Stroheim's own.

There is a lightness of touch and a clearness of character which
is often quite charming. The early scenes between the two girls (Boots
Mallory and Zasu Pitts) and the young men (James Dunn and Terrance
Ray) are delightful. The meal in the Chinese restaurant, the visit to
Coney Island are fast-moving and enjoyable as they delineate the main
characteristics of the people concerned – in particular the brash un-
scrupulousness of Mac and the instability, based on an only half-
acknowledged realization of her lack of sexual attraction, of Millie.
But the most striking thing is the relationship between the other two.
I don't think Stroheim ever directed a more surprisingly satisfying
sequence than that in which Peggy tells Jimmy that she is pregnant.
She expects at best a brush-off; but instead Jimmy reacts with a genuine
fervour of delight and joyfully begins preparations for their marriage.
The melodramatics of the film, when they do come, are tempered by a
powerful realism. The final quarrel and near-tragedy (typically Stroheim,
they occur on Christmas Eve – shades of the murder in *Greed*) are
played out around a registry office, where the lovers miss each other by
passing simultaneously through revolving doors, and in a truly remarkable street scene where, among people scurrying about in a downpour,
they scream at each other against the incessant noise of rain and traffic
– a filmic metaphor for a 'tempest of emotions' which is entirely
effective and magnificently photographed by James Wong Howe.

There are also episodes which bear a more obvious Stroheim

---

[1] For a full analysis of the relationship between *Walking Down Broadway* and *Hello,
Sister*, see Richard Koszarski's admirable article in *Sight and Sound*, Autumn 1970.

[2] It is he who eventually blows up the apartment house, whereas in the Stroheim
version the conflagration was to be started as a result of the jealous girl, in an access of
remorse, trying to commit suicide by gas.

signature, such as Mac's attempt to rape Peggy, climaxed as they crash into the middle of her wardrobe, which somehow recalls the rape scene in *The Wedding March*, just as Terrance Ray's appearance somehow recalls Matthew Betz as Schani; the riproaring fight between Mac and Mona the prostitute (Minna Gombell, good), with them rolling down the stairs in an ecstasy of scratching, kicking and vituperation; and the sensational location shots at the end when the house explodes into flames and most of the New York fire brigade rushes to the rescue.

But it is the tenderness of the love scenes between Boots Mallory and James Dunn which seems to show the emergence of a new Stroheim. The sequence in her top-floor apartment where, by standing on the table, they open the skylight and see the skyline of New York, part moonlight, part smoke and fumes, is finely managed, with dialogue both economic and true. Other episodes, like the dog being run over, the image of the Christmas tree in the deserted registry office, or the slow track-in on to the Leonardo reproduction in the doctor's office as he talks about unmarried motherhood – these seem to me to indicate that had he continued as a director Stroheim might have come to the elegiac mood which some scenes in *The Wedding March* were perhaps hinting at. *Walking Down Broadway* would, I think, have been quite a modest film, in tone and in intent, had Stroheim been allowed to finish it in his own way; and this in itself would have been something new. The monsters were becoming human, and the hero can unremarkably but genuinely remark, as he gazes through the skylight, 'I had forgotten there were stars over New York'.

It is saddening that the débacle of this film was by no means (unlike previous cases) of Stroheim's making. He was the victim of an internal quarrel between two Fox tycoons: and it was in such sordid circumstances that this great man's directorial career came to an end twenty-five years before his death. Let someone who may have understood and appreciated him best have the last word:

'Like Asmodeus, he soared over the rooftops of the world and peered into the windows, and what he saw there is partially discernible in the pitifully few fragments that were permitted to remain of his work by those whom he angered or made afraid.'[1]

[1] Herman G. Weinberg, in *Saint Cinema*, DBS Publications, 1970.

V

Stroheim was of course *par excellence* a European. His influence on Hollywood at that time was significant, perhaps prophetic. Soon, paradoxically enough, it would be the despised and impoverished European cinema which would produce films and film artists which Hollywood realized it would be dangerous to ignore. For, despite inflation, slumps, strikes and general political confusion, the European producers (with the notable exceptions of Britain and Italy) found themselves, in a strange way, enjoying certain advantages which were the reverse of those enjoyed by Hollywood. The American producers were quite certain of their captive audiences; they were absolutely certain that their receipts weren't falling. The Europeans, on the other hand, were catering for communities which had been badly shaken – in some cases virtually fragmented – by the war. With the collapse of economic values had come a questioning of moral and political values. There were revolutions and counter revolutions; there were extremities of left and right. And out of all these circumstances was arising the spectre of a second world war.

Amid all this it is not difficult today to accept the romantic agonizing of the Scandinavian cinema – built perhaps somewhat on a neutralist tradition in terms of recent European history – with films like Stiller's *Atonement of Gosta Berling*, Sjöström's *The Phantom Carriage*, and of course, the extraordinary intensity of Dreyer's *Passion of Joan of Arc*, filmed in Paris but none the less typical of its more than talented Danish director.

Nor was it surprising, as Siegfried Kracauer and Lotte Eisner have respectively noted, to see from Germany the spookiness of *The Cabinet of Doctor Caligari*, *Nosferatu*, *The Student of Prague*, *Warning Shadows* and *Waxworks*. Equally unsurprising from Germany were the psychological gloomfilms such as nearly all Pabst's early works, most of which look as modern as all get-out today.

It was equally easy to accept the new Soviet cinema – lively, brutal, iconoclastic (*Strike*, *Potemkin*, *Zvenigora*, *Mother*, *October*) or the occasionally inward-turning work like Room's *Bed and Sofa* or *The Ghost that Never Returns*.

And again French cinema, fizzing with *esprit* as well as a brisk cynicism, seems a natural outcome of the times, with Delluc at the start and René Clair at the end – to say nothing of Cavalcanti, Feyder and the young Renoir.

But there was something more to this postwar European scene. It was not entirely a question of national characteristics in film. It was also a question of internationalism – an internationalism which artists were deeply concerned to find in order to avoid a repetition of the circumstances which lead to war. In nearly all countries they were seeking an artistic synthesis similar to but more soundly based than Diaghilev's aesthetic compendium. And the fact that the film could now be recognized as a synthesis of the arts came to be very important to the young men of the day. The fact that it was without dialogue, was a sort of defenceless blackboard, recommended it still further. For the avant-garde it became both lab and guinea-pig; for the communists, an instrument of mass propaganda.

It was in this situation that the so-called Golden Age of German cinema made its impact. Seen in the perspective of today its achievements appear much more variable than they did at the time; it may well be that certain revaluations are overdue.

For some time there was a tendency to attack or to leap to the defence of German cinema in relation to the theories put forward by Siegfried Kracauer in his famous book *From Caligari to Hitler*. This book, in effect, attempted to show that the progress of German cinema from the end of World War I until Hitler came to power reflected, more or less accurately, the reasons for the rise of Nazism. This was in some senses fair enough for, as Kracauer himself wrote, 'this book is not concerned with establishing some national character pattern allegedly elevated above history, but it is concerned with the psychological pattern of a people at a particular time'. In the end he tended to try to make all films fit a particular thesis, and landed himself with apparently profound statements which turned out to be unfilled sausage-skins, such as 'We are all human beings, if sometimes in different ways'.

Since the publication of *From Caligari to Hitler*, the subject has had the opportunity of being ventilated in a wider temporal perspective. Lotte Eisner by no means wasted her time while, as a refugee from Germany, she concealed herself under an assumed name in the French countryside from the potential attentions of the Gestapo. Her analysis, in *The Haunted Screen*, is certainly more accurate and arguably more deadly. She stresses in particular certain background influences – apart from defeat, despair and economic collapse – and suggests that they go deeply back into the roots of the German *Weltanschauung* of the earlier years of the 20th Century.

Apart from the profound influence of the genius of Max Reinhardt,

Eisner suggests that the whole expressionist movement (first signalled in cinema by *The House Without Doors or Windows*, made in 1914) was especially influenced by the turgid philosophizing of Kasimir Edschmidt and Wilhelm Worringer.

These two gentlemen put forward, in effect, a conception of the interior world of the individual as a defence against the brutal facts of existence. Edschmidt claimed that facts and objects could not from the expressionist point of view be said to exist. What existed was simply and only the interior vision which they caused; therefore only the artist could take possession of them. All this led Edschmidt off into airy phraseologies like 'Dictatorship of the Intellect' or 'The Creative Will'. (What a humourless period this was, whether the philosophizing came from Right or Left!). Meantime Worringer's statements came rather closer to the expressionist background; for him abstraction in German art came from the fact that the Nordic type always felt a veil between himself and nature; or, from another aspect, that abstraction resulted from the extreme agitation and uneasiness felt by Man when surrounded by phenomena the mysterious contexts and relationships of which he feels completely unable to decipher.

These ideas, to say nothing of the influence of Spengler, implanted not so much a specific style but rather a specific mood of expression on the German cinema of this period. It can be seen in works as diverse as *Caligari*, *Nju*, *Metropolis*, *Warning Shadows* and *Pandora's Box*. Looking at it from the vantage point of hindsight, one may conclude that – with the exception of a dissident minority we shall come to later – the dominant artists were not so much the directors as the writers, designers, cameramen and even actors.[1] As far as scripting goes Carl Mayer was the kingpin of the whole period, and in my opinion he was by no means always well-served by his directors. Next to Mayer in influence I would put Erich Pommer, a producer without whose influence a number of directors would not have fully developed their talents; this was specially true of E. A. Dupont. And third I would place that great cameraman Karl Freund, who gave so much more than photography to every film with which he was concerned.

Coming to the directors themselves, it is interesting to note how many of them were one-shot men. Robert Wiene did little of note other than *Caligari* (while his designers, Warm, Röhrig and Reimann, left their mark on many a subsequent film). What notable film did Galeen make

---

[1] Actors who merit this importance, to my mind, include Werner Krauss, Conrad Veidt, Louise Brooks, Brigitte Helm and even Emil Jannings, who perhaps does not completely deserve Lotte Eisner's cruel comment of 'pompous fatuity'.

other than *The Student of Prague*?, Robison other than *Warning Shadows* (1923)?[1] Or, dare one say it, Czinner other than *Nju* (1924)?

The directors with real continuity were G. W. Pabst, Ernst Lubitsch, Fritz Lang and, to a lesser degree, F. W. Murnau, who tended to be (especially in *The Last Laugh*) a translator of the highly original ideas of Mayer and Freund. (It seems almost certain that the then revolutionary camera technique of *The Last Laugh* was devised, at script stage, mainly by them). And of these continuing directors only one, Pabst, remained European. The remainder went to America to build new and enormously successful careers, Murnau's being most regrettably cut off in a motor smash in 1931.

This Golden Age, then, can be seen as something like the Bauhaus – a grouping of talent in terms of writing, photography, scenic design. *The Cabinet of Doctor Caligari* (1919) is an excellent example of this; its weakness is in Wiene's direction, which is at times muddled and indecisive, and at others unduly melodramatic. Some of the scenes in the asylum garden, for instance, border on the ridiculous. Lil Dagover – later (in 1925) to be such a magical figure in *Tartuffe* (she played Elmire) – is seen here in preposterous make-up, and her acting is stilted and uneasy. The impressive moments of the film, on the other hand, come with the action or inaction of Conrad Veidt and Werner Krauss in relation to the startling décor. One remembers in particular the two-shot in which Caligari reveals the immobile Cesare in his coffin-like box; and the Tarquin figure of Cesare moving amid blowing transparent draperies and across the zigzag expressionism of the painted rooftops.

It must not, however, be forgotten that there were other aspects of cinema in Germany. Apart from the flood of B pictures common to all industries, which need not detain us, there were films which did not have roots in the psychological or the psychotic. The spectacular historical films of Ernst Lubitsch simmered with sexual indulgences specially designed to satisfy the demand of his audiences; when later he went to Hollywood he was able to refine and transmute this element into what became known as 'The Lubitsch Touch'.

As for the supernatural elements – these could be brilliant and stunning, as in *The Student of Prague* (1926) – a tale of the Devil and a Doppelgänger marvellously depicted by Krauss and Veidt in sequences involving windswept landscapes, claustrophobic interiors and cracked mirrors. I reckon this film to have had a quality of the supernatural

---

[1] Robison did a third version of *The Student of Prague* in 1935, the year of his death. It appears to have made no great impact.

hardly matched (with due respect to *Vampyr* and *Nosferatu*) until Cocteau's *Orphée*. From the very beginning, when Werner Krauss, as the Devil or his emissary, suavely accoutred in cloak and tall hat, stands on a hilltop and with sweeping, masterful gestures summons certain mortals, from a hunt or from humbler surroundings, to a confrontation which is to lead to fatal conclusions, the whole film moves ineluctably to Baldwin's double showdown with his perilous *alter ego*, first by night in an avenue of uneasy trees, and second before a murderous, a suicidal mirror.

The German films of this time could also be epic in quality, as in the mythopoeic efforts of Fritz Lang in the *Nibelungen Saga* (1922–1924) where the flowery woodland glades and the enormous dragon took on an extra quality because their deliberate studio provenance managed to translate us into a visually formalized world in which the Wagnerian concept became cinematically acceptable. Later Lang veered from the supernatural to the supranational – the world of Mabuse, of the international spy and, let it not be forgotten, a rocket visit to the moon[1] which was sufficiently convincing to scare the pants off certain officials in the British Foreign Office (and perhaps not without reason when you think that Wernher von Braun's V2 rockets were exploding on London within 14 years). By the time he made *M*, however, the Nazis showed signs of feeling that he was getting a little near the knuckle, and Lang passed on to his new and distinguished career in the United States.

Meantime *M* (1931) still remains something of a classic. Apart from the discovery of a great new screen personality in Peter Lorre, whose playing of the psychopathic child-murderer, whistling his gruesome Grieg signature tune, was so brilliantly built up to that frantic moment when we became *sorry* for him, Lang (in a complete reversal of his muddleheaded *Metropolis* approach) took things very much to the edge when he depicted the underworld of crime setting itself up as a tribunal of justice; for by that time Hitler and his gang had, with the Reichstag Trial and so on, done just that.

This may lead us back to the really dissident minority I mentioned earlier. On the periphery, as it seems, of German cinema you had the experimentalists and sociologists, nearly all of them overtly committed to the Left, and none the worse for that. The filmic experiments of Hans Richter, Viking Eggeling and Walter Ruttmann still stand. Less recognized but more important were films of social propaganda which reflected the more forward-looking sociological aspects of the Weimar Republic or, more often, criticized its dilatoriness in the face of the

[1] *Die Frau im Mond*, 1929.

economic crises whose neglect was letting in the Fascist opportunists and their hangers-on. These films had an honesty, a moving human feeling related to immediate problems which tended to be lacking in the more famous 'Golden Age' pictures, where the relations between capital and labour, as seen for instance in *Metropolis* (1926) or *The Last Laugh* (1924), were oversimplified or mawkishly sentimentalized.

Apart from Pabst, whose social consciousness emerged in the melodrama and violence of *Joyless Street* (1925) and *The Loves of Jeanne Ney* (1927),[1] and whose more mature approach, in *Westfront 1918* (1930) and *Kameradschaft* (1931), was yet to come, it may well be that the films of these left wing directors have been consistently underestimated. When we remember that they include the truthful melancholy of Piel Jutzi's *Mutter Krausens Fahrt ins Glück* (1929), a film about the reality of poverty,. Ernö Metzner's *Freie Fahrt* (1928) and *Überfall* (1928) – the latter falling foul of the censor by suggesting the police were not all perfect – and *So ist das Leben* (1929) by Carl Junghans, which pursues a similar theme to *Mutter Krausen*; one may well wonder which, in fact, were the more important films of that era. A dialogue film made later, but in exactly the same mood, was *Kühle Wampe* (1932), directed by Slatan Dudow from a script by Bert Brecht, and with music by Hanns Eisler – a fine film about the fight for life in a society in which unemployment is the rule and in which petty bourgeois values are not only weighing down on the underprivileged but also laying the seeds for the total destruction of democracy. But by 1933 Goebbels was in a position to finish all progressive film-making in Germany; and did so.

By comparison with the Germans, who tend compulsively to put themselves and everyone else into neat categories, the French operate on a somewhat anarchic level. Whatever may have been the stage of 'pourriture' in the French State during the Twenties, there is no question but that the young film directors were revealing through their cameras a world which was a mixture of wit, poetry and political criticism. This was the world in which Jacques Feyder could transform the staid Chambre des Députés into a corps de ballet; in which René Clair could suspend reality in films like *Paris qui Dort* or scandalize everyone with his *Entr'acte* made for the Ballets Suédois. It was a time when Cavalcanti, in *Rien que les Heures*, could make a sociological film on a great city (in fact ante-dating Ruttmann's *Berlin*) into which he introduced that memorable image of a slaughter-house in full swing substituted for

---

[1] Seen today, this film still astonishes by the skill and rapidity of its cutting – made possible by Pabst's brilliant prevision in the multiplicity of his set-ups.

the steak on the plate from which an epicene young man was eating.[1]
As for Clair, his bright early works did not fully presage the genius he
was to reveal after the coming of the talking picture. But his two classic
farces, *Un Chapeau de Paille d'Italie* (*The Italian Straw Hat*) and *Les
Deux Timides* (*Two Timid Souls*), made in 1928 and 1929, displayed a
marvellously witty use of the silent screen. The former is of course an
established classic; the latter has been consistently underestimated and
should be revived if only for the courtroom sequence in which the
principal witness keeps on forgetting things and has to go back to the
beginning of his evidence and start again. Here Clair's visual reversal of
events is a perfect example of the proper use of the pre-talkie cinema, as
is, in *Un Chapeau de Paille*, his brilliant use of the deaf uncle.

As for the larger-than-life Abel Gance, there is little that anyone
can add to the comprehensive and expert analyses to be found in Kevin
Brownlow's *The Parade's Gone By*. Here I would only mention that the
scale of his perception is not confined to bigness, triptych or multiple
screens and the like. There is a sequence in the first part of *Napoléon* in
which the young Bonaparte arrives back unexpectedly at his Corsican
home. It begins with a finely shot but to present-day eyes overly melodramatic recognition scene with his mother – with a lovely balance of
bright sunlight outside and the cooler white light inside the house (and
I don't know if it should be credited to Kruger, Mundwiller or Burel).
Gance is now faced with the problem that the young man has to be
greeted by all the rest of his family, second cousins and all. He solves it
with an almost insolent conceit. A small child upsets a basket of nuts
which scatter over the floor. The camera, high-angled and looking down
onto the flagged floor, shows how everyone sets to picking up the fallen
fruit and so, in a finely judged pictorial composition, are brought
together with the returning Bonaparte. Let me add that despite some
ridiculous exaggerations (the film often seems to be more about *La
Gloire* than about Napoleon himself), despite variable acting performances, despite a Napoleon who, once grown up, becomes too often
a lay figure resembling a cross and constipated Keaton, despite all the
other '*criantes insuffisances*', as Sadoul calls them, Gance's exuberant
and novel use not only of the camera but also of montage (his quick
frame cutting, used earlier in *La Roue*, anticipated the Soviet directors)
results in some really stunning sequences such as the horseback chase in
Corsica, and above all the fracas in the Assembly (with one of the many
cameras swinging from the chandelier) cross-cut with Napoleon, in a
small sail-boat, fighting a tempestuous sea. There is also a less noted

[1] Was this in part the inspiration of Franju's *Le Sang des Bêtes*?

moment, with Napoleon alone, meditating, by the sea. This is presented slowly and majestically in some five superb camera compositions with variations from medium close shot to extreme long shot.

In addition to all this it was France which produced the quint-essential avant-garde, whose work included Man Ray's almost suicidal attack not so much on society as on photography, and apart from Clair, already mentioned, Jean Epstein with his *Fall of the House of Usher* and Germaine Dulac with *The Seashell and the Clergyman*. Add to this the work of Dimitri Kirsanov, an emigré Russian who could pass from perfectly expressed nostalgia in *Brumes d'Automne* to quite savage social comment in *Ménilmontant*; Alexandre Alexeieff and Claire Parker, who devised the famous pin-screen and made that classic of animation, *Night on the Bare Mountain*, haunting, exquisite, unforgettable; and many others like the Léger-Murphy *Ballet Mécanique* and *Anaemic Cinema*, a film by that prince of spoofers Marcel Duchamp.

Then Buñuel threw a casual bomb which finished off the avant-garde for good, a bomb which, to quote Jacques Brunius, 'still makes the aesthetes shudder'. *Un Chien Andalou*, on which Salvador Dali also worked, though he repudiated it later when Buñuel was in difficulties in New York, concentrated in capsule form all the stuff of dreams and surrealism which the others had been toying with for so long. Some of the images, as again Brunius pointed out, were in fact only too real; the Marist priests and the dead donkeys turned up later on in Buñuel's straight and brutal documentary *Land Without Bread* as familiar road-side features in the Hurdano area of Spain. With the explosion of Buñuel's second bomb, *L'Age d'Or*, in 1931, what remained of the avant-garde finally disintegrated. Robert Desnos indited the funeral oration in which he put *Un Chien Andalou* on the same footing as *Potemkin*, *The Gold Rush* and *The Wedding March*, and contemptuously dismissed nearly all the others as 'the cinema of hairs in the soup'.[1]

Incidentally it is worth noting that both at its first showing, and ever since, *L'Age d'Or* has aroused more fury, violence, intolerance, surprise and delight among its audiences than any other film ever made. Today, nearly 40 years after its première, a showing of this film is almost certain to end up with some sort of a scene amongst the spectators. There is here something of the magic of film, since an analysis of *L'Age d'Or* does not reveal images any more shocking, or even as shocking as those in *Un Chien Andalou*. Yet in some way the juxtaposition of images causes a train of reactions in almost every spectator of unprecedented violence. In particular I have often observed that the rocky landscape

[1] Quoted in *Experiment in the Film*, ed. Roger Manvell, Grey Walls Press, 1949.

on the edge of the sea, peopled with skeletons wearing rich ecclesiastical robes, sets normally quiet and gentle people into a state of gibbering rage.

Hollywood could not afford to ignore European developments, however unimportant they might immediately be from the point of view of finance and economics. The tycoons knew box-office when they saw it; and if there was a bandwagon waiting to be jumped on, they deemed it more prudent to purchase the vehicle outright. For all their brave front, too, they were still a little uncertain. Uneducated themselves, they feared that their 500 million audience might turn out to be one jump ahead of them in schooling; so they took out insurances. From Germany they got, as a start, Lubitsch, Murnau and Pola Negri; and then, from an area of chillily romantic film-making, where a bloom of sadness seemed to touch every ripening fruit, two Swedish directors, Victor Sjöström and Mauritz Stiller. With the latter package was included a girl called Greta Garbo.

For many of those beckoned across the Atlantic at that time the transition was not easy. The new world of Hollywood was, in the end, a world of unreality, and it was difficult to adjust. But the money was good, fabulously good; and quite a few European directors sold their birthright for a mess of montage and sank, creatively speaking, without trace.

It should not be supposed that these raids left the European cinema in a state of deprivation. Creative excitement about the film was still mounting. It must be remembered that during the Twenties and well into the Thirties the young were constantly discovering and rediscovering the aesthetic potential of this new medium. For new it still was; and many still refused to recognize it as an art. But, and this was vital, a corpus of intelligent criticism was coming into being. A coterie paper like *Close Up* had an influence out of all proportion to its circulation; and people were beginning to read seriously the film critics of the *Manchester Guardian* and *The Observer*. In 1928 Robert Herring, the critic of the former, felt able to say:

'The cinema alone can answer our growing need to be fully articulate – to have one sense no longer left out in the cold, taken no notice of, told to be good and repress itself. But this sense of movement cannot be repressed because our life is more and more influenced by it . . . Three dimensional painting and stream of consciousness writing are but misdirected attempts to achieve in a static what can be done in a fluid medium. That is why the cinema is an art – because it expresses a part of us that can be expressed in no other way. There *is* such a part of us and the cinema *can*, though does not fully yet, express it.'[1]

And a little later the doyenne of all film critics, C. A. Lejeune, made the point that 'Every other form of expression, music, drama, painting, poetry, sculpture, drawing, has its own critical language shaped and understood by usage through the ages; the movie alone is subject to a criticism that has neither established measure nor technical currency'.[2] This very real difficulty is worth remembering today, when the film critic has at his disposal a critical vocabulary at least as rich as in all other arts. Another point about this period which should not be forgotten is that by this stage the number of genuine filmic works of art which had been made since 1895 was still comparatively small. Within one week, perhaps, or ten days, and without undue extension of effort, a student could have seen the lot.

The impact of the film on the young was not confined only to countries with flourishing film industries. In Britain, where cinema was at a very low ebb, apart from some beginnings by Hitchcock, students at the Universities and elsewhere began to look towards film as a form of expression alternative to the other arts. The formation in London of the Film Society by a group which included H. G. Wells, Iris Barry, Sidney Bernstein and Professor Jack Isaacs, enabled people to see many films from all over the world which otherwise would have been denied them by the American-dominated cinema circuits. It was the première of John Grierson's *Drifters* at the Film Society which did a good deal to get British Documentary off to a flying start. The Film Society was indeed the beginning of that minority audience which now, world-wide, can be numbered in millions and from which creative and experimental film-makers can at last expect to receive a modest profit from their endeavours.

VI

In the Twenties, however, the situation was quite simple and clear-cut. Throughout Europe there was among the intelligentsia a reaction against the complacency, sameness, tawdriness and generally

[1] *Films of the Year*, 1927–1928, The Studio Ltd.
[2] *Cinema* by C. A. Lejeune, Maclehose, 1931.

low standards of the average American product; reaction too, therefore, against American monopoly. So the intelligentsia turned to the
films of the German Golden Age, the French avant-garde and, above
all, to the Soviet cinema. All previous conceptions of the film were
being shaken to the roots by the differing but equally iconoclastic
styles of Eisenstein, Pudovkin, Dovzhenko and Dziga Vertov. At this
time the Stalinist dictatorship had not made its appearance, and
Russia was seen, by intellectuals if not by governments, as a brave new
world. The appearance of Eisenstein, Alexandrov and Tissé at the La
Sarraz meeting in 1929 was, to say the least, explosive. Later in the
same year Eisenstein lectured in London with equally explosive force.
As one of those who attended these lectures I can vouch for the fact
that he completely changed one's preconceived ideas about cinema and
substituted a vista of rich, surprising and illimitable possibilities. His
personal impact, as well as that of his films, had the most profound
influence on me as a film-maker (equalled only by that of Grierson,
Flaherty and Dovzhenko) which has lasted all my life, and is now
strengthened by the continuously developed theories regarding montage
on which he never ceased to work until the day of his death. (I do not
for a moment pretend to be unique in confessing his influence.)

At that time, however, the young European film-makers were not
really in a position to evaluate comparatively the different film theories
emerging from the Soviet Union. Thus Dziga Vertov's theory of the
Kino-Eye had a tremendous influence. This Kinoki Theory was based
on the idea that 'the eye obeys the will of the camera'. As presented by
Vertov, this was heady stuff for the youth of the day:

'I am eye. I have created a man more perfect than Adam; I
create thousands of different people in accordance with previously
prepared plans and charts.

'I take the most agile hands of one, the fastest and most
graceful legs of another, from a third person I take the handsomest
and most expressive head, and by editing I create an entirely new
perfect man.

'I am eye. I am mechanical eye. . . .

'. . . I free myself from today and forever from human immobility. I am in constant movement, I approach and draw away
from objects, I crawl under them, I move alongside . . . etc, etc.'

Or again:

'Kino-Eye makes use of all the resources of montage, drawing
together and linking the various points of the universe in a chrono-

logical or anachronistic order as one wills, by breaking, if necessary, with the laws and customs of the construction of cine-thing.

'In introducing itself into the apparent chaos of life, the Kino-Eye tries to find in life itself an answer to the question it poses: To find the correct and necessary line among the millions of phenomena which relate to the theme.'

Looked back at today, in cold blood, it is easy to remark that Vertov's attitude to the camera was a simple example of the pathetic fallacy; and that the whole Kinoki Theory, which had emerged from the newsreel, would eventually return there. It is also easy to point out that the young people (of whom I was one) who revelled in trying to imitate the pyrotechnic montage of *The Man with the Movie Camera* were in fact revelling in the appeal of Kinoki to one's innate laziness – creating one's own cinematic jigsaws in constant motion by concentrating only on the mechanics of editing, the cutting bench being constantly fed with the products of the all-seeing, all pervading and completely mindless camera lens.

By his enthusiasm for the Kinoki idea Vertov obscured the simple fact that he was something of a genius as a film-maker – and perhaps the most brilliant film-editor the world has ever seen. The cutting of *The Man with the Movie Camera* had a bite and attack which had at times a genuinely physical effect on the spectator – the steelworks scenes (if I recollect aright) with their pounding rhythm and steadily increasing tempo, causing members of the audience, including myself, in the Marmorpalast, Berlin, actually to break out in sweat. Moreover, Vertov had a lyrical quality which was seen at its best in his finest film, *Three Songs of Lenin*. This lyrical quality, needless to say, only emerged when Vertov forgot the rules of his own Kinoki theory.

I have spent some time on Vertov because he does not deserve to be one of the forgotten men of cinema; his talent was too important, and the success of his theory, temporary though it was, represented at the time a direct challenge to those of both Pudovkin and Eisenstein. Before he fell foul of Shumiatsky or some other creature appointed by Stalin to censor creative film-making, Vertov came to England with a copy of his sound-film *Enthusiasm*, which he showed to Chaplin, Grierson and Ivor Montagu at a séance at which I also had the fortune to be present (working for Grierson often tended to throw up these sort of perks). Like *The Man with the Movie Camera* the film was physically tremendously impressive; at times the soundtrack volume was nearly lethal. Chaplin had nothing but praise for the film; but he

would not on any account do what Vertov deeply desired – give him
something in writing; a talisman, in fact, against the ineluctable
Shumiatsky. It was a sad moment. What Grierson wrote about
Enthusiasm at the time may serve as a fair criticism and a generous
epitaph:

'It is so full of ingenuities that practitioners like myself will be
feeding on its carcase years from now. Never were workmen so
energised by a camera. . . . It gyros to their movements with a growing
intensity of movement which makes excitement of something most
ordinary. . . . By sheer variety of observation – there never was such
variety before – he turns a plain process into a fairy tale of excited
happening. He has missed, however, the simple things which are
the root of all poetry and mysticism. He has given us everything of
the mechanism and nothing of the people. . . . There is Enthusiasm
and no mistake. But I could not for the life of me tell you whether
the enthusiasm is an empty one or a full one. Vertov has not told us.'[1]

So in this world of Soviet experiment or French and German
avant-garde all was fresh, astonishing, exciting and full of promise.[2]
The real meaning of the savage warnings only partly concealed in
Buñuel's films went more or less unnoticed, despite the violent surface
arguments and quarrels which they provoked.

VII

Meanwhile the discontent with Hollywood was being expressed
by other groups – teachers, educationists and scientists not least. The
value of films to the scientist, first recognized by the surgeon Doyen in
1899, was never forgotten; and in Britain during the Twenties the work
of Dr Canti on the study of cancer cells depended a great deal on his
ingenious use of the film. Agitation by educationists against the Board
of Education's 'passionate lack of interest in the film' led finally to the
setting up (without Government support) of a Commission on Educa-

---

[1] *The Clarion*, February 1931 (quoted in *Grierson on Documentary*, ed. Forsyth
Hardy, Faber and Faber). Another epitaph was provided in 1970 by Jean-Luc Godard
who, with a production unit named 'Dziga Vertov', made a film entitled *Pravda*. Drab,
slipshod, visually and aurally null, this was a cruel and gratuitous insult to the memory of
a great film-maker whose work was invariably noted for its skill and its imaginative appeal
both to the eye and to the ear.

[2] In this respect the remarkable work of Alexander Medvedkin with his Film Train
and his feature film *Happiness* should be remembered.

tional and Cultural Films, whose subsequent Report 'The Film in National Life' led to the setting up of the British Film Institute. Similar efforts were to be seen in a number of other countries.

Eventually, too, Governments all over Europe – with varying degrees of reluctance – had to face up to the demands of their film industries for some sort of protection against the American monopoly. The schemes varied from the fatuous to the flatfooted. In Germany the cinemas got a tax cut in return for showing so-called Kulturfilms – often cheaply filmed travelogues of the direst boredom. In France the slump into which the cinema had been sliding since 1920 was hardly broken or mitigated by the talented early works of Clair and Renoir, or by the gyrations of the avant-garde; but the French cinema survived to enjoy an almost indefinitely prolonged period of glory after the coming of the synchronized film. In Britain a singularly ill-designed Act laid down a quota of British-made films to be shown in all cinemas annually. Unfortunately it made no reference either to cost or quality, and thus opened the way to the notorious quota quickies. These films, shoddy, fatuous and boring (even more so than some of those coming from the Andy Warhol stables today), were as often as not produced by British companies deliberately set up for the purpose by American interests. By further discrediting British film-making they were well on the way to putting paid to British cinema for good, had not the introduction of the Talking Film changed the whole situation and laid the foundation for a great creative renaissance in nearly every film-producing country in the world.

How did this great change come about? By the mid-Twenties Hollywood was enjoying a prosperous monopoly of world cinemas; and a world dominated by American films was beginning also to be dominated by American habits, morals, and, if only wishfully, standards of living. The huge mass audiences had no complaints at the films they were fed. It was a triumph for the tycoons, who had constructed a system of mass public entertainment on a scale never before seen.

Why then, in 1927, did a hitherto prosperous company like Warner Brothers get into such financial straits that it gambled a desperate all-or-nothing on the introduction of synchronized sound? What had gone wrong?

Today the popularly accepted theory seems to be that soon after halfway through the Twenties the great public unaccountably – or not surprisingly, according to taste – wearied of the pabulum proffered by Hollywood and began to drift away from the warm, perfumed, fabu-lously decorated and Wurlitzer-saturated picture palaces. Therefore, with a rapid fall in box-office receipts, Hollywood had to find a new gimmick to tempt its audiences back. A nice theory, and morally very acceptable, but simply not true, even if the discontent of the intelligentsia had infected a minute proportion of ordinary cinemagoers.

Hollywood had no crisis in 1927; its real crisis would come in 1932, long after its survival even of the Wall Street crash. The only crisis was that suffered by the Brothers Warner, and that was due to the jungle-like internecine warfare of the industry which, however vicious, had never before put the whole business in jeopardy. What had happened was that a combination of powerful competitors, including Paramount and First National, had found a means of freezing Warners out of well-nigh all the cinema circuits. With virtually no outlet for the films they produced they found themselves facing almost instant bankruptcy. And, like all film companies when faced with a panicky situation, they snatched desperately at a gimmick, in this case synchronization, which had long been available, just as later on Fox would snatch at the anamorphic lens which the good Professor Chrétien, who invented it, had been hawking around for years.

Anyhow the Brothers Warner – Harry, Albert, Sam and Jack – decided that nothing venture, nothing lose, and equipped a sound studio. From this in 1926 emerged *Don Juan*, a non-talking picture whose only difference from the general run of films was that the sound of the orchestra, instead of coming live from the pit, came booming through the loudspeakers, just like the newly popular radio. This didn't seem all that sensational, even though there was a prologue spoken (slightly out of synchronization) by Hollywood's appointed Pope, Will Hays. The Warner Brothers, however, were now so fully committed by their capital investment in the new studio that there was nothing they could do but press on in faith. Accordingly, in November 1927, they unveiled *The Jazz Singer*, a pretty terrible film in which Al Jolson – one of America's most popular variety artists – spoke a few words and sang a few songs.

Nothing was ever the same again.

Warners' success completely turned the tables on their hitherto triumphant rivals. They only had to wire a hall for sound and the luxurious movie-palaces of the First National group emptied. Independent exhibitors fell over each other in converting to sound; and for a time Warners had a virtual monopoly of production as, apart from Fox Movietone, which in any case was designed only for news and travelogues, they alone had the means of producing full-length synchronized films.

It says a lot for the energy and resilience of the Hollywood executives that they not only survived the traumatic experience of finding that their fairy coach had turned back into a pumpkin, but also, and in double-quick time, found the magic formula to restore it again.

The changeover was of course expensive, involving capital investment on a huge scale; and there were many casualties. On the script side many of the title-writers, and indeed story writers, lost their jobs as skilled playwrights were brought in to deal with the need for competent dialogue. On the distribution side there was also much distress among the theatre musicians. But nevertheless the switch was successfully carried out, and rapidly. And it may well have been the compulsive novelty of the talkies which kept the cinemas filled even at the height of the stock-market panic, thus making the film industry the only area not badly hit.

There is of course no doubt that sooner or later the talking film had to come. Personally I think it would have come sooner rather than later, even if the Warners had not had their crisis, because the non-dialogue film had almost certainly gone about as far as it could. The 'silent' film, depending as it did basically on mime, had reached a point of sophistication which was in fact at the end of a blind alley.[1] It may well be too, as I have already suggested, that the tycoons, isolated in their well-feathered yes-men nests, were getting out of touch with their mass audience. The rapid development of the mass media, beyond the press and into the area of broadcasting as well as film, might well have left them stranded like whales in the shallows of their own ignorance while their audiences passed them by.

But let us be quite clear what happened as a result of *The Jazz Singer*. The public had been offered and had accepted a new toy – the synchronized human voice. Nothing else had really changed, except that the range of other sounds had been extended, and accuracy fully obtained in their relation to the pictures on the screen.

The 'silent' film, of course, had never really existed. The motion picture had always been accompanied by music and, not infrequently, by special effects.[2]

Many of the original inventors and pioneers of cinema sought

---

[1] 'Sans chaleur, sans couleur et sans voix.' (Victor Hugo.)

[2] Apart from film used for notebook purposes by research scientists and the like, the truly silent film has always been a rarity. Certain avant-garde and experimental film-makers have specifically rejected any form of sound accompaniment – notable examples being Stan Brakhage and Maya Deren; the former abandoned sound around 1962, while the latter never used it until her last film, made soon before her untimely death; this was *The Very Eye of Night*, which had a score by Teiji Ito.

sound. Indeed Edison pursued his invention of the moving picture largely because he felt it would be an admirable adjunct to his newly invented phonograph. He originally called it the Kinetograph, but soon changed it to Kinetoscope. His concern with synchronous sound was justified by the fact that, as we have already seen, his plans for the Kinetoscope were, to begin with, exclusively confined to the area of the amusement arcade and the fun fair.

All these early experiments involved the problem of wedding film to the gramophone (phonograph) cylinder or disc (even in 1926 Warners chose the disc), but the difficulty of retaining synchronization, as well as the limitations of playing time of the disc (microgrooves were not yet available), were extremely disadvantageous. Nevertheless it must be recorded that in 1902 Monsieur Gaumont gave an address to the Société Française de la Photographie not in person, but from the cinema screen; and by all reports this pioneer effort was quite successful. It was in the same year that the Yoshiwara Company in Japan set about attempting to synchronize discs to film.

However, the eventual solution to the problem had to be the *photography* of sound, so that picture and sound could be married on the same piece of film and be projected simultaneously through the same machine. As early as 1900 a certain Herr Ruhmer was using what he called 'light telephony' to record sound onto film.[1] But nothing really practicable could be done until John Fleming (1904) and Lee De Forest (1907) produced respectively the thermionic valve and the audion vacuum tube. From then on almost unlimited amplification of sound by comparatively simple electric methods was feasible. Thus the synchronous film, based on the amplifier triode valve, must have been perfectly possible from, say, 1912, if not earlier, had anyone wanted it enough to press on with its practical development.

But apparently no one did. Instead, they lavished their efforts on live accompaniments to the soundless films on the screen. Anyone who went to the movies in those days will remember how important this accompaniment was; will remember too the difference between the small cinema with a solitary pianist, the medium size one with a trio, and the super-cinema with a full symphony orchestra plus an organ, usually a Wurlitzer, equipped with a large range of 'special effects'.[2]

Camille Saint-Saëns' Op 128, for strings, piano and harmonium

[1] See *Sound Recording for Films* by W. F. Elliott, Pitman, 1937.

[2] Archive theatres showing old films – notably the National Film Theatre, London – have benefited much from the experience of veterans of this period such as the late Arthur Dulay, whose virtuoso accompaniment on solo piano to the whole of Gance's *Napoléon* was quite unforgettable.

(a prophetic combo) was written in 1907, with careful cueing instructions, to accompany the Film d'Art production of *L'Assassinat du Duc de Guise*. In Russia Ippolitov-Ivanov wrote special scores for two films made by Vassili Goncharov in 1909 and 1914. In Italy Ildebrando Pizzetti wrote special music for the Pastrone epic *Cabiria*. Quite apart from original composition, endless trouble was taken by directors like Griffith to ensure that suitably selected music was used for every sequence in, say, *Birth of a Nation*, and that properly timed cue sheets were sent out with every copy of the film. Subtitles, incidentally, were extremely useful for cueing. Eventually there grew up a great corpus of musical material, often turned out by hacks, to meet the various mood requirements of cinema. The names of Zamecnik and Becce are imperishably associated with those many brief but repeat-marked items with such titles as 'Enraptured Crowd', 'Moonlit Night', 'Chase', 'Heroic Combat', 'Tribal Menace', 'Oriental Market' and (one of my own favourites) 'Disturbed Nature'.

Later on the use of eminent composers became more and more the thing. The score for Stroheim's *Foolish Wives* was written by Sigmund Romberg, and his *Merry Widow* was not unnaturally accompanied by arrangements from the Lehar score. Fairbanks' *The Thief of Baghdad* (1924) had a special score by one Mortimer Wilson, and Erno Rapee did the same for John Ford's early epic *The Iron Horse*. Eisenstein's *Battleship Potemkin* and *October* were, as is well-known, scored by Edmund Meisel, who also provided original music for Ruttmann's *Berlin*.[1] And Wolfgang Zeller wrote a complete score for Lotte Reiniger's silhouette feature film *The Adventures of Prince Achmed*.

French composers were particularly interested in the avant-garde films of the Twenties. Erik Satie's contribution to the *succès de scandale* of René Clair's *Entr'acte* is of course famous. Apart from this, scores were written by Antheil for Léger's *Ballet Mécanique*, by Milhaud for L'Herbier's *L'Inhumaine*, and by Honegger for two films by Gance, *La Roue* and *Napoléon*; while Jacques Ibert did the score for Clair's *Un Chapeau de Paille d'Italie*. Meantime in Germany Hindemith wrote special music for experimental films by Hans Richter, and in the USSR Shostakovitch wrote a full orchestral accompaniment for Kozintsev and Trauberg's fine film *The New Babylon*.

The bigger cinemas went to endless trouble to provide their patrons with special sound effects as well as music, and these were often extremely well synchronized. In the mid-Twenties, in Calcutta, the film

---

[1] Tragically, Meisel's film scores have vanished, and no recordings of them appear to exist.

director Debaki Bose could have been seen at the première of his film
Flames of Flesh (what a splendid title!) sitting behind the screen with a
group of enthusiastic helpers working to produce the effect of galloping
horses and excited crowds. In the first London run of Rex Ingram's
The Four Horsemen of the Apocalypse, the audience was electrified when,
as the two brothers confronted each other in a shellhole in No Man's
Land, and the skeletal figure of Death appeared, a large maroon was
let off in the cinema to coincide exactly with the visual shell explosion
which destroyed them. Famous too was the elaborate accompaniment
to Fred Niblo's *Ben Hur*; in addition to a large symphony orchestra,
there was a huge battery of effects which, in the sea fight, provided a
terrifyingly real rendering of ships colliding, oars splintering and masts
crashing down; not even a Japanese benshi could emulate this.

As a final illustration of the importance of sound in the so-called
'silent' film, let me adduce the evidence of that distinguished film-maker
George Pearson[1] who, with Cecil Hepworth and a few others, managed
to keep the flag of the British Film Industry fluttering during its lean
days after World War I. The climax of his film *Reveille* (1924) involved
a ceremony, now largely forgotten, by which every year, at 11 am on
November 11th – the time and date on which the 1918 Armistice came
into operation – all traffic and movement in Britain ceased, and for
two minutes the people remembered, in silent homage, all those who
had been killed. Now, had the 'silent' film really been silent, no director
could possibly have conceived of using the organized ceremonial of
the Two Minutes Silence as the dramatic highpoint of his film. In
George Pearson's own words:

> 'Of all the moments in my narrative, the Two Minutes Silence
> was by far the most important, the keystone of the whole structure.
> If that failed, all failed . . . The supreme test came at the film premiere.
> Emotional music had illuminated the film throughout, led by that
> master of his craft, Louis Levy. At the vital instant, his baton
> stopped. Melody ceased with lightning suddenness . . . dead silence
> in that great packed auditorium . . . the screen telling only of things
> that spoke to the heart alone . . . and still, the silence . . . exactly
> two minutes . . . an audience seemingly spellbound. Then Louis
> Levy's baton lifted, struck . . . and the Reveille broke the magic
> of silence.'[2]

---

[1] Died 1973, aged 98.

[2] *Flashback* by George Pearson, Allen and Unwin, 1957. Pearson notes that in the
Sunday Times James Agate wrote, 'This film may not be as great as *The Trojan Women*,
but it is two thousand years nearer the human heart'.

That description may serve as a suitable epitaph for the great formative period of film before *The Jazz Singer* gave the speechless muse a voice. To it we may add a final word by the film critic C. A. Lejeune who in 1931, with kindness and warmth, summed it up as follows:

'If the cinema had evolved no other power than Chaplin and the Soviet directors – the opposite poles of individualism and collectivism – in thirty years, it would have done well. That it has also produced the whole school of slapstick, the impersonal (*sic*) work of Flaherty and Schoedsack, the cartoonists, the abstract experimentalists and the newsreel men, as well as individual masters of their craft like Clair and Griffith, Sennett, and Pommer, Lubitsch and Pabst, is surely evidence of a vitality, an urgency and an adequacy to its generation that has seldom been equalled in the history of art.'[1]

[1] *Cinema*, 1931.

SIGNPOST · 1927

THE YEAR OF 'THE JAZZ SINGER'

IN THE UNITED STATES

Buster Keaton and Harold Lloyd appear in what are perhaps their best films – *The General* and *The Kid Brother*. Frank Capra directs Harry Langdon in *Long Pants*, Joseph von Sternberg makes *Underworld*, F. W. Murnau *Sunrise*, and Victor Sjöström *The Scarlet Letter* (starring Lillian Gish). Ernst Lubitsch directs *The Student Prince*, with Norma Shearer and Ramon Novarro; Cecil B. De Mille makes *The King of Kings* and Paul Leni *The Cat and the Canary*. Erich von Stroheim is working on his production of *The Wedding March*, and Robert Flaherty is on location with W. S. Van Dyke on *White Shadows in the South Seas* (from which production he will shortly resign). Charles Chaplin is completing *The Circus*, while Greta Garbo stars with John Gilbert in *Flesh and the Devil*, directed by Clarence Brown.

Charles Lindbergh flies solo across the Atlantic.

Isadora Duncan is killed in an automobile accident on the French Riviera.

Sacco and Vanzetti are martyred in the electric chair in the State of Massachusetts.

Upton Sinclair publishes *Oil!*, Sinclair Lewis *Elmer Gantry*, Thornton Wilder *The Bridge of San Luis Rey*, and Willa Cather *Death Comes for the Archbishop*.

George Antheil, Frederick Converse and Edgar Varèse compose music which presages the advances acclaimed in the Fifties and Sixties; while Eugene Jolas and Elliot Paul launch their cultural magazine *transition*, which will influentially continue until 1933.

The painter Grant Wood is at the height of his powers.

IN GERMANY

The documentary film *Berlin – Symphony of a Great City*, made by Walter Ruttmann to an idea by Carl Mayer, has a successful première. G. W. Pabst completes *The Loves of Jeanne Ney* based on a novel by Ilya Ehrenburg, while Fritz Lang directs *Spione*

(*The Spy*), and Bruno Rahn makes *Tragedy of the Street* (*Dirnentragödie*), with Asta Nielsen, Hilde Jennings, and Oskar Homolka.

On Friday, May 13th, the entire financial and economic system of the country collapses.

Arnold Zweig writes *The Case of Sergeant Grischa*, Kafka completes his novel *Amerika!*, and Hermann Hesse brings out his *Steppenwolf*.

Richard Strauss composes his opera *The Egyptian Helen*, while at the Baden-Baden Festival there take place the premières of Hindemith's *Hin und Zurück* and of *Mahagonny* by Berthold Brecht and Kurt Weill.

IN FRANCE

Abel Gance completes his great epic *Napoléon*, in which he uses a triple screen; René Clair directs *The Italian Straw Hat*, and Jacques Feyder *Thérèse Raquin*, with Gina Manès. Cavalcanti makes *En Rade*, with Catherine Hessling and Natalie Lissenko, and Germaine Dulac produces her avant-garde *The Seashell and the Clergyman*.

Diaghilev presents the premières of Stravinsky's *Oedipus Rex*, of *Le Pas d'Acier* (Prokoviev, with choreography by Massine), and of *La Chatte*, with Lifar and Nikitina in the main rôles, with music by Henri Sauguet, décor by Gabo and Pevsner, and choreography by Balanchine.

With *Le Temps Retrouvé* Marcel Proust completes his masterpiece; Julien Benda writes *La Trahison des Clercs*; and Henri Bergson receives the Nobel Prize. Three books are published which will in due course be filmed – André Gide's *Voyage au Congo*, Cocteau's *Orphée*, and Mauriac's *Thérèse Desqueyroux*.

Maurice Ravel completes his Violin Sonata.

Chagall, Lurçat, Picabia, Tanguy and indeed Picasso interest themselves in Surrealism, which is now three years old.

IN BRITAIN

Alfred Hitchcock directs *Downhill* (with Ivor Novello), *Easy Virtue* (from the Noël Coward play) and *The Ring* (starring Carl Brisson). Under Bruce Woolfe's producership, Walter Summers completes the filmic reconstruction *The Battles of the Coronel and Falkland Islands.* The Cinematograph Films Act, ill-designed to protect the British film industry against American imports, becomes law.

John Logie Baird demonstrates colour television in Glasgow.

Radio telephone established between Britain and Australia; automatic telephone service instituted in London.

Virginia Woolf writes *To the Lighthouse*, T. S. Eliot *The Journey of the Magi*, E. M. Forster *Aspects of the Novel*, and Wyndham Lewis *Time and Western Man*.

Other books published include T. E. Lawrence's *Revolt in the Desert*, D. H. Lawrence's *Mornings in Mexico*, Edith Sitwell's *Rustic Elegies*, James Joyce's *Pomes Penyeach* and Harley Granville-Barker's *Prefaces to Shakespeare*.

Jacob Epstein completes his *Madonna and Child*.

IN RUSSIA

V. I. Pudovkin directs his *The End of St Petersburg*, Olga Preobrazhenskaya makes *The Peasant Women of Ryazan*, Lev Kuleshov directs *Your Acquaintance*, and Esther Shub completes two compilation films – *The Great Road* and *The Fall of the Romanov Dynasty*. Boris Barnet directs his satirical comedy *The Girl with the Hatbox*, and Alexander Room makes his controversial *Bed and Sofa*.

Shostakovitch's *Symphonic Dedication to the October Revolution* has its première in Leningrad, and in Moscow Glière's ballet *The Red Poppy* is produced.

Trotsky is expelled from the Communist Party and Stalin consolidates his position.

The Soviet Union breaks off relations with China.

Mstislav Rostropovitch is born.

IN AUSTRIA

The Sascha Company produces a film called *Café Electric* featuring the not-yet-famous Marlene Dietrich.

Much internal strife. Unemployment leads to riots, attacks on the Law Courts, clashes between Right and Left, and a general strike.

IN EGYPT

Istefan Rosti's *Laila* and Ibrahim Lama's *A Kiss in the Desert* lay the foundations of a national film industry.

Nahas Pasha becomes leader of the anti-monarchy and anti-British party, the Wafd.

IN INDIA

Debaki Bose stars in and directs his first film, *Flames of Flesh*, which is a huge box-office success.

With Irwin (later Lord Halifax) as Viceroy, and Gandhi as Leader of the Congress Party, the Simon Commission is set up to propose constitutional reforms.

IN JAPAN

Teinosuke Kinugasa directs *A Page of Madness*, a pioneer avant-garde picture comparable to *The Cabinet of Dr Caligari*. Heinosuke Gosho makes *A Tricky Girl*, and Daisuke Ito *A Diary of Chugi's Travels*.

Representatives attend the Naval Disarmament Conference at Washington.

A bank crisis causes the fall of the government.

Japanese forces intervene in Shantung against the advance of the Chinese Nationalists.

CHAPTER 3

1927 - 1939

ALL TALKING, ALL SINGING, ALL DANCING

I

The anguish and breast-beating with which the intelligentsia, including myself, greeted the introduction of synchronization now seems faintly silly. But many people at that time genuinely felt that the mimetic values of cinema were just beginning to reach their greatest heights, while at the same time the vital theories of montage expounded by Kuleshov, Eisenstein, Pudovkin and Vertov had hardly had time to pass beyond the experimental stages. All this, it seemed, was to be destroyed by the introduction of a recording system which imprisoned the camera in a heavy and virtually immovable soundproof booth and made film editing ten times more difficult. It was as though Edison's Black Maria had won out over the Lumières' lightweight apparatus.

It is, of course, true that the first talkies were visually dull and static, and that the angle of vision was changed as little as possible – though in fact the change from long-shot to mid-shot to close-up could still be achieved by switching lenses without moving the camera.[1] It is also true that the novelty of hearing screen characters speak or sing, laugh or cry was, to begin with, a sufficient box-office attraction. So too was the novelty of hearing subtle sound-effects which were far beyond the powers of orchestra or Wurlitzer; the thrill, for instance, of eggs and bacon sizzling in a pan.

On the other hand it is clear that the intelligentsia failed to have faith in the aesthetic validity of cinema as a form of creative expression or in the adaptability of the film-makers themselves. They were, however, soon called to order by a manifesto issued by three Soviet film directors, to say nothing of certain film-making gestures by Hitchcock, Lubitsch and René Clair.

[1] The now universal zoom lens lay some 30 years in the future.

The Soviet Manifesto was signed by Eisenstein, Pudovkin and Alexandrov, and was published in 1928. The writers began by voicing the fears of the intellectuals regarding the threat to film-editing and especially to their own montage principles. Basically then, they argued, there must be a development of montage in terms of the new sound recording possibilities. They admitted the validity of the directly synchronized talking picture, but stressed the danger that the 'virginity and purity' of this first perception of new technical possibilities would soon be forgotten in a rash of 'highly cultured dramas and other photographed performances of a theatrical sort'. Therefore, they continued, the only way to rescue, preserve and develop montage must be in terms of counterpoint. 'The first experimental work with sound must be directed along the line of its distinct non-synchronization with the visual images.' This principle they regarded as an answer to those elements of the old 'silent' film which had always interfered with proper film-editing, namely subtitles and explanatory inserts like letters or calendars.

In fact what the three Soviet directors (especially Eisenstein, for the Manifesto[1] bears every evidence of having been largely written by him) had done was to welcome the creative possibilities of the sound film while at the same time denying the aesthetic validity of the one thing about it that was really important, the direct and accurate synchronization of the human voice with the visual image. Nor is it without significance that, with the possible exception of *Que Viva Mexico!*, the montage plans for which never saw the cutting bench, the signatories of the Manifesto did not in the event develop the theory it promulgated. Any 'contrapuntal' work of that sort was carried out by Dziga Vertov who, however, had arrived at it as a result of ideas and theories of his own. As we shall see later, the only people who went to town on this counterpoint idea were the British documentary film-makers of the early Thirties under the influence of Grierson and Cavalcanti.

However, the Manifesto did give the intelligentsia a chance to stop sneering at the very idea of the synchronous film while remaining critical of current releases which, dull though they might seem, were tremendous box-office successes.

Meantime in nearly all film producing countries people were hastily (and usually scruffily) trying to convert almost completed 'silents' into something looking like synchronized talkies. In the course

[1] The full text, translated directly from the Russian, is in the Appendix to Jay Leyda's edition of Eisenstein's *Film Form*, Dennis Dobson, 1951.

of one of these operations Alfred Hitchcock electrified the culture-vultures by partially following the Soviet instruction manual with his famous piece of 'counterpoint' in *Blackmail*. The reiteration of the word 'knife' during a gossipy discussion about the murder weapon was played against close-ups of the heroine (Anny Ondra), of a breadknife on the breakfast table and suchlike, while the dialogue itself was gradually distorted to a point at which only the fatal monosyllable was intelligible. Later on Hitchcock followed this gimmick by another in which a character's unspoken thoughts were recited over a reflection of himself in a shaving mirror. This was in *Murder* (1930); but by this time we had also seen *Sous les Toits de Paris*, *The Virginian*, *The Love Parade*, and *Hell's Heroes*; and Peter Lorre's whistled extract from Grieg in Fritz Lang's *M* was just round the corner. The liberation of the motion picture from the shackles of synchronism no longer posed any great problems.

In *The Virginian* Victor Fleming used sound not only with ingenuity but with tragic impact. At the climax of the film the sheriff (Gary Cooper) has to carry out the summary execution by hanging of his dearest friend (Richard Arlen). All through their lives these two have signalled to each other by means of a whistlecall which exactly imitates the call of a quail. At the moment when the sheriff is about to give the order for the horse to be whipped up – thus leaving his pal dangling from a tree – we hear this quail-cry. Then, in absolute silence, we see Cooper looking at Arlen, Arlen at Cooper; and then, with stunning effect, an actual quail in the nearby scrub. There is the crack of a whip, the clatter of hooves, and that is all.

In *Hell's Heroes*, a film of frank and frantic sentimentality by William Wyler, an effective *coup de cinéma* occurs when the sound of a church choir and congregation singing Christmas carols is suddenly switched off when the rough old villain staggers up the aisle carrying a baby he has brought across the desert at the cost of his own life. The audience is made to switch its identification from the church scene to the man himself at the point of death. It may sound a corny idea, but it was enormously effective. In a similar vein, incidentally, was the great sad sigh of escaping steam from the locomotive that brought the dead boy home in Nikolai Ekk's *The Road to Life*.

At this point it may be worth anticipating a bit by referring to a film which finally finished off the fashion for these experiments, or rather established them as simply a part of the film director's repertoire. On the theatre-stage Eugene O'Neill's play *Strange Interlude* had its characters speak their conversational dialogues normally; but they also had to speak their thoughts which the audience was to hear but their fellow actors not, and for this purpose they put masks in front of their faces. Robert Z. Leonard made this into a film (with Norma Shearer and Clark Gable) in 1932; and guess what! when the characters talked to each other their lips moved; when they were thinking their lips remained closed but their voices were heard (just like the man shaving in *Murder*). This film was, needless to say, advertised as 'the film in which you hear the characters think'. (I seem to remember the Marx Brothers taking a swipe at *Strange Interlude* in one of their earliest films, perhaps *The Coconuts*.)

II

The great triumph of the synchronous film was of course the Musical – that new and splendid form which could only come into existence with the introduction of the talkies.

One of the earliest musicals was René Clair's *Sous les Toits de Paris*, with the camera floating easily past house-façades and over the chimney tops against the theme-song and giving the spectator a dream-like sense of liberation. Lazare Meerson's sets enchantingly created the mood of a Paris *quartier*, and although when seen today the film has some pretty sticky dialogue passages, it still clearly signals the future delights of *Le Million* and *Le Quatorze Juillet*. And as Sadoul points out, Clair, perhaps aware of the difficulties he was having with his dialogue scenes, tried some slightly satiric 'counterpoints', as when a glass door swings closed on people just as they are beginning to speak. But essentially it was the linking into a satisfactory whole of people and action by the movement of a travelling camera accompanied by a pre-recorded musical soundtrack which was the secret of the film's success in so many countries.

But it had to be in Hollywood, with its tremendous physical and financial resources, that this genre of film-making must chiefly develop. The Hollywood Musical was something special; and so it remained, a continuous source of delight to millions, until very recently. The two directors who between them established the main principles of this new style were Ernst Lubitsch and Rouben Mamoulian.

Lubitsch had come to America from Germany, where he had been a successful director of historical or mythological spectaculars based on Reinhardt's theatre influence and laced with a certain coarse humour and double-meanings of Berlin origin. Out of these he developed in Hollywood the famous 'Lubitsch Touch',[1] and just as Clair's musicals were a development from his witty 'silents' like *The Italian Straw Hat*, so Lubitsch saw the musical as a logical extension of his earlier Hollywood comedies like *Kiss Me Again* (1925) and *So This Is Paris* (1926) – light-hearted pieces full of visual wit presented with impeccable style. I remember going to see *So This Is Paris* about six times, not only for the famous Charleston sequence ('like an animated cubist painting' someone wrote[2]) but also for the precise perfection and timing which Lubitsch extracted from his delightful cast, which included Patsy Ruth Miller, Monte Blue and Lilyan Tashman, throughout the whole film.

Like Clair, Lubitsch wanted no truck with the heavy camera booth and the solemnities of the newly tyrannous sound-recordists. In *The Love Parade*, and again in *Monte Carlo*, he took the operetta and the musical play off the stage and into the true camera freedom of cinema.

These two Lubitsch films, however, were more than technical triumphs, more even than the values of their stars, Maurice Chevalier, Jack Buchanan and Jeanette MacDonald, or of their supporting casts which included Lupino Lane, Eugene Pallette, Ben Turpin (no less), Zasu Pitts and Claude Allister, to name but a few. What they had – maybe for the first time – was the verbal comedy and wit which the cinema had for so long been seeking; and this comedy, this wit preceded, I think, the other element we shall be coming to later – the use of truly dramatic dialogue in a manner which overpasses the normal techniques of the theatre. Writers like Ernest Vajda and Guy Bolton, working closely with Lubitsch himself, provided cinema-goers for the first time with a taste of the joys of sophisticated comedy allied to witty lyrics and delightful music in a truly filmic setting. The electrifying sequence of 'Beyond the Blue Horizon' in *Monte Carlo* was certainly a new experience as Jeanette MacDonald waved her hand from her railway compartment to all Europe and its peasants as it swept by the window. Today such things are commonplace, but it is worth occasionally remembering the pioneers whose vision made them possible.

At this point it may be as well to record Lubitsch's extraordinary versatility. In the midst of this outpouring of musicals and suchlike he directed, at his own express request, a very individualistic anti-war film,

---

[1] In *The Haunted Screen* Lotte Eisner points out that 'in order to perfect his famous "touch", Lubitsch had merely to develop his Germanness'.

[2] *The Lubitsch Touch* by Herman Weinberg, E. P. Dutton, 1968.

The Man I Killed, with Lionel Barrymore and Nancy Carroll. This story of the individual in relation to war and its aftermath was strong meat for the contemporary public, who stayed away. But Robert Sherwood wrote of it, 'Lubitsch has accepted the power of speech conferred upon the cinema by courtesy of the Western Electric Corporation, and he has used it merely as a means of emphasising the fact that the greatest moments in screen drama are those in which there is nothing to be said.'[1] The idea of nothing to be said will remind everyone of the famous Lubitsch sequence in *If I Had A Million*, when the meek bank clerk, played by Charles Laughton, receives a cheque out of the blue for $1 million. He traverses office after office, elevator after elevator, and eventually arrives at the Holy of Holies. He marches in and, on being assured that he really is in the Presence, delivers a certain gesture together with an audible raspberry which was too much for the British censor of that day . . .

Lubitsch also directed *Ninotchka* (1939) for which the publicity slogan 'GARBO LAUGHS' superseded the previous and supposedly greatest slogan of all time 'GARBO TALKS'; and he of course made the famous black comedy with, of all people, Jack Benny, called *To Be Or Not To Be*. This film, which contained the last appearance of Carole Lombard before her untimely death, landed Lubitsch in a lot of trouble because of one line of dialogue in which a Nazi general said of Benny, who was playing a ham actor, 'What he did to Shakespeare we are now doing to Poland'. This, plus some passages in *Cluny Brown*, a film which was made when his health was already failing, represents the only real lapse in a career during which the words 'The Lubitsch Touch' meant an approach to which tastelessness was perfectly alien.

Rival to Lubitsch in pioneering the Hollywood musical was Rouben Mamoulian, whose *Applause* (1929) showed sensitive direction as well as, for that time, revolutionary technique. Mamoulian made the microphone follow the camera or, if this was not possible, used multiple microphones strategically placed. All this, presumably, antedates the playback system which he and Lubitsch, by their approach to synchronous film-making, made absolutely inevitable; for it was essential for the actors and the camera to have complete freedom of movement. Mamoulian's *Applause*, together with King Vidor's *Hallelujah!* (which would certainly not appeal to today's Black Panthers but made a big impact as an all-Negro musical in its time) was made at almost the same time as *The Love Parade*; so that by the end of 1929 the new musical genre had been jointly established by three important directors.

[1] Quoted in *The Lubitsch Touch* by Herman Weinberg.

Mamoulian made three other musicals during the Thirties. In *Love Me Tonight* (1932) he took over Chevalier and MacDonald from Lubitsch and showed himself a match for anyone, including René Clair. His opening sequence, well described as 'a joyous hedge-hop through the streets of Paris as the city comes alive',[1] was absolutely bewitching. The combination of a Rodgers and Hart score with a cast which also included Charles Ruggles, C. Aubrey Smith, Myrna Loy and Charles Butterworth made it, of course, almost foolproof; but Mamoulian really clinched it with the smooth perfection of the script – the story and the set-pieces of song and dance imperceptibly interlacing – and with that gorgeous final sequence with Jeanette MacDonald riding madly, not to the rescue, but to interpose herself between the blue horizon and the train which is carrying her lover away.

Rather less satisfactory was *High, Wide and Handsome* (1937), with Irene Dunne, Dorothy Lamour, Randolph Scott and Akim Tamiroff. Its story of the struggle of small oil-prospectors against the vested interests of railway magnates trying to block the building of a pipeline, was hardly appropriate to a musical. Still, it had style, it had a marvellous circus to act as *deus ex machina*, and a score by Jerome Kern which included 'Can I forget you?'.

But Mamoulian's best (and probably most neglected) musical had already been made the previous year. *The Gay Desperado*[2] contained some pleasant satire (that bugbear of film tycoons), and it had the lightness of touch which goes into the making of a perfect meringue. Against Lucien Andriot's lovely photography of Mexican landscapes and architecture (well worthy of a Tissé) there unwinds a splendidly ridiculous story about some Mexican bandits trying to update themselves to the modern techniques of Chicago gangsterdom, only to find in the event that real gangsters have arrived to take over (some nice parodies here of Raft, Cagney, Robinson, etc). In this film audiences outside the United States were introduced almost for the first time to the strange world of commercial radio; and as the advertising jingles were here visible on the screen, the film also acted, as we can now observe, as a prophetic preview of television horrors to come. There is one marvellous moment when a sister act – three plump Mexican senoritas singing in close harmony – continue their commercial (the words being 'Looky, looky, looky, here comes Cooky' or something like that) while the radio station is in the throes of a hold-up. Leo Carrillo as the chief bandit

---

[1] *Mamoulian* by Tom Milne, Thames and Hudson, 1969; an admirably comprehensive study.

[2] The adjective meant something different in those days.

gives a richly comic performance; there are good performances by Ida Lupino and Harold Huber, and the icing to the cake is added by Mischa Auer who, draped in serape and shadowed under sombrero, crouches broodingly throughout the film disapproving of everything and then, at the end, suddenly rises up and delivers himself of a monster oration of pejorative comment. The only fault of *The Gay Desperado* lies in the fact that Mamoulian only partly succeeded in satisfactorily incorporating into the plot an Italian opera singer, Nino Martini who, no doubt at the behest of the front-office,[1] was required to deliver himself of a number of arias, including 'Celeste Aida'. Nevertheless, it is a delightful film, and overdue for revival.

Like Lubitsch, Mamoulian did not confine himself to musicals. His gangster film *City Streets* (1931) with Gary Cooper, Sylvia Sidney and Paul Lukas, and pellucid camerawork by Lee Garmes, was a film of cool distinction which ended in a car chase over the Los Angeles hills which was not only thrilling but also quite beautiful. His *Dr Jekyll and Mr Hyde* (also 1931), with Fredric March, was an improvement on J. S. Robertson's 1921 version with John Barrymore. But his Marlene Dietrich film *Song of Songs* (1933) was not a success despite the big scene of the smashing of the surrogate statue at the end; in plain fact it was a story that only Stroheim could have satisfactorily directed – and if he had, he could also have played the part of the Baron. On the other hand *Queen Christina*, made later in the same year, was a tremendous success; it is probable that the first image which comes into most people's minds when Garbo is mentioned is that famous and final shot in the film as, all passion spent, she stands gazing forward from the bows of the ship.

Becky Sharp (1935), a reasonably adequate distillation of *Vanity Fair*, made its impact largely because it was the first feature film to be made in Technicolor. In its early days this system produced colours of acid vividness and violence, and Mamoulian, realizing this, controlled and manipulated it. Hence the famous Eve of Waterloo Ball, which began with the entire spectrum and ended with nothing but reds against grey walls and the outer blackness of the night.

Of his other non-musicals, which included a new version of the Fairbanks-Niblo *Mark of Zorro* (1940) and a colour version of Blasco Ibañez' *Blood and Sand* (1941), both with Tyrone Power, as well as a light comedy with Henry Fonda called *Rings on her Fingers* (1942), the most striking was *Golden Boy* (1939). This screen version of the powerful Clifford Odets stage piece about the rise and fall of a boxer was directed

---

[1] The producers were Mary Pickford and Jesse Lasky.

with a straightforward simplicity well suited to the debut of William
Holden as Joe Bonaparte. The rest of the first-class cast, which included
Barbara Stanwyck, Adolphe Menjou and Joseph Calleia, were equally
well deployed, and the New York exteriors and interiors were presented
with stifling accuracy in the photography of Karl Freund and Nick
Musuraca.[1] The climactic fight sequence – brutal, sadistic, coldly
hysterical and at the same time horribly overheated in terms of the
violence of the sheer slugging match which finally develops – is painful
to a degree in its tragic realism.

Mamoulian returned to musicals in the late Forties. *Summer
Holiday* (1947), based loosely on Eugene O'Neill's *Ah! Wilderness*, had
a charm which eluded many, though not Tom Milne, who delighted
in its 'pure Utopia of endless summer days, green grass, flowing
meadows and simple pleasures', nor Charles Higham and Joel
Greenberg, who praised it as 'a formal abstract of American youth and
the beauty of a family life gone for ever.'[2] This was followed 10 years
later[3] by *Silk Stockings*, based in general on the Wilder-Brackett script
for *Ninotchka* and starring Fred Astaire, Cyd Charisse, Peter Lorre and
Jules Munshin. Despite the cast, despite the Cole Porter score (which
included 'All of You'), despite Mamoulian's inspired use of the Cinema-
Scope screen, including the balletic slide along a boardroom table, this
film was coldly received. 'A vulgar and only rarely comic anti-Soviet
tirade' said *Sight and Sound*; yet *Silk Stockings* contains what must
surely be Astaire's best top-hat-and-tails number in 'The Ritz Roll'n
Rock'.

From the mid-Thirties on the musical film divided into two distinct types. On the one hand were the backstage revues which were in
effect theatre musicals translated into the vaster areas of the film
studios. Here not only could many more chorus girls be deployed on
ever larger and more spectacular sets, but also the camera could fly
and swoop and swirl so as to give the spectator dizzying angles and
provocative proximities never possible in a theatre. These films – Fox
Movietone Follies, Gold Diggers of Nineteen Whatever-the-Year,
Broadway This and Broadway That – did indeed have their own
particular stars as well; but the stars, for all their talent, were framed

---

[1] Musuraca was responsible also for the photography of *Curse of the Cat People* and
The Spiral Staircase.

[2] *Mamoulian* (Thames and Hudson); *Hollywood in the Forties* (Zwemmer).

[3] Mamoulian's absence from the screen never meant unemployment. He is a dis-
tinguished producer of opera and drama, having to his credit, among many productions,
Boris Godunov, *Pelléas et Mélisande*, *Die Glückliche Hand* (Schönberg), *Marco Millions*,
A Month in the Country, *Porgy and Bess* and *Oklahoma*.

or set like jewels in the elaboration of the big production numbers.

Dominating this type of musical for many years was the super-choreographer Busby Berkeley. For him the human form – multiplied and combined in endless variations – was part of a formalized aesthetic pattern, whether it appertained to nature as in a flower or to abstraction as in the variations of a kaleidoscope. Disregarding the story-banalities of the film concerned, he concentrated on drilling the chorus to perfection in relation to extremely unusual camera angles and camera movements, so that he could achieve 'the purest combination of visual and sound that had yet come from American studios'.[1] Berkeley's apotheosis came with *The Gang's All Here* in 1943, well described[2] as 'a world of kaleidoscopic patterns of female flesh, dissolving into artichokes, exploding stars, snowflakes and expanding leaves of water-lilies . . . Organ-grinders' monkeys crawl through artificial palm-trees . . . the camera moves across a tropical island set covered in yellow-clad girls who whirl gigantic phallic bananas or turn them into a banana xylophone; finally Carmen Miranda, initially singing the numbɹǝ [The Lady in the Tutti Frutti Hat] on top of a waggon in a hat and corsage of bananas and strawberries, is left in an avenue of strawberries five feet high with a cornucopia of bananas sprouting from her head; can surrealism go further?' The good Dr Goebbels had already tried, according to David Hull[3]; in 1938 Tobis made *The Stars Are Shining*, 'a rather mad attempt to do a Busby Berkeley musical set in a movie studio, with guest appearances by thirty-six Tobis stars, stage and sports personalities. The final reel features a number with girls dressed as signs of the zodiac . . .'

The other type of Hollywood musical involved stars and personalities who partook more of filmic than of theatrical tradition, or who had at any rate not only adapted themselves to, but also identified themselves with the moods and methods of film-making. Prime among these were of course Fred Astaire, Ginger Rogers, Judy Garland, Mickey Rooney, Gene Kelly and Frank Sinatra. These were human personalities involved in human predicaments (however trivial) and even in recognizable stories. Also, largely under the influence of producer Arthur Freed, these musicals were liberated from the studios and emerged into the open air, or at least the appearance of it. Even the talented Vincente Minnelli, known chiefly for studio-bound shooting, contributed two of the best of these footloose musicals, the nostalgic

---

[1] Arthur Knight, *The Liveliest Art*, Macmillan, 1957.
[2] *Hollywood in the Forties* by Charles Higham and Joel Greenberg, Zwemmer, 1968.
[3] *Film in the Third Reich* by David Stewart Hull, University of California Press, 1969.

Meet Me in St Louis (1944) and, of course, *An American in Paris* (1951).

From musicals such as these came, for my money at least, much of the real dream-magic of cinema. The cool and coruscating dancing of Astaire and Rogers in a sort of P. G. Wodehouse country-house summer; the very special world of Judy Garland – sometimes tinged with a bitter nervousness, but always exciting, right from the moment in *The Wizard of Oz* when, on a black and white set, she opened the door of the house and there outside all was Technicolor; and of course the fabulous virtuoso delights of *On The Town*, with Gene Kelly, Jules Munshin, Frank Sinatra and others in a magnificent caper across the streets and skylines of New York. Such films are examples of film-production of the highest order. They combine the great singing, dancing and acting capabilities of their casts with equally great filmic techniques which result, in effect, from ignoring any idea of impossibilities.

Hence the magic, be it big or be it small. In *An American in Paris* Gene Kelly does a dance with a group of small children in the street. (Whether it is a studio street or a real street doesn't matter; the effect is that it is a street). Kelly dances *for* these children, dances *with* them; he never dances *at* them. As the dance progresses an extraordinary intimacy, a kind of complicity grows up between him and the children which is climaxed at the moment when, in a tiny flash of genius, he momentarily becomes Charlie, the universal Charlie, and you can feel the children knowing him, knowing that 'this is who you are'. The conspiracy with the kids is complete.

There is a similar magic in some of the sequences of Stanley Donen's *Seven Brides for Seven Brothers*, notably the house-raising scene, in which a group of young dancers carry acrobatics into choreography and out again the other side; and again when certain songs against a wintry landscape lead nostalgia gently but firmly up an ice-bound path. *Seven Brides*, incidentally, must be one of the most frequently revived of musicals; it has thousands of aficionados (of whom I am one) who see it regularly; and this is true to only a slightly lesser degree of *On the Town* and *An American in Paris*.

For some time now there has been a growing tendency to abandon this imaginative approach to the musical in favour of the transference of stage successes straight to the screen. Thus the later Rodgers and Hammersteins coined money for their producers – *Oklahoma, Carousel, South Pacific* and of course *The Sound of Music*, biggest moneymaker of the lot. Year by year these films have been getting duller and duller; mild little fantasies like that in *My Fair Lady* when Eliza dreams the fates she would provide for the professor seem 'way out' in their humdrum surroundings, while the sensitivity displayed in, say, *Carmen Jones*, is quite forgotten. There is, it will be argued, always *West Side Story*, but this was a thousand times better live on the stage.

However, the long drag of bourgeois successes seemed by the 1970s to be coming to an end. *Star!* and *Dr Dolittle* joined *Zabriskie Point* in helping to run Hollywood's finances finally into the ground. A new style needed to be found, and one with a definite appeal to the young, who now turned out to be the real movie-goers while their elders sat at home with the TV.

Hence no doubt the success of *Woodstock*, *Monterey Pop* and the like, which provided a sense of participation on *cinéma-vérité* lines (to say nothing of more sinister documents like the Rolling Stones' *Gimme Shelter*, with its guaranteed genuine murder by Hell's Angels straight in front of the cameras). Such might well be the end of the Hollywood musical as an art form in its own right, and one of America's greatest contributions to the motion picture – unless a younger generation, fired by multi-media ideas, should hit on a new and exciting approach.

III

In Europe the musical film never developed with anything like the same originality and success as in the United States. There were some minor exceptions, and one major one – René Clair, who would, however, like Lubitsch, pass in due course to other areas of filmic expression. Meantime he followed *Sous les Toits de Paris* with *Le Million* (1931), in which he returned to the mood of *Un Chapeau de Paille d'Italie* and *Les Deux Timides* for a piece whose perfection has become legendary. This story of the chase after a lost lottery ticket framed its lunacies and exaggerations – not least the prolonged opera sequence which gradually evolved into a football match – in a structure of steel-like precision. Not until 1952, and then in a different mood with Gérard Philipe in *Les Belles de Nuit*, did Clair achieve the same controlled fantasy; and not until 1956, with *Les Grandes Manoeuvres* (also with Philipe and in its time one of the most beautiful colour pictures ever made) did he make another film of such undeviating precision of structure, which here underlaid the tendresse and the gently elegant melancholy of a love story of *La Belle Epoque*.

Clair followed *Le Million* with his splendid musical satire *A Nous la Liberté* (1932), with its witty and often cogent comparisons between prison life and mass production factories, with its spoofs on politicians and big-business tycoons, its many *hommages* to Chaplin which were later reciprocated in *Modern Times*,[1] Lazare Meerson's splendid parodies of Art Deco, and Georges Périnal's limpid black-and-white photography ending in that staggering track-shot across the fully automated factory and out to the anglers, the alfresco *bals* and the *fêtes champêtres* by the riverside.

Meantime in Germany Wilhelm Thiele had directed *Drei von der Tankstelle* (1930), a reasonably jolly film about some footloose youngsters who take over the running of a gasoline station; and a year later Erik Charell made his spectacular *Congress Dances*, with Lillian Harvey's triumphant progress in her coach and horses rivalling Jeanette MacDonald's train ride in *Monte Carlo*. Beyond these Germany produced only *kitsch*, mainly in the form of operettas transferred more or less straight from stage to screen, though Ludwig Berger managed to maintain a certain cinematic style.

In the Soviet Union, where the changeover to sound took longer than elsewhere (as indeed Eisenstein and his colleagues had foreseen in their Manifesto), Alexandrov finally came out in 1934 with *Jazz Comedy* (also known as *The Jolly Boys*), a rather heavy-handed and derivative effort, as might have been guessed from the disastrous final sequence of his otherwise elegant 'avant-garde' short made in Paris in 1929 and entitled *Romance Sentimentale*. Some two years after *Jazz Comedy* he made *Circus*, which was something of a failure; but in 1940 he had a big success with *Bright Path*, which was shown in a cut version in America under the title of *Tanya*. In subsequent years another director, Ivan Pyriev, did well with musicals, his *At 6 p.m. After the War* (1944) signalling the fact that Stalin regarded the conflict as won.

In the next year *Arshin Mal-Alan*, a musical from the Baku studios, received a Stalin prize. But in the post-war years films on the pattern of Ivanovsky and Rappoport's *Musical Story* (made in 1940, with Bolshoi opera-singer Sergei Lemeshev) gave way more to the filming of actual performances of opera or ballet, or films, like *Glinka*, about the lives of composers.

As for the British, they have never shown more than a minor talent for true musicals.

[1] When *Modern Times* appeared in 1936, Tobis, the producers of *A Nous la Liberté*, had fallen into the hands of Dr Goebbels, who caused an action to be taken out against Chaplin for plagiarism. Forced into the witness box, Clair turned the tables by making a speech of respect and affection for Chaplin as well as freely acknowledging his own derivations from him, which ensured the complete withdrawal of the Tobis case.

IV

One of the earliest criticisms of the synchronous film was the curb it could put on international distribution owing to the language barrier. At the beginning some producers tried to solve the problem by shooting each scene three times, each with a different linguistic cast. Apart from the creative nullity induced by such a method, the expense was prohibitive, and the idea was soon abandoned,[1] though as late as 1933 Pabst, with the multilingual Chaliapin playing the title part in his *Don Quixote*, doubled the part of Sancho Panza, the English version being played by George Robey – no less – and the French by Dorville; and it is perhaps fair to add that Pabst again, in the French version of *Dreigroschenoper*, produced a passable parallel to the original.

Eventually nearly everyone settled either for dubbing – that is, substituting other voices in the required languages for those of the original actors – or for superimposed subtitles translating just as much of the dialogue as is necessary for comprehension. It has to be admitted that from that time to this neither system has been wholly satisfactory. I have never forgotten the dismay I felt many years ago in Barcelona when from the lips of Laurel and Hardy there emerged strange and unsympathetic voices speaking Spanish; while in the version of *L'Année Dernière à Marienbad* which I saw in Los Angeles the lengthy titles often obscured fully half of the screen image. In some multilingual areas such as Egypt, where three or more titles in different languages and scripts are required, they are projected on to separate screens at the sides and bottom of the main screen, leaving the picture image free. It is a pity that such a system has never been universally adopted.

[1] The full lunacy is well described by Sadoul: 'Paramount, installed in the suburbs at Joinville le Pont, planned to create a European Hollywood. To the stipulations of producers and directors frankly and aggressively Californian there was constructed one gigantic film factory, that rapidly assumed the character of a Tower of Babel. Some of the films that emerged therefrom were made in no fewer than fourteen or fifteen different linguistic versions . . . The same scenes of the same film were played successively, on the same sets, by actors brought from France, Holland, Sweden, Denmark, Spain, Portugal, Czechoslovakia, Poland, Rumania, Hungary, Germany, Yugoslavia, Greece, Egypt, Lithuania, under a director who might or might not be of their own nationality. Subjects were chosen for the cosmopolitanism of their appeal, and determined preference accorded to those whose setting was in the salon or the night club . . . But though this company had on its payroll some men of no little talent – Marcel Pagnol, Marcel Achard, Alexander Korda, Alberto Cavalcanti – nothing could be worse than these Paramount canned-goods. The more artistically endowed directors, indeed, could not stand the ruthlessly commercial pace; a number of them crossed to England, there to take up again, sometimes with brilliant results, careers compromised in Paris.' (*French Film* by Georges Sadoul, Falcon Press, 1953.)

The striking thing, however, was that despite all these problems and disadvantages, international distribution continued to flourish and expand. The Americans never forgot that the film must appeal primarily to the eye, if only in terms of vital statistics; nor, as we have just seen, did they overlook the fact that music is an international language.[1] Again, looking at the situation from a different angle, one can see that the linguistic question was bound, in some degree, to favour and encourage indigenous film production. The rapid expansion of the Egyptian film industry between 1930 and 1937, for instance, was almost certainly due to the demand for vernacular songs and native music.

But perhaps the most dramatic example of the impact of the synchronous film was seen in India. It was twofold. On the one hand it opened up – as we shall see – a vista as rich as that discovered by Phalke when he began making his mytho-religious films. But on the other it propelled the Indian film industry into a crisis of such dimensions that total disaster seemed almost inevitable.

Throughout the whole period of the silent film the Indian producers, centred mainly in Bombay, Calcutta and Madras, could happily share between them an audience of several hundred millions in India, together with Burma and Ceylon. The fact that, even apart from the two last named areas, the number of different languages involved was at least twelve was of no significance; just as in Europe, the making of titles in any number of languages was simple and inexpensive.

The problem which arose with the introduction of the talking film is extremely well expounded by Barnouw and Krishnaswamy in their book *Indian Film*:

'In Bombay, which was leading in production volume, it meant this: located in the Marathi-speaking area of the country, its producers would naturally make films in that language. If so, they would at the start of the 1930s have a potential market of 21 million people, almost all in the region surrounding Bombay and including Poona, Kohlapur, and other cities. But the films would be incomprehensible in the rest of India, in Burma, and in Ceylon.

'In Calcutta, which stood second in production, it meant this: situated in Bengal its producers would naturally make films in the Bengali language, which would give them a market area inhabited by some 53 million, largely in the north-eastern portion of India.

[1] Years later incredulous British distributors found a vast market for the somewhat mediocre George Formby films in, of all places, the Soviet Union – presumably because the Russians liked the ukulele and banjo even better than the balalaika.

Again, the film would be incomprehensible in most other parts of India, in Burma, and in Ceylon.

'In Madras, which had made a hesitant start in film production, it meant this: situated in the Tamil-speaking area of the country, its producers would logically make films in that language, which would give them a potential market area of 20 million people in southern India and some additional millions in Ceylon, Malaya and Africa. But the Tamil language, of Dravidian descent and unrelated to Marathi, Bengali, and other north Indian tongues, would make the films incomprehensible in most of India.

'Would film producers, accustomed to visions of wide, growing markets, now be hemmed into linguistic pockets? Instead of competing in a large area, would they chop it into zones? And could an area of 20 million, or 21 million, or even 53 million inhabitants support a film industry, if costs should rise steeply in the era of sound?'

In addition, as the same authors point out, some language areas had no film industry at all. Who would supply talking films to the 28 million Telegu speakers, to say nothing of the 15 million Punjabi, 11 million Gujerati, and so on down to the one million speakers of Kashmiri? Moreover the vast Hindi-speaking market – mainly in the North – which numbered *at least 140 million souls* – was also without a film-production centre; and in any case there were at least three different sorts of Hindi dialects, mutually incomprehensible.

No one was very surprised, therefore, when Madan Theatres, the largest film organization in India, having converted its studios to sound at great expense, made a few talkies and then collapsed. The problem seemed insoluble.

Yet within a few years the Indian industry was enjoying an unprecedented boom.

Apart from the slight measure of protection against foreign imports which the language barriers now afforded, there was one simple, fundamental reason for this dramatic reversal.

Just as Phalke, with his mytho-religious films, brought to millions of people profound experiences of which they were otherwise bound to be deprived, so the synchronous film – coming at a precisely correct historical moment – was able to extend the current revival of Indian drama from its comparatively small urban theatre audiences to millions more.

Hitherto Indian drama (banned or driven underground by the Moguls) had managed to survive, albeit in debased form, through travelling players who had wandered across the country from village to village performing crude folk dramas which originated from the Sanscrit theatre of a thousand years ago. However crude their performances, these travelling players always had a tremendous following and, at times, considerable social and religious influence.

Now the important thing to note is that Indian drama, like Greek, was invariably combined with song, dance, music. Therefore an Indian film based on an original Indian dramatic theme was bound to be, in the strictest sense, 'All Talking, All Singing, All Dancing'. Once such films had been made, the demand for them became insatiable, and 'the Indian sound-film of 1931 was not only the heir of the silent film; it also inherited something more powerful and broad-based. Into the new medium came a river of music that had flowed through unbroken millenia of dramatic tradition. . . . In 1931 and 1932, at what seemed a dark moment in Indian film history, song and dance – in part derived from a tradition of folk music-drama – played an important role in winning for the sound film an instant and widening acceptance.'[1]

The rate of expansion may be gauged by the fact that in 1931 28 films were produced – of which 23 were in Hindi, 3 in Bengali, and one each in Tamil and Telegu. Four years later the figure had risen to no less than 233 films covering at least ten different languages.

As with the preceding era of the 'silent' film, there is no reason to pretend that the bulk of the product was anything other than pretty shoddy. The dramatic elements were only perfunctorily included, for the great demand was for music, drumming and, above all, song. Mass production of hybrid, that is westernized Indian music, became quite an industry; and it was not unusual for the action of the story to be interrupted by anything up to 40 or 50 songs, drum solos, etc – which explains why the films went on for several hours.

Nevertheless a handful of producers, notably Debaki Bose, Prince Barua, Himansu Rai and Rajaram Shantaram, kept up a certain quality both of content and technique. They also, as in the previous period, continued to develop the 'social' films whose appeal was to the urban middle-class, for whom also they made dance dramas of a more elegant and sophisticated nature; and the dominance of the film stars, from Gohar and Billimoria onward, became ever more powerful.

Over all this hung an insane and complicated censorship system set up by the British with some complicity from the film trade itself. It was a censorship with political as well as moral overtones; sample— 'Dreamed of a day when the government would be a government of the

[1] op. cit., p. 69.

people, by the people, for the people', ordered to be substituted by 'Dreamed of the day when peace and contentment would prevail in the land'. There were too a very large number of tender spots in terms of religion and religious customs which exercised the indigenous population as much, if not more than the occupying power; and it was seldom that an opinion on censorship as enlightened even as the following, by Sir George Dunbar (author of *A History of India*) was expressed:

'A film to be successful in India cannot follow British – still less Hollywood – standards. The innate conservatism of Indian nationalism holds to the dramatic conventions of the Golden Age, fifteen hundred years ago, when Kalidasa wrote his deathless drama. . . .

'The howlers perpetrated by Western film-producers when dealing with Indian subjects would not appeal to a Bengali villager seeing a travelling cinema show. Nor would the Friday afternoon matinees for the benefit of the trans-border tribesmen have a civilizing influence if some of the films seen in this country were shown in Peshawar city. In India a wise censorship is absolutely necessary, more especially for religious and racial reasons. In this matter there is much virtue in the Swadeshi slogan "Indian-made films for India"; and it is hoped that the suggestion made by the Indian Cinematograph Committee in 1928, that scholarships should be founded in India for learning the technique of the industry abroad, may be substantially followed up.'

This was written in 1936. There is now a flourishing Film Institute of India where a number of young film-makers receive expert training; the Government film censorship is, if anything, even dottier than under the British Raj; and, as I write, the BBC is being thrown out of India because they showed on British television a series of personal film reports on the country by the distinguished French director Louis Malle. On the other hand, India did finally throw up a great film director, Satyajit Ray; and a younger generation, from the Institute and from film units both in the governmental and the private sector, is beginning to show a lot of promise.

In Japan the arrival of the talking picture was also fraught with crisis, but in different terms and, one might say, with a certain macabre high-comedy as far as the benshi were concerned. First, however, it must be remembered that, unlike India and other Asian countries, Japan already had an established school of film-making, with directors like Ozu and Mizoguchi well to the fore. The themes of a number of their films – and of others by directors such as Shimazu, Gosho and

Suzuki – were of implied, sometimes overt criticism of social injustice in Japanese society. Such criticism still persists in Japan today, as we shall see later in the films of Oshima and others; it is but one of the pointers to the schizophrenic aspect of a country which still retains a culture of purely oriental origin and, it must be added, great sophistication and aesthetic sensitivity, which acts as a perpetual undertow against the tides of westernized industrialization and organization. (One day someone will make a Zen computer, and POW!). The West, however, for many years to come remained unaware of the value and progress of Japanese cinema, though the magazine *Close Up* did run some stills of Suzuki's *What Made Her Do It?*, curiously translated into the more or less meaningless title of *Why She Must Be Done*.

Anyway it can safely be said that when the talking film arrived, Japanese cinema was at a stage of development comparable – both aesthetically and economically – with that of Europe. The only difference was that the arrival of the synchronous film created a different sort of situation. Whereas in America and Europe the synchronous camera at first produced a sense of constriction, in Japan it produced a sense of liberation. For it meant curtains for the benshi.

But not without a struggle. The more conservative critics immediately complained that the new soundtrack left no leeway for the benshis' explanations. As for the benshis themselves, they, as Joseph Anderson and Donald Richie[1] amusingly point out, were 'thrown into complete confusion by the coming of sound. At first they kept silent, hoping that the talking films would go away. Then they tried to take the offensive and tried to narrate over the sound. This was difficult because they had no public address system and were forced to shout as loud as they could. Soon they learned to cut down the volume to let themselves be heard, and, finally, some benshi turned off the sound altogether, showing the film as though it were silent and, as always, faithfully narrating.'

Meanwhile the imported American talkies were in bad odour because dubbing was found to be totally unacceptable to Japanese audiences; which was one up to the benshi. But in due course an answer was found in subtitling which, by illustrating the soundtrack on the screen, *and in text*, finally cut the ground from under the benshis' feet.

A consortium which included respected film critics and one forward-looking benshi (who must, like a forward-looking exhibitor, have seemed a contradiction in terms) got together and, after study,

[1] *The Japanese Film* by Anderson and Richie, Tuttle, 1959.

subtitled, very carefully and economically, von Sternberg's *Morocco*. This immediately became a smash box-office hit (it also had Dietrich), and it was probably the film which finally persuaded the Japanese producers, however reluctantly, to go in for talkies.

Some companies plumped, like Warners in America, for sound on disc; and as even Warners had found, wished they hadn't. It was the Shochiku Company which went in for sound on film and hit the jackpot – not merely because they used the better and more practical system of recording, but also because, in Heinosuke Gosho, they found a director who realized what would appeal, in terms of synchronism, to the benshi-conditioned Japanese audiences. He made a film – *The Neighbour's Wife and Mine* – which, apart from having a box-office title of genius, did everything which the benshi did not, could not, or did not want to do. To quote Anderson and Richie again, 'Benshi banished, the film could revel in especially recorded silence'. In fact the sound, or lack of it, in Gosho's film arose from a carefully planned script. Girl heroine mad on jazz – therefore plenty of jazz-music, from her record-player, on the soundtrack. Man and wife not on speaking terms – therefore minimal dialogue, with natural sounds like cats, children crying, parties in the house next door used in counterpoint (had Gosho seen the Soviet Manifesto?) to comment on the visual action. The whole film was in fact cinematic because it retained the visual sense and pattern of the 'silent' film while indicating to a degree the real advantages of synchronism as opposed to benshi narration.

The feeling of liberation and relaxation thus achieved by Gosho enabled the Japanese cinema – despite a number of difficulties – to enter the synchronous era with a certain confidence and with a renewed consciousness of the expressive possibilities of the medium in terms of Japanese society and Japanese convictions and conventions. While in India the machinery of sound recording was being used to turn out endless 'epics' of diluted and westernised dance-dramas, the Japanese began to integrate the possibilities of the talking film into a new approach to the patterns (however formalized) of their history, their theatre, and their rapidly changing society. The feudal background of history, the sense of the tragic, the literal acceptance of the reality of the ghostly – these on the one hand gave a number of Japanese directors a valid creative impulse in terms of true cinema; while on the other hand the rapid incursion of Western, and particularly American influences, prevented the Japanese film from getting bogged down in the past with the dramatic conventions of Noh, Kabuki, or Bunraku.

The period of the Thirties, during which the extreme militarists increasingly took over the government of Japan and instituted the invasion first of Manchuria and then of China, saw nevertheless the development of a fine school of cinema, led mainly by Gosho, Ozu, Shimazu and Mizoguchi. It was climaxed by Uchida's *Earth* (1939), a film which could perhaps be compared with Dovzhenko's of the same name, though Uchida, unlike Dovzhenko, was not forced to bring in Communist action-politics. Uchida made an elemental film about those who live on, by, or for the soil – the cycle of nature, the cycle of man's life, of his despair and of his hope. As in so many of the best Japanese films – and this includes moderns like Nagisa Oshima's *Boy* and *The Ceremony*, of which more later – the importance of plot and structure is often minimal, whereas significant visuals, physical feelings, and the acceptance of the extraordinary as ordinary (a clumsy description of an ineffable factor), can be made into a wholly satisfying movie-pattern of man's living and dying.

V

While the Japanese, virtually unnoticed by the West,[1] were finding these new possibilities of creative development, Western film-makers were seeing new possibilities not only in the musical but also in fictional drama and comedy. They began to realize that the dialogue film could be more than a ten-day wonder; it could be a creative step forward of almost illimitable importance. For, despite the scorn for the talking picture indicated in the Soviet Manifesto, it was in fact the newfound *vocalization* of film which was really going to count.

It was not for nothing that one of the greatest publicity slogans of all time appeared in 1930 – 'GARBO TALKS!'. And in fact Garbo's first talkie is an excellent example of the progress made possible by the fully synchronized film. First of all Garbo herself – then, now and forever the greatest of all the stars – was revealed as having hitherto been only half-presented to the world; her voice, husky, musky, perfumed with an elusively fascinating *timbre*, was found to be the other half of her persona, hitherto denied to her public. Secondly, by

---

[1] Apart from the pre-talkie masterpiece *Crossroads*, the only Japanese film to have been shown in the West seems to have been Mikio Naruse's *Wife, be like a Rose*, screened in New York as *Kimiko*, and described by Mark Van Doren in 1935 as 'One of the most moving films I know'.

choosing *Anna Christie* as her first talking vehicle, MGM emphasized that now, at last, the great writers of the world could be brought wholly to the screen; and who better, at this time and in this particular case, than a great American dramatist like Eugene O'Neill?[1]

The stage, as it were, was set. There were fundamentally two main choices open to the film-maker. On the one hand there was the translation of the classics, major or minor, to the screen (or, on a lower level, contemporary best-sellers); on the other there was the writing of original screenplays in which sound and dialogue played a major part so that the subject matter could adequately emerge from the social patterns (trivial or important) of contemporary life. From about 1930 onwards both these channels were explored – in Europe as well as in America – with a prescience which showed that film tycoons were not unable to learn a few lessons.

In Hollywood the classics came up very quickly. By 1929 Pickford and Fairbanks – none quicker to jump onto promising bandwagons – made *The Taming of the Shrew* ('additional dialogue by Sam Taylor' providing the highbrow joke of the day). Contrary to general belief this first talkie of Shakespeare was not at all bad. By its very nature it was an excellent choice to start with – a rip-roaring comedy, type-cast for Doug and Mary, in which accusations of blasphemy against the Bard would be difficult to substantiate. The performances, especially in the wedding scene, were quite admirable. I think that the rather snooty disapproval noted in Britain must have arisen in part from the fact that the English were not yet accustomed to the American accent – or rather to the variety of accents from different regions of the United States. It is sometimes forgotten that it was not until the coming of the talkies that the American language imposed itself on the English tongue. Today of course all English-speaking peoples share their understanding of American, be it dry East Coast or velvety Deep South; and it is only local films, like the British *Kes*, which have difficulty in getting wide distribution because it is assumed that the Southern English can't or won't understand the language of the Northern English.

Following *The Shrew* came *A Midsummer Night's Dream*, for

---

[1] Actually O'Neill, apart from *Strange Interlude* (already referred to) and Mamoulian's *Summer Holiday* (adapted from *Ah Wilderness!*) has not been too well served by film-makers. The screenwriter Dudley Nichols' mistaken venture into direction with *Mourning Becomes Electra* (1947) was, despite a distinguished cast (Katina Paxinou, Michael Redgrave, Rosalind Russell, Leo Genn) something of a disaster; nor could much better be said for Alfred (*Winterset*) Santell's arty and watered-down screen version of *The Hairy Ape* (1944) with Susan Hayward and – in an inevitable piece of casting – William Bendix.

which Max Reinhardt himself was imported from Germany to work with his compatriot and ex-pupil William Dieterle. The film was unduly embroidered with masses of superimposed fairies weaving their ways up, down and around the forest trees, thus ensuring, as John Baxter points out in *Hollywood in the Thirties*, the obliteration of content by form. Nevertheless, the film had a good deal of Shakespearian quality as a whole, and there were memorable performances by James Cagney as Bottom[1] and Mickey Rooney as Puck. As for *Romeo and Juliet*, a lovechild of Irving Thalberg, in which the comfortably mature figures of Norma Shearer and Leslie Howard, inhabiting sets of cataclysmic vulgarity, played the star-crossed child-lovers – nothing need be said save that it contained a virtuoso rendering of the Queen Mab speech by John Barrymore which still remains a real collector's piece.[2] Meantime Britain, more cautiously, confined itself to a somewhat whimsy version of *As You Like It*, directed by Paul Czinner with Elisabeth Bergner as Rosalind and Laurence Olivier as Orlando. Of Bergner's performance James Agate remarked, *inter alia*, that he was not conscious at any moment of establishing contact with Shakespeare's heroine; 'That which is substituted is something else – something German, something *gemütlich*, and something nearer to Wagner's Eva than to Molière's Célimène'.[3] This bit of culture-blinding by the old boy should not, by the way, blind *us* to the dangers of the translation of Shakespeare one way or the other. There is a lot of sensitivity needed and perhaps a lot of luck. Gide's French translation of *Hamlet*, performed on the Marigny stage by Barrault and Renaud, was as unexpectedly triumphant as Kozintsev's film of the play in Russian, with Innokenty Smoktunovsky; while Olivier's film of the same play, despite felicities, was in the end a sad affair.

Hollywood went a bit more gingerly on other English classics. But George Cukor's superb *David Copperfield* (1934) was not only well directed but also had perhaps the finest casting of all time. The savour still remains of W. C. Fields as Micawber, Edna May Oliver as Betsy, Basil Rathbone as Murdstone and Roland Young as Uriah Heep, to name only a few. People who accused Hollywood of type-casting used to forget the other side of the picture; Hollywood could usually find exactly the right person for any part. *David Copperfield* remained un-

---

[1] Not all critics agreed. 'I am not very keen,' wrote one, 'on Cagney's Bottom.'

[2] Let me take this opportunity to draw a tactful veil over two other screen versions of this play, by Castellani (1954) and Zeffirelli (1968). This is obviously not a lucky play for film-makers.

[3] *Around Cinemas* by James Agate, Home and Van Thal, 1946.

surpassed until many years later when the British belatedly[1] entered the field with a series of Dickens films, mostly by David Lean; his *Great Expectations* had a quality of the highest order and, with *Copperfield*, must be rated a secure film classic.

A number of the classic writers had of course been used in pre-talkie days for the sake of their notoriety and for their plot-values; and this continued after the coming of the synchronous film. Tolstoy's *Anna Karenina* (with Garbo of course) is a good example; and others included *Dr Jekyll and Mr Hyde*, filmed several times but never better than by Mamoulian in 1932; Victor Fleming's version of Kipling's *Captains Courageous* with Spencer Tracy in one of his finest parts; *Wuthering Heights*,[2] in which William Wyler directed Olivier, David Niven, Geraldine Fitzgerald and Merle Oberon, with magnificent camerawork by Gregg Toland; and, finally, a surprisingly successful version of *Pride and Prejudice*, adapted by Aldous Huxley, with another admirable cast, under Robert Z. Leonard, which included Greer Garson, Olivier, Edmund Gwenn and Edna May Oliver (1940).

Whatever may have been the relative values of the various screen versions of the classics, they did lead to one very positive result. They started people reading. Just as the coming of broadcasting increased the number of concert goers and record buyers, so the box-office success of the classics (a success due very much, as we have seen, to the correct choice of stars and supporting players) sent people hurrying to the bookshops and to the public libraries. This was particularly so in the United States. This aspect of the motion picture as an educational medium should never be ignored, whether it is due to chance or purpose, especially today, when a TV programme like *The Forsyte Saga* seems to be able to hypnotize the entire English-speaking world, and even beyond.

As far as adaptations from literary works are concerned, the first ten years of the talkies were pretty rich. Bestsellers were regularly snapped up – often in fierce competition – by the tycoons; and the style and construction of the modern novel started to change quite significantly. There were two reasons for this. In the first place, as is well known, the influence of still photography and motion picture photography on the visual arts has for long been very considerable. Posters and illustrations today reflect not only, as an example, Monet's vision

---

[1] A rather undistinguished version of *The Old Curiosity Shop* was in fact made in Britain in 1934.

[2] Tantalisingly, there is a version of this by Buñuel, made in 1953 under the title of *Cumbres Borrascosas* (or *Abismos de Pasión*) which few seem to have seen.

of nature but also the violent visual angles adopted by a film-maker like Eisenstein. Similarly the technique of cinema has been more and more reflected in a tautness and economy of expression, a desire to use fewer words to express more vivid visuals. In the second place there was without doubt the simple discovery that the sale of the film rights of a novel could be more valuable than the normal publishing profits; and this naturally led to the idea of writing books more or less in the style of a film script. Both influences therefore led to the same result, and the contrast between the older and the newer approaches can be especially well seen if we compare the work of Graham Greene and Joseph Conrad in relation to the moving picture.

Greene, it seems to me, was born a child of the film age. The film has introduced a new concept of time into art in which, to quote Arnold Hauser, 'almost all strands of the texture which form the stuff of modern art converge . . . above all the montage technique and the intermingling of temporal and spatial forms in the film . . . The agreement between the technical methods of the film and the characteristics of the new concept of time is so complete that one has the feeling that the time categories of modern art altogether must have arisen from the spirit of cinematic form, and one is inclined to consider the film itself as the stylistically most representative, though qualitatively perhaps not the most fertile genre of contemporary art'.[1] Greene's writing, it seems to me, always had a built-in filmic style; nor was it by chance that he became one of the acutest and best film critics of the 1930s. Indeed his experience as a critic may have helped him to intensify his cinematic approach until it was fined down to the exquisite 'chinese box' flashback technique in a book like *The Quiet American*, a technique which in a sense becomes more elaborate than film, at its present stage, can cope with.

Conrad, on the other hand, wrote a number of books which at first, and indeed at second glance, are temptingly cinematic both from the point of view of story and of location. They constantly defeat the best efforts of screen writers and film directors. Yet Conrad himself constantly uses 'chinese box' flashbacks and the like. The difference is that in Conrad the visual action, the bare plot, is in a sense a disguise, and the reader finds himself participating in deep psychological investigations, often on several different levels, into the nature of human relations and man's struggles with his inner self. It is interesting that it is Greene's 'entertainments' (his own word) that make good films,

[1] *The Social History of Art*, Part 4, by Arnold Hauser, Routledge and Kegan Paul, 1951.

while his big serious novels, such as *The Power and the Glory*, resist filmic treatment. Thus John Ford's version of it, *The Fugitive* (1947), ended up as a nothingness behind a façade of superb photography by Gabriel Figueroa.

The density of Conrad's writing, and the fact that he compels himself, his characters, and us to examine people and acts from different psychological viewpoints and through differing personalities, make it almost impossible for the film-maker to translate the 'feel' of his work to the screen; it might *just* be possible with *Nostromo* or *Under Western Eyes*, and Hitchcock got fairly near the mark in *Sabotage* (1936), which was a screen version of *The Secret Agent*.[1] Conrad certainly defeated John Cromwell, who twice made *Victory* (1930 and 1940), Richard Brooks (*Lord Jim*, 1965), and Carol Reed, whose brave effort at *An Outcast of the Islands* will be discussed later.

Somerset Maugham, on the other hand, whose fantastic skill as a story teller masks a fairly shallow attitude to life, adapts easily to the screen, as witness *The Painted Veil* (with Garbo), *Rain* (with Joan Crawford, who could not however efface the memory of Gloria Swanson in *Sadie Thompson*, directed by Raoul Walsh in 1928), *Of Human Bondage*, in which Bette Davis finally established herself as a star, *The Vessel of Wrath*, with Charles Laughton, and the like.

It is hardly necessary to go into details about all the many plays and novels which were bought and converted into films in this first period of the talking picture. They were of course legion, and perhaps the only point to be made here is that at their best they showed a reasonably high level of taste and, for Hollywood, considerable boldness. I for one will give credit to MGM for buying, however reluctantly, Pirandello's *As You Desire Me* – perhaps the least successful at the box-office of all the Garbo films, but memorable not only for her own performance but also for that of Erich von Stroheim. Although this film was originally to have been made by Feyder it was, in the event, brought to the screen with some hability by George Fitzmaurice.[2]

On the credit side, too, must be added *All Quiet on the Western Front* (1930), which will be fully dealt with in the next chapter; Sidney Franklin's *The Good Earth* (1937) with Paul Muni and Luise Rainer – a transcription of the Pearl Buck novel marred slightly by that exaggeration which comes from an attempt to over-simplify; Cecil B. De Mille's *The Sign of the Cross*, if only for the majestic dottiness of its

[1] Confusingly, Hitchcock's previous film was called *The Secret Agent* but was derived from Somerset Maugham's *Ashenden*.

[2] For Feyder's version of this episode see p. 142.

extravagance and the panache with which it was carried out; *Lost Horizon* (1937), from which, despite its superficiality of conception, Frank Capra distilled a special sort of screen magic and obtained from Ronald Colman the performance of his career; John Ford's *Arrowsmith* (1931) and *The Informer* (1935), particularly the latter – arguably Ford's best film with the exception of *The Grapes of Wrath*; William Wyler's *Dead End* (1937), for its fabulous multiple set, for Bogart, and for the first appearance of the archetypal Dead End Kids; and Frank Lloyd's *Mutiny on the Bounty* (1935), a film which, as few others had before, created a genuine atmosphere of period, of place and of cruelty as well as co-starring (among others) Charles Laughton and Clark Gable. I want to add *King Kong* (1932) made by Schoedsack and Cooper of *Grass* fame, but I am not sure whether it was indeed adapted from a novel or a play. The studio bought Conan Doyle's *The Lost World* on its budget, but this may have been a protection against copyright; perhaps the appended extract[1] from the script will serve as a suitable credential for this, the biggest, the best and so far never equalled of the Monsters:

> 'Fade in on a general view of Skull Island at dawn, with the bridge of the ship in the foreground. Captain Englehorn is leaning over the rail looking out at the grandeur of the spectacle. Sea and jungle are still in purple shadow. But high above, the east has drenched the mountains in the glory of its burning. One by one the columnar peaks of snow are kindling downward, chasm by chasm, each in itself a new morning; white glaciers blaze their winding paths like fiery serpents; long avalanches cast down keen streams, brighter than lightning, each sending its tribute of driven snow, like altar smoke, to the heavens. The rose light of the silent domes flushes (*sic*) that heaven about them until the whole sky, one scarlet canopy, is interwoven with a roof of waving flame and tossing, vault beyond vault, as with the drifted wings of many companies of angels.'

I don't recollect much of this getting into the final version of *King Kong*. Perhaps it got cut out when they remembered that the film was in black and white.

---

[1] Quoted in *Behind the Screen* by Kenneth Macgowan, Delta, 1967. Edgar Wallace has often been credited with this screenplay, but Meriam Cooper pointed out (Letter to *Sight & Sound*, Spring 1972) that he used Wallace's name because he had promised to do so before his untimely death; but 'not one single scene, nor line of dialogue . . . was contributed by him'.

VI

That the talking picture brought a new maturity to the screen was not due only to the freedom of expression provided by the use of words and music; its arrival also happened to coincide with an historical period which the film industry could not ignore or evade. The great Wall Street crash of 1929, and the ensuing disastrous slump did not, as we have already seen, immediately affect Hollywood (whose big crisis was to come in 1932) in the financial sense. But the crash, the election of Roosevelt, and the subsequent launching of the New Deal (which, remember, seemed to quite a few Americans a piece of crimson bolshevism) forced the front-offices to reconsider their position. If the right wing were screaming 'Commie', the little men, suddenly dispossessed, were beginning to think, and to wonder what exactly was meant by the American Dream. Some ten years later, in a really mature Hollywood, Ford and Toland could film, in darkness and in a ditch, the whispered conversation between Ma Joad and her son on who in this sad world could be described as a 'Red'. Now, in 1930, the tycoons felt that politically and socially they could hardly avoid the implications of the New Deal. Artistically they deeply needed respect and respectability; the world of the spoken word opened up possibilities which must have been quite frightening to men whose lack of education had so far been reasonably masked by business acumen and the possession of the equivalent of several goldmines.

Actually the tycoons had already succeeded in breeding a new type – the educated whizz-kid of which wonder-boy Irving Thalberg was the perfect example. Thalberg not only produced good pictures which made money. He also saw the importance and value of the 'prestige picture' – a film, that is, which (given a solvent and well-run organization) could bring in the sought-after respect even if it didn't turn a big profit. Although he died young (at 37) Thalberg had time enough to act like a dose of salts on MGM, and therefore by implication on nearly all Hollywood. He married Norma Shearer, produced, among many films, *The Barretts of Wimpole Street*, *Mutiny on the Bounty*, and *Romeo and Juliet*, brought the Marx Brothers to the screen, sacked von Sternberg, Stroheim, William Wellman and Frank Capra, and provided the model for Stahr in Scott Fitzgerald's *The Last Tycoon*. The Thalberg generation of younger, more talented producers was articulate enough to persuade the older men to let them move ahead. This generation included Walter Wanger, Dore Schary and, to a degree, Darryl Zanuck and David Selznick.

With this new attitude, and in the atmosphere of the New Deal, the first films of social criticism were made. It soon became clear that they would go in cycles, one following the other as soon as the box-office vein had been exhausted. The first cycle dealt with the Gangster, that dangerous phenomenon created largely by the imposition of Prohibition in the United States. It is difficult to determine which particular film actually triggered off this series. It could have been *The Secret Six* (a now almost forgotten film), directed by George Hill and starring Jean Harlow, Clark Gable and Wallace Beery, the last-named having also starred in Hill's previous picture, a rather horrifying melodrama about prison conditions called *The Big House*. But I think it more likely that it was *Little Caesar* (1930), which launched Edward G. Robinson and was directed by Mervyn LeRoy. This was a film which 'realistically and uncompromisingly depicted the rise of an egotist through aggressiveness, ruthlessness, and organized, large-scale racketeering . . . Lack of sentimentality, brutal assault on the nerves with gunplay, violence, chases, tense struggles over big stakes, callousness towards human feelings, appealed to a public *suddenly insecure in their own lives*, faced with a desperate struggle for survival and menaced from all sides.'[1] (My italics.)

Once the tremendous success of this film was realized the gangster films came rolling out at great speed. Notable especially were Wellman's *The Public Enemy* (1931), with James Cagney, and Rowland Brown's *Quick Millions* (1931) which, apart from putting Spencer Tracy well and truly on the map, had a frighteningly laconic realism which some of the other and glossier films failed to achieve. In the last sequence of *Quick Millions* the gangster is due to be rubbed out by his friends and colleagues. Sitting in the automobile with them, and unaware of their intentions, he growls 'Take your elbow out of my ribs'. 'That's not my elbow' is the reply, and the film cuts to a long shot of a street corner as the car, with a squeal of tyres, swerves past, disgorging as it goes the crumpled body of the gangster.

For most people, however, the gangster cycle is symbolized by Howard Hawks' superb *Scarface – Shame of a Nation*, with Paul Muni as Al Capone and George Raft as his henchman. Brilliantly scripted by Ben Hecht and marvellously lit by Lee Garmes, this film hardly put a foot wrong. Robin Wood, in his perceptive study of Hawks as a director, points out that in some senses this film is, while not immoral,

[1] Lewis Jacobs, *The Rise of the American Film*, Harcourt Brace, 1939.

amoral. Some of the most scandalously brutal scenes are shot almost as farce, as in the machine-gunning of the restaurant, and as Wood says, 'The film communicated, strongly, a sense of exhilaration: Hawks actually encourages us to share the gangsters' enjoyment of violence.'[1]

And it was because of this attitude that Hollywood was accused of irresponsibility and the encouragement of violence and crime. Yet how otherwise is one to give a true picture of the psychology as well as the pathology of the gangster? The same issue is still with us in such films as *Bonnie and Clyde* (with the amiable statement 'We rob banks'); and in any case the gangster films of the Thirties were reporting a situation already created by society, and, on the whole, reporting rather belatedly in view of the fact that when *Scarface* was released Al Capone was not dead (as in the film's finale) but alive and well though living in Alcatraz.

The gangster films dragged on through the Thirties, gradually losing momentum, but occasionally throwing up notable works like *The Marked Woman* (1936) in which the underworld was seen, not without horror, from the point of view of the gangster's moll; it contains one of Bette Davis' very best performances in addition to giving us the inside dope on Lucky Luciano.

The cycle was finally finished off by a glorious, rip-roaring black comedy, based on a Damon Runyon story, called *A Slight Case of Murder* (1938), directed by Lloyd Bacon. It is a story based on the nightmare moment (from the gangster's point of view) when Prohibition was repealed and drinking became legal again. Marko, a gentleman gangster who has genteelly made his pile from purveying bootleg beer, decides that the only thing is to go legitimate. Unfortunately his beer is, and always has been disgusting, and was only consumed *faute de mieux* in the bad old days. Hard pressed by creditors, he flees to his country mansion in Saratoga; pausing en route to pick up, for a free holiday, a boy from his alma mater (an orphanage), he finds at his house four corpses, the proceeds of a hold-up of the bookies' funds, a State Trooper preparing to marry his only daughter and – if he but knew it – the murderer still in the house and slipping in and out of bedroom doors. Being a man of action (the part, by the way, is played by Edward G. Robinson), he dumps the corpses on the doorsteps of various local folk he dislikes, only to discover that there is a reward of $10,000 for the recovery of each corpse, dead or alive. He duly has them collected again and shoved into a convenient cupboard; and the complications are finally solved when the lily-livered State Trooper, eyes shut and quaking

[1] *Howard Hawks* by Robin Wood, Secker and Warburg, 1968.

with terror, re-shoots all the corpses through the closed door, and with
a wild final bang kills the murderer who has unwittingly strayed within
range. The film is directed with the crackle of a machine-gun and no
concessions to morality or propriety. My own favourite moment is
when Marko refuses all the star pupils at the orphanage and demands
someone after his own heart – the worst boy in the school. 'Pierre,' says
the headmistress, 'take three of the older boys with you, go down to
the cellar, unlock Douglas and bring him to my study.' And Douglas,
joy of joys, turns out to be none other than Bobby Jordan, the most
louche of all the Dead End Kids. *A Slight Case of Murder* destroyed the
sanctity of the gangster just as surely as Cagney's swipe at Mae Clarke's
face with half a grapefruit put paid, screenwise at least, to the sanctity
of American womanhood.

With the war gangsterdom passed into the realm of the storm-
trooper, and it was not really until the Sixties that the type reappeared,
and then alarmingly transmuted into the sordid realism of *Bonnie and
Clyde*, *In Cold Blood*, *Bloody Mama*, and the like. The immorality of
which these films stand accused is, I feel, much more justified than in
the Thirties. There is a romantic attitude to the filthiest crimes which is
both repulsive and anarchic, much more so than anything you could
find in *Scarface*. In *Bonnie and Clyde* this romanticism is overt, despite
the blood spurts and fellatio. In *In Cold Blood* it is more concealed,
but is there just the same in the great red herring of anti-capital punishment propaganda which obfuscates the last quarter of the film.

Equally if not more important were the films about the injustices
of modern society, official or unofficial. On this level the American
talkies of the Thirties certainly achieved respectability, and more. The
films sometimes borrowed from the theatre, as in *Winterset*, or
originated more or less directly from the studios as with Fritz Lang's
first and splendid American film, *Fury*, made from a Norman Krasna
story based on a real-life episode.

Winterset (1936) was of course adapted from Maxwell Anderson's
stage play on the subject of that permanent scar on the American
conscience, the martyrdom of Sacco and Vanzetti. Directed by Alfred
Santell, otherwise known, before and since, as a maker of competent
routine pictures, it made a terrific impact at the time. Most critics
found the screen version superior to the original; parallels with *Hamlet*
were reverently examined and considered, and the film was almost
unanimously voted a classic. Personally I found it a bit corny, and I
am sure it would seem even more so today; but at that time it hit people
especially strongly because Hollywood had not hitherto been known

for this kind of intervention in public affairs, particularly in such a case as this which involved a legal lynching.

Lang's *Fury*, made in the same year, was about an *illegal* lynching and made a similarly stunning impact. Fortified no doubt by his experience in making *M*, a film about a child murderer, Lang managed to get onto the screen, for perhaps the first time, something of the reality of mob-psychology; it exhibited and diagnosed, as Alistair Cooke pointed out, 'the kind of emotion that unites nice middle-class people in obscene hysteria'.

Quite a few other films on lynching were to come, not least Mervyn LeRoy's *They Won't Forget* (1937) in which, with the help of Claude Rains' unforgettable performance, it was made clear that to excuse lynchers on the grounds that they are human is too glib a solution. It is a film which doesn't bother to ask for a cry of pity, or an appeal to justice; it just gives you a remorseless, piled up documentation of events. The story is simple. In a small Southern town a girl is murdered; who did it we never find out. The District Attorney is ambitious for a big public success; he has his eye on the governorship. A perfect suspect is found, someone who is not only a northerner but also a college teacher. This unfortunate man, virtually condemned before his trial opens, and hounded by a venomous yellow press, is, on evidence at best circumstantial, sentenced to the electric chair. But the Governor commutes the sentence to life imprisonment, whereupon the high-souled citizenry take it on themselves to snatch him from the train which is taking him to prison, and hang him on the spot. And in this way the Attorney achieves his life ambition.

LeRoy presents this hideous story with economy and without flamboyance or hysteria. He just gives it you straight – the narrow nasty conversation of the townsfolk, the chinless sadism of the crime reporter, the shifty unscrupulousness of the District Attorney, with his ratlike eyes, his treacherous mouth mangling a cigar, the brooding atmosphere which infects the sidewalks, the offices, and the tidy little home which the accused man and his wife have managed to get together after several years of labour. Even at the climax LeRoy retains this brutal economy. At the beginning of the film we don't see the murder, in fact we are never told how it was done. And at the end of the film we don't see the lynching; instead, at the critical moment, we see the mail train wrenching a mail-bag off the pickup bar and vanishing into the night with a sickening screech.

Previous to *They Won't Forget*, LeRoy had made a film about another form of social injustice with the self-explanatory title of *I am a*

Fugitive from a Chain Gang (1932). This, with *Scarface,* established Paul Muni as one of the most sought after screen actors of the day. Originally a stage actor, he made the transition to the studios with intelligent ease and soon became the central figure of a new cycle, this time of films about famous men.

These films, as much for their content as for Muni's performances, made a great impression at the time. *The Story of Louis Pasteur* (1936), *The Life of Emile Zola* (1937), and *Juarez* (1939) were genuine attempts to give audiences some idea of the problems and difficulties of genius in various fields of activity – aesthetic, scientific and political. At their best, as for instance in the passages showing Zola's intervention in the Dreyfus Case, they had a genuinely dramatic as well as historic impact. Seen today – and this goes too for *Dr Ehrlich's Magic Bullet* (1940) with Edward G. Robinson – they seem rather stilted and old-fashioned examples of biography without tears. The enthusiasm and support they received at the time, and not least from the British documentarists, stemmed mainly from their broad educational content. 'Civics' was very much an 'in' word in those days, and these films were seen in part as a channel through which the citizenry could be made to feel the significance of great men not only historically but also in terms of community relations and the responsibility of the individual to the community. At their best they did have a sincerity which made up for their frequently sweeping over-simplifications.

Perhaps because it was nearer the American heart and habitat, John Ford's biographical film about Lincoln was by far the best in the series. With Henry Fonda's sensitive performance in the name-part matching Ford's assured direction, *Young Mr Lincoln* (1939) was particularly effective; and, as Arthur Knight pointed out in reference to the Fourth of July fight sequence, 'Ford's cutting and his choice of camera position alike have been dictated by the logic of his material, the flow of its emotion and by his superb instinct of what the audience will want to see from one moment to the next'.[1] It is an extraordinary sequence, dominated by alternations of darkness and the capricious light of the moon among the moving clouds – its emotional atmosphere masking the precise and functional methods of its director.

It was Ford, too, with *The Grapes of Wrath,* who brought to a climax all Hollywood's efforts, since the coming of the talkies, to come to terms with the idea of films discussing problems of social progress and social injustice. This great film about the dispossessed of this earth revealed new dimensions in cinema as did, in a different way, *Citizen*

[1] Arthur Knight, *The Liveliest Art.*

Kane. Early on in *The Grapes of Wrath* there is a long-shot of a road, with telegraph posts stretching flatly and drearily to an infinitudinous horizon. Along it is coming one small figure. Here Gregg Toland, deploying that unique genius which was soon to astonish all of us again in *Kane*, caused his camera literally to burn up the image into a hot shimmer of dusty sunlight, and created an image of loneliness, frustration and despair. This film was about the struggles of the dispossessed dust-bowl farmers fleeing from their ruined lands and the cold tyrannies of the foreclosing banks to the false promises of prosperity of the Californian fruit-farms. The tragic tale of these folk trekking in their thousands across the insane continent, and eventually arriving in a hell which makes their previous purgatory a paradise, is seen through the simple eyes of the Joad family (with Jane Darwell as the magnificent matriarch) and becomes a sincere and searing indictment of man's cruel indifference to his fellows.

Like Robert Flaherty's *The Land* – another cry of outrage against man's greed and stupidity – *The Grapes of Wrath* appeared shortly before Pearl Harbour. Unlike *The Land*, it managed to survive the attacks of pressure groups who wanted it withdrawn. Both films, in a sense, mark the end of an era; soon other forms of greed, other forms of dispossession, would demand attention.

VII

In Britain, on the other hand, the coming of synchronism did not stimulate the film industry in the direction of social consciousness or social criticism. The arrival of the talkies did, as we have seen, cause Hitchcock to develop some pieces of imaginative gimmickry; similarly Anthony Asquith, in his beautiful and probably underestimated *A Cottage on Dartmoor*, which like *Blackmail*, was in production as a 'silent' when the talkies arrived, ingeniously adapted a sequence which took place in a cinema. Shots of the audience and of the chief characters were accompanied by the noise of the soundtrack coming from the always unseen screen.

The basic content of feature films in Britain, at least during the first eight or nine years of the talkie era, was trivial and without contemporary emphasis. From the point of view of the film as an industry it was, of course, an important expansionist period, but, as the eminent critic C. A. Lejeune never tired of pointing out, the producers consistently ignored the interesting and vital subjects to be found on their own doorsteps in favour of a flashy cosmopolitanism, whether of the present or of the past. True, Hitchcock made good use of English townscapes and landscapes in nearly all of his films – but only as backgrounds to his thriller plots; of the real life of the people there were precious few signs.

But as in Europe, so in Britain the arrival of the talking picture did have a stimulating effect on national production. There were two dominating groups – Gaumont-British (under the Ostrers, the Woolfs and the Balcons[1]) and ABC (controlled by the Scots tycoon John Maxwell).

These two groups, aided by the National Provincial Bank which in those days was quite a pioneer explorer in the shifting quicksands of film finance, now entered on an expansionist policy. 'Big' films were the order of the day, but apart from the Hitchcocks – *The 39 Steps, The Man Who Knew Too Much, Sabotage, The Secret Agent*, and the apparently imperishable *The Lady Vanishes* – they are, despite their bigness, more or less forgotten. Yet these films, and others like Walter Forde's *Rome Express* or Lothar Mendes' *Jew Süss* (both with the advantage of a notable star, Conrad Veidt who, disgusted with Hitler, had proclaimed himself a Jew, which he was not, and left Germany) did much to put British cinema on the map at that time. Other refugees from Hitler were also beginning to arrive, notably Berthold Viertel, who directed *Little Friend* to a script written by Christopher Isherwood.

But, as is well known, the real boom in British films began with Korda's *The Private Life of Henry VIII*, a film which, seen today, has little to commend it other than Charles Laughton's performance in the name part and some exquisite black-and-white photography by Georges Périnal. This film cost somewhere between £50,000 and £60,000; it brought in £500,000 and started a filmic gold rush. Korda managed to put the bite on a by no means unwilling insurance company – the Prudential. Studios and laboratories were built at Denham. Talent was imported from all over the place, sometimes to the detriment of the natives, whether actors or technicians. From France came Jacques Feyder to make *Knight Without Armour* and René Clair to make *The Ghost Goes West*, both starring Robert Donat, a really splendid actor whose career was to be crippled and finally terminated by acute and

---

[1] It is worth noting that in the final event it was Michael Balcon and Alexander Korda who turned out to be 'Britain's *only* producers in the American sense . . . men who had spent their lives in films, and were capable of guiding and directing a group of film-directors in the same way that directors themselves guide actors' (*Mr Rank* by Alan Wood, Hodder and Stoughton, 1952).

incurable asthma; and from America and Germany came many more, including William Cameron Menzies, Joseph von Sternberg, Marlene Dietrich, Erich Pommer, Paul Czinner, Elisabeth Bergner, and Fritz Kortner. Again, of the films made few have stood the test of time; though in *The Ghost Goes West* (1935), a film about the removal of a Scots castle, complete with haunting, to America, Clair – apart from providing the delightful sight of a negro jazz band dressed in full Highland regalia – produced a moment of shock in the cinema as breathtaking as the appearance of the convict Magwitch to Pip in the churchyard sequence of *Great Expectations*. The camera tracks steadily across the vast baronial hall at midnight. There is no one about. Gradually the camera comes to rest on a close-up of a large goblet standing on a refectory table. What will happen? Will a ghostly hand come and pick it up, or pour wine into it, or what? Suddenly, to the fortissimo sound of a high violin string being plucked unbearably near to the microphone, the goblet shatters itself into a hundred pieces; and the spectators shoot straight out of their seats.

Returning, however, to Korda; here was someone with wit, charm and good taste. He had been making films since 1914, first in his native Hungary[1] and then in Germany, America and France. He was a master of the grand gesture and the grandiose production programme; and when the crash came it was he who survived, not his many imitators, who had tried to take advantage of the boom in film finance but who lacked both prudence and imagination.

The crash came in 1937, only four years after the success of *The Private Life of Henry VIII*. It left Britain with an industry widely expanded in personnel (most of whom, however, now found themselves unemployed) and also in bricks and mortar in the form of Denham Studios and a number of new super-cinemas showing mainly American films. The prestige of Britain as a film-producing country was undoubtedly higher and, although no one realized it at the time, the coming of war would solve all its problems for quite a few years to come. But, as I have already said, few of the films of the Thirties have really survived; Asquith's screen version of *Pygmalion* (1938) perhaps, Flaherty's *Man of Aran* (1933), the Hitchcock films, and precious little else.[2]

[1] One of his earliest was a screen version of Mark Twain's *The Million Pound Banknote*.
[2] I am talking of intrinsic audience values here. Of course all films made by distinguished British directors during this period – by Asquith, Carol Reed, Michael Powell and so on – are deserving of close and complete study which can be, to my own knowledge, extremely pleasurable and rewarding. Nor should we forget figures like Marcel Varnel whose comedies with Will Hay and The Crazy Gang had real merit.

It was not until right at the end of the Thirties that the real Britain, the Britain of the slump, of appeasement mentalities, of mass unemployment, malnutrition and other social injustices came to be discussed, however tentatively, on the screen. And this could hardly have happened had not MGM arrived in Britain with certain ambitions and a lot of dollars. The MGM films, which among other things did give some employment to British actors and technicians who would otherwise have remained out of work, included *A Yank at Oxford*, with Robert Taylor, and *Goodbye Mr Chips*, with Robert Donat. Neither of these need detain us; but a third film must, a screen version of A. J. Cronin's best-seller *The Citadel*.

This film, produced in 1938 by an Englishman, Victor Saville, and scripted by another Englishman Ian Dalrymple, was directed, under the MGM flag, by King Vidor. The MGM connection gave the film a chance for distribution in the United States which other British films had hitherto lacked. But the really important thing was its subject matter and the way it was treated. Today the film may not seem all that revolutionary, but its impact at the time was considerable.

Virtually the first studio film of social or civic tendency to be made in Britain, *The Citadel* set out to make a study of a specific section of the community, to analyse its problems, to show its excellences and its failings and, like the Muni biographicals, to expound the integrity and the passion of a man of science in the battle against nature on the one hand and social conditions on the other.

The story tells of a young doctor who battles with fearful conditions in a mining village; who hits on the idea that the incidence of tuberculosis among miners must be due to silica in the dust amid which they work; whose laboratory is unjustly wrecked by anti-vivisectionists; who migrates to London and starves until an old college friend tells him of the advantages of the fee-sharing racket in the snob medical market. Despite a rather contrived plot, which smells at times of the Procrustean demands of the box-office, the film in the end rings true – not least because of Robert Donat's supreme performance, ending with an impassioned speech before the Medical Council which has arraigned him for saving a young patient's life by taking him to an 'unregistered' (ie, not in the racket) specialist. *The Citadel* was a big success in the United States, where Lewis Jacobs reckoned it to be King Vidor's finest film. I now reckon that it still is.

In the following year another film, this time wholly British in origin, also tackled a sociological theme. This was *The Stars Look Down*, based, like *The Citadel*, on a best-selling novel by A. J. Cronin, and directed by Carol Reed who thus established himself as Britain's most important director. Although melodramatic in tone, this film was an undisguised piece of propaganda in favour of the nationalization of the coal industry. Its picture of conditions among the mining community was certainly provocative enough, the acting of a large cast led by Michael Redgrave and Emlyn Williams was realistic and convincing, and, in fine, the film was a big box-office success.

Like *The Citadel*, it impressed America. In this regard Pauline Kael makes the interesting point that it is 'because it does not sentimentalise the characters of the working-class community that they have a classic dignity completely unlike workers in American films . . . It does not try to make us believe that workers are all on the side of humanity and progress and a free and noble life. To many of us *The Grapes of Wrath* was a rather maudlin, embarrassing film – and not because we were opposed to working people or because we didn't know working people. It wasn't that we did not know the Joads; to some degree we were the Joads, and that's why we couldn't accept the glorification of the common man. When *The Stars Look Down* appeared, the propagandistic sentimentality was at its height – and a film in which workers were no better than other people could be attacked as an anti-labour film'.

This comment points up a perennial puzzle about films; the fact that their appreciation often results from their exoticism; Miss Kael praises Carol Reed's film for those very qualities which I found in *The Grapes of Wrath*; and what she calls the melodramatics and sentimentality of that film are precisely what I feel flawed, to a certain degree, *The Stars Look Down*. It is this interplay of national characteristics and, if you like, prejudices which makes the film such a marvellous international instrument. Both of these films were propagandist, both of them extremely well-made and well-acted, and both of them received appreciation whose quality and emphasis altered not just according to the politics, but also the nationality of the viewer.

VIII

During the Thirties another and different aspect of the British film claimed, nay insisted on consideration – the Documentary. Historically it is interesting that this particular methodology coincided so neatly with the arrival of the talking picture; for it was largely through their

bold and unusual experiments with the soundtrack that the documentarists succeeded in convincingly putting across their sociological
approach to the use of the film.

An enormous amount has been written about documentary. As
far as this book is concerned I think it best that I should try – as someone
who joined Grierson soon after the première of his film *Drifters* in 1929
and has remained in documentary ever since – to summarize as briefly
as possible what this movement tried to do, and what it has meant to
society.

In October 1969 Peter Hopkinson and I found ourselves in
Poona at a crash course in screenwriting for young Asian film-makers
which was being run jointly by Unesco and the Film Institute of
India. Here we found a considerable confusion about what was or was
not a documentary film. Some seemed to regard it as a rather esoteric,
film-festival, quasi-aesthetic form; others equated it totally with the
classroom film. Feelings among professors and students were running
so high that I attempted to settle things down through an aide-memoire
which I now quote in full:

'1. "Documentary" is only a word, not a magic symbol.
During the Thirties, in fact, the Grierson group felt dissatisfied with
it and tried to change it to "Realist" or "Factual". Unfortunately
we had publicised the word so vigorously that it was already embedded
in people's consciousness, and we had to abandon the attempt.

'2. Documentary is a method. It is a method of approach to
public information. It is concerned with, and is a part of the machinery
of mass communication which, of course, includes all the mass media
without exception. Historically, the film happened to be the medium
most suitable for emphasis in the Thirties and Forties. Were
documentary to begin today, instead of then, the emphasis would
undoubtedly be on television.

'3. The motion picture is a medium of communication similar
to printing. Within the covers of a book you may find philosophy,
poetry, religion, fiction, mathematics, geography, biography, cookery,
and a thousand other things. Within the reels of a motion picture
you may find an equal variety of subjects, no more and no less. In
devising a film or a TV programme the documentarist will no doubt
make a conscious selection from certain areas, such as instruction,
training, classroom-teaching and propaganda (to forestall the usual
criticism of this word, let me recall that it comes originally from the
Jesuits' definition of their method and purpose in religious instruc-

tion). One could perhaps say that the documentarist is selecting from an area covered by the word "Education" used in its broadest sense. That is why documentary can range from *Louisiana Story* at one end of the scale to a Super Eight cassette on, say, astronomy, at the other.

'4. The Fiction or Feature Film is made to entertain with the ultimate purpose of making money. The Documentary film is made to inform, with the ultimate purpose of furthering social progress.

'5. The documentarist will always be something of a revolutionary, because he is using the wonderful medium of the motion picture in an attempt to improve the living conditions, spiritual as well as material, of his fellow men.'

This statement was an attempt to clear my own mind no less than the minds of my students, all of whom were concerned with desperate problems centring on the population explosion, food production, and communication between government and governed. What further needs to be said in this particular book, and at this stage in the book, could be put somewhat as follows.

Firstly, it was the documentary film which gained Britain respect and prestige at a time when the feature film was failing to do so.

Secondly, the great period of the British feature film, which was during and immediately after the Second World War, owed a tremendous amount to the influence and example of the documentary film which was reflected not only in excellent Ealing films such as *San Demetrio – London*, but also in larger scale Rank productions like *The Way Ahead* and *In Which We Serve*. (When he was scripting the last-named, Noël Coward asked me to arrange for him to see some representative programmes of contemporary documentaries, which he studied with close attention.)

Thirdly, the documentarists did not fall into the trap of identifying or being identified with any political party or policy. That their 'moderate' attitude was decried as pusillanimous by some is, to my mind, irrelevant. The success of documentary (nearly all of whose members were, by the way, left wing) was due to the fact that it hit on a source of finance based on the idea of the use of film as a public service – an idea which could appeal to government and industry alike. It is not without significance that we in documentary found that the most difficult people to make films for were the so-called progressives – the trade unions, the co-ops, and socialist administrators. Indeed, the conservatism of socialists when faced with problems of public information has to be experienced to be believed;[1] and this perhaps explains why virtually all the best British documentaries were made under Conservative governments or for large monopoly capital organizations such as Shell or ICI.

Fourthly, documentary built up a true conception of practical internationalism, in which national characteristics and national achievements were seen to form the best basis for the interchange of ideas and the promotion of mutual understanding between peoples. The conception of interchange was first developed by Grierson and myself in a Report which we drew up for the International Labour Office – a specialised agency, by the way, which because of its intrinsic importance survived the demise of the old League of Nations and is still a part of the UN set up. The report was written, after a great deal of research, in 1938, and its implications frequently stressed by Grierson, as for instance in this extract from an article he wrote shortly after:

'Propaganda or education in a democracy must operate on a large number of specialised levels and should be deliberately organized on a large number of levels. There must, of course, be a general spate of information and uplift, affecting the minds of general audiences: and you have the film and radio organized for that purpose. But I like to think that those of us who are interested in special aspects of community life will develop our own systems of communications and that film and radio and other media . . . will do much for us.

'When you see this from the international viewpoint, you will realize how much these specialised services could mean to international understanding and to the expression of the democratic idea . . . We are all divided into groups of specialised interests and we are all, at bottom, interested in the same things. There are the same essential groups everywhere. Here is a group interested in town planning, or in agriculture, or in safety in mines or in stamp collecting. Whatever the different language they speak, they speak the common language of town planning, agriculture, safety in mines and stamp collecting . . . The real internationalism is in the manias we share with each other.[2]

---

[1] A shining exception to this rule was Stafford Cripps, without whom the first and second post-war Labour governments in Britain would probably have had no policy of public information at all.

[2] Some years later I had a vivid illustration of this. I gave a lecture on the educational film in Jerusalem at the time when the imminent British exit from Palestine, and the setting up of Israel, was the occasion for terrorism and bomb-throwing based on bitter racial hatreds. But my audience consisted of 50% Jew and 50% Arab; they were all teachers, and their common interest in education united them.

'How great is the opportunity this provides for the creation of the democratic picture! Several years ago Basil Wright and I suggested a scheme to the International Labour Office. We said, in effect: "Why do you not create a great international interflow of living documents by which specialised groups will speak to their brethren in the fifty countries that operate within your system? You are anxious to raise the common standard of industrial welfare. Why do you not use the film to do it? If France has the best system of safety in mines, let other countries have the benefit of this example. If New Zealand is a great pioneer of ante-natal care, let other countries see the record of its achievement." '

I well remember pursuing this idea further after World War Two when I was working with Julian Huxley and Grierson on the then newly born Unesco. With their encouragement I drew up a world plan under which each nation could, from its own culture and expertise, make a contribution to the pool of common interest, from sewage to *haute cuisine*, from birth control to ceramics, from aeronautics to child-psychology. It was, as I recollect, a fascinating document quite apart from its inner values; given goodwill, it could have formed the basis of the most economical exchange of information between nations and peoples ever devised. It was presented to the Unesco conference at Mexico City in 1948. After that, as far as I know, it was put away in a cupboard, where it still remains.

But the thesis is still valid, and much of documentary was based on it. Nor is there much doubt that it inspired and sustained the immense informational output during World War Two and its aftermath; or that it helped so practically in the setting up of national film units in the newly liberated and newly created countries from 1945 onwards.

Fifthly, it is important to remember that the real secret of documentary's success was that it found and developed a new sort of distribution system. Without Grierson's realization that, if you are thinking in terms of information and education, there are more seats outside the public cinemas than in them, documentary would have got nowhere. With rare exceptions, documentaries are not suited for theatre distribution and are certainly not welcomed by exhibitors; during World War Two the British government used compulsory powers – or the threat of them – to ensure public showing of its informational and hortatory films, many of which, let's face it, were bloody awful.

The conception of documentaries being aimed at and shown to audiences in schools, technical colleges, universities, teaching hospitals, women's institutes, co-operatives and all the diverse professional, trade and craft associations, led, once realized, to the organization of long-term programmes and the possibility of treating important subjects in the form of series instead of cramming everything into one film. Typical of such series were *Your Children and You*, with brilliantly simple coverage of such subjects as *Your Children's Eyes*, *Your Children's Ears*, *Meals*, *Sleep* etc, as well as *Children Learning by Experience* and *Children Growing Up With Other People*; a sports series called *Batting Strokes at Cricket*; and ICI's famous *Technique of Anaesthesia* – no less than fifteen expert and detailed films which, translated into I don't know how many languages, were enthusiastically welcomed and used by teaching hospitals across the world.

The existence of this large non-theatrical audience naturally encouraged government departments and industrial organizations not only to sponsor more and more films but also to set up circulating libraries, many of them gratis (the borrowers only paying return postage on the films). The existence of the system at the outbreak of World War Two was of inestimable value to the Governments of Great Britain and Canada. In the latter country John Grierson ran and developed the National Film Board with spectacular success; the Board is still today one of the most successful organizations of its type in the world, both in continuity and in quality of production.

The scale of non-theatrical distribution may be demonstrated by the fact that during World War Two audience figures for the thousand-odd specially produced informational, hortatory, instructional and educational films *outside the public cinemas* rose to an estimated $18\frac{1}{2}$ million people per year.

Sixthly, and lastly, there is the aesthetic question, round which much misunderstanding and controversy has gathered over the years. There is no doubt in my mind that the pioneer years of documentary in Britain, from Grierson's *Drifters* in 1929 to John Taylor's *The Londoners* in 1939, depended ultimately on the desperate desire of all of us to express our artistic souls through the still comparatively new medium of film. At that time the opportunities for doing this through the British feature film industry were, to put it mildly, limited; so Grierson's ideas, no less than his personality, acted as powerful magnets.

Grierson himself knew as much or more about aesthetics as any-one, and it is sad that so much opprobrium was heaped on him as a result of his determination to keep us youngsters under some sort of control. He knew very well that the secret of ensuring the development of this new sort of film lay in access to non-speculative finance; and this meant, in effect, sponsorship by government, industry, big business. The price to be paid for the privilege of aesthetic experiment was therefore the discipline of public service; and it was Grierson who had to press this point. Hence the apparent violence of some of his attacks on us, such as this:

> 'Of the fifteen hundred tyros who applied for jobs in the EMB Film Unit, fifteen hundred exactly expressed their enthusiasm for cinema, for art, for self-expression, and the other beautiful what-nots of a youthful or simply vague existence. Not one considered this more practical relationship of commissions to be served, nor the fact that Treasury money, and opportunity to make any films at all, were entirely conditioned by these commissions to be served. The point is important. In Britain, as in any other country, there is little or no money for free production. There is money for films which will make box-office profits, and there is money for films which will create propaganda results. These only. They are the strict limits within which cinema has had to develop and will continue to develop.'

Or, on another occasion,

> 'They are too damned arty and post-war to stick their noses into public issues.'[1]

Hence, too, Grierson's sudden switch, around 1936, from the comparative lushness of films like *Song of Ceylon, Night Mail,* or *BBC – The Voice of Britain* to the starkness of the reportage films like *Housing Problems, The Smoke Menace,* and *Enough to Eat?.* These films, which anticipated to a great degree the cinéma-vérité movements of 25 years later, did in my opinion have their own particular aesthetic; certainly Graham Greene, then a film critic, thought so.[2]

On the other hand it was Grierson, often critical of Robert Flaherty's approach, who would invariably spring to his defence, and on aesthetic grounds, if anyone else attacked him. It was Grierson who built a protective wall around me, and stood sentry at the gates, so that

---

[1] Both these statements, written in 1932 and 1933, remain broadly true today, the only difference being that access to the means of production – cameras, sound recorders – has become extremely easy, and much more within reach of the pocket of a lone film-maker. The quality, however, of some of the underground films resulting from these circumstances is not entirely encouraging.

[2] See *The Pleasure-Dome,* Secker and Warburg, 1972.

I could finish *Song of Ceylon* in peace. It was, in fact, Grierson who taught us most of what we knew about the aesthetic of film; and when he called in Flaherty and Cavalcanti, it was because they could bring not only their craftsmanship but also their instinct for the art of the film.

Now that the aesthetic aspect of documentary can be seen in its proper perspective, we can note how important to the movement was its coincidence with the introduction of the synchronous film.

Interestingly enough, the finances available from the Empire Marketing Board for whom, thanks to Stephen Tallents, we worked, did not at first permit of the expense of sound recording, other than on rare occasions and on other people's premises. Our early experiences were therefore mainly at the cutting bench in terms of pre-talkie editing, very often of compilation films constructed from existing film material, for we were also, to begin with, short even of cameras. Grierson was a genius at cutting, as *Drifters* had already demonstrated, and to work with him at the editing bench was a liberal education. He and I used to supplement our meagre EMB wages by working at night on the re-editing of appalling B pictures which a British company, saddled with distribution rights, was trying to market. Slogging away at cutting and re-cutting these 'silents' was an invaluable experience.

The first batch of real and considered documentaries, shot by ourselves, were also edited as silents. Subsequently they were bought by a distribution company who added music and commentary, quite horribly, without our being able to exercise more than token control; and as late as 1933 I was still shooting without access to sound. Not that this meant that we were not interested. Certainly when I went on a film-making tour to the West Indies in 1933 I had in mind various possibilities for soundtracks to be added to what I was shooting, and was of course acutely aware of the Russian Manifesto.

When, early in 1934, we moved into a small sound-studio in suburban Blackheath, Grierson, with a perfect sense of timing, let us all loose in an orgy of experimentation. He allowed us, in fact, to be 'arty and post-war' for about a year and a half; Cavalcanti came in, and Walter Leigh, Benjamin Britten, W. H. Auden, William Coldstream, and Len Lye, and a roaring time was had by all – the results being seen and heard in *Song of Ceylon, Coalface, Night Mail, Rainbow Dance* and the like.

The experiments of yesterday are today's routine; and our documentaries are no exception. Nevertheless that period of creative surge at Blackheath Studios produced several film classics and built really firm foundations for the Documentary Film Movement. Writing in 1935, Grierson summarised the situation:

'The relationship between the artist and the themes of the community, so far from binding the artist, has opened new horizons . . . The documentary of work and workers has found endless possibilities stretching out before it: reaching not perhaps as its forebears did to halcyon horizons but by the nearest hole in the road to engineering masterworks, and by the nearest vegetable store to the epics of scientific agriculture . . . As though to demonstrate how in this seemingly sober world the mainspring of creation lies, it is remarkable how much quicker in the uptake this relatively small group has been in the exploitation of the new sound medium. The G.P.O. Film Unit . . . is the only experimental centre in Europe. Where the artist is not pursuing entertainment but purpose, not art but theme, the technique is energised inevitably by the size and scope of the occasion. How much further it reaches and will reach than the studio leapfrog of impotent and self-conscious art!'

Let me add here a brief note about the non-honouring of prophets. In 1970 a happening called Cinema City was mounted in London by *The Sunday Times* and the National Film Archive in honour of the 75th anniversary of the motion picture. Included in this was a printed programme containing a list of *150 Makers of the Cinema*. This, while including Theda Bara, Clara Bow and Mae West, made no mention whatever of Grierson; it also omitted Delluc, Kuleshov, Vertov and Pommer.

IX

The documentary film was not, of course, entirely a British invention, though the word itself, taken from the French, was in fact coined by Grierson when he reviewed Flaherty's *Moana* for the New York *Sun* in 1926. Films previous to this which now merit the description include Ponting's famous film of Scott's last expedition to Antarctica and Schoedsack and Cooper's *Grass*, a magnificent and often beautiful film about a migrating tribe in Iran. And by the end of the Twenties films answering to the documentary definition were being made in many parts of the world.

There was, however, one thing which distinguished British documentary from the rest of the world – its tight-knit organization. For some twenty years from 1929 on, members of the British documentary group – under whatever auspices they were working – were always in touch with each other, always worked to a common policy (agreed after careful discussions), and therefore were always able to present a united front against all attacks on them or their films. In other countries a more individualistic tradition prevailed – the tradition, if you like, of the great Flaherty himself. In Holland there were Joris Ivens, John Ferno and Helen van Dongen, in Belgium Henri Storck and Charles Dekeukeleire, in Germany Walter Ruttmann, Gerard Rutten and Wilfrid Basse, in France Cavalcanti, Jean Lods, Eli Lotar; nor must one forget George Hoellering who directed *Hortobagy* (1935), a film about the life of the horses on the great Hungarian plains, with its marvellous spatial sense (later recaptured by Jancso), its frank and majestic presentation of a stallion mounting a mare, and its tender analysis of the birth of a foal. Hoellering later became one of Britain's most enlightened exhibitors (the triple Academy Cinema in London is his) and in 1951 he made a respectful but somehow emotionally remote film of T. S. Eliot's *Murder in the Cathedral*.

In general it can be said of these extremely talented film-makers that they belonged to no consistent group, and had no real focal point. They made what films they could as circumstances allowed. If they had allegiances they were political; if political, they were usually attached to international communism, of which one of the finest film-makers of them all, Joris Ivens, was the cinematic high-priest. Ivens' film *New Earth* (1934), about the Dutch reclamation of the Zuider Zee, remains a classic. The tremendous dynamics of that long sequence shot from countless angles, including the air, of the final closing of the gap between the two main polders, with the force and rhythm of Hanns Eisler's score exactly fitting the visual montage, are as thrilling today as they were when the film first appeared. What is too often forgotten is the final sequence – cut from many copies for political reasons – in which Ivens, with an angry sarcasm, shows how the completion of the dykes coincided with the bursting of the world economic depression, so that no market existed for the rich crops springing from the newly reclaimed soil. The bitter truth of this sequence, attached as it was to a film which was a paean to man's foresight, energy and technical bravery, made of *New Earth* an example of the documentary film at its finest.

Between them Ivens, Storck and Ferno were responsible for films as far-ranging as China (*The 400 Million*), the South Seas (*Easter Island*)

and of course Spain, in the Hemingway-narrated film on the Civil War, *Spanish Earth*. The British group and the continental film-makers kept in regular touch with each other throughout the Thirties; I remember, for example, spending an Easter holiday in Brussels helping Storck (under an armed guard) in the making of a film against the Nazi political campaign being run in Belgium by the traitor Léon Degrelle.

As far as the Soviet Union was concerned, the documentary concept was not, in the final event, approved by the authorities. There was one pure documentary, *Turksib* (1929), made by Viktor Turin, which had a profound effect on the British documentarians. The English version of this pre-talkie film was prepared by Grierson who, if anything, increased the effect of the subtitles which Turin had used in differing type sizes and different lengths as part of the essential rhythmic montage of the film. *Turksib* dramatically brought to life an economic, social and geographical problem: two communities – Turkestan and Siberia – each needing the other's products to make life viable, but separated by a howling wilderness. The solution – a railway. Simple; but in Turin's hands an exciting and inspiring film. His images, in terms of communities seen largely through individual and personal needs, were built up through crosscutting, not merely shot by shot but also sequence by sequence, to a point when a sudden shot of a locomotive starting off in a cloud of hissing steam seemed not just a solution but a veritable god from heaven.

Thereafter – except for the 'deviations' of Dziga Vertov which I have already discussed – a true documentary approach (at any rate in the Griersonian sense of the word) hardly existed in the Soviet Union. When so-called documentaries were made they tended to be newsreel in character, and concerned with the reporting of facts rather than their interpretation.

In a certain way the documentary film is something essentially to do with democracy. It implies the right to disagree and the right to criticize. It cannot therefore flourish in a totalitarian atmosphere. Thus Leni Riefenstahl's *Triumph of the Will*, for all its impressive shooting and brilliant editing, remains not much more than a jumbo soap-opera. Moreover, like so many of its kind, it can be blown to pieces by one piece of unnoticed truth. Amidst all the thousands of worshipping spectators greeting Hitler's arrival in the streets of Nuremberg, we see one very small girl, hand to mouth, with a look of doubt, perhaps even the dawning of fear, on her face. Riefenstahl could easily have cut it out; perhaps she didn't notice it. But this one brief shot makes something of a nonsense of the whole two reels, or whatever, of that rapturous welcome; perhaps god might not in fact be god. Again, Riefenstahl's lengthy and supremely well shot film on the Olympic Games must now be critically compared with more recent efforts, not least Kon Ichikawa's from Japan. However striking the photography, including all the slow-motion stuff, of the German film, all one really remembers now is something it didn't show – the point at which Hitler left the stadium in a nasty temper when that great non-aryan athlete Jesse Owens won one race too many.

It may also be here noted that the only Iron Curtain country that ever produced documentaries containing elements of controversy or social criticism was Poland – where the communists can only success-fully exist by coming to terms with the Roman Catholics. Even so, the so-called 'black' films made under Film Polski in the mid-Fifties were temporary phenomena. Although in these films 'the directors established a much closer contact with life and were not afraid to show . . . the many difficult complicated problems, alerting, calling attention to, reminding of the things which were still evil and that called for special care and attention'[1] there was no tendency to continue such a series in later years.

As for the Soviet Union, it is a long, long time since the days of Vertov, Turin, and such films as Ekk's on juvenile delinquents, *The Road to Life*. Today the so-called Documentary Studios under the intelligent, admirable and charming Alexander Zguridi, make nothing more imaginative than straight educational films or factual studies such as *Life in the Soviet Arctic*.

The nearest thing to a creative documentary approach must be seen in the work of Alexander Dovzhenko – probably the greatest poet of cinema the world has ever seen. He revealed where the documentary idea could go – could have gone, rather, had anyone taken the narrow jungle path which led to pure lyricism. I am not claiming him as a documentary director – he was indeed *sui generis* – but his example, with that of Flaherty, was the primordial impulse behind the whole documentary idea. His early experimental film *Zvenigora* (1928) is still as exciting, puzzling and invigorating as when it was first shown.

But it is Dovzhenko's *Earth* (1930) which has many people's vote as (if the idiotic choice must be made) the best film, so far, in cinematic history. This film, thanks to the devoted efforts of people like Henri Langlois, Olwen Vaughan, and presumably, someone in Moscow, is now at last available in the form in which Dovzhenko originally com-pleted it, a form which, as Grierson said at the time, 'is tied to the

---

[1] *Contemporary Polish Cinematography*, Polonia Publishing House, Warsaw, 1962.

Bolshevik idea as usual, but in some strange manner manages to escape from it'.

Of Eisenstein, as of Dovzhenko, I shall be writing later, and at some length.[1] At this stage the only point I want to make is that his theories of montage, as much as the actual examples of his own films, probably had more influence on documentary film-makers than anything else, which is interesting when you consider that his two great and final masterpieces of montage, *Ivan the Terrible, Part I* and *II*, had no more to do with documentary than Sternberg's *The Scarlet Empress*.[2]

The question about Pudovkin is whether he does or does not diminish in hindsight. His two really great films were early works – *Mother* (1926) and *Storm over Asia* (1928); after that, apart from *Deserter* (1933), which for all its merits must be regarded as a masterpiece *manqué*, I see nothing of real greatness in his work. Grierson here shows a curious and unusual ambivalence. At one point he called Pudovkin 'only D. W. Griffith in revolutionary garb', adding that 'the pastures of his art are old pastures, eaten to the roots'. But at another, and writing of Eisenstein, he remarked that 'he is not a poet like Pudovkin, whose conceptions are themselves emotional and uplifting'. The latter statement is the fairer. After all, the old pastures were once new; and when we first saw *Mother* it appeared as much, much more than a follow-on to Griffith.

Pudovkin was in no way a complex man; he was, to use the title of one of his films, 'a simple case'. He once said that 'the cinema, directly derived from dramatic art, in its development departs from the drama and comes closer in essence to the novel.'[3]

When you read the race-course episode in *Anna Karenina*, you do not at the time realize the incredible ingenuity of timing, suspense and construction which Tolstoy expended in leading up to Anna's confession to Karenin. You are simply carried away by the events, the feelings, the relationships between the people concerned. In the work of Pudovkin (who incidentally once told me that *Anna Karenina* was a film he would very much like to make) you may find similar examples. One of the best could be that in *Storm over Asia*[4] involving the bungled execution of Bair by the nervous soldier at the very moment when the general and

[1] See chapter 6.

[2] In 1964 Henri Langlois, after seeing *The Scarlet Empress* belatedly for the first time, cabled Sternberg 'What a grand film. All *Ivan Grozny* comes from your film. All my respect and admiration.' Even allowing for Langlois' delightful tendency to hyperbole, this seems to me to be going a bit too far!

[3] *Anglo-Soviet Journal*, Autumn 1952.

[4] This film is frequently known by the alternative title of *The Heir to Genghis Khan*.

his officers are discovering his potential value as a puppet ruler, with the resultant panic-stricken *bouleversement* into the fantastic operation by which Bair is brought back to life.

But if Pudovkin deeply needed the scope of the novel, he also hung on like grim death to the best the theatre could give him – the power of the actor. Unlike Eisenstein he used actors right from the start. A follower of Stanislavsky, he believed that the ultimate 'realism' he sought must come not only from the immediate use of purely filmic technique, but also from an intensity of expression created by the right actor working with the right director. He said: 'The whole point about the actor is to use the emotional values at the right moment . . . The object, when you actually come to the shot, is to achieve the maximum from your actor, and this is impossible if either the director or the actor are thinking about the machinery. You must block yourself off from the mechanical apparatus around you. That is a great moment – when only the director and the actor exist – the two of them combining to present the maximum of truth, the maximum of drama, the maximum of emotion and reality . . . The rehearsals will be intimate; everything will be calculated, everything foreseen, against the only moment which counts, which is when the camera starts turning . . .'[1]

The other great quality in Pudovkin's work is his sense of space. Few directors have achieved such a sense of distance, of immensity, as he does in *Storm over Asia*. Possibly no director except Flaherty possessed, with this sense, the ability to relate man so intimately to his environment. Nearly all Pudovkin's best sequences depend on spatial contrasts – the alternation of an opening up and a closing down of the images. The hunt for the silver fox with which *Storm over Asia* begins is a fine example of this. Even more so, and in the same film, is the visit of the English interventionist general and his staff to the Grand Lama (who turns out to be a baby). The suffocating atmosphere of the Lamaserai, crowded with priests and images seen through a haze of incense fumes, is broken into by a series of shots in total contrast, as partisans fight with soldiers on a vast prairie pullulating with stampeding cattle. Pudovkin finally links these two elements through a shot of the courtyard of the Lamaserai, which earlier we have seen swirling with ceremonial dances. Now it is empty save for the tiny but significant figure of a soldier running across it. But in the foreground of the shot there is the elaborate ornamentation of the palace roof, and this relates directly to the complex ornamentation of the audience-hall. As the background is completely blank until the ant-like soldier runs in, there

---

[1] Interview with the author, Moscow, 1937.

is a moment when our sense of space is deceived, and we don't know whether we are under the wide sky or among the intricately carved and somewhat claustrophobic decorations of the audience chamber; and this disorientation is further compounded, in an unanalysable way, when, surrounded by all the pomp and vapourings of prelates, politicians and staff officers, the baby Grand Lama decides, after prolonged thought, to laugh . . .

A director with a similar approach to that of Pudovkin, and one who probably owes him a good deal, is Mark Donskoi who, on the strength of the *Gorky Trilogy* alone, must be rated as one of the world's truly great film-makers.[1] The trilogy consists of *The Childhood of Maxim Gorky* (1938), *My Apprenticeship* (1939) – also known as *Out in the World* or *Among People* – and *My Universities* (1940). The first two, which were produced at the Children's Film Studio, are in fact one very big film split into two. The third, dealing as it does with Gorky's early manhood, differs in a number of respects from the other two, although the production team (Pyotr Ermolov, camera – I. Stepanov, art direction – Lev Schwartz, music) remains the same throughout. But the whole trilogy is a remarkable achievement in its solving of the problem of putting an autobiography, and a very famous one at that, onto the screen. The great quality of the Trilogy is that it contains no ideological 'types'. Donskoi, with Gorky, shows that it is not only wicked to be wicked: it is also sad.

The first two parts are in fact dominated by Gorky's grand-parents – the man vain, stupid, brutal and hysterical, the woman an image of eternal simplicity, instinctively understanding what life is, and able to describe it as beautiful even in the moment of her greatest suffering. The playing of these two characters, by Mark Troyanovski and Varvara Massalitinova, is a rare privilege to observe. Thanks to the grandfather's frenzied stupidity the family goes into a steady decline; and against this movement towards poverty and destitution the boy Gorky reacts, constantly seeking escape, seeking above all the rescue which can come from education.

It is this conflict between Maxim's ambition and the fatal course of events in which it is so nearly submerged that dominates Donskoi's construction of the films. He takes a series of episodes and treats them in one of two ways, either elaborating them into long and carefully-

---

[1] Previous to the Trilogy, Donskoi co-directed *Song of Happiness* (1934) with Legoshin (who subsequently made the utterly delightful *Lone White Sail*). Donskoi's later films include *How the Steel was Tempered* (1942), *The Rainbow* (1944), *A Village School-teacher* (1947) and *Mother* (1956).

built sequences (and these form the backbone of the work) or, in contrast, using an extraordinary filmic shorthand which makes a momentary but extremely cogent impact – such as the extreme long shot in which a young apprentice falls and is crushed by the huge Cross he is carrying; in this single shot resides most of the history of Russia. To all this, and especially in the first two parts, he adds the domination of the 'majestic river', the great Volga, with its constant traffic and its din of ships' sirens which, even more than Lev Schwartz's admirable music, becomes the theme-song. Over and over again Donskoi brings his characters to the banks of the Volga for scenes of great import; and there are too the episodes on the river itself. In one, where the boy Maxim is a dishwasher on a Volga steamer, the cook, an immensely fat and sentimental character, sits entranced as the boy reads *Taras Bulba* aloud to him while a sneakthief waiter throws the recently washed glasses back into the swill. In another the desire of man for the simple dignity of a job is superbly shown in a long sequence where the down-and-outs get unexpected employment in unloading sacks of grain from a sinking barge. It is raining in torrents, but as they work on (in a passage remarkable for the rhythm of its cutting) a watery sun breaks through the clouds, and they salute it with the dignity and pride with which mythological heroes of past times might have saluted the Sun God in his chariot.

The immense richness of episode and detail in *The Childhood of Maxim Gorky* and *My Apprenticeship* is saved from chaos by the characters of the grandparents and by the images of the Volga. As *My Apprenticeship* ends, all these elements are brought together. Young Gorky is leaving, and as the huge paddlesteamer pulls away from the jetty the grandfather, senile, childish, petulant, turns away; but grandma, with a smile of infinite sweetness, waves gently to the departing Maxim and says, 'I shall never see you again'. Massalitinova here is sublime.

In the third part of the Trilogy, *My Universities*, there is a considerable change in style, and the film as a whole is less satisfactory. Donskoi no longer tries to control the episodic nature of the story and, indeed, uses a large number of linking subtitles which become irksome. The character of Gorky himself, which until now has been played to perfection by the boy actor Alexei Lyarsky, is taken over by Y. Valberg, a young man who has neither the same acting ability nor the same sympathetic qualities. So, save for a few sequences, Gorky becomes too much of a lay figure. And, apart from the opening and concluding sequences, the film is very claustrophobic. In a sense this may be deliberate, since it is mainly concerned with the famous bakery, and

Donskoi is no doubt right to lock us up with the workers in the stuffiness and the flour-dust. But when we emerge it is only to be locked up again – less justifiably – with the liberal intellectuals, whom Gorky learns to despise, in their equally stuffy parlours.

Yet the bakery scenes give us one of cinema's really great characters – the boss Semyonov (played with the genius of a Raimu by Stepan Kayukov), an upstart with a simple cunning and a cunning simplicity, wandering around in a striped nightgown, fondling his prize pigs in the yard, hurt and upset when his attempts to act the bully end in Maxim twisting his ear; arguing with Gorky at midnight among the sleeping bakers, trying to find out why this youth who is causing so much trouble won't accept the simple 'fact' of exploiter and exploited; matching his own cunning against Gorky's determination and never for a moment thinking of sacking him. All this builds to the magnificent culmination when the men walk out on strike – and are joined by the boss while they are celebrating in the local pub, in a sequence which celebrates that pure joy of humankind which can surge up even in the darkest gloom.

Thereafter the film loses grip. The ideas behind the attempted suicide and the subsequent episodes in hospital are no doubt admirable, but I sense in Donskoi's direction here a certain and perhaps understandable fatigue. And the final sequence, in which Gorky helps to deliver a peasant woman of her baby on the shores of a great lake, only shows what the director was *trying* to do. The immense images of the ocean smashing itself against the rocks, with which Donskoi intercuts the woman's labour, are magnificent to look at but too pompously symbolic. They are no substitute for the vastnesses, for the superabundant permeations of love and life with which the Volga inundated the earlier parts of this magnificent trilogy.

X

Although much of the history of American documentary has been clouded by the inability of the film-makers to organize themselves and to work together to agreed policies and purposes, this does not mean that films of importance and distinction were not made. Moreover, for a comparatively brief period, there did exist a lively centre of documentary film-making under the direct auspices, not unnaturally, of the New Deal. It was a beginning which could perhaps have flowered into a long-term and soundly based organizational system as useful as the E.M.B. and G.P.O. film units in Britain. It was associated with the name of one man, Pare Lorentz.

Lorentz succeeded in adapting to his purposes the existing, small, loose and hesitant film-making system of the Federal Government which had grown up, almost by mistake, through the Department of Agriculture and the Department of the Interior. Under the New Deal the President wanted to 'alert the public to certain frightening conditions in the United States, the land of plenty. Almost without notice, large areas of cities had degenerated into overcrowded, unhealthy, filthy slums; farmers were being driven off their land; drought, winds and floods were ravishing the soil . . . The land and the forests were wasting away through misuse.'[1] Under the Resettlement Administration a number of methods of publicizing this situation and the action needed to put it right were discussed, including the use of films.

Owing to the Federal structure, which involved jealous guardianship of their own rights by the individual States; owing too to the jealousy of Hollywood of any film-making – especially governmental – which might in any way threaten its monopoly, all matters of official film-making had to be approached with kid gloves.

When Pare Lorentz – a talented writer and film critic – was brought in to make a film on the Dust Bowl situation in 1935, he decided against the sort of saturation non-theatrical coverage which the British were just beginning to develop, in favour of a direct attack on distribution through the public cinemas. The products for this purpose were to be, in his own words, 'films of merit'. He felt that 'government films should be good enough technically to bear comparison with commercial films and be entertaining enough to draw an audience'.[2]

In the event Lorentz made three of these 'films of merit' himself – on soil erosion, on the Mississippi Valley, and on maternity in terms of public health. He also started, but was unable to complete, a film on unemployment to be called *Ecce Homo*. During his regime he also brought in Joris Ivens to make a film on rural electrification called *Power and the Land* (which was very well received at the time but today has dated badly), and Robert Flaherty who, in *The Land*, made his most important if not his finest film.

Pare Lorentz was a fine film-maker, and his first film for the Federal Government created a sensation. It was made on a shoestring

---

[1] *Pare Lorentz and the Documentary Film* by Robert L. Snyder, University Press, 1968.
[2] op. cit., p. 25.

and in the teeth of a good deal of opposition and even of attempted sabotage.[1] But it received the unqualified approval of President Roosevelt and, after a great struggle, managed to get theatrical distribution.

The Plow that Broke the Plains was indeed a new sort of American film – the stress being on *American* in the sense that it was not an imitation of the then much admired style of British documentaries. Lorentz approached his subject with a certain violence which suited the rough circumstances with which it dealt. He showed filmically how the appalling effects of soil erosion on human decency and dignity arose from man's greed and stupidity. With brutal frankness he showed the resultant wilderness, a land of natural richness and fertility which was now, as the narration said, 'baked out, blown out, and broke'. As contemporary reviews pointed out, the film 'was permeated with a sense of the richness and vastness of the central great plains and of the tragedy of history's majestic march to the disaster of thousands . . . This film is not self-congratulatory, pleased at ingenious advertisement. It is an appeal to the American nation. "The wind still blows, and the sun still bakes the land".'[2]

Lorentz's second film, *The River*, was more controversial. It was built visually onto a lush verse commentary, frequently incantatory, which impressed some people and infuriated others. It was a similar story in that it was concerned with the failure to conserve natural resources; and it had in it a series of sequences about the great floods which happened to occur while Lorentz's unit was shooting; these certainly give an actuality which the film might otherwise have lacked. Seeing *The River* again today, I find it less cogent, less interesting, even than *The Plow that Broke the Plains*.

Both films, incidentally, had the propaganda message tagged on to the end, like an appendix to a book, instead of it being integral to the film as in most British documentaries; by this I mean that Lorentz dramatized the appalling problems and circumstances; but he did not dramatize the solutions or even the attempts at solutions. Nevertheless, the mere statement of the problems in terms of stark poetic realism was in itself of tremendous value.

The Fight for Life (1940) – a full-scale dramatized documentary using real actors – is by far Lorentz's best film. It is the story of the doctors' struggles with the human problems of pregnancy and child

---

[1] He needed stock shots from Hollywood, but the door of every company was locked against him. It was only through King Vidor's personal help that he got what he wanted.

[2] *World Film News*, January 1937.

birth amid the dirt, disease and despair of the Chicago slums. In it
Lorentz used all his know-how and all his fearlessness of experiment –
bringing in, for instance, a background of jazz music at an apparently
inappropriate point, and triumphantly getting away with it. As he
himself said, 'The picture opens with death. My concern was that the
audience would see and say "that's that" and go home. For that reason
we had the night walk (of the young doctor walking through the slums
in the rain) and jazz music. You have a woman die but a big, vital,
roaring city with two million souls, and that background music would
lift the audience's attention and they wouldn't be so distressed that they
would lose interest.' An interesting point, this, for Lorentz is expressing
a typically commercial point of view – the point of view of pure box-
office; very few British film-makers would have come to a similar
conclusion, and if they had done so they would have rationalized it
into some form of sociological theory.

Later in the film the young doctor walks again through the slums,
this time in daylight. This time the childbirth has been successful – but
as he looks around him he wonders why he should bring life into such
a world. At this point Lorentz used a full orchestra (original score by
Louis Gruenberg) and of this Lorentz said, 'the thing that pleases me
about the soliloquy sequence . . . is that it has, I feel, a three-dimensional
quality. The voice of the young interne expresses his personal feelings,
the shots of those miserable tenements holler at you from the screen,
but the music sings a ballad of people and tells the courageous story of
those who live behind the ugly walls and to whom life is still important.'[1]

Unlike the two previous films, *The Fight for Life* had a good and
comparatively easy theatrical release both in the United States and
overseas. It was, however, banned by the Chicago police, and was not
seen in that city until 21 years later.

But despite the undoubted success of the film – to say nothing of
its social value – Congress almost immediately, and in the teeth of
opposition from the White House, abolished the Federal Government's
film services. In this they had the willing co-operation of the film
industry, whose attitude was succinctly expressed by an eminent
exhibitor: 'Contaminating our business – or any business – with politics
is destructive of the sound and fundamental principles of free
government'.

It was a sad ending to a great experiment from which much good
had come. It was doubly sad in that within a few months the United
States government 'was soon to need films to explain the defence

[1] op. cit., p. 115.

mobilization to the people. The Government ignored the accomplishments of Pare Lorentz, the lessons learned by his crews about producing factual films, and the talents of expert and recognized documentary film-makers'.[1] Throughout the war, the government had to turn to Hollywood, which thus celebrated its triumph over Lorentz by raking in profits from the commercial circulation of Government sponsored films.

XI

The coming of the talkies caused a revolution in the world of comedy films, which, unlike the musicals, had right from the beginning (with the Lumières' squirting hose) been one of the mainstays of cinema. As I have already said, it was the comics who raised the art of cinematic mime, on which the presynchronous film so absolutely depended, to its greatest height. To get an idea of this, take a look at some film clips, not of the obvious greats, but of someone like Larry Semon . . .

Quite a few famous screen names, in all departments, failed to survive the change-over, often because of unsuitability of voice or accent, though as Alexander Walker has pointed out, the case of John Gilbert (the most often quoted example) was due less to the quality of his voice than to petty-minded revenge. But the comedians, depending on mime plus sight-gags, should have had every chance of survival as opposed to the dramatic or melodramatic mimes who must, in these new circumstances, face the problems of dialogue. Yet quite a few of the comics went under, though I doubt very much that their public would have deserted them just because they didn't chatter. After all, Chaplin's first synchronous film *City Lights* (1931) was a tremendous success although it contained not a word of intelligible dialogue; but it did have some brilliant pieces of synchronism such as the idea of indigestion resulting from swallowing a whistle. One can't really see any prima facie reason why Harry Langdon, Buster Keaton or Raymond Griffith couldn't have made the transition quite easily. It may perhaps have been partly psychological – a feeling that this new gimmick *must*

[1] op. cit. It should be added that a number of talented individuals have continued to make important documentaries to this day. Of these Irving Jacoby is notable in that he has acted as producer, and therefore as a focal point, for other directors as well as making his own films (latterly mainly on psychology) such as *Angry Boy* (1951) and *The Lonely Night* (1954).

be used if they were to continue to be successful; at which point one can see, in a sense, why Langdon and Keaton, in particular, quailed at changing a technique which was after all the essence of silence, of communication by *other* means. Sad, though, to see how at the end of his life Keaton, in Samuel Beckett's *Film*, could turn all his old original techniques to splendid, even tragic purpose; what a waste of the years between! Harold Lloyd, on the other hand, found the transition quite simple; his gradual disappearance from the screen was his own choice and for other reasons. It could perhaps be said of his few talking pictures that the dizzy speed of some of his earlier films got slowed down; on the other hand in a film like *The Milky Way* he achieved a new dimension through the rapid wisecracking of his co-players Adolphe Menjou and Verree Teasdale.[1]

As for Laurel and Hardy – already established as a superb comedy team by 1927 – they seized on the new development with the greatest enthusiasm. There was no hesitation here. The voices were of course perfect – Stan with a touch of the Fred Karno, and Hardy with that element of refinement which he built up from the underlying softness of a Southern accent. Aided no doubt by production colleagues such as James Parrott and James Horne, they found in, and released from, the treasure chest of synchronism a veritable cornucopia of comic sound effects. No screen comedians, not even Chaplin, have ever made such subtle and brilliant use of sound and dialogue both; in song and dance too, as witness the famous 'Lonesome Pine' sequence in *Way Out West*, their skill and timing leave one lost in admiration. Stan Laurel, of course, was the genius of the two, always full of ideas. I had the privilege of meeting him towards the end of his life, when Hardy was already gone, and it was amazing to realize that he remembered every detail, but each and every detail, of all the films. More than this, he still found them funny, so we spent an afternoon falling about with laughter as one or the other of us recalled sequences from this or that film. The only thing which saddened him was when the films were shown on TV, and the exquisite timings were broken into, regardless, for the sake of the commercials. 'It makes you weep' he said.

There were other artists whose screen success just could not have been achieved before the coming of the talking picture. Some of these, like theatre stars such as Jolson and Eddie Cantor, found a new life

---

[1] In regard to fast wisecracking, be warned that early talkies such as Milestone's *The Front Page* (also with Menjou), which at the time left one breathless and bewildered, seem today to be fairly leisurely; so much have the passing years attuned our ears both to strange accents and increasing speed of verbosity.

not merely by adapting but by developing their existing tec iniques; nou in fact very difficult, this, since their films were nearly all backstage musicals, and thus involved no more than an enlargement of scale. On the other hand the Marx Brothers, who equally came from the vaudeville world, rapidly became high-priests of the talking picture – Chico's fingers on the piano keys, Harpo's hands on the strings, and the sinister agitation of Groucho's cigar as he rasped his mysterious cracks or hurled honeyed insinuations at the imperishable Margaret Dumont.

Even more dramatic was the transition of W. C. Fields.[1] Here was the greatest comedy-juggler of all time (on this the experts unanimously agree) who became one of the great screen comics of all time without benefit of his juggling talent, other than a few sequences such as his famous exhibition on the pool table in *Six of a Kind* while he was explaining how he came to be known as 'Honest John'. At his best Fields, by some sort of osmosis, characterized what film is all about, including its dream-magic – that element of surrealism which is perhaps found more easily in the comics than anywhere else.

Laurel and Hardy raised the physical situation-comedy beyond slapstick to a pinnacle of near, sometimes complete impossibility; it stemmed originally from Méliès' *Voyage à travers l'Impossible*, and like the spectators of Méliès' days we were ready and anxious to suspend our disbelief, to recognize areas of experience which went just beyond the practicable but in which we could, as though dreaming, participate. W. C. Fields led us into a similar dream-world. Levitation is common in dreams, and it is with little hesitation that we empathize with him as he dives, parachuteless, from an aircraft in pursuit of a dropped bottle of gin.

The same sort of elements are found, too, in the Marx Brothers, being especially associated with Harpo. I remember a single shot, unrelated to what came before or after it, in one of their films; across the moonlit lawn of a stately mansion, in long shot, fled a screaming blonde pursued relentlessly by Harpo on a bicycle festooned with balloons – the wish-fulfilment syndrome neatly encapsulated. In *Monkey Business*, Harpo takes over a children's Punch and Judy show, and suddenly, again as in a dream, something rather sinister begins to creep in, something to do, perhaps, with the real and cruel meaning behind the story of Mr Punch. It is quickly turned aside, but not before we have looked over Harpo's shoulder at something supernatural and

---

[1] Fields made a number of silent films, but his real screen impact wasn't felt until his two-reel shorts like *The Dentist* and *The Pharmacist* in which sound played an important part.

gruesome, as when, in the Brothers Grimm story, we eavesdrop on Rumpelstiltskin's secret as he dances in the forest glade.

So much has been written about Chaplin that it would be impertinent of me unduly to add to it. I would only like to say one thing. It seems to me that the decline in his later films is easily explicable if you reckon that an artist may reach a point when he has nothing more to say – or no more than fresh variations on what he has already said. Some, like E. M. Forster, feel, rightly or wrongly, that they have reached this point, and voluntarily abstain. (Did Garbo, perhaps, do the same?) All Chaplin's major works, at least from *The Kid* onwards, have a developmental progression as well as a progression in *maîtrise*; when, in *Monsieur Verdoux*, he deliberately changes his *persona*, it is because a final statement is to be made. Having done this, he cannot return to the original Charlie; and, if he continues, he cannot achieve anything better than a pallid evocation of the shade of Verdoux. Hence *Limelight*, *A King in New York*, and the final nullity of *A Countess from Hong Kong*, from which the *persona* has totally vanished.

One can now see the inevitability of Verdoux. Chaplin had to arrive at this stage because of *The Great Dictator*, in which he brought the best and the worst together in the same image. Hitler's mistake of wearing Charlie's moustache left Chaplin no choice but to seize on this one gorgeous opportunity and at the same time to realize the logical consequence, which was that, having so gloriously exploited it in the name not only of comedy (in the word's highest sense) but also in the name of suffering humanity, it was necessary for Charlie, the Little Fellow, to be put back, like a ventriloquist's dummy, into his box for the last time.

In *Monsieur Verdoux* Chaplin, exercising his full virtuosity as a serious director for the first time since *A Woman of Paris*, summarized the whole philosophy which underlies his lifework.[1] Banal, if you like, certainly sublimely simple, it celebrates the human as individual in his perpetual conflict against the human as organization, so that the many corporate systems of government – political and religious – which make up history and which are necessary and inevitable, must, like the steamroller, be treated with a giggle and a pinch of salt as well as with respect.

The hatred which *Monsieur Verdoux* aroused, particularly in the

---

[1] It may be noted that *A Woman of Paris* has a foreword in the form of a subtitle which says, 'Humanity is composed not of heroes and villains, but of men and women, and all their passions, good and bad, have been given them by God. They sin only in blindness, and the ignorant condemn their mistakes, but the wise pity them.'

United States, was of course the hatred of Caliban seeing his face in the mirror. The film both symbolizes and criticizes the veneer of civilization which, all through time, has masked – sometimes more, sometimes less – the beast beneath. Verdoux's calm vindication of his behaviour reflects all our suppressed sense of communal guilt. His behaviour itself makes *doppelgängers* of us all. That column of smoke in the garden of Verdoux's villa – what is it but the smoke of Nanking, Coventry, Auschwitz, Lidice, Oradour, Hamburg, Dresden, Hiroshima?

In technique *Monsieur Verdoux* is conventional, but in content it is not; it endangers our peace of mind. And it never lets up. Most people remember as the last line of the film Verdoux's reply to the priest's 'May God have mercy on your soul' – 'Why not? After all, it belongs to Him'. But this is *not* the last line. Just before the guillotine they offer Verdoux the traditional drink of rum. He refuses – but then changes his mind. 'Just a minute,' he says, 'I've never tasted rum.' This ghostly echo from the Little Fellow, the Underdog, fittingly concludes Chaplin's *oeuvre*. The films which came after are but footnotes to a lifework.

XII

Two other genres of film-making which benefited greatly from the coming of synchronism were the horror, and the animated or cartoon film.

Apart from the obvious value of a whole range of neatly placed eerie sounds, from the creaking of a vault door to the cry of a werewolf, the horror film really did need the human voice. It in a curious way is one of the most literary of film-styles. In the Thirties it certainly depended on those archetypal figures cooked up by Mary Shelley, Edgar Allan Poe, Robert Louis Stevenson, and even, on a somewhat lower level, Bram Stoker. It may be noted that these archetypal stories are seldom, if ever, ghost stories in the strict sense. True ghost stories are much more subtle than horror stories. The latter set out openly to horrify; the former creep up behind you, they are more subtle, they frighten you by leaving too much to your own imagination. On the whole ghost stories need to be recited or read; the horror is in the fact that we fill in the pictures ourselves.[1]

[1] There are only a very few exceptions to this, such as the sequence about the ventriloquist directed by Cavalcanti in *Dead of Night*, certain episodes in *The Innocents*, Jack Clayton's film of Henry James' *Turn of the Screw* and most of Nicolas Roe *Don't Look Now*.

The baroque visions available from those screen adaptations of *Frankenstein, Jekyll and Hyde*, or *Dracula* were and are cinematic. From the moment when James Whale launched Frankenstein's monster onto the screen in the person of Boris Karloff, the horror film could be said to have come of age. It has remained consistently popular ever since, with few variations from automata, vampires and zombies. Many, maybe most horror films are too explicit, too obvious, and therefore liable, in the event, to tumble into farce. They cannot, even at their best, give one the fright one gets from reading a story alone, at night, in a dark house. Imagination is tarnished by the explicit vision; far more terrifying, surely, are the situations evoked in *Sorry, Wrong Number* or *Night Must Fall*, when the terror comes from the darkening of the commonplace by something sinister.

The same may apply to recent additions to the repertoire in terms of 'Things From Outer Space', who are only too often the old vampires and zombies re-dressed. The best of this genre are films concerned more or less directly with science fiction – such as the enormously successful *Quatermass* series which did such pioneer work in this field and came, significantly enough, from television. And with Kubrick's *2001, A Space Odyssey*, the imaginative ideas of Arthur Clarke carry us into another dimension of experience, profoundly disturbing not only for its familiar exploration of the unknown but also for its plethora of philosophical and psychological booby-traps.

The animated film (whether cartoon or puppet) had always been waiting for synchronized sound. This fulfilment enabled the pictures to be planned to the split-second accuracy of a prerecorded soundtrack, and the efflorescence of Walt Disney and Max Fleischer was immediate. Both of these artists had been active in pre-talkie days – Fleischer particularly with his repellent vamp Betty Boop. Now came Popeye; and Disney's *Skeleton Dance* (1929) – perhaps the best thing he ever did – was followed by Mickey Mouse, Donald Duck and the rest. Nor was it long before inflation set in, Fleischer and Disney vying with each other with feature cartoons like *Snow White and the Seven Dwarfs, Gulliver's Travels, Pinocchio* and suchlike. Disney, who started off with undoubted genius,[1] gradually turned himself into a corporation, and his fantasy world coarsened into clumsy anthropomorphism; then came mixtures of real-life figures with cartoons, competing with nature films whose brilliant shooting was vitiated by the constant use of the

[1] The last of Disney as a true artist was seen in the Forties, with *Dumbo, Bambi*, and that enchanting rag-bag or sketchbook of ideas, *The Reluctant Dragon* – one of his best and most neglected works.

pathetic fallacy; and finally uneasy adaptations of children's classics. It was a busy factory, with lots of by-products in terms of toys and corn-flake packs well to the fore. Today, *si monumentum requiris*, there is Disneyland, a visit to which not even Comrade Khrushchev could escape.

This is no place for a long disquisition on a specialized subject like animation which has been covered at length in a number of excellent books.[1] But let us note that several highly individual graphic artists found inspiration from the introduction of synchronism. Early on Oscar Fischinger made a series of films in which he used abstract shapes in motion to 'illustrate' well-known pieces of music – an idea taken up later by Disney in parts of his extraordinary *Fantasia* (1941), a mélange of brilliant imagination and plodding vulgarity which still has power to attract, repel, tantalize and irritate.

By the mid-Thirties both Len Lye and Norman McLaren were interesting themselves not only in animation but also in *eliminating the use of the camera* by painting direct onto film. Len Lye's *Colour Box* (1935) was the pioneer of this new type, and for a while – typically enough under the aegis of John Grierson and therefore of Britain's General Post Office – he pursued a number of experiments along these lines until his restless genius led him off into a series of other explorations, none of them less valuable and rewarding; at this writing he is noted for kinetic sculpture wired for sound.

Norman McLaren, of course, passed from drawing images direct onto celluloid to drawing *sounds* by a similar method. Installed since 1940 at the National Film Board of Canada, he has not only trained and inspired many individual cartoon film-makers, but has himself built up a corpus of work in which virtually no possibilities of the motion picture medium have remained unexplored. To my mind he is one of cinema's purest geniuses, and in much of his work the relationship between film-magic and dream-magic comes so close that they virtually combine. I am thinking particularly of his comparatively early *L'Aviron* (1945), in which the prow of a little boat takes us forward and forward forever towards a receding horizon until our perception of reality is blurred into a waking dream from which, as after seeing *Orphée*, we find it difficult to emerge.

The extraordinary versatility of this man's genius is also well illustrated by the results of his visit to China with a Fundamental

---

[1] Among others, I note *Animation in the Cinema* by Ralph Stephenson; *The Art of Walt Disney* by Robert D. Field; *Design in Motion* by John Halas and Roger Manvell; *Shadow Theatres and Shadow Films* by Lotte Reiniger; and *Le Dessin Animé* by Lo Duca.

Education team sent there by Unesco in 1949. Faced with a situation in which materials and commodities of all kinds were either in short supply or non-existent, McLaren nevertheless managed to set up a complete visual aids department and to lay down methods, and a training scheme, which could be quickly learnt by the least educated people. He left behind him a little pamphlet on 'How to make Filmstrips without a Camera' which, as I remember, began with the necessary and beautiful simplicity of, 'First is needed a chair (for the artist to sit on). Second, a table (for the artist to sit at)', and gradually going on, step by step, each one visually illustrated, until the whole home-made apparatus was revealed, ready to be operated.[1]

Also in the Thirties came the fabulous screen made of a million separate pins by Alexandre Alexeieff and Claire Parker. Each pin being separately movable in or out of the screen, it was possible, by the use of side lighting, to 'draw' images of considerable complexity; and by this method they made, to Mussorgsky's music, their classic *Night on the Bare Mountain* (1933), one of the greatest imaginative achievements of the animated film. The pin-screen can achieve a visual quality equivalent to etchings or lithographs in motion, the effect of which is often disturbing and hypnotic. Working the pin-screen is a desperately slow job, and the number of films[2] made by Alexeieff and Parker is small. But *Le Nez* (1963), after the Gogol story and with an improvised percussion score by a Vietnamese musician, is an unquestioned masterpiece – frightening, macabrely comic, dreamlike, exquisite; though it must be added that these attributes seem to have caused even the most progressive of specialized distributors (who should know better) to fight shy of showing it.

Nearly ten years later Alexeieff and Parker completed their third major pin-screen film, based, like their first, on the music of Mussorgsky. *Pictures at an Exhibition* (1972) is certainly the climax of their work in this slow and difficult medium. As in their other films, they do not aim at illustration of the original theme but rather at evocation. In *Pictures at an Exhibition* they use two pin-screens (the smaller of them revolving so as, *inter alia*, to produce a negative as well as a positive image without visual interruption) to evoke from three episodes, finely played on the piano by Alfred Brendel, adumbrations of the composer's younger

[1] A complete report on this is to be found in Unesco's *The Healthy Village: An Experiment in Visual Education in West China*, a document of the greatest interest and value to anyone concerned with the possibilities of the visual media.

[2] The screen can of course also be used for 'still' work for book illustrations etc; the titles at the beginning and end of Orson Welles' *The Trial* were made by Alexeieff on the pin-screen.

days, such as his relations with his mother, with a domestic who was a combination of mother-figure and witch, with household pets who are also links with an outside world of the wild beasts of Russian fact and legend, with his first experience of epilepsy, and of the links between his traumatic experiences at military college and his first sweet but vain tastings of love. In this, as in all their films, the makers not only divulge much of the mysteries of the Russian soul, they also partake of and celebrate the mysteries of the passing of time. Over and over again in their films the sun may rise and fall twice or thrice during what should be a simple temporal episode. For them time either stands still or is out of control. Their work is often mesmeric, always lyric, poetic.[1]

Parallel, and often similar in mood and approach to the work of Alexeieff and Parker was Berthold Bartosch, whose feature length animated film *L'Idée* (1934), based on woodcuts by Masereel, symbolized mystical aspirations concerned with freedom and justice, with a sound-track by Honegger who, among other things, achieved some stunning sound effects by the use of the electronic Ondes Martenot. I have always felt privileged that my own film, *Song of Ceylon*, was premiered by the Film Society in London in the same programme as *L'Idée*.

Lotte Reiniger rejoiced equally in the soundtracks she was now able to create for her delicate silhouette-films. Her feature-length *The Adventures of Prince Achmed*, made in pre-talkie days, had in fact a specially composed orchestral score by Wolfgang Zeller; but of course it was the wide range of the synchronized soundtrack which enabled her to take her fairy-story technique into the world of opera, of folk-song, and of children's tales.

To sum up, the fascination of the animated film lies mainly in the fact that all is possible. In some of the earliest cartoons a sort of surrealism certainly prevailed, there being no distinction between night and day; and a question-mark above a character's head turned conveniently into an umbrella or parachute. In *Night on the Bare Mountain*, Alexeieff makes his Baron Samedi doff not only his high hat but his head as well. And latterly, in the mad worlds of Hubley and Bosustow, Yoji Kuri,[2] Jan Lenica, Bob Godfrey and many others (to say nothing of the persistent *Tom and Jerry*) we observe the most extraordinary distortions, perversions, diversions and contradictions. Animation

---

[1] For reference to the work of Alexeieff and Parker in fields of animation other than the pin-screen, see *Animation in the Cinema* by Ralph Stephenson, Zwemmer, 1967.

[2] Kuri is probably the most successful shocker in the animation world, as anyone who has seen no more than his *Tongue Inside a Matchbox* will confirm. And his films about the battle between men and women begin where James Thurber left off.

may be a small area in relation to the whole world of motion picture, but if the present trend against realism and towards multi-media technique continues, it may well turn out to be an expanding one, as witness Halas & Batchelor's full-length film from George Orwell's *Animal Farm* (1954) and the Beatles' *Yellow Submarine* (1968)

XIII

To nearly all national cinema industries, the basic and most far-reaching effect of the coming of the talking picture was that it opened up a whole field of shared social experience, from the domestic human comedy of everyday life to the exaggerations and wish-fulfilment fantasies of high society. For it was the expressive quality of dialogue which made it easy to bring to life the 'sophisticated' or 'middle class' comedy which now began to flood the screens. Hitherto the sophisticated style had been the province of a very few directors with an acute sense of visual construction and visual relations such as Lubitsch, D'Abbadie D'Arrast, and Mal St Clair. Now anyone with a good dialogue-writing script-man could get away with it.

In part the style of these films, especially those from Hollywood, stemmed from the social melodramatics of the theatre of Belasco, Sardou and Pinero. But because of the enormous polyglot audience which was the American people, something else, a common factor, had to be added. This was that quiddity known as 'The American Dream, or How to Stand on the Other Feller's Face and Get at the Ice Cream First'.[1] This conception of a universal goal produced both the sophistication of the Thin Man and the instant identification of Judge Hardy's family.

At this time few directors could afford, or were allowed, to specialize. As John Ford remarked,

> 'It's a constant battle to do something fresh. First they want you to repeat your last picture. . . . Then they want you to continue whatever vein you succeeded in with the last picture. You're a comedy director, or a spectacle director, or a melodrama director.

---

[1] At that time Britain was still enjoying the Imperial Dream, which included violence against colonial inhabitants, a means test for undernourished unemployed at home, and the conception of Europeans as 'far away people of whom we know so little'.

You show 'em you've been each of these in turn, and effectively too. So they grant you range. Another time they want you to knock out something *another* studio's gone and cleaned up with. . . . There's a new kind of public that wants more honest pictures.'[1]

There was, however, one director at this time who could identify with the American dream – true or false – and who had the wit and know-how to bring it off so successfully that no one, not even Harry Cohn, dare say him nay.

To older folk like myself the titles of the films of Frank Capra are like candles lit to represent one's visits to the movies in the 1930s. Many of them are still legendary. There was *It Happened One Night* (1934), which nearly ruined a section of the clothing industry when Clark Gable removed his shirt and revealed he was wearing nothing underneath. There was *Mr Deeds Goes to Town* (1936), in which Gary Cooper showed how honest simplicity could defeat the city slickers and their lawyers, and also perpetuated the words 'doodling' and 'pixillation'. There was *Mr Smith Goes to Washington* (1939), in which James Stewart showed how honest simplicity could defeat the wicked congressmen and their lawyers. There was *Lost Horizon* (1937), in which Ronald Colman showed symbolically on the Roof of the World how honest etc etc could defeat wicked etc etc. There was *You Can't Take It With You* (1938), in which Lionel Barrymore revealed that the reason for the title was the iniquitous working of the US Federal Income Tax system. After which, apart from an adaptation of the stage success *Arsenic and Old Lace* (1944), Capra more or less faded out as a topline director – though not before he had, as we shall see, made a most valuable and distinguished contribution to the US War Effort by producing the *Why We Fight* series.

Capra is perhaps the prime exemplar of the Hollywood director reflecting the basic attitudes of the American people – or at least the Americans of the cities and small towns. He was of course a professional to his fingertips. Before the talkies came he had been responsible for the direction of Harry Langdon's best films – *The Strong Man* and *Long Pants*. He was a master of mood as well as of timing. Even in a film which today dates as badly as *It Happened One Night*, we can still appreciate how the exchanges between Gable and Claudette Colbert in the crowded and cluttered sets of Greyhound buses and tourist cabins were shot (in almost continuous close-up) and timed for editing with an absolute precision of touch. Indeed Capra's craftsmanship is

[1] Quoted in *The Rise of the American Film* by Lewis Jacobs.

what so cleverly conceals the sticky sentimentality in which all but his very best work is ultimately embedded.

Other directors who, like Ford, made all sorts of films and did not keep to any set pattern were the imperishable William Wyler, with films like *Dodsworth* and *These Three*; and William Wellman who, in 1937, turned his hand to mild forms of satire in two films, *A Star is Born* and *Nothing Sacred*. Satire is box-office poison, but in *A Star is Born* it was masked by some glamorous sentimentality, and in *Nothing Sacred* by some wonderful comedy acting by Carole Lombard and Charles Winninger. However slow and old-fashioned this film may seem today, the latter's description of journalists (script by Ben Hecht) surely deserves preservation.

'You know what I think, young feller? I think yer a newspaper man. I can smell 'em. Excuse me while I open the windows. I'll tell you briefly what I think of newspaper men. The hand of God reaching down into the mire couldn't elevate one of them to the depths of degradation. Not by a million miles.'

There were also Gregory La Cava with *My Man Godfrey* (1936), George Cukor with *Dinner at Eight* (1933), Wesley Ruggles with *True Confession* (1937), and so on. They and their peers represent the tip of the iceberg. Underneath that tip lay the great mass of mediocre, bad, or even squalid pictures, mostly made to fill the screen in the name of the double-feature programme which was for so many years the bane of picture-going. On their own, most of these B and C pictures (however low their budgets) would not have made money had they not been forced on the exhibitors by systems of blind- or block-booking; in order to be sure of getting one top level picture they had to agree to take six others. This was an almost universal system, and was just as prevalent in Britain, France and Germany as in the United States. But it was basically imposed by Hollywood, which must take the blame for a great dreary mass of tasteless, ill-made films which debased the spectators if they didn't send them to sleep.

Yet, to be fair, there used to emerge from time to time out of the morass a few promising low-budget films, often by young directors getting their first chance, which were modest in intent but succeeded either through an unwonted freshness and sincerity or by a new approach to a conventional subject. Such films, in my recollection, were Stuart Heisler's *The Biscuit Eater* (1940)[1] – a film about a small boy (Bobby Lee) and his dog which avoided all mawkishness and was

---

[1] Also known as *God Gave Him a Dog*.

shot with skill, perception, and economy; *Sing and Like It* (1934), by William Seiter, a marvellous parody of the gangster film with a cast like a box of diamonds – Zasu Pitts, Edward Everett Horton, Ned Sparks, Nat Pendleton; *Rynox* (1933), a British quota quickie which revealed a new directorial talent in the shape of Michael Powell; an off-beat British comedy directed by Randall Faye, somewhat un-disciplined, about a spy scare, entitled *Mr Stringfellow Says No* (1937), with that sadly forgotten comedian Claude Dampier; and a beautifully modulated story, directed by Elliott Nugent, about a bourgeois family during the US Depression called *Three Cornered Moon* (1933) which included an exceptionally sensitive performance by Richard Arlen.

XIV

In whatever country with a developed film industry, it was the tip of the iceberg which counted for quality. Only the best French films were exported to England, and vice versa. It used to be a traumatic experience for the young English cinéaste, his mind full of Clair and Renoir and Duvivier, to visit Paris and see a series of films whose vile inefficiency reminded him strongly of home.

But as I have said the Europeans also had the common experience of being exposed to the block-booking system imposed by the Holly-wood tycoons, who nearly always had the whip hand, if only because the local producers could not deliver enough films per year to fill their own cinemas – a situation perpetuated by the Americans dumping their own cheap pictures on them to fill the gap.

In France the coming of the talking picture intensified the financial and economic crisis which the industry had been trying to cope with ever since the end of the First World War. Although, as in America, the first talking films were a big box-office success, the industry was still suffering from franc-starvation owing to the failure of the French financiers adequately to support it during the Twenties. By now Charles Pathé had left the firm he had originally founded and had continued so long to nurture. It was taken over by a certain Monsieur Bernard Nathan, who had begun his career by making pornographic films and was to end it, a few years later, in prison for embezzlement whence, during the Occupation, he was removed to the gas chamber by the Nazis; a sad story and, as Sadoul pointed out, one which ended in a less optimistic dénouement than René Clair had postulated in *A Nous la Liberté*.

The real problem for France in those first days of the talkies was that there was no indigenous sound system. The Americans and the Germans, both with systems of their own (Western Electric and R.C.A. in the one case, and Tobis Klangfilm in the other), were able to move in and make their killings. In the event it was the Germans who proved more prescient than the Americans who, as I described earlier in this chapter, foolishly tried to build up a huge multilingual Hollywood at Joinville.

Tobis went in for a quieter and more restrained programme; and it was from their new studios at Epinay that there emerged Clair's *Sous les Toits de Paris*, after which Clair went from strength to strength with *Le Million, A Nous la Liberté* and *Le Quatorze Juillet*. The success of his films did in fact mask to a degree the continued financial instability of the French industry; and when Tobis, by now in the clutches of Dr Goebbels, got cold feet over *Le Dernier Milliardaire* (this was also the France of Stavisky and the Cagoulards), Clair, discouraged, joined Korda in England where he made *The Ghost Goes West*.

Yet despite this economic crisis, which soon affected most aspects of French life, and not only the film world, there now began a creative period in French film-making which was to be of tremendous importance in the whole history of cinema.

This period is linked indissolubly with the names of Renoir, Feyder, Duvivier and Carné (Gance, alone of the great ones, spent this period in eclipse; and Vigo was already dead), to say nothing of Grémillon, Benoit-Lévy, Pagnol. And, just as in Germany of the 1920s, this renaissance was linked with the names of writers. The roll-call of the scripts of Charles Spaak is very nearly the roll-call of French cinema of the mid-Thirties – Feyder's *Pension Mimosas* and *La Kermesse Héroique*; Duvivier's *La Bandéra, La Belle Equipe, La Fin du Jour*; Renoir's *Les Bas Fonds* and *La Grande Illusion*; Grémillon's *La Petite Lise* and *L'Etrange M. Victor*; he is only rivalled by Jacques Prévert.

What in general were the characteristics of this renaissance?

For France as a whole this was a time which could only be described as politically and economically disastrous. Here, as in England, defeatists were trying to undermine the moral structure of the country, and in the event were going to enjoy a success which would be denied their British counterparts. France would fall; Britain not. On the other hand, it may be said that the prevailing sense of anarchy, the sniff of treachery in the air, brought the artistic mentality to a high degree of sensitivity – this being redoubled by what was happening in Germany, from which France, unlike Britain, was not separated by the sea, to say nothing of events in Abyssinia and Spain, where most of the hopes and fears of mankind were then so sharply focused.

But if these were the immediate impulses in French cinema in the Thirties, there was also another factor, more prolonged and permanent. The Frenchman has a very precise, very passionate, very formal sense of the history of his country. For the French artist 'La Gloire' includes not only military, religious and philosophical traditions, but also culture, *les beaux arts*. Despite the romantic influence of Hugo, the formality with which the Frenchman regards his heritage – the passionate formality (to use a contradiction in terms) of a Racine, an Ingres, of the Comédie-Française – gives him a certain balance, a certain poise, even a certain coolness with which to temper the heat of his inspiration. Even in Hugo the romantic untidiness of a Dickens is lacking.

The United States lacks, or has not had time to crystallize, a heritage from which this sort of supreme cool confidence can derive. The only basic tradition in its short history is British; one has only to look at the myths and legends of the War of Independence to see that. It was only later that the United States became the melting pot of many nationalities; and in the Twenties and Thirties it was certainly too early for this great mixture of Slavs, Latins, Teutons, Scandinavians and Orientals to produce a really rooted common tradition; while behind everything lay the haunting guilt and the traumatic memories of slavery and the Civil War. Those who blame the Americans for brashness, for lack of subtlety, for forgetting, even, that the West is opened up and there are no further horizons into which to escape, might well reflect on the difficulties faced by a still young nation which has had perforce to cram into less than two centuries what other countries have evolved at leisure over twenty. With only a few exceptions, American films are not concerned with subtleties or formalities; and this may very well be the reason why so many of the best French film directors have not been wholly at ease when working in the United States.

In a sense the great French film renaissance of the 1930s may have been signalled by the return of Jacques Feyder from America. Finally disillusioned by his Hollywood experience, he set to work with Spaak and with his wife, the great actress Françoise Rosay, and directed in quick succession *Le Grand Jeu* (1934), *Pension Mimosas* (1935) and *La Kermesse Héroique* (1936).

Le Grand Jeu was about the Foreign Legion, but not from the

Beau Geste point of view; it was nostalgic, heavy with atmosphere, claustrophobic. The theme, as Sadoul rightly pointed out, was Pirandellian: 'Can one ever be certain of the person with whom one is in love?'. Here Feyder had Marie Bell play both of the two women involved in love affairs with the same man; only for the second woman, a prostitute, he had a different voice dubbed on; and, interestingly enough, this ambivalence in picture and sound, used to express doubts about reality or the blurring of psychological attitudes, arose from Feyder's final experiences in Hollywood.

He had directed Garbo in her last pre-talkie film, *The Kiss* (1929). Now he wanted very much to direct her in Pirandello's *As You Desire Me*, which the studio had recently purchased. This story of a perplexing and enigmatic personality was worrying the Front-Office a great deal. 'They felt it impossible,' said Feyder, 'to send the audience away from a film without precise knowledge of the *exact identity* of the heroine, so that they still didn't know whether she was herself or someone else . . . I had had the idea of giving Garbo a different voice from her own, for part of her performance. This would have been done by dubbing, thus taking advantage of a generally odious technical method to achieve a special effect in dramatic expression. But I had to give up the project owing to Hollywood's obstinacy.' However, the final result of the episode was seen in *Le Grand Jeu* 'in which the same person, who is perhaps two different persons, keeps the same physical appearance but has two different sorts of voice'.[1]

Feyder continued his career, notably with *La Kermesse Héroique*, a legend of the days of the occupation of the Low Countries by the Spanish. This, his most famous film and visually the most splendid, provoked violent riots in Belgium and Holland. His last film in France was *Les Gens du Voyage* (1938), notable for a splendid performance by Rosay as a tamer of tigers; previous to that, as we know, he had made one film for Korda in England, *Knight Without Armour*.[2] He retired to Switzerland during the War and died in 1948.

Julien Duvivier had made a number of films, none of them of any note, during the Twenties. The coming of the talking picture seems to have inspired him, and in 1932 he leapt to fame with *Poil de Carotte*, based on a Jules Renard story and starring the child actor Robert Lynen (killed, alas, during World War Two while fighting for the

---

[1] *Le Cinéma, Notre Métier* by Jacques Feyder and Françoise Rosay, Cailler, Geneva, 1946.

[2] Of this film I wrote at the time that 'Neither the irresponsibility of the scenario nor a richly comic performance by Marlene Dietrich can disguise the fact that *Knight Without Armour* was made by a great director'.

Resistance against the Nazis). Like so many films dealing with cruelty and indifference to children, this film, a tear-jerker if ever there was one, had a great international success; I shall discuss it in more detail when we come to *Germany Year Zero* later in the book.

From now until 1939 Duvivier made a number of very distinguished films of which the best known, though perhaps not the best, was *Un Carnet de Bal* (1937), the darling of the film societies and the art houses. This episodic film showed how a woman visited all the men whose names she found on her dance card from her 'coming out' ball; it had a faultless all-star cast and, on the soundtrack, the exquisite *Valse Grise* by Maurice Jaubert,[1] one of the best composers of film music who ever lived. Previous to this film Duvivier had, in 1936, made *La Belle Equipe*, a subject which Renoir had wanted to make and which reflected something of the successes and failures of the Front Populaire. There was also the super gangster film *Pépé le Moko* (1937), which finally established Jean Gabin as a great star; and the very much underrated *La Fin du Jour* (1939), a sad and touching film, directed with extreme skill and delicacy, about a home for retired actors and actresses. After this Duvivier, a rather chameleon-like director perhaps, made a number of films in America, England and France which in general lacked distinction and made little impact. He died in 1967.

Out of the world of Feyder and Duvivier emerged the figure of a younger director, Marcel Carné. With the frequent collaboration of Jacques Prévert, another scenarist to whom French film-makers (including Renoir and Grémillon) owe a great debt, Carné made such classics as *Quai des Brumes* (1938), *Hotel du Nord* (1938), and *Le Jour se Lève* (1939), in which Gabin, as the man trapped in a small bedroom by the police, gave perhaps his finest performance. Carné remained in France during the Occupation, during which he made *Les Visiteurs du Soir* (1942) and his acknowledged masterpiece *Les Enfants du Paradis* (1945). The former film suffered perhaps from the circumstances of its making. It began as a dreamlike evocation of a medieval fairyland, with Arletty and Alain Cuny appearing as damned souls of fatal beauty sent to earth in order to destroy a high betrothal. Nothing could be finer than the sequence in which they come to the castle as minstrels; with a remote but frightening seriousness they sing – and then, with a rustle of guitar strings, bring to immobility all the dancing lords and ladies

---

[1] His other scores included Vigo's *Zéro de Conduite* and *L'Atalante*, Clair's *Quatorze Juillet* and *Le Dernier Milliardaire*, Carné's *Quai des Brumes* and *Le Jour Se Lève*. In the mid-Thirties he came to London and scored documentaries for Grierson and Cavalcanti. He was killed in action against the Germans in June 1940.

and lead their chosen victims apart. This, and the grave romance of
the settings seen against the nightmare grotesquerie of the little dwarfs
whose faces are so hideous we may not behold them, makes for a magic
which we fear to break even by moving in our seats. But then, alas, the
spell is broken by the director himself. Up pops Mephistopheles in the
shape of Jules Berry – a magnificent performance but in a totally
different key. The solemnity and the magic are destroyed by a febrile
if brilliant wit. The clue to this change in the atmosphere in the film is,
no doubt, to do with Carné's attitude to the Germans; and his French
audiences may well have appreciated this delineation of a suave but
frustrated Satan. But it destroyed the shape of what could have been a
film of genius and exceptional enchantment.

As for *Les Enfants du Paradis*, I think that despite its self-
indulgent length it stands the test of time. It is a film of ideas as well as
of grown-up people acting (in every sense of the word) in a grown-up
way. Its types are archetypes – the clown, hovering as ever between the
Commedia dell'Arte and madness; the courtesan, trapped by her own
easiness; the aristocrat, destroyed by a new outlook on life which he
despises[1] because, rightly, he cannot accept its first appearance in the
form of a perversion; and the genuine original nihilist – Stavrogin
perhaps – brought for the first time to the screen. All that Carné says
in this film is presented, as in Gance's *Napoléon*, on a vast canvas
quivering with ideas; and the last sequence is unforgettable, as the
clown (Jean-Louis Barrault) vainly pursues his lost love through an
immense crowd of white-clothed carnival-makers. In this whole snowy
scene of pierrots, masks, confetti, one black object – her coach –
relentlessly gains ground as the crowd gradually overwhelms him until,
with a last despairing cry, he sinks into the sea of human foam.

In the post-war years Carné, despite a number of quite high-
powered efforts, including *Les Portes de la Nuit* (1946) and *Les
Tricheurs* (1958), became something of an extinct volcano; in some
curious way, and despite obviously brave attempts, he did not seem to
be able to keep up with the times.

It is about time that someone wrote a really comprehensive study
of Jean Renoir and his work.[2] He is undoubtedly one of the most
important directors in the history of cinema. The range of his work
spans some fifty years, and its variety, both in subject and treatment, is

---

[1] This character, played beautifully by Louis Salou, recalls in some respects
Stroheim's von Rauffenstein in *La Grande Illusion*.

[2] A good start has recently been made by Leo Braudy with *Jean Renoir: The World
of his Films*, Doubleday, 1972.

fantastic; his influence on younger film-makers has always been profound, and continues so to be. His late brother Pierre was a very distinguished actor; and his nephew Claude is a top cameraman (*Une Partie de Campagne, The River, Le Mystère Picasso*).

For my present purpose I must confine myself as far as possible to Renoir's contribution to the political and social situation in the France of the Thirties. By that time he already had behind him such silent films as *Nana, Tire au Flanc* and *La Petite Marchande d'Allumettes*, and had thus also presented to the world the elusive, disturbing and fascinating character of his first wife Catherine Hessling (famed also for her fantastic performance for Cavalcanti in *En Rade*).

Renoir did not react particularly for or against the arrival of the talking film. He seems just to have taken it in his stride and got on with his work.

One of his early successes in the synchronous medium was *Boudu Sauvé des Eaux* (1932), with Michel Simon, as an incorrigible anti-social layabout, anticipating in a certain sense his superb characterization of the bargehand in Vigo's *L'Atalante*. But Renoir's first overt intervention in contemporary problems was *Le Crime de Monsieur Lange* (1936). This film was a sort of parable about the dishonesties and dissimulations of public and private life in France at the time[1] – the time of the fascist Croix de Feu, of the Stavisky scandals and of the foundation of the Front Populaire. Its simple story concerns the situation which arises when workers take over a printing works whose proprietor has decamped with what was left of the assets. By publishing the books of their neighbour, a M. Lange, they make a big success; but when the original owner turns up again and tries to take over, there is a tragic dénouement. Like several of Renoir's films of this period – and this was something he shared with Vigo – *Le Crime de Monsieur Lange* shows signs of lack of adequate finance; the dialogue in particular, recorded on a cut-price 'pirate' sound system, is frequently distorted into unintelligibility.[2] Indeed Renoir did not have an easy time in his film-making of that period. His Simenon film *Nuit du Carrefour* (1932) was issued incomplete, and his screen version of *Madame Bovary* (1934) was minced up in the true *Greed* tradition. Nor did Renoir make his own life any easier by following up *Le Crime de*

[1] In perspective today it could also be regarded as a sort of trial run for *La Règle du Jeu*.

[2] Soon after the coming of the talkies the three major sound systems set up a world-wide monopoly; it was difficult to avoid using RCA, Western Electric or Tobis, and it was equally difficult for low budget films to afford their royalties (the GPO Film Unit in Britain suffered from this situation also).

M. Lange with a film directly financed by the French Communist Party called *La Vie est à Nous*, made in documentary style.

Renoir's involvement in politics was a natural, even logical process which probably went back to his father's reminiscences of the Commune when his friend Courbet was a firebrand of the Left. *La Vie est à Nous* was a bit rough at the edges, but it had a freshness and boldness which subsequent documentary developments have tended to obscure. It also led to a further political experiment some two years later, when Renoir was invited by the Central Trades Union council to direct a film, to be made on a co-operative basis, about the French Revolution and entitled *La Marseillaise*. In this the people of Paris were invited not only to subscribe their cash but also to appear in person, and on the exact historical locations, in a reconstruction of the main events of the Revolution. On top of this Renoir enlisted a distinguished cast to play the principal historical rôles, including Pierre Renoir who, as Louis XVI, gave one of his greatest performances. There are marvellous things in *La Marseillaise* – not merely crowd movements and an interesting feeling for the interlocking of past and present which Renoir built up from his use of actual locations. Beyond this he took the opportunity to present the Revolution with the advantage of having a second and later Revolution, that of Russia, with which to compare it. Owing to the current political situation, including the collapse of the Front Populaire, the film was never properly completed, and must be regarded as a *chef d'oeuvre manqué*, but through no fault of its director. It still has great qualities, and for me the big crowd scenes in Paris and Marseilles, excellent though they are, must cede to the very human portrayals of the individual revolutionaries, simple men learning their principles during the bitter actions of each succeeding day, and of the Royal family, learning gradually their fate by the same process.

In the meantime Renoir also made a film of Gorky's *The Lower Depths* (1936) which one would like to view today in conjunction with Kurosawa's magnificent 1957 version; and *Une Partie de Campagne*, another unfinished film which did not see the light of day until after World War Two when, tidied up by Marguerite Renoir, it was released with enormous success – so much so that it must, surely, have encouraged Renoir to pursue something along the same lines, though in deeper and earthier terms, when he made *Le Déjeuner sur l'Herbe* some twenty-three years later. Renoir's really extraordinary output during the Thirties makes it difficult to follow him strictly chronologically, and it is now necessary to remember that *La Grande Illusion* (which will be dealt with in the next chapter) was made before *La Marseillaise*, and that after *La Marseillaise* he made *La Bête Humaine*, a brutal and melodramatic piece, with Gabin, which seems somewhat of an interruption when you realize that his next film was *La Règle du Jeu*. This film is very much a companion piece to *La Grande Illusion*, and will also be considered in the next chapter.

So, with French cinema at the height of its influence, with British cinema in the doldrums, German films in the grip of Nazism, Russian directors ideologically bewildered by the German-Soviet Pact, Japanese film-makers like Mizoguchi seeking escape from militarism in the historical past, and the United States about to launch what was to be the greatest box-office success of all time, *Gone With the Wind* – the world was ready to plunge into the most disastrous of wars. In this the film was to play a not insignificant part.

SIGNPOST - 1939

THE YEAR OF 'GONE WITH THE WIND'

IN THE UNITED STATES

Ernst Lubitsch directs Greta Garbo in *Ninotchka*. Frank Capra stars James Stewart in *Mr Smith Goes to Washington*, and Paul Muni plays the name part in *Juarez*. A girl called Judy Garland makes her name in Victor Fleming's Technicolor *The Wizard of Oz*. Cecil B. De Mille directs *Union Pacific*, William Wyler *Wuthering Heights*, and John Ford produces some of his best work in *Young Mr Lincoln* and *Stagecoach*. Charles Chaplin is working on *The Great Dictator*, with its parodies of two of the men who are about to plunge the world into war; meantime the Marx Brothers are seen *At the Circus*, and Laurel and Hardy appear in *Flying Deuces*. Walt Disney completes his second feature animation film, *Pinocchio*. A consortium of documentarists, Joris Ivens, John Ferno and Robert Capa, return from China with the material for their impressive feature *The 400 Million*, while Herbert Kline, shooting dangerously, covers the Czech and Polish crises with his reportages *Crisis* and *Lights Out in Europe*. A young man named Joseph Losey is making commercial shorts. Scott Fitzgerald and Budd Schulberg visit Dartmouth College to obtain script material; this episode will become the centrepiece of Fitzgerald's unfinished novel *The Last Tycoon*. Nathanael West publishes his satire on Hollywood *The Day of the Locust*, to which Schulberg's *What Makes Sammy Run?* will be a parallel nearly twenty years later.

President Roosevelt seeks specific assurances of non-aggression from the dictators in relation to thirty-one named countries. He also signs the 'Cash and Carry' bill to facilitate the supply of arms to Britain and France.

King George VI and Queen Elizabeth visit the President and Mrs Roosevelt at the White House.

Pan American Airways inaugurate regular trans-atlantic flights by flying boat.

Igor Sikorsky constructs the first really successful helicopter.

John Steinbeck's *The Grapes of Wrath*, soon to be filmed by John Ford, is published, as are Thomas Burke's *The Web and the Rock*, Robert Frost's *Collected Poems*, Raymond Chandler's *The Big Sleep*, and William Saroyan's *The Time of your Life*.

W. H. Auden and Christopher Isherwood arrive in the United States, where they will remain.

Virgil Thomson composes his ballet music for *Billy the Kid*.

The Man Who Came to Dinner, by George S. Kaufman and Moss Hart, is successfully staged.

Grandma Moses, primitive painter, is 'discovered'.

Ethel M. Dell and Zane Grey die.

IN FRANCE

Marcel Carné directs *Le Jour se Lève*, in which Jean Gabin gives his finest performance to date. Pierre Chenal makes *Le Dernier Tournant*, a film based, as will be Visconti's *Ossessione* a few years later, on the James Cain novel *The Postman Always Rings Twice*. Julien Duvivier directs his touching film on old age – *La Fin du Jour*. G. W. Pabst is in Paris making potboilers. Jean Renoir completes his masterpiece *La Règle du Jeu*, which is howled down at its première.

Albert Lebrun becomes President, and Prime Minister Edouard Daladier visits Algeria, Tunisia and Corsica in an attempt to counter Mussolini's colonial ambitions.

The Communist Party is proscribed for supporting the Nazi-Soviet Pact.

After the invasion of Poland, France, with Britain, declares war on Germany, and the 'Drôle de Guerre' begins.

Frédéric Joliot indicates the possibility of splitting the atom of U235.

After much controversy Cocteau's *Les Parents Terribles*, featuring his young friend Jean Marais, is having a successful run. Fokine creates *Paganini* for the De Basil Ballet.

Picasso is painting at Antibes.

Arthur Honegger composes his *La Danse des Morts*.

André Gide publishes what will be the penultimate volume of his *Journals*, and Jean-Paul Sartre completes *Le Mur*.

IN BRITAIN

Hitchcock completes *Jamaica Inn*, and the American Sam Wood directs (for MGM's British subsidiary) *Goodbye Mr Chips*, starring Robert Donat. Carol Reed consolidates his reputation with *The Stars Look Down*, a film about the coal-mining industry, starring Michael Redgrave and Emlyn Williams. Paul Robeson appears in another mining film, *The Proud Valley*, directed by Pen Tennyson, soon to meet an untimely death on Active Service. Geoffrey Bell and Arthur Elton make (for the Shell Film Unit) their classic and still influential expositional film, *Transfer of Power*.

A military mission is sent to Moscow too late to prevent the Nazi-Soviet Pact.

Parliament approves independence for Palestine by 1949.

Radar is developed.

The Government brings in conscription and an excess profits tax.

With France, Britain recognizes the Franco regime in Spain and, after the invasion of Poland, declares war on Germany.

The Royal Air Force drops propaganda leaflets on Germany, and HMS *Royal Oak* is sunk by a U Boat in Scapa Flow.

The Battle of the River Plate takes place off Montevideo.

T. S. Eliot's play *The Family Reunion* is staged, as also is George Bernard Shaw's *In Good King Charles's Golden Days*; and Ivor Novello stars in his own musical *The Dancing Years*.

Jacob Epstein completes his large statue *Adam* which causes a scandal.

Other artists who have come to the fore are Henry Moore, Graham Sutherland and John Piper.

Arthur Bliss composes his Piano Concerto, William Walton his Violin Concerto, and Michael Tippett his Concerto for Double String Orchestra.

W. H. Auden and Christopher Isherwood collaborate on a record of their visit to China, *Journey to a War*; and Isherwood publishes his own *Goodbye to Berlin* which will be translated to stage and screen, first as *I Am a Camera* and then as *Cabaret*. Aldous Huxley writes *After Many a Summer*, and Graham Greene *The Confidential Agent*.

Stephen Spender publishes *The Still Centre*, and Dylan Thomas *The Map of Love*; and Cyril Connolly founds the magazine *Horizon*.

The great Sutton Hoo Burial Ship is discovered and excavated.

W. B. Yeats and Ford Madox Ford are dead.

IN RUSSIA

Alexander Dovzhenko completes his epic *Shchors*, Mark Donskoi finishes the second part of his Gorky Trilogy, *Out in the World*, Kozintsev and Trauberg direct

The Vyborg Side with a score by Shostakovitch, and Pudovkin completes his *Minin and Pojarsky*. Other films of the year include Romm's *Lenin in 1918*, Ermler's *A Great Citizen*, Sergei Gerasimov's *Teacher*, and Vasili Petrov's *Peter the First, Part II*, with Nikolai Cherkasov. Ivan Pyriev follows his successful musical *The Rich Bride* with another, *Tractor Drivers*; both films have the same singing star, Marena Ladynina.

Molotov succeeds Litvinov as Commissar of Foreign Affairs, and in due course he and Von Ribbentrop sign, on behalf of Stalin and Hitler, the Nazi-Soviet non-aggression pact.

Russia and Germany invade and partition Poland.

Russia is expelled from the United Nations.

Dmitri Shostakovitch composes his Sixth Symphony.

Isaac Babel is arrested and taken to the Lubyanka Prison where, it is revealed later (1954), he is executed in 1941.

IN GERMANY

With the entire industry under the control of Goebbels, Veit Harlan makes a romantic period-biography about the inventor of the pocket watch, *The Immortal Heart*, and then embarks on his infamous version of *Jud Süss*, to be released the following year together with the most odious film of all time, Hippler's *The Eternal Jew*. Heinz Hilpert makes *Unholy Wishes* (based on Balzac's *Peau de Chagrin*), starring Olga Tschehova and with music by Wolfgang Zeller. Combat cameramen on land and in the air shoot the material for *Feldzug in Polen*, later released as *Baptism of Fire* and used widely by Goebbels to soften up neutrals through its terrifying pictures of the Nazi *blitzkrieg* techniques.

Hitler annexes Czechoslovakia, denounces the 1935 Anglo-German Naval Agreement, signs the 'Pact of Steel' with Mussolini, does his deal with Stalin, and invades Poland.

The deportation of Polish Jews to Lublin begins.

Heinkel flies the first jet plane.

After Britain's declaration of war, a Nazi U Boat sinks the liner *Athenia*, which is evacuating children to Canada, with heavy loss of life.

Amongst many exiled Germans, Thomas Mann writes *Lotte in Weimar*; Ernst Toller and Sigmund Freud are dead.

IN ITALY

Under Fascism Mario Camerini makes *Heartbeat*, Alessandro Blasetti *The Black Mask* (a film about Salvator Rosa) and Mario Soldati *Two Million for a Smile*. Augusto Genina makes a not unsympathetic story film about the Spanish Civil War – *The Siege of the Alcazar*.

Mussolini invades Albania and is visited to no avail by Neville Chamberlain and Lord Halifax.

Cesare Pavese is engaged on translating Gertrude Stein's *Three Lives* and Herman Melville's *Benito Cereno*.

Benedetto Croce, strongly opposed to the Fascist regime, continues to live in strict retirement.

IN JAPAN

Tomu Uchida directs his classic *Earth*, and Kenji Mizoguchi completes *The Story of the Late Chrysanthemums* (about a *kabuki* actor). Tomotaka Tasaka makes two war films, humanistic in intent, *Five Scouts* and *Mud and Soldiers*, both with Isamu Kosugi. Yasujiro Shimazu directs *Older Brother, Younger Sister*, and Hiroshi Shimizu makes *Four Seasons of Children*.

Troops occupy Hainan and blockade the British concession at Tientsin.

The Japanese militarists install Wang Ching-wei as their puppet ruler in Nanking.

CHAPTER 4

1939 - 1945

WAR

I

To the artist war brings – at least to begin with – instant simplification. Issues are no longer in doubt, or at any rate are not seen to be so. One knows what to do.[1] Wartime films are therefore ideologically and emotionally very simple. Their value in later times tends to be historical rather than aesthetic. There are of course some exceptions – mainly from World War II rather than World War I; but on the whole the great war films are made when the wars are over.

On the other hand war films do very strikingly reflect the changing nature of war and attitudes to war. The films made during the first World War are almost without exception valueless. Films made after it, however, present a wide variety of serious thinking and aesthetic merit, contrasting sharply in mood and attitude to many of those made after World War II. The films about World War I, made during the twenty-two years after its ending, are represented by titles such as *The Four Horsemen of the Apocalypse*, *The Man I Killed*, *J'Accuse*, *All Quiet on the Western Front*, and *La Grande Illusion*. World War II, in a period so far of twenty-five years, has produced a much larger and more varied crop (complicated also by such compilation series for TV as *Victory at Sea*) in which, with the passage of time, changes of mood are prominent. But although Korea, Vietnam, etc may seem to cloud the straight war issues, there still continue to be made films on an historical level about World War II exclusively; *Patton – Lust for Glory*, *Is Paris Burning?*, and *Tora, Tora, Tora* are obvious examples. But in the years immediately following one can see in the films a marked difference of

---

[1] The dangers are obvious; and the existence of conscientious objectors is as essential to a war as is the existence of at least one neutral country. I am also aware that World War II may have been the last time when general agreement on aims existed. The new perspectives arising from Korea, the Congo, and Vietnam belong to a later chapter.

153

approach from that of World War I. The emotional and ideological
attitude to mutual guilt in terms of crimes against humanity is more
sharply focused; and quite apart from the shadow of the Bomb being
something with which the earlier film-makers did not have to cope,
this can be seen from such works as *Paisa, Germany Year Zero, Orders
to Kill, Les Jeux Interdits, Eroica, Memorandum*, and *The Burmese Harp*
– to name a few almost at random.

As for the films made *during* the Second World War, we have to
remember that the cinema had by now grown up very considerably,
that the illusions with which nearly everyone started in 1914 were
completely absent in 1939, and that both the nature of the combat and
the issues involved were, if I may so put it, ultimately more *acceptable*
than in the previous holocaust. Therefore the films made during the
hostilities by the Americans and the British deserve a measure of
respect when we study them; this is the case too in at least some of the
Soviet wartime films. As for Germany and Japan there are, as we shall
see, special and differing significances to be taken into account.

There is one thing that both World Wars have in common. They
were comprehensively recorded *on a factual level* by the movie camera.

It is perhaps not realized what a tremendous amount of the
1914–1918 War reposes in the archives of Britain and the United
States. Material from Britain's Imperial War Museum was being used
as early as 1922 to make feature length compilation films such as *The
Somme*. There is not so much variety of material as in the later war, if
only because the Western Front was strategically static, with gigantic
artillery barrages converting the battlefields into seas of viscous mud in
which whole armies bogged down and drowned. But the coverage was
there; and in the 1939–1945 war, Governments needed no convincing
of the importance of the film-camera as a recorder – strategic as well as
historical – of combat on land, sea and in the air; though the day had
not yet come when a war like that in Vietnam could be fought, atrocities
and all, publicly, daily and in colour in everyone's parlour.

This combat use of movie was, for security reasons, often kept
somewhat apart from other film-uses – hortatory, training, informational
– and tended only to be released by the authorities when the subject
matter was a *fait accompli*, as in Allied films like *Desert Victory* or
Memphis Belle. Goebbels used newsreel-type material to make those
terror films with which, early in the war, he tried, not without success,
to soften up morale in countries which were next on Hitler's list.

The use of the newly developed techniques of documentary has already been touched on, at least as far as Britain is concerned, and I shall

go into a little more detail later in this chapter. In general terms here let me remark that John Grierson built up in Canada a wartime information service, using film as a major spearhead, which was a model of its kind. The acute political and strategic thinking behind film series like *Canada Carries On* and *The World in Action* was extremely important. These films helped some of us in Britain to point out to the Ministry of Information the laxity and parochialism of so much official thinking on the level of global strategy. Indeed Grierson twice hauled me over to Canada for indoctrination. In 1943 I travelled through most of the country studying opinions and attitudes; as a result, on my return to England, I found myself writing articles for *The Spectator* not on cinema but on such things as Canada's relation to the grand strategy of the war in terms of Polar air routes and suchlike.

The Frank Capra films for the US War Information Service were similar in style though not in content, being concerned mainly with the indoctrination of enlisted men, many of whom, unlike their European counterparts, had very little idea as to what the war was all about.

Capra's name in this connotation emphasizes the general absence of an organized documentary system in the United States thanks, as we have already seen, to Congress strangling it more or less at birth. So, while no one could find anything useful for the great Robert Flaherty to do, the experience and talents of Hollywood directors such as Wyler, Ford, Huston and Capra could be and were deployed as necessary. The jealousy with which the tycoons prevented anyone else muscling into their Hollywood preserve thus led to a curious situation in which these eminent directors were switched from fiction to reality and back again. William Wyler's *Memphis Belle* and *The Fighting Lady* contrast strangely with his mawkish and unreal study of wartime Britain, *Mrs Miniver*, with Greer Garson, as the Establishment, keeping a stiff upper lip during the Blitz.[1] Meantime John Huston turned from *The Maltese Falcon* to combat-documentaries like *The Battle of San Pietro* – a film of a comparatively small episode of the Italian campaign which was so true and vivid that the Top Brass tried to have it suppressed. Among other things they were upset by some of the narration as when, just after we have seen some troops killed (and for real), the commentator remarks that 'the lives of these men were valuable – valuable to their country, to their loved ones, *and to the men themselves*'. This suggestion, as Richard Griffith mordantly pointed out, was 'almost unprecedented in a culture which habitually viewed war casualties in terms of their

[1] It is only fair to say that this film is supposed to have had a great influence on viewers in the US, many of whom it converted from an anti- to pro-British attitude.

damage to the feelings of female relatives'.[1] *The Battle of San Pietro* still remains a classic. Its moment by moment depiction of a real battle from inside and from the point of view of civilians as well as combatants has a truth to it which is searing and inescapable.

This is a good moment to pay tribute to the bravery and devotion of combat cameramen on all fronts during the war. It requires a special bravery to go through a battle shooting with a totally non-lethal weapon. Without them, and their rather high casualty rate, a whole aspect of great importance to wartime information and propaganda would have gone by the board. Right at the end of the war two films appeared which exemplified what they could achieve. *The True Glory* – a feature-length compilation film – was the fruit of US–UK collaboration under the joint direction of Garson Kanin and Carol Reed; it celebrated with humour, as well as drama and dignity, the Liberation of Europe. *Le Retour*, shot by cameramen of the US Signal Corps, was a most moving account of the freeing of prisoners from the French POW and concentration camps. One of those freed was the great still photographer Henri Cartier-Bresson, who joined with Richard Banks of the Signal Corps in the direction of the film. The scenes of reunion at a Paris railway station, which were shot on a hand-camera by Cartier-Bresson himself, never fail to move me to tears; as in the Huston film, the human documentation of reality – *cinéma-vérité* in fact – proves how the movie can strike home to the heart.

So much for the raw material of actuality. The next thing to consider is the relation of the creative film artist to the idea of War – its splendours and miseries, its fearful arbitraments.

To do this we must go much further back. The first twenty years of cinema coincided with the twenty years during which the Powers moved steadily nearer and nearer to collision course, and finally crashed into a struggle whose disastrous outcome was totally unanticipated.

II

On the outbreak of war in 1914, film had not yet fully found its feet as an art form. The full impact of *The Birth of a Nation* was not really felt until 1915; that of *Intolerance* not until 1918. *The Cabinet of*

[1] *Documentary Film* by Paul Rotha, Sinclair Road and Richard Griffith, Faber and Faber, 1953.

Dr Caligari appeared in 1919 – the same year as Abel Gance's *J'Accuse*, perhaps the only film of distinction to arise directly *and immediately* from the conflict (unless we include Chaplin's *Shoulder Arms*, made in 1918, in which he reduced the whole thing to its proper idiocy by capturing the German Crown Prince single-handed).

It has to be remembered, too, that civilized Europe emerged from the First World War stunned and in a state of shock. This condition was exacerbated by events in the aftermath such as the successful defence of the Russian Revolution against the White interventionists, the starvation of thousands of women and children in Austria and Germany (due not just to inflation but to the intransigence and bloody-mindedness of the victorious Allies), and the devastating pandemic of pneumonic influenza which killed more people than had perished in the war itself (it is estimated that by the end of 1918 no less than 20 million had died from influenza alone).

Out of despair, anger and cynicism arose movements which marched under the banners of Expressionism, dada, Surrealism and the like. The German cinema turned in on itself (if it had not already started to do so) and began to search deeply into the dark places of the Teutonic soul. The French cinema experimented with attitudes of anarchy. The British cinema, in the grip of its American landlords, struggled to keep itself alive by making mediocre films reflecting an age which had already vanished and ignoring the realities of the General Strike and mass unemployment. The Soviet cinema alone, in a fantastic surge of experimentation, celebrated the success, the history and the immediate problems of its Revolution.

Only America remained relatively unscathed. She had entered the conflict late, and at its close she was at a peak of prosperity, with virtually all European countries her debtors. Her intellectuals – partly at least owing to the War – had discovered the joys and attractions of European, especially French and Italian, culture. For the Americans indeed it was a world of optimism and excitement; and this was clearly reflected in the vast majority of the films which now poured from the studios of Hollywood.

In this climate could blossom the genius of a von Stroheim, a Lubitsch, a Chaplin. In this climate it was possible, in the name not of genius but of supershowmanship, to promote a steady raising of standards of technical production (in which Cecil B. De Mille was a pioneer) and, even more important, standards of ideas, values and screenwriting. Hollywood could afford to buy the best; and in June 1921 Paramount was advertising that:

'The greatest living authors are now working with Paramount. Sir James Barrie you know; and Joseph Conrad, Arnold Bennett, Robert Hitchens, E. Phillips Oppenheim, Sir Gilbert Parker, Elinor Glyn, Edward Knoblock, W. Somerset Maugham, Avery Hopwood, Henry Arthur Jones, Cosmo Hamilton, Edward Sheldon, Samuel Merwin, Harry J. O'Higgins – all these famous authors are actually in the studios writing new plays for Paramount Pictures, advising with directors, using the motion picture camera as they formerly (*sic*) used a pen'.

The scene in the studio canteen at lunchtime must have been extremely impressive; I would especially like to have seen how Barrie fitted in. No doubt he sat next to the seventy-year-old Henry Arthur Jones and asked him who Harry O'Higgins was.

Thus the basis of an indigenous American industry was established, and by the mid-Twenties it was beginning to be able to digest as well as absorb new influences and new directors from the Old World.

It is against these circumstances that we must evaluate the War films – European and American – which now began gradually to emerge from the ideological chaos of the immediate post-war period. And it becomes clear that, apart from the debatable *J'Accuse*, the first serious films of comment on the war came from the United States, beginning in 1921 with Rex Ingram's *The Four Horsemen of the Apocalypse*, the film which finally established Rudolph Valentino as a great star. I daresay this film might look overly melodramatic today, but at the time it had a very powerful effect. I remember much of it vividly; I was only 14 at the time, and it was the first experience which brought home to me, for true, that war was wicked as well as wasteful. I was taken to see it by my grandfather – who up to that time had been no fervent filmgoer but found in this film something which powerfully reflected his own anti-war sentiments. A self-made man and an ardent Gladstonian Liberal, he never forgot this example of the film's powers of persuasion. In later years he used to command a cousin of mine who ran a large girls' school in North London to bring her Sixth Form to various private film shows, ranging from documentaries made by my colleagues and myself to one of his favourite films, Laurel and Hardy's *Big Business* in which, arising from their attempt to sell an emblem of goodwill, namely a Christmas tree, to James Finlayson, there is an orgy of mutual destruction including a house and an automobile. This film my grandfather not unjustifiably regarded as a parable about escalating warfare; I am only sorry he didn't live long enough to see

Norman McLaren's *Neighbours*, in which the same theme is developed to its ultimate horror. (It is interesting, by the way, that McLaren himself censored this film after it had been in circulation for quite a long time; the scene where the two neighbours kill each other's wives and babies has now been cut.)

Then in 1926 came two films which, each in its own way, crystallized the purely American as opposed to the European attitude towards the recent World War. It is worth remembering at this stage that this had been widely publicized as the war to end wars; and at this particular time our mental balances had not yet swung towards the idea that there might well be another and worse global conflict in the not too distant future. Thus the two films in question – *The Big Parade* and *What Price Glory?* – could be seen as attacks on the evil of war designed to strengthen support for the peace-keeping programme of the newly formed League of Nations, and for the resultant pacts aimed at outlawing war as an instrument of policy. (The Locarno Pact was signed in 1926 and Germany was admitted to the League in the following year.)

In the case of *What Price Glory?* I have always found myself somewhat of an odd man out in that I liked and was impressed by it when others, while admitting its eloquent gutsiness, rejected it as an anti-war film. True, it was a translation to the screen of a successful stage-play; true, as Paul Rotha remarked, it was 'notorious for its military discrepancies'; yet at that time, and now in memory, it seemed to me to be a splendid send-up of war. It deglamorized the recently completed conflict with an honest coarseness and vulgarity; it was I suppose the equivalent of today's *Catch 22* or *M*A*S*H*, though in those old-fashioned days sick humour and violence-for-a-giggle hadn't been invented. *What Price Glory?*, apart from making a star of the beautiful and talented Dolores del Rio, was written by Maxwell Anderson and Lawrence Stallings[1] – neither of them amateur dramaturges. As for its director, Raoul Walsh, he may not have been the most polished of his clan but he could go ten rounds, and his other great film of the period – *Sadie Thompson* (based on Somerset Maugham's *Rain*), with Gloria Swanson and Lionel Barrymore – is equally memorable. In the case of both these films by the way, the absence of synchronism was used as a splendid method of avoiding the censor. The things said on the set and before the camera by Victor McLaglen, Edmund Lowe and Gloria Swanson belonged very much to the four-letter word fashions of our present permissive society, and 'lip-reading became obligatory for full enjoyment . . . The language of the players . . . was too hot for any

---

[1] Stallings also wrote the book on which *The Big Parade* was based.

titles. Gloria Swanson was able to ride all her censorship problems . . .
by sandwiching discreet titles between honest-to-goodness Anglo-Saxon
delivered silently – but scorchingly for lipreaders. The new sport became
known as the "cussword puzzle".[1]

Very different from and, I admit, much superior to *What Price
Glory?* was King Vidor's *The Big Parade*. This was a full-scale picture
about the American army in France. It was a big film, and the scenes
of troops on the move or in combat were not to be surpassed until the
coming of *All Quiet on the Western Front*. It was also a film which was
all-out against war; and this attack, as Vidor himself admitted, was
carried out by the use of deliberate tear-jerking sentimentality. It
worked. Few could resist at least a snuffle when Renée Adorée ran
vainly after the truck which was taking her doughboy out of her life
forever. *The Big Parade* not only put King Vidor on the map and paved
the way for his great film *The Crowd*; it also put war films into the high
box-office bracket. During its pre-release run at a New York theatre
(the Astor) it grossed at least twice its production cost, thus making
the world safe for *What Price Glory?* which cost four times as much.
It also made the world comparatively safe for a number of other films
whose budgets began to soar into the empyrean.

So war-spectaculars became the order of the day, entering at the
same time a new and romantic element, the sky. Stunts involving
jumping from planes to trains or vice versa had of course long been
popular, but now that a war had been fought at least partly in the air
the stunts could become an integral and legitimate part of the films.
Hence William Wellman's *Wings* (1927), Howard Hawks's *The Dawn
Patrol* (1930) in which a wide-screen system called Magnascope was
used to great effect, and, of course, *Hell's Angels* (1930), on which
Howard Hughes spent some four million dollars by the time he had
converted it from a silent to a talking film and boosted it by the introduction of Jean Harlow in her first starring rôle. (It was indeed in this
film that, clad in an exiguous and filmy nothing, she excused herself
from the boy-friend's presence in order to put on 'something more
comfortable.')

These spectaculars, which more or less coincided with the changeover to the talking film, are interesting today largely for their employment of large-scale aerial manoeuvres rather than for their emotional
or aesthetic content, though, however frightening, some of the dogfights
against orthochromatic cloud-scapes did have a beauty of their own.
In this respect *Wings* was probably the best of them, while *The Dawn*

[1] *The Parade's Gone By* by Kevin Brownlow, Secker and Warburg, 1968.

Patrol, with the added element of a psychological situation involving Richard Barthelmess and Douglas Fairbanks Junior, was a good second. In the violence of *Hell's Angels* real lives were lost; and beyond its spectacle it was an epic of vulgarity.

During all this period, as we have already seen, the European cinema produced little that was directly connected with the war. In Britain, apart from sentimental melodramas of little importance, the only war films of note were the historical reconstructions made under Bruce Woolfe at British Instructional Films, the best of these being *Zeebrugge* (1924) and the *Battles of the Coronel and Falkland Islands* (1927). These had in their day a definite honesty and distinction; seen now, they still justify their position in the archives. In France there was Gance's *J'Accuse*, and very little else, unless we include Léon Poirier's so-called documentary reconstruction of the battle of Verdun made in 1928. Entitled *Verdun, Visions d'Histoire*, and inspired by the noblest of pacifist intentions, this film always seemed to me to have an intolerable mawkishness and sugary sentimentality. The use of symbolic images (which even the great Gance cannot always get away with) was particularly irritating.[1]

During the Thirties, however, the European situation began to change. The impact of the American war films – and not least of *All Quiet on the Western Front* – encouraged European producers to enter the field, a further impulse being given by the increasing realization that there was the gravest danger of another war. From the era of the synchronous film, therefore, we can point to *All Quiet* and *La Grande Illusion* as the two Greats; but before coming to these let us look at a number of admirable if more limited efforts.

In *Westfront 1918*, made in 1930, G. W. Pabst sought, in a sense, to provide a German counterpart to *All Quiet*. It was, to my mind at least, a curiously pedestrian job. Pabst seemed to be trying to present the miseries of war through details of its drabness. He showed the boredom of war, but somehow missed both heart and horror. Far better was his subsequent *Kameradschaft* (1931), a story about a mine disaster on the frontier between France and Germany. Here, with great humanity, and with superbly convincing studio reconstructions of the mine, Pabst created a parable of war and peace in which, under the imperative needs of human disaster, all barriers fall. Particularly striking was the ironic sequence at the end when, crisis over, the frontier

---

[1] Some of Poirier's straight documentary work was admirable, especially *La Croisière Noire* (1926), the record of an African journey undertaken for the Citroën automobile company. A sound version of *Verdun* was issued in 1931.

guards busy themselves re-erecting the barriers and re-opening the customs.

At the same time as *Kameradschaft* there appeared another anti-war film called *War Is Hell* (also known as *Niemandsland* and *Hell on Earth*). This strange allegorical film, directed by Viktor Trivas, was very much the reverse of *Westfront 1918*. Its object was to batter at our emotions. Trivas put a German, a Frenchman, a Briton, a Jew and a Negro into an abandoned ruin in No Man's Land. Under the pressure of this proximity, their artificially stimulated prejudices break down and common humanity re-asserts itself; the barriers of nationality, class and race all collapse. Here Trivas, at least in intention, initiates the same discussion, if not the same conclusion, as Renoir in *La Grande Illusion*, in which film we see that in the event certain barriers or prejudices will in fact re-emerge. Trivas, however, in *War Is Hell*, having satisfactorily established the brotherhood of man in a well-directed film, made obviously on a shoestring, now found himself in the situation of not being able to find a logical ending. He had landed us in a nobly emotional situation which we accepted because of the engagement of our feelings in a thesis whose good intentions could not be denied. But the actual situation on the screen was in fact virtually impossible. Despairingly, Trivas has his characters set out together, marching shoulder to shoulder across the shell-torn hell of No Man's Land towards . . . what? Kracauer rather cruelly suggests Shangri-La.

Somehow, though, this remains a memorable film, largely because the passionate intensity of the direction cannot fail to heighten one's normal antagonism towards war. But by oversimplifying his theme, by rendering it down, as it were, into a concentration of emotional relationships, he defeats his own ends. As long as you are watching, the magic persists; once out of the cinema and into the street, the falsity of the premise cancels all the passion and sincerity. The film remains a noble failure, but by no means deserves oblivion. It obviously cannot have had much appeal for Dr Goebbels, and Trivas prudently withdrew to the United States where he worked on such scripts as *The Song of Russia* and *The Stranger*. He died in America in 1970 – one of a number of somewhat mysterious characters who have flickered across the screen of cinematic history.

In Britain, meantime, a large-scale war film was embarked on by Anthony Asquith in collaboration with Geoffrey Barkas.[1] This was

---

[1] Barkas had worked with Bruce Woolfe on the filmed war-reconstructions already referred to.

Tell England (1931), a film adapted from Ernest Raymond's novel about the ill-fated Gallipoli campaign. No film of Asquith's could be without distinction, but *Tell England* suffered badly owing to its need to depict the late Edwardian glow and the naïve Rupert Brookian patriotism of the early days of the war. By the Thirties this was not merely out of fashion, it was actively unpopular. The brilliance and sweep of the reconstruction of the Gallipoli landings – better of their kind than anything achieved by any British director up to that time – could not efface the essential falsity of the story. Like Trivas, Asquith finally ended up with something in which people would not believe.[1]

A film with certain affinities with *Tell England* was *Journey's End* (1930), adapted from the enormously successful stage play by R. C. Sherriff. This quintessentially English piece was made in Hollywood with an English producer, George Pearson, and an English director, James Whale (who remained in America and started off the Horror cycles with the original *Frankenstein*). *Journey's End*, also like *War Is Hell*, tried to concentrate the essence of war into a narrow space – in this case a dug-out; but in mood it was about as far away from Trivas as could be. It was almost painfully English, and I cannot believe that the strangulated emotions which resulted can have meant much to audiences outside the English-speaking world.[2]

It was at this time that Lubitsch in America made *The Man I Killed* which I have already referred to in the previous chapter. Let me add here that this fine film about a French youth who, after the war, goes to make his peace with the family of the German he killed, justly deserved John Grierson's encomium: 'I cannot remember a film so beautifully made, so completely fine in its execution.'[3]

The Man I Killed was not box-office. Universal's production of *All Quiet on the Western Front* most certainly was. Lubitsch dealt with recollections of guilt. *All Quiet* was about immediacies of conflict. The situation, involving individuals caught up in a mass war, is simpler, more direct, easier to understand. In this sense it must be counted more effective with the public than the Lubitsch film; whether it is philosophically as valid is another question. But the plain fact is that *All Quiet* hit the heart and imagination of the public in a way no other war film did.

It was an adaptation by Maxwell Anderson and George Abbott

[1] Twenty-eight years later, in *Orders To Kill*, Asquith was to make one of the most powerful anti-war films of all time.

[2] In 1972 the original play was revived on the London stage with enormous success.

[3] *Everyman*, June 1932, quoted in *Grierson on Documentary*.

of the best-selling novel by the German writer Erich Maria Remarque. It was directed by Lewis Milestone, known up till then as not much more than an average director, though *Two Arabian Knights* (1927), a comedy with William Boyd, had made a certain impression.[1]

Milestone realized that the coming of the talking picture did not mean that a 'literary' approach to film-making – however powerful the novel concerned might be – should affect the essential visual elements of movie. This particular book was narrated in the first person by its hero, who also spoke in the present tense. Milestone had of course to personalize the hero – to observe his narration from the outside, right up to the point where he was killed by a bullet. In the book Remarque did the death scene by a literary trick; he kept to his hero's present tense and, assuming a voice from beyond death, made him say 'Then I know nothing more'. For the film director, whose camera, however subjectively used, must in the end be an observer, such a short-cut is impossible. Robert Gessner has rightly noted two stages in Milestone's visual perception of this problem.[2] The script as written called for five final shots in the film – one showing the hero Paul stumbling away from the dead body of his dear friend Kat; one of the French sniper sighting his rifle; one, in close shot, of Paul crossing the battlefield, and over this superimposed a series of troops of different nationalities marching at different angles and identified by the sounds of their national anthems; this shot broken into by Paul crying 'No! Stop! No more! No More!'; then one shot, from high angle, designed to break into the continuity of the 'vision', showing Paul, the sniper's bullet having done its work, rolling gently over, 'asleep' and smiling; and finally on to this, to the sound of a typewriter, the superimposition of the words 'All Quiet on the Western Front'.

The version eventually shot and edited by Milestone went as follows: after the scene in the dressing station when Paul finds that his dear friend Kat is dead, the image changes to the trenches, where troops are digging in a vain attempt to get rid of the mud and water. Nearby, Paul is at a lookout post, with a rectangular hole in the parapet through which no man's land may be observed. (The whole sequence is in close-up.)

    1. Paul sits near the observation hole.

---

[1] After *All Quiet* Milestone made another very successful film, *The Front Page*, but thereafter his film career was irregular in quality, only occasionally bringing in winners like the Steinbeck *Of Mice and Men*, and, later, *The Strange Love of Martha Ivers* and *A Walk in the Sun*, a not undistinguished film about World War II (both made in 1946).

[2] *The Moving Image* by Robert Gessner, Cassell, 1968.

2. On the other side of the parapet a brightly coloured butterfly has settled.[1]

3. Paul sees the butterfly and is impelled to look closer.

4. A French sniper spots Paul's movement and raises his gun.

5. Paul, leaning closer and rising slightly so as to get nearer to the butterfly, makes himself even more conspicuous.

6. The sniper takes aim.

7. In big close-up, Paul's hand starts to move gently towards the butterfly.

8. In big close-up, the sniper prepares to fire.

9. Paul's hand comes near to the butterfly. There is a sharp whining crack of a bullet. The hand jerks, then very slowly subsides, turns slightly over, and becomes quite still.

10. The ghosts of Paul's comrades, marching diagonally away from the camera, turn their heads accusingly, one by one, towards us, the audience; and the film ends.

After the crack of the bullet there is not a single other sound, no play-out music, nothing.

There have been many criticisms of the final shot on grounds of sentimentality, of piling on the agony, of underlining the obvious and so on. I personally did not like it when the film was first shown; now I am less sure. The shot, like so many others in the film, is a sort of reprise or link with another – in this case a shot of the young soldiers marching when they get to the Front for the first time; and perhaps, after the butterfly and the dead hand, the broader sense of accusation is effective.

In any case the final sequence is an interesting example of how an imaginative director can transform a 'literary' concept into an entirely filmic effect produced (apart from the last shot) by the use of no more than three starkly simple visual images.

In general terms of construction *All Quiet* as a whole is quite fascinating. Milestone repeats things in threes throughout. There are, for instance, three big revelatory moments involving the opening of doors or gates to show large-scale action beyond; indeed the film begins this way. Three times, also, during the film the fact that a person is dead is revealed by the attempt to give him a drink of water.

[1] The butterfly motif has already been established. When Paul is on leave he and his sister are seen together in his bedroom looking at a framed showcase full of butterflies. She points at this particular type and reminds him of a childhood quarrel they had had over it.

Again, just before the final sequence, Kat's death is accomplished in an almost formal pattern of three bombs dropped from an idly circling French plane – the final one killing Kat while Paul is carrying him on his shoulders to the dressing station, where the orderly tells him he could have saved himself the trouble.

And of course the main battle scenes form a triptych. The first shows the French attack on the German lines; the second shows the German counter-attack; and the third concentrates on the mad muddle of war in the attack-counter-attack sequence in the graveyard, and ends with Paul in the shell-hole with the *poilu* whom, in savage panic, he has mortally stabbed.

The first two battle sequences share a basically similar technique. The audience is involved in the *movement* of the conflict – all the more effectively after the static quality of the war scenes up to this point. (There has already been a passage of high hysteria because of the lack of action combined with the remorseless bombardment of camp, canteen and billet.) The spectator is caught up in rapid camera movements, tracking or panning, skilfully intercut[1] with close shots of machine-gunners swinging their weapons from side to side and spraying bullets on to the attackers. At the climax of the first battle a vast barrage of shellfire, exploding with hideous realism and moving from background to foreground, smashes up the French advance. In the second battle (the counter-attack) the action is varied by hand-to-hand bayonet fighting. In the third, which comes much later in the film, when the situation and predicament of the men is more brutally understood, Milestone shows the awful confusion among the graves from either a very high angle, mainly of the general action, or from a very low angle, indicating individual viewpoints from among the shellholes which appear, as it were, as instant graves. And this in due course brings us right down to Paul's terrible confrontation with the dying, then dead Frenchman – his vain remorse reminding us that it was from this sort of situation that Lubitsch stemmed *The Man I Killed*.

Throughout the film Milestone also uses, to great effect, the contrast between sound and silence. At that time, when audiences were as yet unused to the possibilities of the synchronous film and to the often quite unexpected degree of amplification now available, the result was sometimes shattering – not least when, after what seemed an eternity of fortissimo shellfire, the barrage stopped as suddenly as it had begun. In the ensuing vacuum there was something heartrending

---

[1] It seems almost certain that Milestone had seen and studied some of the Soviet films like *Potemkin* or *October*.

in the wide-eyed, frightened looks which passed between the young and inexperienced soldiers.

Basically *All Quiet* is the story of men trying desperately to survive under the hideous conditions of trench warfare. It is only incidental to the film that they are Germans; for this film must have been the first to take the attitude that all the soldiers involved in the war, on whatever side, were in the same boat.[1] It is full of human detail, and its visualization often makes it superior, in terms of reality, to Remarque's own writing. The dialogue sequences, in what now seems to us their naïve schmaltziness, are the weakest element in the film, despite their obvious sincerity. The power of the visual over the verbal image, already noted, is seen particularly strongly in the sequence following the acquisition of the coveted boots from the dying Kemmerich, in which, with dreadful brevity, we see, image by image, the rapidity with which their ownership continues to change.

All Quiet was revived shortly after the end of World War II, and although the type of combat it showed looked rather antediluvian compared with the variety available in the more recent conflict, its truth in simple terms of the human predicament still came through, despite the shadows of Auschwitz and the Final Solution which were bound in some sense to darken in hindsight our attitude to the nationals of the film.

There was too, by then, a whole change of attitude which tended to distort people's reactions to the film. This was neatly pinpointed at the time by the late Campbell Dixon who wrote,

'The last scene . . . is as shattering as ever, but it isn't, perhaps it never was, really tragic. It is merely the logical end to an existence which has ceased to have meaning. Remarque's point is not that the war of 1914–18 meant a military defeat, not even that it meant the blotting out of a whole generation. His point is that all the fury and agony were meaningless, a tale told by an idiot signifying nothing. . . . Its whole teaching is that patriotism is an empty phrase, that war is futile, that the bureaucrats and generals who started it should be left to fight it out among themselves. Well, there may have been some men on both sides who did not know what the war of 1914–18

---

[1] Films about the second World War were different because the issues were different. Pauline Kael, after remarking that perhaps it was easier to make *All Quiet* because it was about the Germans, adds 'War always seems like a tragic waste when told from the point of view of the losers. It would be an altogether different matter to present the death of, say, RAF pilots in World War II as tragic waste'. This point is partly answered, however, by stress on the individual problem as presented in a film like *Orders To Kill*.

was all about. . . . Today everybody knows; and the hour when the
nation's – and the United Nations' – existence depends on our
willingness to serve, not for the aggrandisement of one but for the
freedom of all, seems an odd one to revive a film designed to kill the
idea of service altogether.'[1]

I have quoted this passage not because I entirely agree with it,
but because it reflects the rapid changes of historical perspective
among which we live. Dixon was expressing ideals and aspirations for
the post-World War II period which now seem to us to have something
of the starry-eyed dreaminess of the Rupert Brooke generation of 1914
– the ideals shown in *Tell England* in fact – the delusion that ultimate
perfectibility could somehow emerge from such a thing as a universal
war. If *All Quiet*, seen in 1950, seemed to voice a cynicism unsuitable
for expression in the face of the ideals of the newly formed United
Nations, what does it seem to represent today in view of subsequent
events in Korea, the Congo and Vietnam?

In *All Quiet*, when Paul goes on home leave (and this is quite
late in the film) he is faced by the total incomprehension of everyone.[2]
His father and his cronies are besotted by maps and grand strategies
and have no time for his individual experience. His mother warns him
against women and begs him to be 'careful' during battle. And his
chauvinist schoolmaster, whose simmering patriotism had indeed been
the cause of Paul and his classmates joining up, is appalled and out-
raged when Paul, addressing the class, states that 'It is dirty and painful
to die for your country'. If his ideals had been destroyed then, so today
have those of the young men fighting in Vietnam. But Paul's world
was in some ways more innocent; he knew nothing of such things as
Green Berets, My Lai or the Black Panthers.

The film, like the world, is forty years older; and it is possible to
feel that nothing has really changed for the better. But the persistence
of *All Quiet* in one's visual memory is a great tribute to Milestone's
talent. If we see the film again today we should remember to note that
the young Germans it presents were not in essence so different from
their successors in the Thirties and Forties; it is just that the successors
were seduced and perverted by evil doctrines purveyed in part, indeed
in great part, by films specially made for the purpose. If *All Quiet*
seems a little naïve and oversimplified today, it does in essence contain
something of that *saeva indignatio* without which violence and brutality

[1] Written in October 1950 and quoted in *Shots in the Dark*, Allen Wingate, 1951.
[2] Here, incidentally, we have another triptych; the incomprehension is shown from
precisely three different points of view.

can never be adequately opposed. We may also remember that it was not made in Germany, but in the United States.

The other great anti-war film, *La Grande Illusion* (1937), is a very different kettle of fish, if only because it raises much subtler issues than the Milestone film. Does its title, by the way, relate directly to the book of the same name by Norman Angell which, published shortly before World War I, claimed that in the modern world no one could win a war and that all would be losers?

I note that, writing about *La Grande Illusion* in 1938, I accused Renoir of 'trying to say in film terms something which is too subtle for the larger crudeness of cinema'. I added that the subject needed the spaciousness which could be accorded to it in a novel, that as a film it was too long, and that it had three distinct endings. As a result, 'what Renoir wished to say has become obscured, not by any lack of sincerity or by technical defection, but purely by the very over-simplification which is cinema's birthright and this story's death certificate'.

I now pay my tribute to the lasting quality of Renoir's work by withdrawing these remarks. They may, prissy though they were, have seemed valid at the time, if only because no one, not even Renoir, could sense the prophetic quality of this film. To us at the time it was basically a discussion of certain social implications which underlie, often unnoticed, the general idea of war. We can see now that these implications projected themselves forward and far beyond the fractures in society which were revealed, in a limited way, in the situation posed by the film. This takes place chiefly in a series of German prison camps, and revolves round continuous efforts to escape. But beyond the story of men patiently tunnelling their way out – only to be moved to another camp the day before their tunnel is complete, beyond the frenzied efforts at normality, at amusement, at any sort of occupation, beyond all the well-observed phenomena of this strange and artificial creation of a senseless war, is a basic and important theme. Class distinctions persist, says Renoir. In your prison camp – locate it where you like – your upper classes, your bourgeoisie, your workers, separate out into their own compartments. In fact, your camp would be the ordinary capitalist cosmos were it not for a further distinction imposed by war itself – the distinction of rank, the discipline of officers and men. Yet the intolerable circumstances of war are grinding away at these distinctions; the rise of class-consciousness is a sign of the coming collapse, of a conflict which will carry through into the hectic years of ill-planned peace which are to follow.

Von Rauffenstein, German aristocrat, smashed in an air crash, spine gone, silver plate in the head, hands disfigured by fire, in charge of a prison camp as the only job left to him; de Boeldieu, French aristocrat, a prisoner under the German's vigilance; down what corridors of time, from what mediaeval vistas of *schloss* and *château* have they travelled to this meeting, this discussion in an empty chapel as they realize that the world they belong to is vanishing in the rattle of the machine-guns? De Boeldieu, rigidly conscious that there is a great gulf fixed between himself and his fellow officers and fellow prisoners, unable to be really friendly with Maréchal the machinist and Rosenthal the wealthy Jew, only fulfils his fate by sacrificing his own life (to a bullet fired in cold horror by von Rauffenstein) to cover their escape. But even in escape the problem of relationship remains, and in a remarkable coda, in which Maréchal as near as dammit leaves his Jewish pal to freeze to death in the snow, there is an intense sequence when the escapees take refuge in the mountain farm of a German peasant woman who has been deprived of husband and brothers by the war. There is love between her and Maréchal, but the urge to escape is paramount, and the two men trudge off across the mountains in search of the safety of neutral Switzerland.

The film is full of marvellous images – the English officers, in drag, dancing the can-can at the Christmas party; a little Frenchman translating Pindar in his draughty fortress cell; and the Russian soldiers burning the packing case of books sent them by the Czarina herself (they would have preferred vodka).

Writing years later, Georges Sadoul suggested that *La Grande Illusion* 'might be considered as a last, sincere, but already hopeless appeal to the German people not to go to war again. It called upon individual Germans to remember the spirit of international sympathy that existed at the end of the last war, and to prevent their warmongering masters from launching another world conflict'. If this idea was in Renoir's mind during the making of this film, I think it was to fade soon after it was finished;[1] because what is absolutely clear is that *La Grande Illusion* leads directly and logically to the last film he was to make in France before the war. *La Règle du Jeu* makes it perfectly evident that Renoir quickly abandoned the idea of any 'last sincere

---

[1] In 1962 Renoir, replying to questions as to which films on peace and war he found most effective, and what films on those subjects ought now to be made, said, 'In 1936 I made a picture named *La Grande Illusion* in which I tried to express all my deep feelings for the cause of peace. This film was very successful. Three years later the war broke out. That is the only answer I can find to your very interesting query.' (*Film Book 2*, edited by Robert Hughes, Grove Press.)

appeals' either to the dictators or to the ruling classes of his own country. He now saw France and the whole Western world on the brink of a war which was largely due to the continuous and insidious collapse of the moral structure of society. In *La Grande Illusion*, as we have seen, a certain solidarity persisted, largely in terms of class; in, that is, the accepted (perhaps God-given) stratification of society. But this – a structure on which nearly everyone had learned more or less to depend – was now found to be suffering from an incurable internal disease.

In *La Règle du Jeu* Renoir reveals how advanced was this *pourriture* in French society of the late Thirties. He does it in the form of a brilliant and highly enjoyable film about a house-party in the French countryside – a house-party whose guests are invited to take part in a shoot and unwittingly also find themselves taking part in a shooting. Unlike the prison camp of *La Grande Illusion*, this château has no rules. The rules of the game, in fact, are null. As Pauline Kael perceptively pointed out, 'The concept of honour has disappeared (the honour that meant so much to a von Rauffenstein, a de Boeldieu); dishonour is just another name for indiscretion.'[1]

All standards have been abandoned except those of cash and casuistry. The aristos take a perverse pleasure in entering into apparently warm, but actually insincere relationships with the 'lower classes' – particularly those connected with 'La Chasse'. When a wronged gamekeeper suddenly takes the whole charade seriously, the total moral confusion of this world is suddenly and alarmingly revealed for what it is. It is a confusion which will continue until the Nazi invasion forces the issue with the choice of being either a collaborator or a resister.

How brilliantly Renoir focuses the confusion! The rather fusty luxury of the *château*, the constant, mindless slaughter of wild animals, the minuets of adultery and seduction, the gavottes of mutual hatred or mistrust – all these built up to the final fancy dress ball which, like the opera house sequence in Clair's *Le Million*, turns gradually into a classic chase. (The cutting of this sequence is a treasure-house for the student.) The point about the chase, of course, is that everyone takes it for a joke, except for the gamekeeper with the gun, who is, for good reason, dead serious. Like reality, he breaks in inconveniently in the hard cold light of early day.

It is significant that Renoir himself plays an important part in the film, that of the 'old family friend'. It is even more significant to note the costume he chooses for the fancy dress ball. It is that of a bear, that

[1] *Kiss Kiss Bang Bang* by Pauline Kael, Calder and Boyars, 1970.

great big furry, huggable, lovable creature which is in fact the cruellest and most dangerous of beasts. Who now is the family friend? Where will we next meet the bear? In the maquis?[1]

It hardly needs to be added that the film, when premiered in 1939, was a disastrous failure. There were noisy demonstrations against it in the cinemas; the distributors mutilated it; and eventually it was banned by Pétain and Laval. The negative was destroyed in an allied air raid, and it was only by the devotion of two young cinéastes that the film was reconstructed, from stray prints and so on, into the exact shape in which Renoir had completed it.

La Grande Illusion and *La Règle du Jeu* together represent a unique statement about the sickness of Western society on the brink of World War II. No other director anywhere came near Renoir's perception and filmic capability.[2] The debt owed to him by many directors in many countries has perhaps never been fully acknowledged. Yet without his example, particularly in these two films, where would be Fellini, Antonioni, even Bergman?

During the Occupation there appeared a remarkable companion piece to *La Règle du Jeu*. This was *Lumière d'Eté*, directed by Jean Grémillon in 1943. It was, in effect, a restatement of Renoir's thesis in the light of the sharper implications arising from the German invasion and occupation. The sickness of the France of Pétain and Laval could now be exposed in relation to a renewed patriotism and to a faith and hope in ultimate liberation. What Grémillon in fact did was to restage the house-party of *La Règle du Jeu*, but in a different landscape and connotation. Grémillon's landscape shimmers in the bright, arid sunlight of the Midi, and there is, contiguous to the château, a new and menacing symbol. Thousands of men are building a gigantic dam for a hydro-electric power scheme. This is not only a (pretty obvious) symbol of the times; it also represents a direct political confrontation, and as the film proceeds the decadent society of the *château* crumples up in face of it. With this message Grémillon hoped to hoodwink the Pétainists and hearten the Resistance; for the decadents could be taken as representative of those who had got France into its present mess.[3] On the other hand, patriots could see in this film how the rottenness of

---

[1] There is a fantastic passage in which he desperately tries to take the costume off and is absent-mindedly helped by two other guests who are entirely wrapped up in their own *affaires*.

[2] Buñuel could have, but between *Land Without Bread* (1932) and *Los Olvidados* (1950) he was not heard from.

[3] He only just got away with it. The authorities, according to Sadoul, at one time thought of banning it.

the collaborators could be set against the positive ideas of hope for victory and a reconstructed society.

This vastly underrated film is beautifully directed and photographed, and has remarkable performances by, among others, Pierre Brasseur, Madeleine Renaud and Paul Bernard. The mood is tenser, more hysterical than that of *La Règle du Jeu*, in which society did in fact accept a situation in which the terms of reference were openly dishonourable. Here, in *Lumière d'Eté*, the rules have become neuroses, the terms of reference basically unacceptable. The pathologically twitching *entretiens* between these rich and idle people are marvellously contrasted with the work on the dam; and the light, the summer light itself, never ceases to show up their garish emptiness. The fancy dress ball which climaxes the film – in which the characters appear as historical or literary personages reflecting their own natures, a boozy Hamlet, a de Sade, and so forth – ends in a dawn sequence in which the rising sun cruelly exposes the whole stupid orgy as the Dance of Death it really is (there is a gruesome automobile crash), as the last excuses for survival are stripped from all but one of the château's house-party.[1] It would be a splendid experience to see this film and the Renoir in a double bill.

The inner tensions and breakdowns of society were less reflected by film-makers in other European countries. The Germans had done it all in the Twenties with their pictures based on the Inflation period; and by now the German cinema had become the personal property of Dr Goebbels. Under Mussolini nothing very interesting was made; the best work was probably that of Blasetti who, however, would find the post-war period much more to his liking. De Sica at this time was a successful actor, but had not yet taken up direction. There was, however, an expertly made feature-length documentary on the invasion and conquest of Abyssinia which became involved in a delightful piece of skullduggery on the part of the Film Society in London. It so happened that a team of Soviet film-makers had been at work in Abyssinia during the invasion; and, largely at Ivor Montagu's instigation, the society borrowed this film as well as the Italian one (which was grandiloquently entitled *The Path of the Heroes*).[2] The films were then shown to the audience alternately, reel by reel, so that for instance the aerial sequences of the Italian 'heroes' dropping their bombs were immediately followed by the Russian sequences showing bombed Red Crosses, civilians with mustard

[1] There is something of this film in Godard's *Weekend*.
[2] It was edited from material shot by combat teams under the leadership of Luciano De Feo.

gas burns, and the like. These mounting contrasts had a cumulative effect, and the audience were soon aware that reality, however inefficiently shot (the Russians worked under great difficulties) had a bite which all the panchromatic posturings of Mussolini's propaganda could not rival. The Italians were, of course, furious, but the damage was already done and they had no redress legally; the Film Society had done nothing wrong.

In Britain, however, one film made in the Thirties took an almost unique point of view towards the question of war. Instead of the usual anti-war message based on showing how terrible the last one had been, the Korda-H. G. Wells epic, *Things To Come*, looked to the future, both immediate and more remote. This film was made at the time when the people of Britain were being prepared for Munich by such phrases as 'the bomber will always get through' and pronouncements about the virtual certainty of the use of poison gas against civilian populations. Wells, a prophet not without honour in his own country and, with Jules Verne, joint patron of all science fiction, was asked by Alexander Korda to deliver himself of a great prophecy about what was likely to happen if, as now seemed most probable, a Second World War broke out. The resulting script he entrusted to an American director, William Cameron Menzies, largely because of his immense experience as an art director and set builder. This was, in fact, reflected in the finished film; the sets were superb, but the handling of a cast of distinguished actors and actresses sadly inept.[1]

However, it is the prophetic intent of the film with which we are here concerned; and it is interesting to compare comments on it at the time of its release, as well as the forecasts it made, with what actually happened during and after the second world war.

Some of the contemporary critics concentrated on its visions of the far future and omitted reference to the more immediate picture of a destroyed world depicted in the first half of the film. The American critic Don Herold, for instance, made no reference to the war scenes, but accused Wells of choosing 'practically to ignore any possible evolution of the human soul' and of prognosticating 'almost entirely in terms of so-called technical progress'. He praised its 'marvellous trick photography of giant mechanical whatsits. It is an amazingly ingenious technical accomplishment, even if it does hold out small hope for our race.'

---

[1] This film also marked the beginning of the pioneer work of Muir Mathieson who, by persuading Arthur Bliss to write the score, made film music respectable, and from then on attracted to the recording studios all the most talented composers of the era.

Alistair Cooke attacked the film for its bad acting and bad psychology and went on to point out that the wonderful technological world of the future depicted in *Things To Come* was sadly contemporary.[1] He remarked that 'according to Mr Wells, in another hundred years, after the intervening holocaust, the relation of artist and scientist will still be at the stage it has now (1936) got to in our country in the sixth forms of schools'. Later he adds that the film 'shares with most Utopias the primary error of making today the premise, of pretending that new civilizations do not differ in kind but only in the degree of decoration, luxury, leisure and so on'.

All this is very true; and in fact since then we have seen dramatic developments which have changed much of the outward décor of civilization – including the new languages of the spacemen and of the computers, more practical than those of the film who talk with platitudinous airiness about 'Wings Over The World' and suchlike; nevertheless it still interests me that contemporary critics like Cooke paid so little attention to the war scenes of which a great part of the film was made up. Did we all at that time find the future so bodeful that we shied away?

The story of the film is explicit enough and, to begin with at any rate, near enough to the knuckle. Just before Christmas 1940 a world war breaks out. It drags on, horribly, for thirty years, at the end of which Western civilization has totally collapsed. There is Plague. The mechanical and scientific knowledge of centuries is utterly lost. Petty chiefs wage guerilla war against each other with primitive weapons. (One chief is posh enough to travel in a Rolls Royce drawn by a mule.)

Then, out of the Middle East, comes a new force, a new race of super-scientists who have taken over where the politicians and the generals have failed. They inhabit a clean and clinical world, and their eyes are already turning towards the firmament. The film ends, in fact, with a quarrel and a query. Shall a young man and girl be offered up as a scientific sacrifice in a dangerous rocket journey to the moon?

The passage of time has in part answered the query; and the world war of the Forties turned out differently from the Wellsian prophecies, for by hook or crook, or luck, the world managed to save itself from total collapse; the surface crust of civilization remains, though we may not be sure how much weight it will bear.

One of the reasons for the difference between Wells' prognostications and the reality was, in fact, the time factor. Reviewing the film at the time, John Grierson put his finger on it. 'Can patriotism,' he

[1] True, the costumes of the Future started a fashion in beach wear that very year.

asked, 'be mobilized to its own evident destruction over thirty years? Is the human spirit so craven as to endure the destruction of civilization in the name of whatever patriotism? On a more practical and political level, would an armed proletariat stand for it?'[1] He goes on to point out that by the end of the 1914–18 war the breaking point (of the will to win) had already been reached; the Allies were lucky in that the breaking point of their troops was a fraction later than that of their enemies. He adds, finally, that *Things To Come* 'is no more intimate in its human reference than a spectacle by De Mille'.

This is very true. Indeed nearly all the criticisms were valid; I made them myself, as did many others, at the time. It was in essence a film without heart, and this may be why it, together with certain others from the Korda stables was, as Arthur Knight points out, 'strange and unacceptable fare to the vast American public'.[2]

Yet this film (a superfilm of its day, costing the then unheard-of sum of £260,000) did, as we can now judge from hindsight, get a few things right. Travelling through the Ruhr in the spring of 1945, where it was often impossible to determine even where the street or road was supposed to be, the landscape of ruin and rubble exactly reminded me of scenes from *Things To Come*. And in our day we have seen the rockets fly and men have walked on the moon. It was perhaps no bad thing for at least one group to make a film looking to the future just at the time when man was on the verge of a new world war. But the real horrors, the Bomb and the Final Solution, went beyond even Wells' imagination; he lived to see them, despaired, and wrote Mankind's obituary before his own.

III

As I have already remarked, films made under the immediate urgency of war tend to lack the deeper comprehensions, and to snatch at the curious ephemeral quality which comes in when soldier and civilian alike may at any moment be within a hair's-breadth of violent death. Seen in later days, war films have a nostalgic quality for those who were there; for those whose memories don't go back that far they can, I suspect, be something of a bore. In the long run it is the non-war

---

[1] *Grierson on Documentary*, ed. H. Forsyth Hardy.
[2] *The Liveliest Art* by Arthur Knight, Macmillan, 1957. Apart from content, there is no doubt that the English accent was also unacceptable.

films made during a war which have the lasting power; and, with a few exceptions, this may well be true of both America and Britain in World War II.

Up to 1939 Britain had hardly established a recognizable school or style of cinema (other than documentary, whose influence was not fully realized). Apart from Hitchcock, Asquith, Korda and Carol Reed (and the first-named was already in the United States), the film-makers now associated with the successes of the Rank empire or of Ealing had not yet made their mark.

Hollywood, on the other hand, was rich, monopolistic, and firmly established. The rôle of the film industry in relation to the economic and social problems of the nation had, as we have already seen, been explored and cautiously exploited. And although the fear of being drawn into a world conflict inhibited the making of more than a very few films about the struggle for freedom or against dictatorship, the better producers and directors were realizing that world events were about to force the industry to grow up, and fast.

The same events brought British cinema even more quickly to maturity. Johnson's[1] proposition that the prospect of imminent execution concentrates the mind wonderfully was in a sense true of the British people from the summer of 1940 onwards. Dunkirk and its aftermath had made that hitherto mysterious area 'The Continent' a vivid and contiguous reality. So the film-makers, like the rest of the nation, put themselves wholly at the disposal of the Government, and, after a too long period of muddle and stupidity and a good deal of prodding, were rewarded with a reasonably decent deployment of the use of film in the national effort.

By the nature of their work the documentarists were expert in matters of propaganda, and it was not unnatural for the feature film-makers to turn in their direction. Michael Balcon, in particular, swung his organization at Ealing sharply into the documentary style; and nearly all producers, willingly or unwillingly, kept a close eye on documentary and, in particular, on the Crown Film Unit at Pinewood Studios, where the Government also concentrated most of its other film-making activities, including those of the Armed Services. As a result, one may observe some interesting duplications in some of the films made. The documentarists at Crown made a film about submarine crews; so did the feature producers, and in similar style. Charles Frend's vividly realistic feature about the Merchant Navy, *San Demetrio London*, was matched by Pat Jackson's super-documentary in

[1] Samuel, not Lyndon.

colour, *Western Approaches* (known in America as *The Raider*); and so on.

The Americans, on the other hand, with a civilian population still far removed from the physical proximity of an enemy, needed to whip up some sort of fervour in people whose national loyalties could be painfully divided. The situation of first or second generation German-Americans or Italian-Americans could be fraught with embarrassment and difficulty; while the treatment of the Nisei (well-established Japanese-American families) after Pearl Harbour by the U.S. Government is now recognized by most Americans as virtually a crime against humanity. On the whole, then, the American feature films about the war and its issues tended to oversimplification, from the appalling *schmaltz* of films like *Since You Went Away* or *The Mortal Storm*[1] to the crude depiction of Nazi cruelty and violence in such films as Lang's *Hangmen Also Die* (about Heydrich, Gauleiter of Czechoslovakia) or Renoir's *This Land Is Mine*. Even more oversimplified were the films in which the dreaded Reds or Commies had to be temporarily depicted as loyal and brave allies; I doubt if any of these could stand resurrection – certainly not *Song of Russia* and probably not *North Star*, directed though it was by Lewis Milestone. Finally, there were the combat films, set in Burma, North Africa, the Pacific or Occupied Europe. Many of these, while no doubt excellent for America's internal morale, put a certain strain on relations with her allies by depicting campaigns being apparently won singlehanded by Humphrey Bogart, Alan Ladd and the seemingly ubiquitous Errol Flynn.

The real films about World War II were to be made later, in the years following the end of hostilities, when men in all countries had had time to realize the full horror of the crimes they had committed at Belsen, Hamburg, Lidice, Dresden, Hiroshima, Oradour.

Meantime, during the war, there was a certain schizophrenia in Hollywood. If films on war subjects were childishly oversimple, films on other subjects were becoming significantly more adult, if only because Hollywood, perfectly naturally, was growing up.

In this wartime period cinema suffered the loss of W. C. Fields – who departed in a final blaze of glory with *The Bank Dick* and *Never Give a Sucker an Even Break*. Audiences were also, though they did not yet know it, seeing the last of Garbo on the screen; she withdrew from films after her not too successful *Two-Faced Woman* (1941). At this time too Elia Kazan made his bow with *A Tree Grows in Brooklyn*;

[1] It must be recognized that a film like this, despite overblown sentimentality, did play a part in getting across to people the real nature of Nazi racism and anti-semitism.

and a young man called Joseph Losey was making documentary and 'Crime Does Not Pay' shorts. And finally there was the extraordinary rise and fall of that controversial figure, Preston Sturges.

Sturges, already experienced as a screen writer, wrote a script for Paramount for free on condition that he should also direct the film. The result was *The Great McGinty* (1940) which launched a barbed but comic attack on corruption in politics; it had a *succès d'estime* but not much more. After a couple more films which showed a talent for the humorous but no great directorial personality, Sturges, in 1941, suddenly smashed his way through with *Sullivan's Travels*.

This tremendous ragbag of a film, starring Veronica Lake and Joel McCrea, was held together by its satiric intent. It is the story of a film director who, seeking the truth or, rather, THE TRUTH, leaves the comparative safety of the studios to study life in the raw. His various adventures cause him to return to the film fold, convinced now that what most people need from life is good straightforward escapism and that the box-office therefore is the answer to all the problems of existence. The film is funny, cruelly satirical, often melodramatic and sentimental. It fizzes with a life of its own, and it's only later that you find the fizz has subsided, leaving exposed the weakness of Sturges' philosophy, so well summarized by Richard Griffith: 'His is an inverse kind of satire. He is not interested in crushing infamy, but in recording it and implying that nothing can be done about it.'[1]

This weakness also infects his subsequent successes, none of which to my mind had the bite of *Sullivan's Travels* except possibly *Hail the Conquering Hero*, which must have made a lot of publicists and parlour patriots pretty hot under the collar.

The Preston Sturges star began to wane after this film and he had little further success, despite teaming up with Harold Lloyd in 1946 for a film originally called *The Sin of Harold Diddlebock* but wisely re-christened *Mad Wednesday*.

Some people, including myself, could never get over an uneasy feeling of falsity in Sturges' work. I used to try to rationalize this as insincerity, but the fact is that the ultimate fascination of his work arose from the fact that it *was* sincere. It was perhaps the sincerity of someone who was capable of seeing life in the round but not as a whole. There resulted a gap in comprehension; his work tended to leave a sour

---

[1] *The Film Till Now.* Sturges' approach can be exemplified in the following exchange of dialogue: *Sullivan* (to dumb blonde who has expressed admiration for several of his more trivial films), 'But don't you think that with Europe devastated by war a film director could be better employed than in making this sort of trash?' *Dumb Blonde*, 'No.'

taste behind. But he could be side-splittingly funny and he directed his actors and actresses beautifully.

He made a comeback, in fact, in 1948 with a splendid comedy notable for the simplicity of its idea as well as of its treatment. *Unfaithfully Yours* (which for some reason was savaged by the critics) starred Rex Harrison as an eminent British conductor married to an American (Linda Darnell in one of her very best rôles). Seized with suspicions of her fidelity, he plots three different ways of dealing with her, ranging from murder to the Great Unselfish Sacrifice, according to the music he is conducting at the time – Rossini, Wagner and Tchaikovsky, in that order. There is then a final variation, this time for real in their apartment, and this involves what must be the most brilliant, prolonged and elaborate piece of slapstick involving one single person ever perpetrated on a helpless audience. Harrison discovers more methods of tripping over a telephone cable than one can count, and his efforts to falsify evidence through a recalcitrant tape-recorder are as funny as anything thought up by Clair in *A Nous la Liberté* or by Chaplin in *Modern Times*.[1] In addition to all this there are, early in the film, some scenes of orchestral rehearsals (not I think without an eye to Sir Thomas Beecham) which edge almost impercept-ibly into fantasy; and some superbly comic performances by Lionel Stander,[2] Rudy Vallee and Edgar Kennedy. And at one point in *Unfaithfully Yours* Sturges has his camera track right across a concert hall into one of Harrison's eyes in a somewhat backhanded *hommage* to Hitchcock's *Young and Innocent*.[3]

While Sturges flashed comet-like across wartime Hollywood, other new talents continued to emerge. The screenwriter John Huston, with his first film *The Maltese Falcon* (1941), set a fashion for tougher, franker, tauter and more sophisticated crook or gangster tales. This new attitude led to such excellent jobs as Preminger's *Laura* and Wilder's *Double Indemnity*. But for a time the great Hitchcock seems (with the single exception of *Shadow of a Doubt*) to have had difficulty in adjusting himself to this new and much faster style of presentation. He retired into private experiments like *Lifeboat* and *Rope* in which he set himself excruciatingly difficult production problems (in the first a cramped and limited location, and in the second the abandonment of all editing), or into fascinating but essentially bogus fantasies like *Spellbound* and

---

[1] A film which – reissued in 1972 – turned out still to be the work of genius one remembered from its first release.

[2] Stander, an all-too-underestimated actor, with a voice like calico being ripped up in an empty cistern, made a welcome reappearance in 1966 in Polanski's *Cul de Sac*.

[3] Retitled for America as *The Girl Was Young*.

Notorious which served up Ingrid Bergman on a lordly if psychotic dish. It was not until *Strangers on a Train* (1951) that he returned to his true metier and to top form, where he has indeed remained ever since.

The symbolic figure of the new thriller technique triggered off by *The Maltese Falcon* is Humphrey Bogart. He had been around for quite a time, and made his grade with Bette Davis in *The Marked Woman* (1937); but he now became an archetypal figure with his appearance in Michael Curtiz's *Casablanca* (1942), a position which he finally clinched by his performances in *To Have and Have Not* (1944), a screen version of Hemingway's best, because most laconic, novel, and *The Big Sleep* (1946) – both directed by Howard Hawks, and both co-starring the sultry and talented Lauren Bacall.

Indeed this was the time when those who wanted to become Sacréd Monsters had to start jockeying for position. Joan Crawford finally sloughed off her Flaming Youth image in favour of the more mature approach of *A Woman's Face* and *Mildred Pierce*. *A Woman's Face* (1941) was directed by George Cukor with a skill that was badly needed in coping with a melodramatic story of a woman determined to revenge herself on the world for a scarred face received in early childhood. In this film the tigerish inner passion, the stoked fires behind the eyes, which are the emblems of the Crawford we now know, were first fully deployed; they became permanently established in Michael Curtiz's *Mildred Pierce* (1945/6), where Crawford's portrayal – against a most authentic Southern Californian setting – of a ruthlessly ambitious and wholly American woman put her firmly on a pedestal of equal height to that which Bette Davis had mounted after her appearance in *Now Voyager* in 1942. Of the latter film Charles Higham and Joel Greenberg justly remark, 'This piffle is directed by (Irving) Rapper with mesmerising skill.'[1] A few years later Davis played twins in *A Stolen Life*, a whizzbang double-part, and all was set for the apotheosis of *All About Eve* (1950), directed by Joseph Mankiewicz from his own script about an unscrupulously ambitious actress; one line from this film, spoken by guess who, passed into history – 'Fasten your seat belts, its gonna be a rough evening', uttered, as Alexander Walker points out, 'with a matchless sense of someone used to sniffing blood on the wind'.[2]

The non-war film output of this period is mainly interesting in that for the first time Hollywood appeared to be building up a genuine corpus of criticism of American society as a whole; not merely the

[1] *Hollywood in the Forties*, Zwemmer, 1968.
[2] *Stardom*, Michael Joseph, 1970.

American Dream or the One Nation Myth, but some sort of an analysis of those differences despite which the Federal structure managed to cohere. For the first time the outsider was able to observe that the customs and habits of the East Coast were more 'foreign' to people in the Mid-West or on the Pacific Coast than they were to most Europeans.

The traumatic experience of Pearl Harbour may, at any rate subconsciously, have turned film-makers towards these analyses of a contemporary society which, after all, the United States was fighting to save, European traditions and all. Was it altogether coincidental that the year the war ended also saw the completion of *The Lost Weekend*? Billy Wilder's faithful transcription of Charles Jackson's vivid and sympathetic study of an alcoholic brought everything full circle from the days of Slump and Prohibition. The prognosis for the drunk at the end of this film was no more and no less hopeful than that for the nation, which, willy-nilly, had for the first time got itself completely involved in global affairs and the resulting power politics.

During the war period, too, a new and more subtle sort of horror film was evolved, largely thanks to the producership of Val Lewton. The prototype was *Cat People* (1942), which intimated supernatural possibilities of transmogrification against, usually, a commonplace city background, thus adding to the spectator's apprehension. This was quickly followed by *I Walked With a Zombie*, *The Seventh Victim* and *Isle of the Dead*. The last-named, directed by Mark Robson, has been claimed by some to be the most frightening film ever made.

The popularity of these horror films, which has continued unabated to this very day, is presumably due to the fact that they are a convenient form of escapism from the omnipresent horrors of actuality which surround us daily. Against the massacres of Biafra or Jordan or Vietnam, the catastrophes of Pakistan, and the realities of drug-induced ritual murder, these mythical and romantic horrors provide a happy bolt-hole (so long, of course, as they remain untrue).

On a more cheerful note came a cavalcade of musicals, including *The Gang's All Here* and *Meet Me in St Louis* to which I have already referred. Particularly memorable was *Cover Girl* (1944), in which Rita Hayworth starred at the top of her form opposite Gene Kelly. A masterpiece of escapism this, combining the world of the fashion model with a conventional backstage story. I well remember how Jack Beddington, then director of the Films Division of the British Ministry of Information, used to run this film early in the morning, before the day's work started, to revive his own and his staff's morale. *Cover Girl's* director,

Charles Vidor, created a freshness, a zing, which remained unmatched until Stanley Donen and Gene Kelly unleashed *On The Town* (1949), a trial run for which had appeared in the Kelly-George Sidney 1945 musical *Anchors Aweigh* (also about sailors), which is specially memorable for the brilliant trick sequence in which Kelly danced with a cartoon.

Let it be noted too that it was in 1941, the year of Pearl Harbour, that Joseph von Sternberg made his finest film, *The Shanghai Gesture*, based on the John Colton play about a brothel in Shanghai. Sternberg's fantastic mastery of décor and atmosphere (compare also *The Scarlet Empress* of 1934) here reached its zenith. To satisfy the morals (so-called) of the Hays Office, the brothel had to be changed to a gaming house, but Sternberg's intense direction 'evoked', as Herman Weinberg remarks 'a descent into the Maelstrom of iniquity'; and the feeling of people trapped in a series of evils not all of their own making hung over the film like a thundercloud. This film, curiously described by no less a critic than Richard Griffith as 'ludicrous', seems to me to have a directional intensity which inspires the actors and transposes what otherwise might be clichés or banalities into a higher key. As *The Scarlet Empress* had already shown, Sternberg was one of the few people who could afford to overdo things almost to the point of tastelessness, and triumph in so doing. The cast of *The Shanghai Gesture*, incidentally, was quite superb, and included Ona Munson (as the Madame), Gene Tierney, Albert Basserman, Maria Ouspenskaya, Walter Huston, Eric Blore, Victor Mature and, somehow surprisingly, Marcel Dalio.

Apart from his strange and unsatisfactory Japanese venture, *The Saga of Anatahan* (1953), von Sternberg never completed another film on his own.[1] Neither *Jet Pilot* (1950) nor *Macao* (1951) can be considered as his, since they were altered, cut and generally messed about after completion and without his being consulted. He was a strange and somewhat rebarbative person, as I discovered when I met him very late in his life at the Mannheim Festival; but during the retrospective of his work there I had occasion more than once to bow low at his feet. He was a master film-maker and never doubted what he was doing. As he himself said, 'All art is an exploration of an unreal world';[2] in exploring that world he deliberately made of himself a lonely man. His best work has genius, is *sui generis*.

At this stage another but younger genius who flashed into prominence during the war years can no longer be kept out – that

[1] Except for one wartime short made for the US Office of War Information.
[2] *Joseph von Sternberg* by Herman Weinberg, Dutton, 1967.

enfant terrible of the radio programme, *The War of the Worlds*, who came into movies to astonish, infuriate and frighten Hollywood with *Citizen Kane* (1941). Today, some thirty years later, we can note that the effervescence of the *enfant terrible* masked something deeper. The pattern of Orson Welles' thought can be viewed in the perspective of time, and we can see *The Immortal Story* as a threnodic coda to *Citizen Kane* as well as a beautiful diadem to crown all the work that has gone between.

It can, of course, be said that Welles, like Stroheim, makes films about monsters. I should now qualify this by remarking that what we are concerned with is that not unknown factor of the *hero* as monster; the situation in which we pass from a reaction to the nature and the dilemma of the monster to the crisis at which the monster becomes romantic, then sympathetic and, in the final climactic issue, sacred.[1] And it is in some such perspective that we can now view Welles' chief characters – Kane, Haki, Kindler, Elsa Bannister, Macbeth, Othello, Arkadin, Quinlan, Hastler, Falstaff, Clay.

Only one of the films stands out as an exception, *The Magnificent Ambersons* – a film which Welles gives the impression of having tired of before it was complete (though this may have been due to the troubles he was having with his employers, RKO), and which was certainly issued in an incomplete and partly mutilated form which Welles could surely not have approved. He had of course left on his disastrous and sometimes tragic South American venture before the film was finished; and in more recent years he has been known to express a desire to remake the ending of the film.[2]

If this film does not, like all the others, feature one single monster, it does nevertheless have a collective monster – the Amberson family themselves; it is the mythical family story from Greek tragedy which has so often been revived in modern times, notably by T. S. Eliot and Eugene O'Neill, out of whose *Mourning Becomes Electra* Dudley Nichols made a disastrous screen version in 1947. It is a story of hubris, to be told either in the grand manner or deviously through psycho-pathological approaches. It was the second alternative which Welles chose for his screen version of the Booth Tarkington novel.

The film of *The Magnificent Ambersons* is about a wealthy family in a small American town at the beginning of this century – the story of

[1] In his magnificent series of sculptures, paintings and writings, Michael Ayrton has, over a period of years, given an impressive delineation of this process, and beyond.

[2] Details may be found in the Appendices of Charles Higham's admirable book *The Films of Orson Welles*, University of California Press, 1970.

a new aristocracy whose corruption and perversion arises from an indigestion of money rather than from inbreeding and traditions tarnished through time. The family destroys itself, as it is fated to do, and all its marvellous material possessions – collected, displayed, polished, arranged and collated in scene after scene – become as dust, just as in the last moments of *Greed* all is seen to be dust, all that is left is a man handcuffed to his dead enemy, a spill of useless gold, and a pet bird, freed at last from its cage, dying in the pitiless heat. Of the Ambersons little remains save a man who has killed his mother out of jealousy, and a horrid young lady who is much, much too fond of her father.

Welles found in this story much to appeal to him – themes which run through so many, if not all of his films – the misunderstanding of the nature of power and the dissolution resulting from such a misunderstanding, a failure to accept the reality of death allied to an unreasoning fear of the future, and an inability in human communication arising from an absence of any faith other than in oneself (exact reversals, as we shall see, of the themes which dominate the films of Dreyer and Bresson).

Nevertheless the complexity of the Amberson story was more literary than filmic; the absence of a single, strong focal point led Welles into cinematic exercises of considerable brilliance but with an absence of heart. The exercises are marvellous, though. Nearly every scene is played with a casual perfection which could only come from endless, painstaking planning and rehearsals, and a wonderful sense of timing.[1] The 'horseless carriage' party in the snow – an animation of everybody's old snapshot album; Aunt Fanny's super-hysterics; the long, elaborate tracking shot along the sidewalk as Anne Baxter, her face immutably fixed in a hard yet dazzling smile, elegantly and cruelly rejects her lover; all these are splendid, but capped by the tour-de-force of the kitchen scene – a single take lasting some six minutes, with a set loaded with detail as is the soundtrack with dialogue, and embellished with movements across the set to and from the camera. Yet, for all the skill and the brilliance, *The Magnificent Ambersons* is a film which, unlike some others by Welles, needs warmth and lacks it.

There is one other film which has a similar lack, and that is *The Stranger* (1946). Here Welles takes a perfectly possible situation – the Nazi war criminal who turns up in the USA under a new name and character, and who must in due course be tracked down. This is a good

---

[1] As with *Kane*, the cast was largely recruited from Welles' own Mercury Theatre, and included Joseph Cotten and Agnes Moorehead. It also had a welcome return to the screen from Dolores Costello.

Hitchcock plot and, indeed, the film reminds us frequently of Hitchcock, but not to Welles' advantage. Hitchcock's smooth logicality makes us accept the strangest situations as real – the dead man sprawled across the organ keyboard in *The Secret Agent*, the gulls and ravens gathering outside the schoolhouse in *The Birds*. Welles, on the other hand, can enlist our belief in fantastic matters; but when, as in *The Stranger*, he abandons fantasy for a kind of realism, he fails. Thus the disguised Nazi Kindler (played by Welles himself) makes, during a dinner party, a big anti-German speech which can in fact be taken both ways, and *must* be taken as such by the audience in the cinema, who will therefore ask why his audience on the screen are so stupid, at which point belief in the goings-on suffers a mortal blow. This is unfortunately under-lined by something Kindler says in answer to an interruption: 'But Marx wasn't a German, he was a Jew'. It takes the detective (Edward G. Robinson) well into the next sequence to get the point! Equally unbelievable are Kindler's relations with his wife (Loretta Young), who kowtows to his Prussian bullying and ill-temper in a most un-American manner, even making no protest when he locks her adored retriever in the cellar. It is a film of confused motivations and clumsy effects.

Yet it has a few very good moments – the wife taking off her pearl necklace at the very moment when she realizes what her husband might do to her, the various episodes with the inquisitive, self-engrossed, checkers-playing drugstore man (Billy House), and the wonderful confrontation between the detective and Kindler just after his wife has been told (and tried not to believe), during a screening of Belsen atrocities, who Kindler really is; here the conversation skates menacingly over quotations from Emerson and produces a genuine *frisson*, not least when we later realize that Emerson's 'You cannot draw up a ladder so as to leave no inlet or clue' has given Kindler the idea for the method by which he will murder his wife.

Welles himself gives a powerful performance as Kindler; yet he fails to convince us that the persona he presents could kid everyone in a small American town for so long. The Nazi in him is too prominent for us; why is it not so for the people in the film? Even the reality of the Belsen newsreels – at one point momentarily and strikingly pro-jected onto the interesting map of Edward G. Robinson's face – fail in this context to make their point. Their truth being absolute, they have no place in the relative artificiality of this story, because the artificiality is not covered by artifice as in Hitchcock or, for that matter, in Carol Reed, who in *The Third Man* uses Joseph Cotten and Welles himself to provide a moment of genuine horror in relation to the (unseen) results of tampering with the penicillin supply to a children's hospital.

In a curious way Welles' fantasies like *The Lady from Shanghai* and *Mr Arkadin* are more convincing. In the end Kindler is no monster; he is a snivelling coward and a fool to boot, so that when, in the pay-off line of the film, Robinson wishes Loretta Young a good night and pleasant dreams, the irony is already blunted.

Returning to real monsters, we face the first seminal example – Charles Foster Kane, *Citizen Kane*. Welles began this film as the blue-eyed boy of Hollywood, and ended it as someone who would be thenceforth viewed with fear and suspicion. In relation to *Kane* it is perhaps only fair to remark that Hollywood, and RKO in particular, underwent a terrible pasting from William Randolph Hearst when he recognized himself – not indeed without good reason – as the original.[1] Hearst was powerful enough to put the fear of God (or someone similar) into the distributors and exhibitors who, apart from anything else, depended very much on the advertising and publicity facilities available in his chain of newspapers; in the end *Citizen Kane* was only shown in RKO's own theatres, and then after considerable delay. Whether it would, even under optimum circumstances, have been a big box-office success is another matter. It is now a classic.

Citizen Kane not only contained the basic philosophy which has determined all Welles' work; it also established his cinematic signature once and for all (thus incidentally endearing him to André Bazin in his campaign against montage). This style is based on the creation of a constant, uninterrupted flow of images, on a desire to intensify the *human* eye's experience of seeing, and on a use of chiaroscuro which can only be described as personal to Welles himself.

This flow of images and chiaroscuro was accomplished through the inspired work of his cameraman Gregg Toland, who not only devised means of attaining fantastic depth of focus (sometimes sixteen inches to infinity!), but also invented dissolves made by interference with the light sources on the set itself – a set which, as often as not, was built with a ceiling so that special lighting methods had to be evolved.[2]

Given these innovations, Welles' dominant style emerged fully developed from his first film, and is to be observed, with little or no

---

[1] Charles Higham remarks, however, that Kane could also have been based on the Kodak tycoon Jules Brulatour who, among other things, tried to make his wife a top singer (op. cit.).

[2] Toland, who had already made some remarkable cinematic breakthroughs in shooting Ford's *Grapes of Wrath*, wrote a fascinating description of his work on *Citizen Kane* in *The American Cinematographer*, February 1941, some of which appears in Charles Higham's already mentioned book.

further change, throughout his subsequent work. His use, thanks to
Toland, of the intensification or diminution of light – whether to
establish a strange time-sense through dissolves or to intensify a
psychological point – must have had a profound effect on many
directors, not least, I would guess, on Resnais, from his early art films
to *L'Année Dernière à Marienbad*.

For Welles himself this style was evolved as a means of expressing
his own dream of time – not the eccentric time of the Resnais films,
but the straightforward and ineluctable time which erodes power as
surely as it erodes gold, but more swiftly; the time whose dark wings
can enfold a man before he has learnt love or life. Kane dies sterile of
love ('Can't buy me love, baby') because he never knew that it can
only be obtained by real feeling (at the least); and Clay, in *The
Immortal Story*, dies before the love-search he has just learned how to
institute has come to fruition. For Kane and Clay alike time, power,
cash, all crumble; and both of them end with no comfort beyond a
childlike fetish – a paperweight, a seashell. We are back with McTeague
and his cage-bird.

Of the series of strange fantasy thrillers which Welles made from
time to time after *The Magnificent Ambersons* and the abortive South
American trip, I myself have a preference for *Mr Arkadin*, also known
as *Confidential Report* (1955). Most people prefer *The Lady from
Shanghai* (1947), with its bizarre climax in the hall of mirrors, or the
more realistic and claustrophobic violence of *Touch of Evil* (1957); but
for me *Mr Arkadin* is the quintessence of this aspect of Welles. It is a
film which is not about a single monster, but about a gallery of monsters
in a world where all dreams are nightmares. Like other Welles films it
is built round the idea of a search; but in this case the search itself
wriggles and turns back on its own track like a snake.

Arkadin – a personage suggested perhaps by Kruger or Zaharoff –
has, like Kane, risen to a position of unprecedented wealth and therefore
power by methods which would hardly stand up comfortably to public
examination. To prevent his daughter finding out about this grimy and
disgusting past, he employs a special agent to seek out all those who
were concerned in it, with the intention of ensuring that they are
murdered one and all, including necessarily, and as a final *bonne bouche*,
the agent himself. The film follows the agent's search, which becomes
more and more macabre, until at its conclusion he realizes the brutal
fact of Arkadin's final intention. How he thwarts this is shown in a
tense and extraordinary final sequence with Arkadin circling the sky
alone in a tiny plane and talking by radio-phone to his daughter who

is in the airport control tower. When she tells him that she knows everything he jumps out, and the film, like the plane itself, spirals out of control into a final crash – 'The End'.

The nub of the film is in the series of visits by the agent, Van Stratten, first to Arkadin himself and then to the various ex-collaborators. Arkadin is played by Welles who also, and rather unfortunately, chose to dub his voice onto some of the other characters – presumably a money-saving gimmick.

Van Stratten's first interviews with him take place during a fantastic fancy-dress party in one of those Spanish castles the reality of which it is always so difficult to accept – a touch here from Stroheim's world of *The Wedding March* and *Queen Kelly*. When, briefed by Arkadin, he starts his search, it takes him across the world. In Copenhagen he finds the Professor (Mischa Auer), proprietor of a flea circus, in a scene weirdly dominated by a top hat and a magnifying glass. On then to an antique shop run by Trebitsch – an eccentric played quite unforgettably by Michael Redgrave. In his cluttered den, filthily dirty, wearing a greasily sinister hairnet and surrounded by equally sinister cats, this monster of monsters, with his whining epicene voice, his offbeat nervous movements and his overmastering greed for money, is eventually persuaded to provide the next clue which, by this stage not unsurprisingly, takes Van Stratten to Mexico.

Here again we meet a monster – Sophie, Arkadin's ex-mistress who must indeed know a very great deal too much, impeccably presented by Katina Paxinou – chain-smoking, card-playing, sinister, placid, imperturbable on a sunny terrace by the subtropic sea. At which point, with rupturing effect, Welles flings us across to Munich in mid-winter, where this *totentanz* reaches its climax in perhaps the most grotesque piece of filming ever thought up by Welles. In Munich there is one more personage to be sought, one Zouk (played by Akim Tamiroff even better than his later 'Uncle' in *Touch of Evil*) who, by now poverty-stricken, despairing, is prepared possibly to provide the needed information in return for a meal of *pâté de foie gras*. By this time Arkadin himself has turned up, and he organizes a macabre procession of waiters who rush along the frozen streets from an expensive restaurant bearing with them the coveted goodies; preludes to Zouk's bumping off.

One of the great attractions of *Mr Arkadin* is that the evil in it is fabulous in the strict sense of the word. The monsters in the film are the monsters of fable; thus the evil is at second remove, and the frissons are from a ghost story. The more genuine evil of a Kindler or a Quinlan is miles away. The film is in a sense a mere *jeu d'esprit*, but it is carried out with such imagination and with such a perfectly chosen cast that it is a sort of compendium of Wellesian style. It also reminds one, as I have said, of Stroheim (Trebitsch with his cats and Zouk with his *pâté* come from a *Greed* or *Foolish Wives* sub-plot), and of Buñuel (the procession of waiters could be from *The Exterminating Angel*). The quality of the soundtrack is quite disastrous, but there is a certain grandeur about the carelessness of the film's construction which makes one forget everything except the immediacy of the moment.

It was with *Chimes at Midnight* that Welles finally succeeded in mastering the monster by the simple process of accepting him (Falstaff) as a human being. This is undoubtedly far the best of his three Shakespearean projects. It is clear that Welles fell utterly in love with the character – a love almost identical with that so beautifully expressed by Elgar, a love not unaware of the dangerous depth which may lie beneath the looks and springtime scents of the green landscapes of England. In Falstaff Welles saw 'a man defending a force – the old England – which is going down . . . The film was not intended as a lament for Falstaff but for the death of Merrie England . . . the age of chivalry, of simplicity, of Maytime and all that.'[1] And again, 'What is difficult about Falstaff . . . is that he is the greatest conception of a good man, the most completely good man, in all drama. His faults are so small and he makes tremendous jokes out of little faults. But his goodness is like bread, like wine.'[2]

Whatever one may think about this reading of the character, there is no doubt that it is very effective on the screen. By writing his own script and only using the bits and pieces he really needed from Shakespeare, Welles avoided the infelicities of his *Macbeth*, and for that matter of Olivier's *Hamlet* film; but in so doing he tended towards that self-indulgence which has always been a danger. As James Price remarked at the time, 'I was forced to realize that the Welles I was admiring was the actor, not the film-maker. The creative act at the heart of *Chimes at Midnight* is an act of imaginative impersonation.'[3]

Yet there is much pictorial beauty in the film, and the battle scenes do achieve a real impression of the fighting of those days – chivalry, grotesquerie, slime, blood and savagery – all somehow summed up by the colossal crash when the rope breaks as they are trying to hoist the armoured Falstaff on to his horse. Like the clangour

[1] *Welles and Falstaff* – interview with Juan Cobos and Miguel Rubio, *Sight and Sound*, Autumn 1966.
[2] loc. cit.
[3] *Sight and Sound*, Summer 1967.

of the iron doors in Poe's *Fall of the House of Usher*, the old boy's clamorous fall carries portents beyond the immediate comedy.

Talking about the making of *Chimes at Midnight*, Welles said, 'I believe in the film as a poetic medium . . . There is no picture which justifies itself, no matter how beautiful, striking, horrific, tender . . . it doesn't mean anything unless it makes poetry possible. And that suggests something, because poetry should make your hair stand up on your skin, should suggest things, evoke more than you see. The danger in the cinema is that you see everything, because it's a camera.[1] So what you have to do is to manage to evoke, to incant, to raise up things which are not really there.'[2]

Evocation is the key to Welles' last film to date, a one-hour offering, made for television in colour, based on Isak Dinesen's (Karen Blixen's) *Histoire Immortelle*, *The Immortal Story*. Having mastered his monster by falling in love with him, Welles, after *Chimes at Midnight*, could divine in this exquisite novella – just as Visconti did in Thomas Mann's *Tod in Venedig* – a perfect opportunity to convert the economies of the visual image to the enframed distillation of an elegy. In all elegies, resurrection or no, there must be tragedy; and all elegies must be beautifully framed, for they represent completion.

Certainly, with *The Immortal Story*, Welles has come full circle from *Citizen Kane*. *Citizen Kane* is an obituary; *The Immortal Story* an elegy. Kane dies never having known love; Clay dies on the verge of its discovery. Kane in the end could never reconcile himself to life as he led it, even to life as he *could* have led it. Everything stopped, frozen, at 'Rosebud'. But Clay in *The Immortal Story*, for all that he has spent his life omitting the things which are of real importance, for all his dry bemusement with finance, comes in the end to reckon with other possibilities. In his dusty loneliness he remembers a legend and, in a last exercise of power, tries to make it come true. The legend, like that of the Flying Dutchman, is a myth universal to seafarers. An old man offers a young sailor a bag of gold if he will sleep with his lovely young wife and, hopefully, impregnate her with the son which he himself is incapable of begetting.

In this film everyone is, sadly and in some way or other, flawed by life. Clay's clerk, the appointed go-between, has behind him the ghettos and pogroms of Central Europe. The surrogate wife (for Clay is not married) is an ageing semi-prostitute whose childhood home he

---

[1] This is the danger which Vertov so mistakenly embraced as a truth and on which in fact he based his Kinoki theory.

[2] Interview, *Sight and Sound*, Autumn 1966.

inhabits. And the golden boy himself is a shipwrecked or, more accurately if less romantically, a stranded sailor.

The Immortal Story is made with an economy rare in Welles' work. Simple sets, simple images create the *ambiance*. The huge spaciousness of Xanadu is here reduced, distilled into the tropic roominess (big enough in all conscience) of punkahed verandahs and balconies, living-areas enlarged by mirrors and by trails of curtains in endless vistas of blowing gauze, amid all of which sits Clay, daily desiccating, like a spider.

Why then is the film so infinitely touching? Mainly, I think, because Clay, in exercising the power by which he knows that he can bring about the arrangement he desires, knowing too that he can control, even observe, the events he is causing to happen, learns in the process that there is one secret into which he can never, never enter – the feelings and emotions of the persons involved. Worse still, the situation which his power has so easily created turns out to be one in which all the participants are in doubt. The clerk has only one ambition – to be left alone. The woman, with the wrong end of middle age visible on her face, would be too proud to be thus employed by Clay were she not motivated by feelings of resentment and revenge that he should now be living in her dead father's house. And the young sailor, bust and broke, is hardly able to comprehend what the old man wants (buggery is obviously his first thought), and then, in the flowing dimness of the bedroom which obscures the lines on the lady's face, has to confess to her that he is a virgin. . . .

Clay stands and watches in the shadows outside the bridal chamber; and next morning he sits on his verandah and quietly dies, his 'Rosebud' symbol a conch shell. Nothing else is much changed. One person is dead. The rest, for all that has happened, will remain stranded.

Shot by Willy Kurant in pale tints, with an occasional splash of vividness for contrast; accompanied by Welles' own narration of the Dinesen words and by snatches of Satie's music, as economic in use as they were in composition; and exquisitely performed by Jeanne Moreau, by Norman Eshley (as the sailor), by Roger Coggio (as the clerk) and by Welles himself as Clay – this film, with its beautifully conceived background of dust and sunshine, of hands dealing Tarot cards (the Drowned Sailor comes up of course), and of the discreet movements of black-clad Chinese servants and children, is a contribution to that rare and select list of films which can be truly described as film poetry.

IV

Welles' incursion into the war period with *Citizen Kane* has led me into something of a digression. Returning now to the realities of World War II and to the European arena, we may note that the mood of film-makers in Britain was, at least until after Pearl Harbour, inevitably different from that of their American counterparts. The nearness of the enemy, the actual participation in the conflict by non-combatants caused by the air raids, induced in them a more concentrated if not more dedicated mood. This was, too, a period in which at long last there was money to make films with, thanks mainly to the filmic ambitions of J. Arthur Rank and Filippo del Giudice, the latter having the one thing the former lacked, cinematic ideas.

The distinction between war films and non-war films was less sharp in Britain, not only because of the proximity of the action but also because the crisis of war was forcing the British people as a whole to re-examine some of their national characteristics and, indeed, to question the social and economic structure of the nation. Thus in a film like Carol Reed's *The Way Ahead* (itself based on his Army indoctrination film *The New Lot*) there was a great emphasis on the levelling of class distinctions. The main characters were chosen so as to cover a wide cross-section of the community, and the story of the film was concerned firstly with their personal efforts to adjust themselves to being soldiers, and secondly with the gradual building up of a corporate sense in terms of platoon or battalion. This was all climaxed by the excoriating speech delivered by the Commanding Officer (played by David Niven) to the recruits after they had 'let down' their regiment on manoeuvres, in which he had no hesitation in referring to tradition as well as to personal pride and self-respect; while at the end of the film, the same men, now fully welded together in efficiency as well as comradeship, are seen successfully in real action on the North African front.

Similarly, in Noël Coward's *In Which We Serve*, the flashbacks from the torpedoed crew clinging to their liferaft were mainly concerned with their different social backgrounds. Indeed at one point Coward boldly staged a confrontation in a railway carriage between the upper-class commander (based loosely on Lord Louis Mountbatten and played by Coward himself) and a middle-class petty officer – together with their respective wives. The awkwardness of this encounter, with everyone desperately trying not to say the wrong thing, was brought off with a delicacy of touch which made it moving and not at all embarrassing. Although in the long run this film can be seen to be basically concerned with the traditional structure of the Royal Navy, and therefore with the preservation rather than the modification of class-distinctions, it was, in the short run at any rate, a remarkably effective piece of morale-raising propaganda as well as being a gripping and extremely well-made film.[1] It is interesting to recall Pudovkin's reaction:

'It's a splendid job, overwhelming in its complete and well-thought-out frankness. One of my comrades called it profoundly national, and I fully agree with him. The picture is English through and through. You can see the face of the real England in it. The scene in which the Captain, taking leave, shakes the hands of a whole file of his compatriots, and each conducts himself as though he were like no one but himself, and yet at the same time all are like each other, will remain long in my memory'.[2]

Such elements of social consciousness are to be found, to a greater or lesser degree, in a large number of British wartime films, whether fictional or documentary. One clear example is Anthony Asquith's *The Way to the Stars* (1945) – known in America as *Johnny in the Clouds*. Here, treading the narrowest of tightropes, he presents British and American fliers in all their mutual misunderstandings and agreements with humour, humanity, and not a sign of mawkishness. This film also contains a classic opening sequence, with the camera wandering through an abandoned air-base, peering in at each detail in the nissen huts, the sleeping quarters, the canteens, noting all the time a procession of objects each one of which will have its own special significance in the action of the film.

Cavalcanti, apart from his work as a producer first at the GPO Film Unit and then with Michael Balcon at Ealing, himself directed two wartime films. One was *Yellow Caesar* (1941), a savage and sarcastic compilation film about Mussolini and his gimcrack empire. The other was a feature film from an idea by Graham Greene which aroused considerable controversy when it was shown in 1942. *Went the Day Well?*, made in haste and on a very low budget, postulated the course of events if an English village were to be taken by Germans. The first part showed how the villagers' suspicions were aroused by the behaviour

---

[1] Coward chose as colleagues two more or less unknown youngsters, Ronald Neame and David Lean.

[2] From a letter to Ivor Montagu published in *Documentary News Letter*, Jan/Feb 1944.

of troops who represent themselves to be a unit of the Royal Engineers but who make curious little slips like writing '꒭' instead of '7' and not being able to spell 'chocolate'. The rest of the film followed the villagers' heroic resistance both as a group and as individuals and was, to put it at its lowest, a really exciting adventure story with some good acting performances, not least from Marie Löhr as a lady involved with an unfamiliar object in the form of a hand-grenade. Why this film aroused such passionate feelings, pro and con, it is difficult to say. Perhaps the divisions of opinion were caused by the reactions of different people, at that particular crisis, to the very idea of showing invasion actually in progress – though the film explicitly stated that the German soldiers were only a probing advance-guard of a proposed invasion, and they were in the event roundly defeated. *Went the Day Well?* had a certain quality not to be despised; it would be interesting to revive it today.

On a very down-to-earth level were the films of Frank Launder and Sidney Gilliat; they tended to start in the lower strata of society and work upwards to not much higher than the lower middle-class. These films – especially *Millions Like Us* (1943) and *Waterloo Road* (1945) – showed the reaction of the so-called 'little men', the semi-educated, the tongue-tied – with their memories of unemployment, the Means Test, malnutrition – to the crisis of war. It is in these films that we can most clearly see the reasons why the British people, as soon as the war was over, rejected the Conservatives (including the man who had led them to victory) in favour of men who were less guilty of the neglect, cruelty and incompetence of the ruling administrations between the wars.

Some documentaries of the period, despite Ministry of Information doubts, propounded a similar point of view, as in Paul Rotha's celebrated expositional films *World of Plenty* (1943) and *Land of Promise* (1945). There was also a now almost forgotten film by John Taylor – *Goodbye Yesterday* (1942) – which depicted a group of individuals on whom the war, in comparison with their previous circumstances, had had a positive effect. At the end of the film this group was revealed sitting in a projection room, having (like the audience) just viewed it; they then discussed how they felt about what they had just seen and how they thought the film should now end – the result being a slightly sinister question mark which boded no good for supporters of the *status quo*.[1] The film was never released.

Another phenomenon of the war was the emergence of a pro-

---

[1] This sequence anticipated by nearly twenty years the finale of Jean Rouch's *Chronique d'un Eté*.

duction team called the Archers. This in fact consisted of an Englishman, Michael Powell, and a Hungarian, Emeric Pressburger. Their films, always beautifully made, seldom failed to raise ideological storms of considerable magnitude.

Their first main wartime film, *49th Parallel* (1941), was about six members of an escaped U Boat crew on the run in Canada, who are one by one pursued and captured. The first feature film to be partly financed by the Ministry of Information, it was criticised in some quarters for having a negative propaganda slant. It was argued that Hollywood had so conditioned us to take sides with the hunted rather than with the hunters that our sympathies would be with the pursued Nazis; it was also argued that it was a pretty poor show if enemy personnel could be left at large for so long in hostile territory. It was also complained that Leslie Howard, as a rather defeatist English intellectual, was a less sympathetic character than the ruthless, dedicated U Boat commander played by Eric Portman.

Against all this it was claimed that Powell and Pressburger were doing no more than express general criticisms of the British attitude to the rest of the world and, by showing these to be essentially false, aiming to shock the Americans and Canadians into treating apparent dilettantism with more respect. The whole story and motivation of the film was, indeed, very carefully calculated. In the course of their flight the Nazis met a French-Canadian trapper (Laurence Olivier), a German Hutterite settler (Anton Walbrook), a toughly cynical Canadian soldier (Raymond Massey), and an assortment of Red Indians and Eskimos as well as Leslie Howard's aforesaid dilettante. All this was planned to indicate that in the British Commonwealth there was room for all, regardless of race, language or creed; and the story-line is such that in each confrontation the Nazis come off worst, even when, as an added anti-Hitler stroke, the U Boat commander commits a typically cold-blooded murder. Finally, it is the 'typical' Englishman, apparently so weak and cynical, who gives the knockout to the Nazis.

49th Parallel brought into sharp focus, and quite early in the war, the hair-trigger differences of emphasis in the world of propaganda. In this case I think the balance tipped the right way, and the superiority of the democratic over the totalitarian viewpoint was satisfactorily demonstrated.

One may note, similarly, that the famous Harry Watt-Humphrey Jennings reportage *London Can Take It* (1941) which, by showing the Blitz as it happened, made a deep impression in favour of Britain among the peoples of North America, was also criticised. 'Sure they can take it,' it was said, 'but can they dish it out?'[1] It was fortunate that very soon afterwards – indeed during the same year – the course of the war enabled Harry Watt to make his famous *Target for Tonight* which showed the British doing just that.

Another controversial Archer film was *The Life and Death of Colonel Blimp* (1942—1944). This was a very big film for its time, in length, in production values and (hopefully) in ideological conceptions. Like all the other Archer films it was superbly made from every point of view. Indeed, I think one of the reasons why criticism of the content or motive in these films was always exceptionally violent was exactly because they were tremendously good entertainment and therefore very convincing. Blimp himself – based of course on the figure invented by the cartoonist David Low to symbolize all that was most reactionary in Britain – was here transformed into a real human being as we watched his reactions to the war. He was in fact shown as a sincere though misguided reactionary with a heart of gold; and Powell and Pressburger chose to reveal his behaviour and development through the eyes of a Prussian.

The result was certainly a fascinating if over-long film, but its fatal flaw, as I pointed out at the time, was this very Prussian. By including him as, in the event, a sort of *deus ex machina*, the Archers created a situation in which the English represented what people from the mainland of Europe (and especially Germany) thought they would like them to be – stupid, brave, amiable, kind to animals and domestics and, *au fond*, eminently amenable to reason, particularly from someone of another nationality.

The film, in the end, showed only a narrow cross-section of wealthy upper-class British life. Ordinary people hardly existed, except in that the intention of the film seemed to be to explain to them that Blimp didn't really mean any harm, and would be quite OK after the war and prepared to see their point of view. There was, I think, no reference anywhere in the film to what Blimp was doing or thinking at the time of the Japanese invasion of Manchuria, the Italian invasion of Abyssinia, or the Spanish Civil War.

So for all their efforts the Archers in this case misjudged the firepower of their thesis; despite a number of very fine performances – not least from Roger Livesey as Blimp in a love-hate relationship with Anton Walbrook as the Prussian – the film gently but firmly backfired.

In 1944 Powell and Pressburger made what must have been, from any point of view, the kinkiest film of the war. It was called *A Canterbury*

[1] The title was later changed to *Britain Can Take It*.

Tale, and it was concerned with a dedicated Kentish Justice of the Peace whose extra war-effort involved him in lecturing to the locally stationed troops on archaeology and suchlike. Alarmed at the thought of the men being seduced from these delights by the wiles of the local girls, he takes to going around in the black-out and pouring glue on their hair. Repentance for these psychotic excesses is eventually achieved by the J.P. through a sort of pilgrimage to Canterbury Cathedral in the company of a sweet kind girl, a British soldier and an American ditto. To most people the intentions of the film-makers remained highly mysterious; nor did this picture of British administrators of justice commend itself to the authorities, who showed some reluctance to encourage its export to our allies.

Then just after the end of the war came the Archers' *A Matter of Life and Death*, another mysterious pilgrimage, this time on the part of an airman who, shot down, finds himself in a world part past, part present, part future. Photographed sometimes in colour and sometimes in black and white, this film, though losing its way sometimes in philosophical discussions between historical figures, had a fervour which was lacking in their other works. It compelled attention and created emotion. Thereafter, despite the elaborate sensations of *The Red Shoes* (1948), the Archers achieved nothing significant other than a surprising masterpiece, modest in intent, *The Small Back Room* (1949). Based on a Nigel Balchin novel, this film had, in the dismantling of a dangerous bomb, a suspense sequence of unparalleled fascination; the only equal to it might be Len Lye's terrifying army training film about two snipers stalking each other – *Kill or be Killed*, made in 1943.

The Archers' desire to contribute statements about the war led them into complications, into unexpectedly thorny byways. By contrast, the finest film made in Britain during the war had a pellucid clarity of intention and achievement which still shines out of it when it is shown today. Yet it was produced in an atmosphere of controversy, if not of downright opposition. Its makers were accused of gross extravagance at a time when Britain needed to conserve all her resources; they were criticised for shooting spectacular scenes in a neutral country; they were even accused of irrelevance. The film in question was of course *Henry V*, in word and subject as inspiring a piece of propaganda as any government might wish to be able to circulate at the height of an all-out war.

This beautiful and well-nigh faultless film, directed by Dallas Bower and Laurence Olivier, was the first, I think, to present Shakespeare within genuine terms of cinematic imagination. It was a film which right from the start, when the spectator was pitchforked into the sweaty auditorium of the Globe Theatre, fascinated, tantalized, moved, impressed and delighted. It also, through Shakespeare, summed up what Britain had been up to during the weary years of war in terms not of jingoism but of common humanity. The long sequence at night on the eve of the battle – the young soldier discussing the issues ('But if the King be not in the right . . .') – and the King's own encounters with his men, remain one of the most touching expositions of war's meaning ever put on the screen. Add to this the spectacle – of battles and courtly scenes, especially the French court, an exquisite reconstruction by Roger Furse of *Les Très Riches Heures du Duc de Berri*; add again an almost impeccable cast – and you have something which justifies the tremendous risk taken by Filippo del Giudice in the first place, and in the second place, when money was running out, by J. Arthur Rank.

Henry V cost nearly half a million pounds – a vast budget for a British film at that time – and what's more, it was such a box-office success that it recouped the lot, thus incidentally starting a period of rapidly accelerating inflation in the British film industry which neither del Giudice nor Rank seemed at first to worry about. There can be no doubt that their almost wholly permissive attitude to film-makers (whatever the ultimate financial problems) led to a Golden Age of British films to which many of the old-stagers must still look back with regret and nostalgia.[1]

As I have already mentioned, World War II caused a close rapprochement between feature and documentary film-makers. This is frequently described in terms of one-way traffic, with the feature people learning realist techniques from the documentarists. But the boot was also on the other foot. When the Government took over the then largest studios in Britain – Pinewood – and there installed the Crown (ex-GPO) Film Unit, together with the film units of the Armed Forces, a lot of documentary-makers grabbed with joy at the elaborate film-making facilities available there. As the feature people surged out onto location, the documentarists rejoiced in building complex interior sets of submarines and suchlike on the studio floor. In the end, however, the two elements achieved a good balance. Documentary had always needed *some* studio facilities (the interior of the sorting van in *Night Mail* was a studio reconstruction), and the feature men, by having to face wartime realities in order to convince not only Government officials but also

---

[1] A wit of the period emended Shakespeare's 'crammed with distressful bread' to 'crammed with Rank dough'.

the general public, who were in the course of experiencing those realities, learned not only extra values from location-shooting but also how to achieve greater verisimilitude in the studios themselves.

The situation did at times result in a certain duplication. There was Crown's submarine film *Close Quarters* (1943) and Asquith's *We Dive at Dawn* (also 1943), which were sufficiently similar to make one wonder why both had to be made. But both sides in the end benefited greatly from this shot-gun wedding; so that a film like *Journey Together*, made by John Boulting for the R.A.F. Film Unit, but with an international cast which included Richard Attenborough and Edward G. Robinson, was a felicitous combination of both categories.

There were, of course, the 'pure' wartime documentaries such as Jack Holmes' aerial study of the work of *Coastal Command* and, very notably, Pat Jackson's already mentioned and intensely felt disquisition (in colour) on the perilous life of the merchant seaman – *Western Approaches*. On top of these came the big compilations made from the millions of feet shot by combat cameramen on all fronts – *Burma Victory, Desert Victory, Tunisian Victory* and, to cap all, *The True Glory*, that fantastic story of the invasion of Europe, made jointly by Garson Kanin and Carol Reed, a really brilliant example of collaboration of talent on an international level.

Out of the Crown Film Unit, too, there emerged a unique figure – an individualist as distinct from the general trend of documentary as Flaherty. This was Humphrey Jennings, who found in the circumstance of war an inspiration which exactly reflected his own personal feelings about his country. The films he made, perhaps because they were so *extremely* British – or should one say English? – established for him a significant international reputation.

Jennings, whose career was tragically cut short in 1950, was a man of wide-ranging talents as writer, painter and stage designer[1]; he came into films as an afterthought. His work for the GPO Film Unit before the war was unimportant, except for one film, *Spare Time*. This film arose from the operation of a semi-scientific organization called Mass Observation, founded by Tom Harrisson and Charles Madge for the purpose of studying what ordinary British people did and thought, rather on the lines employed by Margaret Mead and others in their studies of the habits of Polynesians. *Spare Time* was a somewhat depressing picture of the British taking their pleasures sadly – the kazoo

---

[1] At Cambridge, between 1926 and 1929, he created some remarkable sets and costumes, notably for Dennis Arundell's productions of Purcell's *King Arthur* and Honegger's *King David*.

band sequence, with flimsily clad drum-majorettes shivering in the icy
winds of the industrial North, was quite heartrending – but it had a
certain truth about it.

With the War, however, all Jennings' feelings about his country
were intensified, inflamed. His *idée fixe* had always been the England
of the Industrial Revolution, on which he was compiling a vast book
(alas! never to be finished) called *Pandemonium*; and there was a
Blakean quality about him which only stopped short at Blake's sardonic
passions at their most intense. That Jennings drew slightly back where
Blake went over the brink was perhaps typical of his own 'Englishness' –
a tendency to appear not to want utterly to commit oneself (safe,
though, to 'connect'). If then he had a weakness as a film-maker, it
may have been that he tended to put the heat of his feelings through
a cooler in the process of production. But all the same *Listen to Britain*,
Fires Were Started, and *Diary for Timothy* were work of unique and
universal appeal. Indeed when *Fires Were Started* – with its vivid
depiction of firemen at work in the London blitz – was shown in the
Fifties at a British Film Week in Rome, the astonished Italian directors
acclaimed it as a masterpiece of neo-realism, though it had been made
well before *Rome – Open City* or *Shoeshine*.

As for *Diary for Timothy*, this is a film whose effect on audiences
never ceases to produce surprises. In India in 1969, for instance, a group
of young Asian film-makers and film-students who had never been to
England, never experienced air raids or been concerned with moral
issues arising from that war, were impressed, intrigued and fascinated
by the film. For days afterwards they discussed it, asked questions about
it, probed for inner meanings. Somewhere here, for them, lay clues to
the strange mysteries of the British character which no one, during the
long era of the British Raj, had really been able to unravel. The choice
of E. M. Forster to write the narration may have been more significant
than we thought.[1]

As producer of *Diary for Timothy* I spent most of my time, while
Humphrey was shooting, wondering what it was about. From the nature
of the product he had of course the perfect excuse (with which in my
own nature I sympathized) for having no script at all. The film literally
was a diary, not only of the life of the baby and of the arbitrarily
selected real characters such as the locomotive driver, the wounded air
pilot and the equally damaged coalminer – but also of what, unpredict-

---

[1] When he saw the first rough-cut, Jack Beddington propounded two names – Max
Beerbohm and Forster. I often wonder what the film would have been like had the choice
gone the other way.

ably and day by day, was happening during the last months of the
European war.

He was, to put it mildly, not a very communicative director, and
I don't think he told anyone at the time of his intention to crosscut
the graveyard sequence from Gielgud's *Hamlet* with the canteen conversation about V-bombs – bringing them together by the actual
explosion of a bomb. This sequence, neatly planned and dovetailed, is
what in earlier times used to be called a Conceit. Whatever you call it,
it is a stroke of cinematic genius, and it certainly served as a sheet
anchor when the first rough version of the film was projected to the
authorities. It gave a focus to what otherwise tended to look like a rather
tattered sketchbook, and enabled Beddington to talk down a largish
junta of officials who wanted the entire project junked there and
then.

What is the secret of the tremendous pull which this film has on
so many different people? It is, in essence, a rather cosy, liberal, middle-
class statement about some aspects of war. The approach to the staging
and direction of individual episodes is not particularly warm; indeed,
compared with *Fires Were Started* and *Listen to Britain*, it is cerebral.
Some, I think incorrectly, have discerned a touch of patronage in
Jennings' attitude towards some of his characters. In the end, though,
one has to accept that, in a film artificially constructed, with staged
sequences, rehearsed dialogue, and Forster's narration,[1] he communicates an emotional immediacy.

The answer to all this may be found in an affectionate and perceptive analysis of Jennings' work by Lindsay Anderson[2] in which he
points out how 'with dazzling virtuosity, linking detail to detail by
continuously striking associations of image, sound, music and comment, the film ranges freely over the life of the nation, connecting and
connecting. National tragedies and personal tragedies, individual
happinesses and particular beauties are woven together in a design of
the utmost complexity . . . The impressions themselves are rarely
un-memorable, not merely in their splendid pictorial quality, but for
the intimate and loving observation of people, the devoted concentration
on the gestures and expressions, the details of dress and behaviour that
distinguish each unique human being from another.' The word 'unique',
which I see I have used in previous paragraphs, is a good one in relation

---

[1] The ways of film-making are very strange. One of the most admired phrases in the
narration – 'and death came by telegram to many of us on Christmas Eve' – was, with its
surrounding paragraph, written by myself to fill a last-minute gap left by the not-always-
too-industrious Forster.

[2] *Film Quarterly*, Winter 1961/2.

to Jennings. He perceived the unique in all around him, and being himself unique, was its perfect interpreter.

His work after the war was less striking, despite some very fine touches in *Family Portrait*, a film for the Festival of Britain in which he tried to sum up the national character in too short a space – not his fault; like so many of us he was asked to put a quart, nay a gallon, into a pint pot. And because of his untimely death we shall never know how he would have adjusted himself to some of the drabber visions of post-war Britain. But the legacy of his wartime films remains, and Anderson's epitaph is surely just:

> 'They will last because they are true to their time, and because the depth of feeling in them can never fail to communicate itself. They will speak for us to posterity, saying "This is what it was like. This is what we were like – the best of us."'

And to this we might add as a postscript Eric Rhode's interesting comment, 'From a historian's point of view *A Diary for Timothy* is a wonderful illustration of why Britain went labour in 1945'.[1]

There was a second figure of singular interest in the wartime film-making scene. John Eldridge's film *Our Country* (1944) had a reception about as controversial as Cavalcanti's *Went the Day Well?* Hard-boiled film-trade people surprisingly took to it (it opened at the Empire, Leicester Square – one of London's largest cinemas) while normally perceptive critics like Richard Winnington and Arnot Robertson were enraged – a curious reversal of the normal attitude to the products of the documentary movement. *Our Country* was a remarkable experiment in a new kind of screen poetry; as such it was, and is, difficult to describe on paper. The poetry came visually through exquisite camerawork by Jo Jago and through Eldridge's sensitive direction and editing, and aurally through a fine score by William Alwyn allied to a commentary by Dylan Thomas in which he successfully wedded (and in part subordinated) his style to the needs of the medium. The story, if such it could be termed – it was perhaps more a theme – concerned a sailor on leave who wandered through wartime Britain to see and to feel the way life went on. From its opening in Glasgow with

'To begin with
a city
a fair grey day

[1] *Tower of Babel*, Weidenfeld and Nicolson, 1966.

a day as lively and noisy as a close gossip of sparrows . . .
. . . when each man is alone forever in the midst of the masses of men
and all the separate movements of the morning crowds
are lost together in the heartbeat of the clocks
a day when the long noise of the sea is forgotten
street-drowned in another memory'

the film evoked the feeling of a waking dream, a live vision of the
inwardness of our daily life; and this evocation had the effect of removing all sense of the unduly episodic, so that at the end one felt that
everything had been superimposed and yet every facet of the film
remained separate and as clear as crystal – the lorry hitch-hike, the
hop-picking in Kent with the Cockney woman briskly darning the
sailor's socks, the grim Welsh schoolmaster with his pupils, the West
Indians a-dancing and the Scots trawlermen a-boozing and, all through,
a marvellous affection for the landscapes and townscapes and skyscapes
and

'to end with
a quayside
a fair grey day
with the long noise of the sea flowing back
as though never in factory or harvestfield
market or timber temple street or hill
it could have been forgotten . . .'

so that at the end, over the faces of fishermen, Dylan Thomas' words
drew together and summarised all the visual patterns and beauties of
the film.

After the war Eldridge's imagination continued to range. His
Three Dawns to Sydney (1947) was commissioned by BOAC as a
prestige film about their new through-service to Australia. Eldridge hit
on an idea which, as it happens, W. H. Auden and myself had arrived
at in 1938 in planning a film for the GPO Film Unit, the making of
which was cancelled by the outbreak of war – to make the film not so
much about the aircraft itself as about the countries it overflew. To
this Eldridge added a further element – a specific moment in time,
Christmas Eve. As the aircraft made its way across the world it flew
over the hustle and bustle of a small Sicilian town, over a group of
Glubb's Arab legionaries (non-Christians in the land of the Nativity),
over the teeming life of Karachi and Singapore, over the vast Australian
outback with its aborigines to remind us of the dawn of time and, to

end with, the modernity of Sydney and the utter Englishness of its celebration of the Christmas festival. Again this was a film in which a mood of poetry overpassed the mere sense of episodic description; again there was exceptionally limpid photography – this time by Martin Curtis; and again it was graced by distinctive music from William Alwyn.

After making *Waverley Steps* (1948), a film on Edinburgh, episodic in style and built round a series of individual characters ranging from a barrister through a coal-carter to a visiting Danish seaman, Eldridge directed three features for Grierson at Group Three and then, dogged by increasing ill-health, was forced to confine himself to scriptwriting (at which he was most adept) and regrettably died at the early age of forty-three.

Finally there was that prince of filmic miniaturists, Richard Massingham, whose comedic talent for depicting man's constant fight against the recalcitrant bloodymindedness of inanimate objects found an unexpectedly useful outlet in terms of wartime exhortation.

Massingham, a medico who started by making films in his spare time and at minimal expense, rejoiced in a small canvas; indeed he could say more in a shorter space than anyone except perhaps Len Lye. His first film, a macabre and all-too-recognizable account of a visit to the dentist, was *Tell Me If It Hurts* (1934), which had the signal honour of being banned (if only temporarily) by the British censor on the grounds that it might bring dentistry into disrepute.[1] This was followed by an even more harrowing *exposé* of human kind at its lowest ebb – *And So To Work* (1936) – in which the horrors of rising in the morning were vividly portrayed in all their universal truth.

By this time Massingham had come to the attention of John Grierson, and he was quickly enlisted into the service of the General Post Office.[2] Thereafter he poured out a mass of witty and cogent films, particularly during the War. Of these, the best of which ranged in length from $1\frac{1}{2}$ to 15 minutes, many people still remember with joy his propaganda for the bath with no more than five inches of water, for the avoidance of the sneeze, or for not taking more than the permitted currency abroad. Like Lewis Carroll, Massingham could take a logical

[1] A ruling which, if followed in terms of other professions as well, could have eliminated nearly all the best work of Chaplin, Laurel and Hardy and W. C. Fields from the screen (to name but a few).

[2] For the record, the list of those discovered, or given their first chance, or gainfully employed when they most needed it, by Grierson, included – apart from Massingham – Len Lye, Norman McLaren, Humphrey Jennings, Lotte Reiniger, Alexeieff and Parker and Jean Bhownagary.

situation and move it into a mirror-world of illogicality in which the original meaning was not lost but transmuted. When he wished to advise us (on behalf of the Ministry of Transport) not to dawdle on pedestrian crossings, he involved us in the spectacle of himself settling cosily in a large bed in the middle of the road; while to remind of the need to post early for Christmas, he was to be seen tying knots in everything within reach, including the cat's tail.

With a large, moonlike and amiable face – he acted in many of his own films – he endowed his fortunate audiences with delight as well as instruction. He was less happy on large scale film-work, though his children's feature *To The Rescue* (1952), made in collaboration with Jacques Brunius, had many merits.

At the time of his untimely death in 1955, Henri Langlois of the Cinémathèque Française wrote,

'Il est à la fois Méliès et Vigo . . . et . . . si l'on me demandait quel est le metteur en scène anglais le plus près de Buñuel et de Mack Sennett, je répondrais . . .c'est Massingham.'

Remembering the sinister and comic glory of one of his longer films (18 minutes), *They Travel by Air*, made for BOAC in 1947 and still a classic picture of the papering-over of the miseries of flying with a façade of cocktails and false bonhomie, I think Langlois' estimate may be more than just. That Massingham was by any standard a major film-maker there can in any case be not the slightest doubt.

V

Soon after June 22nd, 1941, Eisenstein got some reels of film out of the vaults and remarked, after showing them to two American visitors, 'We think that it will not be much longer before *Alexander Nevski* will be shown in public cinemas again'. This film, which celebrated the defeat of the Teutonic Knights by the Russians, and for which Eisenstein had received the Order of Lenin from Stalin, had had, of course, to be hastily stuffed away in a cupboard after the signing of the Soviet-Nazi Pact (soon after which Eisenstein found himself producing *Die Walküre* at the Bolshoi).

A similar fate had befallen Herbert Rappoport's *Professor Mamlock* (1938), one of the earliest and perhaps the finest of the films designed to expose the horrors of Nazi anti-semitism, with its memorable sequence showing the eminent surgeon, his operating robe newly defiled with smears of 'Jude!', being apologetically requested to perform an emergency operation on a Nazi general.

In Germany, however, the Ribbentrop-Molotov Pact found no anti-Soviet film worth banning. The priorities at the time were for direct anti-semitic films like Veit Harlan's *Jud Süss* and Hippler's disgusting *Der Ewige Jude*; while at the same time the distinguished and highly popular film star Joachim Gottschalk, who happened to have married a Jewess, was driven by Goebbels to kill her, their children and himself[1]; it is today of little comfort to reflect that Goebbels himself found it convenient to choose a similar ending.

While on this unpleasant subject we may recall a further example of the perils of working in films under the Nazi regime. Herbert Selpin, specially assigned by Goebbels to make the superfilm *Titanic* (anti-British and anti-US propaganda) lost his temper with a colleague owing to the bad behaviour of some naval officers who had been instructed to act as extras in the film. Unfortunately Selpin used very heated words which were regarded as insulting to the Wehrmacht as a whole. Arrested by the SS, he was brought before his employer, Goebbels, who asked for an apology. He refused. Whereupon he was taken to jail and, to quote David Stewart Hull, 'two guards went to Selpin's cell and proceeded to tie his suspenders to the bars, then tied the suspenders round his neck and took the bench away. When the unfortunate man could no longer hold on, he was strangled to death . . . With typical thoroughness Goebbels had the death-scene photographed . . .'[2] For Selpin read Carol Reed, Carné, Pudovkin, or William Wyler, to get the full flavour of the good Doctor's ministrations.

Whatever criticisms one may make of the Stalin regime – and there are plenty, fully justified – its film directors were never caught up in this sort of mindless savagery.

The German invasion of the Soviet Union involved nearly the whole Russian film industry in a vast evacuation to Alma Ata and other places out of reach of the Nazi advance. Here, eventually, full feature production was resumed; here indeed Eisenstein continued with *Ivan Grozny*. But by far the most important film work was that of the newsreel and combat cameramen whose coverage resulted in a number of staggeringly effective historical documents.

---

[1] As early as 1937 the popular musical star, Renate Müller, had been similarly hounded to death.

[2] *Film in the Third Reich*, University of California Press, 1969.

The Defeat of the German Armies near Moscow, completed in early 1942, was one of the most widely shown and most successful propaganda films of the war. In America it was re-titled *Moscow Strikes Back*, with a commentary spoken by the ubiquitous Edward G. Robinson. This type of film, Pudovkin pointed out, 'is fully international and can be fully understood anywhere. The commentator's voice may be translated into any language without disturbing the integrity of impression. The montage of visual images does not require translation . . . The task of the artist working in this form is to find more subtle means of artistic communication of simple propositions as well as of their profound development on the philosophic and pictorial planes.'[1]

Alas! for Pudovkin and alas! for other great documents like *The Siege of Leningrad, Stalingrad, Berlin*, and Dovzhenko's superb actualities of the war in the Ukraine. Immediately after the war, Stalin ordered the making of a series of slanted historical 'reconstructions' of all the main war events, in which his erstwhile allies could be black-guarded and cut down to size while his own omniscience was duly exaggerated.

It is indeed a sad thing to compare *The Battle of Stalingrad* (1950) with the grim and convincing realism of the 1943 report. The same goes for *The Fall of Berlin* (1949) compared with the original *Berlin* (1945). But at least some belated justice was done to the brave cameramen who worked on the earlier films. In the course of his famous 'Secret Speech' in 1956, Khrushchev, among other things, said:

'Let us take, for instance, our historical and military films and some literary creations; they make us feel sick. Their true objective is the propagation of the theme of praising Stalin as a military genius. Let us recall the film *Fall of Berlin*. In it only Stalin acts, issuing orders from a hall in which there are many empty chairs. . . . And where is the Military Command? Where is the Political Bureau? Where is the Government? . . . There is nothing about them in the film. Stalin acts for everybody . . . Everything is shown to the nation in this false light.

'Stalin knew the country and agriculture only from films. And these films had dressed up and beautified the existing situation in agriculture. Many films so pictured collective farm life that the tables groaned beneath the weight of turkeys and geese. Evidently Stalin

[1] *Kino* by Jay Leyda. Pudovkin does not appear to have noted that the translation of the narration can be slanted in directions other than those intended by the original film-makers.

thought that it was actually so . . . The last time he visited the countryside was in January 1928 . . .'[1]

Of the Soviet feature films of the war period little of note has survived, *Ivan Grozny* being *hors concours*. Pudovkin's historical film *Suvorov* was completed during the year of the invasion; it had some fine spectacle and a great performance in the name part by Nikolai Cherkasov-Sergeyev. In 1943 Alexander Zguridi completed his excellent educational documentary *In the Sands of Central Asia*, and by the next year the tide had turned so much toward victory that there appeared a very successful musical, no less, directed by Pyriev and entitled *At 6 pm after the War*.

The feature films directly about the war need not now detain us except for those of Mark Donskoi, whose magnificent Gorky Trilogy had been completed with *My Universities* in 1940. The deep human feeling, the compassion, the understanding of these three films became converted, as the war developed, into a white-hot, almost irrational fury. After a perhaps hastily made film[2] paralleling an episode of the Civil War with the current conflict in which, as in Gorky, he built his story on the experiences of a growing boy, Donskoi made, in 1943, *The Rainbow*, one of the most searing and horrible war films ever made, 'directed', as Jay Leyda remarks, 'with all the anger Donskoi was capable of expressing'. *The Rainbow* is a film of atrocities, of the Germans at their lowest and most bestial; indeed the very heroism of the Ukrainian people in these circumstances becomes almost swamped by the horrors.

This film appalled that brilliant and sensitive critic James Agee; he couldn't take it, and his analysis of why not makes interesting reading today in view of some of the things we now so frequently see on our TV news. Agee queried whether anyone had the right to make this sort of film of bestial cruelties 'unless some sort of attempt is made, in the film, to understand them'. He suggested that 'certain dreadful events . . . are so incalculably rich in the possibilities of moral and aesthetic blackmail that they can never be presented naturally or even undeceitfully, and so had better not be represented at all'. And he added 'When you can make such a picture, or watch it with untroubled approval, some crucially important moral nerve has, I believe, gone dead in you'.

Agee was of course intelligent enough to admit that he had not

[1] Jay Leyda, op. cit.
[2] *How the Steel was Tempered*.

gone through the sort of experiences that this and similar films depicted. It seems to me, though, that the deep moral issue which he felt to be involved was precisely that which modern war instantly destroys. In war today the combatants are involved in a mutual descent into bestiality. To 'win' (laughable word) a war today all ideas of humanity, let alone chivalry, even perhaps of ordinary individual courage, must be abandoned. The finger which presses the atomic button will inevitably be that of a coward.

Resnais finished *Nuit et Brouillard* the year Agee died. It is sad that he never saw it because it does, I am sure, answer his problem. Resnais shows the concentration camps today, empty, shot in colour; and in this framework, using the sickening reality of the documentation left behind by the Nazis, he takes us point by point through the catalogue of horrors and involves us in a universal guilt. It is this that Agee finds lacking in Donskoi's fury.

The Rainbow is also an example of the fact that films about war made during a war tend to be of historical rather than aesthetic interest. When all is over and what remains of our morality emerges from the spin-dryer not clean, but at least less soiled, we have the chance to pause, think, and perhaps make better and more useful films, if only because some sort of perspective has returned.

In the post-war years Stalin's shadow hung menacingly over the film scene, though it is good to note that Donskoi returned to the humanitarian mood again with *A Village Schoolteacher* and a remake of Gorky's *Mother*. Otherwise, sensible directors aimed at subjects as non-committal as possible – the lives of famous musicians, elaborately made puppetry, or records of famous ballets. And it was not until after Stalin's death in 1953 that there began, as we shall see, a little renaissance in Soviet cinema signalled, I suppose, by Kalatozov's *The Cranes Are Flying*.

VI

If it were not so essentially sordid, the story of Goebbels' acquisition, control and eventual destruction of the German film industry would have a certain lunatic grandeur. The method by which the good Doctor (known secretly among film people as Mickey Mouse) tightened the Nazi stranglehold and eliminated the Jewish element is told in detail by David Stewart Hull in *Film in the Third Reich*.[1]

[1] See also *The German Cinema* by Roger Manvell and Heinrich Fraenkel, Dent, 1971.

What interests me most is the extraordinarily *self-defeating* quality of the Nazi propaganda machine. Siegfried Kracauer somewhere pointed out that it was propaganda which tended to consume itself; the more material Goebbels poured onto the flames, the faster was it consumed. The main reason for this must have been that the Nazi philosophy (so-called) was unable to raise itself to the power of a lasting religion. It was, *au fond*, a nonsense; as soon as anyone stopped to think, it was finished. Marxism, on the other hand, has become a real and extremely successful religion; and for this reason the Russians, though living under a totalitarian regime, won the war. In the final event they had something to fight for; the Germans, not. The Germans had to prefer the vainglory of defeat to the vainglory of victory. Thus, from Stalingrad on, the Third Reich went down in a display of masochism the like of which the world had never before seen.

To return to the Nazi cinema, one may get some idea of its 'philosophy' by glancing at a few examples.

Karl Ritter – a film-maker who specialized in Hitler Youth subjects (it is estimated that no less than 6 million kids saw his awful films between 1936 and 1939) – was asked why he ended one of his 'heroic' *jugendfilms* with a situation in which friend and foe perished alike. He replied, 'I want to show German Youth that senseless, sacrificial death has its moral value.' Next question.

In 1936 Goebbels said, 'Because this year has not brought an improvement in criticism of the arts, I forbid once and for all the continuance of criticism in its past form, effective today . . . The critic is to be replaced by the arts editor. The reporting of art should not be concerned with values, but should confine itself to description.' But a year later the head of the Reich Press Association remarked that 'Art criticism is not primarily an aesthetic question, but a political one . . . The old idea that there is good art and bad art must be removed.'

After all this it is not uninteresting to recall what Hitler himself thought about the use of film *before* he handed the German industry over to Goebbels. In 1933, speaking very probably off the record, he said:

'I want to exploit the film as an instrument of propaganda, but in such a way that every theatregoer may be clearly aware that on such and such an occasion he is going to see a political film. It nauseates me when I find political propaganda hidden under the cloak of art. Let it be either art or politics. The subject matter strikes me as immaterial. The artistic effect must be 100%.'[1]

[1] *Film in the Third Reich* by David Stewart Hull.

Finally, let it be noted that the success of all the Nazi propaganda efforts may be measured by the fact that in Germany from 1941 onwards 'to make sure that the viewers remained captive, it was common practice to have the doors of the cinemas locked during the projection of newsreels'.

Out of all this lunacy emerges, appropriately, Goebbels' swan-song – the epic of *Kolberg*. This film was first mooted in 1941 as a historical spectacular. The story was of an episode from the Napoleonic Wars in which the small city of Kolberg held out against all odds in face of the French attacks until finally the brave citizenry were overwhelmed. (Note that as early as 1941 the masochist element was there.) The production was postponed, however, probably in favour of the elaborate, dotty and skilfully made *Adventures of Baron Münch-hausen* (itself a very appropriate subject for the Propaganda Ministry); so that by the time it came up for consideration again it had taken on a new importance for Goebbels. He now saw it not just as a spectacular designed to glorify German patriotism, but rather as a powerful piece of pleading for resistance against invasion; propaganda, in fact, for 'promoting popular resistance should the Army be on the defensive.'[1]

Kolberg was made on a truly gigantic scale. The entire town was reconstructed at Neu-Stettin, the budget was 8½ million marks, and nearly 200,000 persons took part in the production in one capacity or another. 'At a time when every soldier possible was needed on the Eastern Front, Goebbels thought nothing of diverting crucial man-power to his insane project. Although the railroad system was in chaos and people were going hungry because it was impossible to ship food-stuffs into the cities, one hundred railcars of salt somehow found their way to the set to provide the necessary "snow".'[2]

After two years' effort *Kolberg* was completed. With great if unexpected historical *savoir faire* it was premiered at La Rochelle, a city which by that time was completely encircled by the invading Allies. The copy of the film had to be dropped into the town by parachute.

That was in January 1945. Two and a half months later Goebbels screened *Kolberg* to his Staff, and followed it up by a lecture urging them all to play their full part in the coming holocaust. He was apparently dreaming of 'a fine colour film describing the terrible days we are living through', and he urged his hearers to choose the parts they would play. 'I can assure you,' he added, 'that it will be a fine and elevating picture . . . Hold out now, so that a hundred years hence the

[1] David Hull, op. cit. Goebbels in this sense was no fool; he never trusted the army.
[2] op. cit.

audience do not hoot and whistle (*sic*) when you appear on the screen.'
In comparison with Churchill's 'finest hour', this invitation to lie down
in front of the advancing Soviet tanks must surely have lacked a certain
cogency.

Two weeks after this speech Goebbels killed his wife, his children,
and finally himself.

Kolberg was directed by Veit Harlan, the most talented director
of the Hitler epoch. The odiousness of most of his films (which include
Jud Süss) does not alter this fact, though it leads one to reflect that the
use of real talent in an evil cause is worse than the use of mediocrity.
But most of the films of the Nazi period are of interest only to the
historian or the psychopathologist – if even to them. Aesthetically there
is an almost total sterility.

Perhaps the only film-maker to emerge from this period with any
respect was Helmut Käutner. His two best films, *Romance in a Minor
Key* and *Die Grosse Freiheit* (the latter also known as *La Paloma*), were
roundly hated by Goebbels who, in fact, banned the latter, a film
supposed to be about German sailors in the port of Hamburg but
cunningly switched by Käutner into a simple waterside-cum-nightclub
romance. Shot in very delicate colour, and directed with perception,
tenderness and absolutely no *schmaltz*, this was an extraordinary film
to have come out of Nazi Germany in 1944. It is indeed difficult to
understand how Käutner survived, as his work stood for everything
Goebbels hated and feared – respect for the individual, the splendours
and miseries of human love, and the reality of psychological crises in
people's lives; it was probably because Käutner was wise enough to
mute the expression of his ideas, while Goebbels was too preoccupied
with rehearsals for *Götterdämmerung* to give his full attention to
these subversive suggestions.

VII

With Germany split in two after the war, and in ruins, it was
bound to be some time before anything like a really creative cinema
would emerge, whether in the West or the East sections. Meantime all
film people were screened and denazified or otherwise, and a period of
drab confusion set in.

The situation in Japan was, fortunately, less depressing. The film directors there fell into two categories – those who went along with the militarist regime, and those who (like the almost solitary Käutner in Germany) did their best to keep away from it. No one anywhere, in wartime, can do so entirely, but a look at the pattern of Japanese war productions shows that the best directors like Mizoguchi, Ozu and Yamamoto only went in for direct war propaganda when forced to. The real sabre-rattling stuff was done by others. The situation was made easier for the dissidents in that part of the military government's policy was the glorification of home and family. Add to this the infinite possibilities of the very popular historical films, and it can be seen that even when someone like Mizoguchi was 'collared and made to create yet another version of the Kabuki perennial, this one all for the war effort and called *The Loyal Forty-Seven Ronin of the Genroku Era*'[1] he still managed largely to avoid contemporary comments.

The difference between Japan and Germany during the war was that in Japan creative freedom persisted, whereas in Germany it was almost entirely stifled. Mizoguchi's film of the Meiji period, *The Story of the Last Chrysanthemum*; Ozu's *There was a Father*, a tender story of a family relationship which entirely ignored the war; Yamamoto's *Horse*, a child-plus-animal tearjerker with semi-documentary motivations; Yoshimura's comedy *South Wind*; Gosho's *New Snow*, in which he 'took a script which was intended to be . . . about a soldier giving up his love for the greater love of his country, and turned it into a nicely sentimental melodrama which only happened to occur in wartime'[2]; all these preserved a sense of dignity, truth and sincerity despite any other war-work they may – as with Yamamoto's documentary-style *The War at Sea from Hawaii to Malaya* – have been pressurised into undertaking.

Thus in July 1945, though much of Japan's exhibition system was in physical ruins, though her studios, more or less undamaged, were prevented from operating properly by the Occupying Power, the creative flame remained unextinguished. Not even MacArthur could dowse it.

All this must be something to do with a deep-rooted and very ancient culture. During the war both Germans and Japanese behaved with barbarous, unforgivable savagery; but the German heritage went under almost completely with the Nazis, and mindlessness prevailed. The Japanese traditions withstood all onslaughts in a manner which we in the West may find hard to understand; the dichotomy of Beethoven and Himmler is difficult enough, but what is one to think when even

---

[1] Donald Richie, *The Japanese Movie*, Ward Lock, 1966.
[2] Richie, op. cit.

today Japan's most distinguished writer, Yukio Mishima, commits public harakiri in the most gruesome manner?

Meantime let us note that it was during World War II that Akira Kurosawa made his first film. *Sanshiro Sugata* (1943) was the story of a Judo champion. That this film established Kurosawa's mastery as a film-maker is undoubted; but it is unfortunate that he made a sequel to it, which according to Richie, was 'nothing but a piece of jingoistic hack work'. Kurosawa, like Yamamoto whose pupil he was, had had to give in to the authorities. But only this one time. By 1945 he had completed *Walkers on the Tiger's Tail* in which he had the boldness to introduce a modern comic into an old Kabuki story, and which also had the distinction of being banned by the MacArthur regime, which also confiscated the negative of Kon Ichikawa's picture *A Girl at Dojo Temple*.

At the end of the Second World War, then, virtually no one in the West had ever heard of Japanese cinema other than as a big industry with a vast output regarded as uninteresting to Occidentals as that of India.

In the twenty-five years which were to come there were to be many revelations, not only from Japan but also from India, Ceylon, and Egypt; while in America and Europe, out of the atomic dust of war, was to emerge an era of creative activity the like of which the motion picture had never known.

SIGNPOST - 1945

THE YEAR OF 'ROME – OPEN CITY'

IN ITALY

Francesco De Robertis makes *La Vita Semplice*, and Vittorio De Sica *La Porta del Cielo*. Luigi Zampa makes *Un Americano in Vacanza*. Both Rossellini and De Sica are preparing masterpieces – the former *Paisa* and the latter *Sciuscia*.

Mussolini and his mistress are executed by partisans two days before Hitler and Eva Braun commit suicide in Berlin.

The Allied Forces having reached Bologna and the Po, the Germans in Italy surrender.

Alcide De Gasperi forms a coalition government.

Ezra Pound is arrested by the Americans at Rapallo and held in custody pending a trial for treason.

IN FRANCE

Robert Bresson completes *Les Dames du Bois de Boulogne* with a distinguished cast including Maria Casarès; Jacques Becker makes *Falbalas*; and Christian-Jaque directs *Boule de Suif*. On the documentary side Henri Cartier-Bresson, released from a prison camp and working with US Army cameramen, makes *Le Retour*; Eli Lotar shoots his slum film *Aubervilliers*; Georges Rouquier is working on *Farrebique*; and René Clément is preparing his actuality-feature film *La Bataille du Rail*.

France becomes one of the four Occupying Powers of Germany.

Despite a swing to the Left in the Constituent Assembly, De Gaulle becomes President; and his visit to Washington ameliorates Franco-American relations.

Laval is executed, but Marshal Pétain's death sentence is commuted to life imprisonment.

French women are given the vote.

As well as *Huis Clos*, Sartre publishes his *Les Chemins de la Liberté* (*L'Age de Raison* and *Le Sursis*).

Jean Genet is completing his *Le Miracle de la Rose*.

Olivier Messiaen composes his *Harawi*, for soprano and piano.

Picasso states that 'painting . . . is an instrument of war for attack and defence against the enemy'.

Paul Valéry dies of throat cancer.

IN BRITAIN

Anthony Asquith directs *The Way to the Stars*, and David Lean makes Noël Coward's *Blithe Spirit* under the author's supervision. Gabriel Pascal completes his unprecedentedly expensive *Caesar and Cleopatra* starring Vivien Leigh and Claude Rains. From the Ealing Studios comes Robert Hamer's *Pink String and Sealing Wax*, together with that now famous compendium of ghost stories, *Dead of Night*. Sidney Gilliat and Frank Launder make *The Rake's Progress*, with Rex Harrison; and from the Crown Film Unit comes Humphrey Jennings' *Diary for Timothy* with a narration written by E. M. Forster.

Winston Churchill attends the Yalta Conference with Roosevelt and Stalin; after Roosevelt's death he goes with Attlee to Potsdam for the meeting with Truman and Stalin.

At the General Election, Labour is returned with a large majority.

Family Allowances are introduced.

At Sadler's Wells the première takes place of Benjamin Britten's opera *Peter Grimes*.

Henry Moore produces his *Family Group* and Stanley Spencer paints his Resurrection Series.

Ronald Duncan's *This Way to the Tomb* is staged for the first time.

George Orwell publishes *Animal Farm*, and Evelyn Waugh *Brideshead Revisited*. Other books to appear include Henry Green's *Loving*, Rex Warner's *Poems and Contradictions*, Arthur Koestler's *The Yogi and the Commissar*, Cyril Connolly's *The Condemned Playground* and H. G. Wells' *Mind at the End of its Tether*.

The deaths of Lloyd George and Charles Williams are made known.

IN RUSSIA

The superb on-the-spot wartime actuality filming of the conflict is climaxed by Dovzhenko's *Victory in the Ukraine* and by *Berlin*, a film of the fall of that city made by Yuli Raizman with the assistance of some forty-five combat cameramen (one of whom is Roman Karmen). Mark Donskoi completes *Unconquered*, and Kozintsev and Trauberg make their last film together, *Plain People* which, however, will be banned from distribution until 1956. Meanwhile Eisenstein, having completed *Ivan the Terrible, Part I* two days before the New Year, is hard at work on *Part II*, completed in 1946 but not allowed to be shown until 1958, ten years after his death.

> The Soviet Army sweeps on to Berlin where Von Keitel surrenders to Zhukov.
> After the dropping of the Atom bomb the USSR declares war on Japan.
> Dmitri Shostakovitch is completing his Ninth Symphony, and Serge Prokoviev is nearly at the end of the composition of his opera *War and Peace*.

IN JAPAN

As a result of the heavy bombing of cities and of the action of the Occupying Powers, film production falls to an all-time low. More than fifty per cent of cinemas have been destroyed, though most of the studios are intact. Akira Kurosawa's *Walkers on the Tiger's Tail*, based on a famous Kabuki play, is banned for containing 'feudal remnants' and will not be issued until the end of the Occupation in 1953. Kon Ichikawa's *A Girl at Dojo Temple* is also banned.

> At Kyushu the Imperial Fleet is defeated by the Americans.
> After fire raids on Tokyo and the dropping of atom bombs on Hiroshima and Nagasaki, the Government, on orders from the Emperor himself, surrenders unconditionally.
> The Allied Control Commission proscribes Shintoism.

IN THE UNITED STATES

The end of the War coincides with the release of John Ford's *They Were Expendable*, William Wellman's *The Story of G.I. Joe*, and Raoul Walsh's *Objective Burma*, in which Errol Flynn is seen to defeat the Japanese single-handed and without help from the Grand Alliance. John Huston follows the searing actualities of *The Battle of San Pietro* with his equally searing film on men suffering psychologically from combat shock, *Let There Be Light* – a film which is instantly and in panic banned by the military authorities who commissioned it. Louis de Rochemont produces his documentary-style feature on espionage, *The House on 92nd Street*, directed by

Henry Hathaway. Other than the War, dramatic subjects include Joan Crawford in *Mildred Pierce*, directed by Michael Curtiz; Ingrid Bergman and Gregory Peck skilfully teamed by Hitchcock in *Spellbound*; Ray Milland in Billy Wilder's nightmare study of alcoholism, *The Lost Weekend*; Renoir's uneasy study of poverty in *The Southerner*; and Fritz Lang's *Scarlet Street* repeats, with Edward G. Robinson and Joan Bennett, the sad viciousness of *The Woman in the Window*. Comedies are scarcer on the ground; but Mitchell Leisen directs a Pygmalion story in *Kitty* with Paulette Goddard, George Marshall concocts some clever parodies of Hollywood styles in *Murder He Says*, and Danny Kaye continues his series for Sam Goldwyn with his *doppelgänger* appearances in *Wonder Man*. Musicals include *Yolanda and the Thief*, by Minnelli and starring Fred Astaire; Gene Kelly and George Sidney's *Anchors Aweigh*; Irving Rapper's *Rhapsody in Blue*, built round the story of George Gershwin, and Charles Vidor's appalling *A Song to Remember*, being the screen biography of a musician called Showpan. Horror films unconnected with the War are frequent; the best are two Val Lewton productions – a version of the Burke and Hare story, *The Body Snatcher*, and Mark Robson's frightening *Isle of the Dead*; and Albert Lewin's stylish *The Picture of Dorian Gray*.

Two months before his death President Roosevelt consults with Stalin and Churchill at Yalta.

Later his successor President Truman attends the Potsdam Conference with the same characters, plus Clement Attlee.

After successful tests at Almagordo in New Mexico, two atom bombs are dropped on Hiroshima and Nagasaki, thus bringing the Japanese war to a rapid and ghastly conclusion – the European war having already ended with Jodl's capitulation to Eisenhower.

San Francisco is the venue of the first United Nations Conference.

President Truman cancels Lend Lease. Later he sends General Marshall to China in an attempt to mediate between the rival factions of Chiang Kai-shek and Mao Tse-tung.

Publications include Sinclair Lewis' *Cass Timberlane*, Robert Frost's *A Masque of Reason*, Henry Miller's *The Air-Conditioned Nightmare*, Richard Wright's *Black Boy*, Scott Fitzgerald's posthumous *The Crack Up* and, more successful (financially at least) than all these, Kathleen Winsor's *Forever Amber*.

Tennessee Williams' play *The Glass Menagerie* is produced and acclaimed.

For his Sextet, Charlie Parker creates his *Groovin' High* in 'transitional jazz' style.

Alexander Calder creates his mobile *Red Pyramid*.

Theodore Dreiser dies.

CHAPTER 5

1945 - 1960

NEO-REALISM, WITCH HUNTS AND WIDE SCREENS

I

As World War II ended, few people fully realized that the world was falling under the domination of two new imperialist superpowers, the United States and the Soviet Union. The former appeared, to begin with, as the more reactionary of the two, but as time went on it was the USSR which (to the despair of the left wing nearly everywhere in the world) moved inexorably in the direction of monolithic fascism. In any case the world had to learn to live under the rivalry of these two powers, which soon took the precaution of pre-empting space elsewhere in the solar system against careless button-pressing. In the meantime, with Europe at last liberated from the Nazi horror, a generous humanitarianism became observable in the work of most film-makers; they had at last the chance to draw the true perspectives of war.

This world of postwar film-making was, I suppose, inaugurated by Roberto Rossellini's *Rome – Open City* (1945), a film about Italian resistance to the German Occupation in which Catholics and Communists made common cause, and which he shot in part under the noses of the Nazis. This film had a big success in the USA and its purchaser, Rod Geiger, made enough profit to return to Italy with finance for the production of Rossellini's second and perhaps most important film, *Paisa* (American title *Paisan*). This, together with De Sica's *Shoeshine*, launched the influential if comparatively short-lived Neo-Realist movement.

The term 'neo-realism' had in fact been applied as early as 1942 to Visconti's *Ossessione*, a powerful screen version of James Cain's novel *The Postman Always Rings Twice*; but in most people's minds the word is associated with the group of films made just after the war by Rossellini, De Sica, Visconti himself, Lattuada, De Santis, Zampa and a few others.

Outwardly most of these films were stories of despair, yet such was the human sympathy with which they were made, so universally recognizable in their suffering were the people who appeared in them, so convincing was the realism with which they were presented, that they were noted more for their celebration of the imperishability of the human spirit than for the grimness of their subject matter.

Contrary to general belief this was not due entirely to the absence of actors. The realism of *Rome – Open City* was not adversely affected by the use of Anna Magnani and Aldo Fabrizi, among others, in the cast; and even in *Paisa* at least four of the cast were amateur actors brought over from America by Geiger. The new realism was something more than this – a further exploration perhaps of the paths opened up by Renoir in *La Grande Illusion* and even by John Ford in *The Grapes of Wrath*.

Rossellini and De Sica had, however, a tougher philosophy than the others; they showed us the wounds before they had been dis-infected or bandaged; and they showed us how Western society can be as callous and cruel to itself as an occupying army. They celebrated, perhaps as never before in cinema (unless by Chaplin) the fact that the human spirit in all circumstances, and never more so than when tragically defeated, remains triumphant – something which can be divined even in the tragic sadness of the last shot of *Bicycle Thieves* as the small boy looks up at his crushed and defeated father.

Paisa occupied a unique position in the neo-realist canon, firstly because of its episodic construction, and secondly because of the tremendous impact it had on audiences when it was first released. That perceptive English critic Richard Winnington felt that it would 'stand as one of the few great comments on the Second World War to be made in the contemporary cinema'; and I note that I myself wrote that '*Paisa* may well prove to be not only the climax of documentary development but also an influence on all types of film production as profound and far-reaching as that of *Potemkin*'.[1]

In retrospect this seems a bit sweeping. Today I would rather say that after *Paisa*, *Shoeshine*, *Germany Year Zero* and *Bicycle Thieves*, cinema could never be the same again. The neo-realist approach became a permanent part of the film-makers' equipment. Its influence can be seen, for instance, in French cinema from Clément, Cayatte and Clouzot to Godard and Truffaut; its influence, direct or indirect, on Japanese directors like Kinoshita, Ichikawa and Oshima must have

[1] I am indebted for the reminder of these two quotations to Ian Johnson's admirable and comprehensive study of *Paisa* in *Films and Filming*, February 1966.

been considerable; and it may well be that the neo-realist example encouraged Satyajit Ray when he embarked on *Pather Panchali.*

The story of *Paisa* is the story of the relations between Italians, British, Americans and Germans during the Allied invasion of Italy. It begins in the extreme South and passes through Naples, Rome, Florence and an unidentified monastery until it arrives at its tragic finale in the riverine marshes of the North. Each episode is separate and self-contained. But all the episodes add up to one accurate sum of human experience, a sum compounded, as Ian Johnson points out,[1] from the six evils of war – injustice, human misery, degradation, universality of suffering, insensitivity through familiarity, and futility.

Uneven in quality, both as regards direction and acting, rough in technique, especially in the final episode which is at times confusing in continuity, *Paisa* nevertheless maintains this unity; it is indeed worth noting in passing that Rossellini had already discovered that a straight cut would just as easily put across a time lapse as a dissolve or a symbolic montage of spring and winter symbols. He had also discovered the alarming emphasis to be achieved by using a wrenching cut to an extreme long shot instead of an expected close-up.

The first episode of *Paisa* is savagely ironic. A peasant girl saves an American platoon from a German ambush by sacrificing her own life. But the Americans think she was killed while trying to betray them. What one remembers most from this is the horrifying but innocent expressions on the faces of some of the GIs. Strangers in a strange land; their incomprehension makes it seem like a Zoo. The second episode takes place in the cruel and hideous confusion of post-liberation Naples and is about the dispossessed of this world, a negro GI and a small boy who steals his boots while he is drunk. Eventually the negro sees the small boy in the street and pursues him to his 'home', a hellhole of a slum crammed with human detritus which makes his own hovel back home seem like a palace.

The third episode – and the weakest – concerns a melodramatic confrontation between a young American officer and a prostitute in Rome. His indifference to her charms is due, as he doesn't hesitate to tell her, to his memories of the beautiful pure girl who welcomed him when the forces of liberation arrived; and guess who that girl was? The sequence – except for some of the bedroom scene – is stiffly directed, and the irony is somehow too obvious to make its point; it would have fitted better into *If I Had a Million.*

Fourthly, we see the frantic and frightening efforts of an American

[1] op. cit.

nurse to cross a Florence in the throes of savage street-fighting in order to get to her Italian lover who is in the Resistance. The apparently empty menace of the Florentine streets and squares as she dodges, waits, hides, dashes desperately forward, is brilliantly projected. Even more so is the almost casual life of others in crisis which she encounters in passing. Then comes the denouement, or rather the non-denouement; casually again, from a wounded partisan, she learns that her lover is dead.

The fifth episode has a purity and beauty of which the film, at this stage, is badly in need. Three US Army chaplains, armed with provisions, billet themselves in a Franciscan monastery; but the joy of the newly liberated monks, and their anticipation of their first really good meal for many months, turns to sorrow when they learn that of the three chaplains only one is a Catholic, and that, worse, the other two are respectively a Protestant and a Jew.

In penance for this situation the monks must refuse the meal, and the three Americans dine alone. There is a charming sadness about all this which arises from the fact that the warmest relationships have developed between all concerned before the discovery of the religious divergences. Here Rossellini creates a marvellous atmosphere of trusting and civilized kindness and has the sensitivity, when the sad discovery is made, to retain the sense of loving, so that the very irony of the situation takes on the quality of a benediction. (It is worth noting, by the way, that throughout *Paisa* all the characters speak their own native language plus as much of other languages as they happen to know. In real life there is no dubbing, and Rossellini leans quite heavily on this fact.)

After this interlude comes the final and horrifying episode among the Northern marshes of the Po. American Special Service men have joined a group of Italian partisans. They are all surrounded by the Germans. They manage to obtain some sorely needed food from a local peasant family who, when the Germans discover this, are promptly slaughtered, with the exception of one small baby which is left on the midden howling for its mother – a spiritual sibling of that Shanghai baby on the deserted station which so shocked everyone (we were more easily shockable then) in the press photographs of the Japanese invasion of China in 1936. Meantime the British try to help by bombing the Nazis, but one of the planes is shot down, and the crew, parachuting, join the partisans and the Americans. Too late. The end of the film, which is so near the end of local hostilities and of the whole European war, is disaster, a mass execution. The Germans move in; and their victims, tied hand and foot, are pushed casually into the river. After a while – and Rossellini makes us wait – there are no more ripples left on the fast flowing waters . . .

Paisa is a very uneven film. Rossellini was clearly not always at ease with his imported 'actors'; sometimes, as in the Rome and Naples episodes, he lapses into a kind of sentimentality. Indeed the late Robert Warshow – a critic somewhat neglected on the European side of the Atlantic – went so far as to accuse Rossellini of rejecting ideas as well as principles, and adduces one of the best sequences in the film to support this view:

'In the Florentine episode, there is a moment when a group of partisans captures two Fascist snipers. A confused knot of men bursts around a corner into the sunny street and moves rapidly toward the camera, growing larger and clearer. One man is dragged by the shoulders, kicking and struggling; another, erect, is propelled by blows that force him to move ahead as if he were part of the group, rather than its object, and shared the general desire to bring matters to a quick conclusion. Just in front of the camera, the men are thrown to the ground and left for a moment inside a small circle, the camera pointing downward at their backs. One of them cries, "I don't want to die!" There is a burst of machine gun fire and the scene is over.

'The scene moves so rapidly that the action is always one moment ahead of the spectator's understanding. And the camera itself remains neutral, waiting passively for the action to come toward it and simply recording as much of the action as possible, with no opportunity for the variation of tempo and the active selection of detail that might be used to interpret the scene; visually, the scene remains on the same level of intensity from beginning to end, except for the increasing size and clarity of the objects as they approach the camera – and this has the effect of a "natural" rather than an interpretive variation.'

Up to this point it seems to me that Warshow has made quite a brilliant analysis of Rossellini's technique, with all its breathless tension of reality. We are meant to participate in the scene with the swift unwillingness with which we might participate in an automobile accident not of our own making. But Warshow goes on to say:

'The speed of the action combined with the neutrality of the camera tends to exclude the possibility of reflection and thus to divorce the events from all questions of opinion. The political and moral distinctions between the snipers and their captors do not appear . . . and the spectator is given no opportunity to assent to the killing. Thus the scene derives its power precisely from the fact that it is not cushioned in ideas: events seem to develop according to their own laws and take no account of how one might – or "should" – feel about them.'

In all this Warshow shows what must be an element of approval as well as an element of doubt. He makes the excellent point that 'American culture demands victory' while the Italian 'neither requires nor dreams of victory . . . From this hopelessness – too inactive to be called despair – Rossellini gains his greatest virtue as an artist: the feeling for particularity.'

But in pursuing this idea further he concludes that Rossellini 'has no intellectual defences, and when he tries to go *beyond the passive representation of experience* (my italics) he falls at once into the grossest sentimentality and falsehood' – of which the monastery sequence is, in his opinion, the most dishonest example. And, curiously enough, he goes on to accuse both Rossellini and De Sica of a tenderness for the Church when, as we all know, it was the Church as much as the politicians which set out to make life impossible for the Neo-Realists.

I think therefore that Warshow, whose analysis of the basic quality of *Paisa* is probably the best ever written, did at this point, perhaps because of an acute *political* consciousness,[1] fail to see what Rossellini was finally up to. What struck me most when I first saw the film was that I had, in a sense, been trapped by the *apparent* use of the camera as a passive recorder of newsreel-like events. It was the sudden realization that the apparent passivity was in fact a calculated representation of active truth which hit one so hard. The hard truths of war are as casual as the hard truths of social cruelty and injustice.

No, it is when Rossellini's episodes lose the aspect of casual truth *and are felt to be contrived* that the film weakens. In this sense I agree with Warshow in what he says about the Naples and Rome sequences:

'In Naples it is not enough that the Negro and the Italian child are both suffering; it must be shown that *even* an American Negro is shamed before Italian misery. In Rome, it is not enough that the prostitute and the soldier are both unhappy; the prostitute must be

[1] Lionel Trilling described him as 'a highly politicalised intellectual'.

the *very same girl* that he remembers from his first days in Rome and has looked for in vain; and at the end we must see him throw away her address with a sneer . . .'[1]

But the monastery sequence, which Warshow so disliked, seems to me to be something different and something the film terribly needs at that stage – a pause, a change of viewpoint, perhaps even the beginning of a call to reason. The impact of war is here shown significantly enough in the appearance of extra rations of food. The American men of God bring symbols of their affluent society to members of another society whose vows, in theory at least, make such luxuries of minor or of no importance. The fact that the monks would have eaten the goodies with great pleasure had they not felt impelled to do penance is ironical in a mild, pleasant, almost charming sense.

It may be worth remembering here that both the Americans and the British took offence at some of the incidents in *Paisa*. The British thought Rossellini was insulting them and sucking up to the Americans when he depicted two British officers, armed with binoculars, discussing the architectural beauties of Florence instead of paying attention to the street battles, or when, in the final sequence, the American OSS man says to the RAF officer, 'These people (the partisans) are not fighting for the British Empire, they are fighting for their lives.' Personally I felt it an almost refreshing surprise to find someone bold enough at that time to look at the British without that idolatry which they had hitherto expected and were, in fact, never again to enjoy. One might feel the same about the implied rebuke to the three American padres,[2] or about the implication of callousness on the part of the young officer in the Rome sequence. Perhaps Warshow may in this case have been nearer the mark when he suggested that *Paisa* represents 'the fantasies of the eternally defeated as he tries anxiously to read his fate in the countenance of a new master'.

Nevertheless *Paisa*, for all its faults, represents, with *Bicycle Thieves* and *Shoeshine*, the essence of the neo-realist movement. The unity from diversity here achieved has seldom been equalled in cinema, except perhaps in the also episodic *Intolerance* where, however, the central theme was clearer and less intractable.

De Sica's *Bicycle Thieves* is, as far as construction is concerned, a complete contrast to *Paisa*. The plot is elaborated, worked out, fictionalized almost, like any studio script; written by Zavattini, the

[1] All Warshow quotations are from *The Immediate Experience*, Doubleday, 1962.
[2] Better described by Pietrangeli, in *La Revue du Cinéma*, May 1948, as 'une absurde mais sublime aspiration à une paix inaccessible'.

eminence grise not only of neo-realism but of most of Italian cinema, and today the proponent of the new theory of Free Cine-Journals, it was in a sense the climax of the neo-realist movement.

Bicycle Thieves is said to have dated, to be felt now to be old-fashioned in style as well as outlook. I find this difficult to accept. When someone alleges that 'the protest which the film makes is exaggerated from a single (!) character and argued badly in abstraction', or that the final sequence (in which the father tries to steal the bicycle) 'has a symbolic weight totally unsuited to it'[1] I am seized of a profound irritability. This is an elaborately scripted film, designed in terms of the utmost realism and concerned with the vain struggle of the individual against society. This struggle, as depicted by De Sica, is only incidentally about the social, political and economic situation in Italy in the late 1940s; it is really about universal injustice, which is found wherever civilization – defined as the organization of society into industrial and urban complexes – exists. It is a communist as well as a capitalist symptom. It is tragic and almost inevitable; and it is especially tragic because no single individual has willed it. What De Sica and Zavattini so triumphantly brought off in *Bicycle Thieves* was to cause our intimate participation in a minor incident (hardly worth three lines in a local paper) which to those concerned was tragic on a major scale. The man and his son, whose predicament is from moment to moment predictable, inescapable, are bound together by fate and society in bonds of affection which one desperately hopes will not, cannot be severed. It is in the very last sequence of the film, when the man, beaten physically and morally, humiliated, cold, wet, hungry, hopeless, lets his will go and begins to weep – it is in this sequence that De Sica tracks us back with him along the street and, dipping the camera to the small boy, indicates perhaps – and how much we wish for certain – that with a look, a pressure of the small hand, he may be able to bring back at least the first stirrings of human dignity.

All the episodes in the film are of course very carefully planned, calculated and placed. The basic theme is simple. Man out of work. Man gets job. Man redeems bike from pawn. Bike stolen. Man searches. Man becomes demoralized. Man runs himself into the ground.

It is what Zavattini has done to the theme that is important. The multifarious incidents are casual, though not quite in the same sense

---

[1] In quoting these extracts from 'The Destruction of Neo-Realism', by Kevin Gough Yates (*Films and Filming*, Sept 1970) let me add that the article as a whole gives an excellent account (long overdue) of the eventually successful campaign run by the authorities, political and religious, against the Neo-Realists – to the point at which finance for their films became very difficult to obtain.

as in *Paisa*, where Rossellini's camera appears to be eavesdropping; here we are more directly involved. The incidents, a conglomeration of the trivialities of a great city, have been fitted together into a pattern of human defeat. Add to this the achievement of De Sica – himself an actor *par excellence* – in eliminating from the film any feeling of acting, and you have something which moves beyond mere realism (neo- or otherwise) into genuine tragedy or, as Richard Winnington put it, 'the small tragedy of poverty' which is 'happening daily in every city in the world, making and moulding the faces and figures of the poor'.[1]

That is why *Bicycle Thieves* doesn't date, and why, when I showed it to my students in India they recognized and understood it at once, for it could have taken place in Bombay, Calcutta or a hundred other cities. Its world is the same world as that of Apu or of Siddhartha in *The Adversary*.

As I have said, De Sica's 'casualness' is more brutally involving than Rossellini's. Yet the feeling of 'being there' that he achieves must in fact have involved every sort of artifice. If you think, for instance, of the sequence in which the man and his son track down the thief in a slum alley and are immediately surrounded, buffeted and chased off by a hostile crowd, what time the thief has a convenient epileptic fit, you will realize that this must have been quite a major operation involving crowd organization, rehearsals and so on. Yet on the screen it is utterly convincing, and the episode, epilepsy and all, which appears rather silly and overdone in cold print, becomes a shared experience and, to quote Winnington again, 'the miracle of the movie camera has brought us close into the feelings and lives of people whose validity we never question and whom we will never forget'.

Bicycle Thieves is certainly unforgettable. The rainstorm; the conflict when the father, desperate, hits his son and the son, desperate, cuts off communication; the scene in the church during the charity 'do'; all these, and others, become part of us, and for good.

Equally dateless is De Sica's *Shoeshine* (*Sciuscia*), which in fact preceded *Bicycle Thieves* by two years, but which I have reserved until now as a kind of archetypal example of the world's cruelty and indifference to children, so well and strikingly dealt with by a large number of film directors. It was of *Shoeshine* that James Agee wrote:

'This is one of the few fully alive, fully rational films ever made. And one of the beauties of it is that its best intelligence seems to have operated chiefly on an instinctual level, forcing the men who made the

[1] *The Cinema*, *1950*, Pelican Books.

film . . . to do better than the best their talents alone might promise them and better, I imagine, than they planned or foresaw. I suspect that all they intended in this story of two street boys who are caught almost by accident into the corrective machinery of the state, and are destroyed, was an effective work of protest, a work of social art; and that it was more out of the aroused natural honesty of their souls, and their complete devotion to their subject, that they went so much deeper. *Shoeshine* is all that a work of social art ought to be, would have to be to have any worth whatever, and almost never is. It is remarkably perceptive and compassionate in its study of authority and of those who embody, serve it, and suffer in and under it. It is also the rarest thing in contemporary art – a true tragedy.'[1]

It is clear that Agee is here using the word tragedy in the strict Aristotelian sense, and correctly. Yet I have often heard people complain that *Shoeshine* is too melodramatic. This is a criticism which can be directed against many films about children. The fact is that children and their emotions *are* melodramatic; physical and psychological cruelty to children *is* melodramatic; our reaction to this *is* melodramatic; and what's wrong anyway with melodrama in the Aristotelian or any other sense?[2]

The tragedy in *Shoeshine* is that what happens is nobody's precise fault: two innocent young boys are destroyed – or caused to destroy each other – by a cumulation of small actions (or inactions) involving indifference, inefficiency, pusillanimity, stupidity, laziness, misunderstanding and selfishness.

Giuseppe and Pasquale have one glorious and romantic ambition – to own a horse of their very own; they even know the very horse they want. Note that their ambition is really great and glorious – the ambition of the child who still believes that dreams *can* come true, but is yet practical enough not to ask for the sun. What they earn as shoeshine boys can, of course, never be enough. But in trying to earn more they become unknowingly involved in the black market. Seized by the police, they refuse to implicate their friends and are sent to a gaol for young persons.

Thus they become the victims of a disorganized and demoralized society which is trying to recover not merely from economic and social dislocations, but also from the traumas of Fascism, of German occupation, and of a disruptive liberation. They have no chance.

[1] *Agee on Film*, Peter Owen, 1963.

[2] In another perceptive passage Agee compares De Sica's 'creative generosity' with that of Verdi – a melodramatic genius if ever there was one.

With mounting horror and pity we watch their doom. The official who consigns them to prison is distraught by overwork, by an avalanche of insoluble problems. The lawyer who is supposed to defend them only acts, reluctantly, from a sense of duty. The prison officers are venial or hypocritical. The innocent candour of these boys (and of how many others?) is helpless against the cynicism, the egoism and dishonesty of the adult world.

The whole thing is brilliantly codified in the sequence where a group of Holy Fathers come to give a film show to the 'delinquents'. Out of the mass of children De Sica picks not only Pasquale and Giuseppe but others as well, notably a boy with acute tuberculosis who has a small ambition – to see the ocean – and who is about to do so at secondhand, thanks to the cinema. And what happens? The projector catches fire, there is uproar, the authorities rush around and the Holy Fathers flap about like ineffectual crows . . .

Shoeshine comes to an end with a dramatic climax so immense, so almost ridiculous in its symbolic and actual horror that Agee's analysis is seen to be the only accurate explanation of how De Sica came to conceive it. The boys are led to believe that the one has betrayed the other. By night, in a romantic landscape, among trees and running water, Pasquale kills his friend.

Then comes a cry of appalling anguish – a cry echoing the anguish of all children who have been neglected, hurt, or murdered – and this cry mingles with the sound of the hoofs of the horse they both loved as it canters into the night. It is one of *the* most unforgettable moments in all cinema.[1]

Shoeshine has some faults, all forgivable. Some of the sequences are too sketchy, or insufficiently worked out. At times the motivations are not absolutely clear, not least in the events leading to the final sequence. But the total effect and message of the film is so clear, so bright, so generous, that we are purged as we should be by the tragedy.

Almost simultaneously with *Shoeshine*, Rossellini too was making a film about a tragedy of childhood. *Germany Year Zero* (dedicated to the memory of his own son) was, however, set not in liberated Italy but in the smashed ruins of a defeated Berlin – a stinking monument to the insanity of all the general staffs of all the participants in the war and, in particular, to the psychopathology of Hitler, Goebbels and Himmler.

Germany Year Zero is a puzzling and sometimes unsatisfactory

---

[1] The anguish of this final scene is of course anticipated in the ending of *The Children Are Watching Us*, where De Sica has the child vanishing in misery down long empty corridors; and it was to be heard again later at the end of Clément's *Les Jeux Interdits*.

film. It succeeds best when Rossellini's horror at the negative nightmare of the ruined city is overpassed by a concentration of sympathy for his boy-hero (if hero is the word) Edmund. Even so, by stressing the boy's solitude and loneliness he tends also to isolate him from the realities of Berlin, isolate him also in the sense that we, the spectators, wonder if we are supposed to be examining him as a specimen in the laboratory. The effect is schizophrenic, and it is a tribute to Rossellini's genius as a director that despite all this much of the film is compulsively moving.

Berlin, and indeed the Ruhr, was in the immediate post-surrender period an area which could not but appal the visitor. The extent of the destruction, the faint sweet smell of death everywhere, the grey pinched-looking people living in the nightmare of nothingness which was all that was left of the 'thousand years' Third Reich – all this Rossellini puts across with remarkable perception. It is within this cage of victims that Edmund wanders.

He lives in a tenement with his family, which consists of an aged father, sick, complaining, reminiscing about the Good Old Days; a sister who has found out the simple method of obtaining cigarettes, chocolates etc from the occupying forces; and a lay-about elder brother who, as an ex-Nazi, prefers to remain gloomily and lazily in hiding.[1] They are all hungry.

Edmund learns to steal food or, if not food, money; the atmosphere in which he is trying to live is well established early in the film when we see in a street a large crowd whose object of interest is, we learn as the camera approaches, a dead horse. Food! The boy moves steadily into the world of black market and corruption. He runs into an ex-schoolmaster of his, who turns out to be a shady queer with a house full of sinister characters including an epicene acrobat walking around on his (or her) hands. As a result of this connection, Edmund gets tied up with a crowd of young gangsters and is finally seduced (so it would appear, but to me the sequence is ambivalent) by a young girl.

Meantime the old father has been moved into hospital for a few days, just to prevent him from starving to death (another example of the 'social service' which destroyed the boys in *Shoeshine*), and Edmund becomes concerned to know what will happen when he comes out. Where will the food come from then? He asks the schoolmaster, who snappishly replies that people like his dad are a drag on society and are better dead. Edmund takes him at his word, steals some poison he finds in the hospital ward, and when the old man returns home, puts it in his tea. The family disperses, and Edmund wanders off on his own,

[1] With the exception of the father, all the parts in the film are played by non-actors.

tormented. He goes to the schoolmaster and tells him what he has done; the middle-aged queer, horror-struck by Edmund's act to which he has unwittingly contributed, strikes him and throws him out of the house. Now totally rejected, the boy climbs to the top of a ruined building and throws himself off.

This final sequence is extremely impressive. The boy is utterly alone; and we are forced to follow him, aimlessly wandering through the city's gritty and repulsive dusk, observe the traces of simple childish interests and play which dimly break into his misery, and feel, in tune with the exclamation of an anonymous passer-by who sees him fall to his death, that it is, obscurely but none the less certainly, our fault.

Technically, *Germany Year Zero* reveals again Rossellini's unusual style. Dialogue sequences are shot in constricted spaces, with both the camera and the characters moving restlessly in varying focal planes. Moments of great significance are pointed by the sudden withdrawal of the camera to extreme long shot – there is a moment when the boy hears an organ playing in a roofless and ruined church, and the camera suddenly shows us the scene in a high angle perspective which recalls Chirico. These technical points arise, invariably, from Rossellini's conception of what the film must say. A good example is the portable gramophone playing a recording of Hitler's broadcast on the defence of Berlin, while the Yanks and the Tommies wander listlessly around the Reichschancellery, and the ruins stretch for mile after mile, masking one knows not how many skeletons or how many living dead: this is not just a clever trick, it is integral to the plot and motivation of the film.

But in the end one has to admit that *Germany Year Zero* is, like the Third Reich, broken-backed. The isolation of Edmund comes to be felt as artificial, if only because no genuinely sympathetic human relationships are established between him and anyone else. He lives in a world of monsters; he lives in a world whose motivations he cannot understand and to which therefore he cannot humanly react. The only thing he does with which we can genuinely sympathize is his suicide. That at least is logical.

Yet it is a film not easy to forget. Despite the unease which the director communicates, despite the over-lush score by Renzo Rossellini, we see fleetingly, as in a splintered mirror, the survival of the German soul. Seen now, in relation to Western Germany's extraordinary prosperity and *gemütlichkeit*, the film seems to come from another world, though if you go to East Germany and walk around areas clear of the rebuilt town centre in a place like Leipzig, you can still get a sniff of what Rossellini was trying to express.

This somewhat artificial isolation of Edmund in *Germany Year Zero* is in a sense comparable with the isolation of the boy in Duvivier's *Poil de Carotte*, made in 1933.[1] The boy in question is a misfit, a bit fey, estranged, and subject to the various sanctions which always surround a redhead. The film is an extraordinary mixture of styles, from heavy ham-fistedness to delicate and exquisite fantasies. Apart from that splendid actor, the late Harry Baur, and Robert Lynen, who plays the boy, the performances range from the mediocre to the just plain awful. Yet the film remains gratefully in the memory. Lynen, in the name part, creates a special atmosphere about himself, a level of intensity which, especially in the scene of the attempted suicide, becomes electrically charged.

This is no ordinary boy; there is something pagan, of Pan and of panic about him; and this is emphasized by the film's most famous sequence – the 'marriage' of Poil de Carotte to his little girl-friend. This episode of naked innocence, of a summer day fluttering with blossoms and sparkling streams, is perhaps Duvivier's finest achievement, with its tender and sympathetic wedding march across the meadows as a climax.

La Maternelle, which was made at the same time as *Poil de Carotte*, has a factual realism which the latter never attempted, and as such comes closer to our hearts and sympathies. Jean Benoit-Lévy and Marie Epstein, in their treatment of the infant school and its staff in relation to the internal conflict which arises, provide a lively and vivid personal experience for the spectator. If *Poil de Carotte* suggests Maeterlinck or even Barrie at times, *La Maternelle* belongs to a real world of potties, nappies, running noses, and not-very-good-looking people who seek desperately to love each other and find that even in this they are unwittingly and unwillingly cruel. The emotional situation arises from a documentary foundation; and the result is a more powerful tear-jerker than *Poil de Carotte*, if only because in *La Maternelle* nobody *wants* to be cruel. The unhappy Rose, who takes up nursery school work as an antidote to having been crossed in love, finds herself betraying her dearest pupil, Marie, when love miraculously comes to her again from the school's visiting doctor. Marie is a not very attractive girl – one of the world's born waifs perhaps – and she is consumed with such grievous jealousy at the thought of losing her beloved Rose that she tries to drown herself. Of all the tear-jerking scenes, the one in which, after the suicide is frustrated, she is persuaded to make friends with her 'rival' the doctor, is the most handkerchief consuming.

[1] This Jules Renard story had already been put on the screen by Duvivier in 1925; it was filmed again by Paul Mesnier in 1952.

La Maternelle is a film which is quite crudely made, and indeed is in every way the reverse of pretentious; but because it persuades us that these are real people with real emotions, we are able to enter into the inner lives of children and grown-ups alike (as we can do in *Shoeshine*, for instance, but not in *Germany Year Zero*). It is impossible to watch *La Maternelle* and remain an observer.

Many years later I saw a TV film-programme made by Danny Kaye for UNICEF. He was touring the world on behalf of its sick and dispossessed children, and at some stop-off – I think Turkey – he came upon a sad little boy who had never been seen to smile. Challenged by this fact, Kaye set to work. His producer warned him that he had no time left; he replied, 'Tear up the schedule', and the battle for the smile continued. I don't know how long it lasted, but to see this great artist trying every trick he knew – almost humiliating himself – until at last a gleam of pleasure, however wintry and reluctant, dawned on the boy's face, was a marvellous experience. It also reminded me of something I had seen before; and some days later I traced it. It was of course the little boy in *La Maternelle* who would never smile either, but whose fate was less happy.

All the children in the film are magical, and none more so than little Paulette Flambert as Marie; with the possible exception of Franco Interlenghi in *Shoeshine*, I don't think the passion of childhood has ever been so superbly expressed. For this, and for Madeleine Renaud's beautiful and unforced acting as Rose, one may forgive the film-makers some mistakes and clumsiness; these came anyhow, I would guess, from difficult working conditions due to inadequate finance – a not uncommon circumstance attendant on many really good films.

Another film of this period was Leontine Sagan's *Mädchen in Uniform*, which I am sure I shall be expected to mention at this point. But I have to confess that I find this film about a mild attack of lesbianism in a Prussian girls' school unconvincing and overblown, despite distinguished performances by Dorothea Wieck and Hertha Thiele. The typically Teutonic symbolism is well summarized by Arthur Knight:[1] 'There is a striking visual contrast between the innocence of Hertha Thiele, dressed always in white and photographed against light backgrounds, and the harsh, black-robed head of the school; while ominous, recurrent shots of the deep stairwell in the institution dramatically foreshadow the film's final tragedy'. It was also noted (by Kracauer) that despite the film's plea for more sympathetic understanding of the young, 'there is no hint of the possibility that

[1] *The Liveliest Art*, Macmillan, 1957.

authoritarian behaviour might be superseded by democratic behaviour'. What happens in *Mädchen in Uniform*, therefore, has to happen against an accepted system; the deliberation of the cruelty resulting from the system diminishes our humanitarian instincts, particularly since the 'good' school-mistress, with her heretical human approach to the pupils, proves in the end to be an essentially weak person who would never think of actively opposing the headmistress and the tyranny she represents.

I suppose the earliest of the films about victimized children was Chaplin's *The Kid* (1921). This was his first full-length feature[1] and certainly his most moving and dramatic until *City Lights* some ten years later. *The Kid*, as Theodore Huff points out in his indispensable book[2], 'is almost straight drama,' and remains 'one of the best remembered and most loved of all motion pictures'.

The story is of course frantically melodramatic; and the plot is developed with an intricate ingenuity of twists and turns and dove-tailings worthy of a Sardou, a Courteline or a Labiche. Underlying this are two serious themes – the dilemma of the unmarried mother in a highly non-permissive society, and the cruelties which can be performed on children by removing them, in the name of the law, from the only persons they have ever learned to love and to trust.

To this Chaplin adds his usual theme of the Little Fellow versus Society. One of the most brilliant sequences is that in which the Kid (Jackie Coogan) goes around breaking windows so that Charlie, as an itinerant glazier, can be sure of continuous business. (Relations with the cops in this and other sequences are clearly developments from *Easy Street*.)

But this film's great stroke of genius is the Vision of Heaven which forms the penultimate sequence. It comes at a moment when Chaplin has reduced us to a deep state of anxiety and emotional crisis – if not to tears. Despite a tremendous struggle the Kid has been separated from Charlie by the authorities; and this after our hearts have been rent by the scene of their all-too-brief reunion in a police-van. Only a genius like Chaplin could at this stage take his *mise en scène* of slums and shabbiness and convert it into a magically white paradise in which little dogs, as well as the Little Fellow himself, have downy angels' wings and can swoop and soar hither and yon at will. (Incidentally the trick work of the dissolve to this scene is technically magnificent.)

---

[1] *Shoulder Arms*, which is often spoken of as a feature, was in fact only just over 3,000 feet in length.

[2] *Charlie Chaplin* by Theodore Huff, Cassell, 1952.

The arrival of the mephistophelian figure of Sin puts paid of course to the dream paradise, and Charlie wakes to the rough shaking of a policeman. Thinking (without much surprise) that he is being arrested, he allows himself to be led off – to the gasping surprise of a reunion with the Kid and his long-lost mother. This happy ending, which belongs to all fairy tales, could hardly have been acceptable without the dream sequence; this supplies just the right element of fantasy to make a non-tragic conclusion acceptable.[1] Otherwise *The Kid* would have had to end more like *Bicycle Thieves*. Indeed, the two films have much in common.

The terrible loneliness of the non-smiler, the child who cannot or will not come to terms with society, is a theme which has been treated in a variety of ways.

Sidney Meyer's low-budget 16mm film *The Quiet One* was made in 1949 as part of an appeal campaign for the Wiltwyck School for maladjusted children near New York (a school in which Mrs Roosevelt took a close personal interest). It ended up in the theatres, rightly regarded as a classic of its kind. With the aid of one of the best narrations ever written (the work of James Agee) it analyses – often with the suspense of a detective story – the reasons for the disturbances in the soul of a negro slum-boy, and shows, without any forced glamorization, how with the help of dedicated teachers he learns to come to terms with himself, and becomes perhaps – only *perhaps* – capable of coping with life in the cruel city to which he must return, alone. (I don't know how true it is, but someone once told me that the story of this boy was based in part on the youth of that great boxer Floyd Patterson.)

The Quiet One shows all the signs of a modestly intended picture which outgrew in conception the capacities of the planned production but which somehow managed to struggle through. Despite this, despite lapses in camerawork and continuity, the whole film compels. The boy himself (Donald Thompson) rings miraculously true; in him we recognize all the others, from *Shoeshine*, from *Les 400 Coups*, from *Kes* and from *Boy*.[2]

For instance, the way a rebellious tension is built up in Donald, eventually breaking out in a great gesture of useless violence, has a moving parallel in the Oshima film in which the boy methodically

---

[1] The author of *Peter Pan* said that he found the dream sequence 'superfluous'!

[2] One might also add the sad, lonely figure from Anthony Pelissier's much under-estimated film of D. H. Lawrence's *The Rocking Horse Winner*, though in his loneliness this boy is (as with the children in *The Innocents*) a victim as much of the supernatural as of the adult world.

destroys a fine snowman (while his young brother watches) -- the movements being gradually slowed down by the camera as we watch. Again, there is that heart-stopping breakaway by Victor in *L'Enfant Sauvage* just at the moment when success seems so near; a moment comparable with the last shot of *Les 400 Coups* when Doinel, faced with the freedom of the wind and the breaking seas, is instantly transfixed into freeze-frame, and stares accusingly at us for ever.

The ultimate pessimism of that great cry of despair with which De Sica ends *Shoeshine* is matched, if not overpassed, by that of Buñuel's *Los Olvidados* (American title, *The Young and the Damned*). This is a film which many people cannot 'take'. It is too much for them, it 'can't be true – things aren't really like that'. Oh no? It is the same story of destruction as *Shoeshine*, but with a more brutally uncompromising outlook.

Los Olvidados (1950) marked the return to the screen of Luis Buñuel after a long absence. The last film we in Europe had seen from him had been *Land Without Bread* (*Las Hurdes*) made in 1932.[1] It was in this film that we had noted with horrified surprise that a number of the so-called surrealist images in *Un Chien Andalou* and *L'Age d'Or* were in actual fact straight documentary observations from the Spanish scene – Marist priests and dead donkeys included. Indeed, just as the Hurdanos are the prisoners not so much of themselves as of natural circumstance combined with the continued neglect of a society totally indifferent to them, so it is with the children in the frightening Mexican slums of *Los Olvidados*.

Buñuel never makes 'easy' films. His 'answers' to the situations and problems he delineates are seldom palatable. The series of twists with which he ends *El Angel Exterminador* are exceedingly alarming, even though in this case they are part of a story which we are not expected to believe. In a way, the twists in *Los Olvidados* arise from more than mere fact, or, better, from a heightening of fact. The dreams of Donald in *The Quiet One* are pallid beside Pedro's terrible nightmares; Buñuel is not here concerned with 'documentary' truth but with ideas and images of suffering of more Freudian dimensions. The world of all his films is a world of anarchy; and they are in some degree prophetic in that in their anarchy they have continually anticipated the move of all Western civilization further towards it. After *The Criminal Life of Archibaldo de la Cruz* and *El Angel Exterminador*, let alone *Los Olvidados* itself, we need hardly be surprised at things like hippie

[1] Actually Buñuel made two features, a musical and a comedy, in Mexico before *Los Olvidados*; but he views neither of them with much favour today.

murders and suchlike. In this sense, perhaps, Buñuel has an eye for reality.

His images, of course, repeat themselves endlessly – smashed-up drawing-rooms, farmyard animals in domestic interiors, reasonless cruelties. The assault on the blind man in *L'Age d'Or*, a motiveless *acte gratuit*, crops up again in *Los Olvidados*, where the boys add their own variation by tipping a legless cripple out of his little cart.[1] The blind man in *Los Olvidados* is incidentally not utterly helpless; he defends himself with a spiked stick, he is an expert rapist, and he devises Jaibo's death.

Buñuel once wrote, 'If it were possible for me, I would like to make films which, apart from entertaining the audience, would convey to them the absolute certainty that they do not live in the best of all possible worlds'.[2] He also said, 'If I employ "violence" it is not violence for its own sake. It is to express something else – perhaps something in the world of ideas'.[3]

When, in *Los Olvidados*, he leads us temporarily out of the nightmare, it is only to lull us into a sense of false security. Pedro is looking into the window of a luxury store. Buñuel places us, the audience, safely inside the shop; we are perhaps the salesman. We look out towards the street – insulated, even from the sound of traffic. We watch a dumbshow: a silky-bearded, neatly hatted old queer places himself next to the boy. Would the boy like some pocket money? Yes, indeed he would; the boy's face lights up. An admonitory hand is raised; no, he can't have it yet – there must be a *quid pro quo*. Come home with uncle first . . . At which point there suddenly appears (still in the aquarium-like silence) a suspicious policeman. Uncle departs and the deal is off.

Then again, later in the film, when Pedro is convicted (falsely) of stealing a knife, he is sent to a nice clean reformatory with a modern and liberal-minded headmaster. Hygiene and reform, to say nothing of decent food, are rife. Now comes the great test. 'We are going to trust you,' says the well-meaning booby,[4] and sends Pedro on an errand with a few pesetas. And trustingly the innocent Pedro runs off – honest and happy in the airy sunlight. Needless to say Jaibo (already a killer, and

---

[1] There are two images from Eisenstein's works which always seem to me to be precursors, if not inspirations, of Buñuel. The first is the legless man in the Odessa Steps sequence of *Potemkin*; and the second is the fearfully wrecked Czarina's boudoir in *October* which looks very much as though Modot has passed by.

[2] *Film Book I*, ed. Robert Hughes, Evergreen Books, 1959.

[3] Interview with Kenji Kanesaka in *Film Culture*, Spring 1962.

[4] This after Pedro has run amok and beaten some chickens to death – surrogates for the men who have convicted and imprisoned him.

sleeping with Pedro's mother), is waiting for him. So much for the pesetas and so much for Pedro's future. In a series of sickening episodes he is forced into the rôles of coward, stool-pigeon, informer and goodness knows what else; and finally he is killed and thrown on a garbage dump.

Buñuel offers us no solutions. He demands only that we be aware of what he shows us. His presentation suggests indifference, but this is not so. Rather, as Raymond Durgnat acutely points out, he *refuses to indulge* in pity. 'Pity is real only as an unsentimental and effective act'.[1] But this does not mean that he does not enlist our emotions, or our sympathies, even if sometimes we may feel that we are being terrified into purgation rather than the reverse. Take Jaibo, for example. Here is a layabout who, emerging from prison, sets about beating to death the boy on whose evidence he was sent there; who re-establishes himself as leader of a gang of kids devoted to sadistic sorties against, preferably, the helpless; who, finally, tends to appear, blood-boltered, in their dreams. Even Jaibo, in the terms in which Buñuel presents him to us, demands our sympathy, for neither he nor we *live in the best of all possible worlds*. And Pedro's terrible dream of his mother, the white hen, the entrails and the blood – what is it but a horrifying image of a universal wound? This is the hook from which Buñuel does not release us.

A similar accusation underlies René Clément's *Les Jeux Interdits* (*Forbidden Games*), which he made in 1952. But he is more catlike, as well as more specific in his approach. He is dealing not only with circumstances of war (though these are not entirely vital to his theme) but also with French society, peasant and bourgeois, which is a very different matter from the lower depths of Buñuel's Mexico. He concentrates on the wall of incomprehension which separates children and adults – a theme valid in all circumstances but here particularly triggered off by the fragmentation of society under the impact of war.[2]

The scripting of the opening sequences[3] of *Les Jeux Interdits* (by Jean Aurenche and Pierre Bost) must be a model for all students of film. It provided the director with a brilliantly devised series of incidents

[1] *Luis Buñuel* by Raymond Durgnat, Studio Vista, 1967.

[2] The fear and suspicion with which society reacted to his ideas is indicated by Clément himself: 'It took me five years of patient negotiations to convince the producer. Then, although the censors never touched it, certain producers and critics tried to scuttle the film: it was refused by the selection committee for the Cannes Film Festival. However, when it was specially invited to the Venice Film Festival, it won the top award . . . It is remarkable that censorship did not block the film, while exterior forces – and far worse ones at that – tried to throttle it.' (*Film Book I*, ed. Robert Hughes, Evergreen Books, 1959.)

[3] The original French version had a short prologue cut for foreign distribution.

by which two small children, who otherwise would not have met each other in a thousand years, were brought inevitably together. This is done not merely by a brilliant evocation of the war situation, but also by a cunningly planned series of 'moves' by which, although we are not aware of the 'chessboard', the desired confrontation is, apparently quite naturally, effected.

The scenes of the bombing and machine-gunning of the refugees are shot with stunning realism. There is, to begin with, a frightening contrast between the formal and beautifully organized movement of the attacking aircraft and the confused mess on the roads below – in particular the panic caused by the impedimenta of flight, the precious personal and domestic possessions, and the vehicles themselves which, by breaking down, become agents of death instead of salvation, and are desperately jettisoned. To the refugees the planes seem like fatal anonymous agents; and to none are they more anonymous or mysterious than the children.

At this point the film begins to close in. A specific location is selected – the classic, key location of the war-game – a bridge. All routes of escape are narrowed into this little area. The planes concentrate on the bridge. A car breaks down. In panic and fury the refugees push it off the road. We are nearer now, can distinguish individual figures – a family, a child, a dog. In a single diagonal line across the screen rips a formalized hail of machine-gun bullets . . . The child now has no parents. They lie before her, dead. But she is too young to react to the real experience of death; and it is not until the end of the film that she does what she should do here and now – cry for her mother.

By now the camera has guided us away from the treachery of the roads and into the less deceptive peacefulness of a rustic landscape. And here Paulette and Michel meet – between them a little pet dog, dead; and around them an adult world which, personally or impersonally, can and maybe will destroy them just as surely as it destroyed Pasquale and Giuseppe.

The little girl Paulette has suffered the fate so often meted out to children by peoples at war. The security of a warm and happy home, the loving presence of her parents, the companionship of her pet – all have been summarily dismissed forever. The boy Michel, although older than Paulette, is not yet old enough to have been infected with the stupidity and narrowmindedness of his family of peasant farmers; but he *is* old enough to sense the need for the love they are too dunderheaded to provide, and old enough, too, to feel deprived of it.

The development of this situation is most delicately carried out by Clément and his scriptwriters. It is all a matter of nuances and details (in exquisite black and white photography by Robert Juillard) so that it is a long, long time – so absorbed are we in their secret ceremonies – before we begin to realize that they are committing, each time in a bigger and bigger way, what the grown-up world regards as blasphemy and/or heresy.

To start with they have to bury the dog. This, they know, means a cross; the *meaning* of the cross, though, is *their* meaning, not that of the adult world. Hence the initiation and motivation of the Games, with the need for the cross becoming confused with need for a death; and the ceremonies become so elaborate, and the need for crosses so urgent, that they steal from the church itself – at which point do we not detect in Michel, if not in Paulette, the arrival of the idea of guilt as a conception in itself rather than as a mere fear of the grown-ups?

The pattern of these beautiful and so intimate episodes is broken into all the time by the thumping clodhoppery of Michel's family. This family is perhaps exaggerated too much at times, so that they begin to appear too stupid to be true. But on the other hand the various motivatory or climactic situations between them and the children are so effective that the exaggeration is forgotten. So, when the boorish relatives squabble at the funeral, with two of them actually wrestling with each other in the open grave; when the priest arrives, his face showing shock and horror at *this* blasphemy, how can we think of the children's blasphemy other than in terms of innocence? This situation is clinched by one of the most lovely and moving shots of the whole film. Paulette puts out her hand and lifts up part of the priest's vestments and, with the inner, completely confident love which comes from her and Michel's 'religion', examines what is there embroidered; it is their own wonderful symbol, a cross. It is *this* image that appeals to her – not the priest or *his* religion.

So we end with the grown-ups' graveyard, like the grown-ups' world, turned into a battlefield; and the forbidden graveyard of the children, so beautiful in its inception and its setting and so sinister in its final implications, stands as a symbol both of their innocence and also of the cruelty of the world which surrounds them and to which they must all too soon belong.

Clément leaves us with two heart-rending final images. Michel, deprived of Paulette and despised by his own clottish family, goes back to the secret place in the mill and makes an offering of her necklace to the old owl, to be kept, he says, for a century; which, for a child, is all

eternity. At this moment we know that he is offering up his own innocence as well.[1] And Paulette, dragged away in a great tide of displaced persons and well-meaning Red Cross workers, looks back at us,
and him, and the whole cruel world, and cries out, as she should have
known how to do on the bombed bridge, 'Maman! Maman!' as she is
engulfed in the crowd. . .[2]

Of films in which the children take their revenge on society there
are only a few. Omitting the determination of Baby Le Roy to destroy
W. C. Fields, which we have in the end to admit to have been a figment
of the great man's imagination, we are left with *Les Mistons, Zazie dans
le Métro, A High Wind in Jamaica, Zéro de Conduite*, and *If . . .*

It is interesting that *Les Mistons* (1958) should have been
Truffaut's first film. *Les Quatre Cents Coups* is admittedly partly auto-
biographical, and as Doinel hardly met his problems with an attitude
of passivity in the face of an unjust world, one may well regard *Les
Mistons* also as a gesture, however mild, of revenge. The infuriating yet
attractive children who so successfully make the lovers' meetings a
misery have something in them of the desire 'to get one's own back';
but there is also, and without doubt, a resentment at being 'left out'.
The kids are in fact jealous because they are not yet old enough to
participate in the world of love and of sex; the facts of life are not
enough. They have of course the usual vague feelings of sexual desire,
but these are undirected or multi-directed and, as Pauline Kael puts it,
they 'look at the adult world greedily but contemptuously; the adult
world pays no heed'.

No one wins in the end. The boys tire of their torment, and when
the affair is over – the man killed in an accident, the girl inconsolable –
they are no longer in the least interested.

What, however, gives the film such value is the surprisingly
lyrical mood which Truffaut achieves with the aid of sensitive performances by Gérard Blain and Bernadette Lafont, and excellent
camerawork by Jean Malige. In a curious way it ends up as a good-
humoured film, and it puts forward an attitude which Truffaut was not
to find again until *Baisers Volés*.

Louis Malle's *Zazie dans le Métro* is a more deliberate piece of
revenge. The essence of the story (from a novel by Raymond Queneau)

---

[1] There is a moment in *Kes*, when the boy clumsily scratches a grave for his bird
which the adult world has so cruelly destroyed, which somehow, in its sense of loneliness
and lost innocence, recalls this scene.

[2] There are enough films on children and the cruel world to fill a book. I have here
mentioned only those which have a very special significance and impact to me.

is the reversal of rôles as between child and adult. It is Zazie who knows better than the adults – even her transvestite uncle – and with a vulgar maturity and a scabrous vocabulary she defeats them all. The film is full of surprises, lightning cuts, unusual clashes of colour, and a deliberate incoherence of plot[1] which defeats its own ends by leaving the audience baffled though giggling. Yet it persists in the memory – impudent, intolerant, anarchic; and its success can be gauged by Bosley Crowther's indignant cry: 'There is something not quite innocent or healthy about this film'. The children's revenge, as in *A High Wind in Jamaica* (of which more later), is complete.

In contrast, and almost too late for this book, I came on Andrei Tarkovsky's *Ivan's Childhood* (1962) – the story of a small boy's savage determination to revenge himself on the Nazi invaders who slew his parents. From the opening sequence in which the twelve-year-old returns from behind the German lines and dominates – indeed virtually bullies – the adult officers who are hard put to it to accept that he is a key secret agent, this film clutches at your heart as it moves towards its tragic denouement, all the more affecting in that it is elliptically presented through the chance discovery of the executed boy's photo in the ruins of a Gestapo bunker in Berlin. This film, passionate and lyrical in true Dovzhenko tradition, is graced by a phenomenal performance by young Kolya Burlyaev, who subsequently appeared, equally phenomenally, as the young bell-caster in Tarkovsky's haunting *Andrei Rublev* (1966).

Children are, I suppose, as anarchic as they are conservative. Like clowns, they are contradictions in terms. Adults fear and mistrust clowns when they escape from the prison of the circus ring; equally they fear and mistrust children outside the context of nurseries, educational institutions or other prisons. The revolt against such grown-up conceptions is well represented by two films, *Zéro de Conduite* and *If . . .*, the latter being much influenced by the former.

Both these films question not the fact but the validity of the institutional system. They are imaginative pleas for anarchy as against the hidebound traditions and hypocritical selfishness of established society; nor do they lack awareness of the destruction of innocence and of the vacuum created by the absence of *tendresse*. Rightly or wrongly, the answer to these problems is seen as revolutionary activity rather than sweet reasonableness.

The Cabinet of Dr Caligari has often been falsely represented as showing the world seen through the eyes of a madman. Similarly

[1] Among other things the Métro isn't working owing to strikes.

Zéro de Conduite has frequently been traduced as a film which shows the world as seen through the eyes of children. It is nothing of the sort. It is the world of children seen by someone who is not only on their side but has also, miraculously, succeeded in re-identifying with them, in remembering exactly what it feels like to be a child. That is why the people who hate this film hate it so passionately. Vigo, they feel, has betrayed the adult world, has joined the enemy; he is a collaborator.[1] It infuriates them that the film isn't 'true', that, for instance, part of the audience at the school prizegiving consists literally of stuffed shirts and that the headmaster is a dwarf, to match the size of his brain. These are of course the important *graffiti* of childhood, and not to be ignored. Unless we accept this particular logic, the whole of *Zéro de Conduite* is incomprehensible, from the opening sequence in the train (where, delightfully, nothing is what it seems), through the dormitory sequence with its pillow fight[2] turning into a religious procession, to the final sequence of riot and mutiny.

Like *Zéro de Conduite*, Lindsay Anderson's *If . . .* is based to a degree on the film-maker's personal experience. The Anderson film has the unique quality of being about every public school there ever was; we all, if Old Boys, see in it our own school[3] – tribute of a sort, perhaps, to the System. The difference between the two films is that although *If . . .* is in many ways a simulacrum of *Zéro de Conduite*, there is a tremendous difference in the ending. The finale of *If . . .* is a real revolution: 'Trust me', pleads the up-to-date modern-minded headmaster, and is promptly shot straight through the head. The Vigo film ends inconclusively with the kids breasting a rooftop and planting their pirate flag like climbers on a fictitious Everest; but *If . . .* ends with both sides, rebels and establishment, at it hammer and tongs with real machine-guns and grenades. Thus Anderson has taken Vigo's anarchy (Vigo's father was imprisoned and subsequently 'suicided' for his anarchism) and driven it to a logical conclusion which Vigo may indeed have contemplated but which in the end he evaded. Anderson himself is puzzled by this, regarding Vigo's background as 'more authentically, politically,

[1] The complete censorship ban on *Zéro de Conduite*, imposed after its first showing in 1933, was not lifted until 1945.

[2] It is interesting to speculate on the relationship between this pillow fight and that in Gance's *Napoléon*; which could also lead us to the three snowball battles – in *Napoléon*, *Le Sang d'un Poète* and *Les Enfants Terribles*.

[3] What the film says to people who have *not* been to a British public school I wouldn't like to guess. It was, I understand, very successful with the young generation in the US; and its *general* questioning of 'authority' probably validates it everywhere, though a good deal will be missed or misunderstood.

violently anarchist' than his own; though he then adds 'or perhaps not
. . . His was a gentle and lyrical soul.'[1]

Anyway, instead of Vigo's stuffed shirts, which are dummies,[2] we
have in *If . . .* the genuine live articles, with bishops, knights and
generals in full rig – all the hot air of the public school 'tradition'
coagulated into one comprehensively nauseating mess.

If . . . is very like *Zéro de Conduite* in its episodic construction and
its variation in levels of fantasy. The beautiful sequence in the gym-
nasium when one boy watches another taking off his sweater has a
tender realism which passes into the dreaminess of adolescence through
the use of slow-motion to prolong the sweetness of the gesture. On the
other hand the sex-scene with the girl in the cheap café is shot with
brutal realism although it is in fact a fantasy of the boy's imagination.
This is done, I take it, in order to create a deliberate confusion on the
psychological level, causing the spectator to take no motivation for
granted, and leaving him uncertain of the ground on which he stands.
Similar is the climactic moment later in the film when the headmaster,
remarking 'I take a very serious view of this', pulls out a desk drawer
in which lies the school padre whom the boys have recently shot on
manoeuvres. With grave ceremony the padre shakes their hands and
accepts their apologies, and is then returned to base. This is a crucial
point in the film. The 'reality' of the public school spirit becomes fused
with the 'fantasy' of the anarchic imagination; the incident questions
the validity of everything, and its implications make the final scenes of
bloody revolution understandable if not acceptable. Vigo's equivalent
is subtler, more evanescent, but equally evocative; it comes when the
bearded dwarf of a headmaster stands on tip-toe in order to enshrine
his bowler hat (or 'melon') under a glass case on the study mantelpiece;
that, and the boy's insult of 'Monsieur le Directeur, je vous dis MERDE'.

II

'Merde' and a good many similar epithets were liable to be flung at the
American film industry by both French and British producers in the
period immediately following World War II. During this difficult
interlude the United States seemed to be making a determined effort

---

[1] From a letter to the author, January 1969.
[2] Which Anderson uses, though, at the end of *The White Bus*.

to corner the world film market again, destroying various indigenous film industries in the process.

The methods employed varied in that the circumstances in France differed from those in Britain. Up till 1939 the Americans had relied on recouping their production and exploitation costs from their home market; their receipts from the rest of the world were therefore money for jam. The Nazi conquest of Europe put paid to this; and from 1940 until the end of the European war no new Hollywood films reached French cinema screens. In 1945 the Americans, not unnaturally from their point of view, sought to flood this parched soil. They had this on their side, too, that the French had been starved of films save for limited home production and the hated propaganda films of Goebbels' organization.

The British were in a different position. They had, of course, continued to import US films during the war, and had even built up a small export of their own films to America. Furthermore the British industry emerged from the war considerably strengthened, not only because of the improvement in quality of the films, but also because of the arrival of the influential millionaire flour-miller, J. Arthur Rank.[1] What Hollywood feared from this situation was a constriction of their market as quality British films got a larger and larger share of screen time in British theatres. The answer to this was, in part, to infiltrate the British industry on the levels of finance and investment. Acquisition of distribution control was especially important, since by this means British product could be prevented from achieving too profitable a circulation. Most of this was in fact nothing new; a similar threat had existed in the pre-war period; but by 1946 it had become much more menacing.

Up to 1939 both the French and the British had tried to protect their home product by regulation. Quotas were fixed by Governments, and these made the annual exhibition of a minimum number of home-produced films compulsory. Such systems had many failings, but they did, to some degree, enable both industries to keep their heads above water during the Thirties. It was not unnatural therefore for Hollywood to attack, among other things, the quota system.

I do not want to go into elaborate detail about all this,[2] but it is sufficiently important to the existence of film as an art to deserve some

[1] Later Lord Rank.
[2] The subject has been fully dealt with in a number of books, including Georges Sadoul in *Le Cinéma Français* (Flammarion, 1962), Alan Wood in *Mr Rank* (Hodder and Stoughton, 1952) and P.E.P's report on *The British Film Industry* (1952).

general mention; for it is the expression of national, not cosmopolitan characteristics which must be the essential basis of film aesthetic, and for quite a few years from 1945 on, American actions came to be felt as a real threat to national film expression in both Britain and France.[1]

The French situation can be generally summed up by the signing of the Blum-Byrnes Agreement of 1946, under which the old quota system was revised very much in favour of the United States. The French industry felt itself vitally threatened, since Léon Blum had succumbed so much to the blandishments of Mr Byrnes[2] that he had agreed to a quota of no less than 400 United States films per annum instead of 120 as previously. Political agitation focused through *ad hoc* Committees for the Defence of the French Cinema eventually had its effect; the agreement was abrogated in 1948, and at the same time the Government set up an Industry Fund based on a new entertainment tax on the theatres. Not everyone was content with this, but it was in the event just enough to save the French cinema. Production began to rise from then on, and during the Fifties opportunities arose not only for the Old Guard but also for a newer generation of film-makers.

In Britain the American problem was tackled by various official commissions whose Reports eventually led in 1947 to an ill-conceived attempt by the Labour government to clobber Hollywood by imposing a swingeing 75% *ad valorem* duty on all foreign films – the ostensible object being the need to conserve dollars. Playing from strength, the Americans simply suspended all shipments of films to Britain whose producers, even if they had had 100% protection, were in no position to fill the distribution gap thus left. Less than a year later the Government had to cave in and re-negotiate, and not really from strength. The French tactic, of giving in first and then negotiating, seems to have been more satisfactory. As it was, the duty was removed and instead an increased quota of 45% (from 20%) was imposed. But the whole episode caused much ill-feeling on the part of the Americans, and this did not help Rank, whose attempts to corner the English market and to break into that of the United States had involved ill-conceived extravagances which were to bedevil the British industry for some years to come.

---

[1] In Italy, at least to begin with, the industry proved rather more resilient, if only because its production costs were extremely low (*Bicycle Thieves* cost only £18,000 or $55,000). Later, however, partly due to official hostility to Neo-Realism, the industry found itself forced to accept governmental paternalism.

[2] It must be remembered that at this time all countries desperately needed dollars in order to survive, so it was not unnatural for the Americans to think they could get away with almost anything.

III

The problems of France after liberation were therefore considerable. One of the results of the Blum-Byrnes episode was that established French directors who had been overseas and now wished to start work again in France found things very much against them. It was to be nearly ten years before Renoir could make a film in his own country; and in the interim he only made two films – his beautiful and loving picture of India called *The River*, and in Italy a coruscating vehicle for Magnani called *The Golden Coach*. As for René Clair, he managed in 1947 to make *Le Silence est d'Or* – a good film but not one of his best – but thereafter was in the wilderness until 1950 when, with *La Beauté du Diable*, he began a series of exquisite and mainly nostalgic films which would cover the next ten years.

The immediate aftermath of the Liberation was, however, marked by the appearance of several important documentaries. I have already written about Henri Cartier-Bresson's work on *Le Retour*, a film which stands on the bridge, as it were, between war and peace. As a follow-up to this came Jean Grémillon's very personal documentary about the Allied invasion of France from D-Day onwards. Although inevitably uneven visually, *Le 6 Juin à l'Aube* had a tremendous atmosphere (much aided by a musical score composed by Grémillon himself), and in particular managed to put across a sense of the persistence of basic values of humanity, as when, amid the explosions and air raids, the peasant farmers continued their immemorial seasonal tasks.

This feeling of attachment to the soil was celebrated in the same year (1946) by the appearance of one of the finest documentaries of all time – Georges Rouquier's *Farrebique*, a film about life on a farm in a little-known part of Central France. There is nothing striking about the landscape, nothing specially picturesque or good-looking about the people. And all the film does, in essence, is to pass in review the events of the four seasons of the year. Plenty of other documentaries have done this sort of thing before; indeed it sounds something of a cliché. But in *Farrebique* Rouquier, not without a certain debt to Flaherty, has really dug himself in. He takes us inside the farm buildings and he also takes us inside the hearts of the peasant farmers themselves. The film is an intense, intimate and very detailed study of the *mystique* as well as of the day-to-day life of those who live by the soil. Here, by the way, is the other side of the medal from Clément's clodhoppers in *Les Jeux Interdits*.

The farm is rather dilapidated, like most farms; and its annual income is low enough to make the question of repairs and improvements a constant matter for discussion and argument. Decisions are taken – and then put off by unexpected turns of events – such as a young man spraining his back at harvest-time and thus reducing the vital labour-force by one. The year passes. A child is born. An old man dies. Electricity is installed. The new buildings remain unbuilt. Life persists.

Rouquier sees to it that we don't just observe these and other events. He makes us live them. He has an intensity of observation which is rare in cinema, though perhaps less rare in French cinema, which can share in the great traditions of Flaubert and Zola. Details are accumulated, then arranged in wonderful patterns, and then, from time to time, exploded in lightning flashes of drama, or poetry, or a sense of 'the sum of things'. The making and baking of bread, filmed not without a tender humour, becomes in the end a ritual, a symbolic act. The old man, mindful of death, talks to his sons about the family hisory; and the long, hard tradition of the farm and its soil, of its sons and its sons' sons, unfolds like a flower. A tree falls in winter, and among its ruined branches we see a bird breathe its last little breath in the snow – just as later we see, in gigantic close-up, the last final pulse-beats in the wrist of the dying man. We see, too, when spring comes, the re-assertion of life, as the young man's eyes look upwards at a girl's skirt billowing in the breeze as she stands at the top of the loft ladder.

In his intensity Rouquier goes beyond these deceptively simple images of the soil. With the coming of spring he mounts a long sequence (admirable music, incidentally, by Henri Sauguet) in which all sorts of camera tricks are employed – stop-motion shots of flowers opening, microphotography of sap rising, everything to bring us that great celebration of the joyous explosion of spring. It is almost a superabundance of imagery, and only by a hairsbreadth fails to defcat the director's purpose by making us conscious of the marvels of scientific photography instead of the warm heartbeat of the earth.

Rouquier also seeks images of time. He gives us, in a few seconds, a day from noon to sunset by showing, again in stop-motion, the shadow of a ladder against a wall changing and lengthening with the passing of the hours. This is a striking example of cinematic as opposed to actual time. The speeding up of the movement of the shadow results in slowing down our time-sense; it is temporarily elongated, and we live literally on borrowed time.

It is a pity that Rouquier has never since then made a major feature.[1] Some of his subsequent shorter documentaries, however, were impressive – notably *Sel de la Terre* with its exquisite vision of the Camargue (rivalling that of Lamorisse) and his honest study of *Lourdes and its Miracles*. *Malgovert* in particular – a film about the building of a hydro-electric dam – had an unusual intensity recalling that of *Turksib*.

In the same year as *Farrebique*, Eli Lotar (Buñuel's cameraman on *Land Without Bread*) made his famous attack – in mood honourably comparable to such works of the Twenties as Kirsanov's *Ménilmontant* – on the horrible slums of Aubervilliers, a district, incidentally, which one used to skirt while on the way to Le Bourget in the airport bus. The slums have long since gone; but the film, as an attack on all slums, still has its own validity. Lotar added to the visual accusation a quite extraordinary sound-track by Prévert and Kosma, of whose popular songs *Les Feuilles Mortes* may perhaps be the most famous. In sweet words and music they promised justice to the 'Petits Enfants d'Aubervilliers', and this refrain, against the savage visual images of the slums, caused an ironic collision well-calculated to arouse generous indignation in the spectator. People like Lotar are not popular with landlords or municipalities.

Unpopularity was also the lot of Georges Franju's first film *Le Sang des Bêtes*, a film which has so horrified people that they have rushed from the cinema halfway through the projection. Yet it is without doubt a poetic film in the true sense of the word; in dealing with the abattoirs of Paris, Franju was taking subject-matter no better or worse than Aeschylus' or Shelley's choice of the daily-eviscerated Prometheus.

Franju's technique in this film is not unlike Lotar's in *Aubervilliers*. He also goes for a complete contrast between visuals and sound, and he too uses music by Kosma – among of course other sound effects such as the striking of twelve noon, through which we are released from the interior of the slaughterhouse to a series of carefully planned images which bring us little comfort but an even greater sense of poetic unreason. Other aural collisions take place, not least that of a childlike voice[2] commentating with the most appropriate inappropriateness while we observe the almost incredible images of the

---

[1] An attempt at a fiction-feature in 1953 was unsuccessful. Later on he appeared as actor in *Pitchi Poi*, the long episodic TV programme made in several European countries about the search for a child lost in the infamous Nazi camps.

[2] The voice, in fact, of Nicole Ladmiral, who played Chantal in Bresson's *Journal d'un Curé de Campagne*.

slaughterhouse in full action, with the animals' fresh blood steaming in the wintry air. This film made an admirable début for a director who was going to make a mark or, should one say, leave a scar on French cinema.

In this same period two other documentarists, milder and less controversial, made their appearance – Jacques Cousteau and Nicole Védrès. Cousteau's underwater films, *Epaves* (1945) and *Paysages du Silence* (1947) laid the foundations for his future films, and not least for his great feature-length *Le Monde du Silence* which, with Louis Malle as co-director, he completed in 1956.

The secret of the fascination one feels for Cousteau's work is that he is a scientist with the heart of an artist. His explorations therefore have a double purpose and a double mood. And his films tend to be quiet, unsensational in the sense that they never 'plug' the often extraordinary material in them, and are filled much of the time with a kind of humble amazement[1] at the marvels which his camera is showing. One of the pleasures gained from Cousteau's films is the sharing of explorations and experiments whose aesthetic attractions are combined with the thought that they are likely to be of very great benefit to the future of the human race, especially in the field of nutrition.

Finally there is Nicole Védrès, whose fascinating film *Paris 1900*, which appeared in 1947, was a unique compilation record – absolutely authentic – of 'La Belle Epoque'. An elegant narration spoken by Claude Dauphin and an impeccable score by Guy Bernard accompany this film of warmth, wit, and social comment. 'Monsieur le Président', bearded, top-hatted, beaming, moves through the film symbolizing those halcyon days when the rich thought that summer would last forever; the city council of Paris is so moved by the appalling conditions in the slums that it votes a large sum of money for the construction of a mosque; and a poor little man makes himself a pair of leather wings and tries to fly from the Eiffel Tower – perhaps the first newsreel scoop, including a close-up of the dent his body made in the ground; meantime Renoir and Manet are seen at their easels, Sarah Bernhardt is the tops, and 1914 is just round the corner. *Paris 1900* remains permanently fascinating, as indeed does Guitry's more specialized *Ceux de Chez Nous*.[2]

Meantime, under the difficulties already described, most features

---

[1] Pauline Kael, with a rare lapse of perception, calls this 'self-congratulation'.

[2] Védrès was to make only two more films before her untimely death in 1965. Both of them, *La Vie Commence Demain* (1950) and *Frontières de l'Homme* (1953), studied the future largely in terms of filmed interviews with eminent contemporaries in the fields of science, politics and the arts

in the immediate post-war period were made by those directors who had stayed on in France during the Occupation. After *Les Enfants du Paradis*, not completed in fact until 1945, Carné went straight on to another major film – or so he intended – *Les Portes de la Nuit* (1946). Despite the brilliantly constructed studio sequence of Paris during the Occupation with which it opened, it failed to please, mainly because in its later stages it passed from realism to symbolism in a way which did not suit the taste of the post-war public.

In this respect it is interesting to note the success of René Clément's *La Bataille du Rail* – a brutally neo-realist film about the Resistance which came out in the same year as the fantasy *La Belle et la Bête*, which he had co-directed with Cocteau. *La Belle et la Bête*, an imaginative interpretation of the fairy tale, with Jean Marais in marvellous *maquillage* as the Beast, was superior even to *Les Visiteurs du Soir* in its sustained, dreamlike and mediaeval mood. The film was made under great difficulties – shortage of technical apparatus, shortage of materials for Christian Bérard's gorgeous décors, shortage of food, and on top of that the almost continual illness of Cocteau and Jean Marais. Yet of all Cocteau's work between *Le Sang d'un Poète* and *Orphée*, it is the only one to make the magical combination of dream and reality, to communicate so intimate a fantasy that we become children again with the universal legend.[1] It is full of images that attract and mesmerize, not least those naked arms which as human candelabras light endless perspectives of shadowy corridors.

A completely different aspect of Cocteau was to be seen in three other post-war films, *L'Aigle à Deux Têtes*[2] (1947), *Les Parents Terribles* (1949) and *Les Enfants Terribles* (1950) – the first two being adaptations from plays and the last-named from a novel. *L'Aigle à Deux Têtes* was highly successful both on stage and screen but it hardly stands up to the test of time, at any rate as a film, in relation to Cocteau's other work. Despite fine performances by Edwige Feuillère and Marais (both repeating their stage success), the film remains stagey and never really gets off the ground.

In this it is utterly different from *Les Parents Terribles*. This had been Cocteau's most successful play, box-office-wise, from the moment it opened in Paris in 1938, although during the Occupation it came under some attack from Jew baiters and collaborationists. In trans-

---

[1] Cocteau himself said that he wanted the film 'to plunge me into a lustral bath of childhood'.

[2] For an amusing discussion of the accent, or otherwise, on the 'à' see Francis Steegmuller's biography of Cocteau (Macmillan, 1970) which also contains much of interest about Cocteau's film work (though the author is less than fair to *Le Testament d'Orphée*).

ferring this claustrophobic play about family conflicts, and in particular about mother-son love-hate relationships, to the screen, Cocteau somehow managed to eliminate all sense of theatre and to force us cinematically into a cluttered, airless world where close-ups dominated and exteriors did not exist. As in *L'Aigle à Deux Têtes* the principals, Yvonne de Bray, Gabrielle Dorziat and Jean Marais, played the same parts as they did on the stage; but not a trace of theatricality remained. De Bray, as the mother, was a monster to outdo all sacred monsters; her death scene at the end of the film is truly memorable.

Les Enfants Terribles was written during one of Cocteau's many 'cures' for the opium habit. It was first published in 1930 and became something of a seminal novel for the young people of that time. Like Auden's *The Orators*, it had a revelatory and releasing effect; it mirrored unspoken ideas and, like *The Orators*, its influence was profound. A study in relationships among young people – familial and otherwise – with attendant confusions of purpose and lost senses of direction, it did not reach the screen until 1949, and then without Cocteau as director, though he worked closely on the script, supplied some passages of narration, and is said to have directed one short sequence. The director he chose was Jean-Pierre Melville, who would subsequently be known for, among other films, *Bob le Flambeur*, *Léon Morin, Prêtre*, and *Le Samourai*. He was on all counts an excellent choice.

This is a film which has never had its due recognition. It was dismissed by nearly all the critics and is not, I think, much in circulation today. To me it is a tremendously exciting work which perfectly reproduces the feeling and atmosphere of the novel. It was shot entirely on location, much of it in Melville's own apartment, where the tangled mess and muddle of the young participants was magnificently displayed. From the snowball fight onwards, the story moves steadily on its erratic and utterly fatal course – with clashes of temperament, clashes of incident, confusions of sentiment, intimations of incestuous fancies and fears, all building up to that irrevocable act when the letter of declared affection and explanation is deliberately flushed down the toilet.

Les Enfants Terribles shares with Bresson's *Un Condamné à Mort s'est Echappé* the use of music (in this case Bach and Vivaldi) in an apparently disorganized and *outré* manner but in fact with stunningly successful impact. The acting of an almost unknown cast of youngsters is superb; nor do I agree with many critics that the doubling of two of the parts is a mistake. Dargelos and Agathe, the two friends of the incestuous brother and sister, are both played by Renée Cosima, and the resultant ambivalence is absolutely right, and intensifies the threat to the 'secret' room to which they bring a disorder more arcane and dangerous than Paul and Elisabeth can ever expect or accept.

During the Occupation Cocteau had written scripts or dialogue for several directors, including de Poligny, Bresson and Jean Delannoy. In the case of the last-named – a very variable director but capable on occasion of fine work – he had written the script of *L'Eternel Retour* (1943), a heavy-handed and not very successful modernization of the Tristan legend which was, to use Sadoul's apt phrase, 'alourdie par des épisodes baroques et gratuits'. But soon after this, at the end of the war, Delannoy turned to a work by Cocteau's rival Gide, and brought to the screen one of his 'purest' novels, *La Symphonie Pastorale*.

This is a beautiful and very moving film. It tells the story of a wild, neglected blind girl who is adopted, *par charité*, by the pastor of a small mountain village. As she grows up, the life of his household is gradually dislocated by the fact – at first neither realized nor admitted – that he loves her. His son also loves her; and when, after a successful operation, she can see for the first time, all the ugly passions from which she had been protected by her very blindness blaze up around her, and tragedy ensues.

At no point in the film are the delicate psychological and emotional situations overdramatized or sensationalized. The relationships are depicted with meticulous sensitivity and a great understanding of the hidden deeps of the heart. There are beautiful performances by Michèle Morgan, Pierre Blanchar and Jean Desailly against the setting of village church and home, and the crisp, crackling landscape of snow and conifers.

In the immediate post-liberation period, the director who perhaps had the most striking impact on the public was Henri-Georges Clouzot. During the Occupation he had made – unfortunately on behalf of Tobis, Goebbels' stooge French production company – *Le Corbeau*, a dark, poison-pen thriller based in part on a real life episode in France. It was a brilliantly conceived and constructed whodunit with excellent performances by, among others, Pierre Fresnay and Ginette Leclerc, and it certainly foreshadowed Clouzot's future successes. But Goebbels got the idea that it could be used as propaganda in occupied and neutral countries to show how decadent the French had become; and although it was a huge success for quite other reasons (people were delighted to see high class film-making again), Clouzot was accused in 1945 of collaboration with the enemy and the film was banned. By 1947, however, good sense had prevailed and he emerged from the shadows with that brilliant *roman-policier*, *Quai des Orfèvres*. The story involves crime and detection in music hall circles, shabby and furtive, and is dominated by a suave performance, reminiscent of Maigret at times, by that lamented actor Louis Jouvet. In this, as in subsequent Clouzot films in black and white, the stylish photography of Armand Thirard was much in evidence.

Following this, Clouzot delivered himself of three remarkable films – *Le Salaire de la Peur*, *Les Diaboliques* and *Le Mystère Picasso*. (I omit here his *Manon*, made immediately after *Quai des Orfèvres*, an updated version of the novel which carried all Clouzot's inspissated pessimism and cruelty but somehow failed to hit the mark; though, to be fair, anyone who saw it will retain squeamish memories of Cécile Aubry's death).

Le Salaire de la Peur (1953) has some claim to be the greatest suspense thriller of all time; it is the suspense, not of mystery but of Damocles' sword. It also convinces because its circumstances and development are built on a human situation to which we can direct a justified social criticism; we identify, as it were, with both hands. The four men who drive off to deliver two truckloads of appallingly unstable nitroglycerine across a rough and inhospitable South American land-scape[1] are impelled by social miseries and economic injustices arising from capitalist, indeed specifically American capitalist, organization.

From the opening sequence of the dusty, dirty little shanty town miles from nowhere, with its naked children and scratching mongrels (there to be stoned), an atmosphere of tension is remorselessly built up. Clouzot's pessimism – induced partly perhaps by the ill-health which has dogged him all his life – is here, as in *Les Diaboliques*, a positive advantage.

Practically the whole film is taken up with the journey of the trucks with their terrible loads. Nevertheless the opening episodes, so essential to the entire motivation of the film, would be useless without Clouzot's intense directorial concentration. The opening shot is of course famous: two beetles are seen in fierce combat; then the camera draws back to show that they are being manipulated on strings held by a small boy ('as flies to wanton boys, are we to the gods'). After this our vision is further enlarged to take in the full scruffiness and discomfort of a so-called trading community several hundred miles from nowhere. All the paraphernalia of 'je-m'en-foutisme' are displayed, and it is no

---

[1] In the two years previous to this film Clouzot had been working on a documentary about Brazil which was not completed. His experiences there must have been of great value in his reconstruction of the South American scene in a French landscape. It is totally convincing.

surprise when a man watches unmoved as his girl friend goes off to have sex with her shabby employer. Who else? It is logical. Nothing matters, points out Clouzot, nothing, except the mirage of Escape.

This once established, the appalling journey takes on an extra dimension. The hair-trigger risk becomes just viable because the need, even for a mirage, is so great. And consequently we are even more implicated in the suspense.

I do not remember ever having felt so nervous, so on edge, in a cinema. Clouzot's close attention to detail means that one is in a constant anguish of apprehension as the trucks gingerly pick their way through a nightmare landscape of rock, sand and mud. Wheels spin, jerk and bump. Any minute, as folk used to say, may be the next. And then of course it happens. One of the trucks goes up in smithereens and it's goodbye to Bimba, the German refugee (Nazi or Red, who cares?) with a passion for cleanliness, and goodbye to his jolly extrovert buddy, the Italian Luigi.[1]

The other two continue their journey, with psychological pressure approaching bursting point. Mario – hero of the film, if hero is the word – is an amoral, perhaps basically criminal type, but with a personality which attracts the adoration of his less stable gangster friend Jo. (The two parts are played to perfection by Yves Montand and Charles Vanel.)

The showdown comes when the truck gets bogged down in a deep gully full of oil. Mario, in his black determination to extricate it, uses Jo as a wheel grip and grinds him into the mud – an episode which has something of the terror of the climax of *Psycho*.

Mario gets through in the end and claims his money. Driving back in triumph and in waltz time to his floozie – the truck now clear of its dangerous load – he carelessly crashes into a ravine and kills himself. The whole thing, the whole frantic escapade, has been to no purpose. Four men have died, and who cares? One would have more feeling for Jaibo, even, than any of these.

Yet Clouzot's genius in concentrating our attention has been such that we have been entirely implicated in their lives, and feel we have actually shared the trigger-atmosphere of their journey and, at least until he murders Jo, fall somewhat for the attractions of Mario; it was presumably no chance that Clouzot chose Yves Montand – France's Sinatra – for the part.

---

[1] I doubt if all this variation of nationalities means as much as Clouzot hoped; we end up by being too deeply interested in the doomed chaps' personalities as individuals to care where they come from.

Les Diaboliques (1955) is by comparison something of a let-down. Here Clouzot has dressed up a murder thriller to make it look like something more important; and in the pay-off, if he doesn't exactly cheat, he makes us feel cheated. This story of an unpleasant school-master murdered yet not murdered by his wife and his mistress is, however, as always with Clouzot, rich in atmosphere. It depends very much on the intimate details of the seedy fourth-rate school, with its inadequate education and uneatable food, its general smell of unwashed children, neglect, hatred and petty perversions. Without all this detail around them, the performances of Simone Signoret and Vera Clouzot would impress without convincing.

It must be admitted that at a first viewing *Les Diaboliques* is pretty compulsive. The necrophilic sequences – notably the 'murder', the nightmare car journey, and the raising of the dead – are really exceedingly disturbing. Clouzot's talent for visually rubbing our noses, as it were, in unpleasantness has seldom been better deployed. It is said that in the school dinner scene the actors were actually forced to eat bad fish while Clouzot's camera recorded their only too genuine reactions. But unlike *Le Salaire de la Peur*, this film cannot rate a second viewing – at least not for enjoyment; once the dénouement is known, interest evaporates.

It is only fair to add that there is a twist at the end of *Les Diaboliques* which not everyone who sees the film manages to pick up. When the whole mystery has been cleared up and all the loose ends tied, one of the schoolchildren makes a remark to a member of the staff which suggests a horrifying implication involving the supernatural – all the more frightening because it relates to the *false* supernatural scares during the main story. The whole thing is thrown away so casually that you wonder whether you heard aright; but if you do get it, it certainly adds an extra dimension to the film.

Human sympathy is a rarity in Clouzot's world, which is a world of multiple disasters leading, all of them, to the one basically unpleasant disaster, death. His characters, seedy, brutal or victimized, are all destined for repellent endings. *Le Mystère Picasso* therefore came as a great surprise. This long documentary study of the Master is full of human warmth; it reveals, tantalizes and delights; and one thinks how wonderful it would be to have such a film about Leonardo, say, or Michaelangelo.

The title itself indicates, of course, Clouzot's typical approach. Just as his *general* approach to life led him to thrillers and *romans-policiers*, so here Picasso is treated as a mystery to be, *if possible,* unravelled; and this treatment, thanks not least to the remarkably relaxed co-operation of its subject, succeeds extremely well. I would put it among the best of the art films – and heaven knows there are enough of them[1] – if only because Clouzot has subordinated his own special talent to the expression of Picasso as a living and lively artist; and as Picasso unhesitatingly accepts that living artists should not expect the respect accorded to dead masters, he goes more than halfway to meet Clouzot's 'detective' technique. He is, after all, a showman as well as a great artist, and in this case he was well aware of the limitations and superficialities of the film medium in this sort of connotation.

Le Mystère Picasso has often been criticized for not doing things which it never set out to do – criticized for *not* getting inside the head of a great artist, for *not* sharing with him the agonies of creation, etc etc. What it does show, for us and for future generations, is the *man*, displaying his techniques and displaying *himself* – some of the time with tongue in cheek – before the camera of that sensitive photographer Claude Renoir, and delighting in adapting himself to its needs when he is not making it adapt itself to his. (There is a very amusing moment when he complains about the size of his 'canvas', and the screen obligingly enlarges itself to Cinemascope size.)

It must also be remembered that this is not the only, nor the definitive film on Picasso; but it is something more than a *jeu d'esprit* in which all the participants know exactly what they are doing and give good value for the money. It is, without being heavy-handed, very revelatory.

In the end of course the mystery is not solved. What happens, however, is that the element of greatness in an artist, so almost if not quite impossible to analyse, does come through as we watch not only the fascinating metamorphoses on the screen but also the movements of hands and fingers which accompany them. Irrelevant, some have said. I wonder? Many years ago I spent a good deal of time with that great violinist Szigeti discussing the idea of making a film about the mystery of *his* art. He was particularly anxious, in all our discussions on the script, to have a sequence showing in detail all the muscular actions involved, arms, fingers, back and so on; it was his hope to be filmed naked to the waist playing, say, Bach's Chaconne, with varying lighting effects and camera speeds. I think among other things he intended to use this for his own personal study.

Anyway, Picasso, Clouzot and Claude Renoir between them have presented an *aspect* of Picasso as a living artist who has become a

[1] See Unesco catalogues passim.

legend in his own time. It is only one aspect of many. It is in one sense somewhat superficial; but in another sense it is, within its limited intentions, very complete. To complain, as John Berger did on its first release,[1] that in it 'Picasso is divorced from reality', or that 'the most gifted artist of our time, whose tragedy has been that he has only occasionally found themes great enough to absorb all his gifts, is turned into a theme unto himself . . . an idol; a conjuror; a dreamer' – this is to belittle not Clouzot but Picasso himself.

For me there is only one falsity in the film, and that is when Picasso sets himself to paint against the clock, or rather against the footage in the camera's magazine – a competition which has no point, is unfair to the camera, not Picasso, and is slightly cheap. Also it is just as well not to pay much attention to the English narration (imposed by the distributors?) which manages to get it all wrong.

During the Occupation four other directors – Robert Bresson, Claude Autant-Lara, Jacques Becker and Jacques Tati – were, one way or another, flexing their muscles. Bresson made *Les Anges du Péché* in 1943 and *Les Dames du Bois de Boulogne* in 1944–1945; I shall be writing about him later in this chapter. Autant-Lara had been an excellent art-director and assistant to René Clair in the Twenties. In the Thirties, apart from a dubbing stint in Hollywood, he had directed films in France and England with little creative freedom – even to the point where his producer took, in three cases at least, directorial credit. Now, in the Forties, he had his chance with a series of films starring Odette Joyeux, of which the most notable was *Douce* (1943), a film about illicit amours in the house of an excessively aristocratic family, with bailiffs and governesses muscling in on the Vicomte's daughter and the Vicomte himself (wooden leg and all), with tragic or, rather, melo-dramatic results. It wouldn't be worth a second's thought were it not for the direction. The great mansion, heavy with decoration and dominated by the newly-installed hydraulic lift with its tortured metal-work (the period is *art nouveau*); the shabby comfort of the almost respectable hotel which hosts the guilty lovers; the almost vicious charity visits of the *grande dame*, who slums luxuriously, as a matter of principle, at Christmas – all this is presented with an intensity of perception and an unerring sense of period which rivets the attention in spite of the ridiculous story. And the acting is dominated by the magnificent Marguerite Moreno, capable of acting anyone, even herself, off the screen.

At the end of the war Autant-Lara completed *Sylvie et le Fantôme*,

[1] *Sight and Sound*, Spring 1958.

with Joyeux, a delicately amusing film about a girl in love with a ghost, which, like *Douce*, depended on the creation and maintenance of a certain atmosphere throughout; after which, in 1946, he made his masterpiece, a film adaptation of Raymond Radiguet's *Le Diable au Corps*.

The precocious Radiguet – a protégé of Cocteau who, come to think of it, crops up almost everywhere when one writes about French cinema – the precocious Radiguet wrote only two novels before dying in rather atrocious circumstances in 1923, the second being *Le Bal du Comte d'Orgel*. The first was *Le Diable au Corps*, the tragic mood of which Autant-Lara succeeded to perfection in translating to the screen.

The story is simple – a love affair between a teenage boy and a young, but older, married woman whose husband is away at the War. It is told in flashback as the boy watches her funeral; for she has died in giving birth to his child, though her husband must think it his own. The boy, utterly alone, cut off by law, by convention, and by fate from her family's modest funeral procession, stands there in the rain, remembering. To add to the irony, the crowds around him are gaily celebrating (and to hell with the rain) Armistice Day – a reminder to him, among other things, of the time when he and she longed for the war to go on for ever so as to delay her husband's return.

In the flashback story the joyous despair of François and Marthe is so delicate in conception that it could be in danger of foundering on the slightest error of taste; but this Autant-Lara never permits. This time it is not just the absolute sense of period which counts; it is the hair-trigger feeling for the loving predicament of these two young people in their tragedy and, implicitly, in their cruelty; for the wronged husband's absence is omnipresent.

From this beautiful film I remember three sequences in particular. The first of course is the bedroom scene, to preserve which from being cut that most enlightened British film censor Arthur Watkins invented the X Certificate.[1] In this sequence Gérard Philipe and Micheline Presle – in all the freshness of their youthful talent – play out the passion and tenderness of the affair – she with some experience, he with none. Never has the discovery by a boy of the commingling of sexual passion with true love been so perceptively shown on the screen, framed in a marvellous combination of lighting and camera movement by Michel Kelber – lamplight, firelight, and shadows like soft velvet.

---

[1] It was the splendid Watkins who refused any certificate at all to Columbia unless they put back into *Le Plaisir* the Maison Tellier episode.

The second sequence is a scene of innocence, in a posh restaurant which François cannot really afford. In an attempt to assert himself he decides that the wine is corked ('Ça sent le bouchon') and sends for the sommelier. The embarrassment, the understanding reaction of the sommelier, the undercurrent of nervous happiness, of a happiness so very precariously poised – all are in perfect balance, and the tears come to your eyes.

The third sequence is of course that in the train. Marthe, already pregnant, tries to escape to her grandmother in Brittany without telling François. But he finds out and follows her onto the train and demands a showdown. 'Wait for me, François,' she says, 'I will be back.' 'Yes,' he replies harshly, 'You will be back – with your husband. And you'll have given him *my* child.' And, putting his hand on her belly, he suddenly feels the full import of her pregnancy and the appalling defencelessness of his own youth. At which point the tension is crashed into by a ticket collector (it is a non-corridor train and the collector arrives, as had François earlier, from the outside running-board, letting in a flurry of steam and smoke). For François this is the last straw – to be caught without a ticket. He whistles furiously while he pays and then, when the collector has gone, becomes almost hysterical, like a spoilt child. He insists that she must tell him quite clearly that she is leaving him. He wants this outright, unadulterated. She understands this and does so, the words tumbling out like a formula. Now all is over, all passion spent. It is quiet. Still like a child, François is resting his head on her shoulder. The train slows, stops at a platform. 'François,' she says gently, 'It is Paris,' as she gets up and pushes him gently away . . .

Autant-Lara never surpassed this film. He tried in a sense to repeat it in his filming of Colette's *Le Blé en Herbe* (1954), but despite a fine performance by Edwige Feuillère, despite some delicate direction, this story of growing love between two teenagers which is interrupted by the boy's seduction by an older woman remains perfectly tasteful but emotionally rather cool.

Le Rouge et le Noir – also with Gérard Philipe (whose early death from cancer deprived the film world of one of its best actors) – was bound to be one of those marathon epics, and despite felicitous touches it defeated Autant-Lara. Since then he seems to have done little of note save perhaps the black comedy of *La Traversée de Paris*, notable mainly for the splendid partnership of Jean Gabin and Bourvil in their attempts to get a black-market pig from one end of the city to the other.

Before World War II Jacques Becker had been assistant to Jean

Renoir for six or seven years. During the Occupation he directed his first films[1] in Paris on his return from two years' imprisonment in Germany. The first of these, *Le Dernier Atout*, was, it is said, no more than a conventional thriller. The second was a melodrama of peasant life called *Goupi Mains Rouges* which made something of an impression; while his third film, *Falbalas*, from an original script and set in a French fashion house, attracted controversial but on balance admiring criticism. He had by now established his own very personal style. This Becker style is concerned with detail – but not so much *attention* to detail as *involvement* in it, an involvement which often ends in a pleasing irony. It is a style which could comprehend the fizzy exuberance of *Antoine Antoinette* or *Rendez-vous de Juillet* equally with the gangsterdom of *Touchez pas au Grisbi*;[2] the elegant social comedy of *Edouard et Caroline* or the dramatic tensions of *Casque d'Or* and *Le Trou*. He will be remembered best, I think, for the last three I have named.[3]

Edouard et Caroline (1951), with Anne Vernon and Daniel Gélin – the latter being in a way Becker's Gérard Philipe – is based on the slenderest of stories. It involves a young married couple who fall into estrangement during a socialite manoeuvre to get him recognized as a concert pianist. For this they enlist the help of Caroline's uncle, who gives a reception which is the real centre-piece of the film; and in the end the young couple are reconciled by the intervention of a Texan millionaire. The great thing about this film is that it is never farcical. Its characters are all real human beings, most of them pretty empty and useless it is true – like those in *La Règle du Jeu*, though less seriously treated by Becker, who delights in the details of intimate crises, as when the young couple are dressing to go to the party. The film is not only funny; it is sometimes touching – and never cold.

As for *Casque d'Or* – what greater contrast could one find? This is a concentrated tragedy about ordinary people who are enlarged to a certain monstrosity by the passage of events and by their own passions. The framework is extremely simple; two lovers, neither of them great shakes morally or socially, get involved in murder and are parted by the guillotine.

Here again Becker is obsessed with detail to a degree where we become utterly convinced by the period sense he builds up and by the combination of brutality and sentiment, lovingness and insensitivity,

---

[1] In 1939 he had begun a feature, *L'Or du Cristobal*, which ran into money troubles and was abandoned; it was later completed by another director for another production company.

[2] A film rather unjustly overshadowed by Jules Dassin's *Rififi*.

[3] Tragically, he died in 1960 at the height of his powers.

which animates his characters. Serge Reggiani, as Manda, gives a fine rendering of a man who is weak when he should be strong, and vice versa, but who in the end is compelled by some unexpected inner compunction to confess to his crimes to save a friend. And of course the splendid Simone Signoret makes of Marie an effulgent and all-engulfing *femme fatale*.

Becker presents much of his story and his people in a sort of glow of sunlight which fits perfectly the period atmosphere of *La Belle Epoque*. There is something almost hieratic in the processional glory of their first passion – the boats on the river, Marie and Manda on the grass and under the trees, and Marie especially, with her full breasts, so intent on giving herself, on taking him . . . All this Becker well contrasts with the intimate sordidity of a fight to the death and, above all, with the final sequence when Marie watches from an upper window the whole shifty, furtive, horrifying ritual of the guillotine. Here is nothing but the dingy chilliness of the dawn which ends Manda's life and leaves her's – where? Poor Marie, with her golden hair-do; truly brightness falls from the air – with the knife.

In *Sylvie et le Fantôme* and *Le Diable au Corps* small character parts were played by an ex-music hall artist called Jacques Tati. Tati had in fact made a number of short films, based on his variety act, during the Thirties,[1] but it was not until 1947 that he made one, *L'Ecole des Facteurs*, which so impressed his producer, Fred Orain, that he encouraged him to expand the idea into a full length film. Hence *Jour de Fête*.

Tati is a rare bird; the mere mention or memory of his films is liable to start people off in a laughing fit. His output is minimal – five feature films over a period of twenty-three years; yet he has a constant world-following. As an artist he is as individual as Chaplin, though narrower in range. Above all he is French; though his films are probably more successful outside than inside France. The village and its people in *Jour de Fête* are seen at the beginning of the film almost from a documentary standpoint. The visual gags are Gallic, just as Chaplin's are Anglo-American; and all, by the clown's strange magic, universal. Indeed the seaside resort in *Les Vacances de M. Hulot*, for all its universality of pleasures and discomforts, could not be anywhere except the North Coast of France. Yet both these films are excellent examples of the internationalism of movie arising from the exploitation of national characteristics.

Hulot himself is extremely real – more so than François the postman. He is also extremely French, not least in his liking for somewhat

[1] One of them is said to have been directed by René Clément.

anglicized clothes and a pipe. And it is from his reality that the funniness arises; the extraordinary things which happen to him are only too possible – they could happen to anyone. Only occasionally does Tati put things to a stretch, as in the gorgeous cemetery scene when the spare tyre from Hulot's car becomes a funeral wreath; but even this is played with a certain factual, deadpan quality, not least when Hulot, anxious not to embarrass the mourners, waits patiently till the end and shakes hands all round before remaining behind to retrieve his tyre. And we all have our Walter Mitty daydreams such as the one which Hulot translates into reality by suddenly developing a tennis service of ineluctable speed and violence which terrorizes all concerned. As for the collapsible canoe, the gobbledegook loudspeaker misdirecting railway passengers, the demented fireworks which take on a life of their own – all the malice, in a word, of the inanimate – these we recognize for and in ourselves.

In *Mon Oncle* (1958) and *Playtime* (1967) Tati may have been inclined to take himself too seriously. They both have the elements of a 'message'. The malice of the inanimate is no longer seen as entirely comic. *Mon Oncle* is a fable which contrasts the merits of the old-fashioned disorganized world with the disadvantages of the so-called efficient modern world with its chromium, its sharp edges, and its gadgetry. *Playtime* is a very elaborate (and costly) series of variations on the same theme – now almost an *idée fixe* – in which, unfortunately, M. Hulot gets almost squeezed out, though there are a few moments of glory as, for instance, in the brand-new modern hotel when he succeeds in reducing everything to that satisfactory anarchy in which he (Hulot-Tati) can feel reasonably comfortable. *Mon Oncle*, too, has a number of lovely gags – aural as well as visual, as witness the extraordinary noises produced by the *batterie* of Madame Arpel's household gadgets; but I can't help feeling that the invisible wasp which so bedevils the cycling postman is purer and more satisfactory.

With *Traffic* (1971) Tati came back on form, despite an exceedingly unfortunate choice of female lead. This story of the attempt to take an ultra-modern 'camping car' from Paris to the Motor Show in Amsterdam[1] contains some splendid vintage Tati scenes of vast and majestic dottiness, like the vista of hundreds of cars stranded like seals during a rainstorm, and forming an obstacle course round and over which a multitude of umbrella-ed pedestrians must make their way.

---

[1] It is pleasing to see from the credits that Tati enlisted the help of Bert Haanstra, who no doubt added his own particular brand of humour to the Dutch sequences, particularly those concerning the Dutch customs posts and the Dutch police.

There is also a multiple crash which parodies Godard's *Weekend*, not least when a Volkswagen, gnashing its teeth, ferociously pursues one of its own wheels. In *Traffic* the contrivance which was too much to the fore in the previous two films is in general concealed (except in the laboured practical joke about the 'dead' dog) by scenes of farcical splendour and in the development of tiny gags into monuments of human suffering and endurance. There is one sequence which begins in the exhibition hall with all the salesmen opening and shutting doors, boots, and sunshine roofs, and then edges down to one poor soul whose bandaged finger tells its own story as, still bravely demonstrating, he tries to conceal his fear of the car as a dangerous and not yet fully tamed monster. As ever with Tati, the film needs neither titles nor commentary. The visuals and sounds – including a neatly multilingual dialogue track – are enough.

One comes back all the time to Tati's close observations of reality: with Massingham he is perhaps the only humorous documentarist. The long and meticulous preparation which he devotes to his films is not just a question of the development and timing of gags; it is, it must be devoted to the observation of human nature – observation sympathetic as well as critical. For there is always sympathy in the background – for the Arpels trapped so willingly in their spin-drier world, for the American matrons who are not to be allowed to see anything of the real Paris other than by mistake, and for the sad motorists whose faces take on the characteristics of their windscreen-wipers . . .

Sometimes regarded as a second generation Tati, Pierre Etaix operates on a slenderer talent and from a less universal outlook. His humour is *par excellence* pessimistic. Its tone was set in his first short film *Rupture* (1961), in which a young man's attempt to carry out a difficult and disquieting task (answering a letter from his girl-friend announcing she has jilted him) is frustrated, Tati-wise, by the inanimate objects – pen, paper, stamps etc – which should be at his disposal, and finally by his rocking-chair which hurls him through the window. Unfortunately Etaix made only one more short – *Heureux Anniversaire* (1961), with an equally funny and equally pessimistic story – before he took to making full-length pictures like *Le Soupirant* (1962), *Yoyo* (1965) and *Tant qu'on à la Santé* (1966), which do not entirely suit his miniaturist talent and therefore seem unnecessarily padded at times. Nevertheless his acid and very individual humour is welcome, and when, as in *Yoyo*, he goes for sequences made in the style of early silent comedy the results – as witness the shoe-fixation sequence – can be quite glorious.

IV

The Occupation and the years immediately following Liberation resulted, as we have now seen, in a number of films of great quality which lay, however, largely outside the area of what one might call commitment, political or otherwise. Apart from *Les Jeux Interdits*, apart from the documentaries of Franju and Lotar, and apart from the work of André Cayatte, to which I am coming shortly, the world of French cinema was escapist in tone. This, during the Occupation, was obviously inevitable; the best way of 'getting by' was to deal in a world of fable or history long past – as Clouzot found to his cost when he made an up-dated film like *Le Corbeau*.

Then in the confusion of the immediate post-war situation it was equally tempting for directors to enjoy and celebrate the return of general freedom, the pleasures of romantic tragedy or of comedy, whether in the hothouse rococo style of Max Ophuls or in the Flaubert-like analysis of human fears and failings in *Casque d'Or*.

It is interesting to note, too, in this period, the gradual diminution of the influence of the screenwriters. Aurenche and Bost still dominate in certain areas, notably the films of Autant-Lara and of course Clément's *Les Jeux Interdits*; and the influence of Prévert is still obvious in the work of Carné and Grémillon. But the main tendency seems now to be towards the *auteur* concept, so-called. Thus we find Becker, Clouzot and Melville constructing their own scripts either alone or with a non-dominant collaborator. We may also note that directors like Becker, Carné, Clair, Renoir and Tati tend to write original stories rather than make adaptations from existing works.

With Becker in particular, and the early short films of Franju, the first faint rumblings of a filmic revolution were beginning to be heard; and at the same time, and not in France only, film-makers were beginning really to tackle subjects about the recent world conflict now that the immediate issues of war had, at least temporarily, receded.

V

The situation was less easy than after World War I. It was, for a start, complicated by the arrival of three major wars in Korea, the Near East, and, eventually, Vietnam. The impact of these came more quickly and, thanks to the new media of communication, more vividly, than the Manchurian and Abyssinian affairs of yesteryear. The events were inextricably tied up with the Cold War (a boiling hot quarrel between the Capitalist and Communist hierarchies), and the agonizing fear of ordinary folk (fomented of course by the Cold War) of nuclear, biological and nerve warfare. These prospective goodies created tension not only internationally but internally; the general unrest of the world became increasingly reflected in civil unrest inside each individual nation.

Before all this had had time to boil up into the confusion in which we now live, there were made, by directors in France, the United States and Britain, a handful of films which approached in simple terms the basic human issues arising from 'modern' war. *Les Jeux Interdits* has already been discussed in a slightly different context; there remain, from the period under review, works by Cayatte and Resnais from the French point of view, by Stanley Kubrick and the Sanders brothers from the American, and by Anthony Asquith from the British.

André Cayatte, trained in the legal profession, set out at this time to be a film-propagandist against injustices arising from the blind operation of State legal systems, as well as against the often unthinking social and familial injustices which thereby arose. His films are unequal in quality though not in sincerity; their value tends to lessen in proportion to the more obvious intrusions of propaganda messages. But when the filmic, dramatic and propagandist balance is achieved, the result can be terrific; and such is the case with *Nous Sommes Tous des Assassins* (1952)[1], a film in which Cayatte combined an attack on capital punishment with the related question about the morality of individual as opposed to mass killing in time of war – a question paralleled by Asquith from a different angle in *Orders to Kill*.

The central focus of Cayatte's film is the capacious condemned cell at the Santé prison, where we are introduced to four convicted murderers. Gino, a Corsican, has killed someone in a blood feud and, without doubt, his execution will be followed by a similar murder; and indeed, we see it happen. Bauchet, a lout from the slums, slew his screaming baby in a fit of temper. Dutoit, a doctor of medicine, has pled not guilty to poisoning his wife but has been convicted just the same. Finally there is René le Guen, who has been sentenced for killing someone in self-defence without knowing that on a certain date his action had become illegal.

A carefully hand-picked lot of dossiers, one could say; too obviously hand-picked perhaps. But it doesn't work out this way. This

---

[1] Two other films, *Justice est Faite*, about jury service, and *Avant le Déluge*, about juvenile delinquency, contained much impressive material but suffered as a whole from too much 'preaching'.

is mainly because in the prison scenes Cayatte establishes his arguments in a horrific atmosphere of suspense which intensifies our sympathies while also sharpening our judicial criticism. The official method of execution is shown early on in the film, with the warders taking off their boots in the corridor so as not to be heard approaching, padding softly to the cell, then suddenly bursting in, seizing their victim, and speeding him (accompanying priest and all) to the waiting knife; all this for humanitarian reasons, so as to 'lessen the agony'. Thus the arguments, the pleas, the difficulties of religion and of priestly ministrations all take place in this deathly shadow, and in the knowledge that on any dawning day the door may burst open and the warders take – who? Who this time?

As far as argumentation goes the scene is dominated by the Doctor – a beautiful performance by Antoine Balpêtré.[1] Urbane, clever, perhaps a little devious, Dutoit never admits guilt; nor does Cayatte ever let us know the truth of the matter. Dutoit goes to his death without our ever knowing whether he is guilty or not. In a moment rather reminiscent of *Monsieur Verdoux* (except that *he* admitted his guilt) Dutoit, seized by the warders and asked by the priest whether he will in his last seconds confess, replies 'Another time, perhaps. These gentlemen[2] are in a hurry'. And down comes the knife.

This ironic quality in the film – and surely it owes a great deal to Cayatte's scriptwriter, none other than Charles Spaak – combined with Jean Bourgoin's sharp, remorselessly accurate camerawork, makes us very much prisoners ourselves. We can almost smell the sourness of the prison cells. There is irony too when we get outside the prison, as when we see Le Guen's younger brother[3] chopping off ducks' heads with a cleaver on the farm where he works; or when Le Guen himself, seized by an internal haemorrhage, is whisked into the prison hospital at Fresnes in case he should die before being judicially killed. In point of fact we never learn whether or not he is executed. Cayatte ends the film as Le Guen's advocate picks up the phone and waits to hear the result of the appeal against the sentence, while Le Guen's young brother – who has rather improbably been adopted by the advocate's rich and conventional parents – hovers in the background.

When all is said and done, and despite the impact of Dutoit's clever arguments, it is Le Guen who dominates the film; the part is taken by Marcel Mouloudji, an actor of great power who seems to have vanished. It is on Le Guen that Cayatte rests his double accusation

---

[1] Balpêtré is also seen as the doctor in *Le Journal d'un Curé de Campagne*.
[2] The English hardly conveys the sarcasm of 'Ces messieurs'.
[3] Played by Georges Poujouly, the small boy in Clément's *Les Jeux Interdits*.

against the legalities of war and of capital punishment. Le Guen is a layabout of limited intelligence (limited, that is, by lack of adequate education and opportunity) who during the war, having as it were nothing better to do, drifts into the Resistance. Here he is taught and encouraged to kill; and the more successfully he kills the more he is praised. When the war ends he continues to ply his trade, and is astonished to find that it is no longer heroic, no longer permitted. In a fantastically exciting sequence the police come to get him. He is lying in his bath, and from here he shoots it out with a sub-machine gun before being arrested. So he is condemned, and so he waits for death. But who could really explain to him the point at which his actions changed in moral terms?

That this issue was the springboard from which Spaak and Cayatte launched the whole structure of their script is indicated by the impressive opening sequence. A wasteland of rubble and detritus such as is found on the outskirts of all cities; drum rolls from German troops (almost toylike sounds) leading to the more sinister noise of rifle volleys – an execution. It is the execution of a man who to the French is a patriot, to the Germans a criminal. *Pro patria mori* or *écrasez l'infâme* – take your choice. But what if your patriot is in fact an uneducated slob with no idea of the issues on hand? Thus Cayatte introduces us to Le Guen, and through him to the cell at the Santé.

It is in wartime Paris that the bulk of Anthony Asquith's *Orders to Kill* takes place; and in fact the film contains a scene of desolation somehow comparable to that at the beginning of *Nous Sommes Tous des Assassins*. This is when Summers, in the rain-soaked Cimitière du Montparnasse, desperately rids himself of the banknotes which he has 'stolen' as cover to the killing he has just committed.

The question posed in this film is quite simple. In wartime, what is the moral difference (if any) between dropping a bomb which will kill hundreds of innocent men, women and children, and killing personally with your own hands one middle-aged civilian? Is there a difference in scale, in number? Summers, the protagonist of *Orders to Kill*, replies, 'There is no difference. Only when I dropped my bombs I wasn't there at the other end to hear someone ask "Why?"'

The film starts rather slowly and uncertainly with a sequence set in the United States. Captain Summers of the USAAF, grounded after the regulation 50 combat missions, fears that he will now be stuck in Washington on a desk job. His mother (played, one notes with delight, by Lillian Gish) uses her influence to get him a more active job, with Intelligence.

He is flown to London, and there he is prepared for an undercover job in Occupied France. Someone is betraying Resistance members to the Gestapo; it is essential he should be rubbed out. At this point the film starts to gather its horrifying momentum. Summers' main instructor is an American (Eddie Albert) who is nothing if not thorough, and subjects him, among other things, to a sudden Gestapo type interrogation which is physically as well as mentally alarming; it is introduced by Asquith in a way which alarms and startles the audience as much as it does Summers himself.

Another instructor – a beautifully modulated performance by James Robertson Justice – is an ex-Naval Commander who has made himself an expert in discreet and silent killing. With suave meioses and cosy family metaphors he leads Summers along murder's treacherous paths. But the realities, the physical realities of killing, are not touched on. All is, as it were, a dancing lesson; no one mentions that the Ball itself may be very different.

Fully trained[1], Summers is deposited in Paris, and the nightmare begins. His destined victim (a fine performance by Leslie French here) appears almost certainly to be innocent. The more Summers insinuates himself into warm and friendly relations with the man, his wife and his small daughter, the more certain he becomes that his superiors have chosen the wrong person. This section of the film is beautifully developed by Asquith against Paris locations in which the images and atmosphere of the Occupation period are convincingly portrayed.

Summers' confidence begins to crack. He goes to his one contact Léonie and, in desperation, breaks security by telling her the full details of his mission; this she had forbidden because, if caught and tortured, she might break down and reveal it. In this sequence, which is crucial to the film, Irene Worth gives a performance of staggering virtuosity and conviction[2] – now like an iceberg, now a caged tiger. It is a long scene, simmering with emotion, in which not only the practicalities of terror, but also basic issues of guilt and innocence are thrashed out to a terrible conclusion. Guilt and innocence have nothing to do with it, she points out. Did he argue this point with his superiors before dropping bombs on innocent civilians? Let him shut up and get on with the job.

He does. But he bungles the murder, and has to finish off the poor little chap with a pair of scissors in one of the most painful episodes I

[1] Paul Dehn, who wrote the screenplay, was himself an undercover agent during the war, and was wounded in the process; he was thus able to ensure absolute and vivid authenticity.

[2] It is a tragedy for cinema that she prefers to confine her art to the theatre. She made a welcome appearance in Peter Brook's film of *King Lear*.

have ever seen on the screen. Here Paul Massie, as Summers, puts across the full psycho-tension of the situation – in particular that element seldom shown, the *distaste* involved in doing a dirty job badly. And before he has managed to finish it, the little man has had time to gasp out a despairing and incomprehending 'Why?'.

To which there is no answer except panic and emptiness. And at this point Asquith speeds up the tempo in a series of episodes which apart from anything else are models of pure film editing of the highest order. Everything goes wrong. A message from Léonie makes it seem certain that he has killed the wrong man. Three times he tries to call her back; and at the third attempt – he is by now drunk – it becomes obvious that she has been caught by the Gestapo. An air-raid warning drives him down into the Métro, and he begins to lose all grip on reality. (There is a marvellous cut-in here, a flash of a few frames, of the victim's daughter showing off her dancing steps, which cracks the heart.) Nothing is now left save the madness of alcohol.

The film virtually ends here. There is a coda in which Summers is found after the Liberation at an Allied hospital where he is being treated for acute alcoholism. Gradually he learns the full truth. His victim was innocent; Léonie is dead. From his back pay he collects the equivalent of the blood-money he stole and hands it over to the widow and her daughter. 'He was', he says, 'a colleague of mine'.

These final sequences are somewhat ambivalent, and the intended irony does not come off very well. But then one may say – and Asquith perhaps felt – that there can never be a satisfactory solution. A cry of rage? A cry of pain? A cowardly whimper? Take your choice.

There is another film, set in France but made in America, called *Paths of Glory* (1957). Directed by Stanley Kubrick, it raises similar issues of responsibility and concerns a singularly stupid staff order for an attack by an infantry company which cannot possibly succeed. When the soldiers retreat, the Commander orders his own guns to fire on them, and when the gunners refuse, there ensues a court martial where all the sordid issues and intrigues, all the excuses and palliatives, all the avoidances of responsibility, whether personal or collective, are argued to a horrible outcome. And as in *Orders to Kill* it is the innocent who suffer. There is a scene reminiscent of the confusion and incomprehension of the murder in that film, when a man condemned to be shot for cowardice fells to the ground the padre who is offering him the Last Sacrament.[1]

A far too little known and neglected film on war issues was made in

[1] For further reference to *Paths of Glory* see chapter 7.

1962 by Denis and Terry Sanders, whose thesis film, *A Time Out of War*,
made while they were students at UCLA, had already become established
as a small classic. In *War Hunt* the war in question is the Korean War.
The period is that in which the Panmunjom negotiations were leading to
a cease-fire. As one of the soldiers remarks, 'It's a funny kind of war';
and it is presented as such, with the propaganda loudspeakers booming
words and music across no man's land, with desultory sniping by day
and savage barrages and attacks by night.

Basically the story is told through the eyes of Loomis (Robert
Redford, in what must have been one of his earliest major rôles), who
has been sent to the front line as a replacement. The opening sequences
are quite a *tour de force* in that the Sanders brothers make us participate
in his confusion and puzzlement without losing our own interest. This
is as well done as in the opening reels of Donskoi's Gorky Trilogy.

Then there emerges the sinister figure of Endore, whose pleasure
it is to go out by night on solitary patrol, face blackened and moving
like a cat. The information he brings back is valuable, but it is not the
real reason for his trips. He is a killer, and he uses a knife. His killings
are ritual, and followed by a sinister dance around the corpse. Attached
to Endore is a small orphaned Korean boy whose village has been wiped
out by napalm. ('It was a mistake,' he tells Loomis.)

Everyone is afraid of Endore ('I'm glad he's on *our* side', says
someone) and none more so than Loomis who, nevertheless, is forced
by conscience to try to rescue the boy from his clutches. He fails. But
of course with Endore everyone fails. The cease-fire comes into operation. Endore ignores it, and this time he takes the boy with him into
the darkness. Next day the military try to persuade him to come back.
But there is a scuffle and he is shot. The boy runs off into the scarred
landscape; and that is all.

War Hunt is a powerful and disturbing film. The psychopathic
Endore, wedded to war – war, that is, in its genuine connotation as an
inflicter of death – wishes to prolong forever his murderous honeymoon. For him peace is the ultimate destroyer, and he cannot face it.
John Saxon's playing of this part is splendid, with a curious withdrawn
quality which makes it all the more terrifying, like an M. R. James
ghost story.

The contrast with Loomis is pointed with some deliberation.
Loomis loves peace and cannot adjust in any way to war. In the midst
of carnage he instinctively seeks civilization. When, during a night
barrage – directed and photographed (by Ted McCord) with brilliant
and savage intensity – he goes chicken and is rescued by Endore, he

has no answer at all to Endore's 'I *like* you this way'. And when he reluctantly forces himself into a confrontation about the boy's future, there is a long moment of suspense, with Endore's knifepoint at his throat, in which we hear nothing but heavy breathing and must wait and watch until – and this is a fine dramatic stroke – nothing happens, but nothing.

The background to *War Hunt* is too sketchy. It is a short film as features go, and there is not enough time to develop the other characters to a sufficient degree.[1] Thus the moving episode of the death of one of the soldiers, Fresno, just before the cease-fire comes into operation, would mean more if the film-makers had had more time to build up his character; as it is, we have not got to know him well enough to feel the full impact of his death.

But this is a minor point in relation to the major impact of the film. In sticking perforce to their main story the Sanders have pulled no punches. This is especially true of the Korean boy, the real sacrificial victim of the war. Here they give us an innocent who is being totally corrupted, and they rub our noses in the harsh logic of corruption. There are two key scenes. In the first the boy decapitates a wounded bird rather than hand it to Loomis. In the second, which is a deliberate sequel to the first, Endore hands the boy a knife, so that he, the child, may give the *coup de grâce* to an enemy soldier, and thus become more surely lost even than Miles was through Quint. There is something so ineffably sad about this episode that tears supersede horror.

War Hunt is a haunting film, and none the less so for the grim authenticity of its combat scenes and for a telling and economical score by Bud Shanks. In showing a breakdown in human communication the film retains deep human sympathy. In the final sequence the Captain and his unit try, helplessly and idiotically, to tempt Endore back with candy and a DSC. 'Come back,' says the Captain, 'Come back, the war is over.' And Endore replies 'Which war?' Which, indeed?

With Alain Resnais' *Hiroshima Mon Amour* we enter an entirely different field in the approach to war and its results, which are here seen in relation to the nature of time and the nature of memory. Compared with Resnais' later work this film is easily intelligible – perhaps deceptively so.

The Frenchwoman who loved a German soldier, who saw him die, and who had her hair cropped as a collaborator; the Japanese man whose family, friends and city were destroyed by the first atom bomb; these two meet here and now, in the present; their love is here, now,

[1] The film was made on a starvation budget, and shot in 15 days.

physical. Yet they are simultaneously drawn together and kept apart by an often incommunicable community of experience.

The opening sequence is vital to the understanding of the film as a whole. The images, implicitly or explicitly, involve the sexual act between the man and the woman, intermingled with the negation of sex in terms of the depilated and mutation-mutilated victims of Hiroshima and, too, of the depilated cranium of the woman herself at the time when she was the victim of a love affair with the 'wrong' person at a town called Nevers in France six months before the bomb was dropped . . .

Vainly do these two search each other; for memory is not easily externally transferable. The man is desperately anxious to understand, to *enter into* her memories. But he can only see them from outside just as she, even though she is now in Hiroshima, cannot enter into his feelings when he returned to the ruined city after the bomb.

During that crucial sequence in the teahouse when, as it were, everything and nothing is said – she suddenly cries out, when the juke-box unpredictably churns out a waltz, 'I was young once!'. And she talks to the man (note here that Resnais chose a not very Japanese-looking Japanese for the part) as though he was her German lover. Then she says, 'He grew cold under me. He took so long to die . . . It was the Liberation. The bells rang.' And soon she screams at the memory of the shaving of her head. And the Japanese slaps her face. And they part, to meet again almost at once in the asepsis of a modern hotel corridor, in the lonely confluence of a railway station, and at the separate tables of an all-night bar. The streets of Hiroshima mingle with the streets of Nevers; but his heart, her heart remain apart and apart.

That is one aspect – the emotional and sentimental aspect, if you like, of the film. It involves human understanding and misunderstanding in terms of the cruel outcomes of total war; though the issues are not put forward in clearcut black and white as in *Nous Sommes Tous des Assassins* or *Orders to Kill*. But what happens in *Hiroshima Mon Amour* is something deeper. Love and hate, guilt and innocence, the passion of suffering and the passion of joy – how can their experience be communicated from one to another when they cannot or have not been shared? What, for him, are her memories of Nevers? How can he touch them? 'Does it rain often there?' he asks. And there is another thing; they are both married, and both, so they tell each other, happily. (In the lighter moments of the film Resnais achieves almost a Tchekovian atmosphere.)

So in a way the question he is asking is both 'How can they remember?' and 'How can they forget?'. Over and over again in the film they come back to this – trying to forget, trying to remember or not remember, accusing each other because of memories which neither can fully comprehend.

For memory involves time and time involves space. Resnais cross-cuts at all critical moments between Japan and France, and we, as spectators, can accept filmic time and filmic geography whereas the lovers, with their own time and space, cannot. The images of Nevers which *we* see are her memories, not his. The images of Hiroshima martyrs which *we* see are primarily his; if they are shared by her as a visitor (she has come there to take part in an anti-war film) it is as exhibits, not memories. Somewhere in this there may be a mistake on the part of Resnais and his screenwriter Marguerite Duras. The rôle of the man, other than as an immediate lover, is curiously passive. Energy, agony, suffering – these are expressed by the woman. He is there. He is alive. But in whose time does he live, his or hers? He feels left out; his only answers tend to be practical, like making love or slapping her face; but this is no way to escape from the trap of time and memory.

Time and memory haunt Resnais' earlier films too. His film about the Bibliothèque Nationale is called, significantly enough, *Toute la Mémoire du Monde* (1956). In this film he shows how libraries are insurances against our inadequate memories; how they are concentration camps for the imprisonment and retention of our ideas; and how the prisoners are as carefully preserved as patients in a hospital.[1] Lying in the background there is the conception of a takeover by the machine, the computer in fact. Implied too is the thought that H. G. Wells' conception of a World Brain could be at best a mixed blessing.

Even more germane to Resnais' feature film work are two other short films of his – *Guernica* (1950) and *Nuit et Brouillard* (1955). In *Guernica* the question of guilt is crystallized, formalized. Because Picasso's painting is self-sufficient; and because, maybe, the crime of Guernica was also self-sufficient in that it was one individual, deliberate incident – a planned rehearsal for horrors soon to come – the soundtrack is deliberately dominated by the precision of Paul Eluard's verse. This is not in the form of comment, but in the form of an elaboration of ideas which may be felt to underlie Picasso's powerful images. These images, through the camera's selective eye, take on extra significances

---

[1] In his book on Resnais, John Ward has pointed out a horrifying parallel with the camps in *Nuit et Brouillard*, where there was constant and careful supervision to facilitate, not prevent destruction.

not only in Resnais' choice of the precise areas to be shown, but also from time to time in dramatic exaggerations of light values.[1]

If *Guernica* is frozen at a certain point in time, *Nuit et Brouillard* certainly is not. Here we face a double time-sense. On the one hand there is 'Now', which is part of our consciousness of present continuity which operates at any time we see or re-see the film. This 'Now' is presented in colour, and shows us the empty grass-grown remains of the concentration camps as they are today. On the other hand there is 'Then', a specific period which ended (theoretically at least) when the Allied Forces opened up the camps and for the first time revealed their full horrors. 'Then' is of necessity in black and white, and records, in film or stills, what happened in the camps. The images are infinitely more horrible, more *painful*, than the very immediate images of *Le Sang des Bêtes* in which the dish is served up piping hot. In *Nuit et Brouillard* the meat is frozen.

The time-streams of 'Now' and 'Then' alternate throughout the film; but this scheme is not so simple as it seems because of the intervention of Michel Bouquet's voice speaking Jean Cayrol's narration. Laconic and merciless, the words spill over from one time area to the other, and they become a sort of danger signal – 'Be careful! You may not be precisely where you think you are.' Gradually the film, by this very structure, implicates us in guilt.

At one point there is what is very near to a conventional run-of-the-mill documentary sequence describing the various uses to which the corpses of the prisoners are put. 'With typical German thoroughness nothing is wasted.' And the hideous procession is passed in review – the neatly stacked spectacles in their thousands, human hair to stuff a thousand sofas, and the ingenious multiple guillotines so well designed for the quick removal of a thousand corpses' heads. What remains after all that, the narrator is kind enough to tell us, 'is boiled down for soap'. Memory, we are later reminded, is sluggish; and the film ends, in a sense, with a denial of hope. For if Auschwitz could happen, *and it did*, then anything is possible.[2]

These images from *Nuit et Brouillard* spill over, of course, into the opening sequence of *Hiroshima Mon Amour*, where the images of the atom bomb victims match exactly with those of the concentration camps. Only here Resnais goes further and further into the dilemma of

[1] Compare Resnais' technique in his films on Van Gogh and Gauguin.

[2] This thought occurs equally cogently (and independently) in *Memorandum*, a film from the National Film Board of Canada made by Donald Brittain, in which *cinéma-vérité* technique is used in combination with images from the past in depicting a visit to Belsen by survivors. This is another film in which one's time-sense is uncomfortably disturbed.

memory and of time. There is one point in the film where the position of her lover's hand lying on the sheets stimulates in the woman the memory of the dead hand of her original German lover. This she can never really communicate to the Japanese boy; but Resnais, through film, can communicate the resemblance, the memory, *and the fact that she cannot communicate it further*, to us, and only to us. And from the complexities arising from this sort of situation come his later works.

L'Année Dernière à Marienbad (1961) contains no moral issues, no questions of general or individual guilt. Its characters are personally time-dislocated; they are almost automats with their clockwork out of gear.

The concept is Bergsonian.[1] There is artificial time (clockwork if you like) which is precisely measured and only goes forward; to it belongs the awful phrase 'putting the clock back'. And there is pure time (intuitional) – the time of the mind and the time of dreams; the time which is past and future as well as present. The dislocations of time suffered by the personages in *Marienbad* are dislocations which most of us can recognize from our own inner experience. The long tracking shots through the hotel corridors are levitational; as in a dream, we are easily, lazily flying. The sudden changes of costume and position on the same location – especially those in the terraced gardens and amongst the statuary – also have the logic of a dream in that when dreaming we find such dislocations entirely natural and, more importantly, acceptable. The 'flash forward' techniques, particularly when the woman is seen sitting on her bed brilliantly overexposed (in the photographic sense) in a series of flashes, each one longer than the previous one, which are cut into the darker images of the hotel lounge, correspond with those flashes of precognition we all experience from time to time, the feeling that we 'have done this (or been here) before', or of 'knowing exactly what is going to happen next'. The hypnotic effect of this film is surely due in great measure to this sense of a shared experience – one perhaps which goes as deep as the Collective Unconscious of Jungian theory. It is, too, about what Whitehead describes when, in considering what he calls the 'coherence of the known', he points out that 'the perplexity we are unravelling *is as to what it is that is known*'.[2]

---

[1] John Ward's book on Resnais (Secker and Warburg, 1968) is based almost entirely on a Bergsonian approach to his work, almost to the exclusion of any other considerations. It is usefully and cogently argued and there is little need for me to add to it here.

[2] My italics. Also implicit in Resnais' approach, no doubt, are the precognitive theories of J. W. Dunne (*An Experiment with Time* etc), and those which postulate a second and reversed time running parallel with ours but from future to past; in which case the meeting might have taken place *next* year in Marienbad.

Quite apart from Resnais, we may note various attitudes regarding
time taken by other contemporary film-makers. Bertolucci's ambivalence
in *Partner*, and his very direct dislocation of time at the end of *The
Spider's Strategy*, are obvious examples; so too is the timelessness
indicated by Pasolini in *Teorema* when the father removes himself from
the concourse in Milan railway station to that nowhere desert of black
dust and slag in which we shall still find ourselves at the start of *Porcile*.
Nearer to Resnais, however, and perhaps the most disturbing exposition
of all, is Chris Marker's comparatively short film *La Jetée*, made in
1962.[1]

Here is a brutal distillation of Whitehead's 'perplexity'. It postulates a to-ing and fro-ing in time, a flow of time in both directions, more
dangerous and frightening than anything in Resnais, with the exception
perhaps of *Je t'Aime, Je t'Aime*. The film begins with a child observing –
on one of the piers at Orly airport – the face of a beautiful girl and,
almost simultaneously, the death of a man. Immediately after this – and
let us be clear that in a film like *La Jetée* it could be equally true to say
immediately *before* this – we are informed of the destruction of the
Western world, and in particular Paris, during the Third World War.
Out of the ruins, and among the catacombs, emerges a dominant race
of scientists engaged in horrible experiments – their generation in
Marker coming, I would think, from those terrible actuality pictures of
men being asphyxiated or frozen in the experimental laboratories of the
Nazi concentration camps – with the object of projecting the human
psyche forward and backward in spacetime. Our hero, in these terrible
and anguished journeys, receives solace from the beautiful girl into
whose continuum it is convenient for his mentors (or tormentors) to
project him; and there comes a point when they nearly, really 'meet'. But
not quite. There is a realization of a suspense in time. She calls him her
'ghost'. He knows she is 'dead'. Yet despite the fact that they are living
in two different channels of time, they get nearer and nearer to each
other until, during one fractional, minimal moment, she looks into his
eyes and they seem to be 'there' . . .

His mentors then ship him into the far future where Beings
accept his presence. These personages of the future have learned how to
travel in time – no doubt in part as a result of the experiments which he
is undergoing – and they invite him to join them in their journeyings.
But his own 'reality', if such it is, urges him back to the moment of
cognition which is all he has to cling to – the episode at the airport. And
so, in one of the most traumatic climaxes in cinema, we watch him

[1] It was not publicly shown until two years later.

return to this solitary certitude and discover that the man he watched falling dead as a child was, in fact, himself.

Simply as a sci-fi story *La Jetée* has a quality comparable with Bradbury or Asimov at their best. The idea of time as a sort of collection of Chinese boxes which will not even keep to their appointed shapes but make their own rules and fit with alarming perfection into all the wrong spaces, is in itself quite frightening. But what really gets you is Marker's treatment of the visuals; for the film is made up from a collection of freeze-frames which in themselves cause a rupture in time. With one exception, every shot in the film is a still. But the stills are not posed photographs; they are fractional moments ripped from the flow of motion-pictures. Each shot is a frozen one-twenty-fourth of a second, a moment of life, of movement (which is life) suspended in time, until we seem to arrive at a glimpse of that infinity in which macrocosm and microcosm merge, light is bent, and time turns in on itself. To this is allied a soundtrack of voices, his, hers, the guttural hypodermic count-downs of the experimenters, the sounds of nature and, above all, the sound of his heartbeats – louder and faster, ever more urgent, until they seem about to burst right out of the screen as the masked faces of the 'surgeons' loom.[1]

The frozen images are, of course, images of action, segments seized brutally and arbitrarily from a flow of motion – the girl's head turning to look at a stuffed monster in the natural history museum where she and he 'meet', the thrust of a hypodermic, or the patterns of running feet.

But then, for one tremendous moment, but only one, Marker restores to us 'real' time, time, that is, as we think we know it. On the bed, as the birds in the garden chorus for a summer sunrise, she opens her eyes, the lids flutter; and from this tiny fragment of living and loving (for it is on him that her waking glance falls) there seems to come a fanfare of glory, a revelation. This is honeydew; this is the milk of paradise.

All this comes about because Marker is taking a poetic as well as a prophetic and philosophical stance. For him the philosopher's stone is not there just to transmute dross to gold; it is there to take the mind or the soul to transcendent experiences, whether nightmarish at the hands of the dread scientists, or into the exquisite regions whose ecstasies

---

[1] An echo here of the appalling Professor Pothimere in Rex Warner's *The Wild Goose Chase*: 'I shall never forget my agreeable perturbation when I first saw a woman roasted. Almost my heart burst. But ah! my friends, this is not love . . . The perversions of the body are interesting, but lasting satisfaction is to be discovered in the perversions of the mind.'

drift like the gossamer spider-threads seen in the sunlight across autumn gardens. That she opens her eyes 'then' means hope; and this moment irradiates a film which otherwise would conjure up only that ghostly monster which lies deep, singly and communally, in the unconscious.

For all that, *La Jetée* is a frightening film. Marker remorselessly adumbrates those points at which, as in dreams, we are released from the bonds of physical time to meet those we know to be dead or those we have never seen save in subconscious imaginings; so that the world of *La Jetée* is a part of our contemporary consciousness, as when we turn the head from the television image of men walking on the moon and look out of the window at the moon itself or, watching the last reel of *2001: A Space Odyssey*, suddenly experience the forgotten panic of that moment when, with how much reluctance, we were expelled from our mother's womb.

This essay in the suspension or dislocation of time was stunningly capped in 1968 when Alain Resnais, having followed *L'Année Dernière à Marienbad* with the somewhat desiccated *Muriel* (1963) and the warmer and more appealing *La Guerre est Finie* (1966), came out with his own extraordinary tale of time-travel, *Je t'Aime, Je t'Aime*.

Like Marker's film, this is not just a science fiction job, though to begin with it pretends to be. No, like *La Jetée*, it relates the problem of time to the very human relationships of men and women. The difference between the two films is in the balance between the temporal and human factors. Marker concentrates, distils; Resnais expands. Marker uses two characters only, but his time travel goes forward as well as back. Resnais is concerned only with the past – a re-lived, not just a remembered past, filled with a number of people whose relationships, inevitably, must centre on and be tied to his protagonistic time-traveller. Of the deaths which end these two macabre journeys, that in the Resnais film is far more shocking and horrifying than that in *La Jetée*.

In bare outline the story of *Je t'Aime, Je t'Aime* is simple. A man recovering from a suicide attempt, and in a mood of absolute neutrality as regards continuing his life, is asked by a group of scientists to take part in an experiment which involves a trip into his own past; they make it clear that this will not just be a recreation in memory but a physical return, so that he will himself be where he was one year ago. They see time as concrete, tangible. Already, they think, they have succeeded in sending a mouse on such a trip; but as the mouse cannot communicate they cannot be sure. Hence the need to send a human being. The experiment is to be under strict scientific control. He is to visit the past for precisely sixty seconds. On his return to the present he must, for technical reasons, remain for four minutes in the time capsule before they release him. He agrees.

The experiment begins. Very soon a disastrous distortion manifests itself. The man is unable to establish a continuity of past time lasting sixty seconds. The past he is living lacks logical order, lacks normal temporal progression. As a result his time gets out of synchronization with that of the scientists, who are unable, during his frequent returns to the present (their present), to extricate him from the capsule in . . . I was going to write 'time', but under these circumstances we seem to need another word. Eventually they are forced to abandon him. 'We have lost him', mourns the professor. He is wrong. The man returns monstrously, and too late.

The man, Claude Ridder, is entangled again in a tragic past. His marriage to a beautiful but clouded girl, his liaisons with other women, his creative frustrations in various boring office jobs – all these lead to a sense of failure, to a lack of communication. On a visit to Glasgow he leaves his wife Catrine asleep in the hotel bedroom. The gas fire leaks, and he returns to find her dead. Exonerated by the police, he nevertheless tells his other girl that he deliberately murdered her because he could 'no longer help her'. Then, unable to live without Catrine, he shoots himself in the heart.

As a story it is not all that thrilling or original; it stands because Resnais clearly cares in depth about his characters, and when he fragments it into the confusion of time-travel, his concern for them as persons rather than superficial figures from a Lelouch movie is vital. In the abysses of time we are still concerned with the gulfs, the impossibilities of communication we find in, say, Bresson's *Une Femme Douce*.

Catrine has in her persona an attraction-repulsion which sometimes sends Claude round the bend. He bursts out into objurgations, throws books about. When she invents a theory that man was created solely to be a slave at the service of cats, he accepts the fancy – they are at the seaside on a day of pale-blue enchantment – but one has the impression that she may well think of herself as a cat. Both Claude and Catrine have acute, overt time-consciousnesses. Her's concern interruptions in time, broken slumbers, broken thoughts, intimations of death which she translates for him into irrational fears and fancies. He on the other hand is obsessed with a static conception of time. 'For me,' he soliloquizes at one point at one of the many office desks he frequents, 'it is eternally 3 p.m.'[1] And he holds intimate colloquies with the talking clock.[2]

This undercurrent of obsession with time helps us to relate to the overall structure of the film, and particularly to Claude's regular though ever useless returns to the time capsule ready to escape back into the present. The capsule itself, which must of course contain both time present and time past, is shaped on the outside like the anatomical exterior of the human brain, and on the inside like both the womb and the ventricular areas of the human heart.

Because the time-travel system has gone wrong, the past, as it existed, comes to Claude, and so to us, in illogical and non-sequential fragments. Episodes repeat themselves, or refuse to get into a 'proper' time-context. It is only after quite a long time that the facts, the locations, the sentiments, the conflicts, become understandable. And all through there comes this handful of crucial images which lead him back into his past – an underwater swim, a wade through the tide to where she lies on the beach, and a snatch of banal chat. It is these – the components of the vital sixty seconds which is the only and precise period which he is supposed to 'live' – it is these fragments which refuse to compose themselves into a sequence of 'real' time. And so the rest of his past – equally fragmented – takes over like a disintegrated jigsaw, part of whose pattern we can vaguely discern. And the scientists lose him.

Towards the end space starts to run out of control as well as time. After we have witnessed more and more frustrating returns to the capsule, with its womb-like couch tending more and more to engulf Claude, who has retired to it exhausted after thrusting vainly against the only partly-yielding walls – browny-pink, fleshy – we come to notice spatial as well as temporal dislocations.

These have been signalled quite early on in a jagged moment when the mouse (which as a seasoned time-traveller has been enclosed in the time-capsule with him) suddenly runs past Claude and Catrine on the beach. To us this is disturbing enough, for we know that Claude on the beach is living a year earlier than Claude in the capsule. But it is also disturbing to Claude. A white mouse. What is a white mouse doing on this wide, sandy beach? And we feel that he, living in the past,

---

[1] 'In the real dark night of the soul it is always three o'clock in the morning.' – Scott Fitzgerald, *The Crack Up*.

[2] Resnais uses telephone soliloquies a lot. The tenderest love scene is that in which we see Claude, in his bedroom at a small seaside hotel, listening on the phone to Catrine telling him what he can see from his window; and this in itself – given the context – creates an equivocation of filmic time and space.

has felt the future through the mouse, that with some ineffable instinct he has recognized it and dimly realizes that time doesn't move, that its apparent movement is an illusion created by ourselves, that it really is 'eternally 3 p.m.'.

Now physical objects begin to add to the nightmare by appearing in the wrong context. At certain moments in the film we join a fragmentary conversation which Claude has with a man in a railroad train in which he tells how he once called at a house and was invited by a young girl to tend her while she had her bath. At another arbitrary moment we see the lead-up to this episode. But now, without warning, we see, as we have seen several times before, the large office, well-staffed, in which Claude works; and there in the middle of it, installed on top of a desk, is the bath with the girl in it, substantial, tangible, actual. Again, the factual interview with the Glasgow police inspector after Catrine's death suddenly repeats itself in terms of sheer nonsense, in the wrong room, with piles of papers instead of chairs, and with the inspector apologizing *in French* for not being able to speak French. And there is one traumatic and inexplicable shot – seen once only – of a heavy iron-barred door, like that of a prison, which is opened for Claude by a small person wearing the mask of what seems to be a mutated goldfish.

But after all this, after other disturbing images (a man in a telephone box full of water, bubbles coming from his mouth like visible sounds), we are suddenly faced with a long, long close-up of Claude, who quietly, softly, explains exactly what happened over Catrine's death in Glasgow. And with the truth (if it is the truth) comes the realization that he cannot go on without her. He puts on the gramophone. No sound comes from it. He sits down on the floor of the sitting-room, takes out a revolver, and shoots himself in the heart . . .

And as he keels over, the blood welling through his shirt, there is a series of rapid flashes of him falling, falling, falling – each time in the open air, and onto gravel or grass – and there comes the horrible realization that this is outside the scientific centre where the experiment has been being carried out. The scientists who have given him up for lost now try to resuscitate him; but it is too late. The suicide from which formerly he was returned to life has been used again by him in a desperate attempt to break through time, to break out of time, to return to a certain point in time and space. His success has cost him his life; he has lost the present as well as the past. The final image is of the mouse, still in the time capsule, seen in gigantic close-up as it reaches up towards the air hole in its glass cage.

Je t'Aime, Je t'Aime is liable to leave one mentally disorientated;

it is a truly remarkable example – and much more specific than *Hiroshima* or *Marienbad* – of the manner in which film can disrupt normal conceptions of time and space. This may well turn out to be Resnais' best film, though there may be quite a few people who will resist, or turn away from it – no doubt for deep but unexplained psychological reasons.

The performances are splendid throughout – especially Claude Rich as Claude and Olga Georges-Picot as Catrine – and Jean Boffety's photography is stunningly effective. The script, with its remarkable dialogue, is by Jacques Sternberg, author of, among other books, *La Brûlure de Mille Soleils*. And Resnais' genius as a director is once again uniquely established.

Another truly unique director, Robert Bresson, is frequently linked with Carl Theodor Dreyer, not so much for the solitudinous non-conformity which he shares with the Dane as for the fact that they both made films on the trial and execution of Joan of Arc. There is, however, a deeper affinity. They are both concerned basically with problems of faith, whether in terms of organized and accepted religion or in more general areas. Religion as a direct manifestation of man's need for faith is seen in Bresson's *Les Anges du Péché*, *Le Journal d'un Curé de Campagne*, and *Procès de Jeanne d'Arc*; and in Dreyer's *Leaves from Satan's Book*, *La Passion de Jeanne d'Arc*, *Day of Wrath*, and *Ordet*. Problems of faith without direct, or at least with only peripheral relation to religion, may be seen in Bresson's *Les Dames du Bois de Boulogne*, *Un Condamné à Mort s'est Echappé*, *Pickpocket*, *Au Hasard Balthazar*, *Mouchette*, and *Une Femme Douce*; and in Dreyer's *The President*, *Mikael* and *Gertrud*.[1]

In either case these two directors share the search for that moment of joy – of certain and absolute joy – which a saint finds in the ecstasy of religious experience and which an unbeliever must stumble on elsewhere. The explicit religious experience is seen at its highest in the two Joan films, in *Le Journal d'un Curé de Campagne*, and in *Ordet*. The other may be seen in, for instance, *Mouchette* and *Gertrud*. Whatever their provenance, these moments are rare and triumphant. Mouchette on the dodgems at the fair; the curé's short journey on the motor-bike pillion; Jost's remark to Fontaine after their escape – 'If only my Mum could see me now!'; the 'recognition' of the miracle by the little girl at the end of *Ordet*; the bare, simple and final page of the curé's diary –

---

[1] Only Dreyer's *Vampyr* (which I have always regarded as a disappointing attempt at an avant-garde film), and perhaps Bresson's *Quatre Nuits d'un Rêveur*, do not fit into either category.

'All is Grace'; Joan receiving the communion wafer in *La Passion de Jeanne d'Arc*; the sudden discovery of love between Anne and Martin in *Day of Wrath*; and even Mouchette's almost sacramental suicide (too cruel a word) wrapped in the torn dress she should have worn at her mother's funeral . . .

Bresson and Dreyer are often spoken of as 'difficult' directors. In certain connotations I suppose they may be. But difficulties surmounted can bring great rewards, and there are certain experiences, emotions, realizations, which only become available if you go more than halfway to meeting their sometimes alarmingly austere approach to film-making.[1]

They are both great rule-breakers. Bresson has a habit of leaving out those very things which any other director would regard as absolutely essential. Dreyer shattered cinema-goers in 1928 by shooting a film almost entirely in close-up, using, as someone remarked, the human face as a landscape; and in his later films he increasingly used longer and longer takes (in *Joan of Arc* 219, in *Ordet* only 69).

Both men's preoccupation with the essential isolation of the human being and with his consequent search for communication – be it with other men or with God – is so profoundly motivated, so pure, so sincere (and I use these words with great deliberation), that the effect is more than idiosyncratic; it is transcendent, unique. They are, if anything, closer to their opposites than to each other – Dreyer to Strohcim, say, and Bresson to Buñuel. Thus in his script for *Day of Wrath* Dreyer sets the scene of the torture of Herlof's Marte with very much the intensity of the director of *Greed*.

> 'The first picture in this scene is a track shot parallel with the long wall where we are standing. We first see the group of priests, then the notary and finally the rack. From the moment the picture fades in a feeling of feverish agitation prevails – as at the end of a thrilling race. The priests are leaning forward or half standing up, in breathless suspense and with shining eyes. The notary's pen races over the paper. The priest, Master Olaus, who is standing at his side, corrects him in a whisper.

> 'And at the rack Master Laurentius and the executioners are "working" under the influence of a tremendous tension resembling that which is found in a hospital during a difficult operation. The whole scene . . . must be characterized by a hectic, forced, ecstatic note.'

[1] I remember rejecting *Les Dames du Bois de Boulogne* out of hand on a first viewing; only after seeing *Un Condamné à Mort* did I return to it and appreciate it.

And similarly Bresson, with the intensity of his scenes of faith in *Le Journal* and *Procès de Jeanne d'Arc*, approaches a contiguity – that of positive to negative – with the Buñuel of *Nazarin* and of *Viridiana*; so much so indeed that one comes to think about *Mouchette* as being a kind of Buñuel anti-masque to *Procès de Jeanne d'Arc*.

Nearly everyone has of course remarked on the similarities between the Dreyer and Bresson Joan of Arc films. Bresson is reported to have said that he has never seen the Dreyer film; in which case the similarities rest solely on the fact that both directors adapted the self-same material for the screen – the *procès-verbal*, in fact, of the trial and of the later rehabilitation. Thus all the main incidents, and the key dialogue, are bound to be the same.[1]

The main difference between the two films is of course that Dreyer's is without a soundtrack. Ebbe Neergaard has stated that Dreyer originally wanted to make *La Passion de Jeanne d'Arc* as a talking film; and the machinery for doing this was of course available in 1928, though cumbersome and not yet fashionable with the intelligentsia. However that may be, Dreyer ended by constructing his film with the aid of subtitles which, as in *October* and *Turksib*, were an integral part of the montage, and which spread out, as it were, the reactions of the interlocutors and their victim in a manner which satisfactorily paralleled the technique of the talking picture. Indeed, the effect is frequently very powerful, as when, like a trapped animal, she recites the Lord's Prayer for her inquisitors; or when she turns on her accusers who are saying she is an agent of the devil and says, '*You* are the devils, you and you and you . . .'; and again when, speaking of her God to Massieu just before her last confession and communion, she says simply, 'I am His child'.

Both films are claustrophobic, and both of them wait until the end, when the bonfire is readied in the market-place, before they open up. Dreyer in fact opens up more than Bresson. He shows a near riot, some of it dramatically reflected in a puddle, and he uses an upside-down effect which tilts strangely and makes the English soldiers look like insects. Bresson, on the other hand, while varying the angles from Joan to the French judges and their English employers, keeps our viewpoint of the final episode fairly constricted. The short, hasty, tiny paces

[1] Equal similarities may be noted in Victor Fleming's *Joan of Arc* (1948) when, after detailing her earlier life, it arrives at her trial and execution. Otherwise one can but say that Ingrid Bergman often looks far too *soigné*, that José Ferrer gives a virtuoso performance as the Dauphin, and that there are, for its time, some fine Technicolor interiors and landscapes with unusually soft pastel shades in blue and green and muted browns and reds.

with which Joan runs towards the stake are shot from close to, and from above, in a long tracking shot, and we see nothing else until she has reached the stake. The pigeons during the burning are seen fluttering about on a wooden cornice, while those in the Dreyer film fly free in the air. Bresson shows us a miserable little dog, tail between legs, coming along the same path that Joan has taken, also shot from above; but Dreyer has a baby at its mother's breast which turns its head and looks beyond Joan, beyond us, towards the whole wide world.

Seen today (with a suitable musical score) *La Passion de Jeanne d'Arc* remains a tremendous, often almost unbearable experience. The spirituality of Falconetti shining out from a face beaded with sweat; the swelling tears which are the interpreters of Joan's origin, of 'her free fields, her home, and the momentum of the inspiration that has urged her into this betrayal';[1] the morning freshness of Massieu's face; the craggy cruelty of Warwick's jaw and of his steel-helmeted head seen always, as are so many other characters, from below; the brutality of the burning almost cancelled by her cry of 'Jesu!' – all these completely survive the passage of time, the changes of fashion, and the super-ventions of new techniques.

Bresson, on the other hand, ends his film with an obscene symbol. The Maid has been utterly consumed in the flames. There remain only the chains that bound her to the stake and the stake itself, seen against the grey sky as a charred, blackened and disgusting phallus. It is a scene of repulsive desolation; but it is repellent in the same manner as the sufferings of the priest in *Le Journal d'un Curé de Campagne* which we identify with the stomach cancer, the sour wine and the sour breath. Behind the repellent images we sense the struggle for faith which ends with 'All is Grace'; and beyond Joan's stake we hear her cry to Jesus and we remember her last vision of the cross held up before her eyes in the smoke until the heat forced its bearer back.

Bresson's technique in *Procès de Jeanne d'Arc* is, like that of her inquisitors, remorseless. His camera focuses dispassionately on her in cell and courtroom over and over again as the official interrogation develops; in the courtroom it swings from her to the inquisitors, especially Cauchon. Little else is shown except for the short journey – again frequently repeated – by stair and corridor between courtroom and cell; and occasionally a brief intervention by Warwick and his colleagues who, like the SS, tell Cauchon and his friends to hurry up and get the required verdict. It is only much later in the film that two

---

[1] Harry Alan Potamkin, in a review written in 1929 and reprinted in *The Emergence of Film Art*, ed. Lewis Jacobs, Hopkinson and Blake, 1969.

variations are made. Firstly, the prelates start to interrogate Joan privately in her cell. Secondly, and arising from this, there is an acidly ill-tempered committee meeting at which certain priests mutiny, on the ground that private questioning is illegal. Bresson gives this episode much more emphasis than does Dreyer; conversely, he virtually throws away the images and threats of torture which, in the Dreyer version, trigger off the whole final drama of confession and recantation.

Bresson uses the English in this film rather as he uses the Germans in *Un Condamné à Mort s'est Echappé*. They are always connected with highly magnified sounds of bolts drawn or closed, of creaking hinges, of footsteps in stone passageways – the background, in fact, against which Fontaine so patiently and faithfully plans his escape. The English are also connected visually with the closing of the door of her cell. This is always shown so that the door also closes on us, the spectators; and it is frequently followed by a shot of Warwick or another officer peering at Joan through a spyhole in the wall, or by a shot of Joan as seen by them – always three-quarters back to camera, sitting stiffly upright on a stool and looking rather like a waxwork. It is a gruesome shot, for it shows us Joan exactly as the English saw her: a dangerous and inconvenient political object and, worse, an object of superstitious fear and hatred. 'I don't want a single hair to remain,' says Warwick, as they collect her clothes and small possessions after the condemnation. There is a striking contrast between the harshness of these visuals and the rare tenderness of certain moments in the courtroom (memorable indeed for their rarity if for nothing else) during which, by discreet and almost imperceptible glances and gestures, Brother Isambart helpfully signals to Joan how to answer the more dangerous questions posed by her inquisitors. He wears a white robe on to which, I suspect, Bresson's cameraman Burel shone a little extra light; this, combined with the expression of sweet and simple sympathy on Isambart's face, gives us, amid the claustrophobic setting, the doubletalk and the threats, some-thing of an understanding of the faith that can animate not only the soul of a martyr but also the heart of someone who has an under-standing of martyrdom as an expression of faith. The way this com-plicity between Joan and Isambart is presented lights up the film momentarily with rays of divine wisdom. And it is Isambart, not Massieu, whom Bresson chooses as one of the two monks who hold up the cross before Joan's dying eyes.[1]

From Isambart the hero of Bresson's finest and perhaps most

---

[1] As Isambart, Michel Herubel provides an excellent example of the perfectionism of Bresson's casting; the delicacy of his performance is beyond praise.

difficult film would, surely, have received the same sweet sympathy and comfort; but there is no one like that in Ambricourt – not even the village girl Séraphita. In *Le Journal d'un Curé de Campagne* Bresson has achieved a unique and wellnigh perfect piece of cinema. He has done this by breaking all the rules of film-making; by refusing to 'adapt' the Bernanos book, by refusing to use actors, by draining his visuals of all warmth and, above all, by withdrawing rather than promoting action and incident. It is a film which sometimes seems to consist almost entirely of omissions, or at least of ellipses; but it is also a film which could justly be described as a religious masterpiece. It has been fully and very perceptively discussed by André Bazin and others, and there is no point in my going over all that ground again.[1] But it is worth noting that Bazin says of it that 'the only film it can be likened to is Carl Dreyer's *Jeanne d'Arc*. The cast is not being asked to act out a text, not even to live it out, just to speak it. It is because of this that the passages spoken off-screen so perfectly match the passages spoken by the characters on-screen . . . What we are asked to look for on their faces is not some fleeting reflection of the words but an uninterrupted condition of soul.'

This is just. The self-martyrdom, if that is what to call it, of the priest leads us to Joan, even to Mouchette, rather than to Johannes in *Ordet*, though theoretically the last-named might seem to be the nearer comparison. But the fact is that for Dreyer Johannes is Christ. Dreyer had always, more than anything else, wanted to make a film on the life of Jesus; indeed, he was still planning this at the time of his death. In *Ordet* Johannes actually raises someone from the dead; therefore he must be seen to partake of the Godhead whose ineffable virtues Joan or the curé only seek to be allowed to imitate.[2] The sufferings of the curé are surely part of the imitation of Christ; and in this humility he succeeds. The sufferings of Johannes are the least of the matter; for he plays his part out as the Christ who came to bring not peace, but a sword. (It is the other members of his family who seek reconciliation – at least until the return of his 'sanity'). Johannes as catalyst, scapegoat, Holy Fool – the trouble with *Ordet* is that come the end of the film we don't believe it. The emotional storms, the violent personal relationships, the 'madness' of Johannes – these hold us. The miracle doesn't; far

---

[1] See *The Films of Robert Bresson*, ed. Ian Cameron, Studio Vista, 1969; Bazin's essay – one of the best things he ever wrote – is a good antidote to Durgnat's stimulating and provocative analysis which precedes it.

[2] Admittedly the miracle in *Ordet* is subjective in terms of the people concerned. But there is nothing in the final sequence to make one think that Dreyer expected his audience to be sceptical.

more compelling is the cross shakily sketched on the last page of the curé's diary.

One of the troubles with *Ordet* is one which is never found in a Bresson film – miscasting. Johannes, played by Preben Lerdorff Rye (so good as Martin in *Day of Wrath*), is convincing as a madman and even more convincing as a religious fanatic who has driven himself mad not in his search for God (he has found Him already) but in his apparent inability to sell his idea of God to others. But, as a product of doctrinal conflicts between friends and relations whom he knows only too well, Johannes needs to do more than persuade us of his own imbalance; he needs to attract our sympathy at least as much as does the aged woman accused of being a witch at the beginning of *Day of Wrath*. (Both films, it may be noted, start in the same way – with people remorselessly on the hunt after someone who is not as others are.) Lerdorff Rye gives us the mad, wild-eyed missionary; but he doesn't give us the human soul which must surely therein reside. The twist at the end of the film by which he regains his sanity before he performs the miracle is almost nullified by the actor and by the way he acts.

Despite this, *Ordet* has fine qualities. There is a beautiful and justifiably symbolic contrast of visuals between the windswept, some-what forbidding dune-landscapes and the glowing, tidy warmth of the Borgens' house which, in turn, contrasts with the austere, almost empty-looking décor of the Skraedders' home. It is a contrast which helps to emphasize the conflicts of religious bigotries. Johannes, preaching across the bare landscape which separates the two, is from time to time impressive; but he never places the human problems of faith and love adequately in balance with the illnesses, the inquisitions, the flawed loves and the unthinking cruelties which somehow crystallize those very attributes in Bresson's best work. It is not perhaps just the fault of the actor; it may well be that Dreyer's own intensity of spirit, so effective in *La Passion de Jeanne d'Arc* and *Day of Wrath*, may here have taken a wrong turning into a cul-de-sac.

It is difficult at this stage not to interpose a film whose characters are by no means mad like Johannes, are the exact antitheses of the Curé and the Comtesse in *Le Journal d'un Curé de Campagne*, but yet are closely concerned with problems of faith. 'If you weren't a priest, would you marry me?' says a woman to a priest; and he, without a word, smacks down an axe on to the block on which he has been chopping wood for her, and leaves the room . . .

Léon Morin – Prêtre (1961), by Jean-Pierre Melville (whose Cocteau film *Les Enfants Terribles* I have already discussed), is a strange patchwork quilt of a film, full of short, sharp sequences often cut off before their thematic development has been achieved, but ultimately held together by the extraordinary tension in the relationship between the two main characters and by the subsidiary tensions which this relationship arouses in others.

The film is set in a small French town during the German occupation. Barny, a young widow whose Jewish husband has been killed in the war, has evacuated herself to this place and is working in the office of a correspondence course. Life is hard and difficult, and she has had to place her little daughter in care with some local farmers. Lonely, left-wing, atheist, attracted strongly to a handsome girl in the office, she decides one day on an impulse, almost for a bet, to attack the falsity of religion by entering the confessional in the local church and shocking the priest by blasphemous remarks. Unfortunately for her she picks on a young Father of peasant stock whose replies are equally provocative. By the time she leaves the box she has somewhat dazedly agreed to perform a small penance.

She is hooked. He lends her religious books to read. She visits him regularly; argues, resists conversion. He for his part never insists. He plays the piano. He shelters maquis men from the Gestapo without question. He provides countless baptismal certificates for Jewish children. He preaches sermons to his bourgeois congregation which end with phrases like 'and for goodness sake brush up your singing'. He is terribly handsome – for he is in fact Jean-Paul Belmondo, who does however so sink himself in the part that it is difficult to think of him in such films as *A Bout de Souffle* or *A Double Tour*.

Then comes what she calls – the film is made in the form of a spoken diary – '*la catastrophe*'. Clearing out the attic one afternoon she is descended on by God. She is converted. When she tells the priest he receives the news with a snort of scepticism; but their relationship inevitably becomes closer, their arguments more complex. And meantime the complications and problems of the Occupation continue to beset everyone. Friends join the Resistance, or become collaborators. Jews are deported. The Maquis blow up the local hotel. The various episodes are sometimes connected with the priest, sometimes not; and when they aren't they become muddled and confusing. Indeed there is one sequence in which Barny gets into an argument with a German sentry at a remote level-crossing whose relevance still escapes me.[1]

---

[1] This is no doubt due to the fact that Melville himself, despite the protests of his producer, cut the film from three and a quarter hours to two hours ten minutes. It was originally 'a sort of great fresco of the Occupation', and Morin did not make his appearance

Out of the confusion there gradually emerges the – to her – appalling knowledge that her conversion is not to God alone, but is the product of her desire, her carnal desire, for the priest. Psychologically this is a well-known syndrome but, apart from its very different treatment in *Nazarin*, and its appearance in reverse in *Rain*, I don't think it has ever been cinematically depicted with such sincerity and frankness. The woman's emotional tensions and agonies are beautifully (and I mean beautifully) expressed by Emmanuelle Riva, and are all the more effective through the emphasis which Melville places, in neo-realist style, on the harsh crudities of her daily existence – the visits to her farmed-out child, the arguments and quarrels in the office, the household chores in her apartment. The film is constructed without pictorial pretensions. Henri Decae often uses his camera as though for a newsreel, with strong contrasts – both exterior and interior – between black and white. The scenes in the church itself – backed as they are by those unexpectedly loud, abrupt, yet very familiar sounds of doors slamming and people muttering – are equally uncompromising.

The basic merit of the film, however, is the way Melville controls the development of Barny's fixation so that while we watch it build up, incident by incident, while we see – nearly always a step ahead of her – her gradual realization of what is happening, we are still hardly prepared for the huge outburst of sexual and spiritual conflict which results. Amid this extraordinary turmoil the priest stands firm. In the whole film there is only one gesture which suggests overtly a dangerous temptation he must recognize in himself – the gesture with the axe I have already mentioned.

This act of violence, for such it certainly is, is followed by a longish anticlimax as the film draws to an end. The priest is leaving for another job which he does not really want but which as a good servant of the Church he will cheerfully accept. In his quarters, now bare and empty, with his few, his very few belongings ready to be packed into his rucksack, Barny and Morin confront each other for the last time. One single tear drifts down her cheek. There is nothing more to say. All was said previously when, at his insistence, she went into the confessional and told God, through him, how she tried to seduce him, to make him forget his priestly vows and to plunge his soul into mortal sin. As the film ends she leaves him standing there, lonely but secure in the physical beauty of his manhood because he has dedicated it to God; and she gropes her way like an old woman down the staircase and into the dark

until the film had been running for an hour and a quarter. (See *Melville* by Rui Nogueira, Secker and Warburg, 1971.)

street. For her, all is not Grace. For him, what victory? He has not entered, and never will enter into the dark conflicts of the Curé of Ambricourt, and it may well be that he is the lesser man for it.

Léon Morin – Prêtre is not, of course, a great film like *Le Journal d'un Curé de Campagne*. But it has the merit of telling, with a sort of documentary honesty, a story about the problems of faith as seen from a secular viewpoint. Morin, for all his 'muscular Christianity', remains an enigma. He withholds his sex from Barny, and yet at the same time forces her to sublimate her deprived lust into at least some shadowy idea of the Divine. At one point in the film she has a fearful vision. She is in bed. He enters her room, comes to her (the scene is finely presented by Decae with a solarization effect), lies on her body and puts his lips to hers. As she starts up from this sweetness which must also be a nightmare, she cries out 'Lord, watch over my dreams!' And at this point, when she is nearer sanctity than Morin himself will ever be, the film has something of the intensity of a Bresson or a Dreyer.

Dreyer's background is of course that of Ibsen, Strindberg, Munk, Bang and Söderberg; Bresson's is not only of Bernanos, Diderot, and Port Royal, but also of that whole French discipline (or indiscipline) which embraces the split between the religious and the secular which took place at the Revolution and has ever since remained built into the structure of French society. I am reminded of a marvellous moment in Marcel Pagnol's *La Femme du Boulanger*, when the village becomes desperate because the baker, whose beautiful young wife has run off with a handsome young satyr of a shepherd, refuses to make any more bread. Eventually an aged fisherman traces the erring lovers to a hideout they have made themselves in the nearby marshes. The young shepherd has by now become more or less identified with Satan himself, and the villagers are agreed that only the *curé* is fit to deal with him. But how is he to get to him through all that mud and water? A truce is called in the conflict between Church and State; and it is on the back of his hereditary foe the schoolmaster that the priest, his skirts well tucked up, journeys across the swamps, shrilling his admonishment over the reeds and the rushes until the shepherd slips like an eel into the water and swims off, leaving the lady to her fate. So she returns, on a large carthorse led by her rescuers while the villagers, discreet behind closed doors and drawn curtains, bolster up the fiction that she has never been away. Thus Pagnol, in his best film and with the aid of Raimu, gave expression to one aspect of this schizophrenia in the French nation. Bresson's point of departure is the same, but he chooses steeper and rockier paths. Like Dreyer, he does not incline to see the humour of things; he is too deeply concerned with the human predicament, which is not just a matter of the conflict between church and state, but of the relations between man and nature, man and man, man and God. The relation between man and nature is, incidentally, nicely summed up in *Au Hasard Balthazar*, where the actions and reactions of the characters – Marie, Arnold, Gérard – revolve round the figure of the poor donkey (the G. K. Chesterton poem comes to mind); and there are, too, elemental qualities in the central section of *Mouchette*.

Of all Bresson's works *Mouchette* is the most affecting. This poor child is Joan of Arc without Joan's advantage – a burning faith to support her in the terrible circumstances in which she finds herself. There is no Isambart to help Mouchette through the cruel experiences she must undergo; nor is she truly aware of a God who might succour her from a station in life to which He surely would *not* have been pleased to call her.

This rather sluttish young girl (for child she no longer is) throws dirt and mud at her schoolmates – Bresson gives us a splendid close-up of a clod landing fair and square on a prized Prisunic scentspray – but her schoolmates, mirrors of the world, ignore her. Her mother is dying; her father is thoughtlessly cruel; all family responsibilities automatically fall on her. Yet she still has to go to school.

It is not for nothing that the film begins with the setting of a snare; the trapping of a bird watched by two pairs of eyes, those of two arch enemies – the poacher and the gamekeeper who are to be the final arbiters of Mouchette's fate; for she will be sucked into their mutual hatred just as Joan was sucked into the mutual hatred of the French and the British. One need not push the analogy too far, but the rape scene in *Mouchette*, with her hair nearly touching the blazing fire, has a certain nightmare affinity with *Procès de Jeanne d'Arc*; it is, too, the sort of sequence, powerful, vivid, incredible yet wholly convincing, which only a Bresson (or perhaps a Buñuel) could bring off.

This film, which like *Le Journal d'un Curé de Campagne* is based on a book by Bernanos, is indeed full of amazing sequences which seem to hit one like a physical blow, like, for that matter, the savage slap in the face with which Mouchette's father terminates her idyllic flirtation with the teenage boy on the dodgems; or that fearful scene when, after the night in the wood – the rainstorm, the fight between Mathieu and Arsène, the epileptic fit and the rape – Mouchette comes home to her dying mother. In pain her mother asks her for gin. Mouchette fetches it from behind the door, gives her the drink, fills up the bottle with water so that her father won't notice, warms the milk and sets to feeding the baby – producing her own breast as well as the feeder. Then, at last, she goes to her mother to try to confide in her, to tell her of her violation by Arsène. But her mother is dead. In cold print the whole thing seems really too much, almost comic in its piling on of horrors. On the screen it is totally convincing, unbearably moving.

It is after her mother's death that, like Joan to her judges, Mouchette begins to answer back. She swears at her father ('Merde'). She goes to get milk for the baby, and on the way a sympathetic female shopkeeper invites her in for a cup of coffee and a croissant. But all is too late. Mouchette is suspicious, resentful. The coffee cup is overturned and broken. The shopkeeper and a friend gaze at Mouchette with eyes like stones. Later, an old lady with a face like a rat beckons her in and offers her a shroud for her mother's corpse, together with a dress she can wear at the funeral. As she sorts out a cupboard jam-packed with dresses and dress material, she says to Mouchette, 'I like the dead. I understand them,' and then, 'Have you ever thought about death, Mouchette?' To which Mouchette replies, 'You disgust me, you dirty old cow.' The question is loaded, however. For the final answer to that question is the *acte gratuit*, the casual suicide. Thus the episode with the old lady is as crucial to the film as is Joan's signature and subsequent recantation to *Procès de Jeanne d'Arc*. But if God was with Joan, he is not, apparently, with Mouchette; like Balthazar, she dies alone, and come to think of it even the donkey *did* have some company – a flock of sheep.

As at the start of the film, she sees men killing animals. A shot hare dies in agony; she is too late to help it die. The new dress given her by the '*sale vieille bête*' gets torn on some thorns. Nevertheless she wraps it round herself and rolls down the grassy slope towards the river. Reeds and bushes stop her on the edge. Continuing the game she goes to the top again, and waves to a man driving a tractor. He does not see her. Again she rolls down the slope. Again the bushes stop her at the edge of the cooling waters. What, now, is meant? Perhaps it is still a game; Edmund, in *Germany Year Zero*, plays the childish game of not-walking-on-the-cracks-in-the-pavement just before he kills himself.[1] Game, or no? True or not true? Very contentedly, Mouchette rolls down the slope again. This time the bushes relent, and the waters receive her. She joins Pedro of *Los Olvidados* and Giuseppe of *Shoeshine*.

From a bald description of this film it would be difficult to receive an impression other than of inspissated gloom and despair. It is a

[1] Since writing this I have noted that Charles Barr, in his contribution to *The Films of Robert Bresson*, has seen the same similarity.

measure of Bresson's genius that somehow he succeeds, in the person of poor Mouchette, in celebrating life. For instance, early in the film there is a singing lesson in the village school. The ill-tempered school-mistress bangs Mouchette's head on the piano keyboard because she sings out of tune. But when Arsène (who will later reward her by a brutal rape) lies on the floor of the hut in an epileptic fit, Mouchette cradles his head in her lap and sings a lullaby in a voice of the utmost sweetness. Even at the moment of the rape itself her arms tighten round Arsène's neck; nor is this an equivocal gesture. The grace sought so assiduously and with such difficulty by the Curé of Ambricourt may, we feel, have been bestowed unasked by the Almighty on Mouchette.

Nadine Nortier, who plays Mouchette, is absolutely perfect (Bresson never makes a mistake in casting). Her performance reveals the depths of life's richness and splendour much as one senses them in Simone Signoret's Casque d'Or. Nortier, indeed, is a classic example of Bresson's use of his material. Be they actors or non-actors he seeks to erase in them anything contrary to his own conception of the character.[1] Writing of *Le Journal d'un Curé de Campagne*, André Bazin remarks, in respect of the way its casting differs so acutely from that of *Les Dames du Bois de Boulogne*, 'Do people really imagine that it was easier to get Maria Casarès to play down her talent than to handle a group of docile amateurs?', and he goes on to add that Bresson's method 'not only rules out any dramatic interpretation by the actors but also any psychological touches either.' In other words, Bresson's theory of '*écriture*' means that he not only imposes on the film a style and interpretation entirely his own, but also that his characters are chosen not only because they look just right but because they will, sooner or later, submit to a kind of progressive hypnosis. By such means he obtains performances which are, filmically speaking, great acting. And here we may note Neergaard's description of the way Dreyer, in *La Passion de Jeanne d'Arc*, worked with (or on) Falconetti;

'Everyone not directly concerned was banished from the set, and absolute silence was demanded . . . When he was describing what he wanted, he would stammer and go red in the face, not from shyness or any hesitation as to what he meant, but simply from eagerness to make his . . . intentions completely understood . . . But

[1] The boy who plays Jost in *Un Condamné à Mort s'est Echappé* was found by Bresson in an orphanage near Paris. During the making of the film he reached his seventeenth birthday, and the production crew put on a small celebration. Whereupon he sobbed, for it was the first time in his life that anyone had even noticed his birthday. Bresson had found a Bresson character ready-made.

just because it seemed difficult for him to express himself clearly . . .
the actress . . . was, as it were, activated into expressing what Dreyer
could not show her, for it was something that could only be expressed
in action, not speech, and she alone could do it, so she had to help
him.'[1]

It is interesting to compare this with the description of Bresson
given by Roland Monod, who played the Minister in *Un Condamné à
Mort s'est Echappé*. Bresson instructed his cast:

'Forget about tone and meaning. Don't think what you are
saying; just speak the words automatically. When someone talks, he
isn't thinking about the words he uses, or even about what he wants
to say. Only concerned with what he is saying, he just lets the words
come out, simply and directly . . . The film actor should content
himself with *saying* his lines. He should not allow himself to show
that he already understands them.'[2]

And Monod goes on to describe how Bresson used to repeat the lines
of the script to himself over and over again 'to get the absolute starkness
and austerity he wanted us to reproduce'; and how Bresson, dissatisfied
with the dialogue directly recorded in the studio or on location ('too
human, too anecdotal'), took his cast into the dubbing theatre and
re-recorded their voices. 'Phrase by phrase, word by word almost, we
spoke our lines after their author – ten, twenty, thirty times over, trying
to match as exactly as possible the intonations, the rhythm, even the
tone of his voice. There is no paradox in saying that in the end Bresson
played every part.'[3]

All this makes it much easier to understand why Bresson, in
Le Journal d'un Curé de Campagne, insisted so much on the voice-off
reciting the words of the diary to match exactly the action on the screen.
It also explains the lapidary quality of all his dialogue sequences, and
thereby his choice of subjects, to which the necessity of dialogue is
minimal.[4]

In *Un Condamné à Mort s'est Echappé* Bresson uses, though less

---

[1] *Carl Dreyer* by Ebbe Neergaard, BFI New Index Series, 1950.

[2] 'Working with Bresson' reprinted in *Sight and Sound*, Summer 1957 from an article
in *Cahiers du Cinéma*, November 1956.

[3] One of the actors in *Gertrud* said, 'There was not a movement that Dreyer did not
supervise and direct. None of the acting was ours, it was all his, expressing his ideas.' Ozu
was the same.

[4] Even in *Les Dames du Bois de Boulogne* the sound of a fountain or (as Bazin points
out) a windscreen-wiper is as significant as the talk – which all leads anyhow to one sentence
– '*Vous avez épousé une grue.*'

convincingly, the diary form of *Le Journal*. Beyond this the amount of exchange of talk in prison is in any case minimal. 'In the shut-in world of prison, it is the objects which strike you most. The object stays: the man who uses it is only there for the time being.'[1]

Inside the prison of Montluc, Bresson uses certain natural sounds precisely and accurately (as indeed he does in *Procès de Jeanne d'Arc*) to indicate solitude, or communication, or menace. The sound of the machine-gun which executes Orsini after his unsuccessful attempt to escape leads to a silence in which Fontaine starts on the most dangerous and tricky move in his own attempt – the making of the hooks for his ladder from the lantern in his cell; 'and it is Orsini's death which pushes him to this brink.'[2]

The extraordinary thing about *Un Condamné à Mort* is that although we know how it will end, it still remains one of the greatest suspense films of all time. The reason is that it is not concerned with the mere Hitchcockian suspense arising from incident and episode; it is concerned, once again, with faith. We are watching a man, a very ordinary man, who finds in himself something he did not know he could possess, and so challenges death in the name of freedom; that is why, when asked how he will escape, he replies simply, 'I don't know'. This is true. He doesn't know; all he knows is that he must.

A blind faith perhaps? No. Bresson's preferred title for this film is *Le Vent Souffle où il Veut*, and this has a certain religious connotation. We are concerned with Divine Providence and with the fall of a sparrow; and the direct comment on Fontaine's 'blind' faith is made to us by Bresson himself in his use – at first glance with staggering inappropriateness – of Mozart's Mass in C Minor. We hear the Kyrie from this glorious work each time the prisoners come down the staircase and into the courtyard to empty their slop-buckets in the morning. We hear it during Orsini's attempt to escape. We hear it again when he is being taken out to be executed. We hear it when young Jost is thrust into Fontaine's cell – thus apparently destroying all his carefully laid escape plans. And finally we hear it when Fontaine and Jost have attained freedom.[3]

We hear it. The people in the film do not. For Bresson is making a contrast and a comparison for us. Fontaine's determination to escape, or inescapably to die (as Orsini in fact does) is set against the generalized

[1] Monod, loc. cit.

[2] Leo Murray, in his admirable analysis of this film in *The Films of Robert Bresson*.

[3] There is an ironic twist here. Fontaine thinks of killing Jost; but in the event, when they make the escape together, it turns out that Fontaine by himself could never have scaled the second wall.

cry of humanity for God's mercy. The implication of the Mozart Mass is that while the prisoner is 'tunnelling like a mole', the bright angels of heaven – though no prayers have arisen from him – are working towards his salvation. By his extraordinary juxtapositions, like the singing and the slops, Bresson makes us feel this. No explanations are needed. The effect is ineffable and of an extreme beauty.

If no explanations are needed for *Un Condamné à Mort s'est Echappé*, this is surely not the case in *Une Femme Douce* (1969), which was Bresson's next film after the pellucid *Mouchette*. Here is Bresson in his withdrawn mood, cool, cryptic, and with his '*écriture*' reduced to shorthand.

A door-handle is turned. A table and a pot-plant on a balcony are overturned. A woman's scarf floats slowly and lazily down past the windows of an apartment block. Car brakes squeal. A girl lies dead on the sidewalk, a trickle of blood flowing from her head.

Such is the opening of *Une Femme Douce* (*A Gentle Creature*), and such too, with certain variations, is its closing. In between, mysteries.

The film is, on Bresson's own admission, about 'the impossibility of communication' – a predicament which leads to suicide. In structure it continues the diary technique so dear to Bresson. In this case it takes the form of the man talking partly to himself and partly to the *concierge* as they wait in the bedroom for the undertakers to come for the body of his wife. He speaks in a soft monotone, all feeling drained from his voice. Only in the flashback sequences in which he speaks directly and synchronously does any emotion appear, and even here it is usually muted; it is a perfect parallel to the forgetting about tone and meaning which we have already noted in relation to *Un Condamné à Mort*.

He is a pawnbroker. A girl – little more than a student – comes regularly to his *mont-de-piété* to dispose of various objects. With an obvious reluctance he finds himself being attracted to her. With little overt show of affection he pursues her, and on a visit to the Zoo (which, with other visits to museums and the like which they make later on, has some strange affinity with similar scenes in *La Jetée*), he asks her to marry him. She says 'No', and it is typical of Bresson that he cuts immediately to the wedding ceremony.

Despite the marriage, despite a nuptial night which she begins in a convulsion of giggles ('I soon got rid of these' he reminisces), she remains mysterious, withdrawn. He too remains outwardly withdrawn. But, as his remembering voice tells us, he becomes increasingly jealous. He begins to spy on her. Yet when he finds her sitting in a parked car with a young man, and commands her brusquely to get out, his memory voice is telling us 'She was virtuous. She had gone to the boy – whose face I didn't even try to see – to revenge herself on me'.

They move further and further apart. A single bed is emphatically installed. She falls ill; a nurse is called. By this time Bresson, by constant visual reiteration, has made us so well acquainted with the rooms and the staircase which leads down to the shop that we know which of the stairboards creaks (for the film, as ever with Bresson, is filled with small, selected, significant sounds).

She has '*une passion pour livres et disques*' and sits on the floor with these around her, together with other objects – *éclairs*, roses – with which to protect herself from reality. Finally, his jealousy spent, he capitulates. He kneels to her. '*Je t'aime*', he says, and then '*Je te désire*'. And that simple phrase, spoken without apparent passion, explodes onto the screen like one of those traumatic surprises which Dreyer produces in *Gertrud*.

It is too late. The moment of true communication was lost somewhere, somehow, some time ago. She covers her face with her hands and weeps passionately. He carries her clumsily to the bed while she cries out to him not to torment her. With a desperate gesture which we all recognize, the cliché which we all use in a crisis, he says they must go away somewhere, must get away from it all. She says at breakfast that she will be his faithful wife and will respect him. He goes out to a travel agency, and while he is there the opening sequence begins again. But this time the scarf, floating lazily down, is seen against a clear, open sky instead of the house façade. From the coffin he raises her beautiful dead face. 'Open your eyes', he pleads. But the coffin lid slides over – in vast close-up as in so many of the shots in this film – and the screws are secured in place . . .

Throughout this strange film Bresson's austere shorthand style produces the feeling that we are separated from the action by a sheet of perspex; and this is accentuated by the almost somnambulistic performance imposed on Guy Frangin by the director. Hallucinatory and often compelling though it is, *Une Femme Douce* leaves one puzzled, unsatisfied. What, one asks, is the point of the performance of *Hamlet* which they attend, and of which we see the last scene acted out in a formal, indeed somewhat strangulated manner? True this leads to a sequence in which she reads aloud Hamlet's advice to the Players, but out of this comes little relevance, though here, as throughout the film, Dominique Sanda's face impresses with a gloriously pure beauty which, moulded in soft colours by Ghislain Cloquet's camera, goes straight to the heart.

In talking about *Une Femme Douce* Bresson has said, in reference to 'the impossibility of communication', that 'I do not mean it is impossible for a couple to get on together, but that it is impossible under the conditions that I am imposing. I believe that once a couple understand each other they can no longer stand each other.' Here, it seems to me, Bresson oversimplifies his explanation if not his position (the phrase 'the conditions I am imposing' is significant), and in so doing tries, wittingly or unwittingly, to prevent us entering into the psyches of his players, or of the persons they represent, in case we should observe a deeper flaw. Thoughts, deeds, desires – these flow naturally towards us from the Curé, or Joan, or Fontaine or even Mouchette. Here Bresson gives us a pair of automata. Is the clue for this to be found after all in what Hamlet says to the Players when he urges, 'use all gently; for in the very torrent, tempest, and, as I may say, the whirlwind of passion, you must acquire and forget a temperance that may give it smoothness'? But if that is the clue, why did Bresson provide it through the girl rather than the man? It seems that in this case, at least, Bresson is not interested in his characters' search for either faith or grace.

Dreyer's *Day of Wrath* provides an absolute contrast. For here he sets faith within a hideous framework of revenge, as though Hélène of *Les Dames du Bois de Boulogne* had been teamed with the tortured Curé of Ambricourt; while for the splendours of Mozart's Mass is substituted the *Dies Irae*, sung by a choir of cool, utterly indifferent boys, which crosses the cruelties and agonies of the film with a visual and aural impact that reveals the affinity of the darker side of Christianity with the Eumenides of earlier legend.

Day of Wrath begins by depicting the physical horrors of witch-hunts, witch-tortures and burnings at the stake. Seldom has the beastliness of human cruelty been so tersely and so horribly put on the screen; the torture scenes in *The Battle of Algiers*, however, do have the same quality, and for the same reason – the cruelties are seen to be justified once a certain code has been accepted. But then what? *The Battle of Algiers* ends at this point. But the remainder of Dreyer's film, with slow and inexorable pace, reveals the destruction of all those who, by action or by lack of action, acquiesced in the original crime. Protected they may be by the sanctions of a religious creed – but the outraging of human decency is a crime from which there is in the end no protection and no escape. So Anne must in her turn confess herself a witch, and the vicious cycle must begin again.

Sombre though it is, *Day of Wrath* has great beauty. The intimacy of Karl Andersson's camerawork, with its unerring manipulation of light and shadow; the contrasts, almost physically violent, between the close, stuffy interiors and the free open fields and rivers; the meticulously economic use of sound – the wind whistling through keyholes and through cracks in window-frames, or a clock ticking, a distant bell or a phrase of music – all these are so similar in technique to Bresson and yet result in something so different, so completely expressive of Dreyer's own extraordinary soul. Bresson may exaggerate a natural sound (the prison bolts and bars in *Procès de Jeanne d'Arc*, the passing trucks in *Mouchette*, and indeed, the very sound of her boots on the dusty road), but for Dreyer the use of sound is logical, absolute, selective. With Dreyer, too, there is a tremendous richness and clarity of camerawork. *La Passion de Jeanne d'Arc* is a vast magnification of the style of *Le Livre des Merveilles*, mingled with effects like microphotographs of the surface, say, of the leaf of a plant. On the other hand *Day of Wrath*, *Ordet* and *Gertrud* tend to remind us of the great Dutch and Flemish painters (both of interiors and of landscapes).[1] Bresson seems to rely less on photographic richness, though it may be noted that of two brilliant cameramen he has preferred L-H Burel for the drained, pallid or 'contrasty' quality that is so effective in *Le Journal d'un Curé de Campagne*, *Un Condamné à Mort s'est Echappé*, *Pickpocket* and *Procès de Jeanne d'Arc*; and Ghislain Cloquet for the exquisite feeling for nature and for the contours of the human face which he brings to *Au Hasard Balthazar*, *Mouchette* and *Une Femme Douce*.

Bresson, thankfully, is still with us; but Dreyer is gone, and without achieving his life's ambition, a film on the Life of Christ.[2] Nevertheless his completed *oeuvre*, which can now be fully assessed, did end with a film which one could justifiably describe as a perfect work of art. It is a film which has that element of mystery which pertains to certain works of great genius that ultimately defy analysis – the mystery of Giorgione's *La Tempesta*, of Shakespeare's *The Phoenix and the Turtle*, of the tapestries of *La Dame à la Licorne*, and of Beethoven's Last Quartets.

Of the fourteen films Dreyer made from *The President* (1919) onwards (fourteen films, note you, in forty-five years – how's that for frustration?), *Gertrud* has an absoluteness which takes it beyond the

---

[1] Let me note for the record that apart from Andersson, already mentioned, Rudolph Maté photographed *La Passion de Jeanne d'Arc* and *Vampyr*, while *Ordet* and *Gertrud* were the work of Henning Bendtsen.

[2] He would, I think, with only a few reservations, have liked Pasolini's *Gospel According to Matthew*.

ordinary approach of film criticism. Indeed, it has been frequently attacked for its so-called 'non-filmic' attitude; and at its Paris première it was subjected to an almost unanimous onslaught of sheer viciousness which was accurately likened by Elliott Stein to 'all the hysteria and insecure aggression of a spontaneous, unexpected lynching.'[1] This incomprehensible episode must have darkened Dreyer's later days. I call it incomprehensible because the film itself is clarity personified; and it can only have been the uncompromising formality by which that clarity was achieved that aroused such hatred and hostility.

Gertrud is, in effect, an opera. It is not by chance that its eponymous heroine was once an opera singer, that her first love was a poet, and that the lover of her middle-age is a young composer. The way the film is shot, the way the scenes are composed, the methods by which the participants communicate with each other – all have the formality, the artificiality, even, if you like – of an opera. It is a formality which the opera itself borrowed from the theatre – the formality of a Racine or a Beaumarchais or even a Goldoni. And yet *Gertrud* somehow partakes of the very essence of cinema.

It is a study of the relations between one woman and four men, of whom three (one of them her husband) have been concerned with her sexually. The relationships between these characters are subjected to all the variations, contradictions, collisions and metamorphoses which could conceivably be imagined. All this is done with a discipline which creates patterns and an overall shape of great beauty.

Gertrud is a *femme fatale* not merely in the old-fashioned sense – that of her effect on her lovers; she is above all fatal to herself, and the tremendous impact of the final sequence of the film comes from our realization that somehow she has rescued herself from that fate. She is alone, sad, proud, unsatisfied – yet self-sufficient, herself to herself; so much so that she can even, softly and kindly, reject the only man with whom she has enjoyed friendship without passion. The film ends with this placid, lingering farewell. The man leaves her with a gentle salute, repeated three times, each time further away; leaves her alone in her scrubbed, hygienic house miles from anywhere, and the door closes on us as well as on all those she has known. The door. Dreyer holds on to this shot. The latch drops slowly into place. Slowly, slowly, and then only after a long pause, the camera tracks back, then stops. And as the door continues to hold Gertrud's secret, now, we know, for ever, the

---

[1] Stein's detailed description of this disgraceful affair (from which only a few critics – notably Georges Sadoul and Henri Chapier – dissociated themselves) may be found in *Sight and Sound*, Spring 1965.

music of a string quartet – cello predominating – gradually creeps in
under the sound of bells – the bells with which Dreyer ends every
episode in the film; church bells, chimes, clocks striking, telephone
ringing – the terminal sound.

The operatic similarities are striking. There are in this film a
series of duets, trios, and quartets involving every possible permutation
and combination between the various characters. There are set pieces
and choruses. There are a few solos, all of grave significance; and inter-
ludes of great import like that when Tosca, after Scarpia's death, moves
in lonely purposiveness around his apartment and places the candles
at his head.

Nothing is left to chance; all is planned. The characters never
interrupt each other; indeed, there is often a noticeable pause before
one replies to the other. When there is to be a change of subject or of
mood, the characters move to another part of the room or of the park,
creating a new pattern and a new atmosphere. From time to time, like
earthquakes, like volcanic eruptions long held back by the strength of
the earth's crust, pent-up emotions break out in explosions of fiendish
intensity – an intensity all the more powerful because it takes the form
of no more than a strangled sob or the tearing up of a photograph,
actions which in this filmic context become cataclysmic.

Gertrud is not, as its critics so brashly claimed, dull and static.
It is a film in which the camera is nearly always on the move, with
elaborate tracking and panning, and combinations of both. It is only
when Dreyer knows he has come to the 'still centre' of an emotional
storm that the movement stops and the camera coldly and impersonally
observes some soul-stripping anguish between a man and a woman
sitting side by side, but slightly apart, on an elegant sofa in a beautifully
decorated room. In *Gertrud* the stopping of camera movement is always
felt as a signal of crisis.

The complexities of *Gertrud* make the intrigues and complications
of *Les Dames du Bois de Boulogne* seem comparatively simple. True, the
Bresson film has a fine formality of shape; true, it has turns of plot and
story which are not without similarity to those of *Gertrud*; true, both
films are built round elements of revenge and of regret. But what shines
out of *Gertrud* is something extra – the vision of a being who, however
wrong-minded, dangerous even, has a generosity of spirit, a single-
mindedness in her love of life (as well as in her fear of it) which overpasses all other qualities and considerations.

For in the final issue *Les Dames du Bois de Boulogne* is about
dishonesty, and *Gertrud* is about honesty. Gertrud is honest. She is

honest when she tells the truth and she is honest when she doesn't. She tells her husband she is going to the opera when in fact she is going to meet her lover. When he finds out she says to him, 'I told you that so that you would not be hurt'; and we know that this is the truth. Right at the end of the film she hands back to her non-lover, her 'true friend', all the letters he ever wrote to her, letters which she must treasure above all else, for him casually to throw on the fire in her own fireplace. And in the centre of the film, when she is ready to give herself to the young composer, she says to him, 'Life is a dream, a long series of dreams which overlap each other', and we know she has taken count of her husband and her previous lover. Then she asks him to play a nocturne (he is an enormously talented, handsome young scallywag), and as he does so she moves, ever gracefully, into the next room, and all is shadow – the shadow of her undressing seen on an exquisitely composed still-life. A chair in the background. In the foreground an oil lamp above which hangs a reproduction of a Greek vase-painting. And the shadow of Gertrud, always so fully clothed – long skirts, buttoned blouse, high-collared neck – unthinkably stripping off to become, as he leaves the piano and moves past us into the shadowed and unseen bedchamber, part of 'the beast with two backs'.

It is typical of Dreyer that he chooses this precise moment to cut to a close-up of her husband (a prim and rather boring chap) being driven in a horse-cab to the opera house to collect her at the end of the performance. He sits there, his lips not moving; but his thoughts tell us what he feels about her already expressed intention of leaving him. This successful lawyer, who has just been offered a post in the Government, thinks 'Life slips from my hands'. And with a vain gesture of affection, vain even if she had been there, he enters the opera house (the work, significantly enough, is *Fidelio*) to be told by the attendant that Madame's box was not occupied tonight. Dreyer cuts back to Gertrud, cool, happy, fully clothed. She takes a cigarette from her lover, says, 'Here with you I've lived again', and, with a coquettish gesture puts the cigarette in his mouth and departs. The young man watches from the window; he is about to betray her more cruelly and brutally than she in her honesty could ever betray anyone.

In Bresson's *Journal d'un Curé de Campagne*, one of the most memorable episodes comes when the Curé has, as it were, saved the soul of the Comtesse. The scene between these two has been, as Bazin remarked, 'unmatched in beauty anywhere in the whole French cinema, perhaps even in all French literature'. Bresson follows it with a sequel of rapier-like cruelty. The Comtesse, suddenly, is dead. In his hands the

Curé holds a letter she wrote him. Was her death the result of her conversion; and if so what Divine motive resided in it and where, in the interplay of those at the château and in the village, could the poor Curé imagine himself now to stand? In the delivery of blows of fate Bresson and Dreyer are equally brilliant and equally ruthless.

The ellipses we have already noted in much of Bresson's work are paralleled in *Gertrud*. It is a film about the past, about the many layers of the past as it affects, in different ways, the feelings of different persons as they meet in the present and find no reconcilement. The layers of the past, recent or long ago, control everything. There is no escape. They are all trapped save, suddenly, Gertrud. And even so she escapes only into another past. The past is merciless. When the film begins, Gertrud is telling her husband that she is going to leave him because, she says, she is only second in his life to his work. 'Do I exist for you at all?' she asks him. The answer seems fairly clear from his reaction. His pride is hurt; he is worried about how her departure might affect his career. His pleas therefore merely confirm the evidence she has already adduced. She does not hesitate to tell him she has a lover; but she will not say who it is. But near the end of the film her husband has reached a deeper and more dangerous desperation. It is not his career which worries him now but one simple, tormenting question. He wants to know only one thing; in all their intercourse did she ever feel real love for him? She replies that she came to him 'already drained of love'. This is not enough. He presses her further. At last, with reluctance, she says that perhaps there was 'at moments, something which *resembled* love'. At which point the suave lawyer explodes, and shouts at her to get out of his house for ever. She goes, cloaked and silent, leaving by a side passage. And as she does so, he, suddenly bereft, calls out her name, as he did at the opening of the film. But as in *A Doll's House*, the only answer is the slamming of a door.

The actors in *Gertrud* are all perfect; perfect not so much in their own way as in Dreyer's; for it is clear that everything in this film, from the positioning of a small candlestick on a shelf to the most heightened moment of Nina Pens Rode's performance as Gertrud, was as much his as everything in *Le Journal d'un Curé de Campagne* and *Un Condamné à Mort s'est Echappé* was Bresson's. This must of course include the camera movements so finely executed by Henning Bendtsen but obviously conceived by Dreyer. These are absolute, with nothing left to chance; yet at times they have the appearance of being beautifully casual. There are two wonderful examples of this in the scenes with Gertrud and her young lover. In one of them he is accompanying her on the piano as she sings one of his own songs. The camera, apparently quite loosely, moves sideways (not panning) in an almost semi-circular track shot, round the piano, on to him, and then back again to its original position. This shot has the air of an improvisation, though of course it was nothing of the sort, and is in acute contrast to Dreyer's treatment of the big dénouement in the centre of the film. Gertrud has been taken ill at the banquet being given in honour of her first love, a portly and handsome poet who still longs for her. Through him she learns, by a devious and odious coincidence for which all three participants are each in their own way to blame, that her *new* lover has boasted of his conquest of her at a drunken late-night party. A few moments later her husband arrives with the young man (knowing nothing of course of the liaison), with a request from the President that she should sing. The boy – nothing yet said, explained or understood – has to accompany her at the piano in a tragic Lied (I think it is Schumann's '*Ich grolle nicht*'). Halfway through her feelings overwhelm her. Her voice is choked by sobs and, with the camera absolutely static and at a slightly low angle, she falls to the ground like a shot bird. The placing of the camera, the simple composition, the dressing of the set – all combine to give the full poignancy of this dramatic moment.

Another example comes in another moment of deception. In the grey, misty park full of birdcalls where she meets her young lover, there is a farewell during which Gertrud demeans herself to a point at which *we* feel the disgust which will shortly overwhelm her. And at this point he blurts out his feelings with all the naïve youthful thoughtlessness which has dominated his attitude to the whole affair, and walks away, the camera casually (as it seems) panning as his feet crunch the gravel. But it is not the end. He returns, to prolong a futile and, to her at least, a shameful discussion and then, with the same casual camera movement, the same crunch of gravel, he walks away – this time for ever.

Dreyer's cuts in *Gertrud* are rupturing. I do not mean his cuts *within* the sequences, for these tend to be few and far between; the shots, except on rare exchanges of close-ups, are of very great length. But as a sequence reaches its appointed end – signalled always, as I have said, by a bell sound and, often as not, by a snatch of chamber music as well – Dreyer cuts to the next sequence absolutely *in medias res*; and because the flow of the whole film is so measured, so, in a sense, remorseless, these cuts serve as deep psychological assaults on the viewer which force him to share in the emotional permutations and combinations of the people in the film who, through the central figure of Gertrud (who would be all woman were she to be, as she is not, a mother), display, undergo and exchange their joys and miseries.

Dreyer had much admiration for the Japanese cinema; the direction and pictorial composition of *Gertrud* sometimes recall Ozu. Nowhere is this more so than in the coda, when we see Gertrud, now old and whitehaired, living a hermit's life in her aseptic, well-scrubbed farmhouse. When her old friend the professor comes to see her, and she greets him with special affection because of their 'friendship which never turned into love', we suddenly realize that *a few shots earlier* we have seen her leaving her husband and on her way to Paris to study psychology with this very same man. Thus in the space of a few feet Dreyer calmly interposes an interval of some 25 years. It is a master-stroke of filmic conception and a master-stroke of timing.

Before passing to other areas, let me record that as far as France is concerned we have reached 1959, the year not only of *Hiroshima Mon Amour* but also of the start of the *Nouvelle Vague* with Chabrol's *Le Beau Serge* and Truffaut's *Les Quatre Cents Coups*; the year of Rouch's *Moi, un Noir*, Franju's *La Tête Contre les Murs* and Camus' *Orfeu Negro*.[1] Of the profound changes in French cinema so signalled I will write later.

VI

In Britain the post-war period saw, in addition to the struggle against Hollywood already described, an internal conflict between two schools of thought about methods of production and distribution. The first, represented by J. Arthur Rank, and to a degree by Korda, stood for high budget productions aimed at breaking into the world, and especially the American, market. The other, led by Michael Balcon, held that British production would remain economically viable only if costs were kept low enough to be recovered from the home market alone. This was of course the principle on which Hollywood had always worked, the only difference being that *its* home market was vast and that it had also built up a near monopoly as far as the world was concerned. Balcon's proposition therefore postulated films of a modest nature.

The Rank system, on the other hand, assumed that the American

[1] Let 1959 also be remembered as the year in which Renoir made his exquisite *hommage* to a style of earlier days in *Le Déjeuner sur l'Herbe*.

market could only be stormed by films made on an American scale. But, apart from anything else, the Americans did not welcome the idea of incursions into their home market; and as the home market in Britain was too small for a big film to recoup its costs, how could Rank's scheme succeed?[1]

Ironically enough, it was Rank who made possible the success of Balcon's policy. Rank had a semi-monopolistic control of cinema houses (the Americans having, more or less, the other half), and it was a distribution arrangement with Rank's General Film Distributors which gave Balcon the home market he required. This, plus some modest production finance (without strings) also from Rank, provided a channel for the stream of films, mostly comedies, which from 1948 onwards poured from Ealing Studios, whose name soon became an international trademark.

Equally ironically it was Balcon's comparatively low-budget pictures which made money in the overseas market far in excess of the earnings of Rank's large-scale productions, which in the five years to 1947 landed him with a loss of something like £6 million. This is not to say that the films were not good. Indeed, one of them, which overshot its generous budget by a third, was Carol Reed's acknowledged masterpiece *Odd Man Out* (1946). As we have already seen, Reed was a well-established director by the end of the Thirties; and he had to his credit by this time *Bank Holiday* (1938), *The Stars Look Down* (1939), *Kipps* (1941) and *The Way Ahead* (1944). But I doubt if anyone suspected the full depth and strength of his talent until it was revealed in the tragic saga of Johnny MacQueen.

An old priest and a shady, seedy little man clutching a bird-cage sit each side of the fire; in slow conversational tones they spar with each other for the body and, no doubt, the soul of a murderer who lies, mortally wounded, in an old hip-bath on a rubbish dump. A crazy, alcohol-soaked and untalented painter wrecks a pub in his attempt to get the dying man as a model; in a studio in a half-ruined house, with snow coming through the roof, he paints away while his friend dresses the killer's wound preparatory to handing him over to the police. The killer opens his eyes. He is delirious. The painter's ugly, unskilful canvases slide from the wall and range themselves before him, row on row, as a nightmare jury.

Those two sequences from *Odd Man Out* give some indication of the flights of creative imagination achieved by Reed in this adaptation

---

[1] When Pascal's *Caesar and Cleopatra* was completed, it was estimated that it might make some £300,000 from the box-office; but it cost £1 million more than that to make.

by R. C. Sherriff of F. L. Green's novel of the same name. The story is, in a way, comparable with John Ford's *The Informer*, similarly based on a novel (by Liam O'Flaherty). Both deal with the hunting down of a criminal on the run. But *The Informer* (one of Ford's best films, incidentally) dealt basically with the hunted man; the plot was personalized in him. *Odd Man Out*, on the other hand, uses the man-hunt as a motivation towards searching the heart of society, to reveal the springs of thought and action which are set flowing by the impact of a man-hunt on a big city. More than this; it is not merely a sordid story of a robbery ending, by an unforeseen error, in a murder. The motives of the original action are deeper. The murderer, Johnny MacQueen, is concerned in political faith, in loyalties to an idea which is in opposition to the power-structure of the society in which he lives.[1] And so the reactions of the people he meets as he stumbles like a frightened, wounded animal through the streets and alleyways and tenements of Belfast are themselves complex, for in Johnny they find a questioning of society. Although they cannot avoid the implications of murder, their actions cannot be so simple as to call for the police; there is some more pressing, more urgent issue, and they compromise – some for one reason, some for another. There is only one character in the film who has an immediate and straightforward reaction – the middle-aged procuress who unhesitatingly betrays Johnny's colleagues to the police.

The film is full of people sometimes seen only for a moment, but remembered, like the two little boys looking out at the falling snow as Johnny lies, near the end of his *via dolorosa*, under the window-sill in their ragged front garden; the silent small girl with the single roller skate who shows Johnny's friend where he is hiding; the panicky scene where his confederates, who have had to leave him in the lurch during the getaway after the unexpected murder, quarrel confusedly in their attempts to justify themselves; and the tremendous filmic stroke in the pub scene, where Johnny's animal cry is cancelled by a great roar from Lukey, the drunken artist, when he recognizes the little shyster Shell. Notable too, throughout the film, is the imaginative use of sound, with the hundred and one noises of the city woven fully into the whole pattern of the film. I remember particularly the continuation of the sound of the factory alarm bell, persisting faintly in the background long after the murder sequence is over; and again, when Johnny's girl-friend has dodged the pursuing police by slipping in and out of a dance

---

[1] The events in Northern Ireland in the late Sixties and early Seventies brought a contemporary significance to this film.

hall, the pop tune (the quintessence of repetitive emptiness) goes on and on as she makes her way to the priest's house. The film also has an excellent score by William Alwyn used climactically throughout and, in the tragic final sequence, with stunning effect. (There is a perceptive analysis of this in *The Technique of Film Music* by John Huntley and Roger Manvell.) And the acting throughout, from top stars to the cream of character actors from England as well as from the Abbey Theatre, is of a perfection rarely seen; it is a film which seems to have stimulated all concerned to rise to the height of their powers.

There are two short sequences in this film which are marred, not ideologically but technically. When Johnny in his feverish dream sees the faces of friends and foes in the bubbles made by the spilt beer on the pub table, the trick effect obtrudes too much. The faces are so obviously, and indeed so cleverly inserted into the bubbles, that we tend to become dispassionate observers of the effect instead of participating in Johnny's delirium. The same thing happens when Lukey's paintings slide off the walls and range themselves before Johnny; though at this stage the tension already built up is so great that the diversion is minimal.

Reed followed *Odd Man Out* with two more films of importance – *The Fallen Idol* (1948) and *The Third Man* (1949).[1] The screen-plays of both of these were by Graham Greene who, years earlier when he was film critic for the *Spectator*, had hailed Reed's second film, a screen version of Priestley's *Laburnum Grove* (1936), as 'at last an English film one can unreservedly praise'. It was an admirable collaboration. Greene's adaptation from an existing short story in the first case, and his original scenario in the second, were both tailor-made to Reed's individual talent.

The Fallen Idol tells how a small boy sees by chance what seems to be a murder (the setting is, by the way, a Grosvenor Square Embassy) and how, thinking the murderer to be the butler (Ralph Richardson) whom he hero-worships, he uses every subterfuge he can to avoid causing the butler's arrest. Ironically enough the evidence he withholds turns out to be the essential information needed to establish the butler's innocence. Such, briefly, is the plot; but the essence of the film resides in the way it reveals the progressive disillusionments of childhood – the sad discovery of the fallibility of the infallible. Reed's direction of the boy Bobby Henrey is remarkable; there is a quite frightening scene between him and Sonia Dresdel in a very sinister rôle; and an electrifying

---

[1] After *Odd Man Out* Reed left Rank, and these two films were made under the producership of Korda.

moment when this small boy, seen from a great height, runs out into the rainsoaked square in his pyjamas while a tremendous surge of music by William Alwyn laments his lost illusions. It is, of course, a hothouse film about supernormality; only a few children are fully bilingual and live in an Embassy; this boy belongs more to the paranormal world of *The Rocking Horse Winner* than to the diurnal miseries of *Bicycle Thieves*.

As with *The Fallen Idol*, so in *The Third Man* the story structure is deceptive – a Hitchcock-type thriller, one thinks at first, set in post-war Vienna. A young American (Joseph Cotten) arrives in the city only to find that the friend he has come to meet has been killed in a street accident. He soon realizes that it was not an accident but murder. Then, as he tries to find out the real facts, his friend is revealed as still alive, and himself a murderer to boot. In the end, after a melodramatic chase through the sewers (the weakest part of the film), he has to shoot him.

But there is a further quality behind the bare story outline; an alarming overtone. The murder in question goes beyond gangster melodrama. It involves tampering with the penicillin supplies to children's hospitals with results which, in a sequence made all the more horrible by the reticence of its presentation, we seek vainly to ignore. The main characters tend to be more than life-size; and if the villain (Orson Welles) – 'Harry Lime Theme' on the zither and all – is a monster, so too, in a disturbing way, is the control officer who tracks him down. This part is played with tremendous power by Trevor Howard, to whom indeed Reed must be incalculably in debt – films like *An Outcast of the Islands* and *The Key* more than repay the chance he gave him in his first appearance on the screen in *The Way Ahead*.

Of *The Third Man* I noted at the time that Reed's tendency to show or create characters larger than life to the point of abnormality or, if you like, supernormality, might overstep itself. 'The villain in *The Third Man*,' I said, 'is certainly abnormal; indeed he should be clearly recognizable as the embodiment of absolute evil. But this embodiment is in the end lost because when he and his "friend" have their first showdown (on the slowly revolving Big Wheel of an almost deserted fairground) the issue in question is not squarely faced. We expect a revelation. We are put off with some clever writing and direction.'[1]

Apart from this, it does seem to me that from this film onwards Reed's work became more diffuse and more erratic (though never

[1] *The Year's Work in the Film* 1949, British Council–Longmans Green, 1950.

less than interesting). Of his subsequent films two, perhaps three if we count *The Man Between*,[1] a piece very much along *The Third Man* lines, were of major importance – *An Outcast of the Islands* (1951) and *The Key* (1958).

That Carol Reed should have made another film about an outcast is no surprise. After Johnny MacQueen and Harry Lime, one came to feel that Reed had a kind of compulsive interest in the hero who is cut off, or who cuts himself off, from society. What Gide calls 'the fatal irresponsible acts of Conrad's heroes' may well have led Reed to Willems. Willems is another sort of outcast. Unlike MacQueen, who is cut off from society as a result of his work for the 'Party', unlike Harry Lime, who cuts himself off cheerfully with the superegoism of the criminal, Willems becomes an outcast through a fatal and perhaps fated ambivalence. The voluntary act – embezzlement – could be wiped out by Lingard's willingness to give his protegé a break. The involuntary act, the final, irrevocable moment of irresponsibility, is Willems' capitulation, through an inner weakness which he fears so much that he cannot control it, to Aissa, the native girl and, through her, to a degradation from which he can never emerge.

As a film *An Outcast of the Islands* builds up to the climactic moment when Willems reaches the point of no return – the horrifying and repellent sequence in which he strings Almayer up in his own hammock and swings him back and forth across the fire. From this moment he forfeits all respect; not merely ours, but also his own. Some critics complained that Reed overstepped the bounds of permitted unpleasantness in this sequence (the bloodbaths of *Bonnie and Clyde*, *Performance* and the like were still far in the future), but in my opinion his brilliant construction brought out the whole dramatic savagery of the episode to perfection.

The whole central section of the film, of which the hammock sequence forms the climax, is magnificent. The river village, which was brilliantly reconstructed in Ceylon from location 'blueprints' shot in Borneo, stands on its stilts over the muddy water, the huts interconnected by crazy catwalks pullulating with children; and as Willems strides along them, lashing out unavailingly at the laughing kids, Reed uses to the full this opportunity for movement and contrast. Between the two focal points – Almayer's bungalow on the one side and the chief's hut on the other – the wretched Willems vacillates like a lunatic pendulum, swinging ever nearer to Aissa, ever further from his only chance of survival. With the exception of the final sequence, all the

[1] In this, as in *Odd Man Out*, James Mason gave a performance of the highest order.

really memorable moments belong to this part of the film – the birthday cake episode, in which Almayer (himself an unpleasant enough representative of 'civilisation') decides, largely because it suits him to do so, that there is nothing more to be done about Willems; the scenes in the dark hut between Willems and Aissa, in which Trevor Howard gives a most frightening delineation of mingled passion and disgust; Almayer's little daughter screaming 'Pig! Pig! Pig!' at Willems as he crosses, finally and forever, the fatal boundary; and the little native boy, sometimes urchin, sometimes almost unearthly, who follows Willems everywhere like a puppy . . . in all these we see Reed's talents at full stretch.

But this is not the whole film. It contains other elements which are disturbingly inapt. This applies particularly to the character of Captain Lingard, cleverly played by Sir Ralph Richardson in a highly stylized manner which could not but be deliberate. This is a figure from a different world. His words are not real. They are from a book. They might be all very well read aloud, but spoken in action they clash with the realism which dominates the other parts of the film.

This formalized approach swamps the whole opening of *An Outcast of the Islands*; and it spreads to other characters – notably the trader's assistant (Wilfrid Hyde White), and it descends to the ludicrous while Lingard speechifies to Willems after he has rescued him from the water. I have the impression that Reed must have got himself tangled up in that peculiarly *literary* aspect of Conrad which Michael Sadleir indicated when he remarked that 'passages occur with words too emphatic for their context, and others where a curious equality of weight is given to words of varying significance'.

It is difficult to see what was Reed's real intention regarding Lingard. Is he supposed to be a frustrated father-substitute, Jehovah, or simply an old bore? It is only in the final sequence, deep in the rain-soaked jungle, that he really seems to mean anything, especially at the moment when Willems lacks the moral power to justify his own evil – if nothing else – by pulling the trigger on him.

Conrad once wrote of himself, 'Those who read me know my conviction that the world, the temporal world, rests on a very few simple ideas . . . It rests notably, amongst others, on the idea of Fidelity.' In Willems, as in others of his heroes, he created, as an artist must, the opposite of that idea. This Reed has faithfully presented; but the idea itself – whether it should be found in the character of Lingard, or in Mrs Almayer, or even in the dumb passion of Aissa – the idea itself is lost.

Like *An Outcast of the Islands, The Key* (1958) sets out to deal in a penetrating and disturbing way with the roots of human behaviour. And, also like *An Outcast of the Islands*, it is weakened by ambiguities and uncertainties which can only arise from the basic conception as well as the shaping of the script (in this case by the very talented Carl Foreman[1]).

The story concerns in the first place a little-known activity of World War II – that of the teams of sea-going tugs which were sent out to rescue ships which, through damage from bombs or U boats, had been left behind by their convoys. In the second place it deals with the life on shore of certain of the tug-captains in relation to a mysterious girl whose apartment becomes the refuge of one after another of them – the key being passed on from man to man only through the cancellation of death. Stella, the girl (Sophia Loren), lost her first and only love on the day before they were to be married; but by some strange inner compulsion she continues to harbour and look after his successors. We are here concerned with two of the captains, Chris (Trevor Howard) and David (William Holden). Chris is the present incumbent of Stella's flat, but it is through David's eyes that we observe the situation. Chris is (inevitably) killed, and David, after a lot of doubts, moves in. A genuine love affair develops, and David becomes a substitute for Stella's first love. But David, following the tradition, has passed on the duplicate key to someone else. He is falsely reported dead – and when he returns Stella feels that he has somehow betrayed her. She leaves for London, and David just misses getting on to the train which is carrying her away. 'I'll find her when I go to London,' he says, and on this equivocal note the film ends.

All this is done with a certainty of touch, a sympathy, and a real sense of the tragicomedy of war which can hardly be faulted. The trouble is that Stella and her relationships represent a different kind of realism from that of the violent actuality of the scenes at sea, which are carried out on a grand and very convincing scale. And they conflict. Indeed, once we are in Stella's flat we are almost as cut off as if we were in Lukey's studio (the hall and the staircase have uncanny similarity); and other shore episodes in a horrible little hotel, or in the smoky, noisy service canteens, have a similar feeling. They are, let me say, all superbly directed, not least the scene in the crowded dance-hall with Chris and David talking to each other in cross-cut close-ups.

But it is still difficult to reconcile these shore episodes with the

---

[1] He had already scripted *Home of the Brave, The Men, High Noon* and *The Bridge on the River Kwai*.

other half of the film; and the difficulty is increased by a suggestion of the supernatural attached (or semi-attached) to the mysterious Stella, and accentuated by some eerie music by Malcolm Arnold. Interestingly enough, the one point in which this element really comes off takes place on the bridge of the tug. David, looking through the window of the wheelhouse, mistakes the ship's 'Sparks' for the ghost of Chris. By a brilliant sideways tracking shot (a fine example of how to use Cinema-Scope properly), the image of Chris, seen through the window, changes to that of the 'Sparks' seen through the adjacent door.

At the same time as Reed was making *Odd Man Out*, the two film-makers who had collaborated with Noël Coward in bringing *In Which We Serve* to the screen were engaged, under the producership of Anthony Havelock-Allan, in filming *Brief Encounter*, another Coward work which was to become a great international success and to rival the best of the Ealing product in bringing the reputation of British film to the fore in many overseas countries. Lean and Neame[1] had already worked together successfully on Coward's *Blithe Spirit* and *This Happy Breed*, and continued to do so up to 1949, with two Dickens films, *Great Expectations* and *Oliver Twist*, and a not very successful screen version of H. G. Wells' *The Passionate Friends*; after which they split up and went their separate ways.

Brief Encounter (1946) was, however, the first film in which the real individual quality of David Lean's talent was fully revealed. From now on he was established as an important film-maker in his own right.

The story of this almost imperishable film, told baldly, sounds rather unpromising, if not ridiculous. Two upper-middle-class persons fall in love after a chance meeting at a railway station. Neither of them is, however, 'free'; and after a furtive but pure affair involving minor deceptions and major frustrations, they 'do the decent thing' and agree never to meet again. It must be added that this story is told in a series of flashbacks as the woman, mentally but not actually, confesses the affair to her extremely understanding husband while a recording of Rachmaninov's Second Piano concerto is being belted out on the gramophone – thus providing built-in background music for the rest of the film.

In fact the film does not emerge just as a tear-jerker. It convinces if only because it makes us feel that upper-middle-class people, with their stiff upper lips and strangulated accents, are in fact human and subject to emotional storms in no way different from any of us. The

---

[1] Neame always as producer.

reason for this is not simply the perfect casting of Celia Johnson and Trevor Howard, but also the hair-trigger sensitivity of Lean's direction.[1] He succeeds in making us identify so closely with the couple that their emotional torment surpasses and swamps the gentility of their social status and surroundings. He concentrates almost exclusively on these two very powerful performers (the rest of the cast is skilful but 'typed' almost to the point of caricature), and makes us realize that the very artificiality and conventionality of their society is in itself a pursuing fate which will inevitably strike them down, not with a dramatic thunderbolt but with some little triviality which arises from failure to observe those conventions by which they are bound.

There is a crucial sequence in which the man tempts the woman to an apartment to which he has access. A cumulation of unimportant incidents and mistimings puts everything out of gear. The owner of the flat returns unexpectedly. The woman has to flee in undignified panic, and she suddenly realizes overtly what subconsciously has been true all along – that she cannot under any circumstances be unfaithful to her husband, dull and dependable though he is. The whole of this episode is controlled by Lean with subtle camera movements (notably in the use of the stairway) and exquisitely timed editing which, allied to the performances of Celia Johnson and Trevor Howard, produce a crushing emotional impact.

When I show *Brief Encounter* to my students in California, I am always delighted to see how, old though it is, it hits them fair and square in what they take to be their tough, cynical and hypercritical hearts. Their criticisms afterwards do their best, in hasty hindsight, to rely on their own convention of anti-bourgeois prejudice; and it pleases me to remind them that James Agee, having remarked that the film 'at its best suggests merely all that woman's-magazine fiction might be at its own best', goes on to add, 'it seems to me that few writers of supposedly more serious talent even undertake themes as simple and important any more; so that, relatively dinky and sentimental as it is – a sort of vanity-sized *Anna Karenina – Brief Encounter* is to be thoroughly respected.'

Lean followed this film with a wholly admirable Dickens adaptation, *Great Expectations* (1946), which was memorable in particular for Martita Hunt's Miss Havisham in her cobwebbed and yellowing bridal

---

[1] *Brief Encounter* has for years been equally popular in revival in America and Europe, and is a constant standby of cine-clubs; in France I would guess that it shares with *Passport to Pimlico* and *Whisky Galore* the greatest popularity and affection among *aficionados* of British films.

dress, for the spectacularly shot sequence of the clash of the paddle steamer and the galley in the attempt to arrest Magwitch, and of course the first startling confrontation between Pip and the convict in the churchyard – a cinematic shock even more traumatic than the breaking of the wineglass in *The Ghost Goes West*. A second Dickens film, *Oliver Twist* (1948), suffered somewhat from the defects of the original, which contains much of its author at his most mawkish and melodramatic; but it was brilliantly made, and dominated by a coruscating performance by Alec Guinness as Fagin – a performance, indeed, which actually caused offence in some Jewish quarters, New York not least.

A number of well-made, successful but not especially distinguished films followed; and then in 1957 Lean entered the blockbuster field with *The Bridge on the River Kwai*; after which, at dates determined by long periods of preparation and meticulously carried out shooting and editing, he delivered *Lawrence of Arabia* (1962) and *Doctor Zhivago* (1966). Unfortunately for myself I am rather out of tune with very lengthy films, but if I have to see one, give me Lean rather than Fellini or Bondarchuk; with Lean the human values are never swamped by spectacle or irrelevant fripperies. It is interesting to note, too, that Lean's productions, with their long preparation and enormous budgets (in excess even of those which helped to put Rank on the rocks) are in fact big box-office successes. His work could perhaps be compared with those unjustly despised academicians such as Lord Leighton and Frith, whose vast, elaborate, meticulously detailed and dramatic canvases fetched such high prices in their Victorian heyday (and will, I suspect, do so again very shortly). David Lean is perhaps the last remaining 'big' director of the old school whose production costs the film financiers can still envisage with some confidence. In 1969 his *Ryan's Daughter* suffered a fearful pasting from the critics, but looked like taking as much money from an enormous and faithful public as any of the others. And if he can still write his own ticket on this level, why not? As he himself has said, 'The producing company puts up vast sums for the making of a movie, and in my personal experience I have little to complain about when I consider commissioned artists in other fields'.[1] Fair enough.

The films from Michael Balcon's studios at Ealing were in genesis and method very different from those of Reed or Lean. The basic policy of modest budgets put a premium on ideas rather than elaboration or spectacularity. Behind the Ealing programme stood a whole team of writers and ideas men (some of whom became talented

[1] *Film Book I*, ed. Robert Hughes, Grove Press, 1959.

directors) who conjured up a display of pyrotechnic brilliance which endured for some fifteen years.

The 'Ealing Formula', as developed in the late Forties by William Rose, T. E. B. Clarke, Robert Hamer, Alexander Mackendrick, Monja Danischewsky, Henry Cornelius and others, was quite simple and owed some basic debt to Lewis Carroll. They took some way-out idea or other which it was just possible to visualize as an actual happening in real life and, however crazy or illogical it might be, they pursued it to a logical conclusion. I suppose the archetype was *Passport to Pimlico* (1948), which arose from a chance reading of a newspaper clip about a hotel suite in Canada being, by Act of Parliament, made part of Holland so that Princess Juliana could have her baby on Dutch soil. Supposing, said T. E. B. Clarke, documents were found proving that Pimlico was an independent state . . .? And under Cornelius' genial direction so it was, to the joy of all.

In a Pimlico street, near London's Victoria Station, the delayed explosion of a German bomb reveals a treasure chamber containing not only gold but also a document (deciphered by a strong-minded and dotty expert gloriously played by Margaret Rutherford) which proves that this street belongs not to the British Crown but to the Duke of Burgundy. As the implications of this discovery gradually dawn on Pimlico and Whitehall, the whole situation develops into a microcosm of the world of diplomacy, politics and local government. Pimlico tears up its ration books and abandons its licensing laws. From all over London the spivs and black-marketeers surge joyously in. Traders and small business men become eligible for valuable 'Export Only' orders.[1] A Burgundian Government is formed; its Cabinet consists of the grocer, the modiste, the bank manager (of course) and the fishmonger. Diplomatic relations with Whitehall become inevitably strained. Whitehall puts up customs barriers. Pimlico retaliates, and all the underground trains passing through Burgundian territory are stopped in the tunnels and boarded by brisk and unmistakably Cockney *douaniers*; this is a superb sequence which nicely epitomizes the whole customs nonsense. Then Whitehall cuts off the water supply (the whole film takes place during a heat-wave), but Pimlico makes a midnight commando raid and turns it on again – too enthusiastically, however, because the food-reserves are submerged and ruined. The Burgundians

---

[1] The film was of course made soon after the war, when rationing and travel restrictions were common in most European countries, and nowhere more so than in Britain. The film certainly has more than local appeal; and would still go over very well wherever people have to cope with irksome, and, it would often seem, idiotic restrictions – which still means almost anywhere in the world.

are faced with starvation, and surrender seems inevitable. But at this point sympathy for the underdog comes to the fore. A 'Bundles for Burgundy' movement is organized (delicate compliment to Britain's American allies here), and there is even an airlift, with helicopters delivering eggs and pigs being dropped by parachute. Finally, after protracted negotiations, an agreement is reached and the Burgundians are re-united with Britain – a fact clearly realized by one and all when the open-air banquet of celebration is broken up, in true English fashion, by a blinding downpour of rain. Needless to say the film was an enormous success in Britain and overseas, especially in France if only, as I noted at the time, because of 'the originality of the idea, the technical skill, and importantly, a certain tender understanding of the real mystique of the Londoner'.

It should be noted, incidentally, that the Ealing mood and method were incomprehensible to a number of the most influential British film tycoons. One of them, told by Balcon that Alec Guinness could and would be made into a star, replied 'You must be out of your bloody mind'. And on the completion of *Genevieve*[1] its executive producer told its co-directors, Cornelius and Danischewsky, not to despair; they would, he was sure, one day make a successful film.

Of the early Ealing comedies one recollects, in addition to *Passport to Pimlico*, Charles Crichton's *Hue and Cry*, made as early as 1946, with its authentic locations on London's wartime bomb-sites, and the splendidly natural acting of the kids which contrasted so well with the elegant exaggerations of Alastair Sim's performance. Crichton followed this in 1951 with *The Lavender Hill Mob*, with a crazily possible plot on Pimlico lines and impeccable performances by Alec Guinness and Stanley Holloway.

It must however be remembered that the comedies were only a part of Ealing's output. Michael Balcon's switch to a documentary style during the actual war-period now continued with such films as Charles Frend's *The Cruel Sea* (1953) – an accurate and vivid transcription of Monsarrat's novel on naval corvettes, and *Scott of the Antarctic* (1948), which apart from its other merits was the begetter of a new symphony by Ralph Vaughan Williams. Frend, incidentally, made in 1950 a charming and much underestimated film about childhood called *The Magnet*, in which the main part was played by a small boy who was later to appear, as James Fox, in such films as *The Servant*, *King Rat* and *Performance*.

The documentary tradition was also carried on by Harry Watt

[1] An 'Ealing' film, if ever there was one, though it was made elsewhere.

who, with *The Overlanders* (1946), did for the Australian Outback what James Cruze, John Ford and others had done in the Twenties for the American West in such films as *The Covered Wagon, The Iron Horse* and *The Pony Express*.[1]

Other films based on a realist or semi-realist approach included Basil Dearden's *The Captive Heart* (1946), a film on prisoner-of-war camps with fine performances by Michael Redgrave and Rachel Kempson; and *The Blue Lamp*, also by Dearden, a police thriller featuring Jack Warner from which, in due course, sprang one of Britain's most successful TV series – *Dixon of Dock Green*.[2] But of all the non-comedy films of the post-war Ealing period, one classic stands out – *Dead of Night*. This collection of ghost stories, linked centrally to one framing story, was made by several of the up-and-coming young Ealing directors under the aegis of Cavalcanti, who also directed the final episode, by which nowadays the film is only too often solely represented. It is of course the best sequence; but the film as a whole is admirably conceived, only one episode, a would-be funny story about golfers, falling flat; and the cumulative effect of the whole film is too valuable to be wasted. It must be admitted though that the Cavalcanti episode is in itself perfection. Michael Redgrave, as the ventriloquist who is literally possessed by his dummy, gives what is probably still the finest performance of his screen career; the mounting horror of this story still leaves me cold and shivering, especially in those shattering final moments when the man no longer speaks with his own voice, but only with that of the malevolent doll.

It was in *Dead of Night* that Robert Hamer had his first chance at film direction (the story about the haunted mirror), after which, with *Pink String and Sealing Wax* (1945) and *It Always Rains on Sunday* (a realist thriller about the East End of London made in 1947) he emerged as a director of exceptional ability and individuality – being challenged in this only by Alexander Mackendrick. These two directors can now, indeed, be seen to stand somewhat apart from their other Ealing colleagues.

Hamer's style in a number of ways reminds me of the Jacques

---

[1] Some years later, in 1954, an Australian, John Heyer, working for Shell, made a different and in some ways more penetrating film on the Outback called *Back of Beyond*. In this he used the journey of a mailman along the Birdsville Trail to frame and often to reconstruct a number of factual and historical incidents.

[2] In later years Dearden's style and ability as a director deepened. *Sapphire* (1959) and *Victim* (1960) dealt with contemporary problems – race and homosexuality – with compassion and with a frankness unusual at the time. He died untimely in a motor-crash in 1971.

Becker of *Falbalas* and *Casque d'Or*; there is the same extreme concentration and the same instinct for creating a specific and overpowering
sense of mood and atmosphere. Hamer, like Becker, sadly died in mid-
career; but not before he had left behind a film to share the classic
laurels with *Dead of Night*.

This, of course, was *Kind Hearts and Coronets* (1949), a film which,
like Mackendrick's *Whisky Galore* (1948), is certain, any day of the
year, to be seen in a public cinema somewhere in the world. It is
adapted from a novel by Roy Horniman, but its real provenance is
partly Wilde's Lord Arthur Savile's crime, and partly Hyacinth
Robinson, the would-be anarchist of Henry James's *The Princess
Casamassima*.

The film takes the form of a confession made from his death cell
by a convicted murderer, Louis Mazzini, who, to obtain a fortune of
which he believes himself to have been robbed by a legal quibble, takes
the law into his own hands and does away with eight members of the
aristocratic D'Ascoyne family. (The murder of which he is convicted
is in fact the only one of which he is *not* guilty.) By a singular stroke of
inspiration, all the members of the D'Ascoyne family who appear in
the film are played by the same person – Alec Guinness – with a verve
and stylishness matched, fortunately, by all the rest of a large and
talented cast, not least Joan Greenwood and, as the murderer, Dennis
Price.

The style, which never for one moment falters, is elegant, neatly
patterned, a touch cynical and always tongue-in-cheek. The characters
move in a formalized manner which exactly matches the panache of
the spoken confession which so delightfully contrives to intrude itself
on the action throughout the film. The funeral of one of his victims,
which Mazzini typically attends with the bereaved wife, gives the whole
quality of the film in encapsulated form.[1]

EXT: Village Churchyard. Mourners are making their way into the
church.
Louis Voice: The funeral service was held in the village church at
Chalfont, prior to interment in the family vault.
EXT: Churchyard Gate. A closed carriage drives up. Louis descends
from within and helps out Edith, in widow's weeds.
Louis Voice: Mrs D'Ascoyne, who had discerned in me a man of
delicate sensibility and high purpose, asked me to accompany her
on the cross-country journey.

[1] This is part of a section of the Final Draft script published in *Sight and Sound*,
October-December 1951.

INT: Church. It is full of monuments to D'Ascoynes already departed, including two busts of the first Duke and Duchess. The Verger shows Edith into the D'Ascoyne family pew.

Louis Voice: I did so, but not as far as the family pew, since I did not feel this a propitious moment to stress my blood relationship.

Louis takes a seat in one of the side pews, facing the nave.

Louis Voice: The occasion was interesting in that it provided me with my first view of the D'Ascoynes en masse. Interesting and somewhat depressing, for it emphasized how far I had yet to travel.

The camera takes in the members of the family as he enumerates them.

Louis Voice: There was the Duke. There was my employer, Lord D'Ascoyne D'Ascoyne, there was General Lord Rufus D'Ascoyne, there was Admiral Lord Horatio D'Ascoyne, there was Lady Agatha D'Ascoyne, and in the pulpit talking interminable nonsense, the Reverend Lord Henry D'Ascoyne.

Louis yawns discreetly behind his hand.

Louis Voice: The D'Ascoynes certainly appeared to have accorded with the tradition of the landed gentry and sent the fool of the family into the church.

One of the things I especially like about this script is that the instructions for the visuals are written in the same poised and formalized style as Louis Mazzini's meditations and, in other parts of the film, the spoken dialogue; the film must have been envisaged right from the beginning as an absolute and unbreakable whole. The passage just quoted cannot fail to remind one of the fate of that poor booby Admiral Lord Horatio D'Ascoyne who, later in the film, saves Louis a good deal of trouble by going down with his ship in an imperishably ridiculous manner.

For me *Kind Hearts and Coronets* is a film which can be seen and seen again with undiminished pleasure. It is made to an unrepeatable formula. It could not and did not set a new fashion. It is just permanently there, not claiming more than a modest satiric intent, but, perhaps because of its very modesty, it is that rarest of objects – a perfectly satisfying film.

Mackendrick's *The Man in the White Suit* (1951) has, like others of his films, a blackness in its comedy, a sting in its implied social comment, which raises it to a different class from the other Ealing comedies – his own *The Ladykillers* always excepted. This film, which also stars Alec Guinness, poses an all-too-almost-possible situation in which a young scientist, by inventing a clothing material that will not wear out, plunges the whole textile industry into panic and confusion. Much of the film is, of course, uproariously funny. The young inventor's apparatus emits, in addition to noxious fumes, a marvellous burbling noise – a veritable masterpiece of *musique homogenisé*, or whatever Paul Schaeffer would call it;[1] and this gradually builds up to a monstrous explosion as the experiment, inevitably and yet again, goes wrong. The moment when it doesn't explode, but instead silently produces the indestructible fabric, is based on a mass of detail and exquisite timing which results in a masterpiece of comic effect.

It is at this point that the film begins to bite. The wonderful new material becomes a dangerous threat to employers and workers alike. The poor harmless scientist finds himself liable to be an object of hatred. He is an ogre – just as much so as the ancient, fur-coated, rattleboned tycoon whose arrival at the factory, after a night ride in a cortège of Rolls Royces, is one of the highlights of the film.

Inner Office of Factory:
For a moment the task of manoeuvring the old gentleman commands all attention. Gently he is lowered into the big chair. The process is hazardous because Sir John is in danger of coming to pieces in their hands. A weakly groping hand asks for something to be given to it. The Chauffeur proffers a bottle of pills. Cranford, irritated, corrects him.
Cranford (in a swift undertone): 'No, no. The asthma atomiser.'
The Chauffeur offers a small object like a scentspray. The hand snatches it. Presently the wheezing abates. The Chauffeur withdraws. This movement unmasks a close shot of the chair's occupant.
He passes the atomiser blindly to Cranford while the old eyes shift across the faces of the men before him. This is our first view of Sir John Kierlaw's face. It is a remarkable face, very lined and wizened with age. Physically there is not much left of the man. But from the bright hard eyes gleams a sharp, vigorous intelligence. Also a sense of humour, a rather cruel sense of humour, for Sir John has a contempt for his inferiors, and everybody in our story is his inferior. He speaks without preamble.
Sir John (wheezing): 'Now. Some fool has invented an indestructible cloth. Right?'

From now on, though the comedy continues, an increasingly sinister thread is introduced into the story, until Mackendrick makes

---

[1] It is said that at some point an ingenious chap used this burble as the basis for a samba.

us face the reality of a mob readying itself for physical violence –
Luddites turning on flesh and blood rather than on machines.

Similarly in *The Ladykillers*, which can be regarded, I suppose, as
the apotheosis of the Ealing Comedy, there is a rather frightening
moment when Alec Guinness, as the gang leader, is suddenly seen as
the Hitlerish maniac he really is, or at any rate would be if the insane
logic of the film was pursued to the fullest extent. He subsides again
into the gentler lunacies of the succeeding episodes; but the acid
flavour remains, and tinges the final scenes on the railway cutting with
macabre overtones which make the transportation of victims by wheel-
barrow and the final 'crowning' by a dropping signal quite *hysterically*
funny.

The Ladykillers indicated that Mackendrick was outgrowing the
Ealing formulae. He went to the United States and made a very black
comedy indeed, with Tony Curtis and Burt Lancaster both at the top
of their form – partly perhaps because they were enjoying the opportunity of acting outside their normal range. *The Sweet Smell of Success*
(1957) was a merciless attack on the rat-race of New York Yellow
Journalism, where human relationships were as shoddy as the end
product of the murderously malicious columnists and publicity-seeking
press agents. Despite its stars, and because, perhaps, of the sharpness
of its often satiric humour, the film was not a real money-maker.
Pauline Kael well summed it up as 'a sweet slice of perversity, a study
of dollar and power worship'.

Ten years later Mackendrick, again with Curtis but minus
Lancaster, took a look at the dotty world of California in *Don't Make
Waves*. Here he was less strict in his judgment, despite the fact that
Los Angeles – the film's setting – boasts a collection of not always
harmless kooks and racists unparalleled anywhere in the world.
Generously enough he kept his comedy on the right side of satire; the
darker side of the dottiness rarely peeps through. The film does, however,
have that grandeur of conception – in this case the publicity parachute
jump – which Mackendrick brings to nearly every subject or sequence
which he thinks worthy of his special attention. It features in particular
his special brand of iconoclasm in which people or objects apparently
of immense importance and indispensability are reduced to ridicule and
cut down to size. There appears in *Don't Make Waves* a Rolls Royce
convertible of ultimate luxury. Early in the film Claudia Cardinale, in
a raging temper, subjects it to the indignity of a deliberate collision
with a fire hydrant. The Rolls bides its time, and towards the end of the
film it takes a complete and satisfying revenge. Cardinale is seen to

arrive at the house in a torrential rainstorm, lank-haired, dripping, and cursing like a trooper because the automatic hood has refused to rise. As she runs from the car to the house we observe the Rolls, with the courtly gesture of an Edwardian gentleman, slowly raise it, like a hat.

But the iconoclasm goes further. *Don't Make Waves* ends, as *A High Wind in Jamaica* begins, with the collapse of that object of ultimate safety – a house. In the former film it is all played for slapstick, and is very funny indeed, though in the long run it cannot stand up to the inevitable comparison with *The Gold Rush*. In *A High Wind in Jamaica*, however, the collapse of the house is dramatic. It triggers off a situation regarding the children in which their confidence in the immutable reliability of home and parents is completely smashed. From now on they take all disasters – however improbable – in their stride. To be captured by pirates is routine. Firm in their newly gained belief that no one and nothing in the whole world is to be trusted, they set about their captors, first diminishing and then destroying them. It is only in the courtroom, back in Britain and with parents rediscovered, that Emily's iron will breaks (too late) as she realizes that she is sending them to the gallows.

Richard Hughes' book – and particularly Emily, its child-heroine, unnervingly played by Deborah Baxter – is fascinating and disturbing. Mackendrick has done all he can not to lose this quality. He would have succeeded totally had it not been for the egregious miscasting of Anthony Quinn as the pirate chief and, to a lesser degree, of James Coburn as his lieutenant. Every time Quinn launches out into a piece of 'larger than life' acting or puts on his special 'pirate's guffaw', the fragile, dangerous truth of Emily and the other children is flawed or cracked.

Nevertheless *A High Wind in Jamaica* has certainly been underestimated'[1] as has, for even less cogent reasons, *Sammy Going South*, which Mackendrick made, with Balcon as producer though not at Ealing, five years after *The Sweet Smell of Success*.

The picaresque film has always tempted directors, despite the fact that it nearly always turns out to be far more difficult than expected. This one is as near as dammit a complete success. It is the tale of a small boy whose parents are killed (by bombs dropped by their own compatriots) during the lunatic Anglo-French attack on Suez. All he knows is the name and address of an aunt in Durban – so he sets off to walk there. The film, episode by episode, shows his adventures on this long, seemingly endless journey. What distinguishes it very much

[1] It is infinitely superior in its *genre* to *Lord of the Flies*.

from the usual film about a lost and lonely child is that it is adult in approach. Nothing is softened at the edges; Mackendrick sticks to his iconoclasm. It is typical of his feel for a situation that immediately after the boy has, at one blow, been deprived of home and parents, safety and certitude, he is led down an alleyway by a much bigger boy – an Egyptian – who proceeds brutally to beat him up as a representative of the hated British invaders.

Furthermore this is one of the few films – the Gorky and Apu trilogies are maybe the only others – in which the child character actually grows up before your eyes. Every event in the film visibly changes Sammy; his looks, movements, behaviour, all are changed and developed – as in life they would be – by his experiences. By choosing a boy (Fergus McClelland) neither angel-faced nor pudding-faced but just very ordinarily average-looking, Mackendrick was able to intensify *our* experience of the boy's experiences.

Nor are Sammy's adventures 'romantic' in the usual sense. The first stage of his journey – across the Egyptian Desert – ends with him in the predicament of McTeague at the end of *Greed*, handcuffed to a corpse. Luckier than McTeague, however, he finds the key, gets free and, having stolen the dead man's money, continues the journey by himself. Arriving at the Colossi of Memnon, he is instantly picked up by an awful American tourist (awfully played by Constance Cummings) who cleans him up and will clearly take him over unless he can give her the slip – which, with ingenuity, he does. And so it goes – episode after episode, each leading to some form of a climax which tests his morale; there is a splendid sequence when, perched high in a tree, he shouts schoolboy jingles in desperate reply to the terrifying noise of the jungle animals at dusk.

Sammy Going South is slightly overbalanced by the central episode which involves Edward G. Robinson, in a kind of Papa Hemingway rôle, as a wheeler-dealer in illicit diamonds. On the other hand he gives a good performance and has some admirable scenes with Sammy, climaxed by a stunningly shot and edited encounter with a fierce leopardess and her cub which, incidentally, invalidates Bazin's theory that such a scene is only convincing when it is *not* achieved by ingenious editing.[1] This long episode comes to a climax after Robinson's arrest, when yet again Mackendrick uses the destruction of a house. In this case the diamond smuggler's house is pulled apart by tractors; and Sammy, now facing the final crisis in his young life (for Robinson

[1] See *What is Cinema?*, Cambridge University Press, 1968, pp. 48–52, especially the footnote to p. 49.

has become a father-substitute and his house the home he has lost), lies down among the ruins and the tumbled furniture and sobs himself to sleep. When he wakes he has, for all his small size, become a man.

In this film, as to a degree in *A High Wind in Jamaica*, Mackendrick has enabled us to enter into the inner feelings of children under stress. He has, too, managed to capture the 'feel' of the East African scene – a curious mixture of strangeness and familiarity – without the tendency to fake adventure to which most other directors have been prone.

Sammy Going South is a much underestimated film as, for that matter, is its director. Mackendrick's problem may be in part his comparatively low output (ten films in twenty years), and in part the deceptively smooth simplicity of his directorial technique. In actual fact he has very recognizable trademarks. Firstly, pace. His films move along with what seems to be the remorseless accuracy of a conveyor belt, although with study one recognizes inner variations of pace which avoid any mechanical monotony. This more or less unnoticeable pace is the reason for the great concentration with which you watch his films; and it is true even of a comparatively minor work like *The Maggie* (1953), in which the crew of a Highland puffer (or small steam-boat) bamboozle, outwit and fluster an American millionaire (Paul Douglas) and his prissy English assistant, played by Hubert Gregg in one of those small supporting performances (compare Edward Everett Horton) which turns out to be quite perfect and absolutely unforgettable.

Mackendrick also has a great affinity for the wide screen. His compositions for this often recalcitrant area are always right and often strikingly beautiful. He has an interesting habit, shared with Yasujiro Ozu, of shooting with his camera lens exactly at floor level; this is used with particularly good effect in *A High Wind in Jamaica*, especially in the shipboard scenes.

Returning more strictly to the period under review, there are a few more directors who made films which stood out from the general level of competent mediocrity.

Paul Rotha in 1950 turned from straight documentary and made a feature film shot entirely on location in Eire and called *No Resting Place*. This tale of a personal war between a family of itinerant tinkers and a vengeful policeman, treated in the style of Italian neo-realism, and particularly of De Sica, only just fell short of being a masterpiece, the reason for this being that at the climactic moments the dramatic and emotional impact seemed to be (subconsciously no doubt) too withdrawn, and therefore to lack the heat of passion and the heat of the moment. But it contains one freezingly memorable shot – a confrontation, in deep focus, at a railway station when the tinker (Michael Gough) and his enemy the policeman (Noel Willman) confront each other over what seems an unbridgeable distance; it is a shot in which a simple object like a pushbike becomes invested with appalling menace.

Two years later Rotha returned to documentary with a film for Unesco, *World Without End*, which I had the pleasure of co-directing with him. This feature length document was one of the few major efforts of the period (Paul Dickson's admirable *The Undefeated* being another), and it was also something of an experiment in that we shot the material half a world apart – Rotha in Mexico and myself in Thailand. The idea was to show the universality of the basic problems being tackled by the various United Nations agencies – malnutrition, ignorance, epidemics and general underdevelopment in community life. The film had a simultaneous première on the screen (at the Edinburgh Festival) and on BBC Television, and seems to have made a considerable impact on the hearts as well as the minds of its audiences. After its first showing on television, many viewers were so affected by the plight of the Thai children suffering from yaws that, unasked, they sent money to the BBC to help towards UNICEF's work.[1]

The twin brothers John and Roy Boulting, emerging respectively with distinguished wartime records from the RAF and Army film units, launched out – after something of a false start with *Fame Is the Spur* – with the successful *Brighton Rock* (1947), a compelling screen interpretation of the Graham Greene book which, among other things, firmly established Richard Attenborough as a fine actor. Three years later they made another winner, *Seven Days to Noon*, based on an ingenious story by Paul Dehn and James Bernard. This must have been one of the earliest screenplays about the mad scientist and his personalized atom bomb. The scientist in this case informs the Prime Minister that, unless all development work on nuclear weapons ceases forthwith, he will destroy London; he gives the Government seven days in which to comply. By using comparatively unknown actors and shooting on empty London locations early in the morning and on weekends, the Boultings built up a tremendously realistic suspense-movie; the search for the scientist, crisscrossed with the evacuation of London and the inexorable approach of the dreaded dateline, was built up with a documentary realism which was quite convincing even though the ending was a foregone conclusion.

The Boultings subsequently settled down to making highly

---

[1] The impact of this film was much helped by Rex Warner's perceptive commentary and a fine score by Elisabeth Lutyens.

successful but filmically not especially important comedies, of which the best were *Private's Progress*, *Brothers in Law* and *Heavens Above*. These were certainly a cut above the routine British film, if only because each of them was a cunning send-up of one or other of Britain's most cherished traditions or institutions.[1]

Another important film was Thorold Dickinson's *The Queen of Spades* (1948), which he directed from an imaginative and skilful adaptation of the Pushkin tale by Rodney Ackland. Quite apart from the successful creation of a truly spooky atmosphere, the film had about it something of the grand manner – a touch of Sternberg perhaps – with its looming, elaborate and dust-laden sets by Oliver Messel. It was dominated too by Edith Evans as the aged and wicked countess, with her terrifying eyes and a face of crinkled parchment – a female counterpart, somehow, to Ernest Thesiger's Sir John in *The Man in the White Suit*. There was also some splendid (and well-directed) acting by Anton Walbrook and a newcomer called Yvonne Mitchell – the latter later starring in another admirable film of the Fifties, Lee Thompson's *Woman in a Dressing Gown* (1958).

There was also *The October Man* (1947), directed by Roy Baker and both written and produced by Eric Ambler, whose thrillers had already provided the scripts for a number of films. This film of psychological suspense, admirably acted by John Mills, Joan Greenwood and others, tells its complicated story with complete clarity. But it is mainly to be noted for its settings, not least the awful middle-class hotel on the outskirts of London where much of the action takes place – a dreadfully accurate exposition of ghastly wallpapers, occasional tables, genteel whatnots and seedy and desiccated guests, all lit (clever camerawork by Erwin Hillier) by dusty 40 watt bulbs.[2] The soundtrack, too, is effective; there is one electrifying moment when the scream of a locomotive whistle emerges unexpectedly from an orchestral crescendo in William Alwyn's score.

Of Anthony Asquith's films of this period I think that, apart from *Orders to Kill*, I would choose *The Browning Version* (1950) as the best example of his long and fruitful collaboration with Terence Rattigan; and his production, in colour, of *The Importance of Being Earnest* (1951), which he daringly, and triumphantly, filmed virtually as a stage play, in the sense that you felt yourself *in the theatre* although the

---

[1] In 1968 they tried their hand at a *Psycho* type shocker called *Twisted Nerve* which, alas, chilled but didn't thrill.

[2] This is only matched by that quintessential hellhole, presided over by a sniffing Irene Handl, in *Genevieve*.

camera angles were cunningly and discreetly varied all the time. It was a film with true style – and for the archives too, since it featured much of the cream of British acting of the era.

Two films largely neglected by the critics, and no doubt now forgotten by everyone except me and the participants, were *Emergency Call* (1952) and *Johnny on the Run* (1953), both by Lewis Gilbert – something of a *régisseur maudit* whose films, through the years, have varied greatly in theme, size and quality, but have had one thing almost always in common – box-office success. At his best Gilbert is an enormously perceptive as well as a technically brilliant director. He has a talent for never imposing his own personality – he never trademarks his films – but at the same time putting across the point of a shot or a sequence with maximum effect and maximum economy. His almost continuous success at the box-office may indeed have aroused jealousy and suspicion, with a result that *Alfie* (1965) turned out to be the most critically underestimated film of its year; yet the abortion scene is to my mind a small classic of direction, of camera movement, and of power-fully restrained acting by Michael Caine and Vivien Merchant.[1]

Emergency Call, made some twelve years before *Alfie*, was virtually what used to be called a 'quota quickie'. Such films are usually disastrous, but this one had an excellent idea and a bold and enthusiastic young director. A child is dying from loss of blood. Its blood-group is extremely rare, and only a handful of people in Britain are known to share it. The problem is to find at least one of them in time. The suspense arises not only from this but from the fact that, when found, various obstacles appear between the blood source and its actual donation. Thus one of the donors turns out to be a negro (fine per-formance by Earl Cameron) who earlier has been mortally insulted because a wounded Nazi prisoner expressed a wish to die rather than be contaminated with non-Aryan blood. In another sequence we share the agony of the searchers as they watch the coveted blood spurting from the nose of a punch-drunk, beat-up boxer taking his punishment in a fight already 'fixed' (a particularly grim touch, this); the boxer, by the way, is beautifully played by the late Freddie Mills. The pace and vigour of this slender film, together with the urgency of its story, give it a quality which should not go entirely forgotten.

In the following year (1953) Gilbert made *Johnny on the Run* for the Children's Film Foundation – at that time in charge of the redoubt-able Mary Field, earlier well known for her producership of Percy

[1] The American critic John Simon was one of the very few who appreciated *Alfie*. His excellent analysis is to be found in *Private Screenings*, Macmillan, 1967.

Smith's remarkable biological films under the general title of *Secrets of Nature*. This was the story of a Polish refugee boy adopted by an Edinburgh woman. Through a mixture of neglect and misunderstood intentions he is impelled to think of himself as guilty of a crime, and so goes on the run in Scotland. His adventures with various people and in various landscapes were presented with humour as well as sympathy; and the suspense values, plus the immense appeal of the Polish boy (Eugeniusz Chylek), took the film out of the children's matinees and into general release. It also contained a nice homage to Eisenstein – a runaway pram with a baby in it[1] . . .

With *The Kidnappers* (1953) and *The Spanish Gardener* (1956), Philip Leacock – a graduate from documentary – also showed a sure ability in handling child-actors, and in the latter film elicited a fine and somewhat unusual performance from Dirk Bogarde in the name part; while Pat Jackson, also from documentary, produced in *Virgin Island* (1958) a sparkling and original real-life story about a honeymoon couple who set up house on an uninhabited West Indian island to whose sunshine and lagoons, as well as to Jackson's direction, the cast – John Cassavetes, Virginia Maskell and Sidney Poitier – beautifully reacted.

I have never been able to go along with Olivier's screen version of *Hamlet* (1948), which seemed to me to be an opportunity almost deliberately missed (a supposition strongly reinforced when Kozintsev's fine version, with Smoktunovski, appeared in 1964); but his *Richard III* (1956) had tremendous verve and panache, with effective supporting performances by John Gielgud, Ralph Richardson, Cedric Hardwicke and Claire Bloom. The main achievement, however, was the complicity which Olivier contrived between himself and the audience; the Irving-type aside, greatly magnified from its theatrical purport, not only button-holed the audience but gave the whole story, not to mention the villainy (partly self-mocking) of Richard himself, an extra dimension.[2]

Two pieces of production initiative turned up during the Fifties; both set out with high intentions, and neither of them, in the event and for very different reasons, proved stayers. They were Free Cinema and Group Three.

Free Cinema was a reaction against what some of the younger generation of cinéastes felt to be the faded conservatism of established

---

[1] A prank later repeated by Bertolucci in *Partner*.

[2] This is not the same thing as the audience-awareness achieved by Dovzhenko in parts of *Aerograd*. The *Richard III* complicity is nearer to a music-hall method of making palatable a melodramatic situation; one may compare Viva's winks at the audience during one of the more scabrous sequences towards the end of Warhol's *Blue Movie*.

documentary film-makers such as myself. Its prophet was Lindsay Anderson, who raised the battle standards in his famous article in *Sight and Sound*, 'Stand Up! Stand Up!'. This passionate demand for commitment was followed by a number of films which were certainly more footloose but equally certainly no more socially conscious than the old-style documentaries. (It interested me that in *Every Day Except Christmas* nothing was shown of those horrifying and Gorky-like lower depths of Covent Garden inhabited by the pea-podders and sprout-strippers). On the other hand Free Cinema's policy of a less doctrinaire approach (which always had my personal and public approval) did result in works like *O! Dreamland, Momma Don't Allow* and *Nice Time*, which certainly didn't follow the 'official' line of current documentary. Moreover, it acted as a necessary stimulus to the British Film Institute's Experimental Production Fund which (with some financial aid from a pretty reluctant industry) had been set up to provide help to would-be film-makers at all levels of cinematic expression.

After a few years Free Cinema rather disappointingly committed public harakiri, and its members occupied themselves elsewhere, more particularly in the theatre. They later emerged, enriched by their experiences and experiments, as important feature film directors during the Sixties. Free Cinema, for all its brief life, had cradled Tony Richardson, Lindsay Anderson and Karel Reisz.

Group Three was an organization set up under the National Film Finance Corporation which, in turn, had been formed by the British Government in the course of various actions it took to combat what seemed to be the tendency of the Rank Organization (with or without American money) to monopolize the British film industry.

Apart from the President of the Board of Trade's[1] initial loan of £2 million (soon increased to £3 million) to the collapsing British Lion company, which more or less crippled the Finance Corporation from the word go, three groupings were formed with the purpose of bene-fiting from the new set up and thus of diluting the strength of Rank's stranglehold, as it was regarded. The first, by a skilful civil service manoeuvre, went to Rank himself; the second went to his powerful rival ABPC; and the third, called Group Three, was specially formed to 'encourage, and to provide facilities, both technical and financial, for the producer who was not yet established in the main feature industry'.[2]

Group Three began under good auspices. Michael Balcon, ever a rebel against monopoly, was chairman; and the two executive pro-

[1] Harold Wilson.
[2] For details see *The British Film Industry*, a PEP Report, 1952.

ducers were John Baxter[1] and John Grierson (no less). For Grierson, who after leaving his wartime job in Canada had spent some time shaping the newly formed Mass Media section of Unesco, this return to Britain was in a rôle which was seen to be just as much a new extension of the documentary idea as Free Cinema. And, like Free Cinema, it didn't last.

The reasons were devious and complex. To begin with the film industry, ever suspicious of government interference, did not like any part of the group idea, and least of all liked the upstart Group Three. Goodwill and cooperation were, to say the least, reluctantly proffered. Then somehow the films – all low budget productions but not necessarily any theworse for that – did not click (with the honourable exceptions of Leacock's film of a Scottish coal-mine disaster, *The Brave Don't Cry*, and Cyril Frankel's sincere *Man of Africa*). It is all the more puzzling in that the ideas for many of the films were excellent, often rather along Ealing lines; but, whatever the reasons, the Group Three experiment quietly faded.

By this time, however, there were signs of the first stirrings of an entirely new impetus in British cinema. John Braine's louts, Kingsley Amis' Lucky Jims and John Osborne's Angries were, like the Aldermaston Marchers, on the move; and it was in 1958 that Jack Clayton, who had made something of a name for himself three years earlier with an engaging short feature called *The Bespoke Overcoat*, directed *Room at the Top*, with Laurence Harvey and the luscious Simone Signoret in the cast. Next year Tony Richardson mounted a screen version of *Look Back in Anger*, and followed it almost immediately with *The Entertainer*, starring Laurence Olivier and Albert Finney. With Karel Reisz's *Saturday Night and Sunday Morning* (also with Finney) already in the wings, all was set for the start of an epoch in British film-making just as significant as the New Wave which was simultaneously breaking over the scene in France.

VII

It took some time for the liberated countries of Europe to throw off the traumata of occupation; they fell, in any case, into two classes –

---

[1] Solid, down-to-earth and economic British film-maker, who, among other films, directed *Love on the Dole* (1940), *Let the People Sing* (1942) and *When We Are Married* (1943).

those who ended up as police states (peoples' democracies) under the surveillance of Stalin, and those who reverted to capitalist-democracies dependent to a considerable degree on the charity of the United States where, however, as we shall see, a mounting and neurotic anti-communist hysteria was to have an inhibiting though fortunately temporary effect on film-making. Leaving Sweden aside for the moment as having remained neutral, the rest of Scandinavia, and the Low Countries, more or less reverted to type, at least as far as films were concerned, after the war.

Norway, which has never had a very big or influential film industry, almost immediately made an excellent film in cooperation with the French. This was *The Battle for Heavy Water* (1947), directed by Titus Vibe Müller in conjunction with Jean Dréville. The mood and atmosphere were definitely Norwegian, and the film used as actors a number of the actual participants in the secret skullduggeries by which the Germans were frustrated in their attempts to get those vital materials which could have helped in the development of the atom bomb. Shot on the actual locations and in the same windswept and freezing conditions as those undergone by the Norwegian partisans and by the glider-borne troops sent in by the Allies, *The Battle for Heavy Water* had a documentary authenticity which enhanced the vivid excitement of the action.

Little else emerged from Norway except that remarkable if amateurishly made film of the *Kon Tiki* Expedition in 1950. The explorer Thor Heyerdahl, in his attempt to prove that South American and Polynesian cultures might well have common roots, drifted across the Pacific on a raft and, like all sensible scientists, took with him a movie camera. The result was an absolutely fascinating colour film – with some heart-stopping episodes with the ocean and its denizens – which would have been even better if Heyerdahl and his crew had taken a more comprehensive training course in the elements of movie-making.

Some explorers had realized early on the value of the film camera – if only as an extremely valuable type of notebook – but it had not really been scientifically accepted as a *sine qua non*. Some pioneers, not unaware of the market for travelogues, had brought back from their travels such admirable films as Schoedsack and Cooper's *Grass* and *Chang*, and Armand Denis' *Dark Rapture*, a rather lush title for a film which contained some marvellous ethnographic studies of life among pygmies and giants in Central Africa – in particular the circumcision ceremonies, and a fascinating sequence of the killing and eating of an elephant.

Despite all this, and despite the penetrating eye of Robert Flaherty which, though not always focused in exactly the right direction, proved conclusively the depths of observation attainable by a camera lens wielded by an intelligent human, there was a general tendency among professional ethnographers and anthropologists to regard the camera as an intruder, as a contaminating influence which by its very presence could infect and even destroy the primitive subject matter which it was there to record.

It took courage and bloodymindedness on the part of people like Jean Rouch, John Marshall, Richard Hawkins, Asen Balickci and others to reverse this attitude. The final victory was won at the Colloquium on Anthropological and Ethnographic Films held under the aegis of Colin Young at the University of California at Los Angeles in 1968. Here even the most hidebound of the Old Guard became convinced of the value not only of the camera but also of synchronized sound, now so easily and cheaply available. During this colloquium a number of scientists showed films which they had made in the interest of their research but which had, as a side bonus, great intrinsic beauty. John Marshall's sound-film of Kalahari bushmen bathing in a much sought after and rarely found waterhole was utterly fascinating, as was his dialogue sequence of a bushman chatting up a young girl with the idea of a date. From Asen Balickci came colour material shot among the Eskimos which included an exquisite little film of an old man singing to his daughter and her baby about his past prowess; and a virtuoso performance by an Eskimo lady – in a vast and crowded igloo – as she cut up an entire seal, blubber and all, and ensured that everyone present, man, woman and child, received a just and satisfying portion; in a curious way it was like watching Toscanini.[1]

Films like this stay gratefully in the mind long after bigger and more pretentious efforts have faded; and it is worth remembering that *Kon Tiki*, in its own way, helped to pave this path to the acceptance of the motion picture as a useful, not to say creative tool in the hands of the scientist. It is also worth remembering that since that time in the early Fifties the television screen has become an avid retailer of such material.

After World War II the film-makers of Belgium, Holland and Denmark, who during the Occupation had had very much to trim their sails to the wind, returned thankfully to the freer world of filmic expression. What this meant was nicely put by Henri Storck in 1950,

[1] The work of Jean Rouch himself, a great film-maker who has allowed his creative ability to outstrip his scientific training, will be dealt with later.

when he remarked that the Belgian film-maker 'has always been characterized by two things; his poverty and his isolation'. In a small country like Belgium this might seem inevitable. In terms of feature films, the influence of the larger industries in neighbouring countries – and with no special language barriers either on the Latin or Teutonic side – must be paramount; and over the years Belgian film-makers have mainly been concerned with avant-garde or documentary films. In the years between the wars Charles Dekeukeleire made a number of avant-garde experiments, of which *Combat de Boxe*, with its then unusual mix-up of positive and negative images, was outstanding; while at the same time Storck made an impressionist short film, *Images d'Ostende*. But by the early Thirties both Dekeukeleire and Storck had become politically implicated in terms of the human misery resulting from world wide unemployment. Storck is, of course, the principal figure in the history of the Belgian film. In 1931 he enlarged his experience by working in France with Grémillon and Vigo (he was an assistant on *Zéro de Conduite*); and it was after this that, returning to Belgium, he made a number of documentaries of social import such as *Borinage* (made in conjunction with Joris Ivens) and *Maisons de la Misère*. It was Storck, too, who sent the young Dutchman John Ferno to the Pacific to make that splendid contribution to ethnography and archaeology, *Easter Island* (1935); in this film Ferno created one of the masterpieces of documentary, with its memorable images of grave, mysterious stone statues pitted by the weather until their visages became almost indistinguishable from the pathetic disfigurations of the men and women in the leper colony nearby. During the war Storck, like everyone else, had to cultivate the art of the possible, and occupied the occupation by making some films (*Symphonie Paysanne* was the best) recording national customs and ceremonies. Then, immediately after the war, he started on a new tack, the analysis of art through the film, in which he enlisted the expertise of Paul Haeserts. This was not entirely a new venture, in fact, since he and André Cauvin had done some tentative experiments before 1940. But the newly revealed experiments in Italy by Luciano Emmer and Enrico Gras[1] had opened up new fields in filmic analysis of the visual arts, and Storck and Haeserts started to carry these ideas much further. On the one hand they followed the didactic techniques already adumbrated by Haeserts, by which animated lines swooped around major areas of the pictorial composition; and on the

---

[1] They will especially be remembered for *Dramma di Cristo* – the story of Jesus taken entirely from Giotto frescoes – and *Paradiso Terrestre*, from the works of Hieronymus Bosch.

other a surrealist approach, as in *Le Monde de Paul Delvaux*, in which
the talents of the composer André Souris and the poet Paul Eluard
were enlisted.[1] Paul Haeserts also worked on his own, making such
films as *De Renoir à Picasso* and *Visite à Picasso* (both in 1950), in
which he anticipated in part some of the technique used by Clouzot in
Le Mystère Picasso. It was also in this period that Storck made for the
European Community a quiet but rather impressive film – *The Open
Window* (1952). This presented the landscapes of England, France and
the Netherlands as seen by great indigenous painters like Rembrandt,
Poussin, Claude, Constable, Turner and the French Impressionists.
Cool and precise, it was also for its time a remarkable feat of accurate
colour rendering.

A younger generation of film-makers was to appear in the
Sixties – Fons Rademakers, Luc de Heusch; but for the present there
was little more to signal on the Belgian front except for a certain preoccupation with the Congo. In the Thirties Dekeukeleire had been to
Africa and, to quote Storck 'brought back images that were strictly
personal and imbued with an extraordinary sense of form'; and in the
Fifties André Cauvin, already noted for his art films and documentaries,
brought back from the Congo what was intended to be a major contribution to the understanding of this area – his feature length *Bongolo*
(1952). This turned out to be a sad disappointment. Setting out to show
the importance of building some sort of bridge between the indigenous
African civilizations and the new cultures now crashing in from the
West, the film ended up – only too prophetically as it turned out – with
the general impression that the best thing for Whitey to do was to
snatch the uranium and get out quick. I only mention this film because
it is an example of a very talented director exercising himself *pour rien
dire*. Its brilliant technique could not cover up the bogusness of the story
of a young dispenser who goes over to the whites, of the attempt of his
girl-friend to join him, and of her being thrown back by the police into
the world of, so it seems, jungle drums and barbaric rituals from which
they both originated. It was sad in that the film contained much fine
material – ethnographically speaking – about the Bakomba tribes; and
particularly sad in that it was yet another example of the danger of a
director making a film from outside looking in, because in doing this,
however much his feeling of goodwill, he will lack an understanding of,
and an identification with, the people he is filming.

Whereas at about the same time the Puerto Ricans – a pretty

---

[1] Detailed articles, with illustrations, on these films may be found in *Films on Art*,
published by Unesco, Paris, 1949.

underprivileged community – were making films for themselves, by themselves and about themselves which were models of their kind. Crude in technique – partly from inexperience and partly from lack of essential apparatus – *A Cry in the Mountain* was a short film made to promote and support a Government campaign against illiteracy. Simple, often indeed naïve, it had a burning sincerity which really made the audience feel the urgency of its message – especially in a brief sequence which showed the confrontation between a big brawny man and a small child. The child was writing out something in the dust on the path. The man was illiterate. Out of this moment – the calmness and certainty of the child, the anger and frustration of the man – there came an almost inexplicable flash of real drama, a moment of truth. A second film, this time of higher technical quality, was *El Puente* (*The Bridge*), directed in 1955 by Amilcar Tirado. A small village is separated from its school by a ravine through which runs a river subject to sudden flash-floods. In one of these a child is drowned. As the authorities will do nothing unless pressed, the villagers get together, form a cooperative, seek advice from experts, and with their own hands construct a bridge which in due course is ceremonially opened by the local mayor. The tragedy of the flood is beautifully staged, with a compelling simplicity which creates a full sense of reality; and many of the village scenes remarkably anticipate the *cinéma-vérité* techniques which others were later to 'discover'.

The Dutch cinema at this time continued to reflect in general the cosy domesticity, the cleanliness, the preoccupation with land con-servation and farming, and the characteristic sense of humour of the people of the Netherlands. However, in the immediate aftermath of the war, John Ferno made *Broken Dykes* and *The Last Shot* (both 1945) in which, returning to his own native and war-torn land, he showed with compassion as well as with indignation the effects of the conflict on the Dutch people, which included the smashing of the dykes and polders, with resultant massive flooding, by Allied Bombers. Ferno did not, however, settle in Holland, preferring a more footloose rôle as a roving film-maker;[1] and it was not until 1967 that he came back to make his remarkable wide-screen work *The Skies of Holland*, in which the camera, high in the air, speeds among the clouds in a comparison

[1] I make no mention here of the distinguished Dutch film-maker Joris Ivens simply because from 1940 he operated internationally and, after the War, identified himself whole-heartedly with the Communist parts of the World. His attacks on Dutch colonialism, including in particular *Indonesia Calling*, made him *persona non grata*, and his Dutch passport was withdrawn; latterly however all has been forgiven, and he is now once again an honoured citizen.

between nature pure and nature as observed by the great artists of the Netherlands.

Meantime in the immediate post-war years, a group of younger directors, including in particular Herman van der Horst, made a number of imaginative films about the reconstruction of their country; among these were *The Dyke is Closed*, by Anton Koolhaas, and Van der Horst's *Houen Zo!* and *Peaceful Conquest*. And at the same time there emerged the genial figure of Bert Haanstra, a brilliant film-maker on international as well as national levels. His first film, *The Mirror of Holland* (1950), was based on a simple but ingenious idea. He showed his country – towns, villages, landscapes, people – reflected in the waters of its canals; and by inverting the images, produced a series of impressions ranging from quietude to fantasy, which were well sustained by a fine score from Max Vredenberg and by Haanstra's own editing discipline, by which the film was limited to ten minutes and thus did not dissipate its effect.

Typical of Haanstra's attitude is the series of shots with which he opens his one feature film to date, *Fanfare* (1958), a tale about the rivalry between two town brass-bands. A lush Dutch landscape of pasture and cornfields is spread before us; across it, standing perfectly still like cardboard cut-outs, move, dignified and majestic, a succession of cows. They are, of course, being transported along the canals by barges invisible to the camera. The effect is not only irresistibly comic; it also in a very brief space tells us a good deal about the geography and economy of Holland. In a short film, *Glass*, made during the same year, there is a sequence of the mass production of bottles. As each one comes through the machine a voice solemnly intones its number. Suddenly, disaster. A bottle breaks and the procession comes to a halt. With increasing desperation the voice continues to repeat its number over and over again until, at last, someone notices what has happened and starts the process off again while the voice, with deep relief, resumes counting. Beautifully photographed in colour, and edited with precise timing to a score by a talented jazz group, *Glass* is a small classic.

Haanstra has also made a major contribution to films on art with *Rembrandt, Painter of Man* (1956), and some admirable scientific and technological films for Shell, of which *The Rival World* (1955), about man's struggle for survival against the insects, is perhaps the most impressive.

Danish cinema has always been somewhat split between the tendency to gloom of the otherwise hygienic and socially progressive Scandinavian north, and the equally hygienic optimism of the Low

Countries. Dreyer is of course *hors concours*, and has been dealt with in detail already; he certainly represents the darker side, however, as can be seen in a short film he made in 1948 for the Danish Government on the subject of road safety. Titled *They Came to the Ferry* (alternatively *They Caught the Ferry*), it was a grim tale of a young motor-cyclist and his girl-friend who were in a hurry to catch a car-ferry. They hastened too much, and so found themselves crossing the Styx in Charon's boat.[1]

During the German occupation Danish film-makers had managed to carry on by making non-controversial informational films, and as a result of this a number of young film-makers were by the time of Liberation fully trained in their craft; this was largely thanks to a civil servant of considerable vision named Mogens Skot-Hansen, who arranged the necessary sponsorships and who also, immediately after the war, imported Arthur Elton from Britain to produce a programme of socially orientated films.[2] Of these the best (no doubt due in part to the fact that Dreyer wrote the script) was Torben Svendsen's *The Seventh Age*, a tender and sensitive film about homes for the aged. This was an extremely human film. The problems of old age were shown through the eyes and persons of aged folk of all sorts. They were in turn pathetic, humorous, vigorous, astonishing and charming; and some were almost repulsive – for this is one of old age's greatest tragedies. The film stated the problems and solutions fairly and clearly, and there was no attempt to gloss over what the Danes themselves regarded as inadequacies; at one point a fine Home for Aged People was deliberately and firmly described as '*not* typical'. *The Seventh Age* could still usefully be shown today in a number of countries – Britain and the United States not least – to their common shame.

Beyond this, and beyond the many competent and more than competent short films made by directors like Theodor Christensen, Hagen Hasselbach, Søren Melson and others, there were the feature films of Bjärne and Astrid Henning Jensen. In 1948 they created a strong impression at the Edinburgh Film Festival with *Ditte, Child of Man* (*Ditte Menneskebarn*) which dealt with the trials and tribulations of an illegitimate girl growing up in a generally hostile community. This was a sincere and genuine film, with a lovely performance by Tove

---

[1] This film was photographed and edited by Jørgen Roos, who later became a skilled director in his own right. His work includes *The Story of My Life* (1955), about Hans Christian Andersen.

[2] Skot-Hansen later joined Unesco in Paris, and finally became the official representative of United Nations interests in Hollywood.

Maas in the name part. Finely shot in the limpid, breeze-swept landscapes of Denmark, it only needed a stronger feeling of indignation and
protest against social injustice to make it a masterpiece. Other films
by this talented couple included *Those Blasted Kids* (*De Pokkers Unger*),
made in 1947 and dealing wittily, whimsically and sympathetically with
the need and problem of finding adequate play-space for children in
large cities. This film, full of verve and variety of incident, often richly
comic, was splendidly acted by the children – not least by a real natural,
a very small boy called Palle. This infant turned out to be the Henning
Jensens' son, who reappeared shortly in their imaginative film called
Palle Alone in the World, which was just that – a daydream in which
the small boy finds that there is no one around in the great city except
himself; after savouring such delights as the fact that all the trams are
at his sole disposal, he finds that solitude has its disadvantages . . .

As a film-making country Austria has tended to be linguistically
and culturally swamped by Germany, and neither in the past nor the
present has possessed an indigenous industry of any significance. Plenty
of films *about* Austria have of course been made; and soon after the
war, Leopold Lindtberg from Switzerland made in Vienna *Four in a
Jeep* (1950), a not unamusing comedy about the Four Power Occupation. Then in 1955 Pabst himself turned up in Vienna. Although he had
remained in Germany during the Nazi period (making among other
things a spectacular on Paracelsus), he seems to have been quickly
cleared by the Allied Authorities, and now set to work on *The Last Act*.
This film about the last ten days of Hitler's life depicted, not unnaturally, a nightmare world in which raving insanity was the norm,
and in which not merely the physical but also the spiritual structure
of a civilization was collapsing into dust and rubble: a powerful,
perhaps necessary film, but scarcely pleasing. The actor who played
Hitler was terrifyingly convincing. In the same year Cavalcanti also
went to Austria and made a screen version of Brecht's *Herr Puntila* –
said by some to be Cavalcanti's best work; over the years I have vainly
sought to see it.

In West Germany a handful of directors – notably Helmut
Käutner and Wolfgang Staudte – tried to make a new start in their
dislocated and disorientated country. The former's *In Jenen Tagen* and
the latter's *The Murderers Are Amongst Us* were, shall we say, good tries
and suitable in the eyes of the occupying authorities. And then, rather
surprisingly, a splendid comedy turned up, called *Film Without Title*
(1948). This *jeu d'esprit*, supervised by Käutner, who also had a hand
in the script, took the form of a script conference between the members

of a film production team. Starting from a typical boy and girl situation, they discussed the various ways in which the script might lead up to it, and how it might thereafter be worked out. On the screen were shown the story developments as suggested by each member of the team from his own idiosyncratic point of view, thus providing admirable opportunities for parodying various film-styles – including Sternberg's *Blue Angel*. A well-chosen cast which included Hildegard Knef, Willi Fritsch, and Käutner himself, acted with obvious enjoyment; Fritsch in particular did a splendid send-up of himself in the would-be rôle of the popular, romantic young star he once was. Rudolf Jugert directed with a lightness of touch unusual in Teutonic cinema, and ended the film with quite a savage bite when the production team decided that there was, after all, no film there at all, thus implying that there was little the old guard could do to salvage something from the awful detritus left by the Nazi régime and by the bombing raids of the British and the Americans.

Otherwise West Germany had perforce to wait for the arrival of a new generation of film-makers with minds clear of the war's ideological rubble; and these, not unnaturally, did not make their real impact until the Sixties.[1] Meantime in East Germany, under the repressive and humourless régime of Walter Ulbricht, little of note was achieved other than the tremendously skilful but stupefyingly boring propaganda compilations of the husband-and-wife team of Andrew and Annelie Thorndike.

During the war a young Greek was working in England on behalf of his country, mainly by doing overseas broadcasts via the BBC. In his spare time he worked away at a screen adaptation of a novel – 'Eroica', by Cosmos Politis – which it was his life ambition to film. Michael Cacoyannis did eventually achieve this ambition in 1959, the film appearing under the title of *Our Last Spring*. This story of the complex relationships amongst adolescents, and about their hostility toward the adult world – complicated by a plot concerning young Greeks and young Britons revolving round the British Embassy – turned out in the end to be a rather turgid and unsatisfactory film except for one or two sequences, of which the stunning and terrifying Funeral Games organized on the seashore by the hero during the passing of his dead friend's cortège was the most remarkable. By the time he made this film Cacoyannis was of course already established, having first made his name with his fresh and enchanting lottery comedy

---

[1] Though it must be admitted that Herbert Vesely's *No More Fleeing* (1955) was certainly a foretaste of the experimental and underground films to come.

Windfall in Athens (1953). After this he launched the volatile Melina Mercouri on her film career in *Stella* (1954), and then, with the equally talented Ellie Lambetti, made two of his best films, *A Girl in Black* (1955) and *A Matter of Dignity* (1957). In both these films he succeeded in revealing the inner conflicts of the Greek character – with its extraordinary pride, its mixture of reticence and violence – in a poetic as well as a realistic manner. *A Girl in Black* was a simple story of frustrated love between a boy from Athens and a girl on one of the Greek islands, climaxed by a tragic episode in which the hostile locals trick the boy into taking charge of a boat-ride for children; the boat is leaky; it sinks, and some of the children are drowned. Shot entirely on location, the film, aided by Walter Lassally's sensitive photography, really took you inside the insular community, with its dark suspicion and hatred of outsiders. In *A Matter of Dignity* Cacoyannis not only used Lambetti's talent to absolute perfection; he also, in an ambience of blacks and greys, told a story of Greek family life (not without resemblance to *The Magnificent Ambersons*) which was deeply convincing and moving. Both these films have a depth of feeling which is missing from Cacoyannis' most successful film *Zorba the Greek* (1965), and his least successful, the black comedy on an atomic theme entitled *The Day the Fish Came Out* (1967).

At the end of World War II the neutral countries, apart from Sweden, had little more to show than they had in peacetime. Switzerland, apart from a modest output of documentaries, has never been a great film producing country, though many a film tycoon or corporation must at one time or another have been in Zurich seeking end-money or other financial help. Nevertheless, towards the end of the war there emerged Leopold Lindtberg, already mentioned for his *Four in a Jeep*, a director with warm human sympathies who, through Praesens Films, made two features of considerable distinction which, in a sense, embodied the ideals of that Swiss-inspired body, the International Red Cross. *Marie Louise* (1944) focused attention on the universal and tragic problem of children whom war deprives of parents, home and often identity. The little girl of the title had an appeal similar to that of Paulette in *Les Jeux Interdits*. Lindtberg's second film was *The Last Chance* (1945). Played almost entirely by amateurs, it showed how a group of Allied soldiers – themselves derelict if indeed not deserters – managed to combine to help a huddle of lost civilian refugees to cross the Alps into the safety of Switzerland. With excellent camerawork by Emile Berna and an effective if sometimes rather overpowering score by Robert Blum, this film, despite certain melodramatics, had a kind of desperate sincerity and truthfulness which would not, I suppose, make it appear out-of-date today. More important than these two films themselves is the fact that their effect in America was such that the producer at Praesens Films, Lazar Wechsler, managed to set up a co-production with MGM in Hollywood. This ended up as *The Search* (1948), which was directed by Fred Zinnemann and gave the late Montgomery Clift his first starring part. It told the story of a small Czech,[1] reduced to dementia by the loss of his mother and a number of other traumatic war experiences, who is picked up by the Americans and gradually brought back by one of them to the semblance of a reasonable life. Although over-sentimental, especially towards the end, when by a series of coincidences the lost mother is found, the film struck home and, although it was not realized at the time, set the beginnings of a pattern of international co-production which Hollywood, as time went on, began to find not all that unattractive.

As for Spain, from which little had been heard since Buñuel's searing *Land Without Bread* in 1932, there were some surprises to come. Despite the Franco regime, the beginnings of a school of film-making appeared in 1952, when Juan Antonio Bardem and Luis Berlanga got together on the production of a modest but extremely pleasing comedy entitled *Welcome, Mr Marshall*. The story is of a village which is told that some Americans representing the Marshall Plan will shortly be coming on a visit. The villagers become determined to put up the best show possible in order to qualify for plenty of American aid, and, like Potemkin for Catherine the Great, they doll the place up into a veritable Stratford-on-Avon; but in the event the Americans do no more than flash through the village in large automobiles and a cloud of dust. Emboldened by the international success of this film, Bardem and Berlanga each developed their own filmic styles. Bardem's *Death of a Cyclist* (1954) was a strong psychological drama. A man out driving with his mistress – a married woman – knocks down a cyclist and, fearful that their affair will come to light, leaves the victim to die. The rest of the film revolves round the question of conscience, and this also reveals class-consciousness and class differences between the Haves, with their automobiles, and the Have Nots, with their bikes. It was suggested at the time that this theme may have caused the censor's scissors to come into action, which would certainly explain some of the confusions in the editing of what was otherwise a darkly impressive film with an implied sourness of approach to the society which it depicted. Bardem followed this with a bigger and more ambitious

[1] Played indeed by a real small Czech of wonderful personality called Ivan Jandl.

production, *Calle Mayor* (1956). This was an extremely well made film about a cruel jest played by local society in a small town on an unattractive but deeply sincere spinster, by which she is led up the garden path and to the very steps of the altar before her soi-disant fiancé confesses that the whole thing is an elaborate joke resulting from an ill-timed bet. Despite a superb performance from Betsy Blair, the motivation of the story simply fails to convince; the situations creak to the point of impossibility. Buñuel might have brought it off by pushing it even further, *à l'outrance*. As it is, one can only admire the skill of the direction, and certain sequences towards the end in which the perpetrators of the 'joke' begin to realize not only its full implications but also the embarrassments (to put it mildly) involved in trying to explain it away.

Berlanga seems to have had much more trouble with censorship than Bardem. Several of his films in the Fifties seem not to have reached the screen at all, and *Calabuch* (1956) did not entirely fulfil the promise of its rather charming story of a nice old professor who comes to live in a small Spanish village and endears himself to the population by his skill in devising sensational firework displays. In the end it turns out that he is an atomic expert who has opted out. Needless to say, the powers that be turn up and drag him back to so-called civilization. Berlanga himself was reported to be dissatisfied with this film; and this could well be because of the casting of Edmund Gwenn as the professor. He never seemed to get really inside the part, and was not, of course, helped by being dubbed into Spanish. But there were some sweet things in the film, notably the sequences about the bogus bullfighter with his suspiciously well-trained bull. Much later, in 1963, Berlanga made *The Executioner*, a grim, powerful and horrifying film about Spain's official garrotter.

The Wheelchair (*El Cochecito*) must count as Spanish although it was directed in 1960 by an Italian, Marco Ferreri, who fully identified, however, with the feeling and atmosphere of the country. The story (written perhaps with a sidelong glance at Guitry's *Roman d'un Tricheur*) deals with the inordinate passion of an old gentleman for the acquisition of a wheelchair supplied by the state to those who, through age or infirmity, cannot get about on their own feet. In his efforts he gets involved in a welter of intrigues, quarrels, confrontations and skullduggeries which climax in his poisoning the whole of his family; and the film ends with his attempted escape down a motorway in the coveted chair, with mobile police in pursuit. This is one of those minor films which has a nutty flavour that lingers long on the palate. José Isbert, as the old man, gives a virtuoso performance, not least in a sequence early in the film when, with nothing to do, he wanders about poking his nose into the daily activities of each member of the family, irritating them extremely, and yet at the same time revealing the pathetic loneliness and vulnerability of the old.

The one neutral country which had a large and well-established film industry before the Second World War was Sweden. It was here that, from around 1914 onwards, Mauritz Stiller and Victor Sjöström established a recognizable style of Swedish cinema. This climaxed in the early Twenties with films which had a strong impact on world screens – Sjöström's *The Phantom Carriage* (1921) and Stiller's *Atonement of Gosta Berling* (1924). Both these directors migrated to Hollywood, Stiller taking with him the young Greta Garbo, and both made distinguished films there, notably Sjöström's[1] *The Wind* (with Lillian Gish) and Stiller's *Hotel Imperial* (with Pola Negri). Their contemporary, Gustav Molander, remained in Sweden and came into world prominence in the following decade with such films as *En Natt* (1931) and the sentimental and very successful *Intermezzo*, made in 1936 with Ingrid Bergman as star.

Not unnaturally Europe knew little of what was happening in Swedish cinema during the war. But soon afterwards one film at least made something of a sensation. This was Alf Sjöberg's *Hets* (*Frenzy*), made in 1944. An intense, psychologically-fraught Strindbergian film about the relationship between a sadistic schoolmaster and one of his students, it contained one tremendous sequence in which the boy, having found his girl-friend dead in her darkened apartment, comes on his sadist oppressor, now mouselike and trembling, hiding in a closet. The performances by Stig Järrel as the master, Alf Kjellin as the boy, and Mai Zetterling as the girl were all, in a sort of larger-than-life fashion, impressive. In 1951 Sjöberg used very much the same heightened style in his screen version of Strindberg's *Miss Julie* – as powerful and as morbid as the original, though veering at times into unintended comedy. He followed this with a biblical story, *Barabbas* (1953), much of which was shot on location in Rome and Israel; but by this time he was beginning to be eclipsed by the rising star of Ingmar Bergman who, incidentally, had scripted *Frenzy*.

Apart from Bergman's steady and rapidly increasing output, two other extremely interesting film-makers emerged during the Forties and

---

[1] Sjöström is also an actor and has appeared in many of his own films. He made a big comeback in 1957 as the old professor in Bergman's *Wild Strawberries*. While in the USA he transliterated his name to Seastrom.

Fifties – Gösta Werner and Arne Sucksdorff. The first film of Werner's to be shown in Britain was *Midvinterblot* (*Midwinter Sacrifice*), made in 1946. This sombre short (Werner is basically a short-film man), made entirely without dialogue or commentary, made an indelible impression on me when I saw it at the Edinburgh Festival; it is a piece of pure cinema, spare, economic, tailored to the barest necessities of the medium. People huddle in the snow against biting winter winds. Roughly carved wooden figures loom menacingly in the night. A hieratic figure, armed. A man sacrificed. His blood, hot and steaming in the cold air, brings hope of spring to men, women and children as the menace of eternal winter is thus turned away. All this is accompanied by drums as remorseless as the heartbeats in Marker's *La Jetée*; the film has a nightmarish terror. Werner's impressionist *The Train* (1948) was less successful; skilfully made and always good to look at, it fell between the stools of straight documentary reporting and sentimental 'human comment'. On the other hand *To Kill a Child* (1952) had the same compelling quality as *Midvinterblot*. The idea is simple. Today a certain child is going to be knocked down and killed by a car. We see the preliminaries, the gradual gathering together of all the persons and circumstances which are going to bring this tragedy about. Although, as in Bresson's *Un Condamné à Mort s'est Echappé*, we know what the ending will be, there is nevertheless just the same kind of suspense. By choosing a beautiful summer day and exquisitely composing all his shots, Werner adds to the gruesomeness.

Writing in 1932 about Ruttmann's *Berlin – Symphony of a Great City*, John Grierson pointed out that this film 'for all its ado of workmen and factories and swirl and swing of a great city . . . created nothing. Or rather, if it created something it was a shower of rain in the afternoon . . . and no other issue of God or man emerged than that sudden bespattering of wet on people and pavements'. He added later that 'no film has been more influential, more imitated . . . and it set a mark for amateurs the world over'.

Arne Sucksdorff's *People in a City* – the first film, I think, by which he became known outside Sweden – would almost certainly not have been made without *Berlin*, and like that film it produces nothing more significant than a shower, though in this case it is accompanied by thunder. It is, of course, much shorter than *Berlin* (which was of feature length), but its main difference is in its visual quality. Ruttmann was using the old orthochromatic film, insensitive to red tones, and liable to result in strong contrasts in the black-white range – referred to by cameramen of those days as 'soot and whitewash'. For much of *Berlin* it was in fact very effective. But by 1947, when highly sensitive types of panchromatic film had long been developed, it was possible for Sucksdorff to translate his love of simple observation into the most delightful photographic impressions. Yet despite these visual beauties the general impression left by the film is one of triviality. It is not much more than a tourist's eye view of Stockholm – a travelogue of the highest class which only hints at greater things once or twice, as when, in huge close-up, a seagull steals his catch from an unsuspecting fisherman; or when, in the dignified religious hush of a vast church a small boy lets fall a shower of marbles with a clatter as startling as the Last Trump.

Sucksdorff comes into his own as a maker of nature films and films about children, as may particularly be seen in *A Divided World* (1948) and *The Great Adventure* (1953). In these Sucksdorff casts a calm and truthful eye on the realities of nature. There is no Disney-like sentimentality here, no pathetic fallacy; nor on the other hand is there any sadism or forced sensationalism. Sucksdorff insists on showing the balance of nature as consisting on the one hand of animals who survive by preying on other animals, and on the other of man who (leave aside his predilection for preying on himself) intervenes in the animal cycle – sometimes well, sometimes ill – for the purpose of safe-guarding his crops or enriching his supply of food, clothing and other goods.

A Divided World shows quite simply a few of the happenings in a forest during a freezing, crackling, bitter night in the Scandinavian winter. A fox stalks a hare and traps it. An owl swoops to filch the hare from the fox. The trees and the snow icily remain. The film's setting makes an interesting parallel with *Midvinterblot*; but instead of the willed bloodspilling, Sucksdorff shows us a nature 'red in tooth and claw' which is in essence innocent. No guilt in animals; therefore they do not have to propitiate an invented God by killing their own kind.

The Great Adventure is a much more ambitious film, since it involves the relationship between children and animals, between adults and animals, and between adults and children. It can be compared with *Louisiana Story* in that its simplicities are similarly touching; and it can be contrasted with it because it has none of the 'faking by montage' like the struggle with the alligator noted by André Bazin. The methods by which Sucksdorff gets his shots of animals are his own secret; they must involve elaborate hides, remote controls, and I know not how many other tricks. The results are always absolutely convincing in their authenticity. That they are not in any way haphazard is proved by the considered beauty of their photographic composition; in this he is undisputed master of his craft.

Accepting all this, we can admit that *The Great Adventure* goes even further. With a mixture of brutality and tenderness it shows how two small boys pass from their fantasy beliefs about animals to a true understanding of the world of nature, being helped in this by a patient and perceptive father. They begin by finding a small otter and attempting, unknown of course to their parents, to bring it up themselves. They encounter endless difficulties, not merely in the matter of concealment but because of the nature of the young animal itself; and in the end it escapes. Impossible, as the narration says, 'to keep a dream in a cage'. The learning of this lesson, which is the entire film, is beautifully played by the two boys – Anders Nohrborg and Kjell Sucksdorff – and by the director himself as the father, against a marvellous tapestry of wild life – foxes, grouse, hares, lynxes, and so on. The course of the seasons, the iron grip of ice and snow giving way to a spring signalled by the cranes in their thousands flying in from the South, all this, with the rest of the film's images, is built up into a message which we, as well as the two boys, may receive loud and clear: firstly that however kind you are to your otter, you cannot properly divert his true natural instincts – so he will go; and secondly that the growth of understanding from childhood to manhood can to a great degree come from an identification with the magnificent annual dramas of the changing seasons. *The Great Adventure* is not only a beautiful and moving film; it is also a wise one. And here it is again close to *Louisiana Story*, that simple and almost perfect work in which Robert Flaherty depicted the meeting of two different worlds in a romantic landscape, the acceptance of each by the other, and the parting of the two – the Cajun boy and the men from the oil rigs – each having learned from the other, each having changed as a result, and yet everything vital remaining the same.

Sucksdorff made some films in India during the early Fifties which, for all their visual charm, give the impression that he did not feel entirely at home. Better than the large scale *The Flute and the Arrow* is the simple *Indian Village* (1951), showing how villagers who have for centuries accepted drought as an inevitable evil are persuaded by visiting engineers to drill down for the water which, all the time, has been lying under the surface of their land.

To jump ahead into the next decade for a moment, there is another film of note by Sucksdorff – *My Home is Copacabana*, made in Rio de Janeiro during 1965. This is a study of the lives of deprived and underprivileged children in the slums and on the beaches, based largely on material obtained from taped interviews with many of them. At its best – when, for instance, the kids on the beach steal the kites being flown by richer people – it has an easy rhythmic naturalness. And again Sucksdorff's wonderful sense of observation through the camera (like Flaherty) constantly bewitches. But this bewitchment does in the end tend to obscure the social comment which he intended. The future of these enchanting kids – black-skinned or white – is in effect nil. The flashing sunlight shines on the luxurious beach houses and the hotels; it flashes on the sordid tumbledown slum shacks. It shines on the kids themselves, who will remain in poverty, who will slide into crime. Yet in the bright sun the cheerful cheekiness of Lici, Jorghino, Rico and the rest dominates all else; and the message of the film is further overbalanced by an overlong sequence about an admittedly fascinating voodoo ceremony on the seashore at night. Compare all this with Pedro's voodoo-like nightmare in *Los Olvidados*, and with the *cruelty* of the sunlight as Buñuel shows it on the dustheaps and the cripples of a metropolitan wasteland, and the superficiality of *My Home is Copacabana* becomes even more marked. If only Sucksdorff had stated his case for Rico and the rest with the clarity of *The Great Adventure* this would have been a wonderful film. As it is it has much beauty, it has the uninhibited charm of childhood, but little else.

There was in fact virtually no really viable industry in Yugoslavia before World War II, and from 1945 on it was a long hard haul to get one going. Indeed the 'new' Yugoslav cinema, as a power to be reckoned with on the international scene, did not really make its mark until the Sixties. Before that, however, there had been, especially in the years immediately after the War, a fair amount of co-production – some documentaries through United Nations Agencies, and visits from directors like Käutner and Autant-Lara which helped to get things started. And there were one or two indigenous directors of whom Fedor Hanzekovic, previously a journalist, was the most important. In 1950 he made *Fra Brne*, a period story set in the last years of the nineteenth century, about monastic corruption in Dalmatia under the regime of the occupying Italians. It is not, however, a film about resistance to the Italians, though this idea pervades the whole background; basically it is concerned with the dilemma of one individual – a young man doomed by family ties and traditions to become a monk, and trying to escape from such a fate.

With uncompromising logic the film depicts the impossibility of escape, and in the end the youth becomes just as ruthless and corrupt as his teachers; he has lost the battle for his own soul. Shot on actual locations in monasteries and against the sombre beauty of the Dalmatian landscape, *Fra Brne*, with its impressive music by Panadopulo adding to the intensity of Hanzekovic's direction, has a haunting quality which can still disturb the memory after some twenty years.

VIII

The maturation of the American film coincided quite neatly with the maturation of the American nation. As we have already seen, the United States was still something of a melting pot at the time of Hollywood's infancy, vast numbers of its population being first-generation immigrants whose familial ties with Europe had not been wholly severed, but who for many reasons accepted the general policy of the Monroe Doctrine. The only permissible embroilment with the Old World was in terms of trade; and the rapidly expanding manufacturing power of the United States made exports an important economic factor, not least as far as films were concerned. The movie-makers realized that films for mass audiences in America were equally acceptable to mass audiences elsewhere; and it soon became clear that not only did the films make money, they introduced to far-away people the American way of life, thus creating a demand for American products, particularly consumer goods. Trade followed not the flag but the film.

But by the end of World War II the United States had grown up, and with it the American movie. As the gap left by the collapse of European imperialism demanded to be filled, the United States found itself stepping in not only with the dollar but also, and increasingly, with a military presence. By 1946 the confrontation between Communism and Capitalism, between the Russian and American power *blocs*, had been quickly spelled out for all to see; and Hollywood began to reflect not only the political climate but also the dominating international influence of American ideology.

For over fifteen years from 1945 on, Hollywood was at the height of its powers; it was only towards the end of this period that there appeared signs of internal and external stress – signs which again paralleled those of the United States as a whole, with its increasing involvement in Korea and Vietnam and the growth of racial and civil strife at home.

We have already seen how the French and the British resisted in some measure the encroachment of Hollywood on their indigenous film industries. But nothing really could (at least for the time being) prevent the basic influence of Hollywood's production and distribution policy from being felt everywhere in the world outside the areas of influence of the Soviet Union and the Chinese People's Republic (the latter, by some insane illogicality, being presumed by the American Government not to exist). The power of Hollywood was well displayed in the way it imposed its policy regarding television and wide screens on practically the whole of the western world.

Nevertheless it must also be remembered that in terms of filmic quality this period reveals American film-making at the top of its form; it was not until the late Fifties that the shadows of impending disaster began to gather. Nor did American domination bring with it to European countries the oppression and censorship which now made film-making in Iron Curtain countries increasingly difficult and dangerous. It was a financial and industrial domination; the ideological conflicts remained largely at home. The development of these, however, was watched first with incredulity and then with increasing horror by European film-makers as the post-war anti-Red hysteria supplanted the uneasy and reluctant alliance between USA and USSR.

A series of witch-hunts afflicted many walks of American life, and not least the film industry, since it made not passive objects but products which expressed ideas. It all began in 1947 with the setting up in Washington of the Committee on Un-American Activities under the chairmanship of the egregious Judge Parnell Thomas, who on one occasion denounced Christopher Marlowe as one of the most unhealthy of contemporary dramatists.

The avowed object of the Committee was to expose communists working in Hollywood and to sniff out (not to say snuff out) communist content in Hollywood films. The resultant Index included *The Best Years of Our Lives* (a paean to capitalism if ever there was one), *The Grapes of Wrath, Boomerang, Crossfire* and *Citizen Kane* – thus making plain the complete lunacy of the whole operation. The situation as regards individuals was more serious, as was evinced in the case of the Hollywood Ten (eight screenwriters, one producer and one director) all of whom invoked the Fifth Amendment and refused to state whether or not they were communists; unfortunately they also attacked the Committee itself in terms which rendered them liable to charges of contempt of court. They were convicted, and after the Supreme Court had rejected their appeals, they were fined $1,000 each and sent to gaol for terms of up to a year.[1] It is pleasing to note that not long afterwards

---

[1] For the record, the names of the Hollywood Ten were: Herbert Biberman, Alvah Bessie, Lester Cole, Ring Lardner Jnr, John Howard Lawson, Albert Maltz, Samuel Ornitz, Dalton Trumbo, Adrian Scott and Edward Dmytryk.

Parnell Thomas also found himself in gaol – for misappropriation of Congressional Funds.

Individual members of the industry split into opposing factions under this situation. The reactionaries included Gary Cooper, Adolphe Menjou, Ronald Reagan,[1] George Murphy,[1] Robert Taylor, Walt Disney, Barbara Stanwyck and Ginger Rogers; while among the liberals were to be found Lauren Bacall, Humphrey Bogart, Charles Chaplin (damned of course for making *Monsieur Verdoux*), Bette Davis, Henry Fonda, Katharine Hepburn, Danny Kaye, Gene Kelly, Myrna Loy, Fredric March, Gregory Peck, Edward G. Robinson, Frank Sinatra, John Ford, John Huston, Lewis Milestone, William Wyler and, of course, the Ten.

Naturally a great many more than ten people lost their jobs and livelihood as a result of this witch-hunt and of the even more disgraceful one conducted by Senator Joseph McCarthy between 1950 and 1954 (in which year he was slapped down by a Senate Select Committee). The front-offices – especially MGM, 20th Century-Fox and RKO – became prey to unreasoning panics, one of the results being a spate of boring and definitely un-box-office anti-communist films like *The Iron Curtain*, *The Red Menace* and *The Red Danube* – offerings which neatly matched the anti-American films which Soviet directors were then turning out on the instructions of the Stalin regime. On the other hand some areas of Hollywood showed considerable resilience and courage; it was during the witch-hunt period that such films as *Naked City*, *Pinky*, *Home of the Brave*, *The Set Up*, *The Asphalt Jungle*, *The Men* and *They Live By Night* were made. But as a result of this resilience a number of distinguished film-makers were hounded out – among them Dmytryk, Losey and Carl Foreman – much to the advantage of European cinema.

The Red Menace eventually faded before another menace much more immediate and dangerous as far as the Hollywood tycoons were concerned – the rapid rise of Television.

In the euphoric conditions of the immediate post-war period, the film companies were too busy unloading their backlog of films on to the liberated countries to worry too much about this new system which was beginning to revolutionize the whole conception of the motion picture by bringing it into everyone's parlour. When finally the implications became clear the tycoons, like the Japanese benshi in face of the talking film, tried to ignore it in the hope that it would go away. When it didn't they declared war. They tried to starve television out by

---

[1] Subsequently Governor of California and a United States Senator respectively.

a blockade under which no films would be made available to the TV networks; thus, as they eventually came to realize, depriving themselves of a large and lucrative source of extra income. But television, though inconvenienced, still continued to attract audiences away from the cinema and back into the house. So Hollywood cooked up another – and more powerful – answer by evolving a gigantism which the small box would not be able to emulate for many years to come.

Thus it was that a mild little scientist called Henri Chrétien, who since 1928 had been unsuccessfully trying to sell his patent anamorphic lens,[1] suddenly found himself the object of Fox's passionate attention; and CinemaScope, together with the anticlimactic splendours of stereophonic sound, came into being. It was followed by a whole gaggle of monster-screen systems including VistaVision, which used double-sized (70 mm) film, and Cinerama which used three cameras and three projectors. By the time the initial ballyhoo had faded and the novelty value rubbed off, it became clear that, on balance, the art of the film had benefited from these forced innovations.[2]

The big screens were there to stay. The other gimmick of the period, stereoscopy, never got much beyond the novelty stage.[3] It had the disadvantage that the spectator had to wear red-and-green lensed spectacles (which quite a few people, rightly or wrongly, thought gave them headaches), and that the effect – apart from the shock tactics of the 'tiger in your lap' variety – tended to be less realistic and less compelling than the good old flat screen or even the illusory stereoscopy of Cinerama. Whether the Soviet system, in which glasses are not used but which demands somewhat precise positioning of the spectator in relation to the screen, is any better I do not know. But the system does not seem to have been widely adopted in the USSR.

The big screens certainly did what TV couldn't do; and they pulled audiences back into the cinemas. But in the ultimate issue film and television – those two halves of the motion picture medium – had to learn to live together, had, indeed, to learn to learn

---

[1] The invention of which was inspired by Chrétien's seeing Gance's *Napoléon* in its full glory at the Paris Opéra in 1927.

[2] In 1955 Glenn Alvey, an American working in England, made a film from H. G. Wells' story *The Hole in the Wall* in which, on a full VistaVision screen, the size and proportion of each shot was varied according to its content and to the mood or emphasis required. Unfortunately this system (known as Dynamic Screen), which was intended to be operated in the camera at shooting stage, could in the event only be carried out expensively and laboriously in the laboratory, and as far as I know no further work was done. Since that time various technical advances have brought Alvey's ideas much nearer fruition.

[3] Not that it was all that new. I saw a stereo film called *Audioscopics* in a Barcelona cinema in 1936.

from each other. Failure to do this had produced several early disasters on the film side. *The March of Time* – that unique pioneer of screen journalism in depth – was one of the first to fall. Its executives, as Peter Hopkinson, who shot millions of feet for them, has several times pointed out, had a dinosaur-like approach. They thought that the series could be easily transplanted into the TV medium by the simple process of photographing for all to see the man whose commentary-voice (and not least its pay-off line, 'TIME – Marches ON'), was everywhere famous. Unfortunately, Mr Westbrook Van Voorhis, the owner of said voice, was, to mix a metaphor, visually unpalatable. A pictorial interview with Hopkinson on a compilation of Indian material in which Hopkinson had to 'mouth a commentary whose banalities stuck in my throat', put paid to the survival of *The March of Time*.[1] By forgetting that TV can, par excellence, provide immediacy and must to a great degree survive on it, the executives missed a great opportunity to grab for themselves the in-depth shows of the TV screens. Nevertheless, the extreme fluidity of television and its ability to provide instant visual trickery which for films requires weeks in the labs; its instant button-holing quality; its omnipresence; its casualness; its ability – so often rebarbative – to be everywhere all the time; all these elements began to have an effect on cinema which today we take for granted in terms of zoom lenses, *cinéma-vérité* techniques, and all the other things *The March of Time* forgot.

Meantime, however, in the palmy days of the late Forties and the Fifties, the American film reached, perhaps, its zenith. Adulthood had certainly been attained and, despite the witch-hunts, film-makers began to probe deeper than ever before into the problems of United States society – even if, as in the case of the negro problem, it was liable to be too late. In only one respect did it lag, and that was comedy; here, with a few exceptions soon to be noted, the great days were over, and there was nothing to match the *joie de vivre* of the Ealing films from Britain or the films of Clair, Tati and, to a degree, Becker in France.[2]

Otherwise Hollywood at this time was exhibiting in all departments that ruthless and brilliant professionalism which no one else has ever really been able to emulate. From pre-planning through casting to final editing, nothing but the best, the most efficient, was admitted. The skill was tremendous, the appeal international, and the success – other

---

[1] See *Split Focus* by Peter Hopkinson, Rupert Hart Davis, 1969.

[2] I do not here include musicals, which I have dealt with earlier and which of course, as in *Seven Brides for Seven Brothers* and *On the Town*, have a fine humour of their own.

than in those lower depths with which all industries must be plagued – continuous and well deserved.

Take Howard Hawks' *The Big Sleep* (1946). With a screenplay adapted from Raymond Chandler by William Faulkner and Leigh Brackett, with glowing camerawork by Sidney Hickox and a hand-tailored score by Max Steiner, it fielded an impeccable team which, in addition to Bogart and Bacall (fresh from the success of Hawks' previous *To Have and Have Not*) meant top-notch performances by Dorothy Malone, Martha Vickers, Regis Toomey, Elisha Cook Jnr and Theodore Von Eltz. The plot may be too complicated for anyone fully to grasp; yet the film works with exactitude of effect in showing the relationships between the various characters in this scabrous night-town in which murder, nymphomania and pornography flourish – relationships which have a curious warmth and genuine sentiment (between Bogart and Malone, for instance) and which cast a velvet rubescence over the sordid proceedings. Seen today, *The Big Sleep* still looks brand new.

Or take Joseph Mankiewicz' fabulous *All About Eve* (1950), which was not just a vehicle for Bette Davis at her very best as a film-star manacled to middle-age and menaced by a young and talented rival, but also gathered together in a series of superbly shot, fast moving episodes a cast which included Anne Baxter, George Sanders, Gregory Ratoff, Thelma Ritter, Celeste Holm and, in a small part, Marilyn Monroe. Someone remarked of this witty, exaggerated, cruel and yet wildly funny film that the secret of its success was the extreme bad taste shown throughout by all concerned (though I hope they didn't mean to include Milton Krasna's tactful camerawork in this).

Or take John Huston's *The African Queen* (1951), with its inspired flinging together of Bogart and Hepburn (to say nothing of Robert Morley's tragi-comic missionary at the start of the film) in a welter of heat and mud and savaging insects through which, and through epic bursts of suspicion, recrimination and general ill-temper, they arrive at a 'special relationship' and finally at the gorgeously improbable torpedoing of a German gunboat. The fact that the feel and atmosphere was kept at such high tension throughout was due not only to Huston's direction, but also to Jack Cardiff's fine colour-photography and to the adaptation of the C. S. Forester novel by James Agee and Huston himself.

Or take George Cukor's screen version of Garson Kanin's *Born Yesterday* (1951), starring William Holden, Broderick Crawford and, above all, Judy Holliday with her corn-crake voice playing the epitome of all dumb blondes and playing, too, that epic and never-to-be-forgotten game of gin rummy, where the timing of the players was perfectly matched by the unobtrusive and skilful timing of the editing.

Or take *Shane* (1953), George Stevens' mesmeric and deadly serious Western, with Jack Palance and Alan Ladd stalking each other along a street electric with suspense; with Van Heflin, Edgar Buchanan, Jean Arthur and Brandon de Wilde in the cast; and with Loyal Grigg's truly dazzling photography, as in that fantastic funeral sequence. Or take *High Society* (1956), in which director Charles Walters achieved a remarkable transmogrification of *The Philadelphia Story* by the simple process of co-starring Sinatra, Crosby and Grace Kelly (with Satchmo on the soundtrack) in a Technicolor nonsense of impeccable verve and timing; this film also contained the funniest and most accurate delineation of a hangover ever to appear on the screen (even surpassing that of Benchley) by that prince of character actors, Louis Calhern.

Finally, take Billy Wilder's *Sunset Boulevard* (1950), in which are enshrined all Hollywood's pristine romantic glories together with the skill, sophistication and know-how of the up-to-date Forties – the whole neatly packaged in a jewelled casket tied with black ribbon. Wilder himself is on record as saying that Louis B. Mayer, on seeing this film, demanded that he should be horsewhipped and run out of Hollywood; but wiser counsels prevailed. *Sunset Boulevard* – the title itself, in its multiple implication, is a stroke of genius – remains a great example of superb entertainment, and therefore a superb piece of film-making, and is also, in its own way, a fascinating piece of history. This story of an unsuccessful scriptwriter who blunders into the decaying palace of an ageing ex-star and finds himself trapped there (not entirely unwillingly) as her kept boy, though ostensibly employed to help her complete the frightful script with which she plans to make her great come-back, is constructed with remarkable economy and neatness; and as a result the larger than life histrionics of Gloria Swanson as Norma Desmond – a performance truly in the grand manner – become doubly convincing (a blowsy script could have destroyed her). Another great thing about the film is that no one is 'sent up'. All is played for true. Thus we have Stroheim playing himself in one sense as an ex-director permanently out of favour, and in another sense as the distinguished and successful actor he still was at the time the film was made; we have that amazing bridge four in which Swanson is joined by Buster Keaton, H. B. Warner (De Mille's Jesus), and the superabundant Anna Q. Nilsson (the 'Q' stands for 'Querentia'); and we even have a personal appearance of De Mille himself playing De Mille.

The contemporary levels of the tale are equally well-presented –

the young man's attempts to keep in touch with his girl-friend as well as his initial distaste at his gigolo rôle ('as long as the lady's paying, why not the vicuna?' murmurs an odious shop assistant); and of course the grim though idiotic logic of his murder.

The only weakness perhaps is in the beginning of the film, with the young gigolo floating dead in the pool. The prolonged flashback which this necessitates seems unnecessary. It was rumoured at the time that it resulted from the threat that the Hays Office would turn against this story of a kept man unless the audience were first apprized of the wages of his sin. Wilder has given his own reasons, which are both more complex and more macabre, and end with the remark that 'the opening as we finally shot it wasn't logical but it was riveting, and as long as something is riveting they will swallow it.'[1]

Sunset Boulevard is indeed easy to swallow; in it Norma Desmond, after viewing one of her early movies, cries, 'They don't make faces like that any more!' Nor films, more's the pity.[2]

Hollywood's postwar period opened with that enormously successful but ultimately bogus film, *The Best Years of Our Lives* (1946), for which Samuel Goldwyn and William Wyler collected a starry cast which included Fredric March, Dana Andrews, Myrna Loy, Teresa Wright and Hoagy Carmichael, all of whom (except perhaps Carmichael) were acted smack off the screen by Harold Russell, an ordinary ex-serviceman who had lost both his hands in combat. He never, incidentally, appeared in another film. *The Best Years of Our Lives* set out to describe the problems of adjustment facing the 'soldier from the wars returning'; it ended up as an exposé of much that was meretricious in American life, especially from the bourgeois point of view. There was only one real and significant sequence, and this was when a veteran visits a junkyard full of Flying Fortresses and relives, through the soundtrack, their and his days of glory; this would have made a fine ending to the film which, unfortunately, went on for several more reels. If *The Best Years of Our Lives* had been as sincere about the aftermath of war as was *All Quiet on the Western Front* about war itself, it could have been a great film. As it was, it was skilfully and cogently made, so much so that it bamboozled many critics into thinking it was a masterpiece. Let me add that Gregg Toland's camera was, as ever, wielded with complete mastery.

Far more important to the period were two films made by

---

[1] Interview with Charles Higham, *Sight and Sound*, Winter 1967–68.
[2] And now I find I haven't even mentioned Michael Curtiz' superb *Casablanca* (1943), with Bogart, Bergman, Lorre and the rest.

comparative newcomers, Elia Kazan and Edward Dmytryk.[1] *Boomerang* (1947) and *Crossfire* (1946) both set out to take a hard look at certain social realities in the United States, and they both signalled the beginnings of a new approach to the filmic analysis of those realities by a handful of directors whose grip, however, tended gradually to loosen with success.

In *Boomerang* Kazan removed all the gilt and gloss from the detective-thriller and, to quite a degree, showed instead the world of police and criminals in its truer perspective of petty sordidness, frightened and frightening brutality, senseless prejudice and the everpresent possibility of injustice. Seen today in relation to its many successors, this film about the investigation of a murder by a District Attorney (Dana Andrews) leading to the clearing of an innocent man may seem quite mild. At the time it had a documentary reality (in the best sense) which was compulsive – all the more so perhaps because it was based on a real-life case.

With *Crossfire*, Edward Dmytryk violated the most delicate taboo of all – anti-semitism. Outwardly the film was just another thriller with a fine performance by Robert Ryan as a psychopathic murderer who deliberately selects a Jew as his victim. Ryan – an excellent actor much in demand for key rôles at that time – in his playing of an ex-sergeant whose mania is masked by bland, butter-won't-melt-in-the-mouth manners, brings an extra note of conviction to a film which, tightly controlled by Dmytryk, as truly uncovers the sordidness underlying the life of a big city as did *Boomerang* that of a small town. Some of its moralizing – mainly by Robert Young as the detective – would today seem somewhat *voulu*; but it remains a brave and important work as a result of which, as I have already indicated, Dmytryk and his producer Adrian Scott were hounded out of America. *Crossfire* was adapted from a Richard Brooks novel in which the victim was not a Jew but a homosexual; it might be interesting today to see it remade on the original lines, though by now that would probably be regarded as old hat.

A film on anti-semitism was also made by Elia Kazan. *Gentleman's Agreement* (1947), despite its sincere intentions, suffered from a too-obviously contrived plot (smoothly concocted by Moss Hart) in which a goy reporter (crumbs! Gregory Peck) poses as a Jew in order to write a series of exposures for his magazine; the film contained a fine performance by John Garfield (himself a Jew) as a Jewish soldier.

[1] Kazan's previous films included *A Tree Grows in Brooklyn* (1944) and *Sea of Grass* (1947); Dmytryk had made a number of routine thrillers of which at least one, *Murder My Sweet* (also known as *Farewell My Lovely*) was significant.

Kazan followed this film with *Pinky* (1949), which dipped half a toe gingerly into the racialist pond. It depicted the problems faced by a negro girl who is to all outward appearance white, and as a result suffers much from prejudice originating, as it were, from both sides of the tracks. *Pinky* was rather overblown in its general effect, though Ethel Waters and Nina Mae McKinney, as non-pinkies, gave good performances; and although it may have made its point – mainly to the converted – its real weakness was summarized by Richard Winnington who remarked that 'perhaps the most cowardly aspect of this film is the casting of a white actress – in view of the love passages with a white man – to play the part of Pinky'.[1]

Kazan followed *Pinky* with a *roman-policier* fraught with social overtones called *Panic in the Streets* (1950). This crackling thriller, set in New Orleans, is built round the discovery that a dead petty thief is riddled with pneumonic plague; the problem for the police is to try to round up all his contacts (who have probably been infected) without revealing to the public the urgency and the potential catastrophe involved. There is an undercurrent of social satire in this fast-moving film, crisply shot by Joe Macdonald mainly on location in the streets and the port districts of New Orleans, and the final chase scenes, whose complexity Kazan manages somehow to reduce to an effect of simplicity, are often breathtaking. The cast, with Richard Widmark and Paul Douglas as, respectively, the public health doctor and the police chief, and with Barbara Bel Geddes and Zero Mostel in supporting rôles, attune themselves perfectly to the sharp, suspenseful atmosphere which Kazan maintains throughout.

Panic in the Streets was a much better film than the much over-praised *On the Waterfront*, which Kazan made in 1954 with the new wonderboy of Method acting, Marlon Brando.

This attempted epic of trades unionism (American style) foundered in a sea of ill-digested politics and indigestible symbolism from which neither Brando nor the beautiful Eva Marie Saint could rescue it. It was of course powerful in effect in a number of sequences but, like *The Best Years of Our Lives*, it bamboozled many critics into regarding it as a masterpiece; someone even compared the series of violences meted out to Brando in the last reels with the Stations of the Cross. It was left to Lindsay Anderson, in a closely reasoned attack, to blow the gaff. He remarked, among other things, that

[1] *Shots in the Dark*, London 1951. A film on the same subject, but with a male as the protagonist, was made in 1949 by Louis de Rochemont and Alfred Werker under the title *Lost Boundaries*.

'On the Waterfront is essentially an extremely artful conjuring trick; underneath its brilliant technical surface, essential conclusions are evaded and replaced by a personal drama whose implications are entirely different. Put another way, one might say that the potency of Marlon Brando – physical, emotional and dramatic – is effectively employed to palm off a number of political assertions, all of them spurious and many of them pernicious.'[1]

Looking back, one can now see that Kazan's talent was really for the intellectually bizarre, the melodramatic, even the theatrical, so that *Boomerang* was, in a sense, a false start. As early as *A Tree Grows in Brooklyn* (1944), James Agee had some questions on its social pretensions, pointing out that its 'attention to poverty and need, though frank as such things go in films, is also temperate compared with the staring facts of poverty and need; the comfortable have always been able to lick their chops over the hunger of others if that hunger is presented with the right sort of humorous or pathetic charm; if certain Christian or Marxian glands are tactfully enough stimulated, they will drool as well'. Thus it turns out that Kazan's best films are *A Streetcar Named Desire* (made three years before *On the Waterfront*), *East of Eden* (1955) and *Baby Doll* (1956).

Although Tennessee Williams' somewhat claustrophobic play might have been expected to translate rather uneasily to the screen, the intensity of Kazan's direction – an intensity which he communicated to all the members of the cast – made of *A Streetcar Named Desire* something firmly memorable. There were those who felt that Vivien Leigh was miscast or, if not miscast, that she miscalculated her effects. I was not among these. It seems to me that she gave to Blanche Dubois just that haunting, rather scary quality that the character demanded. Here is a woman whose desire to escape reality is absolute. At one point she cries out that she wants magic, not reality; that, for her, truth is not how things really are but how she would *like* them to be. But the reality of truth breaks in (quite literally) when Kowalski rapes her. And from this reality the only retreat, the only escape, must be into madness. All this Vivien Leigh subtly and with a perfect sense of timing conveyed. Her performance was matched by Marlon Brando's miraculously accurate Kowalski – even now to be rated as the best thing he ever did. Like so many brutes, Kowalski also has, at times,

---

[1] *Sight and Sound*, January-March 1955. The whole article still makes cogent reading.

surprising charm, even a kind of tenderness; and this Brando put over perfectly. The glands Kowalski stimulated, however, were other than Christian, other than Marxian.

With *East of Eden* Kazan launched onto the world that *puer mirabilis* James Dean, whose violent and untimely death before his third film, *Giant*, had even been released, made of him an heroic legend to frustrated youth on a scale almost as great as that of Valentino to frustrated ladies. Dean was a talented actor, as *Giant*, if nothing else, proved. *East of Eden* set the scene for his rebellious image. I have always been puzzled and slightly resentful at the violent emotional effect I receive from this film; I always end up having a good cry. Yet on the face of it *East of Eden*,[1] with its overblown allegories of Adam and Eve and Cain and Abel, is often stilted, overdramatized and over-sentimentalized. But at the same time much is revealed of true human feeling and behaviour, of communication and of the failure to communicate, of the tragedy of jealousy and of the gap between young and old; and Julie Harris well matches the playing of James Dean as he causes us to experience 'that tender, romantic, marvellously masochistic identification with the boy who does everything wrong because he cares so much,' as Pauline Kael so finely puts it, and as it was to be seen in further magnification in Nicholas Ray's *Rebel Without a Cause*. The highlight of *East of Eden* is the boy's confrontation of his mother after he has discovered her to be the *madame* of a brothel, and the equally painful sequel when, in an access of frustration and jealousy, he introduces her to his brother, with traumatic results all round.

But *Baby Doll* is undoubtedly the most satisfactory of all Kazan's films; satisfactory, that is, as a film in which everything works – narration, casting, tempo, rhythm, dramatic tension. *Baby Doll* is, quite simply, about sex; brutish, lustful, hateful, sweaty sex. As in *A Streetcar Named Desire*, the writer is Tennessee Williams, and much of the film was shot on location in a typical town of his Deep South, centring on the appalling house, which we get to know so extremely intimately, where Baby Doll lives with a husband twenty years older than herself; for she is not only a child-wife in the accepted Southern sense, she has also, like Blanche Dubois, found a way of opting out of reality. She has decided to escape into a permanent childhood, with infantile toys and an infantile cot in which she can loll and suck her infantile thumb while indulging in infantile dreams of eroticisms which as she soon

---

[1] 'And Cain went out from the presence of the Lord and dwelt in the land of Nod, on the east of Eden.' *Genesis* IV, 6. The film is based, however, on part of a John Steinbeck book.

finds out (again like Blanche) have precious little to do with the rip-roaring reality.

Baby Doll is now twenty – the age at which, by previous agreement, her husband will be permitted to deflower her. But by now he is, not unexpectedly one would suppose, an alcoholic; more, in a frenzy of anti-social jealousy against the local community, he becomes an arsonist. His natural enemy comes to the house seeking evidence against him, and finds Baby Doll easy to talk to (there is a virtuoso slow tracking-shot over the waste-ground that stands in for the garden as she tells him about her married life); soon the confrontation develops into a mad chase round the upper stories of the house, with alarming interventions by old rocking horses and mooses' heads. Then the husband returns and is slowly, remorselessly destroyed by the two of them; first his virility, then his dignity and his self-respect (what's left of it). And threaded through all these goings-on is a rather stock Tennessee Williams character in the shape of mad old Aunt Rose, whose unawareness of everything blankets the scene like a veil of cobwebs.

This sort of Strindbergian *totentanz* is beautifully performed by the three main characters – Karl Malden as the husband, Eli Wallach as his enemy, and above all by Carroll Baker as the sluttish, vicious-delicious Baby Doll. Kazan's direction is totally assured, whether he is wandering his camera around the blowsy, flyblown old mansion, or keeping it motionless for what seems an age, though never for a moment too long, on a confrontation between two people on a doorstep. There is perhaps more comment on some of the darker aspects of the American soul in a few moments of *A Streetcar Named Desire* or *Baby Doll* than in the entire fabric of *On the Waterfront*. Sadly enough, from *Baby Doll* onwards Elia Kazan's talent seems to have declined, though *The Arrangement* (1969), based on one of his own novels and presenting a psychological situation through a clever complexity of flashbacks, had a certain compulsion.

The difference between the Thirties and the post-war period in respect of films about American social problems was, in broad terms, the difference between concentration and diffusion. In the Thirties it was in general possible to concentrate on organized crime (to take an obvious example) in terms of gangsterdom which the Volstead Act so nurtured and encouraged, or (to take another equally obvious example) in the simplistic terms of mob law and lynchings in the Deep South. But during the Forties and Fifties the United States was overtaken by a confused and confusing revolution of thought and attitude; and under this rather contradictory situation it became possible for film-makers to adopt a wider view of criminality, racialism and the general bloodymindedness of human beings. This, too, began to cut across society at all levels. The fairly precise patterns of the old gang wars were now re-arranging themselves behind the more respectable façade set up by Cosa Nostra or into the new perspectives of the beat generation and, soon after, of protest. It is easy to descry in this period the roots of contemporary permissiveness, including the drug problem, and of Black Power. But at the time much of the future was clouded, and what may seem to us today undue optimisms or too easy solutions in various contemporary films were not seen or intended as such at the time.

Of all the directors of that time who made more than a few contributions to this area of film-making, Fred Zinnemann was pre-eminent. I have already referred to *The Search* (1948) – his true and touching film about a lost child in a world of displaced persons. In a similar vein was his *The Men* (1950) – the most sincere, truthful and uncompromisingly honest of all immediately post-war films. A combination of talents – for Zinnemann had Stanley Kramer as producer and Carl Foreman as writer, to say nothing of Brando making his first screen appearance – made this a film which dared its audiences to turn their faces away from the screen and, in so doing, compelled them to keep looking. The setting is a military hospital for paraplegics – war-casualties paralysed from the waist down, facing a future of considerable helplessness and, in all probability, sexual impotence.[1] Impotent rage, as well as despair, is, as one might expect, the first and principal reaction to such a prospect. Against the background of this ward, which is organized by the men themselves into a kind of mutual help and self-disciplinary club, Zinnemann depicts the personal dilemma of Ken Wilosek whose girl-friend, albeit in agonies of doubt and misgivings, insists and insists on engagement and then marriage – a fine performance here by Teresa Wright.

Unlike nearly all the 'problem' pictures of this period, *The Men* neither offers easy solutions nor burkes hard unpalatable realities. The only liberty taken is to concentrate on the most difficult of the paraplegics; for while the rest of the men in the rehabilitation ward are building, each in his own way, some form of defence against despair, Ken has utterly abandoned himself to the blackness of the pit. But it is neither unfair nor over-sensational to take him as an example, for all

---

[1] In 1971 Dalton Trumbo, one of the Hollywood Ten, finally succeeded in directing a screen version of his own book *Johnny Got His Gun* (1939) about a war 'basket case' – i.e. a soldier who has lost all his limbs and half his head and cannot even speak. He bangs his head on the pillow in a morse message asking the doctors to kill him.

those seen in the film must at one point or other have had to pass through this particular hell.[1]

The crucial sequence of the film is that of the wedding night. This is supposed to be, at long last, the fulfilment of Ken's reluctant crawl back to life through remedial training as well as through gradually established contacts with 'normal' society (like the hell of being taken to a restaurant for the first time); it is also supposed to be a fulfilment for Ellen, his girl, who herself, in face of uncomprehending parents, discouraging doctors and Ken's own pathological switches of mood, has come near to total breakdown. Here surely, the audience thinks, comes the answer, the happy ending; things are bound to be a bit difficult, of course, but there there, they love each other . . . At which point we witness a quarrel of such viciously soul-stripping violence as to be almost unacceptable in a place of public entertainment were it not in fact so utterly true – true because in the midst of it we become aware that what this boy and girl in their deep distress are doing to each other does arise only, and absolutely, from love.

It is a measure of the skill of Zinnemann and his colleagues that there is nothing anticlimactic about the remainder of the film, which involves Ken leaving his wife and returning to the hospital (as being the evil he at least knows and understands), going off suddenly on a major alcoholic jag and, as a result, being thrown out of the ward by the joint managing committee made up of patients and doctors. It is this final shock which brings him round to an acceptance of the need for responsibility – responsibility to himself and thereby to others. He returns to Ellen and to a future seen as a question mark not without hope.

In only one respect could one criticize the makers of this film; it is too dramatic, too convincing, too all-engrossing to need the over-intrusive 'background' music by Dmitri Tiomkin. In this respect only do Zinnemann and Kramer seem to have lacked the courage of their convictions.

Just before directing *The Men*, Zinnemann had made a black thriller called *Act of Violence* (1949), with Robert Ryan again playing a psychopath along the lines of the ex-sergeant in *Crossfire*. In this story of revenge, the main character Enley (Van Heflin) is remorselessly pursued by the only man to survive from a group he had betrayed to the Germans during the war. A film of darkness and of the sleazy under-

---

[1] A very effective thing about this film was that the men in the wards were for the most part not actors but actual paraplegics, re-enacting their own experiences; to which should be added the fact that the real actors – especially Everett Sloane as the doctor in charge – combined perfectly with the non-actors.

ground life of great cities, *Act of Violence* fitted closely into the pattern of a number of other films of the time. These included Jules Dassin's *The Naked City* (1948), a crime story brilliantly shot by William Daniels mainly on real New York locations; Abraham Polonsky's *Force of Evil* (1949), a fraternal tragedy of the numbers game in a sub-world of viciously mediocre thugs and swindlers, with cleverly drab photography (George Barnes) completely fitting the mood of the film, and fine acting by John Garfield and Thomas Gomez; *Knock on any Door* (1949), by Nicholas Ray, a melodramatic but sincere story, told largely in flash-backs, of a Chicago dead-end kid's progress through the miseries of petty crime and a doomed marriage to murder and the electric chair; *The Asphalt Jungle* (1950), one of John Huston's best films, a story of a crime from the inside in which the interplay of characters – with all their weaknesses and petty treacheries – becomes the sour agency of failure and death (something of a companion piece to Kubrick's *The Killing*, of which more later); and of course Kazan's already mentioned *Panic in the Streets*.

To return to Zinnemann – he followed *The Men* with *Teresa* (1951), another film on marriage difficulties in the aftermath of war. This time, though, the problem involves a young GI who marries an Italian girl and brings her home to the USA. With great warmth of understanding, Zinnemann shows the interaction of two factors which bring the boy to breaking-point – the jealousy of his mother (perceptive acting by Patricia Collinge), and his own guilty memories of a wartime incident in which he was responsible for the death of a friend – memories which are revealed through a very ingeniously placed flashback. After the nervous breakdown, the film peters out in a parade of psychiatry and a somewhat forced marital reconciliation; but the first two-thirds of *Teresa* are absorbing and by no means overdone, with notable performances by Pier Angeli (her first film outside Italy) and John Ericson who, after this fine start and an excellent follow-on in *Bad Day at Black Rock*, somehow failed to fulfil his early promise.

High Noon (1952), which followed *Teresa*, was a supercharged western which, among other things, observed the Unities (though why this should be a particularly virtuous thing for a film to do I'm not really sure) and, thanks to a remarkably intelligent script by Carl Foreman and a cast which included Gary Cooper, Thomas Mitchell and Grace Kelly, became one of the most box-office cliffhangers of all time. And in this case there could be no complaint at all over Tiomkin's music.

Unfortunately I have a blind spot for *The Member of the Wedding* (1953), which seems to me a high-falutin' job in which an extremely successful stage play has just not managed to adjust to the screen. The dialogue, action, camera set-ups even, are stagey; and Zinnemann's over-anxious direction, together with Julie Harris' pert exhibition of a twenty-year-old pretending to be twelve, swamps the moments of down-to-earth reality provided at times by Ethel Waters and, more frequently, by the resplendently gig-lamped Brandon de Wilde.[1]

I don't know whether making this film did something to Fred Zinnemann, but nothing he has made since has had what I can only call the purity of motivation which distinguished *The Search*, *The Men*, *Teresa*, and, up to a point, *Act of Violence*. The neurotic layabouts of *From Here to Eternity* (1953) – a film basically about the nastiness of regular army life in America – are mostly figures of cardboard, though the late and lamented Montgomery Clift, monstrously miscast, manages somehow to give a convincing performance. Otherwise Zinnemann's later work indicated little more than a steady competence which occasionally, as in his more recent *A Man for all Seasons* (1967), rose to a certain distinction.

In 1973 however Zinneman re-emerged with *The Day of the Jackal* – a minatory thriller about the historic attempt to assassinate de Gaulle. Not in the least deterred by the fact that the spectator must know that the attempt is going to fail, Zinneman, with meticulous attention to detail, shows how the Jackal (a superbly icy Edward Fox) proposes to work out his plan and how, in the event, all succeeds until the climax. Incorruptibly evil, the Jackal chills every sequence with a needle-shower of indifference; and the casual murder of his equally casual mistress sums up his contempt for all values, sacred or profane. *The Day of the Jackal* is a rare lesson in film making in the good old Grand Manner; and it is a model of inspired casting such as has hardly been seen since the great days of MGM and Twentieth Century Fox.

In 1948 the talented screenwriter Robert Rossen (he wrote, among many, *Marked Woman*, *They Won't Forget* and *A Walk in the Sun*) produced and directed *All the King's Men*, starring Broderick Crawford. This was a straight political story which barely disguised Huey Long, would-be dictator of the State of Louisiana, under the name of Willie Stark. It was a startling exposure both of the corruption and of the vitality of American politics; and in the character of Stark the change from the political idealist to the roistering bully, from the liberal to the fascist, was, albeit in cinematic shorthand, remorselessly outlined. *All the King's Men* was criticized for mingling studio-type dramatics with

---

[1] Untimely killed in an accident in 1972, aged only 30. He will surely be remembered always for his extraordinary performance as the boy in *Shane*.

realistic locations (for Rossen shot much of his film in Californian small-towns, using the local inhabitants as extras). But Huey Long's personality and career were in truth melodramatic; and if the flamboyant election campaigns (with memories of *Citizen Kane*), the brutal bullying of milder legislators, and of course the sensational assassination at the end, seemed at the time unnecessarily violent and stressful, we today, with our first hand experiences on TV, are more likely to find them quite familiar. Indeed, a real-life episode such as Ruby's shooting of Oswald had certain obvious parallels with that of Crawford by Shepperd Strudwick[1] in *All the King's Men*.

Ace in the Hole[2] (1951), by Billy Wilder, was an equally savage picture, with the camera turned this time onto the cynical unscrupulousness of the world of journalism. Wilder made this film immediately after *Sunset Boulevard*, and his hero Tatum (played by Kirk Douglas at his best) is, like Norma Desmond, a kind of troglodytic throwback. Tatum is a ruthless, hard-drinking journalist who has managed to drive himself steadily downhill until he has reached bottom with an unpalatable smalltime job on a New Mexico local paper. Then a man is trapped in a cliff cave, and Tatum gets the idea of making this into a nationwide sensation (compare Wellman's *Nothing Sacred*). There are two routes by which the man can be rescued, one quick and easy, and another which will take a full week. Through bribery and corruption, Tatum gets the local authorities to adopt the second route. Brilliantly Wilder then deploys all his filmic know-how onto an acid depiction of mass hysteria and the blind quest for sensation which brings to this uninteresting district the crowds with their automobiles and tents, the cheapjacks and petty thieves making their quick killings, the hot-dog stands, the dust, the noise, the loud-speakers. Then comes the story's really savage twist. By the time the week has nearly gone it becomes clear that the trapped man is dying. But by now the quick and easy route has been blocked; *la commedia è finità*. Tatum – his story gone sour on him, his squalid ambitions dashed, and his victim's wife sticking him with a knife – returns to the newspaper office and drops dead; a slumping anticlimax which suits the film curiously well.

Told in a large number of short, sharp episodes, this story never becomes muddled or diffuse, and it is structurally saved by the uneasy love-hate relationship between Tatum and the trapped man's wife. *Ace in the Hole* features a reporter and rightly tells its tale in a sharp reporting style. It is a model of economy and an excellent example of

---

[1] This actor sometimes appears in films under the alternative name of John Shepperd.
[2] Also known as *The Big Carnival*.

Wilder's wide-ranging talent. It flopped in the United States, because, to quote Wilder himself,

> 'Americans expected a cocktail and felt I was giving them a shot of vinegar instead. I read those reviews that said, "How cynical can a director be? How could a newspaperman possibly behave like Chuck Tatum?" And the day I read the reviews I was on Wilshire Boulevard and I was feeling very downhearted, and somebody was run over by a car right in front of me. And a news cameraman came and took the picture. And I said to him, "Come on, let's help this man, he's dying". And he said, "Not me, boy. I've got to get my picture in." And off he went. When we showed the carnival moving in and the songs being composed, and the hot dogs being sold, it was all factual, based on the facts of the actual man in the cave case of Floyd Collins in the Twenties. But people just don't want to see this in a film, the way we really are.'[1]

True enough; people don't particularly want to be shown the dirt which has been swept under the carpet. And the Americans would certainly rather not be reminded of their disgraceful, unforgivable treatment of the Nisei – American citizens originally of Japanese origin – during the senseless panic which followed Pearl Harbour. The story of how these innocent folk, most of whom had never even laid eyes on Japan, were deprived of their livelihood, their homes and thus virtually of their citizenship, and carted off to reservations which were little more than concentration camps, has not been a popular subject for American film-makers.[2] In *Bad Day at Black Rock*, however, the secret uncovered by the inquisitive stranger turns out to concern a facet of this mindless cruelty visited by the inhabitants on an individual Japanese farmer; but the film, being basically concerned with the suspense of discovery, is not overly concerned with the details of social injustice. Nevertheless the film is a study of communal guilt, and none the worse for that. Nor is it any the worse for being one of the best suspense films ever made, so much so that the big fight that finally releases the unbearable tension is something of an anticlimax. John Sturges made this film in 1954 under Dore Schary's producership, and with a script by Millard Kaufman which is a real model of its kind.[3] There are no stars. Even Spencer

---

[1] Interview with Charles Higham, *Sight and Sound*, Winter 1967–68.

[2] According to Pauline Kael a film on this subject was directed by Phil Karlson in 1960 under the title *Hell to Eternity*; but I have been unable to track it down.

[3] Until this, Sturges had made a number of not very distinguished films. Since he has made, among others, *Gunfight at the OK Corral*, *The Old Man and the Sea*, *The Magnificent Seven*, *The Satan Bug* and *Ice Station Zebra*.

Tracy, as the mysterious one-armed stranger, fits his tremendous personality into the film without overweighting it, and there are impeccable performances by Robert Ryan (yet again), Dean Jagger, John Ericson and Walter Brennan. *Bad Day at Black Rock* is a film of brooding silences broken only by the casual and normal sounds of the small, remote township and occasionally by apt and economic musical comments by André Previn. The very restraint of this quite classic thriller enhances the power of its implicit protest against racism.

The other really big anti-fascist film of this period was *Intruder in the Dust* (1950). From various points of view this was a strange and surprising film. For one thing it was directed by the veteran Clarence Brown, known until this point for his lush, glossy and invariably successful offerings starring, among others, Valentino, Garbo, Norma Shearer, John Gilbert, Charles Boyer, Joan Crawford, Clark Gable, and a child actress of some promise called Elizabeth Taylor (in *National Velvet* – 1944). For another, the central character, the proposed victim of a lynching, is a negro who resolutely refuses to be 'sympathetic', who, indeed, refuses to regard himself as any different from the white man and who tends to ignore the wellmeaning efforts of the white liberals.

One of the things which most impresses in *Intruder in the Dust* is Brown's superb direction – based in essence on one elaborate long shot – of the crowd gathering to watch the lynching. As Elspeth Grant wrote at the time,

> 'It is a beautiful, clear summer day. Since before dawn cars have come streaming into a small Mississippi town from all over the country. The central square is thronged with people. A radio blares out a rowdy tune. Men lounge against shopfronts, smoking, chewing and laughing in the sun. Women gossip in groups – pat at their hair, repair their make-up. Bright-eyed young girls stroll up and down in their fresh gingham frocks. Children munch candy, lick at ice-cream cones and blithely wave their watchman's rattles. There is an air of pleasurable excitement and expectancy over the whole crowd. What is it they are waiting to see?
>
> 'It is a lynching . . .
>
> 'The crowd appears to be composed of perfectly ordinary, normal people. It is this that makes one's blood run cold.'[1]

---

[1] From *Shots in the Dark*, edited by Anstey, Manvell, Lindgren and Rotha, Allen Wingate, 1951. There are of course hints of this in *Ace in the Hole* and in Wilder's comments on it just quoted.

The horror felt by Elspeth Grant and thousands of others could aptly be matched by that classic New Yorker short story by Shirley Jackson, *The Lottery*, which appeared round about the same time and which, like *Intruder in the Dust*, cast a bright light on the essential insanity of mob rule and of the acceptance of mob rule as a normal way of life. The casualness of the lynch crowd is crucial, because when, through the efforts of a young man and an old woman, the negro is proved innocent, it is transformed into the shamefacedness of people caught unawares in a shabby sex act and thereby deprived of its climax. In contrast to this stands the freed negro – 'stubborn and insufferable', as one of the whites remark in reluctant admiration. The negro, Lucas Beauchamp (played in proud splendour by Juano Hernandez) 'refuses', as Pauline Kael puts it, 'to accept condescension or patronage, he insists on his right to be no better than the white man, and what is truly intolerable – he acts as if he *were* white'. And all this from a negro arrested for murder who is to be legally executed, if not previously lynched.

Intruder in the Dust, skilfully adapted from William Faulkner's book by Ben Maddow, was photographed by Robert Surtees with an accurate unpretentiousness which was exactly what the story needed. Indeed the reticence of the direction, as well as of the camera-work, succeeds in eliminating undue melodrama – thus giving extra conviction to the night scene of the exhumation by which the boy and the woman prove that Beauchamp could not have fired the fatal shot. The boy, Chuck, who has a love-hate relationship with Beauchamp based on a self-induced inferiority complex, is a character seen in real depth, and is played with unerring instinct by Claude Jarman Jnr, whom Brown had previously directed in that admirable tear-jerker *The Yearling*. And the old lady is played by Elizabeth Patterson with a perfect delicacy which brings no element of typecasting to this portrayal of a woman who, nigger or no nigger, believes in doing what is right.

Looking back, one can now see that *Intruder in the Dust* had an importance which could not be noted at the time. It was prophetic. Itself the climax of the post-war spate of liberal-minded, anti-racial tracts, it reached forward across the next fifteen years of films designed to show blacks and whites learning how to live cosily together and adumbrated the more brutal realities which were to come – Black Power, the Black Panthers and, filmically not least, *Sweet Sweetback's Baad-asssss Song*.

Somewhere in the characterization of Lucas Beauchamp lay the realization that the white man's liberal gestures could be too late. Just as the whites' lynch mentality was to a large degree based on deep-seated guilt complexes arising from slavery and the slave trade, so Lucas' refusal of anything except total and *unquestioned* equality was based on deep-rooted hatreds which no apology or self-abasement (even if considered) on the part of Whitey could ever soften or turn aside.

That was why Lucas was insufferable; and not even the film's only error – an optimistic remark at the end to the effect that 'as long as some of us are prepared to fight it'll be all right' – can cloud its unmistakable message. Another remark in the film came nearer the truth – 'Lucas wasn't in trouble, *we* were in trouble'; but it should have been in the present tense.

Prophetic or no, *Intruder in the Dust* started no fashion. Instead, and for some years to come, the racial scene, as far as Hollywood was concerned, was dominated by what might be termed the Sidney Poitier syndrome.

Poitier, let me quickly say, is handsome, sincere, intelligent and, above all, an actor with a great talent which he has been meticulously developing throughout his career. I would not think of impugning his motives in any way; and I have no doubt that some of his better films may, despite all, have done something along the line of ameliorating the racial situation.

But what emerges from the Poitier Syndrome productions is a failure to face up to the hard facts about the continuing worsening of relations (often now on the initiative of the blacks) between the two sides. And if the initiative of action is passing to the blacks, these liberal do-good films are liable to look ridiculous or, worse, to exacerbate the situation.

To take the Poitier films as examples, we find, at the lowest level, such productions as *Lilies of the Field* (1963), *A Patch of Blue* (1966) and *To Sir With Love* (1967); note the dates. In *Lilies of the Field* Poitier plays a negro simpleton who is conned by a coven of nuns into building them a chapel. All the characters are darlings, sweetness and light are scattered around like confetti, and the final effect is quite nauseating because nothing, but nothing, is for real. *A Patch of Blue* is a whining melodrama about a blind girl with a cruel mum. The girl falls in love with guess who? And of course being blind she doesn't know he's a darky. Oh dear. Not even skilled direction by Guy Green and good acting by Shelley Winters, Elizabeth Hartman and of course Poitier himself can dissolve the uneasy effect of sentiment hoked up into sensationalism. As for *To Sir With Love*, one can only say that

Poitier brings a decent sense of dignity to a situation (only too common) in which a sensitive and compassionate book has been traduced in its translation to the screen. One is reminded of the Stanley Kramer-Mark Robson psychiatric epic *Home of the Brave* in 1949, which was one of the films which triggered the racial cycle off.

Other Poitier films have been more serious in intent and content. Early on[1] there was *A Man is Ten Feet Tall* (1957) – also known as *Edge of the City* – in which a negro dock-worker befriends a crazy mixed-up white colleague (played by the young John Cassavetes) and takes him into the bosom of his home and family. Much of Martin Ritt's direction of this situation is perceptive; the fact that black and white *can* get on together is assumed, not plugged. He has, too, a lightness of directorial touch which makes the domestic scenes natural and pleasing. Unfortunately the rest of the film echoes the overblown atmosphere of part of *On the Waterfront*, and finally blows up into a climax of murder and revenge; the sound of recrimination drowns the cooing of doves – which would not matter if the point had really been taken that it is malevolent groups or cliques (political or otherwise) which lead sections of society into blind prejudice and to the destruction of friendships and affections which should surely, as with children before they are got at, overpass all questions of race or colour.

It is typical that in *A Man is Ten Feet Tall* it is the negro who is murdered, leaving the white, in a fine lather of grief and indignation, to bring the killers to justice. Test lesson: rewrite the script with the white man murdered. The same sort of thing happens in *The Defiant Ones* (1958). This was an 'important' production from Stanley Kramer, using an idea similar to that of Hitchcock in 1935 when, in *The Thirty-Nine Steps*, he had Robert Donat and Madeleine Carroll wander around Scotland handcuffed together, and no key. In this case, however, it is two convicts – Poitier and Tony Curtis – who are thus playfully linked together by a prison warder given to sour jokes; and then the truck they are in runs off the road and they unexpectedly escape. They both hate society, but they hate each other more. The negro is stronger than the white – not only physically, but also morally, thanks, no doubt, to the long inveteracies of slavery and persecution to which his race has been subjected. The trouble is, though, that this element of the noble savage – however well presented by Poitier – produces a falsity of relationships. Unlike Losey's *Figures in a Landscape*, where both characters are shits,

---

[1] Sidney Poitier first made his name in *The Blackboard Jungle* (1955) as a classroom lout; for all its overemphasis, Richard Brooks' direction of this film made of it something streets ahead of *To Sir With Love*, with which it is directly comparable.

The Defiant Ones tilts the scales, for obvious but insufficient reasons, in favour of the black. By the end of the film we are over-conscious of this and, as Pauline Kael points out, 'the joker in *The Defiant Ones* was that although white liberals were pleased at the demonstration of solidarity,[1] Negroes in theatres could be heard jeering at Poitier for sacrificing himself for his white "brother".'[2] It must be added that Kramer's direction and superb performances by Curtis and Poitier made this film a very fetching piece of entertainment.

The whole problem comes to a head in *Guess Who's Coming to Dinner?* (1968). To begin with, this film is an almost perfect example of box-office at its most effective, with a beautifully worked out story (William Rose), craftsmanly and unobtrusive direction, again by Kramer, and a duet of virtuoso screen-acting by two really great stars, Katharine Hepburn and Spencer Tracy – most regrettably his last, though by no means least performance. Even those like myself who feel strongly that the film burkes its issue – mixed marriage – must concede that the suave and skilful treatment gives much pleasure. Cecil Kellaway, as that tiresome Catholic priest who infests so many Hollywood films, manages not to recall Barry Fitzgerald overmuch; and the fiancée is played by Katherine Houghton with an insouciant freshness which is quite delightful.

So there is everything to be said for *Guess Who's Coming to Dinner?* except that it is a bold and imaginative contribution to race relations. This it pretends to be, and it should not. What Rose and Kramer have done is to create a number of elaborate Aunt Sallies, arrange them in attractive patterns, and then dispose of them with the flick of a feather; clichés all. First cliché; that old number about the eminent liberal who now has to face personally a situation which for many years he has supported only in theory. Second cliché; understanding mother who thinks she is prepared for everything but finds herself at a loss when she learns that the darkie parents are coming to dine and then (surprise, surprise!) that it is *they* who strongly disapprove of mixed marriages; there is also a variation of this cliché, with old black mammy housekeeper telling the young man not to marry outside his station or his race. Third cliché; the negro turns out to be smarter, more suave, better educated and probably more successful than everyone else. Fourth and final cliché; everyone gets together on the luxurious Nob Hill patio (didn't it just *have* to be San Francisco?), and under

---

[1] The two men become reconciled, of course, through circumstance and defeat.

[2] *Kiss Kiss Bang Bang*. I note that she uses capitals for Negro and lower case for white liberal.

the guidance of the wise old Cardinal they work everything out to a satisfactory conclusion.[1]

The plain fact is that the situations and personages in *Guess Who's Coming to Dinner?* are about as real as those in *Lady Windermere's Fan*, no more and no less. Within these limits the film could be regarded as acceptable. But the limits cannot in all conscience be accepted, because the theme, or moral, obfuscates the very cause which it is supposed to support; for it is absolutely no good (and wasn't in 1968) to suggest, however obliquely, that the violence brewing between races in the United States can be solved in a 'civilized' manner over the coffee-cups and the vodkatinis.

Even *In the Heat of the Night* (1967), which is perhaps the most sincerely truthful of all the films under discussion, was described by one of its stars, Rod Steiger, as 'a very nice film and a good film and yes I think it's good to see a black man and a white man working together . . . But it's not going to take the tension out of New York City; it's not going to stop the riots in Chicago.'[2] Nevertheless Norman Jewison's working out of a situation in which a white man's prejudices are gradually eliminated, not by sweet reasonableness but by *force majeure* and the full and final fraternity which resides in mutual expertise or 'shop', has a no nonsense attitude which, allied with the excellence of the direction and acting, is highly pleasing. But all the time the sound of *Sweet Sweetback* is creeping nearer, and someone had better listen.[3]

IX

Hollywood was, between 1945 and 1960, dependent mainly on a handful of 'Big' directors and a largish group of 'Reliables'. By 'Bigs' I mean directors or producers concerned with inflated, colossal or super-charged offerings – not all of which, let me add, are to be sneered at; and by 'Reliables' I mean directors of undoubted talent, deployed over a long career, who succeed in making films on a wide variety of subjects and never fall below a certain standard of basic cinematic expression.

---

[1] In this rich and automobile-oriented community the good Monsignor was probably preaching to the Convertible.

[2] Interview on BBC Television, August 1971.

[3] At the time of writing *Sweet Sweetback* has been refused a censor's certificate in Britain. For Sidney Poitier's interesting venture into film direction with *Buck and the Preacher* (1971) see chapter 7.

Of the Bigs during this period, the inimitable and irreplaceable Cecil B. De Mille completed a career which began in 1913 and ended with his death in 1959 after the finishing of *The Buccaneer*. Few of his last films were up to the standards he early set himself in such super-films as *The Ten Commandments* (1923, and again in 1956 – the former version being the better); *The Sign of the Cross* (which I watched with delight in a mainly black audience under the stars in Kingston, Jamaica in 1933, noting that many of them took the religious parts completely *au sérieux*); and *The Plainsman* (1937), one of the more splendid Westerns, with Gary Cooper as Wild Bill Hickok and Jean Arthur as Calamity Jane – a film equalled only by George Marshall's *Destry Rides Again* (1939) with James Stewart, Mischa Auer and the un-forgettable appearance of Dietrich singing 'See what the Boys in the Back Room will have' . . . my goodness, those were the days.

Anyway, in 1950, with *Samson and Delilah*, De Mille flung The Hunk (Victor Mature) and the bountiful Hedy Lamarr in and out of each other's arms until the Temple came crashing down as only the old Maestro could make a temple crash. Then with *The Greatest Show on Earth* (1953), he made a big and most exciting film about circuses, including a train smash of unparalleled magnificence. Then came his swan song, a re-make of *The Buccaneer*, of which he was no more than the supervising producer and which despite Yul Brynner, Charles Boyer and Charlton Heston, emerged from Anthony Quinn's direction as a 'tastefully deflated imitation'[1] of the Master.

Whatever one may think of De Mille's particular brand of hokum, and not least his L. C. D. versions of bible stories, the fact remains that he was a master film-maker and that certain of his images – the crossing of the Red Sea (1923 version), and Claudette Colbert's bath of asses' milk in *The Sign of the Cross*–remain vivid in memory. As Herman Weinberg remarked, 'You have to hand it to De Mille. He may not have been the cinema genius he thought he was, but he always knew what he was doing, even when it was absurd.'

The wide-ranging talent of King Vidor led him, not completely fortunately, to the filming of *War and Peace* in 1956. Anyone is bound to be defeated by this epic, for the complexities of character and moti-vation woven into the historical fabric of the novel cannot really be extricated or simplified. The big party early in the film showed promise; it was shot with a certain cool delight, and Henry Fonda was excellent as Pierre. But in the end the film turned into a battle-spectacular; and the book is not that, any more than it is an historical resumé, apart from

[1] Review, *Monthly Film Bulletin* (British Film Institute).

Tolstoy's pontifications in the final section, which most readers are liable to skip anyhow. What success Vidor's version had was in terms of bigness, and in this respect we may also note a job he did earlier, much under the shadow of his producer David Selznick – the somewhat tasteless epic *Duel in the Sun* (1946) on which two other directors, William Dieterle and Joseph von Sternberg, also briefly worked. For its time this was one of the longest films ever made (almost rivalling that other Selznick spectacular, *Gone With the Wind*). Violence, glamour, the Wild West, heavenly choirs, Gregory Peck, Jennifer Jones, Joseph Cotten, Lionel Barrymore, Lillian Gish – it all added up to a razzmatazz of thunderous naiveté simmering into a kind of majestic dottiness.[1]

Similar troubles beset George Stevens and John Huston when they in their turn ventured to invest their skill and ideas in the megalomania stakes. Stevens, whose admirable *Shane* I have noted, had already made a respectful and not unsuccessful stab at *A Place in the Sun* (1952), based on Dreiser's *An American Tragedy* and featuring Montgomery Clift, Elizabeth Taylor and Shelley Winters; though ever since Chaplin and Martha Raye in *Monsieur Verdoux*, the ghost of a giggle must hover over all those fraught boating 'accidents'. *Giant* (1956) was overshadowed not merely by James Dean's death but also by irremovable reminders of Charles Foster Kane and the Amberson family. Stevens also did a sincere but not overly inspired version of *The Diary of Anne Frank* (1959), before embarking on *The Greatest Story Ever Told*, which he completed in 1965. This, according to the advance publicity quoted by Dwight Macdonald in *On Movies*, was 'based on the Books of the Old and New Testaments, Other Ancient Writings, The Book *The Greatest Story Ever Told* by Fulton Oursler, and Other Writings by Henry Denker'. A good basis, no doubt, on which the scriptwriters could begin their labours. Anyway, huge images on the vast Panavision 70 screen ended up by dwarfing the story; and although Max von Sydow made a not unacceptable Christ (he was certainly better than H. B. Warner in the De Mille *King of Kings*, who looked like a large and amiable dog), the general effect of the film was of confusion and of a kind of showing off.

Meantime John Huston had inserted his neck into a similar noose with a project entitled *The Bible*, which appeared in 1966 but only got as far, in my recollection, as Abraham's attempted sacrifice of Isaac. The figleaves of the Garden were replaced by a profusion of flowering shrubs;

---

[1] Let it be remembered, nevertheless, that, apart from *Gone With the Wind*, Selznick was also responsible for such excellent films as *Nothing Sacred* and Hitchcock's *Spellbound* and *Rebecca*.

the inhabitants of a slime-green Sodom-and-Gomorrah resembled a meeting of Jehovah's Witnesses seen through the bottom of a pint-pot; and the much vaunted crane shot emphasizing Cain's condemnation suffered from comparison with Mizoguchi's finale to *Ugetsu Monogatari*. On the other hand, the centre of the film consisted of an enchanting fairytale version of Noah's Ark and the Flood.[1] This had authentic magic, and was much enhanced by Huston's own playing as Noah.

In general the perspective of Huston's progress from *The Asphalt Jungle* onwards indicates elements of the indiscriminate. The production of *The Red Badge of Courage* (1950–1951), and its overlap with *The African Queen* (1951), was excoriatingly described by Lillian Ross in her book *Picture*, from which one learns much about the combinations of ill-faith, misplaced enthusiasm, double-crossing, sincerity, identification and alienation which made Hollywood such a difficult yet enticing place of employment.[2] *The Red Badge of Courage* still retained some of the intrinsic feelings of the Stephen Crane book, despite its deformation at the behest of the front office; but it is sad that Huston himself does not seem to have fought very hard in its defence, largely, it would seem, because he was already by that time deeply committed to *The African Queen*. There followed *Moulin Rouge* (1953), an expensive travesty of the life of Toulouse Lautrec with a rather sulky performance by José Ferrer in the name-part, but with some stunning period tableaux stunningly photographed by Oswald Morris. Comparison with Max Ophuls' *Le Plaisir* (made two years earlier) and Renoir's *French Can Can* (two years later) is enough to relegate this film to the fourth division.

Then came the crashing disappointment of *Moby Dick* (1956) – a disappointment magnified by the enormously flamboyant flood of advance publicity given to the film. It seemed mad to me, incidentally, for the P. R. boys to explain in such detail how the whale wasn't real at all but made of plastic with a little man or, alternatively, a remote-control radio inside to make it work. I wanted it for real. In fact it was Gregory Peck who needed a direction-finder; his inability even to indicate the enormous passions of Ahab was quite amazing. There are of course some fine things in the film – Orson Welles' virtuoso sermon,

[1] It is only fair to add that the original idea of the Italian producer Dino De Laurentiis was for the Good Book to be shared among a number of directors including Bresson, Fellini, Visconti and Orson Welles, in addition to Huston.

[2] Sample: reference *The Red Badge of Courage*: 'As soon as Mr Schenck saw the picture, we knew it was a flop. Let's just say it was a flop *d'estime*. I guess that's the way Mr Schenck would put it.'

some of the storm scenes and, again, Oswald Morris' strangely
fascinating camerawork, with the vivid original colour being subtly
withdrawn into a magic world nearer to sepia and grey. But this is not
enough. In 1926 Millard Webb made a film of *Moby Dick* called *The
Sea Beast*; in this the big scenes, with real whales, were sensational and
dramatic, and the first glimpse of John Barrymore, as Ahab, stumping
away from the camera along the quayside, provided a supernatural
frisson as memorable as anything in cinema. Nothing in the Huston
film comes within miles of it, or of Melville's intention.

Yet there is so much of Huston's work which cannot be faulted.
The Battle of San Pietro is still possibly the most authentic (and moving)
picture of a real battle ever put on the screen. *The Maltese Falcon*
(made as long ago as 1941) set the pattern for nearly all the crime films
of the subsequent twenty years with its matter-of-fact acceptance of the
inner as well as the outer brutalities of the criminal world. Huston's
direction of a cast which included Bogart, Mary Astor, Sidney Greenstreet and Peter Lorre, was supersensitive to mood as well as to essential
interplays of character; and Arthur Edeson's photography was
marvellously claustrophobic. Later, too, Huston distinguished himself
with *The Night of the Iguana* (1964) and *Reflections in a Golden Eye*
(1967). In the former, despite a certain hogging of the screen by the
iguana itself, Huston really put across the smothering atmosphere of
the sleazy hotel and its equally sleazy occupants, and obtained from
Richard Burton, as the exceptionally frightful reverend (by Maugham
out of Samuel Butler), one of the finest performances of his career. As
for *Reflections in a Golden Eye*, Huston faced up early on to the soon-
to-be-fashionable hetero-homo-triangle with a cool head and a clear
eye and, perhaps, a tongue partly in the cheek; and brought Carson
McCullers' little tale satisfactorily to the screen despite an over-
mannered performance by Marlon Brando which fortunately did not
much mar those by Julie Harris and Elizabeth Taylor. In this film
Huston also used variations in colour, producing a version in which the
original naturalistic tints were reduced to a sort of golden haze laced
slightly with pink. This was highly commended by most of those who
saw it; but, due no doubt to conservatism on the part of distributors
and exhibitors, it was the 'normal' colour version which was generally
shown.

As for the brave and sincere *Freud – The Secret Passion* (1963),
what can one say except that, perhaps inevitably, it failed, despite the
finely devised dream-sequences and a respectful performance by
Montgomery Clift, to indicate the really frightening revolution which

Freud unleashed on to the Western (but not the Eastern) world. After all Pabst's *Secrets of the Soul* of 1926 was, *au fond*, an equal failure.

The biggest and mostest of the Bigs was presumably Mike Todd's *Around the World in Eighty Days* (1956), in which even the bit parts were played by famous stars, thus making it not only a super-spectacular but also a continuous parlour game. It was directed by a thirty-five-year-old Englishman, Michael Anderson, with commendable *sang froid*; the monster images on the Todd-AO screen were quite jolly; and nearly everyone, I would say, enjoyed it. I certainly did. But for all that I doubt its memorability.

As for the Reliables, we can give pride of place to William Wyler and John Ford, who continued the film-making careers they had begun in 1925 and 1917 respectively.

After his two fine wartime documentaries – *The Memphis Belle* and *The Fighting Lady* – Wyler made, as already noted, the highly competent *The Best Years of Our Lives*, and followed this in 1949 with *The Heiress*, a successful version of Henry James' *Washington Square*, starring Olivia de Havilland as the spinster pursued by a suitor more interested in her money than her person. The adaptation was in fact from a play based on the novel, but although the film hardly left the elaborate setting of the Sloper mansion, the effect was never theatrical. Discreet camerawork allied to Wyler's sensitive direction of that Jamesian dialogue in which the *nuance* is all, made this a cinematically enjoyable work even if Montgomery Clift, with a personality as innocent and open as a child's book, did not entirely convince as the crooked fiancé. Miriam Hopkins and Ralph Richardson were excellent in supporting rôles.

Of Wyler's other films there was *Roman Holiday* (1953), with Audrey Hepburn as a runaway royal taking us on a Cook's Tour of Rome in the company of an American newsman (Gregory Peck at his best) and of the percipient cameras of Planer and Alekan; a pleasant job, though on the slow side. There was *The Big Country* (1958), a well-intentioned Western about a dispute between two families over water-rights, with Peck and Charlton Heston in a moonlight fight and good support from Burl Ives, Jean Simmons and Carroll Baker; and there was *Ben Hur* (1959), a Big, of course, but for me not a patch on its predecessor directed in 1927 by Fred Niblo, with Ramon Novarro and Francis X. Bushman in an unsurpassed chariot race as well as the famous sea-fight.[1] Wyler continued into the Sixties with a re-make of *These Three*, his 1936 version of Lillian Hellman's *The Children's Hour*, under

---

[1] The young Wyler was an assistant on this production. See Kevin Brownlow's enthralling description in *The Parade's Gone By*.

which title the 1962 version appeared in America though not here, where it was called *The Loudest Whisper* (why?). It didn't really improve on the original, even though the lesbian element could now be overt. And in 1965 Wyler made an adequate screen version of John Fowles' kinky *The Collector*, with Terence Stamp and Samantha Eggar.

John Ford, having worked on the official *Why We Fight* series during the war, continued his career with ups and downs not dissimilar to those of Wyler. *My Darling Clementine* (1946) and *She Wore a Yellow Ribbon* (1949) were in the vein of those earlier and excellent works *Stagecoach* and *Drums Along the Mohawk* (1939). What a splendid film the last-named was! This tale of the white settlers along the Mohawk Valley fighting against twin enemies – the Indians and the repressive English – had a tremendous billowing life of its own, to say nothing of some breathtaking colour, with the Redcoats glowing against the dark forests and the warpainted Indians creeping through slanting shadows at sunrise; good gutsy characterizations, too, by Henry Fonda, Claudette Colbert and a large cast. It now makes a fine companion piece to *Cheyenne Autumn* (1964), again a pictorial triumph, this time on 70mm Panavision, and the climax of all Ford's work on Westerns. This film is the negative to *Drums Along the Mohawk*'s positive. In *Cheyenne Autumn* '*les héros sont fatigués*'; the once upstanding, wide-ranging riders of the West, making their own law and order and making it well, have become petty and crooked. The film takes the side of the Indians, and the sad, brutal conflicts in the enormous landscapes are presented with magisterial power – not least the battle amid the burning grass – while the story, somewhat confused it must be admitted, includes a black-farce episode in Dodge City where the whites, rather than the Indians, are seen to be the ruffians. Almost a great film, *Cheyenne Autumn* has a superb cast which includes James Stewart as a burnt-out Wyatt Earp; Stewart had also appeared in Ford's penultimate Western, *The Man Who Shot Liberty Valance* (1962), together with John Wayne and Lee Marvin.

In the midst of all this good stuff appeared examples of Ford's strange lack of discrimination, already seen in films like *Wee Willie Winkie* or *The Fugitive* (nominated by Richard Winnington as 'the most pretentious travesty of a modern literary work since *For Whom the Bell Tolls*'). Thus came *What Price Glory?* (1952), a rash and unsuccessful re-make of the 1926 classic, and *Mogambo* (1953), a confected mishmash with Clark Gable as a white hunter entirely surrounded by Ava Gardner, Grace Kelly and assorted gorillas; curiously enough, this film followed immediately after the charming *The Sun Shines Bright*, a relaxed film about the Deep South, with one deeply moving sequence involving the funeral of a prostitute.

Another veteran (first film 1926) is Howard Hawks, one of the darlings of the *auteur* theorists. This director turns out comedies, thrillers, dramas, outdoor action films and what have you with complete *abandon*. At his worst he can perpetrate things like *I Was A Male War Bride* (1949), with Cary Grant in military drag, or an overblown *Gentlemen Prefer Blondes* (1953) in which even the bosomed presences of Jane Russell and Marilyn Monroe could not efface the ever-fresh recollection of Mal St Clair's 1928 version. At his best he can make, as we have already seen, war films like *The Dawn Patrol*, gangster films like *Scarface*, thrillers like *To Have and Have Not* and *The Big Sleep*, and fizzing comedies like *Bringing Up Baby*. In the period under review he made two fine Westerns in a style more realistic and down-to-earth than Ford's – *Red River* in 1948, and *Rio Bravo* ten years later.

The strength of *Red River* lies in the strength of Dunsford's obsession with his cattle and his resultant tyranny over his men. In this part John Wayne gives what must be the best performance of his career, not least in his showdowns with Montgomery Clift, and particularly the one after the spectacular crossing of the river, with its final chilling statement, 'I'll kill you, Matt', as the two men part. Similarly the almost outrageous intensity of the lovers' parting at the start of the film is seen later to be deliberately designed to echo dramatically to another encounter of lovers at the end; so that we have an impression of the film taking its own obsessional shape as it progresses – no mean feat of scripting, this, by Borden Chase and Charles Schnee. As for the final showdown around the depot and the ragged main street of Abilene (and here Russell Harlan's fine photography really climaxes) one can only say that in its slow and skilful build up, no less than in the explosive force of its multiple dénouement, it surpasses that of *Shane*.

George Cukor (first film 1930) has been frequently labelled, quite unfairly, as a 'ladies' director', an ambiguous phrase at best; does it mean that his films appeal mainly to women or that he is better at directing women than men? If the former, the answer is bosh. If the latter, one must admit the implication of titles like *Little Women*, *Camille*, *The Women*, *Susan and God*, *A Woman's Face*, *Two-Faced Woman*, or *Adam's Rib*. But on the other hand Cukor's direction of males like Cary Grant, Spencer Tracy, Broderick Crawford or James Mason can hardly be faulted. Certainly in *Adam's Rib* (1949) he boldly faces up to the battle of the sexes. This comedy, in which Tracy and Katharine Hepburn appear respectively as prosecuting and defence

counsels for a Judy Holliday accused of murder, has the briskest of
timing, polished dialogue perfectly delivered, and situations which overpass in comedy even those of the earlier *The Philadelphia Story*. *Born
Yesterday* I have already dealt with; it came two years before Cukor's
second teaming up of Hepburn and Tracy in *Pat and Mike* (1952).
Here, if the story is cruder than that of *Adam's Rib*, it is certainly
funnier, with Hepburn as a super all-round female athlete taking on all
comers in (among other sports) tennis, golf and boxing (Aldo Ray
splendid here as a grumpy pugilist). She is faultlessly matched by Tracy
as a sports promoter prevented by his staff of petty crooks from
achieving his ambition of pursuing an honest career. The clash, or rather
the crashing together of these characters represents the Tracy-Hepburn
team at the height of its perfection; it had a cool reception on its
release, but certainly does not deserve oblivion.

In *A Star is Born* (1954) Cukor completely eclipsed William
Wellman's hitherto much admired version of 1937, with Janet Gaynor
and Fredric March, good though it was. Quite apart from single
numbers like the thaumaturgic 'Born in a Trunk' or the tense quietness
of 'The Man that Got Away', which still represent the great Judy
Garland at her greatest, Cukor's control of the still comparatively new
CinemaScope dimensions was assured and at times highly imaginative.
From the rest of his cast he elicited fine performances, and not least
from Jack Carson as an appallingly convincing publicity man. James
Mason, playing move for move to Garland's personification, displayed
the cracking façade of a fading star with a fine nervous realism. But it
was, and is essentially Garland's film. The hypnosis of her personality
sometimes made one forget how beautiful she was; but not here.

Cukor was less at ease with *Bhowani Junction* (1956); based on a
John Masters story and starring Ava Gardner and Stewart Granger,
it had about it something of the exhaustion of a scorching Indian afternoon. But he came back on form in 1959 with the elaborate *Heller in
Pink Tights* – Sophia Loren in a blonde wig and *en travesti* – which
pursued with unabated enthusiasm and improbability the adventures of
a travelling theatrical company in the Wild West during the Jesse James
period. Spectacular, witty, funny (Loren as *Mazeppa*, with her horse
on an inadequate treadmill), it had a purely surrealist sequence with
a band of Indians raiding the theatre's wardrobe and dressing themselves up to hitherto unsuspected levels of incongruity.[1] Since then little

---

[1] Early in De Mille's *The Plainsman* (1937) there is a sequence in which Jean Arthur
tries to take some Red Indians' minds off other things by handing them a wide selection
of women's hats.

has been achieved by Cukor apart from the conventional and quite uninspired screen version of *My Fair Lady* (1964) which was, of course, a tremendous success.

Of Billy Wilder's *Ace in the Hole* and *Sunset Boulevard* I have already written. He had begun the post-war period with two aces on the table – *Double Indemnity* (1944), 'one of the highest summits of *film noir* . . . without a single trace of pity or love,'[1] and *The Lost Weekend* (1945), in which, through Ray Milland, the pages of Charles Jackson's terrifying novel sprang one by one to life. From *Ace in the Hole* onwards, however, Wilder became more erratic. *The Seven Year Itch* (1955) was a fair success, being in essence a duologue between Tom Ewell as a middle-aged man afflicted by unexpected lust and the blonde who is the object of his passion; the latter was exquisitely laid before us by Marilyn Monroe, whose definition of classical music as 'It's got no vocal' will long ring in the ears. But *The Spirit of St Louis* (1957) was a sad disappointment. Of course any film showing the problems and dangers of something like Lindbergh's solo flight across the Atlantic is bound to suffer the twin disadvantages that (a) everyone knows how it will end and (b) that James Stewart looks more like himself than Lindbergh. The best of the film lay in the scenes of preparation, the overloaded take-off, and the muted landing at Le Bourget preluding the subsequent hysteria of the welcoming crowds. But in general one feels that Wilder was ill at ease, was making an effort; as he himself has said, 'I'm not an outdoor man . . . I think I should confine myself to the bedroom, maybe'. The 'maybe' is typical.

Wilder certainly ended this period with a bang. *Witness for the Prosecution* (1958) was a thunderingly enjoyable adaptation (by Harry Kurnitz and Wilder himself) of an Agatha Christie novel in which Charles Laughton and Marlene Dietrich had themselves a ball; and *Some Like It Hot* (1959) provided a wide-eyed Marilyn Monroe as the centre of a transvestite romp of curiously innocent and hysterically funny comedy committed by, of all people, Tony Curtis, Jack Lemmon and Joe E. Brown. In its own idiotic way, this was a classic. Sad that it had to be followed by the over-rated *The Apartment*, with Lemmon again, this time as a clerk half-heartedly playing the rôle of a male *madame* in a would-be send-up of the employer class; and by that disastrous cold war 'comedy', *One Two Three* (1961), with James Cagney, as destructively brilliant as ever, covering up for a set of tired old gags emerging from an even tireder Molnar play.[2]

[1] *Hollywood in the Forties* by Charles Higham and Joel Greenberg.
[2] Subsequently Wilder contributed (among other films) *Irma La Douce* (1963), a

It was in his prisoner of war comedy, *Stalag 17* (1953), that Wilder persuaded Otto Preminger to play a Stroheim part. The Academy Award for acting went, however, to William Holden; and Preminger's fame is more likely to rest on his efforts as producer and director. In the Thirties and Forties his films, apart from *Laura* and *Centennial Summer* – the former a grimly effective thriller with Gene Tierney and the latter a minor but pleasant musical with Jeanne Crain – had not made a great impression. In 1954, however, he made *Carmen Jones*, a screen version of the stage show which, thanks to Oscar Hammerstein, had achieved a very successful transference of Bizet's *Carmen* to a modern American *milieu*. Preminger let loose brilliantly on Cinema-Scope, placing his players, whether in action or repose, in admirably composed shots. A solo by Harry Belafonte, in which he was stationed at the extreme edge of a screen otherwise filled with an open landscape, remains visually memorable, as also does the shooting of a chase along the flatcars of a long freight train. Belafonte himself, with Dorothy Dandridge in the name part and Pearl Bailey, gorgeous as ever, as Frankie, brought great vitality to the scene; and this was, I think, the first film in which Saul Bass – using the basic *motif* of a rose – unveiled his peculiar genius as a title designer.

Preminger followed this with a film which contravened the then Hays Office ban on the mention of drugs (O Tempora! O Mores!) – *The Man With the Golden Arm* (1956). Although treated in a rather stilted manner, it had an extraordinarily effective performance by Frank Sinatra as the addict, some heavy lighting which recalled the German cinema of the Twenties, and the most sensational stunt-fall down a staircase I have ever seen. But the following year, presumably in an access of *hubris*, Preminger made the mistake of trying to film Shaw's *Saint Joan*; and about this the less said the better. The name part was played by a hitherto unknown actress, Jean Seberg, who also appeared in his next film, an etiolated version of Françoise Sagan's *Bonjour Tristesse*; in this she was flanked among others by David Niven, Deborah Kerr and Geoffrey Horne, none of whom were ideally adapted to interpreting the modish Gallicism of the original. As Peter John Dyer put it in *Sight and Sound*, they could 'hardly be blamed for sitting squarely on the fence, toying politely with their euphemisms'.

It was at the end of this period that Preminger made his most

---

mixed bag of a musical with the songs removed and with a superb performance by Shirley MacLaine; *Kiss Me, Stupid* (comma optional), a sexpot farce minus Lemmon and Monroe made in 1964; and *The Private Life of Sherlock Holmes* (1969), a film strictly *not* for aficionados.

successful film ever – at least in terms of box-office. This was *Exodus* (1961), whose theme-tune haunts the whole world yet. Adapted by Dalton Trumbo from Leon Uris' novel about the violent birthpangs of the state of Israel, this big scale job had a star-studded cast including Paul Newman, Eva Marie Saint and Ralph Richardson, but an anxiety not to offend anyone (virtually impossible, given the subject) caused the film, despite its pretensions, to say practically nothing at all. This tendency of Preminger to try to be all things to all men was seen even more clearly in *The Cardinal* (1963). Here he tried to outline, solve, or at least explain all the problems faced by the Catholic Church in the mid-Twentieth Century, focusing them on a sort of priest played somewhat uneasily by Tom Tryon. The parade of dilemmas became stupefying, and one would, at the end, have felt no surprise to see a kitchen stove in the confessional. This was a film which split critical opinion right down the middle – all the more so as Preminger was by then a candidate for canonization under *auteur* rules. Whatever else may be said of it, it was extremely well made, with Leon Shamroy's camera as brilliantly trained on religious objects, miraculous or otherwise, as on the visages of John Huston, Romy Schneider, Burgess Meredith, Carol Lynley and the rest. *Sight and Sound* aptly summarized it: 'A victory of form over content: if *mise en scène* means anything, this is it'. But the final fact about *The Cardinal* is that if for one moment you compare it with *Le Journal d'un Curé de Campagne* or *Léon Morin–Prêtre*, it crumbles to dust.

Less ambivalent was *Advise and Consent*, made a year earlier than *The Cardinal*; this was a quite fascinating film about political intrigue in the *coulisses* of Washington, in which Preminger broke yet another taboo, that on homosexuality (O Tempora! O Mores! again). This actually turned out to be a rather pleasing ornamentation to a story of high level skullduggery presented with a great deal of skilful movement, foreground and background, from which emerged, in admirable filmic perspective, such leading players as Henry Fonda, Don Murray, Franchot Tone and, above all, Charles Laughton's fascinating and convincing playing of Senator Cooley, not a very long way after McCarthy; sad that it was to be his last appearance.

Finally it is pleasant to note that in 1965 Preminger came to Britain and made an admirable *film-policier*, *Bunny Lake is Missing*. This story of the hunt for a missing schoolgirl moved vigorously through convincingly real locations and was dominated by a compelling performance from Laurence Olivier as a police detective. Added to this was a fantastic guest-appearance by Noël Coward as an epicene old trot and a chillingly hypnotic sketch by Martita Hunt in the part of a kindergarten headmistress. *Bunny Lake is Missing* had extra entertainment value, due largely, I would think, to the modesty of its intent as well as the skill with which it was carried out.

Talking of Old Reliables, though, what about this?:

1949   *A Letter to Three Wives*
1950   *All About Eve*
1952   *Five Fingers*
1953   *Julius Caesar*
1955   *Guys and Dolls*
1957   *The Quiet American*
1960   *Suddenly Last Summer*.

That is part of the roster of the work of Joseph L. Mankiewicz in the period in question. No wonder that in 1961 he was grabbed in desperation by Fox and given the job of finishing that money-draining epic *Cleopatra*, which he did with considerable success, thanks in part, so it is said, to a number of last-minute script and dialogue improvizations for which his long career as a screenwriter eminently fitted him.[1]

Mankiewicz is too good a film-maker to be remembered mainly (as he too often is) only for *All About Eve*. His next film, *Five Fingers*, was all the more effective as a thriller in that it was based on the almost incredibly dotty goings-on in espionage and counter-espionage which took place in the British Embassy in Ankara during the most critical period of World War II. The basic idiocies were outlined by Mankiewicz with a cynical gusto which became utterly captivating, and he was splendidly abetted in this universal and very exciting send-up by James Mason as the master spy (or so he thinks). His reaction at the end of the film when, in a luxury villa overlooking Rio, he learns he has become the victim of the super-duper double-cross of all time (his reward of English banknotes turned out to consist entirely of forgeries) was quite memorable; the edginess of his laugh in the South American night air still echoes.

Nor should *Julius Caesar* be too glibly written off. In the tent scene between Brutus and Cassius it had one of the best sequences ever seen in a Shakespeare film. Here Mankiewicz realized that he had two great actors, perfectly cast, absolutely sure of their effects and, above all, knowing how to act and react to each other like a couple of trained duellists. So he allowed his camera quietly to eavesdrop, and the effect

---

[1] As far as I know, the only films of his for which he did not write his own script were *Suddenly Last Summer*, which was the work of Tennessee Williams himself and Gore Vidal, and *There was a Crooked Man*, written by David Newman and Robert Benton.

was terrific; John Gielgud and James Mason put on a classic performance which, however, made Marlon Brando's Mark Anthony –
though obviously carefully studied – look somewhat shadowy.

Brando came into his own with *Guys and Dolls*, a screen version
of the Damon Runyon musical still remembered for the gambling
scenes and for 'Luck be a Lady Tonight'. Here Mankiewicz put his
singers and dancers into convincingly realistic perspectives of New York
streets and somehow managed (thanks in part to Michael Kidd's
choreography) to make us accept a fantasy story about a Salvation
Army lass seduced by a crap-playing hood.

With *Suddenly Last Summer*, Mankiewicz for the first time took a
look at the steaming stew of passion and perversion which was just
getting really popular in the world of the arts. Today this story of a
queer who has been eaten by the beach boys he has used will no doubt
seem old hat. In 1960, presided over by no less a figure than Katharine
Hepburn (with some assistance from Elizabeth Taylor), it was a real
shocker. Indeed Mankiewicz played the whole film entirely for shock,
and this at times ran it into the perilous shoals of unconscious humour.
But on the whole the film, with its brittle sunlight and its anguish
about martyred baby turtles, to say nothing of the lobotomy planned
by mother on daughter, held up to whatever Tennessee Williams
intended. It was an interesting film, too, in that it had elaborate set-
speeches, like that in which the mother described a previous summer
spent with her queer son, in which the visuals evoked by the words
mingled curiously with the actual visuals from the camera, thus creating a
kind of psychological superimposition. *Suddenly Last Summer* had, too,
a prophetic touch. Tennessee Williams' imaginings arose, on his own
evidence, from his observations of contemporary life. 'If you just read
the newspapers in America', he said, 'you'll see that my plays are far
from exaggerations.' Within ten years had come the My Lai and
the Hollywood murders. Mankiewicz's insistence, then, was not illogical
– even to the lush exaggerations of Oliver Messel's decor for Mrs
Venables' New Orleans mansion. *Suddenly Last Summer* was in the end
too well written, too well photographed and too well directed to be
dismissed as just nasty; it was a Thyestean festival.

Other Old Reliables were less consistently successful in their
choice or treatment of subjects. We may note however Anatole Litvak,
whose *The Snake Pit* (1948), with its documentary allegations regarding
horrid conditions in American asylums, fitted well with the Tennessee
Williams statement just quoted; but apart from a performance in the
grand manner by Olivia de Havilland, the film foundered in a sensa-

tionalism which, in the very nature of its subject, should have been played down.

On the other hand the sensationalism of Litvak's next film (dated the same year as *The Snake Pit*) was justifiable and very successful. *Sorry, Wrong Number*, dominated by Barbara Stanwyck's virtuoso performance, was about a bed-ridden woman who hears over the telephone the plans for her murder. For mounting, agonizing suspense this film still takes a lot of beating. Litvak splendidly deployed his restless camera in this world of dangerous shadows, until at the end the chilly yet almost orgasmic vengefulness of the husband (Burt Lancaster) seemed to echo Blake's:

'Is it because acts are not lovely that thou seekest solitude
Where the horrible darkness is impressed with reflections of desire?'

In *Decision Before Dawn* (1951) Litvak made another film of considerable distinction. Although the implications of the plot are not followed into the deep waters they certainly signal, the mere fact that it involves the question of what is and is not treason makes for a certain compulsiveness. The matter at hand concerns the use during the latter part of the war of captured German officers as spies on and in their own country. The particular case chosen is that of a Luftwaffe youngster, played with passionate integrity by Oskar Werner, whose first major part it was;[1] he conveyed finely the brief flush of a doomed innocence – the innocence of the betrayed idealist. The film well captured the atmosphere of a ruined country reeling to destruction – Litvak shot it all in bombed cities like Wiesbaden and Munich – and the night scenes were particularly effective, with fine camerawork by Franz Planer. The final conventionality of the story – German gives himself up for execution so that his American colleague (Richard Basehart) can make good his escape – was rather disappointing; but the *Götterdämmerung* atmosphere and a genuine feeling of sympathy for non-Nazi Germans gave the film, in addition to its excitements, a modest honesty.

From the rest of the Regulars let me arbitrarily pick Robert Wise[2] for his unsentimental film *Desert Rats* (1952), in which James Mason appeared as Rommel for the second time – the first having been in Henry Hathaway's[3] by no means unsentimental *Desert Fox* (1951); and

[1] He had previously been in an Austrian film about Beethoven called, with consummate originality, *Eroica* (1949).

[2] Wise (uncredited) was editor on *Citizen Kane* as, too, was Mark Robson.

[3] Hathaway is another long-time stalwart, one of whose films, *Spawn of the North* (1938), set amidst the salmon fisheries of iciest Alaska and featuring Henry Fonda, George Raft, Dorothy Lamour, John Barrymore and Akim Tamiroff, was for me the acme of

for his boxing film *Somebody Up There Likes Me* (1956), in which Paul Newman, as Rocky Graziano, put himself firmly and intelligently into the star class. This film, which offered an alternative and less pessimistic answer to poverty and slums than *Knock on Any Door*, was quite skilfully steered away from mawkishness and towards the Dean-Brando rebel-syndrome. Later Wise directed *West Side Story* (1961).

Equally arbitrarily Henry King may be cited for his genuine if slightly over-intense *Twelve O'Clock High* (1950), with Gregory Peck, as a newly appointed commander of an already demoralized US Bomber base in Britain, trying to force his men back into the aggressive mood, but destroying his own war-morale in the process. In essence an anti-war film, mercifully uncluttered by background music, and with some electric (because genuine) scenes of aerial battles, *Twelve O'Clock High* made cogent viewing even if, in the long run, it made no real enquiry into the mysterious roots of human behaviour on which the situation really rested. Latterly King has made such films as *The Snows of Kilimanjaro* (1952), *Love is a Many Splendoured Thing* (1955), and a travesty of Scott Fitzgerald's *Tender is the Night* (1961); in the last two, as in *The Song of Bernadette* (1943), he was saddled with exceptionally rebarbative performances by Jennifer Jones. In *The Sun Also Rises* (1957), however, with a cast including Tyrone Power, Ava Gardner, Mel Ferrer and Errol Flynn (the last-named giving, at the end of his life, a superb display of real acting), King, through sheer professionalism which it was a delight to observe, managed to overcome the inanity of Hemingway's emaciated story about expatriate Yanks living it up in France and Spain.

Curiously enough Fritz Lang, in the postwar period, made no more than minor contributions to the film scene. *Rancho Notorious* (1951) and *Clash by Night* (1952) were no more than adequate. There was more to be said for *The Big Heat* (1953), in which the famous battle of the scalding coffee tended unfairly to obscure the basic strength of a plot involving a series of deeply personal conflicts between the representatives of law and order on the one hand and organized gangsterdom on the other; the film also contained an excellent early performance by Lee Marvin as a racketeer. In the mid-Fifties Lang left America and made films in India and Germany (including a Mabuse *reprise*), and finally turned up as a larger-than-life version of himself in Godard's *Le Mépris*.

---

box-office entertainment at its best – 'action and thrills, the quickened pulse and the lump in the throat'.

Briefly still, *The Night of the Hunter* (1955) was a solitary incursion into film direction by Charles Laughton; an undeserved failure at the box-office, this is still one of the most spine-chilling films ever made, with a truly great performance by Robert Mitchum. One of the most frightening things about it is the fact, as Pauline Kael pointed out, that the terrible, hypnotic, evil preacher is wholly trusted by adults while children run away from him in hatred and fear. The escape of the children by river in this film has its own particular magic.

And now Hitchcock. As I have already indicated, his wartime films seemed to reflect an uncertainty, even some inner uneasiness which drove him largely into complex experimentations with technique. But in 1951, after some tentative tuning-up on *Under Capricorn* (1949) and *Stage Fright* (1950) – the latter with Jane Wyman playing a rather uneasy lady's maid to Marlene Dietrich – he came back bang on form with *Strangers on a Train*, a very clever story about 'exchange' murderers (Farley Granger and Robert Walker), with plenty of ingenious twists and turns, and a rather sickening climax with Walker being mangled to death by a berserk carousel. From then on nearly every Hitchcock was a winner.[1]

In particular there was *Rear Window* (1954), in which the exercise of immobilizing the principal character by no means led to immobility in the film itself, and which was the second of three consecutive films starring the delicious Grace Kelly; her performance opposite Cary Grant in the third – *To Catch A Thief* (1955) – against a Technicolor *Côte d'Azur* being sufficient to blur the outlines of a not especially efficient plot.

In *The Trouble With Harry* (1956), Hitchcock, unpredictable as ever, made a knife-sharp black comedy and at the same time introduced a new and splendiferous actress, Shirley MacLaine. His own comment on this film was: 'I took melodrama out of the pitch-black night and brought it out into the sunshine'.[2] *Vertigo* (1958) is mainly celebrated for the shot which combined a track-back with a zoom-in – an effect which to acrophobes like myself is as frightening as anything in *Psycho* or *The Birds*; and this was followed in 1959 by the spacious thrills of *North By Northwest*. The brilliance of the sequence in which Cary Grant narrowly escapes murder from an aeroplane skimming over the vast plain was never more sharply pointed than when Antonioni tried

---

[1] *I Confess* (1952) perhaps lacked a little of the master touch; and *The Man Who Knew Too Much* (1955) didn't – at least for me – recapture the excitements of the 1934 original.

[2] *Hitchcock* by François Truffaut, Secker and Warburg, 1968.

to use the same gimmick (though this time as a love gambit) in *Zabriskie Point*, and fell down with a dismal thud.

And so it goes, year by year, with intriguing and often really striking stories, with impeccable casting, and always suspense, always surprise. 'If you've designed a picture correctly,' says Hitchcock, 'in terms of its emotional impact, the Japanese audience should scream at the same time as the Indian audience . . . Assuming that it loses fifteen per cent of its impact when it's subtitled, and ten per cent when it's well dubbed, the image remains intact, even when the projection is faulty. It's your work that's being shown – nothing can alter that – and you're expressing yourself in the same terms everywhere.'[1] Although this statement doesn't seem to allow for butchery by censors or distributors, it is otherwise a fair enough credo in terms both of the box-office and of creative film-making.

It is certainly a credo which applies to what is still Hitchcock's best film – the first he ever made in the United States, and one with an almost entirely English cast – *Rebecca* (1940). It is not just a question of that haunting opening sequence which everyone remembers so well, with the camera travelling up the laurelled drive to the ruins of Manderley while Joan Fontaine's voice, soft yet urgent, begins to recall the events we are about to witness. There is much more to *Rebecca* than that. There is an indefinable atmosphere, part ghostly, part psychological, and arising from the mysterious, absent, and, it is to be hoped, defunct wife, which makes the machinery of the plot less and less important as the film goes on (which is just as well because the 'solution' is, at best, vague). What Hitchcock has done is to create *and sustain* an atmosphere of fear which he communicates to us not merely through Mrs de Winter herself but also, and remorselessly, through what the camera observes for us when she is not there; the beach hut is a good example. And, as Hitchcock himself has pointed out, one of the unnerving things in the film is that the housekeeper, Mrs Danvers, is never seen actually entering a room. Like Mrs de Winter, we hear a slight noise, look round, startled, and there, quiet, menacingly respectful, she stands. Judith Anderson is quite perfect in this part. One is not so much interested in the 'solution' of the story as in the lifting of the cloud of fear which it brings with it; the 'terrible imaginings' are consumed in the flames of the burning mansion. Years later, when he made *The Birds*, Hitchcock left us with a less comfortable finale. When his characters leave the beleaguered house and enter their car, they and we see, all around, immobile for a moment whose duration we don't know and

[1] op. cit.

cannot guess, those myriad, terrible birds. And when the humans drive off it is not to the safeties they have hitherto known; the birds will be everywhere . . .

X

The Forties and Fifties saw great expansion in the world of the ever-ambitious Walt Disney. His feature-length cartoons of famous children's books became amalgamated with live-action jobs showing real children sometimes in real, sometimes in unreal connotations; and in the end the magic world of Mickey and Donald was transformed into a commercial fun-city called Disneyland, where everything, alas, is exactly what it seems, and the lovely mysteries of *Alice* or *The Jungle Book* are to be seen as large as life and moulded in plastic or jello. In the same period Disney also went in for nature films in a big way. He never did anything by halves; endless trouble and patience must have gone into their making, and some of them, especially the earlier ones such as *Beaver Valley* and *Seal Island*, had some of the wonder and integrity of Sucksdorff. But as usual Disney couldn't leave well alone; it was not enough just to observe nature. So, in his first full-length nature film, Disney continued to indulge in what might be called the Bathetic Fallacy – the attachment of irrelevant human comment to the depiction of animal activities; thus in *The Living Desert* (1953) the love-making of scorpions is accommodated to the drill of a square dance, as if the fact that scorpions actually do make love wasn't interesting enough. This technique is a reversal of the cartoon approach, in which the equation of Mickey or Donald with humans is justified by the fact that nothing is real. The reverse is sour, because the animals and birds and insects *are* real, and are not fair game for wisecracks and suchlike of which they could never in nature be conscious; it is like putting elephants in pinafores. The result is that it is we, not they, who are being made fools of.

Disney's other fault was in trying to give his audiences too much of a good thing. *Nature's Half Acre* (1951), for instance, would have been a better and far more convincing film had it confined itself to one specific half-acre instead of becoming a compendium of diverse episodes, many of them apparently chosen (from areas widely separated geographically) for their sensational possibilities. Similarly in *The Living Desert* we are treated to battles between tarantula and wasp, snake and rat, hawk and rattlesnake, tortoise and tortoise, until we begin to think more in terms of the sand-table than of the vast spaces of the desert itself. Indeed the best sequences are those few which indicate a sense of space and distance – as in that of the dramatic rise and surge of flood water which rages across the wilderness, only to be ineluctably absorbed, sucked down, by the insatiable sands. *The Living Desert*, it should also be recorded, contains a remarkable and surely unique study of the brief, beautiful life of the Night-flowering Cereus; and when Disney did something like this, no one ever did it better.

In direct contrast to Disney's variations on reality was the work of Lionel Rogosin who, in 1956, came from nowhere with a film on New York's alcoholics and down-and-outs called *On the Bowery* which, much to the chagrin of the U.S. Consul, won the Gold Medal at the Venice Festival.

On the Bowery is a film made from the inside, like Flaherty's *Nanook*. Rogosin and his associates (who included Richard Bagley, cameraman on *The Quiet One*) seem to have identified themselves as film-makers with the appalling collection of human catastrophes they depict, and nearly all the sequences have a conviction which can only come from inside observation which, in turn, involves time. It took Rogosin years, not months, to achieve this sort of identification.

On the Bowery is only moderately well edited, and there are moments when the music seems an intrusion. But the visuals, no less than the searing casualness of the dialogue, are in themselves so strong that the whole work hangs together with a sort of desperate sincerity. In the bars and on the sidewalks the camera leans sympathetically across a table or a grating towards men and women who have passed the point of no return, for whom, as Dostoievsky put it, 'the sense of their own degradation is as essential to their reckless unbridled natures as the sense of their own generosity'. Ray, one of the principal characters picked out by Rogosin in *On the Bowery*, is in fact an essentially intelligent young man. When we see him in these lower depths we know, as he does himself, that it is not too late, that he still has the capacity to emerge from them, not temporarily but for ever. But Rogosin, in his frightening final sequence of lost souls, refuses to indicate such a happy ending. He leaves Ray as he had first found him – prognosis doubtful, dice loaded, anything goes. Like Ivan Karamazov, it is not God he doesn't accept, only he must respectfully return Him his entrance ticket.

Rogosin followed this film with a bold but scrappy short, made at the sudden behest of Thorold Dickinson – at that time in charge of the United Nations Film Department. *Out*, as it was succinctly called, was shot at points along the Hungarian border at the time of the Soviet suppression of the Uprising. The circumstances were difficult for film-making, and this attempt to give first-hand, vivid impressions of the situation and of the adventures and plight of the refugees was only a partial success.

Much more to the point was *Come Back Africa* (1959), which Rogosin, pretending that he was making a film for tourism, shot under the noses of the South African authorities. Partly dramatized, and in that respect sometimes amateurishly acted, this film nevertheless took the lid off *apartheid* in a big way. The long and lively discussion among the young Africans in the shebeen – magnificently interrupted by a song from a talented and beautiful singer – was as stimulating as anything of similar significance to come out of America or Europe for a long time. But Rogosin's *Good Times, Wonderful Times*, a discussion of the world of the hydrogen bomb, suffered from a diffuseness and a lack of logicality which interfered with its sincerity; but it was at least a proof of the continuity of his intention to use film to discuss the prime issues of our time.

As Rogosin was beginning his work, death ended that of the great father figure of the documentary world, Robert Flaherty who, during thirty years of difficulties and frustrations, completed no more than six films. He still remains one of the great film-makers of all time, and I was proud to be able to call myself his friend.

He was not a complex character. Indeed in many respects he was like a child – perpetually inquisitive, perpetually surprised or delighted by new (and often simple) discoveries. Being uncomplicated can of course mean some limitation in character, and to some Flaherty may have appeared to be too sentimental. In fact, under this appearance lay the hard self-reliance which came from his mining-camp boyhood and his early days of prospecting and exploration in the Far North.

Again, not being complex led to a tendency to over-simplification, and this in turn sometimes led him to make his locations and people fit an ideal conception of his own rather than the actual facts. This was the main basis of the attacks on him by various critics, and in Britain at least, these were mainly provoked by *Man of Aran*. If some of the criticisms were justified, there was just the same a tendency among some critics to forget that Flaherty was not a reporter with a camera but a creative artist. We do not complain that Veronese and others dressed their biblical figures in contemporary clothes; we *do* complain if an essential artistic truth is missing from the result.

Take as example *Moana* (1925). While this film was being made (it took three years), there were a number of social, political and economic changes taking place in the South Seas. These Flaherty completely ignored. He disliked and mistrusted the spread of Western 'civilization' to areas such as Samoa. He was bitter about the diseases and commercialities introduced by traders and missionaries. His expressed intention in making *Moana* was to preserve for all time the habits and customs which were rapidly dying or, at best, deteriorating into tourist attractions. There is nothing basically wrong in such an intention, which indeed he carried out to perfection, producing a beautiful and memorable film. Later documentarians might have preferred a film which overtly drew attention to the dangers threatening the ancient civilization of Polynesia, but this wasn't Bob Flaherty's way. For me *Moana*, as it stands, remains a perfectly valid work of art.

His approach to the Aran Islands was not quite the same, and I find it less easy to justify. Here he deliberately *re-created* the past. The islanders had long ceased to hunt basking sharks. They had now to be taught (and persuaded) to do so. Again, the economy of the islands was no longer a closed one. They were not only strongly linked with the mainland but also, to some degree, with America. Yet the film presented this recreation of the past as though it was valid in a completely contemporary sense; and this was the basic falsity of which the critics, either by instinct, or through direct knowledge, complained.

Nevertheless, when all the criticisms have been made, *Man of Aran* (1934) remains memorable for Flaherty's shooting of the sea. No one but he could have used the lens – and especially the long-focus lens – with such mastery. The violence, the physical impact, the revelation of the smallness of man against those gigantic breakers – all this through Flaherty's camera produces a 'terrible beauty' which never loses its effect.

All the time Flaherty used his camera to make us see things in the image of his own unique and brilliant eyes. He was happiest with a small camera. He wasn't interested in mixes or any other optical tricks. For him the camera lens was an extension of his eye and his arm. Hence that miraculous anticipation of movement observable over and over again in his work, from the climbing of the coconut palm in *Moana* to the feather-like delicacy of the pans and tilts on the potter in *Industrial Britain* (1931).

Flaherty didn't need a script. He needed time and lots of film. And because of this, editing was vital to him, although in plain fact he had no particular appreciation of the theory or practice of montage.

Editing for him was an extension of his work with the camera; and, as all those who worked with him will testify, he edited his films mainly in the projection theatre rather than in the cutting-room itself.

The most important film in Flaherty's development as an artist was *The Land* (1942). It was sad that the experience of this film came to him so late in life; nevertheless it did enable him to achieve afterwards the perfection of *Louisiana Story*. Until *The Land* he had (with the exception of the incomplete and perhaps essentially half-hearted *Twenty-four Dollar Island* of 1927) never concerned himself with subjects in his own North American area. But now, returning from the myths and the realities of far-off places, he made a film on his own country, and on hard facts about it; and in so doing he made a new discovery of himself.

He looked at the contemporary agricultural problems of the United States, and he was appalled. He saw a situation in which the present was more important than the Eskimo or Polynesian or Irish past. He saw the technological age, which could bring untold happiness and prosperity, bringing, under the flags of financial and political greed, only misery. This film was his cry of protest – it is still all the more cogent in that its passionately indignant commentary is spoken by himself – and it is full of unforgettable images, like that of the small boy whose hands move and flutter in his uneasy sleep and whose mother, off-screen, explains, 'He thinks he's shucking peas'.

Without *The Land*, Flaherty's conception of *Louisiana Story* (1948)[1] could not have existed; for here, like Oedipus at Colonus, he found a balance, a certain peace of mind. Here he mastered the equation he had unwittingly been trying to solve all his life – the balance between the pagan, primitive past and the crisply definitive present. If *The Land* is impressive because of its passionate incoherence, *Louisiana Story* is sympathetic and compelling because of its acceptance, at last, of two ways of life. Flaherty worked by instinct, and there is no reason to suppose that he sat down and thought out this acceptance. It was much more than this; it was the end of his lifelong search for a perfect form of expression. *Louisiana Story*, a simple and almost perfect work, was his last film.

---

[1] I give the completion dates of his films. Most of them represent at least two, or more likely three years' work.

XI

So, as the Fifties drew to a close, as New Waves and Angry Young Men joined with Beatniks in new tides of thought; as similar influences spread among young film-makers in the Far East, in Africa and in Latin America, the world of cinema was, however unreadily, about to face a decade in which apparently imperishable symbols of the motion picture industry would collapse, and in which the very fundamentals of the art of the film would be questioned, and savagely questioned, by some of its most gifted practitioners. The curtain was rising on the Big Show-Down.

SIGNPOST - 1956

THE YEAR OF 'PATHER PANCHALI'

IN INDIA

Despite the success of *Pather Panchali*, the Government remains suspicious about the export of films which might, by showing poverty and similar social problems, be regarded as denigratory. Tapan Sinha who, like Satyajit Ray, is a 'graduate' of the Calcutta Film Society, completes his *Kabuliwala*, based on a story by Tagore. Roberto Rossellini arrives with plans for an episodic film to be called *India 58*. Shooting begins on *Pardesi*, an Indian-Soviet co-production jointly directed (not without a measure of conflict) by K. A. Abbas for the Nayar Sensar Co and V. M. Pronin for Mosfilm.

A mutual aid Treaty is signed with Indonesia.
France's former colonies are ceded to India.
The people of Kashmir vote to be an integral part of India.
A massive loan is received from Russia.
Pandit Nehru intervenes in the Algerian crisis and also puts forward an alternative to the United States (Dulles) plan for the Suez problem.

IN JAPAN

Machiko Kyo appears in *Red Light District* (also known as *The Street of Shame*), directed by Kenji Mizoguchi, shortly after which this great master of Japanese cinema dies. Yasujiro Ozu makes *Early Spring*. Shiro Toyoda directs his comedy *A Cat, Shozo and Two Women*, and Masaki Kobayashi reveals scandals in the world of baseball with his *I'll Buy You*. Kon Ichikawa completes his important *The Burmese Harp* and also directs *Punishment Room*, an unexpectedly shocking and sadistic film, as also is Keisuke Kinoshita's *Sun and Rose*.

Under a coalition of Liberals and Democrats the aftermath of defeat finally gives way to rapid social and economic development. Nobosuke becomes Prime Minister.

Japan is admitted to membership of the United Nations.
Yukio Mishima is engaged in writing his *Seven Modern
No Plays*.

IN RUSSIA

Yefim Dzigan, remembered for his fine *We From Kronstadt* of 1936, directs *Prologue*,
a film featuring Lenin and Krupskaya and using the wide screen. Mark Donskoi
makes a version of Gorky's *Mother* in which Alexei Batalov plays the same rôle as
did his uncle Nikolai in the Pudovkin film of 1926. Sergei Yutkevitch directs his
Othello, with Sergei Bondarchuk, and Grigori Chukrai has a success with his first
film, *The Forty First*. With *The First Echelon* the veteran Mikhail Kalatozov gives
little indication of the excellence to come in the following year with his *The Cranes
Are Flying*.

Khrushchev denounces the late Stalin during the twentieth
annual Conference of the Communist Party; with Bulganin
he pays a visit to Britain, as does the Bolshoi Ballet.

Protests are transmitted to the United States over high
altitude photographic spying.

Marshal Tito visits Moscow.

The Democratic Uprising in Hungary is savagely put
down by invading Soviet forces. The Security Council's
resolutions on this, and on Suez, are equally vetoed by the
Russian representative.

Dmitri Shostakovitch is working on his 11th Symphony.

IN HUNGARY

Laszló Ránody directs his *Abyss*, which is a prizewinner at the Karlovy Vary Film
Festival, while Zoltán Fábri makes his remarkable *Professor Hannibal*, much of the
import of which must have escaped the Communists.

In the course of the Russian invasion Imre Nagy, the
elected Prime Minister is, with a number of his colleagues,
treacherously murdered.

Cardinal Mindszenty takes refuge in the United States
Embassy, where he will remain for many years.

János Kadar becomes the head of the new Communist
regime.

IN CZECHOSLOVAKIA

Jiri Weiss makes his subtle family drama, *Life Was the Stake*, while Elmar Klos and Jan Kadar co-direct their colour musical, in which is embedded not a little social criticism, *The House at the Terminus*. Alfred Radok, the experimental theatre director who has pioneered in polyscreen effects and the Laterna Magica (the latter to be a huge success at the Brussels Exposition in 1958), directs his remarkable *Old Man Motorcar* on which, as on the Laterna Magica, Milos Forman works as an assistant. On more traditional lines Otakar Vavra directs the second of his three historical films about Jan Hus and the Reformation – *Hussite Warrior*; and Vaclav Krska makes a screen version in colour of Smetana's opera *Dalibor*.

As a result of Khrushchev's speech to the Communist Congress in Moscow, there are signs of a relaxation of the restrictions on freedom of expression.

Bohuslav Martinu completes his opera *Hecuba*.

IN POLAND

Andrzej Munk's documentary *Sunday Morning* wins an award at the Mannheim Film Festival. Andrzej Wajda directs *Kanal*, the second film of his trilogy about the Polish Resistance, while Jerzy Kawalerowicz makes his political mystery-drama *The Shadow*.

Labour riots in Poznan are quelled by the authorities with considerable loss of life.

The Primate of the Roman Catholic Church, Cardinal Wyszynski, is released from confinement.

The composer Krzysztof Penderecki, later to become one of the most important figures in the avant-garde world, is a student at the State Music Academy in Cracow.

IN EAST GERMANY

Andrew and Annelie Thorndike complete their compilation film of fifty years of German history, *Du und Mancher Kamerad*, or *The German Story*. Slatan Dudow, remembered for his *Kuhle Wampe* of 1932, directs a conventional feature, *The Captain of Cologne*.

A 'National People's Army' is formed by the regime.

The composers Paul Dessau and Hanns Eisler are both writing music for films.

IN WEST GERMANY

Helmut Käutner directs *The Captain of Koepenick* which compares favourably with Richard Oswald's original of 1931. Laslo Benedek makes *Children, Mother and a General.* G. W. Pabst follows his film on the end of Hitler, *The Last Act*, with a perhaps underestimated film about the July Plot against Hitler, with Bernhard Wicki playing the part of Von Stauffenberg, called *The Jackboot Mutiny.*

The Constitution is amended so as to permit of conscription.

A ten-year agreement on atomic cooperation is signed with Britain.

The German Evangelistic Churches set about revising the Lutheran text of the New Testament.

For the first time a Soviet Ambassador is accredited to West Germany.

The second of Karlheinz Stockhausen's *Electronic Studies* is the first of its kind to be published in the form of a score.

IN GREECE

Greg Talas directs *Agoupi*, and Michael Cacoyannis is working on his successor to *A Girl in Black*, to be entitled *A Matter of Dignity.*

The Government demands that the Cyprus question be discussed at the United Nations General Assembly.

Athens broadcasts to Cyprus are jammed by the British.

Nikos Kazantzakis is in the last year of his life.

Yannis Xenakis composes his *Nomos Alpha* for solo cello.

IN SPAIN

J. A. Bardem directs *Calle Mayor*, featuring the American actress Betsy Blair, while Luis Berlanga's *Calabuch* is felt to be something of a disappointment after *Welcome, Mr Marshall.*

The Franco regime finally recognizes the independence of Morocco.

IN SWEDEN

Ingmar Bergman makes one of his finest films, *The Seventh Seal*, which he will immediately follow with a work different in idea but of equal importance, *Wild Strawberries*. Alf Sjöberg directs *The Last Pair Out*, with Bibi and Harriet Andersson. Arne Sucksdorff is in India shooting *Indian Village*, *The Wind and the River* and the feature-length *The Flute and the Arrow*.

In Stockholm scientists working on transuranic elements are on the verge of discovering nobelium (atomic number 102).

The composer Karl-Birger Blomdahl has begun work on his 'space-opera' *Aniara*, which he will complete in 1959.

IN ITALY

Federico Fellini directs *Le Notte di Cabiria*, starring once again his wife Giulietta Masina; for this film Pier Paolo Pasolini collaborates on the script. Luchino Visconti is between *Senso* and *Le Notte Bianchi*, Michelangelo Antonioni is between *Le Amiche* and *Il Grido*, Roberto Rossellini is in India, and De Sica, with no film to make, has returned to acting.

Italy is now a member of the United Nations.

Pier Luigi Nervi, in collaboration with Vitellozi, designs the Palazzo della Sport in Rome.

Luigi Nono composes his *Il Canto Sospeso*, and Arturo Toscanini is in the last year of his life.

IN FRANCE

Robert Bresson completes his great film *Un Condamné à Mort s'est Echappé*, Jean Renoir directs *Eléna et les Hommes*, and Henri-Georges Clouzot rather surprisingly makes his feature length documentary *Le Mystère Picasso*. Luis Buñuel, in a Franco-Mexican co-production, directs *La Mort en ce Jardin*, with Simone Signoret, Charles Vanel, Georges Marchal and Michel Piccoli. Claude Autant-Lara makes *La Traversée de Paris*, Christian-Jaque *Si Tous les Gars du Monde*, René Clément *Gervaise*, and Jean-Pierre Melville *Bob le Flambeur*. Roger Vadim creates a sensation with his first feature, *Et Dieu Créa la Femme*, in which he surrounds Brigitte Bardot with such eligibles as Curt Jurgens, Christian Marquand, Jean-Louis Trintignant and Georges Poujouly. Abel Gance continues to pursue his multiscreen technique with his *Magirama*, featuring polyvision. Albert Lamorisse directs his enchanting *Le Ballon Rouge*, while Alain Resnais follows his *Nuit et Brouillard* with *Toute la*

Mémoire du Monde, Georges Franju makes a short on *Le Théatre National Populaire*, and Jean-Luc Godard has an acting part in Jacques Rivette's *Le Coup du Berger*.

France recognizes the independence of Morocco and Tunisia but not of Algeria; and joins Britain in the Suez *débâcle*.

Guy Mollet forms a socialist administration.

Jean Anouilh's play *Poor Bitos* is produced.

Francis Poulenc is completing his opera *The Carmelites*.

Jean Cocteau, in the company of W. H. Auden, receives a Doctorate at the University of Oxford.

Picasso is working on his *Las Meninas* series; and Le Corbusier is designing the Tokyo Museum. Amongst other works may be noted Jean Dubuffet's *Georges dans le Jardin*, Louis le Brocquy's *Male Presence*, Jacques Villon's *Icarus*, and Georges Braque's *L'Echo*.

IN BRITAIN

Two films deal strongly and honestly with the question of capital punishment – Joseph Losey's *Time Without Pity* (based on Emlyn Williams' play *Someone Waiting*), with Michael Redgrave and Ann Todd; and J. Lee Thompson's grim *Yield to the Night*, with Diana Dors. The brothers Roy and John Boulting bring off a brilliant double with their two comedies *Private's Progress* and *Brothers in Law*, both starring Ian Carmichael. Memories of the war are evoked by Jack Lee's *A Town Like Alice*, Michael Powell's *The Battle of the River Plate*, and Lewis Gilbert's film about the war-ace Douglas Bader, *Reach for the Sky*, with Kenneth More. Some disappointment is aroused by Carol Reed's *Trapeze*, despite a cast which includes Gina Lollobrigida, Burt Lancaster and Tony Curtis. Philip Leacock's more modest and very sensitive *The Spanish Gardener*, with Dirk Bogarde, and Anthony Asquith's elegant short about the Glyndebourne Opera House – *On Such a Night* – are among other productions of the year.

Anthony Eden's government embroils Britain in the Suez fiasco, and petrol rationing is introduced.

The Bank Rate reaches the highest point since 1932 – $5\frac{1}{2}\%$.

Archbishop Makarios is exiled from Cyprus to the Seychelles, EOKA rejects Sir John Harding's surrender terms, and Lord Radcliffe's constitutional proposals are published.

A big new atomic reactor is completed at Harlow, and at Calder Hall a nuclear power station is opened and delivers 65,000 KW.

The Campaign for Nuclear Disarmament organizes a protest march to Aldermaston.

A genteel form of lottery called Premium Bonds is introduced.

Winston Churchill publishes his *History of the English-Speaking Peoples*, and Lord Beaverbrook his *Men and Power*.

A. J. Ayer's *The Revolution in Philosophy* attracts much notice, but not to the degree of Colin Wilson's sensationally successful *The Outsider*.

Other books of the year include Norman St John Stevas' *Obscenity and the Law*, John Bratby's *A Painter's Credo*, and Angus Wilson's *Anglo-Saxon Attitudes*.

Michael Ayrton creates his *Acrobat* series of bronzes, Barbara Hepworth instals her *Orpheus* sculpture at Mullard House, London, and William Holford publishes his plans for the development of the surroundings of St Paul's Cathedral.

William Walton completes his Cello Concerto.

Frederick Ashton creates *Birthday Offering* for the Royal Ballet, with music by Malcolm Arnold.

Brecht's Berliner Ensemble gives a season in London.

Max Beerbohm dies, as do Frank Brangwyn and Walter de la Mare.

IN THE UNITED STATES

Cecil B. De Mille repeats his blockbusting success of 1923 with *The Ten Commandments*; Mike Todd produces, with Michael Anderson directing, his once-for-all-time and star-spangled *Around the World in Eighty Days*; King Vidor makes a brave attempt at *War and Peace*; and Vincente Minnelli makes an equally brave attempt at the life of Van Gogh in *Lust for Life*, with Kirk Douglas in the name part and Anthony Quinn as Gauguin. Elia Kazan magnificently directs Tennessee Williams' *Baby Doll*, Stanley Kubrick places himself in the forefront with *The Killing*, and Alfred Hitchcock surprises with a splendid black comedy, *The Trouble With Harry*. Katharine Hepburn and Burt Lancaster co-star in *The Rainmaker*, directed by Joseph Anthony; Gary Cooper and Anthony Perkins appear as Quakers in William Wyler's *Friendly Persuasion*, while Marlon Brando plays an Okinawan in Daniel Mann's *The Teahouse of the August Moon*; and with *Somebody Up There Likes Me*, directed by Robert Wise, Paul Newman finally establishes himself as a star in his own right. So does Marilyn Monroe in Joshua Logan's brilliant *Bus Stop*, from the William Inge play; other comedies include *The Solid Gold Cadillac*, directed by Richard Quine, with Judy Holliday, and Charles Walters' re-vamp of *The Philadelphia Story*, *High Society*, with Grace Kelly, Frank Sinatra and Bing Crosby. Out West, John Wayne and Rod Steiger evince different attitudes to the Red Indians in John Ford's *The Searchers* and Samuel Fuller's *Run of the Arrow*. Don

Siegel makes his chilling sci-fi horror film, *Invasion of the Body-Snatchers*, while Walt Disney enters the space race with *Man in Space*, a skilful if slight exposition of various aspects of the exploration of the universe.

President Eisenhower, with Anthony Eden, issues the Declaration of Washington on Middle East policy; he also signs an agreement with Britain on atomic development.

The Administration joins Britain in refusing to finance the Aswan High Dam, thus precipitating the Suez Crisis and letting the Russians into Egypt.

Eisenhower is re-elected for a second term.

There is trouble over desegregation in the South, especially at the University of Alabama.

American scientists discover the neutrino and the anti-neutron.

The designs of Eero Saarinen for the new United States Embassy in London are agreed.

James Baldwin publishes *Giovanni's Room* and Truman Capote *Breakfast at Tiffany's* (which will be filmed five years later); meantime Gore Vidal is at work on the screenplay of Tennessee Williams' *Suddenly Last Summer* and Jack Kerouac is completing *On the Road*, soon to become the Bible of the beatnik generation.

The Rock and Roll craze is at its height, with Elvis Presley as its High Priest.

Willem de Koenig paints his *Gotham News*, and Robert Rauschenberg, *inter alia*, his *Gloria*. The action-painter Jackson Pollock dies.

CHAPTER 6

1945 - 1960

IRON CURTAIN AND POINTS EAST

I

Of those countries which fell under the control of the Soviet Union after the War, only Poland managed to make an immediate impression on world cinema. Others had to wait some twenty years before a younger generation could grow up into a field of action which had become somewhat more permissive.

Thus in Hungary between 1945 and 1960 there was not much to report beyond some promising shorts by, among others, Miklós Jancsó, whose first full length film appeared in 1958 but who did not manage to make his mark as a new and important director until some years later. There was indeed a strong Stalinist influence at work, and even that great prophet of the theory of film art, Béla Balázs, had to toe the line.

Writing in 1945 he had pointed out that 'the scenario is no nearer to being literature than the architect's design is to being a painting or a work of graphic art . . . A script is not literature, but, if I may choose a word corresponding to design, a written plan'. But after the Soviet attacks on Eisenstein's *Ivan the Terrible* and Pudovkin's *Admiral Nakhimov* as being formalist works concerned with 'camerawork and similar problems' instead of concentrating on 'literary values', he found himself constrained to write, in 1948, that 'today's script is not a half-finished product . . . it is not a means towards a work of art, but a complete work of art in itself . . . Soon scripts will be more popular reading than drama . . .'[1] The Hungarian directors were similarly constrained to vest themselves in the script as in a straitjacket, so that when a director put into one of his films a shot not included in the

[1] Quoted in Istvan Nemeskurty's compendious history of the Hungarian cinema, *Word and Image* (Corvina Press, 1968).

script ('The lighting of a cigarette and pressing it out in . . . embarrassment') he was regarded by the newspaper critics as a rather daring innovator.[1]

Despite all this there were two directors who succeeded in making some distinguished films. Zoltán Fábri made a reputation for himself with his third feature *Merry-Go-Round* (1955). In this he managed to master a 'correct' script about the problems of agricultural cooperatives through his penetratingly true psychological picture of a young girl's conflict with her reactionary parents and the stormy progress of her love affair with a young peasant, in much the same way as Dovzhenko transformed his 'correct' directives for *Earth* through his passionate love for his native Ukraine. Next, and during the dreadful year of the Uprising, came his *Professor Hannibal* (1956), the story of a harmless schoolteacher whose strongly held theories about the Carthaginian general landed him in big trouble with the Fascists during the White Terror of comparatively recent history. Blown up into the image of a monster, mercilessly pursued and pilloried, he eventually recants his beloved theories at a huge mass meeting; and so fulsome, so utterly abandoned is his surrender to the Fascists that the crowd, which has been pelting him with stones, now gives him a standing ovation. Acknowledging this, bowing nervously, and stepping modestly back, he falls slap off the edge of the stadium and so dies . . . Fortunate for Fábri that Communist officials tend to lack any sense of humour.

The other director was Felix Mariassy, whose *Springtime in Budapest* (1955), a film about the days of death and confusion during the German collapse and the Russian arrival in 1945, created something of an impression outside Hungary. Mariassy's true feeling for the dilemmas of that period – the collapse of class relationships, the casual mass executions, and so on, were noted. Louis Marcorelles, observing that the end of the film was marred by the arrival of 'some model Soviet soldiers, the contemporary knights in shining armour', so that 'again a fine film sinks to the depressingly unconvincing level of a *Fall of Berlin*',[2] may perhaps not have noticed that the Hungarians who emerge from the ruins to greet the Russians with ceremonial music 'do not play the national anthem which begins with "God" or the Internationale which they do not know, but the Hunyadi March'.[3]

In any case both Fábri and Mariassy must be judged in relation

---

[1] Concentration on the written script is of course a convenient method of censorship.
[2] *Sight and Sound*, Winter 1956–57
[3] Nemeskurty, op. cit.

to the conformist necessities of that time. The next generation, Szabó, Kósa and the rest, were to find things less difficult.

In Czechoslovakia during the same period a very similar situation prevailed. Again, some twenty years were to pass before a younger generation could establish itself; but in the meantime the flag was kept flying by veterans such as Jiri Weiss, who returned to his native country after spending the war working for his exiled government and for the Crown Film Unit in England. His film *The Wolf Trap* (1957) had an impressive brooding intensity, while *Romeo and Juliet in Darkness* (1960) was nearly a masterpiece. This story of a boy hiding a Jewish girl from the Nazis and falling in love with her in the process, took place in a large apartment block in Prague; it had a fine *tendresse* as well as fearful suspense, with the darkness full of significant sounds – sounds that meant danger, sounds that meant relief, sounds that were menacingly mysterious; and the parts of the boy and girl were finely played by Ivan Mistrik and Dana Smutna.

Meantime Elmar Klos, having built up the official Czech Film School in the years after the war, joined forces with Jan Kadar, and together they made a number of box-office successes, though some of their films – notably *Three Wishes* – were banned by the Communist regime. Their biggest triumph came much later in 1965 with *The Shop in the High Street*, an extraordinary film about the sinister influence of pro-Nazi elements in a simple Slovak community which began as a kind of Ealing comedy and moved via elements of surrealism to a climax of shattering tragedy.

The only country in Eastern Europe to achieve an almost instant and freewheeling creative surge was, as I have already mentioned, Poland. There were several reasons for this. In the first place the Poles have an exceptionally ferocious sense of independence; they have no love, and little respect for those countries – Russia, Germany and Austria in particular – who over the centuries have taken it in turn to overrun and occupy their land. Secondly, and partly as a result of this, no Communist government can really work in Poland unless it comes to some sort of arrangement with the enormously powerful Catholic Church; and this implies a certain area of permissiveness lying between the two extremes represented by these formidably opposed religions.[1] Thirdly, the making of films about the destruction and suffering in

---

[1] On the way to the Cracow Film Festival, my car was suddenly held up between the airport and the city by two People's Police on motor-cycles. The reason – to allow a Corpus Christi procession, complete with dozens of small children in white dresses, on their way to their first Communion, to cross the road.

Warsaw and elsewhere, and about the atrocious behaviour of the Germans, could hardly be treated as censorable by the Stalinists, even though the horrors of the final uprising (as depicted in *Kanal* for instance) were to a great degree due to the Russian refusal to allow Allied help to get through to the freedom fighters.

The nationalization of the Polish film industry was quickly followed up by the formation of the now world-famous Film School at Lodz. This, under the direction of Jerzy Toeplitz and his colleagues, became the training ground for a new generation of cameramen, editors, art directors, animators, screen writers, directors, actors, and even critics. While this was getting under way some of the older film-makers – members of a pre-war avant-garde group called START – set to work to get the industry going again. Apart from Toeplitz himself, START had included Jerzy Bossak, who now began to build up a formidable school of documentary film-making and whose own film *The Flood* (1947) won the prize for the best documentary at the Cannes Festival; Eugene Cekalski, who had worked in England during the war; Stanilaus Wohl, who had spent the war in Russia; and above all Wanda Jakubowska, whose appalling experiences as a prisoner in Auschwitz and Ravensbruck inspired her large-scale documentary-style feature film *The Last Stage* (1948). The uncompromising realism with which she unveiled the horrors of the concentration camps was at that time meat too strong for many palates – palates which alas! since that time have become more accustomed to supping off such horrors.

In the same immediate post-war period the veteran Aleksander Ford made his mark with *Border Street* (1948), *The Youth of Chopin* (1952) and especially *Five Boys from Barska Street* (1952), which was also the first major Polish film to be made in colour. The story of this film is reminiscent of Ekk's *Road to Life* in that it shows the efforts of society to bring about the rehabilitation of children whom war has turned into rootless, criminal and homeless orphans. Despite the conventional story line usual in this sort of film – bad boys reformed, relapse into crime, return to society – *Five Boys from Barska Street* had a fine dramatic feeling, and the youngsters' acting was marvellous. Later, in 1960, Ford made a heavy historical drama, *The Knights of the Teutonic Order*, which was, in essence, no worse and no better than Eisenstein's *Alexander Nevski* with which, inevitably, it had to be compared.

Meantime a new generation started to emerge from the Film School at Lodz, and this included Jerzy Kawalerowicz, Andrzej Munk, Andrzej Wajda, and the actor Zbigniew Cybulski, whose expertise as a writer and stage-director enabled him to bring much more than his great acting ability to the new Polish cinema.[1]

Kawalerowicz' *A Night of Remembrance* (1953) and *Under the Phrygian Star* (1954) made a big impression, the latter being a sequel to the former, whose title was the same as that of the novel on which both films were based. This long story about the shaping of a young peasant's character under the influence of political and social events was highly complex in structure, with great proliferation of subplots, and it was perhaps not so easily understood by non-Polish audiences as Kawalerowicz' later *Mother Joan of the Angels* (1961), that powerful study of demonic possession in an 18th century religious community in which he captured the look and feel of a period as accurately as did Dreyer in *Day of Wrath*.[2] His *Pharaoh* (1965), on the other hand, was a somewhat sterile exercise in historical film-making, though it gave the young Egyptian film-maker Shadi Abdelsalam, who worked on the art direction, a chance to acquaint himself with aspects of film production which stood him in good stead when he came to make *The Night of Counting the Years*.

Andrzej Munk began in documentaries and continued to make them concurrently with his feature work; one of them at least, *A Walk in the Old Town* (1959), was a film of great distinction, combining the sights and sounds of a city with the reactions of a young girl who, as a budding violinist, has an acute sensitivity to them. Of the three features he made before his untimely death during the production of *Passenger* (which was completed by Lesiewicz), the film best known internationally is *Eroica* (1957).

This strange film is in fact incomplete. It was supposed to have three movements, in the musical sense; but Munk removed the third because he was dissatisfied with it. Although *Eroica* lacks its planned formal shape, the two existing movements nicely balance each other. The first depicts the ironies of fate with humour; the second with a despairing sympathy. In the first we follow the picaresque adventures of its anti-hero Dzidzius, a sort of confidence trickster who tries desperately to take advantage of the confusions attendant on the struggles of the various rival Resistance groups against the Nazis. Always prepared to sell his services to the highest bidder (in cash or in kind), he wanders from the war-torn city to the comparatively peaceful countryside and back again, constantly being caught by the (to him)

[1] It is sad to have to recall that Munk was killed in a car crash in 1961, and Cybulski in a railway accident in 1967.

[2] And a great deal better than Ken Russell in *The Devils*.

unexpected urgencies of conflict. At one point Munk lands him in a sudden confrontation with a German tank which must be one of the biggest and most remarkable belly-laughs in the history of cinema; this episode, with its impeccable angles and timing, is for me a treasured moment of cinema, beyond gold and emeralds.

The second part is a serious study of a prisoner of war camp where *Grande Illusion* rules still apply until the grades of rank and social status are disturbed by psychological conflicts arising from the secret, known only to a few, of the legendary officer who is thought to have heroically escaped from the camp but is in fact hiding (and sick) in the draughty interstices of the barrack roof. The tale ends with an O. Henry-like twist; its irony may be in the idea that heroism may perhaps reside more in what you feel than in what you do. Munk directs economically, with grim contrast between space and confinement; some of the long shots of the prison yard and its perimeter carry a desolating conviction.

Munk's contemporary Andrzej Wajda is best known for his trilogy about the Warsaw Uprising – *A Generation* (1954), *Kanal* (1956) and *Ashes and Diamonds* (1958). *A Generation* is particularly interesting since we can observe its hero's gradual discovery of himself in parallel with Wajda's discovery of himself as a film director. Parts of the film are stickily conventional and tentative in style; but there are other marvellous moments when the director, like finally his hero, comes to terms with and controls the situation. There is the long tracking shot (a foretaste of *Kanal*) of the crowds passing the hanged bodies of partisans; and the rendezvous outside a church from which suddenly a normal and very respectable bourgeois wedding party emerges; there is the terrible, intimate moment when a young man says to his Jewish friend who has come to him for shelter, 'I can't help you. It's your looks'; and the chase and death of the same young man – a hero-manqué known as Cowboy – which ends in high tragedy at the top of the vast circling staircase of an empty mansion.

Wajda's next film, *Kanal*, has the same scriptwriter as Munk's *Eroica*, Jerzy Stawinsky. The authors of *Contemporary Polish Cinematography* suggest that Stawinsky had intended *Kanal* as 'an anti-heroic work' like *Eroica*, but that 'Wajda's romantic temperament overrode Stawinsky's initial intention'. I think this is probably true. There are characters in *Kanal* – notably the sergeant with a penchant for vodka – who could well be Dzidziuses; but Wajda's whole emphasis is on the Thermopylean heroism of his small group of men and women fighting literally to the last gasp in the stinking sewers under Warsaw. Before ever the film gets going Wajda announces, 'These are the heroes. Watch them die'. He then launches into an enormously long and perfectly executed tracking shot as a group of partisans make their way in a hail of rifle and machine-gun fire over the ruins and rubble of Warsaw. It is a shot as sensational as Milestone's in *All Quiet on the Western Front*. Wajda then establishes his grip on us with a violent shock effect. The group arrive at their rendezvous, and one of them starts talking to a wounded girl-soldier on a stretcher. 'Are you badly hurt?' he asks. She somewhat equivocally shakes her head; and at that point, as the stretcher-bearers pick her up, the blanket covering her slides off to reveal the roughly-bandaged stump of her right leg which has been severed above the knee.

The whole of the first part of the film, while they are still above ground, is gripping and powerful, with the guerilla combats, the menacing anonymity of the Nazi tanks, the anomalies of pianos and Empire furniture teetering in gap-toothed buildings on the edge of nowhere. But when the action moves into the claustrophobic sewers some weaknesses quickly become apparent. Wajda's characters tend to take on certain resemblances to all too familiar Hollywood types – a musician who quotes Dante and eventually goes romantically mad, a black-market floozie with a heart of gold, a self-doubting hero, a meticulous orderly, and the drunken sergeant aforesaid. It is all a little too contrived, a little too over-dramatized, as though the actual drama of the situation were not enough. But *Kanal* has some fine moments, not least the final sequence, when Daisy leads the dying Korab to a patch of light and supposed freedom – actually an unbreakable grating through which can be seen a river, and the peaceful but forever un-attainable habitations of men . . .

In his next film, however, Wajda got a strong grip on his romanticism and turned it to splendid account. *Ashes and Diamonds* (1958) is, like Munk's *Eroica*, a film of disillusionment. It is in large part about its anti-hero Maciek's effort to preserve a romantic attitude to life, his failure to do so, and the ensuing disaster which ends with him lashing about in his death throes on a rubbish dump with the same delirious misery as that of the murderer-kulak grinding his own head into the soil in Dovzhenko's *Earth*.

Maciek (a great performance by Cybulski) is a failure not merely because he undertakes too late the assassination he is under instructions to carry out, but also because he is incapable of coming to terms with reality even if he wants to. As Wajda makes us see towards the end of the film, he belongs to that world symbolized in the Vigo-like slow-motion procession to the sound of a Polonaise. And, as Eric Rhode has pointed out, the futility of Maciek's actions 'is parodied by his alter ego Drewnowsky, whose scandal at the banquet, when he sprays the guests with a fire-extinguisher, and his disgrace when he is thrown down the stairs, mime Maciek's machine-gunning of the wrong man and his ignominious death'.[1]

Ashes and Diamonds is a difficult film to write about. Its plot would be hardly intelligible were it not for the fact that it is all ingeniously focused on the small-town hotel, where the confusion of sentiments, the coincidences of meeting or not meeting, the divergence or convergence of paths and purposes, can be placed in some sort of geographic pattern. Maciek would be a total anti-hero were it not for the force of Cybulski's playing and the extraordinarily magnetic attraction of his personality. In the end this is a film whose impulsive gestures vibrate gratefully in the deeper *coulisses* of the consciousness; Wajda here has spoken perhaps not only for his own generation in Poland but for the soul of Poland itself.

The regret for a dying world hinted at in the slow-motion Polonaise at the end of *Ashes and Diamonds* comes right to the fore in *Lotna* (1959). Here Wajda – alternating sepia and colour – tells the simple tale of the Polish cavalry's hopeless stand against Hitler's panzers in 1939. It is a tale built round the beauty of a horse. The simplicity, the startling yet so right images, again recall Dovzhenko – the apples stored in a coffin, the old man dying amid the beauties of his castle, porcelain, gold, silver, tapestries and, there with him in his room, his beautiful white mare which is now to be passed tragically from officer to officer after the fashion of Kemmerich's boots in *All Quiet on the Western Front*, until in the end she meets her own proud death.

While Wajda was making *Ashes and Diamonds*, an even younger generation began to make itself felt with films such as *The Last Day of Summer*, *Two Men and a Wardrobe*, and *Dom*. The iconoclasts had arrived.

These three films are all comparatively short – the longest being *The Last Day of Summer*, which runs to 65 minutes, while the other two are in the ten to twenty minute range. Each film represented a breakthrough in the film-maker's approach to society, and two of them at least introduced new and significant artists – Roman Polanski, Walerian Borowczyk and Jan Lenica.

[1] *Tower of Babel* by Eric Rhode, Weidenfeld and Nicolson, 1966.

The Last Day of Summer (1958) was made by what seems to have been a once-only team consisting of a distinguished screenwriter, Tadeusz Konwicki,[1] and a skilful and sensitive cameraman, Jan Laskowski.

The Poles, as much as anyone, know the extent of the cruelties which men can inflict on nations, on peoples, and thereby on individuals who are, after all, the most precious of God's creatures. This film, a work of mood and mystery about two such individuals, is in fact simplicity itself.

On a deserted, windswept beach, two people – each cut off from life in a loneliness which comes from savage and indifferent blows dealt them by the tyrannies of war and intolerance – try tentatively to come together in peaceful confidence; they find brief happiness and then part, or, it may be, come close together in death under the ocean waves. This beach – 'A place for tired people who don't care if they win or lose' – is a kind of no man's land. It is now empty, though there is plenty of evidence that people have been there before. Overhead from time to time jet fighters scream to remind the woman of her dead husband, who was a pilot. In the distance, fog-horns sound. And from time to time, from a special nowhere, there creeps in the complaint of a melancholy flute.

The woman, sunbathing alone, finds herself being watched by the man. She tells him to go away, even throws stones at him. While she sleeps he builds a sand barricade to keep the wind away from her. She wakes, chases him away again until he runs far, far into the sea; her desired distance switches to proximity as she finds herself rescuing him from drowning; the gruelling difficulty with which she finally manages to drag him ashore is clearly symbolic of childbirth; and the next stage in their relationship has a good deal in it of that between mother and child. And indeed the man, when quiescent (he alternates between violent activity and absolute stillness) nearly always adopts a foetal position. When they get involved in a rather ambiguous tussle it is she who wins, and who says to him, 'You behave like a child'.

They cook some fish. When they eat it the meal is solemnly parodied as a formal luncheon party, amid the preparations for which he suddenly runs off and re-enacts, for himself alone, a shell- or bomb-burst out of which has come the schizoid isolation in which he now lives. Now they begin to confide in each other; and in their mutual isolation they find a mirror:

---

[1] His script credits include *Mother Joan of the Angels* and *Pharaoh*.

'I just wanted to tell you I'm alone in the world.'

'I've always been a failure.'

'In eight hours I will be gone from here.'

'Stay with me . . . I'll show you where we will build our house.'

'Either you stay or I'll go.'

'All men are liars.'

'If ever I say "I love you", it will be to you.'

There is a rainstorm. They kiss. They come together in love. She wakes. He is gone. Past all the places they have been she goes, calling him, seeking him. She thinks she sees him sitting on the shore – but as she approaches she sees it is only a piece of driftwood. And then she sees his footprints. They lead into the sea. She follows – and as the camera withdraws further and further and higher and higher, her diminishing figure disappears into the waves as, once again, the jets, those beautiful, harsh seagulls of danger and loneliness and death, scream past across the grey skies. Surely the summer is over.

In its own particular genre this film is perfect. The limpid photography, the economic but always effective movements of the camera, the simple, unfussy editing – all these set off the beautifully directed performances by Irena Laskowska and Jan Machulski so that, as Paul Rotha wrote when the film was first shown at Venice, its makers 'have drawn upon the poetry of cinematic imagery – sound and visual – to unveil slowly and subtly and with intense beauty . . . the innermost thought-stream of these two tragic people haunted by their experiences of war'.[1]

With Roman Polanski's *Two Men and a Wardrobe* (1958), which he made while still a student at the Polish Film School, the communist scene was invaded by certain forces of illogicality, of social criticism in reverse. Buñuel and Vigo hover near by, helping to point the very non-Marxist questions which are implied rather than stated by the film – a film which could never have got itself made in the USSR, where the diehard traditions of petty-bourgeois aesthetics are, it would appear, permanent and immutable.[2]

The importance of the film (which is a kid's *jeu d'esprit* and no masterpiece) lies in its choice of subject, its treatment of that subject, and in the first revelation of the style of a man who was to make *Knife in the Water* – a subtle psychological triangle drama – before taking off for Europe and America and the production of *Repulsion*, *Cul de Sac*, *Rosemary's Baby* and *Macbeth*.

[1] *Sight and Sound*, Autumn 1958.

[2] Though Tarkovsky's recent and controversial work in part disproves this.

The men who emerge from the sea carrying their wardrobe are of course victims of Society. This clumsy object, so difficult to transport (worse even than a double-bass), must go everywhere with them, for it represents without doubt their preciously held collection of beliefs and values – beliefs and values old-fashioned by 'modern' standards and incompatible with the plastic myths of a monolithic technocracy, whether capitalist or communist.

They suffer with mild good humour both objurgations and violence – which in the climactic episode involving the gangsters and the dead kitten becomes terrifying and macabre – until, defeated, they return whence they came, taking with them their wardrobe and their values and picking their way with infinite care over the veritable jungle of sandcastles built (deliberately to obstruct them?) by a small child. This film only pretends to be a comedy; it is a parable about freedom in an un-free world, and its final impression is that of a melancholy tinged with anger. One wishes nothing but well to them as they rejoin beneath the ocean the man and the woman from *The Last Day of Summer*.

Dom (*House*), also made in 1958, caused a shake-up in the world of animation-film comparable with those caused previously by Len Lye, Alexandre Alexeieff and Norman McLaren; after *Tusalava* and *Colour Box*, after *Night on the Bare Mountain* and *The Nose*, after *Hen Hop* and *Neighbours*, nothing could be quite the same again – and so it was with *Dom*. Here Borowczyk and Lenica perfectly combined their separate talents into an individual style which reflected 'the satiric power, bitter, black humour and tragic irony born in Poland during the last war and other wars before it'.[1]

This sort of film is extremely difficult to describe verbally, as indeed it should be; suffice it to indicate that it purports to be thoughts or reflections concerning an empty house in which a number of objects, not necessarily disturbing in themselves, tend to take on monstrous significances; there is a wig, red in hue, which wanders about eating or engulfing everything in its path . . . With Borowczyk and Lenica – together or separately – nothing is what it seems to be, nothing is safe. Refrigerators are full of flies, letters of the alphabet trip up or bite innocent personages. It is noteworthy that both these men, who now work separately, seem to have found it necessary to visit and work in other countries from time to time, presumably in order to recharge the batteries of their inspiration from sources other than those of a Communist society; it is equally noteworthy that the Polish authorities do

[1] *Animation in the Cinema* by Ralph Stephenson, Zwemmer, 1967.

not seem to have curbed in any way their movements or their freedom of filmic expression.

Later works by Lenica have included *Monsieur Tête* (a head which is Shakespeare and Napoleon but within which may be found a dead mouse and a candle), *Labyrinth* (a collection of disturbing images which it is difficult to put in writing), *Rhinoceros* (notable for the absence of Ionesco) and *A*, that savage and untrustworthy capital letter; while in parallel Borowczyk has made *Grandmother's Encyclopaedia* (beware its apparently innocent entries), *Renaissance*, in which a cosy little world is painstakingly constructed from a diversity of objects and promptly destroyed; *Les Jeux des Anges*, a pregnancy of totalitarian horrors; the remarkable full-length *Theatre of Mr and Mrs Kabal* (a theatre of cruelty, needless to say); and, finally, the non-animation full-length feature, made in France in 1968, called *Goto, Island of Love*.

This film, though perhaps a shade overlong, is as disturbing as anything Borowczyk has given us. With a documentary realism reinforced by the reportorial quality of Guy Durban's camerawork, he unveils an island cut off from the rest of the world since an earthquake in 1877. It is ruled by a dictator who presides over a community dwelling in the ruined complex of a Victorian factory. As in the collapsed world of *Things to Come*, objects whose viability has vanished are still used as symbols of prestige, and the passage of time and memory has twisted the system of justice into parody (criminals are paired in combat against each other, the loser being adjudged guilty). Goto III, the clumsy dictator – in many ways reminiscent of Haiti's Papa Doc – is capricious, cunning, but in the long run stupid enough to be easily bamboozled. Hence the extraordinary scene in which, through the use of a pair of old binoculars,[1] he at last discovers his consort's unfaithfulness with his stable officer and, after long meditation, hands his gun to his trusted henchman (official fly-trapper) who thereupon and unhesitatingly shoots him dead, instead of hurrying off to execute the officer.

The menacing, decaying quality which pervades this film is insidious; the island prison enfolds the spectator and engulfs him in a drab despair. Throughout the film, which is in black and white, Borowczyk suddenly cuts in brief flashes in colour which, we gradually learn, represent the next moves planned by Grozo, the trusted fly-trapper, in his plan to eliminate the dictator and, in supplanting him, to enjoy his consort. These flashes add the final macabre touch which,

[1] By courtesy, no doubt, of Mr Kabal.

allied to the sinisterly effective performances of Pierre Brasseur, Ligia
Branice, Guy Saint-Jean, Ginette Leclerc and the rest, makes of this
film a diabolically convincing nightmare in which all values are
debased or reversed and, as Philip Strick put it, 'our horror . . . comes
simply from not knowing the rules, or, rather, from the recognition that
the rules are mutations from those of our own society'.[1]

The influence of Lenica and Borowczyk has, I suspect, been quite
profound outside cinema; I would not be surprised to learn that
Kienholz was to some degree influenced by them; and here I am not
talking so much about style as about the liberation of shapes within a
certain discipline which results in a method of communication in which
words are no longer prime to the purpose.

Also in Poland, between 1956 and 1958, there occurred the interesting phenomenon of the so-called 'Black Documentaries', in which
some of the younger directors made criticisms of social conditions
rather after the fashion of British films like *Housing Problems* in the
Thirties. Of these the most important were *Isle of Hope*, by Bohdan
Poreba, which, in showing the little patients in a TB sanatorium,
implicitly accused not only the Germans for their genocidal policy but
also the contemporary Polish authorities for acting too little and,
nearly, too late. Similar implications were to be found in Jan Lomnicki's
sad but somehow noble film *A Home for Aged Women*, which forms an
interesting contrast with the Danish *The Seventh Age*. Other similar
films in this series included *Children Accuse* – an attack on parental
alcoholism by Edward Skorzewski, and *Warsaw 56*, by Jerzy Bossak
and Jaroslav Brzozowski, which made a frontal attack on the slow
progress of the housing programme in the capital. The freedom accorded
to these and other directors was almost unprecedented in an Iron
Curtain country, and this, together with the liberal attitude to the
animators and, on the whole, to feature directors, must be counted unto
Poland for good; though it must sadly be added that more recently –
certainly up to and including the Stettin massacres and Gomulka's
demission – a sinister repression has come into existence, most regrettably allied with anti-semitism, which appears to have placed in jeopardy
the livelihood of some of the distinguished persons herein mentioned,
and in at least one case has ended by the stripping of one of the
country's better film and TV directors of his decorations, his job, and
finally of his citizenship.[2]

[1] *Sight and Sound*, Autumn 1969.
[2] This was Tadeusz Jaworsky who, together with his wife, the noted tapestry maker,
ended up in Rome as a stateless person. Thanks to the efforts of various international

II

I indicated in Chapter 4 how, by the end of the war, the Soviet Cinema had entered a dark age. The final years of Stalin's dictatorship were indeed dangerous and terrible for anyone working in any of the arts – but never more so than for the film-maker, dealing as he did with a medium of mass circulation and therefore potentially of mass persuasion. The immediate post-war period was, in effect, dominated by two official policies. The first was directed against 'cosmopolitanism', delightfully defined by one Konstantin Simonov as 'the desire to undermine the roots of national pride because people without roots are easier to defeat and sell into the slavery of American imperialism'.[1] The second, arising automatically from the first, was straightforward anti-Americanism; and this proved to be a bandwagon on to which it was prudent to jump. One should not therefore be surprised (only saddened) to note such names as Alexandrov, Kalatozov, Room and Romm amongst those making anti-United States features; and one may be glad to note that a sudden policy switch saved other proposed films from Ermler, Arnstam and even Dovzhenko from getting beyond script or planning stage. Wiser, perhaps, were those who, in the early Fifties, chose to devote themselves to making straightforward film records of the performances of the great Russian Theatre Schools such as the Maly and the Moscow Arts.

A melancholy period then, and one from which Soviet cinema was to emerge only slowly after Stalin's death. The melancholy was added to by the loss of so many of the pioneer figures of the Russian film, including the two greatest – Dovzhenko and Eisenstein.

A man eating a hunk of bread: for Dovzhenko a sacrament, a celebration of life; for Eisenstein the physical proof of an intellectual concept. These two directors are in character and genius as far apart as Hopkins and Eliot, and yet, like those two poets, in certain respects curiously close together.

There are many similarities between their first films, *Zvenigora* and *Strike*. Both are irresistible gallimaufries of iconoclasms, experiments, new ideas, and general irreverence. Both are suffused with a revolutionary fervour not yet tarnished by the inevitable disappoint-

---

organizations, including the International Association of Documentarists, they were installed in Canada, where Jaworsky made a beautiful and touching little film on dispossession called *Selling Out*, nominated for an Oscar in 1973.

[1] *Kino* by Jay Leyda.

ments which come from experience and the passing of time. If, after
that, their paths diverged, they certainly came close together again in
the intensity of certain situations where the poetry and the drama are
intertwined – as in the confrontation between the partisan and the
traitor in *Aerograd* and that between Euphrosyne and Vladimir in
Ivan the Terrible Part II.

Both Eisenstein and Dovzhenko fell foul of the Stalinist regime.
That their creative powers were regarded with respect as well as with
fear and suspicion can be seen from the fact that both of them, at one
time or another, were summoned to personal interviews with Stalin
himself.[1] In the long run Eisenstein may have suffered more than
Dovzhenko.[2] His intellectual capacity, his desire to look at everything
from as many different points of view as possible, his theoretical
excursions into the problems of montage in terms not of film art alone
but of all forms of art – all these tended to a nonconformism which was
bound to get him into trouble. Dovzhenko, on the other hand, was a
more simple and uncomplicated person – a great artist who happened
to believe wholeheartedly in the Soviet Revolution and in the sacred
soil of his beloved motherland, the Ukraine. In *Arsenal*, in *Earth*, in
Shchors, these two elements, sometimes combined, sometimes opposed,
surge onto the screen in elemental images – and in face of these we
turn hastily away from the cardboard histrionics of *Alexander Nevski*
to the tragic, mysterious fantasies and fancies (woven from historical
fact) with which Eisenstein, in *Ivan the Terrible*, crowned his long and
difficult film-making career.

Also common to both of them in their earlier films are the
revolutionary pronunciamentos, the jargon of the ·day. The faces and
gestures of the intellectuals, the politicians, the bosses and the middle
classes are interchangeable as between *Strike* and *October* on the one
hand, and *Zvenigora* and *Arsenal* on the other. A sardonic visual
approach to the *ancien régime* had of course been originally instituted
by Eisenstein; and it seems likely that Dovzhenko – an older man but
newer to cinema – followed eagerly in his, and for that matter Pudovkin's
footsteps in this respect. And just as Eisenstein would have recognized

---

[1] Of this, writing later, Dovzhenko said, 'The wickedness of Beria – without any doubt
at all this was a sinister and frightening death's head looming over our times. I remember
his devilish expression the time I was taken before Stalin for that severe and terrible
judgment which was pronounced on the unfortunate and inaccurate phrases which,
according to Stalin himself, had crept into my scenario for *The Ukraine in Flames*.'
(*Alexandre Dovzenko* by Marcel Oms, Paris, 1968.)

[2] Apart from anything else he was, over *Que Viva Mexico*, clobbered by the capitalist
as well as by the communist system.

something of his own influence in the fake public suicide sequence of *Zvenigora*, so also Pudovkin might have seen something of the execution scene between Bair and the soldier, in *Storm over Asia*, in the sequence at the start of *Arsenal* between the German officer and the private.[1]

Where Dovzhenko parted company with all other Soviet film-makers was in his deep and mystical love affair with his native land, the Ukraine. A lyric poet by nature, he channelled all the contradictions of love and hate in his heart into the celebration of the black earth of his homeland and the red blood – so often, so bravely and so sadly shed – of its people. He remained always on the side of these people, proud, simple, the salt of the earth. When he was impelled to move into wider fields he became uneasy, searching always to bring the subject back to the elemental, the natural struggle. This happened, I think, in *Michurin*; and of course in this film he faced a challenge to his personal integrity. Stalin's official backing of Lysenko's misinterpretation of Michurin's work brought Dovzhenko to a political confrontation which, seeing the sort of man he was, could only lead to one result. He withdrew, with great dignity, from the production. He never, alas, completed another film.

Nor was it really surprising that *Earth* should run into so much trouble. This – one of the greatest poetic masterpieces in the history of cinema – was, as indeed was Stroheim's *Greed*, full of elements likely to shock the prudish bourgeois mentality of commissar and film-tycoon alike.[2] A tractor runs dry and the young peasants of the commune get it started again by pissing in the radiator. A young girl, her lover murdered in cold blood, strips naked and writhes in a veritable orgasm of grief on her lonely bed.[3] All this was morally as well as politically out of line, and for many years no one ever saw the film as Dovzhenko had completed it. Not that the Soviet regime was the only culprit. In every country where it was shown the censors had a field day, and nibbled away even at what the esurient Shumiatsky had left. It is, indeed, to the great credit of Khrushchev that during his administration *Earth* was at last released as Dovzhenko had made it. It was only then that

---

[1] For the extremely enthusiastic reception accorded to *Zvenigora* by Eisenstein and Pudovkin see Jay Leyda's *Kino*.

[2] We need not, in blaming Soviet policy, forget what Hollywood has done to other artists besides Stroheim. Lillian Ross' *Picture*, the story of Huston's *The Red Badge of Courage*, is a useful reminder.

[3] Eisenstein deeply disapproved of this scene; it failed, he said, to distinguish between representational naturalism and metaphor. My own guess is that, with the prudery seen in many homosexuals, he just felt shocked, and had to rationalize.

one realized the extent of the violations that had been committed on it.[1]
For the first time one realized the real meaning of the terrifying collapse
into madness of the young murderer in the hilltop graveyard. In the
censored version this was intercut only with the beautiful and dignified
procession through the sunflowers of his victim, carried head high
among the blossoms by his friends. Now we could see that Dovzhenko
had made a double intercut, adding that of the girl's agony in her room.
The young kulak circling and rubbing his head in the earth coalesced
with the girl writhing on her bed. And the dead boy, calm and as
though sleeping, passed by in a kind of triumph which was beyond
murder, beyond physical love, beyond revenge. Here Dovzhenko
showed us the tying and the loosing of all the *poicil* threads of life –
storm, sunshine, drought, harvest, crime, sacrifice, the truth and falsity
of death. And after this amazing sequence he comes quietly to a coda –
the apples on which first the rain and then the sunlight fall, a symbol
as sure and certain as that with which he began the film, with the old
man, surrounded by his generations, dying tranquilly amid the myriad
fruits of the black earth of the Ukraine.

Dovzhenko's montage is nearly always based on the contrast
between stillness and action, and beyond this on a feeling for fable and
folk-tale which, like Mizoguchi, he automatically assimilates into the
most outwardly prosaic scenes. Here the contrast with Eisenstein is at
its most marked. In every Eisenstein image movement is implicit when
not explicit. Like atoms, his images must collide, bounce, come together
again in a mathematico-kaleidoscopic pattern; the overlapping of movements in physical time, as in the raising of the bridge in *October*, are a
perfect example of poetry attained by a very difficult mathematic
precision.[2] When they start the cream separator in *The General Line*
(*The Old and the New*) with Martha Lapkina and her family watching,
we are at the start of a virtuoso piece of film-editing by which the
curiosity, surprise and joy of the peasants is given to us through an
intellectual analysis. In the end *their* delight, *their* emotions have been
translated into *our* language. There is something secondhand. When the
young men start up the tractor in *Earth* we are sucked into a situation
in which, willy-nilly, we *share* the intensity of feeling of these Ukrainian
peasants in search of a new and richer life. There is here a glory which
Eisenstein could never find within his own complex soul; and this is

[1] In Russia the original had at least been preserved. Would that the same thing could
be said of Hollywood and *Greed*!

[2] The one thing that makes me believe that Eisenstein *did* have a hand in *Romance
Sentimentale* is the lovely overlap cut of the greyhound lying down. No one but Eisenstein
could have thought of that cut, let alone make it.

perhaps why *The General Line*, for all its brilliance, was and is a failure.

In *Arsenal*, when the workers take their dead friend home to be buried, it is in a wild sleigh-ride across the snow; and to the exhortations, the 'gee-ups' of their drivers, the horses reply, as in a folk-tale, with human voices; just as earlier in the film, the starving horse says to the starving man – 'It's not me you should be beating, Ivan'. And in the same film the portrait of a national hero suddenly comes to life and blows out the ikon candle in front of it. All this is presented quite naturally and in a style already well established in *Zvenigora*; it is not dissimilar to that moment in *Ugetsu Monogatari* when the man goes into a store and sees, not the shopkeeper's wares, but his wife in a setting hundreds of miles away.

Then there is *Aerograd*, a film which, like Dovzhenko's previous *Ivan*, was so mashed up by political interventions that it is not too easy to establish what it is all about. Suffice that it concerns the building of a great new city of youth in the extreme East of the Soviet Union, and the attempts of Japanese interventionists to prevent it. The climax of the film occurs when the young man has to take his best friend, now proved to be a traitor, out into the forest and shoot him (that dual confrontation again). Through the forest they go for what seems hours – the young man deep in thought, and his prisoner, old, exhausted, stumbling after him with no desire to escape. What is said? The young man speaks his inner thoughts. Looking at the trees he says, 'Is there anywhere in the world such beauty?' Next, when the moment has come, he says, 'Trees, rivers, mountains! Behold my grief. I am going now to shoot Glushak, sixty-two years of age, and my dear friend ever since I was a child'. What does the old man Glushak say? In words, nothing. But earlier he has hidden his face in shame from *us* the audience as he passes Dovzhenko's camera; and now, before the gun cracks, he throws back his head and howls – the howl of a wolf (for the traitor), and the howl of a man (for all the injustice of a changing world which he cannot comprehend).

This consciousness of the camera, and thereby of the director of the film, whose creation Glushak in essence is, leading to a complicity on the part of the audience who find themselves entangled in something much more than a macabre jest, is one of the strangest moments in the history of film. It is a form of *cinéma-vérité*, and indeed it reminds me of an extraordinary sequence in *The Things I Cannot Change*, a reportage made for the National Film Board of Canada in 1967 by Tanya Ballantyne. She lived, with her small camera crew, with a very low-income family in a Montreal apartment for three weeks. At one point the husband, a character at once shabby and mercurial, repelling and attractive, has a street fight and subsequently gets involved with the police. He has a long phone talk with a police officer explaining why he doesn't want to come to the police station. This talk (which like everything else in the film is spontaneous and unrehearsed) is cross-cut with an interview, shot on another occasion, in which the man explains to the film-makers certain previous physical and psychological experiences which have produced in him a highly traumatic attitude towards the police. The alternation of these two conversations – or monologues as they essentially are – sets up an almost electric rapport between the spectator and the little man on the screen. As in *Aerograd*, some extra dimension becomes involved. And if films are like dreams, we have here the point at which the dreams are not our own – wishfully accepted – but an enforced eavesdropping on the subconscious of others. In both these cases there is a poetic element; in Dovzhenko it is deliberate, and in the other film it arises from a deliberate interference by the film-maker with the so-called 'purity' of the *cinéma-vérité* technique. I suspect that this type of experience may be sought after more and more by film-makers as the development of synaesthetics continues through the Seventies and into the Eighties.

Another thing about Dovzhenko is that he manages to use symbolism without causing uncomfortable jolts. Compare the symbolic finales of *Storm over Asia*[1] and *Arsenal*. In *Storm over Asia*, his undoubted masterpiece, Pudovkin, one feels, has used symbolism as an escape from the real issues at hand. Bair's elemental rage begins realistically enough by a Kane-like furniture-smashing spree. But he then goes on to a Samson-like destruction of an entire building, and his anger is translated into a mighty roaring wind which is supposed to be blowing away the English interventionists and all the enemies of the Soviet Union. But all we see are raggedy thorns and tumbleweeds. This symbolism proceeds, as it were, from the animate to the inanimate; the heat is turned down instead of up. And for all its greatness, *Storm over Asia* always leaves one feeling let down as the end title comes up.

In *Arsenal*, towards the end, Timoch[2] faces his executioners. They fire at him again and again. He does not fall. They try again. He tears open his shirt; his chest is unmarked. They now view him as someone supernatural; and he, before the final fade-out, says in pride, 'I am a worker – and a Ukrainian'. Here the heat has been turned *on*. The end

---

[1] Also known as *The Heir to Genghis Khan*.
[2] The hero of *Zvenigora* is also called Timoch.

is inspirational; you feel like cheering. Yet even this dramatic symbolism would not have worked had not Dovzhenko prepared for it by the preceding sequence – a long, deliberate build-up in which we see Timoch's comrades and fellow-strikers, sometimes in small groups, sometimes one at a time, being shot down by one single officer. All is photographed in violent chiaroscuro. The movements, especially when the men fall, are slow, hieratic. Into this Dovzhenko begins to intercut shots of mothers and their children, in many different garbs and backgrounds, directing statements and questions straight at the audience. 'The machinist is no more. Why?' 'The shop foreman is no more. Why?' 'The father is no more. Why?' And it is out of this tragedy, this despair, these accusations, that we realize that the human spirit, in justice, must rise again. From this, then, Dovzhenko passes to his symbolism. It is a kind of religious gesture; body and blood are seen also to partake of the spirit.

Eisenstein was not, of course, unaware of the eternal contrast between stillness and movement. Indeed like Leonardo, whom he resembles in so many respects, he was constantly, compulsively conscious of the still centre, of the whirlpool, of the flow of time and energy. The basic difference between his films and Dovzhenko's is that his approach is analytic, cerebral. Even his written scenario of his never-finished *Que Viva Mexico!* has this quality. It is of course to be a film about dignity and beauty, about cruelty and injustice. But it gives the impression that it is also to be encyclopaedic.

The outline written by Eisenstein in 1931 begins as follows:

'Do you know what a "Serape" is? A serape is the striped blanket that the Mexican indio, the Mexican charro – every Mexican wears. And the serape could be the symbol of Mexico. So striped and violently contrasting are the cultures in Mexico running next to each other and at the same time being centuries away. No plot, no whole story could run through this serape without being false or artificial. And we took the contrasting independence of its violent colours as the motif for constructing our film: six episodes following each other – different in character, different in people, different in animals, trees and flowers. And still held together by the unity of the weave – a rhythmic and musical construction and an unrolling of the Mexican spirit and character.'

The same outline ends as follows:

'But the grotesque laughing of the stone heads becomes still more grotesque in the cardboard "piñata" faces – Christmas dolls.

And then becomes voluptuous in the suffering smile of the Catholic polychrome saints. Statues of saints that were erected on the sites of pagan altars. Bleeding and distorted like the human sacrifices that were made on the top of these pyramids. Here, like imported and anaemic flowers bloom the iron and fire of the Catholicism that Cortes brought. Catholicism and paganism. The Virgin of Guadeloupe worshipped by wild dances and bloody bullfights. By tower-high Indian hair-dresses and Spanish mantillas. By exhausting hours-long dances in sunshine and dust, by miles of knee-creeping penitence, and the golden ballets of bullfighting cuadrillas.'

I have quoted these passages not in any pejorative sense, but to emphasize the wide range of visual and aural effects which surrounded all Eisenstein's movie concepts. For him nothing was fixed, all was flux. His was the precise anti-world to Dovzhenko's; indeed, Dovzhenko said of him, and to his face, at the famous meeting of film-makers in 1939,[1] 'If I knew as much as he does I would literally die . . . I'm afraid also that his laboratory may explode from an overwhelming confusion of complicated, mysterious and enigmatic material'. The contrast may be finally pointed by quoting Dovzhenko's description of the theme of *Poem of the Sea* – the film he never lived to complete:

'The president of a kholkoz knows that his village will soon be submerged under a newly made sea.[2] He writes to everyone born in the area asking them to come and say a last farewell to their native land. Some two hundred people turn up. Some of them have left the village thirty or forty years ago. At this gathering I intend to show a cross-section of our people, kholkoz men, workers, truck-drivers, young women, mothers, children, builders, soldiers, civilians, writers, engineers, bureaucrats, officials . . . There will even be an army general. When they are all gathered together, the president of the kholkoz will speak to them: "It is a joyful thing that our village has given our country so many useful and indispensable people. It may well be, however, that some have not always behaved perfectly. Many of us have been scattered across the nation like lizards in the fields. Others have reached high estate, while we, the collective farmers, have been learning new methods of tilling the soil, and learning too how to arouse the sleeping soul of our people. We are glad you have

---

[1] *Sergei Eisenstein* by Marie Seton, Bodley Head, 1952 (p. 337).
[2] Reading this today one is reminded of the dramatic drowning of the whole of Nubia by the new Aswan High Dam.

come to say farewell to your *isbas*. One of you is a painter, so put them on canvas so that people in future days will know what our village looked like before it disappeared under the sea, under our sea, under the sea made by the hands of man . . . So say goodbye to your houses, to the fountains, the wells, the gardens, the places where you experienced your first pleasures and your first loves. For soon their destruction-construction will begin. Tomorrow your village must be reborn, on the shores of this future sea.'[1]

Enough is known of Dovzhenko's development of this theme to make it more than probable that *Poem of the Sea* (which was to be on wide screen) would have been of a beauty exceeding that of *Earth*. Despite his widow's devoted work towards completion, we shall never really know. What is clear is that in this, as in all his work, he approached the structure of society from its intimate inwardness, whereas Eisenstein approached the structure of society from outside. Apart from what might have been in *Que Viva Mexico!*, which we shall never fully know, the reality of human relationships hardly exists in the Eisensteinian world until *Ivan the Terrible*, where in the end he penetrates even beyond what at first seems to be the world of monsters we have met in Welles, in Stroheim, and perhaps sometimes in Sternberg.

I believe that the two parts of *Ivan the Terrible* represent Eisenstein's finest and most important work; I believe that it was only in these two films that he truly found himself as a film-maker by combining for the first time the deep, dark inner resolutions of his subconscious with the brilliant clarity of his theory of montage.

This immense work was to contain a conspectus of a crucial period in Russian history in terms of a power conflict which had continued into his own day; the individual torn between personal ambition, responsibility for the nation he ruled, an ambivalent attitude towards a God in whom, nevertheless, he truly believed, and by the conflicts of policy and of conscience arising from all these factors. To this end Eisenstein devised the film almost in the formalized style of grand opera. Everything was larger than life. The significance of the settings – heavy, ponderous, stalactic with religious images or the savage machineries of war – was nearly equal in significance to the characters themselves. Never indeed have settings and personages been so much part of each other.[2]

---

[1] From a letter to Georges Sadoul, quoted by Marcel Oms, op. cit.

[2] One may note that the failure to achieve such a combination is the major fault of *The Cabinet of Dr Caligari*.

Eisenstein, like Leonardo, was despite (and because) of his genius, a man of his time; and like Leonardo he accepted the sanctions and reprisals of tyrants, secular or religious. That Ivan and his confidant Malyuta could have been seen as figures resembling Stalin and the odious Beria must at some stage have crossed his mind. (Mikhail Romm, writing well after Stalin's death, specifically makes this comparison.[1]) Writing his script and then shooting the film in Alma Ata at the height of the war, he must have wondered from time to time which way Stalin and his creatures would react to this version of the tale of the man who defeated the boyars and laid the foundations of a greater Russia. What he did undoubtedly know was that his version of Ivan must be absolutely personal to himself. He would face up to any 'sins' *after* he had committed them.[2]

The fact is that Eisenstein's version of Ivan the Terrible is neither more nor less accurate than, say, Shakespeare's of Henry V. What is really important about the film is its study of an immense, almost crushing personality (concealing nevertheless gnawing uncertainties from everyone save God) who attempts to come to terms with a situation of almost superhuman, not to say supernatural difficulty. It is of course concerned with Power; the power which defeats Kane and McTeague but which, in this work – if we take the intentions of the un-made Part III into account – is fought at least to an uneasy draw by Ivan Grozny.

Within this framework we may also observe an attempt, mainly subconscious no doubt, to work out Eisenstein's own personal problems which he had had to live with throughout his career. Marie Seton[3] has emphasized the importance of Eisenstein's repression of his homosexual inclinations, and has shown how these (not least in his attitude to his mother) are reflected in the homosexual Vladimir – particularly in those tremendous sequences which begin with the critical meeting with Euphrosyne, continue through the fantastic dance of Fyodor (himself masked and *en travesti*) with the Oprichniks, and end with that staggering confrontation when, thinking that the Tsar lies dead at her feet, Euphrosyne looks up and sees 'the ranks of Oprichniks part . . . to show Ivan, in his monk's habit, advancing slowly from the far end of the cathedral, staff in hand', and then, bending down to the body at her feet, turns it over and realizes that it is her son.

---

[1] *Ivan the Terrible*, Classic Film Scripts, Lorrimer, 1970.

[2] As witness his public 'confession' about the 'mistakes' of Part I, and Cherkassov's unpleasant description of the interview with Stalin.

[3] op. cit.

A further parallel, originally suggested by Marie Seton, has recently been elaborated by Gaston Roberge, a Jesuit from French Canada, in a detailed study entitled *Thou Art Silent – Tsar of Heaven?* which he wrote as his Master's thesis at the University of California, Los Angeles.[1] Roberge suggests that just as all Ivan's problems were eventually focused on his relations with God, the Tsar of Heaven, just as Ivan went from heights to depths in these relations as he struggled with the individuals and groups of the complex, simmering community over which he was trying to impose his authority, so Eisenstein, in the process of making the film, found himself touching on the nature of a religious experience which he had repressed as successfully (or unsuccessfully, according to your point of view) as his homosexuality.

Religion certainly plays a part in all his films. In *The Battleship Potemkin* the phony, bearded old priest who waves his crucifix in a vain attempt to stop the mutiny is said to have been played by Eisenstein himself.[2] In *October* there is the famous iconoclastic sequence of graven images of all world religions. In *The General Line* there is not only the great religious procession to intercede with the Almighty for rain; there is also the fact that Eisenstein himself thought of the cream-separator sequence in terms of the Holy Grail, however 'negatively'.[3] 'Emotive structures applied to non-emotional material . . . When the "pillar of industry" is finally discovered – it is a typewriter . . . It is not the Holy Grail that inspires both doubt and ecstasy – but a cream-separator.'[4] In *Alexander Nevski* the Teutonic Knights bring with them a portable cathedral, a portable organ, and a black-robed priest who somehow suggests Goebbels.

Apart from the last example these religious references may contain a certain ambivalence. Overtly they ridicule religious forms and observances and show how cruelly they play on the superstition and simplicity of ignorant folk. Implicit in them, however, is the ecstatic element. In exposing the emotional and spiritual trappings of a deceitful religion Eisenstein was, willy-nilly, showing his ignorant peasants in the very process of undergoing the experience of a communion of faith. Communion, communism – the words are very close; and it may be said that the world-wide success and attraction of Communism is that it has in fact *become* a religion, with all the faith as well as the bigotry

---

[1] I am obliged to Marie Seton for drawing my attention to this work and for enabling me to meet its author and discuss it with him.

[2] Seton, op. cit., p. 80.

[3] Seton, op. cit., pp. 107–112.

[4] *Film Form*, p. 77.

which the word implies. What is there to choose, *qua* religious experience, between the peasants praying for rain and Lapkina watching the magic of the cream-separator? And are not Dovzhenko's people, whether in factory or field, bound together in a shared experience involving not only the mystique of the soil but the burning fervour of a new and hopeful revolution, in fact being truly religious?

There is a remarkable shot at the end of *Ivan the Terrible Part I* when the procession of the people wends its way to the palace to beg Ivan to return to Moscow. The long cortège, like a black snake, is seen framed in an archway; the figure of Ivan enters and bends down (he is very tall) to watch the procession. With his long beard and lank hair he appears to overhang the procession like a mountain crag. It is a seminal shot. It carries more than menace in its composition. It is the epitome of the loneliness which accompanies kingship, the loneliness which, above all, comes to the worshipped in face of his worshippers. In this one set-up Eisenstein seems to have summed up, in a compositional montage of attraction and repulsion, the whole insoluble problem of the relations between the ruler and the ruled. Later on, in *Part II*, the great religious frescoes which loom oppressively, almost crushingly over Ivan, state the other aspect of the theme – the problem of the relationship between the Tsar of Russia and the Tsar of Heaven. At times the frescoes crush Ivan to the ground; at other times they are to him a source of strength.

In *Part II* the Church's challenge to Ivan in the parable of the burning fiery furnace is dramatically smashed, and ends with the enraged Ivan saying, 'From now on, I will be just what you say I am. I will be – Terrible!' But in *Part III* Eisenstein had designed a sequence of very different import:

'In a corner inside the cathedral the wrathful face of Jehovah stares out of the fresco of the Last Judgment. The heavenly Tsar carries out the Last Judgment . . . and hurls the sinners into the flames of Gehenna. A Monk reads aloud in front of the choir.
"Remember, O Lord, Thy servants
who died before their hour had
sounded, from Adam to the present
day."
About the heavenly Tsar circles the fire: the celestial hierarchies are depicted. The flaming swords are directed downwards by the winged oprichniks of the heavenly Tsar – downwards to where the sinners burn in eternal fire.'

Remorselessly the monk reads out name after name, from parchment after parchment, of all those killed by Ivan.

'Tsar Ivan lies prostrate in the dust. He is dominated by the representation of the Last Judgment: the celestial judge sits enthroned above the clouds. Sparks shoot out of the eyes of Jehovah and his grim face is full of rage . . . The sinners burn in everlasting flame at his feet. But the remorse which burns, tortures and devours the spirit of the earthly Tsar, the Tsar of Moscow, is even more terrifying than the everlasting flames. He ponders his responsibility. Sweat flows down his forehead. Tears flow from between the closed eyelids. The Tsar has lost weight. He looks ill. He has aged twenty years.'

The remorseless reading continues, interrupted now by Ivan's various excuses – that he had to punish treason, that it was for the Motherland, that in war these things must be. But the Eternal Tsar makes no answer. In a fearful climax, Ivan, with a shout of 'Thou art silent – Tsar of Heaven?' flings his jewelled sceptre at the fresco of the Last Judgment, where it shatters to pieces.

Marie Seton is of the opinion that Eisenstein never intended to shoot *Part III*, and she may well be right . . . Lonely, politically insecure, disliked and opposed by his principal actor, uncertain of his friends (even Tissé), he must have felt reluctant to continue a story which, however he treated it, could hardly do other than arouse the suspicion and thereby the ire of the by now completely psychopathic Stalin.

If at the same time his repressed religious instincts were seeking release, that release had already been found in the tragic charade leading to the death of Vladimir. From the moment when Ivan decides to dress Vladimir in the full regalia of the Tsar there begins, as Roberge points out, a kind of parody of the mocking of Jesus before His crucifixion as well as of Ivan's own coronation in *Part I*. This parody, suggests Roberge, 'was the only form of homage that Eisenstein's wounded sensitivity could then express'. The fact that Vladimir is a homosexual, and that Eisenstein had repressed his homosexual equally with his religious inclinations, adds strength, even poignancy, to this suggestion. Moreover Eisenstein particularly marked the importance of this episode by presenting it in colour, so that the feast, including Fyodor's dance, also homosexual, would, in his own words, 'burst like an explosion' onto the plot to kill the Tsar. It may be noted here that Fyodor's dance, and that of the wild Oprichniks – to say nothing of the rest of the episode – is in general shot from low angles favouring the religious paintings of God and His angels on the walls and on the looming ceiling.

The dense and overwhelming richness of *Parts I* and *II* of *Ivan the Terrible* represents something quite different from anything which Eisenstein had attempted before. It is as though all the inwardness of the Jungian Unconscious, including that most dangerous and deeply-lying of all, called by Jung the Shadow, had been called forth to a celebration of dark and terrible magnificence shot through with flickers and flashes of hope and of salvation.

The great thing is that with *Ivan the Terrible* Eisenstein achieved something of his very own after so many years of prevention and frustration. It has to be remembered that the Mexican episode left unhealed wounds. There is no need here to go into any great detail. The sad story is told in Marie Seton's book and in the recently published *The Making and Unmaking of Que Viva Mexico!* by Harry Geduld and Ronald Gottesman.[1] Eisenstein, and to a great degree Upton Sinclair (who in his innocence used to write to Stalin on behalf of *individual* victims of the mass purges!), were sacrificed on the twin altars of film-commercialism and anti-communism. Eisenstein never had the chance of handling the 213,000 feet he shot in Mexico; and when, long after, he saw the three films which had, one way or another, been made from the material, he was seized, from all accounts, with a certain despair. It was good, therefore, that after Mexico, after the political interference with *Bezhin Meadow*, after the successful but in the last resort rather bogus *Alexander Nevski* (for Eisenstein, surely, not much more than an interesting technical exercise, witness the descriptions in *The Film Sense*), after the many projects mooted but not made, that he was able, on the edge of death, to leave us the two parts of *Ivan the Terrible* in which, one may guess, he purged his soul and satisfied his instincts as a great artist.

Eisenstein's theories of montage are in a sense a collection of creatively inquisitive notes *towards* a theory, like those of Leonardo. Dovzhenko's theories, as stated from time to time by himself, are simple and lapidary. To a questioner he once quoted Courbet's famous answer – 'Madam, I am not thinking, I am excited.' On another occasion, in defence of *Zvenigora*, he said, 'The reason why you don't understand it is in yourself.' Dovzhenko had simplicity plus burning faith; and to mitigate this rather awesome combination he had a sense of humour. The fund-raising sequence in *Shchors* is a fine example of this.

[1] Thames and Hudson, 1970.

In a bourgeois theatre – the same one perhaps which was host to the great political argument in *Arsenal* – the middle classes are summoned to hear an appeal to their pockets on behalf of the Bolshevik Party. This is climaxed when an aged Bolshevik, appropriately moustached and shaggy, shambles on to the stage towing behind him a machine-gun. As, in his clumsy, rustic way, he develops his speech on the need for generous giving, he gently manoeuvres the gun into a position where it can rake the stalls . . . and somehow this sequence raises two memories, one tragic and one fantastic; the unsuccessful struggle and subsequent fate of the strikers in *Arsenal*, and the famous theatre scene in *Zvenigora*, in which Pavlo not only swindles an entire audience which has paid good money to see him commit suicide, but also gets away with the cash, which he intends to use for *counter-revolutionary* purposes – only to find, in the long run, a final solution – suicide, this time for real.

I hope that Dovzhenko, with the production of *Poem of the Sea* ahead of him, died a happy man. That he had suffered as much as any from interference with his work by the stupid and the insensitive is, I fear, only too true. What in this way can be done to an artist may be seen in something which he wrote fifteen years after making *Earth* and at a time when his troubles with *Michurin* must have already been brewing:

'For fifteen long years I tilled my land or, rather, our common land. Spared no effort. Thought nothing of time. Ignored holidays. Slept not at night. Thought always – how to gather a better harvest? And my soil gave forth fruit. There was wheat in my field, apples in my orchard, and honey for the pleasure of those who ate, or would eat. Once only the harvest failed. Maybe I hadn't worked as I should, maybe I hadn't sowed where I should, maybe indeed I hadn't said the proper prayers. In any case my heart and my head pained me much.

'Then some wicked men came into my field – that field so lavishly watered by the sweat of my brow. In the middle of my faded garden they put up a hastily-made rostrum, like a scaffold, and set to screaming, "There he is! he who deceived us with his fifteen harvests. He threw dust in our eyes through the beauty of his work. But luck went our way. On the sixteenth occasion he uncovered his true visage. Crucify him! Crucify him! Hate him! Mistrust him! In the name of Almighty God, our Father, crucify him!"

'Then I fell down in silence, and I died. My body was thrown to the dogs. Untilled remains my field. Empty remains my pillaged home.'[1]

In addition to Eisenstein's death in 1948 and Dovzhenko's in 1956, the Soviet cinema also lost Dziga Vertov in 1954 and Pudovkin in 1953. From the unfortunate Vertov no films of note had come since 1937 when someone, Shumiatsky presumably, put the finger on him. Pudovkin, however, had remained steadily in production, though generally without the spark of his earlier work. From *Minin and Pojarsky* (1939) onwards, he turned out conventional and uncontroversial (in the Stalinist sense) historical epics[2] of which one – *Suvorov* (1941) – had some fine cinematic touches, notably in the scenes of the army crossing the Alps. Pudovkin's last film, *The Return of Vassili Bortnikov* (also known as *Harvest*) was made just before his death. The first part of this film was quite impressive, with some very fine colour photography and something of Pudovkin's old verve in the depiction of the Russian countryside and its people; but the story – of a wartime wife unfaithful to her absent husband, and the crisis to be faced when he returns – was rather turgid.

So in terms of real value the Soviet cinema had little to show for the fifteen years from the end of World War II. It is certainly true to say that no great film was made during this period; for Eisenstein's *Ivan the Terrible Parts I* and *II* had in fact been made during the war years. Caution, as I have said, prevailed. There were remakes of famous books; Donskoi, for instance, remade Gorky's *Mother*, but could not efface the memory of Baranovskaia and Batalov in the Pudovkin version of 1926. Soon after Stalin's death Yutkevitch made a not-unsuccessful *Othello* (1956), better in general but less imaginative in detail than that by Welles in 1952, and with a fine performance by Sergei Bondarchuk who, later, was to become Russia's prime director of super-epics (*War and Peace*, *Waterloo*); and in the following year Kozintsev directed *Don Quixote*, with Cherkassov in the name part – a film which for me did not quite come off (am I haunted still by Chaliapin's performance in the not otherwise successful version by Pabst in 1933?), but which interestingly anticipated those ironically formal court scenes which were to contribute so much to the success of Kozintsev's later *Hamlet*.

Towards the end of this period there were signs that film-makers were beginning to express, or to take advantage of, a more permissive

---

[1] Quoted in *Alexandre Dovjenko* by Marcel Oms. (My translation.)
[2] He ran into some ideological trouble, nevertheless, over *Admiral Nakhimov* (1946)

attitude towards the structure and psychology of Soviet society. In a film such as *The Cranes are Flying* (1957) by Mikhail Kalatozov, we at last find a heroine of character, indeed of a certain elegance, very much unlike the puddingy future *hausfrauen* of the cliché-ridden Stalinist cinema. 'When the son of the family goes off to war, his old grandmother makes the Sign of the Cross over him. This gesture . . .is accepted by the other people in the scene as the grandmother intended it; there are no snide inferences of "opium of the people" or "grandmother's dotage".'[1] *The Cranes are Flying*, by the way, also had a technical exuberance one would have expected from a younger man than Kalatozov, who had been making films since 1928; anyhow it brought a badly needed breath of fresh air into the Russian film scene.

It was also encouraging to see another veteran, Josif Heifitz, directing in 1960 the enchanting *Lady with the Little Dog* – a film with magnificent style, recreating past days as convincingly as did those opening reels of Vera Stroyeva's *Generation of Conquerors* in 1936 (the same year as Heifitz co-directed with Alexander Zarkhi that 'youthful film about an old man',[2] *The Baltic Deputy*).

But of all the films of this predominantly unfruitful period of Soviet cinema, the most wholly satisfying and delightful was a modest little picture which does not even get a mention in Jay Leyda's otherwise compendious work. This was *Chuk and Gek*, made in 1954 by I. Lukinsky. It was about children for children; but it was for grown-ups too. It had a humour, freshness and innocence not seen since Vladimir Legoshin's *Lone White Sail* in 1937. Chuk and Gek are two chubby five-year-old boys (almost circular, rather than chubby, when kitted up for the Russian winter) who, having by mistake thrown away an unopened telegram addressed to their mother, accompany her on a long and adventurous journey by train and sleigh to a remote meteorological station of which their father is in charge. They find it empty. The missing telegram had been sent to tell them not to come, as he has had to go away on an expedition. However, they make the best of what meagre provisions he happens to have left behind; and as they wait for his return the boys, helped by their mother, learn something of the practicalities and realities of life. Apart from the simple but ingenious story and the extraordinarily beautiful landscapes so well photographed by Garibyan, this is one of those few films that display an entirely natural relationship between children and adults without at the same time losing that sense of the private fantasy world in which small kids

---

[1] *Soviet Cinema: The New Way* by Cynthia Grenier, *Sight and Sound*, Summer 1958.
[2] *Kino* by Jay Leyda.

live. The boys – Yura Chuchunov and Andryusha Chelikin – possess charm and no cuteness; by now they are, I hope, married and with equally enchanting offspring. *Chuk and Gek* also has the rare merit of being the right length, without the slightest semblance of padding; it runs for just under 50 minutes. And it pairs well with another modest and no doubt equally forgotten film made at around the same time in the People's Republic of China. This was *The Letter with the Feathers*, directed by Shih Hui. The story takes place against the background of the guerilla war against the Japanese invaders. A message of the utmost importance has to be taken to an isolated group of partisans; it is entrusted to a small shepherd boy who, it is thought, will be, in the company of his herd, unsuspected by the Japanese. So with the letter (the feathers mean top-priority) concealed under the wool, to put it mildly, of one of the sheep, he sets off; and the film, in picaresque style, shows all the adventures and dangers he undergoes before he reaches his goal. It is a roughly made film and, if you like, somewhat naïve. But the boy, Ts'ai Yuan Yuan, reacts well to the understanding approach of the director and gives a convincing, and often, in moments of desperate difficulty, a moving performance. Remembering this, and remembering a strangely beautiful Chinese opera film of the same period, with an all female cast, and entitled *Lian Shan-Po and Chu Ying-Tai*, I sometimes wonder if there are hidden riches in China comparable to those which the West stumbled on so late in time in regard to the cinema of Japan.[1]

III

The sudden and sensational success of *Rashomon* at the Venice Festival in 1951 tended to put critics and film-makers alike into an unprecedented flap. It was as though, never having troubled to make themselves aware of the products of the French film industry, they were presented with Clair's *La Beauté du Diable* or Cocteau's *Orphée* (both made in the same year as *Rashomon*) plus a backlog of French cinema stretching for some thirty years. That indeed would turn out to be an Ali

[1] Apart from mainland China there is a vast output from the Hong Kong studios of the brothers Run Run and Run Me Shaw. These noisy and usually spectacular versions of Chinese historical legends or fairy tales have a very large market in all those many lands where Chinese are in business, and have recently become popular with British audiences.

Baba's cave; and thus it was with Japanese cinema, of which few of us have been able to do more than scratch the surface, and that only thanks to guidelines provided by Donald Richie, Joseph Anderson and Arne Svensson. It has to be faced that Kurosawa has made some 25 films to date, and Ichikawa 54; the completed *oeuvres* of Mizoguchi and Ozu number 87 and 56 respectively; while between his *A Page of Madness* (1926) and *Gate of Hell* (1953) Kinugasa made 53 films.

Rashomon impressed not merely because it was a striking and often disturbing enquiry into the nature of truth, not merely because it introduced a director who was instantly recognizable as a master of his craft no less than as a master of his art, but above all because it served to open Occidental minds to the Japanese tenor of life which had hitherto remained concealed by impressions of sunshades and art-nouveau or by an out-dated and highly regrettable militarism. Here was something between *bushido* on the one hand and *ikebana* on the other; a point at which a hitherto strange culture began to become, if not wholly explicable, approachable. *Rashomon* was, in a word, a not unsuitable work through which the West could start its exploration of a new world of film; in particular, the fact that the 'evidence' provided by the murdered husband through the mouth of the medium was given equal value to that of all the living witnesses helps in understanding the blurred outline of the border between the quick and the dead in Japanese thought. Nor could anyone fail to be impressed by the staggering panache of Kurosawa's tracking shots, the rich, luminous photography by Kazuo Miyagawa, and the great intensity of the performances – particularly Toshiro Mifune as the bandit, Fumiko Homma as the medium, and Machiko Kyo as the wife; or by the fact that the finding of the abandoned baby at the end of the film, which anywhere else would appear extremely corny, here seems to be perfectly right and natural.

Kurosawa, like John Ford, whom he is said greatly to admire, likes to range widely in style and subject. Certainly nothing could be in greater contrast to *Rashomon* than *Ikiru*, made two years later. This strange and not entirely successful film is about a dried-up little civil servant trying to face up to the fact that he is dying of stomach cancer. Having done nothing of note during his career (even the youthful exuberance of his memorandum proposing reforms of his department had been filed away long ago in a dusty cabinet), he now seeks, in the brief time remaining to him, some sort of meaning from life. He finds it in the idea of a children's playground to be set up in a slum area. He doggedly fights this to fruition despite every sort of opposition and inertia, and in the end dies happy, sitting on one of the swings as the first winter snow drifts down.

The most striking thing about *Ikiru* is its construction. The first half is a straightforward chronological presentation; but at the point where Watanabe decides to fight for the playground the film switches ahead in time to the wake being held by his family and his civil service colleagues after his funeral. During this, in which, getting steadily drunker and drunker, they pass from belittling his achievement to a maudlin resolve to follow his shining example of integrity and so on, the true relation of his efforts is shown in a series of flashbacks. These, seen against the background of the drunken wake (an extremely accurate representation of Japanese funeral behaviour, by the way[1]), throw into ironic relief the humility with which little Mr Watanabe went about his work – the bowed figure, bowing ever lower and lower, abasing itself, but always there, never budging until the request was granted or the action taken; and the radiant smile which breaks over his face when, threatened with death by a gangster who wants the playground site for a gaming club, he realizes that death is the last thing he now has to fear.

What is wrong with *Ikiru*[2] is that at times, and especially in the wake scenes, it swerves into *schmaltz*, Hollywood-type. The emotional and sentimental stops are pulled out too far. The colleague at the wake who stands up for Watanabe's memory is just that much *too* nice, *too* goody-goody; and the policeman who turns up to pay his respects is just that much *too* honourable. We feel we are being played on, and with a director of Kurosawa's calibre this is not necessary; he should not have doubted our ability to take it straight.

Nevertheless the film is full of wonderful things. Watanabe's effort to 'find out about life' by having a night out on the town comes to a climax in a fantastic shot of a mighty ocean of dancers in which he and his partner become engulfed; it has some affinity with that scene in *Odd Man Out* when Johnny's girl-friend tries to dodge the police by slipping in and out of the dance hall. And there is a real bravura passage in a coffee house which is as fine as anything Kurosawa has ever done. This coffee house is by no means oriental. It is, to meet Japanese taste for occidental up-to-date-ness, a pretty accurate reproduction of the Cadena or Kardomah of the England of *Brief Encounter*, even to the waitresses in black dresses with white aprons. There is also a 'grand' staircase and plenty of potted plants; and a general feeling of English middle-class gentility. In this setting Watanabe has a kind of

[1] Compare Oshima's *The Ceremony*.
[2] It is typically Japanese that this word is translated either as *Living* or *Doomed*.

show-down with Toyo, a girl who used to work in his office and to whom, in a desperation of loneliness and uncertainty, he clings despite her increasing impatience with him. Three things happen. He tells her the truth about his illness. He demands that she tell him how and why she enjoys life. And she – after an instinctive gesture of distaste and disgust at the thought of his stomach cancer – explains that she left her civil service job through boredom and is now happy because, working in a toy factory, she feels 'as though I am friends with all the children in Japan'. In this way his idea for the playground is born.

This is a tremendously tense, tremendously intense sequence, superbly interpreted by Takashi Shimura as Watanabe and Miki Odagiri as Toyo; but Kurosawa intensifies it further. Throughout, in the immediate background, a birthday party is going on – a surprise party given by a group of office girls for one of their friends – chatter, expectation, music. And the music is first *The Waltzing Doll*, then *The Parade of the Wooden Soldiers*, and finally *Happy Birthday to You* as Watanabe, his plan new-born and clutching one of Toyo's toys, runs down the staircase while the pretty little birthday girl mounts it. No *schmaltz* here; the sequence is deeply felt and deeply true, as is an earlier one depicting the gulf of misunderstanding between Watanabe, his son, and his son's wife which ends with Watanabe crawling under the bed-clothes and abandoning himself to a storm of uncontrollable weeping which is a mixture of self-pity and real despair – what time the camera tilts up to a framed testimonial to his 'twenty-five years of devoted service to the department . . .'

Kurosawa spent the next two years making his biggest and most spectacularly impressive film, *Seven Samurai* (1957) – an unbeatable epic, as was proved by the John Sturges Hollywood remake of 1961, *The Magnificent Seven*, which, however admirable, completely missed what might be called the sense of glory achieved by Kurosawa.[1]

The story is of the simplest. The people of a remote village, beset and harassed by bandits, approach some wandering samurai (out of work because of the collapse of the feudal society which had supported them) and ask for their help. The samurai train the villagers to defend themselves, attack and burn the bandits' hide-out, and finally lead the villagers in a pitched battle in which the bandits are wiped out. Of the samurai only three survive; and they, ignored and forgotten by the

[1] It was the biggest film ever made in Japan and took a full year to shoot. The production company at one point got cold feet and tried to abandon the project; but Kurosawa's threat of resignation was enough to bring them to heel. Would that Stroheim had been similarly successful!

peasants who, thanks to them, can now return in peace to their farming,
start out again on their wanderings.

This enormous film bursts with action and emotion. The cameras
are everywhere, photographing through dust, through rain, through the
rising and falling mattock as an old lady bashes at a prostrate and
defenceless bandit's head, through flurries of running feet, horses'
hooves, flashing swords; and – pioneer work this – super-telephoto and
slow motion shots are used by Kurosawa to accentuate and intensify
the violence of the action.

Seven Samurai is obviously much more than a 'Cowboys and
Indians' epic. The villagers are fighting for survival, for the preservation
of an ancient and not undignified life, however humble. The collapse
of the higher reaches of Japanese society, which means that many professional warriors become *ronins*, that is unemployed, is to the villagers
a godsend, for under no other circumstances could they afford to employ
them (even had they deigned to accept the job). The whole story is
therefore pinned to a credible and viable human situation. Amid the
appalling violence, amid the rainstorms, the heat, the dust and the mud,
the huge cast of characters appear not as types but as real persons, in
the round. One remembers in particular the 'crazy samurai' – the one
who doesn't really belong, but wants to – a kind of Dostoievsky/
Dovzhenko figure (and with something of Tobei from *Ugetsu Monogatari* in him as well), whose personality is diffused magnificently
throughout the whole roaring action of the film. Against the action
scenes – some of them quite horrific, as in the slaying of the bandits
outside their burning hide-out – Kurosawa places sequences of deep
tenderness like the love scene between the young samurai and a village
girl among the sunflowers, which is treated not only with an outward
lyricism but with a considerable insight on the psychological level. The
version of *Seven Samurai* released in Europe and America ran for three
hours: the original was some 40 minutes longer, and all those who have
seen it say that the cut was a great mistake; in fact Donald Richie, in
The Japanese Film, goes so far as to suggest that this shortening, and
others made in various places for distribution convenience, may have
prevented *Seven Samurai* from being recognized as 'among the best
films ever made not only in Japan but anywhere in the world'.[1]

[1] Seven years later Kurosawa made a sort of black comedy on a theme similar to
Seven Samurai. In *Yojimbo* – also with Mifune – he gave us one single ronin faced with
the problem of trying to reconcile, or at least pacify, the Montagus and Capulets of a
Japanese village. All concerned are criminal, crooked, cruel (a key shot in the film shows a
dog wandering around with a human hand in its mouth – shades of Buñuel!); there are
balletic, single-handed fights (like *Shane*), and when the samurai finally leaves, the solution

In 1957 Kurosawa made *Throne of Blood* (also known as *Cobweb Castle*). This remarkable film has suffered some indignities at the hands of English-speaking critics because it is based on a play by William Shakespeare called *Macbeth* (as was, incidentally, a rather strange motion picture by Orson Welles). What actually happened, as far as I can see, was that Kurosawa and his screenwriters engulfed the play and, after digestion, regurgitated it in terms of Japanese myth, Japanese historical romance, and Japanese warrior traditions.[1] The translation (I use the word as Peter Quince did) may have been stranger than that carried out by Verdi for the operatic stage; perhaps we should go for wider comparisons – Racine and Corneille adapting the Graeco-Roman classics or, nearer the mark perhaps, *West Side Story* for *Romeo and Juliet*, and *Catch My Soul* for *Othello*.

Kurosawa's 'translation' in *Throne of Blood* consisted mainly of stripping away nearly all the flesh of the drama and presenting it in its bare, skeletal bones. The very settings of the film are, without exception as I recollect, stark. The ride of Washizi (Macbeth) through the dew-misted pine forests (in a series of incredibly brilliant tracking shots) and his meeting with the single, evil-entangled witch; the fantastically empty interiors of the castle – a mat, a bowl, a small lamp in a vast hall; the whitened ghastliness of the mask-like visage of Asaji (Lady Macbeth), who is like a vengeful, icy ghost even before the climax of a still-born child (none of your 'I have given suck' here) drives her into madness; and the final frenetic sequence in which Cobweb Forest (Birnam Wood) comes to the Castle not just as trees but as wooden arrows which, projected by the vengeful and shadowed army, transfix the tyrant a hundred and a hundred times against the log-cabin walls of his stronghold; all these do in the end, and in their own hallucinatory terms, add up to at least the bare bones of the Macbeth story – the inevitable fate awaiting 'vaulting ambition, which o'erleaps itself'. And those who have seen Japanese drama, Kabuki and Noh, will recognize in this film the contrasts between a masked stillness and a sudden crescendo of violence, will recognize too that apparently innocent third-person narrative which (within a frighteningly formal framework) suddenly leaps at your throat . . .

No greater contrast could be imagined than the other film which the prolific Kurosawa made in the same year as *Throne of Blood*. This

---

has not really been found; there are corpses. It is, by the way, quite a film, made with verve and panache, and Mifune is superb.

  [1] How far these differed from Shakespeare and Holinshed's idea of the Scots tribesmen of the Macbeth period it is not easy to say; perhaps hardly at all.

was his screen version of Maxim Gorky's *The Lower Depths* (*Donzoko*).
His transposition of the Russian work to the slums of Edo (Tokyo's
earlier name) around the 1860s was a quite staggering success. It was
made on one single set comprising the central courtyard of a small and
filthy dosshouse, with a few cubby-holes leading off it as well as a
passage-way to the narrow street outside. No starring rôles; Toshiro
Mifune himself was merged completely into the rest of the cast depicting
a group of down-and-outs, or worse, who have congregated here in a
hate-love conflict with each other, with a remorseless landlady, and
with a priest who has come briefly to live among them. They are all
shut into this dosshouse just as they are all (save the priest) shut into
their own inner dream-worlds, their refusal to accept the fact of their
degradation. It is a degradation not entirely of their own making;
society also has a part in it; so in the end the priest can do no more
than tell them, hopefully, that there is always hope – and depart. There
is passion, sordid enough, yet pathetic; and from that there is murder.
Finally, as the old actor kills himself, one of the others, revealing a mad,
imperishable gleam of almost Dickensian humour, says, 'The fool!
What a thing to do just as things are getting jolly'.

　　The Lower Depths would not have its grip and power if Kurosawa
had made it in conventional studio terms. The reason why we enter so
fully, so sympathetically into the sordid lives of this little group (the
actor, the gambler, the travelling tinker, the thief, the old soldier, the
prostitute) is that the director, in order not to miss the point that,
however low, these are still human beings with the human spark, has
forced his cast to become so much one with another that they lose their
outer identity almost entirely.[1] 'The cast and the crew, with lights, full
costume, make-up and camera positions, *rehearsed for forty days* (my
italics), before starting the actual shooting.'[2] Only so could such a unity
be achieved; it reminds me somehow of the magnificent performances
of children in Satyajit Ray's films: no one has ever heard one word he
has said to them during production, but the results indicate secret
understandings of immense significance.

　　There is a Japanese director whose work is so extraordinarily
varied that he almost qualifies for the title 'Anon'. How can one put
a trademark on Kon Ichikawa, the variations of whose directorial work
make him stylistically as elusive as a butterfly, witness, for instance,

---

[1] Whereas in Renoir's screen version of the same work, made in 1936, the dramatic
balance lay between the admittedly superb performances of Jean Gabin as the thief and
Louis Jouvet as the gambler.

[2] *The Japanese Film* by Richie and Anderson.

The Burmese Harp, Odd Obsessions (or *The Key*), *Fires on the Plain*, *An Actor's Revenge*, *Alone on the Pacific* and *Tokyo Olympiad*? I suppose one could say that Ichikawa, like Hitchcock, is a *seductive* director. He pulls you into the film (if necessary feet foremost), enfolds you in it as in a cocoon, and then slowly releases you through a series of experiences which can be puzzling, pleasant or alarming, according to subject and treatment. Personally I have only once resisted this seduction, and this was in the case of *Punishment Room* (1956), a film based on a sensational contemporary novel which rather unpleasantly and sadistically exploited the well-worn subjects of sex, alcohol, drugs and violence among teenage students.

The Burmese Harp (1956) offended some British critics who felt that it was too soft towards the recollections of Japanese militarism, and who particularly disliked the singing of a sentimental British song by a group of Japanese soldiers. Time has no doubt mitigated thes animadversions, which in any case showed a complete misunderstanding of the film. *The Burmese Harp* is a sad, poetic, mystical and semi-religious tale based clearly on certain important elements in the Japanese ethos and the Japanese subconscious. The framework of the story concerns a soldier, presumed missing or dead, trying to make his way back home after the Japanese surrender. Dressed in Buddhist robes given him by a monk who sheltered him, he sees everywhere on his way the corpses of his fellow-countrymen, abandoned, forgotten and un-buried. It comes to him that it is, at the least, his duty to give them burial. And this task soon becomes his life, based on a kind of respect (the dead should be honoured) and a kind of expiation (why should they be dead and he still living?). These self-imposed duties are mingled with flashbacks to various wartime experiences with his unit; and the whole film proceeds on its path in a rather dreamlike manner, until we are willingly drawn into its mood of waking vision – I had almost said sleepwalking – a vision touched with remorse, with regrets. In the end he falls in by chance with members of his old unit. They recognize him, despite his monk's habit, because he still carries the 'harp' from which he was always inseparable. But he does not overtly admit his identity; and in sympathy they let him go on his way. Let the dead bury their dead.

A melancholy film, perhaps, but tinged with grace: Bresson, above all, would understand it. The playing, by Shoji Yasui as the soldier-monk and by Rentaro Mikuni as his company commander, is excellent; and Minoru Yokoyama's muted camerawork exactly fits the mood of the film.

The horrific *Fires on the Plain* was made two years after *The*

Burmese Harp. It is a story of the last days before the final Japanese surrender in the Philippines. The army has disintegrated; troops are wandering about, hopeless, undisciplined, and without supplies. Through Tamura (Eiji Funakoshi), a private suffering from TB, we are introduced to this despairing world, and to a procession of ghastly horrors which include rape, murder and cannibalism. All is beastliness and degradation; and Tamura, in whom at the end some vestiges of humanity are seen to persist – he shoots his cannibalistic fellow-soldier – is killed by a stray bullet just as he is staggering towards safety. The superb photography of the Philippine scene by Setsuo Kobayashi – beautifully composed for Cinemascope – only adds to the horror of the film as, no doubt, it was meant to do. This undeniably powerful film, which engulfs you in its gruesomeness, has been perceptively compared by Pauline Kael to Godard's *Weekend*.

In the same year Ichikawa made another off-putting film, *Odd Obsessions* (also known as *The Key*). This story of the perversions elaborated by a husband whose sexual powers are failing ends up in a melodramatic situation verging on the farcical. Paralysed by a stroke, he is forced to watch his young wife stripping, and dies from frustrated excitement as a result; whereupon an aged retainer poisons everyone else with flykiller. This may be one of those cases in which the attempts of a Westerner to enter into the secrets of Japanese matrimonial life become frustrated; it is certainly impossible to divine the director's intention – how seriously, for instance, are we supposed to take this film?

No difficulties, however, need be encountered in three other Ichikawa films made (I anticipate a little) during the Sixties. *An Actor's Revenge* (1963) is a film in the grand style and acted as such by Kazuo Hasegawa – one of Japan's greatest *onnagata*, or male players of female rôles in the Kabuki theatre. The drama of the story lies in the contrast between the iron will of the man and the delicacy of his appearance and movements as a woman – all seen in a series of fine colour compositions in Cinemascope (a screen proportion which seems particularly well adapted to the Japanese visual style). It is also a satisfyingly simple story from the moment when, from the stage, the actor recognizes a businessman who, with two colleagues, has earlier swindled and ruined his parents to the point of suicide, and the pattern of revenge, interwoven as it were with the 'flower-path' of the Kabuki stage, begins to take its implacable course. Apart from the Kabuki sequences there are some marvellous exteriors (photography by Setsuo Kobayashi), especially at night. Exotic, strangely patterned, *An Actor's Revenge* approaches at moments the stature of classic drama.

From this bravura period piece Ichikawa turned (in the same year) to the reconstruction of a modern real-life saga – the lone voyage of young Kenichi Horie from Osaka to San Francisco in ninety-four days. But *Alone on the Pacific* is much more than a documentary. Drawing on Horie's actual diaries, Ichikawa concentrates on the youth's psychological reactions to solitude and to the perils of the ocean; and he does this in conjunction with a series of brilliantly conceived flashbacks (the construction of the film recalls that of *The Burmese Harp*) through which we see not only the difficulties he had in setting up the expedition, but also the personal reasons which impelled him to conceive the idea and carry it through. Aided by an exquisite perform-ance by Yujiro Ishihara, Ichikawa has created a film whose neat construction is in itself an aesthetic pleasure, and which is also a human document of charm and of a certain passion. Indeed, out of that passionate storm of tears when the typhoon and loneliness leave him soaked, defenceless, self-pitying, the young man gradually develops not merely a renewed belief but also a great strengthening of that very desire for independence, the 'getting away from it all', which was the original *raison d'être* of his journey. Thus at the end of the film, amid all the ballyhoo and razzmatazz of his triumphal arrival at San Francisco, he finds it simple and pleasant to fall asleep.

Alone in the Pacific is the most Western in feel of all Ichikawa's work. It is easy to comprehend the boy's ambition, to participate in his quarrels with his parents, his arguments with his boat-builder, and his rebuttals of the mockery of his friends. We observe here an obsession not with expiation, not with sexuality, not with revenge, but, quite simply, with the delights and dangers of freedom.

These delights must of course rest on some form of achievement, and Ichikawa pursued this idea further in his superb documentary on the 1964 Olympic Games in Tokyo. From the early sequences in which the runners – often seen from the viewpoint of a high-flying eagle – carry the Flame across the magnificent mountains and valleys; through the fabulous telephoto details of the contestants in their intimate personal struggles; and on to that incredible, seemingly unending pan shot of the Ethiopian Bikila winning the Marathon – *Tokyo Olympiad* has the authority of a master film-maker, and at long last matches, indeed supersedes, Riefenstahl's film of 1936.[1]

The prolific Teinosuke Kinugasa seems to have made no films of

---

[1] Since *Tokyo Olympiad* Ichikawa has made an immense serialization of *The Tale of Genji* for television; a co-production, partly animated, with an Italian company; and several documentaries.

particular note since his silent masterpieces of the Twenties – this despite
visits to Germany and to the Soviet Union (where he studied with
Eisenstein) – until in 1953 he made the extraordinary *Gate of Hell* (*Jigokumon*), starring the ubiquitous Machiko Kyo and Kazuo Hasegawa,
later to be the protagonist of *An Actor's Revenge*. The theme is
traditional to the Japanese theatre and therefore to that large area of
Japanese cinema concerned with the past – Mizoguchi's work in particular: the clash between passion and duty, and the redemption of man
by woman's faithfulness and self-sacrifice. Thus in *Gate of Hell* the
wife, learning that the warrior who loves her has reached such a point
of passion that he intends to kill her husband, substitutes herself for
him, so that it is she who is killed. Her lover takes holy orders and
begins a lifetime of expiation for his sins.

The film is played to an approximation of the formal style of
Kabuki – a style with which the Westerner needs to familiarize himself
before he can fully appreciate it. In his London lectures of 1929
Eisenstein pointed out that an actor on the Kabuki stage could by a
gesture create the effect of a close-up on all the members of his audience,
wherever they were sitting. The film can make a simple short-cut to
comprehension by the requisite change of camera position.[1] This may
eliminate some of the actor's skills; but in *Gate of Hell*, by bringing us
into close proximity with the coiled passions of the story, the very
formality of whose presentation adds to their intensity, Kinugasa helps
us to participate in the drama with the same concentration we would
give to, say, Euripides' *Antigone*.

Gate of Hell also made a sensation when it first came out because
of its beautiful colour photography by Kohei Sugiyama, long a master-
cameraman in black and white. This was an early example of the use
of Eastmancolour, a system which quickly proved its advantages over
the garishness of Technicolor and the sometimes too muted pastel
shades of Agfacolor; Sugiyama's patterns and colour-relationships,
deployed always to achieve the maximum simplicity of effect, were often
breath-taking. In hindsight they seem to me to have much in common
with those brought to *Death in Venice* by the photography of Pasquale
De Santis.

During the Fifties two of Japan's most veteran and finest film-
makers came to the height of their respective powers, and both found
in their latter years – as does happen with great artists – some extra
dimension of aesthetic expression. Both are now dead, and although

---

[1] Eisenstein was passionately interested in the relationship between Film and Kabuki.
See *The Film Sense* and *Film Form*, passim.

Ozu's last films were made in the Sixties it seems convenient to consider him and Mizoguchi together at this point, leaving the newer and sometimes disruptive elements in Japanese cinema for discussion in the next chapter.

It would hardly be possible for a Westerner (unless he devoted a very great deal of time to concentrated research) to acquire an adequate knowledge of the works of Kenji Mizoguchi – stretching as they do from the mid-Twenties to the mid-Fifties. But it seems possible to establish that his undoubted masterpiece is *Ugetsu Monogatari* (American title *Ugetsu*) which he made in 1953.

This film, in style and mood so different from *Rashomon* and *Seven Samurai*, created a deep impression when it was shown at the Venice Festival in 1953. Some were impressed by it because it was less directly 'realistic' than Kurosawa's work; though this was not exactly true unless we assume that the Western and Oriental definitions of realism differ fundamentally. *Ugetsu Monogatari* may indeed have much in common with the 'realism' of the medium's evidence in *Rashomon*; and it is interesting to note that Eric Rhode in this context refers to Ibsen's statement that 'Life is a contest between the phantoms of the mind'; he goes on to suggest that this attitude 'goes a long way towards explaining why Ibsen's realism has so much substance'. Thus the apparent insubstantiality of Mizoguchi's film, with its mingling of the ghost world and the real world, is in fact a delusion. Just as we cannot understand the actions of human beings unless we also understand their inner world, with its phantasies which are 'the primary content of unconscious mental processes, and condition the behaviour of even the most "normal" person', so also we cannot understand Mizoguchi's realism unless we realize that his ghostly convention represents 'the manner in which the past, with all its phantom memories, desires and histories, plays a vital part in the present and gives it meaning'.[1] Thus it is absolutely essential to accept the two potters, Genjuro and Tobei, and their families, as real people with real problems; to treat the film as a fairytale is to traduce Mizoguchi's intent entirely.

Ugetsu is, however, a moral tale. It is against the evils which come from war and from misplaced ambition; it is on the side of the artist, the craftsman, the tiller of the soil. Its message is that the mistakes men make, inevitable or no, are part of experience, and that from this comes the choice of loyalty against lying, love against lust. Thus, at

---

[1] Rhode's admirable essay appeared originally in *Sight and Sound* (Winter 1961–62), and has since been reprinted in *Renaissance of the Film*, ed. Julius Bellone, Collier-Macmillan, 1970.

the end of the film, when Tobei and his wife Ohama return home after their adventures (in which he has been the sinner, she more sinned against than sinning), it is she who says, as they re-enter their broken-down hovel, 'Let us now hope that our sufferings will not have been in vain'.[1]

The disruption of normal life by the intervention of outside forces sets the scene for certain departures from virtue which, though in theory they could be rejected, will in fact lead to paths of glory and of disaster; and through these we accompany the characters rather after the fashion of *The Pilgrim's Progress*, only with a great deal less overt moralizing. The great point is that we share in the reactions of the characters to events which are as mysterious or as obvious (and, disturbingly, inter-changeably so) to them as they are to us. At the end of the film, when the other potter, Genjuro, returns to his home, we accept the physical presence of his wife and the way she tends him as in former days. And it is with Genjuro that we wake in the morning to the truth that she is dead. The curious thing here is that we know, as he does not, that she has been murdered by robbers; but even so, the quiet realism by which Mizoguchi presents her at Genjuro's homecoming makes us feel that our eyes perhaps deceived us, that she was never killed at all. What then, is reality? We begin to realize that it involves things which are not what they seem, that there may be mirror realities in reflection or opposition, or even that there is a stream of ghostly existence running as a kind of parallel to our own, with branches reaching out to cross our lives at moments capriciously determined by fate.

Ugetsu Monogatari is a beautifully constructed film. To begin with we have the two potters, living with their wives in a small village, content with their work, content with their lot, humble though it be. But there are wars and rumours of wars. From out of nowhere come bandits who set about the pillage and destruction of the village. Tobei and Genjuro, like the others, go into hiding. When the bandits have left they return to the ruins and find that, by luck, their kilns have been left untouched. All this is portrayed with an almost elegant economy of visuals, especially in that use of the emphatic long-shot at which Mizoguchi is such a master.

This in effect has been the prologue. The destruction of the village triggers off the main action. While the other inhabitants return, as one would expect, to pick up the pieces and restore their homes, Tobei and Genjuro, each fired by hitherto latent personal ambitions, or perhaps

---

[1] I have been told that a different translation makes her say, 'Let us hope your future behaviour will ensure that our sufferings will not have been in vain'.

just daydreams – the one for military glory, the other for perfect love – decide to set off for the nearest town to realize their pots at the highest price instead of leaving them at the mercy of the bandits' next raid. With them go their wives and Genjuro's child. They find a small boat by the lakeside and decide to travel to the town by water. As the voyage begins an atmosphere of menace, of something doubtful and unknown, drifts over the screen like the waters and the mists of the lake itself. And here, with genius, Mizoguchi has his camera lens resting, as it were, on the water itself so that the fragile boat seems somehow to be suspended in a liquid void. Into this scene slides another boat; ghost or real? It is difficult to say at first, for its occupant is dying, having been slashed by pirates. As he dies, he gives them solemn warnings of the dangers of the lake. Appalled, Genjuro disembarks his wife Miyagi and their child and tells them to make their way back to the village. And then Genjuro, Tobei and Ohama continue their journey to the town.

At this point, thanks to skilful scripting by Matsutaro Kawaguchi and Giken Yoda, the film smoothly splits into two sections. To Genjuro, the romantic, there comes what seems to be the answer to all his desire in the form of an aristocratic lady, slender as a reed in the lake, who, with her aged servant, comes to the market, buys his wares, and entices him to carry them to her palace. She, it seems, is seeking to learn the secret of his art as a potter; he of course is seeking to possess her beautiful self, the exquisite Lady Wakasa. In scenes of calm beauty – cool rooms hung with silks, placid bathing pools, carpets of cushiony grass bordered by willow beyond which lies the sheen of the (ever dangerous) lake – the would-be lovers' desires go out to each other like the delicate fronds of a plant, and as the silken scarves and raiment billow in the breeze, Genjuro forgets his wife and child and his village. The Lady Wakasa asks him to marry her, and he agrees. At this very moment Miyagi is slain by robbers near the shores of the perilous lake. And soon Genjuro discovers the truth. The lady and her entourage are all ghosts. He takes his sword and with wide symbolic sweeps of anger and sadness drives all of them from the palace. Then, waking from a swoon,[1] he finds that not even the palace exists; he is in burnt ruins as grim as those of the home and village he has left.

In contrast is the brutal activity of Tobei's adventures. By the sale of *his* wares he makes enough money to buy the armour and accoutrements of a samurai. Stumbling quite by chance on a ceremonial execution he is able to steal and bring to a shogun's camp the head of

---

[1] Like Jean Marais after the first showdown with Death in Cocteau's *Orphée*.

an enemy warrior; and thus he qualifies, as fraudulently as has Genjuro
for his 'marriage', as an officer in the shogun's army. But in the meantime Ohama, like Miyagi, has fallen among thieves. She is set upon,
robbed and raped – a grim scene, with the gold pieces scattered over
her dishonoured body. She escapes with her life and, as Tobei has
deserted her, she becomes a prostitute. Time passes – some sort of time –
an exactness of hours, days, weeks is not required by this film – and
one fine day Tobei visits the whore-house and is accosted by his wife.
They are reconciled and, although there is no sign that Tobei is other
than successful as a warrior, they decide to return to the village together.
There is here, I think, the one flaw in the film's scripting or, alternatively, a motivation which eludes the Occidental mind. We know
Tobei has attained his military ambition by means of a downright
swindle; is he likely, in his success, to be so conscience-smitten?
Reconciliation with Ohama, yes perhaps; return to his ruined, humble
village, hardly.

Be that as it may, the threads are drawn together again; and the
two potters are back at their trade. All seems the same, yet all is
changed. Ohama has been scarred by lust and dishonour. Miyagi is no
more. The men have seen a world they wanted but to which they cannot
belong. Yet at the final moment of the film it is Miyagi's voice we hear,
saying in effect to Genjuro 'Lo! I am with you always, even to the end
of the world' – and, in that famous crane shot, Mizoguchi takes us up,
up into the sky, floats us above the village and field and toiling peasants
. . . . All perhaps, in the heart of eternity, *is* the same.

Magnificently photographed in black and white by Kazuo
Miyagawa, this is visually one of the most beautiful films ever made,
for the images throughout have the quality of being emotionally affecting
as well as compositionally satisfying. The acting is splendid (including
Machiko Kyo once again, as the ghostly Wakasa) and there is a
delicate soundtrack which includes admirable wisps of music by Fumio
Hayasaka.[1]

In the penultimate year of his life Mizoguchi made two colour
films, sometimes regarded as pot-boiling period pieces. This is true, I
suppose, of the first of them, *New Tales of the Taira Clan* (*Shin Heike
Monogatari*), in which Mizoguchi's touch is not all the time discernible –
though there is a marvellous torchlight procession through trees, and
the formal patterns of imperial ceremonials are, as ever, elegantly

---

[1] Hayasaka, one of Japan's finest film composers, also scored many of Kurosawa's
films, including *Rashomon*, *Ikiru* and *Seven Samurai*. He died before completing the score
of *I Live in Fear*.

drawn. The second film, on the other hand, entitled *The Princess Yang Kwei-Fei* (*Yohiki*) seems to me to be, despite a story somewhat perfunctorily developed at times, a film of delicate, elegiac beauty.

Based on an ancient Chinese legend, it contains all the ingredients – Cinderella, Joan of Arc, Haroun al Raschid, the lot. But basically it is the story of a lonely old emperor, enwrapped in the memories of his dead wife. As a result of court intrigues he suddenly finds himself presented with a scullery maid as beautiful as the woman he has lost; and this girl gradually comes to take her place. But in the end the intrigues lead to an uprising against him, and the girl is executed. Alone again with his memories, he can rejoin her only in death.

The trappings of this tale don't bear much examination, and some of the minor parts are played with an insensitivity unusual for a Mizoguchi film. But the relations between the Emperor and his Princess (very finely played by Masayuki Mori and Machiko Kyo – the Genjuro and Wakasa of *Ugetsu*) are excellently set forth, whether in intimate scenes or in set-pieces such as his disguised visit to the annual market and fair – a sequence in which Mizoguchi's unexpected yet quite simple camera angles add much to the feeling of his warm and unexaggerated acceptance by the common people. There is also one heavenly extreme long-shot of their visit to a garden foaming with peach blossom.

But the real meaning and feeling of the film come out in the opening and closing sequences which enframe all its action. At the beginning the camera moves slowly across the vista of a long corridor down which some men are approaching, and sweeps slowly through swaying silk curtains to reveal the aged Emperor, alone. By this time the men have reached the end of the corridor, and now confront the old man with an ultimatum from his son, who holds power in all but name: it is expedient that he should move into another dwelling place. With little hope but with as much vigour as he can muster, the old man, still dignified enough, makes his protest and, once they have withdrawn, turns back to the simulacrum of his lost love; and from here the long flashback action of the film proper begins.

At the end, after we have seen the execution of the Princess, with her touching farewell to her ladies, and her dignity as she gives the executioner her own silk scarf with which to take her life, and after they have brought her body to the sorrowing Emperor, the film comes back to him as the lonely old man in the palace from the opening sequence. From all those memories he receives only a solitudinous despair. He flings himself down on the floor and cries aloud for his lost Princess.

Now comes one of the most magical moments I know in cinema.[1] The camera very gently tilts up from the Emperor, and rests on the empty palace room, with its cool, precise décor. And we hear the voice of the Princess Yang Kwei-Fei answering the old man. 'Yes, here I am,' she says; and we know, without seeing, that the old man is dead. 'Come,' says her voice, 'Come, for now we can be happy together forever.' Then he replies to her, and the hope in his voice soon turns to joy; and the camera starts to move gently across the empty chambers and corridors, following their invisible persons through the curtains which sway slightly in the breeze of their unseen passing, and their voices rise and fall, and dissolve into happy laughter while a leaf drifts lightly along the floor in their wake . . .

When Yasujiro Ozu died in December 1963, Chishu Ryu, the man who had played the leading rôle (there were no stars) in every film he made from 1948 on[2], put down some reminiscences during which he said,

'As to Mr Ozu's way of direction, he had made up the complete picture in his head before he went on the set, so that all we actors had to do was to follow his directions, from the way we lifted and dropped our arms to the way we blinked our eyes. In a sense, we felt quite at home when we were playing in his pictures. Even if I did not know what I was doing and how those shots would be connected in the end, when I looked at the first screening I was often surprised to find my performance far better than I had expected . . . (In another picture) Mr Ozu asked me to play an old man. Although I did my best in making up for this part, every device turned out to be a failure. Mr Ozu happened to be on the set. He called me in, and with a few touches from my make-up things, succeeded in a moment in producing a wonderful figure of an old man. I must confess that I felt then as if I were only the paints or some other materials with which Mr Ozu painted pictures . . . And once a film was completed, even if the actors' performances were poor, Mr Ozu never complained of it. Even when we were sure that he must have had complaints in his mind, he took all the responsibilities on himself and never spoke of them to others. This, alone, gives one some idea of his character.'[3]

This evidence is almost identical with that given by actors who worked with Carl Theodor Dreyer and Robert Bresson, and it is

[1] A moment which is clearly an extension of the idea of the final sequence of *Ugetsu Monogatari*.

[2] He also played some part or other in every film Ozu made with the exception of two.

[3] Article in *Sight and Sound*, Spring 1964.

interesting to note that Dreyer, late in life, expressed a strong interest in Japanese cinema; there are indeed in *Gertrud* quite a few shots taken very much from Ozu's standard camera position; Gertrud's collapse while she is singing at the reception is a notable example.

Most Japanese directors, and certainly Mizoguchi and Kurosawa, found it easy to move from films of contemporary life to period films and back again; for these two genres were the backbone of Japanese cinema, just as in India there were the two categories of the religious or quasi-religious 'musicals' and the 'social' dramas or comedies.[1] But Ozu confined himself, throughout his long and fruitful career, solely to the making of *shomin-geki* pictures – that is, films about modern life in areas ranging from the proletarian to the middle-class; in fact nearly all his films are concerned with the urban middle-class.

For the Japanese themselves his films accurately record the feeling and flavour of middle-class life. They are concerned almost exclusively with home and family life; even love, as Donald Richie has pointed out on several occasions, is for Ozu an element in family relationships rather than an expression of romantic passion. Yet his films, now that, however belatedly, they are getting shown in Western countries, have an appeal which goes far beyond the interest of viewing the social habits of an exotic 'death-oriented people . . . turning toward and confronting in their own way the chaos of living".[2]

Ozu's films, in fact, have an extra appeal to Westerners because they invariably portray aspects of Japanese social and familial life which are by now irrevocably subject to occidental influences while at the same time retaining attitudes which have nothing whatever to do with the West. Apart from the intense pleasure we get from Ozu's personal artistry, we have the additional bonus of seeing the outward trappings of our own social and procedural behaviour from a new and often surprising angle. In the occidental world to be really drunk, as opposed to tipsy, is generally regarded as a social misdemeanour; in Japan no such sanctions exist, as anyone can bear witness having seen respectable Tokyo or Osaka businessmen emerging from the bars they visit at the end of the day's work before they go home. In an Ozu film the head of the family, returning home drunk, receives not a rocket but a certain sympathy, as though he had got caught in a shower on the way; certainly nothing stronger than an expression of gentle reproof.

[1] Japanese cinema, however, has a greater variety of styles and types within these two groups, which originally arose from films reflecting the split in Japanese drama around the turn of the century between Shimpa – period and traditional – and Shingeki – the new theatre.

[2] *The Japanese Movie* by Donald Richie, Ward Lock, 1966.

In this world whose difference to our own is emphasized by its similarities, Ozu, in film after film, plays variations on universal family themes – the relationships between husband and wife, brother and sister, parents and children, and in-laws of all kinds; the problems of courtship, of arranged marriages, of fashion and of finance; and the ceremonies of birth, marriage and death.

It is a world which is conveyed to us through a filmic technique which Ozu has stripped of all elaboration. The camera angle seldom varies, being centred on the action from a position a little above ground level. There are no fades, wipes, dissolves. Each sequence is introduced by a series of simple establishing shots – atmospheric and temporal as well as geographical – presented in a cool and completely unfussy manner. Nor is there any significant variation in editing tempo. Ozu's films tend to proceed at an ambling pace, and at moments of climax they slow down rather than speed up. Once one is accustomed to this unpretentious *andante*, a slight change of pace one way or the other is enough to quicken the nerves.

Why aren't Ozu's films dull? The answer is that he is a wizard storyteller, that he is always in love with all the characters in his films (good and bad alike), and that his scripts are invariably first-class in detail as well as in overall shape. An Ozu film is always intriguing because we share with him the pleasure of discovering the different facets of all the characters and their relationships to each other *at the same time as he does*. There is a continuous process of revelation, and we find ourselves in that real world of human give-and-take in which there is forever some aspect of a person yet to be revealed or, perhaps, to remain forever hidden.

In these films everything and nothing happens. Their plots are slender, to say the least; the cast list isn't overlarge and the relationships between the characters are not noted for their psychological complexities (which, if they are there, are already built-in). Yet the films and the people in them unfold before us like those paper flowers – also Japanese – which open gently to reveal their petals when we drop them into a bowl of water.

An Autumn Afternoon (1962) was his last and perhaps his most perfect film, though some may feel that *Tokyo Story* (1953) runs it very close.[1] It is about a businessman, a widower, with a married son living away from home, and a daughter and a younger son living in his house with him – the daughter looking after him as his wife would do were she

---

[1] The gentle similarities of Ozu's titles can be confusing – *Early Spring*, *Early Summer*, *Tokyo Story*, *Tokyo Twilight*, *Early Autumn*, *Late Autumn*, *An Autumn Afternoon*.

still alive. Talking among his friends, he begins to realize that it is more than high time that his daughter should be married off; he has procrastinated because her 'wifely' attentions have been so convenient. As the arrangements for the marriage gradually develop he begins also to realize – and to see reflected in life around him – the loneliness of old age, or even just plain loneliness, which is liable to creep up after the younger members of a family have 'spread their wings'. Thus it is a film about all of us, about the hurts which come from putting off decisions too long and perhaps from making them too late.

Early in *An Autumn Afternoon* Shuhei, the widower, combines with some of his friends to entertain to dinner their ex-headmaster, now getting on in years. The old boy duly arrives in his best suit and by the end of the evening is well and truly drunk. Shuhei takes him home, only to find that this headmaster, once such an imposing figure to them, is now scratching a living running a cheap noodle restaurant in a working-class district with the assistance of a middle-aged daughter who has sacrificed everything for his welfare and whose chances of marriage are long since passed. Next day Shuhei and his colleagues put together some money for the old man. Shuhei goes back with it to the noodle shop, where now all is sobriety and where the old headmaster is deeply embarrassed at the proposed gift. In the midst of all this (typical Ozu), Shuhei is suddenly accosted by a man who served under him in the Navy during the war and who takes him off to a local bar to carouse and talk of old times; in which bar (again typical Ozu), there is a good-looking woman in early middle-age whom he persuades himself looks like his dead wife. He forms a habit of going to this bar, and eventually takes his sons, who say the lady's not the slightest like their late mother and he must be off his chump. Thus, and in greater proliferation than there is time for here, a whole series of tenuous threads are gradually woven into a web of surpassing beauty, delicacy and strength.

At the end of the film, in the blank aftermath of the wedding breakfast, Shuhei returns home pickled. The house seems to be full of empty rooms. A dog barks. His young student son – the only remaining habitant of the house now that his daughter has gone – advises him to 'lay off the saké', and shortly after remarks 'The hell with it – I'm going to bed' – and does. Sobering slowly, Shuhei sits down to begin somehow to reconcile himself with life, however late it may be. And there, in an extreme long shot as exquisite as anything ever screened by this master of pictorial composition, we leave him and alas, Ozu – perhaps the most complete artist that the Japanese cinema has yet produced.

IV

The Indian cinema was pretty hard hit by World War II. Congress, while naturally abhorring the Nazi philosophy, did not feel like collaborating with the British who were, from the Indian point of view, preventing the millions of the sub-continent from attaining freedom from the tyranny of the Raj. The British set up a film organization to promote the use of films in the war effort, and handed to the British documentary director Alexander Shaw the thankless task of getting this off the ground in the teeth of much opposition from the film people. This he achieved by a superb deployment of diligence, tact and charm. Films were made; but in the long run it became necessary to make their public showing compulsory.

Meantime there was rationing of film stock; and through this the Raj was able (in addition to the existing and still insane censorship system) to exercise a certain control over subject-matter and its treat-ment. Amidst all the black markets (which for Indians, remember, represented a high form of patriotism) was one very specialized manifestation, involving large concealed payments to the film stars; this very soon got out of control with the result that production costs soared to unviable heights.[1] Meantime the industry was thrown into other confusions arising from the Japanese entry into the war; some regarded them as potential liberators from the British, while others thought them to be a threat to India's future.

Out of this confusion, and out of the confusion which followed the coming of Independence in 1947, there eventually emerged a Government Film Unit which was really a continuation of the organiza-tion set up by the British at the start of the war. Rechristened Films Division, this organization has over the years come to play an increasingly important rôle in Indian life. Under producers such as Ezra Mir, J. S. Bhownagary and K. L. Khandpur, and with the assist-ance of outside consultants such as the Canadian James Beveridge, it has built up a huge and wide-ranging system of production and dis-tribution, and has also encouraged to a limited degree the activities of independent non-government film-makers.[2] By 1968 Films Division was making over 142 films and 52 newsreels every year, these being released

---

[1] Budgets in 1939 averaged Rs 90,000 per film; by the end of the war they had risen to around Rs 400,000–500,000. (*Indian Film* by Barnouw and Krishnaswamy, Columbia University Press, 1963.)

[2] Shell, via its Burmah-Shell Film Unit, made some excellent films in the early 1950s including Paul Zils' *Textiles*, Fali Billimoria's *Village in Travancore*, and Hari Das Gupta's *Panchupti*: after which, for reasons shrouded in mystery, it was disbanded.

in 14 different languages to an audience estimated at 30 millions a week. As with the British organization which preceded it, the showing of certain Films Division products is compulsory in all public cinemas. When one considers the enormous problems facing India – food supply and the population explosion in particular – the value of the visual media, and film not least, becomes obvious.

A remarkable and, for India at least, very unusual series of Films Division productions is called *Actual Experience*. In these, ordinary men and women talk direct to the camera about their reaction to and feelings about various forms of contraception and sterilization which they have undergone. Other films of a similar nature are shown widely in rural areas together with series about improvements in agriculture, often through mobile cinemas. For more sophisticated urban audiences experimental films, often of high cinematic interest, like those of Pramod Pati, are made; and on more general levels there are a number of really beautiful films on Indian art – notably *Radha and Krishna* (1957) and *Akbar* (1967), both by Bhownagary; *The House that Ananda Built* (1967), a human and touching document about a humble peasant and his life, directed by Fali Billimoria; S. Sukdhev's coruscating and commentary-less feature length survey of the sub-continent made for the Montreal Exposition, *India 67*, in which *cinéma-vérité* is combined with the very best of Dziga Vertov technique; and *I Am 20*, a fascinating series of interviews with young people from all over India who were born on Independence Day in 1947, and who here talk about their hopes and feelings in relation to their country and to themselves.

Thus from 1948 onwards this form of government film-making – not dissimilar to that undertaken in Britain, Canada, Australia and elsewhere – has existed in parallel with the established entertainment film industry which, despite various ups and downs, has continued to pour out its endless musical films and social melodramas or comedies, all of them featuring stars whose popularity in Indian eyes is as great as was that of the Valentinos and Swansons of yesteryear in the West.

In the meantime a young man living in Calcutta was, in 1956, to astonish both India and the world by making the first of a series of films which established him unquestionably as one of the really great artists in the history of cinema. This was the Bengali Satyajit Ray, and the film, which had taken him five years of desperate and penurious struggle to make, was *Pather Panchali*.[1]

---

[1] At one point, Ray has stated, 'To be able to continue, I sold my library, my art books, my mother's jewellery and my wife's'. (Interview with Georges Sadoul, 1965, published in *Cahiers du Cinéma* and subsequently in *Montage*, Bombay, 1966.)

Interestingly enough, just before this phenomenon, there appeared two John the Baptists, so to speak, to prepare for Ray's coming. In 1953 Bimal Roy directed *Two Acres of Land* (*Do Bigha Zamin*), and in the following year K. A. Abbas made *Munna*.

Both of these films had a truth and sincerity about them which was almost unheard of in the world of Indian entertainment films. *Two Acres of Land* is a straightforwardly heartrending tale of the efforts of a Bengali peasant to hang on – despite disasters of drought and debt – to his small but precious parcel of agricultural land. The only way to do this is to try to earn some money in Calcutta, 'the city that takes everything and gives nothing'; but he and his son, lost and bewildered in the crowded slums, fail. For, by the time they have saved up just enough money to redeem their little farm, they find that it has already been sold up to someone who wants to build a factory. This sad story, very well played by Balras Sahni as the father and Rattan Kumar as the boy, was admittedly influenced (as also later was *Pather Panchali*) by De Sica's *Bicycle Thieves*, and none the worse for that.[1]

K. A. Abbas – already known for a few films which tried to deal with social problems – achieved considerable notoriety with *Munna*, for it was said to be the first Hindi film ever to be made without any singing or dancing. This is a picaresque story about a boy who escapes from an institution for orphans to search the world for a mother who he is sure must somewhere exist. The incidents which occur during his wanderings range from the comic to the tragic; the boy is very appealing, and the film is realistic enough to remind one once again of the Italian neo-realists. In complete contrast, incidentally, Abbas in his next film, *Awara*, launched one of the most successful Indian film stars of all time, Raj Kapoor; the film included a pop song which swept through Turkey, Iran and the entire Arab world as well as the Soviet Union.

Then came *Pather Panchali*. I have never forgotten the private projection at the British Film Institute during which I experienced that shock of recognition and excitement when, all unexpectedly, one is suddenly exposed to a new and incontrovertible work of art. Everything struck home: the scene in the field of flowers when Apu and Durga first lay their eyes on a train – that symbol of hope and ambition which runs through the whole Apu Trilogy; the characterization of Chunibala Devi as Old Indir, especially at the moment of her casually tragic death;

---

[1] Some years later, in 1959, Bimal Roy made a feature on that most difficult of all subjects, the Untouchables. This story of a high caste young man wanting to marry a harijan girl was faced up to with realism and honesty, which made a refreshing change from the average feature film approach, by which this sort of problem was invariably solved by a tragic but conveniently satisfactory death (such as occurs in E. M. Forster's novels).

and the unexpected dénouement (deliberately turned by Ray into a non-dénouement) when, just before the family leaves the village for Benares, Apu happens to find the missing necklace and knows that Durga really did steal it . . . so that we re-live in a different way and in immediate memory poor little Durga's death during that appalling storm – the same storm which cracks and rumbles and pushes against walls and roofs and windows in nearly every film made by Ray as inevitably as mirrors reflect back other dramas, from the cracked one at the start of *Abhijan* through the little one in which Apu, in *Pather Panchali*, admires his Rajah moustache, to the gigantic and tarnished glass in which so much of the tragedy of *Jalsaghar* is reflected.

When *Pather Panchali* was first shown, the full significance of Satyajit Ray's conception was still hidden from the world. It was three years before the Apu Trilogy was complete; for although *Aparajito* (*The Undefeated*) followed closely after *Pather Panchali* in 1956, *Apur Sansar* (*The World of Apu*) was not finished until 1959, two other films having been made in between; *Paras Pathar* (*The Philosopher's Stone*), the story of a poor man who receives the gift of Midas, and Ray's finest film *Jalsaghar* (*The Music Room*).

The three Apu films have often been compared to Donskoi's Gorky Trilogy, and there are indeed certain parallels such as the grand-mothers in *The Childhood of Maxim Gorky* and *Pather Panchali*. But Ray himself has disclaimed being influenced by Donskoi's work, much though he admires it; and the individualities of the two directors, no less than their national *Weltanschauungen*, differ considerably. Gorky's work, and Donskoi's interpretation of it, implies a future revolution. Ray's does not. He is concerned with the past and the present rather than with the future; or to put it another way, he is only concerned with the future as a shadowy projection of the present.[1] In this he truly reflects the outlook not only of his native Bengal but of most of India; and behind lies a whole philosophical and religious attitude in which time catches itself by the tail, in which past, present and future some-times are not distinguished from each other – a perspective in which the importance of death is sometimes eschatologically disregarded.

When Apu's family, and later Apu himself, think of the future it is in terms of the most modest ambition – if indeed the word is not too positive in this connection. The object, really, is somehow to survive. The object is to obtain a modicum of money, a modicum of education, to be able to afford to keep one's wife and to have the good fortune to see one's children grow to adulthood. These hopes, in India, are not so

[1] Though *The Adversary* and *Company Limited* may indicate a change of view.

often realized; but like all true human aspirations they carry with them
an imperishable glory, and it is this which Ray celebrates in his films.
Bound up with this is an indissoluble sense of family. In *Aparajito*
the filmic structure is built round the father's death and, through the
resultant development of Apu as an individual, round the tragedy of
his drawing apart from his mother so that the love and respect he still
bears her are obscured by his own desire to learn, to better himself.
This effect is heightened by the shape of the film. Ray, unusually, has
managed to use restlessness as a method of construction. From Harihar's
death onwards, Apu is always on the move. To begin with there is the
decision to return to the village which will, from Sarbojaya's point of
view, be a fatal mistake; after the big city Apu will not re-adapt, and
'the transformation which comes to Apu with adolescence becomes
intensified when Pinaki Sen Gupta, as the boy Apu, is replaced by
S. Ghosal as the youth Apu, who has captured the interest of his schoolmaster, a teacher utterly different in outlook from the eccentric Pandit-
grocer . . . in *Pather Panchali*'.[1] After this changeover, brilliantly
managed by Ray so that we feel no dislocation in our acquaintanceship
with Apu,[2] his return to the city is inevitable; off he goes, uncomfortable
in lace-up boots he has never worn before and into a house which has
that ultimate of all marvels – electricity. Against this new life Ray plays
the increasing ill-health of his mother of which we, but not Apu, are
aware. He comes home for a holiday and still doesn't notice her illness
(which indeed she does all she can to conceal). He is as thoughtless
and bound up in himself as all young men tend to be at that age.

Here Ray introduces an episode of great psychological subtlety.
When Apu is due to return to the city, Sarbojaya deliberately 'forgets'
to wake him in the morning in the hopes that he may miss the train
(that train again, the arbiter of fate which, with the ubiquitous telegraph
pole and the cricket bat, probably remains as the only lasting contribution of the British Raj to the Indian sub-continent). But Apu
wakes up himself and, angry, rushes off to catch the train. Then suddenly, on a whim it seems, he changes his mind and goes back to the
house to spend one more day with his mother . . . and is it not perhaps
the memory of this that faintly persists as, later, alone and in sadness,
she sits dying under a tree and gazes with unseeing eyes at the myriad
fireflies of the Indian night?

But the episodic restlessness is not yet over. A postcard to

[1] *Satyajit Ray: Portrait of a Director* by Marie Seton, Dennis Dobson, 1971.
[2] Whereas Donskoi's switch to the older Maxim in the last part of the Gorky trilogy
is definitely disruptive.

Calcutta brings Apu hurrying home; and this is the first time he realizes that Sarbojaya is ill. He arrives too late; the funeral pyre is already cold. Apu weeps.

When I said earlier that in India less regard is sometimes felt for the importance of death, I was referring to a general philosophical attitude about death itself and not to the emotions of bereavement. Throughout the Apu Trilogy the impact of death is traumatic, dramatic.[1] Durga's death in *Pather Panchali*, which takes place in a raging storm that wrecks the family home, is followed by a terrible sequence in which Sarbojaya sits mute and stunned until Harihar returns, ignorant of what has happened, and bearing gifts; then she gives one terrible, unearthly cry that seems to tear the world apart. Conversely, when, in *Aparajito*, Harihar breathes his last breath, a swirl of pigeons rises from the Benares roofs and sweeps across the holy city and the holy river – an image that in cold print may sound banal but is pure poetry in the context that Ray places it.

In due course Apu returns to Calcutta and the stage is set for *Apur Sansar*. In this film Ray does so much more than show a young man growing into adult life and eventually accepting its cyclic round of sorrow and joy. Apu's world becomes a parable of the whole world. Without heavy symbolism or sequences deliberately fraught with meaning, Apu summarizes man's desire to create, man's ability to rise above suffering and to face fate in the eyes, and somehow to find, even from his worst mistakes, the path to re-birth; though first of all Apu, utterly stricken by his wife's death, reacts by running away from life (he nearly commits suicide under a train) and, in a sequence of desolating and simple beauty, commits the pages of his novel, one by one, to the wind and the water.

In *Apur Sansar* one can sense that Ray had already reached full maturity as an artist in directing *Jalsaghar*. Otherwise I don't think he could have achieved the extraordinary intensity of the wedding sequence in which Apu is caught up in a grotesque situation only possible in a community which has 'arranged' marriages with no meeting between the participants until the actual day of the ceremony. At the climactic moment the curtains of the bridegroom's palanquin part and reveal him to be a lunatic, a maniac. This is too much, and the girl's parents call off the wedding. Then, as the situation gradually disintegrates, the girl's family beg Apu to take the bridegroom's place because astrologically it is certain that this day, and this day only, is propitious fo

---

[1] Ray once said (to Marie Seton, op. cit.), 'People have asked me why there is much death in my films. I answer this question with "in life there is so much death ".'

her marriage. Apu refuses. 'We are living in the twentieth century,' he says. 'I know that,' is the reply, 'but, Apu, you know and I know that certain things in this country have not changed.' 'But *I* have changed,' answers Apu. Yet, as darkness falls, a number of obscure, uncertain influences begin to operate. Ray shows this by contrasting Apu, slowly and almost against his will, approaching the house again with the mad groom's party, complete with brass band and all the rest of the paraphernalia, trailing disconsolately away. A child is crying. Apu comes back to the house and weds Aparna. The whole strange set-up, and Apu's impulsive gesture, which must be so completely outside occidental experience, is made completely acceptable by Ray's treatment of it; and as time flows on and Apu and Aparna come to grow together in a nigh-perfect relationship, the wedding episode seems to have become the most normal thing in the world.

There are two other unforgettable moments in *Apur Sansar*. The first is that sudden, vicious blow with which Apu strikes the friend who tells him of Aparna's death; it brings home Apu's shock to us with a physical sting like Sarbojaya's terrible cry in *Pather Panchali*.

The second, of course, is the magical sequence at the end of the film which brings together Apu and the son he has rejected because it was his birth that caused Aparna's death. This scene, in a landscape of utter desolation, begins with Kajal throwing stones at this stranger who is in fact his father. And it ends with the heart-grabbing moment when the boy, still ignorant of the truth, but with a sudden change of heart, comes to join up with the stranger who, he begins to believe, may be able to lead him to his father . . .

In the historical sense, and like so many of Ray's films, the Apu Trilogy is about the past – the past of forty or fifty years ago. So too are *The Postmaster*, *Charulata*, *Devi* and *Jalsaghar*. Ray himself has said,

> 'What I look for in a story, primarily, are certain logical aspects of human relationships. Some of them have a timeless quality . . . while others may be more specifically related to a particular period – either in the past . . . or the present.'[1]

and it is interesting to note that he regards the Apu Trilogy as timeless and *Jalsaghar* as related to a period. On the whole his earlier films about the present were less successful; this was certainly so in the case of *Nayak* (1966), filmed entirely on a railway train[2] and consisting of almost continuous dialogue.

[1] Interview in *Montage*, Bombay, 1966.
[2] 'A joke current in Calcutta film circles is that no movie has yet been produced in Bengal that hasn't a train in it. The train is symbolic of missed connections, of forever

In the timeless, period, or nostalgic world of writers like Tagore and Bannerjee, Satyajit Ray seems particularly at home; not that he is a slavish imitator or translator. The madman who administers such a shock to us in *The Postmaster* is a brilliant invention added to the Tagore story by Ray; so too is nearly all of *Samapti* from the wedding night onward, including that incredibly long close-shot of Mrinmoyee as she tries to opt out of life by lying in her room and doing nothing. This shot, with the outside world heard only on the soundtrack, or visible only in the details of people's hands or feet as they come to her room, is a tremendous *tour de force*, and the tragico-farcical ending of it, as someone dangles the corpse of Chorky, her pet squirrel, in front of her eyes, is quite perfect.

Jalsaghar itself is a large elaboration by Ray from a short story by Tara Shanker Bannerjee,[1] and represents, as I have already indicated, Ray's most perfect achievement to date. It is a story about the collapse of a zamindar – a member of the landed gentry – set not in the fine flush of the post-Independence days, but way back in the old days of the British Raj. The period, judging from the automobiles and other evidence, is the late Twenties. *Jalsaghar* is about the attempt of one individual not just to live in the past but actually to try to drag the past into the present with his own bare hands. As for the future – if there ever was one – it has vanished the moment his wife and son are drowned; and, at the very end, it is back into the past that he magnificently rides, proud on a proud horse.

Jalsaghar is a film which carries not one single ounce of spare flesh. In its ninety-five minutes of running time there is not one second of superfluity. Every image, every sound makes its exact contribution – no more, no less – to the tragedy. For, despite the humorous observations and all the varied aspects of household comedy, tragedy it is – the tragedy of a wilful but extremely attractive old layabout who refuses to face facts but, in the final event, reveals all the highest dignity of an aristocrat in the best sense of that often misused word. When he tells his faithful retainer to lay on a big party in the Music Room, the reply is that there is no money. But there *must* be *something*, he imperiously replies. 'There's some jewellery,' answers the servant, 'but it's the last.'

---

continuing goals, of existentially ambiguous meetings and partings. The train, as the contemporary steel *linga*, is apparently a profound phallic symbol, and the Bengali imagination . . . finds much romance and beauty in trains' (from a review of *Nayak* by Professor P. Lal in *Montage*: the same issue contains the entire script of the film).

[1] Not to be confused with the Bannerjee who wrote the novel on which *Pather Panchali* is based.

'Last!' thunders His Honour Biswambhar Roy, 'How can you say "Last"? There's no such word!'

But there is. And that is the tragedy.

The infinitude of detail in this film is not a decoration, but an integral part of its construction to which Bansi Chandragupta's inspired art direction and Subrata Mitra's[1] equally inspired camerawork fully contribute. The vast mirror in which the zamindar can see the reflection of himself and his guests is just that amount tarnished to make its point. On the walls of the almost empty great hall hang the portraits of his family; over that of himself in all the glory of his manhood strolls a large spider. To these portraits (including that of his dead son) he raises his glass as he talks in English of 'the blood in my veins' and, in a final flourish of pride and dignity, drinks a toast 'To you . . . my noble ancestors'. But there are cobwebs on the great chandelier, and as the camera restlessly tracks in, past the edge of a table which has caught the white of the moonlight, a dog barks, bats fly down the corridor, and at last, in the enormous tarnished mirror, Biswambhar Roy confronts his real self . . .

It would be impossible to overpraise the performance of the late Chhabi Biswas in the part. The puffy eyes, the full, rather decadent mouth, the arrogant, selfish poses, the petulance, the dignity – they all come together into a deeply understanding portrait of someone who against all odds demands and receives our love; and our hearts are rent at the sight of this old man sinking more and more inexorably into a suffocating, desolating loneliness. There are three particular highpoints. There is the opening scene, when we see him for the first time in his shabby but once elegant dressing gown, sitting in his shabby (but still gold and brocade) armchair on his shabby roof terrace by his shabby and empty pool; and he says suddenly, 'What month is it?' All loneliness, all solitude, lies in that question. Then there is that terrible moment when, in a landscape as desolate as that in which Apu confronts Kajal, Biswambhar stands with the body of his drowned son in his arms. And above all there is that great moment during the very last party he gives in the Music Room – a party designed for the final putting down of the rich upstart Ganguli. The old glories are revived and the rich rugs are spread. The most expensive and popular dancer of the day (whom Ganguli thought no one but he could afford) is there with her orchestra. Then, as her dance reaches its climax, the upstart

[1] Mitra has photographed all Ray's films except *Rabindranath Tagore*, *Three Daughters*, *Abhijan* and *Kapurush-o-Mahapurush*, which were in the hands of the equally talented Soumendou Roy.

Ganguli makes a move to throw a generous rupee-tribute to her. Down on to his wrist, like a guillotine, flashes the crook of an elegant Bond Street walking stick. With him pinned there, helpless, the old man, with a gesture of ineffable scorn and dignity, tosses across to the singer an elegant bag which we know contains not only a more than generous payment but also the last, the once impossible last, of the zamindar's wealth. And there is another thing we know. It is that Mr Ganguli, for all his wealth, would never have the taste to buy a walking stick like that or, for that matter, to realize the vulgarity of his motor horn which plays 'Colonel Bogey' as he passes, in a cloud of dust, the zamindar's more dignified though no doubt less useful status symbol, an elephant.

I had almost forgotten to add that the film is also about music, and is full of music. The two set pieces in the Music Room are carried out by Ray with a panache which entirely disguises their length; and somehow we come to share and feel the appreciation of music by this man who loved it so much and who 'did all the things with it that make people human, he loved it, he showed it off, he showed off about it, he guarded it and he was selfish'.[1] That is all. One morning, he mounts his horse and rides to the beach. And the last shot is a long, low, sideways track which ends on his unwound, crumpled turban lying in the damp sand.

Six years later Ray travelled even further back in time with *Charulata* (1964), based on a Tagore story. Bourgeois rather than aristocratic (Biswambhar Roy is a million miles away), it is truly Victorian in thought and mood. Ray has superbly recreated the influence of the British Raj on the liberal-revolutionary-yet-Tchehovian-if-not-Jamesian intellectuals of the late 1870s – a period during which the husband, savouring the splendour of his young cousin's proposed visit to England (he never goes, of course), can roll round his tongue talismanic words – 'Macaulay! . . . Gladstone! . . .', and a well-bound book or the smell of newsprint is worth a thousand frangipanni trees.

Also, and above all, *Charulata* is a film of perspectives. An elaborately designed set, involving different levels and some elements of false perspective, enables the characters (and the camera) to move around as freely as the breeze or the sudden storm-wind which billows out the curtains and rattles the shutters. Nostalgic music by Ray himself, Indian in essence but delightfully and curiously reminiscent of Mendelssohn's Scottish Symphony, also drifts breezelike through the film. The people of the story – the husband devoted to his wife but

[1] Review by Nisha de Cunha, lecturer at St Xavier's College, Bombay, in *Montage*.

neglecting her in his devotion to his liberal newspaper; the wife, moon-
ing around the house and peering from windows through opera-glasses
at people passing in the street outside; the bright young cousin who,
entirely by mistake, arouses her love; her brother, brought in to manage
the paper by her husband (to please her) and his rather vulgar wife,
who decamp with the money – all move through the patterns of a
kind of Pinero melodrama and yet remain amazingly true, amazingly
alive.

Charulata is a film of nuances, a film in which what is not said
is more important than what is. It is no chance that at the end, when the
deceived husband (though not really deceived, just aware that a thought
of deception had been there), lying on the beach in grey weather and
with a solitary and slightly ridiculous seabird stalking the sand in the
background, comes to terms with his pretty wife for a new paper to be
run jointly by the two of them – at the end, as their hands stretch
tentatively towards each other, as their fingers are about to touch, the
image is frozen. What Ray is here saying is, I am sure, not 'What will
happen next?' but 'Who now can feel secure?' The embossed Victorian
wallpapers, the hand-embroidered kerchiefs or slippers, the vast bed,
the crockery, the garden, the servants – all are seen, in Penelope
Houston's evocative phrase, as 'an expression of a world which has
stopped waiting for something to happen'.[1] Poor Bhupati! For all his
literary and political skills and enthusiasms he is, like the best, like the
rest of us, 'but shadow'.

If Charulata has not got that curious inner lovingness with which
Ray pervaded Jalsaghar, it does have a gentle evocation of a period and
of people almost playing at living, of ambitions whose fulfilment is not
really desired; and all these are expressed to the full through Chandragupta's designs and set-dressing no less than through the beautiful
movements of Madhabi Mukerjee as Charu and Soumitra Chatterjee
as Amal.

After Charulata Ray's inspiration suffered a brief check. Kapurush-
o-Mahapurush (The Coward and the Holy Man), made in 1965, was by
all accounts a minor work; Nayak I have already referred to; and
Chiriakhana (1967) was a 'detective' film made by a group of Ray's
assistants under his general supervision. He was eventually pressured
into taking directorial credit, but although 'quite pleased' with it,
'thought it unsuited for export'.[2]

But during the next three years Ray came right back on form

[1] Sight and Sound, Winter 1965–66.
[2] Marie Seton, op. cit.

with three films of widely contrasting subjects, styles and treatments. *Goupy Gyne, Bagha Byne* (1968–69)[1] was based on a fairy story written by Ray's grandfather. The fantasy adventures of the two boys Goupy and Bagha – a kind of Laurel and Hardy couple – had an open-air pantomime quality, and the highly episodic structure of the film was held together by Ray's own musical score. This was followed by a slender, tender, dreamy little masterpiece, *Days and Nights in the Forest* (1969–70). The story is of the slightest. Four young men set out for a few days' holiday in the country. Their nicely contrasted characters are seen, separately and together, in relation to the people they meet after settling down in an empty house in the woods. Against the subtle beauties of nature we observe the nuances of a social comedy. The delicacy of Ray's treatment and the disguised complexities of its development recall Renoir's influence on Ray and, for that matter, Renoir's own *Une Partie de Campagne* and *Déjeuner sur l'Herbe*.

Then in 1971 Ray made a film on a serious modern theme. *Pratidwandi*, also known as *The Adversary* and *Siddhartha and the City*, is about a young medical student looking for a job in contemporary Calcutta. Here we have Ray in his most perceptively realistic mood. The film builds up *via* an increasing sense of frustration to scenes of rebellion and violence, interspersed with the young student's personal contacts and in particular his growing love affair with a charmingly unpredictable young lady. It is a film which glows with the warmth of Ray's sympathy for the young, and especially for those many of them who have become the victims of an effete and desiccated bureaucracy; and the final section, in which the boy gives up his ambitions and settles for a minor medical job in a distant country town, is embellished by a ravishing snatch of bird-song which entwines precious moments of love and emotion into a finely patterned *envoi*. In *The Adversary* Ray uses some of the latest technical tricks. His excursions into negative are not always very satisfactory, but his use of flashes is splendid. Apart from flashbacks to memories of childhood, he also uses flash-forwards to indicate a person's thoughts or, indeed, what he or she intends to do – a game also played very effectively by Borowczyk in *Goto, Ile d'Amour*. The film is also graced with a delightful mixture of English and Bengali dialogue. In 1972 Ray followed *The Adversary* with *Company Limited* – a brilliant and sensitive film about the top echelons of the business world and the subtle corruptions endemic therein. Using the old device of exposing the situation through the innocent but accusing eye of a 'country mouse', he succeeded in making a fresh and devastating com-

[1] Also known as *The Adventures of Goopy and Bagha*.

ment on Western capitalism as a whole, while at the same time remaining compassionate in his delineation of the problems of human relationships.[1]

V

At the time when Ray was completing *Apur Sansar*, the first film of another Asian film director made its appearance. Battling, just as Ray had done, against seemingly endless prejudices and difficulties,[2] Lester James Peries in 1959 finally managed to bring his first feature film to the screen. *Rekava* (*The Line of Life*) was a financial disaster, but it won three international awards and put Sri Lanka (then still known as Ceylon) well and truly on the map of world cinema.

The story of *Rekava* anticipates that of Ray's *Devi*. An ordinary mortal is, all unwillingly, credited with miraculous powers, and when these fail becomes the target of the hate and hostility of the disappointed community. The victim in Peries' film is a small boy (in Ray's of course it is a girl), and the discovery of his 'powers' is built up to quite slowly, so that it is almost halfway through before the apparent miracle takes place. This puts the film slightly off balance, though this may perhaps be due also to the fact that *Rekava* was cut by some 55 minutes for export, which involved the removal of various episodes as well as an entire sub-plot.[3] Nevertheless what emerges from *Rekava* is a true feeling for village people and village life as well as a story whose dramatic impact is convincing and very moving. Peries eschewed studio work. He shot his interiors as well as exteriors on location, thus providing his cameraman William Blake with problems similar to those handed earlier to Mitra by Ray; and he used almost entirely amateur actors.

The film begins with a quite magical sequence, with a harlequin-like figure on tall stilts stalking across the landscape followed by a rabble of delighted and delightful children; something here to recall

---

[1] In 1972 Ray made it clear that he regarded *Days and Nights in the Forest*, *The Adversary* and *Company Limited* as a trilogy.

[2] Like India, Sri Lanka has an official Government Film Unit (originally set up under the guidance of the British documentarian Ralph Keene). This has a number of good films to its credit – Nihalsingh's *Bakhti*, a lovely study of prayer, not least – and it is surprising that it actively opposed Peries' efforts at that time. Needless to say it no longer does so.

[3] The cuts were made by Peries himself together with his wife (who edits all his films) with advice and help from Lindsay Anderson. For full details of this and of all Peries' films see Philip Coorey's *The Lonely Artist*, Lake House, Colombo, Ceylon, 1970.

Gelsomina's famous 'march' in *La Strada*. When the stiltman is attacked and robbed by thugs it is one of the kids, Sena, who helps to bring them to justice, and in return, in the hearing of the other kids, he tells his fortune and says, 'You will be a great healer'. (There are other moments of magic, notably an exquisite interlude in which a girl singing a baby to sleep is enclosed by Peries' subtle tracks and pans in a secret garden of maternity.)

The small girl goes blind in a sequence in which the suddenness of the stroke is emphasized by huge close-ups of the puppet show she is watching, and of the gaudy kite from an earlier episode when she suffered from a dimming of eyesight. Then from the moment when she says to Sena, 'Cure me', and he, shyly wiping his hand on his singlet first, places it gently on her eyes, the film gains in momentum and intensity. By a clever stroke, and one which is well designed to emphasize the possibilities of credulity, the healing does not take place at this moment. It happens quite a long time after, when the girl and her mother are coming back by river-boat from seeing a doctor. Suddenly the girl sees the blurred, dancing reflection of the sun on the water and, as it comes into focus, she cries out, 'Sena cured me!' (when, after all, it might have been the doctor who has just been treating her).

So now Sena must suffer the cruelty which comes when people become infected by the twin hysterias of superstition and greed. Sena's voracious father, together with some crooked cronies, persuades the family of a crippled boy that Sena will cure him. Sena, entirely against his will, is brought to the house, and touches the boy's legs. With mindless cruelty they all force the poor sick boy off his bed, force him to walk, he *must* walk somehow, no, don't let him have his crutch, he's got to walk by himself – until, his tormented spirit failing, the sad little figure falls dead in the dust. Peries here spares us nothing of the torture inflicted on a defenceless child by the adult world; and it is no chance that the next sequence – which is the boy's funeral – builds to a grave-yard fight as blasphemously idiotic as that in *Les Jeux Interdits*, and perhaps more appalling, since it takes place by the flames and smoke, the snapping and crackling of a funeral pyre.

In the final sequence of the film, when drought has come to the village, brought, they say, by Sena who must be possessed of a devil, Peries is aided by a performance of staggering power by the boy Somapala Dharmapriya, who had never acted before.[1] His lonely walk through the village – doors and windows closed against him, and occasionally a stone or an old can whizzing at him from nowhere – ends

---

[1] He appeared ten years later as the servant boy in Peries' *Delovak Athara*.

with him casting himself to the ground in a storm of despairing tears which hurt almost as much as that final despairing cry in *Shoeshine*; and later, the dignity with which he undergoes the devil-dancers' attempts to exorcize the devil within him by means of fear and terror is quite magnificent.

The solution comes quite rightly from heaven, which suddenly opens and delivers a tropical downpour to break the drought and prove Sena's innocence. Sena and his mother (a fine performance by Iranganie Meedeniya) walk slowly away from the scene of tribulation as the film ends. But nothing, we somehow know, will ever be the same again.

After making *Sandesaya* (*The Message*) in 1960 – a historical epic about resistance to the Portuguese which had some success but may be chiefly remembered for the impertinence shown by the Czech authorities at the Karlovy Vary Festival who, without the director's knowledge, re-edited it to 'make it more palatable in socialist countries',[1] Peries directed *Gamperiliya* (*The Changing Village*), which he completed in 1964. It is based on a well-known Sinhalese novel of which he himself has said, 'It is the kind of story that hardly dates, and is still topical. It tells of social change; portrays very realistically the decline and fall of village attitudes; is the swan song of the favoured aristocracy of the villages at the turn of the century; . . . (and) is a very subtle and sensitive, realistic and human study of a family.'

All this Peries well brings to the screen. The story of a girl making the usual family marriage, losing a baby, being widowed, and finally, under strange circumstances, marrying her first love, forms a framework for a picture of the changing values in countryside and city.

Like Ray, Peries has an impeccable sense of period; and also like Ray, he never fails to emphasize the importance of the railway and the postman. There is a scene preluding the nervous breakdown of Nanda (the heroine) after she has sent her real love, Piyal, away; she is on the verandah, and beyond it, in extreme long shot and only just visible through the trees, his train clanks away. This is one of several Welles-type deep-focus shots; there is another almost immediately, with the doctor in the foreground and the sick Nanda in the extreme background; it may also be noteworthy that, the doctor failing to effect a cure, the family call in devil-dancers as in *Rekava* and, as in that film, the sequence is climaxed by thunder and torrential rain.

After the marriage of Nanda to Jinadasa, her family's choice,

---

[1] On finding this out Peries very properly walked out of the Festival and gave the story to a London paper. An apology from the Czechs followed; there had been, they said, 'a technical error'

Peries manages to give a clever impression of the passage of time, of the accommodation of the couple to each other (as with Apu and Aparna in *Apur Sansar*) and of the gradual decay of her once powerful family. She has a baby and loses it at once – a sharp, casual tragedy ('Stupid midwife . . . she used rusty scissors') – with a storm of hysterical tears. Then, as family finances get worse and worse, Jinadasa must go off to the North to try to earn some money. When he leaves she bows low to his feet as a dutiful wife; she is never to see him again, alive. For a long time nothing is heard from him save rumours that he has taken up with a woman; eventually, in a curious sequence built with curved wipes moving from the top right to bottom left of the screen, she herself travels in search of him, but fails. Back at home Piyal, arriving rich and successful from the city, approaches her again, hints – in a sequence of beautifully modulated gestures of hands and of subtle expressions – that she might become his mistress . . . and into this situation comes the postman with a letter saying that Jinadasa is dead. So now there is another wedding, this time a posh city affair with a brass band and gracious colonial ladies being rather patronizing; and the couple settle down into a wealthy and bourgeois life in town, with Piyal always rather too conscious of his expensive suits and, in general, something of a shadow between them.

It is at this point that Peries springs his big surprise. Piyal goes on a visit to Nanda's family in her old village home. They are in an increasingly bad way, and he offers to help them. They are too proud, however, to accept his charity, and he drives away in his new status symbol, a car. Nanda gets a telegram saying that he is dangerously ill in a country hospital. She dashes there, but when she arrives it is too late; he is dead. She enters the morgue, and from her point of view we see only the soles of the corpse's feet, the big toes tied together with tape. She moves forward, and through her eyes we suddenly realize that the dead man is not Piyal – but Jinadasa.

This surprising and ironic twist leads to a series of showdowns between Nanda and Piyal. She cannot forgive herself for having, however unwittingly, married him while Jinadasa was still alive. He demands that she accept this trickery of fate. The quarrel mounts. 'How *can* I forget?' she cries. 'You gave him a good funeral with *my* money,' he blurts. She runs upstairs, past curtains blowing in the wind. He follows her. 'I have feelings too,' he says; and then calmly reveals that he knew all along that Jinadasa was alive. He had made her his mistress after all. So, on a half question-mark – for they have already been happy together – the film ends.

Beautifully performed by Punya Heendeniya as Nanda, Henry
Jayasena as Piyal and Gamini Fonseka as Jinadasa, *Gamperiliya*,
despite its essentially episodic nature, impresses as an organic whole
in which the development of human relations within a changing society
is presented with a calm conviction and with a certain warmth – a
quality which *The Magnificent Ambersons*, with which it has some
affinity, ultimately lacked. It is a film which rewards a second viewing.[1]

VI

Finally, one film from Pakistan, whose comparatively small and
somewhat parochial film industry has otherwise made no impact on the
world's screens. *The Day Shall Dawn* (*Jago Hua Savera*) was made in
1959. Its writer-director Aaejay Kardar and his unit were joined by the
Englishmen John Fletcher (as editor) and Walter Lassally, who shared
the photography with Sadhan Roy. It is a tragic film of classic beauty;
like Bimal Roy's *Two Acres of Land*, it is concerned with the appalling
struggle of the exploited and the dispossessed to rise somehow above
the surface of an existence which will otherwise drown them.

The setting is the fishing village of Shaitnol, on the river Meghna.
The waters are rich, and the nightly catches of the fishermen provide
sustenance for millions of people in East Pakistan. But they themselves
possess nothing, are continually exploited. A man's greatest ambition is
to become the owner of a boat – his own, his absolutely own boat;
and we see how two men try to achieve this by saving money. But the
saving of the money has to be done through the very man who owns
the fishery concession and is, as a result, also their wagemaster. One
man, Ganju, finally gets his boat; but in the process he has literally
worked himself to death, and he never sails in it. The other, Mian,
having also saved all his life, now tries to buy Ganju's boat; but the
overseer makes sure that the price is just too high. Defeated, Mian
returns to the daily routine of the underdog.

The Day Shall Dawn is full of intense feeling expressed *through*

---

[1] Unfortunately much of Peries' subsequent work – including his two most successful
films, *Ran Salu* (*The Yellow Robe*) and *Golu Hadawatha* (*The Silence of the Heart*) –
received little or no showing outside Asia. But at the 1972 London Film Festival his
Nidhanaya (*The Treasure*) proved most impressive. This story of a fated and fatal obsession,
as heavy with doom as *Wuthering Heights*, was directed with a chilling intensity matched
by the dedicated performances of Gamini and Malini Fonseka.

the characters rather than *about* them. The opening and closing sequences of night-fishing – visually exquisite – are poignant because from the beginning they reveal a kind of innocent acceptance of an unjust society, and at the end an equally innocent acceptance of the impossibility of fighting it. Yet, who in fact is to blame? Lal Nian, the concessionaire, slave-driver and moneylender, is no Shylock; cheerful, by no means unkind, he follows his own bent, aware that he too is being exploited by the invisible Governmental higher-ups in the distant city. He too is a victim.

There are some shattering sequences – not least that in which Ganju's deaf old mother – locked in herself and never having believed that he would succeed – sits staring into nothingness while he coughs and coughs up what remains of his lungs into the bilge of the so-hoped-for boat which his fellow villagers have gently carried up the hill, shoulder high, and placed on the dusty earth outside his house.

Deeply affecting too is the penultimate sequence when Mian – that not very bright soul (save in honesty) – tries to get together enough cash to buy the boat. The other members of his family, like himself, like nearly everyone on the outer margin of existence, are obsessional savers. Now, ruthlessly, he collects. To his own hoard he appropriates – to her deep anguish – that of his wife. And when this is not enough his small son, who whenever his father was paid has asked compulsively for the spare cent, goes to a hiding place and produces his hallowed hollowed-out bamboo moneybox. But it is no good; and in a heartbreaking moment the boy follows his defeated father up the hill (memories of *Bicycle Thieves*) and, with the just insistence of the cheated, asks for his money back . . .

The Day Shall Dawn, for all the despair implicit in its story, for all its lack of an acceptable solution (political or otherwise), still succeeds in showing how the essential dignity of the human being can rise somehow above the swamp of life. It has, too, what Pauline Kael, writing of *Shoeshine*, called 'a sweetness and a simplicity that suggest greatness of feeling . . .'

Since it was made, East Pakistan – now Bangladesh – has suffered disasters, natural and man-made, which add up to the biggest and most horrifying tragedy of our generation. This finely acted and candidly beautiful film, by showing the heights to which the lowest may rise in love or in hope, may remind us that the film as an art must also be reckoned with as a messenger of social justice, social indignation and social reform.

SIGNPOST - 1960

THE YEAR OF 'A BOUT DE SOUFFLE'

IN FRANCE

Apart from the Godard film, several other contributions to the *Nouvelle Vague* movement make their appearance, notably François Truffaut's disjointed but attractive *Tirez sur le Pianiste*, with Charles Aznavour, Louis Malle's *Zazie dans le Métro*, with its gorgeously scandalous little heroine, and Jacques Rivette's confused, confusing but somehow compelling *Paris Nous Appartient*. Roger Vadim follows his *Les Liaisons Dangereuses* with *Et Mourir de Plaisir*, a Franco-Italian co-production based on Sheridan Le Fanu's vampire story *Carmilla* and starring Mel Ferrer and Elsa Martinelli, while, also in co-production with Italy, the Englishman Peter Brook directs *Moderato Cantabile*, with Jeanne Moreau and Jean-Paul Belmondo, from a script by Marguerite Duras. Jacques Demy directs his first feature film *Lola*, beautifully photographed by Raoul Coutard, which, though not a musical, will be seen to be a sort of rehearsal for *Les Parapluies de Cherbourg*. After his collaboration with Walerian Borowczyk on *Les Astronautes*, Chris Marker comes up with a serious and considered full-length colour documentary on the problems of the emergent state of Israel, *Description d'un Combat*. Of the old guard, André Cayatte makes the not very distinguished *Passage du Rhin* (with Aznavour), while with *La Vérité* Henri-Georges Clouzot involves Brigitte Bardot in a courtroom drama liberally peppered with flashbacks, and Marcel Carné's further attempt to deal with youth problems, *Terrain Vague*, makes little impact.

The Summit meeting in Paris between De Gaulle, Eisenhower, Khrushchev and Macmillan breaks up in disorder as a result of the U2 incident.

De Gaulle institutes negotiations with the Front de la Libération in Algeria; during his visit in December there is much rioting, mainly by Europeans.

The Convention of the Organization for Economic Co-operation and Development is signed in Paris.

Madagascar receives its independence, together with seven other African colonies including the Congo.

Despite strong protests from African and European countries, France explodes a nuclear device in the Sahara, thus becoming the fourth nuclear power in the world.

Jean Cocteau is trying to recover from the second of two serious illnesses.

Pierre Boulez composes *Pli selon Pli*.

476

Alain Robbe-Grillet writes *Dans le Labyrinthe*, and Eugène Ionesco's *Le Rhinocéros* is staged.

Jacques Maritain publishes his *Philosophie Morale*, and Jean-Paul Sartre is completing his *Critique de la Raison Dialectique*.

The Musée Léger, complete with *Jardin d'Enfants*, is opened at Biot.

IN ITALY

A bumper year produces Fellini's *La Dolce Vita*, Antonioni's *L'Avventura*, De Sica's triumphant return to form with *Two Women*, a co-production with France, as is Gillo Pontecorvo's powerful prison-camp film *Kapo* (with Susan Strasberg and Emmanuelle Riva), and Rossellini's colour spectacular on Garibaldi, *Viva L'Italia*. Alberto Lattuada directs *Sweet Deceptions* (*Dolci Inganni*) with Catherine Spaak, Christian Marquand and Jean Sorel, a tender and psychologically perceptive description of a young girl's discovery of love; and Luciano Emmer returns more to the form of *Sunday in August* with *The Girl in the Window*, with Marina Vlady. Ermanno Olmi completes his first feature film, *Time Stood Still* (*Il Tempo si è Fermato*) on semi-documentary lines. Pier Paolo Pasolini works on the scripts of a number of films, including Mauro Bolognini's *Il Bell'Antonio* and *La Giornata Balorda*, as well as on the story-line for Franco Rossi's *Morte di un Amico*.

There are big anti-Fascist demonstrations in Genoa and elsewhere.

Premier Antonio Segni resigns, and after some difficulty Amintore Fanfani forms an administration which is thought to give a chance to an *apertura a sinistra* (an opening to the Left).

The Olympic Games are held in Rome, which is also visited by the Archbishop of Canterbury.

Alberto Moravia, whose *La Ciociara* (*Two Women*) has just been so well filmed by De Sica, and whose *Il Conformista* will later be filmed by Bernardo Bertolucci, writes *La Noia* (*The Empty Canvas*) which receives the Viareggio Prize.

Luciano Berio composes his *Circles* for Voice, Harp and Percussion.

IN SWEDEN

Ingmar Bergman directs his grim XIVth century legend *The Virgin Spring*, with Max von Sydow, and also his less effective fantasy about Don Juan returning from Hell to make an attempt on the virginity of a clergyman's daughter – *The Devil's Eye*, with Bibi Andersson and Jarl Kulle. Alf Sjöberg directs *The Judge* (*Domaren*), about a young man's fight to obtain justice during which he is nearly driven mad. Erwin Leiser makes his film on Hitler, *Mein Kampf.*

Sweden is now a member of the European Free Trade Association.

Despite having all the knowhow, the country resolutely refuses to indulge, like some others, in the manufacture of nuclear weapons.

Thirteen months before his death in an air-crash, the Secretary General of the United Nations, Dag Hammarskjöld, enters Katanga with a force of United Nations troops which includes Swedes, as does the UN Force keeping order in Cyprus.

For the first time women are allowed to be pastors in the Lutheran Church, and three are inducted.

Karl-Birger Blomdahl's space-opera *Aniara* is in the repertory. Bengt Hambraeus is experimenting with new forms of composition for the Organ.

IN HOLLAND

A new director, Fons Rademakers, shows much promise with his film of a young boy's problems, *The Knife* (*Het Mes*).

Holland joins with Britain, France and the United States in a Caribbean Organization for Economic Cooperation.

In a row over the housing question, the Prime Minister, J. E. de Quay, resigns because the Protestants side with Labour.

IN WEST GERMANY

Fritz Lang makes a nostalgic return to pre-Hitler days with *The Thousand Eyes of Dr Mabuse*, featuring Dawn Addams and Peter van Eyck. For Walter Koppel, the Englishman Paul Rotha is making his vast compilation film out of millions of feet of material, *The Life of Adolf Hitler*. In memory of the children of the Hitlerjugend senselessly sacrificed in the last stand against the Allied advance, Bernhard Wicki brings to the screen his terrifying *The Bridge*, while Wolfgang Staudte, in *Fairground*, attacks the persistence of Nazi representation in official posts.

The government comes to an agreement to compensate French victims of Nazi persecution.

A number of antisemitic incidents lead to the banning of Neo-Nazi groups.

Protests are received from the USSR against the equipping of the Bundeswehr with the Polaris missile.

K-H. Hoffman synthesises the pituitary hormone, and R. L. Mossbauer makes important discoveries relative to gamma rays.

Hans Werner Henze completes his opera *Der Prinz von Hamburg*, and Karlheinz Stockhausen composes his *Zyklus* (*Cycle*) for percussion alone.

IN EAST GERMANY

Gerhard Klein directs *One Summer Day Doesn't Mean Love*, to which Kurt Maetzig ripostes with *September Love*. Konrad Wolf, later to make a big success with *I Was Nineteen*, directs *Men with Wings*.

A partial blockade of West Berlin is imposed.

The collectivization of the agricultural system is completed.

President Wilhelm Pieck dies and is succeeded by Walter Ulbricht.

IN RUSSIA

Grigori Chukrai makes his human and relaxed *Ballad of a Soldier*, while the veteran Josif (*Baltic Deputy*) Heifitz makes his enchanting period piece, *The Lady with the Little Dog*. Another veteran, Mikhail Kalatozov, follows up his successful *The Cranes are Flying* with *The Letter that was not Sent*; while Alexander Zarkhi, co-director with Heifitz of *Baltic Deputy*, makes *Men on the Bridge*. Andrei Tarkovsky, soon to make the controversial *Andrei Rublev* and *Solaris*, is directing school films. Tchaikovsky's opera *The Queen of Spades* is admirably transferred to the screen by Roman Tikhomirov.

Nikita Khrushchev visits India, Burma, and Indonesia; and after the U2 incident he breaks up the Summit Conference in Paris.

Leonid Brezhnev replaces Marshal Voroshilov as President.

A manifesto is issued against the dogmatism of Chairman Mao, and the ill-fated Patrice Lumumba is briefly supported.

Two dogs are sent into space, make 17 earth orbits, and are retrieved.

Prokoviev's opera, *The Tale of a Real Man*, banned by Khrennikov (the Shumiatsky of Russian music) in 1948, at last receives its first performance. But meantime all so-called modern music, from Schönberg to Boulez, is officially dismissed.

The great Soviet writer, Boris Pasternak, earlier disgraced for having been awarded the Nobel Prize, dies at the age of 69.

IN POLAND

Jerzy Kawalerowicz directs his film on demonic possession, *Mother Joan of the Angels*, and Andrzej Wajda unexpectedly makes a rather jolly, almost jazzy film, *Innocent Sorcerers*. Aleksander Ford directs his *Knights of the Teutonic Order*, not without a sideways glance at *Alexander Nevski*; and Wanda Jakubowska makes *It Happened Yesterday*. Of the younger generation, Wojciech Has makes *Farewells*, and Jerzy Passendorfer *Return to the Past*. Roman Polanski has graduated from the Film School at Lodz where he made *Two Men and a Wardrobe*, and is preparing his *Knife in the Water*. Jerzy Skolimowski, also fresh from Lodz, is preparing a documentary on boxing.

The government requests the NATO powers to recognize the Oder-Neisse Line.

Krzysztof Penderecki composes, with a number of unusual instrumental effects, his *Threnody for the Victims of Hiroshima*.

IN CZECHOSLOVAKIA

Otakar Vavra directs two films; the first, *Time Gentlemen*, is concerned with working conditions in Prague at the end of the last century and owes not a little to Gorky's *The Lower Depths*, while the second, in colour and cinemascope, is *A Sunday in August* and, on the basis of a successful stage play, deals with the generation gap. Jiri Weiss makes perhaps his finest film in *Romeo and Juliet in Darkness*.

Three years after the taking over of the Presidency by Novotny, the stresses and strains within the essentially inefficient and clumsy Communist regime lead to signs of a certain liberalism which will come briefly to flower in eight years time with the Dubcek government.

Bohuslav Martinu's opera *The Greek Passion*, based on Kazantzakis' *Christ Recrucified*, is about to have its first performance two years after the composer's death.

Among younger composers Jan Cikker is working on an opera based on Tolstoy's *Resurrection*.

IN HUNGARY

Zoltán Fábri makes *The Last Goal*, a war-time prison-camp story based on a true event in which a team of prisoners playing their Fascist guards at football make the mistake of winning and are gunned down for their pains. Felix Mariassy disappoints with *It's a Long Way Home* and *Test Trip*. András Kovács makes his first feature, *Summer Rain*, about divorce among country folk, which does not presage the *cinéma-vérité* style he will later develop. Miklós Jancsó is making shorts and documentaries.

Gyorgy Ligeti experiments with works using dense note-clusters, and will soon complete *Volumina* for Organ, and his orchestral *Atmospheres* which in due course will be used by Stanley Kubrick in *2001*.

IN YUGOSLAVIA

France Stiglic directs *The Ninth Circle*, a grim drama about Jews and Nazis. Velko Bulajic makes *War*, while Vatroslav Mimica and Dusan Vukotic concern themselves with animation.

There are signs of the beginning of an easing of tension between Yugoslavia and the Soviet Union.

Tito agrees with Turkey and Greece to dissolve the Balkan Alliance set up in 1954.

Cardinal Aloizji Stephinac dies.

IN GREECE

Michael Cacoyannis directs *Our Last Spring*, a somewhat uneasy film but notable for the stunning sequence of the funeral games. The American Jules Dassin, aided by the effervescent Melina Mercouri, makes a world box-office hit with *Never on Sunday*.

The Eoka leader Grivas has returned to Athens from Cyprus, and is by no means contented when that country becomes an independent Republic with Archbishop Makarios as President.

The question of Enosis is by no means closed.

IN INDIA

Satyajit Ray directs his controversial *Devi*, about a young woman who is taken to be a goddess. Based on a Tagore story, Tapan Sinha's *The Hungry Stones* is well received, and Rajen Tarafdar's *Ganga*, shot on location among fishermen, will get a showing at the Venice Festival next year. The Government announces its intention to set up a Film Finance Corporation to 'render assistance to film-producers by way of loans'.

Khrushchev visits India.

A Treaty is entered into with Pakistan relating to the development of the waters of the Ganges.

IN CEYLON

Lester James Peries makes his second feature *Sandesaya*.

The newly elected ministry of Dudley Senanayake does not last long. After fresh elections the widow of the assassinated Prime Minister of last year, Mrs Sirimavo Bandaranaike, forms a government, one of the first acts of which is to take over control of the Press.

IN JAPAN

Toshiro Mifune stars in Akira Kurosawa's film about corruption in the high places of government and big business, *The Bad Sleep Well*. A similar background, though very dissimilar treatment, is to be found in two films by Nagisa Oshima, *Cruel Stories of Youth* (also known as *Naked Youth*) and *The Sun's Burial*, both films ending with scenes of gruesome violence. Matriarchy is the dominating factor in both of Kon Ichikawa's films, *Bonchi* and *Younger Brother*. Yasujiro Ozu makes his *Late Autumn*, which is in fact a colour remake of his *Late Spring* of 1949, while in contrast Kaneto Shindo presents his harsh, repetitive but compelling *The Island*.

Rentaro Mikuni, of *The Burmese Harp*, appears in *The Great Road* directed by Hideo Sekigawa, from whose vivid feature *Hiroshima* (1953) Resnais drew some of the material for *Hiroshima Mon Amour*.

The government signs a mutual security Treaty with the United States despite student protests which lead to the postponement of a visit by President Eisenhower.

Hayato Ikeda becomes Prime Minister.

Regular colour television transmissions begin.

At $9\frac{1}{2}$ million, the population of Tokyo overpasses those of London and New York.

IN ARGENTINA

Leopoldo Torre Nilsson puts his country on the cinematic map with his impressive and obsessive *Hand in the Trap*.

It is one hundred years since Buenos Aires and Argentina were formally re-united, and five years since the sacking of Juan Peron.

The Frondizi regime is finding it difficult, however, to stem a renewal of Peronism among the masses.

IN BRAZIL

Glauber Rocha is working on short films and preparing the script for what will be his first feature film, *Barravento*. Ruy Guerra starts on a feature called *Oros* which is never completed.

Janio Quadros is elected President on a somewhat *faute de mieux* ticket by a nation disillusioned by false promises and unaccomplished programmes.

Brasilia is now officially the capital of the country, and its Congress and Museum building, designed by Otto Niemeyer, is completed.

IN MEXICO

Luis Buñuel makes what is, for him, something of a B picture in *Island of Shame* (also known as *The Young One*) with a cast that includes Zachary Scott.

The government's campaign against illiteracy, based on the 'Each one teach one' principle, continues to show progress.

At 5 million the population of Mexico City is approaching that of Moscow.

IN THE UNITED STATES

John Wayne produces, directs and stars in *The Alamo*. A more attractive Western is George Cukor's *Heller in Pink Tights*. The maestro of shocks Alfred Hitchcock gives his audiences in *Psycho* some of the biggest shake-ups ever. Blockbusters include Stanley Kubrick's *Spartacus*, with Laurence Olivier, Charles Laughton and Peter Ustinov as well as Kirk Douglas and Jean Simmons; Otto Preminger's *Exodus*, about the birthpangs of Israel; and John Sturges' surprisingly successful copy of Kurosawa's *Seven Samurai* entitled *The Magnificent Seven*. Elizabeth Taylor appears in a piece of polished nonsense, *Butterfield 8*, reliably directed by Daniel Mann; and Richard Brooks films Sinclair Lewis' *Elmer Gantry* with Burt Lancaster. *From the Terrace*, directed by Mark Robson, provides fine acting from Paul Newman and Joanne Woodward, but Billy Wilder purveys a rather tasteless offering in *The Apartment* with Jack Lemmon and Shirley MacLaine. Disappointments include Elia Kazan's too sentimentally romantic *Wild River* and John Frankenheimer's confused film on teenagers waging gang-war in New York, *The Young Savages*. Important films include Stanley Kramer's Monkey Trial film, *Inherit the Wind*, with Spencer Tracy as Clarence Darrow and Fredric March as William Jennings Bryan and a coating of soothing syrup overall; *One-Eyed Jacks*, with Marlon Brando at his best both as director and actor; and John Huston's *The Misfits*, one of whose stars, Clark Gable, dies before it is released, and of the other two, Marilyn Monroe is to die two years later and Montgomery Clift in 1966. But the most stimulating aspect of the year is in the signs of a real breakaway from Hollywood convention and tradition. John Cassavetes practically singlehanded invents the cinema of improvisation in *Shadows*, while Shirley Clarke with her drug-film *The Connection* shows a real underworld instead of the romanticised gangsterdom of the hack script-writers. Finally, with a great healthy gust of fresh air *Jazz on a Summer's Day*, directed by Bert Stern and documenting the Newport Jazz Festival (Mahalia Jackson, Chico Hamilton, Anita O'Day, Louis Armstrong, among many), blows away the cobwebs from the windows of the front-offices. These new off-beat movies may not yet be in the big league, but just you wait and see.

J. F. Kennedy becomes President after an election campaign in which confrontations between his rival Richard Nixon and himself on television are felt to have added a new dimension to politics.

In protest against segregation, Negro sit-ins at lunch counters and the like begin. The Civil Rights Bill (to protect negro voting rights) is passed by the Senate.

The Administration cuts off aid to Cuba and places an embargo on all shipments to that country.

American relations with USSR are bedevilled by the U2 episode.

The Discoverer satellite is recovered from the Pacific and a radio reflector satellite is launched.

The Piccard-designed bathyscape *Trieste* reaches the bottom of the 35,000 feet Challenger Deep.

The Research Laboratory of Pennsylvania University, designed by Louis Khan, is completed.

Andy Warhol paints a soup can.

John Updike publishes *Rabbit Run.*

Aaron Copland is working on his *Connotations for Orchestra*, composed in Twelve Tone style.

IN BRITAIN

Films from the newer generation (loosely described as Angries) include Tony Richardson's *The Entertainer* from Osborne's play, with Laurence Olivier; Karel Reisz's *Saturday Night and Sunday Morning*, with Albert Finney and Rachel Roberts; and, in more muted key, Jack Cardiff's screen version of D. H. Lawrence's *Sons and Lovers.* Critical opinion divides over the respective merits of *The Trials of Oscar Wilde* (with Peter Finch directed by Ken Hughes) and *Oscar Wilde* (directed by Gregory Ratoff and starring Robert Morley). In lighter mood Anthony Asquith finds a sure-fire box-office formula in *The Millionairess*, with a screenplay from G. B. Shaw and starring Sophia Loren and Peter Sellers with the inclusion of a top-selling song; Tony Hancock depicts the frustrations of a would-be modern painter in *The Rebel*, directed by Robert Day; and for the Children's Film Foundation Cavalcanti turns up with his delightful fantasy *The Monster of Highgate Pond.* Suicide and madness are found behind the stiff upper lip in Ronald Neame's regimental story *Tunes of Glory*, with John Mills, Alec Guinness, Dennis Price and Gordon Jackson, while Joseph Losey's *The Criminal*, with a sharp screenplay by Alun Owen, takes up the theme of prison conditions and features Stanley Baker and Sam Wanamaker. In a co-production with Australia, Fred Zinnemann makes *The Sundowners* – a relaxed though rather shapeless Antipodean period-piece with Peter Ustinov and Glynis Johns. For British Transport Films a newcomer called John Schlesinger makes a prizewinning documentary about Waterloo Station called *Terminus.*

Prime Minister Harold Macmillan visits Ghana, Nigeria, Rhodesia and South Africa, and while in Cape Town makes his 'Winds of Change' speech. Later in the year he addresses the United Nations in New York.

African members abandon their boycott of the Kenya Constitutional Conference.

The Commonwealth Prime Ministers' Conference meets in London.

The Labour Party formulates its Clause IV policy regarding nationalization.

George Woodcock becomes secretary of the TUC and Harold Wilson is defeated in his attempt to replace Hugh Gaitskell as leader of the Party. Labour back-benchers, however, rebel against Gaitskell in a debate on defence.

Profits Tax is increased to $12\frac{1}{2}\%$ and a credit squeeze includes the raising of the Bank Rate to 6%.

Selwyn Lloyd replaces Heathcote Amory as Chancellor of the Exchequer and Alec Douglas Home becomes Foreign Secretary.

The liberal tradition suffers another blow in the demise of *The News Chronicle* and *The Star*. A. J. Ayer publishes his *Logical Positivism*, Lawrence Durrell *Clea*, and John Betjeman *Summoned by Bells*.

Michael Ayrton embarks on his big series of *Icarus* sculptures and drawings.

Interest in Australian art is aroused by exhibitions by Arthur Boyd, William Dobell and Sidney Nolan.

Benjamin Britten composes his Cello Sonata for Mstislav Rostropovitch, and William Walton completes his Second Symphony. Other music includes Arthur Bliss' *Tobias and the Angel* and Humphrey Searle's Third Symphony.

Princess Margaret gets married, and Aneurin Bevan dies.

CHAPTER 7

1960 - 1970

NEW WAVES, ANGRIES AND UNDERGROUNDS

I

This decade saw the fragmentation of cinema as it had been known and accepted since the Twenties. The very concept of film was, by the late Sixties, being seriously questioned. That great Father/Mother figure known as Hollywood disintegrated; and what remained of the fabric was direly threatened by the dry rot of Jean-Luc Godard and the rising damp of Andy Warhol, while the simmering rise of permissiveness, especially in Occidental civilization, was reflected with increasing vividness in the theories, attitudes and products of the younger film-makers. Which country they lived in seemed to make little difference, for each community was sweat-stained with the same mixture of guilt, uncertainty and fear out of which, with some inevitability, arose intellectual and emotional excess. For Britain, with Kenya, Suez, Cyprus and Aden behind, there were still matters involving Nigeria and Ulster. For the United States, the background of Korea, no less than the oppressions supported by dollar diplomacy in Central and Southern America, served to highlight the immediacies of Vietnam and Black Power. For France, after Dien Bien Phu and Algeria, there remained the stupidity of the Pacific atomic tests and increasing tensions between the community and the police. And the Soviet Union, after Korea and Hungary, chose to saddle itself with the invasion of Czechoslovakia and the persecution of intellectuals, artists and Jews. Add to this the boiling anarchy of the general world scene in terms of the Congo, Biafra and later Bangladesh – and you find a situation in which the artist's commitment must take him into a splintered rather than an ordered world of aesthetic.

Meantime the collapse of Hollywood and, with it, of much of the hitherto sacrosanct structure of distribution on a world scale did, apart from anything else, advantage the growth of creative film-making in countries hitherto underprivileged in this cultural sense. To the positive progress already seen in countries like India and Ceylon (to say nothing of Poland and Czechoslovakia), could now be added a broadening area which included Cuba, Argentina and Brazil as well as African states like Senegal.

Nor has fragmentation been confined to production only. The concept of the vast cinematic cathedral designed for mass-worship has gone by the board. The big palaces have been gutted, split into segments, each seating smaller audiences in more modest and more intimate conditions. When new movie-houses are built they tend to contain up to four separate auditoria, each one showing a different film. It is the long despised minority audiences for whom the film tycoons now have to cater. At the other end of the scale there have been signs of the use of movies in conjunction with the other media, in the development of jumbo-size synaesthetic happenings and similar punch-ups which may well turn out to be an important factor in reshaping the idea of the moving picture.

In looking at the Sixties it is essential to take sides, to declare allegiances; and it seems to me that to deny or to try to repel the fragmentations which have been taking place would be quite pointless. One may not like fragmentation – at least until one has had time to distinguish between those of its practitioners who are bogus and those who are for real – but it is essential to make at least the gesture of accommodation; for it may well be that only in this dark situation of virtual anarchy can the true solution, the future of the film, be found.

Whatever criticisms, therefore, I may make of Jean-Luc Godard are made on the assumption that he is a seminal character in the history of cinema who may well turn out to have an importance equal to that of a Griffith or an Eisenstein; when he is being exceptionally naughty or, as in the case of *Pravda*, worse than naughty, one should perhaps remember that it is as much the fault of the times as of himself that he has embarked on a questioning of the very validity of the art in which he can so sensationally excel.

With Warhol, on the other hand, whose influence on various areas of film has also been considerable, we find the reduction of the medium to a nitty-gritty nihilism, accompanied by sloppy, lazy, muddled work which no phrases like 'Minimal Cinema' can cover over; indeed, Warhol's addition of film to the other assets of his Factory have only caused one to look with a much less favourable eye on the campery of the Campbell Soup cans. Why I dislike *Pravda* so much is because it is the only film of Godard's in which he has fallen to the Warhol level. A little more about Warhol will come in its proper place. Meantime, with Godard as the key figure of the decade, let us start off from his country of origin.

II

In France the Nouvelle Vague, or New Wave, is generally supposed to have started with Claude Chabrol's *Le Beau Serge* (1958), which was closely followed by his own *Les Cousins* and *A Double Tour* (1958 and 1959), by François Truffaut's *Les Quatre Cents Coups* (1959), and Godard's *A Bout de Souffle* (1959). The new Wave represented a kind of rebellion which largely stemmed from a group of young critics who were writing for *Les Cahiers du Cinéma*. The rebellion was basically against the current ideological conservatism in the film world, against its failure to face up to or to express the facts of contemporary life. Apart from Godard, Marker and to a degree Truffaut, the movement did not depend entirely on the development of new cinematic techniques. (I omit Resnais and Bresson from the New Wave; each is *sui generis*.)

Le Beau Serge made an instant impression by the brutal immediacy of its presentation of the story of a young man who returns to his village to find that the companion of his boyhood has become an alcoholic. The attempts by François to 'save' Serge – presented, it must be said, with ever-increasing melodramatics – bring to the forefront the dilemmas of individual responsibility and the doubts appertaining thereto. In a film like *Le Journal d'un Curé de Campagne* Bresson will weigh this responsibility against the glories of faith and salvation as well as against immediate and grubbier dangers. But the rough realism of *Le Beau Serge* throws into sharp relief the fact that, in trying to save his friend, François makes a series of clumsy mistakes (leading in one case to rape) and has, by the end of the film, almost become a self-martyr. Indeed, the melodramatic finale, in which François (to the peril of his own tubercular life) forces Serge through a snowstorm so that he may witness the birth of his son, completes the utter change from the neo-realist mood in which the film began.

Chabrol's work after *Le Beau Serge*, however, moved more in the direction of Hitchcock, long a favourite of the *Cahiers* group which tended, perhaps to exaggeration, to concentrate more on the darker side of his work. It is indeed interesting to note that in 1957 Chabrol and Eric Rohmer jointly wrote a book on Hitchcock, and that in 1966 Truffaut published his big book of interviews with the master in which every one of his films was covered. Hitchcock of course tends to push aside or evade the more solemn attributions of his disciples. But the fact remains that the corpus of his work embodies a world of fear – a fear which lies just under the surface of everyday life. The unexpected eruption of this fear through the thin crust of society is the secret of Hitchcock's mastery of suspense, and in some of his later films – notably *Psycho*, *Vertigo*, *The Birds* and *Marnie* – it takes on a deeper significance than that of the thrillers he pretends those films solely to be; though to be fair one must note also that he told Truffaut that 'I take pride in the fact that *Psycho*, more than any of my pictures, is a film that belongs to film-makers, to you and me . . . but I also know that the construction of the story and the way it was told caused audiences all over the world to react and become emotional'. To this we may add Truffaut's statement that in addition to its huge box-office success '*Psycho* . . . in its savagery and uninhibited licence . . . goes much further than those daring 16mm essays by youthful avant-garde film-makers that somehow never get past the censors'.

There can be little doubt that *A Double Tour*[1] was influenced by Hitchcock. It doesn't have the clarity of construction or the under-standing of character relationships presented *visually* which we find in other Chabrol works, but it does have a nervous, often spine-chilling atmosphere, as in the long, menacing tracking-shot through the 'Japanese' room, or the savage fight in mud and water against the background of a field of blood-red poppies. It also has Jean-Paul Belmondo at his best as an unscrupulous, anarchic petty crook attempt-ing to marry into a rich, would-be conventional bourgeois family. Early in the film he makes his own attitude (and perhaps that of the Nouvelle Vague) clear by emerging stark naked from the shower to talk to his fiancée; when she seems shocked, he remarks that he had been under the impression that she was already aware that he was a man.

A Double Tour sticks in the mind more vividly than other Chabrol films, always excepting *Les Biches* (1968) and *Que la Bête Meure*[2] (1969). In particular the last-named, based on the famous Nicholas Blake novel *The Beast Must Die*, about a father determined to track

[1] This film is also known as *Leda* and *Web of Passion*.
[2] Released in Britain as *Killer!*

down the hit-and-run driver who killed his small son, has a depth of feeling and perception beyond anything attained by Chabrol at this stage in his career.

His alterations to the original story are filmically valid and psychologically very successful. Thus we have a dangerously ambivalent situation in which Charles (the father, admirably played by Michel Duchaussoy), having wormed his way into the killer's family, falls into a close and sympathetic relationship with the young son of the house who, as it turns out, also has it in mind to kill his brutally insensitive father (the motivation for this is well built up both aurally and visually). To this Chabrol adds another twist; the intended victim finds Charles' diary in which his intentions are clearly expressed, and he gives it to his lawyer, thus ensuring that if he is killed Charles will be caught. He *is* killed. Charles *is* arrested, on the strength of the diary. But at this point the boy Philippe confesses to the crime, and this puts Charles into a dilemma compounded of psychological, moral and brutal view-points all entangled together.

It has already become clear that Charles' intention to kill Paul (the 'Beast') is, at least unconsciously, weakening. In the crucial scene on the cliff top, where the thing is handed to him on a plate, he finds it impossible not to stretch out his hand to prevent his would-be victim from falling to his death. And when later he takes Paul out for a sail he is in a quandary since the diary, as Paul makes clear, has already been deposited with the lawyer; it is after his safe return from this trip that Paul dies agonizingly from a poisoned dose of medicine.

Now in fact Chabrol ends the film without indicating which of the two, Charles or the boy Philippe, really did commit the murder. Logically speaking, it must surely be the latter, even though his confession could look like a cover-up for Charles, to whom he is very deeply attached (as a father-substitute if not something more). But what happens is that Charles gets into his boat and sails away – presumably for ever. The waters over which he passes are deep. Throughout the film we have, at critical moments, been hearing passages from Kathleen Ferrier's exquisite and unsurpassable rendering of Brahms' *Four Serious Songs* (*Vier Ernste Gesäng*), and in the letter which Charles leaves behind him he quotes from one of them the text from *Ecclesiastes*: 'For that which befalleth the sons of men befalleth beasts; even one thing befalleth them; as the one dieth, so dieth the other'.[1]

---

[1] The French version used by Chabrol runs: 'Il faut que la bête meure, mais l'homme aussi; l'un et l'autre doivent mourir'. This involves an imperative absent from the English text.

Somewhere in this Chabrol is adumbrating the idea of the scape-goat and its Christian development towards the conception of ex-piation. If Charles really committed the murder, but has been cleared of it by Philippe's confession, his expiation is real. If he did *not* commit the murder, and Philippe did (which is undoubtedly the probability), there remains the consideration that he (Charles) must admit to himself that he had all along intended to do it and therefore 'must redeem himself from his "intent to kill" by accepting the blame for Philippe's crime'.[1] This situation, presented through visuals of a passive, un-demanding ocean and accompanied by Ferrier's heavenly voice, produces an eerie semi-religious emotion, a feeling like that of Hamlet about the idea of death, which is quite rare in cinema.

The moral and psychological complexities of *Que la Bête Meure* were exemplified to the extreme in Chabrol's next and probably his best film to date, *Le Boucher*, in which the issues are crystal-clear and which is virtually a duet for two persons played out amid the real people and the buildings and landscapes of a French village.

The great effectiveness of the film arises from the way it steadily contracts from the amplitude of a big wedding celebration down to the narrow and terrible intimacy of the final sequence when the school-mistress Hélène has to drag the murderer she loves out of her house, into her small car, and so to the local hospital – he having gruesomely committed *hara-kiri* (this may sound like Hitchcock, but it isn't). There is here a sense of loneliness and despair which is almost unbearable. From the time when Popaul, the butcher with the killer's compulsion, comes by night to Hélène (whose at first unacknowledged love for him has led her to cover up clues to his identity) and stands outside her window whispering 'Mademoiselle Hélène . . . Mademoiselle Hélène' and she refuses to reply, running from doors to windows locking every-thing – only to find that he is already in the house, the knife in his belly, begging for her love, begging like a small boy for a mother's comforting embrace – Chabrol distils a tragic essence which recalls but is deeper than the crisis at the end of *Le Beau Serge*.

Jean Rabier's discerning camerawork adds to the atmosphere of the film; his early dawn scenes right at the end when Hélène stares unseeing at waters as misty as the tears in her eyes, are exquisite. Jean Yanne follows his Paul of *Que la Bête Meure* with an absolutely impeccable Popaul in this film, putting across with fastidious skill the appalling contradictions of the character; while Stéphane Audran is

---

[1] See *Claude Chabrol*, Studio Vista, 1970, an admirable study by Michael Walker and Robin Wood.

honest and bold enough to make of Hélène a woman of a certain age with a face already marked by past experiences which have rendered her fearful and suspicious of love. Chabrol's direction is more than felicitous. The wedding feast, with the actors mingling perfectly with the real villagers, and with a good deal of highly successful improvisation, is beautifully capped by a slightly tipsy stroll through the village as Popaul escorts Hélène back to the school-house and, with inhibitions obscured by champagne, they move towards the beginning of an affair. All through Chabrol has directed this film with the sort of simplicity which is terribly hard to come by. One may note, too, that the quotation from *Ecclesiastes* fits this film as aptly as the other; and that the production date given for both films is the same – 1969. Chabrol has in fact created two variations on the same theme.

If Chabrol's best work is framed by *A Double Tour* at one end and *Le Boucher* at the other, Truffaut's may in a sense be said to show a similar perspective from *Les Quatre Cents Coups* to *L'Enfant Sauvage* with, in between, the engrossing story of Doinel escaping from childhood, growing to manhood, sowing his oats, and marrying. Truffaut's overmastering love of life, which he has succeeded in creating for himself despite what must have been a number of crippling childhood injuries (psychologically speaking), tends to imbue his films with a sense of buoyancy and light, with a certain innocence too, which is wholly beguiling. Only in that mistaken detour through Godard's *Alphaville* country with *Fahrenheit 451* does he seem to have temporarily lost his sense of direction.

Truffaut is also the only one of the founder-members of the New Wave to emulate Godard in experimenting with cinematic techniques – though, unlike Godard, he did not continue along those lines for long. The technical high-jinks were not crucial to *Les Quatre Cents Coups*, in fact, but in his second and third films, *Tirez sur le Pianiste* (1960) and especially *Jules et Jim* (1961), he discovered new and ravishing possibilities in camera mobility; as Graham Petrie remarks, 'Truffaut conducts an intoxicating love affair with the cinema, determined apparently to exploit every visual source at his disposal, yet the result and purpose are much more than mere stylistic virtuosity'.[1]

I have referred to Truffaut's lightness and innocence. This doesn't mean that I think of his films as jolly little comedies; there is in him an underlying acceptance of the tragedies as well as the joys of life.

One can observe that *Baisers Volés* (1968) is pretty precisely about

[1] *The Cinema of François Truffaut* by Graham Petrie, Zwemmer, 1970.

sheer happiness; but if we look back at *Tirez sur le Pianiste*, with Lena's death in the snow, or at Catherine's plunge to oblivion in *Jules et Jim*, we can note that Truffaut's world is one of proportions, of relationships between different sorts of situations, events, characterizations, which, like the colours of the spectrum, add up to white rather than black. It is this which enables him to move from the crazy, enjoyable pyrotechnics of the first half of *Jules et Jim* into a realization – shared between ourselves and the characters in his story – of the essential falsity of the whole set-up; and he develops this in such a way as not to break the back of the film. He is above all concerned with human values – hence the interchangeability and availability of Doinel-Léaud.

It is not without significance that Truffaut dedicated *L'Enfant Sauvage* (1970) to Jean-Pierre Léaud. Originally, Léaud equalled Doinel, who equalled Truffaut as a boy; all three, as it were, escaped from *les désastres de la jeunesse*; misfits, they managed somehow to come to terms with life. But what if no terms existed? What if the boy was no more than an animal?

The true story of the little brute who came to be known as Victor de l'Aveyron, which happened at the turn of the 18th century, posed and in part answered these questions, and it was perhaps inevitable that Truffaut should turn it into a film. Indeed, so deeply did he become involved in it that he found it impossible to cast anyone except himself in the main part of Dr Itard, the man of vision who undertook the 'education' of the wild boy.

Not a Doinel rebelling against society or circumstances; not even Rousseau's noble savage; simply a human who had never known humanity, a human to all intents and purposes an animal. Captured, brought to Paris as a curiosity and then as an object of scientific research, the poor thing looked like ending its short, brutish life by pining away in what would in effect be a zoo. But at this point Itard stepped in; he believed that because this thing was in fact the offspring of human beings it could, it must in time be made into one; and so set about its education.

Truffaut shows explicitly how a strictly scientific approach would have failed, and how the key to the problem rested on moral, on humanitarian considerations, regardless of the chancy, casual manner by which they were arrived at. The cinematic technique is austere – black and white photography (by Eric Rohmer's cameraman Nestor Almendros), no tricks other than old-fashioned irises in and out, and the avoidance of camera movements unless absolutely necessary, as at the start of the film when the boy is running free and wild in his native woods. The atmosphere is cool, dispassionate. The contest between Itard, aided by his housekeeper and some friendly farmer-neighbours, and the wild boy he has optimistically named Victor, becomes all-engrossing. The style of the film doesn't change; Itard/Truffaut struggles all the time to retain his scientific attitude. But in proportion as Victor begins to show signs of intelligence, of human instead of animal reactions, his heart quickens with ours. Then there comes the heart-breaking realism of the sequences in which Itard tries to make Victor understand the relation between the letters of the alphabet, the words they make, and the things they stand for. And at the end, when the boy 'escapes' back to the freedom he once knew and finds, in the rain and the loneliness, that he can no longer enjoy it, we are left, as he returns to Itard's house and the motherly ministrations of the housekeeper, with a question-mark. Can he go further? He is, as Itard tells him (not without pride) no longer a savage; but, as the film ends, the question is – can he become a man?

There is something of a reminder of Bresson in the masked passion of Truffaut's treatment of *L'Enfant Sauvage*, which, incidentally, leaves quite a number of people cold. For my part I find it a tender and beautiful film, honest in its simplicity and even more honest in its questions, explicitly or implicitly posed, about the nature of freedom, the nature of free-will. Doinel originally managed to come to terms with society because he had, after all, been some sort of a part of it all along. Truffaut raises the question: what if he had not been a part of it, ever?[1] Freedom can be an ugly house, but if you are inside looking out, the scenery may be beautiful. Thus the greatest moment in *L'Enfant Sauvage* comes when Victor (superbly played throughout by Jean-Pierre Cargol), in violent conflict with Itard, reveals that he has come to feel the passions aroused by the sense of justice and injustice; and the stormy tragedy of this discovery is in fact a moment of great triumph.

A third figure from the *Cahiers du Cinéma* stables – and a some-what later developer – was Eric Rohmer. He made a feature film, *Le Signe du Lion*, in 1959, which was not a success, and he returned to film

---

[1] During the interview with the psychologist in *Les Quatre Cents Coups* Doinel, in reply to the question 'Why don't you like your mother?', replies: 'Because at first I had a nurse; then when they had no more money they sent me to my grandmother . . . but she got too old and couldn't look after me, so I went back to my parents when I was eight . . . and I noticed my mother didn't like me much (*he wrinkles his nose*) . . . So . . . also I . . . when there were fights at home . . . (*he keeps his eyes lowered and fidgets with his hands*) . . . I heard that my mother had me when she . . . when she . . . well, when she wasn't married yet . . . and once she had a fight with my grandmother and I found she wanted to have an abortion. (*He finally looks up at the psychologist.*) I was only born thanks to my grandmother.'

criticism while at the same time making a number of educational programmes for French television. Meantime he was carefully working out
the plans for his *Six Contes Moraux* through which, according to his
own avowal, he would seek to lead cinema away from the theatre and
toward the novel; which indeed he has done, and with considerable
success, for his work, though appearing literary if synopsized, is in fact
splendidly cinematic.

Of the six moral tales, only the four most recent are generally
known[1] – *La Collectionneuse* (1968), *Ma Nuit chez Maud* (1969), *Le
Genou de Claire* (1970), and *L'Amour, L'Après-midi* (1972). He has
defined the *conte moral* as 'not a tale with a moral, but a story which
deals less with what people do than with what is going on in their minds
while they are doing it. A cinema of thoughts rather than actions.'[2]
His films are indeed just like that. Rhomer has a tremendous visual
sense, acute in perspective. He manages to convey the everyday complexity of our mental processes by which, while watching a tennis match
and talking to a companion about the situation in Vietnam, we are in
fact thinking about how to get the girl-friend into bed. This sort of
thing is particularly well conveyed in *Le Genou de Claire*, in which even
the coming weather changes signalled by Alpine clouds have their
casual but proper significance.

In a way the key to this film is the realization that Claire and her
knee are incidental to the inner motivation of the story, which is the
two-way predicament in which Jérôme (Jean-Claude Brialy) lands himself in regard to the mature and self-satisfied Aurora (Aurora Cornu)
and the mercurial and uncertain teenager Laura (Béatrice Romand).
Jérôme needs to assert his experienced manhood, firstly against the
boy-friends who surround Laura and Claire, but secondly and urgently
against Aurora's habit of making maddening announcements such as
that she has made three young boys out of five in the course of the week;
she saves till very late the revelation that a rather dim man, glimpsed
only briefly earlier in the film, is her solid Genèvois fiancé.

Jérôme's confusion of sentiments is subtly portrayed by Rohmer
through the device of a diary, which allows for delicious and usually
self-explanatory dislocations of continuity rather similar to those
employed by Alea in *Memories of Underdevelopment*. The great variety
of episodes makes this a rich film, and each episode plays its proper
part in building it into a Proustian whole. There is a ridiculous but also

---

[1] The first two were *La Boulangère de Monceau* (1962) and *La Carrière de Suzanne*
(1963), both made for television. The sixth was too late for discussion here.
[2] Interview with Rui Nogueira in *Sight and Sound*, Summer 1971.

touching attempt at seduction by Jérôme when he takes Laura for a walk on the mountain slopes, in which her balance between childlike naïveté and a newly-found sophistication (she tells the poor chap that she is looking for a father-figure) reduces him to a state of clumsy bafflement. In contrast there is a Quatorze Juillet sequence in which one can sense how Jérôme both resents and delights in the propinquities of the dance-floor. In a similar way the trivial quarrel with a youth club leader about the danger and disturbance of the speedboat takes on traumatic undertones as we feel a growing realization of Jérôme's pusillanimity (it is interesting that in this sequence Rohmer made Brialy improvise his dialogue), and this leads as it were to an unexpected bonus at the very end of the film when Claire and her boyfriend Gilles, whose liaison Jérôme has boasted of having permanently broken during the knee-touching scene, are observed by Aurora (who else?) happily making it up again.[1]

With the exception of Aurora, who is used partly as a narrator and as dramatic catalyst, and thus at times gives the impression of being imposed on the film, the characters in *Le Genou de Claire* are delightfully, recognizably real. The still-handsome widowed mother with an eye for men; the two girls; Gilles, Claire's young man, handsome but *louche* – just the sort to rub Jérôme up the wrong way; they all perform their permutations and combinations in a kind of dreamy Proustian summer (a summer moving towards autumn) which is in absolute contrast to the wintry Clermont-Ferrand of *Ma Nuit chez Maud*, that industrial city of *Le Chagrin et la Pitié* whose harsh outlines not even the beneficent snowfall can soften. *Ma Nuit chez Maud* starts on a fairly high intellectual level which, were it not for Rohmer's sense of just how far to go, might have bogged down in the academic sterilities of the Steiner apartment in *La Dolce Vita*. But by some magic process the argument, based on Pascal's famous bet with the Deity and debated by a Marxist, a Catholic and a Freethinker, runs delightfully on until it ends with Trintignant having to stay the night at Maud's because of the snow. During the small hours his Pascalian chastity deserts him, but freethinking Maud will have none of that, for she doesn't like people who change their minds. Thus the film takes a new turn, and the man becomes involved with his 'true love' Françoise (Marie-Christine Barrault) and, once again because of the snow, spends a night in *her* spare room; which leads to marriage and later on to a dénouement and

[1] Rohmer himself, however, has commented (not untypically), 'Yes, but the boy could be lying'. He adds, speaking in general about his work, 'The endings I find have multiple repercussions. Like an echo.' (Nogueira, op. cit.)

to confessions all round like the tying up of ends in the finale of an
opéra bouffe. *Ma Nuit chez Maud* succeeds not merely because it is a
comedy of manners skilfully constructed, but because the manners are
those of flesh and blood, not of waxworks or automata.

These two films, allied to the triangular sarabandes on beach and
in Mediterranean villa in *La Collectionneuse*, which provides a light-
hearted discourse on the 'être et néant' point of view involving a rather
bogus philosopher, an over-dedicated painter, and a girl who exists as
far as possible without thinking, add up to a marked personal achievement on Rohmer's part. His interest in Hitchcock is seen only in his
ability to put across dialogue scenes by cunning camera placement as
much as by his direction of the characters; otherwise one may discern
in him more than a little of the influence of the Renoir who made
La Règle du Jeu.

A very different, but still major figure of the *Nouvelle Vague* is
Jean Rouch – pioneer of *cinéma-vérité*. Originally trained as an
ethnologist, he began, like so many forward-looking scientists, to use
a movie camera as an essential instrument in his researches and explorations. Soon, I think, he became seduced by the film medium itself –
a fact for which some of his scientific colleagues have never forgiven
him – and he began to make a number of admirable and imaginative
documentaries about African life and customs, notably *Les Fils de l'Eau*
and *Les Maîtres Fous*, the latter being a description of a sort of
embryonic Black Muslim group catering for the poorest of the poor
and focusing, in the name of religion, much of the justified resentment
at the injustice and inequality in the relations between blacks and
whites.

By this time Rouch had realized the enormous interpretative
power available through the lightweight camera and tape recorder, and
moved into what became known as *cinéma-vérité* with *Moi un Noir* in
1958. Rouch in fact does not especially like the definition he originally
thought up (any more than Grierson liked 'Documentary'). He has
said that *cinéma-vérité* was coined 'in homage to Dziga Vertov, who
completely invented the kind of film we do today. It was a cinema of
lies, but he believed simply – and I agree with him – that the camera
eye is more perspicacious and more accurate than the human eye . . .'[1]
Anyway, in *Moi un Noir* Rouch chose to depict the life of a negro dock

[1] American pioneers of *cinéma-vérité* regarded Rouch's attitude as 'impure', dis-
torting or interfering with the reality observed by the camera. Later some of them, notably
Richard Leacock, tended to move more towards his point of view. See the interviews with
Rouch and Leacock in *Documentary Explorations*, ed. G. Roy Levin, Doubleday, 1971.

worker in the port of Abidjan, Ivory Coast; he began by analysing the man's life through the camera, shooting without sound, and then built up a soundtrack by showing the dock worker the material and recording his comments. The resultant interrelation between Rouch, the man *and the film* produced a new factor – a change in the man's attitude to life, a surge, if you like, of new interest in himself, in who he was, and the arrival of a perhaps hitherto unknown pride or self-respect; and he chose himself a new name – Edward G. Robinson. The result, according to Rouch himself, 'is false, it's a film that's acted out, an acted out autobiography, and therefore false'.[1]

Following this, and over a period of several years, Rouch worked on another experiment – *La Pyramide Humaine*, finally completed in 1961. Also made in Abidjan, this film records an attempt to bring together the white and black pupils of a large integrated school who, outside the school grounds, hardly ever mixed at all. Rouch asked the two groups to take part in the production of a film about the problem of making this contact, and in the course of production a considerable amount of integration took place; the mere act of trying to make a film, therefore, had positive social results.[2] The film itself was not very successful, largely owing to the normal character changes of the boys and girls as they grew up and exchanged the spontaneity of childhood for the self-consciousness of adolescence.

From his experience on *La Pyramide Humaine*, however, Rouch was emboldened to embark on what still remains his best full-length film, *Chronique d'un Eté* (*Chronicle of a Summer*), made in 1961. Here, instead of turning his ethnographic camera on Africans, he pointed it at the people of Paris. In close collaboration with Edgar Morin he embarked on a period of shooting during which not only were over twenty hours of film recorded – mostly synchronous – but also the ideas and attitudes of the film-makers themselves changed according to their reactions – conscious or subconscious – to their totally non-fictional subject matter. When edited into a film ninety minutes in duration, the material was revealed as a rich mine of human relationships and

[1] The hero of *Moi un Noir* became a film-maker himself, under his original name, Oumarou Ganda. His *Cabascabo* was shown at the Moscow Festival in 1969.

[2] The family who appeared in *The Things I Cannot Change*, referred to earlier, represent an opposite experience. The film made them an object of scorn and derision to their neighbours – so much so that they had to migrate to another district. Here was the case of a film which was in itself good, and would undoubtedly do good in a broad social field, but yet practically destroyed the very people whose circumstances it was designed to help. The lesson was not lost on the National Film Board of Canada, who now ensure participatory understanding by a whole community *before and during* the production of such films.

revelations which, however raw and direct they emerged from the camera, had somehow become bound together into something of a genuine work of art.

Chronique d'un Eté begins with a routine. Rouch and Morin have arranged for a girl they know, Marceline, to go into the streets and ask random passers by, 'Are you Happy?' Out of this exercise, with its often conventional and predictably humorous replies, there are gradually introduced certain characters on whom – by some sort of osmotic instinct – Rouch and Morin decide to concentrate, one of them being in fact Marceline herself. We are now involved in interviews in depth with, in addition to Marceline, Angelo, a worker in the Renault factory; Landry, an African negro studying in Paris; and Marilu, an Italian girl working in Paris as a typist.

After the development of these interviews all concerned are packed off for a holiday in the South of France, where we observe further developments in themselves and in their relationships with each other; here, despite (or because of?) the would-be catalytic introduction of a number of delightful children, the sequences tend to become diffuse and blurred. The film-makers realize this almost as soon as we do, and they stop shooting; and we find ourselves in a private cinema where all the people of the film (who have, as it were, been seeing it with us) proceed to give their personal reaction to it and in particular to themselves as they appear in it. Some fascinating revelations result.

This is not, however, the end. With total honesty, Rouch and Morin appear by themselves, pacing a gallery and discussing in some detail the errors they have made, the problems aroused by the actual making of the film as well as by the film itself, and various new ideas which may arise from it.

Even if it lacks symmetry, *Chronique d'un Eté* somehow gives the opposite impression – perhaps because it so continuously unfolds the marvels and beauties as well as the ennuis and miseries of the human heart with a breathtaking and innocent naturalism. At one point the film-makers introduce Angelo and Landry to each other. After the exchange of some guarded banalities they become interested in each other, sit down on the stairway, and really start talking. And we watch the formation of a friendship like a stop-motion of the opening of a flower.

Then there is Marilu, the Italian typist, who turns out to be a girl disturbed in her mind by a crushing sense of loneliness. In her first interview with Morin she is, to begin with, fairly conventional. She says she was homesick when she first arrived, but also felt that her small, cold rented room could be a good challenge to her energy and ingenuity. Soon, though, she becomes more open with Morin. Yes, she's fed up. Lonely. What does she do? Well, she says, I drink (*'Je bois, par exemple'*). And so on until she has virtually confessed to being a soul tortured by loneliness and by the absence of love. To another question she doesn't reply. For what seems an hour we watch her face, the working of her mouth, but – nothing. Silence. Nothing. The sense of despair chokes us.

Later in the film she has a second interview with Morin. Something has happened. She has found a lover. Still there are long silences; but they come to an end with the slow dawning of a most exquisite smile – a smile which, as we learn when she at last speaks, she hardly dares to permit herself lest its *hubris* should bring a return of the nightmare of solitude. With that beautiful, hesitant smile and with the arrival of her boy-friend (no great shakes to look at but who cares?) we leave her until the final sequence in the private cinema when, asked what value she sees in the film, she replies, rather cautiously, that she thinks it has something comforting in it for someone who is nervous and alone . . .

Another highlight of this film comes when a number of the participants are grouped together in general conversation; Rouch suddenly breaks into a discussion about the Congo and asks Landry what is the meaning of the number tattooed on Marceline's arm. Landry has no idea. A gimmick? he guesses; her phone number perhaps? Then, quietly, she tells him she is Jewish and that this is her number from the German concentration camp. And Landry is literally struck dumb. At which point Rouch cuts brutally to Marceline walking alone through a deserted Paris at dawn – across the Place de la Concorde and on to Les Halles; and as she walks she speaks aloud about her memories of those days in the camp, where her mother died but she survived; and the melancholy of the past mingles with the melancholy of the present and surges over us as well as her.

This is the sort of point at which many critics accuse Rouch and Morin of ignoring the rules of *cinéma-vérité*, of interfering, intervening, of deliberately setting up situations. In this case of Marceline's walk Rouch has given a succinct answer. 'It's false,' he agrees, 'No one walks along talking out loud. But I suddenly discovered that this released a series of confessions that Marceline had never made during a direct, face-to-face interview, simply because she was suddenly in a totally different element.' He goes on to point out that despite the fact that she was carrying a portable tape-recorder and had a microphone round her neck, so that the set-up was completely artificial, nevertheless 'suddenly, there is in effect no camera, no microphone. There's a revelation, a staggering revelation because it's totally sincere – *and totally provoked*.'[1] To this we may add what Marceline herself says in the discussion at the end of the film – that all the time she thought of herself as an actress portraying herself and that it was only in this way that she felt she could be truly 'true'.

Since then Rouch has done much work on the vast amount of material he shot in Africa during the Fifties; out of this, in particular, have come two feature-length films – *La Chasse au Lion à l'Arc* (1958–65) and the extraordinary *Jaguar* (1953–67), a wild picaresque swoop through Francophone Africa which contains everything from marvellous anthropological observation to sequences of comedy and fantasy which must drive some of his scientist colleagues mad. It is a *jeu d'esprit* well worth seeing.

Better than all this, however, is a short film he shot for the National Film Board of Canada in 1963. *Rose et Landry* – the same Landry from *Chronique d'un Eté* – talk gently about the differences and tensions, overt or hidden, between people, peoples, races and civilizations. That is all; a girl and a boy probing deep problems as best they can, beautifully shot (by Georges Dufaux) on telephoto lenses – as though the camera wished not to intrude too indelicately on their thoughts and visions . . .

Here I must mention Chris Marker's *Le Joli Mai* (1963), which is something of a companion piece to *Chronique d'un Eté*. The difference between the two is striking, because Marker's approach is basically political and iconoclastic. When he pokes his camera into people's affairs he doesn't hesitate to be rude; he examines Paris from a point of view of alienation rather than affection (though here, as elsewhere in his work, his obsession with those super-alienators, cats, softens rather than hardens the line), and above all he dazzles not only with his technique but with the people who (albeit seen less in depth than Rouch's) constantly surprise with a sense of something else, something more lying behind their outward reactions – as witness Marker's negro student compared with Landry, or his Algerian worker with Angelo. The Paris of Marker in *Le Joli Mai* – satirically named for the first Spring 'without war' since 1939 – is seen with poetic as well as political rage; but its sharp edges ultimately fail to cut the stubble off society's chin.

[1] G. Roy Levin, op. cit. My italics.

Political issues increasingly invaded films during this period. Godard I will come to shortly; but apart from Marker – who also made *Cuba Si!* and provided his contribution to *Loin du Viet-Nam* (1967) by organizing and editing all the material[1] – we may note that in retrospective vein Frédéric Rossif made *Mourir à Madrid* (*To Die in Madrid*) in 1962, a remarkable compilation film on the Spanish Civil War in which an inevitable sense of disasters *déja vus* was countered by its celebration of the burning faiths and enthusiasms, however misplaced, however misled, however betrayed, of those terrible days. The narration contains telling quotations from, among others, Mauriac and Bernanos, to say nothing of a savagely dignified speech by Unamuno; and in the English version John Gielgud nobly reads Lorca and Irene Worth magnificently impersonates La Pasionara. In a time when a Lieutenant Calley, perpetrator of acts which make Guernica look like a charity bazaar, can become, if only for a brief period, a national hero, the genuine moralities of Rossif's film come to us across the blood and disaster like a refreshing breeze.

Nearer the present, however, films tend to have their own built-in ordure. Two films by Costa-Gavras, *Z* (1969) and *L'Aveu* (*The Confession*), made the following year, are directly political and hardly bother even to disguise the factual origins of their stories. *Z* is clearly about George Lambrakis and the Greek colonels; *L'Aveu* is equally clearly about the brainwashing systems employed by the Communist party in Czechoslovakia and, more particularly, about the sort of situation (as with Saint-Just and Robespierre in the French Revolution) in which the practitioner of cruelty and repression – in this case Slansky – becomes the victim of the system he has created. Costa-Gavras tends to become so committed to the theme of his film that he overplays his hand; the verisimilitude of his reconstructions is sometimes marred by unnecessary overemphasis and by the overplaying of his *figurants*.

Not so with Gillo Pontecorvo, whose *Battle of Algiers* (1965) is in its own way one of the most astonishing 'documentaries' ever made. Using apparently the whole city and the bulk of its inhabitants, he has encapsulated all the main factors of that savage war between the Arabs, the *Pieds Noirs* and Metropolitan France, from which only Le Grand Charles could find a reasonable means of general extrication, into a feature length 'actuality' of extraordinary convincingness.

It is a film framed in horrifying tortures. It begins with soldiers

---

[1] This omnibus political pamphlet consisted of filmic contributions from Godard, Resnais, William Klein, Joris Ivens, Agnès Varda and Claude Lelouch, as well as much newsreel material.

being nice to what is left of a little man from whom they have just hideously extracted the name of a colleague. And practically at the end of the film the French commanding officer delivers a cogent argument in defence of the use of torture (followed a few moments later by a series of illustrations of a fearfully explicit and sickening nature), during which he refers not only to the bravery of his opponents but also to their having the multiplicity of a tapeworm; and, in a moment of rhetorical bravura, asks 'Why are the Sartres always on the other side?'

Pontecorvo remains remorseless in his presentation. When an Algerian woman plants a bomb in a crowded bar, he makes sure that she, as well as we the audience, takes due note of the young married couples, the small children and all the other innocents who are there. It is of course the simple story of Saigon, Nicosia, Belfast and the rest. Pontecorvo, however, can come to a conclusion. For in Algeria the conflict did end. The French left. Something, not perhaps justice, not even perhaps good sense, and certainly not compassion – but something has triumphed, and the carnage is over. Pontecorvo has made us observe, at least in part, the thrilling, terrifying, horrible cost; and the film is so realistic that although one knows it is a reconstruction, one forgets that simple fact. There has always been a quarrel among documentary people about 'justified reconstruction' – from Flaherty cutting an igloo in half to show how Nanook and his family lived their domestic life, to the building of the railway coach interior in the studio for *Night Mail*; both of those, and many others, I support, and with equal enthusiasm I salute Pontecorvo and his film.[1]

Other important directors of the New Wave period included Georges Franju who, turning from the short films referred to earlier in this book, made a number of features of which the best perhaps was a screen version of Mauriac's *Thérèse Desqueyroux* (1962) – a stifling and often frightening story of bourgeois life in which a wife tries to poison her husband, is found out and, both for the sake of appearances

---

[1] *Le Chagrin et la Pitié* (1970), a four-hour-long filmed television programme by Marcel Ophuls about the behaviour of the French during the German occupation, had something of the same quality. This emerged, however, from the juxtaposition of material shot at the time (largely by the Germans or by collaborators) with the actual participants on either side speaking today in justification, accusation or sheer reminiscence. The contrasts of attitudes during the war and today, between the two peasant farmers, some of the more self-seeking tradesmen of Clermont-Ferrand, Mendès-France (the truest of patriots), and the Comte de Chambrun (Laval's nephew), were engrossing, upsetting, and often tragic. Like the BBC over Peter Watkins' *The War Game*, the French TV authorities refused to show the film; and, also like *The War Game*, it had a great and deserved success in the cinema. One may also remember in this context Michael Papas' film about the Cyprus troubles – *The Private Right* (1966).

and as a grim punishment, is taken back into family imprisonment until, in the end, she is freed by her boorish husband to live on her own in Paris (if it is not too late for freedom). Splendidly played by Emmanuelle Riva as the wife and Philippe Noiret as the husband, this atmospheric film develops its theme in the claustrophobic family mansion and the equally claustrophobic forests and marshes of the Landes. Franju's next film, *Judex* (1963) – a prolonged and elaborate *hommage* to Louis Feuillade – seemed to me, for all its skill and variety, for all the brilliance of its art direction, and for all the compulsive acting by Francine Bergé, Edith Scob and Michel Vitold, to hang fire and to overstay its welcome; terrifying and unforgettable, though, the sequence of the Ball at which all the guests, as well as the sinister host, have the heads of birds above their elegant evening dress – a nightmare from Ancient Egypt entangled with *La Belle Epoque*.

From Louis Malle, whose *Zazie dans le Métro* I have already noticed, came, among others, *Le Feu Follet* (1963) with Maurice Ronet and Jeanne Moreau; *Viva Maria* (1965) with Brigitte Bardot rumbustiously joining forces with Moreau but to little avail; and *Le Voleur* (1967) with Jean-Paul Belmondo and Geneviève Bujold. Of these *Le Feu Follet* (translated for some obscure reason as *A Time to Live and a Time to Die*)[1] was undoubtedly the best. It is curious that it has never had the success it deserves, for, despite its subject – the last hours of an alcoholic bent on suicide – it has a Bresson-like perfection of style and a number of very effective performances dominated by Maurice Ronet as the self-doomed hero, pursued by the probing but sympathetic camera of Ghislain Cloquet.

The suicide-bent Alain Leroy is a destroyed playboy reminiscent of the Scott Fitzgerald era (to which the film indeed makes oblique references); and he has an estranged American wife, the renewal of contact with whom, as suggested by the doctor at the residential clinic where he has been taking his cure, he turns down in favour of a series of visits to cronies of the mad, bad days, during which he can bid them an unspoken farewell. Malle grimly delineates them for us in all their self-centred uselessness; insults to human-kind, they cannot but confirm Alain in his date with death scrawled on his bathroom mirror. Only a lesbian, or would-be lesbian (finely played by Jeanne Moreau) suggests some sympathy with the lonely vacuum to which, through inertia, he has condemned himself. Otherwise all is contempt. Leaving the clinic, he makes the symbolic final gift of his wristwatch to an uncomprehending *femme de chambre*; time must have a stop. The taxi-

---

[1] It was recently re-issued in New York as *The Fire Within*.

driver, receiving from him an enormous tip, remarks 'Quel idiot!' It is a film which could be repellent. But such is the director's sympathy for his fated hero, such is the skill and charm of Ronet as Alain, that we identify, and long to offer other avenues of escape than the blind alley he has chosen and down which we reluctantly must see him vanish. Needless to say, his suicide is hygienic and designed to cause the minimal trouble to everyone.

Le Souffle au Coeur (once again an inexplicable English title – Dearest Love) was made eight years after Le Feu Follet but in some respects may be seen as a companion piece. Here Malle gives us an adolescent seeking to break out from the 'false' life of childhood into the realities of the grown-up world and particularly of sexual experience. Alain found the solution to his problem in death; young Laurent, in Le Souffle au Coeur, finds his in the surprise of an entirely spontaneous and unplanned moment of incest with his comparatively young and extremely attractive mother. This episode is presented with a curiously convincing sense of innocence (and I mean that word); as the mother says afterwards, 'We'll never mention this again' – and we know they won't. The immediate effect of this experience is to trigger off all Laurent's normal stud impulses; he gallops off and lays one of his contemporaries with great success, and the film ends in the early morning when he is caught sneaking back, shoes in hand, to his own room by his father and two elder brothers, who bring up the end titles in a cascade of laughter.

Crowded with incident and observation (randy boys at Mass, a gorgeously ridiculous game of tennis, the pestering of an aged nanny by her ex-charges), the film is also cleverly anchored in time by Malle. It is the year of Dien Bien Phu. People are reading Camus. The gramophone intones Charlie Parker and Sidney Bechet while the radio emits its sempiternal reports on the Tour de France. With excellent performances by a very large cast, Le Souffle au Coeur has a flavour as distinctive as sorrel soup – sharp yet creamy, seductive yet cleansing.

Alain Robbe-Grillet, the novelist who turned script-writer for Resnais on L'Année Dernière à Marienbad, subsequently went into production himself, making in Istanbul the mysterious L'Immortelle (1963), which in its inexplicability recalls the Resnais film but lacks its compelling style. This he followed with Trans-Europe Express (1966) a railway thriller, constructed rather like a Bach mirror-fugue, which landed itself in a lot of trouble – often very surprisingly – with the censors.

Meantime Jacques Demy founded a new, rather touching and

simplistic version of the Musical in *Les Parapluies de Cherbourg* (1962) and *Les Demoiselles de Rochefort* (1967), while Claude Lelouch hit box-office highspots (to say nothing of Top of the Pops) with *Un Homme et une Femme* (1967), in which a Ladies Home Journal story was skilfully dressed up (not least thanks to Lelouch's own brilliant photography and camera-movement) to look like an art film, and automobiles waltzed in elegant time to the starry motions of Anouk Aimée and Jean-Louis Trintignant. In his next film, *Vivre pour Vivre* (1967), Lelouch had Yves Montand and Candice Bergen; but the general effect was little different – treacle this time, rather than honey, perhaps.

Agnès Varda, that comparatively *rara avis*, a female film director,[1] made her name with a short film entitled *Opéra Mouffe* (1958), an impression of a Paris *quartier* seen from the point of view of a pregnant woman. Her *Cléo de Cinq à Sept* (1962) had something of the same observational quality; but her next film, *Le Bonheur* (1965), followed a different course. Here Varda poses not Rouch's question 'Are you happy?', but 'What is Happiness?', and finds the answer in a lyrical abandonment (accompanied by lashings of Mozart) to the idea of the simple life of a carpenter with his wife and children; which would be all very well if it did not involve his mistress as well (an actress) whom, thanks to his wife's death, he is enabled to marry. The film is beautiful to look at (camera by Jean Rabier), but its answer to the question remains in doubt. What is happiness? Certainly not make-believe; Blanche Dubois found that out the hard way quite a time ago.

The insistent Jean-Luc Godard can no longer be put off. The amount which has already been written about him – too much of it blindly indiscriminate praise – makes me inclined to be as brief as possible. Nor do I wish to counter the blankets of praise with vituperation.[2] But the plain fact is that you can neither ignore Godard nor try to brush him off.

[1] In these days of Women's Lib I should perhaps take the opportunity to list some other female directors not mentioned elsewhere in this book, adding in each case at least one of their principal films: Ida Lupino (*The Bigamist*), Barbara Loden (*Wanda*), Lina Wertmüller (*The Lizards*), Olga Preobrazhenskaya (*Peasant Women of Riazan*), Susan Sontag (*Duet for Cannibals*), Muriel Box (*The Truth about Women*), Nelly Kaplan (*La Fiancée du Pirate*), Judit Elek (*The Lady from Constantinople*), Jacqueline Audry (*L'Ingénue Libertine*), Nadine Trintignant (*Mon Amour, Mon Amour*), Nina Companeez (*Faustine*) and, last but not least, that distinguished pioneer Dorothy Arzner who, after graduating from the cutting room where she edited, among other films, *Blood and Sand* and *The Covered Wagon*, became a top director with films such as *The Wild Party*, *Merrily We Go To Hell*, *Craig's Wife* and *Dance, Girl, Dance*.

[2] When it comes to vituperation those who hate Godard really let themselves go. John Simon, film critic of the American *New Leader*, has a tremendous passage in his book *Private Screenings* in which, relative to Andrew Sarris' comparison of Godard's position

When asked whether he did not think that, as a matter of principle, a film should have a beginning, a middle and an end, he is said
to have replied, 'Yes, but not necessarily in that order'. The reply was
not a naughtiness or a *jeu d'esprit*. Godard meant it; nor was he the
first to enunciate the principle: the first was the unknown who created
the flashback.

What Godard basically has done is to codify the various factors
which separate the cinema from the theatre, though not, significantly
enough, from the novel, the frizzling-up of Emily Brontë in *Weekend*
notwithstanding (her behaviour made it virtually an *auto da fé*). He has
also realized, as much as or more than any film-maker so far, the
extraordinary fluidity of the medium in relation to the commingling of
film time and actual time, which is Einsteinian, and of filmic space,
which is multidimensional, as opposed to actual space which is not
(Einstein again, I suppose).

In a Godard film there would at this point be a trick title making
a play on *Eisenstein, Ei(se)nstein, Einstein*.

Over and over again in his films Godard plays tricks on us,
stupefies, impresses, irritates us through his manipulation of these
spacetime relationships. One of the most brilliant things in *Le Mépris*
(*Contempt*), made in 1963, is the manner in which he compresses the
long, gradual breakdown between husband and wife, which must have
been brewing up over a long period, into one tightly organized sequence
of argument during which they wander around, or sit about in their
huge, still unfinished apartment – a simultaneous symbol of a desired
permanence and a suspected love-trap. What they here do or say compresses weeks or months into a few minutes. At one point Bardot
ruptures everything by suddenly wearing a black wig; the effect is
doubly traumatic – on Michel Piccoli as her husband and on us as
audience. He can't do that to *us*, we say (i.e. Bardot can but Godard
'can't'), yet at the same time we notice that Piccoli, taking it in his
stride, is cleverer than we are – so that we now suffer a sort of superimposition of extra annoyance mingled with reluctant admiration. Here
indeed is a fine example of the subtlety of Godard's alienation technique. At a moment when, apart from anything else, we would like to
remain alone with Bardot in the bathroom, he uses an elaborately
convoluted technique to remind us that we are only watching a film.

---

to those of Stravinsky, Picasso, Joyce and Eliot, he remarks 'About the only place where
Godard's position might be comparable to that of the other four is on the toilet seat. But
Godard, alas!, also expels his works from that position.' Nothing rougher has been written
since the première of Dreyer's *Gertrud*.

Another example is in *Deux ou Trois Choses que Je Sais d'Elle*, or *Two or Three Things I Know about Her* (1966). At a moment when – at least as far as I am concerned – he has created a mood of maximum tedium, maximum annoyance, of *ennui*, of *cafard*, he suddenly concentrates everything on to the bubbles on the top of a cup of coffee, and in a split second launches us into a mystical exploration of galactic space while on the soundtrack the urgent-trivial-urgent efforts of man's brain to encompass terrestrial problems are nervously and confusedly adumbrated. It is in this respect that Godard must be seen as a director unique in his understanding of the medium and in his ability to manipulate it. It is annoying that his genius also demands his preoccupation with other matters – existentialism, Maoism, and a general desire to interfere – which leads filmically to unnecessary and sometimes unsavoury *cul-de-sacs*.

Like *Une Femme Mariée* (1964) and *Masculin Féminin* (1966), *Deux ou Trois Choses que Je Sais d'Elle* is a sort of maddening ragbag out of which from time to time Godard snatches some dazzling purple patches which emerge from a lot of deliberately dull 'documentary' shooting or *cinéma-vérité*-type interviews in which he seems to have only a mild interest and from which he switches with relief to something else like a sequence treated in Pabstian manner, when Juliette, in the process of earning her pin-money, picks up or is picked up by a young boy who looks like a Nureyev with acute psoriasis and they go to a hotel where the sex scene is played out like a cold and upsetting mirror image[1] – icily practical and also sad – of the relations between Camille and Paul in *Le Mépris*.

It is a weakness as well as a strength of Godard's attack on Western civilization that it is indiscriminate; and one may say precisely the same about his attacks on cinema. Yet when the two are combined, one can get explosively fabulous concepts – *Les Carabiniers* and *Weekend* for instance – or dust and ashes like *Alphaville* and the coffin-shaped insults of *Pravda*.

In *Weekend* there is a particular episode which throws into sharp relief the ideological carelessness which is the penalty exacted from Godard by his indiscriminate exuberance. In the final section of the film we find ourselves among hippie bandits who indulge, by preference, though not exclusively, in cannibalism ('These are the leftovers of last week's tourists from the Rolls Royce and also, I think, part of your husband'), and he decides to insert scenes of the culinary preparations which are a mixture of sick humour (a girl is literally stuffed with a

[1] They have a row over a real mirror too.

fish before being despatched and cooked) and Rabelaisian humour (the
so-called chef is a vast quivering mixture of Gargantua and an Edinburgh grave-robber, as well as being tremendously inefficient at his job).
Early on in the sequence Godard treats us to the slaughter of a goose
and a pig – the latter being despatched by a bang on the head and the
former decapitated, its liver and lights being removed while its wings are
still flapping. Clearly the implication here is that these are surrogate
killings, presented as vividly as possible because it is *not* possible to
present the actual killing of a human being. Thus the actual killing of
the two animals is used to emphasize a 'lack' or 'failing' in the cinematic
translation of the idea to the screen, and this is true whether or no
Godard has his tongue in his cheek. The effort fails, however, for a
number of reasons, some of which have been cogently stated by Pauline
Kael who, in *Going Steady*, remarks,

'When people are killed in a movie, even when the killing is
not stylised, it's generally OK, because we know it's a fake, but when
animals are slaughtered we are watching life being taken away. No
doubt Godard intends this to shock us out of "aesthetic" responses,
just as his agit-prop preaching is intended to affect us directly, but I
think he miscalculates. I look away from scenes like this, as I assume
many others do. Is he forcing us to confront the knowledge that there
are things we don't want to look at? But we knew that. Instead of
drawing us into his conception, he throws us out of the movie. And,
because we know how movies are made, we instinctively recognize
that his method of jolting us is fraudulent; he, the movie director,
has ordered that slaughter to get a reaction from us, and so we have
a right to be angry with him. Whatever our civilization is responsible
for, that sow up there is his, not ours.'

It is of course possible that Godard took *all* this into account
and that his effect on Miss Kael is precisely what he planned. But the
whole thing still remains something of a nonsense. For it is only a
minority of sensitive, *élite* intellectuals who shudder at such scenes
when they are demonstrably real, as in the abattoir scene behind the
tournedos rossini in *Rien que les Heures* or in virtually the whole of
Le Sang des Bêtes, but who accept them, as in the eyeball and razor
scene in *Un Chien Andalou*, when they are not. (They are probably
more shocked when, in *L'Age d'Or*, Modot kicks a small poodle to
kingdom come.) No, the real nonsense of the pig and the goose is that
in any normal peasant community – Europe, Asia, Africa, America –
the scene of their killing would cause neither shock nor surprise; it is

normal, routine. To eat, one must kill.[1] Nor would it occur to a countryman to avert his eyes like Miss Kael and the rest.

Robin Wood has said – and this relates to the previous paragraphs,

'What makes *Weekend* so much more insupportable is Godard's refusal to see the end of civilization as final. It is insidiously flattering to the liberal-humanist ego to be able to equate the end of western civilization with the end of the world. But *Weekend* is not about the end of the world – it is simply about the end of *our* world.'

This is well said; and one may note that *Weekend* ends with two titles:

FIN DE CONTE

FIN DE CINEMA.

And it is true that Godard, in the very nature of his cinematic genius, has put film at peril. We can never feel quite safe again. But it is also true that by his fragmentation, by his challenge to the validity of the structure we have erected to prove that film is an art, he has forced us to start thinking about movie all over again.

This morning I read the following in the *Sunday Times* Colour Supplement:

'The population in these areas, where traces of the complex cultivation of old still show on the barren hillsides, is dwarfed and enfeebled through generations of malnutrition and servitude. One child in three survives to reach adolescence. Up to 70% suffer from tuberculosis. In some small towns only the mayor can read and write. Here civilization has been powdered to nothingness.'

This is the world of Godard; not merely the Latin American world from which the quotation emerges, but the whole Western world as he sees it in which – to continue the *Times* quote – 'liberalism is dead. There is no longer any middle of the road. All the revolutionaries have turned to Marx.' He must fragment his medium of expression in order completely to identify it with the collapsing edifices, the disintegrating psyches, and the already decaying ruins of the society he is describing and attacking. This fully explains his great output and its mixture of good and bad, success and failure. If only his more adulatory sup-

---

[1] A fascinating sidelight is thrown on this by the goose-stuffing episode in Jiri Menzel's *Closely Observed Trains*. All societies for the prevention of cruelty to animals fight against the system by which a goose's feet are nailed to the floor and it is then forcibly fed so as to swell its liver until it is suitable for the making of *pâté de foie gras*. But the facts remain; we eat *pâté*. And in this case Menzel makes of it a superb and at the same time a touching sexual joke.

porters would admit that he can and does make some terribly bad films, the air would be much clearer.

By the same token his influence on other film-makers has been very varied. It is a moot point whether Bertolucci's *Partner* or *The Conformist* would have been better or worse without it. His effect on Oshima, judging by *Diary of a Shinjuku Thief*, was the reverse of beneficial, though the subsequent (and excellent) *Boy* indicates that it was only temporary. In Latin America itself it has been in general effective if one goes by the Glauber Rocha of *Antonio das Mortes* or the Tomas Alea of the more genial *Memories of Underdevelopment*.

Something of a reply to Godard by one of his contemporaries who is in his own way equally unorthodox came from Dusan Makavejev:

'I see the cinema as a guerilla operation. Guerilla against everything that is fixed, defined, established, dogmatic, eternal. It's not irrelevant that the cinema should be at war, because eventually everything is connected. Hollywood is Wall Street and the Pentagon . . . But that doesn't mean that the cinema must serve the revolution: the revolution has no need of servants. Everyone has to make his own revolution . . .

'Godard has placed himself at the *service* of the revolution. I don't want to serve . . . I think only that fighting in the cinema . . . for a freer, more authentic expression . . . we are waging the same war as those who fight on the barricades. It's always the same job of freeing yourself from authority, of breaking down structures, of opening up doors, opening up paths; in short to create a free, open world where every individual can be himself.'[1] ·

I shall return later to Makavejev's optimistic brand of anarchism; meantime let Godard defend himself through the words he speaks over the close-up of the coffee-cup in *Deux ou Trois Choses que je Sais d'Elle*:

'As every event changes my daily life, as I constantly fail to communicate, to understand, to love, to be loved . . . As I can neither free myself from the objectivity that is crushing me nor the subjectivity that is driving me into exile . . . As I can neither raise myself into life nor fall back into nothingness . . . I must listen. I must look around me . . . at the world . . . where capitalism is beginning to doubt its rights and where the workers are in retreat . . . where the future is more present than the present, where the distant galaxies are at my door.'

[1] *Joie de Vivre at the Barricades* by David Robinson, *Sight and Sound*, Autumn 1971.

And he adds:

'Where does it begin? But where does *what* begin?'[1]

Which partly explains why, despite the destructive titles at the end of *Weekend*, he entitled his next film, in which his characters at least made a positive effort to come to terms with the human predicament, *Le Gai Savoir*.

Godard is still at work, and who knows what will yet come from him? For the time being I would be inclined to apply to him Terence Mullaly's criticism of Picasso on the occasion of his 90th birthday, in which he described him as 'a restless, wayward genius. He is one of the most richly endowed of artists. Yet he is one who, led away by the lack of wisdom and heart of his times, has too often confused gesture with the abiding rôle of the artist, which is to honour man and express his humanity.'[2]

III

It is now high time to return to the Italian cinema, which I abandoned in full flood some chapters back.

Of the original neo-realists, Rossellini continued his astonishing career with films starring Anna Magnani (notably a screen version of Cocteau's *La Voix Humaine* coupled with *The Miracle* in 1948) and Ingrid Bergman in *Stromboli* (1949). As time went on his virtuosity increased rather than diminished, as witness his splendid *Il Generale della Rovere* (1959) – a deceptively raw, rough quickie with a magisterial performance by De Sica[3] as a petty crook who is persuaded by the Nazis to impersonate a Resistance leader (in order to spy on fellow prisoners) and who gradually takes on the genuinely patriotic character of the dead man he is impersonating. In more recent years Rossellini has turned with equal success to the making of films for television – his *La Prise de Pouvoir par Louis XIV* (1966) being particularly admired, not least for its extraordinarily convincing period authenticity.

As for De Sica himself – as director – he followed *Bicycle Thieves*

---

[1] See Robin Wood on *Weekend* in *The Films of Jean-Luc Godard*, Studio Vista, 1967.

[2] *Daily Telegraph*, October 23, 1971. Picasso is now dead, but I doubt if Mullaly would wish to alter his comments.

[3] De Sica has always remained one of Italy's highest paid actors; many will remember his superb performance opposite Lollobrigida in Luigi Comencini's *Bread, Love and Dreams*.

with a rather disappointing mixture of fantasy and realism, *Miracle in Milan* (1950). He followed this, however, with a film which fully stood up to comparison with *Shoeshine* and *Bicycle Thieves*. *Umberto D* (1952) told with grim clarity but also with deep sympathy the story of the loneliness of old age and of the despair of the dispossessed. The chief part was again played by an unknown non-actor. The old man tries desperately to come to terms with a world where his values and his status have been ruthlessly downgraded, and in a heart-grabbing final sequence he comes to the brink of suicide. The film is full of marvellous moments, not least the scene where, with the aid of his only companion, a small fox-terrier, he tries to come to terms with begging in the street. His failure in this is both a tribute to human dignity and as pathetic a moment as any in cinema.

Thereafter De Sica's directorial work became more erratic – *Two Women*[1] (1960), however, and *The Condemned of Altona* (1963) being worthy of note. The former in particular, showing a mother (Sophia Loren) and her daughter (Eleanora Brown) caught in the crossfire of battle and politics in the last days of the war in Italy (they are raped in a church by Moroccan troops of the liberating French Army), was emotionally powerful and convincingly presented; it may be one of his most underestimated films. Latterly De Sica has emerged again with a film on the fate of a Jewish family during the Mussolini regime entitled *The Garden of the Finzi Continis* (1970).

Meantime the glorious Anna Magnani divided her favours among other directors like Jean Renoir (*The Golden Coach*, 1952), Daniel Mann (*The Rose Tattoo*, 1955) and Visconti (*Bellissima*, 1951). But it was back in 1949 that she gave one of her finest performances in Luigi Zampa's *Angelina* (*L'Onorevole Angelina*). Despite a rather contrived happy ending this is a film bursting with life; Magnani, as a policeman's wife who, stung by the corruption of the black market and other local injustices, organizes all the women along the lines of *Ecclesiazusai* rather than *Lysistrata*, is elected to the council, imprisoned, and finally triumphantly released, well deserved Richard Winnington's comment that 'her unclassifiable beauty is a unique fusion of the physical and spiritual'.

In many respects though, Zampa's earlier *To Live in Peace* (*Vivere in Pace*) made in 1946, is a better film. Here he takes neo-realism up a picturesque side road into tragi-comedy. The scene is a remote Italian village during the War; staff are very thin on the ground, and the Axis is represented only by the local secretary of the Fascist

[1] Italian title *La Ciociara*; it is based on a novel by Alberto Moravia.

Party (whose attempts to convince himself rather than his sceptical colleagues that the Germans are winning lead to some rich comedy), and one solitary German NCO.

It is in fact quite a cosy situation, since no one concerned wants to be bothered with the war; they prefer to try to 'live in peace'.

But suddenly there arrive two escaped American prisoners on the run. Old Tigna (Aldo Fabrizi), an influential member of the community, knows that they must be sheltered – no question about that – and his fellow villagers agree. But there is a complication; one of the Americans is a negro, and therefore can't be conveniently passed off as a local. The German NCO arrives on his rounds. The negro (a fine performance by John Kitzmiller) has been hastily concealed in a large wine cellar, where he has proceeded to indulge himself in a really majestic bender which includes a song and dance act. Tigna and friends desperately (and successfully) ply the German with drink in order to distract his attention from the American's performance. But with a crash the negro emerges from the cellar and confronts the German, who is also by now gloriously sloshed. There is a long, long moment of electric, poised suspense. Then, with a mutual roar of laughter and delight, the two fall into each other's arms, stagger singing round the village, open up the Nazi food stores to all comers, and publicly announce that the war is finished . . .

There is rich enjoyment in this sequence which one doesn't often get – W. C. Fields' and Alison Skipworth's holocaust of innocent automobiles in *If I Had a Million* has something of the same flavour – and in the thudding anticlimax, when the German passes out cold, and people realize that dawn will bring the ugly question of what he will do when he wakes up to the cold light of duty with a hangover of the gremlin-boogie type.

Unfortunately the film from now on relapses into melodrama and overdone histrionics (especially by Fabrizi); but nothing can efface that elemental gale of human understanding, of the assertion of life and brotherhood of man, which sweeps through the centre of this film.

In the same period Alberto Lattuada made something of a mark with *Senza Pietà* (*Without Pity*), produced in 1947 – a story about the G.I. deserters who formed an outlaw community near Leghorn in the immediate post-war era. Personalized in the relationship between a negro deserter (Kitzmiller again) and a white girl (Carla Del Poggio), the film created a considerable sensation (not least because of its patent sincerity and *absence* of sensationalism) and also ran into a lot of censorship trouble, especially in the United States. There was, however, a certain frigidity about Lattuada's approach, and this became more apparent in his next film *The Mill on the Po* (1948), a historical story about the beginnings of the socialist movement in Italy framed in the dramatics of a tragic love affair.[1]

Lattuada's fellow graduate from the Italian Film School, Giuseppe De Santis, was very much the opposite – full-blooded, barnstorming and never averse to a spot of eroticism. In *Caccia Tragica* (1947) he showed much talent in handling crowds as well as individuals in a tale of the chaos at the end of hostilities, when various bands of partisans, fleeing Fascists, and groups of Germans refusing to surrender, produced in the Italian scene a virtual replica of the times of the *condottieri*. His following film (1949) was *Riso Amaro* (*Bitter Rice*), which became famous for the juiciness of its well-upholstered peasant girls in the rice-fields no less than for the prodigious panoramas of crowds in action across vast landscapes.

During the whole of the neo-realist period there was one influential, almost controlling figure in the person of the screenwriter and film theorist Cesare Zavattini, who inspired and guided most of the directors of the day with a power comparable to that exercised so tactfully but so effectively by Carl Mayer during the Golden Age of German Cinema. Zavattini became especially well-known for his work with De Sica – *Shoeshine, Bicycle Thieves* etc – but anyone familiar with Italian cinema will know that, quite apart from his credits on other films, his general influence has been constant, positive and pervasive. Unlike some others, he has never abandoned the neo-realist position, but has continued to build on it. Indeed, by the late Sixties he was promulgating the idea of a new method of realist film-making based on the fact that by now the ease of use and the low price of the apparatus (8mm, $\frac{1}{2}$ inch video tape etc) makes it possible for individuals or groups, using modest skills and finances, to express themselves through the making of 'Cinegiornali Liberi' or 'Free Newsreels' which could be independently and locally circulated completely outside the structure of the film industry itself. Zavattini has never ceased to move towards this 'intervention of the film, ever more direct, more immediate, more responsible and influential in relation to the events of our era', and has survived all the so-called burials of neo-realism whether in the name of politics or of fashion.

Meantime, in the Fifties, a second group of directors followed on the pioneer efforts of Rossellini, De Sica and the rest.[2] Of these

---

[1] In 1949 Lattuada co-directed Fellini's first film, *Luci del Varietà* (*Variety Lights*), with among other players, Giulietta Masina, Carla Del Poggio and John Kitzmiller.

[2] Of whom I should also mention Luciano Emmer, who followed his excellent art

the most significant were Federico Fellini (who had worked with Rossellini), Luchino Visconti and Michelangelo Antonioni.

The impact of Fellini's third film, *I Vitelloni* (1953), was considerable, and firmly consolidated the foundations he had already laid with *Luci del Varietà* (*Variety Lights*) in 1950 and *The White Sheik* in 1952. From an unpromising subject – the dull vacuity of middle-class life in a small provincial town – he created a vivid and sympathetic study of the attempts of a few souls to avoid being smothered by boredom and triviality; attempts, sad to say, not by any means always successful. This theme, it turned out, was to imbue most of his later films – especially *La Dolce Vita*, $8\frac{1}{2}$, and *Fellini Satyricon*.

In *I Vitelloni*[1] he takes five young men of varying character who are more or less protected from the necessity of work by the modest incomes of their families, and who are quietly rotting amid the trivialities of the café, the street, the beach, the local theatre and the occasional party. Each of them has some sort of ambition, but none the energy to fight it through until, right at the end, Moraldo – the youngest of them all – takes the fairly equivocal but for him very dramatic decision to leave town and see what he can do in the big city (a beautifully modulated performance, this, by Franco Interlenghi, the Pasquale of *Shoeshine*).

The humour, at once sardonic and sympathetic, with which Fellini invested this film was quite remarkable. There are sequences which remain gratefully and clearly in the memory – the terrible hangover of the lad who has been to a fancy dress ball in drag, and the sequence in which the would-be playwright is tempted nearer and nearer a dark and windswept pier by an aged homosexual actor from whom he expects to extract his Big Chance. Both episodes could be no more than ridiculous, sordid; but Fellini's comic muse tears through them in a gale of laughter.

I Vitelloni was followed in 1954 by *La Strada*, which starred Fellini's magical, enchanting wife Giulietta Masina (who had already been seen in his first two films) as well as Anthony Quinn and Richard Basehart. This film tells the story of a half-witted girl (a 'natural' would perhaps be a better word) who is sold by her mother to a travelling

---

films of the war period with an admirable feature *Sunday in August* (1950); and Renato Castellani and the veteran Alessandro Blasetti – the former for *E Primavera* (1950) and *Due Soldi di Speranza* (1951), and the latter for, in particular, *Altri Tempi* – English title *Infidelity* – made in 1952.

[1] Variously rendered into English, *The Drones* being the most favoured title, though I would prefer *The Mooncalves*.

strong man – brutal and brutish. In the course of their journeyings through small towns and villages they cross the path of a tightrope walker who represents the exact opposite of the brutish Hercules. He is of light-fantastic demeanour, acts as a gadfly to the strong man, and brings to the girl not love, of which she perhaps would never be fully capable, but a feeling of being some part, some necessary part, of the pattern of human existence; there is a scene in the dark when he talks to her of stars and of stones which is the most moving thing Fellini has ever put on the screen. Eventually the strong man kills him in a roadside brawl, disguising the episode as a motor accident and reckoning that the girl's simple-mindedness will protect him. But now the girl, Gelsomina, becomes his travelling conscience, his unknowing fury; he cannot stand it, and deserts her. Years later he comes to a certain town and learns of her death; a surge of conflicting emotions overwhelms him, and he disintegrates rather after the manner of the young kulak in Dovzhenko's *Earth*.

La Strada has at times something of the magic of Vigo's work; Fellini juxtaposes people and events quite ordinary in themselves in such a way that a fantasy results – a fantasy of reality, the point of experience where life becomes a dream and the dream is life. This of course pivots on Masina's wonderful performance as Gelsomina – a delicious series of reminders of Harpo and Charlie and Harry Langdon and Zasu Pitts to which she adds her own particular magic.

For *Il Bidone* (1955), Fellini assembled a cast which, in addition to Masina, included Basehart again, plus Broderick Crawford and Franco Fabrizi. This film was more intense and uncompromising than anything he had so far attempted. His '*bidoni*' – small-time confidence tricksters – are at the start fairly devil-may-care and light-hearted. They find it quite amusing to get themselves up as priests in order the more easily to swindle the peasants. But gradually a sense of inevitable doom builds up like a thunderstorm, and the film ends in a welter of symbolic disasters and outrages which recall Stroheim. In the final sequence Augusto (Broderick Crawford), paralysed from the waist down after being cast off a cliff by his confederates (and for good reason, considering what he has done to a crippled girl), tries to claw his way up an arid slope with his bare hands; unseeing, a group of sweetly singing peasants pass by – a signal, some have thought, of a slender thread of grace by which he might yet rescue himself from a self-made hell. This may be to read too much symbolism into a film which would be more effective with less.

Le Notti di Cabiria (1956) was built round one central character –

a small-time prostitute (played, naturally, by Masina), a Gelsomina-like figure preyed upon and put upon by the world, but yet, as a sacred fool, somehow immune. The film has passages which are enormously appealing – not least the one showing her reactions at a tawdry vaudeville show when, hypnotized by the resident 'magician', she converts all the sordidness into a radiant and innocent beauty, only to be yet again cruelly mocked and betrayed. The film is full of strange and fascinating sequences involving the other prostitutes with their different, violent characteristics, the flashy nightspots of Rome, and the utterly, utterly poor.

However, after *Le Notti di Cabiria* Fellini moved steadily into a mood of often inflated egocentricity which sometimes – in $8\frac{1}{2}$ especially– drifted into autobiography. Nevertheless the theme remained the same – the tragedy of man's self-delusion, 'the dreamer fooled by dreams' as Pauline Kael put it, and the dilemma of the dialectic approach in attempts to come to terms with the spirit. Thus in *La Dolce Vita* (1960) it is Steiner, the man who has everything, with his education and his books and his hi-fi and his nice family and his clever friends and, of course, his wealth, it is he who cannot come to terms with life, it is he who kills his family and himself. Yet there is nothing of tragedy, in the Greek sense, here. The aridity of his life has left no room for pity or for terror. The only person who might have helped Steiner would, one imagines, have been Gelsomina.

In all his films from *La Dolce Vita* onwards, Fellini shows a constantly developing technical brilliance which can command nothing but admiration – from the breathtaking conception of the huge statue of Christ suspended from a helicopter *en route* to the Vatican, through Giulietta's 'vision' on the beach, to the forced homosexual marriage on the sea-sprayed, windswept, dawn-lit deck of the pirate galley in *Fellini Satyricon*.

The trouble with these later and bigger films is that little more is being said than in the more modest earlier ones. All that has happened is that Fellini has gone into overdrive and sped on with the same problems into the stratospheric but polluted area of a dying aristocracy, a proliferating plutocracy, and a half-world of jet-sets and beautiful people. This is not enough, even when, as in $8\frac{1}{2}$, he also invites us to share in his change of life.

Of these later films *Giulietta degli Spiriti* (*Juliet of the Spirits*), made in 1965, is the most interesting because it is, in a way, $8\frac{1}{2}$ seen from the woman's, the wife's point of view – and the woman is of course Masina. Giulietta is in effect having a breakdown within a breakdown, the breakdown of her marriage, and, as Suzanne Budgen points out, 'the spirits . . . are not confined to the occult. The film is full of telephone calls, snatches of radio programmes, and glimpses of television . . . When Giulietta's doctor says, "The air is full of voices", he is referring to radio, but, if the air is full, then maybe Giulietta's voices are as truly present as any, and are only different in the means by which they may be heard.'[1] So, despite its hyperbole, the film manages to attract a sympathy which the others tend to repel.

Fellini Satyricon (1969) is at one and the same time Fellini's most skilful technical achievement and his biggest failure. For none of the pyrotechnics can disguise the fact that it reduces everything to dust and ashes. Fellini has taken a lively and picaresque tale – scandalous, funny, exciting and full of a bubbling *joie de vivre* which rises above the permissive decadence which is the background to all its events – and turned it, with a few exceptions like the fun-in-the-bath sequence with the boys and the coloured girl, into a drab *News of the World* discourse – into a grubby 'facts of life' without love, without romance.

All this is marked, it seems to me, by an extraordinary lack of pace in the editing. However many sausages are stuffed into a roast boar, their cascading emergence when the belly is slit depends on cinematic movement, not mere numbers or bulk; and the same goes for all those orgies of slave girls, unarmed combats and sexual pursuits through Pompeian art galleries. A glance at the big orgy scene in Cecil B. De Mille's *The Sign of the Cross* (1932) will quickly prove the point. Apart from anything else, there is that stunning shot of the Goings-On seen through the waterfall of a woman's silken hair which implies more than any of the explicit statements of the Fellini film.

It is interesting to note that Alberto Moravia, writing in the *New York Review*, made the following comments in reference to Fellini's statement that the film was a 'documentary of a dream'.

> 'He does not recapture the real homosexual passion of Encolpius and Asclytus for Giton that lives beneath the fiction. In Petronius there is psychology, even when changed into eloquence: in the movie it is sacrificed to the dreamlike effect.'

Moravia goes on to indicate that the psychology of dream resides not in the dream figures but in the dreamer who creates them. He continues,

> 'Only in two episodes does Fellini show himself intent on representing a reality that is not dreamlike: the episode of Trimalchio

---

[1] *Fellini*, by Suzanne Budgen, British Film Institute, 1966.

and that of the villa of the suicides . . . The rich man who vulgarly and unrestrainedly enjoys his wealth; and the rich man who not only rejects wealth but also life . . .'

which brings us back to Steiner in *La Dolce Vita*.

Not to end on too sour a note in relation to this very talented director, let me remark on the trivial but delightful comedy represented in his brightly coloured wide-screen contribution to *Boccaccio '70* (1962), entitled *Le Tentazioni del Dottor Antonio* (*The Temptation of Professor Antonio*).[1] This involves the seduction of a conservative, prudish and academic little man (he lectures his boy-scout troop about the dangers of cleavage) by a gigantic poster of a sexpot – Anita Ekberg, no less – which has taken on a life of its own and comes near to engulfing him. Fellini works out the many implications of this situation with a sense of comedy broad enough to enable us to sympathize not so much with Antonio's prudery as with his inability to adjust to modern society in general. He is so left behind by events that even the scurrying nuns and the scarlet-clad priests whizzing about in the background seem to be mocking him.

One of the more uncompromising of the younger neo-realists is Francesco Rosi.[2] His *Salvatore Giuliano* (1961) proceeds on the lines of a sort of documentary reconstruction in describing the life and, more particularly, the death of the bandit-*mafioso* folk hero. It is a film in which the hero himself is perforce absent except in death, the mystery surrounding which is one of the main concerns of the film, which indeed grimly revolves around attitudes, descriptions and opinions on the part of all sorts of persons caught up in the ramifications of his career. A mercilessly effective film, and never more so than in the scene of Giuliano's mother kneeling in grief by his corpse amid the jostling of a curious and unfeeling crowd.

Not dissimilar in style is *The Moment of Truth* (1964), an intimate,

[1] The other two episodes were *Il Lavoro* (*The Job*), by Visconti, with Romy Schneider in a sweet-sour Maupassant *conte*; and *La Rifa* (*The Raffle*) by De Sica, with Sophia Loren as a girl who tries to be her own tombola once too often. (In the original Italian version of *Boccaccio '70* there was a fourth episode, *Renzo and Luciana*, directed by Mario Monicelli.)

[2] Not to be confused with Franco Rossi, director, among other films, of the tenderly beautiful *Amice per la Pelle* (1955) – released in America as *The Woman in the Painting* and elsewhere as *Friends for Life*. This tale of a deep but non-homosexual friendship between two schoolboys from differing *milieux* develops into a near tragedy. The sensitivity of Rossi's direction is only equalled by the sensitivity of the acting (or more accurately *non*-acting) of Geronimo Meynier and Andrea Scire as the boys; different though the circumstances are, they have something of the feeling of Giuseppe and Pasquale from *Shoeshine*.

detailed portrait of a Spanish country kid who becomes a successful bullfighter (perhaps Rosi had El Cordobes in mind?). Not for the squeamish, this close-knit, crowded film, much of it shot with hand-held cameras,[1] really takes you inside the world of bullfighting – a world of greed, ambition, bravado, bravery and, above all, fear.

Between *Salvatore Giuliano* and *The Moment of Truth* Rosi made in 1963 his finest film, *Hands over the City* (*Le Mani sulla Città*), a superbly conceived and constructed film about building rackets and local politics in Naples. It begins with a shattering sequence of the collapse of an old tenement adjoining a new building site, the aftermath of which sets going an *exposé* of all the complications, intrigues and skullduggeries in the world of industry and finance as well as of politics. Rosi casts unorthodoxly, with Rod Steiger (excellent) as the ambitious and unscrupulous industrialist, and a real-life Communist trades-unionist as his main rival on the city council. Like *The Battle of Algiers*, this film gives the impression of genuine actuality throughout, whether it depicts protesting slum-dwellers being evicted, or the chops and changes of the political parties on the floor of the Chamber. Truthful, dramatic in the most surprising contexts, *mouvementé*, *Hands over the City* is totally engrossing from start to finish.

Until *Death in Venice* I had always had a certain feeling of reservation about the work of Luchino Visconti. His immense abilities are unquestionable, and the same goes for his sincerity and his serious-ness of purpose. Yet in his neo-realist essays like *La Terra Trema* and *Rocco and his Brothers* – both made, of course, very much under the influence of Giovanni Verga – I seemed to detect a patrician aloofness which kept him a fraction removed from the real heart of the events and feelings he was depicting. The death of the old man in *La Terra Trema*, for instance, was beautifully represented, but no more; one only has to compare it with the death of the old man at the beginning of Dovzhenko's *Earth* to get the point. *Senso* and *The Leopard* were, with all respect, no more than admirably decorative pageants (the latter flawed by the miscasting of Burt Lancaster); and *The Damned*, stagger-ingly brilliant in its direction, suffered from what it showed – the sordid, unthinking acts of Nazidom which, under a general banner of brutality and cruelty, managed to take in a bit of incest here, and sodomy there. The most awful thing about the Hitler world was its dullness. Amid all the blood, the tortures, the Zyklon gas, the sadistic operations without anaesthetics, one comes most horribly to someone like Himmler who

---

[1] All of the Rosi films referred to here were photographed by that great Italian cameraman Gianni Di Venanzo.

was quite simply dull. The spectacular shooting – and not least the blood-bath at Roehm's weekend party – ends up as a nonsense, because it is, in the end, concerned with what the French newspapers in their crime reports call 'personnages peu intéressants'.

With *Death in Venice*, however, Visconti grabs the heart. We are emotionally involved from beginning to end. This is a film which we must all feel because, like Aschenbach, we too have lost, we too have sought and not found, or, like Clay in *The Immortal Story*, have only learned to seek when it is too late. According to our experience, and therefore to a greater or lesser degree, we share here the frustration and at the same time the imperishability of the creative impulse. Above all, it is about that moment of truth when even that which we have never had will be taken away: it is about *The End*.

A composer of immense and usually soulful works (the character is admittedly based on Mahler), Aschenbach has always been uncertain of his genius, has indeed been constantly attacked and insulted for those very works whose acceptance could have resolved that very uncertainty. Now, in a Venice where an epidemic of cholera is being concealed by the authorities for fear of losing tourism, there appears before him in flesh and blood the very image of his search for genius – an exquisite boy, the *Puer Aeternus* who is also to be the Angel of Death.

When Aschenbach disembarks from the vaporetto (a breathtaking shot of Santa Maria della Salute here) he is greeted on the landing stage by a rouged and painted death's head of a little man, and immediately afterwards is poled towards the Lido by a gondolier who is clearly Charon.

It is worth noting here how closely Visconti follows Mann's story, never traducing it but occasionally making a concentration necessary to the technique of film. Thus the death's head man, in the story, had been introduced previously during the voyage to Venice. 'Aschenbach . . . was shocked to see that the apparent youth was no youth at all. He was an old man, beyond a doubt, with wrinkles and crow's feet round eyes and mouth; the dull carmine of the cheeks was rouge, the brown hair a wig . . .'[1] and so on. On the screen Visconti introduces this character rapidly, and as a shock the significance of which we do not realize until late in the film when Aschenbach goes to the hair-dresser's. The scene with the Charon-gondolier, by contrast, is taken straight from the book: and indeed it is astonishing to note the faithful-ness with which Visconti, nearly all the time, has transcribed Mann's prose; for much of the film it is quite literally exact.

[1] *Stories of Three Decades* by Thomas Mann, Secker and Warburg.

Once arrived at the Hotel des Bains, Aschenbach becomes part of the rich, leisurely pattern of life – a tapestry into which, we soon realize, is woven his own dance of death.

Aschenbach and the Polish boy, Tadzio, never speak, never do more than exchange glances and once, dazzlingly, a smile. Yet the boy is interested, intrigued – is *seen* to be interested, intrigued; there are moments when a confrontation seems possible. But always Fate, in the form of a governess (and how very like a governess Fate is!), intervenes; and Aschenbach is forced into his own dangerous dream world of wishful thinking and of memories.

I cannot remember a film in which flashbacks were so perfectly used. They tend to come almost unnoticed, just as one's own inner thoughts, which take little count of the difference between past and future, are unnoticed among the immediacies of the present moment. It is here that Visconti makes a brilliant departure from the original. In the novella, Aschenbach the writer meditates on the boy in terms of Socrates, the *Phaedrus*, and indeed the whole area of Plato's Dialogues. Visconti, having made Aschenbach a composer, substitutes for these his memories of his past – the premières, his wife, his quarrels with a friend who is also his most violent critic. Thus there comes a point where Mahler's music, which is being dramatically used as *background* music, suddenly surges into the foreground as Visconti cuts to Aschenbach conducting it with a full orchestra in a concert hall, years ago; and this leads to a quite terrible confrontation, first with a booing audience and then with the *odi-et-amo* friend aforesaid.

Another flash comes directly from the book. The agent at Thomas Cook's tells Aschenbach confidentially about the reality of the cholera epidemic. Immediately Visconti cuts to a sequence, bathed in blinding white sunlight, when Aschenbach, on the terrace of the hotel, warns Tadzio's mother of the danger of staying in Venice, and at the same time, with a gentle and tentative gesture, strokes Tadzio's hair. All imagination, of course; it is the filmic representation of a moment's flash of thought. In truth Aschenbach does nothing; why should he hasten the boy's departure?

The psychological degradation suffered by Aschenbach is nowhere more powerfully signalled than in the scene at the railway station, when Aschenbach has decided to leave; he still has enough control of himself to know that this is the only wise thing to do. But the timetable is wrong an d his bags have been misrouted – an excuse to stay, to continue the imaginary colloquy with Tadzio. Imperiously he demands transport back to the Hotel des Bains. The camera comes into close-up, and here

Dirk Bogarde reaches the apex of what is certainly the finest performance of his career, as he smiles and nods to himself in self-congratulatory
complicity, and in that pleasure which all of us who have made the
mistake we want to make will recognize. From this image Visconti cuts
to something which is not described by Mann, though it is implicit in
the story.

There is a poorly dressed man leaning against the wall of the
waiting room. Without warning he slides slowly down and collapses
on the floor. Cholera.

The casting of *Death in Venice* is uniformly perfect. Silvana
Mangano, cool, silken, veiled and exquisite, presides over her family –
two pudding-faced girls in addition to Tadzio – with an affectionate
remoteness only possible in a Polish countess who can afford a really
efficient governess. She and her friends float across the Lido's timeless
light and air, with their enormous hats and sugarspun parasols, while
Björn Andresen, as Tadzio, plays on the beach, a combination of
Antinous and Nijinsky, with his more earthy friends. Bogarde completely engulfs the part of Aschenbach. Among many fine moments is
one when, conned by the hairdresser into a full beauty treatment, he
emerges rouged, dyed, pomaded, buttonholed (like the ghastly man on
the landing stage) and follows the dawdling Tadzio down a narrow
backstreet where, every few yards, the bonfires of pestilence are
burning . . .

The final sequence of the film is partly a straight transcription
of the last two pages of the Mann novella, and partly a justified
elaboration by Visconti, who allows us to see Aschenbach himself,
whereas Mann, once he has settled him in his deck chair, shows us only
what he himself sees.

'The whole beach,' writes Mann, 'once so full of colour and life,
looked now autumnal, out of season; it was nearly deserted and not
even clean. A camera on a tripod stood at the edge of the water,
apparently abandoned; its black cloth snapped in the freshening wind.'

Out of this Visconti, on his wide screen, has made an image of
desolating beauty; and he goes on to show, exactly after Mann's
description, the rather sexy fight on the beach between Tadzio and his
friend. But what Visconti shows on top of this is, first of all, a long shot
from a high angle of the whole formal pattern of the beach huts, in the
midst of which is to be seen the tiny figure of Aschenbach in his deck
chair and, yards away, the two little girls, clad in black making a sand-
castle; near by a woman sings a Polish song of farewell, for Tadzio and
his family will be leaving later today. Secondly, Visconti crosscuts

Tadzio's beach fight with big close-ups of Aschenbach, mortally ill, the pallor showing through his make-up, and the walnut stains from his hair dye running down his face, as he watches with orgasmic frustration the boys tussling in the sand; and then, as Tadzio wades out into the Adriatic shallows, comes that final beautiful gesture described by Mann and so exactly transliterated by Visconti: 'Once more he paused to look: with a sudden recollection, or by an impulse, he turned from the waist up, in an exquisite movement, one hand resting on his hip, and looked over his shoulder at the shore.' And so to a close-up as the poor pomaded genius, reduced to a booby by the dread fury, incontinently dies . . .

In a sense both Visconti and Antonioni (the omission of the latter from these pages being explained in the Preface) represent a kind of bridge between the original neo-realists and the successive new generations of Italian cinema seen in the persons of Olmi and Pasolini, and of Bertolucci and Bellocchio.

Of these Ermanno Olmi has probably attracted least public notice; the respect accorded his films by the critics has not in general been confirmed by wide success at the box-office. This may in part be due to the very virtues of his directorial skill. He is *au fond* a domestic miniaturist. His films celebrate the minor triumphs and defeats of ordinary folk. None of his characters come within a thousand miles of the epileptics and schizophrenes of Bellocchio and Bertolucci – let alone those archetypal emanations from the collective unconscious which, dressed often in Marxist cast-offs, haunt most of Pasolini's films. Perhaps it is because Olmi deals with the little worlds we ourselves know – the breathlessly unimportant hopes and fears, the shame of wearing the wrong socks or forgetting to renew the toilet paper in the WC – that we sometimes reject him; there are times when we like to recognize ourselves, and times not.

If you give yourself to them, his films have a warmth, a glow of humour and sympathy which is unique and irresistible. They succeed in doing what the old Hollywood series like the Hardy Family (with Lewis Stone, Mickey Rooney et al) tried to do, but failed owing to a blind reliance on the obviously cosy, the obviously cute.[1] Even his first full-length film, *Il Tempo si è Fermato* (*Time Stood Still*), a semi-documentary made in 1959 about two men in a small mountain hut overlooking a dam-site of which they are watchmen, is full of simple human relationships. Like all of us, these men examine each other

[1] Latterly of course this *genre*, in various transmogrifications, has been transferred to the television screen, pre-recorded audience reactions and all.

covertly, try to make their preliminary discoveries of each other through side-long rather than direct manoeuvres. Then, the manoeuvres over, and from a push given by a minor crisis, a relationship between the two – one older, one younger – arrives as naturally as spring.

His first two full features, *Il Posto* (*The Job*, incomprehensibly released in America as *The Sound of Trumpets*) and *I Fidanzati* (*The Engagement* or *The Fiancés*), made in 1961 and 1963 respectively, are based solidly on the glories which emerge from the ordinariness of life, glories similar to those celebrated by Arnold Bennett in his best work. The first is about a boy's experiences as he begins a job in an office; the second is about a lovers' quarrel – but no, nothing so fraught as that – about a lovers' problem brought about by everyday circumstances. The two films are very close to each other; one might say that the one grows out of the other. Indeed when, under the titles of *I Fidanzati*, the band tunes up and the very ordinary dancers begin to arrive, we at once recognize that we are in the same familiar ambience as the office Christmas party in *Il Posto*.

All that *Il Posto* does is to show us, through the eyes and heart of Domenico, what it is like to leave school early and get a minor job in a commercial firm in order to supplement family finances. Olmi's camera is in the heart as well as the eyes. The hourly events in the lives of Domenico, of his family, of his new colleagues and their families, are not paraded, they are woven into a deep, rich pattern. The humour is true and not mawkish; of the pathos the same can be said. And Olmi never forgets that small triumphs or defeats are as important as big ones – a dance which goes wrong but suddenly rights itself, or a one-armed bandit which remorselessly fails to respond to the coin.

I Fidanzati goes deeper than *Il Posto* in that it does not have a completely central character like Domenico. Here the human problem is doubled. Giovanni and Liliana are engaged; indeed they have been engaged long enough for it to have become something of a routine. The problem posed is simply that Giovanni is offered promotion, and this means leaving home, leaving Liliana, and going to work at the other end of Italy. True, the film then centres on Giovanni – but Giovanni in relation to his absent girl and family. Olmi in this film uses flashes forwards or back, often unexplained at the time, to emphasize Giovanni's loneliness – not a soul-shattering loneliness, this, but ordinary, rather sad; the dislocation one feels on arriving in a strange place after midnight, with an empty stomach and doubts about dawn. It is a world where the industrial landscapes and their detritus vary little between Sicily and Milan. But Olmi never forgets human hope.

The ending of *I Fidanzati* glows with glory; on a pouring wet Sunday Giovanni, his head meagrely sheltered from the rain by an old newspaper, exults with joy. He has, on an impulse, made a cheap-rate weekend phone-call to Liliana. They have spoken nothing save clichés and banalities, but the inner meaning of these is plain, and it can be seen in Giovanni's eyes.

After a sincere but not very successful tribute to the late Pope John, Olmi returned to his real form in 1968 with *Un Certo Giorno (One Fine Day)*. This is the world of *Il Posto* seen from the other end. *Il Posto* ends with Domenico, like it or not, being confirmed in the office job he has been forced to seek. *Un Certo Giorno* is about a Domenico who, having over the years risen to a top executive position, finds this called in question by an unexpected, extraneous event. It could happen to any of us. His car skids slightly on a patch of ice, and by sheer bad luck bumps into a cart being pushed by two workmen, one of whom is killed. So all the neat protective patterns of the ordered life are broken. In the end all is well; indeed the incident leads to a better relationship with his wife whom he has selfishly neglected but on whom he really relies. (Here Olmi uses flashes again; when the executive, Bruno, is at low ebb, there come these rapid, evanescent visions of a smiling, comforting woman.) In *Un Certo Giorno*, as in his other story films, Olmi has followed De Sica's early example in exclusively using unknown people as actors.[1] He has made his attitude on this quite plain:

'If I use professional actors as intermediaries, I lose the chance to convey the truth, because those actors are followed by the public not for the characters they represent on the screen but because the actors themselves are a model of success in our society . . . In the theatre the actor is the right intermediary for the interpretation of a character. In the cinema as I intend it – which doesn't mean that I exclude others' ways of making films – if I want to show a tree, I take a real tree . . . And if I want a scavenger who makes his living out of digging for scrap metal left over from World War One, then I look for someone who has done that job.'[2]

Which is precisely what he did when he made *I Recuperanti* (1969), a colour film which, it appears, ended up on Italian television in black and white.

Olmi continued the same policy in *During the Summer (Durante*

---

[1] But in *A Man Called John*, a film which he himself regards as a failure, he used Rod Steiger as an anchor figure.

[2] Conversation with John Francis Lane in *Sight and Sound*, Summer 1970.

l'Estate) which he made in 1971. Here he chose as his central character a man called Renato Paracchi who in real life earned his living by colouring maps for a firm of cartographers. So in the film he does precisely that – the only difference being that in the film he romantically insists on colouring the maps the way *he* thinks proper, which never coincides with the intentions of his employers.

The main theme of the film is solitude. This lonely middle-aged man takes refuge in romanticism. Living on his own in the urban desert of industrial Milan, he conjures up dreams in which ordinary people find themselves to be of the nobility. His attempts (however venial they may seem) to translate these dreams into fact by selling people fake coats-of-arms land him eventually in gaol; but not before a surge of genuine romance has come to him through a chance friendship with a pretty girl whose job is the handing out of free detergent samples. Repelled at first by his age and lack of looks (you cannot say 'ugliness' in an Olmi film – he loves people too much), she eventually capitulates to his tranced and mythic nature ('You could well be a real Princess,' he tells her, 'Only you don't know about it yet.')

Their friendship unfolds in a blistering heat-wave and in a Milan emptied by the summer vacations. The pressure of the heat, the pressure from the repellent modern skyscrapers descends like an incubus. The two of them move as in a dream; and there is one marvellous sequence of quiet comedy when they are cut off from food and drink because in this vacant city they cannot find anyone to change a 100,000 *lire* note . . .

After the police have got him (on the charge of swindling an old age pensioner), after the girl has bravely stood up for him in the witness-box, and after he has been committed to gaol, we finally see him gazing out from his prison window at his *Princesse Lointaine*, out there in freedom. It is a moment of pathetic beauty, a little reminiscent of the final confrontation of Chaplin and Virginia Cherrill at the end of *City Lights*; and indeed in this, more than any of his other films, Olmi makes us understand how the most ordinary-looking or unattractive human being can suddenly irradiate the world with a single smile and, in so doing, induce at the same time a healing and liberating cascade of tears.

Pasolini's early work coincided with Olmi's. *Accattone* came out in the same year as *Il Posto*, and *Mamma Roma* antedated *I Fidanzati* by a matter of months. But their styles are poles apart. Moreover Pasolini's first two films lack the certitude, though not the political convictions, of his later work. *Accattone* is a sprawling, shapeless film

redeemed by the extraordinary and candid beauty of the youthful
Franco Citti in the name part, and by one or two sequences in which
the plight of people in poverty is indicated with the cruelty of a Buñuel.
The final reels, too, with Accattone's dream of his own death and the
tragic dénouement in a bungled piece of street banditry, have a strength
and shapeliness of their own which presages films like *Theorem*. In the
present perspective I find *Accattone* preferable to *Mamma Roma* which,
rumbling with melodrama, is concerned with the intense relationship
between a retired whore (Anna Magnani) and her young son. This
seems to have been the turning point at which Pasolini, hitherto mainly
known as a successful writer, decided to concentrate on film-making
and embarked on a film version of the *Gospel According to Matthew*,
significantly omitting the sanctification of its author.

Impressive and beautiful as much of it is, this film, made in 1964,
cannot be counted as entirely successful; it contains warring elements
which may well arise from a conflict between Jesus seen from a Marxist
standpoint and the ever inescapable Jesus of Christian legend and
Christian doctrine. There are sections of the film in which the camera
brings to familiar life the various recognizable traditions and styles of
Italian painting; these are often arresting and moving – the Annunciation
and the Massacre of the Innocents, for instance. Other sequences are
shot in a brutal *cinéma-vérité* style, camera hand-held, a leper almost
casually cured, and the Sermon on the Mount almost thrown away
against the threat of a coming rain-storm. Moreover, after the
Crucifixion the film becomes strangely perfunctory, and Christ's final
farewells resemble those of a man in a hurry to catch his train; they
may, for all we know, have been like that – His next appointment was
pressing and extremely attractive – but film-wise they make a lame
ending. Nevertheless it remains a fascinating film, and the Italian landscapes in whose heart it is played seem traditionally right as portrayals
of the Holy Land; one feels no regret that after actually shooting some
test-footage in Israel, Pasolini decided to return to those Italian
settings in which the great Italian painters from Giotto onwards had
placed the stories of the Bible.

The tragic power which is the essence of the Oedipus story was
for me lacking in Pasolini's screen version, produced in 1967 as *Oedipus
Rex* (*Edipo Re*), although his binding of it to a contemporary episode
was certainly striking and was, too, a forewarning of the developments
which were soon to be seen in *Theorem* and *Pigsty*. I think that the main
trouble was the extreme formalization of the costumes. There is
nothing wrong with treating the Greeks of the period from a rather

prehistoric viewpoint; an archaeological rather than an old-fashioned classical approach could be welcome; but the get-ups were so *outré*, so, as it were, redolent of an aesthetic deliberately devoted to the primitive and brutish, that they took away from the conviction which the admirable performances of Silvana Mangano and Franco Citti should otherwise have carried. Pasolini himself seems to prefer the modern prologue and epilogue to the main central story ('The Prologue in *Oedipus* is one of the best things I have done'), and he has said that he 'wanted all the central part of the film (which is almost the whole movie) to be a kind of dream, and this explains the choice of costumes and settings . . . I wanted to represent the myth like a dream, and I could only present this dream by aestheticizing it; and perhaps this is what is disturbing.'[1]

But with *Teorema* (*Theorem*) in 1968 and *Porcile* (*Pigsty*) in 1969 Pasolini finally established himself as a great film-maker. These films, which may be regarded as closely-conceived companion pieces, have a remarkable purity; they have an entity of style which forbids any clash between idea and décor, between characterization and situation. At the end of *Theorem*, when all the outcomes of the visitation have been revealed and the father, having stripped himself stark naked in the main concourse of the railroad station, is translated to a howling wilderness of black ashes and dust, we are presented with a question-mark whose (provisional) answer comes pat at the beginning of the *Orgia* section of *Pigsty*. Here is the same black and arid landscape, carcassed now and cannibalistic, and seen through a different lesion in time which, in turn, will be reflected in the blackness of mind of the German industrialist's mansion over which hover worse things than the shadow of Dr Strangelove.

One of the more powerful aspects of *Theorem* is that the film proper only really gets going when its motivator is abruptly withdrawn, and withdrawn at a point when a perfectly shapely story has already been unfolded. This disappearance of the mysterious and beautiful young man (Terence Stamp) becomes an almost literal as well as a symbolic *coitus interruptus*. Something has been given, but something has too soon been taken away – and no blessings on the name of the Lord. As Noel Purdon has put it, in a detailed and often controversial article, the hypothesis of the film now works out

'that each member of the house will be brought to a precise awareness of why their lives are unsatisfactory.

---

[1] *Pasolini on Pasolini*; Interviews with Oswald Stack, Thames and Hudson, 1969.

'that their sufferings will become critical and acute, that they will lose their ideas of self.

'that the condition of man is naked and alone, and that whatever his cry may mean, it will be permanent.'[1]

The intensity with which Pasolini presents this predicament gives *Theorem* a mounting, terrifying power. The total degradation of the wife (another fine performance by Mangano), who takes to picking up young men at random, is shown with deliberation and in full sordid detail; as the sex goes on we are made to observe the pile – almost reproachful – of crumpled hastily removed clothing lying on the floor.[2] Even more striking is the fate of the maid (superbly played by Laura Betti), who sublimates her unsatisfied sexual urges to such a depth that she moves towards a revengeful sanctity; her diet of nettles, her levitations, her desire for live burial (an anticipation of the execution of Clémenti in *Pigsty*), all these seem somehow logical and natural – to us as well as to the villagers by whose uncomplicated faith she is surrounded and upheld.

Teorema is an attack on middle-class morals and standards, and thereby also on capitalism. It is only too easy, in a film so full of dramatic incident, of suspense and of sexual excitement, to forget that its credit titles coincide with a straightforward newsreely sequence in which the capitalist father, in a gesture of apparent grandeur, makes his factory over to the workers: a distant echo here of the finale of Clair's *A Nous la Liberté*? Pasolini, though, doesn't deal in caricatures; his bourgeois family is real. In his own words, he hates 'the petit-bourgeois vulgarity . . . of hypocritical "good manners" ' and finds 'their cultural meanness insufferable'; yet for this film 'I chose people who were not particularly odious, people who elicited a certain human sympathy . . . It is only right that I should feel something for all individuals, including bourgeois individuals'.[3]

Right at the start of *Porcile* (*Pigsty*) we find ourselves in the black desert into which the father has fled at the end of *Teorema*. The idea of the bourgeoisie has vanished. The two sections of *Porcile* are concerned with images of humans who have passed beyond the 'normalities' of civilization. On the one hand there is the cannibal who passes from the compulsion of brute necessity to the discipline of ritual; on the other there are the mindless perversions of idea and action which emerge from totalitarianism. And Pasolini's answer to both situations is

[1] *Pasolini: The Film of Alienation*, in *Cinema*, Nos 6 and 7, London, August 1970.
[2] As the father's clothes will be left on the station paving later on.
[3] *Pasolini on Pasolini*, ed. Oswald Stack.

pessimistic. Julian is killed and eaten by the pigs, sexual intercourse with whom had brought him the greatest joy; while the cannibals of the first episode are dealt with by *condottieri* who are probably not much better than they are – but not before their ringleader (Pierre Clémenti) has said that in killing his father, and in eating human flesh, he found transcendent joy.

That statement, incidentally, represents the only spoken words of the cannibal episode; and Pasolini deliberately points a contrast by filling the other episode to the brim with verbiage. The series of verbal smokescreens sent up by Klotz and Herdhitze in the veiled strategies of their mutual enmity provide a macabre counterpoint to young Julian's 'search for God', and in particular to the very deep trance into which he falls at the crucial point of the film.

At the same time the stark colours of the cannibal episode are exchanged for biliously rich hues which are, however, based on the same areas of the spectrum. The interior settings are rich, rich regardless of expense, and perfectly reflect Pasolini's phrase 'insufferable cultural meanness', while at the same time providing an almost incongruent ambience for a world which has reduced even bourgeois values to ordure. The apparent aimlessness, shapelessness even, of this episode is beginning to become annoying when Pasolini suddenly, snappily, draws all the threads together into an extraordinary double dénouement. When Herdhitze counters Klotz's blackmailing attempt in regard to his war-crimes (he was a supplier of Jewish skeletons) by pointing out that he has discovered that his (Klotz's) son is demented about fucking pigs, the deadlock is easily broken by a business merger instead of a takeover. It is casual, horrible, macabrely comic, *and we become aware that Klotz and Herdhitze also see it this way.* Pasolini then twists the screw further when, in the remote and formal pattern of Greek tragedy, a messenger arrives to report that Julian has been eaten by the pigs. Klotz's only reaction is to enquire whether every last little bit of him has been gobbled up. On being assured of this, he puts his finger to his lips and engulfs us all in a frightening complicity with, 'Well then, not a word about all this to anyone' – as Himmler no doubt said to Eichmann.

By cross-cutting the two episodes, and by the common device of the Greek chorus or messenger element, Pasolini has structured this frightening film, with its story-threads constantly reaching out to each other like tentacles, into an experience of tremendous intensity and with, even, a strange beauty of its own.

Bernardo Bertolucci was an assistant to Pasolini on *Accattone*, and his first film, *La Commare Secca* (*The Grim Reaper*), made in 1962, a year later than *Accattone*, was based on a story by Pasolini which had some affinities with *Rashomon*. Five suspects are rounded up by the police in regard to the killing of a prostitute, and the question that arises is – can the truth be determined from the various lies (themselves clues to individual characteristics) with which they try to avoid implication and generally to obfuscate the situation? The film had a warm reception at the Venice Festival.

Bertolucci then directed four films which put him in the forefront of modern Italian directors. Three of them – *Before the Revolution* (1964), *The Conformist* (1970) and *The Spider's Strategy* (1970)[1] are basically lyrical and poetic in mood; the other, *Partner* (1968), is more complex in construction and Godardian in outlook. All four are of great interest, and behind all four lies the trauma of Fascism – the Mussolini era which Bertolucci was too young personally to experience but whose ideological (at least) persistence in modern Italy he more than suspects. He has said that '*The Conformist* is a film on the present. And when I say that I want to make the audience leave with a sense of malaise, perhaps feeling the presence of something subtly sinister, it's because I want them to realize that however the world has changed, feelings have remained the same.'[2]

The Conformist is a film about the corruption and decadence of the Fascist regime. Its final sequence finds its hero, or anti-hero, Marcello, confronting at the same time the downfall of Mussolini and the appearance, in sordid circumstances, of the chauffeur whose homosexual advances years ago he thought he had terminated by a pistol shot. But the chauffeur Lino is still alive – and the film ends with Marcello, in the *louche* shadows of the Colosseum (night-haunt of venal queers), gazing blankly at the naked boy whose seduction by Lino his arrival had interrupted.

Before this point the film is constructed in a series of flashbacks representing Marcello's memories while he is en route to assassinate an anti-Fascist professor. Marcello's conformism in terms of Fascism represents his attempt to escape from the traumatic implications of the chauffeur incident, but it never really works because for him nothing is what it seems (there is at one point a fascinating discussion between him and Quadri, his intended victim, on Plato's Cave), and none of the people he comes into contact with are what he thinks or expects. His young wife confesses on their wedding night that as a girl she was

[1] Italian titles: *Prima della Rivoluzione, Il Conformista* and *Strategia del Ragno*.
[2] Interview with Marilyn Goldin, *Sight and Sound*, Spring 1971.

seduced by a dirty old man. And when Marcello himself falls in love with Quadri's beautiful blonde wife (Dominique Sanda from Bresson's *A Gentle Creature*), he finds that his own wife is also after her; the sequence of the two women doing their Lesbian tango in a Paris dance-hall is one of several highlights in a film full of marvellous human observation as well as superb camera movements.[1] Finally Marcello sits, in frozen helplessness, in a parked car, while others, and not himself, murder not only Quadri but also his lovely wife – a sequence of austere and terrifying beauty in an icy, snow-mantled forest, the girl running and stumbling through the trees screaming in anguished, animal fear before her pursuers gun her down.

While the influence of Godard is seen and heard both in *Before the Revolution* and (in particular) *Partner*, Bertolucci seems deliberately to have rid himself of it in the other two; and this must have been a real break, since the two had been warm personal as well as ideological friends. In fact *Partner* is the only one really to suffer from the Godardian approach, though even without it I feel it would still be a difficult if unevenly brilliant film. The Dostoievsky story, which concerns a young man and his *doppelgänger*, is hardly new. In film terms Henrik Galeen's *The Student of Prague* (1926) remains the classic example. Bertolucci, however, has elaborated the idea with complexities which sometimes lead to muddle. It is fair enough to have Jacob, a young drama teacher, lead an inner life which is all action, courage, revolution and the theatre taken into the streets, while in actual fact he is nervous, timid, living amid vast protective barricades of books under the protection of a landlord who also acts as his nursemaid and valet; it is fair enough to have Jacob create for himself (consciously or unconsciously) an emanation identical in looks but with all the qualities he himself lacks; it is even fair enough to develop a subtle change in their relationship so that in the end the two Jacobs become confused (when both are poised to jump off the roof, we can hardly know which of the two utters the payoff line: 'Jacob! I've had a wonderful idea!').

But it is *not* fair for Bertolucci to confuse this already complicated situation with situations whose provenance is inexplicable. For instance, the *acte gratuit* early in the film in which Jacob, the pre-*doppelgänger* Jacob, it would seem, murders a young man while he is playing the piano, remains a puzzle; even if it is meant as a flash forward it doesn't work, for when we come back to it later in the film the matter is no further resolved – indeed is further complicated in that the trick in the original sequence, by which the audience is made, through the sound-

[1] This cannot but be regarded as a pre-echo of *Last Tango in Paris*.

track, to participate in Jacob wearing cottonwool in his ears, is no longer followed through. As an isolated episode it is finely done, with the circling shadow of a swinging art-nouveau lampshade dominating the set-up; but the disturbance of time (in the second appearance the corpse of the young man is beginning to smell) does not come off because its relevance is not felt or understood. Some other sequences, too, are overlong or irrelevant, such as that concerning the girl selling detergents – a sort of living TV commercial, with false eyes painted on her eyelids, who is, it would seem, rape-murdered by one or other of the Jacobs in a welter of Procter-and-Gamble foam.

On the other hand *Partner* has some moments of splendid comedy – not least the false elopement with, and subsequent seduction of, the doll-like Clara. This takes place in a car which is supposed to be speeding into the night but actually remains stationary, though Jacob's landlord Petrushka, capped and furred like a *droshki* driver, religiously sits in the driving seat making all the suitable noises of engine revvings and gear-changes with the virtuosity of a Japanese *benshi*.

But the obscurity of the film in general is a pity; for there are moments, as in Jacob's efforts to bring his theatre students into action in the Roman forum, and in his parodies of the older professors, when one feels that Bertolucci is trying to tell us something really important. The acting of Pierre Clémenti, as the two Jacobs, is expertly alarming.

Partner, in fact, looks rather like a young man's first film (compare *Strike* or *Zvenigora*), and if one didn't know otherwise one would suppose it to have been made before and not after the more mature *Before the Revolution*. This poetic and limpidly clear work deals, in effect, with the failure of a young man to break away from his middle-class milieu and take part fully in the brave new world of Communism which his teacher friend so cogently preaches. At the start of the film Fabrizio has a romantic fixation on a relaxed don't-care boy called Agostino – a fixation which he extrapolates by trying to persuade or bully Agostino into meeting and listening to his communist pal Cesare. But Agostino, suddenly and casually, is found drowned. From this situation Fabrizio rebounds into an affair with Gina, his young and attractive aunt – herself still only on the way to recovery from an acute psychological crisis. He tries to balance himself, however precariously, between his family, his feelings for Gina, and his relationship with Cesare. (It is noteworthy that Bertolucci keeps Cesare unseen – an influential shadow – until quite late in the film.) But Fabrizio still talks of Agostino, whose hair 'was like the yellow feathers of a canary' (Gina's is black). About halfway through the film, on a visit to an old monastery, they try but fail to come to terms. So significant is this sequence between Fabrizio and Gina, a sequence in which much is said about the mysteries of time and of the passing of the seasons, and in which their situation becomes – though not overtly – precipitous, that Bertolucci suddenly switches the film into colour, what time the two of them become separated not merely by the distance between her in a tower and he in the square below, but also by the added alienation of a camera obscura. This sequence, mysterious, rupturing, returns the film to black and white.

Crises mount; the clash of psyches becomes deafening. Fabrizio introduces Gina to Cesare in a scene in which they all read to each other or tell fables; after which Gina has a big crisis alone in her room, pouring it all out long-distance to her psychiatrist in Milan; after which she provokes Fabrizio to the extreme by deliberately taking up, though not in fact *au sérieux*, with another man.

Finally it becomes inevitable, sexually and socially, that Fabrizio will conform to the bourgeois conventions in which he is trapped. So it is the blonde, dull Clelia he marries, even though her hair has neither the colour nor the texture of Agostino's. At the end of the wedding Gina, in a strangely equivocal gesture, bestows something more than an auntly embrace on Fabrizio's young and comparatively innocent brother.

Before the Revolution is truly rich in incident, with constant switches from love scenes to family scenes to political discussions. Aldo Scavarda's camerawork brings an effective chiaroscuro to the interiors – especially the intimate love-scenes between Gina and Fabrizio – and is particularly fine in the opera-house sequence where, after Fabrizio's engagement to Clelia, he and Gina meet in the corridor and, against a storm of music from Verdi's *Macbeth* (played not in synchronization with the stage action but in relation to *their* emotions), exchange, in a series of violent cuts, banalities which, in this context, take on a deep significance. This powerful cinematic effect will be repeated in the opera house scenes of *The Spider's Strategy*, though in a different and more terrifying context.

It is a pity that Bertolucci retained in the film a rather maddening and irrelevant sequence in which Gina, Fabrizio and Cesare visit an old friend of Gina's – a highly cultured, multilingual landowner nicknamed, for heaven's sake, Puck. This chap has been overtaken by the march of events and the foreclosings of mortgages, and is about to lose all his estates. Against exquisite country landscapes he and they discuss things in a mood of whimsiness – 'Here ends life, here begins survival' – and the only sensible thing that occurs is when Fabrizio asks him: 'Why didn't you think of all this while you still had the money?', for which Gina rewards him with a sharp slap in the face. If Bertolucci shot this sequence with satirical intent, it certainly doesn't register as such.

But in *The Spider's Strategy* Bertolucci brings together all the elements of his previous three films – split personality, Fascism, and the relativity of time. Based on a Borges *conte*[1] originally set in Ireland, this story of a young man's search for the truth about his father has here been transferred to a small Italian town. The son and the father are both played by the same actor (Giulio Brogi) so that, as in *Partner*, there is a strong element of cross-identification. As the film progresses we gradually realize that the director is leading us into a maze where the reality of the past as well as the present is being questioned – a maze, too, which seems to have no centre and in which time is suddenly seen to have ceased to exist.

The story concerns the young man's attempt to find out the truth about the death of his father, who died fighting the Fascist regime. His name, like that of his father, is Athos. In the small town where his hero-father died he finds – thirty years later – evasions, hostility, even violence. Refusing to be put off, he pursues his enquiries until he discovers that the murder of his father was a fantastic put-on. The truth was that Athos senior was found by his colleagues to be a traitor to the anti-Fascist cause; but in his remorse he begged them to execute him in such a way that his guilt would not be revealed and, as a result, the Fascists would not benefit. So an elaborate conspiracy is evolved through which he is to appear to be assassinated by the Fascists themselves during a performance of *Rigoletto* in the local opera house. The whole town becomes a party to the weaving of this web. The murder is played out on two time-scales, that of the past and that of the opera house today, with Athos' son participating, so that it is no wonder that not only the past and the present but also the *personae* of father and son become commingled. No wonder, either, that after all this is over the townsfolk beat up Athos junior in front of his father's statue which, in turn, he defaces.

The upshot is that young Athos decides to leave the truth buried and unrevealed. But when he tries to leave he finds at the railway station firstly that the train is late, secondly that it is not coming, and thirdly that the station has been closed for years and the rails are overgrown with grass and weeds. He is trapped in time.

What is so splendid about *The Spider's Strategy* is that the com-

[1] *Theme of the Traitor and the Hero* by J. L. Borges.

plexity of the story never leads (as in *Partner*) to an irritating confusion. Bertolucci's narration is here absolutely clear, and the whole film is held together by the figure of Dreyfa, the father's mistress – a magnificent performance by Alida Valli, who switches back and forth over thirty years without any change of make-up, and through whom we are enabled to identify with and to recognize both father and son; there is indeed a crucial scene in this respect, when she persuades young Athos to dress up in his father's clothes, with catatonic results. The fact that she never changes (she is of course named after Dreyfus) is not just an anchor point for the narrative. As the film goes on it becomes increasingly clear that her immutability is more than fascinating – it is dangerous: for she is mad. There is a scene where she tries to persuade young Athos not to leave – presented through a brilliantly executed combination of tracking and panning in a curved corridor with a wall covered with paintings of lilies – which creates a feeling of ghostly terror out of, it seems, nothing.

Bertolucci's camera movements are indeed beautifully designed throughout the film; they are functional, vital. It is, too, a film of perspectives, right from that early moment when, as he circles the memorial to his father (and here, as so often in this strange little town, the vistas recall Chirico), we begin to realize that the citizenry are posed, poised, menacing and *ready for him*. Then again there is the fantastic sequence of the escaped lion, with men and animal milling around against endless cloisters seen through a window, which suddenly switches to the lion's head being carried in procession and served up on a lordly dish like that of a boar; or the extraordinary sequence (the mechanism of which recalls the circular pans during the piano recital in the farmyard in Godard's *Weekend*) when the camera, acting for Athos, seeks out the strolling figure of Dreyfa in a wide courtyard full of flowers.

The complex layers of the story, the deceptive folds of time, all are peeling off like onion skins; the apparent illogicalities explain themselves in a manner which is more than disturbing; for we, with the characters, find ourselves uneasily suspended in time. Even the children are ambivalent, like the boy who lives in a dream-world of fairy tales and mediaeval legend, and the other boy in a broad-brimmed hat who, in the event, turns out to be a girl.

There are, too, moments of rich, raw humour, as with the *charcutier* who reminisces about Athos senior while prestidigitating with toothpicks and skewers on his hams and salamis (a sequence which Bertolucci constantly fades out and cuts back into itself, a trick which, within the confines of a single set-up, powerfully accentuates the mood of reminiscence); and another (which incidentally involves a disturbing time-switch) where Athos *père*, strolling with colleagues, is seen imitating cockcrows on a country path, and so triggers off a dawn chorus of chanticleers some thirty years later.

Thus the film is entirely devoted to questioning the nature of time and of truth in relation to human experience. As in *The Conformist*, the main character is deeply concerned to uncover past events; as in *Before the Revolution*, the climax involves the timelessness of music bound up with the formalities of opera and the opera house; and as in *Partner*, the resolution of a duality of identity is crucial – the difference, however, being that in this case the duality is not simultaneous but, on the contrary, widely separated in time.

The crucial mistake made by young Athos at the end of the film is when he returns to the town from the railway station (having been told that his train will be late) in order to try to stammer out to the populace some sort of an explanation of his decision not to expose the true facts of his father's demise. But by now he has something near a split mind; and he makes a speech whose confusions reside in his inability to make coincidence between what he *wants* to say and what his inmost thoughts are urgently indicating. This useless interlude costs him his escape; and Bertolucci rubs in this final lesion in time in a very precise way. We have seen at the start of the film that young Athos' arrival coincides with that of a young sailor on leave. At the end, when Athos makes his first visit to the station, the young sailor is also there, to catch the same train. And he does. He is outside the web. It is only when Athos returns to the station that the web slowly engulfs him as, in a truly cinematic concertina-ing of time, years of closure and decay, of rust and of weeds, creep like a dry tide over all. It is a disturbing, even frightening ending to a film distinguished – apart from its directorial maturity and its faultless acting – by superb photography (Vittorio Storaro and Franco Di Giacomo) and a remarkable score which, in addition to the Verdi, includes a 'popular' song called, significantly enough, 'Il Conformista', and passages from Schönberg's hallucinatory Second Chamber Symphony.

Like all the Bertolucci films so far, *Last Tango in Paris* is concerned with the problem of identity. But whereas *Partner* involved a *döppelgänger*, and *The Spider's Strategy* the same character seen both as father and son, *Last Tango in Paris* (*pace* other critics!) goes back to *The Conformist* and focuses on a single individual. The variation here is that the individual focuses in turn on another whose predicament is comparable but not exactly similar; and the story of the film details how he fails in this focus and so destroys both himself and her (for her triumph at the end is, to say the least, pyrrhic).

The 'sexual scandals' of this film were grossly exaggerated in nearly every review (Pauline Kael being a notable exception). The sexual element is of course vital to the film, for it is one of the means to an end and, indeed, is seen to be, in that end, a self-imposed confidence-trick; it fails, as do all the other means – the insults, the violence, the ill temper and, above all, the paradoxical desire for anonymity as a cure for solitude and loss of *persona*.

The weakness of the film resides in the sub-plot concerning the girl's engagement to a TV producer (played with surprising unease by Jean-Pierre Léaud) which, as far as I was concerned, failed to combine with the main plot; if the dichotomy was deliberate on Bertolucci's part, the effect failed. The two Jacobs in *Partner*, however obscure some of the motivation may have been, were nearer the mark.

Nevertheless, thanks largely to Marlon Brando's necromantically committed performance, *Last Tango in Paris* finally makes one understand – to plagiarize Roger Graef – the space between words; in Brando's outburst in the lobby of the rooming house a universe of despair roars down on us like an avalanche.

Parallel with Bertolucci is another young director with an individual talent at least as powerful – Marco Bellocchio, whose first film, made in 1965, was *I Pugni in Tasca (Fists in the Pocket)*, a work of sensational psychological impact about a family matched in screen terms only by the Ambersons of Orson Welles; Elizabeth, Paul and the rest in Melville's *Les Enfants Terribles*; or the Sakuradas of Oshima's *The Ceremony*.

Bellocchio gives us a family enwrapped in epilepsy. The widowed mother is blind. The adolescent Sandro is epileptic, and his relationship with his teenage sister Giulia is not far from incestuous. His younger brother Leone, also epileptic, lives in a state of listless apathy and is, perhaps, 'not quite all there'. The only normal member of the family is the grown up Augusto, responsible for them all since the father's death, and in this deeply frustrated as he is engaged to be married and wants to get away.

Nearly all the above facts are put across by Bellocchio in a single sequence showing the family at dinner. That the mother is blind becomes clear when the cat, wandering about on the table, eats off her plate; that the rest of the family is at least strange becomes clear when no one seems to bother about the cat. Leone, blank and dull, slurps at a saucerful of coffee. Sandro and Giulia play 'footy footy' under the table. Such is the springboard for a macabre story centred on Sandro, whose normal adolescent frustrations and rebellions are brought to boiling point by the added frustrations and handicaps of epilepsy.

The answer to this is, predictably, an angry violence. Bellocchio – aided by a menacingly brilliant performance by Lou Castel – concentrates everything on the *logic* of this anger and violence. Thus the reason Sandro puts to Augusto for him to fiddle him a driving licence is that then he will be able to drive Leone, Giulia, their mother and himself over a cliff – thus leaving Augusto free to live a reasonable life. Augusto gets the licence. Sandro drives the car insolently around the town; but after these delusions of grandeur he signally fails to go over the cliff. However, he does push his mother off, and after the cold formality of the funeral (her death is made to appear as an accident) there is an extraordinary sequence in which Sandro and Giulia wildly destroy all traces of her. Everything is thrown out, down to the most trivial memento, and everything that can be burnt is burnt while the poor younger brother crawls around bewildered among the rubbish and the ashes.

For some strange reason these goings-on, to say nothing of the macabre remainder of the film which recalls the excesses of *The Duchess of Malfi*, seem completely viable in terms of modern *verismo*. Yet consider what happens. Sandro's *weltschmertz* is by no means relieved by his mother's death; and his ambitions and velleities are exacerbated by his epileptic condition. After a macabre *rencontre* in which a prostitute taunts him for comparing unfavourably in sexual prowess with Augusto, he sets course for a programme of total destruction. He kills Leone, and contemplates doing the same for Giulia who, however, after a fall downstairs is, or is pretending to be, paralysed and remains permanently in bed.

Perhaps because of the very intensity with which Bellocchio presents this monstrous series of events, perhaps because of the uniform excellence of the acting and the admirable black and white photography by Alberto Marrama, there is never so much as a sniff of unintentional comedy. The final sequence encompasses a tragic terror with Sandro, seized with an appalling and surely mortal fit of *Le Grand Mal*, writhing on the floor of his bedroom while Giulia lies passive and motionless in hers, and from the record-player there soars the exquisite sound of 'Sempre Libera' from *La Traviata* . . .

Fists in the Pocket landed Bellocchio in trouble with the Establishment in Italy. A number of Members of Parliament protested against it, and at one point it looked like being banned by the censor. No doubt the reason for this was not so much that it attacked the sacred cow of motherhood and thus the sanctity of the family, but that the attack was so uncompromisingly savage and violent. The anger behind the young man who directed this film makes the world of Jimmy Porter and the rest look like a Presbyterian sewing bee. Bellocchio himself has remarked that the epileptic theme 'meant all the frustrations, all the troubles and weaknesses found in the young'. So through Sandro he expresses his own anger at the rottenness and hypocrisy of the society in which he lives; through Sandro he echoes the cannibal and the pig-lover of *Pigsty*.

Bellocchio ran into further trouble with his next film, *China is Near* (*La Cina è Vicina*), in which he continued his attacks on the idea of the family by combining them with attacks on the shams of the community; the individual convolutions of the family are here entangled, if not identified with, the communal convolutions of Italian politics. A strong desire on the part of the authorities to ban its circulation was, however, frustrated by its acceptance critically as a minor masterpiece, and by the fact that it shared the Jury Prize at the 1967 Venice Film Festival with, interestingly enough, Godard's *La Chinoise*.

In fact *China is Near* is a sharp comedy about sex and politics. Its brilliant script, the result of a collaboration between Bellocchio and his female lead Elda Tattoli,[1] has, like Dreyer's *Gertrud*, strong affinities with opera and not least with the complexities and symmetries of *opera buffo*.[2] The centre of the plot concerns the sexual permutations of Vittorio and Elena – upper class brother and sister – relative to their two employees, Giovanna, a secretary, and Carlo, an accountant, whose mutual love is hardly proof against their individual ambitions. The various gyrations of these four personages are seen against a political background in which bourgeois socialism and Maoist communism meet in head-on collision, thanks to the machinations of the fifth main character, Camillo – Vittorio and Elena's young brother, a sharp and remorseless kid with a sadistic sense of humour who, typically enough, works in a Catholic seminary.

On the personal level Carlo and Giovanna are ruthless enough to betray each other with Vittorio and Elena in order to better themselves; and at the end of the film we see Elena and Giovanna – both

[1] Later on director of *The Planet Venus* (*Pianete Venere*) in 1972.

[2] Operatic influence, particularly that of Verdi, is notable in the films of both Bertolucci and Bellocchio. The opera sequence in *China is Near* appears indeed to be a *hommage* to Bertolucci which, however, was probably not welcomed, as he is said to disapprove of the film.

pregnant by Carlo – sitting placidly together doing their mother-to-be exercises on the parquet of an elegant *piano nobile*. The parallel political plot, meantime, has been developed through Vittorio's efforts to get himself elected councillor on a socialist ticket; these are not helped by Camillo's use of bomb scares and police dogs during his public meetings.

It must be said here that the film really revolves round Vittorio, a character conceived marvellously in the round and played to perfection by Glauco Mauri. Wealthy, ambitious, essentially cloth-headed rather than consciously hypocritical, he pursues his aims with an innocent optimism which somehow survives all his electioneering disasters, to say nothing of familial problems (his failure to persuade Elena to have an abortion – in which for the first and last time he finds Camillo on the same side – is high comedy at its best); and he gives to his few, brief moments of triumph, like the standing ovation accorded to him by his audience when he proposes the nationalization of all pharmacies (at which point Camillo's Alsatians irrupt into the meeting), an epic effulgence.

Bellocchio begins *China is Near* with a series of brief episodes depicting his main characters behaving in manners largely inexplicable to us since we do not yet know them. Thus in the cool greyness of morning we observe two persons (they will be Carlo and Giovanna) sharing a bed improvised from benches in a bare, unpromising room. As the man gets up and drags on his pants, the camera notes that the walls display posters recommending 'Unificazione Socialista'. Soon after this a young man (Camillo) is seen scrawling the film's title on a wall.[1] And then, with a panache which in hindsight is hilarious, there is revealed to us Vittorio (as we shall come to know him) sitting on the WC in the throes of constipation or masturbation – probably the former, but the camera angle encourages ambivalence – and calling urgently on the Almighty for both forgiveness and help.

There are a number of splendid set pieces. Prime among these is Vittorio's open-air election meeting in a village square where everything, at first trivially and then monumentally, goes wrong, and in the end Vittorio's precious automobile is beaten up by the locals; at which point Bellocchio hints that this is just as bad as hitting one's old mum. There is too a subtle scene in the seminary when Vittorio is confronted by a totally obdurate Camillo – the argument taking place during a sort of musical serenade or offering provided, somewhat out of tune, by a

---

[1] Bellocchio has a penchant for background comment in his visuals; at various points in *China is Near* one notes posters advertising such films as *Goldfinger* and *Alfie*.

choir of small boys for the delectation of a sick Monsignor. And there is a sequence in the truest style of classic comic opera when the erstwhile lovers Carlo and Giovanna, now in mutual liaison with Elena and Vittorio, take part in a perfectly timed minuet of bedroom-hopping. Here, as throughout the film, Tonino Delli Colli's camera movements are impeccable.

Despite the fact that it is basically about personal and political betrayals (it is not only the bourgeois Vittorio who betrays socialism, but also the 'workers' Carlo and Giovanna), *China is Near* is a remarkably funny film – funny in the sense that it constantly gives rise to immediate laughter, loud and clear. That Bellocchio, for all his social commitment, can achieve this augurs well both for his own future and that of Italian cinema.

IV

While Chabrol's *Le Beau Serge* was launching the New Wave in France, the appearance in 1958 of Tony Richardson's *Look Back in Anger* and Jack Clayton's *Room at the Top* signalled a similar wave of 'new' film-making in Britain which stemmed largely from the theatre-world of John Osborne and the fiction-world of writers like Kingsley Amis and John Braine. The films themselves were conventional in style. It was their content – a persistent and nagging questioning of national values and morals – which, together with increasing permissiveness of expression, gave them bite and a capacity to shock their public.

During this same period it became increasingly difficult to distinguish between British and American films. The collapse of Hollywood was already being prepared for by the so-called 'runaway productions' which will be dealt with later in the chapter. It will be sufficient at this point to note that the Hollywood people – actors and technicians alike – had begun to price themselves out of the labour market, so that producers found it more economic, if not always more convenient, to transfer their film-making activities elsewhere.

Directors who needed big crowds in big landscapes, and particularly battle scenes, found a welcome in countries like Spain and Yugoslavia, where the authorities did not hesitate to place large sections of the army at their disposal. The advantages to these governments in terms of cash and prestige were considerable, while the producers still found that the price to be paid was far lower than that which they would have had to cough up in the United States.[1]

Meantime, as Hollywood increasingly ceased to be the box-office Mecca, and as the borderline between film and television became increasingly blurred, it was not unnatural that English-speaking film-makers should intermingle more than previously, and that the financial set-up should, to a degree, become more equalized as between Britain and America, instead of the British end being always dominated, or at least threatened, by American interests.

From now on it would be more and more difficult to categorize films on national levels. An English director like John Schlesinger can make a totally 'American' film, *Midnight Cowboy*, and follow it with a totally 'English' film, *Sunday Bloody Sunday*.[2] Peter Watkins' films on totalitarianism have the same style and flavour whether he shoots them in Britain, America or Scandinavia. Conversely Americans make American or British-style films in Britain; Kubrick's *2001* was made in England as well as his *Clockwork Orange*.

V

Look Back in Anger and *Room at the Top* both had a success more than that of scandal on their appearance in 1958. The latter was by far the better film. It was based on the comparatively loose and therefore amenable framework of a novel, whereas *Look Back in Anger* was a translation to the screen of the most successful and sensational stage play of its day. Moreover, the theatre area from which it emerged was that to which the proponents of Free Cinema had transferred their attentions. Jack Clayton, on the other hand, had grown up inside the conventional cinema industry and, after a long, hard slog had managed, in 1955, to create something of a reputation for himself with a short film, based on a Wolf Mankowitz story, called *The Bespoke Overcoat*.

The distinction between the two films may lie in memorability of visuals. *Look Back in Anger*, despite its star-studded cast (Richard

---

[1] British directors like David Lean also availed themselves of these facilities, but for different reasons. America can provide enormous spaces and landscapes; Britain cannot. For a blockbuster like *Dr Zhivago*, Lean needed a good hunk of Spain to convert into a fair semblance of Russia. Economy was for him not the main object, whereas the runaway producers were shopping for space similar to but cheaper than that in the United States.

[2] Few people realize even now that *The Bridge on the River Kwai* is an *American* film.

Burton, Claire Bloom, Mary Ure, Gary Raymond, Donald Pleasence, Edith Evans,[1] George Devine, Glen Byam Shaw), has left on the whole only shadowy memories, while those of *Room at the Top* remain crisp and clear. Of course it did have the inestimable advantage of Simone Signoret at her best; but beyond this the fact remains that the story of Joe Lampton's rise had a brutal, factual realism which eluded the screen version of *Look Back in Anger*. Lampton came at us off the screen as solid as the very tangible muck and brass of his milieu; and beyond this some of the love scenes, no less than those of violence, had a richness recalling *Casque d'Or*, to which – and not only because of Signoret – *Room at the Top* is comparable. Of subsequent films by Clayton one may note a distinguished screen version of Henry James' *Turn of the Screw* called *The Innocents* (1961), which in at least two sequences – by the lake and in the classroom – nobly re-created the supernatural terror of the original; and *Our Mother's House* (1967), a film about some children who, for good reasons of their own, conceal the body of their dead mother and pretend she is still alive.

In general the protest films made by the Angries seem pretty mild in comparison with the more violent attitudes expressed in French and Italian films of the same period;[2] Jack Cardiff's *Sons and Lovers* (1960), Karel Reisz' *Saturday Night and Sunday Morning* (1960) and even the Boulting Brothers' *I'm All Right, Jack* (1959), are comparatively discreet. There is a despairing drabness about these films which neither skilled direction nor fine photography can wholly disguise; and it is only when a flash of fine acting illuminates a shot or a sequence that we feel things for real – some of Burton's outbursts in *Look Back in Anger*, two or three moments of mindless yet supremely cunning stupidity created by Sellers in *I'm All Right, Jack*, and nearly the whole of Olivier's Archie Rice in *The Entertainer*.

Pauline Kael may have put her finger on the whole problem when she wrote that in these films 'the people live without grace'. This is indeed true of one of the best of them – Lindsay Anderson's *This Sporting Life* (1963). This is a well-made film, with some outstanding scenes of pure movie emerging from a script cunningly constructed around flashbacks. It is a film about failure; and it is a failure which arises from a reliance on violence. The rugby-playing hero Machin knows no other reaction,[3] whether in his career on the football field

[1] She splendidly incarnated Ma Tanner who, in the play, was only an off-stage reference.

[2] *This Sporting Life* is an exception.

[3] One may compare the despairing cry of Albert Finney's girl in *Saturday Night and Sunday Morning*, 'Why are you always throwing things?'

(the rugby scenes, with all their dirty play, are superbly conveyed) or in his personal relationships (he strikes Mrs Hammond in the face at the end of the sequence in which they attend a friend's wedding). Mrs Hammond herself, frigid, withdrawn, accepts his sex as a joyless manifestation of violence and when, following the climactic moment after his ghastly behaviour in the restaurant, he finally commits himself with his shout of 'I love you', she finds only one simple answer – to die. Especially memorable here is the scene when Machin, confronted with her corpse, sees a spider on the wall and smashes it with his fist while, from the dead woman's mouth, a stream of haemorrhagal blood blackly congeals. The absence of grace persists.

Meantime Tony Richardson followed *The Entertainer*[1] with *A Taste of Honey* (1961), translated as skilfully from stage to screen as had been *Look Back in Anger*. This film, like Basil Dearden's *Victim*, brought into the open the till then largely unmentionable subject of homosexuality (to say nothing of miscegenation), as well as providing admirable acting parts for Rita Tushingham and Murray Melvin. Richardson followed this with *The Loneliness of the Long Distance Runner* (1963), in which the hard outlines of the original Alan Sillitoe story about a young delinquent were somewhat softened at the edges, though the key sequence, well shot and finely played by Tom Courtenay, of the cross-country race being deliberately, bloody-mindedly lost, had its compelling moments.

Richardson then switched away from the contemporary scene and contemporary problems to a vast, rumbustious colour version of *Tom Jones* (1963), crammed with character actors hamming it up no end in attempts to give 'larger than life' performances and being from time to time wiped clean off the screen by Edith Evans' impeccable balance and sense of timing. This film is now mainly memorable for the famous eating match between Albert Finney and Joyce Redman which became, with mounting acceleration, a hilariously symbolic tour of the works of Krafft-Ebing. It was in *Tom Jones* that Richardson's tendency to overdo things, to pile effect on effect, first came clearly to the fore and pre-figured the kind of excesses which were later to be the hallmark of Ken Russell's work.

In 1961 Bryan Forbes, an ex-actor who had been a successful screenwriter for some ten years,[2] went into direction with a strangely

---

[1] If we omit his excursion to Hollywood to make a screen *réchauffage* of Faulkner's *The Loved One* entitled *Sanctuary*.

[2] His credits include *The Wooden Horse*, *The Angry Silence* and *The League of Gentlemen*.

effective fantasy tale, *Whistle Down the Wind*, in which a group of children, coming on a fugitive murderer in a deserted barn, take him to be Jesus. Although the film became somewhat over-elaborate towards the end, Forbes' working out of the results of the simple, practical faith of the children was convincing and often moving; it was much aided by a fine performance by Hayley Mills. The meticulous scripting of this film was repeated in *The L-Shaped Room* (1962) and *Seance on a Wet Afternoon* (1964); but it was in 1965 that Forbes made his best (and generally most underestimated) film. *King Rat* was set in the notorious Changi prison camp in Singapore during the Japanese occupation, an enclave in which the appalling shortage of food tended to undermine the morale and morals of all but the most dedicated and strong-minded. At the centre of the story is an American corporal named King (played by George Segal) who, gangster-like, has set up a racket with the Japanese guards, and manages to live in comparative luxury, with various fellow prisoners acting as his servants in return for favours rendered. Among other things he breeds rats which he then sells to the officers under the disguise of rare Oriental delicacies. King gradually draws into his orbit a young and very public-school-type Englishman (James Fox) who becomes his devoted follower. In the event he saves the youngster from death by using some stolen drugs which he has acquired for quite other purposes. There is only one other main character – a grim, puritanical, jealous, class-conscious military policeman (Tom Courtenay), whose frustrated disapproval of King's activities adds to the luridness of the sun-drenched scenes of men being reduced to hysteria through hunger.

Forbes' treatment is uncompromisingly brutal. There is a horrible sequence in which King – he is King Rat of the title of course – serves up to his companions a dish concocted from the remains of a pet dog belonging to one of them. What is horrible about this scene is not the disgust and anger with which they at first react to this fact, but the mood of mouth-watering, greedy anticipation which almost instantly supervenes.

Against all this brutal realism the director poses the delicately developing relationship between the American and the young Englishman – a relationship in which disapproval of King's racketeering gradually changes (and not simply through the ministrations of hunger) to the hero worship of a small boy for a school prefect and, in the final event, to a fervent if unexpressed love. The scene at the end when, after the liberation, King (now no more than an ordinary Yank corporal) is taken off in a truck while the thin, handsome English boy stands there lost, bewildered, alone, and with all the values of his upbringing, all the self-reliance of his class, in shredded ruins, and nothing to replace them, has an extraordinary poignancy. It is too, with *The Servant* and *Performance*, an example of James Fox's acting at its very best.[1]

I question whether Forbes ever bettered this film. He went on to make a disastrous version of the Robert Louis Stevenson classic *The Wrong Box* (1966), in which the deadpan matter-of-factness on which the whole joke depended was converted into whimsy and horseplay (as Ken Annakin had earlier done with *Three Men in a Boat*); and among other productions we may note *The Whisperers* (1967), a well-constructed vehicle for a virtuoso performance by Edith Evans (yet again) as a poverty-stricken old woman living in a dream world compounded of a mixture of uneasy fears and delusions of grandeur. In 1969 Forbes became executive head of ABC, one of the largest producing companies in Britain.

Apart from Richardson, the output of the original Angries turned out to be small. After *Saturday Night and Sunday Morning* (1960), whose considerable appeal and success may well have been due to the fact that it was literally a poor man's *Look Back in Anger*, Karel Reisz did a somewhat disappointing remake of *Night Must Fall* (1963), and then, three years later, came up with *Morgan: A Suitable Case for Treatment*. This extraordinary film, which at times echoes Buñuel, involves, in essence, a man's effort to break up his wife's divorce proceedings and, when that fails, her re-marriage. Ambivalently pretending to be mad and later being actually mad, he chooses to identify himself with the law of the jungle by assuming the *persona* of a gorilla. In this guise he plays a series of appalling practical jokes which eventually develop into episodes a great deal more sinister. Tied in with this is a fixation on Marxism and/or Trotskyism (there is a marvellously funny sequence at Marx's grave in Highgate Cemetery), and at the end of the film, when he has finally been certified, we see him, calm and smiling, tending the formal flower-beds in the garden of the mental home; in the last shot the camera draws back to reveal that the design he has made from the lobelias and whatnot is of the Hammer and Sickle.

Morgan is a jerky film, disturbing in construction as well as in content. It is no doubt designed to make us question our own confidence in the society in which we live. Splendidly played by a cast

[1] *King Rat* is another example of the blurring of the dividing lines between British and American production. This very English film, set in a former colony, was in fact made in California, with the whole Changi prison complex reconstructed on an exterior lot.

which includes David Warner, Vanessa Redgrave, Robert Stephens and Irene Handl, it is leavened with some really funny black humour. The smashing up of the wedding reception, followed by Morgan's majestic slow motion entry into the River Thames on his motor bike, is absolutely terrific.

Isadora (1968), also with Vanessa Redgrave, disappointed in comparison with Ken Russell's television programme, but I have it from Reisz himself that the film as released had involved cuts and alterations of which he by no means approved.

Lindsay Anderson's output was even smaller. After *This Sporting Life* he went back to theatre work for several years, and then emerged to make what was planned as part of a trilogy based on three stories by Shelagh Delaney. *The White Bus* (1966), a fantasy which, like *If* . . . later on, was partly in black and white and partly in colour, ran for some 50 minutes; as the other two items (by Tony Richardson and Peter Brook) had been shelved by the distributors, it was left rather out on a limb, being an awkward length for the theatres.[1] This was a pity, for it is an enchanting film which deserves wide circulation.

The White Bus is beautiful, funny, sad, satiric, disturbing, loving. Exquisitely photographed in black and white and colour by Miroslav Ondricek[2] (who later shot *If* . . .), it mixes realism and fantasy in a manner hardly seen since Jean Vigo made *L'Atalante*. The story, such as it is, concerns a girl who leaves the drudgery of an office job in London and returns to her home town in the industrial North. Here she goes on a conducted bus tour led by the Mayor in full regalia (a finely modulated performance by Arthur Lowe), his pompous and not very bright macebearer, assorted citizenry, and, from overseas, a Japanese woman and a Nigerian man. All these Anderson uses as a means of observing and commenting on the industrial scene from a number of points of view – his rather than theirs. After the bunfights, the modern blocks of flats, the old back-to-back houses, the Museum and the Library (after reciting a statistical panegyric on the latter, the Mayor suddenly turns on the librarian and says 'It's full of filthy books'), it comes as no surprise when at the end of a vivid civil defence demonstration – which includes a traumatic cut from a fearsome blaze to a close-up of the Japanese lady – all those present turn out to be no

[1] Previous to the Delaney idea, the Trilogy had been planned for Richardson, Anderson and Reisz; the change of plan took place because in the event Reisz's contribution, *Morgan: A Suitable Case for Treatment*, turned out to need full feature length for its development.

[2] Czech cameraman who had previously worked with Milos Forman, Jan Nemec and Ivan Passer.

more than stuffed dummies like the personages at the prize-giving in
Zéro de Conduite. Only the girl remains flesh and blood. In a remarkable
coda she drifts off through the city at night, glimpsing through lighted
windows simple images of contentment until at the end, in a fish-and-
chip shop where they are piling the chairs on the tables while reciting
a ridiculous litany of not putting off till tomorrow what you can do
today, we leave her, seated, solitary – a question-mark.

Anderson constantly turns the edge of his satire; nor is he afraid
to switch to straightforward jokes, many of them really funny and
splendidly timed. The hard central argument, the spine as it were of
the film's construction, is against the way ordinary folk accept rather
than question or oppose the circumstances of their life and the
organization of the society in which they live. *The White Bus* is *par
excellence* an anti-conformist picture. Anderson's sympathy for these
same ordinary folk gives the film an ambiguity which he is proud to
admit. He has said that 'some people find it a very sad film and some
people find it a very satirical film. I hope it is both. I wouldn't dictate
to anybody how they should receive it.'[1]

In 1967 Anderson was invited to Poland, where he made a two-
reel poetic documentary called *The Singing Lesson*, featuring students
of the Warsaw Dramatic Academy; after which he embarked on *If . . .*,
which I have discussed earlier. He then returned to his second and
equally distinguished career as a theatre producer, returning to films
in 1973 with the interesting but somewhat overblown *O Lucky
Man!*

Apart from the few films of the Angry Young Men group, it is
difficult to discern any specific trends in the British cinema of this
period. Perhaps the nearest example of common ground may be seen
in a developing attitude on the part of a number of film-makers to the
idea of war, as witness a whole string of films taking an attitude to the
subject which differs considerably from that of the war films of the
Forties and Fifties.

After the First World War film-makers were mainly concerned
with disillusionment. After World War II, which no one had approached
with any illusions, but rather with a sense of doom, the appalling aftermath, with its proliferation of local conflicts and an increasing acceptance of the atrocious, quite apart from the existence of nuclear
weapons, was likely to turn the thoughts of many directors and screenwriters into areas of furious cynicism and of appeals for sanity.

Without claiming any overly dramatic moves in such directions,

[1] See *Lindsay Anderson* by Elizabeth Sussex, Studio Vista, 1969.

I think one can find something of the attitude suggested in most of the war films on this list:

> *It Happened Here* (1964)
> *King and Country* (1964)
> *The War Game* (1965)
> *Tell Me Lies* (1967)
> *How I Won the War* (1967)
> *The Gladiators* (1969)
> *Oh! What a Lovely War* (1969)

The story of how Kevin Brownlow – first alone and later in conjunction with Andrew Mollo – spent seven years overcoming every sort of obstacle and discouragement in order to bring to the screen *It Happened Here* has been fully told in his own book,[1] and there is no need to repeat it here. As for the film itself, this 'reconstruction' of what might have happened had Britain been invaded and occupied by the Germans in 1940 remains not only a remarkable piece of film-making (its verisimilitude verges on the miraculous), but also a very disturbing thesis to which the French TV documentary *Le Chagrin et la Pitié* later added further emphasis. The more often one sees *It Happened Here*, the more one wonders which of us would have been collaborators and which would have been in the Resistance. The casual everyday quality of the film, with the Nazi troops, led by a band, marching through Regent's Park; the betrayal of a patriot in a Hampstead flat; a newsreel odiously mouthing propaganda; a Collaborationist rally in Trafalgar Square; and, for good measure, the savage revenge of the Resistance on their ambushed compatriots – all these are sinister enough. But worst of all are the actual statements, made during the production of the film and related to its historical background, in which contemporary British Fascists make it clear that for them nothing has changed. Indeed, these sequences are so convincing that when the film first appeared many people mistook it for Fascist propaganda. After protests from the Jewish authorities a violent press controversy broke out, and eventually Brownlow and Mollo were compelled to agree to the deletion of a discussion among British Nazis which included such statements as 'The Jew is a parasite race . . . a flea on a dog . . . Fleas can live on a dog but fleas cannot live on fleas. Send 'em all to Madagascar, that's the simplest way.'[2]

[1] *How It Happened Here* by Kevin Brownlow, Secker and Warburg, 1968.

[2] As Brownlow has pointed out, it was 'not so much what was said as how it was said that led to the censorship of this sequence. The intensity of expression, and the tenseness of the atmosphere, made the words far more sinister than they appear [in print].'

Leaving aside for the moment *King and Country* and *Oh! What a
Lovely War*, we may note what an admirable companion piece to *It
Happened Here* is to be seen in *The War Game*. The former deals with
what might (perhaps would) have happened in the past; the latter is
concerned with what might (perhaps would) happen in the future. The
history of what happened to *The War Game* is of political as well as
cinematic significance – not least because all of Peter Watkins' subsequent work has undergone similar or comparable treatment.

Watkins, working for BBC Television, made in 1965 a filmed
feature programme called *Culloden*. This acute and perceptive work
exposed with merciless clarity one of the bloodiest blots on the conscience of the English people – the genocide of the Highlanders after
the battle, which was in itself a shambles, since the Young Pretender,
with asinine arrogance and complete remoteness from the reality of the
situation, committed his ill-equipped, starving, undisciplined rabble of
clansmen to a conflict on the wrong terrain against a large, superbly
equipped modern army led by the ruthless Duke of Cumberland.

The trick by which Watkins turned this far-off tragedy into an
unbearably realistic immediacy was that he assumed, for the purposes
of his programme, that at Culloden all the mass media facilities of
today were readily available. Thus he had on-the-spot commentators
before, during and after the battle; direct interviews with Prince
Charles, the Duke, Generals, Captains, common soldiers and Scots
civilians; *cinéma-vérité* type coverage of all aspects of the combat and
of the subsequent atrocities committed by the English. It became a
tour de force in which filmic and televisual concepts were welded
together as never before.

Culloden was a huge success. As a result the BBC gave Watkins
more or less *carte blanche* in the choice of another subject. He decided
to do a similar programme on nuclear war. He was thus dealing not
with the past but with the future, and with a subject which, as he was
soon to find out, was White Man's Big Juju – and Taboo.

The War Game set out to explain what would happen if the
Russians launched a nuclear attack on South-East England. To do this
Watkins used a twofold approach. On the one hand the story-line of the
film consisted of on-the-spot camera coverages, from the time the
authorities became sufficiently alarmed to start the evacuation of
women and children to the point when, after the bomb and ensuing
chaos, the country was moving towards savagery, with summary
executions in the street becoming commonplace. On the other hand
Watkins interspersed this account of the effects of nuclear war with

contemporary statements, as of today's date, illustrated by diagrams, together with interviews with different types of experts and quotations from various sources – political, military, scientific, medical, religious. These interceptions serve to remind us that while the holocaust has not yet taken place, the impending horrors constructed for us on the screen are not guesswork, but factual reconstructions of what did actually happen in Hamburg, Dresden, Tokyo, as well as in Hiroshima and Nagasaki.

The 'reconstructions' are hideously convincing, sometimes to the point of nausea. Against them the calm, factual statements from the screen build up not only to a frightful indictment of nuclear war, but also to an exposition of the idiocy of nuclear strategy and in particular of so-called civil defence. The film quotes an official handbook for civil defence workers, current while it was being made, which includes suggestions for simple meals for refugees after a nuclear explosion; these include things like stewed fruit and custard (and never mind, presumably, about the radiation). In fact *The War Game* made perfectly clear what no one would come out officially and admit – namely that there is no defence unless we consider something like Dr Strangelove's scheme for an *élite* which will retire to deep shelters and there breed for a century.

The shattering effect of *The War Game* at its first private viewings made it an immediate centre of controversy. The BBC flatly refused to show it, despite the fact that it was theirs. One can understand why. It broke a sacred taboo by 'telling it like it is': it was the clear childish voice pointing out that the emperor is actually naked. Everything it showed and said exposed the ineffectiveness and deceit of Authority, which now found itself varying its normally dignified gavotte with convulsive and unexpected somersaults.[1]

In the event the BBC let the British Film Institute take the film over for limited distribution. *The War Game* ran for a total of 26 weeks in London's West End; elsewhere, if it was not always shown in cinemas (and the controversy about it did result in sanctions), it was projected to audiences in church halls, youth clubs, film societies and the like. After one year it was reckoned that $1\frac{1}{2}$ million people had seen it – a small enough figure in terms of mass audiences, but none the less by no means to be despised. In the years since then *The War Game* has been seen by many millions right across the world.

---

[1] It was reported at the time that, during a projection of the film to a select audience of experts, opinion-formers and running dogs, a member of the BBC top brass said, 'I am sure that Peter Watkins would be the first to agree that the greatest compliment we can pay him is not to show his film'. The implications of this remark are worth thinking about.

Ever since *The War Game*, Watkins has truly been a *régisseur maudit*. His subsequent films have been reviled, conspired against or ignored. This is no doubt due to the fact that they all have pursued the same path of excoriating criticism of the Establishment, the eternal 'They' who, we are told, always know best but who are almost invariably wrong.

This is not to say that Watkins' films are necessarily masterpieces or even that they always express their messages satisfactorily in filmic terms. It may well be true that he has never really moved on from the formula he evolved for *Culloden* and perfected in *The War Game*. It may well be, as Michael Armstrong wrote of him, that 'his interests have become so concentrated upon content that he has forgotten form'.[1]

Whether or not that is true, the certainty is that Watkins is a violently sincere propagandist; filmwise there has been no one like him in Europe since André Cayatte. His next film, *Privilege* (1967), in which he depicted the Establishment using a pop star as a means of building and maintaining totalitarian control, was distinguished by the use of a very real pop singer (Paul Jones). While concentrating on the main issue this film (which was in colour) made quite an impression, particularly in the big crowd scenes; but an insistence on 'documentary' technique by breaking into the narrative with TV-style interviews (as in *The War Game*) vitiated the total impact of the film through dissipation.

For *The Gladiators* (1969), also known as *The Peace Game*, Watkins had to go to Sweden for his production finance, but I cannot help feeling that in this case his subsequent distribution problems may have been partly due to the fact that the idea of the film, excellent though it was, didn't come off. This story of how the Great Powers, seeking a substitute activity to avoid the dangers of atomic war, set up a system of miniature warfare something on the pattern of the Olympics and run jointly by a sort of UN team and a not very efficient computer, needs at least some element of fantasy to be acceptable. This is precisely what Watkins does not provide. This is not to object to the realism, similar to that of *The War Game*, by which the brutal facts of this 'Peace Game' are presented; it is simply that the tale doesn't of itself convince. The fantasy characters of *Strangelove* actually strength-

[1] *The Peace Game: A Passionate Plea for Peter Watkins, Myself and You*, in *Films and Filming*, October 1970. Armstrong's long and interesting study unfortunately infuriated Watkins, who replied at length in the issue of February 1971. Both pieces are worth reading. As for form and content, we may note that another bright boy from television, Ken Russell, went overboard in the other direction; though personally I find myself unrefreshed by the chilling hyperbole of films like *The Music Lovers* and *The Devils*.

ened the ferocity of Kubrick's thesis. If Watkins wanted to do it the other way, his people should be more *realistically* convincing. Instead they tend to be cliché types or Aunt Sallies; one sighs for the psychotic Endore (*War Hunt*), the megalomaniac General Mireau (*Paths of Glory*), or even the mute, inglorious Hamp (*King and Country*). Nevertheless *The Gladiators* deserved a wider showing and a more considered critical reception than it actually received when, after a delay of two years (why?), it had its London release. The cinema needs committed young directors like Peter Watkins who will not agree to trim their anger to the standards either of the Establishment or of the Mass Media (if indeed there is any significant difference between the two).

This point is much reinforced by *Punishment Park* (1971), which is undoubtedly Watkins' best film to date. Made in the United States, it postulates a period in the near future when the volume of protest against Vietnam, racism, and so on has reached a point at which the Government has set up arbitrary tribunals to deal with dissidents. Those convicted – and, as it appears, all are – are offered the choice of a long term of imprisonment or an endurance test in a punishment park which involves a fifty mile trek across scorching desert, the goal at the end being the American flag flying over a barren hilltop. Halfway there is supposed to be a water-supply, but in the event this turns out to be a hoax; there is nothing but a disconnected faucet lying in the dust. Those who survive to reach the goal are then told that they are not free but will be detained indefinitely; if they protest against this betrayal, they are mercilessly clubbed or shot down.

In presenting this scarifying 'report', Watkins continues the technique he developed for *Culloden* and has, as we have seen, stuck to ever since. Never, though, has it been so effective as in *Punishment Park*. We witness the trial of a batch of prisoners – the tribunal sits in a makeshift tent on the edge of the desert – and after they have chosen the test rather than imprisonment, we follow their terrible and fatal pilgrimage across the Park. This is cross-cut with the trial of a second batch of prisoners who, at the end of the film, are seen to make the same fatal choice. All this is shown through the television cameras of teams from two networks, one West German and one British, who have been invited by the authorities to record these new judiciary methods. The sense of immediacy thus achieved is frequently shattering – not least at the end when the TV crews come into conflict with the police thugs who have just finished off the prisoners after they reached the goal. The brutal, overpowering sense of hate and stupidity here comes across with hideous clarity. We see more than the America of McCarthyism and racism and Mayor Daley; we see the new violence in societal relations among the European democracies, we see the KGB, we see Rhodesia and South Africa, Brazil and Chile.

Ideologically Watkins plays very fair. If the members of the tribunal are prejudiced and hidebound, some of the accused are equally so. At certain points, as when a passionate but politically naïve kid lets fly at the judges in a uselessly wrong-headed manner, one wants to cry out, 'No, no – not *that* way'. For in the end what we are witnessing is the destruction of innocence as well as of freedom.

Punishment Park is not flawless. There are moments when the impression of reality is weakened; some of the victims, interviewed by TV during their torturing trek, do not look sweaty or breathless enough. But these minor defects are soon swallowed up by the terrifyingly convincing impact of the film as a whole.

Like other Watkins films, it had short shrift from the critics and, sadly, from some of the younger members of the public who could not apparently take the implication that however evil the powers assumed by authority may become, this does not automatically mean that all those in opposition are plaster saints. Of its American reception Watkins remarked, 'Even the supposedly liberal Press became berserk over it, calling it offensive and a paranoid fantasy'.[1] *Punishment Park* is of course offensive – deliberately so. But the paranoia is not so much in Watkins as in the society in which he as a creative film-maker is living, and whose sickness he tries to signal before it is too late.

In the same period there were two other films which, in their own minor ways, suffered from taking standpoints unpalatable to the Establishment. There was nothing emollient about Peter Brook's *Tell Me Lies* (1968) or Richard Lester's *How I Won the War* (1967). The former took the mickey out of the Vietnam War; the latter dared to make jokes not only at the expense of the Top Brass but also of Our Brave Boys in World War II.

Tell Me Lies was a rambling, sometimes incoherent film based on Brook's brilliant and seductive stage piece *US*, which may well be, with the possible exception of his 1971 *Midsummer Night's Dream*, the best thing he has ever done. In *US* he elaborated on Brechtian techniques to the point where alienation began to become indistinguishable from involvement; by filling the first half full of action and physical material, and devoting the second half to direct argument and discussion, he gave to this production a symmetry which enormously increased its political as well as its dramatic impact.

---

[1] Interview with Ray Connolly, *Evening Standard*, February 12th, 1972.

In *Tell Me Lies* the very richness of filmic possibilities, as opposed to those of the theatre, was Brook's downfall. Where *US* had been tight-knit, *Tell Me Lies* was diffuse. The loose picaresque style in which a young actor wanders around London seeking facts and opinions about Vietnam – mainly because he is haunted by the picture of a child-victim – leads to a wide variety of techniques: reconstructions (Norman Morrison burning himself to death), interviews (Kingsley Amis, Stokely Carmichael *et al*), improvisations (Soho strip-clubs for Saigon brothels), dreams (burning down the US Embassy in Grosvenor Square), variety (Royal Shakespeare cast singing songs from *US*) . . . Much of this is skilfully, astutely done; but in the end it has added up to very little – certainly much less than, for instance, *Loin du Viet-Nam*. It is a jig-saw which, put together, yields no satisfactory pattern.

Richard Lester ran into similar trouble with *How I Won the War*. Using once again those techniques of surrealist send-ups which had served him so well in *A Hard Day's Night*, *The Knack* and *Help!*, he proceeded to take apart, not the horror of war itself, but the horror of 'heroic' war movies and even the horror of inadequate or over-sentimental anti-war movies. Like Peter Brook, Lester is so in love with the infinite possibilities of the medium that indiscriminate invention tends to smother sincere intentions.

The most effective episodes are those about the relations between officers and men (Michael Crawford is a splendid 'officer type'), which are effective because they tip over from reality into farce. But in the end all is drowned in the grotesqueries of Jack MacGowran (one sighs for Kubrick's General Ripper), the prankishness of John Lennon, and the failed Falstaffery of Roy Kinnear. Even the cricket jokes fizzle out. Since then we have seen *M*A*S*H* and *Catch 22*, whose black humour and savage laughter come nearer the knuckle and nearer the truth.

Elegant and moving, *Oh! What a Lovely War* was, like *Tell Me Lies*, based on a stage show – Joan Littlewood's coruscating reconstruction of the First World War in terms of a concert party. With a star-studded cast (theatrical knights and all) at his disposal, Richard Attenborough, whose first directorial job this was, took the piece off the theatre boards and on to the Pier at Brighton, thus providing himself with a wider horizon and a wider range of décor. Through the members of an ordinary family, which provides a peg for all the varied events, the disillusionments of the war are paraded one by one in terms of personal reactions as well as in terms of the countless betrayals visited on the small people of Europe by the militarists, the politicians and the capitalists alike. It is of course an anti-war film; but the accusations tend to be wrapped in a nostalgic mist. The sad and beautiful ending, as the only surviving Smith follows an Ariadne thread (red tape) which leads him through the Versailles conference and up, up on to the breezy Downs where the quick and the dead picnic together, until gradually the whole screen becomes a graveyard of little white crosses – this is indeed pure cinema, finely conceived. But the past it is concerned with is too remote for most. It is history.

The same cannot so confidently be said about Joseph Losey's *King and Country* (1964), a film based on a play adapted from J. L. Hodson's World War I novel *Hamp*. Like Kubrick's *Paths of Glory*, made six years earlier, with which it is directly comparable, it concerns the execution for desertion and cowardice which has always been the ultimate sanction and safeguard of an army in war. Today, when other ranks in Vietnam amuse themselves by fragging their officers with hand grenades, these films may look somewhat old hat; yet what they say remains valid. Both are concerned with sacrificial victims. They are sacrificed to a Holy Trinity of Tradition, Discipline and Class. But against the apparently immutable values involved are placed the attitudes of those who have to administer these ultimate, irrevocable sanctions, and who may not be entirely convinced of their justice and validity.

In *Paths of Glory* Kubrick gives himself a fairly wide canvas. His combat scenes open up a good deal in *All Quiet* style, and there are some sensational fast tracking shots through and along the trenches during a barrage and subsequent attack.[1] The issue of the three men, picked on decimation principles to be court-martialled for cowardice allegedly committed by an entire battalion, is thrashed out at a military court in a vast chateau, marble pillared, with a grand staircase. Here, of an evening, the General Staff and their ladies pass their time with the graceful waltz. Kubrick goes out of his way to make this spaciousness, and that of the terrible execution scene in the vast courtyard before the chateau, with thousands of soldiers lined up for the hideous formalities, in itself accusatory. The very dimensions are a crime.

In *King and Country*, on the other hand, Losey goes for claustrophobia – the claustrophobia of that trench warfare which meant mud, mud to live in, mud to die in. Officers and men alike are shut in by this mud. Everyone is in a state of nervous strain near to breaking point. And there's this Hamp, ill-educated, slow-witted, inarticulate, who has,

[1] The camera takes the place of the officer striding along the trench, so that as the men get out of its way they appear to be standing aside for him. This effect, and the combat scenes in the same sequence, are terrific.

with clogged inadvertence, passed the breaking point and must therefore be court-martialled for cowardice and desertion. Note here that Hamp is technically guilty as an individual, unlike the men in *Paths of Glory* who are scapegoats selected at the command of the demented General Mireau (whose final comment – in the great tradition – is 'These things are always grim, but this one had a kind of splendour. The men died wonderfully.')[1] One of his victims, as they wait through their last night on earth, points to a cockroach and says, 'Funny. Tomorrow that will still be alive.' Whereupon his fellow victim grinds it to nothing under his boot.

In that gesture, perhaps, lies the common denominator between the two films. In each case the sufferers are the victims not only of war but of the brute fatality of a society in which class counts above all – this issue, as we may remember, being the peripeteia of *La Grande Illusion*. In the Kubrick film there is no question of the cowardly officer of the opening sequence ever being court-martialled; and in the Losey film the final irony is provided when Hamp's defending officer reveals after the verdict that he has only been doing his reluctant duty and that in his opinion the man deserves all he is getting. Both films brought out the best in several actors. In *Paths of Glory*, Kirk Douglas was entirely convincing as the dissident but ultimately powerless officer, Adolphe Menjou smoothly perfect as a devious GHQ go-between, and George Macready frighteningly convincing as the hysterical traditionalist, General Mireau; in *King and Country*, Dirk Bogarde was excellent as the reluctant 'soldier's friend', while Tom Courtenay totally embodied Hamp, and never more so than at the end when, the firing squad having botched the job, he gasps an apology to the officer who has to administer the *coup de grâce*. *King and Country* is said to have been shot in eighteen days to a budget of £100,000. It is one of Losey's most powerful films, and its quality was well summed up by Penelope Gilliatt as 'impressive . . . black-hearted and implacable'.[2]

Losey, whose enforced exile from America thanks to the anti-Red witch-hunts was a bonus for European cinema, and whose general influence – on Schlesinger as one example – has been admirable, works largely in a socially conscious ambience which fortunately lacks the

[1] There is a full and very perceptive analysis of *Paths of Glory* in *Stanley Kubrick Directs* by Alexander Walker, Harcourt Brace Jovanovich, 1971.

[2] *Sight and Sound*, Winter 1964–65. One could perhaps regard *King and Country* as the other side of the coin to *The Damned*, Losey's strange and not entirely satisfactory film involving radioactive children segregated by authority into a world of their own, but not of their own making. Freya in this film, talking of her sculptures, says 'If I could explain these I wouldn't have to make them'. She might be referring to the kids.

blight of overcommitment which can so easily fall on films made under such banners. While *The Servant, Accident* and *The Go-Between* are serious studies of aspects of the papered-over cracks in various sections of society, there may be found an equally stimulating criticism underlying his fantasy films such as *Modesty Blaise, Secret Ceremony,* and *Boom.*

On his own admission Losey has been much influenced by Brecht. He has said of the characters in his films,

> 'I don't see any of these people either as heroes, or even as anti-heroes, but simply as prototypes, various kinds of prototypes for the things that are done to all of us by ourselves and by each other all the time. This is the essence, for me, of the struggle of understanding life, and of staying alive instead of being dead while alive, and of making use of life before you're too tired to do anything except wither away.'[1]

And in the same context he talks about the problem of

> '. . . how to believe in human beings, and how to believe even in various forms of human existence, recognizing that they are archaic, selfish, barbaric and circumscribed by an enormous clutter of deceptions.'

That the enormous pessimism implicit in this sentence (note the use of 'even') does not inspissate his work is a measure of his stature as an artist.

He is of course a born story-teller, and that is half the battle. When to this capacity is added script-work and dialogue by Harold Pinter, you get the extraordinary concentrations of *The Servant* and *Accident.* Although not made consecutively (the first dates from 1963, the second from 1967), they are both complementary. Both use personal predicaments to illustrate fundamental weaknesses in specific strata of society. In *The Servant* it is the Army/Mayfair/Aristo element whose maladjustment is exposed. The icy insolence with which Susan underlines to Barrett the mistress-servant relationship in at least two key moments in the film is in its way a complete summing up of the reasons why Britain gained and so quickly lost an Empire.[2]

---

[1] Quoted in *The Cinema of Joseph Losey* by James Leahy, Zwemmer, 1967.

[2] I am aware that this interpretation is at variance with Losey's own statement (*Losey on Losey*, ed. Tom Milne, Secker and Warburg, 1968) that 'if she had been . . . "a lady" she would never . . . have had any of the humiliations, because she would only have had to produce a certain accent and a certain attitude to reduce Barrett'. For me, this is precisely what she does – the tragedy being that contrary to all expectations Barrett (after a momentary but very significant hesitation) turns out to be proof even against this. Thus when she strikes him right at the end of the film it is a double confession of defeat, for she has now had to lower herself to his level.

In *Accident*, on the other hand, the microscope is trained on the stains and taints of the middle class intelligentsia, with some especially shrewd sideswipes at the University tradition; significantly enough, Losey introduces into this certain elements from the milieu of *The Servant*, notably when Stephen comes slap up against the implacable fortress of the Upper Classes in the mysterious 'Game' at William's family's stately mansion. Thus Losey doesn't regard the various areas on which he turns his camera as being subject to specific demarcations. They are not studied, in terms of thought and behaviour, without reference to other areas, other groups, so that in the end everything is related to society as a whole.[1] The final example of this is in *The Go-Between*, which I believe Losey chose less for its period setting than for its exposure of a hidden relationship between the two extremities of an apparently settled social pattern. The boy, as messenger of an unthinkable liaison, himself comes from the middle class no man's land in between; against him both sides put up their shutters.

Figures in a Landscape (1970) stands outside of all this. It is separated, enclosed, isolated. Mac and Ansell, the two men on the run, exist only in relation to their mutual need to escape, with which is bound up the need to restrain their mutual antagonism; in this respect the film carries a reminder of Curtis and Poitier in *The Defiant Ones*. But unlike that film, we are here never told from whom or from where the men have escaped or towards whom or where their flight is directed. Linked only by driving necessity – the brute necessity of survival which must often blot out completely their final goal – they go through (like the lovers in *The Magic Flute*) the ordeals of air, fire and water. Their pursuers, a fugue of more than two armed men, helmeted and uniformed, menacing extensions of the helicopters in which they ride, could be agents of the KGB, the Gestapo, the CIA or, indeed, of the elegant figure of Death in Cocteau's *Orphée*. Allied to them on the ground are lesser, ant-like soldiers, brutish and busy, omnipresent. The other personages in the film, villagers, farmers, shepherds, are humans without human rights, to be used, to be killed by pursued and pursuers alike.

Within this particular hell – which consists incidentally of landscapes of great beauty, whether warm with valley crops or chill with grassy uplands leading to rocks and mountain snow – Losey encloses his two characters (excellently portrayed by Robert Shaw, who also scripted, and Malcolm McDowell). Though they have nothing much

[1] Note the ornamentations of the restaurant scene in *The Servant* – the couple of gossiping clergy, the quarrelling Lesbians, etc.

in common save the situation they are in, each can contribute something
to salvation. The elder, coarse, brutish, ill-educated, has guts and
ruthlessness; the younger, quick-witted, slickly but superficially educated
(probably left school early), has a sense of strategy and a streak of
practicality (it is he who produces a can-opener at the critical moment).
And although, in a superbly directed penultimate sequence, both are
reduced to mere animals on a rock ledge remorselessly drenched with
rain, it is in the end the older man who destroys himself at the very
moment when he could achieve freedom. This last episode is crucial to
Losey's meaning. We have seen earlier how Mac has winged a helicopter
– the co-pilot falls out. Now as they reach the frontier post the helicopter
reappears, and Mac chooses to turn back and take another and by now
unnecessary swipe at it; and thus is gunned down. It is not so much a
gesture of defiance as an admission of failure;[1] it could even be suicide.
The incident makes the point that there is probably no difference
between the society they have escaped from and the society towards
which they have fled; in which case all the energy, agony and adventure
adds up to nothing. In this strange country Kafka would feel at home.

Visually *Figures in a Landscape* has an elegant clarity superior to
the photography of any other Losey film,[2] whether Henri Alekan is
revealing the enormous roll of the foothills, the shut-in valley villages
where murder must be done by night, or the flames of a fired canefield
licking round terrified pigs trying to escape. Equally fine is Guy
Tabary's shooting from the helicopter in those rupturing moments when
Losey, with keen calculation, switches our viewpoint from the pursued
to the pursuers.

After this came the convolutions of *The Go-Between* (1971), with
its slow build-up through a sultry, thunderous Edwardian summer to its
scarifying climax. Losey's re-creation of the mood and manner of that
period is splendid,[3] and much aided by a fine cast, with specially notable
performances from Margaret Leighton and Edward Fox. On the other
hand the device by which Harold Pinter tries to transfer to the screen
the reminiscent structure of the L. P. Hartley novel seems forced and
unreal. The brief flash-forwards of the middle-aged, impotent man the

---

[1] In a certain sense *Figures in a Landscape* is a distillation of the dilemmas of Leonora
and Cenci in *Secret Ceremony*: Leonora's stabbing of Albert, and the parable of the two
mice in the milk, are to the point.

[2] And I have not forgotten *Modesty Blaise*.

[3] Though there is one strange exception. The lawns in front of the country mansion –
particularly the croquet lawn – would in Edwardian times look like soft green velvet. Here
they resembled nothing so much as a hastily cut hayfield, and at this point the illusion was
broken.

boy will become, travelling in a hired car to revisit the scene of his youthful sex-shock, are shot in a drab, damp light which is in unfortunate contrast with the sunlight of the main story; also the final interviews with the remaining protagonists are tentative and shadowy, and Michael Redgrave seems uneasy in the part.

John Schlesinger takes for granted, as it were, that structural element in society which Losey is always questioning. He concentrates on individual, personal dilemmas which, while they are of course a product of societal influences or circumstances, are seen by him in terms of an intercourse of souls as well as of bodies. The dilemmas of communication are largely interior. When, as in *Darling*, he enlarges his area of vision to take in a structural view of society, the result is an aesthetic failure.[1] His last two films to date, *Midnight Cowboy* and *Sunday Bloody Sunday*, have on the other hand shown a creative maturity which seems to indicate that Schlesinger is now at the height of his powers.

After *Terminus* (1960), a long documentary made for British Transport Films about Waterloo Station round the clock – a film whose ingenuities, not least of reconstruction and staging, did not disguise the fact that it was ultimately heartless – Schlesinger entered the feature film world with *A Kind of Loving* (1962), adapted from Stan Barstow's book by Keith Waterhouse and Willis Hall. Beautifully acted by Alan Bates and June Ritchie, this story of two lovers trying to understand each other, trying to stay together despite the pressures of provincialism and familial possessiveness, was directed by Schlesinger with a deep concern for their predicament. Again, the social background, the habits of an urban industrial community, are accepted without question; their danger to young love is similar to that posed for Romeo and Juliet in ancient Verona.

They meet, become passionately infatuated, have sex. She becomes pregnant, so he 'does the right thing'. After a hideous wedding they find themselves well and truly in the spider's parlour; for her Mum (splendid Thora Hird) has them trapped. It is only after a painful showdown and his departure that, after a while, they come together again, equivocally, interrogatively, and in the hope that at last they may have reached some relationship which could be cautiously described as 'a kind of loving'.

This is the only early film by Schlesinger which fully forecasts the

---

[1] I am well aware that *Darling* won many awards and was a huge success at the box-office; the fact remains that the truth was never in it and that, seen today, it looks terribly dated.

compassion and humanity of his later work. *Billy Liar!* (1963) was a very different kettle of fish-and-chips. Technically brilliant, Schlesinger's evocation of this Thurber-like character, whose real and dream worlds become increasingly interchangeable, had a sense of movement as well as of comedy (to say nothing of a skilful use of Cinemascope – with Denys Coop at the camera); and Tom Courtenay's Billy was quite splendid. True, the sinister, even sad element behind Billy's fantasies was swamped by the comedic verve, but somehow it never seemed to matter.

After a respectful and visually beautiful version of Hardy's *Far From the Madding Crowd* (1967),[1] Schlesinger embarked on the making of his first masterpiece. In a strange way *Midnight Cowboy* rides on a Stroheim-like mixture of documentary realism and symbolism. The grim, grimy reality of the pad shared by Ratso and Joe is in violent contrast to the TV jackpot's Niagara of nickels at the moment in the woman's apartment when Joe reaches orgasm – in an encounter in which he discovers that he must be the payer and not, as he had dreamed and expected, the payee. Again, there is an extreme contrast between the psychedelic party given by the brother and sister – which becomes half daydream, half nightmare – and the sickening moment of truth when Ratso wets his pants in the Florida-bound Greyhound bus.

Midnight Cowboy is about innocence, about rejection, about the ultimate indifference of a corrupt, falsely rich society whose 'values' are reflected equally from the skysigns of Times Square and the motorway billboards along the Florida freeways. Thus Joe the optimist-stud and Ratso the cough-racked smalltimer complement each other; Ratso woos his tuberculosis all the more ardently as he fails ever more noticeably to bring off even the cheapest dishonesty, while Joe passes from the trauma of losing his beloved transistor to the drama of raising the fare to take Ratso to Florida by the clumsy killing of a guilt-ridden middle-aged queer who thinks all the time of his wife. And so Joe ends in the Promised Land with a dead Ratso and no future; and it is here that Schlesinger proves himself. For this drab finale in the meretricious real-estate landscape of Miami, under its brilliant sun, becomes filled with a compassionate love and sympathy.

Both Joe and Ratso are destroyed because of a misplaced belief in the American Dream; like so many others, they did not know that it had become a legend of the past, a living hope which, once the West had been won and the Pacific coast found to lead to areas like Vietnam,

---

[1] It was photographed in Panavision 70 by Nicolas Roeg, who was soon to become at least the equal of both Losey and Schlesinger as a film director.

had been strangled and destroyed by the monstrous indifference of a corrupt society. In *Sunday Bloody Sunday* (1971) – a pointless title if ever there was one – Schlesinger turns to a communal situation in which corruption is not yet monstrous and in which permissiveness is predicated from the point of view of civilized rather than barbaric behaviourism. Penelope Gilliatt's screenplay postulates a young, handsome boy with some talent and with definite prospects in the world of visual media who shares his sex life with a successful career woman (Glenda Jackson) and an equally successful member of the medical profession (Peter Finch). These two, unacquainted with each other until later in the film, form the base of an isosceles triangle of which this bisexual boy is the apex.

The area they all live in is that of the intelligentsia. One of the film's greatest merits is that it populates this usually arid cinematic area with real people. One may not like the habits of the very progressive family for whom the boy babysits; yet the supposedly awful kids, the parents' reefers within reach and mother's breastmilk left handily in the fridge, the negro kept more or less as a pet, the husband's blinkered intellectualism – in the end this all adds up to a group of perfectly attractive people who are quite content to have trapped themselves in a parlour of *démodé* but euphoric Fabianism. All of these characters, especially the enchanting children, are beautifully played and beautifully directed.

The relationship of the three main characters – charmingly glossed from time to time by extracts from *Cosi Fan Tutte* – is formed into a graceful pattern from which, however, strong emotion is not excluded. Within this pattern a series of fine episodes evolves – the woman, Alex, suddenly having sex with a middle-aged job applicant on the rebound from his wife; Daniel the doctor's long but not uncongenial ordeal at a sensitively presented Bar Mitzvah (full of aunts asking why he hasn't got married yet); the fighting-drunk woman at an otherwise polite party whose behaviour signals a most unwanted row between Daniel and the boy, Bob; and Alex's muted visit to her parents (perfectly played by Peggy Ashcroft and Maurice Denham) in a great chilly house where estrangement is masked by an enforced patience, as when her mother finishes their talk with 'You think it's nothing but it's not nothing'.

There is one intrusive episode – that in which Daniel is accosted in his car near Piccadilly Circus by a hustler from his past, and wilder, sex life. This involves a visit to Boots and a review of the junkies waiting for their fixes; and finally to a small anticlimax. The sequence is sensitively directed, but somehow it breaks into a narrative whose power and significance needs no unnecessary variations.

Peter Finch, Glenda Jackson and Murray Head cannot be faulted in the main parts. The impact of the last-named is felt at its strongest at the end of the film when Bob has already left for America. Alex comes home to find Bob's key and a note saying 'Could you look after the toucan for a bit?' She realizes for the first time the real gap he has left in her life. She stares at the toucan; it stares unwinkingly back. And we may remember Bob's last direct remark to her, 'You keep asking too much', as being in some contrast to his last exchange with Daniel, to whose 'The truth is I don't want to lose you' he replies vaguely, 'I'll be back sometime'.

Schlesinger ends the film with a cleverly sprung surprise. Instead of fading out on the scene in which Alex and Daniel somewhat shyly commiserate with each other over their mutual loss, he adds a final solo for Daniel who, turning from his Italian language lesson on his Hi Fi (he had planned to go on holiday with Bob), talks direct to the audience. 'I miss him that's all. They say he'd never have made me happy and I say, I am happy, apart from missing him . . . But something. We were something. You've no right to call me to account.' And he stares us out as unflinchingly as Bob's toucan does Alex.

Sunday Bloody Sunday is perhaps the most civilized comedy since *China Is Near*. Something of the same quality may be observed in Barney Platts-Mills' *Private Road* (1971) – a simple and perceptive tale of the generation gap in middle-class suburbia, an area which most film-makers tend, apart from farce or parody, to avoid. *Private Road* shows a marked advance in technique from his first film, *Bronco Bullfrog* (1970), in which there were some directorial uncertainties that matched rather uneasily with the inarticulate improvisations of the characters.

Private Road continues the theme of the previous film in the sense that it is concerned with the frustrations, real or imagined, of people trying to escape from the routine patterns of modern life. But whereas in *Bronco Bullfrog* the attempts at escape were in general tied in with material practicalities (Del's motor bike, Wimpy bars, and, at the end, the fantastic parade of stolen goods offered to Del and Irene by Bronco), in *Private Road* the issues are psychologically more complex.

The apparent banality of the story – Peter, a young writer, falls in love with a middle-class girl and comes into conflict with her parents – is soon seen to be a foil against which the very real human reactions of all the people concerned can be shown off and indeed illuminated.

The suburban father, for instance, is marvellously depicted by Robert Brown as a perfectly likeable and not impercipient chap within, that is, the limits of business and subtopian life. The interchanges between him and Peter are some of the best things in the film, and it is fascinating gradually to realize that Peter is being seduced into taking a regular job.

His attempts to shoot off into escape holes with Ann are always sad failures; they also provide opportunities for some superb landscape photography (including some stunning Scots scenes) by Adam Barker-Mill. The feckless muddle of Peter's flat-sharing (which includes a potential junkie) is seen to be as frustrating in its way as his relations with Ann's conventional parents.

Platts-Mills does not seek a tidy conclusion. Ann's pregnancy makes, under the circumstances, a wedding inevitable. So Peter will have to become a breadwinner. But in the meantime neither he nor Ann has found a real answer to their ideas about escape. The film ends on this deliberately equivocal note. Junkie Stephen, desperately hoping to tempt Peter away from dreaded married respectability and back into his disorganized life as a writer, turns up with a stolen typewriter. Handing it to Peter he asks, 'Is there anything else you want?' 'Yes,' replies Peter, and bang! up comes the End Title.[1]

The problems of escape are more brutally dealt with by Ken Loach, another film director who has emerged from television, where his uncompromising documentary features *Cathy Come Home* and *Up the Junction* created a big stir because of their forthright social criticism. He has made two major films to date (I omit the overblown *Poor Cow* as a sad but perhaps inevitable evolutionary error); in the first escape is symbolized by the taming and subsequent death of a bird; in the second the escape is to a living death.

Kes, stupidly held back for a year by its distributors, appeared in 1969. Based on a novel by Barry Hines, it excoriatingly observes the nothingness behind the 'modern' façades of our industrial communities. The schools are new, with all mod cons; the welfare state is in full operation. But the staff are harassed and confused; and one of the high points of the film shows a headmaster doing a total injustice to a small boy which arises from sheer weariness and negligence. Everywhere, and especially for the adolescents, is an emptiness ready to be filled by, at

[1] Like Peter Watkins, Platts-Mills has had distribution troubles. *Bronco Bullfrog* had a meagre and inefficient release, and with *Private Road* he had to choose the unenviable course of doing the distribution himself, including the hiring of a Notting Hill cinema for the first run.

best, petty crime; the careers adviser is simply a bad joke, and presented as such.

The hero, Billy Casper, is a weedy, unattractive little runt who, in the capture and taming of a kestrel, achieves a wondrous beauty. His lecture about Kes to his classmates is a classic moment of effective cinematic simplicity. And when, at the end of the film, we see Billy rescue the bird's remains from the dustbin (his stepbrother has killed it in a fit of temper) and bury them in a shallow, nettle-menaced grave, we feel for the potential destruction of a young soul which had found for itself a momentary glimpse of freedom.

Kes is in a sense a split-minded film. Billy's obsession with the hawk is deliberately kept outside his home and school life. His talk in the classroom is the only point of contact. This separation works very well. And within the school ambiance itself there are some richly comic areas of non-communication, such as the football game in which the sportsmaster whips himself up into a vision of winning the Cup at Wembley, and the changing room, where the comedy turns to pathos in the shower scene.

Family Life (1971),[1] on the other hand, is remorselessly integrated, knit closely into a pattern which allows of no deviations from doom. It can indeed be criticized for weighting the evidence unduly at various points (the liberal psychiatrist is too good, the orthodox one too bad); but the overall description of a schizoid character being driven into the internal and irremediable solitude of her own despair is too powerful and sincere to be gainsaid.

It is typical of the predicament of this girl Janice (played, like the other key figures in the film, by an amateur) that at the really big crises in her life she finds herself forgotten other than as the springboard for other people's selfish intentions. There is a tremendous quarrel (directed with perfect timing and climactic sense by Loach) during a typical Sunday dinner at home, with her elder married sister storming at the parents for their insensitivity and lack of understanding. The battle rises and falls, and amid all the objurgations and counter charges, with father shouting and mother calmly feeding jellies to the kids and equally calmly blackguarding the daughter, Janice sits there at the table, utterly disregarded. Later, when her boy-friend has rescued her from the mental hospital, only to find his rooms besieged by ambulance men and threats of committal and legal actions, it is she who is ignored while he scuffles and argues his own case, not hers, with the authorities. It is

---

[1] Not to be confused with the Polish film of the same name, made in 1970. It might have been better for Loach to use the title of the David Mercer TV play – *In Two Minds*.

only when he surrenders that she is remembered, scooped up onto a stretcher, and removed. Thus it is no surprise at the very end when, in front of a group of bored students in a lecture theatre, she is exhibited as, in effect, a non-person. 'Regression,' remarks the psychiatrist who has helped to destroy her, 'is complete.'

In this film Loach has geared his style to complete naturalism; and improvised dialogue adds to an impression of *cinéma-vérité*. Apart from the singularly beautiful Sandy Ratcliffe as Janice, there is one other character of outstanding, indeed terrifying impact – Grace Cave as her mother. This lady, we are assured, has never acted before; she gives a great performance. Impenetrably fortified behind the conventions of the lower middle class, she mercilessly deploys her social and familial values to the detriment of all concerned. Her convinced *rightness* in all things is awful to behold; at the very moment when she is forcing Janice to have an abortion, she will not allow 'that word' to be spoken in her house. She is the nightmare figure we sometimes detect lurking behind the Thurber woman; she is Mrs Darling and Motherdear and Fate and the Furies.

Originally a cameraman (*Far From the Madding Crowd, Petulia, Fahrenheit 451*, etc), Nicolas Roeg has made two films to date – *Performance* (1968), which he co-directed with Donald Cammell, and *Walkabout* (1970). Both films (superbly photographed in colour by Roeg) have certain dramatic and philosophical depths rare in British films. Filmic in the highest sense of the word, they enter, philosophically and psychologically, deeper waters than are locally expected or accepted. In its consideration of the nature of personality within the area of violence and the 'still centre', *Performance* adumbrates the interchangeability of psyches, while *Walkabout* looks at our conception of what we call civilization in terms of that disturbing contrast mentioned by Lévi-Strauss – the view of the range of human societies in time on the one hand and in space on the other.

Although *Performance* was held up for two years by its producers and, according to Jan Dawson,[1] was recut by seven different editors, it emerged apparently unscathed and with the loss of only three minutes of screen time. Although it is constructed 'straight' and without benefit of flashbacks, it creates a similar perturbation to that found in *Partner* and *The Spider's Strategy*. This relates to the interchangeability of identity already mentioned.

The story is fast-moving – at least to start with – brutal, cruel and visually luxuriant. Chas (James Fox in his finest rôle) is the sadistic

[1] *Monthly Film Bulletin*, February 1971.

henchman of Harry, a big-time undercover racketeer. In the course of various thuggeries he makes the mistake of crossing the path of a betting shop magnate whom Harry has told him to leave alone. The bookie and his pals smash up Chas' flat and, when he returns, smash him up too in a welter of blood and bruising well in excess of Kubrick's efforts later in *A Clockwork Orange*, but matched in time by the gory doings of Polanski's *Macbeth*. In the midst of the struggle Chas grabs at a gun and kills the bookie; and the first part of the film ends with him on the run both from Harry's organization and the police. In the second part he manages, thanks to a casually overheard conversation, to find and insinuate himself into the house of Turner, a wealthy retired pop-singer (Mick Jagger). The story moves into a world of fantasy. For although Chas is really there to hide and to try to get a passport photo, the relations between him, Turner and the two girls, Pherber and Lucy, who live with Turner (and each other), become dangerously complex, not least because the girls set about getting Chas hooked on drugs. Meantime Turner begins to see in the violence of Chas an image of the violent power *he* once wielded over millions of screaming fans. He needs to return to that for a moment, and he puts on a special individual performance for Chas. As a mutual identification, a mutual merging, almost, of personalities is beginning, Harry and the gang track down Chas and arrive at the house. Turner knows exactly what is happening; but so far has he now identified with Chas that he demands that he should be taken for the ride equally. But Chas, like the Student of Prague confronting himself in the mirror, shoots his *alter ego* between the eyes and goes on to his death alone.

It is at the moment of this final act of violence that Cammell and Roeg introduce the last of a number of references to Borges, whose influence here is even more marked than in Bertolucci's *The Spider's Strategy*. In the case of both films the question of identity is the paramount issue. In the former the double character of Athos *père et fils* becomes merged in the figure of Dreyfa, who is in herself time past and time present. In *Performance* the androgyne Turner (a name carefully chosen no doubt) becomes in one of Chas' trips a smoothy version of Harry – a doubly dislocating moment as we witness also a Jagger with ears astoundingly visible and Brylcreem-plastered hair. Such Borgesian images of heroic violence, exchangeable identities, and the constant interflow of dream and reality are of course the very stuff of cinema. Here Cammell and Roeg have exploited them to the full, and with memorable results. If people call the film amoral because the Borgesian point of view hardly admits of the idea of redemption, what must they say of *A Clockwork Orange* – a film about a redemption which doesn't work?

Walkabout directly questions the validity of our so-called Western democratic civilization; by confronting it with the still visible pre-history of the Outback, Roeg shows conventional values at risk. Equally at risk, however, are aboriginal values; it is the noble savage who is destroyed. When in this film Roeg brings us up against a brick wall, the result is not only abrasive, it is concussive; because behind the wall, as we see, are two desolations, not one – the desolation of the city and the desolation of the desert.

A father takes his teenage daughter and small son out for a picnic. He drives them well into the wilderness. Once there, he shoots at them. They run off and hide behind some rocks, whence they see him set fire to the car and then kill himself. They are alone in the middle of nowhere. There is nothing that they can do save try to walk home.

The interesting thing is that no reason is given for this episode. True, the opening sequences have shown unattractive visuals of Australian city life, with a soundtrack mingling inanities of conversation and radio chatter with mysterious and disturbing sounds from Stockhausen's *Hymnen* – but there is nothing more to prepare us for this *acte gratuit*, this kind of madness of despair. Roeg's reasoning regarding the father's madness and suicide in *Walkabout* is, I am sure, that we are to see only what the children see, and to understand it as little as do the children. They have neither the time nor the need to reason. The enormous space in which they find themselves has become an enclosed world. They walk in search of its edge.[1]

They walk. The sands close over their footsteps as though they have never been. Some water. A tree with fruit. The water sinks into the sand. Harpy birds strip the fruit.

Then on the horizon a slender stick of licorice. An aboriginal boy on his endurance test for manhood. And it is he, black and naked, who must lead these ridiculously cluttered creatures – satchel, blazer, school hat, spare mac and all – towards home and safety.

The central part of the film, as these three cross the Outback in a yellow blaze of sun and among an animal kingdom of Hieronymus Bosch creatures sliding and scuttling over rock and scrub, has a torrid fascination. At dawn and dusk the sun's disc, enormous and bloody like the beginning and end of the world, illuminates a landscape into

---

[1] The roots of the story go back a long way to something that really happened. John Heyer, in his fine, imaginative documentary *The Back of Beyond* (1954), reconstructs a similar episode, with three children and a dog, and a tragic ending.

which Roeg suddenly will inject an episode of disgusting sordidity as the small group comes on a community of poor whites or 'no-hopers' with their hideous output of ceramic souvenirs and a raddled woman who makes a pass at the aborigine boy; at which point he, always noble, becomes a virtual Ithuriel.

Then the situation is reversed. The aborigine falls in love. Alone and far from his tribe, he yet performs the necessary ritual which preludes marriage. Like one of the strange exotic birds of the Antipodean landscape he clothes himself in feathers, paints ritual patterns on his skin, and performs his dance of courtship. And the poor little teenage ninny, still living in her world of gym-slips and quotidinous proprieties, understands nothing. Does nothing. Fails to react. So the boy, within his own deep and solemn proprieties, kills himself. As Lévi-Strauss has said,

'A native thinker makes the penetrating comment that "all sacred things must have their place". It could even be said that being in their place is what makes them sacred for if they were taken out of their place, even in thought, the entire order of the universe would be destroyed.'[1]

As it turns out, the boy has brought them near a road, and the two kids stumble back to their civilization, their first greeting being an instruction not to walk on the grass. Here is the brick wall again; but from it Roeg takes us into an epilogue of great beauty – perhaps also a *kontakion* for the aborigine boy. It is years later. The girl has long since grown up. Married to a go-getting businessman (will he one day drive out into the desert and not return?), she is cooking his supper. And into her mind come memories of those long-past days in the desert. The images – of the coolth of water and of seldom-found shade, of the naked bodies of the three youngsters, splashed with the primeval innocence of Eden – are not repeats of scenes we have already seen in the film, when the grey flannel shorts and the elastic bands were omnipresent. Here Roeg gives us a larger, finer memory. Maybe this is a recollection of how it really happened. Maybe the passage of the years has glorified – one cannot say falsified – it in her fond reminiscence. But there is the memory, and its vision is companioned by a voice speaking the words of a fastidious, sophisticated Western poet; and the words fit the images perfectly:

[1] *The Savage Mind* by Claude Lévi-Strauss, Weidenfeld and Nicolson, 1966.

'That is the land of lost content,
I see it shining plain,
The happy highways where I went
And cannot come again.'[1]

So in *Walkabout* Roeg and his colleagues, aided by the beautifully natural acting of David Gumpilil, Jenny Agutter and little Lucien John, have created a despairing but exquisite parable of man's fate. The bridge between *Walkabout* and *2001* crosses a deep gulf in but a few paces, as we can see again from Lévi-Strauss:

'The savage mind is logical in the same sense and the same fashion as ours, though as our own is only when it is applied to knowledge of a universe in which it recognizes physical and semantic properties simultaneously.'[2]

And we may remember, when we come to Kubrick in the next chapter, that he begins his film with apemen from the dawn of time, and that the world of Man began when a connection between use and purpose and the relation between a symbol and a thing led finally, as we see so forcefully in Truffaut's *L'Enfant Sauvage*, to abstract concepts like justice and injustice and so, through centuries, to the negative ideas implicit in the Ludovico Treatment and HAL.

Don't Look Now (1973), a film which entirely fulfils the promise of Roeg's earlier work, did not appear until well after this book had gone to press. Briefly and inadequately then let me remark that its interference with our temporal sense fully matches *La Jetée* and *Je t'Aime Je t'Aime*, that its evocation of Venice in winter (when even the sunlight is the colour of ashes) is thaumaturgic, that its construction is a model of pure filmic conception, that all its actors and actresses give performances which are miraculously right, and that it is one of the most numinous, ominous, haunting and frightening films ever made. Here certainly, 'a terrible beauty is born'.

---

[1] It was the same poet who wrote:
'We for a certainty are not the first
Have sat in taverns while the tempest hurled
Their hopeful plans to emptiness, and cursed
Whatever brute and blackguard made the world.'
(A. E. Housman, *Last Poems*, 1922.)

[2] Lévi-Strauss, op. cit.

VI

In Scandinavia and the Low Countries some interesting new film-makers made their appearance in the Sixties. While Bergman continued with his remarkable output – notably *The Silence* (1963), *Persona* (1965), *The Shame* (1968) and *The Rite* (1969) – two young men, Jan Troell and Bo Widerberg. made an international as well as a local impression with their own individual approach to cinema.

Troell, who is also cameraman on all his films, made a number of shorts between 1960 and 1965; one of them, the successful *The Boy and the Kite*, he co-directed with Widerberg. His first feature, *Here is Your Life* (1966), was followed in 1968 by *Who Saw Him Die?* (*Ole Dole Doff*) – a dark and tragic tale of a schoolmaster's inability to communicate with his pupils, with a fine performance by Per Oscarsson.[1]

Bo Widerberg's *Elvira Madigan* (1967) put him in the forefront of contemporary Scandinavian directors. This visually exquisite work (photography by Jörgen Persson) tells a slight but melancholy tale in which an idyllic love affair is flawed by circumstances, folly and fate, and ends in a suicide pact. The film at times has an other-worldly quality which is much enhanced by the music of Mozart and Vivaldi.

Adalen 31 (also known as *The Adalen Riots*), made in 1969, could hardly be in greater contrast. Based on an historical event – the intervention of the Army in a conflict between strikers and blacklegs which resulted in a number of dead and wounded – the film has a rather conventional fiction framework which doesn't always accord well with the very effective documentary-style reconstructions of the riots themselves or, indeed, with the more intimate representations of actuality among the families of the strikers. Towards the end one of the soldiers remarks, 'We do the shooting all right – but who pays for the bullets?' That the answer is monopoly capitalism Widerberg leaves us in no doubt. In 1970 he made, again on a basis of historical fact, *The Ballad of Joe Hill*, about the singer of that name who emigrated to America and was in due course – most people think unjustly – executed in Utah on a murder charge. The early reels, depicting the wonders of the New World through the eyes of newly arrived immigrants, were wholly admirable; elsewhere, too, Widerberg well captured the feel of the

---

[1] Who in 1969 played a very different sort of schoolmaster in Stellan Olsson's happy and delightful *It's Up to You*.

time of the Wobblies and the private armies of the big employers. But, as Penelope Houston pointed out, 'this is the history of the American labour movement wafted on a haze of romanticism'. She added, 'It's ironic that Widerberg should be celebrating these primitive battles of unionism at a time when it is the all-powerful unions who are themselves seen as . . . agents of reaction'.[1]

The Sixties also witnessed the sex-ridden films of Vilgot Sjöman, notably *I Am Curious – Yellow* (1967) and *I Am Curious – Blue* (1968). These remarkably popular films followed his 18th century period piece on incest, *My Sister, My Love* (*Syskonbädd*) of 1966. Meantime that fine actress Mai Zetterling took up film direction. As early as 1963 she had made in England, for television, a chilling anti-war allegory about two small boys quarrelling over a gun. With the same title as Peter Watkins' subsequent *The War Game*, this short film did not perhaps get the attention it deserved. In the following year, in Sweden, Zetterling made a feature film, *Loving Couples*, ingeniously constructed in flashbacks of the memories of three pregnant women in a maternity home – memories hardly complimentary to the prospective fathers.

Then in *Night Games* (1966) she set out, successfully, to run virtually the whole gamut of sexual anomalies in a series of elaborate orgies of Fellini dimensions whose content tended at times to arouse reactions of unintended laughter. In the end the small boy who has grown up in this somewhat overheated atmosphere gets together with his girl and sends up the film as well as his ancestral home in a gloriously satisfactory conflagration. Zetterling's next film, *The Girls* (1968), was more worthy of her talent, being an Aristophanic attack on men and their wars mounted by three redoubtable women, played by Bibi Andersson, Harriet Andersson and Gunnel Lindblom. There is a splendid moment towards the end when one of the women, during a starchy dinner party, tells her husband she is going to divorce him; typically he replies, 'But – this means war!'

Other interesting Swedish films of this period include Jonas Cornell's 1967 production, *Hugs and Kisses* (*Puss och Kram*), an amusing marital comedy of manners; Kjell Grede's charming film of childhood, *Hugo and Josefin* (1967); and Jarl Kulle's *The Bookseller Who Gave Up Bathing* (1969) which, according to Peter Cowie, depicts with 'gleeful *élan*' the problems arising from an unlikely marriage between two people of a certain age.[2]

---

[1] *Sight and Sound*, Autumn 1971.
[2] See *Sweden 2*, the second of two admirable volumes on Swedish cinema in *Screen Series*, Zwemmer, 1970.

In Belgium, apart from established figures like Henri Storck, the work of André Delvaux drew much attention. This new director made three films involving elliptical and mysterious psychological motivations which for me lacked the magnetic chiaroscuro of Resnais; their titles were *The Man Who Had His Hair Cut Short* (1967), *Un Soir, Un Train* (1968) and *Rendezvous à Bray* (1971).

Much more exciting to me was the *cinéma-vérité* work of a young director, Marian Handwerker, which included some fascinating studies of Turkish workers in Belgium (including a free and frank interview with a Belgian woman married to a Turk). In particular Handwerker's *Poïs Poïs* commanded attention. This is a moving and very truthful picture, lasting just under an hour, of a young Portuguese returning from his job in Belgium for a holiday in his native village. As he wanders around asking people how things are going, or have been going, we get, conveyed with a sweet casualness, a wonderful feeling of the joys and sadnesses of peasant people living a marginal existence in a world which cares for them not at all. But they care for themselves. There is a tremendously touching monologue spoken by an old woman as she tends her husband's grave; and at another point there is a pyrotechnic and revelatory interview with a young soldier back on leave from fighting the revolutionaries in Angola.

In Holland at the same time a new feature director appeared – Fons Rademakers. His first film was *The Knife* (*Het Mes*), made in 1961. This story of a young boy coping simultaneously with problems of family relationships and of puberty had both the faults and the virtues of a first film – a tendency on the one hand to overbalance scenes or sequences in length or emphasis, but on the other a fine tenderness and naturalism in depicting the inner and outer conflicts of the boy (played with remarkable authenticity by Reitze van der Linden). The scenes of his solitude, when he is either bored or indulging in aimless violence as a substitute for sex, are as effective as those in which he tries to come to terms with a widowed mother who is involved in an affair with his tutor.

Rademakers followed this film with *The Dance of the Heron* (1966), a slightly disappointing effort at describing the smash-up of a marriage. Fraught with passions and with Resnais flashes, it never quite struck a balance between fantasy and reality.

In Denmark the most important event of the Sixties was of course the completion of Dreyer's *Gertrud*. This masterpiece is dealt with at length elsewhere in this book. Beyond this there were a few send-ups of the fashionable porn, notably *Danish Blue*, much of which was very funny, including some slapstick; and *Seventeen*, the story of a boy's rapid, joyous and lavish discovery of sexual pleasure which was in many ways charmingly touching. Other notable films included Henning Carlsen's serious and human study, *Hunger* (*Sult*), and Palle Kjaerulff-Schmidt's *Once There Was a War* – both made in 1966.

The latter resembles *The Knife* in that it is concerned with a young boy coping with problems of puberty. Unlike *The Knife*, however, there are no family problems involved. Tim lives in a placid middle-class home with understanding parents; the film is wholeheartedly devoted to showing his attempts, in the end successful, to come to a reasoned and balanced understanding of sex. There are some dream and fantasy sequences which vary from the hilarious – when he becomes a superman – to the moving – when he dreams of his own death – to the misplaced, when he dreams of what he might have done to his girl-friend. The whole story carries an extra punch in that it is set against a Denmark under Nazi occupation. An impeccable cast (including a magical performance by Ole Busck as Tim), and imaginative direction make this an extraordinarily enjoyable though too loosely constructed film.

As we have already seen, West German cinema was slow to recover from the War; but in the Sixties one or two things began to happen. In 1966 Volker Schlöndorff made a more than competent screen version of Robert Musil's gloomy novel *Young Törless*; and Peter Fleischmann's *Hunting Scenes from Lower Bavaria* – a film about the persecution of a homosexual by a peasant community – showed considerable promise.

But the German scene is finally dominated by three new directors, each of whom is in his own way challenging and controversial – Alexander Kluge, Jean-Marie Straub, and Rainer Werner Fassbinder. Kluge first hit the headlines at the Mannheim Festival in 1966 with his *Abschied von Gestern* (*Yesterday Girl*), in which his beautiful sister Alexandra gave a talented performance as a young woman unable to adjust to the 'new' Germany. The Godardian techniques which Kluge so skilfully adapted to his own purposes in this film were, unfortunately, allowed to run to seed in his next, *Artistes at the Top of the Big Top: Disorientated* (*Die Artisten in der Zirkuskuppel: Ratlos*) made in 1968. This story of a widowed circus lady (played with an almost unique lack of charm by Hannelore Hoger) planning and dreaming of a new rôle for the Big Top in the Media World, is portrayed in a series of inconsequent sequences which makes it very difficult for one to raise any interest in what is going to happen next (a sign of late Godard influence this). The characters tend, when overfaced with their problems, to settle down in a bath with a good book; and there are some impressive appearances by a troupe of highly conservative elephants. Let me add that this film has been enthusiastically received in many quarters and that Kluge, like Godard, is someone to be reckoned with, one way or the other.

Jean-Marie Straub is an apostle of minimal cinema. Apart from two shorts, his principal films so far have been *Nicht Versöhnt* (*Unreconciled*), made in 1965; *The Chronicle of Anna Magdalena Bach* (1968); and *Othon* (or *Eyes Do Not Want to Close at All Times*; or *Perhaps One Day Rome Will Permit Herself to Choose in her Turn*, 1969). Richard Roud has written a book on Straub which expresses a positive point of view on his work and thereby also on minimal cinema.[1] To this I will only add from my own point of view that of all Straub's films I find the Bach one the least disagreeable because, despite the director's efforts, the structure of the music itself holds the film together. *Othon* is a version of one of Corneille's most complex and least approachable plays, and therefore presumably ideal for Straub's purpose. He chose to shoot it on location in Rome against a background, visual and aural, of that city's traffic. The actors, with two exceptions, speak French with an alien accent. On occasion some of them are forced to gabble their lines in a monotone. This, according to Roud, 'serves two functions: one of distancing us from the otherwise gentle rocking-horse rhythms of the Alexandrines, and the other of enriching the complexity of the sound tapestry'.[2]

I note that 'distancing' and 'distantiation' are even more important to minimal cinema than alienation. Nevertheless the effort to drain from a film all but a final irreducible semblance of a moving picture can be painful in the extreme: in *Othon* the operation has been almost completely successful.[3]

I note further that, talking of the absolute necessity of making films with direct sound (for obviously guide-tracks or dubbing must be anathema to this sort of film-making), Straub is reported to have said:

'The most beautiful films which exist are the first sound films of Renoir and not only because they all speak with this nice accent from the South of France, but because they are made with direct

---

[1] *Straub* by Richard Roud, Secker and Warburg, 1971.
[2] Op. cit.
[3] I cannot rid myself of a sneaking feeling that the whole thing is a put-on.

sound . . . This sound of the first talkies is for me the best of all existing sound on films. A film like *Man of Aran* was something that impressed me most then.'[1]

This statement does not increase my confidence in Straub, if only because the soundtrack of *Man of Aran* was added in the studios in London and sounded as though it had been recorded in an exceptionally reverberant bath-tub.

    Finally we come to Rainer Werner Fassbinder, a young man with considerable theatre experience who appeared as a player in Straub's short film *The Bridegroom, the Comedienne and the Pimp* (1968). Fassbinder is not a minimalist. His powerful eye for rich cinematic compositions, reminiscent of Gregg Toland, in which he is aided by his admirable cameraman Dietrich Lohmann, together with a sense of humour sometimes quirkish and sometimes satirical, gives to films like *Warum Laüft Herr R Amok?* (*Why Did Herr R Run Amok?*) or *The American Soldier* – both made in 1969 – an extraordinary solidity and cohesion. I say extraordinary because Fassbinder apparently works at tremendous speed.

    The American Soldier is said to have been shot in ten days. Even allowing that Fassbinder follows the current trend (though it goes back to Dreyer) of shooting in very long takes, this is something of a *tour-de-force*.

    The story, such as it is, concerns a person returning from the war in Vietnam who has no hesitation in using a gun, and thus becomes a convenient agent of death, on his own or others' account. From certain aspects the film guys pictures of past days. The visuals hint at Dietrich, Zasu Pitts, Bogart, Peter Lorre. There are some *hommages* to Lang, Pabst, Hawks. The construction is quite formal. Long takes. Punctuations, repetitions. Card games (the faces are pornographic). Telephone calls. Endless car journeys. Elaborate set pieces shot in depth with considerable complexity of lighting.

    Behind the send-ups and the humour there extends a hinterland of sinister uncertainty; one is never sure when the film will turn round and bite. The final scene, the final showdown of many, is in an Alphaville subway setting. The 'American' himself is shot. His 'son' hurls himself onto the dying man and, with 'mother' all in black standing at the top of some steps in a far distant background, the two men roll about together in an increasing sexual frenzy, shot entirely in slow

---

[1] Article by Andi Engel in *Second Wave*, Studio Vista, 1970. Straub is also quoted as saying 'In *La Voix Humaine* you can hear the dolly. That's beautiful!'

motion. It is funny, frightening, insulting, provocative. Maybe Fassbinder will turn out to be the film-maker Germany has been waiting for.

VII

In the Soviet Union during the Sixties, the establishment of a neo-Imperialist policy was naturally reflected in a hardening of the bourgeois attitude of officialdom to the Arts. Any questioning of accepted values led to disapproval and repression. Various noted writers were arrested, sent to Siberia or, worse still, committed to sinister psychiatric hospitals. Although none of this stopped a growing surge of protest and criticism among the younger generation from making itself felt much more than in the Stalinist era, the cinema, by its very nature more exposed to instant censorship than other arts, remained perforce conservative and unadventurous. There was one big row which rumbled loud enough to be heard outside Russia, and that was over Andrei Tarkovsky's *Andrei Rublev*, which for various reasons was held up for three years after its completion in 1966; when it was shown at the Cannes Festival in 1969 it was to the disapproval of the Russian delegation, and it had been mysteriously cut by some forty minutes.[1]

Within these imposed limits Soviet film-makers continued to reveal a high level of skill and competence. The emphasis gradually switched from revolutionary themes or references back to *The Great Patriotic War* (to quote the title of Roman Karmen's film of 1965), to a celebration of contemporary life seen with that warmth and humanity one has always recognized in established directors like Donskoi, Zarkhi and Heifits; or to screen adaptations of Russian literature,[2] more particularly Tchekov, Dostoievsky and Tolstoy. Ivan Pyriev specialized

[1] By 1972 however *Andrei Rublev* had been taken for distribution in the West. In the same year Tarkovsky's beautiful and disturbing *Solaris* (1972) was shown at the London Film Festival. This story of man in space has little in common with *2001: A Space Odyssey* – and a great deal in common with Resnais' *Je t'Aime, Je t'Aime*. Neither pure science fiction, nor purely an experiment with time, perception or identity, this film, with its passages of Tchekovian humour crossed with savage spiritual confrontations, marks its director as a great artist of cinema.

[2] One may note with some sadness that Solzhenitsyn's *One Day in the Life of Ivan Denisovich* had to be made outside Russia. Caspar Wrede's respectful and accurate version with an admirable cast led by Tom Courtenay, somehow gave only the surface of the grim tale and missed those inner revelations which a Soviet director might more instinctively have rendered.

in screen versions of Dostoievsky (who had been frowned on by the Stalinists); he made *The Idiot* (1958) and *White Nights* (1959), but died in 1968 before completing his screen version of *The Brothers Karamazov*. This was the same Pyriev who was previously a successful director of musicals such as *The Rich Bride* (1938), *Tractor Drivers* (1939), *Swineherd and Shepherd* (1941) – shown in the USA as *They Met in Moscow* – and of course the famous *At Six P.M. After the War* (1944).[1]

The Russian classics inspired delightful films like Josif Heifits' *Lady with the Little Dog* (1960) and *In the Town of S——* (1966), in which the character of Tchekov himself was finely played by Andrei Popov; Turgeniev's *A Nest of Gentlefolk* (1968), directed by Andrei Konchalovsky; and Mark Donskoi's *A Mother's Heart* (1966).

Attempts continued to be made to make satisfactory films from *Anna Karenina* and *War and Peace*. The veteran Alexander Zarkhi made a brave attempt at the former in 1967, but fared not much better than a large number of predecessors.[2]

Sergei Bondarchuk, on the other hand, certainly made the biggest and most impressive effort so far to put Tolstoy's epic on the screen. His version of *War and Peace*, lasting all of seven hours, took three years to make and was finally premiered in 1967. The sheer sweep and grandeur of the battle scenes, with cameraman Anatole Petrinsky's virtuosity matching the director's imaginative interpretation, must surely remain unbeatable. Nor should some other and less spectacular sequences be forgotten – the duel for example. But the great difficulty in trying to turn this vast novel into a film is in somehow finding a balance between the vast manoeuvring of armies and the tactics of the commanders as against the highly individual personalities and emotions of a large cast of subtly observed characters. Maybe King Vidor in his 1955 version (with Henry Fonda as Pierre and Audrey Hepburn as Natasha) was – at any rate in the earlier reels – more successful at this than Bondarchuk; but his battle scenes, and his burning of Moscow, are completely eclipsed by Bondarchuk, who incidentally, as James Price has pointed out, used the same simplified skeleton of the story

---

[1] As late as 1951 Pyriev was attacking Eisenstein's memory, saying that he had, through his formalist 'montage of attractions', misrepresented 'reality and the character of the Russian people'.

[2] I don't know how many times this novel has been filmed. Jay Leyda records three other Russian versions, in 1911, in 1914 (directed by Vladimir Gardin) and in 1953 (a straight film record of the Moscow Art Theatre's stage production). Garbo did a silent of it called *Love* in 1927 and a talkie directed by Clarence Brown in 1935. Duvivier directed Vivien Leigh and Ralph Richardson in it for Korda in 1948. Pudovkin told me in 1937 that he would dearly like to do it; but he never did.

as did Vidor. Nothing really can be said in detraction of Bondarchuk's visual richness – that of Borodino not least – which has something of the stop-at-nothing splendour of Gance's approach to *Napoléon*.

But his attempt to repeat all this grandeur in *Waterloo* (1969), in a co-production with Italy, was a sad disappointment. The battle scenes were fine – with some especially effective aerial shots – but the large and star-studded cast seemed more like figures in a local pageant, and Rod Steiger, as Napoleon, unaccountably miscalculated the part and carried his 'Method' style of acting to the point of caricature.

The other outstanding figure of Soviet cinema in this period is Grigori Kozintsev. As young men he and Leonid Trauberg had made that unforgettable silent picture of the Paris Commune, *The New Babylon* (1929).[1] In the Thirties the same partnership made *Alone* (1931), with Elena Kuzmina as a young teacher sent to a distant and poverty-stricken village in the remote Altai area; a tense and revelatory film with a compelling score by the young Shostakovitch. They continued with the three Maxim films (not to be confused with Donskoi's Gorky Trilogy) which told the story of the rise and education of a young communist at the time of the Revolution – *The Youth of Maxim* (1935) and *The Return of Maxim* (1937) being climaxed in 1939 by *The Vyborg Side*, with its memorable performance by Maxim Straukh as Lenin.

At the end of the Second World War, Kozintsev and Trauberg made one more film together – *Ordinary People* (1945). After this the partnership was dissolved. By 1949 Trauberg seems to have fallen into ideological disgrace with the authorities; but Kozintsev went on to forge himself a new place in cinema. In 1957 there came *Don Quixote* which, with its formal period atmosphere, can now be seen to have been a kind of rehearsal for Kozintsev's entry into the world of Shakespeare with his versions of *Hamlet* and *King Lear*, on both of which he lavished long, thoughtful and meticulous preparations.

Shakespeare's universality transcends the problems of translation. Even in Kurosawa's way-out *Throne of Blood* original elements remain; no one who saw the Barrault-Renaud stage production of *Hamlet* in Gide's translation after the war will ever forget it – with Barrault's echoing cries of 'Mère . . . Mère' preluding the closet scene, and the felicities of the translation including '*séduisant sentier de rose*' for 'the primrose path of dalliance'. And, as we shall see later, a Pole filming in the original language can, in *Macbeth*, make all things new.

---

[1] The two youngsters emerged in the Twenties with the experimental theatre group FEKS. Their first film was *The Adventures of Oktyabrina* (1925).

So, with Kozintsev's deeply-studied versions, we are enabled to gain new insights into, and new experiences of, Shakespeare's inexhaustible dramatic possibilities.

The provenance of his *Hamlet* (1964) is well-documented.[1] Like the subsequent *King Lear* (1969), it is a large-scale, majestic and spacious cinematic rendering of the essence of the play, with close attention to the inner characters of the protagonists. Unlike the famous Olivier screen version, it seldom if ever makes one conscious of the studio, the lighting, the movement of the camera, or the careful arrangement of screen composition. Nothing deters from concentration on the drama. As Hamlet, Innokenty Smoktunovsky finely evokes the full vigour of manhood as well as the inner torture of a sensitive soul in a prison 'not of stone or iron but of people', as Kozintsev once put it in an interview given at Unesco: a radically different approach, this, from Olivier's 'tragedy of a man who could not make up his mind'. Both the Kozintsev and Olivier versions can be criticized for alterations and omissions, though those by Olivier are inevitably more noticeable; and as we shall see Kozintsev took considerable liberties with *King Lear*. Both versions rely much on the use of music – for Olivier a score by William Walton, and for Kozintsev one by the same Shostakovitch who scored his first film in 1931. And both versions, interestingly enough, present Hamlet's invasion of Ophelia's room in the form of a mime played to her subsequent description.

Where Kozintsev's version is superior to Olivier's is in its sense of immediacy and of actuality. There are some tremendous moments, as when the Ghost – whose eyes glow with an almost human light – stampedes the horses in the Royal Stables;[2] or when Hamlet, voice over, moves with the 'How weary, stale, flat and unprofitable' soliloquy through the luxurious and crowded courtrooms of Claudius' (but once his father's) palace; or when Laertes and his followers erupt into the palace like avenging furies. To these actions Kozintsev opposes patterns of formality. Ophelia's first appearance, learning a courtly and punctilious dance from her black-clad duenna, is paralleled later in the scene where she is imprisoned in a metal corset (strait waistcoat or *ceinture de chasteté*?) ready for her father's funeral. It is in this terrible framework that she is found, now mad, by the Queen; and in it she subsequently wanders through those same crowded courtrooms as has

[1] See *Shakespeare: Time and Conscience* by Grigori Kozintsev, Dobson, 1967: also *Shakespeare and the Film* by Roger Manvell, J. M. Dent, 1971.

[2] Did Kozintsev lift this idea from *Macbeth*? And if so, did Polanski borrow it back again for his brilliant transposition of the episode to the murder scene instead of its aftermath?

Hamlet previously – distributing her withered herbs to the embarrassed sycophants and hangers-on.

The Castle of Elsinore is, for the exteriors, a real one in Estonia (to which area Kozintsev later returned for some of his *King Lear* locations), and this, with its images of sea and rocks, is bound up intimately with the interiors which, as I have already said, fail to suggest the studio as miraculously as do those of *Ivan the Terrible*. Finally there is Smoktunovsky's Hamlet[1] – a simple, uncomplicated reading of the part which, like Michael Redgrave's superb rendering at the Old Vic in 1949, confronts the inner tragedy with a kind of shining innocence whose final betrayal is stunningly conveyed by the dying Prince's matador-thrust into the bull-like Claudius. Claudius, incidentally, is magnificently played by Mikhail Nazwanov; and one may note here that there is a sly dig at the late Stalin, for the palace is crammed with unattractive statues of the usurper, many of them markedly made of metal.

Kozintsev's *King Lear* is magisterial. As all good directors (or stage producers) should, he has established his own interpretative point of view about the play, has developed and nurtured it and brought it to a fruition which throws something of a new light on this greatest and at the same time most difficult of Shakespeare's tragedies.

He opens the film on a world in ruins, a world of refugees. It is a world of centuries long past; but the ruins and the refugees are not so different from those adumbrated by Peter Watkins in *The War Game*. Even the royal palace, straddled along a rocky ridge and buttressed with timber, is partly in ruins. The film confronts us with a despot who will be reduced in disaster to an equal sharing of misery with the lowest of his people and who, like them,

> 'strives in his little world of man to outscorn
> the to and fro conflicting wind and rain'.

Inside the palace the luxury is minimal. Royal comfort is well illustrated by a shot of His Majesty taken from within a burning fireplace. Beyond that temporary circle of warmth stretch chilly and barren vaults through which the wind hums.[2] One result of all this starkness is

---

[1] Smoktunovsky, one of Russia's most noted stage actors, appeared earlier in Mikhail Romm's *Nine Days of One Year* (1962) playing opposite Alexei Batalov in a story of human dilemmas posed when an atomic scientist accidentally exposes himself to a dangerous level of radiation. He has since, among other rôles, played the name part in *Tchaikovsky* (1971), a sober counterblast by Dmitri Tiomkin (no less) and Igor Talankin to Ken Russell's *The Music Lovers*.

[2] Shostakovitch, with an economy of instrumentation possible only to a genius, produces throughout music which fits the film perfectly.

that the treachery and brutality of Regan, Goneril and the rest becomes more of a side-issue than in the play (and even there it is in all conscience pushed aside at times); and it is Lear sharing the storm not only with the Fool and Edgar but also with the refugees which builds up the pathos and the drama.

There is one shot in which the narrowness of the gap between king and beggar is brutally pointed. The king, hitherto broad and majestic in his great cloak, takes it off, and at that moment is revealed as a sad, skinny old man. Yuri Jarvet, the Estonian actor who so beautifully plays Lear, makes of this moment, and of many others subsequently, a penetrating comment on the frailty of man.

Kozintsev shot this film in black and white. The castle, the landscapes, exist in a land without sunlight. Rays of the sun are to be seen sometimes as distant shafts piercing the omnipresent stormclouds. This consistency of mood, no less than the consistency of the performances of the whole cast, gives the film a compelling authenticity.

It is only towards the end that Kozintsev, in pursuit of this consistency perhaps, has made disturbing alterations to the original. He has abandoned altogether the scene with Gloucester and Edgar on Dover cliffs; and he has overplayed his hand by extending the action after Cordelia's death far further than did Shakespeare. Kozintsev should have ended his film at the point when Lear's agonized cry of 'Never Never Never' is swept with the camera through a ruined archway and out over a grey and angry sea; there was no need to add to this an admittedly marvellous but essentially redundant processional.

But despite these faults it remains a fine film, full of elaborate and often menacing camera movements (of which one, a magnificently carried out rising camera shot, means, alas! nothing at all), and its special interpretation in terms of uprooted humanity,[1] and of the predicament of the despot in relation to the people, has been well described by Kozintsev's contemporary (and director of *Othello*) Yutkevitch:

'Why have they come here? What has driven them across the land? What do they want from the king, sheltering within the endless castle wall? And why does their silence and their dumbness seem to hang so wearily and yet so menacingly? . . . Silently they await the decision of the king's fate; of their own fate . . . They wait for a miracle, but it does not come. Lear renounces his power not because

---

[1] Verdi's brilliant use of the refugee theme in his version of *Macbeth* is an interesting parallel.

he is weary or doubts the rightness of his rule. It is the last whim of a vain man, spoilt by the flattery and hypocrisy of his entourage, persuaded that nothing will change the established order.'[1]

It is the predicament of Ivan Grozny seen from the opposite angle.

There is no such gloss in Peter Brook's 1970 screen version of *King Lear*. Here the emphasis is solidly on the falling and fallen king who, like the other characters, and especially Irene Worth's evil-epitomizing Goneril, is projected as somewhat larger than life. Brook's film, however, shares with Kozintsev's a grim northern landscape creaking and aching with cold. Only at the end, in the Dover beach scenes, does a watery sun illuminate without warming the tragic finalities. The whole production is obviously carefully thought out and thought through – sometimes to the point of some puzzling trans-positions (Edmund's lines on filial relationships are given to Edgar, for example) – and there are some striking juxtapositions in the editing; but in the final resort the result is basically cerebral. We watch admiringly from outside, and it is only towards the end that our hearts are attached – notably in the scene between Lear and Gloucester, which is punctuated by an imaginative long-shot with the two old men in a vast perspective of beach and dune and with Edgar standing apart; and of course the scenes between Lear and Cordelia. It is in these that Paul Scofield, dominantly skilful throughout, at last achieves a sense of pity and terror, aided it must be said in the first instance by Alan Webb's humanistic Gloucester.

The storm passages are unfortunately marred by cinematic con-ceits, including in-and-out-of-focus effects and a curiously separate set-up on Lear's face for the lightning flashes. These tend to take the mind off the matter in hand. But the icy exteriors of Northern Denmark are impressive in Henning Kristiansen's black and white photography, the soundtrack is marvellous, and, *mirabile dictu*, there is not a note of music in the whole film which, for all its faults, was distinguished enough to deserve a better reception than it received in Britain. It is good to know that it fared better in the United States.

[1] *The Conscience of the King* by Sergei Yutkevitch in *Sight and Sound*, Autumn 1971.

VIII

In Poland during the Sixties a number of directors began to show a preference for working in other countries, and the authorities do not seem to have objected to this. Thus the veteran Wajda made *The Gates of Paradise* (1967) in England and Yugoslavia; this film about the Children's Crusade has, however, never been released, and it is said that Wajda himself did not like it. Other films of the Sixties by Wajda were, however, made in Poland. They include *A Siberian Lady Macbeth* (1962), which evoked the atmosphere of 19th century Russia; *Ashes* (1965), a story of the Napoleonic Wars; and what was probably his best film since *Innocent Sorcerers*, a tribute to the memory of Zbigniew Cybulski – *Everything for Sale* (1968).

As for the younger generation – by the early Sixties Roman Polanski was ranging the Western world, and Walerian Borowczyk was working most of the time in France, though he returned to Poland to make *Mazeppa* in 1968. He then went back to France to make *Blanche* (1971), a mediaeval tale – sinister and sensitive and with the exquisite Ligia Branice[1] starring, as she did in *Goto, l'Ile d'Amour* – which somewhat recalls *Les Visiteurs du Soir*, though it goes deeper than the Carné film. Meantime the new wonder-boy, Jerzy Skolimowski, visited Belgium in 1967 to make *Le Départ*, a comedy about a young man with a consuming desire to become a motor rally driver. Of his work outside Poland this is certainly the best so far. The humour is fresh and delightful, and the final sequence in the bedroom between Marc (Jean-Pierre Léaud) and Michèle (Catherine Duport) is, with its surprise dénouement, nicely and tenderly rendered. Skolimowski then returned to Poland and made *Hands Up!* (1967), the third of his films about his largely autobiographical hero Andrzej Leszczyc[2] (always played by Skolimowski himself). Of this he has said, 'It is my best and most mature film, and it is not funny at all'. It was banned *in toto* by the Polish authorities, so remains unseen.

After contributing an episode to *Dialogue* (1968) in Czechoslovakia, he made a period piece for United Artists in Italy – *The Adventures of Gerard*, based on the Conan Doyle book and featuring Peter McEnery, Claudia Cardinale and Jack Hawkins. His next film *Deep End* (1970), set in a public swimming baths in England but

[1] She is Borowczyk's wife.
[2] The first was *Rysopis* (*Identification Marks: None*), made in 1964, and the second *Walkover* (1965).

actually shot in Munich, was a disappointment. Somehow Skolimowski turned his location into a kind of no man's land; and the characters (with the splendid exception of Diana Dors as a lustybusty matron) were *déracinés* and unconvincing.

I think Skolimowski's Polish films are more important. Basically they deal with the generation gap – and specifically the gap between the older people who cannot and *au fond* do not want to forget the traumata of World War II, and the younger folk for whom 'all that' is mere hearsay, who want to live their own 'modern' lives, and who do not necessarily take the Establishment (i.e. doctrinaire Communism) for granted. That last point is pressed home hard in the conflict between Teresa and Andrzej in *Walkover* – a film, incidentally, which is remarkable for its staggeringly prolonged and skilful camera movements which in themselves become integral to the story.[1]

This question of the generations is, *inter alia*, raised again – and to immense effect – in *Barrier* (1966), which followed *Walkover* and preceded *Le Départ*. This is far and away Skolimowski's best film, and probably the best and most stimulating film to come from Poland since Munk's *Eroica*,[2] with the first part of which it has much in common. *Barrier* is a poetic film. In it Skolimowski, stepping outside the auto-biographical rôle, has used an intense, heightened lyrical mode to indicate the social, political and psychological problems of his contemporaries and their elders. With rare perception he uses the movie medium to present us with reality seen as a dream rather than a dream seen as reality. Thus the factual is continually fantasised, and its inner meaning is shown in various distortions or variations representative of the different attitudes of the characters. The basic dilemma – that of Dzidzius in *Eroica* and indeed of Maciek in *Ashes and Diamonds* – is in turn expanded, contracted, crystallized and diffused (the end shot fades into a dazzling whiteness as the tram-driver heroine says 'Get up or you'll catch cold'), while the camera alternates between elaborate sweeping movements (as in *Walkover*) and brusque, almost brutal short takes. No doubt a good deal of the detailed content of the film – psychological and political – may elude a non-Polish audience; it is difficult for outsiders to enter into that long history which has spiritualized as well as brutalized the Poles. But *Barrier* is basically pure movie; so that when it touches on their own problems of youth and age, ideals and disillusion, ambition and despair, it becomes a poetic

[1] There are, according to Michael Walker, only 35 shots in the whole film. (*Second Wave*, Studio Vista, 1970.)

[2] One should perhaps add Wojciech Has' enticing phantasmagoria *The Saragossa Manuscript*.

and universal asseveration of life, open to anyone's understanding. *Barrier* is also full of humour, from simple gags like the exploding cigarettes which are the defecting hero's parting gift from his fellow-students at the Medical School, to the long, elaborate and satirical spoof involving a large run-down restaurant, a singing charwoman, a veteran's reunion, and a middle-aged failure trying to pretend he has saved face by becoming a vendor of a woman's magazine.[1] And there is much *tendresse* as well as stress; near a range of Easter candles the boy and girl crouch by a glowing brazier while, in utter silence, cars pass by in the night street.

Meantime Polanski, removed permanently from Poland, as it would seem, was maturing his control of the movie medium. The uncertainties and exaggerations which had flawed the otherwise effective *Repulsion* (1965) had almost completely disappeared in *Cul de Sac* (1966). This brisk black comedy, set on Holy Isle off the Northumbrian coast, where the tide cuts off the castle from the mainland every day, concerns a horrid little man (Donald Pleasence) with a beautiful wife (the late Françoise Dorléac), on whom descends a gangster (Lionel Stander) who in turn is waiting for a colleague (Godot?) who will in fact never turn up alive. The permutations of the relationships which grow up among the three main characters, and various others who appear as the film progresses, are most skilfully worked out in a script with dialogue by Pinter; Polanski's direction is brisk and positive, and Gilbert Taylor's photography pellucid.

Of Polanski's enormously successful *Rosemary's Baby* (1968), little now remains to be said except perhaps that it is much more than a standard horror film even in the Polanski sense. It is insidiously frightening, if only because for a long time we don't believe what the satanists are doing to Rosemary; even the appalling rape scene can be taken – only too easily indeed – as a terrible nightmare. In this we become in a way identified with Rosemary herself, since she, as Beverle Houston and Marsha Kinder have pointed out, is herself 'trapped in a reality which she cannot believe'. They also point out that the film is about the birth of an antichrist, which for centuries we have believed to be a detestable lie. 'The film is frightening because it forces us to examine the kinds and bases of belief. We confront the idea that the Christian myth is certainly no more believable than its mirror image, and possibly less so.'[2]

---

[1] His apotheosis comes when someone shows him how to make the pages into paper hats which everyone then wears for the remainder of the sequence.

[2] *Sight and Sound*, Winter 1968–69.

Polanski's version of *Macbeth* gave rise to a sharp division of critical opinion. For me it was and is one of the few really successful translations of a Shakespeare tragedy into true film form. It is full of the same sort of felicitous acts of imagination as those which characterized the screen version of *Henry V*, and is only marred by some unnecessary brutalities – physical in the case of Macbeth's rather ludicrous decapitation, and literary in some fearful text-mangling, not least in Act One Scene 2, which is reduced to encapsulated *Reader's Digest* nonsense.

The great thing about this *Macbeth* is that Polanski and Kenneth Tynan seem to have thought the whole play through in cinematic terms, so that not only camera movements but also changes of *venue*, and thus montage, are made to heighten, never falsify, Shakespeare's intent. Thus Macbeth's soliloquies and his arguments with Lady Macbeth over Duncan's fate are cleverly interwoven with scenes of the banquet (offstage only in the play) offered to Duncan after his arrival at Dunsinane. This same sequence also includes the thunderstorm and the stampede of the stabled horses, which in the play are referred to by Ross and the Old Man only after the discovery of the murder. A further *trouvaille* – disapproved of by many but not by me – was the admittedly anachronistic but hugely effective singing by Fleance of Chaucer's 'Merciles Beauté' roundel,

'Your eyen twa wol slee me sodenly,
I may the beauté of hem not sustene'

straight at Lady Macbeth during the banquet.

There are other fine effects. Duncan wakes and recognizes Macbeth before he is killed; the resulting struggle is poignant and enriches our sympathies. When Macbeth 'regrets' the slaying of Duncan's grooms, the pause before Macduff's astounded 'Wherefore did you so?' is elongated by the editing to a degree virtually impossible on the stage. Lady Macbeth's final breakdown is preluded by a scene showing her re-reading Macbeth's letter announcing Duncan's fateful arrival – now simply a 'rooted sorrow' in 'a mind diseased'. Ross is presented as a viciously unscrupulous Von Papen who, after warning Lady Macduff of the danger to her life, casually signals the assassins in as he leaves the castle. Finally, Macbeth's visit to the weird sisters becomes a *tour de force* of evil and terror. The witches are part of a huge coven cavorting naked in the abyss.[1] The appalling potion is brewed before Macbeth's very eyes; then he drinks it, steaming and

---

[1] In Hecate's speech, nearly always cut, the meeting place is specifically described as 'the pit of Acheron'.

reeking, and is launched on a psychedelic trip in which the formal visions become, even to us, a series of shattering experiences.

Gilbert Taylor's Todd-AO photography is outstanding even in an era in which fine camerawork is taken for granted; its tone is set right from the almost tactile pre-credit sequence on the salty seashore. The designs and set-dressings (Wilfrid Shingleton and Bryan Graves) give the story a convincing realism; the castles are also farms, with cattle and middens in the courtyards, and this sense of contemporaneity is increased by the naturalistic soundtrack full of animal and bird noises, with the owl and the cock persistent in their warnings throughout the film. There are, too, constant reminders of the casually accepted brutality of the times; these include the introduction of a bear-baiting sequence (it is the caged bear which is first referred to as 'Here's our chief guest'), triggered off no doubt in the scriptwriter's mind by Macbeth's later reference to himself as a staked bear.

From all this, and from the naturalistic non-actor-managerish performances of Jon Finch and Francesca Annis and a generally excellent cast, I received the full Aristotelian reactions. Shakespeare's shattering genius flooded unimpeded from the screen.

IX

In Hungary during the Sixties a new generation of film-makers appeared, free in general of the fears and preoccupations of older directors like Fábri and Mariassy who had had to suffer the War, the Rákosi-Stalin period, and the Uprising. Not that the younger directors were self-satisfied; like their Polish counterparts they questioned, if they didn't reject, the reminiscent standards of the older generation. Nor were they content with things as they found them; but they were questioning the future even when dealing with the past. Thus, while Fábri continued during the Sixties with, among other films, *Darkness in Daytime* (1963) and *The Paul Street Boys* (1968), and Mariassy made *Goliath* (1964), *Fig Leaf* (1966) and *Bondage* (1968), the main emphasis and interest rested on the younger men like Miklós Jancsó, András Kovács, Ferenc Kósa, and István Szabó.

Of these Jancsó is in truth nearer the age of the Fábri-Mariassy group (he is already 50), but in attitude he is closer to the younger directors, most of whom are still in their thirties. He tends to be interested in the individual only in relation to the group – this in a positive as well as a negative sense. Thus in *The Round Up* (1965), the search for one single person – the hero-figure Sándor – by the pitiless and mysterious military police, takes place within the patterns formed by the various groups of prisoners from whom informers and victims are selected apparently casually but actually according to a sinister and elaborate plan. Even in his earlier film, *My Way Home* (1964), Jancsó makes his two individuals – the Hungarian boy and the young Russian soldier with whom he teams up – victims of some higher and probably mindless military plan. They are used, and disposed of, like pieces in a game.

As his films have progressed, Jancsó has increasingly formalized his group ideas. In *The Confrontation* (1969) the whole story is conveyed balletically, indeed almost operatically, with groups of youngsters moving in patterns of aggression, of assumed triumphs, and of celebration. But the confrontations are not simply between the kids celebrating the reconversion of their country to Communism and their 'reactionary' rivals representing the educational ambitions of the Church; they are confronting a not yet fully realized challenge to their youthful ideals by the inflexible monolithic regime which they now praise for liberating them. As Penelope Houston pointed out,

'Jancsó leaves you feeling the presence of a power behind the scenes, a system which will give everyone the rope to hang himself, will compile the dossiers and note the deviations and in the end negate what look like decisions arrived at by free will.'[1]

Similarly the movements in *Agnus Dei* (1971) – the singing, dancing and banner-flourishing – follow the pattern not just of *The Confrontation* but also of *The Red and the White*, with its rival forces on the wide Hungarian plains intent on merciless showdowns.

Jancsó's genius at conveying this vast sense of space in its relation to the humans who dwell in it, is perhaps summed up by the title of another of his films, *Silence and Cry*. The small buildings set against the flatness of the landscape, often in wide screen composition; the running or riding figures receding from the camera into a series of distances – all these impose horizons. In *The Round Up*, which is the most formal and hieratic of all Jancsó's films, the guard-room or prison walls always and almost visibly mask the space beyond. Every gate, every door, opens onto enormous distances which, however, seldom indicate freedom.

Meantime his films move steadily onwards towards an increasingly

[1] *Sight and Sound*, Summer 1969.

nervous and mysterious symbolism. Already hinted at in *The Confrontation*, it comes into the open in *Agnus Dei* and takes complete charge in *La Pacifista* (1971), which Jancsó made in Italy.[1] Here the ancient palaces, castles and churches which formed a gracious setting to the challenges of *The Confrontation* start crowding in and become metropolitan, overtly political. The girl TV journalist (Monica Vitti) reflects, in an increasingly personal fear, the mysteries of urban conflicts which surround and menace her. Dislocating images of students, fanatics, karate chops, figures in store windows; sudden demonic possessions in public parks (with the Pierre Clémenti of *Partner* and *Porcile* as sinister *compère*), all pile up into a climax of cruelty and death which, if it resolves the fright and the mystery with which Jancsó has drenched this film, does so only at the expense of the idea of personal liberty. It is interesting to me that *La Pacifista* is the only Jancsó film which leaves an impression of blurred rather than vivid visual images. Whether this is because he is less at ease in the claustrophobia of the city – reflected maybe in the long-focus lenses he here so liberally uses – I don't know; the result is a disturbing and not entirely satisfactory film.

Nearest in mood and style to Jancsó is Ferenc Kósa, director of the impressive *Ten Thousand Suns* (1967), in which, incidentally, he uses as principal player András Kozák, the Hungarian boy in *My Way Home*. While concerned with the generation gap, he is especially implicated in the passage of time, in the impingement of history on the small lives of ordinary, unimportant people. In this film he piles image on image, sometimes with surrealist effect, so that we are impelled into a perspective of history distilled into the continuing existence of a small and isolated peasant community. The great martial or political movements of the outside world are here seen as meaning the taking of the livestock, or the food supply, or even the menfolk.

András Kovács, whose student years coincided with the most repressive period of the Rákosi regime (when even Béla Balázs was dismissed from his post at the Academy), not unnaturally found himself concerned filmically with the problem of the individual in relation to the state. A stay in Paris during the early Sixties introduced him to *cinéma-vérité*, and he returned to Hungary to make *Difficult People* (1964), which was in effect a series of direct interviews with inventors whose ideas and machines had been ignored or frustrated by jumped-up bureaucrats. In 1966 he made a film about the massacre of thousands of hostages by the Hungarian Army during World War II – and here again he shaped his film into the form of interviews with soldiers. Then

---

[1] It was jointly financed by French, West German and Italian interests.

in 1968 he made a more arid, possibly Godardian film called alternatively *Walls* or *Lost Generation*; this was a long series of political discussions among various people in a state factory where an engineer-critic of the organization awaits a verdict on his behaviour pending the return of the managing director from a business trip. Here Kovács tried 'to make an intellectual adventure ... which may lure the audience on to paths they did not want – or perhaps dare – to explore. An intellectual experience is often an emotional one, and vice versa.'[1] Since then Kovács has completed for Hungarian Television a feature length *cinéma-vérité* reportage on a wide variety of public attitudes towards pop music and its performers.

The baby of the Sixties period is István Szabó, who made his first feature film, *The Age of Daydreaming*, in 1964 at the age of twenty-six. He is particularly interesting in that not only is he deeply concerned with the rôle of the individual as a member, hero even, of a collective society, but also he is exclusively metropolitan. He is the city-dweller *par excellence*; Jancsó or Kósa country is for him something glimpsed from the window of a coach or a train. His heroes have much in common with those of Skolimowski; they confuse their fantasy lives with the hard realities of living, and thus have difficulty in striking a balance or avoiding an ambivalent attitude to the structure of the society in which they live.

In his best film so far, *Father* (1966), Szabó presents a nicely controlled, sentimental view of a young man growing up in the modern world behind a self-erected fortification – namely the memory of his father, whom he has built up in his mind into a legendary Hero of the Resistance. Szabó builds the youngster's flashback dreams and visions from the cops and robbers simplicities of a boy's imagination[2] into the more serious and psychologically more dangerous fantasies and wish-fulfilments of a young man. There comes a point when it is difficult to tell whether the screen action is daydream or fact, as when the youngster has a terrifying journey across Budapest during the Uprising with a Hungarian flag: we wonder if he is imagining himself as a hero, but in the event the incident not only turns out to be fact, but ends with a slumping anti-climax.

An extremely human film, *Father* eschews neither comedy nor sentiment. The long tracking shot by the river, in which the boy's

---

[1] Statement by Kovács quoted in *Quite Apart from Miklos Jancso*, an admirable and comprehensive article on Hungarian cinema by David Robinson in *Sight and Sound*, Spring 1970.

[2] These are done with a sympathy and humour which recall the similar daydreams of Tim in Palle Kjaerulff-Schmid's *Once There Was a War*.

Jewish girl-friend alternately justifies and accuses herself about her attitude to her own race, is fascinating, wise, compulsive. And when at the end of the film Szabó finally lets his hero off the hook, he does it with tender humour. Having at last decided to stand entirely on his own and to depend no further on memories of his father,[1] he decides to symbolize this decision by swimming across the wide, wide Danube. We see him in close-up as he undertakes this (to him) bold journey, and in voice-over we hear his thoughts on the dangers of the enterprise; and it is only after a good while that the camera draws back to show that behind him there are some fifty other kids also making the crossing. *Father* is a richer and more imaginative film than some critics have made it out to be. In its humanism there is something of De Sica, something of Truffaut.

In *A Love Film* (1970), Szabó concerns himself with memory again, but this time with more affinity with Resnais, in following a love affair from childhood onward. Those who have seen it maintain that it has more than a purely sentimental approach in that it ends with an absolute acceptance of memory as a substitute for the actual presence of the lost loved one. It is also said to be somewhat self-indulgent in terms of length – particularly length of sequences; this may well be true, since this is also a fault found in parts of *Father* and in at least one of Szabó's earlier non-feature films, *You*.[2]

Of other contemporary Hungarian directors one must mention István Gaál, whose *The Falcons* (1970) is a coldly alarming study of a young man's visit to a reserve where the birds are trained, which turns out to be very much the other side of the medal from Ken Loach's *Kes*; Imre Gyöngyössy's *Palm Sunday* (1969) – a mixture of Communist and Christian legend and argument; and *The Upturned Stone* (1968), a partly autobiographical story about a young man's conflict with an unimaginative approach to land nationalization, directed by Sándor Sára, the eminent cameraman who shot so many of the best Hungarian films, including *Ten Thousand Suns* and *Father*.

[1] The young man and his father are beautifully portrayed by András Balint and Miklós Gábor, who also played the main parts in *The Age of Daydreaming*.

[2] Like most communist countries, Hungary has a large and flourishing short film industry which includes experimental as well as cartoon and documentary films. Of a large number of directors in this field one may note Marianne Szemes who, among others, has made some distinguished films on social and psychological problems.

X

The Sixties saw the Czech film-makers developing new and brighter approaches which reflected the growing defensiveness of the Novotny regime (which never fully recovered from the internal cancer indicated by the Slansky/Clémentis trials and executions); the all-too-brief springtime of the Dubcek era was on its way, and before the Soviet invasion and colonization of the country re-established the drab *status quo*, there was a splendid efflorescence of Czechoslovak cinema which, indeed, had somehow survived as a viable entity throughout all the tyrannies and occupations whether from right or left. This was a period which opened with Forman's *Peter and Pavla*, Vavra's *Romance for Trumpet*, Juracek and Schmidt's *Josef Kilian*, and the Kadar – Klos *Shop in the High Street*, and closed with Forman departing to the United States to make *Taking Off*, and the virtual banning of Menzel's *Larks on a String*.

Like the Poles, with whom they share the experience of centuries of oppression from various European powers, the Czechs have a resilience and an inner sense of humour which frequently enables them to bamboozle and satirize their usually humourless tyrants; the Good Soldier Schweik moves undyingly among them no less than the more melancholy shade of Franz Kafka.

In *Josef Kilian* (1964), Pavel Juracek and Jan Schmidt superbly combined both elements. This story, something under feature-length, about a man who hires a cat for the day and then can find no one to return it to, is both funny and frightening; its *aperçus désagréables* of a superinhuman bureaucracy are brilliant. To this a nice companion piece is to be found in *The Party and the Guests* (1966),[1] which indeed had to wait a year before more liberal ideas permitted its release. In the English language at least the words 'Party' and 'Guests' have double connotations which the film certainly reflects.

Some carefree picnickers are spending a day in the countryside. There suddenly appear in the woods a number of sinister persons who agitate them with ridiculous and humiliating requests and commands. Then there emerges an impressive host (somewhat reminiscent of Lenin in appearance) who invites them to an elaborate formal banquet laid out among the birch trees . . . Nothing could be nicer – except that everything starts to go wrong: guests are given the wrong seats, the

[1] Also known as *Report on the Party and the Guests*.

candles in their ornate stands are extinguished, and the baying of blood-hounds is heard in the darkness of the forest . . .

The Party and the Guests, directed by Jan Nemec not without a sidelong glance at the Resnais of *L'Année Dernière à Marienbad*, is a luminiferous piece of film-making which never for a moment abandons its veiled, but none the less savage attack on the *maquillage* of the 'people's police' and the like, which in fact never deceives anyone. Had some of the characterization been more deeply conceived (Nemec's use of non-professionals does not always pay off), this film could have been a masterpiece.

Nemec's next film, *Martyrs of Love* (1967), consisted of three episodes about romantic daydreamers which involved the exercise of a variety of filmic techniques, New Wave style. As a result it got clobbered by the authorities at the same time as Vera Chytilova's charming and footloose *Daisies* (1966); both directors were refused further state funds for film-production because of their 'nihilist' attitude.

Meantime the veterans Jan Kadar and Elmar Klos had jointly produced their masterpiece, *The Shop in the High Street* (1965). I have already referred to this fine anti-Nazi or, as one might say, anti-totalitarian film. Here I add an extra word in praise of Josef Kroner's superb and deeply moving study of an honest, simple man hounded and persecuted not for being a Jew but for sympathizing with one. To a subject which is ever moving to the sensibilities, and one which inevitably tends towards the higher dramatics, this great actor brings an extra dimension of truth.

Another veteran, Otakar Vavra, well-known for a wide variety of films from 1937 onward – including *Humoreske* (1939), *Krakatit* (1948), and three films on the Czech national hero *Jan Hus* (1955–57) – now made *Romance for Trumpet* (1967), a film in which a prolonged flashback delineated the memories of a frustrated romance; illuminated by some intense observations of character as well as of nature, this film, for all its lyricism, seemed a little old hat in relation to the work of the younger directors.

Of these, Menzel and Forman are of course pre-eminent. They both combine a delectable sense of humour with a sharp and some-times satiric eye on the personal and communal problems of the society in which they find themselves. They are great whiskers-away-of-cobwebs.

Forman's first feature film was *Peter and Pavla* (1963), with an extremely slender story-line about a shy boy on his first job as a store detective which was gorgeously embellished by carefully noted con-

frontations with his relations and his employer as well as with a girl.
He followed this with *A Blonde in Love* (1965), by which time his team
(Ivan Passer as writer and Miroslav Ondricek as photographer)[1] was
complete. This film had an absolute certainty of technique which
enabled its hilarious story to develop with no loss of clarity. Again the
whole film is ingeniously developed from a slight and simple story. An
impressionable girl spends the night with a young jazz-player.[2] To her
it is the beginning of a romance; to him something forgettable. She
suddenly turns up at his home, confronting not only him but also his
bewildered parents. From then on it is a question of the various well-
meaning but often blundering efforts of all concerned to solve the
situation. The film also has a sequence involving three bored soldiers
in a dance-hall which has something of Olmi's quality of sympathy with
life's leftovers. Much of the success of *A Blonde in Love*, as indeed of
his other films, is due to Forman's skilful mingling of professionals
with non-actors, and to his gentle insistence on improvisation (usually,
it would seem, without previous warning). Certainly in the dance-hall
the blank desperation of *ennui* on the faces of the three soldiers is
memorably funny in its naturalness.

The Firemen's Ball (1967) is much sharper, much more overtly
critical of, and less kind to, many of its characters. Within the confines
of this petty bourgeois event Forman examines the errors, the foibles
and the vices of humanity. One may also, perhaps, note a certain
attitude of disrespect and mockery towards the Novotny regime, at
that time (if only temporarily) on its way out. It is a film almost
exclusively about the middle-aged. It is also about the disasters which
arise from people taking themselves too seriously. The whole build-up
of the annual Ball is fraught with doom and frustration from the very
start. The cast – again mostly non-professionals – are especially convincing because they seem personally to *feel* the selfishness or foolishness
or pettiness of the behaviour they are portraying. The two set-pieces – a
hysterically comic attempt to run a beauty contest, and the fire which
puts paid to the whole party – are Forman at his best. The effect is as
though he had just happened to be passing by with a camera, and
switched it on.

The Firemen's Ball ends with a truly surrealist scene as an old
man climbs into bed – a bed he must share with a fireman left on duty
in case the blaze starts up again – and settles down for the night. This

---

[1] Passer scripted all Forman's films except *Taking Off*. Ondricek also shot *Taking Off*,
having previously done *The White Bus* and *If* . . . for Lindsay Anderson in Britain.
[2] That enchanting young chap Vladimir Pucholt, who also played in *Peter and Pavla*.

bed, surrounded by various of his household belongings, stands in the snow and open to the night sky. Beyond are to be seen the gutted remains of his home, dank and black, no longer flowering with the flames which are the firemen's enemy and emblem.

After this there was something of a pause, not perhaps without relation to the Soviet invasion. Forman's next work came from America in 1971, and was a deceptively wide-eyed study of the habits of that strange country. *Taking Off* is the generation gap as seen from the parental point of view, so that here, as David Wilson has pointed out, the indignant father who was left speechless in frozen frame at the end of *Peter and Pavla*, at last has a chance to sound off. Poor chap: his American simulacrum has been prescribed a fist-clenching exercise by his analyst in a campaign to stop smoking, and, using it while walking in the street, receives a brisk Black Power acknowledgment from a passing negro. Anyway, the search by mother and father for their wandering daughter lands them in various predicaments, including a boozy night out, a convention of members of the Society for the Parents of Fugitive Children to whom an exceptionally with-it hippie explains how properly to smoke Pot, and finally a game of strip poker which is interrupted by the daughter's return just as Dad (no poker buff he) is standing naked on the table singing a forfeit song.

Forman's observation of the United States here shows something of the tact of a newcomer; the deeper and more serious issues of the generations are omitted. But in its own way *Taking Off* is a re-arrangement of *The Firemen's Ball* in terms of the New World. The middle-aged parents are devotedly played by Lynn Carlin and Buck Henry; and the soundtrack is crammed with the rich and the rare, from the Incredible String Band to the Czech Philharmonic Orchestra playing Dvorak's *Stabat Mater* for a city sunrise stunningly rendered in colour by Ondricek.

It was at the Mannheim Festival of 1966 that there unrolled before the incredulous and delighted eyes of the Jury (of whom I was one) a film with the unpromising title of *Closely Observed Trains*. This was the first full-length feature of a talented Prague stage actor, Jiri Menzel. The story is of a young man (perfectly played by the pop-singer Vaclav Neckar) whose passionate desire to enjoy sex is frustrated by premature ejaculation; of his attempted suicide; and of his serio-comic yet heroic death in a triumphant act of sabotage against the Nazis It. is also concerned with the intrigues, gossip and bureaucratic fiddle-faddle of a small country railway-station, to say nothing of a splendid prototype of Women's Lib who solves the young man's sexual problems in full measure before his aforementioned death which, let it be said, takes place as a signal for the blowing up of a German munition train in an explosion of singular grandeur and magnificence. Even in its wilder moments, as with the station official who lets his various rubber stamps run wild on the body of his girl (and then has to explain the aberration to her mother as well as to a commission of enquiry), *Closely Observed Trains* remains down to earth; the attempt at suicide, in particular, is exceptionally well scripted and directed.

Menzel's *Capricious Summer* (1968) is an enchanting film with something of fable, something of morality-play to it, and – in the figure of the tightrope walker – something of the legends of Mephistopheles and of the Wandering Jew. Relaxedly it recounts the story of three middle-aged men – an Abbé, representing religion, a retired colonel, representing militarism, and the owner of a small riverside bathing-place who, with his wife, represents bourgeois capitalism. The even tenor of their lives is totally disrupted by the arrival – in a sequence very reminiscent of the magical incursion of the commercial traveller in Vigo's *L'Atalante* – of a not very efficient tightrope walker[1] and his beautiful wife. The men's efforts to make this girl all end in their own particular disasters. The sequence in which the Abbé has to have a damaged ear secretly stitched up (with a fish-hook) and is subjected to a lecture on morality at the same time, is a miracle of comedic sensitivity, while at the other end of the scale there is a hilarious scene when the girl, compulsively eating apple after apple as luscious and as juicy as herself, lazily resists being raped by the ex-colonel on his dining-room table.

Since *Capricious Summer* Menzel has directed *Crime in the Night-club* (1968), reported to be a parody of *Tosca* in a cabaret setting; and *Larks on a String* (1969) which, as already noted, was banned. Last heard of, he was back in the theatre as an actor.

XI

As we have already seen, the fecundity of Satyajit Ray continued through the Sixties, climaxing in 1970 with his splendid *The Adversary*. During the same period, in addition to the continued development of the official Films Division and a considerable amount of equally good

---

[1] Played by Menzel himself, who learned tightrope-walking specially for the film.

short film-making in the private sector, a few new names emerged from the general ruck of Indian feature film production. Of these may be noted Tapan Sinha, with his *Atithi* (1966), a charming, inconsequent, touching and funny film from a Tagore book about a runaway boy; and, more particularly, *Bhuvan Shome* (1969) by Mrinal Sen – a Bengali director who was encouraged, no doubt by Ray's example, to break away from the usual formulae.[1] The result in this case is a relaxed, warm comedy somewhat reminiscent of Ealing. It concerns a self-important railway official who decides to take a holiday, to go, indeed, on a hunting expedition to 'shoot some birds'. His ludicrous adventures as he penetrates deeper and deeper into the countryside are neatly intertwined with his coincidental relationship (unknown to himself) with the pretty young wife of a ticket-collector he is proposing to sack for accepting bribes. Shome himself – a major performance by Utpal Dutt[2] (here certainly recalling the British actor Alastair Sim) – has enough inner sense of humour to come to terms with his own deflated pomposity, and this gives the film a human warmth which enwraps its sometimes farcical events. Shome's ride in the bullock cart is an extended sequence of unalloyed joy. His driver (Shekar Chatterjee), who prides himself (erroneously) on being a linguist and at the same time much enjoys misinterpreting all orders, creates crisis after crisis, culminating in a terrified flight from what turns out to be a quietly domesticated water-buffalo. Throughout the film Mrinal Sen has allowed himself freedom of reference. Animated cartoon sequences are suddenly cut in to point a moral (however dubious); early in the film there is even a 'newsreel' of a street demonstration by protesting film-technicians; and there is some imaginative use of freeze-frame, not least in a lyrical passage involving a girl on a swing, where the use of a zoom lens on the frozen image produces a particularly pleasing effect.[3]

But the most striking newcomers to the Indian scene in this period

[1] Previous films by Sen, though based on the standard 'social' formula, had revealed a number of imaginative touches. They included *Punascha*, *Pratinidi*, and *Akash Kussim* – all in the Bengali tongue – and in the Oriya language *Matira Manisha*. *Bhuvan Shome* was made in Hindi, and incidentally to a notably low budget.

[2] A regular player for Ivory, he was the Maharajah in *Shakespeare Wallah*, the musician Ustad in *The Guru*, and the producer Bose in *Bombay Talkie*.

[3] Later Sen, in *The Interview* (1970) and its virtual sequel *Calcutta 71*, indicated a deep implication in sociological and therefore political problems. The former film is comparable in a sense with Ray's *The Adversary*, though more uncompromising in the solution it adumbrates. The latter, using a variety (perhaps too great a variety) of techniques, presents with rage as well as with love the apparently eternal miseries of the people of Calcutta. With his sweeping imagination and strong visual sense, Sen here makes a very sharp impression – not least in a passage showing the predicament of a large family under a leaking house-roof during the remorseless monsoon.

were the Indian Ismail Merchant and the American James Ivory,[1] who
in 1965 astonished the London Film Festival with *Shakespeare Wallah*,
which they had completed during the previous year. This film is a piece
of sustained nostalgia, a poetic lament, almost, for the passing of the
British Raj, here reflected in the gradual run-down of a company of
travelling players (whose patterned and sometimes stilted Shakespearean
performances have begun to brim over into their ordinary lives), and
in their personal relationships with varied Indian friends. With music
by Satyajit Ray and fine black-and-white photography by Ray's
Subrata Mitra (who later also filmed *The Guru* and *Bombay Talkie* in
colour), the film moves at a leisurely pace – sometimes indeed too
slowly – as the love affair between the daughter of the two main players
(Felicity Kendal) and a young Indian (Shashi Kapoor) develops amid
various complications, including the jealousy of a top-of-the-pops
Indian film star; the skill with which the sharp and delicious Madhur
Jaffrey smashes up a performance of *Othello* from the vantage point
of her box is a joy to behold. Other fine things are the dinner party at
the Maharajah's palace, reminiscent at times of *Jalsaghar* with its
delicate balance of decay and memory; and a beautiful Dovzhenko-like
love scene amid the rain of the Himalayan foothills, when the embracing
lovers are gradually blotted out from view by the drifting mist and then,
long after, so it seems, as the mist slowly clears, are still seen to be
locked in the same sweet encounter.

　　The Guru (1968) was both more ambitious and less convincing.
With Michael York as a pop idol visiting India to study the *sitar* and
Rita Tushingham as an English girl vaguely seeking enlightenment (or
something) from the Mysterious East, the film drifts uneasily from conventional patterns of Western film-making into a number of sequences
during which the West is more or less forgotten, thanks to some more
exhibitions of jealousy by Madhur Jaffrey and a smashing performance
from Aparna Sen – the Mrinmoyee of Ray's *Samapti*.

　　The same actress gives a striking performance in *Bombay Talkie*,
a film which has been underestimated and misunderstood. The relationships of the principal characters have been criticized for being
exaggerated, unreal, drowned in clichés. But the clichés and exaggerations are in fact intended and precisely calculated by Ivory to throw
into sharp relief the predicament of the self-torturing American author

[1] The two men had met in the United States, where both of them had been experimenting with film-making at graduate level. They eventually got together to make their
first Indian feature *The Householder* (already with Shashi Kapoor) in 1962. No one took
much notice of it until the success of *Shakespeare Wallah* earned it a belated but none the
less well-merited release.

who comes to India in search of new experiences (spiritual or otherwise), becomes entangled in the film world, and so also in a hot but hopeless love affair which in the end leads to her self-destruction. From the very beginning, with its frantic production number with Les Girls dancing on the keys of a gargantuan typewriter, the film forces all its characters into a frenzied and artificial existence which rages like a malarial fever. Shashi Kapoor, Jennifer Kendal, Zia Mohyeddin and the rest of a distinguished cast undertake this prolonged Trip with the utmost zest and, when real ham is required, provide it in just the right quantities. Jennifer Kendal's big scene on the grand staircase of the Bombay hotel is as justifiably exaggerated as Swanson's great finale in *Sunset Boulevard*; the threesome boozing party is searingly portrayed for the stupidity it is; and in the middle of the film there is a very quiet and maliciously comic episode in which the American lady tries to adapt her flamboyant personality to life in an *ashram*.

Ivory followed *Bombay Talkie* with his first feature film made outside India. *Savages* (1971) was made in America. It is a kind of reversed *Admirable Crichton*, in which a crowd of primitives are lured into an early 20th century mansion – deserted but fully equipped and furnished – and there gradually evolve a pattern of society suitable to the setting. This builds up to an elaborate dinner party in the exact style of the Twenties which is the set-piece of the film; after which, mysteriously, the ephemeral 'civilization' disintegrates, and the characters revert to savagery again. *Savages* had a *succès d'estime* during the Directors' Week at the Cannes Festival in 1972.

XII

It was during the Sixties that a new name from Japan began to impinge on the West. Nagisa Oshima in fact made his first feature in 1959; and since then he has to his credit sixteen more features and a number of television programmes, mostly documentary. Few of his films have been widely seen in Europe or America,[1] but those that have provide enough evidence to indicate that he is an artist of great importance and unique individuality. He is frequently really brutal and horrifying, sometimes with straight realism, as in the suicide image in *The Sun's Burial* (1960), and sometimes on a Godardian pattern (e.g.

[1] He was virtually unknown until *Death by Hanging* was snown (out of competition) at Cannes in 1968.

Weekend) as in parts of *Death by Hanging* (1968) and *Diary of a Shinjuku Thief* (also 1968).

The last named film was indeed made very much under the influence of Godard; its structure recalls *Deux Ou Trois Choses que Je Sais d'Elle*. This, together with its essentially Japanese approach to life, makes it a bewildering film even after several viewings. It becomes easier to understand when you realize that the Kara Juro who appears at the beginning is in fact a real person who runs a modern theatre group which wants 'to take kabuki back to the primitive form in which it originated'.[1] Beyond this, the film, in a sporadic manner, follows the search for a satisfactory mutual orgasm by a boy (with a Jean Genet-disguised name of Birdey Hilltop) who begins by sublimating his sex into book-stealing, and a girl bookstore attendant who catches him at it. Their pilgrimage covers a wide variety of episodes – shot sometimes in colour and sometimes in black and white – which include a splendid observation of activities within a brothel which, among other things, employs three men to sit on the roof with hoses to simulate a rainstorm and thus make the clients reluctant to go home; a gloriously ridiculous interview with a sex-psychologist; and a whizzing street chase ending in violence and rape (committeed incidentally and gratuitously by the three men off the brothel roof) which presages Kubrick's *A Clockwork Orange*. Throughout the film sexual details, particularly those appertaining to menstruation – are explicit. There are also a number of irritating elements such as Godardian subtitles and cutaways to clocks showing the time in different parts of the world.[2] *Diary of a Shinjuku Thief* is powerful and in its own way fascinating; but in the last resort it fails because it lacks heart.

In *Boy* (*Shonen*), made in the following year, the conflicts with society of *Diary of a Shinjuku Thief* are simplified and concentrated into one simple situation, though Oshima's treatment is not so simple as might at first appear. As in the previous film there are dislocations and lapses in continuity; and in one sequence involving a motor accident in which a girl is killed the presentation is so ambivalent as to raise the question of whether we are to understand it as really happening as we see it, or as a subjective experience seen through the eyes and imagination of one of the characters.

Apart from all this *Boy* is a sensitive study of the relationships within a small family living off a simple and repetitive crime. The

---

[1] See Ian Cameron's comprehensive study of Oshima (as far as *Boy*) in *Second Wave* (Studio Vista, 1970.)

[2] But there is a nice moment when the girl goes berserk and smashes one of them.

father, with his son by his first wife, and the second wife, with a smaller son from her previous husband, between them build a rackety pattern of life round their petty trick – that of simulating having been knocked down by an automobile, and thereupon frightening the driver into parting with a lot of hush money on the spot. The elder boy is found by his stepmother to be even better at this job than she is, so he is put on to it whole time. Oshima makes us participate in his childish yet in its small, proud way professional attitude to this difficult and often risky task, as well as in his fantasies about a Cosmic Man or Saviour from Andromeda in Outer Space.

The boy alone: the boy in relation to his little half-brother, to his father, and above all to his stepmother whom, because of their special complicity in the job, he begins to love: the boy as a member of a familial group haunted by the necessity of always moving on before they are rumbled, and bemused by wild dreams of 'having a good time': but above all the boy solitary – Oshima tellingly combines all these factors into a study of a victimized child (marvellously played by little Tetsuo Abe with a deceptively deadpan style which appallingly crumples from time to time into overt emotion).

The film opens with the boy playing a dream-game on his own in a small and deserted temple. Later in the film he runs away in a vain attempt to rejoin his distant granny; he hasn't enough money for the trip and, thrown off the train in a strange town, cries himself to sleep on a darkling beach. (It is typical of Oshima that the next we see of him is back with his family, with no explanation of how.)[1] And at the end of the film, when the family, having given up the racket and settled down to respectability, are at last caught up with by the police, it is he who steadfastly refuses to testify against them. In this his efforts to resolve his solitude by initiatives of action or of imagination all come to naught; and as the family is carted off to justice his small memories are shown to us in flashback. But in fact he has done and said everything earlier when, with his little half-brother, he builds a snowman (the Cosmic Man of course) and enshrines in it his wristwatch and a shoe worn by the girl killed in the car accident. But the symbol and the two talismans fail him. Methodically he sets about destroying the snowman, and here Oshima – using Cinemascope as ever with great mastery – gradually translates the scene into slower and slower motion as Hikaru Hayashi's music slowly fades into a silent desolation equal to that of the visual.

---

[1] I have been told that Oshima meant this sequence to be taken as a dream; it doesn't seem to be shot as such.

Of *The Ceremony* (1971) it may be said that its construction, compared with that of *Diary of a Shinjuku Thief*, is pellucidly simple; but this does not by any means imply that it is an easy film to understand. There is here some sort of a barrier to understanding which earlier directors like Mizoguchi, Ozu and Kurosawa have managed to surmount, so that what they say in purely Japanese terms becomes largely intelligible to the Western viewer with the result that, however superficially, he feels able to identify with the quite exotic culture, customs, and indeed emotions which are being shown. Similarly the *mores* in a film like Shindo's *The Island* (1960) allow of identification. However unbelievable the total acceptance of unrelieved and perhaps unnecessary drudgery may be, the very simplicity of the action, and of the virtual absence of a time-sense outside the constantly repeated actions, makes the behaviourism acceptable. Similarly too, Hiroshi Teshigahara's extraordinary *Woman of the Dunes* – a kind of duologue of doom – comes across to us quite clearly as a parable of the problem of evil and of personal responsibility. And, even though we may miss many *nuances* in Masaki Kobayashi's ghostly *Kwaidan*, the beauty, the fear, and the humour of its fairy-tale stories become universal.

With *The Ceremony*, on the other hand, one has at first the tantalizing feeling of watching the equivalent of the *Forsyte Saga* without having the key to the traditions which inhabit the customs and behaviour of those concerned. Oshima's Sakurada family, seen over a period of twenty-five years, is clearly dominated by the powerful and incestuous figure of the grandfather in whose shadow the film's hero, Masuo Sakurada, grows from childhood into manhood. The saga is related in a series of perfectly comprehensible flashbacks as Masuo and one of his girl cousins travel across Japan to an island house in which another cousin (male) has just committed suicide. There is a great deal of voice-over narration which superimposed subtitles cannot convey in sufficient detail; but on the other hand the general effect is helped by the fact that Masuo's memories are all fixated on climactic ceremonial moments in the life of the Sakurada family. In the end the power of the direction, of the acting by a large cast headed by Kenzo Kawarazaki as Masuo, and of Toichiro Narushima's superb wide screen camerawork, takes complete grip and, even where some precise meaning or motivation eludes us, projects those heightened emotions which are universally recognizable in the celebrations of birth and marriage and death.

The Ceremony is full of memorable images. The young Masuo with his ear to the earth listening for the breathing of his dead (perhaps murdered) baby brother; a girl giving a boy a lesson in sex; and some moments of uproarious humour as when, at a funeral wake, the domineering grandfather forgets the words of his Old School Song, or when the communist bride of one of the Sakuradas bursts out with *The Red Flag* during the wedding ceremony. The final sequence, when the two young people reach the island and find Tadashi's body, has an exquisite dying fall. The girl, simply, almost naturally and with a casual confidence, kills herself beside him. Masuo, alone, gradually populates the shore and the lakeside with images from his childhood on; and, as in the ending of many Mizoguchi films, the fact of death seems somehow to become irrelevant.

Oshima claims that *The Ceremony* is meant to be something of a review or even a questioning of the spiritual development of the Japanese people since the end of the war. He remarks that

'during ceremonies Japanese are possessed of particularly delicate emotions, emotions often completely unrelated to their daily lives. Ceremonies are a time when the special characteristics of the Japanese spirit are revealed. It is this spirit that concerns and worries me; my own spirit, which wavers during such occasions. One might easily reject, both intellectually and emotionally, militarism and xenophobic nationalism in daily life. But these forces, once beyond the realm of daily life, are not so easily denied.'

and it is interesting to note that Eric Rhode, accepting this point of view *en principe*, expresses the view that the film's obscurities are 'necessary rather than wilful', and that 'to have summarised the post-war psychic history of the country in such a fascinating way seems to me both bold and worthwhile'. He adds, not without reason, 'Is *The Entertainer* the best we can achieve along these lines over here?'[1]

Oshima's explanation must of course be accepted, even if it may seem over-simplistic. What is more important perhaps is that from the characters he has created, and from their relationships seen in a fine continuing flow of conflicts, of doubts, of changing personal loyalties or of tentative comings together, he has made the most important Japanese film of this decade and maybe the next.[2]

---

[1] *The Listener*, May 11th, 1972.

[2] In 1971 a new young director appeared who bid fair to overpass with some ease the iconoclasms of *The Diary of a Shinjuku Thief*. Shuji Terayama's *Throw Away Your Books, Let's Go into the Streets* is a fascinating post-Godard, almost post-Makavejev hotchpotch which indicates a real sense of cinema as well as a considerable absence of discipline. Terayama carries alienation and distantiation to agreeably distracting extremes in detailing (sometimes autobiographically) the dilemmas of a young drop-out trying to emulate

XIII

The Third World is a convenient umbrella phrase which, film-wise, can be used equally to cover internally made films, often revolutionary in intent; scientific – and especially ethnographic – studies of native and aboriginal life; and productions by the richer nations, often through the United Nations and its Agencies, which explore and explain the urgent needs of those parts of the world which are overpopulated, undereducated, and therefore almost certainly starving.

Of this latter category countless films, some general and some highly technical, have been and are being made; their extent may be found from the catalogues of Unesco, WHO, FAO and the like, as well as from those of various national information services. Out of all these one, for me, remains outstanding.[1] James Blue's modestly titled *A Few Notes on our Food Problem* (1966–68) has good claim, through the force of its message and its cinematic beauty, to be regarded as one of the few really great documentaries. Its subject is the future (or otherwise) of mankind as seen in terms of food production and the population explosion; its basic object is to draw our attention – and the attention in particular of the governmental and wealthier classes in the developing countries – to the fact that peasants and farmers do not produce few or no crops through stupidity or bloodymindedness but through ignorance and through lack of access to the proper means of production.

Blue, having possessed himself of all the facts and statistics and arguments, constructed his film from original shooting in Africa, Asia and the New World in the form of a poem infused with passion and compassion, anger and hope, and above all a feeling for the real goodness to be found everywhere in ordinary folk. This film never stands outside its subject. African villagers shake hands with the camera and therefore with us. In India a small farmer tells us through an interpreter, and with indignation, how officialdom looks like ruining his new and larger rice harvest by neglect of his needs for such things as fertilizers. With a smile full of warm and loving humour a young

---

Icarus by re-creating the legend in his own terms. Terayama is no fool, and filmically is respectful and old-fashioned enough to understand the value of a carefully placed *coup de foudre*, as witness the staggering visual climax to the sequence in the whore's bedroom. His previous short film, *Emperor Tomato Ketchup*, smothers a good idea in smut.

[1] Though, on a somewhat different level, Peter Hopkinson's *African Awakening* (1963) is, in its imaginative approach, a model of its kind.

South American lab-assistant confides to us the problems of soil analysis.

Blue even illustrates his theme through episodes like that of the little Indian girls who are learning endurance and industry through the intricate *mudras* of their dance. But over all this, throughout the film, is the sense of multitudes of mouths to be fed and of a multitude of men and women longing to bring from a pregnant earth enough produce to satisfy every one of those mouths. *A Few Notes on our Food Problem* is not just a powerful warning of impending disaster; it is also a triumphant assertion of the marvellous potentiality of Man. This beautiful and moving film was financed by the Government of the United States, and all honour to it for so doing. How it can be reconciled with the devastation of Vietnam is another question.[1]

The Sixties saw an uprising of film-making in Africa, where the old colonial information services had, in some areas, established facilities which newly independent governments could take over and use for education, and see to it that exponents of indigenous culture could gain access at last to the means of film production.

Thus it was that in Senegal – with the example and often the physically-present stimulus of Jean Rouch – directors like Ousman Sembéne could start to make movies. Sembéne began with short documentaries like *Borom Saret* (1964), about a day in the life of a barrowboy in Dakar, or *Niaye* (1965), a description of life in a coastal village. Then in 1966 he made a feature film of considerable significance, *La Noire de . . .* This brutally simple story of a Senegalese girl who got a job in France as a domestic and, thanks to various grim incompatibilities, was driven to suicide, was hailed by Georges Sadoul as a presage of a great stride forward in African film-making. Whether this was immediately achieved is another matter. Sembéne's next film, *Mandabi* (1968), was a somewhat clumsy comedy about the problems of cashing a money order in face of a barrage of red-tape; while from other African nations not much has emerged, though in 1970 the distinguished Nigerian poet and dramatist Wole Soyinka announced that he was teaming up with the American negro Ossie Davis[2] on a major

---

[1] Another noble documentary is Noriaki Tsuchimoto's *Minamata* (1972), a long and remorseless description, much of it in *cinéma-vérité* style, of the hideous sickness and death brought to a fishing community by mercury effluent from a near-by factory. As terrifying in its implications as the Thalidomide scandal, *Minamata* shows how, over a period of years, the victims gradually managed to organize themselves to seek justice, and in the end invaded a shareholders meeting dressed in funeral robes.

[2] Davis, remembered for his powerful performance in Lumet's *The Hill*, turned up, as we shall see later, as a director in *Cotton Comes to Harlem*.

production called *Kongi's Harvest* – a screen version of Soyinka's play about a once sincere African politician being changed by the corruption of newly-found power into a ruthless dictator and then, in due and predictable course, being thrown out by the Army. This by now familiar story would need, no doubt, a certain tact as well as the imagination and skill which the principals could doubtless supply.

From other African nations there was little to report, other than locally useful but run-of-the-mill documentaries from the Government Film Units of countries such as Ghana, Kenya and Uganda. As for South Africa, nothing had emerged from that unhappy country since Lionel Rogosin's *Come Back Africa* of 1959, until there appeared in 1970 *Phela-Ndaba* (*End of Dialogue*), made equally secretly by members of the Pan African Congress. *Phela-Ndaba* is about the working of apartheid as seen exclusively from the point of view of the black. With a sort of cold anger which is all the more effective for its restraint, it specifies visually – partly in colour and with camerawork which is, not surprisingly, variable – some of the operations of this quintessentially stupid and eventually self-destructive system. The images do not deal with violence, though the film ends with a long, sad rollcall (in blood-red letters) of the many Africans done to death in Afrikaans gaols. The images are effective just because they reveal the virulence of the system through the small, everyday commonplaces. What comes across even more tellingly than the contrasts between servants and masters or the notices on park seats, railway compartments or toilets, is the appalling insensitivity and sometimes the obvious sense of suspicious insecurity seen on the faces of the so-called whites (usually an unpleasant shade of puce) registered by concealed African cameras as they pass along urban streets. That a film like *Phela-Ndaba* can still somehow get made and distributed is one of the hopes and glories of the motion-picture.

One of the more dramatic developments of this decade was the proliferation of movies in Latin America. From Argentina in 1960 came Leopoldo Torre Nilsson's *The Hand in the Trap* (*La Mano en la Trampa*), a bodeful, atmospheric and sometimes melodramatic film of bourgeois society which established his particularly obsessive and obsessing style, seen subsequently in *The Roof Garden* (1963) and in particular *The Eavesdropper* (1965), a claustrophobic study of the mind of Fascism as expressed in the person of a young terrorist hiding out from the police in a dilapidated old hotel full of equally dilapidated guests.

Torre Nilsson's influence was reflected to a degree in Edgardo

Cozarinsky's compulsive study of a priest with ultra-right-wing views – so ultra that even his own church rejects him. This film, maddeningly entitled "...." and made in 1971, has passages during which, as in *The Ceremony*, one feels one is missing something through not understanding certain nuances of Argentinian social life; but, also like *The Ceremony*, it remains visually interesting and often exciting.

In Cuba soon after the Revolution there appeared a number of not unnaturally rather tentative films, plus some celebrations from directors from other countries, notably Chris Marker's *Cuba Si!* The production of feature films soon developed, however, and in 1968 a really remarkable film emerged, bearing the rather unpromising title of *Memories of Underdevelopment*. With a highly personal style (and perhaps with a sidelong look at Godard), Tomas Gutierrez Alea here studied a Laodicean member of the Cuban middle-class who, unlike most of his fellows, did not flee to the fleshpots of Florida but remained behind to see what would happen and whether he could adjust himself to the new situation. Wandering around his luxury flat or through Havana streets, Sergio – with an endearing tendency to yawn – relives in his mind's eye some fiendish rows with his estranged and absent wife, indulges in some velleities regarding the girl who cleans the flat, picks up a girl in the street and beds her, attends political meetings and indulges in desultory arguments with others and with himself.

Much of the film is very funny, not least when the girl's family charge him with rape. During a climactic and hysterical (in all senses) court scene, Sergio, voice over, meditates '*I* am too educated to be innocent. *They* are too ignorant to be guilty.' He is acquitted, though.

Alea uses his camera, and especially the zoom, in a fascinatingly relaxed manner. Indeed the fact that the film is extremely leisurely but never boring or over-long is one of its greatest merits. It is also much to the credit of the Castro regime that it accepted the making of a film of this sort, which deliberately doesn't take sides, and which discusses the difficulties of a bourgeois intellectual in coming to terms with a people's revolution; there is incidentally a very amusing sequence when two officials – a man and a woman – come to enquire about the occupancy of his apartment and, while rather sniffily casing the joint, make it quite clear he won't be living alone there much longer.

Alea properly ends the film on a question-mark. The Cuban Missile Crisis is at its height. Sergio's mind is dark with doubt and confusion (earlier in the film he has remarked, 'I keep my mind clear – a disagreeable emptiness'); and there we leave him, uncertain still, as dawn breaks over Havana – a dawn which, for all he knows, may herald a nuclear war.[1]

Meantime from Brazil emerged a whole new school of film-makers on whom, for once, Godard's influence seems to have been positive and beneficial. Ruy Guerra's *The Guns* (*Os Fuzis*), made in 1964, compressed into a small and crowded area a whole compendium of communist theory and practice. The story of a small group of soldiers sent to a provincial town to prevent hungry peasants from eating food supplies earmarked for the Big City, it is violent, action-packed and unequivocal. Guerra followed this with a strange, slow film, made apparently as a Panamanian-American co-production, called *The Sweet Hunters* (1969). It was badly received at Venice, though described by Tom Milne as 'haunting, unhurried, operatic; a masterpiece or a disaster, depending on how it hits you'.[2] Next year Guerra returned to the style of *The Guns* with a magnificently photographed study of the conflict between two powerful landowners in the Nordeste area of Brazil – *The Gods and the Dead* (*Os Deuses e Os Mortos*).

But the most important of the Latin American directors is without doubt Glauber Rocha. Savage, comic, violent, tragic, his films are infused with a burning sincerity which his enormous film-making talents can superbly (though sometimes at too great a length) express. Michel Ciment has pointed out that 'a film by Rocha is at once a story and a poem',[3] and it is as well to approach his films, like Dovzhenko's, with this in mind. To combine the poetry and the story he often uses Godardian techniques – fragmenting his images, juxtaposing them against true time and order, but keeping them always understandable because rooted in the sense of a people's, a nation's tragic and turbulent past. The conflicts, past and present, between landowners and peasants, church and communism, bandits and police, are all enveloped by Rocha in the great cloak of folk-history – its legends, its symbols and above all its music.

Martins, the hero of *Terra im Transe* (1967), begins where Sergio in *Memories of Underdevelopment* leaves off. Sergio is trying to come to terms with the new life around him. Martins, a poet, is suddenly faced with the agonizing fact that the events of his life – the things he

---

[1] From Cuba, also in 1971, came Manuel Octavio Gomez' *The Days of Water*, a story of a woman with apparently miraculous powers which, like Ray's *Devi* and Peries' *Rekava*, had poignancy as well as some highly dramatic episodes. Meantime in 1971 Alea came up with a satire – *Death of a Bureaucrat*.

[2] *Sight and Sound*, Autumn 1969.

[3] *Second Wave*, Studio Vista, 1970.

has done and the things he has lived through – have been illusory or wrongly understood. 'Now' he seems to say, 'now and only now I can see it all' – and the film is in fact a fantastic jigsaw of his memories of political and other happenings and of his too-late desire to alter or adjust them, at least in relation to his own attitudes. Sometimes strictly realistic, sometimes symbolic in the sense that Buñuel in *L'Age d'Or* is symbolic, *Terra im Transe*, with its contradictions, its black humour, its restless camera and cutting, its characters reminiscent of the people used to represent Capitalism or Militarism in early Soviet films, grips you from start to finish not so much by the elbow as by the throat.

Antonio das Mortes (1969), Rocha's first film in colour (ravishingly realized by Alfonso Beato), is in effect a sequel to his *Black God, White Devil* (*Deus e o Diablo na Terra del Sol*) made four years earlier. Both films are set in the Sertão area of the Nordeste, and both are concerned with facts and legends about the *cangaceiros*, the 'honourable bandits', who were finally wiped out by the Brazilian authorities in 1940. It is in *Black God, White Devil* that Antonio das Mortes, who kills *cangaceiros* for cash, finally slays the blond Corisco, himself a disciple of the greatest *cangaceiro* of them all, Lampiaio. But who is really dead, and when? At the beginning of the film entitled *Antonio das Mortes*,[1] we find Antonio – huge, sinister, dark-cloaked – setting off once again into the Sertão, with the full approval of the authorities, to find out whether, as it is rumoured, there still remains there a solitary follower of Lampiaio. The film is built around this quest, and around the legend of Saint George who slew the Dragon and rescued the Lady. Veering from the 'reality' of a village morality play to melodramas of intrigues and mindless murders, with the daggers of *Macbeth* multiplied a hundredfold and massacres in a whorl-like convolution of rocky nature from which the camera zooms back to show it as a cockle-shell in the whole landscape of hell, *Antonio das Mortes* confronts you with the 'Aesthetic of Violence' propounded by Rocha:

'The most authentic cultural manifestation of hunger is *violence* . . . Violence is the normal behaviour of a hungry man, but the violence of the hungry is not primitivism; the aesthetic of violence, before it is primitive, is revolutionary. It is the moment when the colonizer first notices the existence of the colonized.'[2]

Thus Rocha's mauve-clad Lady Macbeth moves among the sordid village houses in intrigues with her protector, an old blind landowner,

[1] Its alternative title is *O Santo Guerreiro Contra O Dragoa da Maldade*, that is, *The Holy Warrior Against the Dragon of Evil*.
[2] *Second Wave*, Studio Vista, 1970.

her lover, a shabby police-chief, and a tipsy educationist, all of whom belong in their own ways to the worlds of Dostoievsky, of Tchehov and of Joseph Conrad. And none of it is illogical. *Antonio das Mortes* carries you along on a torrent of visuals and sounds (the track is of almost incredible richness), and leaves you illuminated by gorgeous images such as that of the tall negro Saint George, clad in scarlet silk and riding a white horse with the Holy Lady on his crupper, thrusting his lance not at a real dragon but at a fading and blind old capitalist – and all this during a gun-battle on a sloping village square which overlooks an infinity of stunning landscape.

A year later, on the other side of the world, there appeared from, of all countries, Egypt, a film which, just as surely as did *Pather Panchali*, announced the appearance of a major new film-maker. This was *The Night of Counting the Years* (also known as *The Mummies*), completed in 1970 by Shadi Abdelsalam under difficulties very similar to those experienced by Satyajit Ray nearly twenty years earlier – indifference, jealousy, and official opposition. Had it not been for the vigorous pressures exercised by Rossellini (to whom Abdelsalam pays generous tribute in his credit titles), this film might never have reached the screen.[1]

It is interesting to note that Vachel Lindsay, the first serious film critic, saw the cinema at one point in relation to the Pharaonic caves and hieroglyphs of Ancient Egypt. Writing in 1915 he said of the movie theatre:

> 'Now we have a darkness on which we can paint, an unspoilt twilight . . . There is a tomb we might have definitely in mind, an Egyptian burying place where with a torch we might enter, read the

---

[1] The comparatively large Egyptian film industry – established in the early 1920s and nationalized in 1952 – has for many years fed the Levantine world with films whose quality has not led to their circulation in wider fields (the Levantines themselves are now reported to be getting restless); the films are made to well-worn formulae and often with well-worn stars. Exceptions have been films made by outside directors like Jacques Baratier with his admirable *Goha* (1956), various documentaries from Shell and similar sources before the Revolution and, more recently, two films by the New Zealander John Feeney – *Fountains of the Sun* (1967), a finely shot cinemascope documentary feature on the Nile, and *The Eighth Wonder* (1972), being the story of Abu Simbel. From indigenous sources may be noted Yusuf Shahin's admirable and sincere *The Land* (1970). It was Shahin who discovered and nurtured Egypt's gift to romantic cinema, Omar Sharif, who had made some 22 films in Egypt (including *Goha*) before appearing in Lean's *Lawrence of Arabia*. One may also note some promising short films of recent date, such as A. Fahmi's footloose picture of modern youth, *A New Life*; *The Flute*, a beautiful musical evocation by I. Farghal (since alas killed in a road accident); and, not least, films made by students of the High Cinema Institute, such as Ahmad Yassin's very sensitive and moving *Round Trip*, and Atiat Abnoudi's *Horse of Mud*.

inscriptions, and see the illustrations from the Book of the Dead on the wall, or finding that ancient papyrus in the mummy-case, unroll it and show it to the eager assembly, and have the feeling of return. Man is an Egyptian first, before he is any other type of civilized being. The Nile flows through his heart. So let this cave be Egypt, let us incline to revere the unconscious memories that echo within us . . . Egypt was our long brooding youth. We built the mysteriousness of the Universe into the Pyramids, carved it into every line of the Sphinx.'[1]

In a strange and powerful way Abdelsalam has brought Lindsay's allegory to real cinematic life. From its opening sequence of the experts in conference under shaded lights around a baize table, with Mario Nascimbene's eerily appropriate music – a succession of long held chords – backing the archaeologists' talk, *The Night of Counting the Years* moves with absolute assurance of purpose and total command of technique. Abdel Aziz Fahmy's colour photography, whether of the dark cave interiors or of the shattering light contrasts of the desert and the river and the rocky hills, is of the highest order, and the direction of a fine cast led by the young and talented Ahmed Marei is magisterial. And, in addition to Nascimbene's score, the soundtrack is marvellous – lacerated by the desert winds, dozing in the lapping of the great river, and urgent with the constant, insistent bird songs amid the gigantic ruins.

The story is set at the end of the 19th century and is based on fact. A tribe has for years been living on the proceeds of grave robberies from a vast mountain cave into which many mummies of the Pharaohs had been secretly moved, centuries ago, to protect against this very eventuality. After the funeral of their father two brothers are initiated into the secret, but are horrified when they see their uncle desecrate one of the mummies and realize that this is the source of their communal prosperity. The elder brother protests and refuses to accept this way of life. To preserve the secret, they murder him. Wanniss, the younger brother, wanders away torn with conflicting thoughts – unstable, anxious, guilty.

The predatory antique-dealers from Cairo (who are only too anxious to doublecross each other) arrive on their annual visit, and

---

[1] *The Art of the Moving Picture* by Vachel Lindsay (New Edition by Liveright, New York, 1970). In connection with this quotation it may be interesting to note that Abdelsalam's epigraph for his film comes from the Egyptian *Book of the Dead*, as follows:

'Though Thou Goest . . . Thou Comest Again
'Though Thou Sleepest . . . Thou Wakest Again
'Though Thou Diest . . . Thou Livest Again'

approach Wanniss, whom they know to be the heir to the mysterious source of Pharaonic gems. Meantime Wanniss becomes friendly with a young stranger who is looking for a job with the Effendis from the Cairo Museum – an Egyptologist and his mounted police-guard – who have come to try to uncover the thieves.

After a series of intrigues the young stranger gets beaten up. Wanniss makes up his mind that he cannot countenance his tribe's and his family's sacrilegious way of life. And then he learns of his brother's murder. He confronts the chief Cairo dealer and says he is going to blow the gaff. For this he in his turn is badly beaten up. Nevertheless, he approaches in fear and trembling the great, brightly lit, effendi steamboat, is admitted aboard, and tells the whole story. The hoard is found by the Egyptologists, and they decide to remove the mummies to the boat at once. There ensues a fantastic pre-dawn procession across the rocky crags and down to the river; and the film ends with Wanniss alone, bloodstained, shivering in misery on the banks of the Nile. He has lost his family and his tribe. He is of no further interest to the Effendis sailing off back to Cairo in their shining vessel with their precious finds. His small figure wanders slowly away as the wash of the steamer slaps lazily against the reeds on the river bank in the foreground. Justice has been done, but not to him.

All this is unfolded by Abdelsalam in a slow, majestic, hieratic pace which in other hands might be unbearable, but under his discipline is both thrilling and suspenseful. The moments of crisis and action, which occur without warning and are often underplayed or truncated in mid-movement, come on us as shockingly as those in *Gertrud*. In one particular instance, the beating up of Wanniss is cut off almost as soon as it has begun, and we are switched to a shot of him lying spread-eagled, unconscious and alone on the sand; the shot is taken vertically from above and from a considerable height, and the effect is shattering, not least since in this flat location by the river the shot seems a physical impossibility and therefore has an almost supernatural quality.

After *The Night of Counting the Years*, Shadi Abdelsalam made a two-reeler called *The Eloquent Peasant*, again with Marei in the chief part. This actual story from an ancient papyrus had all the qualities of the other film, including the extraordinarily effective camera angles, as when Abdelsalam plunges his camera into the sand, just as in *Ugetsu Monogatari* Mizoguchi plunges his camera into the surface of the lake water.

Another new director who, despite initial approval seemed to be without honour in his own country, was the Iranian Daryush Mehrjui, whose *Gav* (*The Cow*) created a great impression at the Venice and London Festivals in 1968, and of whose *Postman* (1971) Alexander Walker wrote, 'Mehrjui's gift lies in marvellously human sympathies with his characters and the funny-pathetic side of their obsessions. Not since Michael Cacoyannis came into sight in the 1950s have I met a more prodigiously talented newcomer'.[1]

XIV

In the Sixties the process of natural selection finally caught up with Hollywood. The tycoons who had for so long dominated the American, and indeed the world's screens, had for some time been a dying race. Now only a few were left[2] and, like the dinosaurs of old, they could do no more than continue their own way of life, even though it was by now self-destructive.

During the long conflict with Television some accommodations had been arrived at – not least in terms of the sale of old movies to the networks at, to begin with, grossly inflated prices. Simultaneously there grew up in Hollywood a second movie industry concerned with the production of series films which appeared in packages of mystical numbers – 13, 26, 39. The highspeed approach to film-making which these series required was something to which established producers found it difficult to adapt. By 1962, out of some one hundred filmed TV series produced in Hollywood, only twenty-six came from the old majors like Warner, Columbia, MGM and Twentieth Century-Fox. It was the big Agent companies (originally the representatives of top actors, directors, writers etc, but now consolidated into much wider areas) like MCA – through its subsidiary Revue Productions – or new TV whizz-kids like Lucille Ball and Desi Arnaz (who astonishingly acquired the RKO Studios and renamed them Desilu) who were the real exploiters of this new and highly profitable mass market. Thus the sort of money which the old companies had for so long made from a steady supply of B pictures – the real bread and butter of the industry – was being diverted before their eyes, changed in form but not in content (unless somewhat for the worse), into other hands.

But the tycoons and their current successors still believed that

---

[1] *Evening Standard*, May 18th, 1972.
[2] Including Zukor, who in 1973 celebrated his 100th birthday.

the big profits were in the big pictures. Behind them in the Fifties lay the memories of the big gambles – some successful, like CinemaScope, VistaVision and Cinerama, some failures, like 3 D – and ahead of them lay a prospect of increasing uncertainty; for the big picture always involves a gamble at the box-office. 'If *Ben Hur* had failed, MGM would have gone bankrupt. If *Spartacus* had failed Universal would have been in a very shaky condition. The budget of *Cleopatra* carried with it the fate of Twentieth Century-Fox.'[1]

Despite a contracting foreign market, despite the huge successes of low-budget pictures like *Marty* and *Twelve Angry Men*, despite the increasing tendency of runaway producers to make their pictures on comparatively inexpensive overseas locations instead of in costly California, the dinosaurs still persisted in their old ways. And by the mid-Sixties it even looked as though they might be right.

In 1962 Twentieth Century-Fox had lost nearly $40 million – this on top of a $48 million loss during the previous three years – and was keeping going by selling real estate. Meantime 'in Rome, production had started on *Cleopatra*[2] which began to sop up money faster than Fox could pour it in . . . Bankruptcy threatened, the sound stages were closed, the parking lots were empty. Spyros Skouras was fired as President, and Darryl Zanuck . . . was elected to take his place and save the sinking ship.'[3]

Five years later Zanuck presided over a stockholders meeting at which the gross revenue of Fox was reported as over $225 million, with net profit after taxation at $12\frac{1}{2}$ million. Current capital investment ncluded 30 feature films at various stages of production; while for Television (for Fox had at last caught up with this new market) there were ten shows covering nine hours of prime-time viewing. A dividend of $4.28 on each share in the company left the stockholders, to say the least of it, content.

[1] See *Hollywood in Transition* by Richard Dyer McCann (Houghton Mifflin, 1962) for a general study of the situation during the Fifties and at the start of the Sixties. McCann points out, among other things, that in those days producers were still banking on the mirage of Pay Television, that 'chance for colossal box-office returns in a single night . . . with its wonderful prospect of bypassing the costs of prints and distribution to theatres'. Now, years later, the talk is of Cassettes.

[2] An example of how *not* to organize a runaway production. Before Rome, Fox had built Alexandria on the lot at Pinewood Studios, England, and very sad the buildings looked in the cold damp fog of November. It is impossible to imagine how grown men could have landed themselves in such a piece of lunacy.

[3] *The Studio* by John Gregory Dunne, W. H. Allen, 1970. Dunne, a worthy successor to Lillian Ross, provides a scarifying and sometimes highly comic play by play description of the period during which Fox was involved in making, among others, *Dr Dolittle, Star!*, *The Boston Strangler, Hello, Dolly*, and *Valley of the Dolls*.

Behind this dramatic reversal of fortune lay in fact just one film – the most successful film ever made (overpassing even *Gone With the Wind*). By 1967 *The Sound of Music* had already grossed nearly $100 million and was still going strong. Its production cost had been $18 million.

Four years later, at an annual general meeting at which a net profit for the first quarter of 1971 of $4½ million, plus a vague forecast of some further profit in the full year, had to be placed against losses of $25 million and $77 million in 1969 and 1970, the stockholders threw the Zanucks, *père et fils*, off the Board, and handed the affairs of Twentieth Century-Fox to an expert company lawyer, who instituted a regime of low-budget movies – thirteen at $3 million or less each, and one at 'approximately' (there we go again!) $5 million.

Meantime MGM was also in poor shape, having revealed a loss of $35 million the previous year; part of this, though, was due to the cancellation by MGM's latest new broom, James Aubrey, of fifteen films already in production (including Malraux's *Man's Fate* on which Fred Zinnemann had already spent $3 million) as 'poor box-office risks'. By 1970 most of MGM's studio space had been disposed of, and there was a nostalgic sale of costumes and props, with entries like 'One Hat – Greta Garbo' or 'Dress, blue/white gingham – Judy Garland, *Wizard of Oz*'. In 1972 David Gordon of *The Economist* estimated that the total write-offs of the major Hollywood companies over the previous few years amounted to no less than $422 million.

What had happened? In the case of Fox (and it was in general typical) the answer was quite simple. Blindly, faithfully, Zanuck, on the strength of *The Sound of Music*, led his colleagues and stockholders towards a promised land of more and greater musicals, each one of which would cost around $20 million and each one of which would make a vast profit. Unfortunately the promised land wasn't there. The musicals were *Doctor Dolittle* (1967), *Star!* (1968) and *Hello, Dolly* (1969); and to these must be added the equally expensive and disastrous co-production with Japan, *Tora! Tora! Tora!* (1969). Even if all or any of those films were eventually to get itself out of the red, the day of the blockbuster must soon be over, and for good. It is a solemn thought that the great success of more modestly budgeted Fox pictures of the same period, for example Franklin Schaffner's *Planet of the Apes* or George Roy Hill's *Butch Cassidy and the Sundance Kid*, could not avert disaster.

Of course the lesson to be learnt – or rather relearnt – from the Sixties was the obvious one; good stories, good screenwriting and direction, and low or modest budgets could provide the answer to any company's problems. But the lesson was still not learnt.

Peter Fonda and Dennis Hopper came up with a film called *Easy Rider* – a picaresque drift by motor-bike across the United States, ending in savagery and horror with a dramatic and breathtaking helicopter shot. This film cost $400,000, won the hearts of a generation, and is estimated to have grossed some $30 million. The big boys had a look at this phenomenon and tried to do the same thing. One of the results was *Zabriskie Point*,[1] which was not only very expensive but was also made by a middle-aged Italian who was not really able to identify with the audiences which had taken *Easy Rider* to their hearts because in style, subject and attitude it identified exactly with their feelings.[2] *Zabriskie Point*, technically superb, remained outside.

Not all the small budget successors to *Easy Rider*, with their often rough technique, their extremely unglamorous leading players and stories, were successful either. But enough of them made the grade for Hollywood to realize that 'Make it for under a Million' might be a good motto. When Al Ruddy and Sidney Furie were making *Little Fauss and Big Halsy* (1970), they thought of shooting a motel scene in the Paramount studio. They found it would cost $6,000–$8,000. 'Instead, we rented a couple of rooms at a Los Angeles motel. It cost us $100 and, even better, the set was real.'[3] Since then, we may note, Ruddy has come up with one of the biggest box-office successes of the past ten years – *The Godfather*, a story about the Mafia directed by Francis Ford Coppola.[4]

There is another point to remember. Mike Nichols' film *The Graduate* (1967) had no really important box-office names. But it made a star out of Dustin Hoffman and it grossed $43 million. Hoffman received $20,000 for his performance. As a result of this and similar examples, as well as of increasing tightness in the supply of production money, both front-office and actors have tended to go for modest fees plus a good percentage of the take should the film be successful. It is said that Sidney Poitier's 10% of the gross on *To Sir with Love* may be as much as $3 million; on this reckoning, if Dustin Hoffman had had a similar arrangement on *The Graduate* he would have got even more.

---

[1] Another was a campus story, *The Strawberry Statement* (1970), which also missed the point by going mushy.

[2] In 1970 it was estimated that 62% of movie-goers were between twelve and thirty years of age. (*Newsweek*, December 12th, 1970.)

[3] Interview in *Newsweek*, December 7th, 1970.

[4] This film in 1972 alone grossed $8½ million in nine months and may turn out to be an even bigger money-maker than *The Sound of Music*.

The fact still remains that, despite all the madness and anarchy, Hollywood in the Sixties still managed – as ever – to turn out a number of really good films. In a previous chapter I have already drawn attention to the supreme skill and professionalism which lay behind such imperishable works as *The Big Sleep, All About Eve, The African Queen, Sunset Boulevard* and the like. Those were in the Fifties, but I find little difficulty in finding similar examples from the Sixties and into the Seventies.

Take Blake Edwards' *Breakfast at Tiffany's* (1961), with its offbeat story finely delineated by Audrey Hepburn and George Peppard, and George Roy Hill's *Butch Cassidy and the Sundance Kid* (1969), a kind of beautifully fantasised *Bonnie and Clyde* – both of them films which have left the extra bonus of a song apiece, 'Moon River' and 'Raindrops Keep Falling on my Head'. Take *The Hustler* (1961) and *Cool Hand Luke* (1967), in which Paul Newman, an actor of exceptional talent and intelligence (there was *Hud* too), impersonated two men who were doomed not so much by circumstances as by fatal flaws in their inner selves (one remembers the breaking of the pool hustler's hand, so coldly done, and the appalling egg-eating and sweatbox scenes in *Cool Hand Luke*). Robert Rossen's steely direction of *The Hustler* reminds us that he directed *All the King's Men*;[1] in the other film Stuart Rosenberg – a recruit from television – showed a sympathetic control far in advance of his previous films. Take Elliot Silverstein's *Cat Ballou* (1965), a marvellously affectionate send-up of the Western, with a superb double performance by Lee Marvin, especially as a drink-sodden cowhand-gangster snorting and pawing like a buffalo before the shooting starts. Or take *The Graduate* (1967) in which, by reversing 'boy gets girl' into 'woman gets boy', Mike Nichols built a fresh and gorgeously comic epic of offbeat seduction. Or *Bullitt* (1968), which backed its famous automobile chase (still not surpassed, even by Gene Hackman's race with the El in *The French Connection*) with some nice location intimacies of San Francisco. And finally take *Bonnie and Clyde* (1967), Arthur Penn's Pied Piper film whose attraction for the kids remained unchallenged until the coming of *Easy Rider*.

Bonnie and Clyde may by today's standards seem quite mild. But it should not be forgotten that in effect it started the craze for explicit violence in movies – much more so than *In Cold Blood* (also based on historical fact) which was made in the same year. The latter, shot in black and white and directed by Richard Brooks with a restraint which

---

[1] *The Hustler* was his penultimate film; he died in 1966.

emphasized rather than minimized the factual horrors of the story, was somehow too chilling to incite to violence.[1] *Bonnie and Clyde*, on the other hand, seemed to equate a bloodbath with a love-feast, while at the same time having the honesty to show *in colour* what a man's face looks like when shot at point blank range. And it was this honesty which set the fashion. Until the later appearance of *Easy Rider*, no film for years had aroused such strong and spontaneous enthusiasm among young people, who besieged the first-run house in London long before the press criticisms had appeared.

Anyway the cult of violence – not perhaps without reference to the sickening realities of the newscasts seen on TV screens – continued to escalate during the Sixties. Controversy raged over the moral intent of such films; and it was interesting to note that the most vocal opposition from morality groups increasingly lumped together sex and drugs with the depiction of violence. The real point was that the borderline between fantasy and reality was becoming blurred.

Roger Corman, for instance, who had started off as a splendid horror fantasist based largely on Poe,[2] began to change his tune in the mid-Sixties. *The Wild Angels* (1966) was about gangs of motor-cycle roughs, their blasphemies, swastikas and aleatory violations. *The St Valentine's Day Massacre* (1967) documented a well-known historical episode of gratuitous gangster savagery. *The Trip* (1968) elaborated on the psychedelic effects of drug-taking, especially LSD. However damaged by censorship-cuts, these films hardly indicated that Corman was better at depicting the immediate realities of a sick society than the imaginary nightmares of Poe. With *Bloody Mama* (1970), however, he moved not unsuccessfully into the *Bonnie and Clyde* country. Based on actual people and events of the Thirties, this saga of Ma Barker and her appalling family is presented with an uncompromising realism hardly seen in Corman's previous work.

Another area invaded was the Western. It is indeed curious that this *genre*, based as it is on lawlessness, savagery and the remorseless mutual cruelties of white men and Red Indians, had until now been subject to a formality and a whole pattern of conventions by which the grim and gory actualities of shoot-ups, punch-ups, scalpings and torture were conveniently masked or disguised.

---

[1] Its overall effect was marred by the final reels, which switched the direction of the film into a disquisition on capital punishment and the nature of guilt. Morally impeccable though this may have been, it smothered the general effect.

[2] *The Fall of the House of Usher* (1960), *The Pit and the Pendulum* (1961) *The Premature Burial* (1961), *The Masque of the Red Death* and *The Tomb of Ligeia* (both 1964).

No longer. With films like *The Wild Bunch*, *Soldier Blue* and *A Man Called Horse*,[1] the long-accepted legend vanishes and the factual horrors are rammed into our faces. Moments of particular nastiness are prolonged by slow motion, nothing is left to the imagination, and any intention to raise our indignation at past criminalities tends to be swamped by nausea. Memories of John Ford and Howard Hawks grow sweeter, and John Wayne's halo glows brighter; but to no avail.

Sam Peckinpah, who may well supplant Hawks in the eyes of the *aficionados* of the auteur theory, can, we know, make good films without indulging in the multiplication of overt atrocities. *Ride the High Country*[2] (1961) is witness to that, as is more recently the fascinating and sometimes quite surrealist *Ballad of Cable Hogue* (1969). Moreover, one can appreciate his desire to correct or even contradict the legend of the movie Western, based on the fact that by 1913 'the stories of the Indian Wars and the Gold Rush and the Great Gunfighters had become either bar-room ballyhoo or front-porch reminiscences'.[3] But the trouble is that an exaggeration in the opposite direction tends to defeat its own ends. It is because of what is *not* shown in, say, *Paisa* or *Two Women* that their messages come across so powerfully and permanently; and it is the *innocence* of the children's blasphemy in *Les Jeux Interdits* which points up the horror and the cruelty. Even in *Los Olvidados* Buñuel stops short of the ultimate in the explicit; and it is the rigid discipline of his most *outré* scenes which makes them so effective.

By 1970 everyone was in on the act, including Kubrick, who set out to formalize the idea of violence in current society, just as the earlier directors had formalized the idea of guns and scalpings in the Westerns; and by the same token Peckinpah transferred his interest to the rusticity of England's Cornwall, whose inhabitants were seen to treat American visitors with, to put it mildly, scant courtesy.

The outcry against 'sex and violence' which was raised in Europe and America in the Sixties and early Seventies was often bedevilled by the tendency of many occidentals to regard all sexual variations as perversions (if not all sex as sin), whereas in other areas of the world a bisexual attitude is quite commonplace, and elaborations of sexual technique felt to be as pleasurable as eating and drinking. One of the

---

[1] How could the director of *Cat Ballou* let himself in for this one?

[2] Also known as *Guns in the Afternoon*.

[3] This quotation is from a narration planned to be spoken over the opening scenes of *The Wild Bunch*. It wasn't used. That explicit brutality is *not* a *sine qua non* may be seen in *Tell Them Willie Boy Is Here* (1969), that admirable and cogent work by Abraham Polonsky – one of the most shabbily treated members of the Hollywood Ten.

most enlightened acts of the then film censor in Britain, John Trevelyan, was the passing of *W.R. – Mysteries of the Organism* without cuts.[1] Here was a film which proclaimed sex as joyful and turned its indignation against those who, with wider and more impermissible sanctions, clamped down on human freedom in general.

There is, of course, a complication. There is a common ground on which the perpetration of injustice and the act of sex meet and intermingle; sadism and masochism, two facets of cruelty, are also sexual perversions. Sadism, in particular implies sexual satisfaction achieved by hurting an unwilling victim. Those who attack sexual permissiveness on the screen should confine themselves to this angle only; and those who attack violence on the screen should examine extent and intent on the same lines. What Luke and others suffer in Stuart Rosenberg's *Cool Hand Luke* may be seen as acceptable because it is related to a genuine criticism of injustice as it is organized in an allegedly democratic society, and because it does, however sentimentally, depict the utter solitude of the individual in penal circumstances which, in the end, can lead to the appalling tribulation of the scapegoat. On the other hand the casual, almost mindless violence which enwreathes that brilliantly made and tremendously exciting film *The French Connection* seems to me to be far less permissible.[2] That it is shown to be an accepted way of life is bad enough; that it is also shown as accepted police routine is going too far, especially since there is nothing in the film which really criticizes or attacks this situation; nor is this helped by the fact that the chief drug-smuggler is explicitly stated to have escaped arrest. I am personally against all censorship except what the artist voluntarily imposes on himself; but if I were forced to make an exception it would be in regard to realistic, gratuitous and socially accepted violence – a very different thing from the fantasies of James Bond, Barbarella and the rest.

After which digression, let me return to the general picture of the American product during the Sixties to note that the representatives of the old Hollywood tradition, many of whom were discussed in Chapters 4 and 5, continued on their way, if somewhat diminished in

[1] Though of course with the X Certificate expressly designed by his predecessor Arthur Watkins for such cases.

[2] I will discuss later the possibility that the gratuitous horrors of *Straw Dogs* and *A Clockwork Orange* have certain side effects; the former because it collapses into unintended comedy, and the latter because it may, up to a point, have a philosophical validity. Meantime it may be noted that William Friedkin's direction of *The French Connection* puts him high in the roster of newer directors, and certainly far higher than his handling of *The Boys in the Band* (1970) suggested.

numbers – which were however to a degree replaced by members of the younger generation.

Robert Aldrich, for example, continued his procession of pessimistic but usually gripping and suspenseful films, which had started in the Fifties with works like *Apache* (1954), *Kiss Me Deadly* (1955), and *The Big Knife* (1955). He now moved into a bigger league with films starring some of the more prominent sacred monsters. With *What Ever Happened to Baby Jane?* (1962), he enshrined in a *Grand Guignol* frame two virtuoso performances by Bette Davis and Joan Crawford, with the former, as an ex-child star, keeping the latter in revengeful durance vile, what time the suspense built up to a climactic and horrifying last-minute confession. Both of those imperishable stars gave all they had got and yet somehow, and convincingly (given the story), managed to play it straight.[1] An attempt to repeat the formula in 1964, this time without Crawford but with Olivia de Havilland, Mary Astor and Agnes Moorehead, was less successful, perhaps because some of the *monstres* were *moins sacrés*. Anyway, *Hush . . . Hush Sweet Charlotte* had the whole box of tricks – including the return of a dripping corpse straight from Clouzot's *Les Diaboliques* – but horrors piled on horrors reduced Bette Davis' participation to some grand exits and entrances and a wide variety of not ineffective screams. Nor was *The Killing of Sister George* (1968), a Lesbian would-be shocker picked up from the London stage, much better; a tendency to over-emphasis and over-exposition (as in the sequence of the Lesbian bar) made the film seem heavy and overlong. Pauline Kael cruelly remarked that it was 'as fresh as Joan Crawford's smile'.

Aldrich had almost as big a success – at least in the United States – with *The Dirty Dozen* (1966) as he had had with *What Ever Happened to Baby Jane?*. With an admirable cast (Robert Ryan, Lee Marvin and Telly Savalas among others), this story of a group of convicted military prisoners sent on a pre-D Day operation against a German staff head-quarters was in effect a crochet work of war-film clichés ('We've made it!' cries one of the characters, and is instantly shot dead) which was at times made to seem convincing by skilful direction; but nothing in the film equalled the terrifying opening sequence involving an execution by hanging. *Too Late the Hero* (1969), with Michael Caine, Cliff Robertson, Denholm Elliott and Harry Andrews, followed something of the same line, only this time in the New Hebrides in the war against

[1] 'Bob Aldrich is a genius,' Bette Davis is said to have remarked on his decision to co-star her with Crawford, 'Joan, the greatest glamour star and me, I've no glamour, I'm an actress.' Take cover!

the Japanese; competently made, it was, for all its length and pretension, no more than a routine war-film.

There was indeed something of a rundown in the number of films about World War II. Franklin Schaffner, rather surprisingly after *Planet of the Apes*, made *Patton: Lust for Glory* (1969) – a whacking big film with George C. Scott in the name part recalling only too often his General Turgidson in *Dr Strangelove*. This effective exposition of an eccentric yet successful misfit in the military machine was in strange contrast to *The War Lord* (1965), an earlier and romantic piece (with Charlton Heston) set in 11th century Normandy and carrying some echoes of *La Belle et la Bête*.

There was, too, Darryl Zanuck's would-be super-blockbuster *The Longest Day* (1962), in which Ken Annakin,[1] Andrew Marton and Bernhard Wicki, under the close supervision of the maestro himself and with the collaboration of practically everyone in Spotlight and its French and German equivalents, made a singularly unmemorable film about the invasion of Europe. There was also Anthony Mann's *Heroes of Telemark* (1965), a film on the same theme as the Norwegian-French co-production *The Battle for Heavy Water* discussed earlier in this book. *Heroes of Telemark* was a somewhat laboured film in comparison with Mann's large-scale and De Mille-like epics (which seemed to come more easily to him) like *El Cid* (1961) and *The Fall of the Roman Empire* (1964).[2]

More interesting in this period was a newly iconoclastic attitude to World War II, paralleling in part British efforts like *Oh! What a Lovely War*. *Catch 22* and *M*A*S*H* took hold of the horribleness of the last war in the same way that Kubrick in *Dr Strangelove* took hold of the terrors of the future – by seizing at the situation in terms of black humour. Robert Altman's *M*A*S*H* won out (narrowly) over Mike Nichols' *Catch 22* – they were both made in 1969 – largely because it did not suffer comparison with a super-best-selling original. There were times in *Catch 22* when the literal translation of Joseph Heller's work to the screen went sour – as in the episode of the young officer on the

---

[1] Who did better on his own in 1965 with *The Battle of the Bulge* – a rattling good account of the German counter-attack in the Ardennes, with Henry Fonda, Robert Shaw and Robert Ryan.

[2] Anthony Mann, who sadly died in 1967 before completing *A Dandy in Aspic*, is not to be confused with two other Manns – Daniel, who made *Butterfield 8* (1960) with Elizabeth Taylor, *Ada* (1961) and *Five Finger Exercise* (1962); and Delbert, director of *A Gathering of Eagles* (1963) and of *Fitzwilly* (1967) – also known as *Fitzwilly Strikes Back* – notable mainly for Edith Evans' performance as a dotty dowager. His first film, *Marty*, is dealt with elsewhere.

bathing raft being cut in half by a plane buzzing him for fun; though on the other hand Orson Welles' excoriating General Dreedle, with his pneumatic nurse companion, splendidly overpassed the writer's conception.[1] In *M*A*S*H*, on the other hand, the concentration of sick humour within a canvas pullulating with gore and yet, like a Bosch painting, well content to remain within its frame, gave a singular authenticity to the horrible comedies through which the inmates of the hospital masked or diverted their daily, hourly confrontation with ghastly realities.

A prime representative of the older traditions of Hollywood is of course Stanley Kramer, long noted for his production and, frequently, direction of *soigné* and distinguished films. In 1961 he came up with the immense and star-studded *Judgement at Nuremberg*, which he directed himself. As in his later *Guess Who's Coming to Dinner?* Kramer leaves as many options open as possible (he always wants his audience to have its cake and eat it), and the film, with a smoothly mobile camera and a penchant for chiaroscuro in the close-ups, leans over backwards to be fair and liberal while at the same time accepting the historical facts. The trouble with this sort of film is that all the guest stars remove from it the reality it is supposed to be recreating. Spencer Tracy as the presiding judge therefore gives a polished performance as Spencer Tracy as the presiding judge. But there are exceptions; in the mind, long afterward, remain the images of Judy Garland, strained and taut as a German victimized by the Nazis, and of Marlene Dietrich, superb, delicately poised on a dangerous dignity, as the widow of an already executed German general.

As director as well as producer, Kramer also made *It's a Mad Mad Mad Mad World* (1963) and *Ship of Fools* (1965) – the former an attempt to make a 'comedy to end all comedies', which fell over without even benefit of pratfall,[2] and the latter a screen version of Katherine Anne Porter's best-selling parable on war guilt, or, as Pauline Kael succinctly put it, 'Original Sin Meets Mr Fixit'.

The extraordinary thing about Kramer's work is that the bigger and more important it tries to be, the more forgettable it becomes. Who now remembers his much-trumpeted anti-nuclear film from Nevile Shute's novel *On the Beach* (1959) with, for heaven's sake, Fred Astaire,

---

[1] In addition to this film, and *The Graduate*, Nichols of course directed *Who's Afraid of Virginia Woolf?* (1966), a magnificent cinematic version of the Edward Albee play, with fine performances from George Segal and Sandy Dennis as well as from Elizabeth Taylor and Richard Burton.

[2] Of this film J. B. Priestley remarked, 'There is in it not a glimmer of affection for anybody or anything'.

Ava Gardner and Gregory Peck? And what remains in recollection about *Inherit the Wind* (1960), about the Scopes 'monkey trial', other than a strange isosceles triangle consisting of Fredric March, Spencer Tracy and, for heaven's sake, Gene Kelly? Somebody once said that Kramer was always being praised for his intentions rather than for his films. This might be so in the sense that the precautions he takes to present his subject in absolutely safe box-office terms may blunt original inspiration as well as aesthetic achievement. I think he will be remembered in the end for his more modest efforts – his producership of Zinnemann (and especially *The Men*), of Mark Robson (*Home of the Brave*), of Laslo Benedek (*The Wild One*), of Edward Dmytryk (*The Caine Mutiny*), and indeed of Roy Rowland's *The 5000 Fingers of Dr T*, a children's film of high fantasy and superb invention which has never had the recognition it deserves. As a director he is seen at his best in a quiet and efficient film like *Guess Who's Coming to Dinner?* which, despite the poshed-up pusillanimity of which I have earlier accused it, must stand as a beautifully constructed vehicle for Hepburn, Poitier and, in an especially inventive and touching swan song, Spencer Tracy; this film I place second to *The Defiant Ones*, which is certainly the cleanest and clearest job to Kramer's name to date.

Meantime the unpinnable-down Vincente Minnelli made *Two Weeks in Another Town* (1962), a colour film about the inner secrets of the film industry, but in Rome's Cinecittà rather than Hollywood. Featuring Kirk Douglas, Edward G. Robinson and Claire Trevor, this was a sort of throwback to the earlier *The Bad and the Beautiful* (1952), from which indeed he here quoted – Lana Turner and all. This, together with *The Sandpiper* (1965) – an appalling film with Richard Burton as a clergyman[1] repressing volcanic sexual desires in face of an atheistic Elizabeth Taylor – was a sad comedown for the maker of *Meet Me in St Louis*, *Father of the Bride*, *The Long Long Trailer*, *The Pirate*, *Gigi* and *An American in Paris*. Nor was his reputation completely restored by his 1970 musical *On a Clear Day You Can See For Ever*, with Barbra Streisand. Beautiful in design and colour, and with some first-class musical numbers by Burton Lane, it still somehow lacked that filmic zizz which sent his earlier musicals soaring.

Mark Robson, originally a graduate of the Val Lewton horror academy (his first film, in 1943, was *The Seventh Victim*), and also, as we have just seen, a quondam protégé of Kramer, was still in business in the Sixties. A more than competent commercial director (his output

---

[1] A rôle he had played to much, much better effect two years earlier in *The Night of the Iguana*.

in the previous decade included *The Bridges at Toko-Ri*, *Phffft*, *The Harder They Fall*, *Peyton Place* and *The Inn of the Sixth Happiness*[1]), he now embarked on a film about Gandhi's assassination. This was *Nine Hours to Rama* (1963), and, however noble the intentions, this version of an event as shattering as the assassination of John Kennedy or of Martin Luther King ended up as a sad mishmash. Against some evocative camerawork of Indià by Arthur Ibbetson and the moving authenticity of J. S. Casshyap's assumption of Gandhi's *eidolon*, there stood ranged a totally unconvincing gallery of dressed-up, pancake-plastered Europeans and American actors of whom only José Ferrer, as a top police officer, managed to look and act at all convincingly. The actual crowd scenes around the murder were, however, very well done; and compared with *Valley of the Dolls* (1965) – Robson's contribution to Fox's disaster period and 'a Golden Treasury of Hollywood clichés . . . which don't clitch'[2] – *Nine Hours to Rama* could almost be reckoned a masterpiece.

Only in *Von Ryan's Express* (1965), with Trevor Howard and Frank Sinatra, did Robson seem to recapture some of his earlier sensibility. The beginning section of the film, set in a prisoner of war camp, was a little turgid, but the bulk of the film, a rip-roaring journey on a stolen train with the Germans in full pursuit, was Hollywood expertise at its best. Doubt only creeps in when it is compared with John Frankenheimer's *The Train*, made in the previous year. This admirably directed film has a breathless motivation in that the cargo the train carries is practically the entire contents of the *Jeu de Paume*, so that with every crisis the heart is in the mouth for the Renoirs, the Monets and the Sisleys. Nor is the chase, which involves one super-spectacular smash, the only thing. The film is also about obsession. The German colonel (fine performance by Paul Scofield) is utterly determined to get the Impressionists back to Germany. Labiche, his opposite number (Burt Lancaster), is not really interested in the paintings but rather, and solely, in an absolute resolve to have his own way and to scupper whatever the German wants to do. With a supporting cast largely French, including Jeanne Moreau and Michel Simon – the latter as a locomotive driver whose clumsy try at sabotage finally triggers off Labiche's obsession – *The Train* has a cogency which is very much Frankenheimer's hallmark.

One of the younger generation – he is in his early forties, compared with Robson's sixty-odd – Frankenheimer emerged from TV at

---

[1] In this film that great but doomed actor Robert Donat made his last appearance.
[2] Raymond Durgnat in *Films and Filming*, March 1968.

the end of the Fifties with *The Young Stranger* (1957), a James Dean-ish story of conflict between a kid and his parents which had at times a raw and affecting reality. But he really made his mark in 1962 with *Bird Man of Alcatraz*, based on the true story of the prisoner who became a world-known expert on avian life; and with *The Manchurian Candidate*, a political story involving brainwashing plus the general atmosphere of a reality just slipping over the edge into an uncontrollable tumble[1] (as in the last reels of *Dr Strangelove*), and with a magnificent performance by Angela Lansbury, who had already worked with Frankenheimer in *All Fall Down* (1961), opposite Karl Malden as her husband and Warren Beatty as their idolized, spoilt son who is ruined not only by his parents but by himself.

Frankenheimer's most effective film is probably *Seconds* (1966). This macabre, chilling thriller grips right from its opening, with its extremely high-angle camera directed on to scurrying crowds at a railway station, and then isolating two persons, one of whom passes a packet to the other, which triggers off a sequence of alarming over-the-shoulder-looking suspense. The subsequent story concerns an organization which undertakes (via a little euphemism called Cadaver Procurement) to provide a person with a new body and a new personality. The character who falls for this treatment (well portrayed by Rock Hudson) is thereby converted from a conventional and prosperous banker into an unconventional but equally prosperous artist. He settles in a congenial Californian community, but eventually finds out, via some Frankenheimer scenes of rococo fancies (including a dotty wine-trampling episode), that his neighbours are not at all what he thinks; and in a frightening dénouement he himself becomes fodder for Cadaver Procurement. Brilliantly photographed (often into alarming distortion) by the veteran James Wong Howe, *Seconds* belongs more to the nightmare moments of *The Manchurian Candidate* than to the adventurous obsessions of *The Train* or to the more prosaic factualities of *Grand Prix* (1967) and *The Gypsy Moths* (1969).

In *Grand Prix* Frankenheimer treated the Monaco automobile race with the detailed and expositional elaboration that the subject demanded; and as usual in these cases, the human element tended to end up as no more than some trimming on the side. It is the sleek machines which dominate, leaving Toshiro Mifune, Eva Marie Saint, Yves Montand and the others to play their dutiful parts as puppets of

---

[1] The great public found this a 'difficult' film, not least the dream sequence in which the camera panned a full circle. As its co-producer George Axelrod remarked, 'It went from failure to classic without ever passing through success'. (*Sight and Sound*, Autumn 1968.)

Michelin and High Octane. Much more attractive are the preoccupations of *The Gypsy Moths*, a tale about a travelling circus of sky-divers, into which with considerable skill is woven a love affair between one of the birdmen (Burt Lancaster at his best) and a small-town married woman (Deborah Kerr) which has a tender realism reminiscent of De Sica.[1] This film was a welcome return to form after the turgid sentimentality of *The Fixer* (1968), about the persecution of a Jew in pre-revolution Russia. Frankenheimer shot this in Hungary with a largely British cast that included Alan Bates and Dirk Bogarde; no stone was left uncast, and the film gradually drowned in the treacly flow of Maurice Jarre's music. Nor was the subsequent *The Extraordinary Seaman* (1968) much of an improvement; despite some moments of satiric comedy, and a good performance by David Niven as the ghost captain of an agéd vessel on duty in the Pacific during the Japanese war, the film hardly got off the ground. It needed perhaps the zany touch of a Richard Lester.

Generally speaking, though, Frankenheimer brought a briskly individual breath of air into the American film scene. In this he was paralleled, though in slightly different terms, by Sidney Lumet, who also came from the world of TV and who made his name in movies, in the same year as Frankenheimer, with *Twelve Angry Men*, that small, claustrophobic and classically addictive movie about the deliberations of a jury, which at that period rivalled only Delbert Mann's *Marty* in proving that low budget pictures without famous stars can, if well made, score at the box-office. True, *Twelve Angry Men* was rather pegged to Henry Fonda; but in the other film Betsy Blair and Ernest Borgnine were as unglamorous and as unknown as all get-out.

Lumet's approach to film is pretty catholic, though one may note a certain interest in making screen versions of stage plays, as witness *A View from the Bridge* (1961), *Long Day's Journey into Night* (1962), and *The Seagull* (1968). The last-named, with a cast which included James Mason, Vanessa Redgrave, Simone Signoret and David Warner, tended to be too muted and respectful in its approach – in contrast to his treatment of the O'Neill six years earlier, in which, with equal respect and less spatial freedom, Lumet managed to allow the illuminations of this great play to flow unimpeded from the screen.

But Lumet's abilities are best seen in his more precisely filmic offerings. *Fail Safe* (1964) was a true and honest piece of movie-making, with a fine performance by Fonda as a President locked in a lonely isolation. It couldn't eclipse *Dr Strangelove*, however, because it treated

[1] For the record, one of the other sky-divers was played by Gene Hackman.

the whole idea of the Bomb gone maverick dead straight, while Kubrick had realized that the horror of the idea made it essential to treat it with a wry and twisted smile edging towards madness. Near the end of *Fail Safe*, however, Lumet, through the phone talk between the US staff officer and his Soviet counterpart, did manage to indicate the absolute insanity of nuclear war.[1]

With *The Pawnbroker* (1966), Lumet made a brave and bold attempt at a film of deep human significance. The story is about the sole survivor from a family immolated in a Nazi concentration camp, who sets up business in New York with his mistress (widow of another Nazi victim), and an erratic young Puerto-Rican assistant through whom he gets involved in the world of gang warfare, and by whom, in a sacrificial gesture, he is saved from a hoodlum's bullet. This narrative is interrupted throughout by Resnais-like flashbacks to the camps, and even to idyllic and idealized memories of life before Hitler, paralleling in a curious way those creamy dreams of the world as it might be with which Klos and Kadar interrupt the final tragic reels of *The Shop in the High Street*. It is all done – as ever with Lumet – with tremendous skill, and Rod Steiger pulls out all the Method stops in the chief part. But, despite some brief and moving moments of memory (the long line of hands, from the fingers of which the Nazis are removing rings, has a terrifying suggestion of nameless horrors), *The Pawnbroker* suffers in the end from over-emphasis. The truth of suffering – present or remembered – is lacquered over with facile melodrama; and the emotions aroused fade as the house-lights come up.

Nearer to reality was the often horrifying *The Hill* (also 1965), in its way a foretaste of Peter Watkins' *Punishment Park*. The hill concerned is a sand-mound in the African desert, and is part of a military prison run on a personal penal system by a dyed-in-the-wool RSM (Harry Andrews). His system is wrecked by the arrival of two NCO assistants, whose overt and active sadism leads to the death of one of the prisoners, and finally to open revolt by the rest. Although the ending is a little obvious and facile (the revolt is begun all too predictably by a negro soldier), the remorseless repetition of the punishment exercises and the equally remorseless exhibition of the pusillanimity or stupidity of all the other staff concerned – from a shifty Medical Officer (Michael

---

[1] Something of a companion piece to this film was Frankenheimer's *Seven Days in May* (1964), a sort of follow-up to *The Manchurian Candidate* in which the military try to engineer a palace revolution against the occupant of the White House. With its constant pattern of media machines, not least the omnipresent TV screens, this film suggests a dangerous dehumanization in which the scientist may find himself losing control.

Redgrave) whose only interest is in viewing the men's parts, to the hidebound Sergeant who is on the wrong side of the fence (Sean Connery) – builds up a powerful and sweaty indictment of the injustices which can occur within the confines of a so-called discipline.

Passing over *The Group* (1966), an efficiently made film with a number of good performances (especially from Candice Bergen and Shirley Knight) which nevertheless watered down – partly no doubt for fear of censorship – the acid sexual disillusionments which were so important to Mary McCarthy's novel, we come to what may well be Lumet's best film so far, *The Deadly Affair* (1967) – a spy thriller very well adapted from the John Le Carré book by Paul Dehn. Lumet's offbeat colour atmospherics of a seedy London admirably frame the undercover skullduggeries and, particularly, the discovery by the spy (James Mason) that one of his associates has changed sides. To this may be added a powerful and affecting performance by Simone Signoret as an ex-concentration camp inmate, and a horrifying sequence involving a stage presentation of the murder of Edward II in Marlowe's play of that name. *The Deadly Affair* put a steely grip on the spectator which was lacking in a film of an earlier Le Carré story, efficiently though it was directed by Martin Ritt[1] – *The Spy Who Came in from the Cold* (1965) – or for that matter Sidney Furie's by no means undistinguished version of the Len Deighton story, *The Ipcress File* (1965).

Of Arthur Penn it might be said that he put his thumb-print on nearly all of American cinema from 1967 onwards, when *Bonnie and Clyde* launched a new era of permissive violence and violent permissiveness. He had in previous films – notably in his version of the stage play about Helen Keller, *The Miracle Worker* (1962) – shown a talent for laying on scenes which burn themselves into one's visual memory. With *Bonnie and Clyde*, realistic, but *really* realistic, in its dusty yet pastoral colour photography (Burnett Guffey) of exclusively location episodes, in its at that time appallingly explicit bloodletting, and in its remarkable identifications (rather than performances) by Faye Dunaway, Warren Beatty, Michael Pollard, Denver Pyle, Gene Hackman, Estelle Parsons and all the other supporting players without exception; in all this the whole pattern of the crime film, whether pastoral or metropolitan, was

---

[1] Ritt's *Hud* (1962), with Paul Newman as a classical prairie layabout, and with classical photography by the great James Wong Howe, bid fair at one point to become the *Urfilm* of the Sixties, but was beaten to the post by *Bonnie and Clyde*. Latterly Ritt made *The Molly Maguires* (1969), a grim, often effective, but *in toto* indeterminate film about the conflict between an Irish-influenced secret society and repressive mineowners in the coalfields of Pennsylvania.

fundamentally changed. For the first time since the arrival of the Hawks/
Bogart/Bacall era of the Forties, a total change of style was imposed.

Penn followed on with a quite magical screen transmogrification
of Arlo Guthrie's LP dreamorama, *Alice's Restaurant*. Penn's embroider-
ings and variations of the original moved sometimes into a Vigo-like
area in which the screen visuals defy adequate description, and, as in
Vigo, cold shadows interpose, like the moment in *L'Atalante* when
Dasté destroys the treasures in Michel Simon's cabin; so here, amid
the dreams and the dropouts and the pot, a cold wind will suddenly
blow – and not least in the last scene of Alice as the sun slides behind a
cloud. After this *Little Big Man* (1970) was somewhat of a disappointment. For me at least Dustin Hoffman didn't quite fit into the part of
an anti-legendary legendary hero (if that's the way to put it). Some
splendid stuff though, with lots of banging about with Custer (Richard
Mulligan) and Wild Bill Hickok (Jeff Corey), and still, as with the
other films, a real feeling for the picaresque.[1]

Unlike Penn, who came to Hollywood from TV in the Fifties,
Don Siegel comes from the way-back movie days of the Forties. Of
the long roster of his films since *The Verdict* (1946), two have certainly
stuck in the mind – *Riot in Cell Block Eleven* (1954) and *Invasion of the
Body Snatchers* (1956). The latter in particular, though a low-budget
film (on the face of it), had a chilling science fiction story in which
influences from outer space began to take over human beings and turn
them into virtual vegetables, and which began to seem too real for
comfort: the hints of mass brainwashing were too near the knuckle,
and the realism made quite a few people turn away. Then, over ten
years later, Siegel came up with *Madigan* (1967), a film of considerable
perception despite a clogged and sometimes over-moralistic script
(Henry Fonda has some terrible lines). Next year, in *Coogan's Bluff*
(with Clint Eastwood as the bluffer, and a splendid first line of dialogue,
spoken in the desert to a ravaged-looking Apache, 'OK Chief, put your
pants back on'), he made a more elaborate and better scripted film,
alternating between the landscapes of Arizona and the townscapes of
New York, and with admirable performances by Betty Field and
Lee J. Cobb.

Siegel's *Dirty Harry* (1971) was set, like so many crime thrillers,
in that most attractive of all cities, San Francisco, and again starred

[1] In the same year as *Little Big Man* there appeared a ninety minute film about Arthur
Penn by Robert Hughes which was revelatory, documentary and at no point slavish,
mawkish or fanatical. Interviews and discussions were interwoven with extracts from the
films, and out of all this emerged an honest and valuable analysis of the director. Hughes,
a talented critic and interpreter, died suddenly, and young, in 1973.

Clint Eastwood. It was concerned, *inter alia*, with the question of the use by police of rough and unscrupulous methods, and these not just in terms of interrogation. The speeding plot builds up to a somewhat ridiculous climax in which a murderer tries to blackmail a whole community by holding a busload of children as hostage; yet Siegel's treatment of this climax is nicely edgy. Of the final scene, when Harry, having solved the problem by disobeying the orders of his superiors and thus destroying the killer, takes off his police badge and throws it after the corpse which is floating slowly away downstream, one may well say that the moral issue has been raised and then well and truly burked.

Of the younger generation of American directors, Norman Jewison, who like a number of others came into films via television, made five or six films in rapid succession, none of them (except perhaps *The Cincinnati Kid* of 1965) of much note, and then came up with *The Russians Are Coming, the Russians Are Coming* (1966) which was, apart from anything else, a reminder that Hollywood used to be the centre for comedy and high-spirited humour, and could be again. Unlike Kramer's *It's a Mad Mad Mad Mad World*, this film didn't set out to bludgeon you into laughter. It had in it something of the Ealing comedy spirit[1] in that it escalated a real possibility from the edge of fantasy to beyond, and this within a normal realistic setting. The small New England community apparently invaded by Soviet forces (the scene is a coastal island with no Sunday ferry connection to the mainland) reacts with splendid inconsequences as well as predictabilities. With Carl Reiner, Alan Arkin, Michael Pollard and the glorious Ben Blue, this was one of the few really funny films of the decade. Another was also by a newcomer, Francis Ford Coppola, whose *You're a Big Boy Now* (1967), though somewhat self-indulgent (there were sequences, such as the night-time romp through New York streets, which a good producer would have cut to length), had wit, slapstick and some great belly-laughs connected in particular with one of those beds which folds up into the wall. Coppola showed in this film a real gift for passing from fantasy to reality, and vice versa, without dislocating the sensibilities, so that his hero (Peter Kastner), who uses free-association of ideas and action in order to escape from his oppressive family (his mom puts locks of her own hair in the letters she writes to him), can be put in and out of almost any situation without much ado.

Jewison and Coppola both went on to land themselves with large-

---

[1] It was scripted by William Rose, an ex-Ealing man; but as he also wrote *It's A Mad Mad Mad Mad World* this doesn't prove much.

scale musicals – the former with *Fiddler on the Roof* (1971), and the latter with *Finian's Rainbow* (1968). Both films were highly successful; but by now the magic of the real musicals of the Thirties and Forties had been lost. In contemporary terms perhaps only *Cabaret*, which apart from all its other merits was the most brilliantly edited film in many years, belonged to the real *genre*. From *Finian's Rainbow*, Coppola rebounded into something stylistically much more up-to-date. *Rain People*, a film which he said was very personal to himself, chronicled a rather sad journey along the motelled highways of the United States; scrappy, sincere, it had good performances from Shirley Knight and James Caan. As for Jewison, he had previous to *Fiddler on the Roof* brought off the admirable *In the Heat of the Night* (already discussed) and, in 1968, *The Thomas Crown Affair*, a film about an ingenious and baffling bank robbery which gradually turns into a battle of wits, and then of love between the organizer of the raid (Steve McQueen) and the investigator employed by the insurance company (Faye Dunaway). As in *In the Heat of the Night*, Jewison focuses our total attention on the interrelationship between two characters. This film, like *The Boston Strangler*, made some tentative but not overly significant use of multiple screen images.

It is no small compliment to Alan Pakula to say that *Klute* (1971) almost effaces Peter Yates' excellent *Bullitt*.[1] As a psychological thriller *Klute* excels because it is redolent of the fears and weaknesses, the sense of imbalance and insecurity, which constantly seem to erode the structure of our urban civilization. Klute himself – in a truly magnificent portrayal by Donald Sutherland – is wellnigh schizophrenic. Like Dirty Harry, he has withdrawn from the organized police so as to free himself for an investigation into the highly mysterious disappearance of a noted and apparently respectable scientist. To investigate one must spy; and with sometimes almost intolerable emphasis, Pakula insists on our complicity in this process, degrading though it may be. All this is underlined by the violent chiaroscuro of Gordon Willis' photography – eye-aching brilliance against shadows whose dark depths seem almost tangible. Thus the screen images themselves become schizo, and it is only occasionally that Pakula relaxes the tension, and then in strange and unexpected ways, as when the ambiguous girl Bree – clue surely to the mystery – almost forcibly seduces Klute when through circumstance

---

[1] Let me emphasize the 'almost'. The car chase in *Bullitt* is inimitable. But psychologically *Klute* is far superior, though we must remember that Yates had to his credit *One Way Pendulum* (1964) before he went to America, and that later (1969) he made the not undistinguished *John and Mary*.

he has to put her up for the night. To all this, and on top of the sinister and constant underflow of the spying tape-recorders, Pakula adds the tightrope existence of Bree herself (Jane Fonda at her best); and one of the most brilliant things about this gorgeously written film is that throughout the action we accompany her in a psychoanalysis which she is undergoing in an attempt to escape from what may in fact be her real vocation – that of a call-girl.

Round about the same time as *Klute* there arrived Gordon Parks' *Shaft* (1971), a fast-moving thriller in which the private-eye hero is a negro engaged on investigating internecine conflicts involving black gangsters, Black Muslims, and black stool-pigeons, with the Mafia intervening. Central to the story is a love-hate relationship between Shaft and a much put-upon white lieutenant of police. Richard Roundtree and Charles Cioffi are exceptionally good in these exchanges; at one point the lieutenant picks up a ballpoint pen and says to Shaft, 'You ain't so black' – to which Shaft, picking up a coffee cup, replies, 'You ain't so white'. *Shaft* keeps up a standard of whizzing speed remarkable even in relation to films like *Bullitt* and *The French Connection*. The pace is set right from the opening sequences whose urgent, breathless movement is arrogantly increased by Isaac Hayes' superb score. Quite a few I know turned up their nose at this film on the grounds that it was being overpraised for racial reasons. Certainly there is no reason to glorify it simply because it was an all-black job (including the publicity department).[1] Nevertheless it was and is a portent, especially taken in conjunction with Ossie Davis' *Cotton Comes to Harlem*, made a year earlier and concerned – on a fairly light-hearted level – with conflicts between negro gangsters and negro police. *Shaft* is a vastly superior film, however, and is enriched by moments of lovely comedy – the sight of the great tough gangster weeping over his vanished daughter, and a superbly prolonged sequence, all the better for being vital to the plot, in a homosexual bar. Only in the last reels, when Shaft and his gang suspensefully prepare, *Rififi*-style, to rescue the kidnapped girl from the hotel room in which she is immured, does the film slow down too much and go sadly off the boil.

Anyway, *Shaft* and *Cotton Comes to Harlem* were just two bits of evidence that the all-black film was no flash-in-the-pan. For in the

---

[1] Parks himself said, 'It's just a Saturday night fun picture which people go to see because they want to see the black guy winning'. Parks, though, in his first film, *The Learning Tree* (1968), dealt with the problems of a young negro growing up in the United States into a gradual realization of the reality of racism. At least two sequels to *Shaft* have already been made.

meantime there appeared the pioneer figure of Melvin Van Peebles.[1] His *Watermelon Man* (1970), though it did not completely come off, had a deadly serious undertow to its sick-joke surface comedy about a brash, unthinking racialist Wasp who wakes up one morning to find he has turned into a negro (excellent performance by Godfrey Cambridge). After that came the phenomenon of *Sweet Sweetback's Baadasssss Song* – at this writing not yet seen in Britain – which kicked off straightaway by grossing over $10 million (some $4 million more than the highly successful *Shaft*). These, and other films like *Soul to Soul* – about a tour of Ghana by Wilson Pickett and other top pop singers – or *Black Jesus*, in which Woody Strode impersonated the martyred Congo leader Patrice Lumumba, are basically films made by blacks for blacks however successful they may be (and are) with the whites. According to *Newsweek*[2] the success of these films is partly due, in the riot cities at least, to a change in living patterns. Since the Chicago and Detroit riots, for instance, the whites have tended to retire to the suburbs where brand new movie-houses spring up to serve them, while 'the blacks have inherited the city centres and most of the downtown theatres' while 'in New York the polarization between the East Side art houses and the West Side houses that have had to scrounge for "mainstream" movies as production declines has created a vacuum into which black movies and audiences have poured'. Meantime Van Peebles has gone on to other triumphs, and in particular has conquered Broadway with a cruel and fantastic stage musical (ending with a Voodoo curse on the audience) called *Ain't Supposed to Die A Natural Death*.

One may also note with gratification that ·the Sidney Poitier syndrome referred to in Chapter 5 has been exorcised by Poitier himself. With *Buck and the Preacher* (1971), of which he was the director as well as one of the leading players, he teamed up with the talented Harry Belafonte[3] to make a fairly lighthearted movie which had, as in *Watermelon Man*, a substratum of real seriousness (the film is dedicated to 'those whose graves are as unmarked as their place in history'). The story dates back to the time of the Liberation of the Slaves and to the efforts of unscrupulous whites virtually to re-enslave the negroes in the

---

[1] 'What a name
To fill the speaking trump of future fame!' (Byron.)

[2] Issue of September 6th, 1971.

[3] Together with a large and well-chosen cast including Ruby Dee and, from TV's *High Chapparal*, Cameron Mitchell. By 1972 Black Movies were proliferating – one of the more notable being *Superfly*, starring Ron O'Neal and taking the drug scene very much for granted.

name of cheap labour. Told as an action-packed adventure story on Western lines, *Buck and the Preacher* has a glorious twist at the end when it is the Indians who ride to the rescue.

The makers of black cinema will no doubt have to face the problems common to all movie-makers, including the embarrassment of a lot of greedy people climbing onto the bandwagon and turning out a lot of worthless crap. But black cinema is no longer just a portent; it is a permanency.[1] Behind it, make no mistake, looms the ultimate conflict between white and black which Le Roi Jones so powerfully symbolized in *Dutchman*. Anthony Harvey's chilling screen version of this play – a summation of the hatred and the failures of communication which stretch from the days of the Slave Trade through South African apartheid to the Saga of the Soledad Brothers – peels off layer after layer of festering skin and diseased flesh until two stark skeletons, which one would surely hope would now share at least a common anonymity, continue still, with tragic inevitability, to mete out death and to receive it.

The other portent of the Sixties was a great resurgence of the old avant-garde, now dressed up in the rather pointless guise of something called the Underground, the sinister implications of which word were in general belied by the triviality of the product.

This subject has been exhaustively and admirably covered by Parker Tyler and Sheldon Renan (among others), and I have no particular wish to go on about it at great length. I only want to point out the difference between the original avant-garde tradition, which, whatever else it did, accepted the idea of the film as art, and the Warhol tradition which basically questions that acceptance.

It is in fact very important that the bulk of the films from the Warhol factory are bad in technique as well as being weak in content. The importance resides in the fact that their nullity forces all of us to look closely all over again at the bases of the art of the film which it has not occurred to us to question over the past thirty or forty years. In this sense, but no other, Warhol and Godard may be seen as stable-mates. Otherwise the nothingness of most of the Warhol canon (excepting some of the Morrissey material, which bears resemblance to cinema) seems to me to be based on a gross miscalculation. In the other visual fields he is able to achieve real effects by sheer size and by multiplication.

---

[1] Another contemporary black film, *Reggae*, was made by West Indians in London and Jamaica. This was followed by *The Harder They Come*, the first all-Jamaican feature film, directed by Perry Henzel; simple, sometimes naïve, it nevertheless had the ring of truth to it.

When I went to his big show at the Tate in London I was indeed moved
to reluctant admiration, even among the Campbell Soup cans. But this
effect can only occur physically and spatially. A reproduction of the
Tate gallery show in a newspaper would be meaningless; whereas a
reproduction of, say, a Magritte show would not. This is one of the
reasons why the Warhol films don't work.

It is I suppose conceivable that if Warhol could, Campbell soup-
wise or Presley-wise or Monroe-wise, project *The Chelsea Girls* onto a
whole battery of screens, a more impressive effect might be achieved.
As in a large-scale affair like the Tate show, the magnification of form
might draw the attention away from the lack of content (and I don't
accuse the Campbell Corporation in this respect).

Apart from the human touches in the Morrissey films, and I don't
mean the beer-bottle in *Trash* but things like Joe Dallesandro crawling
about the floor with his baby in *Flesh*, what of interest has Warhol to
offer? His superstars tend to be repellent to the eye (have you seen
Viva in *Blue Movie*?), and his cinematic technique seems to be a
deliberate insult to spectators and film-makers alike. Yet he manages to
sell it. In Montreal I overheard a young cinéaste explaining earnestly to
his companion how good it was to get 'the real nitty gritty' into the
camera – never clean the gate and never wipe the lens.

All right then – we are back to the brute question, what is movie?
Strip off all the properties which we, poor fools, have so far relied on,
and you are left with a camera, some film, a projector, and a screen or
wall. Then forget or reject the achievements and traditions of the past
75 years, approach the minimal machinery with an aleatory cynicism,
and there you are.

By such methods Warhol and his shop stewards look like managing
to bamboozle audiences into acceptance of their shabby renderings of
campery, transvestism, casual porn and, above all, inactivity. The
popularity of all this rests essentially on that sense of despair one so
frequently detects today in the young (and with which one sympathizes)
but which, when detected in the mature, tends to be put down to a
hardening of the arteries or alternatively a determination to be With It
at all costs. Boredom is all.

Warhol and Godard have questioned the very nature of the film
medium; and this, as I have already said, is no bad thing in itself.
Godard is a film-maker *par excellence*, whatever naughtiness he may
from time to time commit. Warhol is not, and even if he were,
Makavejev would by now have made him unnecessary. Gregory
Battcock has pointed out that Warhol's 'use of film as a device to

torment its audience may be understood as an intellectual challenge', and he adds later in the same essay,[1] 'In stripping the cinematic medium of its pretensions and decorations, Warhol has produced an art statement (*sic*) that is likely to be acceptable to the very few'. *Verb sap* and *Deo Gratias*.

Turning now to the real avant-garde as understood, and properly understood, by critics like Parker Tyler (see his send-up of Warhol in the final chapter of his book),[2] we can see the distinction between the true cinéastes – the people who have a *feel* for the medium (at the least) – and those who, to quote Tyler, 'are headed as fast and as far as possible toward more commercial success and a revised formula based (humorously) on the new supertolerance to nudity and sex-display'.

One is not of course talking about subject matter but about filmic treatment. Brakhage on masturbation is an artist trying his damnedest to express an experience in cinematically aesthetic terms, using the medium to its best advantage. He is to my mind one of the very great avant-gardists; I put him above Kenneth Anger and even – though perhaps more tentatively – Maya Deren. Brakhage is always opening up the medium while Warhol and his followers, who are legion, are trying to close it down. With Brakhage you only have to see that moment of pure joy, that ravishing moment of human experience when, in *Window Water Baby Moving*, the baby comes and his wife snatches the camera from him to record the joy on *his* face; you only have to look at the winter lyricisms of *Sirius Remembered* and *Dog Star* – a kind of Tennysonian evocation of a once-loved dog lying there stiff outside the house in the snow – to understand what cinema is really about.

So, with friendly salutes also to the Mekas Brothers (especially for *Hallelujah the Hills* and its tracking shots); to the Whitney family for their bold ventures with computerised movies; to James Broughton, who poetically delights in breaking even avant-garde rules so as to give pure pleasure[3] (*Four in the Afternoon, Loony Tom, The Bed*); to Sidney Meyers and Frank Simon for their affectionate and compassionate *The Queen*; to Samuel Beckett and Alan Schneider for *Film*, with Keaton's last magical appearance on the screen; and, if they will accept positions in this *galère*, to John Cassavetes for the marvellous and pioneer relaxations of *Shadows* and to Shirley Clarke for the jolts of *The*

[1] 'Four films by Andy Warhol' in *The New American Cinema*, Dutton, N.Y., 1967.

[2] *Underground Film* by Parker Tyler, Secker and Warburg, 1971.

[3] The sophisticated innocence of this director is perhaps paralleled only by that of Labi Siffre, with his songs, his unique voice, his guitar and his impeccable (when he needs it) backing.

Connection and *Portrait of Jason* -- with these salutes we say, like James Fitzpatrick, farewell to the underground, area of experiments and surprises though, to be truthful, there have not been many of the latter since Cocteau and Buñuel.

Buñuel, though, is still with us, and continues to run circles round everyone, and not only the avant-garde and the underground. After his harsh and frightening *The Exterminating Angel*, the unpredictability of which was established right from the start when he sarcastically repeated his opening sequence; after the customary savageries of *Diary of a Chambermaid*, he pretended to be decelerating into a maturer and softer mood, befitting, no doubt, old age. Hence the comparative reticence of *Belle de Jour*, *The Milky Way* and, above all, of the almost tranquil *Tristana*. Needless to say it was all a trap. In 1972 Buñuel pounced. *The Discreet Charm of the Bourgeoisie* is as explosive a film as *Un Chien Andalou* or *L'Age d'Or* – though the behaviour of the ecclesiastics no less than the contents of grand pianos have now become much more sinister and macabre.

Shocking, uproarious, disturbing, temporally dislocating, this film is not only about a dream within a dream – it is about the dreams of the dreamers within the dream (and who will wake up in time?). It has the assault of a well-trained guerilla group armed with the very latest offensive weapons. It is magically funny, jam-packed with practical jokes and booby traps. It is startling and often fearful. It restores the avant-garde to its primacy and, if, which fate forbid, it is Buñuel's last film, it will surely be seen as the crowning glory of his astonishing career.

SIGNPOST - 1970

THE YEAR OF 'WOODSTOCK' AND 'GIMME SHELTER'

IN THE UNITED STATES

The wardrobes and props of MGM's Los Angeles studios are sold by auction. Twentieth Century-Fox announce a loss for the year of $77 million, while a low budget picture called *Easy Rider* is reportedly grossing $30 million. Huge successes are achieved by *cinéma-vérité* records of pop festivals (in addition to *Woodstock* and *Gimme Shelter*, there are *It's Your Thing, Nashville Sound, Elvis – That's the Way It Is*, and the short but sweet *Blues Like Showers of Rain*) which are the negation of the old traditions of Hollywood. Production increasingly moves out of the studios and onto location; and the age-level of audiences continues to drop. Joseph von Sternberg dies, as do Iris Barry, Charles Ruggles and Edward Everett Horton. In contradiction to the fashion for violence and permissiveness comes one single tear-jerker, *Love Story*, directed by Arthur Hiller; this is a smash hit, but fails to stem the tide. From the open-air world comes a steady from Howard Hawks, *Rio Lobo*, while Sam Peckinpah makes the unusually quiet and lyrical *Ballad of Cable Hogue*, much in contrast to Ralph Nelson's *Soldier Blue* with its revolting massacres. Fantasies come in all sizes, from the transvestite *Myra Breckinridge* (saved from disaster by the magnificent Mae West), *Black Flowers for the Bride* with Angela Lansbury and Michael York, and Arthur Penn's hassle with history and Dustin Hoffmann, *Little Big Man*, to the crashing Icarus of *Brewster McCloud* and the more old-fashioned *The Angel Levine*, made by the exiled Czech Jan Kadar with Harry Belafonte and Zero Mostel. Science fiction is represented by two first class and chilling glimpses into the future – George Lucas' *THX 1138* and Robert Wise's *The Andromeda Strain*. Thin on the ground are musicals (*Song of Norway, On a Clear Day You Can See For Ever*) and comedies (*Loving, The Landlord, Catch 22* and *The Boys in the Band*), but there are a number of admirable films on the human predicament (satirical or otherwise), of which the more outstanding are Barbara Loden's roughly made, inexpensive but convincing *Wanda* (made without assistance from her husband Elia Kazan), John Cassavetes' superb improvisations in *Husbands*, Martin Ritt's boxing story *The Great White Hope* based on the life-story of Jack Johnson, and Bob Rafelson's admirable *Five Easy Pieces* starring Jack Nicholson who, in turn, directed the equally admirable if sometimes confusing *Drive He Said*. The rise of the Negro cinema is further signalled by Melvin van Peebles' *Watermelon Man* and Ossie Davis' *Cotton Comes to Harlem*.

President Nixon presents a *New Strategy for Peace* to Congress, visits Italy, Spain, Eire and Great Britain, and later puts forward five-point proposals for peace in Vietnam. But his administration's murderous policy towards that unhappy country continues unabated, and the bombing is extended to Cambodia.

The Apollo Thirteen Moon Mission narrowly escapes disaster.

A number of students are killed and injured in riots at Kent University, Ohio, Jackson College, Mississippi, and in Augusta, Georgia.

The New York City Opera successfully mounts Donizetti's *Roberto Devereux*, with Beverly Sills as Elizabeth I, and Jerome Robbins evolves his third Chopin *oeuvre*, *In the Night*, for the New York City Ballet.

The Metropolitan and Boston Museums of Art celebrate their centenaries, and the untimely deaths are announced of Mark Rothko and Barnett Newman.

Saul Bellow publishes *Mr Sammler's Planet*, Dean Acheson releases his memoirs under the title of *Present at the Creation*, and Robert Lowell issues a volume of poetry entitled *Notebook*. Charles Reich and Charles Silbermann start controversies with *The Greening of America* and *Crisis in the Classroom* respectively. John Dos Passos dies.

On November 29th 76,000,000 persons across the United States view on television John Wayne's Sunday Night Special *Swing Out, Sweet Land*.

IN GREAT BRITAIN

A spate of classics includes *David Copperfield* and *Jane Eyre*, both directed by the American Delbert Mann; Robert Fuest's *Wuthering Heights*, Stuart Burge's modest *Julius Caesar*, Peter Brook's icily impressive *King Lear*; and a musical version of *A Christmas Carol* directed by Ronald Neame and entitled *Scrooge*. Period pieces include Ken Hughes' *Cromwell*, with Richard Harris in the name part and Alec Guinness as Charles I, and *The Last Valley*, James Clavell's fine and intelligent tale of the Thirty Years War, starring Michael Caine and Omar Sharif. The world of fantasy is represented by a screen version of Joe Orton's *Loot*, directed by Silvio Narizzano with Richard Attenborough, Hywel Bennett and Lee Remick; Billy Wilder's rather overdone *Private Life of Sherlock Holmes*; and Ken Russell's extremely overdone *The Music Lovers*, with Richard Chamberlain as Tchaikovsky. David Lean's new super, *Ryan's Daughter*, is panned by the critics and is a vast success at the box-office. Crime films are represented by Richard Fleischer's necrophilic *10 Rillington Place*, and Tony Richardson's outback epic with Mick Jagger, *Ned Kelly*. Two newcomers impress. Barney Platt-Mills, with an unknown cast and much improvisation, makes in *Bronco Bullfrog* a convincing film of frustrations attendant on life in the East End; while Anthony Scott's macabre but poetic *Loving*

Memory augurs well for his future career. The most striking films of the year are probably Christopher Miles' intense screen version of D. H. Lawrence's *The Virgin and the Gypsy* with Joanna Shimkus and Franco Nero; *Bartleby*, Anthony Friedman's sensitive interpretation of the Herman Melville story, with Paul Scofield and John McEnery; Lionel Jeffries' pellucid and charming version of the E. E. Nesbit classic *The Railway Children*; and Joseph Losey's hermetic film of pursuit, *Figures in a Landscape*.

The Government, whether Tory or Socialist, continues its equivocal if not hypocritical actions in relation to South Africa and Rhodesia; but strong popular protests against the visit of the South Africans cause the authorities to bring pressure on the Cricket Council to cancel the tour. Meantime the collapse of Biafra relieves Whitehall of the necessity of continuing its pusillanimity.

Shortly after visiting Ottawa and Washington, Harold Wilson makes the mistake of calling a General Election which the Conservatives, under Edward Heath, win with a majority of thirty.

The administration continues to blunder about amid the admittedly difficult situation among the warring tribes of Northern Ireland, but the full horror of what is to come is not suspected. The MP Bernadette Devlin is imprisoned for six months but returns to her seat in the Commons on her release.

Three new operas are staged – Michael Tippett's *The Knot Garden*, Richard Rodney Bennett's *Victory*, and Nicholas Maw's *The Rising of the Moon*.

Frederick Ashton retires from the direction of the Royal Ballet and is succeeded jointly by Kenneth MacMillan and John Field.

A kaleidoscope of indelicacy called *Oh! Calcutta* opens at the Round House and is later transferred to the West End.

In the theatre proper John Gielgud and Ralph Richardson enjoy great success in David Storey's *Home*; Terence Rattigan launches his play *Bequest to the Nation*, about Nelson and Lady Hamilton; and Harold Pinter produces a double bill with *Tea Party* and *The Basement*. Anthony Shaffer finds a new twist for the whodunnit in *Sleuth*; and Peter Brook, for the Royal Shakespeare Company, produces a breathtakingly beautiful version of *A Midsummer Night's Dream*.

Having meanly abolished free milk in schools, the Tory Government turns its attention to art, and seeks to abolish free entry to public museums and galleries.

Among successful exhibitions are a big Rodin show and a comprehensive conspectus of Kinetic Art.

C. P. Snow completes his *Strangers and Brothers* series with *Last Things*, and Lawrence Durrell publishes *Nunquam*, a sequel to *Tunc*. The centenary of Dickens' death is celebrated, among many books, by Angus Wilson with *The World of Charles Dickens* and by F. R. and Q. D. Leavis with *Dickens the Novelist*. Other publications of the year include Antonia Fraser's *Mary Queen of Scots*, Angus Calder's *The People's War*, John Fowles' *The French Lieutenant's Woman*, John Henning's *The Conquest of the Incas*, and Bernice Ruben's *The Elected Member*.

Roy Fuller receives the Queen's Medal for Poetry. The deaths are recorded of John Barbirolli, E. M. Forster, Air Chief Marshal Dowding (of the Battle of Britain), Bertrand Russell, Basil Liddel Hart, Laura Knight, Adeline Genée and, tragically, soon after his appointment as Chancellor of the Exchequer, Iain Macleod.

IN AUSTRALIA

The Canadian director Ted Kotcheff makes his brutally vivid film about the physical and mental deserts of *The Outback*, while with equal felicity the Englishman Nicolas Roeg directs his touching and beautiful *Walkabout*.

Although public opinion polls and demonstrations indicate continued opposition to the Vietnam conflict, the Federal Government under Premier Gorton remains largely hawkish.

The number of fatal automobile accidents is among the highest in the world, and various States bring in legislation, including compulsory seat-belts and breathalyzer tests.

A decline in the Wool industry leads to the formation of an Australian Wool Commission.

The Royal Family visit the Commonwealth on the occasion of the Bicentenary of its discovery by Captain Cook. The Pope pays an ecumenical visit to Sydney.

The Australian Ballet, whose director Peggy van Praagh becomes a DBE, presents *Don Quixote*, with Nureyev and Lucette Aldous.

Philip Roth's book *Portnoy's Complaint* is declared obscene by a court in the State of Victoria.

The death occurs of Field Marshal Slim, Governor of Australia from 1953 to 1960 and previously the hero of the Burma Campaign of World War II.

IN CANADA

Apart from the continuing progress of the seemingly imperishable National Film Board, Donald Shebib makes *Going Down the Road*, an inexpensive and convincing film about the adventures of two country boys seeking the good life in Toronto; John Trent makes a whizzing quickie about spare-part surgery – *The Only Way Out Is Dead*, with Burl Ives and Sandy Dennis; while David Cronenberg directs *Crimes of the Future*, a sci-fi fantasy about the collapse of genetics through over-use of cosmetics. Meantime Kerry Feltham effectively turns into a film, entitled *The Great Chicago Conspiracy Circus*, the Toronto Theatre Workshop's production of *Chicago 70*, in which the Chicago Conspiracy Trial is truly sent up in a hilarious parallel with the trial scene in *Alice in Wonderland*. Allan King, of *Warrendale* fame, makes *A Married Couple*, an intimate and of its nature sometimes rebarbative *cinéma-vérité* job about a family. Claude Jutra begins work on what is to be French Canada's *Pather Panchali*, the superb and moving *Mon Oncle Antoine*.

The year is bedevilled by the activities of the FLQ (*Front de la Libération du Québec*) which involve several kidnappings including that which ends with the sadistic murder of the Minister of Labour, Pierre Laporte. The Federal Government, under Premier Trudeau, proscribes the FLQ under Public Order Regulations 1970 which allow for wide powers of search and arrest. Despite attacks from opposition parties, this action receives massive (87%) public support.

Proposals at both Federal and Provincial levels to fight inflation by pegging prices and incomes run into trouble with Capital and Labour alike.

By unilateral action, and to the strong disapproval of the United States, Canada establishes a one hundred mile pollution control zone seaward in the Arctic.

Diplomatic relations are established with the People's Republic of China. The British Government's supply of arms to South Africa is strongly opposed, but trade between Canada and South Africa continues unabated.

A report by a Senate Committee on the Mass Media recommends steps to avoid monopoly, secret controls and the like.

At Expo 70 in Tokyo the Canadian Hall of Mirrors is regarded as an architectural triumph.

IN CHINA

Films made available to the West include one of the new-style Peking Opera called *Taking Tiger Mountain by Strategy*, and a long documentary, extremely well made, about peasants creating a vast new irrigation scheme and entitled *Red Flag Canal*.

Both films appear to have been made on a cooperative basis as no directors' names are given.

The rebuilding of the Party, begun after the 1969 Congress, continues apace, and the positions of the top men, including Mao, Lin Piao and Chou En-lai, seem assured.

Economically the emphasis is on light industry and small local units, while in agriculture a good harvest follows successful investment in irrigation, education and land reclamation.

The first Chinese satellite is launched into orbit.

Work starts in Africa on the Tanzania-Zambia Railway, which is being financed through a £169 million interest-free loan from the Chinese government.

A delegation is sent to Britain to discuss the purchase of civil aircraft.

IN JAPAN

Akira Kurosawa returns rather to the mood of *The Lower Depths* with his study of the dispossessed, *Dodeska-den*. Two directors devoted to social criticism, Shinsuke Ogawa and Shohei Imamura, continue their work, the former with *Winter in Narita*, which is the second part of *Liberation Front*, a film about the refusal of farmers to sell their land for the construction of an airport; and the latter with *Postwar Japanese History*, a personal story emphasizing the hardship of life in Japan after the end of the War. Meantime the prolific Nagisa Oshima is working on *The Man Who Left His Will on Film* and *The Ceremony*.

Expo 70 is an impressive success with total attendances estimated at 64 million; unlike most international exhibitions, it makes an operating profit equivalent to £19 million.

A Japanese satellite is put into orbit for the first time.

There is a dramatic increase in trade with China, with exports rising to nearly $4 million, and an equally dramatic increase in atmospheric pollution, notably from automobile fumes.

On the day on which he has completed his four-volume novel *The Sea of Fertility*, Yukio Mishima, one of Japan's finest writers, invades Military Headquarters with members of his 'Private Army' and attempts a coup. When this fails he and a companion disembowel themselves in the General's office.

The fourth economic conference with the USSR leads to plans for the modernization of Soviet ports in the Far East.

IN INDIA

A blazing row breaks out over the content of a Television Series shot for the BBC by the French director Louis Malle, which the Government regards as both derogatory and inaccurate. James Ivory makes his admirable and much misunderstood colour film *Bombay Talkie*.

Having run into difficulties, particularly over the privileges, financial or otherwise, of the former Rajahs, Indira Gandhi dissolves the Lok Sabha (Lower House) and in the ensuing General Election considerably consolidates her position.

In Maharashtra there are serious communal disturbances between Hindus and Muslims; of the latter 130 are killed and 34,000 made homeless.

The quarrel with the Sikhs over Chandrighar is solved by a compromise. Chandrighar goes to the Punjab while the new State of Haryana gets federal funds to build itself a new Capital.

An official report reveals that despite legislation the Harijans (Untouchables) still suffer discrimination and persecution.

IN EGYPT

Shadi Abdelsalam follows his masterly *Night of Counting the Years* with a beautiful and cogent short film, *The Eloquent Peasant*. At the same time the veteran director Youssef Shahin – the discoverer of Omar Sharif – completes his *El Ard* (*The Land*) which is generally regarded as his finest film. Much promising work is in evidence in the documentary field and among the students at the High Cinema Institute.

The crisis with Israel continues despite attempts by both the United States and the Soviet Union to calm things at United Nations level.

The country is thrown into mourning and confusion by the sudden death of President Nasser, who is succeeded by Anwar Sadat.

The new Aswan Dam comes into full operation, delivering no less than 2 million kilowatts.

IN BRAZIL

Ruy Guerra continues to share the _cinema novo_ movement with Glauber Rocha, and follows the latter's _Antonio das Mortes_ with another film about the Nordeste, _Os Deuses E Os Mortos_, a drama of conflict between landowners regardless of the festering discontent of the peasants.

Civil unrest proliferates, and accusations of police torture continue; they appear to be well-founded and are protested by various church dignitaries.

Kidnapping, as elsewhere, remains fashionable, and victims – all in due course released – include the West German and Swiss Ambassadors, and the Japanese Consul General in Sao Paulo.

The Nordeste area is plagued not only by drought but by the ruin of the coffee crop due to a new disease.

The Government signs an agreement on technical cooperation with Japan.

IN RUSSIA

Grigori Kozintsev parallels Peter Brook's English production with his noble and intelligent version of _King Lear_. On the other hand Igor Talankin, under the production of the expatriate Dimitri Tiomkin returning to Russia for this purpose shortly before his death, directs, with Innokenti Smoktunovsky in the name part, a respectful film on _Tchaikovsky_ which has nothing at all to do with Ken Russell's British extravaganza _The Music Lovers_. In the world of filmed music there is a remarkably skilful version of Borodin's _Prince Igor_, brought to the screen by Roman Tikhomirov. In a co-production with Italy Sergei Bondarchuk fails, in his spectacular _Waterloo_, to match the emotional conviction of _War and Peace_.

The centenary of the birth of Lenin, who once said 'For us cinema is the most important of the arts', is marked by an official hardening against any form of liberalism in the arts. A bust of Stalin appears over his Kremlin grave. Alexander Tvardovsky is expelled from the editorship of _Novy Mir_, while Alexander Solzhenitsyn is violently attacked for having been awarded the Nobel Prize and is inhibited from going to Stockholm to receive it. His cause is strongly defended by the great cellist Mstislav Rostropovitch, but attacks on him, as well as on Tarsis, Kuznetsov and Amalrik continue; and in due course the latter is consigned to a labour camp for three years. In general, and despite protests by the distinguished nuclear physicist Andrey Sakharov and others, the detention of intellectuals in prisons or, worse, in sinister 'psychiatric' hospitals run by the KGB, continues.

Meantime Brezhnev and Kosygin visit their colonial territory of Czechoslovakia to consolidate the position of the puppet regime. In Romania on the other hand the government insists on a measure of autonomy, and Brezhnev, miffed, refuses to head the Soviet delegation to Bucharest for the signing of a new Treaty of Friendship.

The cosmonauts Nikolaev and Sevastianov create a record by remaining in orbit round the earth for eighteen days. Luna 16 brings back the first samples of moon-rock; and the moon-vehicle Lunokhod 1 travels over the moon's surface.

The deaths are announced of the great film pioneer, Lev Kuleshov, and of Marshal Timoshenko, who in 1941 halted the Nazi's blitzkrieg advance at the gates of Smolensk.

IN CZECHOSLOVAKIA

The reactionary puppet regime set up by the Russians puts paid to the renaissance of Czech cinema. Jiri Menzel, whose last two films have been banned, returns to his career as a stage actor (though how long his theatre will remain active is open to question), while Milos Forman and Jan Kadar are working in the United States where they make *Taking Off* and *The Angel Levine* respectively. In Prague Jaromi Jires directs a not entirely successful fantasy, *Valerie and her Week of Wonders*

The regime abolishes the Film and Television Artists Union, and on the wider front the whole question of the renewal of Party cards comes up for official consideration, what time warnings are issued regarding signs of 'unhealthy liberalism' (sic). There are some signs too of growing anti-semitism, and the recently revived Boy Scout and Girl Guide movements are once again abolished.

Dubcek is finally disgraced by being removed from his post as Ambassador to Turkey.

IN HUNGARY

Miklós Jancsó follows his *The Confrontation* with the impressive *Agnus Dei* in which he returns to his earlier style. István Szabó makes *A Love Story*, and István Gaál, with *The Falcons*, directs a powerful film in which realism and allegory are remarkably combined.

In eastern parts of the country floods cause much damage and loss of life.

Brezhnev pays two visits to the country and appears to approve the cautious liberalism of the Kadar regime.

The appearance of Maoist cells is said to be causing official concern.

IN POLAND

Some directors are notable for their absence; Skolimowski is making *Deep End* in Munich, and Polanski is in Britain planning with Kenneth Tynan his screen version of *Macbeth*. Andrzej Wajda is completing his *Landscape After a Battle*, based on stories by Tadeusz Borowski and dealing with the attempts of released concentration camp prisoners to adjust to life after their liberation. Kazimierz Kutz's *Salt of the Black Earth*, about the Silesian uprising against the Germans after World War I, is reported to be a masterpiece.

Popular protests about work and living conditions are followed by riots which are savagely repressed. They bring about the downfall of Gomulka, who has just promulgated closer relations with West Germany. He is replaced by Gierek.

The intelligentsia continue to protest about the difficulties of contact with the outside world.

Adam Rapacki, architect of the Warsaw Pact, dies, as does General Anders, commander of the Polish forces during World War II.

IN YUGOSLAVIA

Vatroslav Mimica directs *The Event*, a melodramatic and extremely effective film based on a Tchehov *conte*. Meantime Dusan Makavejev is at work on what will turn out to be a liberating masterpiece, *W.R. – Mysteries of the Organism*, the making of which involves a good deal of shooting in the United States.

President Tito makes two visits to Africa, and President Nixon visits Yugoslavia.

There is a certain amount of industrial unrest, with which student bodies express sympathy.

IN WEST GERMANY

Peter Fleischmann's *Hunting Scenes from Lower Bavaria*, while ostensibly concerned with the persecution of a homosexual by narrowminded country folk, is really an attack on the persistence of anti-semitism, as too is Rainer Werner Fassbinder's rather less accessible *Katzelmacher*. Ulrich Schamoni directs *Wir-Zwei*, a kind of love story; and an admirable documentary of a performance of Bach's B Minor Mass is filmed in the Klosterkirche at Diessen by Arne Arnbom.

Despite much political chopping and changing the administration headed by Willy Brandt remains reasonably stable.

After some two and a half years, the lawsuit against the manufacturers of Thalidomide is settled by the payment of nearly £12 million to the victims of the drug.

Brandt visits Nixon in Washington to discuss proposals for a reduction in Nato and Warsaw Pact forces.

The Stuttgart Ballet under John Cranko mounts Scriabin's *Poème de l'Extase* with Fonteyn, and the Dusseldorf Ballet produces an impressive version of *Le Sacre du Printemps*.

Wolfgang Wagner's new staging of *The Ring* at Bayreuth meets with a mixed reception.

The designs, some of them remarkable, for the Olympiad building complex at Munich are made public.

German television carries out experiments – notably with the Rolf Harris Show – in co-production with the BBC.

Uwe Johnson's *Jahrestage* is the most discussed novel of the year; and the Georg Büchner prize goes to Thomas Bernhard's *Das Kalkwerk*.

IN SWEDEN

Ingmar Bergman has another success with his quite simple love story *The Touch*. On the sex front Mac Ahlberg makes a modern version of Zola's *Nana* (*Take Me, Love Me*) which seems strangely old-fashioned; but with *Blushing Charlie* Vilgot Sjöman, of *I Am Curious* fame, produces a not unsatisfactory *mélange* of sex, pregnancy and political commitment.

At the General Election, held under a new voting system, the ruling Social Democrat Party loses its overall majority but deems it unnecessary to seek a coalition.

A 'conscript parliament', got together at public expense and with the cooperation of the Minister of Defence and the Commander in Chief, is encouraged to express and discuss grievances in Army life.

In regard to the European Community, the Minister of Trade reiterates Sweden's general policy of neutrality, but indicates interest in a customs union and approval of EEC agricultural policy.

Elsa Marian von Rosen becomes Director of the Gothenburg Ballet; and Connie Borg forms a new Dance Company which performs at The Place in London.

IN DENMARK

Ole Søltoft, in *Bedroom Mazurka*, continues his surely over-prolonged initiation into the joys of sex. On the other hand Bent Christensen, in a co-production with Panama and USA, tells within the framework of one family the noble and impressive story of the rescue by the people of Denmark of nearly all the Jewish population condemned to extinction by the Nazis; despite moments of clumsiness this film, *Oktober-dage* or *The Only Way*, is honest and worthwhile.

Parliament votes by a massive majority for membership of the European Community.

With over 24,000 foreign workers in the country, the Ministry of Labour bans further admissions other than from Scandinavia for at least the duration of the winter.

Student bodies protest against statutes designed by the Ministry of Education to regulate the running of the Universities.

The Faroe Islanders complain that their representation on EEC is through the Danish delegation and not independently.

Peter Shaufuss of the Royal Danish Ballet appears as guest star in the London Festival Ballet.

IN SPAIN

In a co-production with France and Italy, Luis Buñuel makes his surprisingly tender, almost elegiac *Tristana*, beautifully performed by a cast which includes Catherine Deneuve, Fernando Rey and Franco Nero. Despite the autumnal glow, the film ends on a harsh note and with an echo of *The Exterminating Angel*.

Opposition to Franco continues to be voiced by the Falangists, who object to him naming Juan Carlos as his successor; they also make much capital out of the Matesa export firm scandal, in which several members of the Government appear to be implicated.

President Nixon visits Madrid. Under new arrangements the United States retains bases at Rota, Zaragoza and Madrid.

The Burgos Trial, in which some of the accused are priests, is accompanied by the kidnapping of the West German Consul who, however, is released on Christmas Day, what time six of the accused, found guilty of the murder of a police inspector, have their death sentences commuted to life imprisonment.

IN FRANCE

Claude Chabrol perceptively directs *Que la Bête Meure* (*Killer!*) based on a Nicholas Blake thriller. François Truffaut continues his Doinel saga with Jean-Pierre Léaud in *Domicile Conjugal* (*Bed and Board*) which seems somewhat stiff and laboured after the joys of *Baisers Volés*. With the fifth of his *Contes Moraux* Eric Rohmer, in *Le Genou de Claire*, makes further advances in the almost Proustian subtlety of his direction. Costa-Gavras follows his terrifying *Z* with his equally terrifying *L'Aveu*. With *Trafic* Jacques Tati is right back on form, while in *Vent d'Est* Jean-Luc Godard continues his desiccated and sometimes splenetic lectures on left-wing dilemmas. Chris Marker returns to Cuba with his not unimpressive *La Bataille des Dix Millions*.

General de Gaulle dies and the world pays tribute at his funeral.

President Pompidou visits Washington, Moscow, and Bonn.

Jean-Jacques Servan-Schreiber creates a sensation by whisking Mikis Theodorakis out of the Colonel's Greece in his private plane.

Five Israeli warships escape from Cherbourg and sail safely to Haifa.

Despite protests, France continues the programme of nuclear tests in the Pacific.

At the Grand Palais Pierre Schneider mounts a definitive exhibition of Matisse. There are also important retrospectives of Chagall and Giacometti, and an exhibition of some sixty magnificent Goyas in the Orangerie.

Jean-Louis Barrault produces his vast, roaring stage production of *Rabelais*.

Maurice Béjart celebrates the tenth anniversary of his Dance Company.

In the world of literature, De Gaulle's Memoirs are naturally a great success. Michel Tourneur wins the Prix

Goncourt with *Le Roi des Aulnes*, and François Nourrisier
is awarded the Prix Fémina for *La Crève*.

The deaths occur of Jean Giono, François Mauriac and
ex-Premier Daladier.

IN ITALY

Pasolini completes his *Decameron*, in which he himself plays the part of Giotto in
some of the more effective sequences. Elio Petri impresses with his *Investigation of a
Citizen above Suspicion*, and Vittorio De Sica returns to form with his delicately
probing tale of the persecution of the Jews in Fascist Italy – *The Garden of the Finzi
Continis*. Other films include Dino Risi's *The Priest's Wife* and Duccio Tessari's
Death Occurred Last Night; but the year is dominated by Bertolucci's brilliant,
disturbing and often beautiful films, based on the traumata of Fascism, *The
Conformist* and *The Spider's Strategy*.

One hundred years have passed since the Unification of
Italy.

Crises in the Government are additionally bedevilled
by rows with the Vatican over new divorce laws, which are
eventually passed in a modified form.

The Pope makes a visit to the Far East and escapes an
assassination attempt in Manila.

Diplomatic relations are established with China.

The sensational production of *Orlando Furioso* by the
Teatro Libero di Roma is taken to Edinburgh, Paris and
New York.

The composer Luciano Berio completes his important
Laborintus 2.

A novel by the veteran film director Mario Soldati,
L'Attore, becomes the year's best-seller.

Forty English martyrs are canonized in St Peter's.

CHAPTER 8

WHATEVER NEXT...?

I

In the last and indeed uncompleted interview which he gave before what, despite his great age, must be described as his untimely death, Igor Stravinsky was asked, 'Does the state of the arts really depress you?' He answered,

> 'Oh no. We live in a very exhilarating time, a little short of a golden age perhaps, but, well, consider, in the visual arts, the recent Warhol retrospective at the Tate; in the dramatic arts, Broadway category, the revival of the Betty Boop period; in literature, the new genre of reality recalled on tape (bestselling fall title: "Manson's Love Life As Told By His 'Family'"); and in music, the increasing involvement of everybody except the composer. And these developments have in turn produced a great critic, Jimmy Durante, who described it all very accurately when he observed that "Everybody is getting into the act".'[1]

Behind this sardonic and alarmingly accurate statement lies the whole question of the future of the Arts in, at least, our Western democratic civilization, which may well be collapsing, via decadence and totalitarianism, into a confusion as ignoble as that of Gibbon's Roman Empire.[2] The particular case of the moving picture may present more rather than less confusion than some of the other Arts; for we are concerned not only with aesthetic problems, but also with questions

---

[1] *New York Review of Books*, July 1st, 1971. The interview was dated March 17th; Stravinsky died on April 6th.

[2] '... the cycle so often repeated in the case of individual nations – Idealism, Disorder, Famine, Tyranny'. (Halford Mackinder, *Democratic Ideals and Reality*, 1919.) The totalitarianism I refer to above could include computers and a mindless bureaucracy.

of extraordinarily rapid technological developments in terms not only of the craft of the moving picture but also – and particularly – of its dissemination.

In so far as one can separate the mechanics of mass-communication from the inspirationalism of art itself, it seems sensible at this stage to begin a survey of future possibilities in terms of the audiences now available to the motion-picture maker and of the methods by which they can be reached. Even here the situation is by no means cut and dried, since the development of Super 8 and of half- or even quarter-inch videotape has in some areas brought about a complex within which audiences are in fact producing their own films.

As we have seen in the previous chapter, the long established and hitherto apparently immutable pattern of the production and distribution of the entertainment film spectacularly collapsed during the Sixties. Hollywood has virtually disappeared as a world centre, and has become only one of a number of broiler-houses designed to mitigate if not to satisfy the inordinate gluttony of television. Meantime – and in all this there is much interaction between the various elements involved – the mass audience has dwindled; it has begun to divide into smaller cells, like those minority groups which earlier were provided for by art-houses, specialized cinemas, film societies and that whole non-theatrical complex of educative, scientific, informational and similar interests, whose existence had been consistently ignored by film people until John Grierson pointed out that in seating capacity they outnumbered all the cinemas in the world. These minority groups have recently – though to a more limited degree – been noticed by television (schools programmes, *Sesame Street*, the *University of the Air* and *The Space Between Words*); and it is now only a matter of time before the videocassette, working on outright purchase or library subscription, will be able to supply myriad packages of visual information – from Eisenstein or De Mille through historical actualities to the History of Art, Newton's *Principia* illustrated, serializations of classics, or a conspectus of *Peanuts* – direct to people in their own homes, there to be shown and reshown at will.

The implications of this enormous new world of communication have not yet perhaps been fully realized by film-makers. Their essays in a new technological freedom are as yet tentative, in the sense that they are preoccupied with permissive concepts in terms of politics (anarchic or otherwise), supersex, or an overt desire to opt out of a disintegrating civilization by destroying the very medium through which alone they can express themselves. Hence Godard's diminution since *Weekend*; hence Warhol's exclusive preoccupation with the Muses' fundaments; and hence the arid bombinations of the minimal-cinéastes.

Yet the motion picture still remains one of the most powerful weapons in the battle to prevent the disintegration of our world through overpopulation and pollution, or destruction by the proliferations of nuclear 'strategy'. Ignorance, malnutrition and disease (each one of which breeds and multiplies from the others) can in terms of direct human approach on a large scale, be more easily combated by the visual/aural method than by any other, since film and television can communicate clearly and succinctly with people of all ages, sex and race, even if they have never learned to read or write. This fact is none the less important because it is a truism. It is one of the symptoms of decadence that it disregards the obvious.

Putting aside for the moment the question of aesthetics,[1] let us consider in broad outline the methodology and organization pre-requisite to a properly planned informational use of the visual media in the world today. We instantly come up against a significant problem, which is that those areas which most need mass visual media are those which are least equipped to use them.

While I was in India in 1969 I chaired a seminar at the National Film Institute in Poona during which the users of informational films confronted the producers and directors (actual and potential) who would be expected to supply them. There were the usual lively and important arguments about form and content, but what came constantly to the fore was the question of how to get simple but vital messages across to a population of some 550 million (and still growing) with some twelve totally different languages.[2] Apart from the obvious use of communal radio and the development of cheap transistor receivers (which, though both of them very valuable, lack the focusing of attention unique to the moving picture), two main solutions were presented. Firstly, the Indian Government had already acquired, at very considerable cost, a TV Satellite which, stationed high over the subcontinent, could beam during its lifetime of two years continuous and multiple programmes of education, information and exhortation to the populace. Secondly there was the question of travelling cinemas and

---

[1] I omit here the obvious fact that any informational film which does its job properly is bound to provide some sort of aesthetic satisfaction as well. The rules of box-office apply to the non-theatrical as elsewhere.

[2] Films Division, the Indian Government's official production centre, makes its newsreels and documentaries in Assamese, Bengali, English, Gujerati, Hindi, Kannada, Malayalam, Marathi, Oriya, Panjabi, Tamil, Telegu and Urdu.

the stationing of static film projectors (suitably serviced and regularly supplied with films by mail) in central village areas.[1]

From all this came the question – how many TV sets, how many cinema vans or static projectors must be deployed if an educational campaign was to have a chance of success, granted that this would mean blanket coverage of the entire population in a comparatively short space of time? At this point I remember enquiring how often a village in a remote area could be expected to see a travelling film show. The answer was once in three or even five years. Thus the magnitude of the problem was simply revealed. The Seminar recommended that in general the travelling vans should be used intensively in areas of easy access, and that for the wider necessities fixed projection spots in groups of villages should be set up; the simplicity of use of Super 8 projectors being an important factor here – allied to the fact that in any community one can find someone with a mechanical bent to whom the well-being of the apparatus can be entrusted (just as in any community one can always find a natural discussion leader). In due course, though at a fearful capital cost, television sets could be similarly installed.

Thus India's priority problems, notably the need for a huge increase in agricultural production and a huge decrease in population, depend in part on capital investment in the means of communication so large as to be liable to eat up some of the capital needed physically to promote the Green Revolution and Family Planning. It is as usual easier to reach the more sophisticated urban or suburban populations than those at the end of the road, the railway, and the electric pylons. God knows the 'sophisticates' need the information too, as anyone who has seen Bombay or Calcutta can testify; but there remains the problem of the other countless millions who are hardly in contact at all. 'Don't you realise,' said an Indian friend to me, 'that there are many who haven't even heard of Gandhi?'

The example of India is, with minor variations, repeated through-out Asia, Africa and Latin America. As the capital investment is far too large for the developing countries to envisage, there is an urgent need for the rich countries to partake in a world effort, channelled no doubt through the Specialized Agencies of the United Nations, by which apparatus and expert personnel could be properly deployed. Unesco and other bodies have already done fine pioneer work on these lines, but the scale (determined of course by finance) is far too small.

---

[1] It must be remembered that in India the word village connotes a large population grouping. The village of Desu, near Poona, where I filmed with my students, had, as I recollect, some 13,000 inhabitants.

It is not for me to labour these points much further; but when we talk about the possibilities for the motion picture in the Western world, we should never forget the problems which exist elsewhere. In one of the last articles he ever wrote John Grierson pointed out that

'. . . in India there is a special imperative for decentralising the film-making process. All the mass media together reach to only a hundred million of the population, leaving four hundred and fifty million to word-of-mouth, local educators, and itinerant entertainments of native origin. Obviously the biggest rôle in economic and social progress of all kinds will be with the local educators, making it necessary to add, in every way possible, to their local powers of persuasion.'

And, after pointing out that the varying languages also imply different ethnic and cultural backgrounds, he goes on:

'Film-making at district level is . . . a logical development; and one to which various foreign aid programmes should soon be giving their attention. This means . . . the appearance of peripatetic teachers of film-making, moving modestly from district to district, teaching the doctor-teachers and other local educationists how to hold their cameras and shoot simply *as their own native powers of exposition direct them. That would be a real 8mm revolution, anchored in necessity.*'[1]

These points he made additionally to a study of the potentialities of these new visual aids in areas like Europe and North America. Having noted the general decentralizing impulse initiated by Super 8 and videotape, and the Free Cine-Journals already adumbrated by Zavattini (mentioned earlier in this book), he issued a warning against taking this mechanized revolution too easily. If many people regard the '8mm revolution' as a magical path to self-expression, he pointed out that 'there are times . . . when self-expression means self-indulgence and this often at the expense of others. This matters . . . where self-indulgence means public hurt. Perhaps it doesn't matter in the midst of North American affluence . . . In poor countries self-indulgence, involving the selfish use of a valuable means of public instruction and expression, presents a simple and nauseous example of bad taste'.

Further than this, Grierson points out that there is an increasing danger that we may forget the old-established documentary principle of

---

[1] *A.I.D.News* (Bulletin of the International Association of Documentary Film-Makers: No. 2, November 1971).

making films not *about* people but *with* them (e.g. *Nanook of the North*, *Housing Problems*); and he adds that the decentralizing process has not yet gone far enough:

> 'The cinéastes may make their films *with* the people and *in* the villages, but they are soon off and away *from* the people and the villages to their normal metropolitan milieu. The old unsatisfactory note of faraway liberal concern for humanity-in-general creeps in . . .'

This can be true not in terms of visits to distant and exotic lands, but in terms of areas not far from one's own doorstep. And in this respect the *Challenge for Change* and allied programmes developed by the National Film Board of Canada (that impressive and constantly self-renewing monument to Grierson's genius and vision) represent a move very much in the right direction. The participation of the community, or sections of the community, in the making of a film can of itself become creative.

Of recent years there have been many examples of this in Canada, where widespread encouragement has been given to the development of film and TV programmes made *for* themselves and *about* themselves by local community groups. The vital elements here are two new factors in the realm of the mass media – VTR and Cable TV. The former – Video Tape Recording – involves the use of a small, simply operated sound/picture TV camera using comparatively cheap magnetic tape. The latter is a simple system by which highly localized TV programmes can be piped into people's homes, carrying not only national or provincial network material but also anything which the local owner or licensee of the Cable TV cares to disseminate.[1] This system, it should be noted, also carries with it a permanently available closed circuit system.

A pioneer Canadian experiment in these new techniques was a film called *VTR-St Jacques* (1968), when the Film Board made available some half-inch videotape equipment to the St Jacques Citizens Committee – an action group which had been formed in a low-income area of Montreal. The film shows how the Committee formed a group to learn how to use the new medium; and it is fascinating to observe these ordinary men and women going into the streets and talking and arguing with passers by on issues which really concern them. The people respond in various ways, usually positively in terms of matters

---

[1] Naturally there are many problems, including political considerations, which are involved. By the time this book has appeared these will no doubt have been fully discussed in print and otherwise. At the time of writing they are reasonably well covered by various *Challenge for Change* Newsletters from the National Film Board of Canada, and by *Challenge for Change* representations made to the Canadian Radio and Television Commission.

which affect them personally – bureaucracy, price of food, etc – but the fascinating point comes when the material obtained, roughly edited, is shown at various public meetings. When people see themselves talking they lose their inhibitions and, in relation to the visuals they have just viewed, take an ever more articulate part in the discussions. Later in the film there is a splendid moment in a press conference given by the Committee during which a journalist from a local paper speaks in the strongest terms against his face and voice being recorded; he fails to realize that he is in fact complaining about the roots of his own profession.

Another National Film Board experiment, by Anton Karch, took place in a coal-mining community where, among other things, a series of tape interviews with young folk was undertaken. The key point here, again, was the effect of the viewing of the VTR images by groups of young people, many of whom had been concerned in the interviews. As Karch makes clear,

> 'It very quickly brought large numbers of youth to view edited tapes of random youth interviews and created an intense level of dialogue. The willingness of the youth present at the first showing (about 30) to share their honest feeling with outsiders was surprising to me. The outcome of the first showing was a second invitation to meet with the Youth Club and share the tapes that had already been done with the Club executive.
>
> 'The young people were anxious to view tapes of themselves and their friends. The conversation that followed did not dwell on the contents of the tape, but rather took off from them. The tape then provided a focal point, and precipitated an openness that would not have been possible had I related to the group without the use of VTR.'[1]

Similar work has of course been carried out in the United States, as witness the *Catch 44* programme in which a Boston station gives the air to community groups for peak periods to use as they please. And of course 16mm or 8mm films can also achieve a good deal along the same lines, as witness *The Troublemakers* (1966) by Robert Machover

---

[1] As Colin Low, in charge of *Challenge to Change*, has pointed out, the dialogue essential to problem-solving in society 'requires that the speaker and listener reverse rôles'; and this is especially true in the relationship between an individual and an organization. The fact that this happens *visually* is, it is clear, exceedingly important. The other point is the simplicity of the VTR apparatus. My friend George Stoney (who earlier made that classic documentary *All My Children*) tells me he edits his video films in the subway on the way home.

and Norman Fruchter. This was a modest and fairly crudely made film about a group in Newark N.J. trying to improve local living conditions by community action, largely in relation to the local authorities. This film, by its sense of total participation by all concerned, and by the honest way it shows the mistakes as well as the successes as they eventuate, remains gratefully in the mind.

So, just as Grierson envisaged for India 'the peripatetic teachers of film-making', in the fully developed countries it is becoming increasingly possible for people to depend less on material supplied to them from centre, and more on material which they themselves can evolve from their own grass-roots. This means that in addition to national TV networks, any community can evolve its own local, intimate programmes and projects (as modest, if you like, as a parish magazine) which can be locally supplied through the use of 8mm cameras or VTRs whose use is no more, indeed less difficult to master than a typewriter. To quote the Canadian argument again, 'Community television can ensure the right to be informed and the right to inform. Communication becomes a two-way street, and feedback is built into the media.' In the end videotape may turn out to be cheaper and easier than film; but whichever you use you will be bringing together human beings in terms in which they can together find the growing points which may lead to a better life.

That all these innovations could be subject to abuse by ambitious or unscrupulous organizations or individuals is obvious. In Canada and the United States plans have already been laid for the establishment of charter systems by which operators of Cable TV can be kept under reasonable control. And the more the smaller communities can have access to the major media, the less easy it should be for the malevolent or the power-seekers to creep up on society.

Another encouraging aspect of this new availability of the means of production is the increasing production of films by school-children, both as a means of self-expression in itself (especially for the youngest age-groups), and as a means of expressing youngsters' newly discovered attitudes to the community, the nation, the world – and of course each other. It may be no bad thing for kids to learn the disciplines – however minor – of these means of expression instead of waiting until, in the joint explosions of puberty and political consciousness, they start to lose their creative bearings in orgies of intolerance or self-indulgence. I note in passing that in every session of children's films I have seen, the best were those in which the influence of the teacher was least discernible.

All of this means that the difference between the professional and the amateur is tending to become blurred. In terms of the use of basic apparatus for the recording of visuals and sound, the amateur can show a basic technical performance much nearer to that of the pro and often, in purely mechanical terms, equal. But as in all arts, there is more to it than that. There is a place for *bricolage*, of course, as such admirable annual events as the Amateur Film Festival at Glasgow so pleasantly testify; and the *bricoleur*, as we have already seen, may also become a community leader in media terms. But the real thing involves whole-time, lifelong devotion and struggle; and here the dividing line, however easy the machinery, is spiky and strict. There is no short cut to a Portinari Triptych or a Ninth Symphony.

II

What we are today seeing is, in effect, a two-way split in the world of the moving picture. In one direction lies the microcosm of the small screen; the picture in the parlour, even the portable picture. And however large the size of the parlour screen becomes it will still be small in essence; one may make the comparison with what art-dealers call 'gallery paintings' – canvases too extensive to fit on the wall of an average room since there is simply no space to stand back and take them in.

In the other direction lies the macrocosm of new conceptions going beyond wide and/or multiple screens, perhaps taking the moving picture out of the theatre and into the open, perhaps developing a new world of kinetics and synaesthetics which may still await its first Diaghilev.

It must be noted here that the split is no longer between film and television; it is between two different approaches to the use of the moving picture. It is no longer valid to think of the machinery of television as small and that of cinema as big. As we have already seen, film-makers are increasingly using 16mm and even 8mm film and apparatus, to say nothing of videotape – the possibilities of which are only just being explored.[1] The financial savings are of course obvious –

---

[1] It is worth remembering Gance's use of the camera in *Napoléon*, as in the sequence in the Assembly with the swinging chandelier; also that as early as *Paths of Glory* Kubrick was personally shooting key sequences with a hand-camera, just as he did more recently in *A Clockwork Orange*.

and not least in terms of the work of students at film schools. On the other hand television is no longer confined to small screens; during Expo 70 in Japan coloured television images, projected through crystals by laser beams, were shown on fourteen foot screens with little or no loss of definition.

Thus the idea of large-scale synaesthetic 'happenings' could well involve televisual as well as cinematic techniques. The difference between our pictorial macrocosm and microcosm is not mechanical but intellectual; that is, it involves attitudes of mind about visual communication in aesthetic, philosophical, social, educational and political terms.

The conception of a series of 500 films covering the whole history of world art available on video-cassettes is in its own way macrocosmic. On the other hand the conceptions underlying the pullulating production line of the Warhol factory – double-screens and all – are nugatory; their ideology could be writ large on the point of a pin.

In looking forward towards new possibilities for the motion picture, one needs to see which contemporary directors are thinking ahead in practical and creative terms. From such a viewpoint I reckon that it is the Bertoluccis, the Kubricks, the Makavejevs and the Roegs who are moving forward; while the Godards, the Straubs, the Peckinpahs and the bulk of the so-called Underground are standing still, if not moving backward.

It saddens me to say this of Godard who, as I have already said, I regard as a cinematic genius. But he seems to have got himself stuck in an ideological impasse in which he hasn't left himself enough room to turn round and so come back. The trouble with *Pravda* and *Vent d'Est* is that for all their toying with the dismantling of the *status quo* and the establishment of the *status mao* – all in the name of pure Marxism-Leninism – they are films which collect dust while we are watching them. The costumed girls in *Vent d'Est* are no more than *simulacra* of the Emily Brontë of *Weekend*, whom Godard immolated, no doubt, because her escapism was 'not a mere departure from conditions she hated, like that of many romantics, but a positive attainment of ideal conditions, of that union with nature which she prayed above all to achieve, even before the deliverance of death would secure her a "mutual immortality" with the earth she loved'.[1] However that may be,

---

[1] *Emily Brontë* by Winifred Gerin, Clarendon Press, 1971. I am aware that the main provenance of the Brontë episode is the last sequence of Truffaut's *Fahrenheit 451*; but, as so often with Godard, what begins as a somewhat back-handed *hommage* develops into something deeper.

it has become rather tiring to participate in Godard's ideological crises presented in the form of filmic notebooks. And in *Vent d'Est*, even when he brings himself to a choice of routes – and in this there should be at least an element of drama – he turns his back on the issue; and yet in his earlier works he had shown himself to be no Laodicean. Has he got himself stuck in that Marxian world which is 'a web of relationships, extending through space and time, into which we can break only with difficulty, and whose isolated bits, physical or ideational, always contain within themselves the severed connections to other parts of the totality from which they were forcibly wrenched?'[1] This would in part explain why in *Vent d'Est* he continually destroys every thesis he himself advances and every argument he himself puts up. The jokey Western setting and style cannot disguise the fact that he has reached something approaching a state of nihilism or even despair.

Godard himself has said, 'There is really a tremendous cleavage between cinema and politics: those who understand politics don't understand cinema, and the lack of comprehension is reciprocal'. To which Colin J. Westerbeck Jnr, in an interesting analysis of the Godardian dilemma, adds, 'If this is the case, he may have to give up film-making after all, as he said he would'.[2]

It is interesting to note that both Bertolucci and Makavejev are escapees from the Godard fold. Even Glauber Rocha, who appears at the crossroads in *Vent d'Est* vainly indicating the choice between aesthetic exploration or the harsh reality of the Third World, proves in his own work that the choice is in fact other: a commitment to the needs and urgencies of the Third World does not *ipso facto* negate the idea of aesthetic experiment. Whatever their faults, *Terra im Transe* and *Antonio das Mortes* transmit their revolutionary message through cinematic techniques as challenging and exciting as those evolved by Godard in earlier days.

[1] *Through the Marxian Maze* by Robert L. Heilbroner, New York Review, March 9th, 1972. In the same article Heilbroner remarks that 'the persistent attraction of Marxism, in the face of its confusing vocabulary, is . . . evidence that Marx manages to assert himself by the reverberations of his thought even when his argument escapes us'.

[2] *A Terrible Duty is Born*, Sight and Sound, Spring 1971.

III

It would seem therefore that for the genuine growing points we shall have to regard Godard as a non-runner.[1] The breaking away of directors like Bertolucci and Makavejev represents a swing back to a warmer, more human response to the internal and external problems of the individual's relations to society and, indeed, to mankind as a whole. The Borgesian approach adopted by Bertolucci – paralleled in part by Roeg in *Performance* – concerns itself, of course, not only with questions of identity but also with questions of time. If in *Partner*, when he was still under the influence of Godard, Bertolucci over-concentrated on the anarchic aspect of the *doppelgänger* or the split-personality, he proceeded thereafter, in *The Conformist* and *The Spider's Strategy*, to a more straightforward approach to the major issue of the individual as a victim of other people's pasts as well as of his own, and the resulting responsibilities which fall on him in his closest human relationships.

Thus in *The Spider's Strategy*, the living Athos junior and the dead Athos senior are in a sense both shipwrecked on the immutable rock of Dreyfa, who is an integral part of both of their lives. The web of time from which the young sailor escapes, but young Athos does not, is of her making. Similarly Roeg, moving beyond the mainly Borgesian conception of *Performance*, shows in *Walkabout* how the brash yet old-before-its-time white civilization of Australia is liable to be trapped in the vast prison of the island continent because of a failure to consider, or even to try to understand, the million-year aspects of the vegetation, the animals and the aborigines on whom they have only in part succeeded in imposing themselves. That Housman cry about 'lost content' at the end of *Walkabout* is not merely a lament for the never-to-be-recaptured joys of youth; it is also a despairing acknowledgment of that brick wall with which Roeg physically represents the barrier which the technocrat has erected against the dangerous intrusion of historical and cultural reality.[2] And Kubrick's *volte face*

---

[1] Though he might find salvation in something like what Dostoievsky's Grand Inquisitor said, *inter alia*, to the returned Jesus: 'Dost thou know that the ages will pass, and humanity will proclaim by the lips of their sages that there is no crime and therefore no sin; there is only hunger. "Feed men, and then ask of them virtue!" – that's what they'll write on the banner which they will raise against thee.'

[2] Writing to *The Times* during a controversy over a BBC Series about the defunct British Empire, an Australian, Professor Bruce Ryan, hinted at this in pointing out that 'vast areas of Australia are littered with the abandoned vestiges of settlement . . . and,

from *2001* to *A Clockwork Orange* may indicate a concern not only with time (which may be running out as well as running on), but also with the more immediate desolations of a cultural wilderness.

Meantime, whooping like a Red Indian brave, Makavejev gallops round the ideological encampments of both East and West, and in his encirclement shows them to be in many ways indistinguishable from each other. A prophet of joy rather than doom, he points out the idiotic and masturbatory bases of this era of the concentration camp and the closed mind. Prophet of *joie de vivre*, he hands to Jeremiah a box of balloons, streamers and fireworks; to Ezekiel a do-it-yourself taxidermist's kit. Where Godard constipates, Makavejev induces a blessed liberation in the bowels.

He has invented his own technique of cinematic collage, the effectiveness of which has increased film by film, and perhaps came to fruition in *W.R. – Mysteries of the Organism*. It is a system which allows him to juxtapose almost anything with anything; and there has probably been nothing like it in cinema since Eisenstein's orgiastic *Strike*, Dovzhenko's kaleidoscopic *Zvenigora*, and Buñuel's first two bombing attacks on the Establishment – *Un Chien Andalou* and *L'Age d'Or*.

Makavejev has said that he sees the cinema as 'a guerilla operation. The guerilla can use whatever weapons he likes, paving stones, fire, bullets, slogans, songs. The same with movies. We can use everything that comes to hand, fiction, documents, actualities, titles. "Style" is not important. You must use surprise as a psychological weapon . . . We can even use material taken from the enemy.'[1] He adds,

> 'You needn't be violent to be effective. To fight in the street with paving stones is to talk the same language as the police of the bourgeois society, it is to rediscover the values of aggression and violence on which this society is built. On the other hand, to act like the hippies, to offer flowers to the cops, forces the cops to find a new way to react. If you are patient, and offer them flowers for long enough, there must come a moment when they give in: there is nothing they can do but weep, go mad, or kill themselves.'[2]

although the present population pursues a very different life style in a very different urban environment . . . thousands of Australians undertake safaris into this desolate country . . . searching like lost children for their origins, however illusory the quest may be'. (*The Times*, March 14th, 1972.)

[1] As he does with such devastating effect in *W.R. – Mysteries of the Organism* when he juxtaposes Gelovani's priggish portrayal of Stalin in *The Vow* with the polystyrene reproduction of the phallus of the editor of *Screw*.

[2] I am indebted for these quotes to David Robinson's excellent article, *Joie de Vivre at the Barricades*, in *Sight and Sound*, Autumn 1971.

From his first film, *A Man Is Not A Bird* (1966), in which he peppered a story film with *cinéma-vérité* shots and a screen lecture by a hypnotist, Makavejev has steadily developed his collage technique. In *Innocence Unprotected* (1968), he took hold of a naïve film made during the German Occupation by and about the life and adventures of a well-known strong-man, and entwined it decoratively with garlands of reminiscence, hand-tinted effects, contemporary newsreels and the like; most charming of all was the picnic party enjoyed by the surviving cast of the film on the grave of the actor who had played the villain in it.

As for *The Switchboard Operator*, made in 1967 – a year before *Innocence Unprotected* – this can now clearly be seen as a sort of preliminary sketch for *W.R. – Mysteries of the Organism*. Like its successor, it pretends at the outset to be a lecture on sex; then it pretends to be a story about a telephone girl's faithless adventures with two boy-friends – adventures which lead to episodes of death which in turn lead to another lecture, this time on criminology . . . and so to documentary disquisitions on rat-catching, cooking, copulation and, to cap all, a series of *tableaux vivants* illustrative of mythic sex. In fact Makavejev here never stops pulling the rugs from under our feet; and this is a fault, for we tend to end up with too many bruises on our metaphorical bums for comfort.

In *W.R. – Mysteries of the Organism* (1971) this imbalance is corrected. Not only does the film have a definite sense of construction, it also propounds a thesis which seems to satisfy a definite inner need of a majority among its audiences. Just as VTR and Cable TV can be combined to make it possible for audiences to produce, participate in, watch and discuss their own films, so here, working from outside, Makavejev suddenly manages to clarify and even dissipate the foetid atmosphere of ideologies and obsessions, national and international, civilized and barbaric, by which so many of us are obfuscated and which seep unceasingly at us from printing press, screen, and all the other manifestations of the media.

We see, we listen afresh. Here is a codification aimed at the heart as well as at the intellect. The passages which ought to be shocking – Nancy Godfrey and Buckley's erection; Andric and Kaloper having it off all over Dravic's apartment; the intercutting of Nazi experiments on the mentally sick with American women moaning and groaning as they perform their orgasmic Reichian exercises – are not shocking in the obscene sense. The shock is that of a cold shower, of a sudden clearing of the brain.

The film is not, of course, a defence of the actual orgone theory.

However valid Reich's earlier philosophy may have been,[1] the delusion that orgone- or bio-energy were actually 'universally present and demonstrable visually, thermoscopically and by means of Geiger-Müller counters'[2] led him into unnecessarily improbable byways and, finally, into gaol. Here Makavejev noted, no doubt, that Reich's fate at the hands of American justice bore some resemblance to that being meted out currently to dissident Soviet intellectuals who are incarcerated in 'mental hospitals' for 'special treatment'. Certainly Reich, after his imprisonment in 1954 for contempt of court (he refused to withdraw his claims for his orgone boxes which the courts had ruled fraudulent), 'was diagnosed paranoid and transferred to Lewisburg, which was the only penitentiary with psychiatric treatment facilities, where he was however declared "legally sane and competent" [2].

Makavejev's pity for Reich causes him to end the film with a stroke of real genius. After the all-out attacks on the Isms of this world, on the artificial separation between sex and societal organization and on the mindless injustices resulting therefrom, he mounts a macabrely ridiculous climax and instantly melts it into a coda of elegiac loveliness. Earlier we have attended on Dravic's constant attempts to seduce Vladimir Ilich, the pretty-boy Soviet ice-skater, which climaxes in his striking her because she is grabbing at his genitals. The next thing we know is that after an orgy of sex with her (the post-mortem reveals so much semen in her that the possibility of mass-rape is considered), he has decapitated her with one of his skates. While her severed head, on the mortuary slab, still proclaims the joys of sexual passion, we see him, lonely, lost, *but free at last*, wandering in subtopian scrublands amid the unfinished artefacts of modern engineering and among groups of the dispossessed sitting round extempore fires, while he sings a song to Almighty God. The song outlines to God the simple needs of men and women and begs Him to grant them; and at the end of each verse comes the refrain, 'and please spare a small thought for me'.[3] And as he

---

[1] It was, put briefly, 'Make love not war'. One may note also that Reich's earlier theory of Vegetotherapy was based, not unreasonably, on the idea that the Unconscious is to be found in the parasympathetic system – i.e. those areas of our nervous system 'which are not capable of being directly affected by acts of will' (*Reich*, by Charles Rycroft). See also A. T. W. Simeons' point that 'Modern man is so overwhelmed with his cortical achievements that he has forgotten that his body is still functioning on a level that was normal before the dawn of culture. The diencephalic reactions of his body, which no longer make sense to his cortex, he misinterprets as disease, and thereby lays down the pattern that eventually leads him into psychosomatic suffering.' (*Man's Presumptuous Brain*.)

[2] Rycroft, op. cit.

[3] This song, be it noted, is by the Soviet underground poet Bulat Okudjava; entitled 'Ode to François Villon', it is sung on the soundtrack by Okudjava himself.

wanders to the sound of this extremely beautiful song, Vladimir Ilich finds himself face to face with a white horse – lone, unharnessed – and somehow this confrontation brings a feeling of tearful liberation and a purging of prejudice and anger.[1]

All of us, I suppose, are looking for a suitable prophet, while at the same time being well aware of how prophets are honoured. There are certainly a number of people who view Makavejev as a disgusting and boring director, just as there are others who feel the same about Stanley Kubrick. I am for Kubrick equally with Makavejev. The sense of liberation obtained from the latter is reinforced by the former's ability to convey the idea of a mysterious, dangerous, but possibly beautiful future. Thus I find myself as equally *en rapport* with the end of *2001 – A Space Odyssey* when the foetus of the star-child appears, as with the slow dissolve from Dravic's severed but triumphant head, still spouting the joys of sex, to a close-up of Reich. Behind each of these cinematic gestures lie the riddles of Time, of Jung's Collective Unconscious, of Freud's mysterious conversion of Ego and Id into 'a form of science fiction',[2] and of the incredible continuity of the aborigine. In the finales of these two films (and indeed elsewhere in them)[3] there resides that essence which the Bushmen of Africa, who believe it is acquired at the very moment of birth, call *now*. It is supernatural, uncontrollable – but under certain circumstances can be tapped and used.

'It is a supernatural essence that forever after connects the person born with certain forces in the world around him: with weather, with child-bearing, with the great game antelope, and with death . . . *Now* is intangible, mystic and diffuse, and Bushmen . . . do not know how or why *now* changes the weather but only that it does. They watch the changes carefully, though, and by observing have discovered the limits of their own *nows*. When the fluid from a

[1] The dominant figure of Makavejev must not be allowed to obscure other Jugoslav directors, in particular Vatroslav Mimica, who combines animation work with feature films, the most important of the latter probably being *The Event* (1961), a chilling and melodramatic film based on a Tchehov short story with, among other things, a woodland fight to the death which is a sort of reversal of the assassination scene in *The Conformist*; Aleksander Petrovic, best known for his fine and humanistic *I Even Met Happy Gipsies* (1967); Zvonimir Berkovic, whose *Rondo* (1966) played interesting intellectual variations on the eternal triangle in terms, partly, of chess; and of course Dusan Vukotic, one of the world's most original and perceptive animators (*Concerto for Machine Gun, Substitute* etc) who has latterly moved into live action pictures like *The Seventh Continent* (1966), and combinations of live action and cartoon as in *A Stain on the Conscience* (1968).

[2] Rycroft, op. cit.

[3] We might add *Walkabout, La Jetée* and *Je t'Aime, Je t'Aime*.

mother's womb falls upon the ground the child's *now* is determined, and it is partly for this reason that birth is such a mighty thing.'[1]

In the last moments of *2001*, is Bowman (Sagittarius), who has perhaps passed his whole life in that Louis XVI bedroom dreaming from Apeman to Hal to Jupiter, is Bowman waiting on that strange common threshold of life and death for the spilling of the precious fluid? That the tender globule in which the starchild stirs is also perhaps the spacepod in which Bowman was imprisoned is another possible factor in Kubrick's haunting and puzzling ending to a film which, like Teilhard de Chardin, considers whether 'life will not perhaps one day succeed in ingeniously forcing the bars of its earthly prison, either by finding the means to invade other inhabited planets or . . . by getting into psychical touch with other focal points of consciousness across the abyss of space'.[2]

In Kubrick's rupturing cut from the apeman's bone cast into the air to the space vehicles waltzing among the spheres there is a further echo of de Chardin's picturization of

'. . . mankind labouring under the impulsion of an obscure instinct, so as to break out through its narrow point of emergence and submerge the earth; of thought become number so as to conquer all habitable space, taking precedence over all other forms of life; of mind, in other words, deploying and convoluting the layers of the noosphere.[3] This effort at multiplication and organic expansion is . . . the summing up . . . of all human prehistory and history, from the earliest beginnings down to the present day.'[4]

There are those today who seriously propound theories that before our presently known prehistory there lies hidden another history of our world inhabited by men (indigenous or from outer space) who knew well those great secrets of the universe which we ourselves are only now approaching.[5] Perhaps they destroyed themselves; perhaps, like men today, having discovered the means of incinerating this globe, they moved farther out into space. Kubrick's monolith in *2001* belongs to an infinite continuum belying time. Our actual moon vehicles and

[1] *The Harmless People* by Elizabeth Marshall Thomas, Vintage Books, 1965.

[2] *The Phenomenon of Man*, Collins, 1959.

[3] The noosphere is defined by Julian Huxley as 'the sphere of mind, as opposed to, or rather superposed on, the biosphere or sphere of life, and acting as a transforming agency promoting . . . progressive psychosocial evolution'. (de Chardin, op. cit.)

[4] Op. cit.

[5] See *We Are Not The First* by Andrew Tomas; also *Chariots of the Gods and Return to the Stars* by Erich von Daniken (all published by the Souvenir Press).

Kubrick's further projections of them underline the utter need for an escape route from the finale of *Dr Strangelove*, with its insane cackle of 'Mein Führer – I can walk!' followed by the explosion of the dooms-day machine.

Kubrick's eclecticism needs no stressing. Of the nine feature films he has made since 1953 four, however, seem to me to be progressively linked in message and intention. *Paths of Glory* is concerned with the *internal* elements of mutual human destruction within the fairly narrow historical perspective of a war which, more than any other, staggered under the burden of its own anachronism; *Dr Strangelove* is involved in a survey of man's very real ability for self-destruction so horrifying that it must be treated as farce; *2001* questions the ultimate destination reserved for man in his attempted escape towards the stars and space; and *A Clockwork Orange* is, as far as I can guess, designed as a con-temporary warning to all of us in the shape of a kind of regressive anti-masque to *2001*. Thus memories of Poole and Bowman's conflict with Hal are disturbingly aroused by Alex being 'wired for sound and vision' by the practitioners of the Ludovico Treatment. Similarly the 'functional'[1] costumes of Alex and his droogs, the desolate urban land-scapes where the basic ideas of Use have become antiquated and useless, and above all the hideous interior of the Cat Woman's house where she and Alex fight to the death with Beethoven bust and plastic phallus – all these look like ghastly parodies of the spacecraft interiors or of Clavius; while Alex's relations with his parents have something in common with Poole's complete lack of interest in the birthday TV message from his mother and father. But what is outstanding about *A Clockwork Orange* is its complete pessimism. For, having established that to be brainwashed into vegetabilism is worse than living in violence with freewill, Kubrick leaves us with . . . violence; the anti-masque becomes really vicious. There is no softening as at the end of *Paths* of *Glory* when Dax sees the German girl singing to the troops; there is no efflorescence as at the end of *2001* with the appearance of the starchild. Alex is resurrected into cruelty and violence; he has become Strangelove.[2]

[1] In the third paragraph of Burgess' book the purpose of each item of apparel is clearly specified.

[2] It would seem that Anthony Burgess added an extra chapter to his book at some stage. At any rate my 1970 copy of *A Clockwork Orange* ends with Alex meeting his old droog Pete, who has now completely settled down into married respectability. Into his own mind there then comes the seductive thought of a wife and, subsequently, a son. True, he expects that his son will grow up to behave like he himself did. But in this instinct to retire into a more bourgeois ambiance he may, by the exercise of his own will, escape into a quiet but non-Ludovico world – grey perhaps, but not without grace. This solution Kubrick, in the film, certainly ignores.

Kubrick's influence on the use of the motion-picture arises from his concern for the future of mankind. It is therefore dangerous to try to ignore *A Clockwork Orange*. Not only does it show a world so nearly our contemporary one that we cannot draw away from it, it also re-establishes the prophetic nightmares of those seminal works of the Thirties – Auden and Isherwood's *The Dog Beneath the Skin* and Rex Warner's *The Wild Goose Chase* and *The Aerodrome*.

If, as I have just suggested, it runs in a recidivist parallel to *2001*, we must try to accept and understand it as such. Filmwise *A Clockwork Orange* is splendidly *mouvementé*. Speed, or its reverse, is of the essence. I don't personally approve of the high-speed double-fuck to Rossini's *Thieving Magpie* overture; this would-be clever visual joke traduces the appalling reality of the book when the two girls, who are only ten years old, 'this time . . . thought nothing fun and stopped creeching with high mirth, and had to submit to the strange and weird desires of Alexander the Large which, what with the Ninth and the hypo jab, were choodessny and zammechat and very demanding . . .' This, like some other sequences (in the prison and with the reformers), tends to soften up our attitude to Alex, to get us, just a little even, on his side. This doesn't happen in the book.

Other interferences with the time factor are effective. The switch to slow-motion at the swimming pool – especially in the cutting of Dim's wrist – is not just a trick but a demonic emphasis; even more so is the single super-slow-motion shot of Alex being bashed with the milk bottle outside the Cat Woman's house.

Kubrick uses other methods of involving us. As in *Paths of Glory* and *Dr Strangelove*, he uses flat-on longshots leading to a vanishing point by which we are pinned to a 'physical sense of things irrevocably on the move', as in the execution no less than the battle scenes of the former, or as in the 'continuing ride into nightmare' of the bomber in *Dr Strangelove* which 'accelerating in depth anticipates the cosmic ride into the unknown in *2001*'.[1]

Thus in *A Clockwork Orange* the deserted casino in which the two gangs fight it out; the set-ups in which Alex is compelled to watch the Ludovico horror film; and in particular the singular horror of the 'Singing in the Rain' sequence, with its brutal rape and the filthy kicking, in time to the music, at the skull of the helpless egghead – all these represent a style of cinema from which everything superfluous has been removed. It is a distillation.

[1] All these quotes are from Alexander Walker's *Stanley Kubrick Directs* (Harcourt Brace Jovanovitch, 1971).

Where the film loosens – as in Alex's vision of his rôle during Christ's walk to Calvary (which in any case Buñuel would do so much better) – or in the introduction of the police inspector from Joe Orton's *Loot* dressed up as Hitler-Himmler – we become disturbed because the film loses its style. It is only the Nadsat dialogue, as formal as that of Restoration comedy, which brings it back into line and so to the structured cinematic pattern through which Kubrick seeks to impose on us the inwardness of the predicaments and problems of our times.

The technical innovations, or perhaps more accurately the new applications of established techniques used by both Makavejev and Kubrick, should not be underestimated. Makavejev's collage system is deceptively simple; it is by no means an indiscriminate magpie's hoard. He succeeds over and over again in superposing or mingling series of ideas or statements in such a way that our oversimplifications or, if you like, conditioned reflexes regarding sex, society and ideological conflicts, are dissipated in favour of a sharper, more disturbing and more acid outlook. No sooner have we begun to savour a savage joke at the expense of Joe Stalin than we are forced to examine the implications of Warhol's repellent transvestite Jackie Curtis swishing through Times Square licking an ice-cream, and this in relation to the hideous experiments in the Nazi concentration camps. It is perhaps a logic first invented by Buñuel, but Makavejev uses it in his own brusque way to jostle us off the road and into the nettles at the side of the track. He has certainly overpassed Godard's effort in the same direction, though of course the latter more or less abandoned this sort of approach after making *Weekend*.[1]

As for Kubrick, it is hardly necessary to stress further the fantastic brilliance of his space visuals in *2001*. Without the absolute conviction carried by the special effects, the inner conviction of the story would be utterly lost.[2] Only perhaps on the cosmic 'trip' do the effects – explosively abstract colours – disappoint slightly, perhaps because others have worked over this technique before. Again, in *A Clockwork Orange* the *outré* use of super-wide-angle sometimes catches us with a

[1] The enormous superiority of Makavejev and Kubrick over film-makers like Peckinpah is that in their world of cruelty there is no unconscious humour; whereas in *Straw Dogs* the would-be superhorrific scenes – the foot shot off, the head in the mantrap – tend to relapse into the comic. In *The Graduate*, where Dustin Hoffman plays exactly the same part of the worm who turns, Mike Nichols, in the final sequence when the crucifix is used as a door blocker and a weapon, makes the act, despite the comedy, more immediately shocking than a lot of the rustic skullduggery in *Straw Dogs*.

[2] Some of the methods used are explained and illustrated in *The Making of Kubrick's 2001*, edited by Jerome Agel (Signet, New York, 1968). See also *Expanded Cinema* by Gene Youngblood (Studio Vista, London, 1970).

real shock – not only for instance in the fight with the Cat Woman, but at the moment later in the film when the intellectual who has been crippled for life by Alex after witnessing the brutal rape of his wife suddenly realizes who he is. Shot from a low ultra-wide-angle, the man's face seems to swell and distort like that of a test pilot subject to high G factors during a power-dive. What gives this grotesque close-up its unique horror is the fact that it shows Alex's original Evil being transferred to another human; a soul is seen being lost. In a curious way this moment is similar to Bowman's destruction of Hal, except that *A Clockwork Orange* never really recovers, whereas *2001* takes off at that point into new explorations and mysteries.[1]

Writing in 1946, in an essay entitled *Dostoievsky and the Collapse of Liberalism*, Rex Warner described as the greatest problem of our time 'the conflict between science and religion, between the individual and the State, between the original mind and the fetters of a hampering environment, between the child and the parent. It is a problem which, to some extent, has exercised every human being and every society throughout the ages; yet in our times it has been posed with especial force and our failure to deal with it has been attended with unprecedented catastrophe'.[2] Today the problems remain very much the same; the aesthetic of the film-maker must in the end depend on a critical standpoint towards the society in which he lives, bearing in mind however the danger implicit in 'the rapidity with which generally accepted ideals of the early Twentieth century such as toleration, kindliness, objective truth, freedom, have been replaced in many people's minds by their exact opposites'.[3] Thus the somewhat negative plea on behalf of freewill which lies behind the horrors of *A Clockwork Orange* needs to be answered by more reasonable approaches to the human condition such as those adopted by a director like Eric Rohmer; or by an asceticism by no means devoid of love and faith such as that evinced by a director like Bresson, whose view of the relation of the individual to society and to God, not only in a film like *Le Journal d'un Curé de Campagne* but also in *Une Femme Douce*, are just as important to us as the sincerity of Peter Watkins' warning sirens and remorseless police, the exquisite pessimisms of Nicolas Roeg, the fascinating temporal experiments of Resnais and Bertolucci, or the despairing yet

---

[1] It is interesting to note that early versions of the screenplay give no indication whatever of all the richness which in fact follows the killing of Hal. In particular, the final sequence is absent; and it is clear that the imaginations of Clarke and Kubrick were working all out up to the last minute.

[2] *The Cult of Power*, Bodley Head, London, 1946.

[3] Ibid.

acrobatic navel-gazing of Godard. But all of these artists, together with various contemporaries of the calibre of Pasolini, Olmi, Bellocchio Malle, Ray, Abdelsalam, Oshima, Menzel, Polanski, Glauber Rocha – to name a few – all face the same problem in their desire to extend the limits of cinematic expression: that of a continuing self-control in the use of a medium whose debasement in the vast market available to it has only too often been more than an empty threat. In this respect a statement by George Steiner seems to me to strike a sharp and significant note:

'I wonder whether the primacy of language as we have known it in human civilisation, as well as many of the dominant syntactical features of language, are not the embodiment of a particular view of man's identity and death. The trinary set, past-present-future, the subject-object function, the metaphysics and psychology of the first person pronoun, the conventions of linguistic repeatability and variation on which we found our techniques of remembrance and, hence, our culture – all these codify an image of the human person who is now under attack. A "happening", an aleatory piece of music, an artefact made only to be destroyed, are strategic denials of the future tense, even as the derision of precedent, the unsaying of history or a contemptuous indifference towards it, are a refusal of the past. In the grammar of the freak-out and the wrecker it is always today . . .

'. . . Totalitarian politics, the long erosion of fear, tend to collectivise men and women, to reduce as far as possible their sanctuary of private identity. So do the conditions of standardised desire, of noise level, of programmed efficacy in a "free society" . . . Under the piston-stroke of the mass media, of open and subliminal advertisement, even our dreams have grown more uniform.'[1]

This seems to me an admirable yardstick by which to estimate the value of current motion-picture production, and not least the output of the Warhol factory and the minimalists.

The element of despair underlying so much of this sort of film-making has of course been seen before (though to a lesser degree) in the Germany of the Twenties; but the current decadence in thought and in technique, with its 'strategic denials of the future tense', is surely unparalleled in the history of the motion picture.

In his book on the Underground, Parker Tyler constantly tries to separate the reals from the phonies – a task not always easy in this day and age; he surmounts it quite well, so that the truths that are in, say,

[1] From *The Language Animal*, published in *Encounter*, 1969.

Stan Brakhage, are distinguished from the – not lies, not falsehoods –
but bored neutralities of the 'best' work of Warhol, whom indeed he
treats with a modicum of respect, though only, I think, as a phenomenon.
To the current generation of film-makers he makes himself absolutely
clear at the end of the book:

> 'If the history of the Underground Film[1] . . . has one essential
> message, it is that the film medium, to achieve its destiny, must not
> only be pure, free of all commercial taints, it must also have scope
> of vision and an implacable aesthetic character.'[2]

He adds later the point that in film the poetic imagination is
historically in the keeping of the international avant-garde, so that 'in
turn, the *historical duty* of the international avant-garde, is to consider
the poetic imagination as in its keeping'.

With the means of production becoming, as we have already seen,
every day cheaper to buy and easier to operate, it is even more necessary
to guard jealously these basic aesthetic values, and never more so than
when we start to look into some of the more way-out experiments of
the day.

IV

The world of kinetics and synaesthetics is not all that new. In his
Lives of the Artists, Giorgio Vasari gives a long and detailed description
of a representation of the Annunciation put on by Filippo Brunelleschi
in the Carmine Monastery, Florence. This involved the construction
of a hemisphere in the roof of the main hall, with cross-structures
enabling brackets to be installed, 'on each of which . . . stood a child
of about 12 years . . . so safely secured . . . that it could not fall even
if it had wanted to. There were twelve of these *putti* . . . dressed as
angels . . . and when it was time they clasped hands, waved their arms
and, especially as the ball itself was continually turning and swaying,
they seemed to be dancing together. Inside the hemisphere above the
heads of the angels were three circles . . . of lights . . . and from the
ground these lights looked like stars, and the [wooden] beams, which

---

[1] Which he dates back to 1915 for Gance's *La Folie du Docteur Tube* and Feuillade's
Les Vampires.
[2] *Underground Film* by Parker Tyler, Secker and Warburg, London, 1971.

were covered with cotton wool, seemed like clouds'. In addition to all this Brunelleschi had devised other platforms and brackets, moving up and down vertically beneath the hemisphere and similarly equipped with other children as well as a 'copper *mandorla* or circle of lights . . . and so Paradise was realistically depicted by the heaven, the garland, the God-the-Father and the *mandorla*, accompanied by countless lights and the most harmonious music'.[1]

Ludwig of Bavaria, encouraged by Wagner, installed one of the first electric power stations through which arc lamps were used to illuminate a rainbow machine in the Tannhäuser Grotto 'while the lake and cascade were fed by a complex of water pipes'.[2]

In more recent times Luca Ronconi put on a vast production of *Orlando Furioso* in a hall with stages at both ends in which the audience, unseated, were completely caught up in the swirl of the action. 'Knights on sheet metal steeds go rocketing through the fields . . . Mythical monsters flap their metal wings and soar high above the crowd', and 'the audience is part of the show as a dreamer is part of his dream . . .'[3]

From all this it is but a short step to such fantasies as Otto Piene's sky ballets of balloons and other inflatables in Pittsburgh, which, also in 1970, included a 1,500 foot polyethylene helium-filled bright red tube floating over the city, to say nothing of a manned helium sculpture made of ten 250 foot lengths of clear polyethylene tube, 40 helium tanks, 3 searchlights and 8 floodlights, to which was attached (shades of Brunelleschi's *putti*) a seventeen-year-old girl who rose some sixty feet above the ground to become the centre of Piene's 'plastic chrysanthemum'.[4] To this we may add Rockne Krebs' network of lasers called *Night Passage*, created for the Los Angeles County Museum of Art, which mixed 'a blue-green laser beam knifing down from a thirty-one storey building . . . with several pulsing up from the museum itself'.[5] And in the same year Eric Rhode, in the *Sunday Times*, described the Steel Pavilion at Japan's Expo 70 'with its 1300 amplifiers and ballet of laser beams probing the darkness like searchlights of an almost unimaginable agility'.[6]

[1] *Lives of the Artists* by G. Vasari; a selection translated by George Bull, Penguin, 1965. The whole passage, which takes up several pages, makes fascinating reading, not least because, as Vasari says, it all 'came to grief and the men who could have described it from their own knowledge are dead . . . and what is more the monastery of the Carmine was ruined because the machinery pulled down the timbers supporting the roof'.
[2] *Times Literary Supplement*, November 20th, 1970.
[3] *Newsweek*, November 16th, 1970.
[4] *Time*, May 4th, 1970.
[5] *Newsweek*, May 31st, 1971.
[6] Earlier than this, Albert Speer had arranged for the Nazi Party Rally of 1937 a

Similar combinations of moving structures and light-forms had preoccupied some of the young artists in the Soviet Union during the Twenties. Of these one of the most notable was Vladimir Tatlin, famous for his Tower; and although he and his group fell into Stalinist disfavour, their ideas remained behind. Thus we may note two huge constructions erected in Moscow and Leningrad in 1966 by Lev Nusberg and a number of colleagues. In one, *Cosmos*, a vast wheel revolved to the accompaniment of electronic music 'to give an impression of signals being sent into outer space', while the other, *Atom*, was an equally impressive construction celebrating the marvels of the microcosm.

From Germany's *Bauhaus* in the Twenties and early Thirties there emerged one of the great kinetic geniuses in the person of stout, amiable Laszlo Moholy Nagy, whose masterpiece, the Light-Space Modulator, which took him eight years to construct, was used as the basis for his film *Light Display: Black White Grey* (1931), as well as for many other experiments. The original, which over the years had deteriorated through disuse, was recently restored to working order; and at least two duplicates have been constructed. It may well remain for many years the seminal reference point for anyone concerned with the essence of the visual in motion. Moholy Nagy's conception of an architecture of light leading to a 'total theatre' with no actors, consisting simply of a synthesis of light, motion and sound effects, was as positive in approach as the mobile designs of Marcel Duchamp were neutral, and the more recent self-destroying machines of Jean Tinguely are negative (though none the less comic and delightful).[1] Today direct descendants of the Moholy Nagy initiative are to be seen in workers like Jordan Belson (who has carried the affair into colour as, of course, Moholy Nagy would have done had he lived), and the Whitneys, who use cybernetic techniques including computers.

Moholy Nagy's modulator was one of the first products of a deliberately organized collaboration between art, industry and engineering; his colleagues included an architect, an engineer, and various experts from a large electrical cartel. In today's world such collaborations are commonplace, and certainly the multiscreen marvels at

---

battery of 130 anti-aircraft searchlights whose vertical beams were 'visible to a height of . . . 25,000 feet, after which they merged into a general glow. The feeling was of a vast room, with the beams serving as mighty pillars'. (Albert Speer, *Inside the Third Reich.*)

[1] I am not unaware of the practical joke side of Duchamp and Tinguely; the latter would have had Kubrick's Hal commit suicide. As regards films, it should not be forgotten that there were a good few experimental film-makers in Europe during this period who were working on abstract design in light and shade – notably Viking Eggeling, Eugène Deslaw, Francis Brugière and Oswell Blakiston.

Canada's Expo 67 would have been impossible without them, not least the National Film Board's *Labyrinth* – a multimedia construction whose visual images rode above, below and around the visitor, and which provided a series of experiences involving at times a quite alarming feeling of disorientation:

> 'To begin with the audience found itself grouped around a series of tiered balconies . . . watching a short film on two 38 by 28 foot screens . . . One screen was set into the floor of the building and the other rose at right angles at one end. From the beginning the viewer's eye was disorientated and from that point it never had a chance . . .

> 'Sometimes the two screens were used simply to extend space, as an acrobat somersaulted right across them both. Sometimes we were presented with cause and effect. A man smiled down from one screen at the new-born child on the screen below; a child threw a piece of bread which was snapped up by a fish on the second screen . . . This first part of *Labyrinth* changed the texture of film space and particularly of film time . . .

> 'The next experience came in the third . . . chamber, an orthodox auditorium with five screens arranged in the shape of a cross . . . The theme of the film . . . was of less significance than the technical virtuosity involved in the endlessly flowing series of images which grouped and splintered on the five screens. Sometimes the images were all of a kind, then one would change to a different mood and . . . either slowly or suddenly . . . affect the rest . . . But invariably the screen would fragment again seconds later, leaving the mind to find its focus.'[1]

Similar, but not particularly better, effects were achieved by the Japanese in Expo 70, as in the Mitsubishi pavilion 'where you glide on a slowly moving conveyor belt through caverns in which mirroring walls, floor and ceilings, back-projected film and stereophonic sound give the impression that you are passing through typhoons and volcanic eruptions or, more peacably, journeying through outer space'.[2]

The ballet, that quintessentially synthetic art, has also been concerned in these new developments. Quite apart from the use of electronic and other new forms of music, various choreographers have been

[1] *Beyond the Frame* by Harry Day in *Sight and Sound*, Spring 1968 – a long, admirable and detailed article on all the multimedia cinematic experiments and displays at Montreal.

[2] Eric Rhode in *The Sunday Times*, May 1970. He added that elsewhere the Exhibition relapsed into 'snack-bar taste' with 'gardens made up of plastic tulips, unconvincing cuckoo sounds, cosy homes inhabited by emaciated men and women constructed out of wire'.

attracted by the extraordinary ease by which TV can, at the touch of a button, achieve effects which used to take the film-makers days or weeks to achieve. Thus in 1971 Alvin Nicolais produced, in collaboration with BBC London, an electronic ballet in which some remarkable spatial perspectives were achieved; but this was eclipsed later the same year by Birgit Cullberg's television ballet for Swedish Television – *Adam and Eve*. In this she achieved something of the space magic of *2001*. At times the background moved – sideways, forward or backwards – *against* the formal movements of the dancers; at other times the dancers were put into alarming infinitudes of perspective; and there were some extraordinary moments when the dancers, seen vertically from above, were placed in front of moving backgrounds covered horizontally by the cameras.

Music, too, has been invaded by more than the fragmented and aleatory work of men like Karlheinz Stockhausen. George Newson's *Arena*, giving during the Promenade Concerts in London under Boulez in 1971, employed narration, spotlights, newsreels, and a chorus disposed among various sections of the audience. Even more striking was the happening or event laid on in 1969 at the University of Illinois by John Cage. This, entitled HPSCHD (computerese for Harpsichord), in addition to including several of those instruments, was also involved with

'52 tape machines, 59 power amplifiers, 59 loud speakers and 208 computer-generated tapes. The visual contributions to the performance employed 64 slide projectors showing 6,400 slides and 8 moving picture projectors using 40 cinematographic films . . . In the middle of the circular sports arena were suspended several parallel sheets . . . each 100 by 400 feet; and from both sides were projected numerous films and slides . . . Running round a circular ceiling was a continuous 340 foot screen, and from a hidden point inside were projected slides (of) outer space scenes, pages of Mozart's music, computer instructions and nonrepresentational blotches. Beams of light were aimed across the undulated interior roof. In several upper locations (*sic*) mirrored balls were spinning, reflecting dots of light in all directions.'[1]

This whacking *Gesamtkunstwerk* must have made Scriabin stir in his grave; and it comes interestingly from the hand of a composer one of whose most famous works consists of four minutes and thirty-three seconds' worth of absolute silence.

[1] From a long article by Virgil Thomson entitled *Cage and the Collage of Noises*, New York Review, April 23rd, 1970.

Meantime, where now do we stand, motion picture-wise, in this new world in which all the arts assault the eyes with aleatory happenings that include blinding strobe or laser effects, and the ears with electronic assaults?

V

There is little doubt that the motion picture will, to a degree, need to make similar experiments to those just described. In an increasingly permissive society it is not only Content to which licence is freely granted; and while the coming together of film and TV on the small screen in terms of Super-8, VTR and Cassette means, among other things, a revolution in education and the exchange of information, the creative worker will still want to explore existing and future possibilities on a scale (and I use the word to indicate largeness of conception rather than mere size), which may well involve multiplication and division of image as well as combination of the recorded and the actual.

In 1971 the National Film Theatre in London ran an evening of twin-screen films which ranged from serious and interesting experiments to pointless and ridiculous exercises. The programme included a stop-motion study of cloudscapes made by two cameras facing east and west respectively, each one taking a single exposure every ten seconds from dawn to darkness. The simultaneous projection of the two resulting films on side-by-side screens showed that the contrasting images, as a result not only of the accelerated movement (nothing new in that), but also of a certain dislocation in time caused by their opposed orientation, created in the spectator a curious psychological tension.

A second small and simple experiment also involved temporal concepts. The same sequence – of someone opening a door and coming into a kitchen – was projected on to twin screens. On one of the screens the identical action started slightly earlier (or later, according to which screen you favoured) than the other. The effect was of seeing a specific action in space and time being called into question; for which of the two films was now to be thought of as *now*? Or, since both no doubt had a common origin in a negative shot previously, why should they arouse in us a dislocating temporal clash? The disorienting effect of this simple little effort was quite shocking; one trembles to think what Resnais might do with it.

A more elaborate example was seen at UCLA, California, in 1968, when Richard Hawkins, having returned from an ethnographical visit to Chile during which he and his team had filmed in depth an immense religious festival, had his rushes (which were copious and covered some 36 hours' running time) assembled into three separate sections, the subject content being roughly divided between them. The sections were then projected simultaneously on to three parallel screens. At certain points – and as the material was rushes, the impact was largely aleatory (though identity of subject did provide possibilities arising from the contiguity) – some extraordinary effects were achieved, as when action on the left-hand screen would start to drift across on to the centre screen and then relate, without further movement, to another action on the right-hand screen. On another occasion the three screens provided a development from the Gance triptych in *Napoléon.* The centre screen showed an annual pilgrimage by one individual devotee through miles of city streets to the great Cathedral in the centre of the town – a journey which he made entirely on his knees. While this painful but rapt Odyssey went on, the left-hand screen depicted the pilgrim's wife, in her homely kitchen, being interviewed by the press; while on the right-hand screen the pilgrim himself was seen in his every-day life plying his normal trade as a barber.

This simultaneous compression of different times and geographies resulted in a kind of super-montage over and above the individual cutting (such as it was) possible to the individual assemblers of the three different reels. One may imagine a triple screen film deliberately conceived and planned, with the aleatory factor removed or at least confined to occasional overtones, in which new devices of story-telling, new complexities of emotional and psychological relationships, might be achieved. A tense situation, for instance, could be shown simultaneously through the eyes and consciousnesses of three different persons; and from this their individual choice of action or inaction could be charted, depicted and, in a climactic crisis, brought together on to one single screen in one single conclusive action.[1]

Yet these and many other ideas, involving new flash-frame tech-

---

[1] I am reminded here of a gimmick launched by the Czechs at Expo 67 and elsewhere. In this, at a certain point in the story, the projection is halted and the audience votes – by pressing buttons attached to their seats – on what course of action a certain character should now take. The filmic action subsequently proceeds according to the majority vote. The Czech films, though quite lighthearted, involved a moral choice; and most of the group votes indicated an alarmingly footloose attitude to morals and honesty. The fact was that they voted not for what they felt right but for what they liked. The persons on the screen didn't represent reality but, as those old tycoons in Hollywood knew so well, wish-fulfilment.

niques as in Antony Stern's *San Francisco*, or strobe effects as in Burton Gershfeld's *Now That the Buffalo's Gone*, all in fact assume a quite old-fashioned system of communication based on the architecture of the current movie house. This is, in effect, an architecture based on the old proscenium theatre which long ago superseded Shakespeare's 'Wooden O'. The only modification made by cinema architects to the theatrical design evolved to meet the needs of 18th century playwrights has been a broadening of the auditorium so as to minimize the number of people who have to view the screen from an oblique viewpoint.

In other words the film has remained, however unspokenly, an offshoot of the drama – itself a prisoner of the comparatively recent proscenium arch. And just as modern producers and playwrights have gone into revolt against the proscenium theatre (while still recognizing its validity for plays deliberately written for it), so the time may come when film-makers will no longer be content with a single formula for movie-house design.

Here indeed they will find themselves at one not only with theatre people but with painters and sculptors, who are currently altering conceptions about the layout and function of the gallery – as well as moving towards a synaesthetic approach with participatory and tactile techniques, including objects which may stroke you or engulf you – and who are continuing Moholy Nagy's work on the relationship between shapes in movement and controlled light.[1]

In any case there is no *a priori* reason for the film-maker always to conceive of his work in terms of projection in the proscenium cinema. As we have already seen, films for international exhibitions provide film-makers with golden opportunities to get away from this straitjacket. It may well be that we shall soon see movie-houses in which the spectators no longer sit in serried rows facing the screen.[2] There are indeed endless possibilities of differing spatial relationships between the audience and the film image. We have already seen the Soviet system in which the audience stands in or strolls around a circular hall in which films are being projected continuously on a 360° screen; true, it was not much more than a travelogue gimmick, and the problem of colour-matching the images shown by the multifarious 16mm projectors

---

[1] The big exhibition of Kinetics mounted in 1971 in the Hayward Gallery, London, by the Arts Council of Great Britain, was a remarkable exposition of this sort of work. Its huge and detailed catalogue remains a most valuable work of reference.

[2] The most grotesque example of this is of course the Drive In, where rows and rows of automobiles, like patient animals, stand facing a gigantic screen under the open canopy of a night sky.

was by no means solved – but the possibility was established.[1] Alternatively the audience could surround a central circular screen and both, or either, could revolve.[2] Or it could be left to the spectator to choose his own spatial position in relation to the screen or screens; perhaps, as in an art gallery, he would move around and, when he felt like it, sit down on seats provided at strategic intervals. Again, as in the Montreal *Labyrinth*, the image need not only be part of the wall; it can be part of the floor and the roof as well.

How far the people commercially concerned in the motion picture would go for such ideas is another question. So far the timid split-screen technique used, for example, in *The Boston Strangler*, has not advanced much beyond Gance's experiments of the now distant past. It may well be that no genuine advance will be made until the picture industry becomes as desperate for a new gimmick as were the brothers Warner in 1927, or 20th Century-Fox in 1953 when, in face of television, they launched CinemaScope with *The Robe*.

VI

In 1972 a curious phenomenon was observable in the entertainment field. Producers began to make films based on successful television series; and the films proved to be highly successful at the box-office. This could only mean that a reasonably large section of the population (mainly from the middle-age group?) wanted to combine their desire for an evening out with assurance that whatever they saw at their local movie-house would not differ in any great degree from what they would have seen had they stayed at home with their faithful old telly. This incestuous relationship between movie and TV (like the Pharaonic inter-marriages of brother and sister) was also seen – mainly in the United States – in reverse, with movies being specially made for showing on TV. These offerings, usually ninety minutes but sometimes two hours long, were, according to *Newsweek*,[3] 'the result of the networks' desire to

[1] This system was subsequently followed up by Disney, though without any imaginative advances.

[2] Such an idea, involving a translucent revolving cylinder showing action and décor filmed from a series of angles covering 360°, projected by apparatus revolving at the same speed, was proposed as early as 1936 by Dallas Bower. (See his *Plan for Cinema*, Dent 1936.)

[3] April 10th, 1972. These films appeared on BBC TV under the general title of 'Hollywood Première' – which to old film buffs must have seemed like having your dust and ashes and eating them.

cash in on the resurgence of interest in cinema (especially among the young), to assure a steady supply of films that were less expensive[1] than the "used" Hollywood products, and to recoup development costs by packaging series "pilots" into original "movies"'.

Such agglomerations would be unlikely to bode well for the creative future of either aspect of the visual medium, though the idea of a 'resurgence of interest in cinema' was gratifying in an insulting sort of way. Meantime, however, the real future was beclouded by confused arguments over form and content; and these were additionally bedevilled by quarrels over the censorship system for films and the desirability or otherwise of some sort of external censorship on TV – especially the BBC, which is frequently accused (the row in 1972 over *Echoes of Britannia's Rule* being a prime example) of eating away the vitals of the Establishment from the inside. The cries of *Quis Custodiet*? drown those of *Quo Vadis*?

One fact must, however, be faced. There is now (or very soon will be) no practical difficulty in showing TV images in the same size and proportions as those seen on the biggest cinema screens. Apart from anything else this will mean that McLuhan's famous but always fluffy distinction between the 'hot' and 'cold' media will now be cut down to size, if not mercifully forgotten, since the reference will be to a comparison between the *use* of visuals rather than their source.

The options for the small screen have already been discussed. For the larger screen, or rather for the ambience of the communal meeting-place at which motion pictures are shown to large numbers of people, there seem to be three main possibilities:

1. A multiplication of the present system of production and distribution, which would continue the trend towards an increased number of small cinema halls catering for a greater variety of audiences whose interests cover a wide variety of subject matter, styles and countries of origin.

2. A deliberate reversion to the making of more blockbuster films in an attempt to reiterate the contrast between the largesse of the Big Screen and the tiny intimacies of the Parlour Cathode. The demise of Hollywood makes it unlikely that this will happen. The present output is probably just about what the market can bear.

3. The gradual emergence of a hybrid system using something of the best of all aspects of movie and video (which as I have said have in this sense already merged) in order to provide on the one hand areas with a wide choice of visual and aural variety, and on the other super-

---

[1] The networks were paying as little as $375,000 for one of these 'movies for the tube'.

events and happenings involving all the senses as well as combining instant 'live' effects with video elements previously recorded and therefore frozen in time. Such affairs could take place in areas specially constructed for the purpose or, as in the various examples already mentioned, be superposed on existing landscapes or cityscapes, thus willy-nilly involving an entire community whether all its individuals wanted it or not.[1]

It seems to me that the first and third of these possibilities will emerge in coexistence from the present situation. The proliferation of movie-halls will continue because the motion picture *as film* is now wholly accepted as an art form. Moreover, it now has a historical backlog which younger generations want to catch up with in the same way as they want to catch up with writings or paintings of the past.[2] The current output of films is no longer tied to a limited number of national production centres or language groups; and as the means of production continue to become cheaper and simpler, the output will undoubtedly be increased by offerings from various African and Latin-American countries, to say nothing of the South Seas, New Zealand, Australia and certain ethnic groups within other countries which have not yet had their say, such as the Eskimos and Red Indians (to whom already, I believe, Canada's National Film Board has extended production facilities). These possibilities will no doubt be speeded up as the ethnographers and anthropologists, in addition to using the motion picture themselves, learn also to place it in the hands of the so-called primitive communities they are studying. It will surely be extremely useful for the aboriginals and suchlike to use the simple means of Super 8 or VTR to express what they feel not only about the inwardness of their own community but also about the teams who have come from outside to enter into relationships with them.

As for the third option, it is worth remembering that the film as big spectacle was established by the Italians before the First World War and brought to a top level of achievement by Griffith before that war was over. And within a few years his ideas were taken up and dramatically developed by the new Soviet directors, notably Eisenstein.

---

[1] Nor is this a new idea. In the bright, brash early Twenties in the USSR there were public symphonies of factory hooters and sirens designed and orchestrated across Leningrad or Moscow by young musicians; and it may be noted that more recently Peter Brook mounted a happening called *Orghast* on a vast rocky landscape in Iran, and had a special new language invented for it to boot.

[2] In most countries National Film Archives are beginning to meet this need. Pioneer of this field is Henri Langlois, whose magical Musée du Cinéma in Paris is tangible evidence of the vitality of the medium.

In an interview on BBC Television in 1970 John Grierson made this claim:

'I believe Eisenstein to have been the greatest master of public spectacle in the history of the cinema, and I am forgetting neither D. W. Griffith nor Cecil B. De Mille. He was a superb exponent of that tradition of collective art which is represented by the pageants of ancient Egypt, by the circuses in Rome, by the surroundings of the Roman Catholic Church, and by all the many and varied collective manifestations of faith. That he has also come to represent novelties in film technique is less important for me than his membership of an ancient theatrical tradition that was to be found once again in the work of Leni Riefenstahl, or in the Duke of Norfolk's presentation of the Coronation, or in the colossal resources of the Army, Navy and Air Force at the funeral of Winston Churchill. It was Eisenstein who could attack the Winter Palace with several hundreds of the citizens of Leningrad, who could fire the first shot of the Revolution from the *Aurora* herself, who in *Battleship Potemkin* could use the Black Sea Fleet . . . But he was also very much a man who reacted to all the forces of his time, and especially to the great new world of industry and technology; and in his art he sought to mirror the colossal power and resources of this world.'[1]

This viewpoint on a man who, as Grierson also said on the same occasion, 'truly belongs to the history of art as a whole rather than to the brief history of cinema', may at this stage be a useful corrective to that more fashionable attitude which concentrates on the *minutiae* of Eisenstein's theoretical writing. The prospect of bigger and better spectacle inherent in the latest technical developments in the visual media could mean the opening up of marvellous new areas of endeavour, provided always that the spectacle was matched by an *aesthetic* grandeur of conception. It was this grandeur of conception which De Mille ultimately lacked and which Griffith and Stroheim possessed. In Eisenstein it is seen not only in the attack on the Winter Palace[2] but also in *Ivan the Terrible*, in which film Grierson believed that 'Eisenstein was most gloriously, most truly himself'. He added,

'It remains in my memory as something not only visually memorable but vastly quiet; and when a great artist who is so full of

---

[1] *Omnibus* programme on Eisenstein produced by Norman Swallow; this excerpt was reproduced in the *Listener*, April 13th, 1972, shortly after Grierson's death.

[2] Or indeed even earlier in the Cossack invasion of the tenement building in *Strike*.

energy – a Michaelangelo for instance – can be so quiet, he is a great artist indeed.'

This reference to another aspect of grandeur of conception is particularly apt; for just as Michaelangelo could produce those late and often unfinished sculptures, at once magisterial and intimately, emotionally *bouleversant*, of slaves and *piètas*, as well as the thunder-blast of the Sistine Chapel, so Eisenstein in his last work often concentrated his feel for the immense into the confines of a single close-up.

In this sense his montage theory is by no means separate from his sense of spectacle. Indeed it may be seen as a bridge between the epic element of *Potemkin* or *October* and the poetic intimacies of parts of *Old and New* (for instance Lapkina and the cream-separator), or the terrifying but deeply moving relationship between Euphrosyne and Vladimir in *Ivan the Terrible*.[1]

It is therefore to Eisenstein that the director of the future synaesthetic spectaculars should turn for guidance; for here he will find not only the montage of collision and conflict, but also the montage of poetry which can come from those rare and inspired moments when a film-maker juxtaposes certain images in such a way (temporal and spatial) that they produce something more than a new 'concept', something which overpasses the sum of the content of the visuals concerned to an unanalysable effect to which Eisenstein, *faute de mieux*, gave the title of Overtone.

The development of the spectacular not for its own sake but with a deliberate purposiveness of expression has been the hallmark of certain great directors. Apart from Griffith, Stroheim and Eisenstein we may note other examples such as, for instance, the extraordinary and memorable power of Godard's traffic-jam in *Weekend*.[2] In the same way Kubrick in *2001* is Eisensteinian; certainly that cut from the thrown bone to the spacecraft could not have come about without him, any more than the song at the end of *W.R. – Mysteries of the Organism* could have happened without the examples set by that other great

[1] In his *Omnibus* talk Grierson also made the interesting distinction that he and his documentary group were more influenced by this aspect than by the 'violent montage' of *Potemkin* or *October*. 'If you want to know where the courage of poetry in *Song of Ceylon* came from, or the courage of poetry in *Night Mail*, then you must go for your answer to *Old and New* or to *Romance Sentimale*.' I am glad to note here that Grierson, like myself, felt that the latter film showed Eisenstein's hand – certainly in the cutting; the rather childish final sequence is, on consideration, an aspect of Eisenstein's love of clowning which is also seen – and again not always to advantage – in *Old and New*.

[2] Compare it with Tati's monster jam in *Traffic*, which is no more than a brilliantly inflated gag. Godard's is, apart from anything else, a savage and unforgettable criticism of Western civilization.

genius of cinema, Dovzhenko, as in the ski-ing boy in *Aerograd* or the grieving father in *Earth*.

I do not think that the motion picture – whatever new shapes it may be going to take unto itself – need look much further for its grammar and syntax than those basic principles of montage first put forward by Griffith, developed and enlarged by Eisenstein and Dovzhenko, and subsequently elaborated over the years by many directors such as Vigo, Resnais, Godard and Dreyer.

The world of the moving picture is based on the collision of images and their control; and as in the universe the collisions can be microcosmic, as in the atom, or macrocosmic, as in the nebulae, so in the visual media are to be found similar contrasts. There will be room for artists working on every scale. I am not a prophet, and don't wish to probe further; for what we are waiting for is some new genius who will know how to use and organize the new technical perspectives with a certitude of aesthetic discipline through which, no doubt, new forms of montage may be evolved on the bases on which so far all of us, whether on screen or tube, have learned and must continue to learn to work.

As to the question of where the motion picture has got to so far, would, in looking back over my own sixty years of film-going, be inclined to choose one single sequence to justify its existence and development as an art. Many sequences parade in memory, and the world of filmic recollection is rich and full. I shall choose the ending of Mizoguchi's *Ugetsu Monogatari*, where the threads of all the joys and sorrows of human life, of nature, and of the supernatural are magically woven together in a montage which floats gently and compassionately into a continuity, an infinity, and finally into an ineffable peace.

THE END

A NOTE ON THE DATES

As everyone who reads or writes film books knows, the question of dating is a perennial vexation. Variations of up to three years in the date of a given film are not uncommon. These discrepancies are due to several factors. There is the difference between the date of a film's completion and the date of its first public showing. If these coincide in the same year, all is well. But if, as so often happens, they don't, the date will vary from one book to another according to which occasion the author has chosen. Furthermore, films sometimes suffer long delays between completion and release, in which case anyone who uses the release date can be grotesquely inaccurate.

I cannot expect to have done better than my many predecessors. For the record, though, let me explain that I have relied wherever possible on the admirable *Monthly Film Bulletin* published by the British Film Institute and on the filmographies found in expert books about individual film directors or national cinemas. To give an example, in the case of Japan I have used the dates given in Donald Richie's two books *The Japanese Film* and *Japanese Movie*, cross-checking these with Arne Svensson's *Japan* in the Screen Series edited by Peter Cowie; while in the cases of Kurosawa and Oshima, I have further checked with Richie's *The Films of Akira Kurosawa* and with Ian Cameron's chapter on the latter in *Second Wave*.

In cases where the documentation is less specific and where details are hard to come by, I have either taken an average or by my own research arrived at a date which seems to me the most likely. Corrections will be gratefully received.

SELECT BIBLIOGRAPHY

HISTORY

Allister, Ray. Friese Greene: Close Up of an Inventor (Marsland, 1948).

Anderson, Joseph L. and Richie, Donald. The Japanese Film (Tuttle, 1959).

Armes, Roy. Patterns of Realism: a Study of Italian Neo-Realist Cinema (Tantivy Press, 1971).

   French Film. (Studio Vista, 1970).

   French Cinema. Vols I & II (Zwemmer, 1970).

Baechlin, Peter. Histoire Economique du Cinéma (Paris, 1947).

   see also under *Schmidt*.

Balcon, Michael. Twenty Years of British Film (with Ernest Lindgren, Forsyth Hardy and Roger Manvell) (Falcon Press, 1947).

   Michael Balcon Presents – A Lifetime of Films (Hutchinson, 1969).

Bardèche, Maurice and Brasillach, Robert. The History of the Film, translated by Iris Barry (Allen & Unwin, 1938).

Barnouw, Erik. The Image Empire: Vol III of A History of Broadcasting in the United States (Oxford, 1970).

Barnouw Erik and Krishnaswamy, S. Indian Film (Columbia University Press, 1963).

Battcock, Gregory (Ed). The New American Cinema (Dutton, 1967).

Baxter, John. Hollywood in the Thirties (Zwemmer, 1968).

   Hollywood in the Sixties (Zwemmer, 1972).

   Science Fiction in the Cinema (Zwemmer, 1970).

   The Gangster Film (Zwemmer, 1970).

Brownlow, Kevin. How It Happened Here (Secker & Warburg, 1968).

   The Parade's Gone By (Secker & Warburg, 1968).

Bryher. Film Problems of Soviet Russia (Pool, 1929).

Butler, Ivan. To Encourage the Art of the Film (Robert Hale, 1971).

Cameron, Ian (Ed). Second Wave (Studio Vista, 1970).

Capra, Frank. The Name Above the Title (W. H. Allen, 1972).

Carter, Huntly. The New Spirit in the Cinema (Shaylor, 1930).

Cowie, Peter, in collaboration with Svensson, Arne. Sweden, Vols I & II (Zwemmer, 1970).

Danischewsky, Monja (Ed). Michael Balcon's 25 Years in Films (World Film Publications, 1947).

Datt, Gopal (Ed). Four Times Five (Govt. of India Films Division, Bombay, 1969).

De La Roche, Catherine. see under *Dickinson*.

Dewey, Langdon. Outline of Czechoslovakian Cinema (Informatics, 1971).

Dickinson, Thorold and De La Roche, Catherine. Soviet Cinema (Arno, 1971).

Drinkwater, John. The Life and Adventures of Carl Laemmle (Heinemann, 1931).

Eisner, Lotte. The Haunted Screen (Thames & Hudson, 1969).

El-Mazzaoui, Farid. Cinema in the U.A.R. (Ministry of Culture, Cairo, 1970).

Geduld, Harry M. and Gottesman, Ronald. The Making and Unmaking of 'Que Viva Mexico!' (Thames & Hudson, 1970).

Gish, Lillian. The Movies, Mr Griffith and Me (W. H. Allen, 1969).

Goldwyn, Samuel. Behind the Screen (Doran, 1923).

Gow, Gordon. Hollywood in the Fifties (Zwemmer, 1971).

Hampton, Benjamin B. History of the American Film Industry (Dover Publications, 1970). This was originally published in 1931 under the title History of the Movies.

Hardy, H. Forsyth. Scandinavian Film (1952 edition reissued by Arno 1971).

Hepworth, Cecil M. Came the Dawn (Phoenix House, 1951).

Herring, Robert. Films of the Year 1927–28 (The Studio, 1928).

Higham, Charles, and Greenberg, Joel. Hollywood in the Forties (Zwemmer, 1968).

Higham, Charles. Hollywood Cameramen (Thames & Hudson, 1970).

Houston, Penelope. The Contemporary Cinema (Penguin, 1963).

Hull, David Stewart. Film in the Third Reich (University of California Press, 1969).

Jacobs, Lewis. The Rise of the American Film (Harcourt Brace, 1939).

Jacobs, Lewis (Ed). The Emergence of Film Art (Hopkinson & Blake, 1969). The Documentary Tradition (Hopkinson & Blake, 1971).

Jarratt, Vernon. The Italian Cinema (Falcon Press, 1951).

Khan, M. Introduction to the Egyptian Cinema (Informatics, 1969).

Knight, Arthur. The Liveliest Art (Macmillan, 1957).

Klaue, Wolfgang and Lichtenstein, Manfred. Filme Contra Faschismus (Staatliches Filmarchiv, DDR, 1965).

Kracauer, Siegfried. From Caligari to Hitler (Dennis Dobson, 1947).

Leprohon, Pierre. The Italian Cinema (Secker & Warburg, 1972).

Leyda, Jay. Kino, a History of the Russian & Soviet Film (Allen & Unwin, 1960).
   Films Beget Films (Allen & Unwin, 1964).

Low, Rachel and Manvell, Roger. The History of the British Film 1896–1906 (Allen & Unwin, 1948).

Low, Rachel. The History of the British Film 1904–1914 (Allen & Unwin, 1949).
   The History of the British Film 1914–1918 (Allen & Unwin, 1950).

The History of the British Film 1918–1929 (Allen & Unwin, 1971).

Lunatscharsky, A. W. Der Russische Revolutionsfilm (Orell Füssli, Zurich, 1929).

McCann, Richard Dyer. Hollywood in Transition (Houghton Mifflin, 1962).

Macgowan, Kenneth. Behind the Screen (Delta, 1967).

Mac Liammóir, Micheál. Put Money in Thy Purse: the Diary of the Film of Othello (Methuen, 1952).

Manvell, Roger. Film (Penguin, 1944).

Manvell, Roger with Fraenkel, Heinrich. German Cinema (Dent, 1971).

Manvell, Roger (Ed). Cinema 1950 (Penguin, 1950).

Manvell, Roger (Ed) with Baxter, R. K. Neilson. Cinema 1951 (Penguin, 1951). Cinema 1952 (Penguin, 1952).

Manvell, Roger. see also under *Balcon, Michael, Halas, John,* and *Low, Rachel.*

Montagu, Ivor. With Eisenstein in Hollywood (Seven Seas Books, 1968).

Moussinac, Léon. Panoramique du Cinéma (Au Sans Pareil, 1929).

Naumberg, Nancy (Ed). We Make the Movies (Faber & Faber, 1938).

Nemeskurty, Istvan. Word and Image: History of the Hungarian Cinema (Corvina Press, 1968).

O'Dell, Paul. Griffith and the Rise of Hollywood (Zwemmer, 1970).

O'Laoghaire, Liam. Invitation to the Film (Kerryman, 1945).

Pearson, George. Flashback (Allen & Unwin, 1957).

Pickford, Mary. Sunshine and Shadow (Heinemann, 1956).

Ramsaye, Terry. A Million and One Nights, Vols. I and II (Simon & Schuster, 1926).

Renan, Sheldon. The Underground Film (Studio Vista, 1968).

Richie, Donald. The Japanese Movie (Ward Lock, 1966).
Japanese Cinema (Secker & Warburg, 1972).
see also under *Anderson, Joseph L.*

Robinson, David. Hollywood in the Twenties (Zwemmer, 1968).
World Cinema (Eyre Methuen, 1973).

Rondi, Gian Luigi. Italian Cinema Today: 1952–1965 (Dennis Dobson, 1966).

Rotha, Paul. The Film Till Now (Jonathan Cape, 1930).

Rotha, Paul with Richard Griffith. The Film Till Now, revised and enlarged (Spring Books, 1967).

Rotha, Paul. Documentary Film (Faber & Faber, 1935).

Rotha, Paul with Richard Griffith, and Sinclair Road. Documentary Film, revised and enlarged (Faber & Faber, 1953).

Rotha, Paul. Celluloid: the Film Today (Longmans Green, 1931).
Movie Parade (The Studio, London, 1936).

Sadoul, Georges. L'Invention du Cinéma: 1832–1897 (Editions Denoël, 1946)
Les Pionniers du Cinéma: 1897–1909 (Editions Denoël, 1947).
Le Cinéma Français (Flammarion, 1962).
Histoire du Cinéma Mondiale (Flammarion, 1968).

Schmidt, Georg with Schmalenbach, Werner and Baechlin, Peter. Der Film (Holbein Verlag, 1947).

Schnitzer, Luda & Jean with Martin, Marcel. Cinema in Revolution (Secker & Warburg, 1972).

Sinclair, Upton. Upton Sinclair Presents William Fox (published by the author 1933).

Slide, Anthony. Early American Cinema (Zwemmer, 1970).

Sternberg, Josef von. Fun in a Chinese Laundry (Secker & Warburg, 1966).

Tallents, Stephen. British Documentary (Film Centre, London, 1968).

Tyler, Parker. Underground Film (Secker & Warburg, 1971).

Vallance, Tom. The American Musical (Zwemmer, 1970).

Various Hands. The Film in National Life: Report of the Commission on Educational and Cultural Films (Allen & Unwin, 1932).

   Soviet Cinema (Voks, 1936).

   The Film Index, Vol I: Film as an Art (Museum of Modern Art Film Library, 1941).

   Contemporary Polish Cinematography (Polonia, 1962).

   The Arts and Man (Unesco, 1969).

Waldekrantz, Rune. Le Cinéma Suédois (Stockholm, 1953).

Walker, Alexander. Stardom (Michael Joseph, 1970).

Wolf, Steffan (Ed). Der Tschechoslowakische Film (Mannheim, 1965).

Wood, Alan. Mr Rank (Hodder & Stoughton, 1952).

Zalman, Jan. Films & Film Makers (Orbis, Prague, 1968).

THEORY

Arnheim, Rudolf. Film (Faber & Faber, 1933).

   Film As Art (Faber & Faber, 1958).

Balazs, Bela. Theory of the Film (Dennis Dobson, 1952).

Bazin, André. What Is Cinema? Vols I & II, tr Hugh Gray (University of California Press, 1967 and 1971).

Benoit Lévy, Jean. Les Grandes Missions du Cinéma (Parizeau, Montreal, 1945).

Eisenstein, S. M. The Film Sense, tr Jay Leyda (Faber & Faber, 1943).

   Film Form, tr Jay Leyda (Dennis Dobson, 1951).

   Notes of a Film Director (Lawrence & Wishart, 1959).

Elliott, Eric. Anatomy of Motion Picture Art (Pool, 1928).

Grierson, John. Grierson on Documentary, ed H. Forsyth Hardy (Faber & Faber, 1966).

Lindgren, Ernest. The Art of the Film (Allen & Unwin, 1948).

Lindsay, Vachel. The Art of the Moving Picture (Liveright, 1970 – reprint of revised 1922 edition).

Nilsen, Vladimir. The Cinema as a Graphic Art, tr Stephen Garry (Newnes, 1936).

Pudovkin, V. I. Film Technique and Film Acting, tr Ivor Montagu (Lear, 1949).

Spottiswoode, Raymond. A Grammar of the Film (Faber & Faber, 1935).

Strasser, Alex. The Work of the Science Film Maker (Focal Press, 1972).

CRITICISM

Agate, James. Around Cinemas (Home & Van Thal, 1946).

Agee, James. Agee on Film (Peter Owen, 1963).

Anstey, Edgar (Ed) with Manvell, Roger, Lindgren, Ernest and Rotha, Paul. Shots in the Dark (Wingate, 1951).

Barry, Iris. Let's Go to the Pictures (Chatto & Windus, 1926).

Bellone, Julius (Ed). Renaissance of the Film (Collier Books, 1970).

Betts, Ernest. Heraclitus, or the Future of Films (Dutton, 1928).

Chiarini, Luigi. Cinema: Quinto Potere (Laterza, 1954).

Cooke, Alistair (Ed). Garbo and the Night Watchman (Cape, 1937 – Secker & Warburg, 1972).

Davy, Charles (Ed). Footnotes to the Film (Lovat Dickson, 1937).

Durgnat, Raymond. Films and Feelings (Faber & Faber, 1967).

   A Mirror for England (Faber & Faber, 1970).

Epstein, Jean. Esprit de Cinéma (Editions Jeheber, 1955).

Farber, Manny. Negative Space (Studio Vista, 1970).

Gessner, Robert. The Moving Image (Cassell, 1968).

Greene, Graham. The Pleasure Dome (Secker & Warburg, 1972).

Hillier, Jim. see *Lovell, Alan.*

Kael, Pauline. I Lost it at the Movies (Cape, 1966).

   Kiss Kiss Bang Bang (Calder & Boyars, 1970).

   Going Steady (Temple Smith, 1970).

Lejeune, C. A. Cinema (Maclehose, 1931).

   Chestnuts in her Lap (Phoenix House, 1947).

Lovell, Alan and Hillier, Jim. Studies in Documentary (Secker & Warburg, 1972).

Macdonald, Dwight. On Movies (Prentice Hall, 1969).

Manvell, Roger. A Seat in the Cinema (Evans, 1951).

   Shakespeare & the Film (Dent, 1971).

   see also under *Anstey, Edgar.*

Manvell, Roger (Ed). Experiment in the Film (Grey Walls Press, 1949).

Rhode, Eric. Tower of Babel (Weidenfeld & Nicolson, 1966).

Rotha, Paul. Rotha on the Film (Faber & Faber, 1958).

   see also under *Anstey, Edgar.*

Seldes, Gilbert. The Seven Lively Arts (Harper, 1924).

   An Hour with the Movies & Talkies (Lippincott, 1929).

   Movies for the Millions (Batsford, 1937).

Simon, John. Private Screenings (Macmillan, 1967).

Tyler, Parker. Sex, Psyche Etcetera in the Film (Horizon, 1969).

Warshow, Robert. The Immediate Experience (Doubleday, 1962).
Weinberg, Herman G. Saint Cinema (DBS Publications, 1970).
Winnington, Richard. Drawn and Quartered (Saturn Press, 1949).
Wollen, Peter. Signs and Meaning in the Cinema (Thames & Hudson, 1970).

DIRECTORS
Anderson, by Elizabeth Sussex (Studio Vista, 1969).
Antonioni, by Ian Cameron and Robin Wood (Studio Vista, 1969).
Bardem, by Marcel Oms and others (Premier Plan, Lyon, 1962)
Bergman, by Robin Wood (Studio Vista, 1969).
Bergman on Bergman, tr Paul Britten Austin (Secker & Warburg, 1973).
Bresson. The Films of Robert Bresson, by various hands (Studio Vista, 1969).
Buñuel, by Raymond Durgnat (Studio Vista, 1967).
        by Freddy Buache (La Cité, 1970).
Cavalcanti, ed. by Wolfgang Klaue (Staatliches Filmarchiv, DDR, 1962).
Chabrol, by Robin Wood and Michael Walker (Studio Vista, 1970).
Chaplin, by Theodore Huff (Cassell, 1952).
   My Autobiography (Bodley Head, 1964).
Clément, by André Farwagi (Seghers, 1969).
Cocteau, A Biography by Francis Steegmuller (Macmillan, 1970).
   La Belle et la Bête, Journal d'un Film (du Rocher, Monaco, 1958).
   Entretiens autour du Cinématographe, ed Fraigneau (Andrè Bonne, 1951).
Dovzhenko, by Marcel Oms (Serdoc, Lyon, 1968).
Dreyer, The Cinema of: by Tom Milne (Zwemmer, 1971).
Eisenstein, by Marie Seton (Bodley Head, 1952).
   By Yon Barna (Secker & Warburg, 1973).
Fellini, by Suzanne Budgen (BFI Education Dept, 1966).
Flaherty, ed Wolfgang Klaue & Jay Leyda (Henschelverlag, Berlin, 1964).
   The World of Robert Flaherty, by Richard Griffith (Gollancz, 1953).
   The Innocent Eye, by Arthur Calder Marshall (W. H. Allen, 1963).
Franju, by Raymond Durgnat (Studio Vista, 1967).
Godard, by Richard Roud (Secker & Warburg, 1970).
   a critical anthology, ed Toby Mussman (Dutton, 1968).
   on Godard, tr Tom Milne (Secker & Warburg, 1972).
Grémillon, by Henri Agel (Seghers, 1969).
Hawks, by Robin Wood (Secker & Warburg, 1968).
Hitchcock, by François Truffaut (Secker & Warburg, 1968).
Ivens, ed Wolfgang Klaue (Staatliches Filmarchiv, DDR, 1963).
   The Camera and I (Seven Seas, Berlin, 1969).
Kubrick: Stanley Kubrick Directs, by Alexander Walker (Harcourt Brace
        Jovanovich, 1971).
   The Making of Kubrick's 2001, ed Jerome Agel (Signet, 1970).
Kurosawa, the Films of, by Donald Richie (University of California, 1970).

Lorentz: Pare Lorentz & the Documentary Film, by Robert L. Snyder (University of Oklahoma Press, 1968).

Losey, by Tom Milne (Secker & Warburg, 1968).

   The Cinema of, by James Leahy (Zwemmer, 1967).

Lubitsch: The Lubitsch Touch, by Herman G. Weinberg (Dutton, 1968).

Mamoulian, by Tom Milne (Thames & Hudson, 1969).

Melville, by Rui Nogueira (Thames & Hudson, 1971).

Murnau, by Lotte Eisner (Secker & Warburg, 1973).

Pasolini, by Oswald Stack (Thames & Hudson, 1969).

Peries: The Lonely Artist, by Philip Coorey (Lake House, Colombo, 1970).

Polanski, the Cinema of, by Ivan Butler (Zwemmer, 1970).

Prévert, Les (Jacques and Pierre), by Gérard Guillot (Seghers, 1966).

Ray, by Marie Seton (Dennis Dobson, 1971).

   by various hands, Special Edition of *Montage* (Anandam, Bombay, 1966).

   The Apu Trilogy, by Robin Wood (November Books, 1972).

Renoir: the World of his Films, by Leo Braudy (Doubleday, 1972).

Renoir, by Pierre Leprohon (Crown, 1971).

Resnais, by John Ward (Secker & Warburg, 1968).

Rossellini, by José Luis Guarner (Studio Vista, 1970).

Sternberg, by Herman G. Weinberg (Dutton, 1967).

   The Cinema of, by John Baxter (Zwemmer, 1971).

Straub, by Richard Roud (Thames & Hudson, 1971).

Stroheim, by Joel W. Finler (Studio Vista, 1967).

Truffaut, the Cinema of, by Graham Petrie (Zwemmer, 1970).

Vigo, by Pierre Lherminier (Seghers, 1967).

   by John M. Smith (November Books, 1972).

   by P. E. Salles Gomes (Secker & Warburg, 1972).

Visconti, by Geoffrey Nowell-Smith (Secker & Warburg, 1967).

Warhol, by Peter Gidal (Studio Vista, 1971).

Welles, the Films of, by Charles Higham (University of California, 1970).

Wilder, by Axel Madsen (Secker & Warburg, 1968).

SOME SCRIPTS AND SCREENPLAYS

Anderson. If . . . (Lorrimer, 1970).

Antonioni. Screenplays (Orion, 1967).

   Blow Up (Lorrimer, 1972).

Bellocchio. China Is Near (Orion, 1969).

Bergman. The Seventh Seal (Lorrimer, 1967).

   Wild Strawberries (Lorrimer, 1968).

Buñuel. Viridiana, The Exterminating Angel and Simon of the Desert (Orion, 1969).

   L'Age d'Or and Un Chien Andalou (Lorrimer, 1968).

   Belle de Jour (Lorrimer, 1971).

   Tristana (Lorrimer, 1971).

Carné. Les Enfants du Paradis (Lorrimer, 1968).
  Le Jour se Lève (Lorrimer, 1969).
Clair. A Nous la Liberté and Entr'acte (Lorrimer, 1970).
De Sica. Bicycle Thieves (Lorrimer, 1968).
Dreyer. The Passion of Joan of Arc, Vampyr, Day of Wrath, Ordet (Thames & Hudson, 1970).
Eisenstein. The Battleship Potemkin (Lorrimer, 1968).
  Que Viva Mexico, with introduction by Ernest Lindgren (Vision Press, 1951).
  Ivan the Terrible (Lorrimer, 1970).
Ford. Stagecoach (Lorrimer, 1972).
Godard. Alphaville (Lorrimer, 1968).
  Le Petit Soldat (Lorrimer, 1968).
  Pierrot Le Fou (Lorrimer, 1968).
  Weekend, Wind from the East (Lorrimer, 1972).
Ivens. Zuiderzee (Poligono, Milan, 1945).
Kurosawa. Ikiru (Lorrimer, 1968).
  Seven Samurai (Lorrimer, 1970).
Lang. M (Lorrimer, 1968).
Menzel. Closely Observed Trains (Lorrimer, 1971).
Olivier. Hamlet, the Film and the Play, ed Alan Dent (World Film Publications, 1948).
Pabst. Pandora's Box (Lorrimer, 1971).
Pasolini. Oedipus Rex (Lorrimer, 1972).
Reed. The Third Man (Lorrimer, 1968).
Renoir. La Grande Illusion (Lorrimer, 1968).
  La Règle du Jeu (Lorrimer, 1970).
Schlesinger. Sunday Bloody Sunday (Corgi, 1971).
Sternberg. The Blue Angel (Lorrimer, 1968).
Stroheim. Greed, ed Joel W. Finler (Lorrimer, 1972).
  Greed, ed Herman G. Weinberg (Arno, 1972).
Truffaut. Les Quatre Cents Coups (Grove Press, 1969).
  Jules et Jim (Lorrimer, 1968).
Warhol. Blue Movie (Grove Press, 1970).
Welles. The Citizen Kane Book (Secker & Warburg, 1971).
  The Trial (Lorrimer, 1972).
Wiene. The Cabinet of Dr Caligari (Lorrimer, 1970).

GENERAL
Ackland, Rodney and Grant, Elspeth. The Celluloid Mistress (Allan Wingate, 1954).
Anderson, Lindsay. Making a Film (Allen & Unwin, 1952).
Blakeston, Oswell. Through a Yellow Glass (Pool, 1928).

Bower, Dallas. Plan for Cinema (Dent, 1936).

Brownlow, Kevin. How It Happened Here (Secker & Warburg, 1968).

Buchanan, Andrew. Films: The Way of the Cinema (Pitman, 1932).

Cameron, Ken. Sound and the Documentary Film (Pitman, 1947).

Carrick, Edward. Designing for Motion Pictures (Studio, 1941).

Charensol, G. Panorama du Cinéma (Editions KRA, 1930).

Delluc, Louis. Cinéma et Cie (Paris, 1920).

Dickinson, Thorold. A Discovery of Cinema (Oxford, 1971).

Duca, Lo. Le Dessin Animé (Prisma, 1948).

Dunne, John Gregory. The Studio (W. H. Allen, 1970).

Elliott, W. F. Sound Recording for Films (Pitman, 1937).

Ernst, Morris. The First Freedom (Macmillan, 1946).

Ernst, Morris and Lorentz, Pare. Censored (Cape & Smith, 1930).

Everson, William K. The Films of Laurel and Hardy (Citadel Press, 1967).

Feyder, Jacques and Rosay, Françoise. Le Cinéma Notre Métier (Cailler, 1946).

Field, Mary and Smith, Percy. Secrets of Nature (Faber & Faber, 1934).

Fitzgerald, Scott. The Last Tycoon (Grey Walls Press, 1949).

Ford, Richard. Children at the Cinema (Allen & Unwin, 1939).

Geduld, Harry M. Film Makers on Film Making (Indiana University, 1967).

Gelmis, Joseph. The Film Director as Superstar (Secker & Warburg, 1971).

Guback, Thomas H. The International Film Industry (Indiana University, 1969).

Halas, John and Manvell, Roger. Design in Motion (Studio, 1962).

Hopkinson, Peter. Split Focus (Rupert Hart Davis, 1969).

Hughes, Robert (Ed). Film Book I: The Audience & the Film Maker (Grove Press, 1959).

Film Book II: Films of Peace and War (Grove Press, 1962).

Huntley, John. British Film Music (Skelton Robinson, 1947).

Jarvie, I. C. Towards a Sociology of the Cinema (Routledge Kegan Paul, 1970).

Kitses, Jim. Horizons West (Thames & Hudson, 1969).

Latham, Aaron. Crazy Sundays: Scott Fitzgerald in Hollywood (Secker & Warburg, 1972)

Legg, Stuart and Fairthorne, R. Cinema and Television (Longmans Green, 1939).

Legg, Stuart and Klingender, F. D. Money Behind the Screen (Lawrence & Wishart, 1937).

Levin, G. Roy (Ed). Documentary Explorations (Doubleday, 1971).

London, Kurt. Film Music (Faber & Faber, 1935 – re-issued Arno Press, 1970).

Lovell, Alan (Ed). Art of the Cinema in Ten European Countries (Council of Europe, 1967).

McCabe, John. Mr Laurel and Mr Hardy (Doubleday, 1961).

McCann, Richard Dyer. Film and Society (Charles Scribner, 1964).

Manvell, Roger and Huntley, John. The Technique of Film Music (Focal Press, 1957).

Mayer, J. P. Sociology of the Film (Faber & Faber, 1946).

Montagu, Ivor. Film World (Penguin, 1964).

The Political Censorship of Films (Gollancz, 1929).

Nizhny, Vladimir. Lessons with Eisenstein, tr Ivor Montagu & Jay Leyda (Allen & Unwin, 1962).

Notcutt, L. and Latham, G. The African and the Cinema (Edinburgh House, 1937).

Orrom, Michael and Williams, Raymond. Preface to Film (Film Drama, 1954).

Powdermaker, Hortense. Hollywood the Dream Factory (Secker & Warburg, 1951).

Quigley, Martin. Decency in Motion Pictures (Macmillan, 1931).

Reiniger, Lotte. Shadow Theatres and Shadow Films (Batsford, 1970).

Reisz, Karel. The Technique of Film Editing (Focal Press, 1953).

Richter, Hans. Filmgegner von Heute – Filmfreunde von Morgen (Reckendorf, 1929).

Rosenthal, Alan. The New Documentary in Action (University of California, 1971).

Ross, Lillian. Picture (Gollancz, 1953).

Schulberg, Budd. What Makes Sammy Run? (Transworld, 1958).

Smith, Percy, Durden, J. V, and Field, Mary. Cine-Biology (Penguin, 1941).

Spottiswoode, Raymond. Film and its Techniques (Faber & Faber, 1951).

Starr, Cecile. Discovering the Movies (Van Nostrand Reinhold, 1972).

Stephenson, Ralph. Animation in the Cinema (Zwemmer, 1967).

Stephenson, Ralph and Debrix, J. R. The Cinema as Art (Penguin, 1965).

Temple, Lt.-Col. Sir Richard. The Cinema in India (All India Radio, 1938).

Thorp, Margaret Farrand. America at the Movies (Yale University, 1939).

Unesco. The Arts and Man (Unesco, Paris, 1969).

Wagenknecht, Edward. The Movies in the Age of Innocence (University of Oklahoma, 1962).

Weidenfeld, A. G. (Ed). The Public's Progress (Contact, 1947).

West, Nathanael. The Day of the Locust (Grey Walls Press, 1951).

Wickham, Glynne (Ed). The Relation between Universities and Films, Radio and Television (University of Bristol, 1956).

Wysotsky, Michael Z. Wide Screen Cinema & Stereophonic Sound, tr A. E. C. York (Focal Press, 1971).

Youngblood, Gene. Expanded Cinema (Studio Vista, 1970).

SOME BACKGROUND READING

Broszat, Martin. see under *Krausnik, Helmut.*

de Chardin, Pierre Teilhard. The Phenomenon of Man (Collins, 1960).

Farr, Eugene. see under *Hubbard, Hugh W.*

Gombrich, E. H. The Story of Art (Phaidon, 1967).

Gregory, R. L. The Intelligent Eye (Weidenfeld & Nicolson, 1970).

Hauser, Arnold. The Social History of Art (Routledge & Kegan Paul, 1962).

Hubbard, Hugh W. with Farr, Eugene, McLaren, Norman and others. The Healthy Village (Unesco, 1951).

Jung, C. J. Psychology of the Unconscious, tr Beatrice Hurkle (Kegan Paul, 1946).

Krausnik, Helmut and Broszat, Martin. Anatomy of the SS State (Paladin, 1970).

Langer, Suzanne K. Feeling and Form: A Theory of Art (Routledge & Kegan Paul, 1953).

Lévi-Strauss, Claude. The Savage Mind (Weidenfeld & Nicolson, 1966).

Mackinder, Halford. Democratic Ideals and Reality (Penguin, 1944).

McLaren, Norman, see under *Hubbard, Hugh W.*

McLuhan, Marshall. Understanding Media (Sphere Books, 1967).

Piaget, Jean. Structuralism, tr Chaninah Maschler (Routledge & Kegan Paul, 1971).

Rycroft, Charles. Reich (Fontana, 1971).

Shattuck, Roger. The Banquet Years (Cape, 1969).

Simeons, A. T. W. Man's Presumptuous Brain (Longmans, 1960).

Sontag, Susan. Styles of Radical Will (Farrar Straus & Giroux, 1969).

Speer, Albert. Inside the Third Reich (Sphere, 1971).

Steiner, George. Extraterritorial (Faber & Faber, 1972).

Tallents, Stephen. The Projection of Britain (Faber & Faber, 1932).

Thomas, Elizabeth Marshall. The Harmless People (Vintage Books, 1965).

Tomas, Andrew. We Are Not the First (Souvenir Press, 1971).

Vasari, Giorgio. Lives of the Artists, tr George Bull (Penguin, 1965).

Warner, Rex. The Cult of Power (Bodley Head, 1946).

Wilenski, R. H. Modern French Painting (Faber & Faber, 1963).

Wilhelm, Richard. The Secret of the Golden Flower (Kegan Paul, 1947).

Wilson, Edmund. To the Finland Station (Secker & Warburg, 1941).

REFERENCE

Annual Register of World Events (Longmans).

Art in Revolution: Soviet Art & Design Since 1917 (Arts Council, 1971).

British Cinema: Guide & Index, by Denis Gifford (Zwemmer, 1968).

The British Film Industry (P.E.P., London, 1952).

Chronology of the Modern World, by Neville Williams (Barrie & Rocklifl, 1966).

Cinéma 64 (containing *Le Cinéma Chinois*) (C.I.B., 1964).

Deutscher Kultur- und Dokumentarfilm Katalog (VIP Wiesbaden, 1964).

Eastern Europe: Film Guide & Index, by Nina Hibbin (Zwemmer, 1969).

Encyclopaedia of Dates & Events, by L. C. Pascoe, A. J. Lee and E. S. Jenkins (English University Press, 1968).

The Factual Film (P.E.P., London, 1947).

Feature Films on 8mm & 16mm Available for Release or Sale in the United States, compiled by James L. Limbacher (R. R. Bowker, New York, 1971).

Films on Art (Unesco, Paris, 1949).

Films on Art (Unesco, Paris, 1951).

Films of Britain: 1947–50 (British Council, 1950).

The Filmgoer's Companion, by Leslie Halliwell (MacGibbon & Kee, 1970).

The Film Industry in Six European Countries (Film Centre for Unesco, 1950).

Film Society Programmes 1925–1939, with introduction by George Amberg (Arno, 1971).

France: Guide & Index, by Marcel Martin (Zwemmer, 1971).

Georges Méliès, Centenary Catalogue (Cinémathèque Française, 1961).

International Encyclopaedia of Film, ed Roger Manvell & Lewis Jacobs (Michael Joseph, 1972).

International Film Guide (Tantivy Press).

International Motion Picture Almanack (Quigley Publications).

Japan: Guide & Index, by Arne Svensson (Zwemmer, 1971).

The Literary Life: 1900–1950, by Robert Phelps & Peter Deane (Chatto & Windus, 1969).

A Long Look at Short Films, by Derrick Knight & Vincent Porter (Pergamon Press, 1967).

Press, Radio, Film: Report of the Commission on Technical Needs (Unesco, 1947).

60 Ans de Cinéma (Cinémathèque Française, 1955).

The Times History of Our Times, ed Marcus Cunliffe (Weidenfeld & Nicolson, 1971).

The Visual Arts (P.E.P., London, 1946).

World Encyclopaedia of Film, ed Cawkwell & Smith (Studio Vista, 1972).

The Year's Work in the Film: 1949 (British Council & Longmans Green, 1950).

The Year's Work in the Film: 1950 (British Council & Longmans Green, 1951).

PERIODICALS (Select List)

A.I.D. News – Bulletin de l'Association Internationale des Documentaristes (France).

British Film Academy Journal, subsequently *Journal of the Society of Film and Television Arts* (UK).

Biografbladet (Sweden).

Bulletins de l'IDHEC (France).

Cahiers du Cinéma (France).

Challenge for Change Newsletter (Canada).

Cinema Quarterly (UK).

Close Up (UK).

Close Up (India).

Contrast (UK).

Documentary News Letter, subsequently *Documentary Film News* (UK).
Experimental Cinema (USA).
Film (UK).
Film Art (UK).
Film Culture (USA).
Film and TV Technician (UK).
Films and Filming (UK).
Focus on Film (UK).
Hollywood Quarterly, subsequently *Film Quarterly* (USA).
Indian Documentary (India).
Kinematograph Weekly (UK).
Monogram (UK).
Montage (India).
Monthly Film Bulletin (UK).
Movement (India).
Objectif (Canada).
Penguin Film Review (UK).
Picturegoer (UK).
Revue du Cinéma (France).
Sequence (UK).
Sight and Sound (UK).
Skoop (Netherlands)
Variety (USA)
World Film News (UK).

INDICES

Note: From the *Signpost* sections only direct filmic references are included.

1. INDEX OF FILMS

A

Abhijan, 461, 466n
Abismos de Pasión (Wuthering Heights), 93n
A Bout de Souffle (Breathless), 291, 476, 489
Abschied von Gestern, 579
Abyss, 401
Accattone, 529–30, 533–4
Ace in the Hole, 369, 371n, 285
Accident, 562–3
Act of Violence, 366–7
Actor's Revenge, An, 445–6, 448
Actual Experience, 459
Ada, 67n
Adalen Riots, The, 575
Adalen, 31, 575
Adam's Rib, 383–4
Admiral Nakhimov, 408, 436n
A Double Tour, 291, 489–90, 493
Adventures of Baron Munchäusen, The, 212
Adventures of Gerard, The, 589
Adventures of Goupy and Bagha, The, 469n
Adventures of Oktyabrina, The, 584n
Adventures of Prince Achmed, The, 4, 63, 135
Adversary, The, 228, 469, 470n, 602, 603n
Advise and Consent, 387
African Awakening, 610n
African Queen, The, 379, 623
Aerograd, 332n, 422, 425–6, 694
Age d'Or, L', 53, 237–8, 510, 615, 644, 671
Age of Daydreaming, The, 596
Agnus Dei, 594–5, 653
Agoupi, 403
Aigle à Deux Têtes, L', 252–3
Akash Kussim, 603n
Akbar, 459
Alamo, The, 484
Alexander Nevski, 206, 411, 422, 431, 434, 480
Alfie, 331
Alice's Restaurant, 636
Alice in Wonderland, 14n, 394
All About Eve, 181, 357, 388, 623
All Fall Down, 632
All My Children, 665n
All Quiet on the Western Front, 153, 160–1, 165, 167–8, 359, 414–15, 560
All the King's Men, 368–9, 623
Alone, 584
Alone on the Pacific, 445, 447
Alphaville, 493, 509
Altri Tempi, 516n
American in Paris, An, 80, 630
Americano in Vacanza, Un, 216
American Soldier, The, 580
American Tragedy, An, 378
Amiche per le Pelle (Friends for Life), 521n
Amiche, Le, 404
Among People, 121
Amour l'Après-Midi, L', 496
Anaemic Cinema, 53
Anchors Aweigh, 183, 219
Andrei Rublev, 243, 479, 581

Andromeda Strain, The, 645
And So To Work, 205
Angel Exterminador, El (Exterminating Angel, The), 237
Angel Levine, The, 645, 653
Angelina, 514
Anges du Péché, Les, 259, 284
Angry Boy, 127n
Angry Silence, The, 548n
Animal Farm, 136
Anna Christie, 91
Anna Karenina, 93, 119, 317, 582
Année Dernière à Marienbad, L', 10–11, 14, 83, 188, 277, 280, 284, 506, 599
A Nous la Liberté, 81, 140, 180, 532
Antoine et Antoinette, 262
Antonio das Mortes, 512, 615–16, 652, 669
Apache, 627
Aparajito, 461–3
Apartment, The, 385, 484
Apropos de Nice, 40n
Apur Sansar, 461, 463–4, 470, 473
Apu Trilogy, The, 327, 460–1, 463–4
Ard, El (Land, The), 651
Around the World in Eighty Days, 381, 406
Arrangement, The, 364
Arrowsmith, 96
Arsenal, 422–3, 425–6, 435
Arsenic and Old Lace, 137
Arshin Mal-Alan, 82
Artisten in der Zirkuskuppel: Ratlos, 579
Artists at the Top of the Big Top: Disoriented, 578
Ashes, 589
Ashes and Diamonds, 413–15, 590
Asphalt Jungle, The, 354, 367, 379
Assassinat du Duc de Guise, L', 6
Astronautes, Les, 476
As You Desire Me, 40, 95, 142
As You Like It, 92
Atalante, L', 145, 551, 602, 636
Atithi, 603
Atonement of Gosta Berling, The, 46, 347
At 6 p.m. After the War, 82, 209 583
At the Circus, 148
Aubervilliers, 216, 250
Audioscopics, 355
Au Hazard Balthazar, 284, 294, 302
Autumn Afternoon, An, 456–7
Avant le Déluge, 267n
Aveu, L', 503, 659
Aviron, L', 133
Awara, 460

B

Bach's B Minor Mass, 654
Back of Beyond, The, 321n, 573n
Bad and the Beautiful, The, 630
Bad Day at Black Rock, 368, 370–1
Bad Sleep Well, The, 482
Baisers Volés, 242, 493, 657
Bakhti, 470n

Ballad of a Soldier, 479
Ballad of Cable Hogue, The, 625, 645
Ballad of Joe Hill, The, 575
Ballet Méchanique, 53
Ballon Rouge, Le, 404
Baltic Deputy, The, 437, 479
Bambi, 132n
Bandera, La, 140
Bank Dick, The, 178
Bank Holiday, 309
Baptism of Fire, 151
Barabbas, 347
Barbarella, 14n
Barnaby Rudge, 24
Barravento, 483
Barretts of Wimpole Street, The, 97
Barrier, 589–90
Bartleby, 647
Bas Fonds, Les, 140
Bataille des Dix Million, 657
Bataille du Rail, La, 216, 252
Batting Strokes at Cricket, 112
Battle for Heavy Water, The, 335, 628
Battle of Algiera, The, 301, 503, 522
Battles of the Coronel and Falkland Islands, The, 67, 161
Battle of San Pietro, The, 155–6, 218, 380
Battle of Stalingrad, The, 208
Battle of the Bulge, The, 628n
Battle of the River Plate, The, 405
Battleship Potemkin, The, 29, 46, 53, 63, 166n, 221, 238n, 431, 693
BBC – The Voice of Britain, 113
Beau Geste, 142
Beau Serge, Le, 308, 489, 492, 545
Beauté du Diable, La, 248, 438
Beaver Valley, 394
Becky Sharp, 77
Bed and Board, 657
Bed and Sofa, 46, 68
Bedroom Mazurka, 656
Bed, The, 643
Before the Revolution, 534–7, 540
Bel Antonio, Il, 477
Belle de Jour, 14n, 644
Belles de Nuit, Les, 81
Belle Equipe, La, 140, 143
Belle et la Bête, La, 14n, 252, 628
Bellissima, 541
Ben Hur, 64, 381, 620
Berlin, 208, 217
Berlin – Symphony of a Great City, 51, 63, 66, 348
Bespoke Overcoat, The, 334, 546
Best Years of Our Lives, The, 353, 359–61, 362, 381
Bête Humaine, La, 147
Bezhin Meadow, 434
Bhowani Junction, 383
Bhuvan Shome, 603
Bible, The, 378
Biches, 490
Bicycle Thieves, 221, 226–8, 236, 247n, 312, 460, 475, 513–14, 516
Bidoni, Il, 518
Bigamist, The, 507n
Big Business, 158

Big Carnival, The, 369n
Big Country, The, 381
Big Heat, The, 391
Big House, The, 98
Big Knife, The, 627
Big Parade, The, 159–60
Big Sleep, The, 181, 357, 383, 623
Billy Liar, 566
Birdman of Alcatraz, The, 632
Birds, The, 186, 392–3, 490
Birth of a Nation, The, 20, 23, 28, 35, 63, 156, 318
Biscuit Eater, The, 138
Bitter Rice, 516
Blackboard, The, 374n
Black Flowers for the Bride, 645
Black God, White Devil, 615
Blackmail, ix, 72, 103
Black Mask, The, 152
Blanche, 589
Blé en Herbe, Le, 261
Blind Husbands, 32, 39–40
Blithe Spirit, 217
Blonde in Love, A, 600
Blood and Sand, 77, 507n
Bloody Mama, 100, 624
Blow Up, 14n
Blue Angel, 343
Blue Lamp, The, 321
Blue Movie, 332n, 642
Blues Like Showers of Rain, 645
Blushing Charlie, 655
Bob le Flambeur, 253, 404
Boccaccio '70, 521
Body Snatchers, The, 219
Bombay Talkie, 603n, 604–5, 651
Bonchi, 482
Bondage, 593
Bongolo, 338
Bonheur, Le, 507
Bonjour Tristesse, 386
Bonnie and Clyde, 99–100, 313, 623–4, 635
Boom, 562
Bookseller Who Gave Up Bathing, The, 577
Boomerang, 353, 360, 362
Border Street, 411
Borinage, 337
Born Yesterday, 357, 384
Borom Saret, 611
Boston Strangler, The, 620n, 638, 689
Boucher, Le, 492–3
Boudu Sauvé des Eaux, 145
Boulangère de Monçeau, La, 496n
Boule de Suif, 216
Boy, 90, 236, 512, 606
Boy and the Kite, The, 575
Boys in the Band, The, 626, 645
Brave Don't Cry, The, 334
Bread, Love and Dreams, 513n
Breakfast at Tiffany's, 623
Breathless (A Bout de Souffle), 476, 489
Brewster McLeod, 645
Bridegroom, the Comedian and the Pimp, The, 580
Bridge, The, 339, 478
Bridge on the River Kwai, The, 315n, 318, 546n
Bridges at Toko-Ri, The, 631
Brief Encounter, 316–17, 440
Brighton Rock, 329
Bright Path, 82
Bringing Up Baby, 383
Britain Can Take It, 197n
Broadway Melody, ix
Broken Dykes, 339
Bronco Bullfrog, 568, 569n, 646
Brothers in Law, 330, 405
Brothers Karamazov, The, 583
Browning Version, The, 330
Brumes d'Automne, 53
Buccaneer, The, 377
Buck and the Preacher, 640–1
Bullitt, 623, 638–9
Bunny Lake Is Missing, 387–8
Burma Victory, 200

Burmese Harp, The, 154, 400, 445–7, 483
Bus Stop, 406
Butch Cassidy and the Sundance Kid, 621, 623
Butterfield 8, 484, 628n

C

Cabaret, 638
Cabascabo, 499n
Cabinet of Dr Caligari, The, 46, 48–9, 156, 243, 429n
Cabiria, 18, 20
Caccia Tragica, 516
Caesar and Cleopatra, 217, 309n
Café Electric, 68
Caine Mutiny, The, 630
Calabuch, 346, 403
Calcutta '71, 603n
Calle Mayor, 346, 403
Camille, 383
'Canada Carries On' Series, 155
Canterbury Tale, A, 197
Capricious Summer, 602
Captain of Cologne, The, 402
Captain of Koepenik, The, 403
Captains Courageous, 93
Captive Heart, The, 321
Carabiniers, Les, 509
Cardinal, The, 387
Carmen, 23
Carmen Jones, 81, 386
Carnet de Bal, Un, 143
Carousel, 80
Carrière de Suzanne, La, 496n
Casablanca, 181, 359n
Casque d'Or, 252, 266, 322, 547
Cat and the Canary, The, 66
Cat Ballou, 623, 625n
Catch My Soul, 443
Catch 22, 159, 559, 628, 645
Cathy Come Home, 569
Cat People, 182
Cat, Shozo and Two Women, A, 400
Cenere, 18, 25
Centennial Summer, 386
Ceremony, The, 90, 440n, 541, 608, 650
Certo Giorno, Un, 528
Ceux de Chez Nous, 251
Chagrin et la Pitié, Le, 407, 504n, 553
Champion, The, 23
Chang, 335
Changing Village, The, 472
Chapeau de Paille d'Italie, Un, 52, 63, 81
Charulata, 464, 467
Chasse au Lion à l'Arc, La, 502
Chelsea Girls, The, 642
Chemineau, Le, 24
Cheyenne Autumn, 382
Chien Andalou, Un, 53, 237, 510, 644, 671
Childhood of Maxim Gorki, The, 121–2, 461
Children Accuse, 420
Children Are Watching Us, The, 230n
Children Growing Up With Other People, 112
Children Learning by Experience, 112
Children's Hour, The, 381
Chimes at Midnight, 190–1
China is Near, 543–5, 568
Chinoise, La, 543
Chiriakhana, 468
Chronicle of Anna Magdalena Bach, 580
Chronique d'un Eté, 195n, 499–502
Chuk and Gek, 437–8
Cid, El, 628
Cina é Vicina, La, 543–5
Cincinnati Kid, The, 637
Ciocara, La (Two Women), 514
Circus, 82
Circus, The, 66

Citadel, The, 106–7
Citizen Kane, 43, 102–3, 184, 187, 191, 193, 353, 369, 390n
City Lights, 127, 235, 529
City Streets, 77
Clansman, The, 28
Clash by Night, 391
Cléo de Cinq à Sept, 507
Cleopatra, 388, 620
Clockwork Orange, A, 546, 572–3, 606, 626n, 667n, 671, 676–9
Closely Observed Trains, 511n, 601–2
Close Quarters, 200
Cluny Brown, 75
Coalface, 114
Coastal Command, 200
Cobweb Castle, 443
Cochecito, El (Wheel Chair, The), 346
Coconuts, The, 73
Collector, The, 382
Colour Box, 418
Combat de Boxe, 337
Come Back Africa, 396, 612
Company Limited, 469, 470n
Collectioneuse, La, 496, 498
Commare Secca, La (Grim Reaper, The), 534
Concerto for Machine Gun, 674n
Condamné à Mort s'est Echappé, Un, 253, 284, 285n, 288, 296n 297–9, 302, 306, 348, 404
Condemned of Altona, The, 514
Confession, The, 503
Confidential Report, 188
Conformist, The, 512, 534, 540 658, 670, 674n
Conformista, Il, 534n
Confrontation, The, 593–4, 653
Congress Dances, 82
Connection, The, 484, 644
Contempt, 508
Coogan's Bluff, 636
Cool Hand Luke, 623, 626
Corbeau, Le, 254, 266
Cottage on Dartmoor, A, 103
Cotton Comes to Harlem, 611n, 639, 645
Countess from Hong Kong, A, 130
Coup du Berger, Le, 405
Covered Wagon, The, 321, 507n
Cover Girl, 14n, 182
Cow, The, 619
Coward and the Holy Man, The, 468
Craig's Wife, 507n
Cranes Are Flying, The, 210, 401, 437, 479
Crazy Page, A, 35
Crime de Monsieur Lange, Le, 145–6
'Crime Does Not Pay' Series, 179
Crime in the Night Club, 602
Crimes of the Future, 649
Criminal, The, 485
Criminal Life of Archibaldo de la Cruz, The, 237
Crisis, 148
Croisière Noire, La, 161n
Cromwell, 646
Crossfire, 353, 360, 366
Crossroads, 35, 90n
Crowd, The, 160
Cruel Sea, The, 320
Cruel Stories of Youth, 482
Cry in the Mountains, A, 339
Cuba Si!, 503
Cul de Sac, 180n, 417, 590
Culloden, 554, 556–7
Cumbras Borrascosas (Wuthering Heights), 93n
Curse of the Cat People, 78n

D

Daisies, 599
Dalibor, 402
Damaged Goods, 23

Dames du Bois de Boulogne, Les,
    216, 259, 284, 285n, 296, 297n,
    301, 304
Damned, The, 522, 561
Dance, Girl, Dance, 507n
Dance of the Heron, 578
Dandy in Aspic, A, 628n
Danish Blue, 578
Darkness in Daytime, 593
Dark Rapture, 335
Dark Victory, 14n
Darling, 565
David Copperfield, 92–3, 646
Dawn Patrol, The, 160, 383
Day of the Jackal, 368
Day of Wrath, 284–5, 290, 301–2,
    412
Days and Nights in the Forest, 469,
    470n
Day Shall Dawn, The, 474
Days of Water, The, 614n
Day the Fish Came Out, The, 344
Dead End, 96
Deadly Affair, The, 635
Dead of Night, 131n, 217, 321–2
Dearest Love, 506
Death by Hanging, 605n, 606
Death in Venice, 448, 522–6
Death Occurred Last Night, 658
Death of a Bureaucrat, 614n
Death of a Cyclist, 345
Decameron, The, 658
Decision Before Dawn, 390
Deep End, 589, 654
*Defeat of the German Armies Near
    Moscow, The,* 208
Defiant Ones, The, 374–5, 563, 630
Déjeuner sur l'Herbe, Le, 146,
    308n, 469
Delovak Athara, 471n
Demoiselles de Rochefort, Les, 507
Dentist, The, 129n
Départ, Le, 589, 591
Dernier Atout, Le, 262
Dernier Milliardaire, Le, 140, 143n
Dernier Tournant, Le, 149
De Renoir à Picasso, 338
Description d'un Combat, 476
Deserter, 119
Desert Fox, 390
Desert Rats, 390
Desert Victory, 154, 200
Destry Rides Again, 377
Deus e o Diablo na Terra del Sol,
    615
Deuses e os Mortos, Os, 614, 652
*Deux ou Trois Choses que Je Sais
    d'Elle,* 509, 512, 606
Deux Timides, Les, 52, 81
Devi, 464, 470, 614n
Devil's Eye, 478
Devil's Passkey, 40
Devils, The, 412n, 556n
Diable au Corps, Le, 260, 263
Diaboliques, Les, 255–9, 627
Dialogue, 588
Diary for Timothy, 201–3, 217
Diary of a Chambermaid, 644
Diary of Anne Frank, The, 378
Diary of a Shinjuku Thief, 35, 512,
    606, 608, 609n
Diary of Chugi's Travels, 69
Difficult People, 595
Dinner at Eight, 138
Dirnentragödie, 67
Dirty Dozen, The, 627
Dirty Harry, 636–7
*Discreet Charm of the Bourgeoisie,
    The,* 644
Ditte Child of Man, 341
Ditte Menneskebarn, 341
Divided World, A, 348
Do Bigha Zamin, 460
Dodeska-den, 650
Dodsworth, 138
Dog Star, 643
Dolce Vita, La, 477, 497, 517, 519,
    521
Dolce Inganni, 477

Dom, 415, 418
Domaren, 478
Domicile Conjugale, 657
Don Juan, 60
Don Quixote, 83, 436, 584
Don't Look Now, 575
Don't Make Waves, 325
Donzoko, 444
Double Indemnity, 180, 385
Douce, 259
Downhill, 67
Dracula, 132
Dramma di Cristo, 337n
Doctor Dolittle, 81, 620n, 621
Dreigroschenoper, Der, 83
Drei von der Tankstelle, 82
Dr Ehrlich's Magic Bullet, 102
Drifters, 108, 112, 114
Drive He Said, 645
Dr Jekyll and Mr Hyde, 77, 93, 132
Drones, The, 517n
*Dr Strangelove, or How I learnt to
    Stop Worrying and Love the
    Bomb,* 628, 632–3, 676–7
Drums Along the Mohawk, 382
Doctor Zhivago, 14, 318, 546n
Duel in the Sun, 378
Due Soldi di Esperanza, 516n
Duet for Cannibals, 507n
Du und Mancher Kamarad, 402
Dumbo, 132n, 183
Durante l'Estate, 528
During the Summer, 528–9
Dutchman, 641
Dyke Is Closed, The, 340

E

Early Autumn, 456n
Early Spring, 400, 456n
Early Summer, 456n
Earth, 90, 118, 152, 409, 414,
    422–4, 429, 434, 518, 522, 694
Easter Island, 116, 337
East of Eden, 362–3
Easy Rider, 623–4, 645
Easy Street, 235
Easy Virtue, 67
Eavesdropper, The, 612
Ecce Homo, 124
Ecole des Facteurs, L', 262
Edge of the City, 374
Edouard et Caroline, 262
8½, 14n, 517, 519
Eighth Wonder, The, 616n
Eléna et les Hommes, 404
Eleventh Hour, The, 34
Elmer Gantry, 484
Eloquent Peasant, The, 618, 651
Elvira Madigan, 575
Elvis, That's the Way It Is, 645
Emergency Call, 331
Emperor Tomato Ketchup, 609n
End of Dialogue, 612
Enfant Sauvage, L', 237, 493–5,
    575
Enfants du Paradis, Les, 143–4, 252
Enfants Terribles, Les, 244n, 252,
    290, 541
Engagement, The, 527
En Natt, 347
Enough to Eat?, 113
En Rade, 145
Entertainer, The, 334, 485, 548,
    609
Enthusiasm, 57
Entr'Acte, 51, 63
Epaves, 251
Eroica, 154, 390n, 412–13, 590
Et Dieu Créa la Femme, 404
Eternal Jew, The, 151
Eternelle Retour, L', 254
Et Mourir de Plaisir, 476
Etrange Monsieur Victor, L', 140
Event, The, 654, 674
Every Day Except Christmas, 333
Everything for Sale, 589
Ewige Jude, Der, 207
Executioner, The, 346

Exodus, 387, 484
Exploits of Elaine, The, 23
Exterminating Angel, The, 190,
    237, 644, 656
Extraordinary Seaman, 633

F

Fahrenheit 451, 15, 493, 571, 668n
Fail Safe, 633–4
Fairground, 478
Falbalas, 216, 262, 322
Falcons, The, 596, 653
Fallen Idol, The, 311–2
Fall of Berlin, 208, 409
Fall of the House of Usher, The,
    53, 624n
Fall of the Roman Empire, The, 628
Fall of the Romanov Dynasty, The,
    68
Fame is the Spur, 329
Family Life, 570
Family Portrait, 203
Fanfare, 340
Fantasia, 14n, 133
Fantômas, 20
Farewell My Lovely, 360n
Farewells, 480
Far from the Madding Crowd, 566,
    571
Farrebique, 216, 248–9
Father, 596–7
Father of the Bride, 630
Faustine, 507n
Feldzug in Polen, 151
Fellini Satyricon, 517, 519–20
Femme Douce, Une, 281, 284,
    299–302, 679
Femme du Boulanger, La, 293
Femme Mariée, Un, 509
Feu Follet, Le, 505
*Few Notes on Our Food Problem,
    A,* 610–11
Fiancée du Pirate, La, 507n
Fiancés, Les, 527
Fidanzati, I, 527–9
Fight for Life, The, 125–6
Fighting Lady, The, 155, 381
Fiddler on the Roof, 638
Fig Leaf, 593
Figures in a Landscape, 374, 563,
    564n, 564, 647
Film, 128, 643
Film Without a Title, 342
Fils d'Eaux, Les, 498
Fin du Jour, La, 140, 143, 149
Finian's Rainbow, 638
Fires Were Started, 201–2
Fires on the Plain, 445
Fire Within, The, 505n
Firemen's Ball, The, 600–1
First Echelon, The, 410
Fists in the Pocket, 541
Fitzwilly, 628n
Five Boys from Barska Street, 411
Five Easy Pieces, 645
Five Finger Exercises, 628n
Five Fingers, 388
5000 Fingers of Dr T, The, 630
Five Scouts, 152
Fixer, The, 633
Flames of Flesh, 64, 69
Flesh, 642
Flesh and the Devil, 66
Flood, The, 411
Flute, The, 616n
Flute and the Arrow, The, 350, 404
Flying Deuces, 148
Folie du Docteur Tube, La, 24,
    681n
Foolish Wives, 40–1, 43, 63, 190
Fool There Was, A, 23
Force of Evil, 367
Forty First, The, 401
Forty Ninth Parallel, The, 196
For Whom the Bell Tolls, 382
Fountains of the Sun, 616n
*Four Horsemen of the Apocalypse
    The,* 64, 153, 158
400 Million, The, 116, 148

Four in a Jeep, 342, 344
Four in the Afternoon, 643
Four Seasons of Children, 152
Fra Brne, 351–2
Frankenstein, 132, 163
Frau im Mond, Die, 50
Freie Fahrt, 51
French Can Can, 379
French Connection, The, 623, 626n, 639
Frenzy, 347
Freud – The Secret Passion, 380
Friendly Persuasion, 406
Friends for Life, 521n
From Here to Eternity, 368
From the Terrace, 484
Frontières de l'Homme, 251n
Front Page, The, 128n, 164n
Fugitive, The, 95, 382
Fury, 100–1
Fuzis, Os, 614

G

Gai Savoir, Le, 513
Gamperiliya, 472, 474
Ganja, 482
Gang's All Here, The, 79, 182
Garden of the Finzi-Continis, The, 514, 658
Gate of Hell, 448
Gates of Paradise, The, 588
Gathering of Eagles, A, 628n
Gav, 619
Gay Desperado, The, 76
Generale della Rovere, Il, 513
General, The, 66
General Line, The, 424–5, 431
Generation, A, 413
Generation of Conquerors, A, 437
Genevieve, 320, 330n
Genou de Claire, Le, 496–7, 657
Gens du Voyage, Les, 142
Gentle Creature, A, 299, 535
Gentleman's Agreement, 360
Gentlemen Prefer Blondes, 383
George V Durbar, 20
German Story, The, 402
Germany Year Zero, 143, 154, 221, 230–4, 295
Gertrud, 284, 297n, 300, 302, 455, 507n, 542, 578, 618
Gervaise, 404
Ghost Goes West, The, 104–5, 140, 318
Ghost That Never Returns, The, 46
Giant, 363, 378
Gigi, 630
Gimme Shelter, 81, 645
Girl at Dozo Temple, A, 215, 218
Girl in Black, A, 344, 403
Girl in the Window, The, 477
Girls, The, 577
Girl Was Young, The, 180n
Girl With the Hatbox, 68
Giulietta degli Spiriti, 519
Gladiators, The, 553, 556
Glass, 340
Glinka, 82
Go-Between, The, 562–4
Godfather, The, 43n, 622
God Gave Him a Dog, 138n
Gods and the Dead, The, 614
Goha, 616n
Going Down the Road, 649
Golden Boy, 77
Golden Coach, The, 248, 514
Goldfinger, 544n
Gold Rush, The, 53, 326
Golem, The, 20, 25
Goliath, 593
Golu Hadawatha, 474n
Gone With The Wind, 14, 28, 147–8, 318, 378, 378n, 621
Goodbye Mr Chips, 106, 149
Goodbye Yesterday, 195
Good Earth, The, 95
Good Times, Wonderful Times, 396
Gorky Trilogy, The, 121, 209, 272, 327, 461, 584

Gospel According to Matthew, The, 302, 530
Goto, I'le d'Amour, 469, 589
Goto, Island of Love, 419
Goupi Mains Rouges, 262
Goupy Gyne, Bagha Byne, 469
Graduate, The, 14, 622–3, 629n, 678n
Grande Illusion, La, 40, 140, 144n, 146, 153, 161–2, 169, 170–1, 221, 413, 560
Grandes Manoeuvres, Les, 81
Grand Jeu, Le, 141–2
Grandmother's Encyclopaedia, 419
Grand Prix, 632
Grapes of Wrath, The, 96, 102–3, 107, 188n, 221, 353
Grass, 115, 335
Great Adventure, The, 349–51
Great Citizen, A, 151
Great Chicago Conspiracy Circus, The, 649
Great Dictator, The, 130, 148
Greatest Show on Earth, The, 377
Greatest Story Ever Told, The, 378
Great Expectations, 93, 105, 316–17
Great Gabbo, The, 40
Great McGinty, The, 179
Great Patriotic War, The, 582
Great Road, The, 68, 483
Great White Hope, The, 645
Greed, 41–4, 145, 185, 190, 285, 327, 423, 424n
Grido, Il, 404
Grim Reaper, The, 524
Grosse Freiheit, Die, 213
Group, The, 635
Guernica, 275–6
Guerre Est Finie, La, 280
Guess Who's Coming to Dinner, 375–6, 629–30
Gulliver's Travels, 132
Gunfight at the OK Corral, The, 370n
Gun Sudari, 33
Guns, The, 614
Guns in the Afternoon, 625
Guru, The, 603n, 604
Guys and Dolls, 388–9
Gypsy Moths, The, 632–3

H

Hail the Conquering Hero, 179
Hairy Ape, The, 91n
Hallelujah!, 75
Hallelujah the Hills!, 643
Hamlet, 92, 100, 190, 332, 436, 584–5
Hand in the Trap, 483, 612
Hands Over the City, 522
Hands Up!, 589
Hangmen Also Die, 178
Happiness, 58n
Hard Day's Night, A, 559
Harder They Come, The, 641n
Harder They Fall, The, 631
Hardy Family Series, 526
Harvest, 436
Heartbeat, 152
Heavens Above, 330
Heiress, The, 381
Heir to Genghis Khan, The (Storm Over Asia), 119n, 426
Heller in Pink Tights, 384, 484
Hello, Dolly, 620n, 621
Hell on Earth (War Is Hell), 162
Hello, Sister, 40, 43
Hell's Angels, 160–1
Hell's Heroes, 72
Hell to Eternity, 370n
Help!, 559
Hen Hop, 418
Henry V, 198, 592
Here Is Your Life, 575
Heroes of Telemark, 628
Herr Puntilla, 342
Heureuse Anniversaire, 265
Hets (Frenzy), 347

High Noon, 315n, 367
High Society, 406
High Wide and Handsome, 76
High Wind in Jamaica, A, 242–3, 326–7
Hill, The, 611n, 634
Hiroshima, 483
Hiroshima Mon Amour, 2, 11, 73, 274, 276, 284, 308, 483
Histoire d'un Crime, 17
Hole in the Wall, The, 355n
Holy Warrior Against the Dragon of Evil, The (Antonio das Mortes), 615n
Home for Aged Women, A, 420
Home of the Brave, 315n, 354, 374, 630
Homme et Une Femme, Un, 507
Horse, 214
Horse of Mud, 616n
Hortobagy, 116
Hotel du Nord, 143
Hotel Imperial, 347
Houen Zo!, 340
House (Dom), 418
House at the Terminus, The, 402
Householder, The, 604n
House on 92nd Street, The, 218
House That Ananda Built, 459
House Without Doors or Windows, The, 48
Housing Problems, 112, 420, 664
How the Steel Was Tempered, 121n
How I Won the War, 553, 558–9
Hud, 623, 635n
Hue and Cry, 320
Hugo and Josefin, 577
Hugs and Kisses, 577
Humoreske, 599
Hungry Stones, The, 482
Hunting Scenes from Lower Bavaria, 579, 655
Hurdes, Las (Land Without Bread), 237
Husbands, 645
Hush . . . Hush Sweet Charlotte, 627
Hussite Warrior, 402
Hustler, The, 623

I

I am a Fugitive from a Chain Gang, 101
I am Curious – Blue, 577
I am Curious – Yellow, 577
I am Twenty, 459
Ice Station Zebra, 370n
I Confess, 392n
Idée, L', 135
Idiot, The, 583
I Even Met Happy Gypsies, 674n
If . . ., 242–4, 551–2, 600n
If I Had a Million, 75, 222, 515
Ikiru, 439–41, 452n
I Live in Fear, 452n
I'll Buy You, 400
I'm All Right Jack, 547
Immortal Heart, The, 151
Immortal Story, The, 184, 188, 191, 523
Immortelle, L', 506
Importance of Being Earnest, The, 330
Ipcress File, The, 635
Incident at Owl Creek, 14n
In Cold Blood, 100, 623
India '58, 400
Indian Village, 350, 404
India '67, 459
Indonesia Calling, 339n
Industrial Britain, 397
Infidelity, 516n
Informer, The, 96, 310
Ingénue Libertine, L', 507n
Inherit the Wind, 484, 630
Inhumaine, L', 63
In Jenen Tagen, 342
Innocence Unprotected, 672

Innocent Sorcerers, 480
Innocents, The, 131n, 236n, 547
Inn of the Sixth Happiness, The,
  631
Intermezzo, 347
Interview, The, 603n
In the Heat of the Night, 376, 638
In the Sands of Central Asia, 209
In the Town of S——, 583
Intolerance, 29–30, 156, 226, 318
Intruder in the Dust. 371–3
Invasion of the Body Snatchers, 407
  636
Investigation of a Citizen Above
  Suspicion, 658
In Which We Serve, 109, 193, 316
Irma La Douce, 385n
Iron Curtain, The, 354
Iron Horse, The, 63, 321
Isadora, 551
Island, The, 482, 608
Island of Shame (The Young One),
  483
Isle of Hope, 420
Isle of the Dead, 182, 219
Isn't Life Wonderful?, 28, 30
Is Paris Burning?, 153
Italian Straw Hat, An, 52, 57, 74
It Always Rains on Sundays, 321
It Happened Here, 553–4
It Happened One Night, 41, 137
It Happened Yesterday, 480
It's a Long Way Home, 481
It's a Mad Mad Mad Mad World,
  629, 637
It's Up To You, 575n
It's Your Thing, 645
Ivan, 425
Ivan Grozny (Ivan the Terrible),
  119n, 207–9, 588
Ivan's Childhood, 243
Ivan the Terrible, 119, 218, 408,
  429–34, 436, 586, 692–3
I Walked with a Zombie, 182
I Was a Male War Bride, 383
I Was Nineteen, 479

J

J'Accuse, 153, 157–8, 161
Jackboot Mutiny, The, 403
Jaguar, 502
Jalsaghar, 461, 463–4, 468, 604
Jamaica Inn, 149
Jane Eyre, 646
Jane Shore, 24
Jan Hus, 599
Jazz Comedy, 82
Jazz on a Summer's Day, 484
Jazz Singer, The, 60–1, 65
Je t'Aime, Je t'Aime, 11, 278,
  280–3, 575, 582n, 674n
Jetée, La, 11, 278–80, 299, 348,
  575, 674n
Jet Pilot, 183
Jeux des Anges, Les, 419
Jeux Interdits, Les, 154, 230n
  239–42, 248, 266–7, 268n, 344,
  471, 625
Jew Süss, 104
Jigokumon, 448
Joan of Arc, 286n
Job, The, 521n, 527
John and Mary, 638n
Johnny Got His Gun, 365n
Johnny in the Clouds, 194
Johnny on the Run, 331
Joli Mai, Le, 502
Jolly Boys, The, 82
Jour de Fête, 263
Journal d'un Curé de Campagne,
  Le, 250n, 268n, 284, 286–7, 289,
  290, 293–4, 296–8, 302, 305–6
  387, 489, 679
Journey's End, 163
Journey Together, 200
Jour Se Lève, Le, 143, 149
Joyless Street, 51
Juarez, 102, 148
Judex, 505

Judge, The, 478
Judgement at Nuremberg, 629
Judith of Bethulia, 20
Jud Süss, 151, 207, 213
Jules et Jim, 493–4
Juliet of the Spirits, 14n, 519
Julius Caesar, 388, 646
Jungle Book, The, 394
Justice est Faite, 267n

K

Kabuliwala, 400
Kameradschaft, 51 161–2
Kanal, 402, 411, 413
Kapo, 477
Kapurush-o-Mahapurush (Coward
  and the Holy Man, The), 466n,
  468
Katusha, 27
Katzelmacher, 655
Kermess Héroique, La, 140–2
Kes, 91, 236, 242n, 569–70
Key, The, 312, 315, 445–6
Kid, The. 130, 235–6
Kid Brother, The, 66
Kidnappers, The, 332
Killer!, 490n, 657
Killing, The, 367, 406
Killing of Sister George, The, 627
Kill or Be Killed, 198
Kimiko, 90n
Kind Hearts and Coronets, 322–3
Kind of Loving, A, 565
King and Country, 553–4, 556,
  560–1
King in New York, A, 130
King Kong, 96
King Lear, 270n, 584–8, 646, 652
King of Kings, The, 66, 378
King Rat, 320, 549, 550n
Kipps, 309
Kiss, The, 142
Kiss in the Desert, A, 69
Kiss Me Again, 74
Kiss Me Deadly, 627n
Kiss Me Stupid, 385n
Kitty, 219
Klute, 638
Knack, The, 559
Knife, The (Mes, Het), 478, 578–9
Knife in the Water, 417, 480
Knights of the Teutonic Order, 411,
  480
Knight Without Armour, 104, 142
Knock On Any Door, 367, 391
Kolberg 212–13
Kongi's Harvest, 612
Kon Tiki, 335–6
Krakatit, 599
Krishna Jalna, 16
Kühle Wampe, 51, 402
Kwaidan, 608

L

Laburnum Grove, 311
Labyrinth, 419, 684, 689
Lady from Constantinople, The,
  507n
Lady from Shanghai, The, 187–8
Ladykillers, The, 323, 325
Lady Vanishes, The, 104
Lady with the Little Dog, The, 437,
  479, 583
Lamb, The, 23
Land, The, 103, 124, 398, 616n,
  651
Landlord, The, 645
Land of Promise, 195
Landscape After A Battle, 654
Land Without Bread, 53, 172n,
  237, 250, 345
Lanka Dahan, 16
Larks on a String, 597, 602
Lact Act, The, 342, 403
Last Chance, The, 344
Last Days of Pompeii, The, 18
Last Goal, The, 481
Last Day of Summer, The, 415–16,
  418

Last Laugh, The, 49, 51
Last Pair Out, The, 404
Last Shot, The, 339
Last Stage, The, 411
Last Tango in Paris, 540–1
Last Valley, The, 646
Late Autumn, 456n, 482
Late Spring, 482
Laura, 180. 386
Lavendar Hill Mob, The, 320
Lavoro, Il, 521n
Lawrence of Arabia, 318. 616n
League of Gentlemen, The, 548n
Learning Tree, The, 639n
Leaves from Satan's Notebook, 284
Leda, 490n
Lenin in 1918, 151
Léon Morin, Prêtre, 253, 290, 293,
  387
Leopard, The, 522
Letter That Was Not Sent, The,
  479
Letter to Three Wives, A, 388
Letter With The Feathers, The, 438
Let the People Sing, 334n
Let There Be Light, 218
Liaisons Dangereuses. Les, 476
Lian Shan-Po and Chu Ying-Tai,
  438
Liberation Front, 650
Life and Death of Colonel Blimp,
  The, 197
Lifeboat, 180
Life in the Soviet Arctic, 118
Life of Adolf Hitler, The, 478
Life of Christ, The, 16
Life of Emile Zola, The, 102
Life Was the Stake, 402
Light Display: Black White Gray,
  683
Lights Out In Europe, 148
Lilies of the Field, 373
Limelight, 130
Line of Life, The, 470
Listen to Britain, 201–2
Little Big Man, 636, 645
Little Caesar, 98
Little Fauss and Big Halsey, 622
Little Friend, 104
Little Women, 383
Living Desert, The, 394–5
Lizards, The, 507n
Loin de Vietnam, 503, 559
Lola, 476
London Can Take It, 196
Londoners, The, 112
Loneliness of the Long-Distance
  Runner, 548
Lonely Night, The, 127
Lonely Villa, The, 31
Lone White Sail, 121n, 437
Long Day's Journey Into Night,
  633
Longest Day, The, 628
Long, Long Trailer, The, 630
Long Pants, 66, 137
Look Back in Anger, 334, 545–8
  550
Loony Tom, 643
Loot, 646
Lord of the Flies, 326n
Lost Boundaries, 361n
Lost Generation, 596
Lost Horizon, 96, 137
Lost Weekend, The, 182, 219, 385
Lotna, 415
Loudest Whisper, The, 382
Louisiana Story, 109, 349–50, 398
Lourdes and its Miracles, 250
Love, 382n
Loved One, The, 547n
Love Film, A, 597
Love Is a Many Splendoured Thing
  391
Love Me Tonight, 76
Love on the Dole, 334n
Love Parade, The, 72, 74–5
Loves of Jeanne Ney, The, 51, 66
Love Story, A, 653

Love Story, 645
Loving, 645
Loving Couples, 577
Loving Memory, 646
Lower Depths, The, 35, 146, 444, 650
Loyal Forty Seven Ronin, The, 20
Loyal Forty Seven Ronin of the Genroku Era, The, 214
L Shaped Room, The, 549
Luci del Varietá, 516n, 517
Lumière d'Eté, 172–3
Lust for Life, 406

M

M, 50, 72, 101
Macao, 183
Macbeth, 190, 417, 571, 584, 592–3, 654
Madame Bovary, 145
Mädchen in Uniform, 234–5
Madigan, 636
Mad Wednesday, 179
Magi, The, 328
Magirama, 404
Magnet, The, 320
Magnificent Ambersons, The, 184–6, 188, 344, 474
Magnificent Seven, The, 370n, 441, 484
Maisons de la Misère, 337
Maitres Fous, Les, 498
Malgovert, 250
Maltese Falcon, The, 155, 180–1, 380
Mamma Roma, 529–30
Man and a Woman, A, 14n
Man Between, The, 313
Man Called Horse, A, 625
Man Called John, A, 528n
Manchurian Candidate, The, 632, 634n
Mandabi, 610
Man for All Seasons, A, 368
Man I Killed, The, 75, 153, 163, 166
Man in Space, 407
Man in the White Suit, The, 323, 330
Man Is Not A Bird, A, 672
Man Is Ten Feet Tall, A, 374
Mani sulla Città, Le (Hands Over the City), 522
Mano en la Trampa, La (Hand in the Trap), 612
Man of Africa, 334
Man of Aran, 105, 396–7, 380
Manon, 255
Man's Fate, 621
Ma Nuit Chez Maud, 496–8
Man Who Had His Hair Cut Short, The, 578
Man Who Knew Too Much, The, 104, 392n
Man Who Left His Will On Film, The, 650
Man Who Shot Liberty Valance, The, 382
Man Who Stayed At Home, The, 24
Man With the Golden Arm, The, 386
Man With the Movie Camera, The, 57
March of Time, The, 256
Marie Louise, 344
Marked Woman, The, 99, 181, 368
Mark of Zorro, The, 77
Marnie, 490
Married Couple, A, 649
Marseillaise, La, 146–7
Marty, 620, 628n, 633
Martyrs of Love, 599
Masculin, Feminin, 509
M*A*S*H, 159, 559, 628–9
Masque of the Red Death The, 624n
Maternelle, La, 233–4
Matira Manisha, 603n

Matter of Dignity, A, 344, 403
Matter of Life and Death, A, 198
Mazeppa, 589
Meet Me in St Louis, 80, 182, 630
Mein Kampf, 478
Member of the Wedding, The, 367
Memorandum, 154, 276n
Memories of Underdevelopment, 496, 512, 613–14
Memphis Belle, The, 154–5, 381
Men, The, 315n, 354, 365–8, 630
Menilmontant, 53, 250
Men on the Bridge, 479
Men With Wings, 479
Mépris, Le (Contempt), 391, 508–9
Merrily We Go To Hell, 507n
Merry-Go-Round, The, 41, 409
Merry Widow, The, 43, 63
Mes Het (Knife, The), 478, 578
Message, The, 472
Metropolis, 48, 50–1
Michurin, 423, 435
Midnight Cowboy, 546, 565–6
Midsummer Night's Dream, A, 91
Midvinterblot, 348–9
Mikael, 284
Mildred Piece, 181, 219
Milky Way, The, 128, 644
Million, Le, 73, 81, 140, 171
Million Pound Bank Note, The, 105n
Mill on the Po, The, 516
Millionairess, The, 485
Millions Like Us, 195
Minamata, 611n
Minin and Pojarsky, 151, 436
Miracle, The, 513
Miracle in Milan, 514
Mirror of Holland, The, 340
Misfits, The, 484
Mistons, Les, 242
Miss Julie, 347
Moana, 115, 397
Moby Dick, 379–80
Moderato Cantabile, 476
Modern Times, 82, 180
Modesty Blaise, 562, 564n
Mogambo, 382
Moi un Noir, 308, 498
Molly Maguires, The, 635n
Moment of Truth, The, 521–2
Momma Don't Allow, 333
Mon Amour, Mon Amour, 507n
Monde de Paul Delvaux, Le, 338
Monde du Silence, Le, 251
Monkey Business, 129
Mon Oncle, 264
Mon Oncle Antoine, 649
Monsieur Tête, 419
Monsieur Verdoux, 130, 268, 354, 378
Monster of Highgate Ponds, The, 485
Monte Carlo, 74, 82
Monterey Pop, 81
Mooncalves, The, 517n
Morgan: A Suitable Case for Treatment, 550
Morocco, 89
Mortal Storm, The, 178
Morte di un Amico, 477
Mort dans ce Jardin, La, 404
Moscow Strikes Back, 208
Mother, 46, 119, 121n, 210, 401, 436
Mother Joan of the Angels, 412, 416n, 480
Mother's Heart, A, 583
Mouchette, 284, 286, 294, 299, 302
Moulin Rouge, 379
Mourir à Madrid, 503
Mourning Becomes Electra, 91n, 184
Mr Arkadin, 187–8, 190
Mr Deeds Goes to Town, 137
Mrs Miniver, 155
Mr Smith Goes to Washington, 137, 148
Mr Stringfellow Says No, 139

Mud and Soldiers, 152
Mummies, The, 616
Munna, 460
Murder, 72–3
Murderers Are Amongst Us, The, 342
Murder He Says, 219
Murder in the Cathedral, 116
Murder My Sweet, 360n
Muriel, 280
Music Lovers, The, 556n, 586n, 646, 652
Musical Story, 82
Music Room, The, 461
Mutiny on the Bounty, 96–7
Mutter Krausens Fahrt ins Glück, 51
My Apprenticeship, 121–2
My Darling Clementine, 382
My Fair Lady, 89, 385
My Home Is Copacabana, 350
My Man Godfrey, 138
Myra Breckinridge, 645
My Sister, My Love, 577
Mystère Picasso, Le, 145, 255, 257–8, 338, 404
My Universities, 121–2, 209
My Way Home, 594–5

N

Naked City, 354, 367
Naked Youth, 482
Nana, 145
Nanook of the North, 664
Napoléon, 52, 62n, 63, 67, 144, 244n, 355, 584, 667n, 687
Nashville Sound, 645
National Velvet, 371
Nature's Half Acre, 394
Nayak, 464, 468
Nazarin, 286, 292
Ned Kelly, 645
Neighbours, 159, 418
Neighbour's Wife and Mine, The, 89
Nest of Gentlefolk, A, 583
Never Give a Sucker an Even Break, 178
Never on Sundays, 481
New Babylon, 63, 584
New Earth, 116
New Lot, The, 193
New Snow, 214
New Tales of the Taira Clan, 452
Nez, Le, 134
Niaye, 611
Nibelungen Saga, 50
Nice Time, 333
Nicht Versöhnt, 580
Nidhanaya, 474n
Niemansland, 162
Night Games, 577
Night Mail, 113–14, 199, 504, 693n
Night Must Fall, 132, 550
Night of Counting the Years, The, 412, 616–18, 651
Night of Remembrance, A, 412
Night of the Hunter, The, 392
Night of the Iguana, The, 380, 630n
Night on the Bare Mountain, 53, 134–5, 418
Nine Days of One Year, 586n
Nine Hours to Rama, 631
Ninotchka, 75, 78, 148
Ninth Circle, The, 481
Nju, ix, 48–9
Noire de . . ., La, 611
No More Fleeing, 343n
No Resting Place, 328
North Star, 178
Nose, The, 418
Nosferatu, 46, 50
Nothing Sacred, 138, 369, 378n
Notorious, 181
Notte Bianchi, Le, 404
Notte di Cabiria, Le, 404, 518–19
Nous Sommes Tous Des Assassins, 267, 268n, 269, 274
Now That the Buffalo's Gone, 688

Now Voyager, 14n 181
Nuit du Carrefour, La, 145
Nuit et Brouillard, 210, 275–6, 404

O

Objective Burma, 218
October, 46, 63, 166n, 238n, 286, 422, 424, 431, 693
October Man, The, 330
Odd Man Out, 309–11, 313n, 316, 440
Odd Obsessions, 445–6
O! Dreamland, 333
Oedipus Rex, 530–1
Oktober-dage, 656
Of Human Bondage, 95
Of Mice and Men, 164n
Oh! What a Lovely War, 553–4, 559, 628
Oklahoma, 80
Old Curiosity Shop, The, 93n
Old Man and the Sea, The, 370n
Old and New, The (General Line, The), 424, 693
Older Brother, Younger Sister, 152
Old Man Motorcar, 402
Ole Dole Doff, 575
Oliver Twist, 316, 318
Olvidados, Los, 172n, 237–9, 295, 351, 625
Olympic Games, 118
On a Clear Day You Can See Forever, 630, 645
Once There Was a War, 579, 596n
One Day in the Life of Ivan Denisovich, 582
One Eyed Jacks, 484
One Fine Day, 528
One Summer Day Doesn't Mean Love, 479
One Two Three, 385
One Way Pendulum, 638n
Only Way, The, 656
Only Way Out Is Dead, The, 649
Onorevole Angelina, L' (Angelina), 514
On Such a Night, 405
On the Beach, 629
On the Town, 80, 183, 356n
On the Waterfront, 361, 364, 374
Open Window, The, 338
Opera Mouffe, 507
Orders To Kill, 154, 163n, 167n, 267, 269–71, 274, 330
Ordet, 284–5, 289, 290, 302
Ordinary People, 584
Or du Cristobal, L', 261n
Orfeu Nègre, 308
Oros, 483
Orphans of the Storm, 30
Orphée, 11, 14, 50, 133, 252, 438, 451n, 563
Oscar Wilde, 485
Ossessione, 149, 220
Othello, 401, 436, 443, 587
Othon, 580
Our Country, 203
Our Last Spring, 343, 481
Our Mother's House, 547
Out, 396
Outback, The, 648
Outcast of the Islands, An, 95, 312–5
Out in the World, 121, 150
Overlanders, The, 321

P

Pacifista, La, 595
Page of Madness, A, 35, 69
Page Out of Order, A, 35
Painted Veil, The, 95
Paisa, 154, 220–6, 625
Palle Alone in the World, 342
Palm Sunday, 597
Paloma, La, 213
Panchupti, 458n
Pandora's Box, 48
Panic in the Streets, 361, 367
Paradiso Terrestre, 337n

Parapluies de Cherbourg, Les, 476, 507
Paras Pathar, 461
Paracelsus, 342
Pardesi, 400
Parents Terribles, Les, 252
Paris 1900, 251
Paris Nous Appartient, 476
Paris Qui Dort, 51
Partie de Campagne, Une, 145–6, 469
Partner, 278, 332n, 512, 534–6, 539–41, 571, 595, 670
Party and the Guests, The, 598–9
Passage du Rhin, 476
Passenger, 412
Passion of Andrei Rublev, The, 582
Passion of Joan of Arc, 46, 284–7, 289–90, 296, 302
Passport to Pimlico, 316, 317n, 319–20
Pat and Mike, 384
Patch of Blue, A, 373
Pather Panchali, 222, 400, 459–64, 463–4, 616, 649
Path of the Heroes, 173
Paths of Glory, 271, 556, 560–1, 667n, 676–7
Patton – Lust for Glory, 153, 628
Paul Street Boys, The, 593
Pawnbroker, The, 634
Paysages du Silence, 251
Peaceful Conquest, 340
Peace Game, The, 556
Peasant Women of Riazan, The, 68, 507n
Pension Mimosas, 140–1
People in a City, 348
Pépé le Moko, 143
Performance, 313, 320, 550, 571–2, 670
Persona, 575
Peter and Pavla, 598–9, 601
Peter the First, 151
Petite Lise, La, 140
Petite Marchande d'Allumettes, La, 145
Petulia, 571
Peyton Place, 630
Phantom Carriage, The, 46, 347
Pharaoh, 412, 416n
Pharmacist, The, 129n
Phela-Ndaba, 612
Pffft, 631
Philadelphia Story, The, 358, 384, 406
Philosopher's Stone, The, 461
Pickpocket, 284, 302
Pictures at an Exhibition, 134
Picture of Dorian Grey, 25, 219
Pigsty, 530–3, 543
Pink String and Sealing Wax, 217, 321
Pinky, 354, 361
Pinocchio, 132, 148
Pirate, The, 630
Pit and the Pendulum, The, 624n
Pitchi-Poi, 250n
Place in the Sun, A, 378
Plain People, 218
Plainsman, The, 39n, 377, 384n
Plaisir, Le, 260, 379
Planet of the Apes, 621, 628
Planete Venere, 542n
Playtime, 264
Plow that Broke the Plains, 125
Poem of the Sea, 428–9, 435
Poil de Carotte, 142, 233
Pöis Pöis, 578
Pokkers Unger, De, 342
Pony Express, The, 321
Poor Cow, 569
Porcile, 278, 531–2, 595
Porta de Cielo, La, 216
Portes de la Nuit, Les, 144, 252
Portrait of Jason, 644
Postman, 619
Postmaster, The, 464
Posto, Il, 527–9

Postwar Japanese History, 650
Power and the Land, 124
Pratidwandi, 469
Pratinidi, 603n
Pravda, 58n, 488–9, 509, 668
Premature Burial, The, 624n
President, The, 284, 302
Pride and Prejudice, 93
Priest's Wife, The, 658
Prima della Revolutione, 534n
Primavera, E, 516n
Prince Igor, 651
Princess Yang Kwei-Fei, The, 453
Prise de Pouvoir par Louis XIV, La, 513
Private Life of Henry VIII, The, 104–5
Private Life of Sherlock Holmes, The, 385n, 646
Private Right, The, 504n
Private Road, 568
Private's Progress, 330, 405
Privilege, 556
Procés de Jeanne d'Arc, 284, 286–7, 294–5, 298, 302
Professor Hannibal, 401, 409
Professor Mamlock, 206
Prologue, 401
Proud Valley, The, 149
Pskovityanka, 25
Psycho, 256, 330n, 392, 484, 490
Public Enemy, The, 98
Puente, El, 339
Pugni in Tasca, I, 541
Punascha, 603n
Punishment Park, 556–7, 634
Punishment Room, 400, 445
Puss och Kram, 577
Pygmalion, 105
Pyramide Humaine, La, 499

Q

Quai des Brumes, 143
Quai des Orfèvres, 254–5
'Quatermass' Series, 132
Quatorze Juillet, Le, 73, 140, 143n
400 Coups, Les, 236–7, 242, 308, 493, 495n
Quatre Nuits d'un Rêveur, 284n
Queen, The, 643
Queen Christina, 77
Queen Kelly, 32, 189
Queen of Spades, The, 330, 479
Que la Bête Meure (Killer!), 490, 492, 657
Que Viva Mexico!, 71, 422n, 427, 429
Quick Millions, 98
Quiet American, The, 94, 388
Quiet One, The, 236–7, 395
Quo Vadis, 20

R

Rabrindranath Tagore, 466n
Radha and Krishna, 459
Raffle, The, 522n
Raider, The (Western Approaches), 178
Railway Children, The, 647
Rain (Sadie Thompson), 95, 159, 292
Rainbow, The, 121n, 209–10
Rainbow Dance, 114
Rainmaker, The, 406
Rain People, 638
Rajah Harischandra, 16
Rake's Progress, The, 217
Rancho Notorious, 391
Ran Salu (Yellow Robe), 474n
Rashomon, 35, 438–9, 449 452n, 534
Reach for the Sky, 405
Rear Window, 392
Rebecca, 14n, 378n, 393
Rebel, The, 485
Rebel Without a Cause, 363
Recuperanti, I, 528
Red and the White, The, 594
Red Badge of Courage, The, 379 423n

Red Danube, The, 354
Red Desert, The, x
Red Flag Canal, 649
Red Light District, 400
Red Menace, The, 354
Red River, 383
Red Shoes, The, 198
Reflections in a Golden Eye, 380
Reggae, 641n
Règle du Jeu. La, 145n, 147, 149, 170–1, 172–3, 262, 498
Rekava (Line of Life, The), 470, 614n
Reluctant Dragon, The, 132n, 183
Rembrandt Painter of Man, 340
Renaissance, 419
Rendezvous à Bray, 578
Rendezvous de Juillet, 262
Renzo and Luciana, 521n
Report on the Party and the Guests, 598n
Repulsion, 14n, 417, 591
Retour, Le, 156, 216, 248
Return of Vassili Bortnikov (Harvest), 436
Return of Maxim, The, 584
Return to the Past, 480
Reveille, 64
Rhapsody in Blue, 219
Rhinoceros, 419
Richard III, 332
Rich Bride, The, 151, 583
Ride the High Country, 625
Rien Que Les Heures, 51, 510
Rifa, La (Raffle, The), 521
Rififi, 262n, 639
Ring, The, 67
Rings On Her Fingers, 77
Rio Bravo, 383
Rio Lobo, 645
Riot in Cell Block 11, 636
Riso Amaro, 516
Rite, The, 575
Rival World, The, 340
River, The, 25, 145, 248
Road to Life, The, 72, 118, 411
Robe, The, ix, 689
Rocco and his Brothers, 522
Rocking Horse Winner, The, 236n, 312
Romance for Trumpet, 598–9
Romance in a Minor Key, 213
Romance Sentimentale, 82, 424n, 693n
Roman d'un Tricheur, 346
Roman Holiday, 381
Rome Express, 104
Romeo and Juliet, 92, 97, 443
Romeo and Juliet in Darkness, 410, 480
Rome – Open City, 201, 216, 220–1
Rondo, 674n
Roof Garden, The, 612
Room at the Top, 334, 545–7
Rope, 180
Rose et Landry, 502
Rosemary's Baby, 14n, 417, 591
Rose Tattoo, The, 514
Roue, La, 52, 63
Rouge et le Noir, Le, 261
Rough Seas at Dover, 2
Round Trip, 616n
Round Up, The, 594
Run of the Arrow, 406
Rupture, 265
Russians Are Coming, the Russians Are Coming, The, 637
Ryan's Daughter, 318, 646
Rynox, 139
Rysopis (Identification Marks: None), 589n

S

Sabotage, 95, 104
Sadie Thompson (Rain), 95, 159, 292
Saga of Anatahan, The, 183
Saint Joan, 386
Salaire de la Peur, Le, 255–7

Salt of the Black Earth, 654
Salvatore Giuliano, 521–2
Samapti, 465, 604
Sammy Going South, 326–8
Samourai, Le, 253
Samson and Delilah, 377
Sanctuary (Loved One, The), 548n
San Demetrio – London, 109, 177
Sandesaya, 472, 482
Sandpiper, The, 630
Sang des Bêtes, Le, 52n, 250, 276, 510
Sang d'un Poète, Le, 244n, 252
Sanshiro Sugata, 215
Santo Guerreiro Conta o Dragon da Maldade (Antonio das Mortes), 615n
Sapphire, 321n
Saragossa Manuscript, The, 590n
Satan Bug, The, 370n
Saturday Night and Sunday Morning, 485, 547, 548n, 550
Savages, 605
Scarface, Shame of a Nation, 98–100, 102, 383
Scarlet Empress, The, 119, 183
Scarlet Letter, The, 66
Scarlet Street, 219
Sciuscia, (Shoeshine) 228
Scott of the Antarctic, 320
Scrooge, 646
Sea Beast, The, 380
Seagull, The, 633
Seal Island, 394
Séance on a Wet Afternoon, 549
Sea of Grass, 360n
Search, The, 345, 365, 358
Searchers, The, 406
Seashell and the Clergyman, The 53, 67
Seascape, 2
Seconds, 632
Secret Agent, The, 95, 104, 186
Secret Ceremony, 562, 564n
Secret Six, The, 98
'Secrets of Nature' Series, 332
Secrets of the Soul, ix, 381
Sel de la Terre, 250
Selling Out, 420n
Senso, 404, 522
Senza Pietà, 515
September Love, 479
Servant, The, 320, 550, 562–3
Set Up, The, 354
Seven Brides for Seven Brothers, 80, 356n
Seven Days to Noon, 329
Seven Samurai, 441–2, 449, 452n
Seventeen, 579
Seventh Age, The, 341, 420
Seventh Continent, The, 674n
Seventh Heaven, 41
Seventh Seal, The, 14n, 404
Seventh Victim, The, 182, 630
Seven Year Itch, The, 385
Shadow, The, 402
Shadow of a Doubt, 180
Shadows, 484, 643
Shadows of the Yoshiwara, 35
Shaft, 639
Shakespeare Wallah, 603n, 604
Shame, The, 575
Shane, 358, 368n, 378, 383, 442n
Shanghaied, 23
Shanghai Gesture, The, 183
She Wore a Yellow Ribbon, 382
Shin Heike Monogatari, 452
Ship of Fools, 629
Shoeshine, 201, 220–1, 226, 228–31, 234, 236–7, 295, 472, 475, 514, 516–17, 521n
Shonen (Boy), 606
Shop in the High Street, The, 410, 599, 634
Shoulder Arms, 157, 235n
Siberian Lady Macbeth, A, 589
Siddartha and the City, 469
Siege of Leningrad, The, 208

Siege of Sevastopol, The, 20
Siege of the Alcazar, The, 152
Signe du Lion, Le, 495
Sign of the Cross, The, 95, 377, 520
Silence, The, 575
Silence and Cry, 594
Silence Est d'Or, Le, 248
Silence of the Heart, The, 474n
Silk Stockings, 78
Since You Went Away, 178
Sing and Like It, 139
Singing Lesson, The, 552
Sin of Harold Diddlebock, The, 179
Sirius Remembered, 643
Si Tous les Gars du Monde, 404
Six Contes Moraux, 496, 657
6 Juin à l'Aube, Le, 248
Six of a Kind, 129
Skeleton Dance, 132
Skies of Holland, The, 339
Slight Case of Murder, A, 99–100
Small Back Room, The, 198
Smoke Menace, The, 113
Snake Pit, The, 389
Snows of Kilimanjaro, The, 391
Snow White and the Seven Dwarfs, 132
Solaris, 479, 582n
Soldier Blue, 625, 645
Solid Gold Cadillac, The, 406
Somebody Up There Likes Me, 391, 406
Some Like It Hot, 385
Somme, The, 154
So Ist Das Leben, 51
Song of Bernadette, 14n, 391
Song of Ceylon, 10, 113–14, 135, 693n
Song of Happiness, 121n
Song of Norway, 645
Song of Russia, The, 162, 178
Song of Songs, 77
Song to Remember, A, 219
Sons and Lovers, 485, 547
So This Is Paris, 74
Sorry Wrong Number, 132, 390
Souffle au Coeur, Le, 506
Souls on the Road, 35
Soul to Soul, 640
Sound of Music, The, 80, 621, 622n
Sound of Trumpets, 527
Soupirant, Le, 265
Sous les Toits de Paris, ix, 72–3, 81, 140
Southerner, The, 219
South Pacific, 80
South Wind, 214
Spanish Earth, 117
Spanish Gardener, The, 332
Spare Time, 200
Spartacus, 484, 620
Spawn of the North, 390n
Spellbound, 180, 219, 378n
Spider's Strategy, The, 278, 534, 537–40, 571–2, 658, 670
Spione, 66
Spiral Staircase, The, 78n
Spirit of St Louis, The, 385
Springtime in Budapest, 409
Spy, The, 67
Spy Who Came in from the Cold, The, 635
Stagecoach, 148, 382
Stage Fright, 392
Stain on the Conscience, A, 674n
Stalag 17, 386
Stalingrad, 208
Star!, 81, 620n, 621
Star Is Born, A, 138, 384
Stars Are Shining, The, 79
Stars Look Down, The, 106–7, 149, 309
Stella, 344
Stolen Life, A, 181
Storm Over Asia, 119–20, 423, 426
Story of G.I. Joe, The, 218
Story of Louis Pasteur, The, 102
Story of the Late Chrysanthemum, The, 152, 214

Strada, La, 471, 517–18
Strange Love of Martha Ivers, The, 164n
Strange Interlude, 72–3, 91n
Stranger, The, 162, 185–6
Strangers on a Train, 181, 392
Strategia del Ragno, 534n
Strawberry Statement, The, 622n
Straw Dogs, 625n, 626n, 678n
Streetcar Named Desire, A, 362–4
Street of Shame, The, 400
Strike, 29, 46. 421–2, 536, 671, 692
Stromboli, 513
Strong Man, The, 137
Student of Prague, The, ix, 20, 46, 49, 535
Student Prince, The, 66
St Valentine's Day Massacre, The, 624
Substitute, 674n
Suddenly Last Summer, 388–9
Sullivan's Travels, 179
Sult, 579
Summer Holiday, 78, 91n
Summer Rain, 481
Sun Also Rises, The, 391
Sun and Rose, 400
Sunday Bloody Sunday, 546, 565, 567–8
Sunday in August, 477, 480, 516n
Sunday Morning, 402
Sundowners, The, 485
Sunrise, 66
Sun's Burial, The, 482, 605
Sunset Boulevard, 40, 358, 369, 385, 623
Sun Shines Bright, The, 382
Superfly, 640n
Susan and God, 383
Suvorov, 209, 436
Sweet Deception, 477
Sweet Hunters, The, 614
Sweet Lavender, 24
Sweet Smell of Success, The, 325–6
Sweet Sweetback's Baad-assss Song, 372, 376, 640
Swineherd and Shepherd, 583
Switchboard Operator, The, 672
Sylvie et le Fântome, 259, 263
Symphonie Pastorale, La, 254
Symphonie Paysanne, 337
Syskonbädd, 577

T

Take Me, Love Me, 655
Taking Off, 598, 600n, 601, 653
Tale of Genji, The, 447n
Taming of the Shrew, The, 91
Tant Qu'on a la Santé, 265
Tanya, 82
Tartuffe, 49
Taking Tiger Mountain by Strategy, 649
Target for Tonight, 197
Taste of Honey, A, 548
Tchaikovsky, 652
Teacher, 151
'Technique of Anaesthesia' Series, 112
Tell England, 163, 168
Tell Me If It Hurts, 205
Tell Me Lies, 553, 558–9
Tell Them Willie Boy Is Here, 625n
Tempo si e Fermato, Il (Time Stood Still), 477, 526
Temptation of Professor Antonio, The, 521
Ten Commandments, The, 377, 406
10 Rillington Place, 646
Tentazioni del Dottor Antonio, Le, 521
Ten Thousand Suns, 595, 597
Teresa, 367–8
Terminus, 485, 565
Terra im Transe, 614–15, 669
Terrain Vague, 476
Terra Trema, La, 522

Testament d'Orphée, Le, 252n
Test Trip, 481
Tête Contre les Murs, La, 308
Théatre Nationale Populaire, Le, 405
Theatre Mr and Mrs Kabal, The, 419
Theorem, 530–3
Thérèse Desqueyroux, 504
Thérèse Raquin, 67
There Was a Crooked Man, 388n
There Was a Father, 214
These Three, 138, 381
They Came to the Ferry, 341
They Live by Night, 354
They Met in Moscow, 583
They Travel By Air, 206
They Were Expendable, 218
They Won't Forget, 101, 368
Thief of Baghdad, The, 63
Things I Cannot Change, The, 425, 499n
Things to Come, 174–6, 419
Third Man, The, 186, 311–13
Thirty Nine Steps, The, 104, 374
This Happy Breed, 316
This Land Is Mine, 178
This Sporting Life, 546n, 547, 551
Thomas Crown Affair, The, 638
Those Blasted Kids, 342
Thousand Eyes of Dr Mabuse, The, 478
Three Cornered Moon, 139
Three Daughters, 466n
Three Dawns to Sydney, 204
Three Men in a Boat, 550
Three Songs of Lenin, 57
Three Wishes, 410
Throne of Blood, 443, 584
Throw Away Your Books, Let's Go into the Streets, 609n
THX 1138, 645
Time Gentlemen, 480
Time Out of War, A, 272
Time Stood Still, 477, 526
Time to Live and a Time to Die, A (Feu Follet, Le), 505
Time Without Pity, 405
Tire au Flanc, 145
Tirez sur le Pianiste, 476, 493–4
Titanic, 207
To Be Or Not To Be, 75
To Catch a Thief, 392
To Die in Madrid, 503
To Have and To Have Not, 181, 357, 383
To Kill a Child, 348
Tokyo Olympiad, 445, 447
Tokyo Story, 456
Tokyo Twilight, 456n
To Live in Peace, 514
'Tom and Jerry' Series, 135
Tomb of Ligeia, The, 624n
Tom Jones, 548
Tongue Inside a Matchbox, 135n
Too Late the Hero, 627
Tora! Tora! Tora!, 135, 621
To Sir With Love, 373, 374n, 622
To the Rescue, 206
Touchez Pas Au Grisbi, 262
Touch of Evil, 188–9
Toute la Mémoire du Monde, 275, 404
Town Like Alice, A, 405
Tractor Drivers, 151, 583
Traffic, 264, 657, 693n
Tragedy of the Street, 67
Train, The, 348, 631–2
Trans Europe Express, 506
Transfer of Power, 150
Trapeze, 405
Trash, 642
Traversée de Paris, 261, 404
Treasure, The, 474n
Tree Grows in Brooklyn, A, 178, 360n, 362
Trial, The, 14, 134n
Trials of Oscar Wilde, The, 485
Tricky Girl, A, 69

Tricheurs, Les, 144
Trip, The, 624
Tristana, 644, 656
Triumph of the Will, 117
Trou, Le, 262
Troublemakers, The, 665
Trouble With Harry, The, 392, 406
True Confession, 138
True Glory, The, 156, 200
Truth About Women, The, 507n
Tunes of Glory, 485
Tunisian Victory, 200
Turksib, 117, 250, 286
Tusalava, 418
Twelve Angry Men, 620, 633
Twelve O'Clock High, 391
Twenty Four Dollar Island, 398
Twisted Nerve, 330n
Two Acres of Land, 460, 474
Two Arabian Knights, 164
Two-Faced Woman, 178, 383
Two Men and a Wardrobe, 415, 417, 480
Two Million for a Smile, 152
Two or Three Things I Know about Her, 509
2001: A Space Odyssey, 8, 14, 132, 280, 546, 582n, 671, 674–9, 693
Two Timid Souls, 52
Two Weeks in Another Town, 630
Two Women, 477, 514, 625

U

Ueberfall, 51
Ugetsu Monogatari, 35, 379, 425, 442, 449–53, 454n, 618, 694
Ukraine in Flames, The, 422n
Ultus, the Man from the Dead, 24
Umberto D, 514
Unconquered, 218
Undefeated, The, 329, 461
Under Capricorn, 392
Under the Phrygian Star, 412
Unfaithfully Yours, 180
Unholy Wishes, 151
Union Pacific, 148
Unreconciled, 580
Un Soir un Train, 578
Up the Junction, 570
Upturned Stone, The, 597

V

Vacances de M. Hulot, Les, 263
Valerie and her Week of Wonders, 626
Valley of the Dolls, 620n, 631
Vampires, Les, 24, 681n
Vampyr, 50, 284n, 302n
Variety Lights, 517n, 518
Vent d'Est, 657, 668–9
Vent Souffle Où Il Veut, Le, 298
Verdict, The, 636
Verdun, Visions d'Histoire, 161
Verité, La, 476
Vertigo, 392, 490
Very Eye of Night, The, 61n
Vessel of Wrath, The, 95
Victim, 321n, 548
Victimes de l'Alcöol, 17
Victory, 95
Victory at Sea, 153
Victory in the Ukraine, 217
Vie Commence Demain, La, 251n
Vie de Notre Seigneur Jesus Christ, La, 20
Vie Est à Vous, La, 146
View from the Bridge, A, 633
Village Schoolteacher, A, 121n, 210
Village in Travancore, A, 458n
Virgin and the Gypsy, The, 647
Virginian, The, 72
Virgin Island, 332
Virgin Spring, The, 477
Viridiana, 286
Visite à Picasso, 338
Visiteurs du Soir, Les, 143, 252, 288
Vita Semplice, La, 216

Vitelloni, I, 517
Viva l'Italia!, 477
Viva Maria!, 505
Vivere in Pace, 514
Vivre Pour Vivre, 507
Voix Humaine, La, 513, 581n
Voleur, Le, 505
Von Ryan's Express, 631
Vow, The, 671n
Voyage à Travers l'Impossible, 8, 129
VTR – St Jacques, 664
Vyborg Side, The, 151, 584

W

Walkabout, 571–5, 670, 674n
Walking Down Broadway, 40, 43–5
Walkers on the Tiger's Tail, 215, 218
Walk in the Old Town, A, 412
Walk in the Sun, A, 164n, 368
Walkover, 589n, 590
Walls, 596
Wanda, 508n, 645
War at Sea from Hawaii to Manila, 214
War Game, The, 504n, 553–6, 577, 586
War Hunt, 272–3, 556
War Is Hell, 162–3
War Lord, The, 628
Warning Shadows, ix, 46, 48–9
War and Peace, 261, 377, 406, 436, 583, 652
Warrendale, 649
Warsaw '56, 420
Warum Laüft Herr R Amok? (Why did Herr R Run Amok?), 581
Waterloo, 436, 584, 652
Waterloo Road, 195
Watermelon Man, The, 640, 645
Waverley Steps, 205
Waxworks, 46
Way Ahead, The, 109, 193, 309, 312
Way Down East, 28, 30
Way Out West, 128
Way to the Stars, The, 194, 217
Web of Passion (A Double Tour), 490n
Wedding March, The, 40, 43, 45, 53, 189
Wedding of Himmet Aga, 26
We Dive at Dawn, 200

Weekend, 173n, 265, 446, 508–9, 511, 513, 539, 606, 661, 668, 678, 693
Wee Willie Winkie, 382
We From Kronstadt, 401
Welcome Mr Marshall, 345, 403
Went the Day Well?, 194, 203
Western Approaches, 178, 200
Westfront 1918, 51, 161–2
West Side Story, 81, 391, 443
Whatever Happened to Baby Jane?, 627
What Made Her Do It?, 88
What Price Glory, 159–60, 382
Wheelchair, The, 346
When We Are Married, 334n
Whisky Galore, 317n, 322
Whisperers, The, 550
Whistle Down the Wind, 549
White Bus, The, 244n, 551–2, 600n
White Nights, 583
White Shadows in the South Seas, 66
White Sheik, The, 517
Who's Afraid of Virginia Woolf?, 639n
Who Saw Him Die?, 575
Why Husbands Go Astray, 33
'Why We Fight' Series, 137, 382
Wild Angels, The, 624
Wild Bunch, The, 625
Wild One, The, 630
Wild Party, The, 507n
Wild River, 484
Wild Strawberries, x, 14, 347n, 404
Wind, The, 347
Windfall in Athens, 344
Wind and the River, The, 404
Window Water Baby Moving, 643
Wings, 41, 160
Winter in Narita, 650
Winterset, 91n, 100
Wir-Zwei, 655
Without Pity, 515
Witness for the Prosecution, 385
Wizard of Oz, The, 80, 148, 621
Wolf Trap, The, 410
Woman in the Painting (Amice per le Pelle), 521n
Woman in a Dressing Gown, 330
Woman in the Window, 219
Woman of the Dunes, 608
Woman's Face, A, 181
Woman of Paris, A, 130
Woman Standing in the Light, A, 35

Women, The, 383
Wonder Man, 219
Wooden Horse, The, 548n
Woodstock, 81, 644
'World in Action' Series, 155
World of Apu, The, 461
World of Plenty, 195
World Without End, 329
Wrong Box, The, 550
W.R. – Mysteries of the Organism, 626, 654, 671–2
Wuthering Heights, 93, 148, 646

Y

Yank at Oxford, A, 106
Yearling, The, 372
Yellow Caesar, 194
Yellow Robe, The, 474n
Yellow Submarine, 14n, 136
Yesterday Girl, 579
Yield to the Night, 405
Yohiki, 453
Yojimbo, 442n
Yolanda and the Thief, 219
You, 597
You Can't Take It With You, 137
Young and Innocent, 180
Young and the Damned, The, 237
Younger Brother, 482
Young Mr Lincoln, 102, 148
Young One, The, 483
Young Savages, The, 484
Young Stranger, The, 632
Young Törless, 579
Your Acquaintance, 68
Your Children and You, 112
Your Children's Ears, 112
Your Children's Eyes, 112
Your Children's Meals, 112
Your Children's Sleep, 112
You're a Big Boy Now, 637
Youth of Chopin, The, 411
Youth of Maxim, The, 584
Yo Yo, 265

Z

Z, 503, 657
Zabriskie Point, 81, 393, 622
Zazie dans le Métro, 242, 276, 505
Zeebrugge, 161
Zéro de Conduite, 143n, 242–4, 337, 551
Zorba the Greek, 344
Zvenigora, 46, 118, 421–3, 425, 426n, 434–6, 671

2. INDEX OF NAMES

A

Abbas, K. A., 400, 460
Abbott, George, 163
Abdelsalam, Shadi, 412, 616–8, 651, 680
Abe, Tetsuo, 607
Abnoudi, Atiat, 616n
Achard, Marcel, 83n
Ackiand, Rodney, 330
Adorée, Renée, 160
Agate, James, 64n, 92
Agee, James, 209–10, 228–9, 230, 236, 317, 357, 362
Agutter, Jenny, 575
Ahlberg, Mac, 655
Aimée, Anouk, 507
Ainley, Henry, 24
Albee, Edward, 649n
Albert, Eddie, 270
Aldrich, Robert, 627
Alea, Tomas Gutierrez, 496, 512, 613
Alekan, Henri, 281, 564

Alexandrov, Grigori, 56, 71, 82, 412
Alexeieff, Alexandre, 53, 134–5, 205n, 418
Allister, Claude, 74
Almendrov, Nestor, 494
Alvey, Glenn, 355n
Alwyn, William, 203, 205, 311–2, 330
Ambler, Eric, 330
Amis, Kingsley, 334, 545, 559
Anderson, Hans Christian, 341n
Anderson, Joseph, 88, 439
Anderson, Judith, 393
Anderson, Lindsay, 202–3, 244, 333, 361, 470n, 547, 551–2, 600n
Anderson, Maxwell, 100, 159, 163
Anderson, Michael, 381, 406
Andersson, Bibi, 404, 478, 577
Andersson, Harriet, 404, 577
Andersson, Karl, 302
Andresen, Björn, 525
Andrews, Dana, 359–60

Andrews, Harry, 627, 634
Andric, Miodrag, 672
Andriot, Lucien, 76
Angell, Norman, 169
Angeli, Pier, 367
Anger, Kenneth, 643
Annakin, Ken, 550, 628
Annis, Francesca, 593
Antheil, George, 63
Anthony, Joseph, 406
Antonioni, Michelangelo, x, 172, 404, 477, 526
Arbuckle, Fatty, 31
Archers, The, 196–8
Arlen, Richard, 72, 139
Arletty, 143
Arkin, Alan, 637
Armat, Thomas, 1
Armstrong, Louis, 484
Armstrong, Michael, 556
Arnaz, Desi, 619
Arnbom, Arne, 655
Arnheim, Rudolf, 21

Arnold, Malcolm, 316
Arnstam, Lev, 421
Arthur, Jean, 358, 377, 384n
Arundell, Dennis, 200n
Arzner, Dorothy, 507n
Ashcroft, Peggy, 567
Asimov, Isak, 279
Asquith, Anthony, 103, 105, 162–3, 177, 194, 200, 217, 267, 269, 270–1, 330, 405, 485
Astaire, Fred, 78–80, 219, 629
Astor, Mary, 380, 627
Attenborough, Richard, 200, 329, 559, 646
Aubrey, James, 621
Aubry, Cécile, 255
Auden, W. H., 114, 204, 253, 677
Audry, Jacqueline, 507n
Aurenche, Jean, 239, 266
Auer, Mischa, 77, 377
Autant-Lara, Claude, 279–61, 266, 351, 404
Axelrod, George, 632n
Ayrton, Michael, 184n
Aznavour, Charles, 476

B
Bacall, Lauren, 181, 354, 357, 636
Bacon, Lloyd, 99
Bader, Douglas, 405
Bagley, Richard, 395
Baker, Carroll, 364, 381
Baker, Roy, 330
Baker, Stanley, 485
Balasz, Bela, 408, 595
Balchin, Nigel, 198
Balcon Brothers, The, 104
Balcon, Michael, 104n, 177, 194, 308–9, 318, 320, 326, 333
Balickci, Asen, 336
Balint, András, 597n
Ballantyne, Tanya, 425
Ball, Lucille, 619
Balpêtre, Antoine, 268
Bang, Herman, 293
Banks, Richard, 156
Bannerjee, Bibhuti, 465n
Bannerjee, Tara Shanker, 465
Bara, Theda, 115
Baratier, Jacques, 616n
Bardem, J. A., 354–6, 403
Bardot, Brigitte, 404, 456, 505, 508
Barkas, Geoffrey, 162
Barker, Will, 20, 24
Barker-Mill, Adam, 569
Barnes, George, 367
Barnet, Boris, 68
Barnouw, Erik, 84
Baranovskaia, Vera, 436
Barr, Charles, 295n
Barrault, Jean-Louis, 92, 144, 584
Barrault, Marie-Christine, 497
Barrie, James, 158, 233
Barry, Iris, 55, 645
Barrymore, John, 77, 92, 380, 390n
Barrymore, Lionel, 75, 137, 159, 378
Barstow, Stan, 565
Barthelmess, Richard, 161
Bartosch, Berthold, 135
Barua, Prince, 86
Basehart, Richard, 390, 517–8
Bass, Saul, 386
Basse, Wilfrid, 116
Basserman, Albert, 183
Batalov, Alexei, 401, 586n
Batalov, Nikolai, 401, 436
Bates, Alan, 565, 633
Batchelor, Joy, 136
Bathing Beauties, The, 22
Battcock, Gregory, 641
Bauer, Harry, 233
Baxter, Anne, 185, 357
Baxter, Deborah, 326
Baxter, John, 92, 334
Bazin, André, 187, 289, 297n, 305, 327, 349

Beatles, The, 136
Beato, Alfonso, 615
Beatty, Warren, 631, 634
Beaumarchais, P. A., 303
Becci, G., 63
Bechet, Sidney, 506
Becker, Jacques, 216, 259, 261–3, 266, 322, 356
Beckett, Samuel, 128, 643
Beddington, Jack, 182, 201n, 202
Beecham, Thomas, 180
Beerbohm, Max, 201n
Beery, Wallace, 98
Beethoven, L. Van, 390n
Belafonte, Harry, 386, 640, 645
Belasco, David, 136
Bel Geddes, Barbara, 361
Bell, Geoffrey, 150
Bell, Marie, 142
Bellocchio, Marco, 526, 541–5, 680
Belmondo, Jean-Paul, 291, 476, 490, 505
Belson, Jordan, 683
Benchley, Robert, 358
Bendix, William, 91n
Bendtsen, Henning, 302n, 306
Benedek, Laszlo, 630
Bennett, Arnold, 158, 527
Bennett, Hywel, 646
Bennett, Joan, 219
Benny, Jack, 75
Benoit-Lévy, Jean, 140, 233
Benton, Robert, 388n
Bérard, Christian, 252
Bergé, Francine, 505
Bergen, Candice, 507, 635
Berger, John, 259
Berger, Ludwig, 82
Bergman, Ingmar, x, 172, 347, 404, 477, 575, 655
Bergman, Ingrid, 219, 286, 347, 359n, 513
Bergner, Elisabeth, 92, 105
Bergson, Henri, 277
Beria, Lavrenti, 422n
Berkeley, Busby, 79
Berkovic, Zvonimir, 674n
Berlanga, Luis, 345–6, 403
Berna, Emil, 344
Bernanos, G., 289, 293–4, 503
Bernard, Guy, 251
Bernard, James, 329
Bernard, Pierre, 173
Bernhardt, Sarah, 18, 251
Bernstein, Sydney, 55
Berri, Jules 144
Bertolucci, Bernardo, 278, 332n, 512, 526, 533–41, 543n, 572, 658, 668–70, 679
Bessie, Alvah, 353n
Betti, Laura, 532
Betz, Matthew, 45
Beveridge, James, 458
Bhownagary, Jean, 205n, 458–9
Biberman, Herbert, 353n
Billimoria, E., 86
Billimoria, Fali, 458n, 459
Biswas, Chhabi, 466
Bitold, Michel, 505
Blain, Gérard, 242
Blair, Betsy, 346, 403, 633
Blake, Nicholas, 490, 657
Blake, William, 201, 390, 470
Blakeston, Oswell, 683n
Blanchar, Pierre, 254
Blasetti, Alessandro, 152, 173, 516n
Bliss, Arthur, 174n
Blixen, Karen, 191
Bloom, Claire, 332, 547
Blore, Eric, 183
Blue, Ben, 637
Blue, James, 610
Blue, Monty, 74
Blum, Robert, 344
Boffety, Jean, 284
Bogarde, Dirk, 332, 405, 525, 561

Bogart, Humphrey, 39, 96, 178, 181, 354, 357, 359n, 380, 581, 636
Bognàr, Cecil, 20
Bolton, Guy, 74
Bolognini, Mauro, 477
Bondarchuk, Sergei, 318, 401, 436, 583–4, 652
Borges, J. L., 538, 572
Borgnine, Ernest, 633
Borodin, A., 652
Borowski, Tadeusz, 654
Borowczyk, Walerian, 145, 418–420, 469, 476, 589
Borzage, Frank, 41
Bosch, Hieronymus, 337n, 573
Bose, Debaki, 33, 64, 69, 86
Bossac, Jerzy, 411, 420
Bost, Pierre, 239, 266
Bosustow, Steven, 135
Boulez, Pierre, 685
Boulting Brothers, The, 547
Boulting, John, 200, 329, 405
Boulting, Roy, 329, 405
Bouquet, Michel, 270
Bourgoin, Jean, 268
Bourville, 261
Bow, Clara, 115
Bower, Dallas, 198, 689n
Box, Muriel, 507n
Boyd, William, 164
Boyer, Charles, 371, 377
Brackett, Charles, 78
Brackett, Leigh, 357
Bradbury, Ray, 15, 279
Brahms, J., 491
Braine, John, 334, 545
Brakhage, Stan, 61n, 642, 680
Brando, Marlon, 361–2, 365, 380, 389, 406, 484, 541
Branice, Ligia, 420
Brasseur, Pierre, 173, 420
Brecht, Berthold, 51, 342, 562
Brendel, Alfred, 134
Brennan, Walter, 371
Brenon, Herbert, 18, 23
Bresson, Robert, 185, 216, 250n, 254, 259, 281, 284–90, 293–302, 304–6, 347, 379n, 404, 445, 454, 489, 493, 495, 505, 535, 679
Brialy, Jean-Claude, 496
Brisson, Carl, 67
Brittain, Donald, 276n
Britten, Benjamin, 114
Brogi, Giulio, 538
Brontë, Emily, 508, 668n
Brook, Louise, 43n
Brook, Peter, 270n, 476, 551, 558–9, 652, 691n, 646
Brooke, Rupert, 168
Brooks, Richard, 95, 360, 374n, 484, 623
Broughton, James, 643
Brown, Clarence, 66, 371–2, 583n
Brown, Eleanora, 514
Brown, Joe E., 385
Brown, Robert, 569
Brown, Roland, 98
Brownlow, Kevin, 52, 553–4
Bruckner, A., x
Bruguière, Francis, 683n
Brulatour, Jules, 187n
Brunelleschi, Filippo, 681–2
Brunius, Jacques, 53, 206
Bryan, William Jennings, 484
Brynner, Yul, 377
Brzozowski, Jaroslav, 420
Buchanan, Edgar, 358
Buchanan, Jack, 74
Buck, Pearl, 95
Buckley, Jim, 672
Budgen, Suzanne, 520
Bujold, Geneviève, 505
Bulajic, Velko, 481
Buñuel, Luis, x, 53, 93, 172n, 190, 206, 237–9, 249, 285–6, 294, 345, 404, 417, 442n, 483, 530, 550, 615, 625, 643, 656, 671, 678
Burel, L-H, 52, 302
Burge, Stuart, 646

Burgess, Anthony, 676n
Burlyaev, Kolya, 243
Burton, Richard, 380, 547–8, 629n, 630
Busch, Mae, 41
Busck, Ole, 579
Bushman, Francis X. 381
Butler, Samuel, 380
Butterworth, Charles, 76
Byam Shaw, Glen, 547

C

Caan, James, 638
Cacoyannis, Michael, 343–4, 403, 481, 619
Cage, John, 685
Cagney, James, 39, 92, 98, 100, 385
Calhern, Louis, 358
Caine, Michael, 331, 626 646
Cain, James, 149, 220
Calleia, Joseph, 78
Calley, Lieutenant, 503
Cambridge, Godfrey, 640
Camerini, Mario, 152
Cameron, Earl, 331
Cameron, Julia Margaret, 5
Cammell, Donald, 571–2
Camus, Albert, 308, 506
Canti, Dr, 58
Cantor, Eddie, 128
Capa, Robert, 148
Capra, Frank, 32, 41, 66, 96–7, 137, 148, 155
Cardiff, Jack, 357, 485, 547
Cardinale, Claudia, 325, 589
Cargol, Jean-Pierre, 495
Carlin, Lynn, 601
Carlsen, Henning, 579
Carlyle, T., x
Carmichael, Hoagy, 359
Carmichael, Ian, 405
Carmichael, Stokeley, 559
Carné, Marcel, 140, 143–4, 149, 207, 252, 266, 476, 589
Carroll, Lewis, 205, 319
Carrillo, Leo, 76
Carroll, Madeleine, 374
Carroll, Nancy, 75
Carson, Jack, 384
Cartier-Bresson, Henri, 156, 216, 248
Casarès, Maria, 216, 296
Cassavetes, John, 332, 374, 484, 643, 645
Casshyap, J. S., 631
Castel, Lou, 542
Castellani, Renato, 92n, 516n
Cauvin, André, 337–8
Cavalcanti, A., ix, 46, 51, 67, 71, 83n, 114, 116, 131n, 143n, 145, 194, 203, 231, 342, 485
Cave, Grace, 571
Cayatte, André, 221, 266–9, 476, 556
Cayrol, Jean, 276
Cekalski, Eugene, 411
Chabrol, Claude, 308, 489, 490–3, 544
Chaliapin, Feodor, 25, 83, 436
Chamberlain, Richard, 646
Chambrun, Comte de, 504n
Chandler, Raymond, 357
Chandragupta, Bansi, 466, 468
Chabrier, Henri, 303n
Chaplin, Charles, ix, 18, 22–3, 31, 38, 57, 65–6, 80, 82n, 127–8, 130–1, 148, 157, 180, 205n, 221, 235–6, 263, 354, 378, 518, 529
Charell, Erik, 82
Charisse, Cyd, 78
Chase, Borden, 383
Chatterjee, Shekar, 603
Chatterjee, Sumitra, 468
Chelikin, Andryusha, 438
Chenal, Pierre, 149
Cherkasov-Sergeiev, Nikolai, 209
Cherkassov, Nikolai, 151, 430n, 436
Cherrill, Virginia, 529

Chesterton, G. K., 294
Chevalier, Maurice, 74, 76
Chirico, Giorgio de, 539
Chrétien, Henri, 60, 355
Christiensen, Bent, 656
Christensen, Theodor, 341
Christian-Jacque, 216, 404
Christie, Agatha, 385
Chuchunov, Yura, 438
Chukrai, Grigori, 401, 479
Churchill, Winston, 213, 692
Chylek, Eugeniusz, 332
Chytilova, Vera, 599
Ciment, Michel, 614
Cioffi, Charles, 639
Citti, Franco, 530–1
Clair, René, ix, 46, 51–3, 59, 63, 65, 67, 70, 73–4, 76, 81, 82n, 104, 139, 140, 143n, 171, 180, 248, 259, 266, 356, 438, 532
Clarke, Arthur, 132
Clarke, Mae, 100
Clarke, Shirley, 484, 643
Clarke, T. E. B., 319
Claude, 338
Clavel, James, 646
Clayton, Jack, 131n, 334, 545–6
Clémenti, Pierre, 532–3, 536, 595
Clément, René, 216, 221, 230n, 239, 241, 248, 252, 263n, 266, 404
Clift, Montgomery, 345, 378, 380–1, 383, 484
Cloquet, Ghislain, 300, 302, 505
Clouzot, Henri-Georges, 221, 254–8, 266, 404, 476, 627
Clouzot, Vera, 257
Cobb, Lee J., 636
Coburn, James, 326
Cocteau, Jean, 11–12, 252–4, 290, 438, 451n, 513, 563, 644
Coggio, Roger, 192
Cohn, Harry, 32, 137
Colbert, Claudette, 137, 377, 382
Coldstream, William, 114
Cole, Lester, 353n
Colette, 261
Collinge, Patricia, 367
Colman, Ronald, 96, 137
Colton, John, 183
Comencini, Luigi, 513n
Commandon, Professor, 7, 20
Companeez, Nina, 507n
Conan Doyle, Arthur, 96, 589
Connery, Sean, 635
Conrad, Joseph, 94–5, 158, 313–4, 616
Constable, John, 338
Coogan, Jackie, 235
Cooke, Alistair, 101, 175
Cook, Jnr, Elisha, 357
Coop, Denys, 566
Cooper, Gary, 72, 77, 137, 354, 367, 377, 406
Cooper, Merriam, 96, 115, 335
Coppola, Francis Ford, 622, 637–8
Cordobes, El, 522
Corey, Jeff, 636
Corman, Roger, 624
Cornelius, Henry, 319–20
Cornell, Jonas, 577
Cornu, Aurora, 496
Cosima, Renée, 253
Costa-Gavras, 503, 657
Costello, Dolores, 185n
Cotten, Joseph, 185n, 186, 312, 378
Courbet, Auguste, 146
Cowie, Peter, 577
Courtenay, Tom, 548–9, 561, 566, 583
Coutard, Raoul, 476
Courteline, 235
Cousteau, Jacques, 251
Coward, Noël, 67, 109, 193, 217, 316, 380
Cozarinsky, Edgardo, 613
Crain, Jean, 386
Crane, Stephen, 379

Crawford, Broderick, 357, 383, 518
Crawford, Joan, 95, 181, 219, 371, 627
Crawford, Michael, 559
Crazy Gang, The, 105n
Crichton, Charles, 320
Cripps, Stafford, 110n
Cromwell, John, 95
Cronenberg, David, 649
Cronin, A. J., 106
Crosby, Bing, 358, 407
Crowther, Bosley, 243
Cruze, James, 321
Cukor, George, 92, 138, 181, 357, 383–5
Cullberg, Birgit, 685
Cummings, Constance, 327
Cuny, Alain, 143
Curtis, Jackie, 678
Curtis, Martin, 205
Curtis, Tony, 325, 368, 374–5, 385, 405, 563
Curtiz, Michael, 26, 181, 219, 359n
Cybulski, Zbigniew, 411, 412n, 414, 589
Czinner, Paul, ix, 49, 92, 105

D

d'Abbadie d'Arrast, H., 136
Dagover, Lil, 49
Dali, Salvador, 12–13, 53
Dalio, Marcel, 183
Dallesandro, Joe, 642
Dalrymple, Ian, 106
Dampier, Claude, 139
Dandridge, Dorothy, 386
Danischewsky, Monja, 319, 320
Darnell, Linda, 180
Darrow, Clarence, 484
Darwell, Jane, 103
Das Gupta, Hari, 458n
Dassin, Jules, 262n, 367, 481
Dasté, Jean, 636
Dauphin, Claude, 251
Da Vinci, Leonardo, 257, 429
Davis, Bette, 14, 95, 99, 181, 354, 357, 627
Davis, Ossie, 611, 639, 645
Dawson, Jan, 571
Day, Harry, 684n
Day, Robert, 485
Dean, James, 39, 363, 378, 632
Dead End Kids, The, 96, 100
Dearden, Basil, 321, 548
de Bray, Yvonne, 253, 268n
Decae, Henri, 292
de Chardin, Teilhard, 675
Dee, Ruby, 640n
De Feo, Luciano, 173n
De Forrest, Lee, 62
De Gaulle, Charles, 368
De Havilland, Olivia, 381, 389, 627
de Heusch, Luc, 338
Dehn, Paul, 270n, 329, 635
Dekeukelaire, Charles, 116, 337–8
Delannoy, Jean, 254
Delany, Shelagh, 551
De Laurentiis, Dino, 359
d'Aveyron, Victor, 494
Del Giudice, Filippo, 193, 199
Delluc, Louis, x, 46, 115
Deighton, Len, 635
Del Rio, Dolores, 159
Delli Colli, Tonino, 545
Del Poggio, Carla, 515, 516n
Delvaux, André, 578
Demeny, Georges, 6
De Mille, Cecil B., 34, 39, 66, 95, 148, 157, 176, 358, 377, 378, 384n, 406, 520, 660, 692
Dempster, Carol, 30
Demy, Jacques, 476, 506
Deneuve, Catherine, 656
Denham, Maurice, 567
Denis, Armand, 335
Denker, Henry, 378
Dennis, Sandy, 629n, 649

de Poligny, Serge, 254
Deren, Maya, 61n, 643
De Robertis, Francesco, 216
de Rochement, Louis, 218, 361n
Desailly, Jean, 254
De Santis, Giuseppe, 220, 516
De Santis, Pasquale, 448
De Sica, Vittorio, 40, 173, 216, 220, 226–30, 237, 328, 404, 512–4, 516, 521n, 597, 633, 658
Deslaw, Eugène, 683n
Desnos, Robert, 53
Devi, Chunibala, 460
Devine, George, 547
De Wilde, Brandon, 358, 368
Dharmapriya, Somapala, 471
Diaghilev, Serge, 47, 667
Dickens, Charles, 141, 316
Dickinson, Thorold, 330, 395
Dickson, Paul, 329
Diderot, D., 293
Dieterle, William, 92, 378
Dietrich, Marlene, 68, 77, 105, 142n, 377, 385, 392, 581, 629
Di Giacomo, Franco, 540
Dinesen, Isak, 191–2
Disney, Walt, 132–3, 148, 183, 354, 394, 407, 689n
Di Venanzo, Gianni, 522n
Dixon, Campbell, 167
Dmytryk, Edward, 353, 360, 630
Donat, Robert, 104, 106, 150, 374, 631
Donen, Stanley, 80, 183
Donskoi, Mark, 121, 123, 150, 209–10, 218, 272, 401, 436, 461, 582–3
Dorléac, Françoise, 591
Dors, Diana, 405, 590
Dorville, 83
Dorziat, Gabrielle, 253
Dostoievsky, F., 395, 442, 535, 582, 616, 670n
Douglas, Kirk, 369, 406, 484, 561, 630
Douglas, Paul, 328, 361
Dovzhenko, Alexander, 56, 118, 150, 208, 217, 243, 332n, 409, 414–15, 421–9, 431, 434–6, 442, 518, 522, 614, 671, 694
Doyen, Dr, 7, 20
Dravič, Milena, 672–4
Dreiser, Theodore, 378
Dréville, Jean, 335
Dreyer, Carl Theodor, 46, 185, 284–90, 293, 296–7, 300–8, 341, 412, 454, 507n, 543, 579, 581
Duchamp, Marcel, 53, 683
Dubcek, A., 598
Duchaussoy, Michel, 491
Dudow, Slatan, 51, 402
Dufaux, Georges, 502
Dulac, Germaine, 53, 67
Dulay, Arthur, 62n
Dumont, Margaret, 129
Dunnaway, Faye, 635, 638
Dunbar, George, 87
Dunn, James, 44–5
Dunne, Irene, 76
Dunne, John Gregory, 620n
Dunne, J. W., 10, 277
Dupont, E. A., 48
Duport, Catherine, 589
Durante, Jimmy, 659
Duras, Marguerite, 275, 476
Durban, Guy, 419
Durbin, Deanna, 14
Durgnat, Raymond, 239, 289n, 631n
Duse, Eleanore, 18, 25
Dutt, Utpal, 603
Duvivier, Julien, 139, 142, 149, 233, 583n
Dvorak, A., 601
Dyer, Peter John, 386
Dzigan, Yefim, 401

E

Eastwood, Clint, 636–7

Edeson, Arthur, 380
Edison, Thomas A., 1, 2, 5, 7, 19, 62, 70
Edschmidt, Kasimir, 48
Edwards, Blake, 623
Eggar, Samantha, 382
Eggeling, Viking, 50, 683n
Ehrenburg, Ilya, 56
Einstein, Albert, 508
Eisenstein, S. M., 15, 29, 36, 56–7, 63, 70–1, 94, 119, 120, 206, 208, 218, 238n, 408, 411, 421–2, 423n, 424, 427–36, 448, 488, 508, 583n, 660, 671, 691–4
Eisler, Hanns, 51, 116
Eisner, Lotte, 30, 46–7
Ekberg, Anita, 521
Ekk, Nikolai, 72, 118, 411
Eldridge, John, 203–5
Elek, Judit, 507n
Elgar, Edward, 190
Eliot, T. S., 116, 184, 421, 508n
Elton, Arthur, x, 150, 341
Eluard, Paul, 275, 338
Emmer, Luciano, 337, 477, 516n
Epstein, Jean, 53
Epstein, Marie, 233
Ericson, John, 368, 371
Ermler, F., 151, 421
Ermolov, Pyotr, 121
Eshley, Norman, 192
Etaix, Pierre, 265
Evans, Christopher, 13–14
Evans, Edith, 330, 547, 548–50, 628n
Ewell, Tom, 385

F

Fabri, Zoltan, 401, 409, 481, 593
Fabrizi, Aldo, 221, 515
Fabrizi, Franco, 518
Fahmy, A., 616n
Fahmy, Abdel Aziz, 617
Fairbanks Jnr, Douglas, 161
Fairbanks Snr, Douglas, ix, 23, 37, 63, 77, 91
Falconetti, Maria, 287, 296
Farghal, I., 616n
Fassbinder, Rainer Werner, 581–582, 655
Faulkner, William, 357, 372
Faye, Randall, 139
Feeney, John, 616n
Fellini, Frederico, 172, 318, 379, 404, 477, 516n, 517–21, 577
Feltham, Kerry, 649
Ferno, John, 116, 148, 337, 339
Ferrer, José, 286, 379, 631
Ferrer, Mel, 391, 476
Ferrer, Kathleen, 491–2
Feuilliade, Louis, 20, 24, 505, 681n
Feuillière, Edwige, 252, 261
Feyder, Jacques, 46, 51, 67, 95, 140–3
Field, Betty, 636
Field, Mary, 331
Fields, W. C., 92, 129, 178, 205n, 242, 515
Figueroa, Gabriel, 95
Finch, John, 593
Finch, Peter, 485, 567–8
Finlayson, James, 158
Finler, Joel, 42
Finney, Albert, 334, 485, 547n, 548–9
Fischinger, Oscar, 133
Fitzgerald, Barry, 375
Fitzgerald, Geraldine, 93
Fitzgerald, Scott, 97, 148, 282n, 391, 505
Fitzmaurice, George, 95, 142n
Fitzpatrick, James, 644
Flaherty, Robert, 56, 65–6, 103, 105, 113–16, 118, 124, 155, 200, 336, 351, 395–9, 504
Flambert, Paulette, 234
Flaubert, G., 248
Fleischer, Max, 132

Fleischer, Richard, 646
Fleischmann, Peter, 578, 655
Fleming, John, 62
Fleming, Victor, 72, 93, 148, 286n
Fletcher, John, 474
Flynn, Errol, 178, 218, 391
Fonda, Henry, 77, 102, 354, 377, 382, 387, 390n, 583, 628n, 636
Fonda, Jane, 639
Fonda, Peter, 622
Fonseka, Gamini, 474
Fonseka, Malini, 474n
Fontaine, Joan, 393
Forbes, Bryan, 549–50
Ford, Alexander, 411, 480
Ford, John, 63, 95–7, 102, 136, 138, 148, 155, 218, 221, 310, 321, 381–3, 406, 439, 625
Forde, Walter, 104
Foreman, Carl, 315, 354, 365, 367
Forman, Milos, 402, 551n, 598–601, 653
Formby, George, 84n
Forrester, C. S., 357
Forster, E. M., 130, 201–2, 217, 460n
Fowles, John, 382
Fox, Edward, 368, 564
Fox, James, 320, 549–50, 571
Fox, William, 19, 30–1
Franju, Georges, 52n, 250, 266–7, 308, 405, 504–5
Frankel, Cyril, 334
Frankenheimer, John, 484, 631–3, 634n
Franklin, Sidney, 95
Freed, Arthur, 79
Frend, Charles, 177, 320
Fresnay, Pierre, 254
Freud, Sigmund, 473
Freund, Karl, 48, 78
Friedkin, William, 626n
Friedman, Anthony, 647
Friese-Green, William, 5
Frith, W., 318
Fritsch, Willi, 343
Fruchter, Norman, 666
Fuest, Robert, 646
Fuller, Samuel, 406
Furie, Sidney, 622, 635
Furse, Roger, 199

G

Gaál, István, 597, 653
Gabin, Jean, 39, 143, 261, 444n
Gable, Clark, 73, 96, 98, 137, 371, 382, 484
Gábor, Miklós, 597n
Gai, A. Ivanov, 25
Galeen, Henrik, ix, 48, 535
Ganda, Oumarou, 499n
Ghandi, Mahatma, 631, 662
Gance, Abel, 18, 24, 52, 62n, 63, 67, 140, 144, 157, 161, 244n, 355, 404, 584, 667n, 681n, 687, 689
Ganguly, Dhiran, 35
Garbo, Greta, 38, 40, 54, 66, 75, 77, 90, 93, 95, 130, 142, 148, 178, 347, 371, 583n, 621
Gardin, Vladimir, 583n
Gardner, Ava, 382, 384, 391, 630
Garfield, John, 360, 367
Garibaldi, G., 477
Garibyan, A., 437
Garland, Judy, 79–80, 148, 384, 621, 629
Garmes, Lee, 77, 98
Garson, Greer, 93, 155
Gauguin, P., x, 276n, 406
Gaumont, Léon, 62
Gaynor, Janet, 384
Geduld, Harry, 434
Geiger, Rod, 220–1
Gélin, Daniel, 262
Gelovani, Mikhail, 671n
Genina, Augusto, 152
Genn, Leo, 91n
George, Maude, 41

Georges-Picot, Olga, 284
Gerasimov, Sergei, 151
Gershfeld, Burton, 688
Gershwin, George, 219
Gessner, Robert, 164
Ghosal, S., 462
Giannini, A. H., 32
Gide, André, 92, 253, 313
Gielgud, John, 202, 332, 389, 503
Gilbert, John, 66, 127, 371
Gilbert, Lewis, 331, 405
Gilliatt, Penelope, 561, 567
Gilliat, Sidney, 195, 217
Giorgione, 302
Giotto, 337n, 530, 658
Gish, Lillian, 29–30, 66, 269, 347,
    378
Gish Sisters, The, ix
Glyn, Elinor, 158
Godard, Jean-Luc, 58n, 173n,
    221, 265, 391, 405, 446, 476,
    487–9, 493, 503, 503n, 507–13,
    535, 539, 543, 580, 606, 609n,
    613–14, 641–3, 657, 660, 668–
    671, 678, 680, 693–4
Goddard, Paulette, 219
Godfrey, Bob, 135
Godfrey, Nancy, 672
Goebbels, J., 79, 82n, 140, 151,
    154, 162, 207, 210–13, 245, 254,
    612
Gogol, Nikolai, 134
Gohar, 33, 86
Goldoni, C., 303
Goldwyn, Samuel, 19, 219, 359
Gombrich, E. H., 12
Gomez, Manuel Octavio, 614n
Gomez, Thomas, 367
Gomulka, W., 420
Goncharov, Vassili, 63
Gordon, David, 621
Gorki, Maxim, 21, 210, 444, 480
Gosho, Heinosuke, 69, 87, 89–90,
    214
Gottesman, Ronald, 434
Gottschalk, Joachim, 207
Gough, Michael, 329
Gough Yates, Kevin, 227
Graef, Roger, 541
Granger, Farley, 392
Granger, Stewart, 14n, 384
Grant, Cary, 383, 392
Grant, Elspeth, 371–2
Gras, Enrico, 337
Graves, Bryan, 593
Graziano, Rocky, 391
Grede, Kjell, 577
Greenberg, Joel, 78, 181
Green, F. L., 310
Greene, Graham, 94, 113, 194,
    311, 329
Green, Guy, 373
Greenstreet, Sidney, 380
Greenwood, Joan, 322, 330
Gregg, Hubert, 328
Grémillon, Jean, 140, 143, 172,
    248, 266, 337
Grierson, John, x, 55, 57–8, 71,
    108, 110–15, 117–19, 133, 143n,
    155, 163, 175, 205, 334, 348,
    663–4, 666, 692, 693n
Griffith, D. W., ix, 20, 22–3,
    29–32, 36, 39, 63, 65, 119, 488,
    691–4
Griffith, Raymond, 127
Griffith, Richard, 155, 179, 183
Griggs, Loyal, 358
Grimm, The Brothers, 130
Grossmith, George, 38
Gruenberg, Louis, 126
Guerra, Ruy, 483, 614, 652
Guffey, Burnett, 635
Guinness, Alec, 318, 320, 322–3,
    325, 485, 646
Guitry, Sacha, 251, 346
Gumpilil, David, 575
Guthrie, Arlo, 635
Gwenn, Edmund, 93, 346
Gyöngyössy, Imre, 597

H

Haanstra, Bert, 264n, 340
Hackman, Gene, 623, 633n, 635
Haeserts, Paul, 337–8
Halas, John, 136
Hall, Willis, 565
Hamer, Robert, 217, 219, 321–2
Hamilton, Chico, 484
Hamilton, Cosmo, 158
Hammerstein, Oscar, 80, 386
Hancock, Tony, 485
Handl, Irene, 330n, 551
Handwerker, Marian, 578
Hanzekovic, Fedor, 351–2
Hardwicke, Cedric, 34, 332
Hardy, Oliver, 128
Hardy, Thomas, 565
Harlan, Russell, 383
Harlan, Veit, 151, 207, 213
Harlow, Jean, 98, 160
Harris, Julie, 363, 368, 380
Harris, Richard, 345
Harrison, Rex, 180, 217
Harrisson, Tom, 200
Hart, Lorenz, 76
Hart, Moss, 360
Hartley, L. P., 564
Hartman, Elizabeth, 373
Harvey, Anthony, 671
Harvey, Laurence, 334
Harvey, Lillian, 82
Has, Wojciech, 480, 590n
Hasegawa, Kazuo, 446, 448
Hasselbalch, Hagen, 341
Hathaway, Henry, 219, 390
Hauser, Arnold, 13, 94
Havelock-Allan, Anthony, 316
Hawkins, Jack, 589
Hawkins, Richard, 336
Hawks, Howard, 98–9, 160, 181
    357, 383, 581, 625, 636, 645
Hay, Will, 105n
Hays, Will, 31, 60
Hayasaka, Fumio, 452
Hayashi, Ikaru, 607
Hayes, Isaac, 639
Hayward, Susan, 91n
Hayworth, Rita, 182
Head, Murray, 568
Hearst, William Randolph, 187
Hecht, Ben, 98, 138
Heendeniya, Punya, 474
Heflin, Van, 358, 366
Heifits, Josif, 437, 479, 582–3
Heilbroner, Robert L., 669n
Heisler, Stuart, 138
Heller, Joseph, 628
Hellman, Lillian, 381
Helm, Brigitte, 48n
Hemingway, Ernest, 117, 181, 391
Henning Jensen, Astrid, 341–2
Henning Jensen, Bjärne, 341–2
Henreid, Paul, 14
Henrey, Bobby, 311
Henry, Buck, 601
Henry, O., 413
Henzel, Harry, 641n
Hepburn, Audrey, 381, 582, 623
Hepburn, Katherine, 354, 357,
    375, 383–4, 389, 406, 630
Hepworth, Cecil, 24, 64
Herlie, Eileen, 311
Hernandez, Juano, 372
Herold, Don, 174
Herring, Robert, 54
Herubal, Michel, 288n
Hessling, Catherine, 67, 145
Heston, Charlton, 377, 381, 628
Heyer, John, 321n, 573n
Heydrich, R., 178
Heyerdahl, Thor, 335
Hickox, Sidney, 357
Higham, Charles, 78, 181, 187n
Hill, George, 98
Hill, George Roy, 621, 623
Hiller, Arthur, 645
Hiller, Erwin, 330
Hilpert, Heinz, 151
Himmler, H., 522, 533

Hindemith, Paul, 63
Hines, Barry, 569
Hippler, Franz, 151, 207
Hird, Thora, 565
Hitchcock, Alfred, ix, 55, 67, 70,
    72, 95, 103–5, 149, 177, 180,
    186–7, 219, 312, 374, 378n,
    392–3, 406, 445, 484, 490, 492,
    498
Hitchens, Robert, 158
Hitler, A., 50, 104, 118, 130, 212,
    342, 403, 522
Hodson, J. L., 560
Hoellering, George, 116
Hoffman, Dustin, 622, 636, 645,
    678n
Hoger, Hannelore, 579
Holden, William, 78, 315, 357
    386
Holliday, Judy, 357, 384, 406
Holloway, Stanley, 320
Holm, Celeste, 357
Holmes, Jack, 200
Homolka, Oscar, 67
Homma, Fumiko, 439
Honegger, A., 63, 135
Hopkins, Gerald Manley, 421
Hopkins, Miriam, 381
Hopkinson, Peter, 108, 356, 610n
Hopper, Dennis, 622
Hopwood, Avery, 158
Horne, Geoffrey, 386
Horniman, Roy, 322
Horton, Edward Everett, 139,
    328, 645
Hosoya, Kiyomatsu, 27
Houghton, Katharine, 375
House, Billy, 186
Housman, A. E., 575n, 670
Houston, Beverle, 591
Houston, Penelope, 38, 577, 594
Howard, Leslie, 92, 196
Howard, Trevor, 312, 314–15,
    317, 631
Howe, James Wong, 44, 632,
    635n
Huber, Harold, 77
Hubley, John, 135
Hudson, Rock, 632
Huff, Theodore, 235
Hughes, Howard, 32, 160
Hughes, Ken, 485, 646
Hughes, Richard, 326
Hughes, Robert, 636n
Hugo, Victor, 141
Hui, Shih, 438
Hull, David Stewart, 79, 207, 210
Hunt, Martita, 317, 388
Huntley, John, 311
Hus, Jan, 402
Huston, John, 155–6, 180, 218,
    357–8, 367, 378–81, 387, 423n,
    484
Huston, Walter, 183
Huxley, Aldous, 93
Huxley, Julian, 111, 675n
Hyde-White, Wilfrid, 314

I

Ibañez, Blasco, 77
Ibbetson, Arthur, 631
Ibert, Jacques, 63
Ibsen, Henrik, 293, 449
Ichikawa, Kon, 118, 215, 218, 221,
    400, 439, 444–7, 482
Imamura, Shohei, 650
Inge, William, 406
Ingram, Rex, 64, 158
Ingres, J. D., 141
Interlenghi, Franco, 234, 517
Ionesco, Eugène, 419
Ippolitov-Ivanov, M., 63
Isaacs, Jack, 55
Isbert, José, 346
Isherwood, Christopher, 104, 677
Ishihara, Yujiro, 447
Ito, Daisuke, 69
Ito, Teiji, 6 1n
Ivanovsky, Alexander, 82

Ivens, Joris, 116, 124, 148, 337, 339n, 503n
Ives, Burl, 381, 649
Ivory, James, 604, 651

J

Jackson, Charles, 182, 385
Jackson, Glenda, 567-8
Jackson, Gordon, 485
Jackson, Mahalia, 484
Jackson, Pat, 177, 200, 332
Jackson, Shirley, 372
Jacobs, Lewis, 106
Jacoby, Irving, 127n
Jaffrey, Madhur, 604
Jagger, Dean, 371
Jagger, Mick, 572-3, 646
Jago, Jo, 203
Jakubowska, Wanda, 411, 480
James, Henry, 131, 322, 381, 546
James, M. R., 272
Jancso, Miklos, 116, 408, 481, 593-6, 653
Jandl, Ivan, 345n
Jannings, Emil, 48n
Jarman Jnr, Claud, 372
Jarre, Maurice, 633
Järrel, Stig, 347
Jarvet, Yuri, 587
Jasset, Bernard, 16n
Jaubert, Maurice, 143
Jaworsky, Tadeusz, 420n
Jayasena, Henry, 474
Jeffries, Lionel, 647
Jennings, Hilde, 67
Jennings, Humphrey, 196, 200-203, 205n, 217
Jewison, Norman, 376, 637-8
Jires, Jaromil, 653
Johnson, Celia, 317
Johns, Glynis, 485
Johnson, Jack, 645
John, Lucien, 575
Johnson, Ian, 221n
Johnson, Lyndon B., 177n
Johnson, Samuel, 177
Jolson, Al, 60, 128
Jones, Henry Arthur, 158
Jones, Jennifer, 378, 391
Jones, Le Roi, 641
Jones, Paul, 556
Jones, R. E., 12
Jordan, Bobby, 100
Jouvet, Louis, 255, 444n
Joyce, James, 508n
Joyeux, Odette, 259-60
Jugert, Rudolf, 343
Juillard, Robert, 241
Julian, Rupert, 41
Jung, C. J., 9, 11, 674
Junghans, Carl, 51
Juracek, Pavel, 598
Jurgens, Curt, 404
Juro, Kara, 606
Justice, James Robertson, 270
Jutra, Claude, 649
Jutzi, Piel, 51

K

Kadar, Jan, 402, 410, 598-9, 634, 645, 653
Kael, Pauline, 107, 167n, 171, 242, 251n, 325, 363, 370n, 372, 375, 392, 446, 475, 510-11, 519, 541, 547, 627, 629
Kafka, Franz, 564, 598
Kaloper, Jagoda, 672
Kalotozov, Mikhail, 210, 401, 421, 437, 479
Kanin, Garson, 156, 200, 357
Kaplan, Nelly, 507n
Kapoor, Raj, 460
Kapoor, Shashi, 604-5
Karch, Anton, 665
Kardar, Aeejay, 474
Karloff, Boris, 132
Karlsen, Phil, 370n
Karmen, Roman, 218, 582
Karno, Fred, 128

Kastner, Peter, 637
Kaufman, Millard, 370
Kaütner, Helmut, 213-14, 342-3, 351, 403
Kawalerowicz, Jerzy, 402, 411-12, 480
Kawarazaki, Kenzo, 608
Kawaura, Kenichi, 20
Kaye, Danny, 219, 234, 354
Kayukov, Stepan, 123
Kazan, Elia, 178, 360-4, 367, 406, 484, 645
Keaton, Buster, x, 22, 52, 66, 127-8, 358, 643
Keene, Ralph, 370n
Kelber, Michel, 260
Kellaway, Cecil, 375
Kellerman, Annette, 18, 23
Kelly, Gene, 14, 79-80, 182-3, 219, 354, 630
Kelly, Grace, 358, 367, 382, 392, 406
Kempson, Rachel, 321
Kendal, Felicity, 604
Kendal, Jennifer, 605
Kennedy, Edgar, 180
Kennedy, John, 631
Kennedy, Joseph P., 32
Kern, Jerome, 76
Kerr, Deborah, 386, 633
Keystone Cops, The, 22
Khandpur, K. L., 458
Khrushchev, N., 133, 208, 423
Kidd, Michael, 389
Kienholz, Edward, 420
Kinder, Marsha, 591
King, Allan, 649
King, Henry, 391
King, Martin Luther, 631
Kinnear, Roy, 559
Kinoshita, Keisuke, 221, 400
Kinugasa, Teinosuke, 35, 69, 439, 447
Kipling, Rudyard, 23
Kirsanov, Dimitri, 53, 250
Kitzmiller, John, 515, 516n
Kjaerullf-Schmidt, Palle, 579, 596n
Kjellin, Alf, 347
Klein, Gerard, 479
Klein, William, 503n
Kline, Herbert, 148
Klos, Elmar, 402, 410, 598-9, 634
Kluge, Alexander, 579-80
Kluge, Alexandra, 579
Knef, Hildegard, 343
Knight, Arthur, 102, 176, 234
Knight, Shirley, 635, 638
Knoblock, Edward, 158
Kobayashi, Masaki, 400, 608
Kobayasha, Setsuo, 446
Konchalovsky, Andrei, 583
Konwicki, Tadeusz, 416
Koppel, Walter, 478
Korda, Alexander, 20, 26, 83n, 104-5, 140, 142, 174, 177, 308, 311n
Kortner, Fritz, 105
Kósa, Ferenc, 410, 593, 595-6
Kosma, Joseph, 250
Kosugi, Isamu, 152
Kotcheff, Ted, 647
Kovács, András, 481, 592, 594-5
Kozák, András, 595
Kozintsev, Grigori, 63, 92, 150, 218, 332, 436, 584-7, 652
Kracauer, Siegfried, 46-7, 162, 211, 234
Krafft-Ebing, R., 548
Kramer, Stanley, 365, 366, 374-5, 484, 428-9
Krasna, Milton, 357
Krasna, Norman, 100
Kraus, Henri, 24
Krauss, Werner, 48n, 49-50
Krebs, Rockne, 682
Krishnaswamy, S., 84
Kristensen, Henning, 588
Kroner, Josef, 599

Krska, Vaclav, 402
Kruger, J., 52
Kubrick, Stanley, 132, 267, 271, 367, 406, 484, 546, 560-1, 572, 575, 606, 625, 634, 667n, 668, 670, 674-9, 683n, 693
Kuleshov, Lev, x, 36, 68, 70, 115
Kulle, Jarl, 478, 577
Kumar, Rattan, 460
Kurant, Willy, 192
Kuri, Yoji, 135
Kurnitz, Harry, 385
Kurosawa, Akira, 146, 214, 218, 439-44, 452n, 455, 482, 484, 584, 608, 650
Kutz, Kazimirz, 654
Kuzmina, Elena, 584
Kyo, Machiko, 400, 439, 448, 452-3

L

Labiche, E., 235
La Cava, Gregory, 138
Ladd, Alan, 178, 358
Ladmiral, Nicole, 250n
Ladynina, Marena, 151
Laemmle, Carl, 19, 23, 30-2
Lafont, Bernadette, 242
Laila, Istefan, 69
Lake, Veronica, 179
Lama, Ibrahim, 69
Lamarr, Hedy, 377
Lambetti, Ellie, 344
Lambraki, George, 503
Lamorisse, Albert, 249, 404
Lamour, Dorothy, 76, 390
Lancaster, Burt, 325, 390, 405-6, 484, 522, 631, 633
Lane, Burton, 630
Lane, Lupino, 74
Langdon, Harry, x, 22, 66, 127-8, 137, 518
Langer, Suzanne, 10, 12
Lang, Fritz, ix, 49-50, 66, 72, 100-1, 178, 219, 391, 478, 581
Langlois, Henri, 118, 119n, 206, 691n
Lansbury, Angela, 632, 645
Lardner Jnr, Ring, 353n
Laskowska, Irena, 417
Laskowski, Jan, 416
Lasky, Jesse, 31, 77n
Lassally, Walter, 344, 474
Latham, Woodville, 2
Lattuada, Alberto, 220, 477, 515-516
Laughton, Charles, 95-6, 104, 385, 387, 392, 484
Launder, Frank, 195, 217
Laurel and Hardy, 83, 128-9, 148, 158, 205n, 469
Laurel, Stan, 128
Laval, Pierre, 172, 504n
Lawrence, D. H., 236n, 485, 647
Lawson, John H., 353n
Laydu, Claude, 268n
Leacock, Philip, 332, 334, 405
Leacock, Richard, 498
Lean, David, 93, 194n, 217, 316, 318, 546n, 616n, 646
Léaud, Jean-Pierre, 494, 541, 589, 657
Le Carré, John, 635
Leclerc, Ginette, 254, 420
Lee, Bobby, 138
Lee, Jack, 405
Le Fanu, Sheridan, 476
Léger, Fernand. 53, 63
Legoshin, Vladimir, 121n, 437
Lehar, Franz, 63
Leighton, Margaret, 564
Leighton, Lord, 318
Leigh, Vivien, 217, 361-2, 583n
Leigh, Walter, 114
Leisen, Mitchell, 219
Leiser, Erwin, 478
Lejeune, C. A., 55, 104
Lelouch, Claude, 281, 503n, 507
Lemeshev, Sergei, 82

Lemmon, Jack, 385, 484
Lenica, Jan, 135, 415, 418–20
Lenin, V. I., 401
Leni, Paul, 66
Lennon, John, 559
Leonard, Robert Z., 73, 93
Le Prince, Louis, 5
Lerdorff Rye, Preben, 290
Le Roy, A. J., 6
Le Roy, Baby, 242
Le Roy, Mervin, 98, 101
Lesiewicz, Witold, 412
Lester, Richard, 559, 633
Lévi-Strauss, Claude, 7, 8, 574–5
Levy, Louis, 64
Lewin, Albert, 219
Lewis, Sinclair, 484
Lewton, Val, 182, 219, 630
Leyda, Jay, 209, 437, 583n
L'Herbier, Marcel, 63
Lindberg, Charles, 385
Lindblom, Gunnel, 577
Lindsay, Vachel, 21, 23, 37, 616–7
Lindtberg, Leopold, 342, 344
Lissenko, Natalie, 67
Littlewood, Joan, 559
Litvak, Anatole, 389–90
Livesey, Roger, 197
Lloyd, Frank, 96
Lloyd, Harold, x, 66, 128, 179
Loach, Ken, 569–71
Loden, Barbara, 507n, 645
Lods, Jean, 116
Logan, Joshua, 406
Löhr, Marie, 195
Lohmann, Dietrich, 581
Lollobrigida, Gina, 405, 413n
Lombard, Carol, 75, 138
Lomniki, Jan, 420
Long, Huey, 368
Lorca, Garcia, 503
Lorentiz, Pare, 124–7
Loren, Sophia, 315, 384, 485, 514, 521n
Lorre, Peter, 50, 72, 78, 359n, 380, 581
Losey, Joseph, 148, 179, 354, 374, 405, 485, 560–4, 565n, 647
Lotar, Eli, 116, 216, 250, 266
Low, David, 197
Lowe, Arthur, 551
Lowe, Edmund, 159
Loy, Myrna, 76, 354, 359
Lubitsch, Ernst, 49, 54, 65–6, 70, 73–7, 81, 136, 148, 157, 163, 166
Lucas, George, 645
Ludwig of Bavaria, King, 682
Lukas, Paul, 77
Lukinsky, I., 437
Lumet, Sidney, 611n, 633–5
Lumière, Louis and Auguste, 1, 6, 7, 19, 70, 127
Lumumba, Patrice, 640
Lupino, Ida, 77, 507n
Lutyens, Elisabeth, 329n
Lyarsky, Alexei, 122
Lye, Len, 114, 133, 198, 205, 418
Lynen, Robert, 142, 233
Lynley, Carol, 387
Lysenko, T., 423

M

Maas, Tove, 342
MacArthur, General, 215
McCann, Richard Dyer, 620n
McCarthy, Joseph, 354
McCarthy, Mary, 635
McClellan, Fergus, 327
McCord, Ted, 272
McCrea, Joel, 179
McCullers, Garson, 380
MacDonald, Dwight, 378
MacDonald, Jeanette, 74, 76, 82
MacDonald, Joe, 361
McDowell, Malcolm, 564
McEnery, John, 647
McEnery, Peter, 589
MacGowran, Jack, 560
Machover, Robert, 665

Machulski, Jan, 417
Mackendrick, Alexander, 319, 321–8
Mackinder, Halford, 659n
McLaglen, Victor, 159
MacLaine, Shirley, 385n, 392, 484
McLaren, Norman, 133–4, 159, 205n, 418
McLuhan, Marshall, 690
McKinney, Nina Mae, 361
McQueen, Steve, 638
Macready, George, 561
Maddow, Ben, 372
Madge, Charles, 200
Maeterlinck, M., 233
Maetzig, Kurt, 479
Magnani, Anna, 221, 247, 513–14, 530
Magritte, René, 641
Mahler, Gustav, 523
Makavejev, Dusan, 512, 609n, 642, 654, 668–74, 678
Malden, Karl, 364, 632
Malige, Jean, 242
Malle, Louis, 87, 242, 251, 476, 505–6, 651, 680
Mallory, Boots, 44–5
Malone, Dorothy, 357
Malraux, André, 621
Maltz, Albert, 353n
Mamoulian, Robert, 73, 75–8, 93
Manès, Gina, 67
Manet, Edouard, 25
Mangano, Silvana, 525, 531–2
Mankiewitz, Joseph L., 181, 357, 388–9
Mankowitz, Wolf, 546
Mann, Anthony, 628
Mann, Daniel, 406, 484, 514
Mann, Delbert, 628n, 633, 646
Mann, Thomas, 191, 523, 525–6
Manvell, Roger, 311
Marais, Jean, 253, 451n
March, Fredric, 77, 354, 359, 384, 484, 630
Marchal, Georges, 404
Marcourelles, Louis, 409
Marei, Ahmed, 617–8
Marey, Etienne, 6
Mariassy, Felix, 409, 481, 593
Marker, Chris, 278–80, 348, 476, 489, 502–3, 613, 657
Marlowe, Christopher, 353, 635
Marrama, Alberto, 542
Marquand, Christian, 404, 477
Marshall, George, 219, 377
Marshall, John, 336
Martinelli, Elsa, 476
Martini, Nino, 77
Marton, Andrew, 628
Marvin, Lee, 382, 391, 623, 627
Marx Brothers, The, 73, 97, 129, 148
Marx, Chico, 129
Marx, Groucho, 129
Marx, Harpo, 129, 518
Masereel, Frantz, 135
Masina, Giulietta, 404, 516n, 517, 519
Maskell, Virginia, 332
Mason, James, 39, 313n, 383, 388–390, 633, 635
Massalitinova, Varvara, 121–2
Massey, Raymond, 196
Massie, Paul, 271
Massingham, Richard, 205–6, 265
Masters, John, 384
Maté, Rudolph, 302n
Mathieson, Muir, 174n
Mature, Victor, 183, 377
Maugham, W. Somerset, 95, 158–159, 380
Mauri, Glauco, 544
Mauriac, François, 503–4
Maxwell, John, 104
Mayer, Carl, 48, 66, 516
Mayer, J. P., 14
Mayer, Louis B., 19, 358
Mead, Margaret, 200

Medvedkin, Alexander, 58n
Meedeniya, Iranganie, 472
Meerson, Lazare, 73, 82
Mehrjui, Daryush, 618–19
Meisel, Edmund, 63
Mekas Brothers, The, 643
Méliès, Georges, 8, 15–17, 19, 26, 129, 206
Melsøn, Soren, 341
Melville, Herman, 380, 647
Melville, Jean-Pierre, 253, 266, 290, 404, 541
Melvin, Murray, 547
Mendes, Lothar, 104
Mendès-France, P., 504n
Menjou, Adolphe, 78, 128, 354, 561
Menzel, Jiri, 511n, 598–9, 601–2, 652, 680
Menzies, William Cameron, 105, 174
Mercer, David, 570n
Merchant, Ismail, 604
Merchant, Vivien, 331
Mercouri, Melina, 344, 481
Meredith, Burgess, 387
Merwin, Samuel, 158
Messel, Oliver, 330, 389
Mesnier, Paul, 233n
Metzner, Erno, 51
Meyerhold, V., 25
Meyers, Sidney, 236, 643
Meynier, Geronimo, 521n
Michaelangelo, 257, 693
Michurin, I., 423
Mifune, Toshiro, 439, 442n, 444, 482, 632
Mikuni, Rentaro, 445, 483
Miles, Christopher, 647
Milestone, Lewis, 128n, 164, 166, 169, 178, 414
Milhaud, Darius, 63
Milland, Ray, 219, 385
Miller, Patsy Ruth, 74
Mills, Freddie, 331
Mills, Hayley, 549
Mills, John, 330, 485
Milne, Tom, 78, 614
Mimica, Vatroslav, 481, 654, 674n
Minnelli, Vincente, 79, 219, 406, 630
Mir, Ezra, 458
Miranda, Carmen, 79
Mishima, Yukio, 215
Mistrik, Ivan, 410
Mitchell, Cameron, 640n
Mitchell, Thomas, 367
Mitchell, Yvonne, 330
Mitchum, Robert, 392
Mitra Subrata, 466, 470, 604
Miyagawa, Kazuo, 439, 452
Mix, Tom, 38
Mizoguchi, Kenji, 35, 87, 90, 147, 152, 214, 304, 379, 400, 424, 439, 449–53, 455, 608, 618, 694
Modot, Gaston, 238, 510
Moholy-Nagy, L., 683, 688
Mohyeddin, Zia, 605
Molander, Gustav, 347
Mollo, Andrew, 553
Molnar, Ferenc, 385
Monet, Claude, 93
Monicelli, Mario, 521n
Monod, Roland, 297
Monroe, Marilyn, 357, 383, 385, 406, 484
Montagu, Ivor, 57, 173, 194n
Montand, Yves, 256, 507, 632
Montserrat, Nicholas, 320
Moorehead, Agnes, 185n, 627
Moravia, Alberto, 514n, 520
Moreau, Jeanne, 192, 476, 505, 631
Moreno, Marguerite, 259
Morgan, Michèle, 251
Mori, Nasayuki, 453
Morley, Robert, 357, 485
Morris, Oswald, 379–80

Morrison, Norman, 559
Morrissey, Paul, 641–2
Mostel, Zero, 361, 645
Mouloudji, Marcel, 268
Mozart, W. A., 298, 507, 575
Mukerjee, Madhabi, 468
Mullaly, Terence, 513
Müller, Renate, 207n
Müller, Titus Vibe, 335
Mulligan, Richard, 636
Mundwiller, J., 52
Muni, Paul, 95, 98, 102, 106, 148
Munk, Andrzej, 402, 411–14, 590
Munk, Kaj, 298
Munshin, Jules, 78, 80
Munson, Ona, 183
Murata, Minoru, 35
Murnau, F. W., 49, 54, 66
Murphy, Dudley, 53
Murphy, George, 354
Murray, Don, 387
Murray, Leo, 298n
Musil, Robert, 579
Mussolini, B., 174, 195, 514
Mussorgsky, M., 134
Musuraca, Nick, 78
Muybridge, Eadward, 5

N
Narizzano, Silvio, 646
Naruse, Mikio, 90
Narushima, Toichiro, 608
Nascimbene, Mario, 617
Nathan, Bernard, 139
Nazimova, Alla, 38
Nazwanov, Mikhail, 589
Neame, Ronald, 194n, 316, 485, 646
Neckar, Vaclav, 601
Niergaard, Ebbe, 286
Negri, Pola, 54, 347
Nelson, Ralph, 645
Nemec, Jan, 551n, 599
Nemeskurty, Istvan, 408n
Nero, Franco, 647, 656
Nesbitt, E. E., 647
Newman, David, 388n
Newman, Paul, 387, 391, 406, 484, 623, 635n
Newson, George, 685
Newton, Isaac, 660
Niblo, Fred, 64, 77, 381
Nicolais, Alvin, 685
Nichols, Dudley, 91n, 184
Nicholson, Jack, 645
Nichols, Mike, 622–3, 629n, 678n
Nihalsingh, D. R., 470n
Nielsen, Asta, 25, 67
Nillson, Anna Q., 358
Niven, David, 93, 193, 386, 633
Nogueira, Ruy, 496n
Nohrborg, Anders, 349
Noiret, Philippe, 505
Nortier, Nadine, 296
Navarro, Ramon, 66, 381
Novello, Ivor, 67
Novotny, J., 598
Nugent, Elliott, 139
Nusberg, Lev, 683

O
Oberon, Merle, 93
Odagiri, Miki, 441
O'Day, Anita, 484
Odets, Clifford, 77
Ogawa, Shinsuke, 650
O'Higgins, Henry J., 158
Okudjava, Bulat, 673n
Olmi, Ermanno, 477, 526–9, 600, 680
Oliver, Edna May, 92–3
Olivier, Laurence, 92–3, 190, 196, 198, 332, 334, 387, 484–5, 547, 585
Olsson, Stellan, 575n
Ondra, Anny, 72
Ondricek, Miroslav, 551, 600
O'Neal, Ron, 640n

O'Neill, Eugene, 72, 78, 91, 184, 633
Ophuls, Marcel, 504n
Ophuls, Max, 266, 379
Oppenheim, E. Phillips, 158
Orain, Fred, 263
Ornitz, Samuel, 353n
Orton, Joe, 646, 678
Orwell, George, 136
Osborne, John, 334, 485, 545
Oscarsson, Per, 575
Oshima, Nagisa, 35, 88, 90, 221, 236, 440n, 482, 512, 541, 605–9, 650, 680
Ostrer Brothers, The, 104
Oswald, Richard, 403
Oursler, Fulton, 378
Ouspenskaya, Maria, 183
Owen, Alun, 485
Owens, Jesse, 118
Ozu, Yashiro, 87, 90, 214, 308, 328, 400, 439, 449, 454–7, 482, 608

P
Pabst, G. W., ix, x, 46, 49, 51, 65–6, 83, 149, 161, 342, 381, 403, 436, 581
Pagnol, Marcel, 83n, 140, 293
Pakula, Alan, 638
Palance, Jack, 358
Palette, Eugene, 74
Papas, Michael, 504n
Paracchi, Renato, 529
Parker, Charlie, 506
Parker, Claire, 53, 134–5, 205n
Parker, Gilbert, 158
Parks, Gordon, 639
Parnell Thomas, Judge, 353–4
Parrott, James, 128
Parsons, Estelle, 635
Pascal, Blaise, 497
Pascal, Gabriel, 217, 309n
Pasionara, La, 503
Pasolini, Pier Paolo, 278, 302n, 404, 477, 526, 529–34, 680
Passendorfer, Jerzy, 480
Passer, Ivan, 551n, 600
Pastrone, Giovanni, 63
Pati, Pramod, 459
Patterson, Elizabeth, 372
Patterson, Floyd, 236
Pathé, Charles, 139
Paul, R. W., 2
Paxinou, Katina, 91n, 189
Pearson, George, 24, 64, 163
Peck, Gregory, 219, 354, 360, 378–9, 381, 391, 630
Peckinpah, Sam, 625, 645, 668, 678n
Pelissier, Anthony, 236n
Pendleton, Nat, 139
Penn, Arthur, 623, 635–6, 645
Pens Rode, Nina, 306
Peppard, George, 623
Peries, Lester James, 470–4, 482, 614n
Périnal, Georges, 82, 104
Perkins, Anthony, 406
Persson, Jörgen, 575
Pétain, Marshal, 172
Petri, Elio, 658
Petrinsky, Anatole, 583
Petrovic, Aleksander, 674n
Petrov, Vassili, 151
Phalke, Dadasaheb, 16–17, 20, 26, 33, 37, 84
Philbin, Mary, 41
Philipe, Gérard, 81, 260, 262
Picasso, Pablo, 257, 275, 508n, 513
Piccoli, Michel, 404, 508
Pickett, Wilson, 640
Pickford, Mary, ix, 9, 23, 31, 37, 77n
Piene, Otto, 682
Pinero, Arthur, 24, 136
Pinter, Harold, 562, 564, 591
Pirandello, Luigi, 25, 95

Pitts, Zasu, 44, 74, 139, 518, 581
Pizzetti, Ildebrando, 63
Planer, Franz, 381, 390
Platts-Mills, Barney, 568–9, 646
Pleasence, Donald, 547, 591
Poe, Edgar Allan, 131, 191, 624
Poirier, Léon, 161
Poitier, Sidney, 332, 373–5, 376n, 563, 622, 630, 640
Polansky, Roman, 180n, 415, 417, 480, 572, 585n, 589, 591–2, 654, 680
Pollard, Michael, 635, 637
Polonsky, Abraham, 367, 625
Pommer, Erich, 48, 65, 105, 115
Pontecorvo, Gillo, 477, 503–4
Ponting, Herbert G., 115
Popov, Andrei, 583
Poreba, Bohdan, 420
Porter, Cole, 78
Portman, Eric, 196
Porter, Katherine Anne, 629
Potamkin, Harry Alan, 287n
Poujouly, Georges, 268n, 404
Poussin, N., 338
Powell, Michael, 105n, 139, 196–198, 405
Power, Tyrone, 77, 391
Preminger, Otto, 180, 386–8, 484
Preobrazhenskaya, Olga, 68, 507n
Presle, Micheline, 260
Pressburger, Emeric, 196–8
Prévert, Jacques, 140, 143, 250, 266
Previn, André, 371
Price, Dennis, 322, 485
Price, James, 190, 583
Priestley, J. B., 311, 629n
Pronin, V. M., 400
Psilander, V., 26
Pucholt, Vladimir, 600n
Pudovkin, V. I., 36, 56–7, 68, 70–1, 119–20, 151, 194, 207–9, 401, 408, 422–3, 436, 583n
Purcell, W., 200n
Purdon, Noel, 531
Pushkin, A., 330
Pyle, Denver, 635
Pyriev, Ivan, 82, 151, 209 582

Q
Queneau, Raymond, 242
Quine, Richard, 406
Quinn, Anthony, 326, 377, 406 517–18

R
Rabier, Jean, 492, 507
Rachmaninov, S., 316
Racine, J., 141, 303, 443
Rademakers, Fons, 338, 478, 578
Radiguet, Raymond, 260
Radok, Alfred, 402
Rafelson, Bob, 645
Raft, George, 98, 390n
Rahn, Bruno, 66
Rai, Himansu, 86
Raimu, 293
Rainer, Luise, 95
Rains, Claude, 101, 217
Raizman, Yuli, 218
Ramsaye, Terry, 5, 29–30
Rank, J. Arthur, 193, 199, 246–7 308–9, 311n, 333
Ránody, Laszló, 401
Rapee, Erno, 63
Rapper, Irving, 181, 219
Rappoport, Herbert, 82, 206
Ratcliffe, Sandy, 571
Rathbone, Basil, 92
Ratoff, Gregory, 357, 485
Rattigan, Terence, 330
Ray, Aldo, 384
Ray, Man, 53
Ray, Nicholas, 367
Ray, Satyajit, 87, 222, 400, 444, 459–70, 482, 602–4, 614n, 616 680
Ray, Terrance, 44–5

Raye, Martha, 378
Raymond, Ernest, 163
Raymond, Gary, 547
Reagan, Ronald, 354
Redford, Robert, 272
Redgrave, Michael, 91n, 107, 149, 189, 321, 405, 565, 586, 635
Redgrave, Vanessa, 551, 633
Redmond, Joyce, 548
Reed, Carol, 95, 105n, 107, 149, 156, 177, 186, 193, 200, 207, 309–16, 405
Reggiani, Serge, 263
Reich, Wilhelm, 673–4
Reiner, Carl, 637
Reinhardt, Max, 47, 92
Reiniger, Lotte, 4, 63, 135, 205n
Reisz, Karel, 333–4, 485, 547, 550–1
Remarque, Erich Maria, 164, 167
Remick, Lee, 646
Renan, Sheldon, 641
Renard, Jules, 142, 233n
Renaud, Madeleine, 92, 173, 234, 584
Renoir, Auguste, 251
Renoir, Claude, 145, 258
Renoir, Jean, x, 46, 59, 139–40, 143–7, 149, 162, 169–72, 178, 219, 221, 248, 261, 266, 308n, 379, 404, 444n, 469, 498, 514, 580
Renoir, Marguerite, 146
Renoir, Pierre, 145–6
Resnais, Alain, 10–11, 188, 210, 267, 273–8, 280–1, 282n, 404, 483, 489, 503n, 506, 577, 582n, 599, 679, 686, 694
Rey, Fernando, 656
Reynaud, Emile, 5
Rhode, Eric, 203, 415, 449, 609, 682, 684n
Rich, Claude, 284
Richardson, Ralph, 311, 314, 332, 381, 387
Richardson, Tony, 333–4, 485, 545, 547–8, 551, 646
Richie, Donald, 34, 36, 88, 215, 439, 442, 455
Richter, Hans, 9, 50, 63
Riefenstahl, Leni, 117–18, 447, 692
Risi, Dino, 658
Ritchie, June, 565
Ritt, Martin, 374, 635, 645
Ritter, Karl, 211
Ritter, Thelma, 357
Riva, Emmanuele, 292, 477, 505
Rivette, Jacques, 405, 476
Robbe-Grillet, Alain, 506
Roberge, Gaston, 431, 433
Roberts, Rachel, 485
Robertson, Arnot, 203
Robertson, Cliff, 627
Robertson, J. S., 77
Robeson, Paul, 149
Robey, George, 83
Robinson, Edward G., 98–9, 186–187, 200, 208, 219, 327, 354, 499, 630
Robison, Arthur, ix, 49
Robson, Mark, 182, 219, 374, 390n, 484, 630–1
Rocha, Glauber, 483, 512, 614–15, 652, 669, 680
Rodgers, Richard, 76, 80
Roeg, Nicolas, 565n, 570–5, 648, 668, 670, 679
Rogers, Ginger, 79–80, 354
Röhrig, Walther, 48
Rogosin, Lionel, 395–6, 612
Rohmer, Eric, 490, 494–8, 679
Rolling Stones, The, 81
Romand, Béatrice, 496
Romberg, Sigmund, 63
Rome, Stewart, 24
Romm, Mikhail, 151, 421, 430, 586
Ronconi, Luca, 682

Ronet, Maurice, 505
Room, Alexander, 46, 68, 421
Rooney, Mickey, 79, 92, 526
Roos, Jørgen, 341n
Roosevelt, Eleanor, 236
Roosevelt, F. D., 97, 125
Rosay, Françoise, 141–2
Rose, William, 319, 375, 637n
Rosenberg, Stuart, 623, 626
Rosi, Francesco, 521–2
Ross, Lillian, 379, 423n, 620n
Rossellini, Renzo, 232
Rossellini, Roberto, 220–6, 230–2, 400, 404, 477, 513, 516, 616
Rossen, Robert, 368, 623
Rossi, Franco, 477, 521n
Rossif, Frédéric, 503
Rossini, G., 180, 677
Rosti, Istefan, 69
Rotha, Paul, 195, 328–9, 417, 478
Rouch, Jean, 195n, 308, 336, 498–502, 507, 611
Roud, Richard, 580
Roundtree, Richard, 639
Rouquier, Georges, 216, 248–9
Rowland, Roy, 630
Roy, Bimal, 460, 474
Roy, Sadhan, 474
Roy, Soumendou, 466
Ruddy, Al, 622
Ruggles, Charles, 76, 645
Ruggles, Wesley, 138
Ruhmer, H., 62
Runyon, Damon, 99, 389
Russell, Harold, 359
Russell, Jane, 383
Russell, Ken, 412n, 548, 551, 556n, 586n, 646, 652
Russell, Rosalind, 91n
Rutherford, Margaret, 319
Rutten, Gerard, 116
Ruttman, Walter, 50–1, 63, 66, 116, 348
Ryan, Bruce, 669n
Ryan, Robert, 360, 366, 371, 627, 628n
Ryu, Chishu, 454

S

Sadleir, Michael, 314
Sadoul, Georges, 5, 52, 73, 83n, 139, 142, 170, 253, 303n, 359n, 611
Sagan, Françoise, 386
Sagan, Leontine, 234
Sahni, Balras, 460
Saint, Eva Marie, 361, 387, 632
Saint-Jean, Guy, 420
Saint-Saëns, Camille, 62
Salou, Louis, 144n
Sanda, Dominique, 300, 535
Sanders Brothers, The, 267, 272
Sanders, Denis, 272
Sanders, George, 357
Sanders, Terry, 272
Santell, Alfred, 91n, 100
Sara, Sandor, 597
Sardou, V., 136, 235
Sarris, Andrew, 507n
'Satchmo' (Louis Armstrong), 358
Satie, Erik, 63, 192
Sauguet, Henri, 249
Savalas, Telly, 627
Saville, Victor, 106
Sawamura, Haruko, 35
Saxon, John, 272
Scavarda, Aldo, 537
Schaeffer, Paul, 324
Schaffner, Franklin, 621, 628
Schamoni, Ulrich, 655
Schary, Doré, 98, 270
Schenck, N., 379n
Schlesinger, John, 485, 546, 565–8
Schlöndorff, Volker, 579
Schmidt, Jan, 598
Schnee, Charles, 383
Schneider, Alan, 643
Schneider, Romy, 387, 521n

Schoedsack, Ernest, 65, 96, 115, 335
Schoenberg, Arnold, 540
Schulberg, Bud, 148
Schumann, R., 307
Schwartz, Lev, 121–2
Scire, Andrea, 521n
Scob, Edith, 505
Scott, Adrian, 353n, 360
Scott, Anthony, 646
Scott, Captain, 115
Scott, George C., 628
Scott, Randolph, 76
Scott, Zachary, 483
Scriabin, A., 685
Seastrom, Victor, 347n
Seberg, Jean, 386
Segal, George, 549, 629n
Seiter, William, 139
Sekigawa, Hideo, 483
Sellers, Peter, 485, 547
Selpin, Herbert, 207
Selznick, David, 98, 378
Sembene, Ousman, 611
Sen, Aparna, 403
Sen Gupta, Pinaki, 462
Sen, Mrinal, 603
Sennett, Mack, 65, 206
Scofield, Paul, 588, 631, 647
Semon, Larry, 127
Seton, Marie, 430, 431n, 433–4
Shahin, Youssef, 616n, 651
Shah, Chandulal, 33
Shakespeare, W., 190, 199, 302, 443, 584
Shamroy, Leon, 387
Shanks, Bud, 273
Shantaram, Rajaran, 86
Sharif, Omar, 616n, 646, 651
Shaw, Alexander, 458
Shaw, G. B., 386, 485
Shaw, Robert, 568, 628n
Shaw, Run Me, 438n
Shaw, Run Run, 438n
Shearer, Norma, 66, 73, 92, 97, 371
Shebib, Donald, 649
Sheehan, Winfield, 45
Sheldon, Edward, 158
Shelley, Mary, 131
Shelley, P. B., 250
Shepperd, John, 369n
Sherriff, R. C., 163, 310
Sherwood, Robert, 75
Shimazu, Yasujiro, 87, 90, 152
Shimizu, Hiroshi, 152
Shimkus, Joanna, 647
Shimura, Takashi, 44
Shindo, Kaneto, 482, 608
Shingleton, Wilfrid, 593
Shostakovich, Dmitri, 63, 151, 584–5, 586n
Shub, Esther, 68
Shumiatsky, Boris, 57–8, 423
Shute, Nevile, 629
Sidney, George, 183, 219
Sidney, Sylvia, 77
Siegel, Don, 407, 636–7
Siffre, Labi, 643n
Signoret, Simone, 257, 263, 296, 334, 404, 547, 633, 635
Sillitoe, Alan, 548
Silverstein, Elliot, 623
Sim, Alastair, 320, 603
Simenon, Georges, 145
Simeons, A. T. W., 673n
Simmons, Jean, 381, 484
Simon, Frank, 643
Simon, John, 331n, 507n
Simon, Michel, 145, 631, 636
Simonov, Konstantin, 421
Sinatra, Frank, 79–80, 358, 386, 406, 430
Sinclair, Upton, 434
Sinha, Tapan, 400, 482, 603
Sjoberg, Alf, 347, 404, 478
Sjöman, Vilgot, 577, 655
Sjöström, Victor (Seastrom), 41, 46, 54, 66, 347

Skipworth, Alison, 515
Skladanowsky, Max, 2, 6
Skolimowski, Jerzy, 480, 589–90, 596, 654
Skouras, Spyros, 620
Skorzewski, Edward, 420
Skot-Hansen, Mogens, 341
Sloane, Everett, 366n
Smetana, B., 402
Smith, C. Aubrey, 76
Smith, George Albert, 18
Smith, Percy, 332
Smoktunovsky, Innokenty, 92, 332, 585–6, 652
Smutna, Dana, 410
Söderberg, Hjalmar, 293
Soldati, Mario, 152
Søltoft, Ole, 656
Solzhenitsyn, A., 582n
Sontag, Susan, 507n
Sorel, Jean, 477
Souris, André, 338
Soyinka, Wole, 611
Spaak, Catherine, 477
Spaak, Charles, 140–1, 268–9
Sparks, Ned, 139
Speer, Albert, 682n
Spengler, Oswald, 48
Stalin, J., 57, 82, 206–10, 335, 421–3, 430, 434, 436, 586, 671, 678
Stallings, Lawrence, 159
Stamp, Terence, 382, 531
Stander, Lionel, 180, 591
Stanislavsky, Konstantin, 120
Stanwyck, Barbara, 78, 354, 390
Staudte, Wolfgang, 342, 478
Stawinsky, Jerzy, 413
St Clair, Mal, 136, 383
Steegmuller, Francis, 252n
Steiger, Rod, 376, 406, 522, 528n, 584, 634
Steinbeck, John, 164n, 363n
Sternberg, Jacques, 284
Stein, Elliott, 303
Steiner, George, 680
Steiner, Max, 357
Stepanov, I., 121
Stephens, Robert, 551
Stern, Antony, 688
Stern, Bert, 484
Stevens, George, 358, 378
Stevenson, R. L., 131, 550
Stewart, James, 137, 148, 377, 382, 385
Stiglic, France, 481
Stiller, Mauritz, 41, 46, 54, 347
Stockhausen, Karlheinz, 573, 685
Stoker, Bram, 131
Stone, Lewis, 526
Stoney, George, 665n
Storaro, Vittorio, 540
Storck, Henri, 116–17, 336–8, 578
Strasberg, Susan, 477
Straub, Jean-Marie, 579–81, 668
Straukh, Maxim, 584
Stravinsky, Igor, 508n, 659
Streisand, Barbra, 630
Strick, Philip, 420, 624
Strindberg, A., 293, 347
Strode, Woody, 640
Stroyeva, Vera, 437
Strudwick, Sheppard, 369
Sturges, John, 270, 484
Sturges, Preston, 179–80
Sucksdorff, Arne, 348–51, 394, 404
Sucksdorff, Kjell, 349
Sugiyama, Kohei, 448
Sukdhev, S., 459
Summers, Walter, 67
Surtees, Robert, 372
Sutherland, Donald, 638
Suzuki, Shigeyoshi, 88
Suzuki, Denmai, 35
Svendsen, Torven, 341
Svendsson, Arne, 439
Swallow, Norman, 692n
Swanson, Gloria, 32, 95, 159–160, 358

Szabó, Istvan, 410, 593, 596–7, 653
Szemes, Marian, 597n
Szigeti, Josef, 258

T

Tabary, Guy, 564
Tagore, Rabindranath, 400, 465, 603
Talankin, Igor, 586n, 652
Talas, Greg, 403
Tallents, Stephen, 114
Tamirov, Akim, 76, 189, 390n
Tarafdar, Rajen, 482
Tarkington, Booth, 185
Tarkovsky, Andrei, 243, 417n, 479, 582
Tasaka, Tomotaka, 152
Tashman, Lillian, 74
Tattoli, Elda, 543
Taylor, Alma, 24
Taylor, Elizabeth, 371, 378, 380, 389, 484, 628n, 629n, 630
Taylor, Gilbert, 591, 593
Taylor, John, 112, 195
Taylor, Robert, 106, 354
Taylor, Sam, 91
Tchehov, A., 582, 616, 654, 674
Tati, Jacques, 259, 263–6, 356, 657, 693n
Tatlin, Vladimir, 683
Tchaikovsky, P. I., 180, 479, 586n
Teasdale, Verree, 128
Tennyson, Pen, 149
Terayama, Shuji, 609n
Teshigahara, Hiroshi, 608
Tessari, Duccio, 658
Thackery, W., x
Thalberg, Irving, 41, 92, 97
Thesiger, Ernest, 330
Thiele, Hertha, 234
Thiele, William, 82
Thirard, Armand, 255
Thomas, Dylan, 203–4
Thompson, Donald, 236
Thompson, J. Lee, 330, 405
Thomson, Virgil, 685n
Thorndike, Andrew, 343, 402
Thorndike, Annelise, 343, 402
Thurber, James, 135n
Tierney, Gene, 183, 386
Tikhomirov, Roman, 479, 652
Tinguely, Jean, 683
Tiomkin, Dimitri, 366–7, 586n, 652
Tirado, Amilcar, 339
Tissé, Edward, 56, 76, 433
Titian, x
Todd, Ann, 405
Todd, Mike, 381, 405
Toeplitz, Jerzy, 411
Toland, Gregg, 43, 93, 97, 103, 187–8, 359, 581
Tolstoy, Leo, 15, 27, 93, 119, 378, 582
Tone, Franchot, 387
Toomey, Regis, 357
Torre Nilsson, Leopoldo, 483, 612
Toscanini, Arturo, 336
Toulouse-Lautrec, H. R., 380
Toyoda, Shiro, 400
Tracy, Spencer, 14n, 371, 375, 383–4, 484, 629–30
Trauberg, Leonid, 63, 149, 218, 584
Trent, John, 649
Trevelyan, John, 626
Trevor, Claire, 640
Trilling, Lionel, 225n
Trintignant, Jean-Louis, 404, 507
Trintignant, Nadine, 507n
Trivas, Viktor, 162–3
Troell, Jan, 575
Troyanovski, Mark, 121
Truffaut, François, 221, 242, 308, 476, 489–90, 493–5, 575, 597, 657, 668n
Trumbo, Dalton, 353n, 365n, 387
Tryon, Tom, 387

Tschehova, Olga, 151
Tsuchimoto, Noriaki, 611
Turgenev, I., 583
Turin, Viktor, 117–18
Turner, Lana, 630
Turpin, Ben, 74
Tushingham, Rita, 548, 604
Twain, Mark, 105n
Tyler, Parker, 641, 643, 680
Tynan, Kenneth, 592, 654

U

Uchida, Tomu, 90, 152
Ulbricht, W., 343
Unamuno, M., 504
Ure, Mary, 547
Uris, Leon, 387
Ustinov, Peter, 484–5

V

Vadim, Roger, 404, 476
Vajda, Ernest, 74
Valberg, Y., 122
Valentino, Rudolph, 38–9, 158, 371
Vallee, Rudy, 180
Valli, Alida, 539
Van der Horst, Hermann, 340
Van der Linden, Reitze, 578
Van Dongen, Helen, 116
Van Doren, Mark, 90n
Van Dyke, W. S., 66
Vanel, Charles, 256, 404
Van Gogh, Vincent, 276n, 406
Van Peebles, Melvin, 640, 645
Van Voorhis, Westbrook, 356
Varda, Agnès, 503n, 507
Varnel, Marcel, 105n
Vasari, Giorgio, 681, 682n
Vaughan, Olwen, x, 118
Vaughan Williams, R., 320
Vavra, Otakar, 402, 480, 598–9
Védrès, Nicole, 251
Veidt, Conrad, 48n, 49, 104
Verdi, G., 229n, 443, 537, 587n
Verne, Jules, 174
Verga, Giovanni, 522
Vernon, Anne, 262
Veronese, Paolo, 396
Vertov, Dziga, 9, 10, 56, 58, 70–1, 115, 117–18, 191n, 436, 459, 498
Vessely, Herbert, 343n
Vickers, Martha, 357
Vidal, Gore, 388n
Vidor, Charles, 183, 219
Vidor, King, 75, 106, 125n, 160, 377–8, 406, 583–4
Viertel, Berthold, 104
Vigo, Jean, 40n, 140, 143n, 145, 206, 244–5, 337, 414, 417, 551, 602, 636, 694
Visconti, Luchino, 149, 191, 220, 379n, 404, 514, 521n, 522–6
Vitti, Monica, 595
Viva, 332n, 642
Vivaldi, A., 253, 575
Vlady, Marina, 477
Von Eltz, Theodore, 357
Von Stauffenberg, Count, 403
Von Sternberg, Joseph, 41, 66, 89, 97, 105, 119, 183, 330, 343, 378, 645
Von Stroheim, Erich, ix, 32, 39–46, 63, 66–7, 95, 97, 142n, 144n, 157, 184, 189–90, 285, 358, 386, 423, 441n, 518, 692–3
Von Sydow, Max, 378, 477
Vredenberg, Max, 340
Vukotic, Dusan, 481, 674n

W

Wagner, Richard, x, 180, 682
Wajda, Andrzej, 402, 411, 413–15, 480, 589, 654
Walbrook, Anton, 197, 198, 330
Walker, Alexander, 38, 127, 181, 619
Walker, Michael, 590n
Walker, Robert, 392
Wallace, Edgar, 96n

Wallach, Eli, 364
Walters, Charles, 358, 406
Walton, William, 585
Walsh, Raoul, 95, 159, 218
Wanamaker, Sam, 485
Wanger, Walter, 98
Ward, John, 275n
Warhol, Andy, 59, 332n, 487–9, 641–3, 661, 668, 680
Warm, Herman, 48
Warner Brothers, The, 19, 59–62
Warner, David, 551, 633
Warner, H. B., 358, 378
Warner, Jack, 321
Warner, Rex, 279n, 329n, 677
Warshow, Robert, 224–6
Waterhouse, Keith, 565
Waters, Ethel, 361, 368
Watkins, Arthur, 260, 626n
Watkins, Peter, 504n, 546, 554–8, 569n, 586, 634, 679
Watt, Harry, 196–7, 320
Waugh, Evelyn, 548n
Wayne, John, 382–3, 406, 484, 625
Webb, Alan, 588
Webb, Millard, 380
Wechsler, Lazar, 345
Wegener, Paul, 25
Weinberg, Herman G., 42, 183, 377
Weiss, Jiri, 402, 410, 480
Welles, Orson, 40, 134n, 184–93, 312, 379, 436, 443, 541, 629
Wellman, William, 41, 97–8, 138, 160, 218, 369, 384
Wells, H. G., 2, 55, 174, 176, 275, 316, 355n
Werker, Alfred, 40, 361n
Werner, Gosta, 348
Werner, Oskar, 390
Wertmüller, Lina, 507n
West, Mae, 115, 645

West, Nathaniel, 148
Westerbeck Jnr, Colin J., 669
Whale, James, 132, 163
White, Chrissie, 24
White, Pearl, 23
White, T. H., 183
Whitehead, A. N., 277–8
Whitney Family, The, 643, 683
Wicki, Bernhard, 403, 478, 628
Widerberg, Bo, 576–7
Widmark, Richard, 361
Wieck, Dorothea, 234
Wiene, Robert, 48–9
Wilde, Oscar, 322
Wilder, Billy, 78, 180, 182, 219, 358, 369–70, 371n, 385–6, 484, 646
Williams, Emlyn, 106, 149, 405
Williams, Tennessee, 362, 363, 388n, 389, 406
Williamson, James, 18
Willis, Gordon, 638
Willman, Noel, 329
Wilson, Harold, 333n
Wilson, Mortimer, 63
Winninger, Charles, 138
Winnington, Richard, 203, 221, 228, 316, 382, 514
Winters, Shelley, 373, 378
Wise, Robert, 390–1, 406, 645
Wodehouse, P. G., 80
Wohl, Stanislaus, 411
Wolf, Konrad, 479
Wood, Robin, 98, 511
Wood, Sam, 149
Woodward, Joanne, 484
Woolf Brothers, The, 104
Woolfe, H. Bruce, 67, 161, 162n
Worringer, Wilhelm, 48
Worth, Irene, 270, 503, 588
Wrede, Caspar, 581
Wright, Basil, 111

Wright, Teresa, 359, 365
Wurtzel, Sol, 45
Wyler, William, 72, 93, 96, 138, 148, 155, 207, 354, 359, 381–2, 406
Wyman, Jane, 392
Wynd, Oswald, 34

Y
Yamamoto, Kajiro, 214–15
Yanne, Jean, 492
Yassin, Ahmad, 616n
Yasui, Shoji, 445
Yates, Peter, 638
Yokoyama, Minoru, 445
York, Michael, 604, 645
Yoshimura, Kozaburo, 214
Young, Colin, 336
Young, Loretta, 186–7
Young, Robert, 360
Young, Roland, 92
Yuan, Ts'ai Yuan, 438
Yutkevitch, Sergei, 401, 436, 587

Z
Zamecnik, J. S., 63
Zampa, Luigi, 216, 220, 514
Zanuck, Darryl, 98, 620–1, 628
Zanuck, R., 621
Zarkhi, Alexander, 118, 437, 479, 581–2
Zavattini, Cesare, 226–7, 516, 663
Zecca, Ferdinand, 15n, 17
Zeffirelli, Franco, 92n
Zeller, Wolfgang, 63, 135, 151
Zetterling, Mai, 347, 577
Zguridi, Alexander, 118, 209
Zils, Paul, 458n
Zinneman, Fred, 345, 365–8, 485, 621, 630
Zola, Emile, 248, 655
Zukor, Adolph, 23, 31, 619n

3. GENERAL INDEX

A
Abbey Theatre, The, 311
ABC, 104, 550
ABPC, 333
Academy Cinema, The, 116
Adam and Eve, 685
Admirable Crichton, The, 605
Aerodrome, The, 677
Agfacolour, 448
Ah! Wilderness, 78
Ain't Supposed to Die a Natura Death, 640
Aldermaston Marchers, The, 334
Alice in Wonderland, 649
Alma Ata Studios, 207, 430
Amateur Film Festival (Glasgow), 667
Angry Young Men, 399, 485, 549, 552
Arena, 685
Army Film Unit, 329
Art of the Motion Picture, 21–3, 617n
Arts Council of Great Britain, 688
'Auteur Theory', 383, 625

B
Bal du Comte D'Orgel, Le, 260
Ballet Suèdois, 51
Bauhaus, The, 49, 683
BBC Television, 329, 554–5, 651
Beast Must Die, The, 490
Beatniks, 399
Benshi, The, 22, 34–5, 88, 354
Biograph, 30–1
Bioscope, 2
'Black' Documentaries, 420

Black Jesus, 640
Black Panthers, The, 372
Black Power, 372
Blum-Byrnes Agreement, 247–8
BOAC, 204, 206
Board of Trade, The, 333
Book of the Dead, The, 617
British Film Institute, 59, 333, 555
British Lion Co, 333
British Transport Films, 485, 564
Bunraku, 89
Burmah-Shell Film Unit, 458n
Bushido, 439
Bushmen, The, 674
British Instructional Films Co, 161
Brûlure de Mille Soleils, La, 284

C
Cable TV, 664, 666, 672
Cahiers du Cinéma, Les, 489, 495
Calcutta Film Society, 400
Canadian Radio and Television Commission, 664
Cannes Film Festival, 239, 411, 582, 605
Carmen, 386
Carmilla, 476
Cassettes, ix, 620n, 686
Catch 44, 665
Challenge for Change, 664
'Charité' Disaster, 6
Chicago '70, 649
Children's Film Foundation, 331, 485
Children's Film Studio, 121
Christmas Carol, A, 646

Cinecitta (Rome), 630
Cinema City, 115
Cinegiornali Liberi, 516
Cinerama, 355, 620
CinemaScope, 78, 355, 384, 386, 566, 620, 689
Cinémathèque Française, La, 206
Cinematograph, 6
Cinematograph Film Acts, 68
Cinéma Vérité, 81, 113, 156, 276n, 356, 425, 459, 481, 498, 501, 509, 554, 571, 578, 595–6, 611n, 645, 649, 672
Collective Unconscious, The, 277
Columbia Pictures, 260, 619
Comédie Française, La, 141
Committee on Un-American Activities, 353
Commision on Educational and Cultural Films, 58
Cosi fan Tutti, 567
Cosmos, 683
Crack Up, The, 282n
Cracow Film Festival, 410n
Crown Film Unit, 177, 199, 200, 217, 410
Czech Film School, 410
Czech Philharmonic Orchestra, 601

D
Dame à la Licorne, La, 302
Day of the Locust, The, 148
Denham Studios, 104–5
Desilu Studios, 619
Director's Guild, The, 32
Disneyland, 133, 394

Dixon of Dock Green, 321
Documentary, 107, 118, 123–7, 498
Dog Beneath the Skin, The, 677
Doll's House, A, 306
Dostoievsky and the Collapse of Liberalism, 679
Dynamic Screen, 355n

E

'Ealing Formula', The, 319, 325
Ealing Studios, 109, 177, 194, 217, 309, 318, 320, 334, 357
Eastmancolour, 448
Ecclesiastes, 491, 493
Echoes of Brittania's Rule, 690
Economist, The, 621
Edinburgh Film Festival, 329, 341, 348
EMB Film Unit, 113, 124
Empire Marketing Board, 114
Eroica, 343
Essanay, 31
Ethnographic and Anthropological Films (Colloquium on), 336
Experiment with Time, An, 10, 277
Experimental Production Fund, 333
Expo 70, 668, 682–3
Expo 67, 684, 687n

F

Fall of the House of Usher, The, 191
FAO, 610
FEKS, 584n
Festival of Britain, 203
Fidelio, 305
Film Booking Office of America, 32
Films d'Art, 18, 63
Films Division (India), 458–9, 602
Film Finance Corporation (India), 482
Film Institute of India, 87, 108
Film Polski, 118
Film Society, The, 55, 135, 173–4
First National, 31, 60
Forsyte Saga, The, 93, 608
Four Serious Songs, 491
Fox Movietone, 60
French Impressionists, The, 338
Front Populaire, 145–6
Free Cine Journals, 227, 516, 663
Free Cinema, 331–4, 546
Free Newsreels, 516

G

Gaumont British, 104
General Film Distributors, 309
Glyndebourne Opera House, 405
Government Film Units, 612
GPO Film Unit, 115, 124, 145n, 194, 200, 204
Group Three, 205, 332–4

H

Hamlet, 202, 300, 584
Hamp, 560
Hays Office, The, 386
Hayward Gallery, The, 688
High Chapparal, The, 640n
High Cinema Institute (Cairo), 616n, 651
Histoire Immortelle, L', 191
Hitler Jugend, 478
Hitler Youth, 211
Hollywood Ten, The, 353, 365n, 625n
HPSCHD, 685

I

ICI, 110, 112
Ikebana, 439
Imperial War Museum, 154
Incredible String Band, The, 601

International Association of Documentarists, 420n, 663
ILO, 110–1
International Red Cross, 344
In Two Minds, 570n
Italian Film School, 516

K

Kabuki, 89, 214–15, 418, 443, 446, 448
Karlovy Vary Film Festival, 400, 472
Khodinka Disaster, 21n
Kinetics, 688
King Arthur, 200n
King David, 200n
Kinemacolour, 20
Kinetograph, 62
Kino Eye, 9, 56–7
Kinoki, 9, 56–7, 191n
Kinetoscope, 1, 5, 6, 7, 62

L

Lady Windermere's Fan, 376
Laterna Magica, 402
Light-Space Modulator, The, 683
London Film Festival, 474n, 481n
Lord Arthur Savile's Crime, 322
Lost World, The, 96
Lottery, The, 372
Loved One, The, 547n

M

Macbeth, 443, 587n
Madan Theatres, 85
Magic Flute, The, 563
Magnascope, 160
Maly Theatre, The, 421
Manifesto on Sound Film, 71
Mannheim Film Festival, 402, 601
Marshall Plan, The, 345
Mass Media, 334
Mass Observation, 200
MCA, 619
Mercury Theatre, The, 185n
MGM, 91, 95, 97, 106, 345, 354, 368, 619–21, 645
Minimal Cinema, 488, 580
Ministry of Information, 155, 182, 195–6
Ministry of Transport, 206
'Moon River', 623
Moscow Art Theatre, 421, 583n
Mosfilm, 400
Musée du Cinéma, 691n
Mutual Film Co. 31

N

Nana, 655
National Film Archive, 115, 691n
National Film Board of Canada, 112, 133, 276n, 425, 499n, 649, 664–5, 684, 691
National Film Finance Corporation, 333
National Film Institute of India, 660
National Film Theatre (London), 686
Nayar Sensar Co, 400
Neo-Realism, 181, 201, 220–32, 247n,
New Deal, The, 97–8, 124
Newport Jazz Festival, 484
Newsweek, 640, 689n
New Wave, The, 334, 399, 489, 504, 544
Night Passage, 682
Nisei, The, 370
Noh, 89, 443
Nostromo, 95
Nouvelle Vague, 308, 476, 489–90, 498
Now, The, 674

O

'Ode to Francois Villon', 673n
Old Vic, The, 586
Ondes Martenot, 135

Orators, The, 253
Order of Lenin, 206
Orghast, 691n
Orlando Furioso, 682

P

Panavision 70, 378, 382, 566
Panoptikon, 2
Paramount Pictures, 19, 60, 157–8, 179, 622
Patent Company, The, 19, 30
Pathé, 30
'Peanuts', 660
Peter Pan, 236n
Phoenix and the Turtle, The, 302
Pinewood Studios, 177, 199, 620n
Polish Film School, 411, 417, 480
Polyvision 404
Postman Always Rings Twice, The, 149, 220
Power and the Glory, The, 95
Praesens Films, 344–5
Princess Casamassima, The, 322
Prudential Insurance Co, 104
Psychology of the Unconscious, The, 9

R

RAF Film Unit, 200, 329
'Raindrops Keep Falling on my Head', 623
RCA, 140, 145n
Resettlement Administration, 124
Revue Productions, 619
RKO, 32, 184, 187, 354, 619

S

Sacco and Vanzetti, 100
Screw, 671n
Sesame Street, 660
Shell, 110, 321n, 340, 616n
Shell Film Unit, 150
Sherman Anti-Trust Act, 19
Shimpa, 455n
Shingeki, 27, 455n
Shochiku Co, 89
Shomin-geki, 455
Sight and Sound, 78, 333, 386, 387
Socialist Realism, 21
Someone Waiting, 405
Soviet Manifesto, 89, 90, 114
Soviet-Nazi Pact, 206
Space Between Words, The, 660
Specialised Agencies (UN), 329, 662
Spectator, The, 155, 311
Sri Lanka Government Film Unit, 470n
'Stand Up! Stand Up!', 333
START, 411
Stavisky Scandals, The, 140, 145
Stereoscopy, 355
Sunday Times, The, 115, 682
Super Eight, 660, 662–3, 686, 691

T

Tarot, The, 193
Technicolor, 448
Tempesta, La, 302
Theme of the Traitor and the Hero, 538n
Thieving Magpie Overture, The, 677
Third World, The, 610
3D, ix, 620
Tobis Klangfilm, 79, 82n, 140, 145n, 254
Todd AO, 381, 593
Tod in Venedig, 192
Toronto Theatre Workshop, 649
Turn of the Screw, The, 131, 546
20th Century Fox, 19, 23, 60, 354, 368, 388, 619–21, 645, 689

U

UCLA, 272, 336, 431, 687
Under Western Eyes, 95

UN Film Department, 396
Unesco, 108, 111, 134, 329, 334, 338, 341, 610, 662
United Artists, 31
Universal Pictures, 19, 23, 41, 620
University of Illinois, 685
University of the Air, 660
US, 559
US War Information Service, 155, 183n
US Signal Corps, 156

V

Valse Grise, La, 143

Vegetotherapy, 673n
Venice Film Festival, 239, 395, 438, 449, 482, 534, 543, 614, 619
Video-tape, 516, 660, 663
VistaVision, 355, 620
Vitascope, 2, 7
VTR, ix, 664–6, 672, 686, 691

W

Wall Street Crash, The, 97
Warner Brothers Pictures, 89, 619, 689
War of the Worlds, The, 184

Warsaw Dramatic Academy, 551
Washington Square, 381
Wayang Kulit, 4
Western Electric, 75, 140, 145n
WHO, 609
Wild Goose Chase, The, 279n, 677

X

'X' Certificate, The, 260, 626n

Y

Yoshiwara Co, 62